HISTORICAL
DICTIONARY
OF THE
SPANISH
CIVIL WAR,
1936-1939

Spain: Regions and Provinces

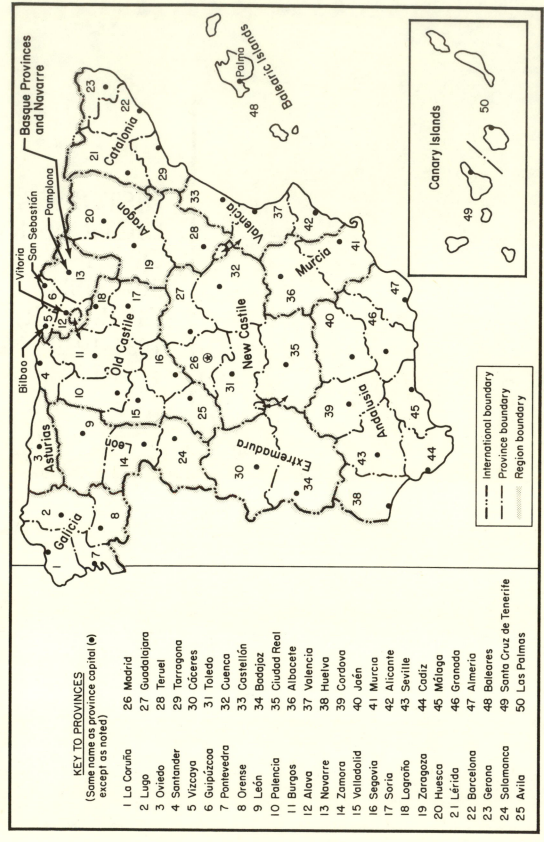

KEY TO PROVINCES
(Same name as province capital (•)
except as noted)

1 La Coruña	26 Madrid
2 Lugo	27 Guadalajara
3 Oviedo	28 Teruel
4 Santander	29 Tarragona
5 Vizcaya	30 Cáceres
6 Guipúzcoa	31 Toledo
7 Pontevedra	32 Cuenca
8 Orense	33 Castellón
9 León	34 Badajoz
10 Palencia	35 Ciudad Real
11 Burgos	36 Albacete
12 Alava	37 Valencia
13 Navarre	38 Huelva
14 Zamora	39 Cordova
15 Valladolid	40 Jaén
16 Segovia	41 Murcia
17 Soria	42 Alicante
18 Logroño	43 Seville
19 Zaragoza	44 Cadiz
20 Huesca	45 Málaga
21 Lérida	46 Granada
22 Barcelona	47 Almeria
23 Gerona	48 Baleares
24 Salamanca	49 Santa Cruz de Tenerife
25 Avila	50 Las Palmas

Legend:
- – · · – International boundary
- – · – Province boundary
- – · – Region boundary

Source: Eugene K. Keefe et al., *Area Handbook for Spain* (Washington, D.C.: U.S. Government Printing Office, 1976), p. 51.

HISTORICAL DICTIONARY OF THE SPANISH CIVIL WAR, 1936-1939

Edited by JAMES W. CORTADA

GREENWOOD PRESS
WESTPORT, CONNECTICUT
LONDON, ENGLAND

Library of Congress Cataloging in Publication Data
Main entry under title:

Historical dictionary of the Spanish Civil War, 1936-
    1939.

   Bibliography: p.
   Includes index.
   1. Spain—History—Civil War, 1936-1939—Dictionaries.
I. Cortada, James W.
DP269.H54   946.081′03′21   81-13424
ISBN 0-313-22054-9 (lib. bdg.)   AACR2

Library of Congress Catalog Card Number: 81-13424
ISBN: 0-313-22054-9

First published in 1982

Greenwood Press
A division of Congressional Information Service, Inc.
88 Post Road West
Westport, Connecticut 06881

Printed in the United States of America

10 9 8 7 6 5 4 3 2 1

Contents

Acknowledgments

A large number of people enthusiastically supported this project and contributed their talents throughout its development. Jim Sabin, vice-president of Greenwood Press, must be credited for conceiving the idea of this dictionary, while Stanley G. Payne provided me with continual advice throughout its growth into a publishable text. Angel Viñas examined the list of entries from the perspective of appropriate balance across all topics, and Ray Proctor did the same for military themes. Robert Kern helped to ensure that the complex story of left-wing and Republican political issues was adequately described, and indeed, he wrote many entries. Victor Alba contributed his talents in the area of domestic history, advising and writing while both in Spain and in the United States. Joan C. Ullman advised on how to develop the appendices on sources. David Wingeate Pike was very helpful in identifying potential contributors in France. As I was completing the manuscript, Robert Whealey helped finish portions so that the book could be sent off to the publisher quickly. My father, James N. Cortada, aided in the translation of some Spanish entries into English. Each of the contributors would also like to acknowledge the help of their colleagues, librarians, and secretaries for making this project possible.

As the general editor of the dictionary, I was profoundly pleased by the universal support with which this project was received by specialists in Spanish history. The long list of contributors is testimony to this encouragement. I would like to thank each author for writing entries and for advising me on material and in finding other contributors. I must also acknowledge the patience of my wife who saw me spend too many hours away from our family to work on the dictionary.

At Greenwood Press Betty Pessagno had the difficult task of copyediting our manuscript, no simple task by any means. Anne Kugielsky efficiently moved the book through production. Both made a large manuscript a manageable book.

Introduction

The Spanish Civil War continues to excite the reading public, despite the fact that the conflict ended over forty years ago. This enthusiasm is in itself one of the most intriguing aspects of the war. Historians, novelists, journalists, and television and radio commentators have described the Civil War as a battle between good and evil, democracy and fascism, civilization and chaos, and the forces of light and darkness. So it was also perceived during the 1930s. The republics of the world saw in the Spanish struggle the potential for blocking the advance of fascism, Hitler, and authoritarian governments in a world they thought should be governed by democratic systems.

The intellectuals who rushed forward to serve in the International Brigades felt that the progress of European civilization depended on their success. To them, as well as to many nonintellectuals, the very concept of progress might therefore be invalidated, fostering the birth of a new Dark Ages. It was a war in which, for many, good lost out to evil. Fascism, dictatorship, and Hitler's allies won, while the military consequences of that victory brought millions of Europeans to their deaths in World War II. Although this line of reasoning was simplistic, it remained popular and is still evident today.

The Spanish Civil War remains a popular subject of study precisely because of its relationship to World War II. Many argue that through a simple process of linear thinking, the democracies' inability to stem the tide of fascism in Spain encouraged Italy and Germany to create the conditions necessary for World War II. Historians indicate that this reasoning ignores other pre-Civil War factors operative in European affairs, although they do admit that events in Spain altered Hitler's views of Western European democracies. Historians argue that the events in Spain were among the many factors that influenced Germany's decision to invade Poland in September 1939, resulting in the start of World War II. Many serious students of the 1930s and 1940s saw a direct link between events in Spain and World War II. They viewed World War II as a continuation of the conflict against fas-

cism, with only a temporary lull during the summer of 1939 from the time Spain's Civil War ended (in late March) and the start of the invasion of Poland (early in September). Today, however, historians discount the link as being specifically linear, arguing that the causes of World War II were much broader than the events in Spain. Moreover, modern-day interpretations of the causes of Spain's Civil War minimize international factors and stress purely internal Iberian forces.

The Civil War has also continued to draw attention because of the Franco regime. From the earliest months of the Civil War, General Francisco Franco was labeled a fascist and a military dictator of the same stripe as Hitler and Mussolini, while others saw him as a crusader saving Europe's civilization from liberalism and communism. He never quite lost the reputation as a dictator, throughout nearly forty years of rule. The fact that many writers on the Civil War sympathized with the losing side, the Republicans, insured his unfavorable press. The Caudillo himself contributed to the problem by constantly reminding his public about the Civil War. Nationalist veterans were given government jobs, the day the Civil War started became a national holiday, many Republicans remained in jail for decades, and publications favorable to the Republic seldom appeared in Franco's Spain.

The victors of World War II, like many of those outside of government who wrote favorably about the Spanish Republican cause, therefore, felt they had a mission to destroy the remnants of fascism and its associated dictatorships. They collectively believed that Franco was one of the last of these rulers who should be gotten rid off at an early opportunity. Circumstances made this goal impossible to achieve; nonetheless, for decades there were constant calls for his ouster from power. Consequently, as long as he remained the Caudillo, Spain suffered a number of economic setbacks. The legacy of the Civil War made Spain's initial bid for membership in the United Nations a failure, and years later both the Common Market and the North Atlantic Treaty Organization forbade its formal inclusion among their ranks. It was not until the mid-1970s, on the eve of Franco's death, that Europe began to soften its attitude toward the Spanish government. Yet even as late as 1981, at the time of this writing, Europe awaited proof that democracy would gain a sincere foothold in Spain.

Much of the imagery of that authoritarian government of the 1939-1975 period grew out of the turmoil of the Civil War. The Franco regime constantly harked back to events of that earlier period. For more than thirty-five years that never changed, while the long shadow of Spanish history stalked young King Juan Carlos later in his bid for constitutional monarchism. Following the reestablishment of a parliamentary monarchy in Spain, interest in the Civil War continued. An attempted coup against the government by military police with the tacit support of some army officers in February 1981 conjured up ghosts from the 1930s. Despite this dramatic event, interest in the Civil War continued because many felt that the true story of the earlier conflict, especially the Republican version, had never been told in Spain, so long as Franco had ruled.

Current events in Spain provide a fourth reason for interest in the Civil War. With the legal recognition of such groups as, for example, the Communist and Socialist parties, and the return to Spain of some of the key protagonists of the conflict, such as Dolores Ibarruri (La Pasionaria) and Juan José Tarradellas, memories of the political life of the 1930s came back. It appeared as if the intervening forty years had been a pause in Spanish history. Ibarruri went back to the Cortes as a delegate, Tarradellas once again ran the newly recreated Catalan government (Generalitat), while Santiago Carrillo (a communist youth leader in the 1930s) took charge of the Communist party in Spain. People who had been silent for many years on the Civil War now spoke more openly about their role. The most vivid proof of this last development is Ronald Fraser's recent book, *The Blood of Spain*, which contains a large collection of personal anecdotes from both sides. Commentators on present-day political events in Spain constantly compare the king to his predecessors, and the role and attitude of Spain's army to that of an earlier age, and they forecast the future with a respectful backward glance at pre-Franco Spain. Even the results of Spain's first free elections after Franco's death resulted in a distribution of votes across several parties reminiscent of those in February 1936.

With more archival material being opened to historians all over Europe and particularly in Spain, the quantity and quality of research on the Civil War are improving rapidly. Over the past few decades, significant archival and library collections have been established in the United States, Great Britain, France, Switzerland, and Spain dedicated to the subject of the Civil War. Materials in Spanish governmental archives which had remained closed until after Franco's death in 1975, along with the private papers of many key individuals whose families were previously reluctant to discuss the role of their ancestors, now made it possible to study subjects considered off limits in the past.

Today research is being conducted on all the political, military, economic, and social activities of the 1930s. Substantial work continues, as it has for the past two decades, on preparing important biographies, military histories, and economic studies. Currently, there are over 10,000 different books, pamphlets, and articles dealing with the 1930s, and, in Spain, a minimum of a half dozen new books appear in print each month on this theme. In the English-speaking part of the world alone, many major new books come out annually. Well over a hundred historians are currently writing books on the Spain of the 1930s, and over half the volumes published on Spanish history since 1900 deal with the 1930s alone. These volumes deal primarily with regionalism, political parties and elections, biographies, and a host of memoirs.

Despite all of these studies, our knowledge of the Civil War remains fragmented. Major archival research, especially in Spanish government papers, has yet to be completed. Biographies of key individuals (such as Juan Negrín) await their historians, and sociological histories about the life of people, provinces, classes, and specific communities remain to be written. Institutional studies on various government agencies, the political life of Nationalist Spain, Franco's early government, domestic economics, and various military units are still not appreciated. But we are at the start of a major growth in our knowledge of the subject. Opportunities for research and writing are so great now that basic reference tools are needed.

It is because of this surge in research that our project evolved. Along with some excellent one-volume histories of the subject and bibliographic guides, this dictionary is designed to serve as a convenient reference to many aspects of the Civil War. It consists of over 800 different entries written by specialists familiar with the topics, and it is enhanced with bibliographic references throughout, reflecting the latest available information. The appendices, especially the chronology, Civil War cabinets, and military history of the conflict, are intended to give the reader rapid access to information of various types.

To help insure that the information presented in the dictionary represents the latest collective knowledge of those who best know the Civil War, forty leading specialists, from Spain, the United States, France, Great Britain, and Canada, among other nations, have been chosen to write the entries. Thus, this dictionary represents a unique collective comment on all major aspects of the subject. Some entries have never been discussed in print before, such as the role of teachers and monetary policy, and others present views that have received very little discussion in the past. Some essays, on themes such as the origins of the Civil War and the Nationalist Army, are written by highly regarded specialists who are sharing their views, many for the first time. Others present novel material and novel interpretations. More traditional and well-trodden territory is also amply represented in this work. The group of scholars drawn together for this project reflects every historical interpretation and faction that exist on the Civil War. In addition, there is a balance between senior scholars and young ones. Senior historians were asked to audit the project throughout its development to insure that all major issues would be discussed. Young historians who have yet to publish their first major works were given an opportunity to present the results of their current research so as to avoid leaving out new and important perspectives.

Because of space restrictions, many entries are quite short. The objective of this dictionary is not to provide a definitive, detailed history of the Civil War, but rather, to offer a quick reference on a broad range of material for those interested in basic information. Despite the limitations of space, the dictionary offers more than just information. It also presents the current thinking on many subjects and a collection of writings unique in contemporary Spanish historiography. These authors' careful attention to bibliographic references further insures the usefulness of the dictionary.

The best way to use this dictionary is to go directly to a particular entry of interest, all of which are in alphabetical order. Entries are cross-referenced to suggest other related topics. Asterisks indicate that the item in question is the subject of its own entry. If the reader wishes to see all references to a certain subject, regardless of location in the dictionary, he or she should use the index. Because of the controversy that still surrounds the Spanish Civil War, each entry is signed so that the reader can identify the source of various interpretations and comments. When possible, we have attempted to avoid having any one author dominate all the entries dealing with any particular theme in order to provide a variety of views. Whenever accurate data were available on birth and death dates, along with place of birth and death, these facts were included in biographical entries since biography remains one of the least researched aspects of the Civil War.

July 1981   *James W. Cortada*

Contributors

Abella Bermejo, Rafael *Planeta, S.A.*

Alba, Victor *Kent State University*

Alpert, Michael *Polytechnic of Central London*

Bertrand de Muñoz, Maryse *University of Montreal*

Blinkhorn, Martin *University of Lancaster*

Bolloten, Burnett *Hoover Institution*

Boyd, Carolyn P. *University of Texas*

Bricall, Josep M. *Centre d'Estudis de Planificació*

Broué, Pierre *Institut d'Etudes Politiques*

Cortada, James W. *IBM Corporation*

Coverdale, John F. *Northwestern University*

Edwards, Jill *University of Reading*

Eguidazu, Fernando *Spanish Ministry of Commerce*

Esenwein, George *Hoover Institution*

Fleming, Shannon E. *Social Security Administration, U.S. Government*

Foard, Douglas W. *Ferrum College*

Frank, Willard C. Jr. *Old Dominion University*

Fraser, Ronald *London, England*

Fredricks, Shirley F. *Adams State College*

Harper, Glenn T. *University of Southern Mississippi*

Holtby, David V. *University of New Mexico*

Irwin, William J. *Bowie State College*

Johnson, Peter T. *Princeton University*

Johnston, Verle B. *Federal Reserve Bank, U.S. Government*

Kern, Robert W. *University of New Mexico*

Malefakis, Edward *Columbia University*

Meaker, Gerald H. *Northside College*

Payne, Stanley G. *University of Wisconsin*

Pike, David Wingeate *Latin American Yearly Review*

Pike, Fredrick B. *University of Notre Dame*

Pilapil, Vicente R. *California State University*

Preston, Paul *University of London*

Proctor, Raymond L. *University of Idaho*

Rosenstone, Robert A. *California Institute of Technology*

Sánchez, José M. *Saint Louis University*

Slaughter, Jane *University of New Mexico*

Southworth, Herbert R. *Roche, Concremiers, France*

Thornberry, Robert S. *University of Alberta*

Voltes Bou, Pedro *University of Barcelona*

Whealey, Robert H. *Ohio University*

Frequently Used Abbreviations

BOC — *Bloque Obrero y Campesino* (Workers and Farmers Bloc)

CAMPSA — *Compañía Arrendataria del Monopolio de Petróleos, S.A.*

CEDA — *Confederación Española de Derechas Autónomas* (Spanish Confederation for Autonomous Rights)

CEPSA — *Compañía Española de Petroleos*

CNT — *Confederación Nacional del Trabajo* (National Labor Confederation)

CTV — *Corpo Truppe Volontarie* (Italian Expeditionary Corps)

FAI — *Federación Anarquista Ibérica* (Iberian Anarchist Federation)

FIJL — *Federación Ibérica de Juventudes Libertarias* (Iberian Federation of Libertarian Youth)

FJS — *Federación de Juventudes Socialistas* (Socialist Youth Federation)

GEPCI — *Federación Catalana de Gremios y Entidades de Pequeños Comerciantes y Industriales* (Catalan Federation of Guilds and Organizations of Small Merchants and Industrialists)

HISMA — *Compañía Hispano-Marroquí de Transportes* (Hispano-Morrocan Transportation Company)

IB — International Brigades

JAP — *Juventud de Acción Popular* (Catholic Action Youth Movement)

JCI — *Juventud Comunista Ibérica* (Iberian Communist Youth) (See also POUM)

JL — *Juventud Libertarias* (Libertarian Youth)

JONS — *Juntas de Ofensiva Nacional-Sindicalista* (National-Syndicalist Offensive Juntas)

JS — *Juventudes Socialistas* (Socialist Youth)

JSU — *Juventudes Socialistas Unificadas* (United Youth Movement)

MAOC — *Milicias Antifascistas Obreras y Campesinas* (Urban and Rural Antifascist Militia)

NKVD — People's Commissariat for International Affairs

PCE — *Partido Comunista Española* (Spanish Communist party)

PCOE — *Partido Comunista Obrero Español* (Spanish Communist Labor party)

PNV — *Partido Nacionalista Vasco* (Basque Nationalist party)

POUM — *Partido Obrero de Unificación Marxista* (Workers' Marxist Unification party)

PSOE — *Partido Socialista Obrero Español* (Spanish Socialist party)

PSUC — *(Partito Socialista Unificat de Catalunya)* (United Socialist party of Catalonia)

ROWAK — *Rohstoffe-und-waren-Einkaufsgesellschaft* (Raw Material and Goods Purchasing Company)

SEU — *Sindicato Español Universitario* (Spanish University Union)

SIFNE — *Servicio de Información del Nordeste de España* (Information Service of Northeast Spain)

SIM — *Servicio de Investigación Militar* (Service for Military Investigation)

SIPM — *Servicio de Información Política y Militar* (Political and Military Information Service)

UGT — *Unión General de Trabajadores* (General Workers' Union)

UME — *Unión Militar Española* (Spanish Miltary Union)

UMRA — *Unión Militar Republicana Antifascista* (Republican Antifascist Military Union)

Maps

Proportion of Impoverished Entrepreneurs in Rural Proletariat in 1936

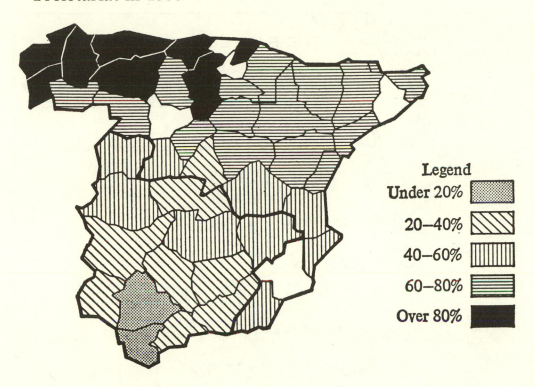

Legend

Under 20%

20–40%

40–60%

60–80%

Over 80%

Proportion of Tenants and Sharecroppers among Impoverished Entrepreneurs in 1936

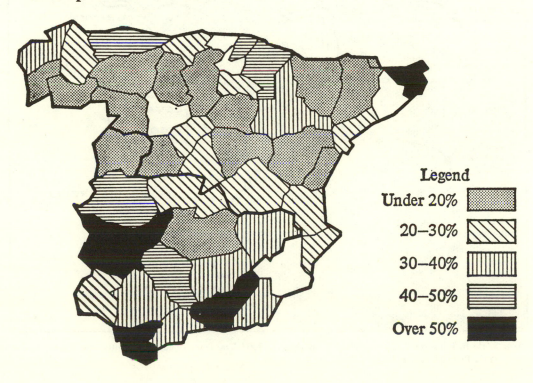

Legend

Under 20%

20–30%

30–40%

40–50%

Over 50%

Source: Edward Malefakis, *Agrarian Reform and Peasant Revolution in Spain* (Yale University Press, copyright © 1970 by Yale University).

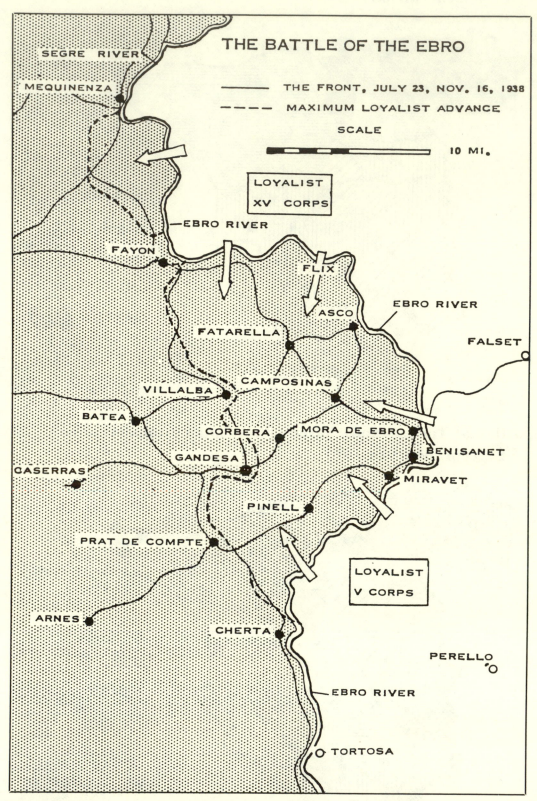

Source: Verle B. Johnston, *Legions of Babel* (copyright © 1967, The Pennsylvania State University Press, University
Park, Pennsylvania 16802), p. 138.

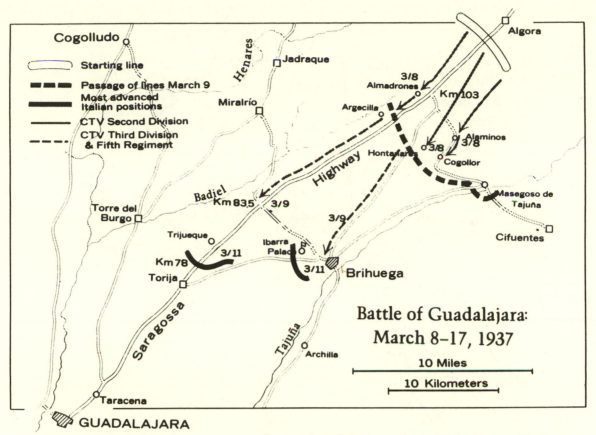

Source: John F. Coverdale, *Italian Intervention in the Spanish Civil War* (copyright © 1975 by Princeton University Press), p. 226. Reprinted by permission of Princeton University Press.

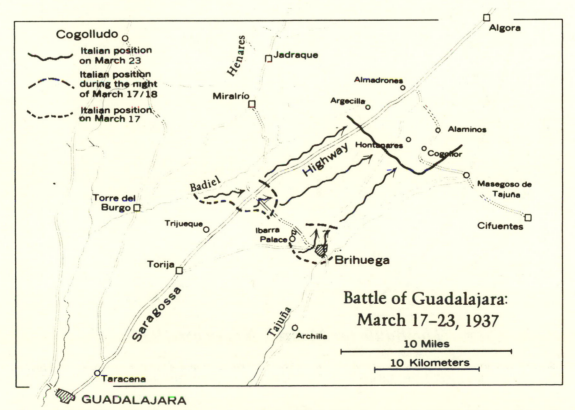

Source: John F. Coverdale, *Italian Intervention in the Spanish Civil War* (copyright © 1975 by Princeton University Press), p. 244. Reprinted by permission of Princeton University Press.

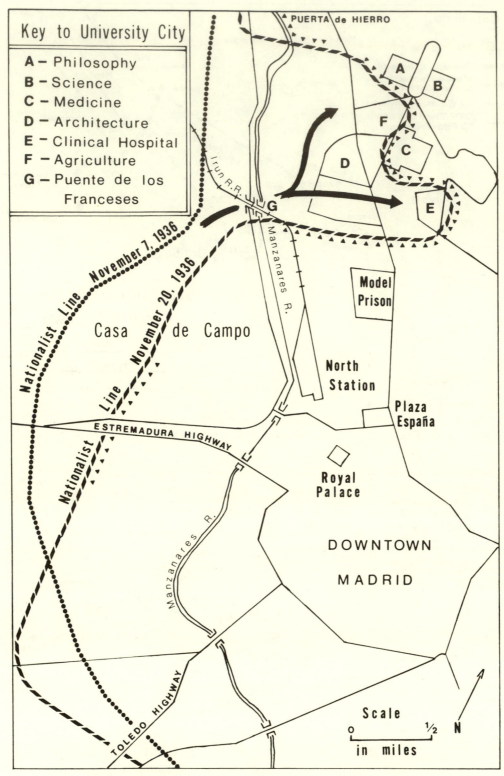

Key to University City

A – Philosophy
B – Science
C – Medicine
D – Architecture
E – Clinical Hospital
F – Agriculture
G – Puente de los
     Franceses

PUERTA de HIERRO

Nationalist Line November 7, 1936

Line November 20, 1936

Nationalist

Irun R.R.

Manzanares R.

Casa de Campo

ESTREMADURA HIGHWAY

Manzanares R.

TOLEDO HIGHWAY

Model Prison

North Station

Plaza España

Royal Palace

DOWNTOWN MADRID

Scale
0   ½
in miles

N

The Battle for Madrid, November 1936

Source: This map appeared on p. 200 of *Red Years/Black Years: A Political History of Spanish Anarchism, 1911-1937* by R. W. Kern, Philadelphia © Institute for the Study of Human Issues (ISHI) Publications, 1978.

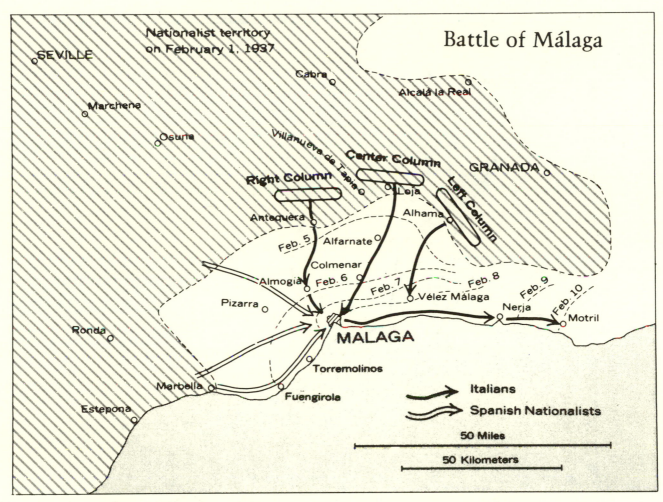

Source: John F. Coverdale, *Italian Intervention in the Spanish Civil War* (copyright © 1975 by Princeton University Press), p. 208. Reprinted by permission of Princeton University Press.

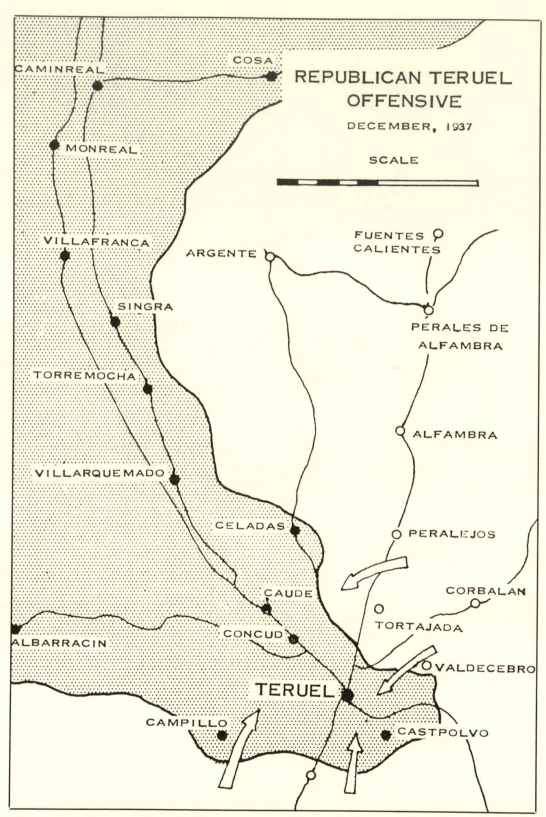

REPUBLICAN TERUEL OFFENSIVE

DECEMBER, 1937

SCALE

COSA

CAMINREAL

MONREAL

VILLAFRANCA

ARGENTE

FUENTES CALIENTES

PERALES DE ALFAMBRA

SINGRA

TORREMOCHA

ALFAMBRA

VILLARQUEMADO

CELADAS

PERALEJOS

CAUDE

CORBALAN

TORTAJADA

ALBARRACIN

CONCUD

VALDECEBRO

TERUEL

CAMPILLO

CASTPOLVO

Source: Verle B. Johnston, *Legions of Babel* (copyright © 1967, The Pennsylvania State University Press, University Park, Pennsylvania 16802), p. 128.

Spain: Spanish Civil War, 1936-1939

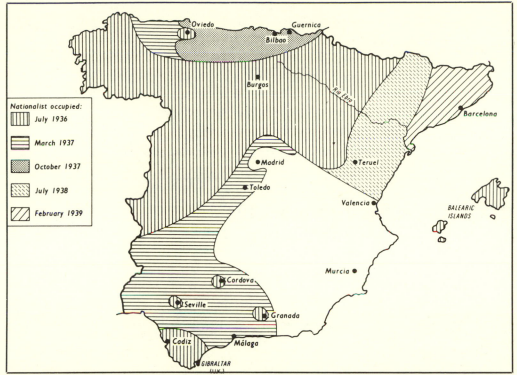

Nationalist occupied:
- July 1936
- March 1937
- October 1937
- July 1938
- February 1939

Source: Eugene K. Keefe et al., *Area Handbook for Spain* (Washington, D.C.: U.S. Government Printing Office, 1976), p. 43.

The Madrid Front

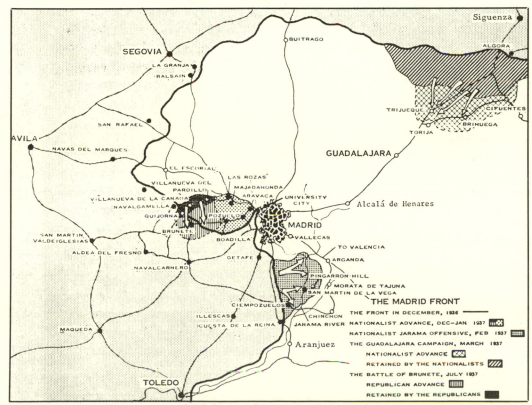

THE MADRID FRONT
- THE FRONT IN DECEMBER, 1936
- NATIONALIST ADVANCE, DEC-JAN 1937
- NATIONALIST JARAMA OFFENSIVE, FEB 1937
- THE GUADALAJARA CAMPAIGN, MARCH 1937
- NATIONALIST ADVANCE
- RETAINED BY THE NATIONALISTS
- THE BATTLE OF BRUNETE, JULY 1937
- REPUBLICAN ADVANCE
- RETAINED BY THE REPUBLICANS

Source: Verle B. Johnston, *Legions of Babel* (copyright © 1967, The Pennsylvania State University Press, University Park, Pennsylvania 16802), p. 40.

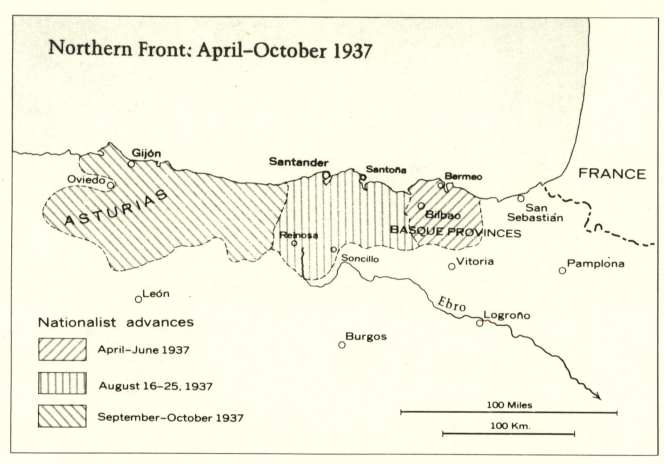

Northern Front: April–October 1937

Nationalist advances

April–June 1937

August 16–25, 1937

September–October 1937

100 Miles

100 Km.

Source: John F. Coverdale, *Italian Intervention in the Spanish Civil War* (copyright © 1975 by Princeton University Press), p. 278. Reprinted by permission of Princeton University Press.

Aragon & Levante
Offensives:
March–July 1938

March 9–May 26

May 26–July 20

50 Miles

50 Km.

Source: John F. Coverdale, *Italian Intervention in the Spanish Civil War* (copyright © 1975 by Princeton University Press), p. 348. Reprinted by permission of Princeton University Press.

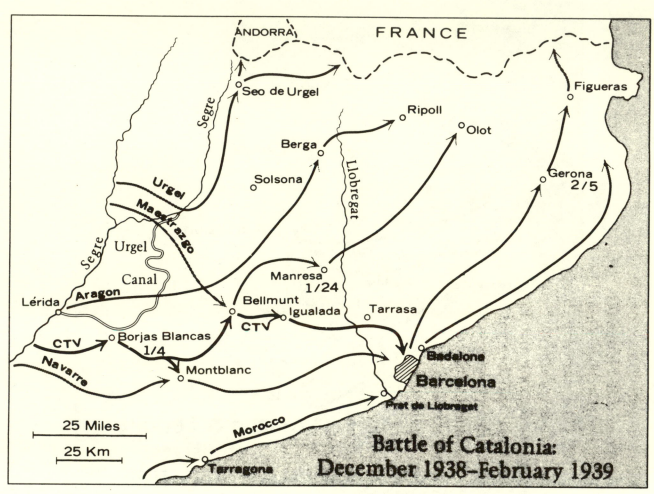

Battle of Catalonia: December 1938–February 1939

Source: John F. Coverdale, *Italian Intervention in the Spanish Civil War* (copyright © 1975 by Princeton University Press), p. 377. Reprinted by permission of Princeton University Press.

Dictionary

A

ABAD DE SANTILLÁN, DIEGO (1897-). Abad de Santillán, the anarchist, was born in Spain, raised in Argentina,* and educated in Madrid.* Bright and capable, he graduated in 1916 from the University of Madrid and drew almost immediate attention to himself for writing several early works, including *El derecho de España a la revolución* (1916) and *Psicologia del pueblo español* (1917) as part of the large and influential regeneration movement begun by Joaquín Costa in the 1880s. During Abad de Santillán's later years, he was one of the leading figures of the anarchist movement, both in Spain and Argentina, and his importance to the Civil War era was as a theorist, journalist, and leader of the *Federación Anarquista Ibérica* (FAI).*

The event that led Abad de Santillán to abandon liberalism and adopt anarchism was the General Strike of August 1917, the first in Spanish labor history. After the strike was crushed by the army, the young scholar's contacts with radical affairs led to a short sentence for disrupting the public order. In 1918 he left for Argentina, where he taught and wrote for the *Federación Obrera Regional Argentina* (FORA), a huge anarchosyndicalist organization that led a series of crippling strikes in Argentina during the 1920s. He represented the FORA in France* and Germany* in 1921-1922 in the formation of the International Workingmen's Association as the anarchosyndicalist international to compete with the Comintern, and he was the first Latin American representative on its executive council. In this capacity, he traveled to Mexico* to assist the Mexican *Confederación General de Trabajadores* in the wake of Ricardo Flores Magon's death. There he met Buenaventura Durruti,* Francisco Ascaso,* Gregorio Jover,* and several other Spanish anarchist militants who, fleeing the Spanish dictatorship of General Primo de Rivera and the possibility of extradition from France, had ended up in Mexico.

Bank robbery rather than politics forced the Spaniards out of Mexico, and although Abad de Santillán was not involved, the Mexican government may have also called for his departure during the 1920s. He returned to Argentina and was soon reunited with the others in Buenos Aires. A new period of fervent agitation and strike activity ensued, punctuated by several more bank robberies, which forced Durruti and Ascaso to flee again, while Abad de Santillán had to remain in hiding for some time. His writings in the Argentine anarchist newspaper *La Antorcha* and various activities among Spanish and Italian immigrants in Argentina did much to increase the FORA's membership, and he became a noisy partisan in the debate over the Argentine government's efforts to extradite Durruti and Ascaso for the murder of a bank guard. By 1930, however, the Uriburu dictatorship in Argentina, reacting against the FORA's many strikes and its unsettling influence, forced Abad de Santillán to flee again, this time back to Europe.* He entered Spain almost as soon as the Second Republic* was proclaimed in April 1931.

He was soon an active member of the FAI, the more purely anarchist branch of the Spanish anarchosyndicalist movement, although his associates in Barcelona,* the *Grupo Acción*, were evidently as much communist as anarchist. This tendency characterized his work until the founding in 1934 of the communist-leaning *Partit Socialista Unificat de Catalunya*,* when he drew away from the communists. In any case, Abad de Santillán's editorship of *Tierra y Libertad*, an anarchist periodical, brought him into the agrarian crisis that dominated 1932 and 1933. Exposure to rural life and the bitter attitudes of many Spanish peasants drastically changed many of his ideas. Ever since the General Strike of 1917, he had focused upon the organization of industrial labor, but now the old regenerationist ideas of his student days returned in more radical form. He began to place greater emphasis on the physical improvement of the countryside by creating peasant communes, obtaining rural social reorganization through maximum peasant solidarity. Such a formula left out the wider social class cooperation earlier envisaged by Joaquín Costa, the premier Spanish modernizer.

Abad de Santillán's first major opportunity to take charge of the anarchist movement came in the fall of 1935, when he began editing a new periodical, *Tiempos Nuevos*, and wrote the first draft of *El organismo económico de la revolución: cómo vivimos y como podríamos vivir en España*, perhaps his most important work. Much of the argument of his book was inspired by the ideas of Peter Kropotkin, whose *The Conquest of Bread* was the intellectual predecessor of *El organismo económico*. Abad de Santillán gave Spanish anarchism an economic theory that provided the movement with a much stronger economic base than the Bakuninist revolutionary violence of the past four or five decades, although he owed much of his collectivist sensitivity to research conducted by a wide range of social theorists.

Abad de Santillán's mutualist system depended upon council communism to link factory councils and syndicates of trade and industry to a federal economic council, which would direct the country towards becoming a society of producers and consumers based upon the principle of social justice. Councils of production among farmers were linked to the development of national councils in various agricultural sectors, all prepared to aid local groups without dictating policy in a governmental fashion. The many details of his plan were sometimes indistinct, but he nevertheless provided a clear picture of what he considered to be a workable libertarian society. Most Spaniards had long wondered about the society which the anarchists* had struggled so long to produce, and now there was an ambitious model.

The genesis of the book came only a short time before the Popular Front* elections of February 1936,* which brought the Left to power. Abad de Santillán's responsibilities in the FAI grew as confrontation and political division polarized Spain, and he found himself entrusted to organize FAI cells in factories and rural areas in preparation for the revolution that now seemed inevitable. His writing assumed the necessity of a class war, and the outbreak of the Civil War found him acknowledged to be one of the Left's most active writers and organizers in Catalonia,* Aragón,* and the Levante.*

The early part of the war was dominated by Abad de Santillán's participation in the Antifascist Militias Committee* and the Economic Council, both of which were instrumentalities of the ad hoc government created by the Civil War in the northeast. While the regional government had been controlled by Catalan separatists, the militia that was sent towards Saragossa* was composed mainly of anarchists, so that militants like Abad de Santillán had to be given places on the committee, a special governing body that only minimally resembled the old Generalitat.* As a member, Abad de Santillán wrote a series of new laws that supported the war effort, developed industrial freedom, simplified the economy, and provided cheaper

foodstuffs. He also provided the theory behind the *talleres confederales*, which were the agencies that collectivized many industries. They provided a centralized workers' council that drew together all of the workers in a particular industry as a means of control, in order to develop a common policy among all of the individual workers' councils in each plant. During the period from July to mid-September 1936, he acted as the temporary economic tzar of Catalonia, indefatigable in his efforts but ultimately unsuccessful because of Madrid's hostility, growing Soviet demands for control, and the sheer impossibility of fashioning a functional economy in a war-torn, highly disrupted situation.

Abad de Santillán, along with others, actively considered resistance to the sudden antirevolutionary threat, playing a major part in a plot to rob the gold reserves of the Bank of Spain* in early October 1936, for instance, and organizing major protests against the Catalan separatist government's weakening of the Antifascist Militias Committee. He quarreled strenuously with fellow FAI members Federica Montseny* and Juan García Oliver,* who accepted cabinet positions in November, comparing them to the much more conservative *Confederación Nacional del Trabajo* (CNT)* (Confederated Workshops) leaders like Juan Peiró Belis* and Juan López Sánchez* who also took places in Francisco Largo Caballero's* government.

In early 1937, Abad de Santillán was acutely discontented, publishing bitter anticommunist attacks in *Tiempos Nuevos* and participating actively in conferences and emergency meetings to preserve the economic enterprises controlled by *incautación* (direct workers' control) and the agricultural communes, particularly when Madrid began to exercise greater control over them. He, among others, pressed for greater development of the syndicates and the old CNT industrial commissions, but on a much more active basis than before. In another area altogether, he fought Luis Companys* and the Catalan separatist government, calling them "treasonable" for their actions in ways he said undermined the Militia Army of Aragón.* Caught in the midst of the May 1937 riots* in Barcelona (May 4-8, 1937), he was the most vociferous advocate of continuing the armed battle against the communists, Republicans, and separatists who attacked the CNT-FAI. He was critical of Montseny and García Oliver for their roles in obtaining a truce in Barcelona, just as he castigated them for becoming so deeply compromised in the mire of Republican politics in the first place. At the same time, he himself had been unsure of proper tactics and amply demonstrated the difficulties of being attuned to the distinctly different calls of social revolution and anti-fascism.

After May 1937, Abad de Santillán lived a kind of half-life, still writing and editing, caught up in efforts to salvage some of the earlier success of the anarchist movement. However, he was also a constant critic of the communist-sympathizing cabinets of Juan Negrín,* for which he occasionally had to avoid the secret police. Much of his later writings reexamined the economics of the revolutionary period of the Civil War in justification of the anarchists' actions. He returned to Argentina in 1939 and resumed a more normal scholarly career, which included authorship of several Argentine national histories. He also continued his career as a libertarian philosopher and so became an important force in the Argentine Left.

For further information, Robert W. Kern, *Red Years/Black Years: A Political History of Spanish Anarchism, 1911-1937* (Philadelphia, 1978); and see Abad de Santillán's later works, which include a number of recent works, such as *Historia del movimiento libertario español* (Madrid, 1976), a considerable portion of reprinted works, and a projected autobiography.

Robert W. Kern

ABC (1903-present). The Madrid* newspaper *ABC* was founded as a weekly publication in 1903. Two years later, it began to publish each morning, and an afternoon edition was soon added for sale in the provinces, often after an overnight train trip from Madrid. Starting in 1929, a separate Andalusian edition was published in Seville.* Prior to the fall of the monarchy, *ABC* was distinguished mainly by its advanced use of photography rather than by controversial political content.

During the Republic, *ABC* was known primarily for its staunchly monarchist stance, but also for its advocacy of clerical policies. These editorial positions, coupled with its national distribution, brought the paper into political prominence as the unofficial organ of the overtly monarchist Right. This prominence, in turn, often brought down upon it the wrath of both Republican mobs and the Azaña* government. Its Madrid offices were burned in the rioting of May 1931, as were its Seville offices in August 1932 after the Sanjurjo* revolt in which a number of army officers and monarchists attempted to overthrow the Republic. For its part, the government suspended *ABC* briefly on both occasions. During the elections of both 1933 and 1936,* *ABC* supported the Right. As the Civil War approached, however, it gave its editorial support to politicians who were plotting to overthrow the

Republic; among the conspirators was the Marqués de Luca de Tena,* owner of *ABC*.

From 1936 to 1939, the fortunes of war determined the paper's fate. The Madrid offices of *ABC* were closed down after Calvo Sotelo's* murder; when they reopened several days later, a Republican paper emerged! Throughout the war, the Madrid version of *ABC* supported the Left Republican position in the various political crises. By February 1939, its editorials admitted defeat and called for the end of the lost war. Although the paper shortage in Madrid forced a reduction in the number of pages and an end to the graphics for which *ABC* was famous, the quality of writing did not diminish markedly. *ABC* never became a mere propaganda sheet.

ABC of Seville supported the Nationalists.* Like its counterpart in Madrid, the quality of the paper remained high by wartime standards. It was one of the best sources of news in the Nationalist zone, and by the end of the war, it claimed the highest circulation of any newspaper in Spain.

After the Civil War, the Luca de Tena family, which had controlled the paper from the beginning, regained control of the Madrid edition. It was supportive of the Franco* regime and now backs the constitutional monarchy. It is the oldest, although no longer the largest, of the Madrid dailies.

For further information, see Jean Michel Desvois, *La prensa en España (1900-1931)* (Madrid, 1977); Henry F. Schulte, *The Spanish Press, 1470-1966* (Urbana, Ill., 1968); and Manuel Tuñón de Lara, *Prensa y sociedad en España (1820-1936)* (Madrid, 1975). A microfilmed copy of the Seville edition is available for the Civil War period from Harvard University.

William J. Irwin

ABRAHAM LINCOLN BATTALION. The Abraham Lincoln Battalion consisted of volunteers* from the United States* fighting for the Republic. The first organized contingent of Americans to volunteer for the International Brigades* sailed from New York City on Christmas Day of 1936, crossed the border from France* into Spain in early January, and reached their training camp in Villanueva de la Jara, not far from Albacete,* a few days later. In the next fifteen months, they were followed by some 3,000 countrymen, the vast majority of whom would see action as members of the 14th International Brigade. While their first and best known unit was the Lincoln Battalion, Americans also filled the ranks of the shortlived George Washington Battalion* and made up the majority of the Mackenzie-Papineau Battalion.*

The U.S. volunteers were a heterogeneous group. While they may not have been as representative of the population as battalion spokesman liked to claim, they did spring from a variety of backgrounds. Over 1,000 had worn blue collars—primarily as miners, steel workers, longshoremen, or seamen—and another 500 were students or teachers. More than 30 percent came from Jewish families, but almost every ethnic group in the nation was represented. Seventy percent of the Lincolns were between twenty-one and twenty-eight years of age. While every region of the nation contributed young men to the ranks, the bulk hailed from large industrial, urban areas. Politically, they were radicals, for more than half were members of either the Communist party or the more loosely structured Young Communist League, but this hardly means they were revolutionaries. Veterans of picket lines, strikes, and unemployment demonstrations of the Great Depression years, they were less committed to Marxist analysis than to a generalized Popular Front* mentality. Few, if any, went to Spain as a way of furthering socialism; instead, their aims were largely defensive. Knowing little of Spanish politics or Francisco Franco,* they were internationally minded enough to believe that anyone supported by Hitler* and Mussolini* was an enemy of civilization, and they wholly subscribed to the wishful slogan that Spain would become "the tomb of fascism."

Compared to their European counterparts, the men of the Lincoln Battalion were much less likely to have undergone any previous military training. The first battalion commander, Robert Merriman, an ex-University of California at Berkeley teaching assistant in economics, was appointed on the basis of four years of college ROTC. Later commanders such as Oliver Law,* perhaps the first black man to lead white Americans into battle, mining engineer Hans Amlio, and twenty-two-year-old Milton Wolff all received their positions after extensive on-the-job training. The same pattern applied to political commissars, with the exception that for such posts Communist party membership was also a prerequisite. The highest commissars, men like Steve Nelson and Dave Doran, both of whom achieved that position at brigade level, were long-time party activists. Such men had to tolerate a good deal of grumbling and dissension in the ranks, for the Americans, true to the national stereotype, did not take easily to even the mildest forms of military discipline.

Lack of military background and the hasty, inadequate training received in Spain did not prevent the Lincolns from compiling a substantial military record. Taking part in three of the four major Loyalist offensives, the battalion—like all the Internationals—sustained heavy casualties;* over the course of the war, slightly over one-third of the American volunteers lost their lives. No action was more disastrous than the first. Rushed to the front to help defend the Valencia Road during the crucial battle of Jarama* in mid-February 1937, the Lincolns spearheaded an ill-advised "suicide" attack on February 27 against rebel forces deeply entrenched on Pingarron Hill. On that single afternoon, three-quarters of the 400-man battalion were injured; this included more than 100 killed.

The next major action for the Lincolns came in the blistering July heat on the plains near Brunete.* Along with the newly formed Washington Battalion, they helped capture Villanueva la Cañada and reached the limits of this the Loyalists'* major push west of Madrid.* Casualties were so high that on July 14 the two American units were merged. Late the following month, the battalion was in the thick of the Aragón* offensive, storming first through the streets of Quinto and then engaging in house-to-house combat in the capture of Belchite.* At the beginning of January 1938, the Americans learned about the icy rigors of winter warfare as they spent a month in a vain attempt to hold the provincial capital of Teruel.* In mid-March, the battalion was shattered during the collapse of the Aragón front that saw rebel troops reach the Mediterranean and cut Republican Spain in two. After three weeks of confused retreats, improvised rearguard stands, and solitary flight, the surviving soldiers escaped only by swimming the swollen spring waters of the Ebro River, for all the bridges across it had been blown.

Rebuilt with Spanish personnel, the battalion numbered 700 by midsummer, but only 150 of these were Americans. Morale, remarkably good for most of the conflict among these highly political men, had now degenerated to the point that commissars worried over the trustworthiness of their troops. Rumors that the International Brigades were about to be withdrawn from Spain were already current when the Lincolns crossed the Ebro in boats late in July as part of the Republic's last-gasp offensive. Again the Americans reached the limits of the advance, but they were unable to seize their objective, the town of Gandesa.* Soon rebel aircraft and artillery dominated the battlefields. In the almost lunar landscape of the Sierra de Pandols, they held on for several weeks until, on September 24, they were removed from battle for the last time.

For further information, see Alvah Bessie, *Men in Battle* (New York, 1939); Cecil Eby, *Between the Bullet and the Lie* (New York, 1969); Arthur H. Landis,

The Abraham Lincoln Brigade (New York, 1967); Edwin Rolfe, *The Lincoln Battalion* (New York, 1939); and Robert A. Rosenstone, *Crusade of the Left: The Lincoln Battalion in the Spanish Civil War* (New York, 1969; republished Washington, D.C., 1980).

Robert A. Rosenstone

ACCIÓN ESPAÑOLA. In the words of its founders, *Acción Española* constituted "a school of modern counterrevolutionary thought." Its founder was Eugenio Vegas Latalpié,* a monarchist journalist from Burgos. Its members were effectively the general staff of the extreme anti-Republican Right before the Civil War. They elaborated a body of authoritarian, anti-Marxist, and antidemocratic thought that provided both the justification for the military rising of July 18, 1936, and the ideological substance for the national syndicalist state founded by the victorious rebels.

Acción Española grew out of the urgent desire of a number of supporters of General Miguel Primo de Rivera to combat the rise of liberalism and republicanism throughout 1930. When republicanism triumphed, on April 14, 1931, ex-ministers of the old dictatorship of José Calvo Sotelo,* José María de Yanguas y Messía, and the Conde de Guadalhorce met with authoritarian monarchist theorists Eugenio Vegas Latalpié, Ramiro de Maeztu, and the Marqués de Quintanar to decide on ways to recapture lost ground. Out of that meeting and with money provided by aristocrats, landowners, and industrialists, an effort was made to create a body that could spread the idea of the legitimacy of a rising against the Republic, especially within the army, and to build a party that would be a legal front for meetings, fund-raising, and conspiracy.

The journal *Acción Española* appeared on December 15, 1931, and the cultural society of the same name was founded on February 5, 1932. In both articles and meetings, they advocated a blending of traditionalism with more modern authoritarianism to produce a government along the lines of the Primo de Rivera regime. Attempts to ally with the Carlists* were hampered by dynastic considerations. Nevertheless, they shared a hostility to the democratic regime and took part in the preparations for the abortive military coup of August 10, 1932, known as the *Sanjurjada*. That failure strengthened the group's determination not to make the same mistakes again, and a conspiratorial committee was set up to organize the next coup. In addition, since the failure led to the expulsion of *Acción Española* members from the Catholic right-wing organization *Acción Popular*,* a political party known as the *Renovación Española** was created in March 1933.

The *Renovación Española* had thirteen deputies elected in the Cortes* elections of November 1933, who thought it their mission to propagate the ideas of *Acción Española* and to undermine democracy. In May 1934, a political amnesty permitted the return of Calvo Sotelo,* a charismatic figure who attempted to unite all elements of the Right into a national bloc committed to the imposition of an authoritarian corporative state. He had little success with the *Confederación Española de Derechas Autónomas* (CEDA)* in power, but after the Popular Front* victory in the elections of February 1936* he came into his element. While *Acción Española* members provided the finances and the organizational facilities for a military rising, Calvo Sotelo and the other *Renovación Española* deputies worked hard to persuade the middle and upper classes that only an insurrection could save them from annihilation. This ensured that the counterrevolutionary doctrines of *Acción Española* received nationwide publicity.

The assassination of Calvo Sotelo on July 13, 1936, provided a rallying cry for the conspirators. *Acción Española* members were rewarded for their contribution to the rising by appointments to important posts in Franco's* early ministries. The notion of the national bloc was put into effect by the so-called *unificación* of all right-wing forces in April 1937. Thus, in many respects, the rising and the state that grew from it carried the imprint of *Acción Española*.

For further information, see Raúl Morodo, *Acción Española: orígenes ideológicos del franquismo* (Madrid, 1980); and Paul Preston, "Alfonsine Monarchism and the Coming of the Spanish Civil War," *Journal of Contemporary History* 7, Nos. 3/4 (1972).

Paul Preston

ACCIÓN POPULAR. *Acción Popular*, a right-wing, Catholic party started during the days of the Second Republic (1931-1936),* was closely allied and became fused with the *Confederación Española de Derechas Autónomas* (CEDA),*, the party formed by José María Gil Robles.* In combination with CEDA, the *Acción Popular* represented the largest coalition of monarchist conservatives in the Second Republic. By the time the Civil War started, the party had faded into nonexistence as factions on the right emerged. It called constant attention to the fact that hundreds of thousands of Spaniards found fault with the policies and programs of the Republic. From its core of followers would later emerge many supporters of the Nationalists.*

For further information, see Richard Robinson, *The Origins of Franco's Spain* (Newton Abbot, England,

1970); José María Gil Robles, *No fue posible la paz* (Barcelona, 1971); and Javier Tusell, *Historia de la democracia cristiana en España*, 2 vols. (Madrid, 1974).

                                        James W. Cortada

ACRACIA (1933(?)-1939). *Acracia* was an anarchist newspaper founded in Lérida* by José Peirats.* The paper was closely associated with the *Confederación Nacional del Trabajo* (CNT)* and reflected many of its views. It was a primary mouth piece for the CNT in many Catalan communities during the Civil War, often containing more propaganda than news. Yet, like many Spanish papers of the time, its mission was to rally support for the cause of the Republic.

For further information, see José Peirats, *La CNT en la revolución española*, 3 vols. (Toulouse, 1951-1953), and *Los anarquistas en la crisis política española* (Buenos Aires, 1964).

See also Anarchists.

                                        James W. Cortada

AFRICANISTAS. *Africanista* was the sobriquet applied to those young Spanish Army officers who spent the formative years of their careers involved in the pacification of Spain's Moroccan Protectorate (1909-1927). Indirectly influenced by the 1898 defeat, the actions and attitudes of this group were also shaped by (1) eighteen years of colonial war; (2) the immediate, difficult, and prolonged nature of their Moroccan combat service; (3) a marked antipathy for what they judged to be the weakness of the parliamentary system and the restoration political parties;' and (4) a defensive attitude concerning Spain's Moroccan involvement and the army's role in Spanish society.

While a few of these individuals enthusiastically supported the establishment of the Second Republic* (Vicente Rojo* and José Miaja,* for instance), most were skeptical of it and championed viewpoints that stressed domestic law and order and a resurgent nationalism. Many of these *africanistas* (Emilio Mola,* Manuel Goded,* José Enrique Varela,* Juan Yagüe,* and Antonio Aranda*) were either involved in the plotting of the military revolt of July 1936, held command positions in the Nationalist forces, or were appointed to political positions in the Francoist governments.

For further information, see Julio Busquets, *El militar de carrera en España: Estudio de sociología militar*, 2d ed. (Barcelona, 1971); and Stanley G. Payne, *Politics and the Military in Modern Spain* (Stanford, Calif., 1967).

See also Army of Aragón (Nationalist); and Morocco, Spanish.

                                        Shannon E. Fleming

AGRICULTURE. *See* Catalonia; Economy, Nationalist; Economy, Republican; Institute for Agrarian Reform; Libertarian Movement; Peasantry, Aragonese; and Workers, Catalan.

AGRICULTURE, NATIONALIST POLICY. Agrarian policy in Nationalist Spain during the Civil War should be analyzed based on two considerations: first, in contrast to the Republicans,* the Nationalists* did not have to face grave food* supply problems; and second, the Republic's liquidation of agrarian reforms had an impact on the populace.

With respect to production, at the beginning of the conflict the area under rebel control included the great wheat zones of central Spain, as well as the principal producers of many other essential foodstuffs. Thus, from the first moment, the Nationalist side could depend upon more than two-thirds of the wheat and bean output, half of the corn crop (from Galicia*), a substantial part of sugar production (Andalusia,* Aragón,* and Castile*), and important percentages of potatoes, cotton, and other crops. Of the important agricultural products, only citrus products (Valencia*), olives (Andalusia), rice (Valencia), and truck crops from other Mediterranean coastal areas remained under Republican control. In terms of total agricultural production, it may be estimated that the rebel side could count on more than 70 percent of the net value of Spain's agricultural output to furnish food to an initial population* of some 12 million (slightly less than half the nation's census). Moreover, this population was more dispersed than that of the Republicans, for the rebel zone was rural in contrast to the urban Republican zone. If control of Galicia, Estremadura,* Old Castile, and Navarre* is also added in, the Nationalists were assured access to a substantial portion of available livestock. What is more, the dairy industry fell into Nationalist hands in the northern sector during 1937. Unlike the Republicans, then, the Nationalist population* had an assured food supply.

One of the key features of Nationalist agrarian policy was the liquidation of the Republic's reforms. These reforms, stemming from legislation in 1932, had not been implemented intensively, especially during the period 1933-1936, until the triumph of the Popular Front* in February 1936. It was in March of that year that programs of agrarian reform began to be implemented. Even so, it may be estimated that at the time the Civil War began, the seizure of lands in accordance with agrarian reform plans did not affect more than 400,000 hectares. It was not until after the start of the war that expropriations and occupation of properties reached important levels.

It was evident that the military rebels could not support the principles of the Republic's agrarian reform. On the other hand, the expropriations effected up to the moment the Civil War began, especially those that were in process or that could be implemented in the Republican zone, required energetic neutralizing measures. Thus, one of the first directives of the new Nationalist regime (August 1936) was to suspend implementation of reform plans that had not yet been effected. A short time later (September 1936), a much more drastic decree nullified seizure of all properties after February 1936, which constituted the greater majority. Before that date, the area seized had not exceeded 120,000 hectares.

The new regime did not limit its agrarian policy to the annulment of the Republican agrarian reform. The Nationalists developed a new "reform" program for the agricultural sector. According to Ramón Tamames, their agrarian policy supposed passage of a sociojuridical reform for the purpose of distributing lands to laborers. The objectives of this technical reform were internal colonization of certain areas of Spain, expanded irrigation, and improved export facilities.

In order to terminate Republican agrarian reforms and implement new policies, the Nationalist regime created the *Servicio Nacional de Reforma Económica Social de la Tierra* (National Service for Economic Social Land Reform) in April 1938. Among this agency's objectives were the study of agricultural structures and the development of specific agricultural reform programs; the allocation of agricultural plots; the nationalization of productive resources; and irrigation. It was given responsibility for reforming transportation, structuring the family farm, and establishing a program for rural beautification. For a long time, however, the service's activities involved only the return of seized properties to their former owners.

The service continued functioning until the end of the Civil War, at which time it was replaced (October 1939) by the *Instituto Nacional de Colonización* (National Institute of Colonization). With the Republic's agricultural reforms totally eliminated, the new regime implemented its agricultural policy through lot concentration in regions characterized by minifundia (small farms) in order to exploit appropriate land sizes most economically; irrigation of lands in dry areas, making these properties available for purchase by set-

tlers on easy credit terms; assistance in the mechanization of agriculture and improved agricultural methods; and, in general, an increase in lands under cultivation, with improved output through more effective methods. Such a program had irregular results and was continued throughout the 1940s and 1950s.

Another problem confronting the Nationalists concerned lands found abandoned in new territories that came under their control. The owners of these lands had fled, fearing imprisonment or execution. For the purpose of exploiting these properties, in May 1938 Nationalists created the *Servicio de Recuperación Agrícola* (Agricultural Recuperation Service) which would reap the crops, operate abandoned equipment, and manage the farms and industries associated with them. For this reason, all abandoned agricultural properties, or those about which there was some question of ownership, provisionally remained seized by the state, with operating responsibility resting in the service.

Nationalist agrarian policy was also concerned with the regulation of wheat. Initially, the basic problem centered on the issue of grain surpluses. In August 1937, a decree-law was promulgated which was designed to assure the wheat producer a minimum fair price, regulated wheat production and distribution, and provided control for the purchase and distribution of the grain. In accordance with these norms, the newly created *Servicio Nacional de Trigo* (National Wheat Service) established the amount of land to be cultivated, acquired total production from the farms, sold the wheat to the mills, fixed prices for purchase and sale, and, in general, directed the entire wheat economy.

During 1937-1938, the Nationalists' military advances led to the addition of large masses of population. As a result, supply needs accelerated sharply, and it became necessary to allow the expansion of wheat production. A new decree in October 1938 granted a premium to farmers who increased their output in the sum of 5 pesetas for each metric quintal of increase over their previous crop. The National Wheat Service formulated a grain policy which, with some variations, lasted throughout the Franco* regime. Although the policy was theoretically conceived to regulate cultivation, rationalize supplies, and help the small farmer, it soon became an instrument favoring large producers.

For further information, see Ramón Tamames, *Estructura económica de España*, 2 vols. (Madrid, 1978) and *La República: La Era de Franco* (Madrid, 1973); and Hugh Thomas, *The Spanish Civil War* (New York, 1977).

See also Daily life, Nationalist Zone.

Fernando Eguidazu

AGUADO MARTÍNEZ, VIRGILIO (1900-1936). Aguado, a career Civil Guard* officer, sided with the Nationalists.* He commanded men sent to Teruel* in the early days of the revolt (1936) to stop the advance of the Republicans* through Valencia,* but he was killed in the process. The Loyalists* were unable to capture Valencia.

For further information, see Ricardo de la Cierva, *Historia ilustrada del la guerra civil española*, 2 vols. (Barcelona, 1970).

James W. Cortada

AGUIRRE Y LECUBE, JOSÉ ANTONIO (1904-1960). Aguirre was a leading Basque Nationalist politician and president of the Basque government during the Civil War. Trained as a lawyer, he formed his first government of the Republic of Euzkadi in October 1936 and then pledged its support to the Spanish Republic in exchange for local home rule. He had mixed results in running the little Basque republic. Industrial production remained low during the Civil War, Basque soldiers were integrated into Republican armies, and the Nationalists* kept invading Basque territory, slowly seizing it all. His relations with the Republican government at Valencia* were usually strained because of conflicting interests. Valencia wanted more control over Basque affairs and simultaneously suspected that the Basques were trying to negotiate a separate peace with the Nationalists. Aguirre's republic was the only part of the Republican zone that remained conservative and Catholic and that kept its churches open. Consequently, there were always doubts about Basque loyalty to the Spanish Republic.

In June 1937, the Nationalists attacked Bilboa* where Aguirre chose to take a stand, but, soon after, it fell to the insurgents, thereby bringing the Basque republic to an end. Aguirre moved his "government-in-exile" out of the Basque country to Barcelona.* He remained president of the Basque government until his death in 1960. After his move to Barcelona in 1937, however, he never again had a significant role in Spanish affairs.

For further information, see José Antonio Aguirre y Lecube, *De Guernica a Nueva York pasando por Berlín* (Buenos Aires, 1944); and Stanley G. Payne, *Basque Nationalism* (Reno, Nev., 1975).

See also Basque Nationalism.

James W. Cortada

AID, FOREIGN MILITARY. Foreign military aid was essential to the war effort of both sides. Generals Mola* and Franco* individually requested Italian and German aid during July 19-22, 1936. With the consent of Mussolini* and Hitler,* the first German aircraft were dispatched on July 27 and Italian aircraft on July 29. Republican premier Giral* pleaded for French aid on July 20, and the first French aircraft were sent on August 4. Aid shipments steadily increased, and each side became completely dependent on their continuance.

Aircraft shipments to each side were in rough balance in August 1936, but France* soon curtailed its aid as it followed a course of nonintervention. By late September, the USSR* replaced France as the main supplier of arms to the Republicans,* and by early November Soviet aid was rising to match the increased flow to the Nationalists* from Italy* and Germany.* The Axis nations were dispatching more aircraft, but Soviet fighters (I-15, I-16) were superior. The Soviet Union sent many more heavy guns and tanks (T-26, BT-5), the best of the war.

Following the Nationalist failure to capture Madrid* in November 1936, Italo-German aid rose to stay ahead, the German Condor Legion* being formed in November and the Italian *Corpo Truppe Volontarie* (CTV) in December. In early 1937, the preponderance of foreign aid increasingly favored the Nationalists. By mid-March, 54,000 men of the CTV had been sent to Spain. German and Italian air legions continued to outnumber those of their opponents, and the newer models (S.79, He-111, Bf-109) outclassed Soviet aircraft. The Soviets remained superior only in tanks. The Nationalists received sufficient supplies of American oil and trucks, and the Republicans of Soviet and Rumanian oil.

To offset the increased flow of arms to Franco, the Soviet Union stepped up its shipments, which peaked in May and June and perhaps tilted the balance by July or August 1937. A major campaign against Soviet supply lines, including Italian clandestine naval war in August-September and increased Nationalist naval attacks in September-October, resulted in the Soviet abandonment of the mediterranean route in October. Soviet shipments were resumed in December 1937, following a cumbersome northern route to France, and overland to Spain when French politics allowed. In 1938, military aid to Franco became significantly greater and more reliable than that to his opponents.

Although the total accumulated military aid to each side produced a rough balance, its total value favored the Nationalists. Approximate total shipments to the Republic included 1,200 aircraft, 380 tanks, 1,800 artillery pieces, and 4 fast motorboats. Perhaps 39,000 foreigners served the Republic, 36,000 of whom were members of the International Brigades* and 3,000

Soviet personnel. No more than 18,000 served at any one time. Total aid to the Nationalists included about 1,500 aircraft, 300 tanks, 2,000 artillery pieces, four destroyers, two submarines, and nine fast motorboats, the Italian contribution exceeding the German. At least 96,000 foreigners served the Nationalists, including 79,000 Italians and 16,800 Germans. Except in early 1937, no more than 46,000 served at any one time. These figures do not include Moroccan troops or the crews of Italian and German warships engaging in clandestine naval warfare.

For further information, see Jesús Salas Larrazábal, *Intervención extranjera en la guerra de España* (Madrid, 1974).

See also Merchant Marine, Spanish; and Submarines, Foreign.

Willard C. Frank, Jr.

AIGUADÉ MIRÓ, ARTEMIO. Aiguadé served in the Catalan government, known as the Generalitat,* as head of the interior, a cabinet-level position. He was a leading member of the Esquerra* party and thus ran into conflict with more radical elements such as the *Partido Obrero de Unificación Marxista* (POUM)* and the *Confederación Nacional del Trabajo* (CNT).* As councillor for internal security, Aiguadé held considerable police* authority between 1936 and 1937. He left office after the Spanish Republic regained control over Catalonia* following the May 1937 riots* in Barcelona.*

For further information, see Carlos Pi Sunyer, *La república y la guerra* (Mexico, 1975).

James W. Cortada

AIR FORCE, NATIONALIST. The Nationalist Air Force grew out of those men and aircraft that either joined or happen to be in insurgent-held territory. The air force was commanded by army officers and was in fact a part of the Spanish Army. At the start of the Civil War, fewer than 100 of the 200 or so working aircraft were in Nationalist hands. At first, Franco* had no full fighter squadrons, perhaps only as many as ten fighters. Each side divided fairly evenly miscellaneous other aircraft. Neither had substantial supplies of bombs, while out of a total of 240 pilots,* ninety fought with the Nationalists.* Within days of the war's start, the Germans agreed to supply the Nationalists with additional aircraft of various types: troop transports, fighters, and bombers. Nine German Junkers and eight Italian Savoias were quickly brought into action, allowing the Nationalists to control the air space in lower Andalusia* in the early days of the Civil War.

By the fall, Italian Fiat fighters and German bombers arrived in quantity, making it possible for the Nationalists to extend their control over air space in southern and central Spain. Moreover, properly trained German pilots in the "Pedros and Pablos" squadron—made up of foreign pilots—outperformed Republican and French pilots, thereby expanding Nationalist air control over Estremadura* and the Tagus front by the fall of 1936. By the end of the year, the Nationalists had nearly 400 planes, of which about 100 were piloted by members of the German Condor Legion,* another 150 by Spaniards, and 120 by Italians. Aircraft included the Fiat CR-32 fighter, the Italian Savoia 79 bomber, Germany's* Heinkel 111 bomber, and the more famous Messerschmitt 109. The last-named was by far the most superior fighter aircraft in Spain by the spring of 1937, faster and more flexible than Republican or Russian planes. It had powerful armament and bullet-proof gas tanks.

By July 1937, the Republicans* had lost both their numerical and technical superiority over the Nationalists. Throughout the war, the Nationalists used a total of 1,300 airplanes, while the Republic operated approximately 1,500. (Both were large air forces by contemporary European standards.) With the superior quality of the Nationalist aircraft, Franco could control the air space over Spain from the spring of 1937 onward, making it possible for land battles to be supported effectively with aerial attacks and bombings. The Germans shipped approximately 600 planes to Spain, of which 136 were the fast Messerschmitts, a variety of bombers, and sixty-three Junkers 52. Italy* sent Franco 660 planes, of which 350 were the Fiat CR-32 and about 100 Savoias 79. German and Italian aid to the Nationalists therefore played a major role in the Civil War.

Nationalist pilots participated in every major battle of the Spanish Civil War, often determining the outcome of ground fighting. They bombed Madrid* almost from the first days of the Civil War and, later, other major Republican urban centers such as Valencia* and Barcelona.* With the encouragement of the Germans, they experimented with new aerial warfare, employing such tactics as bombing cities as a means of breaking enemy morale (which failed). Condor Legion pilots bombed Durango* (March 1937) while they conducted a similar attack next on Guernica* (April). They fought at Jarama,* Vizcaya,* and Brunete* (where the Republicans lost nearly 100 airplanes and the Nationalists twenty-three), in the Basque Campaign, in the Aragón* and in the

Levante,* at the battle of the Ebro,* and finally in the Catalan campaign.

Nationalist ace pilots emerged as heroes, many having flown nearly 500 sorties and having participated in over forty combat missions each. The most famous were Joaquín García Morato,* Angel Salas Larrazábal,* and Carlos de Haya González.*

For further information, see Juan Antonio Ansaldo, *Para Que?* (Buenos Aires, 1951), a pilot's account; Joaquín García Morato, *Guerra en el aire* (Madrid, 1940), a pilot's account; José Goma, *La guerra en el aire* (Barcelona, 1958), a more "official" Nationalist history; José Larios, *Combat Over Spain* (London, 1966), a pilot's account; Jesús Salas Larrazábal, *La guerra de España desde el aire* (Barcelona, 1969), the best account; and Graf Max von Hoyos, *Pedros y Pablos* (Munich, 1941), another pilot's account.

James W. Cortada

AIR FORCE, REPUBLICAN. At the beginning of the Civil War, the Republican Air Force was stronger than the Nationalist Air Force but played a less important role in the fighting. The Republican Air Force, a branch of the army, began the war with fifty fighters and nearly 100 aircraft for reconnaissance, along with thirty planes that could be classified as light bombers. The Republican Navy* had approximately 100 aircraft, the majority of which were seaplanes. Given the fact that nearly a third of the Republican planes were not serviceable in July, this left a total force of approximately 200 (private and military) craft in contrast to the approximately ninety-six in the employ of the Nationalists.* Four fighter squadrons remained in Republican hands, along with four De Havilland Dragon bombers and an additional four Douglas DC2s and miscellaneous pieces of equipment. Of the some 240 military pilots in July, 150 remained with the Republic and the other ninety joined the Nationalists. As the war progressed, others in retirement and in civilian life joined with recruits on both sides, while additional volunteers for the Republicans* (primarily from France* along with some Soviets) joined the fighting. Most of the Republican forces were based in and around the metropolitan areas of Barcelona* and Madrid.* Neither side had any significant supplies of bombs, machinegun bullets, or fuel to support their forces at any of the bases.

In the first months of the Civil War, Republican and French pilots* attempted to provide defensive support for Madrid, while Nationalist pilots flew aggressively and with modern planes brought in from Italy* and Germany.* Thus, air superiority in central

Spain increasingly passed to the Nationalists. Yet, the Republic recognized the importance of aircraft. In the first days of the war, it asked the French government for planes and encouraged pilots to volunteer for service in Spain. By September, a number of reorganizations within the Republican government reflected the needs of war. One of the most important involved the appointment of Major Ignacio Hidalgo de Cisneros* as commander of air units, who now took charge of a general staff reporting to the cabinet.

During 1937, while the Soviets provided additional support by sending over 100 aircraft to Spain, Republican units expanded their forces. The two most widely used Soviet fighters were the Chato I-15 biplane and the I-16 monoplane nicknamed the "Mosca." At the time, they were reputed to be the fastest aircraft in Europe (the Chato flew up to 220 miles per hour), with the ability to drop 25-pound bombs. Supplies of these craft continued to arrive during 1938 as well. These planes continued to be improved, with some models traveling at 300 miles per hour and with greater maneuverability than many other comparable aircraft. In most instances, as with the German planes flown for the Nationalists, the pilots flying them came from the same country as the planes. In addition, the Soviets provided the Republic with a number of bombers and technical crews. The Soviet fighters were superior to the German planes, while the Italian Fiat, although not as fast, provided some outmaneuverability to the Chato. The introduction of large quantities of Soviet airplanes returned air superiority to the Republic for brief periods of time during 1937 and 1938.

The situation in the air can be summarized as follows: the Republic began with air superiority, although the introduction of a few French planes and pilots hardly bolstered this force. Russian aircraft gave the Republicans clear air superiority again during the winter of 1936, while the influx of Italian and German planes insured that the Nationalists would dominate the skies more often than not in 1937 and 1938 throughout Spain and invariably over Madrid and Barcelona.

The Republic failed to maintain air superiority for a number of reasons. First, Soviet aircraft and pilots were used conservatively, even sparingly, while Republican pilots essentially fought a defensive war. Second, there were considerable losses of aircraft and pilots on the Republican side, despite the fact that each side had a similar number of planes in the war (approximately 1,300 for the Nationalists and 1,500 for the Republicans as compared to 2,000 in Germany, 1,500 in Great Britain,* and 3,000 in the French Air Corps). The air force was divided between central and northern Spain, and as the war progressed, more power was concentrated around Madrid and to the northeast of the capital. By early 1937, for instance, of the 450 Republican airplanes, 200 were fighters and 100 bombers, with Spanish pilots flying in north central Spain, under the command of Hidalgo de Cisneros.* The majority of the pilots working in central Spain, near Madrid, were Russians under the command of Soviet officers. Many of the Spanish pilots who began replacing Soviets after May 1937 were communists and had been trained in the USSR.* By mid-1937, Russian influence was also evident in the number of planes being used. Of the 200 fighters, 150 were Russian; sixty out of 100 bombers were also made in the Soviet Union.

Republican air units participated in each major campaign of the war. Around Madrid they warded off Nationalist bombers, although not effectively, and at the battle of the Jarama* (February 1937) they maintained air superiority against all types of Nationalist aircraft, despite the uncanny accuracy of the German 88-millimeter anti-aircraft guns. At Guadalajara* in March, the Republican Air Force hampered the effectiveness of the Italian ground forces, and to Mussolini's great embarrassment, his men lost this battle. Few of these aircraft were used in the campaigns in the north during 1937 as they were needed in central Spain. Bombers had the additional problem of insufficient range to travel to the northern fronts, drop their bombs, and come back to their bases. Thus, they remained concentrated in the fighting in and around Madrid and in the Levante* to the east.

As the war continued, the balance of power in the air shifted first in the number of bombers, with the Nationalists gaining the upper hand. The Nationalists' heavy use of bombers in the Basque country (at Durango* and Guernica,* for example) and in destroying portions of Madrid and Barcelona, attest to these changing circumstances by the end of 1937 and early 1938. The Italians' heavy bombardment of Barcelona in March 1938 was hardly challenged by Republican fighter pilots. At the time, internal dissension within various Republican agencies and confusion over command and use of fighter planes made it impossible for the Catalan city to receive proper protection from the Nationalists. Thereafter, most Republican aircraft were relegated to coastal defense as the amount of surface land in Spain under Loyalist control shrank rapidly in 1938.

The last major campaign of the war, that of Catalonia,* began at Christmas time in 1938, when the Nationalists began their final push toward Barcelona and the French frontier. In this fight, they had air superiority which the Republicans challenged with only some eighty aircraft in the north and with a shrinking staff of enthusiastic but inexperienced pilots. The final act of the Republican Air Force was to fly various groups of government officials out of Madrid and Mediterranean coastal towns to exile in France.

For further information, see Oloff de Wet, *Cardboard Crucifix* (London, 1938), a Republican memoir; Andrés García, *Mitos y verdades* (Mexico, 1974), a Republican pilot's account; André Malraux, *L'Espoir* (Paris, 1937), a novel covering Malraux's contribution, along with that of his volunteer French pilots; Salvador Rello, *La aviación en la guerra de España*, 4 vols. (Madrid, 1969-1971), technical details of the war; Jesús Salas Larrazábal, *La guerra de España desde el aire* (Barcelona, 1969), a complete history of the air war; Miguel Sanchís, *Alas rojas sobre España* (Madrid, 1956), technical details of the war; and F. G. Tinker, *Some Still Live* (New York, 1938), a Republican memoir.

See also Malraux, André.

James W. Cortada

AIZPÚN SANTAFÉ, RAFAEL. Aizpún Santafé, a well-known lawyer, represented Navarre* in all three legislatures of the Second Republic.* He was elected as an independent rightist in 1931, even though he had well-known ties to the Carlists,* and as a member of the *Confederación Española de Dereches Autónomas* (CEDA)* in 1933 and 1936. In addition, he served as minister of justice from October 1934 to April 1935, and as minister of industry and commerce from May to September 1935, both under Prime Minister Alejandro Lerroux.

Like many members of the CEDA, Aizpún Santafé despaired of a peaceful solution to Spain's political crisis of 1936. He vehemently opposed the actions of the Azaña* and Casares Quiroga* governments, and he attended the final session of the *Diputación permanente* of the Cortes* in order to cast his vote of no-confidence in Prime Minister Casares Quiroga. A number of accounts portray him as an emissary from the CEDA, offering party funds to General Mola* to aid in preparing the uprising.

During the war, Aizpún Santafé resumed his law practice in Pamplona.* In 1938, he was named to the tribunal headed by Ildefonso Bellón to demonstrate the illegality of the Popular Front's* activity once it assumed power in 1936. After the Civil War, he continued his law practice in Madrid* and Pamplona, and he eventually published a work on his favorite academic subject (the *fueros*—laws and rights—of Navarre*). He died in obscurity in 1975.

For further information, see Rafael Abella, *La vida cotidiana durante la guerra civil: La España nacional* (Barcelona, 1978), on Aizpún Santafé's wartime activities; Gil Robles, *No fue possible la paz* (Barcelona, 1968); Alexander Leroux, *La pequeña historica* (Madrid, 1963); and Richard Robinson, *The Origins of Franco's Spain: The Right, The Republic and the Revolution* (Newton Abbot, 1970), on Aizpún Santafé's political activities.

See also Basque Nationalism.

William J. Irwin

ÁLAVA. Álava, one of the Basque provinces of Spain, is located to the east of Navarre* in the northern part of the Iberian Peninsula and just below Vizcaya* and Guipúzcoa.* Like its sister provinces in the Basque country, it shared a language and culture indigenous to the region and alien to Spanish Castile.* Its people identified with the Basque nationalist movement both before and during the Civil War. These mountain people were invariably poor, highly religious members of the Catholic Church,* and stood apart from the main political events of early twentieth-century Spain. As in most Spanish provinces in pre-Civil War Spain, illiteracy posed a considerable problem by making it less possible for culture to travel via the printed word into this area. Before 1936, residents of Álava, like their Basque brethren in other provinces, were hostile to any possible infractions over local customs and rights of political and administrative autonomy posed by the central government in Madrid.*

In July 1936, the Basque population* in northern Spain remained within the Republican camp. The one glaring exception was Álava. Its capital city of Vitoria* fell to the Nationalists* under the command of General Angel García Benítez* with the help of Colonel Camilo Alonso Vega,* an old friend of General Francisco Franco,* who was then head of the Nationalist offensive in Andalusia.* The capture of Álava dictated that it would not play the same role in the war as did the other Basque areas which remained in Republican hands until completely overrun by the rebels in the following year. Both sides campaigned for over a year in this province. Republican forces would, for example, overrun a village and execute Nationalist supporters, while, more frequently, rebel forces did the same, often decimating the male population of pro-Republicans. Yet, for all intents and purposes, the province remained in Nationalist hands from the early days of the war. The only real threat to the rebels came in December 1936, when troops under the command of General Llano de Encomienda* launched an offensive against local Nationalist forces led by Alonso Vega. The rebels maintained control over the province in spite of this one military adventure.

For further information, see José Martínez Bande, *El final del frente norte* (Madrid, 1972); and Stanley G. Payne, *Basque Nationalism* (Reno, Nev., 1975). *See also* Basque Nationalism.

James W. Cortada

ALBA, DUKE OF (Jacobo Stuart Fitzjames y Falcó) (1878-1953). The Duke of Alba (Jacobo Stuart Fitzjames y Falcó), a member of a distinguished family of politicians and diplomats, was born in Madrid* and grew up in Europe* and Latin America.* During the Civil War, he served as the Nationalist agent in London. Throughout the war, he kept communications open between the Franco* and London governments. However, he made no significant headway in obtaining British recognition until the end of the war. He then officially became Spain's ambassador to Great Britain,* remaining there throughout World War II. In addition to his political activities, he was an historian and wrote various books on the Spanish nobility.

For further information, see Círculo de Amigos de la Historia, *Diccionario biográfico español contemporaneo* (Madrid, 1970), Vol. 3; and William L. Kleine-Ahlbrandt, *The Policy of Simmering: A Study of British Policy During the Spanish Civil War, 1936-1939* (The Hague, 1962).

James W. Cortada

ALBACETE. Albacete, a province located in southeastern Spain in the region of Murcía* and south of Valencia,* was in Republican hands throughout most of the Civil War. Pockets of rebellion developed in July 1936. The most important opposition came from a group of Civil Guards* in the city of Albacete, but they were overcome on July 25, 1936. The area soon became the locale for a Republican military camp to which members of the International Brigades* were brought for training and where they had a headquarters. Soviet advisers and tank groups also came here. It was conveniently located approximately halfway between Madrid* and Valencia and was usually safe from Nationalist attack.

Thousands of volunteers* from other countries were trained for the Republican Army* almost entirely in Albacete where such commanders as Emilio Kléber* and André Marty* commanded troops. The actual number at Albacete will never be fully known; however, of the 35,000 to 40,000 who came to Spain, over half of these men trained in Albacete during the first eighteen months of the war. The camp manager was a Frenchman, Vital Gaymann, who eventually fled the area after embezzling funds, leading to the appointment of General "Gómez" (Wilhelm Zaisser),* the previous commander of the 13th International Brigade. The camp had volunteers from over a dozen nations, with a multitude of languages and national prejudices to complicate life in Albacete. Communists attempted to dominate the group, while various national elements (for example, the Germans and French) quarreled among themselves. The base finally moved to Barcelona* in March 1938 when it became certain that the Republican zone would be divided in two by the Nationalists.* By the end of the month, Franco's* troops had occupied the entire province.

Franco's army next sought to rid the area of Republican sympathizers. Public officials were arrested and many shot. The local civil governor, Julío Martínez Amutio, later commented that at his trial in December 1939, of the thirty-six co-defendants, thirty-two were executed.

For further information, see Andreu Castells, *Las brigades internacionales de la guerra de España* (Barcelona, 1974); Jason Gurney, *Crusade in Spain* (London, 1974); José Manuel Martínez Bande, *Los cien últimos días de la república* (Barcelona, 1972); and José Sánchez Sánchez, *Elecciones y partidos en Albacete durante la II Republica, 1931-1939* (Albacete, 1974).

James W. Cortada

ALBAR, MANUEL. Albar was a minor leader in the Socialist party* during the Civil War and a devoted follower of Indalecio Prieto y Tuero.* During the Civil War, while Prieto was minister of war in the Republic, Albar worked within his ministry coordinating the activities of various agencies. Albar was also associated with the *Partido Obrero de Unificacíon Marxista* (POUM).

For further information, see Burnett Bolloten, *The Spanish Revolution: The Left and the Struggle for Power During the Civil War* (Chapel Hill, N.C., 1979). *See also* Socialist Party.

James W. Cortada

ALBIÑANA Y SANZ, JOSÉ MARÍA (1883-1936). Albiñana, a doctor, was born and raised in Valencia.* He founded one of the first proto-fascist parties in Spain, the Nationalist party, in Burgos* in 1930, receiving considerable attention at the time for his or-

ganization which was also known as the *Legionarios de España*. At the start of the Civil War, he was arrested in Madrid* and soon after executed.

For further information, see Círculo de Amigos de la Historia, *Diccionario biográfico español contemporaneo* (Madrid, 1970), Vol. 1.

James W. Cortada

ALBORNOZ Y LIMINIANA, ÁLVARO DE (1879-1954). Albornoz, the Republic's ambassador to France* during the Civil War, was born in Luarca in the province of Oviedo* and became a lawyer. He joined the Radical Republican party, served in the Cortes* during the 1920s, was minister of production in the Republic's first cabinet in 1931, and subsequently became minister of justice. Between 1936 and 1939, he attempted to minimize the negative impact of the French policy of nonintervention in Spain and to gain support and supplies for the Republicans.* He proved unable to alter fundamentally French diplomacy, but he did develop a great deal of public support for the Republic which resulted in some supplies and volunteers* coming to Spain.

For further information, see David W. Pike, *Les Française et la guerre d'Espagne, 1936-1939* (Paris, 1975).

James W. Cortada

ALCALÁ DE HENARES. Alcalá de Henares, located approximately 20 miles from Madrid,* was the birthplace of Cervantes and Manuel Azaña,* president of the Second Republic.* It served as home for a Russian air base in the Civil War. During the fighting around Guadalajara* and other points near Madrid, Republican Air Force* planes used this town as a base of operations. It also became one of the first villages to be bombed by German airplanes for the Nationalist cause.

For further information, see F. Bravo Morata, *Historia de Madrid* (Madrid, 1968), Vol. 3; and Robert Colodny, *The Struggle for Madrid* (New York, 1958).

James W. Cortada

ALCÁZAR, THE. The Alcázar, the Spanish Army's school for infantry officers since the 1800s, was the scene of a dramatic siege during the early months of the Civil War. When the fighting broke out in July 1936, rebel forces in Toledo* experienced some early successes, forcing Republican units to concentrate on securing the city. Nationalist forces commanded by

Colonel José Moscardó,* director of the gymnastics school and the local military governor, retired into the fortress-like structure overlooking the Tagus River* and the city and soon after was barricaded in by the Republicans* (July). The Nationalists* numbered about 1,300, only six of whom were cadets at the academy (the rest being in vacation), 800 members of the Civil Guard,* 100 or so officers, some 200 political rightists, 600 women and children, and a few hostages. Meanwhile, Toledo remained under Republican control.

Various Republicans attempted to convince Colonel Moscardó to surrender, but he refused. On July 23, a Republican lawyer, Cándido Cabello, telephoned Moscardó, threatening to execute the colonel's son if he did not surrender. Moscardó, after instructing his son to "die like a hero," told Cabello that he would never surrender and hung up the telephone. Such events quickly made the siege a tale of heroes throughout Nationalist Spain. Meanwhile, food* supplies dwindled, although water was plentiful. The Republicans bombarded the structure and fired at it with rifles and cannon but to no avail. The 1,000 to 1,500 Republican militia laying siege to the Alcázar met with no success throughout July and August and never attempted to storm the building. The defenders, however, could not leave and had to hang on, surrounded by the Republicans. Nationalist airplanes periodically dropped news into the fortress to lift the defenders' spirits.

By September, the Nationalists had to decide whether to relieve the Alcázar or to push on to Madrid,* both of which were nearby, Toledo being only 25 miles away. On September 20, Francisco Largo Caballero,* the Republican prime minister, arrived in Toledo insisting that the Alcázar be captured immediately. The next day, Franco* ordered his forces to march on Toledo, regardless of the possibility that this diversion might cost him the opportunity to seize Madrid by giving the Republicans additional time to prepare the capital's defenses. Franco believed that the rescue of the Alcázar would provide a tremendous psychological advantage and a morale booster for his followers. Republican forces grew in number in Toledo, and they blew up one of the main towers of the Alcázar. On September 27, Nationalist relief forces could be seen on the horizon, Toledo was cut off from the north, and the Republican militia was broken. By the end of the day, Franco's Army of Africa* had relieved the Alcázar. The next day, Moscardó reported to General José Varela Iglesias,* commanding the relief forces, that everything was normal (*sin novedad*).

This military diversion did indeed cost the Nationalists their opportunity to seize quickly the city of Madrid. But Franco believed that if Moscardó had been allowed to die with his men, the Nationalist cause would have lost enormous prestige and support. As it turned out, the episode was heroic and was treated as such in both Nationalist propaganda and foreign newspapers. Toledo suffered a blood bath at the hands of the Nationalists. Varela's troops took no prisoners* as they occupied the city, Republican officials died, and the Moors,* serving Franco, killed wounded militiamen in the local hospital.

For further information, see Cecil Eby, *The Siege of the Alcázar* (London, 1966).

James W. Cortada

ALCÁZAR DE SAN JUAN. Alcázar de San Juan is a small town in the province of Ciudad Real* where, during the early months of the Civil War, many Republican atrocities were committed against religious and pro-Nationalist citizens. A locally elected council of administration was established there in 1936 for the purpose of collectivizing land and industry. What makes these events significant, even though they were repeated in countless other communities, is that this particular town is often cited by historians writing on the subject of the Civil War. The atrocities committed here were given considerable press coverage at the time and editorial writers cited the events as typical of other occurrences in Spain. For these reasons, it has continued to be seen as both a symbol and an example of events of this type.

For further information, see Hugh Thomas, *The Spanish Civil War* (New York, 1977).

James W. Cortada

ALFONSO XIII (ALFONSO DE BORBÓN) (1886-1941). Alfonso XIII, whose departure from Spain in April 1931 ushered in the Second Republic,* was born king in Madrid* following the death of his father, Alfonso XII, some six months previously. He came officially of age in 1902, at the age of sixteen, and thereafter he sought as active a role as his constitutional powers allowed, displaying a taste for political intrigue and marked sympathy towards the military. In 1923, with little alternative but equally little reluctance, he accepted Primo de Rivera's coup d'état. Thus began his progressive abandonment by much of Spain's political and intellectual elite and a significant part of the officer corps. Between the dictator's fall in January 1930 and April 1931, as the governments of General Damaso Berenguer and Admiral Aznar* tried to steer Spain back to constitutionalism, Alfonso's personal position deteriorated still further. The municipal elections of April 12, 1931, while ultimately producing a nationwide monarchist majority thanks to the notoriously manipulative politics of rural spain, nevertheless returned antimonarchist majorities in most Spanish towns and cities where it was generally acknowledged that elections were fairer and therefore more representative of opinion. Alfonso, persuaded by most of his advisers that only his discreet withdrawal from Spain could prevent large-scale violence and perhaps, in the long run, preserve the crown, left for exile on April 15. In doing so, he insisted that he was not abdicating.

The Second Republic was declared on April 14. Alfonso instructed his supporters not to obstruct the new regime, but he was stung when in November 1931 the Constituent Cortes* tried him *in absentia*, found him guilty of high treason against the Spanish people, declared his property confiscated, and banished him for life. In exile, Alfonso received frequent visits from sympathetic politicians; from autumn 1932 onwards, he showed a willingness to countenance monarchist conspiracies, but he consistently displayed greater confidence in the gradualist tactics of Gil Robles* and the *Confederación Española de Derechas Autónomas* (CEDA),* with the Carlist pretenders, Don Jaime and Don Alfonso Carlos, aimed at ending the century-old dynastic rift, came to nothing between 1931 and 1934, but Alfonsine-Carlist relations improved as Alfonso himself adopted more openly authoritarian opinions.

When the Civil War broke out, Alfonso's sympathies naturally lay with the insurgents. Nevertheless, Franco,* after assuming the headship of state within Nationalist Spain in September 1936, announced that no monarchical restoration could be expected in the foreseeable future and that Alfonso XIII himself could never resume the throne. By the end of the war, Alfonso, now living in Rome, was seriously ailing. During the 1930s, the eldest son of his marriage in 1906 to Victoria Eugenia of Battenberg had died, and his second son had renounced his rights to the throne. Consequently, when Alfonso XIII formally abdicated shortly before his death in February 1941 it was in favor of his third son, Don Juan. The present king of Spain, Juan Carlos I, is Alfonso XIII's grandson.

For further information, see Julián Cortes Cavanillas, *Confesiones y muerte de Alfonso XIII*, 2d ed. (Madrid, 1951); and Vicente Pilapil, *Alfonso XIII* (New York, 1969).

See also Carlists; Monarchism.

Martin Blinkhorn

ALIANZA INTERNACIONAL DE TRABAJADORES (AIT). The *Alianza Internacional de Trabajadores* (AIT) (International Alliance of Workers) was a small labor organization associated with the *Confederación Nacional del Trabajo* (CNT)* in southern Spain. Before July 1936, it advocated the use of strikes to gain better working conditions for its members. After the Civil War began, it controlled some agricultural collectives, particularly in the region of La Mancha.* Little is known about this group, its membership, its role in agricultural politics and economics, or its impact within the CNT organization.

For further information, see Edward Malefakis, *Agrarian Reform and Peasant Revolution in Spain* (New Haven, Conn., 1970); and José Peirats, *La CNT—la revolución española*, 3 vols. (Toulouse, 1951-1953).

James W. Cortada

ALICANTE. Alicante, a province located in southeastern Spain next to Murcía,* had one of Spain's most important southern ports. The port of Alicante became a strong center of Republican support from the first days of the Civil War; most of the province also remained in the hands of the Republicans* until the very end of the war. In addition, José Antonio Primo de Rivera* was detained in Alicante's jail in June 1936. It was in this city that he went on trial and died by firing squad on November 20, 1936, giving the Nationalists* a popular martyr. The Nationalists wreaked a heavy vengeance on the city when they overran the province in March 1939, in part because of José Antonio's death. In the final weeks of the Civil War, thousands of Republican refugees* poured into this province—the last Republican zone in Spain—hoping to escape from the Nationalists by sea. While some did, many were trapped in the port city when, on March 30, the Nationalists captured the remaining portions of the province, bringing the Civil War to an end.

For further information, see Emilio Chipont Martínez, *Alicante, 1936-1939* (Madrid, 1974); and Vicente Ramos, *La guerra civil en la provincia de Alicante*, 3 vols. (Alicante, 1974).

James W. Cortada

ALLEN, JAY (1900-   ). Allen, an American journalist in Spain writing for the *Chicago Tribune*, was particularly noted for the reports he filed on the mass executions by the Nationalists* at Badajoz* in mid-August 1936. By taking the city, Franco* was able to unite the northern and southern armies of the Nationalists on Spanish soil without the use of Portuguese territory. Allen reported the details of the battle for the city and described the execution of thousands of prisoners in the local bullring (approximately 1,800 may have actually been killed). His account of this event was reprinted around the world and led many to believe that the Nationalists were harshly conducting the war. Allen was also the last journalist to interview José Antonio Primo de Rivera* prior to the Spaniard's execution on November 20, 1936.

For further information, see Robert Payne, *The Civil War in Spain, 1936-1939* (New York, 1962).

James W. Cortada

ALMERÍA. Almería, a province located in the southeastern corner of Spain on the Mediterranean Sea due east of Granada,* was in Republican hands throughout most of the Civil War. On July 20, 1936, pro-Nationalist *Carabineros* (Carabineers, or Customs Guards) commanded by Colonel Toribio Crespo Puerta, occupied some public buildings in the provincial capital. Soon after, he surrendered after Republican troops arrived from Granada backed up by the Spanish destroyer *Lepanto* which threatened to bombard the rebels. Thereafter, the area remained a Republican stronghold. Pro-Nationalists were rooted out and the Catholic Church* persecuted. Almería's bishop, for example, was one of twelve in Spain killed by the Republicans.* Many of the labor groups in Almería, especially the organized dock workers in the provincial capital, were communist. Most of the large farms and many businesses were collectivized from the earliest days of the war.

The fighting came to Almería in earnest in 1937. Together with Jaén,* Almería made up the entire Republican zone in southern Spain in the second half of the Civil War. On May 31, 1937, Germany's* pocket battleship, the *Admiral Scheer*, accompanied by four destroyers, bombarded the city, killing nineteen people and destroying approximately thirty-five buildings. The Germans had taken the action as reprisal for Republican attacks on their naval vessels. The Nationalists* turned their attention to Almería in the spring of 1939, occupying the port city on March 31. On the way through this area in March 1939, the Nationalists caught up with approximately 50,000 Republican refugees* trying to escape Spain by way of the Mediterranean Sea.

For further information, see José Manuel Martínez Bande, *Los cien últimos días de la república* (Barcelona, 1972).

See also Navy, German.

James W. Cortada

ALMIRANTE CERVERA. The Nationalist cruiser *Almirante Cervera* (7,475 tons standard, 8-152mm [6 in] guns, 33 kts.) was launched in 1925. It was in drydock in El Ferrol* during the uprising of July 1936. The ship surrendered after fierce fighting, becoming the only cruiser immediately available to the Nationalists.* At first she operated in the Bay of Biscay bombarding the coast, especially in support of the besieged Simancas Barracks in Gijon.* The *Almirante Cervera* next participated in the decisive battle of Cape Espartel* (September 29, 1936), damaging the Republican destroyer *Gravina* and opening the Straits of Gibraltar* to Nationalist traffic. She remained in Mediterranean waters from October 1936 to March 1937, sinking two Republican patrol boats, supporting the capture of Málaga,* raiding Republican supply lines and coastal targets, and defending Nationalist convoys from Italy.* The ship returned to the Bay of Biscay from April to October 1937 for her busiest and most delicate operation: preventing British blockade runners from gaining Republican ports under escort by the British Navy.* There were numerous naval confrontations, most of which the Royal Navy won. Returning to the Mediterranean in November 1937, the *Almirante Cervera* again operated against Republican coasts and shipping lanes. She was damaged in a Republican air attack on February 22, 1938, and was present at the battle of Cape Palos* on March 6, 1938.

See also Navy, German; and Navy, Spanish.

Willard C. Frank, Jr.

ALONSO VEGA, CAMILO (1889-1971). Alonso Vega was born on May 29, 1889, in El Ferrol* (Corunna*) and graduated in 1910 as an infantry officer from the Spanish Military Academy along with his good friend and fellow Galician, Francisco Franco.* Throughout their lives, they remained close associates and very warm friends. From military school they were both posted to El Ferrol, and then in 1912 they were sent to the fighting in Spanish Morocco.* They returned to Spain with established reputations: Franco as a man of bravery and dash, and Alonso Vega as a methodical officer. When Franco was assigned to assist Lieutenant Colonel Millán Astray* in the creation of the Spanish Foreign Legion* in 1920, he requested that Alonso Vega join him again in Africa. They were to serve with distinction in the Riff campaigns, where once again most of the glory went to Franco. In 1927, General Franco was directed to establish a new Military Academy at Saragossa.* He requested that Alonso Vega (now an infantry major) be appointed to the academy staff. Shortly thereafter, Alonso Vega was promoted, through seniority, to the rank of lieutenant colonel; he held this rank at the time of the uprising in 1936.

Alonso Vega immediately cast his lot with the Nationalists,* and in the Civil War to follow he was both tested and proven as a combat officer. Early in the conflict, he assisted in the capture of Vitoria,* which was to become a vital base for Nationalist operations in the north. In December 1936, he was promoted to brevet colonel and was given command of the newly formed 4th Navarre Brigade. He quickly made this brigade one of the outstanding units of what was to become the Navarre Division. His force fought well in the Bilbao* campaign and gained much respect not only from the Nationalist command but also from the German air units which supported the offensive.

Alonso Vega's military records take note that during the Bilbao operation his command captured Villareal and Nafarrate. These victories were followed by taking the *Puertos* of Banazar and Zumelzu. With his brigade he captured Elgueta and Monte Gorbea, Llodio, Oquendo, and Valmaseda. These towns are in the Basque regions of Guipúzcoa,* Álava,* and Vizcaya.* In April 1937, he was promoted, for meritorious service, to the rank of colonel of infantry. His brigade was now marked as one of the forces to continue on in the offensive in the north.

The Popular Front* offensive of Brunete* (July 6, 1937) brought a quick change to these plans. With surprising efficiency Alonso Vega and the other brigades that were rushed into the threatened area made a rapid change of front. By late July, not only was the enemy offensive contained, but also the lost territory was recaptured. The Brunete operation, while costly for the Nationalists, was even more so for the forces of the Popular Front.

Alonso Vega's brigade was again moved into the northern sector. There it joined the Navarre* force commanded by General Solchaga.* This was one of the divisions constituting the Nationalist Army of the North* which was now commanded by General Dávila.*

Colonel Alonso Vega led his brigade through the difficult fighting in the Cantabrian Range and the capture of Santander.* Shortly after this operation, he was promoted to brevet brigade general and was given command of a Navarre Division. He moved this division south for the Nationalists' massive offensive of the Aragón* and their breakout on the coast of the Mediterranean Sea. After fighting again through rugged mountains, Alonso Vega led his division into the fishing village of Vinaroz on April 15, 1938. The enemy forces were cut in two. He then turned south and captured the picturesque villages of Peñiscola and

Castellón.* Further south, the Nationalist offensive against Valencia* had to be broken off because of strong defenses, high losses, and the powerful enemy offensive across the Ebro River to the north.

To the north, the Nationalists experienced major reverses on a front extending from Fayón to Mora la Nueva in the direction of Gandesa.* In the heat of August 1938, General Alonso Vega's division was thrown into the Nationalist counteroffensive. His division fought through the slate mountains known as the Sierra de Pandols on the southern sector of the breakthrough. There the Navarrese suffered heavy losses in the face of determined enemy counterattacks. At great cost, the Nationalists finally shattered and reversed the enemy offensive of the Ebro River. In February 1939, Alonso Vega was promoted to brigade general of infantry.

General Alonso Vega was considered a very quiet, austere, methodical, and dedicated commander. His brigade, and then division, was considered one of the outstanding units of the Nationalist Army.* It conducted itself brilliantly in battle, and the critical Germans regarded it as a highly trained, disciplined, motivated, and very well-led force. They viewed Alonso Vega as a fighting general.

Politically, General Alonso Vega was often viewed as ultraconservative and, by some people, as being reactionary. After the Civil War, he continued to serve the Nationalist government. In 1957, he was appointed minister of the interior. During this time, he demonstrated sympathy and support for the *Opus Dei.* In 1969, he was named *Capitán General del Ejército.* He died two years later, on July 1, 1971, in Madrid.

For further information, see José Manuel Martínez Bande, *La guerra en al norte* (Madrid, 1969) and *La ofensiva sobre Segovia y la batalla de Brunete* (Madrid, 1972).

See also Álava; and Abro, Battle of.

Raymond L. Proctor

ALTO DE LEÓN PASS, BATTLE OF. The battle of Alto de León Pass, the first real battle of the Civil War, took place in late July 1936 northwest of Madrid* at a pass through the mountains deemed critical to the defense of the capital. The pass was held by Republican soldiers and militia. The Nationalists* marched and attacked the pass on July 22, inflicting heavy casualties* on their enemy. Both sides fought hard, executing wounded and prisoners.* The Republicans* had to retreat toward Madrid, in large part because of the confusion within their ranks as to who was to command troops at the battle since at this early stage of the war there was no discipline among these mixed units. The murderers of Calvo Sotelo* died in this battle, as did a famous Falangist, Onésimo Redondo. With the loss of this mountain pass, the Republicans* gave the Nationalists access to the plains near Madrid.

For further information, see José Manuel Martínez Bande, *La lucha en torno a Madrid* (Madrid, 1968) and *La marcha sobre Madrid* (Madrid, 1968).

James W. Cortada

ÁLVAREZ ARENAS ROMERO, ELISEO (1882-   ). Álvarez Arenas Romero, a career army officer, sided with the Nationalists* and commanded troops throughout the Civil War. In 1939, when the Nationalists occupied all of Catalonia,* he became the military governor of the region. He was responsible for eliminating enemies of the new state, establishing a new currency, destroying separatist and radical literature and posters, printing new newspapers, and reestablishing peace and order in the area.

For further information, see Raymond Carr, *The Spanish Tragedy: The Civil War in Perspective* (London, 1977); and Hugh Thomas, *The Spanish Civil War* (New York, 1977).

James W. Cortada

ÁLVAREZ BUYLLA Y LOZANO, PLÁCIDO (1890-1938). Álvarez Buylla, born in Oviedo,* spent most of his life in the diplomatic service. Prior to the Second Republic,* he had worked primarily in German and Belgian posts. From 1931 to 1933, he held the political position of director-general for Morocco* and the colonies. Out of office from 1933 to 1935, he served as minister of industry and commerce under Prime Ministers Azaña,* Casares Quiroga,* and Giral* in 1936. He resumed his diplomatic activity during the Civil War, representing the Republic in Uruguay and France* before dying in Paris in 1938.

For further information, see Norman J. Paddleford, *International Law and Diplomacy in the Spanish Civil Strife* (New York, 1939); and Francisco Virgilio Sevillano Carbajal, *La diplomacía mundial ante la guerra española* (Madrid, 1969), the diplomacy of the war.
See also Latin America.

William J. Irwin

ALVAREZ DEL VAYO, JULIO (1891-1974). Álvarez del Vayo was a member of the Socialist party* and one of the principal diplomats of the Second Republic* during the Civil War. He began his career as a journalist and owed a great deal of his rise in politics, just prior to the war, to Largo Caballero.* He also had longstanding ties to the communists. Before the war, he had visited the USSR* as part of the effort made by some Spaniards to decide whether or not to affiliate with the Comintern. After the fighting started in July 1936, he increasingly supported the Communist party in Republican politics.

On September 4, 1936, Álvarez del Vayo joined the Republican cabinet as its foreign minister. He remained in that position until May 17, 1937, only to come back on April 5, 1938, staying until the end of the Civil War. Thus, he had the primary responsibility for developing and implementing Republican foreign policy. Its objectives were to deny any international support to the Nationalists* and especially to block any legal or diplomatic recognition while gaining as much political, economic, and military aid as possible for the Republic. For Álvarez del Vayo personally, this meant spending a great deal of time at Geneva arguing the Republic's cause before the League of Nations* while privately negotiating with the French, British, and Russians for support.

Soon after becoming foreign minister, Álvarez del Vayo made a speech before the League of Nations in which he argued that in effect the Non-Intervention Agreement made the Republicans* and Nationalists* equal before the international community. He stated the Republic's case for buying arms outside Spain while denying the same right to the Nationalist "rebels." Nothing came of the meetings in Geneva as the Non-Intervention Agreement remained in force. Meanwhile, Álvarez del Vayo developed close political relations with the Russians—so much so that Largo Caballero reprimanded him in front of the Soviet envoy saying, "you (Álvarez del Vayo) ought to remember that you are a Spaniard, and minister of foreign affairs of the republic, instead of arranging to agree with a foreign diplomat to exert pressure on your own Prime Minister." Largo Caballero even advised Manuel Azaña,* president of the Republic, to dismiss Álvarez del Vayo on the grounds of disloyalty. Azaña did not do so, possibly because of Álvarez del Vayo's strong communist support. Increasingly, Álvarez del Vayo ignored the reprimand and sided with the communists in internal Republican politics against Largo Caballero. His support of the communists probably had little to do with the amount of aid the Russians gave the Republic since he felt a new social order was needed in Spanish society along the lines articulated by the political left.

In December 1936, Álvarez del Vayo went before the League of Nations to protest Germany's* and Italy's* recognition of the Nationalist government. The league failed to condemn Berlin and Rome. When Álvarez del Vayo left the Foreign Ministry as a result of a change in cabinets, he remained the Republican representative at Geneva where he continued the fruitless task of supporting the Republic's international position. He protested German and Italian aid to the Nationalists just before the Nyon Conference* (September 1937) was held. At that meeting, all the major powers agreed to curtail naval intervention in the Civil War that had caused the destruction of neutral shipping (mainly by the Italians). On May 13, 1938, he again spoke to the league, protesting that nonintervention was not being honored. While his call for action received much sympathy, little came of the gesture. In September 1938, when it rapidly became apparent that the Republic might lose the Civil War, he made one last appeal.

Then in February 1939, Álvarez del Vayo approached the British to see if a mediated settlement of the Civil War could be negotiated. Simultaneously, he arranged for the removal of the Prado Museum's holdings from Spain. Within days he left Spain, but he continued to negotiate a settlement from Paris. The Nationalists rejected all of his overtures, insisting on the Republicans' complete and unconditional surrender. After the war ended, Álvarez del Vayo went into exile in New York, living there until his death in 1974.

Álvarez del Vayo was perhaps Spain's least effective head of the Foreign Ministry in this century. He paid little heed to his administrative responsibilities within the ministry, and despite his eloquence at Geneva, he failed to persuade any government to alter its respective foreign policies toward Spain. A more serious failing was his excessive attention to internal politics within the Republic. He sided with the communists to such a degree that after the Civil War the Spanish Socialist party expelled him from membership. As commissar of war, he filled many Republican positions with communists, often causing other Loyalist leaders to question his allegiance to the government. While in exile, Álvarez del Vayo wrote extensively in defense of his actions and the cause of the Republic, and about the inevitability of democracy and freedom returning to Spain.

For further information, see Julio Álvarez del Vayo, *Freedom's Battle* (New York, 1940), *Give Me Combat* (New York, 1973), Álvarez del Vayo's memoirs, and *The Last Optimist* (London, 1950); Burnett Bolloten, *The Spanish Revolution: The Left and the Struggle for Power During the Civil War* (Chapel Hill, N.C.,

1979); and Dante Puzzo, *Spain and the Great Powers, 1936-1941* (New York, 1962).

See also Communist Party, Spanish.

James W. Cortada

AMADO Y REYGONBAUD DE VILLEBARDET, ANDRÉS (1886-1964).
Amado became the first finance minister of the Franco* regime, chosen by Ramón Serrano Suñer* in January 1938. He served until August 1939 when Franco reorganized his cabinet.

After acquiring a law degree, Amado became director of the tax department in the Ministry of Finance in 1923. Its minister, José Calvo Sotelo,* promoted him to one of the directorships of *Campañía Arrendataria del Monopolio de Petróleos, S.A.* (CAMPSA),* the state oil monopoly established in 1927. He served in that capacity until 1930 when the fall of the cabinet weakened his position.

On the eve of the Civil War, Amado still allied himself politically with the quasi-reactionary and quasi-fascist nationalist founder of CAMPSA, Calvo Sotelo. Amado became one of the early conspirators working to overthrow the Republican government even before Calvo's assassination on July 13, 1936. After the army's uprising in North Africa, he turned Falangist and served the Nationalist *junta* in Burgos* as financial commissioner until his official appointment in January 1938.

A major problem for Amado was how to pay for foreign war supplies when Franco lacked both gold and sufficient foreign exchange generated by exports of raw materials. In this connection, as finance commissioner Amado made a secret visit to Lisbon in August 1936 to deposit 30 million pesetas ($3.6 million) for war purchases. He had to ration foreign exchange carefully in order to purchase the maximum war materials from Great Britain* and the United States* as well as from the Axis. He believed in the fascist theory of economic self-sufficiency and pay-as-you-go barter agreements. Throughout the Civil War, he advocated rejection of all foreign credits and loans, particularly from Britain, fearing that Spain would thereby sacrifice her independence. The Germans had little use for Amado, believing he understood little about finance. In the interest of national pride, he rigidly opposed devaluation of the peseta* as a necessary cost for the war. When Franco fired him on August 10, 1939, both Britain and Germany* viewed his departure with satisfaction.

For further information, see Ramón Serrano Suñer, *Entre silencio y propaganda* (Barcelona, 1977); Angel

Viñas, *El oro de Moscú* (Barcelona, 1979); and Robert H. Whealey, "How Franco Financed His War, Reconsidered," *Journal of Contemporary History* 12 (January 1977): 133-52, and "La diplomacía española del petróleo: De junio de 1927 a abril de 1931," *Cuadernos económicos de información comercial española* 10 (Madrid, 1979): 511-31.

See also Foreign Trade, Nationalist; and Portugal.

Robert H. Whealey

AMBOU, JUAN. Ambou was one of the few communist leaders in Asturias* who advocated resistance against the Nationalists* during the latter stages of Franco's* campaign in the area in September-October 1937. He was overruled by local authorities who ordered a general retreat, thereby clearing the way for the Nationalist takeover of Asturias.

For further information, see Ramón Salas Larrazábal, *Historia del ejército popular de la república*, 4 vols. (Madrid, 1974).

See also Communist Party, Spanish.

James W. Cortada

ANARCHIST BRIGADES. On July 24, 1936, the Antifascist Militias Committee,* set up in Barcelona* immediately after the suppression of the rebellion, dispatched a 3,000-man column under Durruti* and Pérez Farras* to eastern Aragón,* in an unsuccessful attempt to take rebel-held Saragossa.* The column was soon joined in Aragón by the anarchist Ortiz and Ascaso Columns (the latter at Huesca*). Other *Confederación Nacional del Trabajo* (CNT)*-*Federación Anarquista Ibérica* (FAI)* units of varying size in Catalonia* and Aragón included the Roja y Negra, Negus, and the column under Captain Bayo* which undertook an unsuccessful invasion of Majorca.*

Within a few days of the rising, over 100,000 joined CNT-FAI militias,* which were instrumental in securing many areas for the Republic, including Toledo,* Guadalajara* and Alcalá de Henares.* In the Levante,* anarchists* formed the Torres-Benedito Column and the Iron Column, many of whose 3,000 members were hardened criminals. In Guadalajara, Cipriano Mera,* leader of the Madrid* CNT construction workers, organized the Rosal Column, while thousands joined the CNT-FAI militia in Santander* and Asturias* (including the Hignio Carrocera Column) as well as in Estremedura* and Andalusia* (including the Maroto Column).

In response to pleas for assistance, the Catalan Militias Committee sent 3,000 men under Durruti to Madrid in mid-November. Demanding its own sector, the unit broke under a Nationalist attack but then held, and Durruti was killed in fighting on November 20. At least 10,000 CNT-FAI adherents were now fighting on the Madrid front and in addition to Durruti's contingent included a dozen or so small to battalion-sized units, including the Lopez Tienda, Libertad, Aguilas de Libertad, Milicias Vascas, Milicias Libertad, Juventil Libertario, Sargento Vasquez, Andres y Manso, El Aguila, and Triana.

Beginning in September, the Valencia* government issued a series of decrees designed to transform politically affiliated militias into regular units—battalions, brigades, and divisions—of a People's Army. Envisioned by some as a specific means of diminishing anarchist influence, the conversion to regular units encountered strong resistance in the CNT, which feared a regular army, particularly with its growing communist influence, as a threat to the social revolution. However, the decision to pay and supply only militias that subjected themselves to unified command and structure, and recognition by a number of anarchists themselves of the need for disciplined units, influenced a reluctant rank-and-file. The CNT endeavored to retain hegemony over their units and in May 1937 claimed to have an army of 33,000 under its own commanders just on the Madrid front (constituting one-third of the strength of the Army of the Center*). However, the process of dilution was underway. A Soviet tabulation of fifty newly organized brigades in the Army of the Center in mid-1937 indicated only two that were overwhelmingly CNT in composition and only five others in which the CNT accounted for between 25 and 85 percent of the effectives. Nevertheless, the principal CNT brigades in the Republican Army,* many formed from the earlier militia units, appeared to be in the 5th Division during the battle for Madrid, the 3d Corps at Jarama,* and Cipriano Mera's 14th Division at Madrid, Guadalajara,* and Brunete.* The 16th Brigade (34th Division) at Brunete had a large CNT contingent, and CNT elements were particularly numerous in many of the thirty-six brigades of the Catalan Army of the East,* especially in the 25th Division which fought at Belchite* and Teruel,* and the 26th (Ascaso), 30th, 43d, and 44th Divisions. CNT elements also predominated in the 149th Brigade, which suffered heavy casualties* in the attack on Huesca in June 1937, and in the 16th and 83d Brigades (the latter the old Iron Column) of the 64th Division in the Army of the Levante.*

Anarchists were also numerous in the various units of the Army of the North* prior to its collapse, especially the 16th and 17th Corps (including the 55th

Division) of Asturias. They were well represented in the 7th and 8th Corps (especially the 28th Division) of the Army of Estremadura, but apparently were less numerous in the 9th Corps of the Army of Andalusia* (which did include elements of the earlier Maroto Column). Although in command of six of twenty-one army corps in mid-1938, anarchists commanded only nine of seventy divisions, and thirty-three of 196 brigades, with two-thirds of these in the armies of the Levante and Estremadura. In spite of their large numbers in the Army of the East, anarchists commanded only one of its nine divisions and five of its twenty-seven brigades. There is evidence that communists and *Partito Socialista Unificat de Cataluñya* (PSUC)* elements harassed and purged CNT cadre at various times during the war.

In the last action of the war, in Madrid, Cipriano Mera's 4th Corps, including several of Mera's original brigades, acceded to the orders of the CNT leadership to support the Casado* *Junta* and defeated the communist-led lst, 2d, and 3d Corps.

For further information, see D. Abad de Santillán, *Por que perdimos la guerra* (Buenos Aires, 1940); Burnett Bolloten, *The Spanish Revolution: The Left and the Struggle for Power During the Civil War* (Chapel Hill, N.C., 1979); Editorial Codex, *Crónica de la guerra de España*, Nos. 31, 37, 46, 78, 87, 96 (Buenos Aires, 1966-1968); José Manuel Martínez Bande, *La lucha en torno a Madrid* (Madrid, 1968); Stanley Payne, *The Spanish Revolution* (New York, 1970); Vicente Rojo, *Alerta los pueblos* (Buenos Aires, 1939); and *España heróica* (Buenos Aires, 1942).

Verle B. Johnston

ANARCHISTS. Anarchists attempted to create a revolutionary society in Catalonia* and Aragón* just as Nestor Makhno had done in the Ukraine in 1919 before being crushed by the Bolsheviks. Spanish anarchists had identified with the Russian Revolution, even though the militants totally rejected the party politics of the USSR.* At the same time, the anarchists themselves were forced to take charge of administrative positions in order to keep their revolution from being captured by other political groups. Increasingly, anarchists played a part in Republican Spain's political life, sometimes to the despair of the most orthodox groups who, like many foreign anarchists, felt that the Spanish movement had lost its bearings and was being absorbed into the Republic's government.

The sectarian differences that arose were often bitter, and as a consequence, the anarchists usually found themselves surrounded by controversy. Their position on the issues of the Civil War changed many times, but after the May riots* of 1937 in Barcelona,* anarchist representatives were excluded from the Popular Front* and their fortunes declined. However, they did continue, under heavy pressure, to demand revolutionary solutions to many of Spain's problems. The movement refashioned itself quite drastically in this latter stage, but the military defeat of the Spanish Republic forced the anarchist organizations into exile. To a great extent, the international anarchist movement collapsed in 1939 and 1940 because of the loss of its Spanish branch and pressure from fascism and communism.

Many aspects of Spanish anarchism impinge upon the Spanish Civil War. From its beginnings in 1868, the movement took on numerous forms, changing from a peasant-dominated protest group to an anarchosyndicalist labor organization strong among Catalan textile workers, and from an illegal network of terrorists to the *Confederación Nacional del Trabajo* (CNT)* and the *Federación Anarquista Ibérica* (FAI).* The movement encompassed militant feminists like Federica Montseny,* classical nineteenth-century positivists like Anselmo Lorenzo, firebrands like Fermín Salvochea, organizers with great ability like Salvador Seguí, and moderate labor union leaders like Juan Peiró* or Angel Pestaña. During the Civil War era, however, the greatest single figure of Spanish anarchism was Buenaventura Durruti,* a charismatic leader who had been in turn a terrorist, anarcho-Bolshevik, fugitive and political exile, insurrectionist and, finally, militia general.

The peasant origins of anarchism may have come from the "primitive rebel" syndrome which has been so aptly described by Eric Hobsbawm—the dilemma of a precapitalist people caught up in a Spain newly capitalized by the triumph of the liberals after 1836-1837. Michael Weisser, however, argues that peasant discontent was much older (dating back to the sixteenth century) and lay not with a reaction against modernity but in a defense of rural values that stressed collectivism, hostility toward the Church's social neutrality, and defense of local independence.

Whatever the cause, the 1870s found Spanish peasants in difficult straits as land confiscated by liberals to finance public works bond issues often led to the purchase of common lands and ecclesiastical estates by influential politicians. Conditions sometimes changed drastically. At the turn of the century, 0.1 percent of the population owned 33 percent of all arable land, while at the same time 547,548 landless laborers existed in Andalusia* earning less than 1 peseta* a day. These peasants, displaced by capital concentration and the destruction of self-sustenance agriculture, drifted to the cities in slow stages, becoming the industrial proletariat of the early twentieth century.

Like many other European groups, particularly artisans further north, the rapid changes that overcame the Spanish peasants soon had political consequences. Francisco Pi y Margall's federalist doctrines, based upon the anarchist ideas of Pierre-Joseph Proudhon (1809-1865), a Frenchman who attacked the centralized state as the defender of property owners and the chief obstacle to closer cooperation among people, attracted brief attention in 1873. At that time, Pi headed a shortlived cabinet during a period of great turmoil in the midst of an eight-year Bourbon interregnum. But the real center of attention in early Spanish anarchist history was the Russian anarchist Michael Bakunin (1814-1876) whose ideas of spontaneous revolution appealed strongly to the disorganized chapters stimulated by the visit of the Italian, Giuseppi Fanelli, a disciple of Bakunin who brought the anarchist gospel to Spain in October 1868. The possibility of sudden change held out by Bakunin and the discovery of comrades seeking such change in the First International led to a wave of violence which so threatened Spanish society that rival groups of liberals and conservatives soon put aside their differences and united in the restoration of 1876. The *Mano Negra*, or "Black Hand," continued southern Spain's efforts at revolution for almost a decade.

Long after the *Mano Negra* was put down, "propaganda of the deed," a euphemism for individual acts of terrorism,* continued in Barcelona (where a theatre, cafés, and a Corpus Christi procession were bombed) during the 1890s; in groups like *Solidarios** which actively sought revolution in the post-World War I period, going so far as to assassinate the archbishop of Saragossa* in 1923; and culminating with the formation of the FAI in 1927. Members of the FAI kept the Bakuninist tradition alive during the Second Republic from 1931 to 1933 by leading revolts at Alto Llobreget, Casa Viejas, Barcelona, and Saragossa against Republican governments far less oppressive than those in the liberal period from 1876 to 1923. At the start of the Civil War, a good deal of violence against priests, landowners, and the middle class in Catalonia, Aragón, and the Levante* came from this same source. Bakuninism represented the rage of an inarticulate and powerless minority within the movement which could find no other way to express its frustration.

At the other end of the spectrum, Spanish anarchism also possessed an intellectual tradition of sorts. Anselmo Lorenzo's *El proletariado militante* set the sentimental tone, while Federico and Federica Montseny (Urales) added intellectual depth to the movement by the publication of *La Revista Blanca* (1923-1934). Numerous artists and writers shared in the idealistic, yet often surrealistic and zany, qualities of anarchism. Its followers shared bits of popular science, positivism, folklore, and a form of civic religion that was at once optimistic about individuals and pessimistic about many types of institutions. This forced them to create entirely new life-styles such as "life-long companionship," a way around state-registered marriages, or the workers' schools of Francisco Ferrer, the Catalan educator (executed in 1909) who created a very modern form of "alternative" education.* In a traditional country like Spain, urban anarchists represented odd sophistication in a society that was otherwise clerical, awkwardly middle class (because of the fragility and recentness of modernization), or simply out-of-touch. During the Civil War, the profusion of murals (one, in a building occupied by anarchists in Barcelona at the start of the war, was four or five stories high), poster art, revolutionary workers' theatre, and the endless journalistic activity of papers like *Solidaridad Obrera,** *Tierra y Libertad*, and dozens of others all testified to anarchist intellectual efforts.

Somewhere in the middle of the anarchist movement was the labor activity of the CNT. Propaganda of the deed and surreal art did not organize great masses of workers and peasants. Bakuninist philosophy, in fact, isolated the anarchists from the masses by forcing the movement underground, into illegal activities, which prevented contact between the movement and the people in any useful way. Shortly after the turn of the century, Spanish anarchists began to absorb French syndical ideas of creating large industrial unions as a way, Daniel Guérin has said, of winning back popular support and of more deeply influencing the working classes. A new stress came to be placed upon the development of institutions that would serve the mutual interests of the working class and society in general—an influence of Peter Kropotkin (1842-1921), another exiled Russian anarchist whose ideas about the importance of popular institutions rivaled Bakunin's stress on violence. The CNT was not Kropotkin's creation, but its founding in October 1911 did begin a move of the Spanish anarchists away from isolation and the individual desperation of the assassin's calling.

The CNT was the central institution of Spanish anarchist life from 1911 to 1927, when the FAI was created as a more specifically anarchist vehicle. The CNT became the largest labor federation in Spain by 1917, far larger than the socialists' *Unión General de Trabajadores* (UGT).* Electrified by news of the Russian Revolution, the CNT joined the UGT in Spain's first nationwide general strike in August 1917 and was alienated by the UGT's quick capitulation when faced with authority. The postwar years were marked by growing CNT-UGT hostility and a failure to maintain a united front against the series of weak liberal governments which did not have the support of King Alfonso XIII* or the army. Miners left the CNT's first national congress in 1919 for the UGT, leaving the anarchosyndicalists with the textile workers, stevedores, and teamsters to many small artisan groups. There were also loose ties with a southern peasant union, but the bulk of the CNT's activity was urban, not rural. At the national level, Manuel Buenacasa and Salvador Seguí struggled for control of the confederation with contending revolutionary and labor-oriented policies, while on the streets "action" groups of young anarchists fought the government and the police violently. Strikes at the Río Tinto Mines and at La Canadiense Electric illustrated the declining economic conditions that sparked the violence. It was during this period that several self-styled anarchists assassinated Eduardo Dato, the prime minister, while the *Solidarios*, which contained a number of young anarchists destined to become well known in the movement, killed the archbishop of Saragossa. The CNT enabled Catalan workers* to survive the lockout by the Catalan Employers Federation and the establishment of rival *sindicato libres*, but at the cost of many deaths and thousands of arrests between 1919 and 1923.

During this time, the CNT adopted the *sindicato único* as its organizational hallmark. This was the local union that organized all workers of the area into one organization, while also including anarchists, peasants, and any other interested persons. Industrial commissions within the CNT concentrated on the problems of certain industries, but the membership of the locals was not organized around craft affiliation in most cases. CNT unions were open to a very broad range of members, very much like the American Industrial Workers of the World.

In order to organize and negotiate properly, the CNT had to act like a labor union by staying in place to represent the interests of the workers it organized. This was done with some success before 1923, the year when the Primo de Rivera dictatorship was created by the cooperation of the army with the king to cover up military scandals in Morocco.* No further CNT activity was possible until the creation of the Second Republic in 1931. Moderate syndicalists like Juan Peiró and Angel Pestaña then clashed with more revolutionary anarchists over the future direction of the CNT, which would have to continue behaving like a labor union if it was to compete with the UGT's power in the new Republican government.

It was at this point that the Jekyll and Hyde personality of the Spanish anarchist movement caused serious problems. Moderation was not a part of anarchism's tradition. The idea of spontaneous revolution still remained uppermost in the minds of men like Buenaventura Durruti, the son of a railway worker whose involvement in the 1917 general strike had led him into the *Solidarios*, exile, and a belief in permanent insurrection, which he amply demonstrated from the moment he returned to Spain in April 1931.

Behind Durruti was the FAI, the latest of numerous groups that had sought immediate revolution through belief in Bakuninist doctrine. The *Solidarios* had typified the various groups in Spain after World War I which sought to duplicate the Russian Revolution. Some left the CNT to join the new Spanish Communist party,* but many genuinely rejected the party-oriented philosophy of Marxism-*Leninism. Others, like Durruti's group, were so caught up in the struggle against the king and state that philosophy made very little difference, but by 1927 the toll taken by the dictatorship's repression forced the creation of the FAI. This organization was conceived of as a fully Iberian anarchist organization, with affinity groups rather than cells. It essentially took anarchists out of the CNT, even though most still remained in the CNT. But the real purpose of the FAI in 1931 was to take over the CNT in an attempt to use it against the Second Republic. The FAI's hostility to Manuel Azaña's* government was created by the dictatorship's repression, socialist cooperation with both Primo de Rivera and Azaña, and fear that reform would remove any chance of revolution. Wildcat strikes led by FAI members consequently disrupted the CNT's new policy of guarded cooperation with the Republic.

The upshot of this confrontation was the writing of the Declaration by thirty moderates from the CNT who hinted at severing the CNT from the FAI. The FAI reacted by seizing CNT newspapers, offices, and locals. For a time it seemed possible that the two groups would physically battle for supremacy, but the insurrection at Alto Llobregato led by Durruti in January 1932 distracted the FAI members from completing their assault on the CNT. Anarchism had triumphed but at the price of dividing anarchists and syndicalists.* The CNT's "syndicates of opposition" resisted *faísta* radicalism, while the FAI went off on a binge of violence over land reform (Casa Viejas) and forced labor arbitration (Saragossa). The schism unsettled Republican politics and discredited Azaña's statecraft, which allowed the Right to triumph in the elections of November 1933.

This breach within anarchist organizations was never completely healed. Throughout the Civil War, both organizations remained suspicious of one another even while officially united. The tension between "revolutionaries" and labor-oriented anarchists occasionally kept these factions apart, more frequently limited the impact of a unified CNT-FAI, and caused some anarchosyndicalist moderates to move closer to the UGT (largely because of Francisco Largo Caballero's* radicalization) or the small and openly parliamentary-oriented Syndicalist party that flourished briefly.

But in 1935 the FAI finally became so exhausted by its insurrectionalism that it ceased harassing the CNT and was forced underground by the Right. Only Diego Abad de Santillán's* *El organismo económico de la revolución: cómo vivimos y como podríamos vivir en España* and a growing recognition of the need to refurbish anarchist ideas signaled any progress within the movement. What had been low ebb after more than sixty years of anarchist activity slowly began to disappear as the mutualism of Kropotkin replaced the Bakuninist spirit of the Spanish militants. Abad de Santillán's workers' councils, industrial commissions, and plans for large rural communes, while not new, represented a new "possibilist" tendency. Anarchists supported Popular Front candidates in the elections of February 1936* and worked with the UGT in many organizing campaigns on shop floors everywhere. The old violent quality was still there, since *faístas* (members of the FAI) and *cenetistas* (members of the CNT) fought daily in the streets against rightists in the months before the Civil War. But the CNT organized new locals more effectively than before, and the FAI dropped its clandestine character to work for what the Peninsular Commission called "radical solidarity." Without this recovery, the CNT-FAI could never have reacted so militantly at the outbreak of the war.

The anarchists were better prepared than many Republicans* to fight Nationalist rebels in the streets on July 18 and 19, 1936. Durruti and other *faístas* played a particularly strong role in Barcelona, capturing the San Andres and Atarazanas* strongpoints. Atarazanas, however, cost the life of Francisco Ascaso,* creating the FAI's first martyr. The hero, Buenaventura Durruti, was more important, however. He was made commander of a militia army to challenge the Nationalists* for possession of Aragón and its capital, the city of Saragossa. The military history of the Spanish anarchists was bound up in the Army of Aragón,* a rag-tag collection of political activists from numerous parties and factions, all of whom responded resolutely to the revolutionary romanticism of Durruti, the guerrilla leader *par excellence*. Organized into columns with names like *Solidarios* and *Tierra y Libertad*, the anarchist army operated with a minimum of hierarchy but a strong sense of revolutionary discipline. Unfortunately for the army's purpose, the perception of this discipline was frequently diffused by each unit's ideological values.

Of the most serious nature was the lack of trained noncommissioned officers. Few lasted very long, although Durruti did attempt to recruit former regular officers. Equally difficult was the supply problem. As long as Barcelona could provide reserve supplies the army had firepower, but these did not last long. Enterprises that had been placed under direct workers' control (*incautación*, as it was called, a policy of the FAI) did what they could to convert to military production, but Barcelona, industrial as it was, did not have direct communications with the Basque provinces and so lacked durable goods. The government in Madrid, negotiating with the USSR and aware of the Non-Intervention Committee's* hostility to it, blocked all requests for import licenses or funds that could be used to smuggle military equipment into the country. Anarchists dreamed of robbing the Bank of Spain's* gold reserves, but no scheme could relieve the difficulties facing the Army of Aragón.

These difficulties came from the failure to seize Saragossa and Huesca,* which forced the anarchists into a long campaign that an irregular army was ill prepared to conduct. The political power that Aragón's fall would have given the CNT-FAI might have allowed the anarchists a really secure power base, particularly since Catalonia was a region that had to be shared with the Catalan separatists, who did not share the anarchists' zeal for a social revolution. Stalemated by General Cabanellas'* brilliant defense of Saragossa, Durruti was forced in October 1936 to accept greater control from Republican military officials and a loss of autonomy. His death on the Madrid front at the height of the battle for the capital left the army leaderless and seemed to be a portent of eventual disaster.

In early 1937, Ricardo Sanz, Durruti's successor at the head of the anarchist army, tried twice to resume the Aragón campaign, but effort did not make up for missing supplies. The anarchists' military effort faltered badly and quickly tarnished the movement's earlier heroic reputation. Foreigners and communists assumed that all members of the militias* were anarchists, but particularly in the south of Spain the term "anarchist" was almost generic for any peasant fighter. Nominally anarchist leaders like El Campesino (Valentín González),* caught squarely in the path of the Nationalists, accepted communist aid without reservation. In Madrid,* where Cipriano Mera* had led anarchist militiamen in a successful defense of Madrid in July 1936, the collapse of Republican lines south of the city in October and November 1936 led to harsh criticism of undisciplined and ill-trained "militiamen." All of these men were presumed to be anarchists when many were not. Communists and Republicans criticized them as detrimental to the war effort, an obviously biased charge.

The political issues surrounding the anarchists centered upon the charge that they had attempted to conduct a revolution in the midst of an antifascist civil war. George Orwell's* *Homage to Catalonia* (1938) and Burnett Bolloten's *The Grand Camouflage* (1961) discuss the rise and fall of the Spanish anarchist movement as a tragic contest between a populist force and Stalinism at its worst. The actual combatants, however, were socialists and middle-class Republicans who felt threatened by the anarchist revolution in parts of Catalonia and Aragón, and the Catalan separatists who feared the mass appeal of the CNT-FAI. All found it impossible to accept the anarchists as members of local and national governments.

The Spanish anarchists' political role developed suddenly and spontaneously at the beginning of the Civil War. Members of the CNT-FAI, determined to fight for their revolution, bore so much of the early struggle that the weight of their participation forced the creation of antifascist revolutionary committees in Barcelona, Valencia,* and Aragón. The Barcelona committee, certainly the most important, existed to supply the militia, or so the anarchists proclaimed, thereby accepting the myth that the committee was not in fact a government. Nevertheless, it replaced the Catalan regional government for three months until September 26, 1936. The Popular Executive in Valencia had a shorter duration, but the Council of Aragón* continued functioning until September 1937. Unbelievably, anarchists, those haters of governments, now occupied administrative positions of political importance.

Most surprising of all, the FAI participated in these committees with greater alacrity than the CNT. The militia connection with the Antifascist Militias Committee* dictated a very early *faísta* role, with Durruti, Juan García Oliver,* Federica Montseny, and Diego Abad de Santillán all occupying crucial positions. The FAI concentrated on economic and legal affairs in Barcelona, thus contributing a great deal to the Catalan Economic Council as well as taking clear control of the controversial *petrullas de control* (patrol squads) which was a central agency in the administration of Catalan revolutionary justice. Both organizations collectivized bank accounts, industrial property, housing (but not completely), and the securities market, while at the same time using the judicial and police* apparatus to enforce revolutionary mores. The rich

sometimes scrubbed floors, priests were shot, and militiamen occasionally received encouragement to handle justice in their own way. Conversely, the institution of rehabilitation, improvement of prison facilities, and a new philosophy of compassionate treatment for prisoners set a standard that Spanish criminology has not yet surpassed.

The unique character and uneven tenor of the anarchist revolution created many opponents. Socialists, Basque and Catalan separatists, Left Republicans, and other Loyalists* insisted that the time devoted to the revolution by the anarchists weakened the antifascist struggle. Soviet spokesmen insisted that anarchist revolutionary provocations fragmented Republican unity and destroyed national resolve to oppose Franco.* This backlash led to the restoration of normal local government in Catalonia and control by the national government in Valencia. Some influential anarchists reluctantly agreed that the CNT-FAI had to drop its revolution until the war against the Nationalists was won. This attitude prevailed when Madrid's fall seemed imminent, especially because the crisis presented the opportunity of allowing anarchists to recoup their losses by accepting Largo Caballero's offer of four seats in an all-faction Popular Front cabinet. García Oliver and Montseny of the FAI and Peiró and Juan López* of the CNT occupied the ministries of Justice, Health, Commerce, and Industry, respectively. The last two positions previously had been combined in the same office, but despite the doubling Peiró and López could do little to delay the nationalization of the previously collectivized industries under local, regional, or workers' control. Only García Oliver and Montseny succeeded briefly in formulating more vigorous policies.

Federica Montseny's ministry became a whirlwind of activity. She created a council on sanitation and social assistance, a council on medicine, new homes for the blind, rehabilitation centers, and the outline of a full-fledged welfare program that was three decades ahead of the times but that could not be financed in the middle of the war. Even today she is the only woman to have served in a Spanish cabinet, though that may change rapidly. Likewise, Juan García Oliver must have been the only felon to become minister of justice in any European country during modern times. He followed anarchist philosophy as best he could in establishing an elaborate series of economic crimes, while deregulating many aspects of life and removing the state from the administration of justice. Instead, Popular Tribunals* democratized justice, allowed the people to nominate judges and lawyers from among themselves, decriminalized criminal acts caused by need, and allowed judgments to be made according to socioeconomic background. Few of these changes lasted very long, but both Montseny and García Oliver presided over the temporary realization of long-cherished anarchist goals which seemed to portend a bright future.

In fact, the future was growing very dim at the very moment that anarchist values were becoming law. The rise of communist influence, based upon Soviet aid, clashed with the CNT-FAI at every turn in early 1937. The fall of Málaga* was unfairly blamed upon the anarchists for indiscipline, and this reflected badly upon the Aragón front, which had still not received adequate supplies to break out of the siege warfare that continued. Pressure to curb the anarchists also built up in Catalonia, where Juan Casanoves, president of the Catalan parliament, demanded that Luis Companys* take action against them. Even after Casanoves failed and was forced to flee, new communist officials in Catalonia like Artemio Ayguadé,* minister of internal security, and Eusebio Rodríguez Salas,* commissioner-general of police, pressed the CNT-FAI to disarm their members in the rearguard. CNT members of the Catalan government walked out on March 12, 1937, and scattered fighting between anarchists and other political groups took place at Fatarella, Seo de Urgel, Asco, Puigcerda, and Molins de Llobregat. Heavy fighting broke out in Barcelona on May 4 at the telephone exchange, an incident anarchists blamed upon communist provocations. The CNT-FAI was linked with Trotskyism and with a profascist attitude by the coalition of separatists, socialists, and communists ranged against it in Catalonia. The anarchist headquarters on the Vía Durruti was almost overrun, and only a truce on May 8 prevented further losses. This loss of political unity caused the collapse of Largo Caballero's cabinet a week later and led to the resignation of the anarchist ministers of state. An era was over.

The CNT-FAI, once more in the opposition after the formation of Juan Negrín's* new cabinet, which was more sympathetic to the communists, faced the inevitable consequences of their year in power. The Council of Aragón lost independence in September; the militias faced immediate absorption in communist units; and many militants died mysterious deaths, disappeared, or could now work only clandestinely. Even the International Workingmen's Association, the worldwide anarchist organization, condemned the CNT-FAI at a special meeting in December 1937 for having participated in a nonrevolutionary government. As one member said, "Anarchists in government will and must act like all officials and ministers." The exiled American anarchist, Emma Goldman, observed sadly that anarchism faced extinction under the double pressure from fascism and communism.

But the Spanish anarchists refused to admit defeat. The movement quarreled internally but publicly defended its actions as appropriate for the situation at the Civil War's start. Negrín faced steady criticism for his dependence upon the communists; anarchists believed that the many military setbacks suffered in 1937 and 1938 came from the people's disappointment over loss of revolutionary gains. Their solution was to make the FAI into a revolutionary workers' party, with the CNT as its labor union base. Both were guided by the *Comité Ejecutivo del Movimiento Libertario,* an executive composed of Spain's leading anarchists. It was hoped that this group would guide the movement more intelligently than before, with greater reference to anarchist principles. When Negrín decided to reopen the Cortes* in 1938, the FAI ran a large slate of candidates, an act that cooled the premier's enthusiasm for the legislature. But not everything undertaken during this period was successful, since too many actions had been taken which antagonized old enemies in the CNT and FAI, and fewer and fewer syndicate members, youth, and former leaders had time to purge the movement of its many contradictions. Among the younger members particularly, the various communist groups made heavy inroads. "Cheka" action by secret political police and military losses cut heavily into the ranks of the anarchists. Only a few made it into exile at the end of the war, and many of Franco's* political prisoners were anarchists. The severity of punishment which the movement suffered, however, guaranteed its continuation to the present.

For further information, see Murray Bookchin, *The Spanish Anarchists: The Heroic Years 1868-1936* (New York, 1977); Daniel Guérin, *Anarchism* (New York, 1970), general reference; Eric Hobsbawm, *Primitive Rebels* (New York, 1961); Robert Kern, *Red Years/Black Years: A Political History of the Spanish Anarchists, 1911-1937* (Philadelphia, 1978); César Lorenzo, *Les anarchistes espagnols et le pouvoir 1868-1969* (Paris, 1969); Max Nettlau, *La Première Internationale en Espagne* (Dordrecht, 1969); and Michael Weisser, *The Peasants of the Montes* (Chicago, 1976).

See also Communist Party, Spanish.

Robert W. Kern

ANDALUSIA. Andalusia, a large agricultural region in southcentral Spain made up of the provinces of Cádiz,* Málaga,* Granada,* Almería,* Jaén,* Córdoba,* Seville,* and Huelva,* was located directly in the path of Franco's* armies heading from North Africa northward to Madrid.* The region had some of Spain's most important cities (Seville, Córdoba, Cádiz, Málaga, and Almería) and large numbers of poor agricultural workers. Loyalties were mixed during the Civil War; however, the Nationalists* were able to dominate much of the area in the early days of the fighting. By August 1936, they occupied Cádiz, Seville, Huelva, parts of Granada, and Córdoba—in short, western Andalusia—with hardly a fight. By March 1937, they had completed the conquest of Málaga and had added additional territory from Granada, Jaén, and Córdoba. The situation did not change much until July 1938, when almost all of Córdoba came under Nationalist control. The far eastern portion of Andalusia remained Republican until late March 1939 when the rest of the region fell to the Nationalists. Eastern Andalusia remained in the hands of the Republicans* for so long because it was simply too far removed geographically from the Nationalist path northward to Madrid for Franco to conquer.

Those portions of Andalusia which came under Nationalist control early in the Civil War proved useful to Franco. Seville, for example, housed a Nationalist radio station directed toward Republican Spain, while Cádiz was a port through which the Germans and Italians could supply Franco. Andalusia under Franco's authority remained Catholic, while Republicans were purged and workers' unions disbanded. In eastern Andalusia, the opposite took place: Nationalist sympathizers were eliminated, collectives established, and the Catholic Church* persecuted.

The fact that large portions of Andalusia came under Nationalist control early in the Civil War enabled Franco to prosecute the war with increasing strength. The capture and use of the radio station in Seville made it impossible for the government in Madrid to deny the existence of a major revolution, while the land mass now under Franco's occupation served as a base for subsequent operations. Without the acquisition of major portions of Andalusia, therefore, Franco would not have been able to prosecute the war successfully in its early stages and thereby gain the necessary confidence of other Spaniards who could rally to the cause or obtain any substantial foreign aid* from Germany* and Italy.* The remarkable development was the speed with which the south fell to the Nationalists. In Seville, General Gonzalo Queipo de Llano* took the city without significant fighting on July 18, 1936. Cádiz came under Nationalist control very quickly as well. In Granada, it took a while longer because of hesitations and a stalemate, although again there was no serious fighting. In Córdoba a short battle took place. Other communities, such as Jeréz* and Algeciras, rallied to the Nationalists quickly.

After the purges of pro-Republicans in the Nationalist sectors, properties were restored to their original owners and virtual military law imposed. More interesting was the life-style in the Republican portions of Andalusia. Heavily anarchist in strength and sentiment, most towns and cities operated autonomously of each other and, in some cases, even without the use of money. Properties (both farms and businesses) were collectivized, usually under the control of labor unions and anarchist groups. Communities interfered in each other's political affairs and often had heated discussions, on occasion, even leading to hostilities. Socialists and other moderate leftists were virtually excluded from any political power, and less attention was paid to the Madrid government than in any recent time. The *Unión General de Trabajadores* (UGT)* exercised some power in Jaén, while elsewhere members of the old landed aristocracy and middle classes vanished. Laborers were often not paid money but were simply issued food* and other supplies from central repositories located in nearly villages. Police* activity usually became the responsibility of the political party ruling an area. Agricultural production continued despite the interference of war as the central government pressured local authorities to ship food to its armies.

For further information, see Ronald Fraser, *Blood of Spain* (New York, 1979), on life in Andalusia; Antonio Garrachón Cuesta, *De Africa a Cádiz a la España Imperial* (Cadiz, 1938), on Cádiz; Juan Martínez Alier, *La estabilidad del latifundismo* (Paris, 1968); José Manuel Martínez Bande, *La lucha en torno a Madrid* (Madrid, 1968), on military affairs; and Luis Romero, *Tres días de julio* (Barcelona, 1967), on military affairs. *See also* Appendix B.

James W. Cortada

ANDINO, JOSÉ. Andino was head of the Falange* party in Burgos* and a supporter of Manuel Hedilla* at a time when Hedilla was trying to expand his control over the movement (early to mid-1930s). He faded into obscurity by the time General Franco* had established his government in Burgos in October 1936.

For further information, see Maximiniano García Venero, *Falange en la guerra de España: la unificación y Hedilla* (Paris, 1967).

James W. Cortada

ANDRÉ MARTY BATTALION. The André Marty Battalion was part of the 12th International Brigade.

It was formed in November 1936 to fight for the Republic, drawing on French and Belgian volunteers* recruited by André Marty. Before the war was over, nearly 10,000 Frenchmen served in Spain, a large number within this battalion. It saw combat in the early battles around Madrid* and at the University of Madrid in 1936 and later at Jarama* in 1937.

For further information, see Henri Dupré, *La "Légion Tricolore" en Espagne* (Paris, 1942); and *L'Épopée d'Espagne* (Paris, 1957).
See also International Brigades.

James W. Cortada

ANGLO-ITALIAN MEDITERRANEAN PACT (1938).

The Anglo-Italian Mediterranean Pact of 1938 was the result of months of negotiations initiated by Great Britain* to curtail international intervention into Spain. Concluded on April 16, it stipulated that Italy* would withdraw its troops from Spain once the war ended. At that point, each government would help preserve the status quo in the Mediterranean Sea. Through this agreement, Britain hoped to draw Italy away from German influence by increasing Mussolini's* power to implement policies independent from Hitler's* in Southern Europe.* Italy saw this agreement as a simple way of seeming to advocate the conclusion of its international involvement while gaining London's acquiescence in keeping Italian troops in Spain.

For further information, see John F. Coverdale, *Italian Intervention in the Spanish Civil War* (Princeton, N.J., 1975).
See also Germany; and Non-Intervention Committee.

James W. Cortada

ANSALDO VEJARANO, JUAN ANTONIO (1901-1958).

Ansaldo, born in Arechevaleta (Guipúzcoa),* was a member of the Corps of Military Justice. In the 1920s, he acquired prominence as an aviator. A lifelong monarchist, he retired from the army after the proclamation of the Republic in 1931. The following year he sought support in Italy* for General Sanjurjo's* *pronunciamiento* against the government. In July 1936, General Mola* sent Major Ansaldo to pilot Sanjurjo from Lisbon to Burgos,* but his plane crashed at takeoff, killing Sanjurjo instantly. Ansaldo survived and next flew in the northern offensive of 1937. After the war, he represented the Franco* regime as air attaché in Paris and London, but Franco's failure to restore the monarchy led him into a conspiracy to overthrow the regime in 1942. The remainder of his life was spent in exile in Portugal* and France.*

For further information, see Juan Antonio Ansaldo, *¿Para qué...? De Alfonso XIII a Juan III* (Buenos Aires, 1951).

Carolyn P. Boyd

ANTICLERICALISM.
See Anarchists; Catholic Church, Spanish; Communist Party, Spanish; and Libertarian Movement.

ANTIFASCIST MILITIAS COMMITTEE, CENTRAL (CAMC).

The Central Antifascist Militias Committee (CAMC) came into existence during the first week of the Civil War and served as an ad hoc ruling body in Catalonia* until it was officially dissolved on October 3, 1936. The military uprising of July 18, 1936, unleashed a far-reaching and profound revolution in the Republican zone. Not least of the changes that took place virtually overnight was the shift in the source of political power from the Popular Front* government to the workers' organizations. In countless villages and towns, antifascist militias* sprang up, sometimes completely taking over the legislative and executive functions of the *ayuntamientos* (municipal governments), which had either disappeared or ceased activity. Perhaps the best known of all these was the CAMC set up in Barcelona.*

It was in Catalonia that the strength and influence of the anarchosyndicalists were predominant and that the effects of the revolution were most pronounced. Beginning on July 19, when General Goded* spearheaded the revolt against the Catalan government (Generalitat),* the anarchosyndicalists proved to be by far the greatest popular force resisting the rebels. After hours of bloody fighting, they succeeded in subduing the military barracks both at San Andres, the main armory of Barcelona, and at Atarazanas,* emerging the next day as the masters of the city. The struggle itself had provoked a mass defection of forces from the Civil Guard* (*Guardia Civil*) and the Assault Guards* (*Guardia de Asalto*) which considerably reduced the government's traditional means of exercising power. In view of this, Luis Companys,* the president of the Generalitat, met with the leaders of the anarchosyndicalist *Confederación Nacional del Trabajo* (CNT)* and the *Federación Anarquista Ibérica* (FAI)* and offered either to resign his post or to continue governing through a power-sharing scheme. Under his plan, his government would exist alongside a newly created political body, the Central Antifascist Militias Committee.

Although for the first time in their history the anarchosyndicalists faced the opportunity to abolish the state, the CNT-FAI leadership refused to seize power, choosing instead to collaborate with the government. No doubt because they realized that their decision compromised the dominating position of the anarchosyndicalists, leaders such as Abad de Santillán* and Juan García Oliver* later felt compelled to justify their action. They argued that to have done otherwise would have meant establishing a libertarian communist dictatorship, something that flagrantly repudiated the most sacrosanct principles of their anti-authoritarian creed. On the other hand, Helmut Ruediger, the International Workingmen's Association representative in Barcelona at the time, explained that the CNT-FAI did not impose its own dictatorship primarily because they lacked a program for using power, any economic plan and experience in running a government.

For whatever reasons they agreed to Companys' plan, the anarchosyndicalists still found themselves occupying a strong position on the CAMC. This committee was composed of seven representatives from the CNT-FAI, three each from Companys' Left Republican Esquerra* and the *Unión General de Trabajadores* (UGT),* and one each from the *Acció Catalana*, the *Partido Obrero de Unificación Marxista* (POUM),* and the recently formed communist-backed *Partit Socialista Unificat de Catalunya* (PSUC).* To facilitate its operations, the CAMC was divided into various subcommittees, the most important of which (those of war, public order, and transportation) were headed by CNT-FAI members.

Despite their diverse political backgrounds, the CAMC delegates were at first guided by common objectives. Their main work lay in maintaining a rearguard as well as preparing militia forces for the defense of the Aragón* front. In this way, the CAMC rapidly became the de facto ruling body of the region, with the Generalitat merely serving as a rubber stamp for its decrees.

Through their militias* and police squads (*patrullas de control*), the anarchosyndicalists controlled the streets, thus replacing the Civil and Assault Guards as the symbols of public order. Among other things, the anarchosyndicalists were instrumental in curtailing so-called revolutionary excesses, such as the macabre nightly *paseos* (figuratively, taking for a ride), under the veil of which numerous fascists, suspected enemies, and known opponents of workers' groups were spirited away and summarily executed.

The anarchosyndicalists' presence was also felt in the CAMC's military campaign. One of their remarkable achievements in this regard was their organization of militia columns according to libertarian principles. Militias, like the militia formed by Durruti* during the first days of the war, stood in marked contrast to those of the traditional army: there was no saluting, no regimentation, and no centralization of authority.

In the economic sphere, the anarchosyndicalists channeled their energies into a thoroughgoing collectivization program. Under their direction, the CAMC conducted the reorganization of industry and agriculture along collectivist lines. By August, the CNT had assumed administrative and technical control of a number of factories, public transportation facilities, and agricultural enterprises.

On September 4, 1936, the formation of a new Popular Front government under the Socialist Largo Caballero* paved the way for the reestablishment of a centrally directed Generalitat. Since early August, Companys and his party had devoted themselves to rebuilding the state machinery that had collapsed in July. They were supported in their efforts by the middle-class *Acció Catalana* and the PSUC, both of which not only favored returning authority to the Generalitat, but also sought to roll back the gains of the revolutionary programs begun under the CAMC. At the same time, these groups assailed the anarchosyndicalist-inspired policies of the CAMC, arguing that the chaos that resulted from the improvised militia columns, the decentralized factories and agricultural collectives, would inevitably lead to disastrous defeats for the Republican forces.

On another level, the central government in Madrid* increasingly pressed for the dissolution of the CAMC and all other revolutionary bodies that posed a challenge to its authority. According to Abad de Santillán, the government in Madrid effectively undermined the CAMC's position by threatening repeatedly to cut off Catalonia's supply of war matériel and to withhold from it foreign currency needed to purchase arms and raw materials from abroad. Given these conditions, Abad de Santillán and other anarchosyndicalists who believed that the war effort was to be supported at any price, had little choice but to dissolve the CAMC and join the Generalitat.

On September 26, Companys formed a new government containing representatives from all the workers' parties and unions. The anarchosyndicalists offered no resistance to this development insofar as they accepted posts in the Councils of Economy, Supply, and Health. A few days later, Barcelona's brief experiment in revolutionary government ended when the president issued a decree that annulled the CAMC.

For further information, see Diego Abad de Santillán, *Por qué perdimos la guerra* (Buenos Aires, 1940); Burnett Bolloten, *The Spanish Revolution: The Left and the Struggle for Power During the Civil War* (Chapel Hill, N.C., 1979); John Brademas, *Anarcosindicalismo y revolución en España (1930-1937)* (Barcelona, 1974); Juan García Oliver, *El eco de los pasos* (Barcelona, 1978); and Abel Paz, *Durruti* (Paris, 1972), which also appears in an English translation, *Durruti* (Montreal, 1976).

See also Communist Party, Spanish; and Socialist Party, Spanish.

George Esenwein

ANTONIUTTI, MONSIGNOR ILDEBRANDO (1898-1967). Monsignor Antoniutti, an apostolic delegate, represented the Vatican* at Burgos* as the pope's chief diplomatic contact with the Nationalists.* The Vatican had extended recognition to Franco's* government at Burgos on August 28, 1936. Monsignor Antoniutti, although not a *nuncio* (Vatican ambassador), worked diligently to expand the role of religion and of the Catholic Church* in the affairs of Nationalist Spain. For example, he made it possible to reinstate bishops and cardinals who had been resident on Republican soil or critical of Franco while consolidating the Church's political and administrative position in Spain. In June 1938, the Vatican appointed a *nuncio* to call on Franco's government—a clear and final signal that full recognition was being extended to the Nationalists—at which point Monsignor Antoniutti returned to Rome and other responsibilities.

For further information, see Juan de Iturralde, *El catolicismo y la cruzada de Franco* (Bayonne, 1955). As of this writing, there is no diplomatic history of the Vatican's role in the Spanish Civil War.

James W. Cortada

ANTONOV-OVSËENKO, VLADIMIR ALEXEIVICH (1844-1937). Antonov-Ovsëenko was the Russian consul general in Barcelona* during the Civil War. Stalin* eventually had him purged, along with the bulk of his diplomatic corps. During the war, the consul general helped the local Russian advisers in assisting the Republic while expanding the influence of the USSR* in Republican affairs. He was an old revolutionary, having led the Red Guard which attacked the Tsar's Winter Palace in 1917, and he opposed Trotsky* in the 1920s before serving Stalin in diplomatic capacities at Prague and Warsaw. Antonov-Ovsëenko proved to be one of the leading Russian influences in Republican Spain. His efforts, for example, led to a significant Russian influence in the political and police affairs of Barcelona.

For further information, see David T. Cattell, *Soviet Diplomacy and the Spanish Civil War* (Berkeley, Calif., 1957); and Isaac Deutscher, *The Prophet Unarmed* (London, 1959).

James W. Cortada

ARAGÓN. Aragón was the site of much fighting during the second half of the Civil War as the Nationalists* pushed east around Madrid* toward the Mediterranean coast. Franco* intended, and finally accomplished, the division of the Republican zone into several pieces, primarily isolating Catalonia* from Central Spain where the battles for Madrid continued until the final days of the war but without the Republicans* getting much help from northeastern Spain in the fight for the capital. Thus, the area east of Madrid and south of Catalonia, made up of the three provinces of Huesca,* and the two large provinces of Saragossa* and Teruel,* became a battleground.

Almost from the first days of the war, a north-south battlefront was established in Aragón. Two major campaigns took place there. The first was a Republican offensive in 1937, and the second was a Nationalist offensive in 1938. The purpose of the Republican offensive, beginning in June 1937, was to draw away from Bilbao* Nationalist forces which were then attacking the far north. Starting the campaign at Huesca with troops that outnumbered the Nationalists, the Republicans failed with about 1,000 casualties.* Hence, it only momentarily diverted Franco's attention from his campaign in the Basque country. Before the end of the month, Bilbao had fallen, bringing to an end the shortlived Basque government.

Fighting on a less intensive scale continued after the Republican offensive, and the battle lines remained fairly intact where they existed since only key points were held by troops, the rest being a line on battle maps with patrols roving through the area. During the summer additional warfare occurred with other Republican offensives. Historians believe that, apart from the need to hurt Nationalist forces, Republican activity continued in order to break the power of the Council of Aragón* by the central government. The council had decided to act autonomously, often ignoring the will of the central government. The council was staffed primarily with anarchists,* while their rivals, the socialists and communists, dominated the central government. The fighting that took place in August 1937, with the enthusiastic backing of the socialists and communists within the Republican government, thus had both a political and military objective. Enrique Lister* commanded 11,000 men sent to the

Aragón* front, along with forces from the 27th and 45th Divisions, the 5th Army Corps, and some units from the International Brigades.* The council was squashed, members arrested, and about a third of that year's wheat crop destroyed by military action. Many of the farming collectives were also dismantled in the process, which meant a major loss of food* and of growing capability for the Republic.

A large attack against the Nationalists began on August 24, 1937, at eight different points along the Aragón front from areas north of Saragossa to points south of the city. Eighty thousand Republican soldiers with approximately 100 tanks and possibly close to 200 planes initially experienced some victories, only to be stopped by fierce Nationalist resistance. Heavy fighting took place near the town of Belchite* and at the city of Huesca. Although the campaign continued until October, by the end of August most of it was over. The Republic captured less than half a dozen towns at a heavy price in casualties, leading Indalecio Prieto,* head of the Socialist party,* to criticize General Sebastián Pozas,* commander of all troops in the area. The military effort failed to block Nationalist advances in the north and only led to internal political bickering within Republican circles.

After the battle of Teruel (December 1937-February 1938), Franco looked eastward, planning his next attack into Aragón. Under the command of General Dávila Arrondo.* Nationalist forces began a massive campaign in March through Aragón and the Levante,* pushing to the Mediterranean coast by early April, thereby cutting Catalonia off from central Spain. The campaign ended in July with the fall of areas along the coast southeast of Teruel. Fighting took place from the French border to a point north of Valencia* on a north-south axis. Nationalist forces pushed from points as far west as Huesca eastward to Balaguer, Lérida,* Tortosa, and down to the coast. Fighting began on March 7, with Nationalist forces attacking Republican troops tired after the battle of the Ebro.* Resistance was minimal and advances quick. Each day new towns fell while the Nationalists pushed eastward.

Good leadership, effective use of aircraft on the flat plains of Aragón, and an enthusiastic attitude led the Nationalists to many victories in this campaign. The Republican forces were routed and mingled with the thousands of refugees* from collectives and towns streaming northward into Catalonia by the end of the campaign. With the Catalans cut off both to the west and from parts of the Pyrenees,* electrical supplies to Catalan industry were terminated, further weakening the Catalan industrial complex. The Republic, now cut in two by April 3, when the first Nationalist troops

arrived at the Mediterranean, found it difficult to maintain good communications between central and northeastern Spain, let alone to pass supplies, men, and armaments back and forth. All of this in all probability contributed to shortening the war. In possession of 40 miles of shoreline, while having pushed the Aragón battle lines eastward a similar distance into Catalonia, General Franco had won a major victory over the Republic. From then on, most Nationalists, many Republicans, and almost every foreign government had no doubt that Franco would win the war. The only way he could have been stopped would have been if some foreign government had decided to become involved (as Negrín* hoped the democracies of Western Europe* would and did not).

For further information, see José Manuel Martínez Bande, *La gran ofensiva sobre Zaragoza* (Madrid, 1973), on the campaign of 1937, and *La invasión de Aragón y el desembarco en Mallorca* (Madrid, 1970), on the campaign of 1938; Luis María Mezquida, *La batalla del Ebro*, 2 vols. (Tarragona, 1963) and *La batalla del Segre* (Tarragona, 1972); and Ramón Salas Larrazábal, *Historia del ejército popular de la república*, 4 vols. (Madrid, 1974).

James W. Cortada

ARANDA MATA, ANTONIO (1888-1979). Aranda, born on November 13, 1888, in Leganes (Madrid*), was the son of a Spanish Army corporal. He gained a reputation as one of Spain's most brilliant infantry general staff officers with the Spanish forces in Morocco,* and during the Civil War, he became highly respected as a combat field commander.

In the bloody Riff Wars, Aranda helped prepare the amphibious landings in the Bay of Alhucemas (near the headquarters of the wily Abd-el-Krim) and helped bring this long, costly campaign to a close. In 1926, at the age of thirty-eight, he was promoted to colonel of the general staff for meritorious service in war.

Aranda was a rotund, bespectacled man with a broad sense of humor and optimistic nature. While he was known for his jovial and ebullient personality, he was also said to be ambitious and crafty. Politically, he was moderately liberal and a supporter of the Republic. He was on close personal terms with Alexander Lerroux and his radicals, and it has been suggested that Lerroux wanted to make him minister of war. In addition, it is said that Aranda was a Mason, although he was considered to be politically discreet. In the first years of the Republic, he was involuntarily placed on the retired list because he could not be trusted as politically reliable and was not returned to active duty until 1933 when the moderates came to power.

When the Popular Front* assumed direction of the Republic, Aranda was permitted to remain in his post as the garrison commander of Oviedo.* This was possibly because of his "liberal" attitude or his alleged Masonic connection. Soon after Manuel Azaña* came back into the government, he ordered the reduction of the garrison of Oviedo. Aranda went to Madrid in a futile attempt to convince Azaña not to reduce his command, citing the Left uprising in the area in 1934 as a good reason. With the military revolt of July 1936, its leadership assumed that Aranda would secure Oviedo and its environs on behalf of the Popular Front. Thus, the events that occurred there came as a surprise to the Nationalists* and angered, as well as distressed, the Popular Front.

Immediately with the uprising, the Left-led Asturian miners descended upon Oviedo, which was the bastion of their own Left revolt against the Republic in 1934. Colonel Aranda took the position that he could well serve their cause with his men and that the miners were far more needed in Madrid. Surprisingly, the miners' leadership agreed with him. Now several thousand miners, entrained for Madrid under the assumption that Oviedo was firmly in the hands of the Popular Front. That same evening Aranda announced his garrison for the revolt and issued a declaration of martial law.

His garrison was added to by men from the Assault Guards,* Civil Guards,* and the Falange.* Aranda had a little over 3,000 men, of whom about 1,000 were civilian volunteers.* The Nationalists considered his move a surprising and delightful ruse, but the Popular Front saw it as treachery. Very quickly Oviedo was placed under siege.

It was not until the militia forces of the Popular Front were able to overwhelm the Nationalist garrison in defense of Gijón* that they were able to concentrate adequate forces about Oviedo in an attempt to take it by storm. The siege was long and bitter, and it appeared that eventually the attacking forces, which numbered about 15,000, would annihilate the defenders as had been the case of the Simancas Barracks in Gijón. Still, Colonel Aranda daily broadcast cheerful and optimistic messages to Spain. The Nationalists determined (as in the case of the Alcázar* of Toledo*) to save Aranda and his men. During the siege, his long-awaited promotion to brigade general of infantry arrived. General Mola's relieving forces* were augmented by a *bandera* (regiment) of the Foreign Legion* and a *tabor* (batallion) of Moors.* With 60 percent of the officers and 40 percent of his men cas-

ualties,* food* and coal exhausted, drinking water rationed, and plagued by an outbreak of typhoid fever, Aranda's confidence broke. He notified Mola that "the only thing left for us is to die like Spaniards." However, on October 16, 1936, the relieving forces managed to fight their way on to the heights over Oviedo, and the next day Oviedo was saved for the Nationalists. The siege had lasted ninety days. Aranda was now known as "the Hero of Oviedo."

General Aranda was named a field commander in the Army of the North* and shortly was able to prove his skill on the offensive in the Asturian campaign in September 1937. Through rugged mountains and bitter cold, as well as determined enemy resistance, his forces joined with those of General Solchaga* at Infiesto in mid-October. They then captured Gijón on October 21, 1937.

Aranda was given command of a newly organized army corps known as the Corps Galicia and moved into the Huesca*-Saragossa* sector in preparation for a new offensive in the area of Guadalajara.* These plans were upset by the enemy offensive against Teruel* in mid-December 1937. Aranda's Corps Galicia, along with the Corps Castile of General Valera,* initiated the Nationalist counteroffensive on December 29. The fighting was most bloody and took place in the bitter cold of subzero weather and blizzards very typical of the Teruel area, but the Nationalists defending the city were overrun on January 8. Aranda and Valera finally captured the strategic ridge of La Muela de Teruel, then with a Nationalist attack over the Alfambra River to the north the city was encircled, and friendly forces were able to fight their way into the ruined city.

The next test of Aranda's Corps Galicia was the large offensive (March 1938) through Aragón* to the Levante* coast. The purpose was to divide the Popular Front forces of Catalonia* from Valencia.* Aranda was given the southernmost wing of the offensive through the difficult craggy mountains of the Maestrazgo,* a fact that left him rather bitter because of the high losses and suffering of his men. On Good Friday, April 15, 1938, his division, commanded by General Alonso Vega,* crashed out to the sea and captured the village of Vinaroz.

Aranda was then ordered to expand the breach to the south, and on June 14, in the face of determined defenses, managed to take Castellón.* But he was not able to break Valencia's defenses, and at the same time had to divert some of his divisions to the north in the face of the massive enemy offensive across the Ebro River in his rear. The enemy attack was contained, and the Nationalists crashed through their lines to capture Catalonia. In January 1939, Aranda was promoted to division general, and in the spring of that year the Nationalist troops marched into Valencia. The war was over.

During the war, and after, Aranda never shielded his dislike for the Falangists who responded to his open hostility. When he was made military governor of Valencia, he incurred anger in some quarters for releasing former enemy prisoners. He was outspoken in his views that Spain should remain neutral if Germany* should become embroiled in a war. However, once he did lead a large Spanish delegation to Berlin. In 1941, he was named director of the Superior War College, and it has been suggested that this was done to remove him from a direct command position. He was known to be very pro-British. On one occasion, the Spanish foreign minister (and Franco's brother-in-law) Ramón Serrano Suñer* complained to the German ambassador that Aranda was the leader of a military faction against himself and was close to organizing a military plot to give a change of direction to Spain's foreign policy, which Serrano Suñer at the time professed to be strongly pro-Axis. Aranda was no longer destined to play a major role in Spanish affairs. At his death, on February 8, 1979, in Madrid, he held the rank of lieutenant general of the army in reserve.

For further information, see General Antonio Aranda, "Sitio y defensa de Oviedo," *Ejército*, No. 8 (August 1940); and Louis de Armiñan, *General D. Antonio Aranda Mata* (Ávila, 1937).

Raymond L. Proctor

ARANGUREN ROLDÁN, JOSÉ (1875?-1939).

Aranguren was a brigadier general in the paramilitary Civil Guard.* He had occupied first place on the list of colonels when promoted by the Popular Front* government on March 27, 1936. He was appointed to command the highly sensitive 5th Zone of the Civil Guard, with headquarters in Barcelona.*

The army coup in Barcelona failed largely because the forces of public order remained loyal to the government, and for this Aranguren was ultimately responsible. He was appointed commander of the army division after the dismissal of the previous incumbent, Llano de la Encomienda,* but since all the troops had followed their rebellious officer, there was no longer a military structure. The body known as the Antifascist Militias Committee,* in which the anarchist *Confederación Nacional del Trabajo* (CNT)* was dominant, assumed control of military operations and the dispatch of columns to fight the rebels.

Aranguren thus played little part and remained very much a figurehead. When the riots of May 1937* had been settled and the authority of the government had been restored, he was replaced in his command by General Sebastián Pozas* and took military command of the Valencia* division on May 14, 1937. With the abolition of the prewar divisions, he became military commander of the city on November 13, 1937, and then of the inland area of the central-southern zone in May 1938.

Aranguren was a traditional officer of conservative views. He adhered to his oath of loyalty to the Republic and gave evidence against the rebel generals Goded* and Fernández Burriel* when they were court-martialed after their coup failed on July 19, 1936. As they were executed together with a large number of officers of the Barcelona garrison, Aranguren must have realized that, as commander of the Civil Guard, he would receive partial blame for their deaths and for the failure of the uprising in the capital of Catalonia.* Nevertheless, he remained at his post in Valencia, refusing an offer of asylum from a Latin American embassy. He was court-martialed and executed by the victorious Nationalists* in 1939.

For further information, see F. Lacruz, *El Alzamiento, la revolución y el terror en Barcelona* (Barcelona, 1943); and Ramón Salas Larrazábal, *Historia del ejército popular de la república*, 4 vols. (Madrid, 1974).

Michael Alpert

ARAQUISTÁIN Y QUEVEDO, LUIS (1886-1959).

Araquistáin was born in the province of Santander,* became a writer and socialist politician, and one of Largo Caballero's* closest advisers. He was Republican ambassador to Paris in July 1936, and was responsible for purchasing arms for the Republican Army* as director of the Arms Purchasing Commission. When he returned to Spain during 1937, the Communist party* sought to remove his political influence and even had him imprisoned. After 1939, he lived in exile in France.

For further information, see Burnett Bolloten, *The Spanish Revolution: The Left and the Struggle for Power During the Civil War* (Chapel Hill, N.C., 1979); and Círculo de Amigos de la Historia, *Diccionario biográfico español contemporaneo* (Madrid, 1970), Vol. 1.

See also France.

James W. Cortada

ARGELÈS REFUGEE CAMP. The Argelès refugee camp was established by the French government on the French side of the Pryenees* to receive Republican military refugees* and to prevent their movement deeper into France.* This was one of fifteen camps established for that purpose, and it was not much more than enclosed sand dunes. The camp went into use in February 1939 and remained open until nearly the end of World War II. During its existence, it held approximately 40,000 people.

For further information, see Guy Hermet, *Les Espagnols en France* (Paris, 1967).

James W. Cortada

ARGENTINA. Argentina was officially neutral during the Spanish Civil War, although many of its officials were pro-Nationalist. Most of Argentina's Spanish population had recently migrated and thus were very interested in the conflict. This community overwhelmingly favored the Republic, as did the local Argentine political opposition to the government in power. Argentine diplomats were active in the diplomacy of the war. Saavedra Lamas, for example, was president of the League of Nations* Assembly where he cautiously attempted to minimize the opportunities of the Spanish Republic to voice its protests against the Civil War. However, in conjunction with the Argentine ambassador to the Spanish Republic, Daniel García Mansilla, he offered mediation and help to refugees* in an attempt to humanize the conflict. During the summer and fall of 1936, the major democratic powers rejected proposals for mediation by Argentine diplomats to bring an end to the fighting. They either had their own mediatory plans or were unwilling to become involved in any efforts. After the Civil War ended, Argentina joined most other Latin American countries in extending recognition to Franco's government.

For further information, see José Robert Juárez, "Argentine Neutrality, Mediation and Asylum During the Spanish Civil War," *The Americas* 19, No. 4 (1963):383-403.
See also Latin America.

James W. Cortada

ARIAS NAVARRO, CARLOS (1908-   ). Arias was born in Madrid,* studied law at the Central University of Madrid, and worked as a lawyer for the national government. During the Civil War, this official of the Ministry of Justice spent six months in jail for opposition to the Republic in Málaga.* When the city was captured by the Nationalists,* General Franco*

appointed him city prosecutor. He is best known as the prime minister of Spain in the last days of the Franco regime, appointed in 1973 after a full career as district attorney. He held other various high-level administrative and legal positions in the government.

For further information, see Círculo de Amigos de la Historia, *Diccionario biográfico español contemporaneo* (Madrid, 1970), Vol. 1.
See also Málaga; and Terrorism.

James W. Cortada

ARMY, NATIONALIST. Prior to the revolt of July 1936, the Spanish defense structure consisted of the army, navy, and air force, as well as the internal paramilitary police forces of the Civil Guards* (*Guardias*), Assault Guards* (*Asaltos*), and Customs Guards (*Carabineros*). The Spanish Army had two distinct forces: the Peninsular Army (including the forces of the Balearic Islands* and the Canary Islands*), and the Army of Africa* in the Moroccan* Protectorate.

The Peninsular Army was, in the main, a poorly trained conscript force with a paper strength in July 1936 of 8,851 officers (in all grades) and 112,228 men from warrant officer through recruits. Chroniclers vary in their estimates of the army's actual on-hand strength and the resulting division at the moment of the uprising. Furthermore, in the first several days of bitter fighting, an individual or unit might have been caught, at a given moment or location, and fight with that side, but individually and by units would cross over at the first opportunity.

The Peninsular Army was very much understrength with units at less than half-force, and the battalion commander who could muster a total of 200 troops was fortunate. The ration-records reveal that over 40,000 men were on leave. The on-hand troops (below the rank of lieutenant) constituted about 51,300. Of the 8,851 officers, 4,660 stood for revolt and were joined by nearly 19,000 men of other ranks. Of the remaining 4,191 officers, 2,000 cast for the Popular Front,* with close to 3,000 officers being imprisoned or killed by either side. In the lower ranks, 32,365 men remained with the government.

Spain's truly professional force was the Army of Africa, led by many tough, experienced, and battle-scarred veterans of the Riff Wars. It was also understrength with a force of 24,000 officers and men. In its vanguard were six *banderas* (comparable to battalions) of the spirited, disciplined, and dedicated 4,200 men of the Spanish Foreign Legion.* There were ten *tabores* (batallions) of the tough and determined mercenary Moorish *Regulares* (regular army) who were also led, for the most part, by Spanish officer veterans of the African wars. In addition, there were seven Spanish infantry battalions, six Spanish cavalry squadrons, and six batteries of field artillery. With the revolt, the African force was augmented by 6,000 men from the *Mehalla* (Moorish counterpart of the Civil Guards). Only a handful of the African officer corps rejected revolt, and they were quickly arrested or disposed of. The combined African Army stood at nearly 30,000 and, without question, was the best equipped, experienced, trained, disciplined, and led in Spain. Of the 30,000 men available, only about 17,000 could be marked for operation on the mainland; to have done otherwise would have left the protectorate without even a measure of safeguard.

It is difficult to assess the status of the Spanish Navy.* There were some 484 naval and 1,223 army officers posted to that command. Constituting the ships' crews were about 11,000 seamen with a like number in the shoreforce. It is estimated that 80 percent of the fleet officers stood behind the revolt, with the same percentage of the seamen being staunch supporters of the Popular Front. The result was that seamen-cells quickly seized most of the ships of the fleet and disposed of their officers. (It is estimated that nearly 75 percent of the fleet officers were killed.) As a result, only a few ships were able to join the insurrection.

The Spanish Air Force was manned by approximately 500 pilots,* with nearly 200 joining each side. The remainder were disposed of by one side or the other. It was equipped with about 200 obsolete or obsolescent aircraft, and because of their location most of these fell to the Popular Front.

The very elite paramilitary police* force of the Civil Guard was authorized 34,320 men and officers. Its exact strength, at that moment, has not been determined, but 14,000 cast their leather-hats with the revolt and 20,000 remained with the government.

The status of the Assault Guards (*Asaltos*), created by the Second Republic,* is also difficult to assess because included in their count are the departments of the Spanish secret police. The total number might have been as high as 30,000. Most reliable sources state that only Assault Guards joined the revolt, with nearly 3,500 remaining under orders. Both the Civil Guard and the Assault Guards were highly mobile and very well trained.

Less mobile and reliable, regardless of the side initially chosen, were the units of Customs Guards (*Carabineros*). Its force of 14,790 found 6,000 joining the revolt or being caught up in the insurrection zone. The balance remained with the Popular Front.

On the mainland, the Popular Front could count a force close to one-third larger than that of the rebels. However, the complete defection of the Army of Africa brought the figures near to equal, with most of the dedicated professionals in the rebels' ranks. Still, the government controlled almost the entire fleet and a large share of the aircraft, and dominated heavily populated urban and industrial regions, as well as Spain's total monetary reserves. It controlled the main depositories of war impedimenta. The fact that each side was quickly reinforced by militia units and volunteers* greatly changed the structure of the opposing forces.

If timidity, vacillation, and poor planning could have been replaced by resolution and boldness of action, more regular army units would have successfully cast for revolt. The hesitation in many locations permitted thousands of Popular Front militiamen to be armed and to converge on the military barracks before the troops were called out. In Barcelona* (outnumbered four to one), the soldiers of the 4th Division were quickly overrun. Much the same thing occurred with the 3d Division in Valencia.* In Andalusia,* the insurgents lost the isolated units of the 2d Division. But the rebels could count on the 7th Division (Valladolid*), a large part of the 5th Division (Saragossa*), along with about two-thirds of the 6th Division (Burgos*). Part of the 8th Division (Galicia*) cast for revolt, but the units in Asturias* were lost. The understrength Madrid* 1st Division and cavalry units in that sector were quickly destroyed by thousands of armed militiamen.

The uprising temporarily succeeded in Guadalajara,* Alcalá de Henares,* and Albacete,* but in each location succumbed in a few days. In other locations rebel redoubts, reinforced by civilian volunteers,* were established, such as the Alcázar* of Toledo, Oviedo* under Colonel Aranda,* the garrison of Gijón,* and the redoubt of Santa María de la Cabeza. Some managed to hold out against seemingly impossible odds for months until they were relieved, but others, such as the last two, were to be carried by storm with a sizable slaughter. A week following the uprising, the rebels tentatively held in the north of Spain the provinces of Galicia, León,* Navarre,* and large parts of Old Castile* and Aragón.* In the south, they controlled the areas near Cádiz,* Seville,* Córdoba,* Granada,* Huelva,* and Cáceres.* In all, the rebels held about a third of the Spanish land mass.

Immediately in the zone controlled by the Popular Front, almost all regular army units were disbanded with many of its members politically suspect. Thus, in this zone, military power passed to the political party and union-controlled militias.* In Catalonia,*one such force was to exceed 50,000 anarchists.*

On the other hand, in the rebel zone, the original *organic* divisions to come under rebel control (although in no way considered tactical forces) retained their identity within their respective territorial regions and became the base upon which the rebels were to build a new Nationalist army.* This was specifically the case in respect to the 5th, 6th, 7th, and 8th Divisions. Quickly the divisional headquarters, along with their regimental headquarters, became administrative and logistical support centers for the early tactical battle-columns operating through or in a specific geographical region. They also became centers for voluntary and compulsory recruitment and the processing of personnel.

The value of militia units and volunteer formations might be open to debate, but in the case of the rebels they were a very important positive factor. Because Spain had had a conscript system, it can be assumed that, other than for the very young, most of the men up to the age of forty-two knew the rudiments of military training and possessed a limited familiarity with simple weapons. The ranks of the regular troops were quickly increased by volunteers from the Falange* and monarchist parties (Carlists* and their bitter foes the Alfonsists), as well as other volunteer groups and youth organizations. In the early days, the effort was enthusiastic but haphazard. In the first twenty-four hours in Álava* and Navarre, over 7,000 excited Carlists in their red berets appeared on the scene and were organized into *banderas* for the tactical battle-columns. These *banderas* were eventually to grow into brigades, divisions, and then into a full army corps. The records of the *Brigadas Carlistas* eventually proved that they must be considered in the ranks of the select troops of what became the Nationalist Army.

Falangist volunteers were quickly organized into sections, companies, and *banderas*. Initially, many were incorporated into the ranks of the regular army, and some of the rebel field commanders were skeptical as to the dependability of such forces. For example, Colonel Yagüe,* although sympathetic to the Falange, did not want such units attached to his battle-columns for fear they would prove to be a disruptive, undependable political element that would reduce the combat effectiveness of his small professional force. For the most part, the Falangist *banderas* conducted themselves properly and with military distinction.

It is difficult to assess the motives of each individual volunteer to a specific *bandera*. True, many were from the old ranks of the Falange, but others moved onto the rolls after the birth of the Popular Front. Many

were disillusioned Left-party members which included a sizable number of former anarchists. On the other hand, a young college student might have attached himself to a specific *bandera* because it was the only unit in his area which he could join to fight against the enemy. It was not unusual that if he had some qualities of leadership he would soon become a section or even company commander. When the rebels established themselves into an organized government, this same volunteer might have been selected as an officer-candidate and sent to school. With completion of training, he would be commissioned into the ranks of the regular army or the provisional force. As a whole, the Spanish officer corps had only limited sympathy for the Falange and its proposed syndicalist-socialist objectives. It is only natural that the officer-candidate would reflect these views and come to look upon himself as a member of the professional officer class and thereby divest himself of association with the Falange or any other political action group. Forty years after the conflict, many of the highest placed Spanish military figures had such a history.

The initial rebel tactical field forces were the battle-columns. These columns were formed from the ranks of the old numbered divisions and quickly organized volunteer groups. The size of the mixed force of the battle-columns ranged from 200 to over 2,000 men. Rapidly formed, they were dispatched to seize strategic locations such as mountain passes and vital communication centers. They were lightly armed, a few had field pieces, and they were supported with very limited supplies. They hoped that by sheer audacity and determination they would be able to seize a specific location and defend it until reinforcements of men and supplies could arrive.

Following the independent battle-column type operation that had been adopted so extensively in the African war, the rebel columns quickly fanned out from centers of strength. During the first week, eleven battle-columns of varying size were organized in Pamplona.* Of these, seven columns drove into Guipúzcoa* with the objective of securing the rebel right flank and sealing the border with France.* Two columns headed for the mountain passes dominating the approaches to Madrid, and the columns from the 5th Division (Saragossa) drove into Aragón to organize resistance against the Popular Front forces forming in Catalonia. In Aragón, the columns were split into defensive sectors that were supported largely by local organized civilian volunteer units with the help of mobile elements of the Civil Guard.

The first battle-columns in the north numbered about 5,000 men. The columns advancing on the pass approaches to Madrid ran into far superior numbers and determined resistance. As a result, their ranks were reduced. In addition, they were critically short of munitions.

In the south, General Queipo de Llano's* small rag-tag columns of soldiers, Civil Guards, and civilian volunteers were reinforced by the arriving small detachments from the Foreign Legion and Moorish *Regulares*. As other African troops crossed the Straits of Gibraltar, they were quickly formed into battle-columns and began their fighting drive to the north. The objective was to destroy the Popular Front militias organizing before them, along with the ultimate aim of linking with the battle-columns in the north.

Two small battle-columns consisting of a *bandera* of the Legion and a *tabor* of Moors* (equipped with three light field guns) departed Seville on August 3 and 4, 1936. A third column was organized and left on August 9. The combined strength numbered less than 3,000 men. When the remnants of the advance column reached Mérida* on August 11, Colonel Yagüe assumed command. The columns had moved north by every conceivable means of automotive transport that could be requisitioned or seized. All columns depended upon audacity, discipline, and rapid movement to shatter the numerically superior militia forces deploying before them. When faced with resistance, the combat-columns would fan out in skirmish lines and place automatic weapons on their flanks which, with raking fire, could dominate the roads to the rear of the defenders. The core of the battle-column would then strike hard with its limited artillery, improvised armored cars, and, if available, aircraft. Faced with the cool fury and skill of the professionals, the poorly trained and led militia units, more often than not, would break their ranks and flee down the road to their rear, only to be cut down by machinegun fire from the rebel flanks. The retreat would become a bloody rout. Sizable amounts of munitions would then be added to the rebel column's supplies.

The battle-columns would quickly regroup and press on to the next objective. Many skirmishes were bitterly contested, and the battle-columns came under aerial attack. Their ranks began to thin. At the same time, more columns, as well as replacements, were being organized as more troops arrived from Africa.

By September 1, 1936, nearly 9,000 men with basic materials had been ferried to the mainland by a few German Ju-52 transport aircraft in the first major airlift in military history. Spanish and Italian aircraft, as well as surface ships, added to the total. Some of the newly arriving troops would fan out in different directions, but the concentration was the drive to the north. By the time Colonel Yagüe's battle-columns arrived at Mérida, the force numbered 4,500 tough professionals. These rebel battle-columns, along with those in the north, were to evolve eventually into brigades, divisions, and ultimately into the army corps of the Nationalist Army.

In the first hectic days of revolt, and without a centralized command, the commanders in specific areas were left to their own initiative and resources, the latter being very limited. But even in those days, the nucleus of what would be an army was taking form. In Seville, Queipo de Llano almost immediately called up the draft quotas for 1931-1935 and only a week after the rising mobilized all men with driver permits for the Nationalist transport service. In early August, the Burgos *Junta* mobilized the draft of 1935, which brought 20,000 into the ranks of the Army of the North.* In the middle of the month, the Nationalists* on Majorca* had called to the colors contingents of the previous six years. At the same time, General Mola* estimated that the forces in revolt numbered 100,000 in his northern sector and 60,000 in the south. Many of these were volunteers, with an estimated 20 percent in the south and 60 percent in the north. In the latter case, most came from the rolls of the Carlists.

The Nationalist Burgos *Junta* fully recognized that the struggle would most likely be a long and costly one, and as a result a greatly expanded force would have to be created to reach even a parity with the forces being mobilized on the other side. Thus, on August 26, 1936, it issued a decree mobilizing portions of the classes of 1931 through 1934. When this callup was completed, in early 1937, some 270,000 men were added to the colors. This decree, however, had no impact upon the status of the forces that were driving north and south on Madrid at the time.

By August 11, 1936, the Nationalist battle-columns fought their way into Mérida and established a weak link with the outer columns of General Mola to the north. They were able to resupply him with desperately needed ammunition. Colonel Yagüe now turned part of his battle-column westward to seize the important fortified border city of Badajoz.* Although outnumbered by well-positioned and armed defenders, the column took the city by storm in a bloody battle. The 16th Company of the legion's 4th *Bandera* decimated itself against defending machineguns to open a breach in the defenses.

With the communications to Portugal* secure and the left flank protected, Yagüe rejoined the main column to press on to Talavera de la Reina* in the dash to relieve the beleaguered Nationalist redoubt of the Alcázar in Toledo. It was heavy fighting all the way, with high costs to the Nationalists in both men and material as well as total exhaustion of the troops and their officers. In one short period, Franco* estimated his losses at 1,600 dead and wounded, but at the same time 16,000 of the enemy were killed.

The battle-columns were not able to relieve the Alcázar until October 1, the same day that Franco assumed command of all Nationalist forces. By the end of the month, the Nationalists were sorely feeling the impact of 14,000 casualties.*

The now combined Nationalist general headquarters was established in October 1936 at Salamanca.* In November 1937, it was moved to Burgos where it remained until the war was over. Franco frequently moved his battle-staff to threatened areas or to oversee a determined Nationalist offensive. This mobile headquarters was known as "Terminus." General Dávila* was made chief of the general staff. Although unified under a single commander, the respective area commanders continued to enjoy a large degree of independent action other than for overall strategy and logistical support which were increasingly brought under the control of the central battle-staff.

The battle-columns converging for an assault upon Madrid in the Army of Africa and the Army of the North were now joined under the command of General Mola. In spite of their determination and professionalism, their limited numbers and scarcity of reserves raised doubts as to the possibility of success. It is calculated that the entire Nationalist force available in the area was nearly 20,000, but only 4,500 men could be committed for the first assault. In defense, the Popular Front had more than 40,000 men supported by heavy Russian tanks firing cannons and covered from the air by high-performance Russian aircraft. The offense versus defense ratio was hardly a desirable one for the attack. Those who questioned the wisdom of the assault and its probable success proved justified.

As noted, many weeks before the creation of the supreme command, the Burgos *Junta* had established the machinery to call tens of thousands of volunteers and conscripts to the Nationalist colors. It is one thing to have a manpower pool, but to mold it into a trained and properly led force quickly committed to battle is another matter. This the Nationalist leadership fully appreciated as well as their shortage of company grade officers to lead an expanding force. In early September, as the battle-columns were still fighting along the approaches to Toledo, the *Junta* initiated a crash program of officer training. In the eyes of the military professional, the program might be considered not only inadequate but also downright pathetic; but to a

surprising degree it worked. The first prospective officers were selected from the ranks of enthusiastic volunteers in the twenty to thirty year age group who had professional papers or the equivalent of a college degree. Training schools were established in Seville and Burgos for what would be known as *Alféreces Provisionales* (provisional second lieutenants). The first class totaled 250 candidates, and after a terribly short fifteen days (October 3) 183 *Alféreces* were commissioned to join the ranks of the expanding force. The *Alféreces* were eligible for commissions in the army, if they proved themselves, and could be promoted to the rank of colonel. As haphazard as this procedure might seem, the system was greatly expanded and did produce many fine and dedicated officers for the growing Nationalist Army.*

In November 1936, additional schools were opened at Xauen, Santa Cruz de Tenerife, and Majorca.* In January 1937, the lower age limit was reduced to eighteen years and, in addition, the educational requirement was cut considerably. The training period was extended to twenty-four days. However, at least sixty days of previous active line service were required of the selectee. To some of the combat veterans the officer schools, as demanding as they were, took on the aspects of a finishing school. The training of conscripts and volunteer troops was a little more realistic thirty days.

Many of the instructors for the *Alféreces*, as well as the schools established for noncommissioned officers, were active and reserve officers of the German Army. Of the eventual 22,963 *Alféreces* to be commissioned, 10,463 became army first lieutenants and 497 became captains. As a single group, their proportional losses were the highest of Nationalist forces. The noncommissioned officer schools eventually graduated 19,700.

In October 1936, shortly after Franco became Generalissimo, foreign assistance to the Nationalists took on a new form. In the first week of the conflict, a purely Spanish affair was projected into an international event with countries and political movements coming to assist each side. The initial limited Italian/German aid to the insurrection came about in the last week of July with the arrival of a small number of aircraft to assist in the airlift of the Army of Africa. The Germans contributed twenty Ju-52 transport and six antiquated He-51 fighters for protection and training. The crews were all German and were supported by small detachments of communications and a few anti-aircraft batteries. The Germans were under strict orders to remain in a support function and were directed to avoid any possible combat role. At the same time, nine Savoia Italian bomber/transports arrived in Africa. Three others crashed en route. By the end of August, Berlin had slightly increased its aircraft support and had granted the German military permission to engage in a direct combat function. The Italian commitment also continued to escalate, and the two nations began to act in concert.

Late in August 1936, Lieutenant Colonel Walter Warlimont of the German general staff was posted to Spain as head of the small German force, senior economic representative, and chief military adviser to the Nationalist command. Shortly after his arrival, in early September, he suggested to Berlin that the Nationalists were in grave need of at least a German tank battalion. Berlin responded by sending a single battalion (commanded by Major Wilhelm von Thoma) of light tanks armed with only machineguns from the German infant *panzer* force. The battalion was not intended as a combat force but as a training unit for Spanish tank crews.

Before the *panzer* battalion could be formed at Cáceres (October 1936), General Franco informed Warlimont that intelligence channels had just revealed that heavy Russian cannon-firing tanks had arrived on the other side. Warlimont was now in opposition to any increase in German personnel in Spain and so advised Berlin. Shipment of German equipment, however, was encouraged. Unknown to either Franco or Warlimont, in Berlin the decision was made to increase direct German military involvement in the form of a unique air group to be known as the Condor Legion.* It would also absorb all German personnel and equipment already committed.

The Condor Legion was a force of about 100 aircraft with the necessary support functions and personnel. It had a constant strength of about 5,000 men. Lead elements of the force did not begin arriving at Cádiz and Seville until November, and its aircraft could not be committed fully until it was apparent that the efforts to take Madrid were a complete failure. Its initial aircraft were far outperformed by the Russian equipment on the other side. Eventually, higher performance aircraft were to arrive from Germany,* with the result that air superiority began to pass into the hands of the Nationalists.

At the same time, Italian assistance to the Nationalists continued to increase. In December 1936, Mussolini* ordered Italian ground combat troops sent to Spain. The first elements arrived in January 1937 and would eventually become full divisions totaling 32,000. In March 1937, they were incorporated into the *Corpo Truppe Volontarie* (CTV). In time, the CTV was to include Spanish troops under Italian officers.

When General Mola assumed command of the combined columns converging on Madrid (October 1936), he reorganized the forces along the territorial basis of the old organic divisions for administrative and logistical support. The tactical forces remained the battle-column with the battalion as the major unit. However, some of these were now being enlarged and were taking on the form of expanded or reinforced brigades. To the divisional structure Mola added the new Soria and Ávila Divisions. While the battle-columns were still struggling on the outskirts of Madrid, he created the so-called Madrid Division which was a haphazard collection of the battle-columns, *banderas*, and brigades that existed in the Madrid sector.

Also in December 1936, what had already been generally accepted in practice became a matter of law. All militia units were made subject to the military code and were placed fully under military command. By the end of the year, about 200 volunteer battalions (or the equivalent), led by regular officers, had been added.

The volunteer militias gained added emphasis after the shotgun wedding of the Carlists and Falange during the political Unification Decree of April 1937. Although he was to retain active command of his field cavalry forces, General Monasterio* was named to head the Armed Militia and immediately assigned into their *banderas* many of his experienced cavalry officers.

Even though mobilization procedures had been set in motion in the midsummer of 1936, by the early weeks of 1937, they still had only a limited impact on the Nationalist combat forces. Their professional ranks continued to be reduced through casualties. Some writers believe that the rebel lines were so sparse about Madrid that a determined attack, by even a few enemy brigades, would have shattered the Nationalist front.

The lack of Nationalist immediate reserves was fully demonstrated in February 1937 with the Jarama* offensive. It developed into the most bloody single engagement of the war to that date. The Nationalists lost 6,000 and the Popular Front 10,000. Many of the finest units on each side were badly mauled.

In the early spring and summer of 1937, the government continued to enjoy such a sizable superiority in men and equipment that it was questionable if the Nationalists would be able to narrow the gap, much less gain parity, as massive shipments of supplies continued to arrive in Russian convoys. By spring 1937, the Popular Front central zone had organized 153 brigades in forty-seven divisions and thirteen army corps. This was a force of 500,000 with 1,465 guns and 400 aircraft.

On the other hand, by March 1937, the Nationalists had mobilized 350,000 recruits. On March 25, their effort gained momentum with the decree creating the Mobilization, Instruction, and Recuperation Bureau (MIR) under Franco's associate and able administrator, General Orgaz.* Orgaz increased the number of training schools to twenty-two and added more German instructors to their staffs. In March, the draft classes from 1927 to date were called, and all healthy males between twenty-one and thirty-one years of age were mobilized. In the following months, the minimum age was continually lowered and more classes called, with the result that tens of thousands were added to the Nationalist rolls.

The spring of 1937 also witnessed Nationalists' reorganization of their battle-columns from a various collection of battalions, brigades, or *tabores* into tactical divisions. The effort had little impact until the costly enemy offensive of Brunete* was contained and the Nationalists' painfully slow offensive in the Basque provinces and the north were concluded in late 1937. At that time, a general reorganization took place, specifically in the Army of the North which was now commanded by General Dávila. At the same time, large sections of the newly conscripted force were ready for commitment. The total strength was nearly 600,000, with between 300 and 400 batteries of artillery (much captured) and a combined air force of about 400 aircraft. The quality of their armor was far inferior to that of the enemy. At this time, the enemy numbered 800,000.

In the reorganization, the enthusiastic, and so frequently committed, tough Navarre Brigades were formed into divisions. These divisions evolved into army corps. As they were in this process, they were once again thrown into an enemy breakthrough, this time the bloody battle of Teruel.*

By early January 1938, the Nationalists had a field army that had grown from the battle-columns into the army corps of Navarre, Castile, Galicia, Aragón, Morocco, the Corps Valiño (which later became the Army of the Maestrazgo*), and the Italian-Spanish CTV. At first, these army corps had a direct, close connection to the regions that gave them their names. In time, these close ties were weakened but never completely severed.

These same army corps were committed to the massive and brilliant Aragón offensive (March 1938) which shattered the Popular Front forces in the Nationalist drive to the Mediterranean Sea. In 1938, the Nationalist Army of the Center* was formed which included the 1st Army Corps, along with additional divisions or brigades that did not constitute a full army corps.

The Nationalist Army of the South went through several reorganizations, and by late 1938 it constituted the 2d, 3d, and 4th Corps, as well as several reserve battalions or brigades. Then in November 1938, the Army of the Levante* was created, under General Orgaz, constituting the Corps Galicia and Castile. This was followed the next month with the creation of the Urgel Army under General Muñoz Grandes* which was to operate east through northern Catalonia. Included in its files were four divisions and twelve additional battalions or *banderas*.

The major problem in organizing a draft force in a civil war is determining the political reliability of those called. The recruit might support the side that called him, be bitterly opposed and desert at the first opportunity, or feel that a plague should be cast on both houses. Such problems might be solved by intensive training, stern discipline, and a feeling of camaraderie within specific units. This could be developed if the men were from the same geographical area, spoke the same dialect, and enjoyed the same food and drink. In a country such as Spain, which is so divided sectionally, this was a matter of major importance and was well understood by the Nationalist general headquarters. Discipline in the Nationalist Army far exceeded that of the earlier monarchy. Many foreign observers considered it not only stern but excessively harsh.

In late 1937, some of the conscript units were ready for deployment. Still, the Nationalist general headquarters was reluctant to commit such divisions to major engagements until 1938. For the most part, they had been used in rear zones and performed security functions. When they were sent into the line, with few exceptions these divisions performed well. The shattering of one such division during the enemy offensive of the Ebro River should not be looked upon as representative of all units. In this instance, a raw division had to bear the brunt of a massive assault which would have been difficult for the most experienced troops to contain.

The Nationalist general headquarters' concern with the reliability of the conscript divisions to hold before a determined enemy attack or to sustain a fighting offensive of their own reinforced the Nationalist propensity of relying mainly on the experienced, disciplined, and well-led select units of its army. These were mainly the professional and the dedicated volunteer formations. Included were the *banderas* of the Legion, the *tabores* of the *Regulares*, the brigades of the spirited and repeatedly proven Carlists, the dogged *banderas* from Galicia, as well as the tested *banderas* of the Falange. This constant calling upon the same units to stem vicious enemy attacks or to spearhead a Nationalist offensive led to their disproportionate losses, and may of these select units had to have their total strength replaced two or more times.

The Nationalist answer to this problem was to have a constant recruitment program to maintain the select units. To support its demands the Army of Africa, besides drawing from Morocco, encouraged the enlistment of former militia men of the Left-parties, including anarchists.* These men were offered the spirit and mystique of the Spanish Foreign Legion, and the chance to serve in such tough, disciplined shock forces was one way they could prove their new loyalty. Former enemy troops were given the same sort of inducement to "volunteer" for the shock brigades of the Falange. In one period, as Professor Stanley Payne notes, the Army of Africa added to its ranks 12,312 men in eighteen infantry battalions, 5,600 in eight *banderas* of the Legion, 38,000 *Regulares* in fifty-five *tabores* (including 6,800 Europeans), 2,200 in artillery batteries and engineer companies, and 5,893 replacements.

There was a calculated risk in forming units predominantly from the ranks of the former enemy. However, these troops fought well and accepted the spirit and pride of their new organizations. In 1937, one problem did develop in Saragossa where a large group of the *Confederación Nacional del Trabajo* (CNT)* joined the Legion and one *bandera* of such volunteers plotted a mutiny. The plot was discovered before any damage was done, and reportedly the mutineers were handled accordingly.

It has been written that more than two-thirds of what had been the Popular Front Army of the North* were to serve out the war fighting under the flag of the Nationalists. There are no exact figures available, and the estimate may seem excessive, but there is no doubt that thousands of former enemy did serve the Nationalist side—after they had been politically screened.

Among the select units, the Moorish *tabores* continually had to be brought back to strength. In the spring of 1937, over 35,000 *Regulares* had been committed, and before the war was over 80,000 Moroccans had served. They proved to be superb front-line troops with a fantastic ability to withstand grueling hardships. An exact count of their losses is difficult to determine, but they were likely considerable. Among the shock forces of what became the Corps Morocco were the 12th Division (Asensio), 13th Division (Barrón*), and 14th Division (Jesus López Bravo).

Volunteers from all provinces of Spain served in the Nationalist select units. Included in their ranks were the two largest political action groups (in Nationalist Spain), the Carlists and the Falangists. The Carlists and similar monarchist groups provided a total of 62,722 volunteers from all of Spain. The Falangists

committed 116 *banderas* of 207,933. The two groups were to count over 16,000 dead and 80,000 wounded.

The mainland provinces of Navarre and Galicia contributed the largest percentage of troops to the elite brigades, divisions, and then army corps. The select forces to evolve from Navarre were the Navarrese divisions of the 1st Division (Garcia Valiño*), the 4th Division (Alonso Vega*), and the 5th Division (Juan Bautista Sánchez*). They were called upon repeatedly to perform most difficult tasks, both on defense and offense, and suffered accordingly. The region of Galicia followed by contributing 237,385 troops (almost a quarter of the Nationalist total). Many were to be formed into the divisions of the Corps Galicia of General Aranda. In its files were the 82d Division (Delgado Serrano*), 83d Division (Martín Alonso*), and the 84th Division (Alfredo Galera). General Aranda maintained that they suffered nearly 30,000 casualties.*

The claim that the Nationlist Army was a far more popularly supported army than is generally supposed is given weight by Professor Stanley G. Payne's evidence that civilian volunteers constituted about 25 percent of the total mobilized force. These volunteers suffered about 6 percent killed and 30 percent wounded.

Guerrilla bands operated within the Popular Front zones, but to date no study of these shadowy forces has been made. Some did operate in the regions of the Sierra Moreno and the Montes de Toledo, as well as in Catalonia. They cannot be calculated in the strength of the Nationalist Army.

The total mobilized force for Nationalist Spain was slightly over 1,020,000. Of these, the Nationalists' figures report 70,000 killed and 300,000 wounded. On the other side, the Popular Front's dead is calculated at about 125,000. The total of wounded, or those who died of wounds, is impossible to calculate.

In the early days of the insurrection, the Nationalist cause seemed doomed to failure. It would be presumptuous to point to a single factor which made their victory possible. Most of the combatants on both sides were Spaniards, and they fought equally hard. The Nationalists did have the greater share of the professional soldiers, and the former battle-column leaders proved they could handle army corps of tens of thousands. The high leadership, although with some internal political differences, was united in its dedication to defeat the Popular Front. This unity was solidified with the creation of a supreme commander and a centralized government. Very important was the fact that the Nationalists did not destroy the structure of the former Spanish Army but used it as a base for building a new army in the midst of a war. Most observers agree that the forces fielded by the Nationalists were better trained, disciplined, and led at all levels than their opponents.

As expected, military critics frequently fault some of the tactical and strategic decisions of General Franco and his general headquarters. If they are correct, it is entirely possible that the Nationalists could have captured their victory earlier and at less cost.

For further information, see Ricardo de la Cierva, "The Nationalist Army in the Spanish Civil War," *The Republic and the Civil War in Spain*, ed. R. Carr (London, 1971); Rafael García Valiño, *Guerra de Liberación española* (Madrid, 1948); José María Iribarren, *El general Mola* (Madrid, 1945); Alfredo Kindelán, *Mis cuadernos de guerra* (Madrid, 1945); and Stanley G. Payne, *Politics and the Military in Modern Spain* (Stanford, Calif., 1967).

Raymond L. Proctor

ARMY, REPUBLICAN. The Republican Army, or *Ejército Popular de la República*, was the name given to the army with which the Second Republic* fought against the Nationalist rebels.

When the boundaries between the rebel and government zones became clear in the last week of July 1936, the Republic had retained about half of the 65,000 men in barracks that summer, as well as considerably over half of the forces of public order. However, the rebels possessed well over half of the infantry units, and the Republic's equivalent in numbers came from the auxiliary units, mainly in Madrid.* The Republic had dissolved those regiments whose officers had rebelled. Unsure of the loyalty of any army formation, the Giral* government had distributed arms to the rapidly constituted trade union and political militia. Although small army units did form part of militia columns for some time, they were haphazardly formed and were rarely commanded by their own officers. Conscripts were affected by the undisciplined militia spirit and thus were of little use as trained troops to the Republican war effort.

The Republican Army was formed from a combination of militia battalions and successive intakes of conscripts. Political and trade-union militias* were formed on all fronts. They shared broadly similar characteristics, being heterogeneously armed, uniformed and organized, and untrained. Their performance was in general undistinguished, although untrained militiamen performed may acts of heroism in engagements with professional rebel troops. In Aragón,* the militias, drawn from Barcelona* and the urbanized areas of Catalonia,* formed large columns, the best known of which were those led by the anarchists* Durruti,*

Jover,* and Antonio Ortiz, a leader of the *Solidarios*. Other political groups, the *Partido Obrero de Unificación Marxista* (POUM),* *Partito Socialista Unificat de Catalunya* (PSUC),* and the Catalan nationalists, formed their own columns. These bodies, together with columns from Valencia,* consisting of about 30,000 men in all, attempted to carry out a social revolution in the areas they occupied, but were unable to penetrate the rebel lines, which were held by a combination of militias and the trained and properly officered garrisons of Huesca,* Saragossa,* and Teruel.* Militarily, the Republican militias were of little value, and for almost a year there was no centralized campaign planning on the eastern front. In the Basque provinces, the militias were organized mainly by the nationalist (regionalist) parties. Seventy-eight battalions of varying size had been created by the end of 1936. Even though they were almost completely lacking in professional officers, their discipline was good. In general, the militias were able to hold the conscript forces of the rebels at bay, but not to advance against them.

In central Spain, which at the height of the militia period was defended by as many as 90,000 militiamen, they were organized by the War Ministry under the immediate supervision of the *Comandancia General de Milicias* from October 20, 1936. This body insisted that battalions be properly constituted with a minimum of 330 men and with a properly appointed paymaster. There was a large number of battalions, of varied political and syndical hue, but the largest groups were the volunteer battalions, decreed by the government on August 3, 1936; the largely anarchist *Columna Anadalucía*; and the communist Fifth Regiment,* which contributed a large number of relatively well-trained and disciplined men to the later army and insisted on discipline and standard military organization.

After the formation of various numbered brigades, the militias were dissolved in January 1937. Every attempt was made to suppress the militia spirit. Names were forbidden to be used by the units, political differences were to be ignored, and proselytization was forbidden, but in many cases, the military units that had emerged from the primitive militias maintained their original coloring and political tendencies. These ideological differences hampered the unity of the army throughout the Civil War.

The disastrous defeats of the militias in Estremadura* led to the fall of the Giral government and the appointment as prime minister on September 4, 1936, of Largo Caballero,* who also took over the war portfolio. Aided by Colonel José Asensio,* whom he promoted to general and who served as commander of the central theatre of war and then as undersecretary, Largo Caballero proceeded to militarize the militias and to create an army. He did so by establishing a single command (except in Aragón); recreating a staff from various officers who offered their services, one of whom was Vicente Rojo,* later to be chief of staff of the army; appointing generals to command delineated theatres of war; establishing schools for training temporary officers, bringing militias under military law on September 30, 1936; forming brigades from October 18, divisions from November, army corps from December 31, and armies from February 1937; and creating a corps of political commissars on October 16, 1936. The political commissars would ease the tension between soldiers and professional officers, serve as education officers for soldiers who might not comprehend the full significance of a war against fascism or the need for discipline when they were defending a social revolution, and solve difficulties in relations with the rear. They were to countersign any order given by an officer before it was valid. The commissars and the later-appointed education officers (*milicianos de la cultura*) produced a large number of unit newspapers of varying quality and strove to look after the physical and moral welfare of the troops, a great many of whom were illiterate. Their efforts were undoubtedly bound up with political propaganda, and they were often a vehicle for the propaganda of the conflicting aims of different groups in Republican Spain.

The characteristic unit of the army was the Mixed Brigade, which already existed in the Spanish Army and was not, as has sometimes been claimed, introduced by the Russian advisers. It was composed of four battalions with a variable number of artillery, transport, cavalry, signals, and medical troops. It corresponded to the model approved by advanced military thought of an autonomous fighting unit, but it was probably too small, and usually too undermanned, to support its second échelon troops. As a result, it was often no more than a column of infantry with inadequate services. Within the brigade, the smaller units were organized according to standard tables established by staff bureaucrats in spite of the shortage of experienced noncommissioned officers. This happened because the accepted political view was that Spain was not in revolution and that the Republic was to be defended by a regularly formed army. This view, approved by the communists, was accepted by the anarchists,* once they had overcome their opposition to any form of organization and discipline. It was considered the only way to defeat the rebels, who paradoxically were somewhat less wedded to traditional forms. Guerrilla warfare, undertaken in the latter

part of the Civil War on a limited scale, was generally a success but was kept very much as a sideline. Whether or not the Civil War should have been fought on a less formal guerrilla basis remains a subject for debate.

By the end of 1936, brigades had been formed into divisions, and by early 1937 there would be, at least on the central front, a scheme of army corps and armies. In 1938, there would be two army groups, in the central and eastern zones, into which Republican Spain had been split, and a total of over seventy divisions, each in theory consisting of three brigades of about 4,000 men each. It is noteworthy that formal organization proceeded in the Republican Army when men and matériel were lacking. Thus, units would exist on paper when their constituent brigades, for instance, would consist of only two or three battalions, often half armed and unready for combat.

The pyramidal organization of the Republican Army required a large number of officers to command and staff its units. Although some officers, of progressive sympathies, had formed the *Unión Militar Republicana Antifascista* (UMRA)* before the Civil War in response to the right-wing *Unión Militar Española* (UME)* and had given some training to socialist militias, in particular the *Milicias Antifascistas Obreras y Campesinas* (MAOC),* the majority of army officers stationed in Republican Spain had either taken part in the rebellion or were under suspicion or in hiding, or had found their way to rebel lines. Very few officers came back to Republican Spain from the Nationalist zone. A considerable number of officers, through loyalty to their oaths of allegiance, or through political conviction, or through personal reasons, as well as some retired officers, offered their services to the Republican Army. The number of professional officers of the approximately 16,000 who had been on the active list before the war and who served the Republic cannot be stated until the records of their postwar courts-martial become available. Even then, the records will not include those who were killed in battle or who left Spain after the Civil War and did not return. Suggested figures vary widely, but 2,500 is a likely maximum. The resulting shortage of officers led to mass promotions of noncommissioned officers and junior officers and to the recognition of the ranks that had been appropriated by militia commanders. However, they were restricted to a separate list from the professionals and were limited to the highest rank of major until 1938, after which a few became lieutenant colonels. Enrique Lister* and Juan Modesto,* the communists who commanded the 5th Corps and the Army of the Ebro,* became colonel and general, respectively. A few thousand officers were produced by the People's War Schools (*Escuelas Populares de Guerra*), although they failed to produce officers as efficiently and in the same volume as their Nationalist equivalents. Professional officers felt that they were frequently under suspicion, especially in the early days of the Civil War when militia units thought that officers were about to betray them. The officers, in turn, were uncomfortable faced with militia indiscipline. For this reason the communist militias, which accepted the need for formal discipline and insisted on respect for an officer even if he were not politically progressive, attracted professional officers who not infrequently became members of the Communist party.

The activities of the Information and Control Office (*Cabinete de Información y Control*), set up to investigate the background of officers, created difficulties for a number of them and generally hampered the supply of leaders to the units. The result was a shortage of officers at all times in the army. Units at all levels were commanded by men who were unable to handle such responsibilities. Few of the Mixed Brigades,* for instance, were commanded by officers who had been on the active list in 1936, and many divisions and even corps were commanded by militia officers. If some of these, such as the communists Modesto, Lister, and Tagüeña,* and the anarchists Jover, Ricardo Sanz, and Miguel García Vivancos, were competent commanders, they could not be compared with the experienced infantry colonels who commanded Nationalist divisions. And there were militia commanders who, for political reasons, led units they could not handle. The supply of staff officers was so short that the militia and junior professional officers, ex-sergeants and Civil Guards* who so often commanded brigades and battalions, fought a largely amateur war. This was so regularly commented on by senior commanders that it became a truism.

In order to create the army, the Republic resorted to conscription. By the end of the Civil War, the classes of 1917 to 1942 inclusive had been called up, effectively mobilizing men in the eighteen to forty-five age group. The only troops available to the Republican Army besides the militias and conscripts were the five International Brigades* which, together with extra battalions and base troops, may have totaled 60,000, although at any one time the International Brigades probably had no more than 40,000 foreign members in Spain.

At the beginning of the war, the Republican Army held the larger part of the available arms. Since these were quite insufficient to fight even a short war, the government made immediate representations to France* to supply more. Before the Non-Intervention Agree-

ment made the supply of arms difficult, the Republic had received a certain number of French aircraft. The rifles, artillery, and other ground equipment held in depots were exhausted in the defeats of 1936 and were gradually replaced by material bought on the international arms market or supplied by the USSR.* There is no agreement on the total amount received by the Republic, but the quantities would not appear to be significantly different from those received by the Nationalists from the Axis powers. The probable exception is heavy artillery, which the Axis supplied in large quantities to break Republican resistance in late 1938 and early 1939. The evident shortage of aircraft suffered by Republicans* at vital moments is still to be explained, as is the lack of success of the tanks they received from the Soviet Union. The answer probably lies in considerations of the rate and regularity of supply, the suitability of the equipment for the use to which it was put, and the skill of the men who were to use it and the commanders who directed its use.

The Republican Army had to obtain its supplies wherever it could, which created difficulties of spares and ammunition. The Nationalists,* on the other hand, were armed almost entirely with German and Italian equipment, supplied officially by those countries rather than through arms dealers, at a rate and at times that were appropriate. It was also likely that the chaos and indiscipline of Republican Spain, in comparison with the authoritarian centralism of the Nationalist zone, was responsible for as much waste of valuable material as the sinking by Nationalist ships and Italian submarines* of ships consigned to Republican harbors.

That the Republican Army was highly politicized is evident. Given that the military rebellion led to a social revolution in the Republican zone, barely concealed by the reassertion of central authority by the Largo Caballero and Negrín* governments, it is hardly surprising that political consciousness was so developed in the army. This was the more so because the first reaction to the rebellion was one of antimilitarism.

Within the army, the form that military organization would take was the major issue between the various political forces that contributed to the militia effort of the early months and that remained identified with the regular military formations later. Very few of the Spanish working class understood or had any sympathy for standard military organizations, uniforms, salutes, hierarchies, and so on. This attitude was widespread not only among the anarchists and those who shared their views but also among the socialists. It was only when it became evident that the militia system was unsuccessful that the nettle of militarization was seized, as part of the effort to reassert government authority generally. The only organization to have interpreted the military position as requiring a disciplined and hierarchical army was the Spanish Communist party,* which had demonstrated its views in its own Fifth Regiment. Communist views coincided with the Popular Front* policy of demonstrating that there was no revolution in the Republic but a national army defending bourgeois legality.

The anarchists had to accept this and so lost considerable ground to the communists. Anarchist efforts were devoted to persuading the militants in the brigades, formed from the *Confederación Nacional del Trabajo* (CNT)* militias, that formal organization must be accepted. In the process, they fell behind in obtaining commissars' appointments and officers' commissions for their leaders. The CNT expended a great deal of effort in campaigning against the feared communist domination of the army. This was particularly so in Aragón, where the militarization process had been slower and where it was part of the government and communist drive against the separatism and revolutionary character of the social and economic institutions established since the beginning of the Civil War.

Given the contrasting attitudes towards army organization, it was natural that professional officers should gravitate to the Communist party. Even so, their membership in it must be taken either as an attempt at self-protection or as a recognition that the communist position was right, rather than as an acceptance of Marxism* in general. The few army officers who were friendly to the CNT were so motivated either by anticommunism or by longstanding personal friendships with anarchist leaders dating back to the 1920s.

The extent of foreign influence in the Republican Army should be considered. In October 1936, shipments of Russian tanks and, later, of aircraft were accompanied by a number of tank-drivers and pilots,* as well as by some high-ranking Russian officers. It is doubtful whether there were more than 800 or 900 of these advisers, pilots, technical personnel, and interpreters in Spain. Most of them had left by the summer of 1937, either because their job was considered completed or because their presence in Spain was too risky from the international point of view, as the USSR* was a signatory to the Non-Intervention Agreement. Russians played an important role in providing crews for tanks and aircraft and in training Spanish personnel. The Republican Army's lack of success in handling tanks was probably a reflection of its amateurishness. Hence, Russian aid was not as effective as it might have been, although the Soviet advisers might

also have been unable to adapt their advice to the military idiosyncrasies of the Spanish war. Russian aircraft played a vital role in giving the Republic air superiority in the autumn, winter, and spring of 1936-1937 and was largely responsible for the Nationalists' failure to cut Madrid off from its supply lines.

Although the few Russian generals who were in Spain and who also managed to survive the purges and the early weeks of the war against Germany* claim in their memoirs to have played important parts in leading the Republican Army, it is doubtful whether they did more than advise. Given the particularist nature of the Spanish military and its dislike of interference, Russian advice, even if requested, was unlikely to have been given a great deal of weight. However, it does seem that in some battles Russian officers took over field command at certain critical moments.

A well-publicized contribution to the army was the International Brigades,* which were numbers eleven to fifteen of the Mixed Brigades, plus certain other battalions or units. The first two International Brigades came into action in the defense of Madrid in November 1936. While they contributed considerably to their particular sectors, it would be untrue to say that they alone saved Madrid. Likewise, although the International Brigades fought in the vanguard of most of the major offensives of the Republic and suffered high losses, their reputation as crack units was not borne out by their performance. Furthermore, by the summer of 1937, their ranks were steadily being filled out by Spanish conscripts. Nevertheless, their contribution in heroism and as an example of proletarian solidarity must not be undervalued.

Militarily, the Republican Army's performance steadily improved as it gained experience, organization, and discipline. In attack it demonstrated skill and élan, aided by the efficient staff work of Chief Vicente Rojo, who was arguably the best tactician in the Spanish Army. It was also increasingly competent in counterattack and defense. However, its very conservative structure and its lack of experienced junior officers made it less efficient at exploiting breakthroughs, and many of its initial victories were soon bogged down. This was characteristic of the battles of Brunete* (July 1937), Belchite* (August 1937), and the Ebro* (July-November 1938). If some of its units were stubborn in defense, as in stopping Franco's* drive on Valencia* in the summer of 1938, its inflexibility could also lead to disastrous routs, as in the Nationalist drive to the Mediterranean in the spring of 1938.

Republican forces were defeated in the north, in Aragón and Catalonia,* but not on the central-southern front where there was relatively little movement after the failure of Nationalist attacks in 1937. Nevertheless, it is doubtful whether a stubborn resistance in 1939 could have done more than postpone the inevitable defeat, with all its dire consequences to the civilian population, once the rest of Spain had been overrun by the Nationalists. For this reason, the majority of senior officers in the zone, led by Colonel Casado,* commander of the Army of the Center,* decided to establish a National Defense Council (*Consejo Nacional de Defensa*) and negotiate surrender, with the aim of securing time to evacuate those in greatest danger. With the exception of some communist-controlled units, against whom a brief and bloody internal battle was fought, the Republican Army accepted the Casado coup. When the Nationalists refused to accept anything but immediate and unconditional surrender, to the surprise of their erstwhile comrades in arms, the fronts collapsed and the troops abandoned their positions, allowing the Nationalists peacefully to occupy the remainder of Republican Spain in the last days of March 1939.

Two Republican armies, those of the East and the Ebro, had crossed into France* at the beginning of February 1939. A large number of their troops recrossed the frontier to join the several hundred thousand of the Armies of the Center,* Levante,* Estremadura,* and Andalusia,* in prisoner-of-war camps. The majority of those who were not required for trial were released, but service in the Republican Army was not considered as discharging the obligation for military service and many men spent at least two more years in the Spanish Army.

Volunteers,* militia officers, commissars, professional noncommissioned officers, and any soldier who was more than a simple conscript were court-martialed for military rebellion. The number of death sentences was high, although many were commuted. Some men were released in a short time; others were held for many years, sometimes with the threat of death hanging over them for a year or more. While all professional military and paramilitary men were dismissed from their services, some began to receive pensions within a few years. Only recently have the ranks achieved within the Republican Army been recognized for pension purposes. In 1980, Republican war-wounded were at last granted disability pensions.

The Republican Army was characterized by a high degree of formal organization once initial indiscipline had been overcome. But the inflexibility of the army's organization masked a large amount of incapacity and inner conflict created by political conflict. The absence of a common spirit is indicated by the communists' immense propaganda and educational efforts.

The Republican Army was permanently short of the arms it needed at the right time and place, and it lost a large quantity through inexperience. It also lacked good commanders, both to lead its higher formations and to command its field units. It did, however, produce some remarkable leaders from the militias. The presence of the International Brigades and Russian advisers did little to remedy this lack of leadership.

For further information, see Diego Abad de Santillán, *Por qué perdimos la Guerra* (Buenos Aires, 1940); Michael Alpert, *El ejército republicano en la guerra civil* (Barcelona, 1977); S. Casado, *Así cayó Madrid* (Madrid, 1968); A. Cordón, *Trayectoria* (Paris, 1971); D. Ibarruri et al., *Guerra y Revolución en España* (Moscow, 1967-); E. Lister, *Nuestra Guerra* (Paris, 1966); Malinovski et al., *Bajo la bandera de la España republicana* (Moscow, n.d.); José Manuel Martínez Bande, series of monographs on the war (Madrid, 1968-); J. Peirats, *La C.N.T. en la revolución Española* (Toulouse, 1951-1953); V. Rojo, *Así fue la defensa de Madrid* (Mexico City, 1967); L. Romero, *El final de la guerra* (Barcelona, 1967); and Ramón Salas Larrazábal, *Historia del ejército popular de la república* (Madrid, 1974).

See also Appendix B.

Michael Alpert

ARMY OF AFRICA. The Army of Africa consisted of those Spanish Army units based in Spain's Moroccan Protectorate. In July 1936, this force numbered 34,047 men and was composed of regular Spanish Army units, the Spanish Foreign Legion,* and the *Fuerzas Regulares Indígenas.* As a rule, the last-named was manned by Moroccan enlisted men and led by Spanish officers. On July 19, 1936, General Francisco Franco* assumed command of this force and oversaw its airlift to the Iberian Peninsula. During the first two months of the war, approximately 10,500 men were flown across the Straits of Gibraltar.* By November 1936, this number had reached 23,400 and by early 1937, 63,000. This was an important factor in ensuring Nationalist control of southwestern Spain at the beginning of the war.

Originally organized into five vanguard columns, the Army of Africa participated in the conquest of Andalusia* and Estremadura,* the relief of Toledo,* and the siege of Madrid.* As the Civil War lost its initial momentum in late 1936, the African units, particularly the Foreign Legion and the *Regulares*, were parceled out as shock troops to other Nationalist divisions and corps. In the course of the war, these troops acquired a reputation as excellent if brutal soldiers.

For further information, see José María Gárate Córdoba, *La guerra de las dos Españas* (Madrid, 1976); and Ramón Salas Larrazábal, *Historia del ejército popular de la república* (Madrid, 1974).

See also Army, Nationalist; and Seville.

Shannon E. Fleming

ARMY OF ANDALUSIA (REPUBLICAN). The Army of Andalusia (Republican), a designation for a relatively inactive Republican military force assigned to southern Spain, was under the command of Colonel Adolfo Prada Vaquero.* Although it operated in southcentral Spain, its activities were minor. At one time, however, this army consisted of sixteen brigades, five divisions formed into two corps.

For further information, see Michael Alpert, *El ejército republicano en la guerra civil* (Barcelona, 1977).

James W. Cortada

ARMY OF ARAGÓN (NATIONALIST). The Army of Aragón (Nationalist) consisted of various divisions and brigades pulled together during the second half of the Civil War by Franco* for the purpose of seizing control of Aragón.* It was under the command of General José Moscardó Ituarte,* hero of the siege of the Alcázar.* His army was part of a larger force whose overall purpose was to push Nationalist control eastward toward the Mediterranean coast from the Pyrenees* to southern Spain. It participated in the conquest of Catalonia* after Christmas 1938, fighting until it came to the French frontier in February 1939.

For further information, see José Manuel Martínez Bande, *La compaña en Cataluña* (Barcelona, 1979).

See also Army, Nationalist.

James W. Cortada

ARMY OF ARAGÓN (REPUBLICAN). The Army of Aragón (Republican), was composed largely of anarchists* and was originally led by the colorful and controversial Buenaventura Durruti.* It was created by the anomalous Antifascist Militias Committee,* and it carried the main thrust of the Republicans' military efforts against the Nationalists* on the northern front between Huesca* and Saragossa* from August 1936 to July 1937, when it was abolished and absorbed into the regular Loyalist army and its units scattered throughout Spain or dissolved completely. As one of the most partisan and active units in the Civil War, debate about the Army of Aragón polarizes between admira-

tion for the extraordinary effort it made to create a citizens' army from scratch, and hostility towards its loosely organized, highly "libertarian" style and its failure to take Saragossa, the major objective of its efforts.

The army originated in the anarchist defense of Barcelona* against the troops of General Goded* on July 19 and 20, 1936. When elements provided by the *Confederación Nacional del Trabajo* (CNT)* and the *Federación Anarquista Ibérica* (FAI)* triumphed, Luis Companys,* premier of the Catalan Regional State, had no choice but to put these groups in charge of raising a militia army to oppose an expected attack from the West, in the direction of Saragossa, where General Mola,* Nationalist commander of the north, operated in strength. Buenaventura Durruti, one of the most famous anarchist militants and the veteran of numerous uprisings for almost two decades, was named commander-in-chief. Major José Salavera, a former regular army officer, took charge of training and local defense, and other officers, mainly Catalan, lent an element of professionalism to the militia army. The bulk of original volunteers* came from radical political groups in Barcelona*—the CNT, FAI, socialists, communists, and Trotskyists. They were formed up into columns bearing the grandiloquent names of Proudhon, Bakunin, Lenin, *Tierra y Libertad*, and Carlos Marx.

The early campaign, marred by political executions, spread through western Catalonia,* the militias* seizing Lérida* on July 25. At this point, Durruti split his forces in two, which was perhaps a mistake, and continued the advance along both the Huesca and Saragossa highways. Despite Nationalist disorganization, neither column was able to seize its objectives. Mola reinforced his lines with Navarrese *Requetés* (militia) and placed the capable General Miguel Cabanellas* in command of Saragossa's defenses. The hurried nature of the militia's creation, lack of supplies, military inexperience, and the division of forces (which, if it had been able to capture only Saragossa, would have put a significant industrial city with a large radical population at the disposal of the Republic) soon forced the Army of Aragón back from the city's edge on August 12, 1936, after which it dug in.

Reinforced by still more volunteers (many of them foreign, like the Englishman George Orwell,* who arrived some months later and who would later write about the army movingly in *Homage to Catalonia*) and given charismatic leadership by Durruti, the army resumed the offensive again on September 14 by making a feint towards Piña del Ebro on the southern flank as a preliminary to another unsuccessful attack upon Huesca. This time lack of supplies and of sophis-ticated armaments hurt the army badly, and Barce-lona and Madrid* bitterly quarreled over the lack of support given by the Republican government. The Nationalist convergence upon Madrid deprived Aragón* of needed supplies, and in early November, Durruti and 5,000 of his best soliders rushed to the capital as the siege of Madrid began. They anchored the line by the Hospital-Clinic and bore the brunt of the Nation-alist attack, although they were later criticized for allowing Franco's forces across the Manzanares River.* Their greatest loss, however, was the death of Durruti, who died by a sniper's bullet on November 20, 1936.

Durruti's successor was Ricardo Sanz, one of his associates. Much as Durruti's old 26th Division tried to avenge his death by seizing Saragossa, Sanz failed to take the city on December 21, 1936. He again failed in mid-January 1937, when anarchist elements inside the city attempted to sabotage major fortresses but did not succeed, leaving the Army of Aragón tantalizingly close in Fuendetodos. Before another ef-fort could be made, the Republican government in Madrid, eager to centralize administration in the Loyalist zone (a campaign that had already seen the abolition of the Antifascist Militias Committee on Sep-tember 26 and the beginnings of militarization three days later), close to the USSR* militarily and hostile to anarchist stress upon revolution rather than antifascism, withdrew what little it had been giving since Novem-ber 1936. After the resignation of the four anarchist members of the Popular Front* cabinet, and of Fran-cisco Largo Caballero,* the premier, on May 16, 1937, over the rioting between anarchists* and communists in Barcelona, the Army of Aragón was totally absorbed by the Republican military, which was strongly procommunist. Soviet sympathizers like Vicente Rojo* and General Kléber* joined its staff; Trotskyist units were disbanded and jailed; anarchists were scattered; and a new antirevolutionary, antifascism spirit per-vaded the militia.

After these major changes were accomplished, the new socialist minister of defense, Indalecio Prieto,* pressed the Army of Aragón back on the offensive one last time in August 1937, with attacks upon Quinto, Codo, and Belchite,* which fell on September 6. The southern approaches to Saragossa were momentarily threatened, and Republican lines moved 15 kilometers northwest, but the advance was too costly to continue, and by mid-September the Nationalists counterattacked at Teruel* and Jaca. This led to prolonged fighting at the far southern end of the army's line and to the collapse, in the spring of 1938, of the line altogether, thus dividing the Republic in two and setting the stage

for the final campaigns of the Civil War along the Ebro* and into Catalonia.

For further information, see Robert Kern, *Red Years/Black Years: A Political History of Spanish An-archism, 1911-1937* (Philadelphia, 1978); Ricardo Sanz, *Los que fuimos a Madrid: Columna Durruti 26 Divi-sion* (Toulouse, 1969); and Hugh Thomas, *The Span-ish Civil War* (New York, 1977).

See also Army, Republican; May 1937 Riots; and Militias.

Robert W. Kern

ARMY OF CASTILE (NATIONALIST). The Army of Castile (Nationalist) consisted of Navarrese Brigades, North Africans, members of the German Condor Le-gion,* some Italian units, and regular Nationalist sol-diers, all under the command of General Fidel Dávila Arrondo* reporting directly to Franco.* The army was made up of two smaller groups, known as the Army of Castile and the Army of Galicia, respectively, under the commands of Generals José Enrique Varela Iglesias* and Antonio Aranda Mata.* They fought at the battle of Teruel* between December 1937 and February 1938, blunting the Republican offensive. Many of these soldiers had been part of an earlier force that, during the second half of 1936, had conquered most of southern Spain for the Nationalists.* Later, between March and July 1938, this army participated in the campaigns in Aragón* and the Levante,* push-ing the Republicans* eastward from points running north and south from Huesca* down to Teruel and east-ward to points running south from north of Balaguer and Lérida* down to the coast above Valencia.*

For further information, see José Manuel Martínez Bande, *La batalla de Teruel* (Madrid, 1974), *La inva-sión de Aragón y el desembarco en Mallorca* (Madrid, 1970), and *Los cien últimos días de la república* (Bar-celona, 1972).

See also Catalonia.

James W. Cortada

ARMY OF CATALONIA (REPUBLICAN). The Army of Catalonia (Republican) was established to man the Catalan Republican zone in the early weeks of the Civil War. It remained in existence until it became part of the Army of the East* in the spring of 1937. Locally, however, it was called the Army of Catalonia during most of the war. Its men fought in all the major campaigns in the area, including the battles for Huesca,* Saragossa,* the Ebro,* and, finally, in the retreat to the French border in January-February 1939.

For further information, see José Manuel Martínez Bande, *La compaña en Cataluña* (Barcelona, 1979); and Ramón Salas Larrazábal, *Historia del ejército popular de la república*, 4 vols. (Madrid, 1974).

See also Aragón; and Catalonia.

James W. Cortada

ARMY OF THE CENTER (NATIONALIST). The Army of the Center (Nationalist) was one of three major groups formed by the Nationalists* during the mid-period of the Civil War (1937-1938). The other two were the Armies of the North* and the South.* In total, all three comprised approximately 500,000 men, less than what the Republic claimed it had. The Army of the Center was under the command of General Andrés Saliquet Zumeta.* He commanded this army in central Spain as the primary attack group against Madrid.* Thus, his force participated in most of the major battles of the Civil War, including Brunete* (July 1937) in which his men took a heavy toll of Republican lives, even though it failed to conquer Madrid at that time. By mid-1938, this army had continued to grow in size as Franco* placed increased emphasis on seizing Madrid.

For further information, see José Manuel Martínez Bande, *La lucha en torno a Madrid* (Madrid, 1968), *La marcha sobre Madrid* (Madrid, 1968), and *La ofensiva sobre Segovia y la batalla de Brunete* (Madrid, 1972).

See also Army, Nationalist.

James W. Cortada

ARMY OF THE CENTER (REPUBLICAN). The Army of the Center (Republican) was one of the major Republican forces of the Civil War. Its primary responsibility throughout most of the war was to defend Madrid*; thus, it participated in every battle and campaign in central Spain. It successfully prevented the Nationalists* from capturing Madrid for nearly three years, and it was responsible for all the Republican offensives associated with the defense of the capital in central Spain. Its first commander, General Sebastián Pozas Perea,* commanded the army in the early months of the fighting. He led its troops in the battle of Madrid (November 1936), Boadilla,* and Corunna Road* (December). Later, this army repulsed the Nationalist offensive at the Jarama* in February 1937. By the spring of 1937, General José Miaja Menant* had taken over command of this army which now comprised five army corps. Miaja had previously been responsible for the defense of the capital with troops stationed within Madrid's city limits, while Pozas com-

manded soldiers outside it. Under Miaja's command, the Army of the Center still maintained a strength of several hundred thousand and defended central Spain from the Nationalists, although it constantly lost ground. It finally collapsed as a fighting unit in late March 1939 before the forward push of a better equipped, larger, and more successful Nationalist Army.*

For further information, see Michael Alpert, *El ejército republicano en la guerra civil* (Barcelona, 1977); Robert Colodny, *The Struggle for Madrid* (New York, 1958); and Ramón Salas Larrazábal, *Historia del ejército popular de la república*, 4 vols. (Madrid, 1974).

See also Army, Republican.

James W. Cortada

ARMY OF THE EAST (REPUBLICAN). The Army of the East (Republican) was created by the Republic early in the Civil War to operate in Catalonia* and in Aragón* and to help defend the central zone. It was initially under the command of General Sebastián Pozas Perea* who also held command over the Army of the Center.* It had three corps consisting of twenty-five brigades and eight divisions. The Army of the East fought in all the battles and campaigns in Aragón and later in Catalonia. Headquartered in Barcelona,* it contained many of the old militia units evident in the early months of the Civil War such as those from the *Partido Obrero de Unifacación Marxista* (POUM),* *Confederación Nacional del Trabajo (CNT),* Unión General de Trabajadores* (UGT)*, and the Communist party.* It had been known as the Army of Catalonia* prior to being reorganized as a regular army by the spring of 1937 with men from various parts of Spain. After its reorganization, many Catalans considered it an army of occupation heavily influenced by the communists.

This army suffered severe losses between December 1937 and February 1938 as a result of the Nationalist offensives near Teruel.* Following the defeat of Republican efforts in Aragón, the army was once again reorganized under the command of General Juan Hernández Saravia* in the spring of 1938. Along with the Army of the Ebro,* also under his overall command, Saravia commanded approximately 300,000 men in the Catalan campaigns of the last few months of war.

For further information, see José Manuel Martínez Bande, *Los cien últimos días de la república* (Barcelona, 1972) and *La compaña en Cataluña* (Barcelona, 1979).

See also Army, Republican.

James W. Cortada

ARMY OF THE EBRO (NATIONALIST). The Army of the Ebro (Nationalist) was the name given to the Nationalist forces that fought at the battle of the Ebro* between July and November 1938 and that continued campaigning in northeastern Spain, ultimately arriving at the French border in February 1939. During the campaigns at the Ebro River, it halted Republican offensives and retook ground, leaving 10,000 to 15,000 Republicans* dead. The Army of the Ebro lost only 6,500 men. This military force relied heavily on the use of artillery to capture territory while the army occupied land. It also used aircraft extensively, at one point dropping over 10,000 bombs daily.

For further information, see José Manuel Martínez Bande, *La compaña en Cataluña* (Barcelona, 1979); and Luis María Mezquida, *La batalla del Ebro*, 2 vols. (Tarragona, 1963).
See also Army, Nationalist.

James W. Cortada

ARMY OF THE EBRO (REPUBLICAN). The Army of the Ebro (Republican) was formed by the Republic in the summer of 1938 in order to protect Valencia* from the Nationalists.* The proposal was to draw Nationalist forces into fighting at the Ebro River and then to reestablish ground communications between isolated Catalonia* and the central zone. This new army, under the command of Colonel Juan Modesto Guilloto,* the ex-commander of the famed Fifth Regiment,* consisted of 80,000 soldiers, over seventy field batteries, and nearly thirty anti-aircraft guns. All of the army's top commanders were communists and did a good job in holding onto their geographical area of control throughout 1938. This army initiated the offensive that became known as the battle of the Ebro* which lasted from July into November 1938 with mixed results. The army battled against the Nationalists who, after Christmas 1938, successfully invaded Catalonia* and occupied the entire area by the end of February 1939, thereby destroying the Army of the Ebro.

For further information, see José Manuel Martínez Bande, *La compaña en Cataluña* (Barcelona, 1979); and Luis María Mezquida, *La batalla del Ebro*, 2 vols. (Tarragona, 1963).
See also Aragón.

James W. Cortada

ARMY OF THE LEVANTE (NATIONALIST). The Army of the Levante (Nationalist) operated in southeastern Spain primarily to capture Valencia* which became the capital of the Republic midway through the Civil War. Even after the Republican government moved to Barcelona,* this army continued its efforts to seize the province and its port city. On July 5, 1938, it launched a major offensive against the city, employing approximately 900 cannon and 400 airplanes. The city finally fell in the last days of the war.

For further information, see Hugh Thomas, *The Spanish Civil War* (New York, 1977).
See also Aragón; and Catalonia.

James W. Cortada

ARMY OF THE LEVANTE (REPUBLICAN). The Army of the Levante (Republican), under the command of General Juan Hernández Saravia,* was headquartered in Teruel.* This Republican army consisted of approximately 100,000 men by December 1937, organized into three corps. Its major campaign of the war was the battle of Teruel, from December 1937 to February 1938, in which it initiated an offensive against the Nationalists,* only later to be pushed back. Although the army remained in existence until nearly the end of the war and frequently in combat, it did not play as significant a role later as it had at Teruel.

For further information, see José Manuel Martínez Bande, *La batalla de Teruel* (Madrid, 1974).
See also Army, Republican.

James W. Cortada

ARMY OF THE MAESTRAZGO (NATIONALIST). The Army of the Maestrazgo (Nationalist) consisted of four divisions of Franco's* forces fighting during the battle of the Ebro* (July-November 1938). The army was under the command of General Rafael García Valiño* who was once a Navarrese brigade commander and later served in one of Franco's postwar cabinets. This small group recaptured territory originally occupied by the Republicans* at the start of the Ebro campaign. Its efforts, particularly at Caballs in late October and early November, represented a substantial setback for the Republicans since this area was the geographical high point of the entire battlefield. This army next participated in the Nationalist campaign to occupy all of Catalonia,* successfully completing its mission. Throughout all of March 1939, many of these same soldiers fought in central Spain, helping to destroy the Republican Army of the Center.*

For further information, see José Manuel Martínez Bande, *La compaña en Cataluña* (Barcelona, 1979);

and Luis María Mezquida, *La batalla del Ebro*, 2 vols. (Tarragona, 1963).

See also Army, Nationalist; and Madrid.

James W. Cortada

ARMY OF MOROCCO (NATIONALIST). The Army of Morocco (Nationalist) was put together by Franco* in 1937. It saw its first major action as the Army of Morocco during the battle of Teruel* between December 1937 and February 1938 while under the command of General Juan de Yagüe Blanco.* This army, composed of veterans of earlier campaigns in Spain and of fighting in North Africa, experienced a series of military successes throughout 1937 and 1938. During the second half of 1938, it participated in the campaign and battle of the Ebro,* and in 1939, it fought in the final campaign to eliminate the Republican zone in southeastern Spain.

For further information, see Ramón Casas de la Vega, *Teruel* (Madrid, 1975); José Manuel Martínez Bande, *Lo cien últimos días de la república* (Barcelona, 1972); and Luis María Mezquida, *La batalla del Ebro*, 2 vols. (Tarragona, 1963).

See also Army, Nationalist; and Appendix B.

James W. Cortada

ARMY OF NAVARRE (NATIONALIST). The Army of Navarre (Nationalist) was the name given to the forces under the command of José Solchaga Zala.* Originally composed of men serving in the Navarrese divisions in the early days of the war, this army fought in the Asturian campaign (September-October 1937), later in Aragón* and in the Levante* (March-July 1938), and finally in Catalonia* (December 1938-March 1939).

For further information, see José Manuel Martínez Bande, *La guerra en el norte* (Madrid, 1969) and *La compaña en Cataluña* (Barcelona, 1979).

See also Asturias.

James W. Cortada

ARMY OF THE NORTH (NATIONALIST). The Army of the North (Nationalist) was created by General Emilio Mola Vidal* at the start of the Civil War. When, in July 1936, the Nationalists* revolted against the Republic, they were divided into two groups: those operating in the south (under Franco*) and those in the north (under Mola). In the early months of the war, both Mola and Franco had equal stature within the rebels' ranks (and some think Mola was more im-

portant). Thus, Mola's forces, known as the Army of the North, established its own priorities and even contacted Germany* for aid without coordinating with Franco. This army's ranks were originally made up of Navarrese militia, Carlists,* regular army personnel, Falangists, and others who supported the Nationalists. Its early campaigns centered on expanding control over all of northern Spain and simultaneously on marching toward Madrid.* Throughout 1936 and part of 1937, this army occupied most of the north while pouring men into central Spain for the campaigns around Madrid. Varying in size throughout the war, forces fluctuated in strength from several thousand in the early weeks of the war to hundreds of thousands a year later. After Mola died in an airplane accident in 1937, command of this army went to Fidel Dávila Arrondo* who could be counted upon to be more loyal to Franco and to work more closely in concert with his overall strategies. Under Dávila's command, the Army of the North occupied the Basque country and Bilbao.* It next fought in a series of battles in northern Spain (for example, in the Asturian campaign between September and October 1937) and, subsequently in 1938, in Aragón* with over 300,000 men and approximately 500 airplanes and a similar amount of artillery. In short, it was one of the largest armies in Spain. Finally, it participated extensively in the last campaign in Catalonia.*

For further information, see José Manuel Martínez Bande, *La compaña en Cataluña* (Barcelona, 1979), *El final del frente norte* (Madrid, 1972), and *La guerra en el norte* (Madrid, 1969).

See also Appendix B.

James W. Cortada

ARMY OF THE NORTH (REPUBLICAN). The Army of the North (Republican), under the command of General Francisco Llano de la Encomienda,* was charged with preserving northern Spain for the Republic. It fought in Asturias,* in the Basque country, and in Navarre,* constantly losing ground to the Nationalists* throughout 1936 and 1937. As of early 1937, this army had a paper strength of some 150,000 men, although these soldiers and their supplies were scattered all over northern Spain, making them a less powerful force than these statistics might indicate. Its inability to be organized into one unified command made it impossible for the Republic to defend the north adequately against better organized, though not necessarily larger, Nationalist forces. By the fall of 1937, all of the north had fallen to the Nationalists with the exception of Catalonia* to the far east.

For further information, see Michael Alpert, *El ejército republicano en la guerra civil* (Barcelona, 1977); José Manuel Martínez Bande, *La guerra en el norte* (Madrid, 1969), and *El final del frente norte* (Madrid, 1972); and Ramón Salas Larrazábal, *Historia del ejército popular de la república*, 4 vols. (Madrid, 1974).

See also Bilbao.

James W. Cortada

ARMY OF THE SOUTH (NATIONALIST). The Army of the South (Nationalist) was the major Nationalist force in southern Spain. In the early months of the Civil War, the Nationalists* had two primary military groups, the Army of the North and the Army of the South. After several months of personally commanding the southern force, Franco,* in October 1936, named Queipo de Llano* as its commander while Franco assumed the duties of Generalissimo in charge of all Nationalist efforts against the Republic. This Army of the South, which had conquered most of southern Spain during the first two months of the war, administered newly acquired land while expanding its holdings northward. Franco also expected this growing army to seize Madrid* and thereby bring a quick end to the war.

Throughout 1936 and 1937, the Army of the South expanded its control over southern Spain. For example, in January 1937, it began an extensive campaign to seize southeastern Spain, which resulted in the fall of Málaga* in February. By this time, it had three corps with a total of nine divisions operating in southern Spain. Of these units, approximately 40,000 men were Moroccan, another 40,000 Italian, and an additional 5,000 German. Yet, by the middle of 1937, its major fighting in the south was over. The army continued in existence, fighting as well, but stalemated before Madrid. Late in the war, it finally sublimated the last Republican zone in southeastern Spain.

For further information, see Joaquín Arrarás, *Historia de la cruzada española*, 35 folios (Madrid, 1940-1943); and Hugh Thomas, *The Spanish Civil War* (New York, 1977).

See also Army, Nationalist; Seville; and Appendix B.

James W. Cortada

ARMY OF THE SOUTH (REPUBLICAN). The Army of the South (Republican) was formed in late 1936 under the command of General Fernando Martínez Monje.* It launched a small offensive against Córdoba* at the end of 1936 but with little success. Many of the men serving in this army soon after became part of the Mixed Brigades.* The Army of the South also had a number of Russian advisers, the most important of whom was Kiril Meretskov, later to become a marshal. During the spring of 1937, the Nationalists* launched an attack against Málaga,* which was then under the protection of the Army of the South. These Republican forces were unable to protect the city, and consequently, it fell to the Nationalists in February. Throughout 1937 and 1938, this army continued fighting in southeastern Spain, gradually giving up territory to the Nationalists. However, it had the distinction of being the last Republican army to surrender since until the end of March 1939 it held territory along the Mediterranean coast in eastern Spain. During the war, the Army of the South had three commanders: Martínez Monje (December 18, 1936-January 27, 1937); José Villalba Rubio* (January 27, 1937-March 1, 1937); and Gaspar Morales Carrasco (March 1, 1937, to the end of the war).

For further information, see Michael Alpert, *El ejército republicano en la guerra civil* (Barcelona, 1977); and Ramón Salas Larrazábal, *Historia del ejército popular de la república*, 4 vols. (Madrid, 1974).

See also Army, Republican.

James W. Cortada

ARMY OF URGEL (NATIONALIST). The Army of Urgel (Nationalist) consisted of a number of Nationalist units that joined together in late 1938 as part of the final effort of the Civil War to conquer Catalonia.* Under the command of General Agustín Muñoz Grandes,* it was stationed at the northern end of the north-south battle line. It had primary responsibility for fighting near the Pyrenees* and for moving eastward toward Gerona* and the French border. Beginning in December 1938, this army marched into Catalonia, arriving at the Mediterranean on February 7, 1939.

For further information, see José Manuel Martínez Bande, *La compaña en Cataluña* (Barcelona, 1979).

James W. Cortada

ARRANZ Y MONASTERIO, FRANCISCO (1897-   ). Captain Arranz served in the Nationalist Air Force* and is remembered for his dealings with Germany during the first days of the Civil War. On July 23, Franco* sent him along with Adolf Langenheim (the Nazi chief in Tetuán*) and Johannes Bernhardt* (a German businessman) to Germany* for the purpose of persuading Hitler* to sell or give him ten transport aircraft with which to bring Nationalist troops from Africa to Spain. On July 26 or 27, Hitler agreed to extend aid to the Nationalists.*

For further information, see José Escobar, *Asi empezo* (Madrid, 1974).

James W. Cortada

ARRARÁS IRIBARREN, JOAQUÍN (1898-   ). Arrarás came from Pamplona.* In 1936, this promonarchist journalist sided with the Nationalists* and helped organize a news bureau that served as a propaganda arm for Franco's* cause. In 1937, the Nationalists made him director-general of the press. In that same year, he wrote the first biography of General Franco and later served as editor for the massive *Historia de la cruzada española*, published in forty-four volumes between 1940 and 1943. During the Civil War, he militantly defended the Nationalist position and controlled much of the information that foreign journalists could obtain from the government at Burgos.*

For further information, see Joaquín Arrarás Iribarren, *Franco* (Buenos Aires, 1937) and *Historia de la segunda república española*, 4 vols. (Madrid, 1956-1964), one of the first large histories of the Republic; and Círculo de Amigos de la Historia, *Diccionario biográfico español contemporaneo* (Madrid, 1970), vol. 1.

James W. Cortada

ARRIBA ESPAÑA (1935-present). *Arriba España*, the official newspaper of the Falange* party, reflected the perspectives of the Falangists and had considerable autonomy to express its views, even when they contradicted the opinions of other Nationalist supporters. "Arriba España" was also the Falangist salute used at public meetings and when greeting fellow members.

For further information, see Stanley G. Payne, *Falange: A History of Spanish Fascism* (Stanford, Calif., 1961).

James W. Cortada

ART. Both sides in the Civil War used art for political purposes, the Republicans* for international and domestic advocacy, and the Nationalists* for domestic propaganda.

The principal international forum for the Republic was the *Exposition Internationale des Arts et Techniques*, held in Paris in the summer of 1937. The Republic had received an invitation to that international exhibition in 1935, and following the outbreak of the war they were careful to ensure that the entries from Spain would call attention to the Republic's plight. In January 1937, the Republic commissioned Pablo Picasso* to paint a mural for the exhibit hall. He was asked to depict in one image the struggle of the Republic against fascism. The bombing of Guernica* by the Germans on April 26, 1937, gave him the theme for his creation. Less than a week after the attack, Picasso was absorbed in preparing sketches for "Guernica." At the Paris exhibit, the foyer was dominated by "Guernica," facing a large photograph of the assassinated poet García Lorca* on the opposite wall. Both framed an open area where Luis Buñuel* presented a continuous program of documentary films on the war. Other politically inspired art works displayed in Paris were "Montserrat" by the sculptor Julío González and "Pages catala i la revolucio" by the painter Joan Miró.

"Guernica" was neither well received nor widely reviewed at the Paris show, but a decade later it was universally hailed as the quintessential artistic interpretation of the Civil War. For two years after the Paris exhibition, "Guernica" was shown on behalf of Spanish refugee relief agencies in Paris and London, with its tour completed in the spring and summer of 1939 with showing in Hollywood, San Francisco, Chicago, and New York City. Another service to the refugees* which Picasso and other artists provided in 1937 and 1938 was the preparation of posters displayed and sold in numerous countries as an appeal to aid the children of war-torn Spain.

The outbreak of the war led to a flurry of public art, including the painting of train cars, walls, and improvised placards. This street art was a spontaneous expression of support for the Republic, but the use of posters soon became a purposeful part of the campaign to mobilize public sentiment. The posters were intended to fix in the public's mind antifascist slogans, to maintain the citizens' resolve, and to urge attention to public health and civil defense. The ebb and flow of military campaigns was accompanied by the creation of posters by the various political groups urging solidarity, patriotism, and aid for those fighting at the front.

Josep Renau, head of the fine arts in the Ministry of Education and a well-known artist, was responsible for much of the Republic's poster art in 1937 and 1938. He commissioned pieces, encouraged fine art students to contribute designs, and furnished his own work on occasion. For example, he prepared illustrations for the thirteen-point government policy announced by Juan Negrín* to rally domestic and international support to the fledgling Republic in late April 1938.

The Nationalists also used art as propaganda to rally the populace around the cause of national defense. As in the Republican zone, public art in the territory controlled by Franco's* forces was a combination of spontaneous expression and Nationalist urging, especially by the Falange* in the first year of the war. With the formation of the Ministry of Education in 1938, propaganda in art became an important part of the placards displayed in streets and in schools. The Nationalists did much to preserve the art treasures in the area they controlled. For instance, in Toledo* they succeeded in preventing the destruction of many painting after the city fell into Nationalists' hands. When Luis Bolín* initiated tours of Spain in 1938, he was particularly interested in showing the visitors the art works preserved in the north and in Andalusia.*

After the war, the Nationalists manipulated an issue relating to art into part of the regime's "black legend" about the Republic. Specifically, they charged that the Republic had plundered and despoiled the nation's art treasures. In fact, while art was lost on both sides during the war, especially in the attacks on churches in the Republican zone in the summer of 1936, the Republic's record in preserving the artistic heritage of the country was good. A decree of July 23, 1936, supplemented by the issuance of *De Incautación y Protección del Patrimonio Artístico* ten days later, oversaw the removal of private art collections to public museums in cases where Republican troops occupied the residences of supporters of the insurrection. In this manner, the duke of Alba's* art at his palace of Liria was preserved. When in early November 1936 it was apparent that Madrid* would soon be under attack, art treasures and books were transferred from the Prado, Biblioteca Nacional, and Academia de San Fernando. Their move to Valencia* started on November 11, and the bombing of these buildings, which the Republicans insisted was a deliberate act, occurred on November 14 and 25. The logistics of the move to Valencia were incredible, and later, the Prado collection was sent to Geneva. Following Franco's victory, the Prado collection was returned to Madrid.

For further information, see V. Bozal and T. Llorens, eds., *España vanguardia artística y realidad social, 1936-1976* (Barcelona, 1976).

David V. Holtby

ASCASO BUDRIA, DOMINGO (? - 1937). Ascaso Budria, born in Tarragona,* was a baker by profession. He is best remembered as a militant anarcho-Bolshevik leader. With his brothers, including Francisco,* and other leaders such as Buenaventura Durruti* and Juan García Oliver,* he belonged to the revolutionary

*Solidarios** during the 1920s, the group that evolved into the famous *Nosotros** affinity cluster of the *Federación Anarquista Ibérica* (FAI).*

As a member of the FAI, Ascaso Budria agitated for the social revolution, even during January and February 1936 when many leftist groups chose to support the Popular Front* concept. When the Civil War began, he fought with Durruti. After Francisco Ascaso Budria and Durruti were killed, Domingo quarreled with Joaquín Ascaso Budria,* his brother and a leader in the formation of the Aragonese Council of Defense and commander of the Francisco Ascaso Column, jointly inflicting significant damage on the Nationalists.* Domingo was killed at the barricades on the Gran Vía in Barcelona* during the May 1937 riots.*

For further information, see Hans Magnus Enzensberger, *El corte verano de la anarquía. Vida y muerte de Durruti* (Barcelona, 1973); Robert W. Kern, *Red Years/Black Years: A Political History of Spanish Anarchism, 1911-1937* (Philadelphia, 1978); Joan Llarch, *La muerta de Durruti* (Barcelona, 1973); and Abel Paz, *Durruti le peuple en armes* (Paris, 1972).

See also Anarchists.

Shirley F. Fredricks

ASCASO BUDRIA, FRANCISCO (? - 1936). Ascaso Budria was a leading anarchist leader in Catalonia* during the 1930s along with his brothers Domingo* and Joaquín.* Before the Civil War, he worked closely with another famous anarchist, Buenaventura Durruti,* expanding the activities of the anarchists* in northern Spain. Ascaso Budria had been a carpenter, a member of a textile syndicate, a teamster, and then a political activist. He frequently relied on assassination as a political instrument. The most famous of these acts occurred on June 4, 1923 when he helped kill Juan Soldevila Romera, the Archbishop of Saragóssa—a long-time enemy of both the CNT and UGT. At the start of the war in July, he fought with other anarchists against rebel army units in Barcelona,* helping to defeat them. He was killed during this fighting.

A reflective man capable of leading strikes and, in July 1936, of combat assaults on troops, Francisco is best remembered for his leadership role in the Spanish anarchist movement. Many historians believe that had he lived longer, the anarchist movement might have been better organized and have worked more effectively with other factions in Republican Spain.

For further information, see Robert W. Kern, *Red Years/Black Years: A Political History of Spanish Anarchism, 1911-1937* (Philadelphia, 1978).

James W. Cortada

ASCASO BUDRIA, JOAQUÍN (? -1939?). Ascaso Budria became the president of the Council of Aragón* in 1936. This anarchist, brother of Francisco Ascaso Budria,* a leading anarchist, thereby gained almost total power over Aragón in the early months of the Civil War. The Republican government recognized the authority of Ascaso Budria's anarchist regime as the only effective ruling body in the area. During his tenure, the collectivization of agriculture continued, although the communists charged that Ascaso Budria ruled with a heavy hand. Joaquín was energetic and extremely violent. He irritated Republican and Catalan officials almost from the first day in office. When agricultural and mining production failed to match prewar levels, many questioned his administrative abilities. By July 1937, local communists began a campaign to discredit him, confiscating truckloads of food, criticizing him in the press, and persuading officials and politicians that his administration hurt the war effort. Finally, in August, Ascaso Budria's Council of Defense was dissolved and another established without him even as a member. Anarchists* throughout Aragón were subject to arrest; Joaquín was charged with smuggling. His decline in power paralleled the demise of the anarchist movement in Republican Spain. After the May 1937 riots* in Barcelona,* the Republic broke the power of the anarchists, removed them from government and all positions of authority, and arrested many. From August 1937 onward, Ascaso Budria played no role in the war.

For further information, see Robert W. Kern, *Red Years/Black Years: A Political History of Spanish Anarchism, 1911-1937* (Philadelphia, 1978); and Juan Zafon Bayo, *El Consejo Revolucionario de Aragón* (Barcelona, 1979).

James W. Cortada

ASENS, JOSÉ. Asens, a leading member of the *Confederación Nacional del Trabajo* (CNT),* became a CNT representative on the Antifascist Militias Committee,* established to govern Barcelona* in July 1936. As a member of the powerful Department of Investigation and Vigilance, created by the committee, Asens directed the *patrullas de control* (police patrol squads). The commission and the patrols, heavily staffed with anarchists,* were charged with maintaining revolutionary law and order, with monitoring the actions of police* groups in the city, and with controlling war profiteering. To this end, they were authorized to make inquiries, conduct searches, and arrest suspects. When the Central Telephone Exchange was attacked during the May 1937 riots* in Barcelona, it was under Asens' leadership that the patrol squads saved the *Telefónica* for the CNT.

For further information, see Diego Abad de Santillán, *Por que perdimos la guerra* (Madrid, 1975); Pierre Broué and Émile Témime, *The Revolution and the Civil War in Spain* (Cambridge, Mass., 1970); and Robert W. Kern, *Red Years/Black Years: A Political History of Spanish Anarchism, 1911-1937* (Philadelphia, 1978).

See also Catalonia.

Shirley F. Fredricks

ASENSIO CABANILLAS, JOSÉ (1896-1970). Asensio, who led the uprising in Tetuan* in July 1936, fought in all major campaigns of the Civil War as commander of the 12th Division. Frequently referred to as one of the most brilliant commanders of the Spanish Army, he later served as army chief of staff and minister of war until his retirement in 1963.

After the successful uprising in Africa, Asensio, in command of a *bandera* of Spanish legions and a *tabor* of Moroccan regulars, moved to Seville* with Yagüe's* Army of Africa,* arriving there on August 5. By August 10 the army had moved north, and Asensio, on the left flank, gained the town of Mérida* on August 10. By August 14 they had moved west to control Badajoz,* where Asensio was involved in the infamous "massacre" when supposedly hundreds of prisoners were killed. Marching up the Tagus River* Valley, his units were involved in heavy fighting. The town of Talavera de la Reina* finally fell to Asensio on September 2. A slight halt in the advance was followed by the move on Toledo,* where under the command of General Varela,* Asensio took part in the relief of the Alcázar* on September 26-28. Afterwards, he returned to Yagüe's command, moving into the Madrid* area and occupying Navalcarnero on October 21.

In the first assault on Madrid (November 6), Asensio unsuccessfully attempted an attack in the suburban area, Casa de Campo, and then on November 15 he fought in the Ciudad Universitaria where a little more ground was gained, even though Asensio's major function was to fortify and hold. With army reorganization in December, his units, which then consisted of three battalions, two *tabores* of regulars, and a *bandera* of the Foreign Legion,* became part of the *Division Reforzada de Madrid* under Varela and continued to fight in the same area until early January 1937.

In the battle of the Jarama,* Asensio's abilities were more evident as he commanded the right flank, taking San Martín de la Vega on February 11 and successfully assaulting the difficult area of the Pingarron

Heights on the other side of the river on February 12. Casualties* were heavy in this sector, but, as would be the case during the entire war, the general command recognized Asensio's talents and quickly reinforced his units with as good recruits as were available.

Asensio maintained a defensive position in the Madrid area, and, in the summer of 1937 with another army reorganization, his units became the 12th Division. After the Republican attack at Brunete* in July, Asensio was moved to that sector and was involved in the counterattack on July 24. In addition to his military activities, in April 1937, after the party unification decreed by Franco,* Asensio was named the Falangist military representative to the government. His political sympathies, then and later, were pro-Falangist, pro-German, and antimonarchist.

By June 1938, another army reorganization put Asensio and his division in the Navarre Army Corps headed by Solchaga.* The forces were shifted to the new Levante* front where Asensio again showed his exceptional abilities of command in the Pena Juliana sector in July 1938, and at Flix-Granadella in December 1938. By that point he was promoted to general and subsequently was involved in the final move in the Levante area, from Lérida* to Tarragona* in January 1939.

After the end of the conflict, Asensio was promoted to brigadier general and appointed high commissioner of Morocco,* a post he held until May 1941 when Franco brought him back to Spain as chief of the general staff. This move was intended to balance certain promonarchist sentiments in the government and military at the time. In September 1942, Asensio was named minister of war, perhaps because Franco also wished to retain a certain pro-German interest, since he had just dismissed Ramon Serrano Suñer* as a sacrifice to other military objectives. Asensio was replaced as minister in 1945 but continued to serve in the army. He operated as chief of Franco's military household, and in 1955 he was once more named chief of staff. Asensio clearly symbolizes the more capable as well as the politically involved military officers of Nationalist Spain.

For additional information, see Manuel Aznar, *Historia militar de la guerra de España*, 3 vols. (Madrid, 1969); Luis María de Lojendio, *Operaciones militares de la guerra de España, 1936-1939* (Barcelona, 1940); and Stanley Payne, *Politics and the Military in Modern Spain* (Stanford, Calif., 1967).

See also Catalonia; and Madrid.

Jane Slaughter

ASENSIO TORRADO, JOSÉ (1892-   ). Asensio was a member of the élite Staff Corps and had been a colonel since the early age of thirty-four as a result of field promotions. The beginning of the Civil War found him in Málaga* and as first chief of staff to General Miaja's* column operating against the rebels in Jaén* and Córdoba.* On August 8, 1936, he was summoned to command columns fighting the rebels in the mountains north of Madrid.* He was successful in logistics and organization but not in establishing discipline within the militia. Himself smart and well-uniformed, he disdained to wear the overalls which many career officers donned to avoid the suspicions of the militia.

When Largo Caballero* took over the government and the War Ministry on September 4, 1936, he immediately promoted Asensio to general and appointed him to command the central theatre of operations. However, attempts to retake lost ground failed in spite of the wealth of men and equipment used. The militias* were simply not skilled enough, and the professional officers who led them were either unreliable or thought to be so. The enemy advanced despite Asensio's ability and despite reports that he imposed draconian discipline, executing a number of militiamen. It was at this point that the anarchists* and communists began to dislike Asensio. The communists, while respecting his technical ability, came to believe that he had little sympathy with their vision of a people's army. Thus, when his counterattack at Illescas failed in the face of the steady rebel advance, Largo Caballero was forced to replace him. Nevertheless, the prime minister retained his administrative skills by appointing him undersecretary for war on October 22, 1936, and it was here that he made his greatest contribution to the Republican Army.* He was in charge of the rapid militarization of the militias and the creation of the army. He insisted on proper uniforms and hierarchy. He unified military education and set up the officers' schools which had previously been the fief of the political parties and trade unions.* He was also the impeller of the mass mobilization system and of the main artillery and signals schools.

Some sources indicate a certain rigidity in Asensio's views. To some he appeared to be superficial and fatalistic in view of the lack of skill of the militia. In his own defense, written while under arrest, Asensio claimed that his self-possession was mistaken for indifference.

It was Asensio who personally typed the instructions to Generals Miaja and Pozas* on the night of November 6, 1936, when Madrid seemed about to fall. The instructions were to defend Madrid to the extreme limit, but reasonable fallback orders were also given.

The fall of Málaga in February 1937 brought the downfall of Asensio. The Communist party* and press attacked him as part of their attack on Largo Caballero. Asensio was reported to be in a Valencia* night club on the night before Málaga fell. He was said to have abandoned the city and to have been responsible for a munitions shortage. Other evidence suggests that this was not so and that militia disorganization in Málaga had made the city indefensible, however much matériel was sent there. Asensio's dismissal may be interpreted as a political necessity. Evidently, he was greatly mistrusted and pessimistic about the militias' powers.

Asensio was removed from the undersecretaryship of war on February 20, 1937. More than once the Basque president, Aguirre,* asked that he be sent to the north, but the request was always turned down. There were also fears of assassination, which Asensio expressed in a letter to Indalecio Prieto,* the defense minister after Largo Caballero's fall.

Asensio was arrested in September 1937 and held in prison awaiting trial on charges connected with the loss of Málaga. The main accusation was that he had remained passive while aware of the perilous situation in Málaga. The charges were evidently dropped before trial, but in a book published in 1938 Asensio defended himself, giving details of armaments dispatched and orders he sent to Málaga. On his release in 1938, he requested a command but the chief of staff, General Rojo,* demurred, considering him an intriguer. Asensio was appointed to investigate the loss of territory by the Estremaduran Army in July 1938 and produced a long and interesting report on the conditions of that front.

On January 15, 1939, he was appointed military attaché to the Spanish Embassy in Washington, D.C.; he remained in the United States in exile after the end of the Civil War. He subsequently engaged in speaking tours and other political activity.

For further information, see Michael Alpert, *El ejército republicano en la guerra civil* (Barcelona, 1977); José Asensio, *El General Asensio, su lealtad a la república* (Barcelona, 1938); and Ramón Salas Larrazábal, *Historia del ejército popular de la república*, 4 vols. (Madrid, 1974).

See also Army, Republican.

Michael Alpert

ASSAULT GUARDS (*ASALTOS***).** The Assault Guards were special police* units created by the Spanish Republic in 1931 to combat urban violence. They are not to be confused with the Civil Guard* (*Guardia Civil*) which had responsibility for fighting crime in the countryside. At the start of the Civil War, the *Asaltos* had approximately 18,000 members. About 12,000 elected to remain loyal to the Republic while another 5,000 sided with the Nationalists.* Their virtual disintegration, following the large turnover of men who left to join Franco,* insured that the remaining units loyal to the Republic would play a relatively minor role in the war. Other, larger groups of armed men, such as the worker militias,* exercised greater police control in towns and cities through their use of vigilantes. However the *Asaltos* helped put down the Nationalist uprising in Barcelona* in July 1936, and in May 1937, approximately 4,000 of them assisted in restoring order to the same city. Historians believe that the Assault Guards were involved in the assassination of José Calvo Sotelo,* which helped trigger the start of the war.

For further information, see Michael Alpert, *El ejército republicano en la guerra civil* (Barcelona, 1977); and Ramón Salas Larrazábal, *Historia del ejército popular de la república*, 4 vols. (Madrid, 1974).

See also Army, Republican; and May 1937 Riots.

James W. Cortada

ASTIGARRABÍA, MANUEL. Astigarrabía served as secretary general of the Basque Communist party.* He joined the provisional government of the Basques (formed in October 1936) as minister of public works and as head of the local Communist party. In June 1937, when the Basque government retreated from Bilbao* during the last stages of the Nationalist assault on the area, Astigarrabía remained behind as part of a defense *Junta* for the city. After Bilbao fell to the Nationalists,* the Communist party tried to blame him for the defeat. He had been at odds with the Spanish Communist party,* often supporting local Basque nationalist aspirations which led the party to condemn him for backing the "reactionary and bungling policy" of the Basque government.

For further information, see Stanley G. Payne, *Basque Nationalism* (Reno, Nev., 1975).

See also Basque Nationalism.

James W. Cortada

ASTURIAS. Asturias, a region in northwestern Spain facing the Bay of Biscay, was rich in coal deposits and sources for zinc and copper. The Asturian miners were politically militant during the 1930s, attempting a revolt against the government in Madrid* in 1934. General Franco* commanded the troops that suppressed the bloody uprising, hailing the end of a threat to the

Republic by the extreme political Left. When the Civil War came in July 1936, this region overwhelmingly supported the Republic against the more conservative Nationalists.* Pockets of Nationalist rebellion in the region were squashed with memories of 1934 to inspire the miners. Radical leftist politicians assumed control over local governmental affairs, often acting independently of the regime in Madrid. *Juntas* and defense committees came into existence, often staffed with workers. Such groups directed the siege against Nationalist rebels in Oviedo,* capital of the area, where they were sheltered in a few buildings against the miners for many months. Members of the *Unión General de Trabajadores* (UGT),* the *Confederación Nacional del Trabajo* (CNT),* and the Spanish Communist party* worked together in local administration. They collectivized various mining operations which were controlled with committees heavily represented by miners. Coal was supplied to Republican zones and was also sold to other countries in exchange for foreign currencies and supplies. When the Nationalists cut off Asturias from the rest of Republican Spain, less coal could be shipped out, especially to Barcelona.* Then the Nationalists had ships stationed off the coast, making exports even more difficult.

Asturias was cut off from the rest of Spain by the end of 1936, which encouraged it to develop its own government and even a separate currency. The war came to Asturias soon enough, however. During the first winter of the war, over 45,000 Republican troops operated in the region. By spring 1937, portions of western Asturias were in Nationalist hands. Franco decided then to complete the conquest of the north, going after the Basque country, Vizcaya,* and Asturias. Nationalist troops in the north numbered over 100,000 (possibly as many as 150,000), while there were just over 100,000 Republican soldiers. Serious fighting occurred in September when the Nationalists began their major effort to occupy Asturias totally. Their advance, although slow, was effective. Discontent, lack of supplies, and declining military strength weakened the Republicans* and made it possible for the Nationalists to continue their campaign. By the end of the third week of October 1937, Asturias had fallen to the Nationalists. The ultimate reason for their success was that the three Republican regions in the north—Asturias, the Basque country, and Santander*—never worked together for their defense.

The acquisition of the north gave Franco large coal reserves, Basque arms factories, 1.5 million people, and well over 40 percent of the national production of all mineral supplies (coal, iron, zinc, and copper, for example). Some 65,000 Nationalist troops could now

be devoted to other campaigns. In all three areas combined, the Republicans suffered about 33,000 fatalities; in addition, over 100,000 men were wounded, and another 100,000 were taken prisoners. Nationalist losses totaled about 100,000 (dead, wounded, and captured). A severe purge of Asturias took place for several months after October, with many Republicans arrested and sent to concentration camps* or work camps, and others executed.

For further information, see José Manuel Martínez Bande, *El final del frente norte* (Madrid, 1972); and Hugh Thomas, *The Spanish Civil War* (New York, 1977).

See also Bilbao; and Appendix B.

James W. Cortada

ATARAZANAS BARRACKS. The Atarazanas Barracks in Barcelona,* located at the foot of the Ramblas in the largest worker neighborhood in the city, became the scene of some of the heaviest fighting of July 19, 1936, when troops from the installation rebelled in favor of Franco's* cause. Anarchists* eventually took over the facility and suppressed the rebellion. With the fall of this strategically important position, the Nationalist rebels could not hope to dominate the lower part of Barcelona and thus a major city in northern Spain. In the early months of the war, guns from this facility were distributed to anarchist militia units. Later, the barracks served as home for Republican soldiers, militia units, and, on occasion, a hospital, particularly in late 1938 and early 1939 when Barcelona experienced continuous bombings.

For further information, see Robert W. Kern, *Red Years/Black Years: A Political History of Spanish Anarchism, 1911-1937* (Philadelphia, 1978).

James W. Cortada

ATTLEE, CLEMENT (1884-1967). At the time of the Spanish Civil War, Attlee was head of the British Labour party and, therefore, in opposition to the government of Neville Chamberlain* and to the views of other conservative politicians. Attlee supported the Spanish Republic, urged the sale of arms to it, and called the policy of nonintervention a "farce." He supported all efforts to aid the Republic and took great interest in the International Brigades.* In December 1937, he toured Republican Spain and spoke with British brigaders. A year later, when they returned to Great Britain,* he again met with them. In Parliament he called for the elimination of the British naval blockade of Bilbao* on the grounds that the Republic should be helped and that those who wished to sail ships into the port would do so in defiance of the navy. His party placed considerable pressure on the British government throughout the war not to appease Franco* or the governments of Italy* and German* on the question of Spain.

For further information, see C. R. Attlee et al., *What We Saw in Spain* (London, 1937); and K. W. Watkins, *Britain Divided* (London, 1963).
See also League of Nations.

James W. Cortada

AUDEN, W[YSTON] H[UGH] (1907-1973). Wyston Hugh Auden, in Spain from January to March 1937, returned to England to pen "Spain," which is perhaps the best known single poem about the Spanish Civil War. Auden went to Spain amid the cheer of headlines in the *Daily Worker* that "Famous Poet to Drive Ambulance in Spain," but once he arrived he merely visited Barcelona* and Valencia* and then quietly returned home. In Valencia, he wrote a piece for the *New Statesmen* (January 30, 1937), giving his impression of the Republican cause as a spirited defense of personal freedom. Back in England in the fall of 1937, Auden joined the group of leftist intellectuals* organized by Nancy Cunard* in urging writers to take sides in the war.

Auden's poem "Spain" was the fifth pamphlet in a series published by Cunard entitled "Poets of the World Defend the Spanish People." The poem is a psychological rather than a political interpretation of the difficulty of moral choices in wartime. George Orwell* used "Spain" in "Inside the Whale" as an example of political naiveté among leftist intellectuals. In later years, Auden rejected his Marxist sympathies of the 1930s and repudiated "Spain" as "trash" he was "ashamed to have written."

For further information, see Samuel Hynes, *The Auden Generation: Literature and Politics in England in the 1930s* (London, 1976).
See also Literature.

David V. Holtby

ÁVILA. Ávila province, the state located directly west of Madrid* in Old Castile,* quickly sided with the Nationalists* in the first few days of the Civil War and remained under the insurgents' control for the remainder of the fighting. The first major battle of the war was fought in the province at the Alto de Léon Pass* in July 1936, a conflict that the Republicans* lost, retreating toward Madrid and thereby exposing the plains near the capital to the insurgents. Throughout the next two and a half years, troops passed back and forth through the province as the Nationalists attempted to capture Madrid, often using the city of Ávila as army headquarters.

For further information, see José Manuel Martínez Bande, *La lucha en torno a Madrid* (Madrid, 1968).
See also Army, Nationalist.

James W. Cortada

AZAÑA Y DÍAZ, MANUEL (1880-1940). Azaña was born in Alcalá de Henares* on January 10, 1880. The Azaña family had a liberal heritage dating back to Manuel's great grandfather, who was a member of the first constitutional council of Alcalá de Henares in 1813-1814, and a grandfather, who was a militia captain in the Revolution of 1854. Manuel's father, however, favored the Bourbon restoration of 1874 and helped defend it against a republican threat in 1886. For this service, the family would have received a title of nobility, were it not for the objections of the ex-militia man forebear. Manuel's father would also be remembered as the author of *Historia de la ciudad de Alcalá de Henares*. His mother came from a moderately well-to-do family. The Azaña family had made significant strides upward by the time of Manuel's birth. Later, when he was already a prime minister, Manuel Azaña described himself as "an intellectual, a liberal, and a bourgeois"—traits rooted in his family background.

Azaña was orphaned early—his mother died in 1889 and his father the following year. His early schooling was at the *Colegio Complutense* and the *Instituto del Cardenal Cisneros* of his hometown. At the age of thirteen, after receiving the *bachillerato* from the latter institution, he was sent to study at the *Real Colegio de Estudios Superiores*, run by the Augustinian Order in the Escorial. In 1898, he examined and obtained his licentiate in law from the University of Saragossa, with a *sobresaliente* (excellent) mark. Returning home, he published his first articles in *Brisas del Henares*, edited by some friends. In the fall of 1898, he started studies at the *Universidad Central* in Madrid* toward a doctorate of laws, which he obtained two years later with the presentation of a thesis entitled "Las responsabilidades de las multitudes." Following common practice, he became apprenticed to an important law firm. At the same time, he contributed articles for *Gente vieja* and became involved in the activities of the Academy of Jurisprudence, where, in 1902, he delivered a lecture on "Freedom of Association." He balked at exploiting this successful discourse and taking one step further into the ranks of the establishment. Moreover, the family was suffering certain economic reverses, and so he returned to Alcalá de Henares for five years.

Returning to Madrid, he took the competitive examination for a post in the Registry Office of the Ministry of Justice and became a minor bureaucrat. The job provided income and leisure time. In 1911, he received a six-month scholarship from the *Junta para Ampliación de Estudios e Investigaciones Científicas* to study civil law in Paris. While there, he wrote articles for Spanish publications, an activity he continued after his return to Madrid in 1912. He contributed to such publications as *La Correspondencia de España, El Imparcial*, and *España*, as well as to the French *Le Figaro*. In 1920, he helped publish a monthly, *La Pluma*. When this ceased publication in 1923, he joined the editorial board of *España*, the journal founded by José Ortega y Gasset, which ceased publication in 1924 as a result of the Primo de Rivera censorship. His contributions to *La Pluma* and *España* were later published in book form as *Plumas y Palabras*.

Azaña published his first book in 1918, part of a projected three-volume study of French politics, of which only the first volume, *La política militar*, was completed. The topic he wrote on was to have a significant bearing on the choice of Azaña as war minister in the provisional government of the Second Republic.* Actually, his focus in this work was the same as that in his doctoral dissertation and other studies: individual liberty versus the needs of society.

In 1926, Azaña's writing ability received recognition, when he won the National Prize for Literature for "Vida de Don Juan Valera." The work was not published (one author claims that Azaña had made an agreement with Valera's daughter not to publish the whole work until after her death), but substantial portions of it were published in the form of articles, prologues, and pamphlets. In 1927, Azaña published his semi-autobiographical novel, *El jardín de los frailes*, whose anticlerical content drew attention. His first play, *La corona*, was published in 1928. Representations of the work were failures, even though Anzaña had by then become prime minister. In addition, from 1920 to 1932, Azaña translated nine French and English works into Spanish, the most important of which was the three-volume translation of George Borrow, *The Bible in Spain*. Despite all of this activity, his literary fame was not widespread. For that reason, Unamuno* could later say that Azaña was a writer without readers who was capable of creating a revolution in order to be read.

Important for Azaña's political future was his association with the Ateneo, the haven for intellectuals* and liberals. Here Azaña studied, gave lectures, and participated in various scholarly activities, especially in the period after his return from France.* His dedication to the institution, together with the right patronage, resulted in his election as first secretary of the Ateneo in 1913. He made a good impression by the able discharge of the post, which he kept until 1920. It was in one of his interventions in a gathering at the Ateneo that Azaña discovered he had the gift of oratory.

Azaña's desire to become an officer of the Ateneo was related to a general plan to enter politics. In 1913, he joined the Reformist party, recently created by Gumersindo Azcárate and Melquíades Álvarez, republicans disposed to accept the monarchy in return for an English-style, parliamentary government pledged to work for democratic reforms. The party's program especially appealed to the so-called Generation of 1914, to which Azaña belonged. In 1913 and 1914, Azaña explored the possibility of running as a Reformist candidate for the Cortes,* but political circumstances in his hometown were unfavorable. He became a candidate from the province of Toledo* in 1918 and 1923, but lost.

Interest in politics involved Azaña in new activities. He lectured on political topics such as the one in 1917 at the Ateneo attacking the Germanophiles, a subject on which his tours to the battlefields of France and Italy* had given him first-hand knowledge. He also spoke to crowds and became engaged in political organization. In 1914, he actively supported the *Liga de Educación Política Española*, whose aim was to galvanize the intellectuals to bring about national reform. In 1918, he organized the *Unión Demócratica Española*, in collaboration with those intellectuals who supported the Allies during World War I, again with the aim of furthering the democratization of Spain. These were civic associations. As to political party, Azaña still belonged to the Reformist party, until the years following World War I showed the mistaken hopes of that party. The establishment of Primo de Rivera's dictatorship provided a catalyst. The defense and furtherance of individual liberty, Azaña concluded, could not be achieved under the aegis of the monarchy. Thus, in 1925, he founded a political party, *Acción Republicana*, dedicated to republicanism but rejecting the historic Republican party of Alejandro Lerroux. Azaña complained about the lonely struggle endured by those who fought Primo de Rivera's dictatorship; on the personal side, in 1929 he married Dolores Rivas Cherif, sister of one of his closest friends.

The fall of Primo de Rivera in 1930 strengthened Azaña's political position; partly as a result, he was elected president of the Ateneo that same year. This was the highest office Azaña held under the monarchy; it was also a stepping stone to officialdom in the Republic.

The *dictablanda* rule of General Dámaso Berenguer allowed various conspiracies against the monarchy to operate actively within the country. As representative of the small, intellectually oriented, Madrid-based *Acción Republicana*, Azaña met in August 1930 with leaders of other antimonarchist parties. The Pact of San Sebastián was the result. The signatories pledged to work together to bring about the overthrow of the monarchy, by force if necessary. They established a Revolutionary Committee that would become the provisional government upon the arrival of the Republic. In the apportioning of seats, Azaña was designated minister of war, for the simple reason that he was the only one in the unmilitarily minded group who had made studies of military matters. Azaña's Ateneo was the scene of further meetings and activities of the Revolutionary Committee, which decided on December 15, 1930, as the date of uprising. However, Captains Fermín Galán and Angel Hernández of the Jaca garrison, in their desire to steal the thunder, precipitated the rebellion by three days. The government easily quelled the rebellion and arrested the signers of the Pact of San Sebastián. Azaña escaped capture by conspicuously attending a theatrical performance the night of the revolt and then silently slipping away. While news was circulated that he had fled to France, Azaña hid for four months in the homes of friends and relatives and finally in his own home where he reasoned the police* would least suspect him to be. While in hiding, he worked on *Fresdeval*, a novel published posthumously. Because the government did not consider Azaña big game, he was able to stay in hiding, but his political enemies would later use this as evidence of cowardice, a charge often leveled against him during the Civil War.

The municipal elections on April 12, 1931, showed the great strength of antimonarchist forces in urban areas, and, on April 14, Alfonso XIII* decided to leave the country. Azaña literally came out of his hiding place to take possession of the Ministry of War, where he speedily drafted decrees for military reform. On April 25, a mere eleven days after the establishment of the Republic, Azaña took measures to reduce the inordinate number of officers in the army by offering retirement with full pay for those who would do so within a specified period. More than half of the officer corps took advantage of the generous offer, but most die-hards and incompetents stayed on. In subsequent weeks, Azaña issued decrees for restructuring and reorganizing the army, not so much for

technical reasons as for democratizing the army and removing it from politics. These considerations lay behind the closing of the General Academy of Saragossa,* a better blow to its director, General Francisco Franco.* On July 17, 1931, ironically five years to the day of the later outbreak of the Civil War, Azaña declared before the Cortes that Spain had an army ready to die for the Republic. More military reforms were yet to follow. Azaña's decrees received praise in the Constituent Cortes; even military officers shared the opinion of the need for reform. The resentment felt by the military—many of whom had at least passively accepted the Republic—was due to the drastic extent of the reforms, especially the spirit with which Azaña set about carrying the task. He publicly stated that his aim was to "pulverize" the army; his other comments were denigrating to the institution.

Aside from the army, Azaña considered the Catholic Church* as the institution most responsible for Spain's backwardness. It was his intervention in the religious question that confirmed him as the leader of the new regime. He became the "revelation"—later the "personification"—of the Republic. He brought to the regime the gifts of his superior intellect, his moral probity, and his incisive oratory. He also brought to it weaknesses arising out of lack of political experience, his personal and intellectual hauteur, and his tactless—even vindictive—disposition.

When the burning of religious buildings occurred in May 1931, Azaña led the opposition within the provisional government to the use of the Civil Guards* to put a stop to the violence. He reasoned that the burning of all the convents in Spain was not worth the life of a single Republican. Later, when the Constituent Cortes—to which he was elected as a delegate from Valencia*—encountered its thorniest problem in dealing with the religious articles, Azaña intervened decisively in the famous speech of October 13, 1931. He defended the elimination of special privileges for the Church on the grounds that Spain had ceased to be Catholic. This statement was meant to refer to the national ethos and culture, but was understood in a wider sense that Azaña made no efforts to rectify. He also favored preventing the religious orders* from engaging in nonreligious education,* a sphere where he found their influence most injurious. Azaña faced squarely the contradiction posed by the abrogation and curtailment, as far as the orders were concerned, of rights guaranteed in the projected Constitution. He argued that it was not a question of liberty but of the public health of society and the safety of the Republic. Hours after this speech, Article 26 of the Constitution was passed.

Prime Minister Niceto Alcalá-Zamora and Interior Minister Miguel Maura resigned their posts, as they had warned they would in the event of the passage of Article 26. The first cabinet crisis of the new regime was resolved by the election of Azaña as prime minister on October 16, 1931. One of his first acts in that office was to obtain from the Cortes the Law for the Defense of the Republic. The exceptional police powers which the law conferred on the government were again justified by Azaña in terms of the security of the regime. When the new Constitution was passed on December 9, Azaña proposed and carried through the election of Alcalá-Zamora as first president of the Republic in an effort to heal the rift created by the debates on the Constitution. In turn, Alcalá-Zamora asked Azaña to continue as prime minister.

At this point, Alejandro Lerroux, Radical party member of the cabinet, forced Azaña to choose between his party and the socialists. Azaña opted for the socialists, partly out of antipathy toward Lerroux and partly out of the consideration that his position would be stronger in a coalition with the socialists, who had no other possible allies. The clearly leftist government headed by Azaña followed a moderate path on socioeconomic issues, whereby it failed to incorporate the working classes into the Republic. In the Cortes, Azaña's government made little headway in passing bills relative to agrarian reform and regional autonomy. However, the bungling military revolt attempted by General José Sanjurjo* on August 10, 1932, rallied support around the government. For the rest of the year, Azaña was at the height of his popularity. In September, the Cortes passed the Agrarian Reform Bill and the Catalan Statute. Although Azaña was not much interested in the agricultural bill, he had worked hard and staked his prestige on the question of Catalan autonomy. Fittingly, his trip to Catalonia* to deliver the statute of home rule passed by the Cortes was a triumph.

In January 1933, the prestige of the Azaña government plummeted because of the Casas Viejas affair when unfounded rumors were circulated that Azaña had personally given a crude command to the Assault Guards* to mow down the anarchist rebels with gunfire. Azaña's coalition government weathered the challenge from the *Lerrouxistas*, but the sense of loss of moral legitimacy remained. The results of the municipal elections in April 1933 showed the decline in the groups supporting the government. Azaña's disdainful labeling as "rotten boroughs" of those towns where monarchist candidates were triumphant could not hide the signs of popular disaffection. Moreover, his government had trouble with growing labor violence that summer. There was criticism from the most moderate

section of his *Acción Republicana* party. Still, Azaña survived Alcalá-Zamora's first attempt to find an alternative government in June 1933. The final blow came in September, during the elections for the Tribunal of Constitutional Guarantees, when local government leaders voted two to one against candidates identified with the Azaña coalition. President Alcalá-Zamora withdrew his confidence from Azaña; new elections were called for November 1933.

The second parliamentary elections under the Republic were won by the *Confederación Española de Derechas Antónomas* (CEDA)* and Radical parties. *Acción Republicana*, together with other leftist Republican groups, was nearly wiped out. Azaña's party gained only five seats. Azaña spent the years in the opposition in literary activity and in rebuilding the leftist Republican coalition. In 1934, he published *La invención del Quijote y otros ensayos* and a two-volume collection of speeches, *En el poder y en la oposición*. His political activity was equally fruitful. In April 1934, Azaña succeeded in uniting his party with that of the Radical Socialists and the Gallegan Autonomists, resulting in the creation of *Izquierda Repúblicana* under his presidency.

In the summer, there was much talk of revolutionary violence. There was little doubt that Azaña condemned revolutionary procedures and had actually the prescience to realize that military dictatorship would be the result of such violence, but his public pronouncements were vague and threatening. It was the same kind of posturing as when he talked of pulverizing the army and declared that Spain had ceased to be Catholic. The issue of revolutionary opposition came to a head in October 1934, when the inclusion of CEDA ministers in the Lerroux cabinet became the occasion of an uprising, particularly in Barcelona* and Asturias.* At the time of the uprising, Azaña was in Barcelona, having gone there a few days previously to attend the funeral of Jaime Carner, who had served as minister of finance under him. Azaña was apprised of the revolutionary plans of Luis Companys,* and he counseled against them. He was not heeded; the government put down the Barcelona revolt without difficulty.

The Lerroux government, unscrupulously and unwisely accusing Azaña of involvement in the rebellion, arrested him on October 7 and interned him on a ship in the Barcelona harbor. Despite the fact that the military investigator could find no evidence of Azaña's guilt, the government refused to release him until December 28, while the case went to the Tribunal of Constitutional Guarantees. The illegality of detaining, without indictment, a member of the Cortes, the government's foolhardy determination to prosecute Azaña despite the lack of evidence, and the senseless persecution of a former prime minister aroused protest, notably from the intellectuals who wrote an open letter to the government. Nonetheless, some rightist members of the Cortes, discomfited by the lack of evidence linking Azaña with the rebellion in Barcelona, seized on the possibility of prosecuting him for the supply of arms to the Asturias insurrectionaries. In March 1935, the matter was debated in the Cortes, where Azaña ably defended himself in a three-hour speech. On April 6, 1935, the Tribunal of Constitutional Guarantees acquitted Azaña. He recounted the whole episode in *Mi rebelión en Barcelona* (1935), which sold widely.

The travails he had endured and the correctness of his counsel against violence restored Azaña to the position of leadership among the opposition. On April 12, 1935, Azaña, representing the *Izquierda Repúblicana*, together with Martínez Barrio* for the Republican Union party* and Sánchez Román for the *Partido Nacional Repúblicano*, issued a manifesto setting forth common principles and a unified program. It was for this program that Azaña made three notable speeches before huge crowds in Valencia,* Bilbao,* and Madrid. He spoke for a return to the program of the first biennium, for a regathering of the liberal and Left forces, and an end to the corrupt and repressive governments under Lerroux. In the Madrid speech of October 20, 1935, before a crowd variously estimated at between 200,000 and 500,000, Azaña had his apotheosis as the orator of the Republic. In November 1935, the Republican Front was formed; it became broadened into the Popular Front* on January 15, 1936, when new parliamentary elections were announced.

The elections of February 16, 1936,* were a victory for the Popular Front. Inasmuch as the old cabinet refused to continue in power until all election results were in, Azaña was hurriedly called upon to form a government on February 19. In those tumultuous days, Azaña acted to calm down the victorious Left and to rein in the extreme Right. He amnestied all political prisoners, suspended farm rents in southern Spain, forbade victory parades, restored the regional government in Catalonia, transferred Generals Franco and Goded* to posts outside the peninsula, outlawed the Falange* party and arrested its founder, and postponed the municipal elections. In presenting his legislative program to the Cortes on April 4, Azaña followed strictly the lines agreed upon in the Popular Front pact, and appealed to the Left to cooperate with this government and to the Right to accept the result of the elections. However, before any legislation could be introduced, the Cortes was faced with a constitutional issue that resulted in the removal of Alcalá-Zamora

from the presidency. On May 10, Azaña was elevated to that office, the only candidate with the support of all the parties that composed the Popular Front.

Controversy surrounds Azaña's decision to accept the presidency, which deprived the Republic of his leadership at a crucial period. Certain factors apparently influenced him: his dismay at the socialist decision not to form part of the government and the policies being followed by the maximalist wing of that party; his anticipation that Indalecio Prieto* would be the successor to the prime ministership; and his wish to be above political squabbling and to exercise the moderating-power prerogative of the new office. Since Prieto had to decline the charge to form a government, Azaña appointed the ailing Santiago Casares Quiroga,* who accepted the post out of personal loyalty to the president. The ineffective ministry saw the polarization of the country and the military conspiracy against the Republic grow apace.

When the military revolt broke out on July 17, 1936, Azaña proposed a government of concentration, but the socialists continued in their refusal to participate. Azaña then asked Martínez Barrio, who represented the most conservative wing of the Popular Front, to form a government that would negotiate with the rebels rather than risk a proletarian revolution by arming the people. The negotiation effort failed. José Giral,* an intimate collaborator of the president, became the next prime minister. He had no choice but to legalize the distribution of arms to the labor syndicates and political organizations.

The outbreak of the war was a bitter blow for Azaña, for it meant the end of the use of reason for bringing about reforms. Increasingly, he became pessimistic of the prospects of Republican victory—a feeling that was heightened by the adoption of a nonintervention policy by France* and Great Britain.* The storming of the Model Prison in Madrid on August 23, 1936, and the ensuing massacre of its political prisoners, including Azaña's former chief and leader of the Reformist party, strengthened his desire to resign the presidency. But his friends counseled him to subordinate his personal desires to his role as symbol of the Republic. Even the revolutionary Left wanted to keep him in power in order to maintain the appearance of a democratic Spain. For the rest of the war, the burden of being president of one group of Spaniards trying to militarily defeat another group of Spaniards weighed heavily on Azaña. Even the thought of victory became distasteful, for it would mean the victory of Spaniards over Spaniards. Developments on the Republican side, which he was powerless to stop, added to his feelings of consternation, anxiety, and isolation.

As the Nationalist forces approached Madrid, Giral resigned, and Azaña had to call on the socialist Francisco Largo Caballero* to form a government. Largo Caballero, despite Azaña's qualms, included two communist ministers in the cabinet. Azaña's more forceful protest at a later ministerial reshuffling, which brought anarchosyndicalist representatives into the government, was likewise ignored. After the fall of Toledo,* Azaña left Madrid for Barcelona in October 1936. A move that would have been considered prudent in a physically more forceful man was interpreted as a sign of cowardice when undertaken by Azaña, who, moreover, refused to tour battlefronts. When the government also decided to leave Madrid for Valencia on November 6, Azaña stayed on in Barcelona. However, distance between the government and Azaña was more than a physical one.

Azaña used some of the time in Barcelona for writing *La velada en Benicarló*, a book in dialogue form that could not be published until after the war, for it was essentially an indictment of the Republic by its president, who was full of misgivings about the war. A great embarrassment was the appearance of portions of the diary Azaña kept in 1931-1933, which the Nationalists* had gotten hold of and publicized. It appeared later in book form under the title of *Memorias íntimas de Azaña*, in 1939. It showed Azaña's caustic wit and contained malignant descriptions of his colleagues.

On May 7, 1937, government forces rescued Azaña from Barcelona when the anarchist-communist conflict engulfed that city in a civil war. Shortly after his arrival in Valencia, the rift between Largo Caballero and the Communist party* approached a breaking point. Azaña was actively involved in the resolution of that crisis, which resulted in the entrusting of power to Juán Negrín* on May 15. Initially, the two were able to collaborate, but relations between Azaña and Negrín soured before the end of 1937. Hostility and even contempt characterized their relationship for the rest of the war. At bottom lay different analyses of the Republican situation. Negrín was determined to see the war through to victory and, when prospects of victory were extremely dim, he worked to prolong the conflict in the hope that a general European war would rescue the Republic. Azaña, on the other hand, doubted Republican victory, was fearful that the obsession with victory would result in the sacrificing of the Republic, and felt repulsed by the continued fratricidal conflict. He wanted to negotiate peace as soon as possible. Actually, before Negrín assumed the prime ministership, through Julian Besteiro* Azaña had already communicated to the British government a desire for a negotiated peace.

In December 1937, Azaña again returned to Barcelona, following a similar move made earlier by the government. In August 1938, the disagreement between Azaña and Negrín reached the point where Azaña sought to oust the prime minister. Negrín rallied the support he had from the communists and the armed forces to foil Azaña's plan. Friends advised Azaña to resign, but he stayed on apparently in the hope that he could still be instrumental in negotiating peace. He hoped that the Franco side would also be moved by compassion and would see that the victory of brothers over brothers was sterile. On July 18, 1938, the second anniversary of the war, Azaña gave his fourth and last wartime speech. He addressed all Spaniards, the past as well as future generations, reminding them in magnificent language that the message of the fatherland to all its children was "Paz, Piedad, y Perdón."

Barcelona fell on January 26, 1939; Azaña and the government moved to Perelada and La Bajol, close to the French frontier. From there, on February 5, Azaña, his wife, some relatives, personal attendants, and a military escort crossed over on foot to France. Later, he resided at the Spanish Embassy in Paris, declining Negrín's requests that he return to Madrid to continue the struggle. When he knew that France and Britain were preparing to recognize the Nationalist government, he resigned the presidency. In his letter of resignation of February 27, 1939, which he addressed to the president of the Cortes, he claimed that the war having been "hopelessly lost," he did not wish Spaniards to make further useless sacrifices.

Azaña lived in Collonges-sous-Sàleve until two months after the outbreak of World War II, at which time he moved to the south of France and settled near Bordeaux. He suffered a heart attack in February 1940 and was gradually recovering when the capitulation of France to Nazi Germany forced another move by ambulance to Montauban. Bedridden and in financial straits, he lived on for nearly five months, his plight alleviated somewhat by the help of the Mexican government. Another stroke left him partially paralyzed and hardly able to talk. His wife and the archbishop of Tarbes affirmed that he had received the last rites of the Catholic Church when he died on November 3, 1940. Azaña was buried in Montauban.

For further information, see Emiliano Aguado, *Manuel Azaña* (Madrid, 1978); Joaquín Arrarás, ed., *Memorias íntimas de Azaña* (Madrid, 1939); E. Giménez Caballero, *Manual Azaña* (Madrid, 1978); Juan Marichal, ed., *Obras completas de Manuel Azaña*, 4 vols. (Mexico City, 1966-1968); Cipriano Rivas Cherif, *Retrato de un desconocido* (Mexico City, 1961); Carlos Rojas Vila, *Diez figuras ante la Guerra Civil* (Barcelona, 1973); Marcos Sanz Agüero, *Manuel Azaña* (Madrid, 1976); and Frank Sedwick, *The Tragedy of Manuel Azaña* (Columbus, Ohio, 1963).

See also Origins of the Spanish Civil War.

Vicente R. Pilapil

AZCÁRATE GÓMEZ, GUMERSINDO DE (1878-1938). Azcárate served in the Republican Army* as head of the Corps of Engineers. He was a cousin of Pablo de Azcárate,* the Spanish ambassador to London from 1936 to 1939. Azcárate had close ties to the Communist party,* which was unusual in an army that almost to the end of the war had less communist representation than any other major sector of Republican Spain. He served as a lieutenant colonel during the war and was executed in 1938 after being captured while inspecting the Basque Army.

For further information, see Michael Alpert, *El ejército republicano en la guerra civil* (Barcelona, 1977).

James W. Cortada

AZCÁRATE Y FLOREZ, JUSTINO DE. On the night of July 18-19, 1936, Azcárate was asked to serve as foreign minister in the Second Spanish Republic* by President Azaña.* This moderate politician was unable to do so because he momentarily was in León* which fell to the Nationalists* before he could leave for Madrid.* He remained in a Nationalist jail until exchanged in October 1937 for a Republican prisoner, Raimundo Fernández Cuesta,* the prewar secretary-general of the Falange.* His health broken, Azcárate went to France* after he was released.

For further information, see Hugh Thomas, *The Spanish Civil War* (New York, 1977).

James W. Cortada

AZCÁRATE Y FLOREZ, PABLO DE (1890-1971). Azcárate was the Spanish Republic's ambassador to London from 1936 to 1939 and was thus one of the most important Spanish diplomats serving the Loyalists.* He was born in Madrid* on July 30, 1890, and studied at the universities of Saragossa* and Madrid, and later at the University of Paris, primarily in the area of public administration. In 1918, he was elected deputy from León* to the Cortés.* In 1922, he joined the staff of the League of Nations,* worked with Salvador de Madariaga,* and in 1932 was named adjunct secretary general of the league. In August, 1936,

he was appointed ambassador to London with the mission of obtaining diplomatic support and arms for the Republic.

Azcárate brought a number of fine qualities to the job as ambassador. He was a political liberal with considerable diplomatic experience and thus an attractive match for the British Foreign Office. For years he had been a close friend of Juan Negrín* who influence him in his views of Spain and hence could be trusted by the Republic to carry out its wishes. Azcárate's support of Negrín's policies eventually led Madariaga to charge that this diplomat had become a philo-communist. Azcárate quickly established close relations with Sir Anthony Eden* and other members of the British government, in large part because he so closely identified with the thinking of the Republic's leadership.

In the early days of the war, this experienced diplomat sought unsuccessfully to convince the British to support the Republic and at least allow the sale of arms to it. By the late fall of 1936, he had concluded that the British would not stand clearly on the side of the Republic. For him the establishment of the Non-Intervention Committee* represented a setback for the Republic. Throughout 1937 and 1938, Azcárate sought to encourage the British to take a firmer stand against German and Italian intervention on the Nationalists'* side. During this period, he worked closely with political elements within and outside the British government that wanted to aid the Republic. His efforts were to no avail since few in England wanted to do anything that might cause the fighting in Spain to expand into a general European war.

When, in the early months of 1939, Negrín attempted to solicit international help in negotiating an end to the Civil War, Azcárate became a central figure in the negotiations. He made a number of suggestions in support of a British plan calling for mediation. For example, in February 1939, the Spaniard thought that the only condition for peace should be freedom from reprisals, a position Negrín accepted. Nothing came of the negotiations inasmuch as the war ended soon after with the total victory of the Nationalists. With the end of the war, Azcárate turned over his embassy to the British who then gave it to the new Spanish government. Throughout the war, Azcárate was in the center of the democratic powers' diplomatic negotiations regarding the Spanish war.

In the years following the Civil War, Azcárate served on various commissions and United Nations agencies, especially with regard to the Middle East from 1948 to 1952. After his retirement, the ex-ambassador devoted his attention to writing books on Spanish history.

For further information, see Azcárate, *Mi embajada en Londres durante la guerra civil española* (Madrid, 1976), his important diplomatic memoirs and the only significant recollections by a Spanish diplomat of the period; and William L. Kleine-Ahlbrandt, *The Policy of Simmering: A Study of British Policy During the Spanish Civil War, 1936-1939* (The Hague, 1962).

See also Great Britain.

James W. Cortada

AZNAR, AGUSTÍN. Agustín Aznar, one of the younger, more volatile, and emotional followers of José Antonio Primo de Rivera,* gained prominence as a leader of the Falangist militia, and consistently upheld the principle of the independence of his party, a fact that always made Franco* suspect his loyalties.

In 1933, Aznar commanded a *centuria* (approximately 100 soldiers) from the Medical Faculty of the University of Madrid, which was one of three fighting units in the *Sindicato Español Universitario* (SEU). In 1934, he was involved in a number of violent clashes with opposing university student groups, and by 1935 he had become a member of the national directorate of the Falange,* serving as head of the Madrid* militias.* Because of his activities, he was arrested in the spring of 1936, confined in the Model Prison, and then shifted to the prison in Vitoria,* where, on the day of the July uprising, he was freed by local Falange units.

The chief of the Falange military was killed in Madrid in the first days of the war. Aznar took over first as provisional head, and then, after the National Council meeting at Valladolid,* on September 4, 1936, he was named chief of the National Militias. Devotion to Primo de Rivera and insistence on the independence of the Falange characterized most of Aznar's activities thereafter. In September and October 1936, he was the moving force in two unsuccessful attempts to free Primo de Rivera. After the death of his leader in November and moves by military leaders to centralize the Nationalist forces, Aznar found it more difficult to uphold his idea of Falangist autonomy. His only solid support in the party came from the old Madrid militia fighters, as most provincial militia leaders found him impetuous and inefficient.

In late 1936 and early 1937, discussions began between Falangist and military leaders on incorporating the militia into the regular army structure under the direction of General Yagüe.* In addition, plans were afoot to unify the Falangists and *Requetés.* Aznar opposed both moves and thus was not involved in the planning. In the divisions and confusions in the Falange in March-April 1937, Aznar opposed Manuel Hedilla's* leadership and in fact attempted a coup that would install a triumvirate to govern the party. His plan failed; Hedilla remained party head and Aznar lost his position as militia chief, as well as his seat on the National Council. Aznar was imprisoned for inciting civil disorder, and when Franco took over the unified movement on April 19, Aznar was accused of treason and sentenced to five years in prison.

Franco released Aznar from prison and in October 1937 even appointed him to the weak National Council of the Falange, but Franco never considered him reliable. In the spring of 1938, Aznar began to talk of creating a labor front that would establish obligatory work service along military lines. For that purpose he held discussions with various Nationalist military commanders. Franco found these activities suspicious, and when in June 1938 he heard rumors of a plot by old Falangist leaders to reassert their independence, Aznar was one of his prime suspects. Aznar was arrested again, accused of conspiracy, and served a brief prison sentence. Although restored to circulation in 1939, he did not exercise any influence on Spanish politics after that time.

For additional information, see Maximiano García Venero, *La Falange en la guerra de España: la Unificación y Hedilla* (Paris, 1967); and David Jato, *La rebelión de los estudiantes: Apuntes para una historia del alegre SEU* (Madrid, 1953).

See also Burgos.

Jane Slaughter

B

BADAJOZ. Badajoz, a province located in the region of Estremadura* in southern Spain bordering on Portugal,* was in Republican hands in the early days of the Civil War. Unlike the garrison in nearby Cáceres* province to the north, the garrison in the provincial capital city of Badajoz proved loyal to the Republic. Under the command of General Luis Castelló Pantoja,* the town of Badajoz was saved for the Republic in July. Meanwhile, Nationalist troops pushed northward from Seville,* arriving at nearby Mérida* on August 10, 1936. A few miles north was the southernmost line of the Nationalist zone in the north, with Badajoz separating the northern and southern rebel zones. General Juan de Yagüe Blanco* decided to take Badajoz, assigning 3,000 Nationalist troops (many of them Moors*) to do the job. The city, defended by Colonel Ildefonso Puigdendoles Ponce de León, had approximately 8,000 men. The Nationalists* attacked the city, crossing the River Guadiana on August 14. Bitter fighting took place in the streets, house by house, with severe losses on both sides. By the end of the day, the city was in Nationalist hands. The Moors were reported to have killed anyone carrying weapons, and stories leaked out to the world press about a "massacre" at Badajoz where over 1,000 people died. More people were killed when the Republican refugees* who had escaped into Portugal were returned to the Nationalists by Salazar.* The Portuguese border was now closed to Republicans* wishing to escape from southern or central Spain.

For further information, see Hugh Thomas, *The Spanish Civil War* (New York, 1977).
See also Andalusia.

James W. Cortada

BAHAMONDE Y SÁNCHEZ DE CASTRO, ANTONIO. Bahamonde was chief of propaganda for General Queipo de Llano* in the early months of the Civil War. He was responsible for developing much of the press image relating to the general's activities. Later, in 1939, he reported on the number of atrocities and executions carried out under the orders of General Queipo de Llano by Nationalist troops, especially in Seville.*

For further information, see Antonio Bahamonde y Sánchez de Castro, *Memoirs of a Spanish Nationalist* (London, 1939); and the Spanish edition, *Un año con Queipo de Llano* (Madrid, 1938).
See also Radio, Spanish.

James W. Cortada

BALDWIN, STANLEY (1867-1947). Baldwin was prime minister of Great Britain* from 1935 to May 1937, during which Britain developed its policy of nonintervention in Spain. Along with the majority of his cabinet, Baldwin believed that the Spanish Civil War should not be allowed to expand into a general European war. Therefore, he supported the arms embargo imposed by his government on the sale of weaponry to either Spanish side on July 31, 1936, and approved of the efforts of the Foreign Office soon after to establish the Non-Intervention Committee.* His concern was primarily to establish a new order of international peace with Italy* and Germany* in Europe*; thus, Spain became a pawn in the larger scheme of international politics.

Baldwin's government worked closely with the Non-Intervention Committee, which in 1936 he called a leaky dam but "better than no dam at all." Although he had no great interest in foreign affairs, he proved adamant in wanting to develop and implement a combined Anglo-French policy towards Spain. Underlying his policy was his belief that denial of aid to either side in the war would ensure peace in Europe. Germany would not be threatened by any Anglo-Russian alliance that might have emerged from British help to the Spanish Republic, while allowing Italy to take over Abyssinia might satisfy Mussolini's territorial demands.

Stanley Baldwin was not deeply involved in foreign affairs at this time and so Anthony Eden at the foreign office took greater initiative than Baldwin in carrying out British foreign policy. Their relationship was not always smooth since Eden repeatedly advocated more independent action of Paris or Berlin in resolving the Spanish crisis. Yet, by the time Baldwin left office in 1937, British policy was firmly established with its program of nonintervention and non-recognition of belligerency status for either Spanish faction. Therefore, the British preserved his policies until the end of the Civil War.

For further information, see Keith Middlemas and John Barnes, *Baldwin, A Biography* (London, 1969). *See also* League of Nations.

James W. Cortada

BALEARES. The Nationalist cruiser *Baleares* (10,282 tons standard, 8-203mm [8in.] guns, 33 kts.) was under construction in El Ferrol* in July 1936. Commissioned in December 1936, the *Baleares* spent most of her career in the Mediterranean bombarding the coast, attacking Republican fleet units, raiding Republican supply lines, and defending Nationalist convoys. She was deployed with the blockade forces off Santander* in July 1937. Her greatest exploit was singlehandedly attacking a Republican convoy of two cruisers, seven destroyers, and four loaded transports in the battle of Cherchell off the Algerian coast on September 7, 1937. The *Baleares* was damaged, but she succeeded in preventing the convoy from reaching its destination. The cruiser was sunk in the battle of Cape Palos* on March 6, 1938, with a loss of 736 men.

For further information, see Hugh Thomas, *The Spanish Civil War* (New York, 1977). *See also* Navy, Spanish.

Willard C. Frank, Jr.

BALEARIC ISLANDS. The Balearic Islands are located off the northeast coast of Spain. The largest of these islands is Majorca.* The Balearics were a center for Nationalist attacks on the Catalan sector of northeastern Spain. The Italian Air Force, working with the Nationalists,* had a base in the Balearics from which aircraft took off to bomb the city of Barcelona* and other Catalan industrial towns. Nationalist naval forces periodically used ports on these islands as rest stops and depot centers. The Balearics fell to Nationalist forces during the first month of the Civil War, and, despite several attempts to retake them, particularly Majorca in August 1936, they continued to be Nationalist strongholds for the duration of the war. The Balearics were the only strategically favorable locations for the Nationalists off the Mediterranean coast of Spain throughout the war. French ports were not available to the Nationalist Navy, nor were the naval facilities in British Gibraltar.*

As the war progressed, the Balearics became increasingly important for the Nationalists. At first, they were used by the Nationalist Navy, followed by the expansion of Italian ground, naval, and air units used for campaigning in eastern Spain. By the end of 1937, German supply ships and German and Italian submarines* were also using the conveniently located ports of the Balearics. During 1938, bombings by Nationalist forces from these islands over eastern Spain intensified enormously. The Italians' bombardment of Barcelona, for example, during the early months of 1938 and again toward the end of the year, were the prelude to General Franco's campaign to conquer Catalonia.* During the last sixty days of the war, Catalonia was completely overrun, effectively bringing Spain's civil war to an end.

For further information, see José Manuel Martínez Bande, *La invasión de Aragón y el desembarco en Mallorca* (Madrid, 1970); and Josep Massot i Muntaner, *La Guerra civil a Mallorca* (Montserrat, 1976). *See also* Air Force, Nationalist; Air Force, Republican; Navy, German; Navy, Italian; and Navy, Spanish.

James W. Cortada

BANK OF SPAIN. The Bank of Spain, the major central Spanish bank, was founded in 1782. The Republican Constitution of 1931 left the administration of the bank basically untouched. The primary function of this essentially privately owned and managed bank was to lend the government money in exchange for regular payments of interest based on the state's taxing power. Spain's largest private banks—including the *Banco de Vizcaya* and the *Banco de Hispano Americano*—nominated almost half of the directors of the Bank of Spain. Luis Urquijo, representing Spain's richest family, held a major share of stocks. The state also regulated the coining and printing of money and therefore had a voice in nominating the Bank of Spain's directors and management.

The Depression of 1929 forced the bank to export almost 50 ingot tons of gold ($35 million) to the Bank of France between June and September 1931. This guaranteed a French loan to Spain to halt the decline of the peseta* on the international foreign exchange market and tied Spanish currency to the franc. Lagging repayments on this loan and the failure of the conservative government of Joaquín Chapaprieta to provide for new taxes in December 1935 led to the famous Popular Front* elections of February 1936.*

The Bank of Spain maintained a very conservative reserve policy, requiring a 40- to 50- percent backing of gold to printed notes. Therefore, in the spring of 1936, Spain had the fifth largest gold reserves in the world (after the USSR,* and more than those of Italy* and Germany* combined), a total of $725 million.

When the Civil War erupted in July, the bank's directors and stockholders split the institution into two organizations. Sub-governor Pedro Pan, Luis Urquijo, and three-fourths of the stockholders fled the capital and set up a new Bank of Spain in Burgos,* while the gold reserves remained in Madrid.* The Burgos bank, under the control of the army, remained a poor off-spring. It only held £400 thousand ($2 million) and £30 million in paper peseta notes ($3.6 million) deposited in Lisbon in August. Eventually, Franco's* troops collected some 124 million pesetas ($14,880,000), mostly in silver, from provincial banks and a little gold from the donations of a few rich individuals in territories that Nationalist armies controlled at the end of the war.

In March 1938, Franco appointed banker Antonio Goicoechea,* one of the major conspirators of the July uprising, as governor of the Bank of Spain. The bank's officials, who were known in international banking circles, made various legal claims in London, Paris, and New York that the (Loyalist) Bank of Spain, as a private institution, could not, under prewar Spanish law, export gold and silver. The suits were sufficient cause for some foreign banks to hesitate to accept gold exported by the Madrid branch of the Bank of Spain or the Republican Ministry of Finance.

Meanwhile, between July 1936 and March 1937, the Madrid branch spent 26.5 percent of Spain's gold reserves in France* for arms. Luis Nicolau de Oliver, a Catalan appointed governor of the Bank of Spain in March 1936, administered the Republican branch of the bank until the end of the war. The administration was transferred to Valencia* during the Nationalist siege of Madrid in November 1936 and then to Barcelona* in November 1937. But Nicolau was a mere figurehead, lacking any real power.

Control of the assets of the Madrid Bank of Spain was entirely transformed by the decrees of the socialist government of Francisco Largo Caballero* in September and October 1936. The bank was not nationalized, but the government, using wartime emergency powers, regulated the bank's assets. On September 13, 1936, as insurgent troops were converging on Madrid, President Manuel Azaña,* Prime Minister Largo Caballero, and Finance Minister Juan Negrín* transferred 510 tons of gold (1,586,236,800 gold pesetas or $518 million), 72.6 percent of the original reserve, to Cartagena.* About a month later, Largo Caballero and Negrín sent this gold to the Soviet Union, ostensibly for safekeeping, but in reality to pay for the continuing war. Three Bank of Spain officials accom-

panied the four Soviet transports; their duty was to oversee the counting of the gold in Moscow. The Soviets sent at least $340 million of that gold during the year 1937 to Paris to the *Banque Commercial pour l'Europe du Nord* for Spanish Republican purchases and support of the International Brigades.* Gold worth $131.5 million was spent for war supplies in the Soviet Union during 1937. Approximately $36.2 million in gold was allocated by Stalin's* regime for Spanish Republican expenses in both Moscow and Paris in 1938. By fall, the gold was exhausted. Meanwhile, in 1938, the Negrín government used the Bank of Spain's silver reserves of $20 million for purchases in France and the United States.*

As the war progressed and Franco's troops took territory, the Nationalists'* paper bills increased in value. As the Republicans* spent their gold and lost ground, their pesetas lost value. Throughout the war, the Bank of France refused to turn over to either side the 1931 deposit of $35 million in gold, which had increased 59 percent in value through the U.S. devaluation in 1934. This gold was finally returned to Spain, to the Franco regime, in July 1939. By then, the directors of the Bank of Spain had moved from Burgos back to the empty coffers in Madrid. They still faced a major problem of inflation, which lasted well into the late 1960s.

For further information, see Francisco Franco Salgado, *Vida con Franco* (Barcelona, 1977); Juan Sardá, "El Banco de España (1931-1962)," in *El Banco de España* (Madrid, 1970); and Angel Viñas, *El oro español* (Madrid, 1976) and *El oro de Moscú* (Barcelona, 1979).

See also Foreign Trade, Republican.

Robert H. Whealey

BARÁIBAR, CARLOS DE. Baráibar was editor of the socialist newspaper *Claridad** during the Civil War. He was also a close friend and adviser to Francisco Largo Caballero,* the prime minister of the Republic from 1936 to 1937. Baráibar was particularly influential with the prime minister in regard to military affairs. In 1937, he became undersecretary of war. In his position in the Ministry of War, he attempted to bribe Moroccan forces to revolt against General Franco,* an effort that failed.

For further information, see Burnett Bolloten, *The Spanish Revolution: The Left and the Struggle for Power During the Civil War* (Chapel Hill, N.C., 1979).

See also Socialist Party, Spanish.

James W. Cortada

BARAJAS AIRPORT. The Barajas Airport, located just outside of Madrid,* served as a Republican Air Force* base throughout the Civil War. The French novelist and volunteer pilot André Malraux* brought his pilots* and airplanes here for a while. The base became the site of officer training, and toward the end of the war it became a constant target for Nationalist air raids.

For further information, see Jesús Salas Larrazábal, *La guerra de España desde el aire* (Barcelona, 1969).

James W. Cortada

BARBA HERNÁNDEZ, BARTOLOMÉ (1895-   ). Barba led the military conspiracy against the Republic in Valencia* in July 1936. He was also the national head of the *Unión Militar Española* (UME), a group of conservative junior army officers which plotted against the Republic prior to 1936. The initial revolt at Valencia in July 1936 failed, forcing Major Barba to leave the city. All the members of his organization, like himself, went over to the Nationalist cause. Barba spent the rest of the war on unimportant military assignments.

For further information, see Gabriel Araceli, *Valencia 1936* (Saragossa, 1939).

James W. Cortada

BARCARÈS REFUGEE CAMP. The Barcarès Refugee Camp was located on the French side of the Franco-Spanish border to collect refugees* coming from the Republican zone in the last two months of the Civil War. The French government established three major camps and several minor ones quickly, housing 400,000 refugees. Eventually, fifteen camps were established, with little shelter or sanitary facilities for the Spanish. Living conditions remained poor, and the camps were not finally closed until nearly the end of World War II. During World War II, agents of the Franco* regime and of the Nazis periodically went through the camp arresting persons they perceived to be political opponents. Some were sent to Spain for trial, imprisonment, and execution.

For further information, see David W. Pike, *Vae Victis!* (Paris, 1969).
See also France.

James W. Cortada

BARCELÓ JOVER, LUIS (1896-1939). In July 1936, Barceló held the command of the infantry battalion in the Ministry of War as major and served as an aide to the prime minister, Santiago Casares Quiroga.* A member of the Communist party* and of the *Unión Militar de Republicana Antifascista* (UMRA),* he channeled arms to the militias* during the first days of the war and, together with Colonel Julio Mangada,* set up summary courts-martial in the Casa del Campo to condemn captured rebels. Subsequently appointed inspector of militias in the War Ministry, he was the leader of an unsuccessful militia attack against the Alcázar* in Toledo.* Promoted to lieutenant colonel, he led Republican forces at Boadilla,* at the Corunna Road,* and in March 1937, at Guadalajara.* Two months later, he led the 2d Division against the forces of General Varela* at Segovia.* In 1939, as the colonel in charge of the 1st Army Corps in Madrid,* he opposed the rebellion of Colonel Casado,* shooting three of Casado's staff officers and declaring himself head of the Army of the Center.* Arrested at Casado's orders and tried for military rebellion, he was executed on March 15, 1939.

For further information, see Ramón Salas Larrazábal, *Historia del ejército popular de la república*, 4 vols. (Madrid, 1973); Hugh Thomas, *The Spanish Civil War* (New York, 1977); and Cristóbal Zaragoza, *Los generales del pueblo* (Barcelona, 1977).
See also Army, Republican; and Appendix B.

Carolyn P. Boyd

BARCELONA (CITY). During the period of the Republic, Barcelona was both the firmest supporter of the new regime and the source of most of its contentions. The Catalan Right had its followers in Barcelona as did the *Confederacion Nacional del Trabajo* (CNT). Barcelona was the capital of autonomous Catalonia,* and its parliament was known as the Generalitat.* On October 19, 1934, for a number of hours Barcelona was capital of the resistance to the reactionary forces that had entered the government at Madrid.* On February 16, 1936, Barcelona, as well as all of Catalonia, gave a majority to the candidates of the Leftist Front (the name adopted in Catalonia by the Popular Front*) and reestablished the autonomy lost in October 1934. On July 19, 1936, the victory reached by the Republican forces, consisting primarily of workers from the *Confederación Nacional del Trabajo* (CNT)* and the *Partido Obrero de Unificación Marxista* (POUM)* with Catalan police,* caused the failure of the military to rebel successfully in half of Spain. The CNT was the majority popular force at that time. Labor collectivized enterprises whose owners had fled because of their partisanship for the military without even waiting for orders from their unions. They immediately organized a militia committee with representatives from all the major parties and unions to constitute the military force that would venture forth to face the fascists advancing from Saragossa* and would be halted in Aragonese territory. They also organized war industries that were needed to support the effort at the front. Labor action extended the powers of the Generalitat (known in Spanish as the Generalidad) to foreign trade, banking controls, defense, pardons for those condemned to death, and property. As a matter of fact, with Madrid threatened and the Spanish government refuged in Valencia,* Barcelona was the capital of the Spanish revolution.

But in Barcelona a new party emerged, the *Partito Socialista Unificato de Catalunya* (PSUC).* It was made up of the fusion of small groups on July 22 which adhered to the Communist International and which attracted the middle class because it opposed collectivization and all of the revolutionary measures associated with it. This union with the middle class was made possible by the fact that Moscow had instructed the communist elements in Spain to support evolutionary change rather than revolutionary upheaval and to cater to middle-class interests as part of an international effort by the USSR* not to upset the bourgeois republics of France* and Great Britain.* After collaborating in the government of the Generalitat with the CNT, anarchists* took advantage of the need for Russian arms being sent to the Republic, to impose their policies. Meanwhile, the communists did the same, supporting the conservative policies outlined by the requirements of Russian foreign affairs. This approach led to brushes with the more radical CNT and POUM, which culminated in a violent protest by CNT workers on May 3, 1937. The city was covered with barricades, and during the next five days, anarchists and police* fought (the police on behalf of the communists). George Orwell,* in his *Homage to Catalonia*, explained what happened. With the lack of concrete objectives and the fall of the Largo Caballero* government, the mini civil war ended with the communists victorious and now participating in the government of Dr. Juan Negrín.* Through the government, they immediately initiated a persecution of the CNT and the POUM, many of whose members were assassinated. The Soviet police (the People's Commissariat for International Affairs—NKVD) directed *sub rosa* this repression of the anarchists and other rivals of the communists in Barcelona.

The communist Negrín government dismantled the collectivizations, curtailed the powers of the Generalitat in Barcelona, and, as a result, provoked the resignation of the Catalan cabinet and numerous protests by

the Generalitat. As Franco's* forces advanced in the north and east, Barcelona was subjected to bombardment by airplanes from the Balearic Islands* with each attack more intense than the earlier one—a veritable precursor of the battle of London a few years later. On some days the city experienced as many as twenty bombardments and suffered in excess of 1,500 deaths within twenty-four hours.

When the Nationalists* advanced over Catalonia towards the end of 1938, the country was demoralized by the communist policy and could not offer serious opposition in Barcelona. The Catalan government, as well as that of Spain, withdrew to Figueras and from there crossed the Pyrenees.* Hundreds of thousands of refugees* passed through Barcelona and northern Catalonia into France where they were placed in concentration camps* along the Mediterranean beaches.

The Civil War caused considerable damage to the city of Barcelona. The government of General Franco took advantage of this circumstance in order to create plazas and parks, but at the same time removed Catalan street names and prohibited the use of the Catalan language. This government gave a free hand to builders and speculators, permitting them to build as they wished without taking into account aesthetic considerations or urban requirements. As a result, Barcelona began to lose the personality it had before the Civil War and its orderliness. Today it is a chaotic city with the greatest population* density in Spain, perhaps in Europe,* and with tremendous financial urban, and demographic problems. Half of its almost 3 million inhabitants are immigrants from the south of Spain who do not speak Catalan and do not feel rooted in Barcelona, a situation that increases the seriousness of the problems common to any city.

If indeed during the Francoist period opposition to the regime was more dynamic in Barcelona than in the rest of Spain, the city is less the center of the Spanish labor movement than in decades past and no longer has a monopoly on the Left as it had until 1937 when the communists forced a more conservative policy on the city.

For further information, see J. Arias Velasco, *La Hacienda de la Generalitat, 1931-1938* (Barcelona, 1977); F. Artal et al., *El pensament econòmic català durant la República i la guerra, 1931-1939* (Barcelona, 1976); Josep María Bricall, *Política econòmica de la Generalitat, 1936-1939. Evolució i formes de la producció industrial* (Barcelona, 1970); Manuel Cruells, *El separatisme català durant la guerra civil* (Barcelona, 1975) and *Els fets de maig. Barcelona, 1937* (Barcelona, 1970); José Antonio González Casanova,

Elecciones en Barcelona, 1931-1936 (Madrid, 1969); Isidre Molas, *El Sistema de partits polítics a Catalunya, 1931-1936* (Barcelona, 1972); and Hugh Thomas, *The Spanish Civil War* (New York, 1977).

See also Communist Party, Spanish; and Companys, Luis.

Victor Alba

BARCELONA (PROVINCE). Barcelona province, making up one of the four states of Catalonia* in northeastern Spain, remained in Republican hands until February-March 1939 when the Nationalists* finally overran the Catalan region. This province had as its capital the city of Barcelona* which also served as the seat of the Catalan government. It was Spain's largest city and one of its principal points of entry for foreign goods. The province itself was made up largely of fishing villages along the Costa Brava and small agricultural holdings inland. Principal towns were usually involved in the textile industry and some manufacturing of machinery and production of hydroelectric power devices. The province, like its capital city, supported the Republicans during the Civil War. It provided food, industrial and war supplies, and soldiers for the cause. The area was under the control of the Generalitat,* Catalonia's government throughout the war, with increased Republican control after May 1937. Anarchist and communist influence in the province proved significant, with anarchist influence declining rapidly by mid-1937. Businesses and farms were collectivized along the pattern developed within the city of Barcelona and throughout Aragón* to the west. The Catholic Church* was persecuted, as were pro-Nationalist sympathizers.

The most dramatic period in the province's life during the war came after Christmas 1938 when the Nationalists began their final campaign to conquer Catalonia. As the Nationalists moved northward and eastward, refugees* from the occupied zones poured into Catalonia, Barcelona, and eventually north to the French border passing through the province of Barcelona. By February 1939, traffic northward to France* was a solid mass of people and vehicles until the Nationalists closed off the frontier. Following this event and the capture of the city of Barcelona, Franco's* forces purged the area of Republican sympathizers and Catalan nationalists. The pogrom took several years to complete, but the effort was as thorough as in any other part of Spain. The large number of refugees, former anarchists,* and communists, along with thousands of soldiers from the Republican armies captured in the province, were eventually arrested, executed, jailed, or

released in the subsequent months and years. Damage to the province had been severe as it was stripped of all its food* supplies, many of its inland villages destroyed or damaged, its crops and agricultural economy ruined, and many of its citizens wounded, killed, or displaced. The province's industrial production declined steadily during the war and came to a virtual standstill during the last four months of hostilities.

For further information, see Josep María Bricall, *Política económica de la Generalitat* (Barcelona, 1970); José María Fontana, *Los catalanes en la guerra de España* (Madrid, 1951); Carlos Pi Sunyer, *La república y la guerra* (Mexico, 1975); and Carlos Semprún Maura, *Révolution et contre-révolution en Catalogne* (Tours, 1974).

James W. Cortada

BARCÍA Y TRELLES, AUGUSTO (1881-1961). Barcía, born in the province of Asturias,* became a jurist, writer, and politician. During the Civil War, he tried to remain neutral in the conflict while living outside Spain, where he felt it would be easier to remain uninvolved. Before July 1936, he served as Spain's representative to the League of Nations,* minister of foreign affairs, and briefly as president of the Council of Ministers in the Republic. He was a freemason and an historian who, after the Civil War, reconciled himself to and supported Franco's* government. Thus he became, in the years following the Civil War, a symbol of how someone, with pro-Republican sympathies, could acknowledge the value and significance of the Nationalist regime. He spent the last few years of his life writing articles and books on historical themes and diplomacy.

For further information, see Círculo de Amigos de la Historía, *Diccionario biográfico español contemporaneo* (Madrid, 1970), Vol. 1.

James W. Cortada

BARKER, GEORGE (1913-   ). Barker is a British poet. Like most intellectuals* in Western Europe, he enthusiastically supported the Spanish Republic, viewing its fate as a struggle for the survival of Western civilization. He wrote poems in favor of the Republic and critical of Franco.* The best known is his "Elegy for Spain," which laments the Nationalist bombings.

For further information, see Stanley Weintraub, *The Last Great Cause* (London, 1968).

See also Literature.

James W. Cortada

BARLETTA. The Italian naval auxiliary *Barletta* (launched in 1931, 1975 gross tons, 2-120mm [4.7in] guns, 14 kts.) was on Non-Intervention Committee* control duties when damaged by Soviet bombers in the harbor of Palma de Majorca* on May 26, 1937, killing six officers and causing an international incident. Disguised as a Nationalist auxiliary cruiser, the *Barletta* engaged in blockade duties in August-September, 1937, capturing the British *Burlington*. The *Barletta* transported Italian troops to Spain.

For further information, see Hugh Thomas, *The Spanish Civil War* (New York, 1977).

See also Navy, Spanish; and Non-Intervention Committee Sea Observation Scheme.

Willard C. Frank, Jr.

BARRERA LUYANDO, EMILIO (1869-1943). Barrera was born in Burgos,* graduated from the General Military Academy in 1889, and then entered the staff corps. Nearly continuous service in Morocco* led to his rapid promotion; he was a brigadier general in 1916 and a division general in 1922. For his support for the *pronunciamiento* of General Primo de Rivera in 1923, he was promoted to lieutenant general and was appointed captain general of Barcelona,* a post he retained until 1930. A staunch monarchist who had served in the king's military household on several occasions, Barrera conspired constantly against the Republic, which passed him to the reserve in 1931. Hostile to the Catalan Statute, he coordinated the unsuccessful rebellion of General Sanjurjo* in 1932. He escaped abroad and in 1933 sought aid from Mussolini* for a monarchist restoration. Expelled from the officer corps in absentia, Barrera was amnestied after the Right's electoral victory in November 1933. After the departure of Gil Robles* from the War Ministry in December 1935, he began to conspire with other monarchist generals and with the right-wing leadership of the *Unión Militar Española* (UME).* He was arrested in Guadalajara* in July 1936 and released when the military revolt was initially successful there. But on July 22, Republican militiamen and aviators recaptured the city. Although most of the military rebels were executed, Barrera was able to escape to Nationalist Burgos. He played no other role in the war.

For further information, see Guillermo Cabanellas, *Cuatro generales*, 2 vols. (Barcelona, 1977); and Hugh Thomas, *The Spanish Civil War* (New York, 1977).

Carolyn P. Boyd

BARRIO NAVARRO, JOSÉ DEL. Barrio was a Catalan leader in the *Unión General de Trabajadores* (UGT).* He served on the Antifascist Militias Committee* which, in effect, provided Barcelona* with government at the start of the Civil War. This committee reflected Catalan national aspirations and acted independently of the Republic. Barrio soon after became a militia army officer. Later, when the Republic consolidated various militias* into its army, Major Barrio became commander of a communist unit. He fought in most of the major battles in northern Spain in and around Catalonia* and in 1938 took charge of the 18th Army Corps, which was part of the Army of the Ebro.* He thus became one of the highest ranking communist military commanders in the Republican Army.*

For further information, see Michael Alpert, *El ejército republicano en la guerra civil* (Barcelona, 1977).

See also Aragón.

James W. Cortada

BARRÓN Y ORTIZ, FERNANDO (1892-1952). Barrón was born in 1892 and graduated from the military academy at Valladolid* at the age of twenty. Assigned as a lieutenant to the *Regulares de Larache* in Morocco* in 1913, he joined the *Regulares de Melilla* in 1918 and subsequently was promoted to commandant for meritorious service against the Riffs. A skilled horseman with a passion for the cavalry, he later served as professor in the Army Cavalry School and participated in international equestrian competition.

Commander of the *Regulares de Melilla* on July 17, 1936, Barrón, now lieutenant colonel, occupied the airport at Tauima and in September took command of one of the four lead columns making up the Army of Africa* under General Varela.* His column (No. 2), consisting of some 1,200 Moroccans and Legionnaires in the 1st and 2nd *Tabors* of Melilla, and the 1st *Bandera* of Tercio, participated in the conquest of Toledo.* In the subsequent march on Madrid,* it took Illescas, successfully repulsing heavy Republican counterattacks led by then Major Vicente Rojo.*

In the opening phase of General Varela's assault on Madrid on November 7-8, Barrón led a diversionary attack on Carabanchel.* Elements of his column then joined the fighting in the University City on November 12. Barrón commanded one of four brigades in the Nationalists,* attempt to sever the Corunna Road* in January 1937. During the battle of the Jarama* in February, his brigade led the crossing of the Pindoque Bridge and reached the heights west of Arganda before being pushed back several kilometers to lines that stabilized on February 27. In July, Barrón's recently constituted 13th Division, still made up predominantly of Moroccans and Legionnaires, bore the brunt of the Republican offensive in the Brunete* pocket and retook Brunete itself in the Nationalist counteroffensive.

Following his promotion to general, Barrón unsuccessfully attempted to relieve Belchite* following its envelopment by the Republicans in August, but he helped stop the advance south of the Ebro. His 13th Division participated in the retaking of Teruel* in January-February 1938. As one of three divisions in the Moroccan Army Corps during the Nationalists' Aragón* offensive in March and April, it crossed the Ebro at Quinto, swept north, and took Lérida* after a week's hard fighting against El Campesino's* 46th Division.

After participating in the battle of the Ebro* in July-November, the 13th Division took part in the Catalonia* offensive, taking Tortosa and Tarragona* and participating in the capture of Barcelona* on January 26, 1939. Reassigned to the Army of the South* with other units of the Moroccan Army Corps, Barrón commanded the 13th Division in its last action of the war, taking Jaen* on March 26 and then proceeding south to occupy Almería* on the coast. Following the war, Barrón held various military posts and avoided overt political activity. He died in 1952.

For further information, see Robert G. Colodny, *The Struggle for Madrid* (New York, 1958); Editorial Codex, *Crónica de la guerra española*, various issues, including No. 42 (Buenos Aires, 1966); and José Manuel Martínez Bande, *La marcha sobre Madrid* (Madrid, 1968), and *La lucha en Torna a Madrid* (Madrid, 1968).

See also Appendix B.

Verle B. Johnson

BARROSO Y SÁNCHEZ-GUERRA, ANTONIO
(1893-   ). Barroso came from Pontevedra, had a career as an army officer, and served as military attaché in Paris at the start of the Civil War. He resigned his commission as major rather than buy arms for the Republic in France,* electing to join Franco's* side. At the time of his resignation, he announced to the French press that France was attempting to sell arms to the Spanish Republic. This created a momentary political uproar as local newspapers hostile to the government in power talked of an "arms traffic" to Spain. Barroso, who was a personal friend of General Franco, quickly joined his small staff, serving with him to the end of the war as an efficient soldier. By 1939, he had been promoted to colonel. He continued his military career in postwar Spain, rose to the rank of general in

1943, and from 1957 to 1962 served as minister of the army, retiring as a lieutenant general.

For further information, see Círculo de Amigos de la Historia, *Diccionario biográfico español contemporaneo* (Madrid, 1970), Vol. 1.
See also Blum, Léon.

James W. Cortada

BARTOMEU Y GONZÁLEZ LONGORIA, MAXIMIANO (1888-   ). Bartomeu, a career army officer, was a commander of a Navarrese brigade that, in June 1937, made up part of the Nationalist Army of the North* which invaded the Basque country and eventually Bilbao.*

For further information, see José Manuel Martínez Bande, *El fin del frente norte* (Madrid, 1972) and *La guerra en el norte* (Madrid, 1969).

James W. Cortada

BASQUE CHILDREN'S RELIEF COMMITTEE.
The Basque Children's Relief Committee was established by the British with support from the local Roman Catholic Church* during 1937. It accepted 4,000 children evacuated from the area in and around Bilbao* when it was under attack by the Nationalists in 1937.*

For further information, see Yvonne Cloud, *Basque Children in England* (London, 1937); and Hugh Thomas, *The Spanish Civil War* (New York, 1977).
See also Refugees, Republican.

James W. Cortada

BASQUE COMMUNIST PARTY. The Basque Communist party, the Basque branch of the Spanish Communist party,* did not always align fully with the national organization since it represented regional aspirations as well. It was thus typical of all Basque branches of national organizations. Its significance as a political force diminished dramatically by the summer of 1937 when Nationalist forces redivided the geographical area in which the party could function.

For further information, see Stanley G. Payne, *Basque Nationalism* (Reno, Nev, 1975).
See also Basque Nationalism.

James W. Cortada

BASQUE NATIONALISM. The role and fate of Basque nationalism in the Civil War can be understood only in terms of the recent history, cultural context, and structure of the Basque provinces, in conjunction with

their relationship to modern Spanish government and politics. According to the 1930 census, their total population* was nearly 1 million, divided unevenly between Vizcaya* (500,000), Guipúzcoa* (311,000), and Álava* (105,000). Vizcaya and Guipúzcoa had become the two most heavily industrialized provinces in Spain (with the possible exception of Barcelona*), while Álava remained primarily rural and agrarian. Unlike the situation in much of the rest of industrialized Europe,* however, the Basque population retained a great deal of its cultural tradition, and the native Basque population (which still made up a heavy majority of the region at the time of the Civil War) was the most strongly Catholic of any major region of Spain.

The Basque nationalist movement was founded in the 1890s by an upper middle-class ideologue, Sabino de Arana Goiri. Its chief organization, the *Partide Nationalista Vasco* (PNV),* only emerged fully as a mass movement under the Second Republic.* The goal of the PNV was almost complete autonomy for the three Basque provinces as well as Navarre,* which had a partially Basque population. In constitutional and socioeconomic questions, the orientation of the movement was essentially Christian democratic.

The emergence of nationalism as a mass movement, concentrated primarily in Vizcaya and Guipúzcoa, did not automatically win for Basque nationalism the political hegemony of the region. Loyalties and voting support under the Second Republic were triangulated between the Republican leftist groups (especially the *Partido Socialista Obrero Español* [PSOE]* in the industrial regions), the Right (mainly Carlists*), and the nationalists in the Center. Only in 1933 did the PNV achieve a temporarily dominant position. For the Popular Front* elections of 1936* the PNV stood alone and saw its share of the popular vote in the four provinces drop to 28 percent (or 35 percent in the three Basque provinces proper). Navarre and Álava were still essentially rightist and Carlist, while in Vizcaya and Guipúzcoa the Basque nationalists faced the competition of the Republicans* and the Left.

Between 1931 and 1936 there were four different attempts to negotiate an autonomy statute under the Republic. The first had to be abandoned because it conflicted with Republican anticlerical legislation. The second, a four-province autonomy plan, was rejected by Navarre in 1932, while a three-province plan was in turn spurned by conservative interests in Álava in 1933. A fourth proposal was in process of elaboration during the spring and summer of 1936.

The PNV had tried to maintain a centrist position equidistant between Left and Right throughout the Second Republic. The outbreak of the Civil War created a profound dilemma. The Spanish Right led by Franco* was vehemently opposed to regional nationalism and autonomy, while the Left was socially revolutionary and violently anticlerical. During the first weeks of the conflict, the PNV thus adopted a neutralist position, appalled by the excesses of leftist revolutionaries on the one hand but having few illusions about the policies of the Right on the other.

The uncertainty of nationalist policy reflected the ambiguities expressed by the Basque population in general. The eventual Basque president, José Antonio de Aguirre,* later observed that about one-third of the Basques supported the Republic and Basque nationalism, one-third the Spanish Nationalists, and the remainder were more or less neutral. In practice, however, sentiments and loyalties were much more concentrated by region. Navarre and Álava were rightist strongholds, and there local nationalist centers were quickly closed. Most Basque nationalists in those two provinces supported the Spanish Right, some voluntarily, some enthusiastically, but others strictly under duress. Hoping that Basque nationalists in Vizcaya and Guipúzcoa would follow suit, General Mola* did not officially outlaw the PNV in insurgent territory until September 18, 1936, two months after the beginning of the war.

Although the PNV did not at first fully and enthusiastically commit itself to the Republican cause even in Vizcaya and Guipúzcoa, it did join the ad hoc *Juntas* that assumed governmental responsibilities in those two provinces soon after the conflict began. It thus became the only nonleftist party to share political responsibility in any part of the Republican zone, a situation that in fact continued to make some nationalists uneasy. Like other political groups, the PNV also began to organize its militia units.

The role of nationalism and the issue of Basque autonomy finally came to a head after Spanish Nationalist forces captured most of Guipúzcoa in September 1936. By that time, little was left of a Republican Basque country save the province of Vizcaya. The PNV held two of the ten seats in the *Junta de Defensa de Vizcaya*, but that was a gross underrepresentation compared with the nationalist vote of nearly 40 percent in that province earlier that year. Aguirre later admitted that the "Red Terror" in Vizcaya had a "disastrous effect" on PNV morale. Party headquarters maintained intermittent contacts with Spanish insurgent agents, as well as representatives of the British government who might serve as future intermediaries.

The lukewarm relationship between Basque nationalism and the Republican wartime regime was finally transformed after the Largo Caballero* government assumed power in Madrid* on September 4. Since none of the nationalist leaders would participate in Largo Caballero's cabinet until the question of autonomy had been resolved, a special Basque commission was soon summoned to Madrid to hammer out the details of a formal autonomy statute, theoretically applicable to all three provinces. Its general terms were similar to those granted Catalonia* in 1932, but Basque nationalists sometimes dubbed it the *Estatuto de Elgueta*, because by the time it was concluded the small district of Elgueta in western Guipúzcoa was the only piece of Basque land outside Vizcaya that had not been conquered by the Spanish Nationalist Army.* The statute was formally approved by a rump meeting of the Republican Cortes* meeting in Valencia* on October 1, 1936.

Thus, when an autonomous Basque government was finally organized that month in Bilbao,* its effective rule was limited to little more than the province of Vizcaya. Even that was threatened by Franco's forces. The PNV's thirty-three-year-old leader, José Antonio de Aguirre, was the unanimous choice for the first *Lendakari* (president) of the new government, and a cabinet was formed consisting of four Basque nationalists, three socialists, two representatives of the middle-class Republican Left, and one communist.

The new government quickly reorganized the administration of affairs in Vizcaya, making that province the most orderly, least revolutionary part of Republican Spain during the next nine months. Revolutionary excesses and atrocities, already more limited than elsewhere, were brought under control, except for the massacre of 224 rightist prisoners by a mutinous socialist battalion in January 1937. A series of Popular Tribunals* were organized to conduct legal discipline and repression, in accord with the policy elsewhere, but their administration in Vizcaya was moderate.

During its nine months of autonomous existence, Vizcaya enjoyed greater political harmony than any other part of the Republican zone. Under the nationalist hegemony, direct conflict was largely averted, and relations with the communists and other leftist groups were generally amicable. The only exception to this generalization was one or two incidents with the Vizcayan *Confederación Nacional del Trabajo* (CNT),* but these were not of major proportions. Discord more commonly occurred in relations with other parts of the northern Republican zone, the Republican military command, or the central Republican government itself.

The collectivist revolution that swept major parts of the Republican zone scarcely affected Vizcaya. The new Basque government did establish state regulation (*intervención*) over industries related to military production, but official collectivization or the more limited *incautación* (direct workers' control) was virtually unknown. The new system did greatly expand the local government bureaucracy amid wartime controls and regulations, so that complaints were soon being heard about the excess of functionaries and the inefficiency of bureaucratic administration.

The autumn of 1936 was devoted in large measure to the creation of a new Basque army, but its strength was severely limited by lack of matériel, technically qualified leadership, or integration with the other two Republican provinces remaining in the north, Santander* and Asturias.* Although a unified northern Republican Army* command was established under General Llano de la Encomienda* in November, the Basque forces remained almost completely autonomous. Their first major military operation was a local offensive under difficult conditions against the town of Villarreal in Álava to the south, beginning on November 30 and continuing intermittently for two weeks. For lack of organization, training, and firepower, it proved a complete failure and produced high casualties,* including 1,000 dead in the Basque forces. Later, seven Basque battalions were transferred to Asturias for the final unsuccessful Republican assault on Oviedo* in February 1937.

The Basque military strategy was essentially defensive, investing considerable resources in the attempted construction of a *cinturón de hierro* (a sort of Basque Maginot Line), south and east of the greater Bilbao district. Republican military authorities urged greater integration with the broader war effort, even though they in turn failed to provide badly needed supplies for the northern front. Lieutenant Colonel Buzón Llanes, an intelligence officer for the Republican general staff in the north, later complained in an official report that "in Vizcaya one had the feeling of not being at war."

The participation of the ardently Catholic Basque nationalists on the side of the anticlerical and revolutionary Republic was a source of perturbation for both the revolutionaries and the Catholic Nationalists on Franco's side. The only bishop of the Basque country, Múgica* of Vitoria,* was not a nationalist himself, but neither was he very sympathetic to the authoritarianism and centralism of the new Franco regime. He was finally forced, apparently by Church authority, to endorse the Spanish insurgents in September 1936, and then he was recalled to Rome. A public exchange of letters occurred in January 1937 between Archbishop Gomá,* head of the Catholic

Church* in Spain, and President Aguirre, in which they criticized each other's stand on the duty of Catholics in the Civil War. Despite the bitter feeling among most Catholics and Catholic leaders against the Basque nationalists, the Spanish Church hierarchy did not issue its famous pastoral formally blessing Franco's struggle as a crusade until July 1, 1937, a fortnight after the fall of Bilbao.

The final offensive against Vizcaya was launched by Mola's northern forces on March 31, 1937. It was supported by the bulk of the German Condor Legion* as well as the special Italian artillery unit. This final phase of the conflict, as much as or more than earlier ones, also constituted a civil war among Basques, since the main shock units of the Spanish Nationalists consisted of the Carlist brigades recruited in Navarre and Álava. Although a Basque army of approximately fifty battalions was under arms, it lacked firepower and sophisticated weaponry, and was especially weak in the face of aerial attack.

Nonetheless, Mola's troops only began to make significant progress during the latter part of April. On April 26, 1937, there occurred the most famous incident of the Vizcayan campaign: the incendiary bombing and partial razing of the historic "foral center" of Guernica* by German planes of the Condor Legion. On May 5, Aguirre himself took over direct command of the military operations to firm up resistance. For a week or so, there was some optimism that an effective defense line could still be held, but the aerial reinforcements from the Republican central zone arrived in small units of little utility. With each passing day it became increasingly clear that the Basques lacked the strength and resources to hold out. By the beginning of June, the Basque forces had suffered a total of approximately 35,000 casualties* since fighting began. Although some 40,000 troops were still under arms, they were now outnumbered and heavily outgunned. A direct assault against the *cinturón de hierro* (iron belt) began on June 11 and completely breached the hastily conceived, incomplete defense line within thirty-six hours. This meant that the fall of Bilbao and the end of Basque resistance was at hand.

Throughout the spring, a series of maneuvers had been underway to mediate a separate peace and detach the Basques from the Republican cause. Archbishop Gomá was particularly active, working with the Spanish Nationalist government, the Vatican,* and Italian authorities. There is some indication that the Franco forces twice offered special terms to the Basques, terms that were somewhat more lenient than those available to leftist and other Republican groups. Italian diplomatic representatives also encouraged the Basques to use Italian influence in arranging moderate peace terms, and after the fall of Bilbao on June 19, it was officially decided to try to make use of Italian mediation. After the remnant of Basque units had withdrawn westward into Santander,* a two-man Basque delegation headed by one of Aguirre's advisers, P. Alberto de Onaindía, arrived in Rome on July 6. Although no deal could be made with Franco, a vague understanding was reached that arrangements would be made by the Basque forces in Santander to surrender to local Italian units on lenient terms.

This very imprecise agreement proved extremely difficult to implement, and Aguirre himself preferred to avoid dealing with the Italians at all. A midsummer lull ensued on the northern front, which was used to evacuate thousands of Basque civilians, children, and troops who had formed part of the exodus westward. When Franco's final offensive against Santander began on August 13, time ran out. Leaders of the PNV Vizcayan provincial committee under Juan de Ajuriaguerra arranged to surrender the remaining Basque forces in the Laredo-Santona District to Italian units on August 26 (the so-called capitulation of Santona), but nine days later Spanish Nationalist forces took charge. Since Basque nationalists had rejected the separate terms which Franco had offered earlier, those captured were subjected to the same harsh treatment meted out to leftist prisoners.

The Civil War in the Basque country came to a complete end in the summer of 1937. But the autonomous Basque government under Aguirre transferred its place of residence via France* to the new Republican capital in Barcelona, where it resolutely supported the Republican resistance until the end of the Civil War. Several thousand Basque troops were also repatriated by way of France and served in the main Republican Army.* One of the top PNV leaders, Manuel de Irujo,* had entered the Republican cabinet as minister of justice in September 1936 and played a major role in regularizing and moderating judicial proceedings in the Republican zone during 1937-1938. Aguirre and the PNV cooperated closely in political affairs with the Catalan Esquerra,* supporting the Esquerra's protest against the government centralization measures of 1938. Nonetheless, they cooperated with the Republican authorities down to the final evacuation in February 1939.

After Franco's conquest of the Basque country, all expressions of nationalism were proscribed, and the last vestiges of autonomy were stripped from Vizcaya and Guipúzcoa. Conversely, Álava and Navarre were allowed to retain certain local fiscal privileges and a limited degree of corporative self-administration in recognition of their signal assistance to the Spanish Nationalist cause.

For further information, see Stanley G. Payne, *Basque Nationalism* (Reno, Nev., 1975); and Hugh Thomas, *The Spanish Civil War* (New York, 1977).
See also Socialist Party, Spanish.

Stanley G. Payne

BASQUE NATIONALIST ACTION. The Basque Nationalist Action was a small regional party formed during the early 1930s. Its only claim to national fame was that Tomás Bilbao, a member of the party, received an invitation to join Negrín's* cabinet in 1938 as minister without portfolio.

For further information, see Stanley G. Payne, *Basque Nationalism* (Reno, Nev., 1975).

James W. Cortada

BASTICO, ETTORE (1876-1952?). Bastico, the Italian commander of Mussolini's* army units in Spain, led the Italian contingent at the battle of Brunete* during July 7-26, 1937. The following month he participated in the Nationalist conquest of the Basque country around Santander* and thus became an overnight hero in the Italian press. In October, he returned to Italy* and to other assignments. In 1941, he became the Italian governor of Libya and retired from military service at the end of World War II.

For further information, see John F. Coverdale, *Italian Intervention in the Spanish Civil War* (Princeton, N.J., 1975).

James W. Cortada

BATALLA, LA (1924-1939). *La Batalla* was the newspaper of the *Partido Obrero de Unificación Marxista* (POUM),* an anti-Stalin Catalan party made up primarily of ex-members of the Spanish Communist party.* Throughout the Civil War, the POUM competed for influence in Catalonia* with the communists. The Communist party inflicted a severe blow on the POUM when it convinced the Republican government to close down the editorial offices of *La Batalla* and forbid its publication after May 28, 1937. Issues continued to appear sporadically, however, until the end of the Civil War.

For further information, see Andrés Suárez, *Un episodio de la revolución española: El proceso contra el POUM* (Paris, 1974).

James W. Cortada

BATET MESTRES, DOMINGO (1872-1936). Batet, a Catalan career army officer, arrested Luis Companys* in 1934 for an attempted revolt against the central government. General Batet remained loyal to the Republic in July 1936 and within days became a prisoner of the Nationalists.* He was executed seven months later, despite pleas by some Nationalist generals to Franco* that he pardon the soldier.

For further information, see Hugh Thomas, *The Spanish Civil War* (New York, 1977).

James W. Cortada

BAYO GIRÓN, ALBERTO (1894-1967). Bayo, an air force captain, supported the Republicans.* On August 28, 1936, he landed on the island of Ibiza* with an expeditionary force and seized it from the Nationalists.* He commanded nearly 8,000 like-minded men in this campaign. Republican forces later abandoned Ibiza and then returned, killing hundreds of people in retribution.

For further information, see José Manuel Martínez Bande, *La invasión de Aragón y el desembarco en Mallorca* (Madrid, 1970).
See also Catalonia; and Majorca.

James W. Cortada

BEIGBEDER Y ATIENZA, JUAN LUIS (1888-1957). Beigbeder was born on March 31, 1888, in Madrid.* In September 1902, he entered the *Academia Militar de Ingenieros* in Guadalajara,* but given his intellectual precocity he soon transferred to the prestigious *Escuela Superior de Guerra* (Staff College) in the capital. Graduating as a captain of the general staff, Beigbeder volunteered for colonial duty in 1909 and served in Spanish North Africa for the next thirteen years. During this period, he participated in the occupation of Tetuán* (February 1913), the campaigns against the Djebalan rebel, Raisuni (1913-1921), and the sanguine war against the Riffian nationalist, Abd-el-Krim.

In addition to his military duties, Beigbeder took an interest in Muslim culture, acquiring a knowledge of Arabic and a number of Berber dialects. In 1922, Major Beigbeder's scholarly propensities were further encouraged when he was sent to study Arabic and Berber dialects at the School of Oriental Languages in Paris. Following a three-year academic sojourn, Beigbeder served as military attaché to Spanish embassies in Germany,* Australia, and Czechoslovakia.* In 1934, Lieutenant Colonel Beigbeder was ordered back to Spain's Moroccan Protectorate and attached to the high commissioner's staff in Tetuán. He was serving in this post when segments of the Spanish Army revolted against the Republic on July 17-18, 1936. Beigbeder played an important role in this uprising. He personally seized control of the Office of Native Affairs and was instrumental in guaranteeing the cooperation of the caliph, the caliphate bureaucracy and guard, and the sixty-nine tribal *caides* (chiefs) for the Nationalist cause.

Aware of his capabilities, General Francisco Franco* made Beigbeder deputy to the protectorate's high commissioner, General Luis Orgaz,* and chief liaison with local German "businessmen." Beigbeder made the initial Nationalist contact with the Germans on July 23, 1936 when he requested ten planes to transfer troops from North Africa to Spain. When the high commissioner was reassigned to Spain in late 1936, Franco appointed Beigbeder interim high commissioner. During his tenure, Colonel Beigbeder succeeded in maintaining a continuous flow of Moroccan recruits to the Nationalist ranks in Spain as well as securing the protectorate for rebel training activities.

As a reward for these accomplishments, Franco appointed Beigbeder foreign minister in August 1939. He served in this office until October 1940 when the Generalissimo's brother-in-law, Ramón Serrano Suñer,* and replaced him. Through the first difficult year of World War II, Beigbeder reflected Franco's thinking well by keeping Spain on a neutral course—albeit one of decided Axis sympathies.

Following his civilian service, Beigbeder returned to active military duty in the protectorate. In January 1943, he was promoted to brigadier general and attached for a year to the Spanish Embassy in Washington, D.C. Upon his return to Spain, Beigbeder retired from active military service and devoted the remainder of his years to Arabic and Moroccan scholarship and private business interests. He died in Madrid on June 6, 1957.

For further information, see Charles R. Halstead, "A Somewhat Machiavellian Face: Colonel Juan Beigbeder as High Commissioner in Spanish Morocco, 1937-1939," *The Historian* 37 (November 1974): 46-66, and "Un Africain meconnu: le colonel Juan Beigbeder," *Revue d'histoire de la deuixiéme guerre mondiale* 83 (July 1971): 31-60.

See also Morocco, Spanish.

Shannon E. Fleming

BELCHITE, SIEGE OF. The siege of Belchite refers to the Republican attack on this Aragonese town during the Loyalist offensive between August and October 1937. The Republicans* were attempting to push the Nationalists* westward and at the fortified town of Belchite (population 3,800), Franco's* forces held out against large numbers of enemy soldiers. These soldiers survived without water and food* for days, but, finally, on September 6, they surrendered to the Loyalists.* The siege ultimately halted the Republican offensive after early successes.

For further information, see Manuel Aznar, *Historia militar de la guerra de España, 1936-1939* (Madrid, 1940).

See also Aragón.

James W. Cortada

BELGIUM. For generations, Belgium had quietly invested heavily in the Spanish lumber industry, railroads, and subways, and Asturian coal mines. When the Civil War began, the Belgian government sought to protect these interests, yet remain neutral in the conflict. Belgium had no alternative but to follow the British and French lead in neutrality, and, so participated in the Non-Intervention Committee.* Many of the minor powers (Belgium included) performed much of the day-to-day work of the committee, while the larger nations, France* and Great Britain* in particular, established questions of policy. Belgian relations with the Spanish Republic were never cordial, however, because in December 1936, its first secretary of the embassy, Baron Hans Beimler de Borchgrave, was assassinated, probably by agents of the War Ministry. The Spanish Republic later acknowledged that it had failed in its legal responsibility to protect diplomats.

Belgian citizens fought in the International Brigades,* while engineers sent by the French Communist party joined the Basques during the campaign at Irún* in August-September 1936. Despite heated debate at home on which side to support, the Belgian government maintained its low profile of neutrality. It deviated from its position only slightly by not blocking the transportation of some arms and munitions by private citizens to the Republic. These small quantities of help were particularly important in Catalonia* since they aided the establishment of munitions manufacturing facilities. At he end of the war, the Belgian government agreed to accept between 2,000 and 3,000 refugee children from Spain.

For further information, see Arnold J. Toynbee, *Survey of International Affairs, 1937* (Oxford, 1938), Vol 2.

See also League of Nations; and Refugees, Republican.

James W. Cortada

BELLIDO, JESÚS. Like many other intellectuals,* Bellido, a professor of medicine* at the University of Barcelona,* was active in Republican politics. On December 9, 1938, he became commissar-in-chief of a newly established commissariat of religion, established by the Republican government to provide priests for those Republican Army* units that requested them. While the start of the Catalan campaign soon made any such reforms impossible to implement, it was an example of religious activity within the Republican zone. Little else is known about Bellido.

See also Catalonia; and Catholic Church, Spanish.

James W. Cortada

BELLIGERENT RIGHTS. Belligerent rights are granted to a military power in time of war under international law. In a civil war, the rebellious side gains recognition as a belligerent when other nations formally acknowledge the ability of the insurgents to control a large sector of a nation or have the real possibility of achieving victory. In the case of Spain, the Nationalists* sought recognition as a belligerent power almost from the beginning.

Great Britain* proved reluctant to grant such a status for fear of irritating France,* which did not want to harm the Spanish Republic by extending any form of recognition to Franco.* The British were motivated to grant such status, particularly after Franco declared a naval blockade around the Republic in 1937 which could not be honored without belligerency status. By recognition, Britain would no longer have to patrol the waters off Spain to protect English shipping from search by Nationalist vessels, which with belligerency would have the right to do so. At various times during the Civil War, the British government discussed the issue of granting such recognition within its cabinet. The cabinet was divided on whether or not to allow Franco to search ships and was concerned about the negative impact belligerent rights might have on the Spanish Republic and public opinion in Britain. The British never recognized Franco's belligerency during the war and blocked the Non-Intervention Committee* from so doing. Consequently, Franco did not receive belligerency status from the Western republics, thereby insuring the continuation of the policy of nonintervention by the major democratic powers.

For further information, see Patricia A. M. van der Esch, *Prelude to War: The International Repercussions of the Spanish Civil War, 1936-1939* (The Hague, 1951); and Francisco Virgilio Sevillano Carbajal, *La*

diplomacía mundial ante la guerra española (Madrid, 1969).

See also League of Nations.

James W. Cortada

BELTRÁN CASAÑA, ANGEL (-1960). Beltrán, born in Jaca, acquired his nickname, El Esquinazado (The Dodger), as a smuggler in Canfranc. In December 1930, he supported the failed rebellion of Captains Francisco Galán* and Angel García Hernández in Jaca; he joined the *Izquierda Republicana* in 1931. In July 1936, Beltrán joined the Republican militia and subsequently, the Communist party.* He acquired prominence as head of the 43d Division, which was under siege in the Pyrenees* for three months in 1938. He later fought at the Ebro* and in Catalonia.* After the war, he lived in the USSR* and fought in the French Resistance before breaking with the communists and serving as an intelligence agent for the American Embassy in Madrid. He died in Mexico.*

For further information, see Michael Alpert, *El ejército republicano en la guerra civil* (Barcelona, 1977); and Ramón Salas Larrazábal, *Historia del ejército popular de la República*, 4 vols. (Madrid, 1973).

See also Army, Republican.

Carolyn P. Boyd

BEN MIZZIAN, MOHAMED (1879-1975). Ben Mizzian was born on February 1, 1897, in the north Moroccan tribe of Mazuza, which is adjacent to the Spanish enclave of Melilla.* Son of a tribal *caid* (chief), he was educated in Melillan schools, and in August 1913 he was sent to the Infantry Academy in Toledo* to prepare for a military career. In 1916, he concluded his studies, and as a newly commissioned second lieutenant he volunteered for duty in Spanish Morocco.* Ben Mizzian served in various indigenous units in Spain's Army of Africa* and saw considerable combat in both the pacification efforts of 1919-1921 and the Riff Wars of 1921-1927. This service earned him a promotion to captain as well as a reputation for bravery and competence and the friendship of such *africanista** officers as Francisco Franco,* José Varela,* and Rafael García Valiño.*

When sections of the Spanish Army rose up against the Republic in July 1936, Major Ben Mizzian quickly sided with the rebels. On July 19, 1936, he was one of a handful of officers to greet Franco at the Tetuán* Airport when Franco arrived from the Canary Islands.* In August 1936, he was assigned to the *Grupo de*

Regulares Indígenas de Alhucemas and accompanied these troops to the peninsula where he participated in the conquest of southern Spain, the occupation of Talavera de la Reina,* and the siege of Madrid.*

In February 1937, Lieutenant Colonel Ben Mizzian was put in charge of the *Fuerzas Regulares Indígenas* * *de Ceuta* which fought in the Asturian sector during most of 1937. At the conclusion of this campaign, he was promoted to colonel and placed in command of a brigade in the recently created 83d Division. His unit participated in the "liberation" of Teruel,* the battle of Alfambra, and the march to the Mediterranean Sea. In late 1938, he assumed command of the 1st Navarre Division, units of which fought in the battles of the Ebro* and Catalonia*—the concluding campaigns of the Civil War.

After the war, Ben Mizzian was promoted to general and served in various protectorate and peninsula military posts. He reached the apex of his "Spanish" career when he was promoted to lieutenant general and appointed the captain general of the VIII Military Region (Galicia*). In spite of his long and distinguished Spanish Army service, General Ben Mizzian always maintained his Moroccan citizenship. Consequently, in March 1957, when King Mohammed V called upon him to participate in the Moroccan cabinet and to help organize the armed forces, Ben Mizzian unhesitantly resigned his Spanish Army commission and returned to Morocco.

Political and military service was not Ben Mizzian's only forte. In February 1966, King Hassan II named him ambassador to Spain, a difficult post given Spanish-Moroccan tensions in the late 1950s and early 1960s. He died in Rabat on May 1, 1975.

For further information, see Teresa Suero Roca, *Los generales de Franco* (Barcelona, 1975) and "Ha fallecido el Mariscal Mizzian," *Africa* 402 (June 1975): 232-233.

See also Andalusia; and Asturias.

Shannon E. Fleming

BENEDITO LLEO, JOSÉ. Lieutenant Benedito held considerable military power in Valencia* during July 1936. He was a member of the autonomist Left party of Valencia and head of the local defense committee. He controlled Valencia for the Republic but under a revolutionary regional authority.

For further information, see Alfons Cucó, *El valencianismo político, 1874-1939* (Barcelona, 1977).

James W. Cortada

BERGAMÍN Y GUTIÉRREZ, JOSÉ (1895-   ). Bergamín was a Spanish poet, editor of *Cruz y Raya* (an important Catholic publication), and a leading Catholic intellectual who sided with the Republic. This communist Catholic spent much of the war writing poems and editorials bitterly critical of the Nationalists.

For further information, see Aldo Garosci, *Gli intelletuali e la guerra di Spagna* (Turin, 1959); and Stanley Weintraub, *The Last Great Cause* (London, 1968).

See also Intellectuals; and Literature.

James W. Cortada

BERNAL GARCÍA, CARLOS (1874-194?). Bernal, commissioned in the Corps of Engineers in 1889, subsequently entered the Aviation Service. Promoted to brigadier general in 1935, he was head of military railways and of aviation before being given a bureaucratic post in March 1936. During the Civil War, he served the Republican Army* in several administrative capacities: undersecretary of the War Ministry briefly in July 1936, commander of the training center for the Mixed Brigades* and International Brigades* in late 1936, chief of transport services in 1937-1938, and head of the naval base at Cartagena* in 1939. Opposed to continuing the war effort, he relinquished his command on March 4, 1939, and was appointed military governor of Madrid* by Colonel Casado* on March 15. Arrested by the Nationalists* later that month, Bernal died in prison after the war.

For further information, see Ramón Salas Larrazábal, *Historia del ejército popular de la República*, 4 vols. (Madrid, 1973); and Hugh Thomas, *The Spanish Civil War* (New York, 1977).

See also Army, Republican.

Carolyn P. Boyd

BERNANOS, GEORGES (1888-1948). Bernanos, a French Catholic writer, was living in Majorca* at the start of the Civil War, and in 1938 wrote about the arrests and executions by the Nationalists* there during August-September 1936. During the war, on various occasions he attempted to negotiate prisoner exchanges while publicizing Nationalist atrocities. He was one of a few Catholic writers in Europe* willing to criticize Franco,* and for this reason he was widely read at the time.

For further information, see Georges Bernanos, *Les*

Grands cimetières sous la lune (Paris, 1938), a novel on Nationalist repression in Majorca.
See also Intellectuals.

James W. Cortada

BERNERI, CAMILLO (1897-1937). Berneri was an Italian anarchist, intellectual, and writer who was arrested and killed in Barcelona in 1937, possibly by the *Partit Socialista Unificat de Catalunya* (PSUC).* This important Italian anarchist was in Barcelona gathering information documenting ties between Italian fascists and Catalan nationalists and may well have been killed by pro-Russians in the Catalan capital wishing to silence him.

For further information, see comments by his wife in *Lezioni sull'antifascismo* (Bari, Italy, 1962).
See also Anarchists; and Intellectuals.

James W. Cortada

BERNHARDT, JOHANNES EBERHARD FRANZ (1897-). Bernhardt was instrumental in securing Hitler's* support for the Nationalist cause and subsequently played a dominant role in German-Spanish economic relations. A native of Osterode, East Prussia, Bernhardt served during World War I in both France* and the Ukraine. Following Germany's* defeat, he participated in the Free Corps movement in Hamburg and in the nationalist and monarchist National Association of German Officers. Simultaneously, he became active in the economic life of the city, and by the mid-1920s headed a prosperous commercial firm with branches in the Baltic states, the USSR,* and Brazil. In 1929, however, this enterprise collapsed, and Bernhardt moved with his family to Spanish Morocco.*

Bernhardt prospered in Morocco. As an employee of a firm that provided supplies for many of the Spanish garrisons, he established contacts with influential officers. He also became a member of the Nazi party and a close associate of Adolf P. Langenheim, the local leader. When the Spanish Civil War began in July 1936, Bernhardt, without hesitation, cast his lot with the insurgents and on July 23, at Franco's* request, flew with Langenheim to Germany to plead with Hitler for support. His plea successful, he returned to Morocco and on July 31 organized the *Compañía Hispano-Marroquí de Transportes* (HISMA)* to arrange for German deliveries and for Spanish payments. Throughout the Civil War, Bernhardt dominated German-Nationalist economic relations, and his influence remained strong until about 1943. He remained in Spain after World War II.

For further information, see Glenn T. Harper, *German Economic Policy in Spain During the Spanish Civil War, 1936-1939* (The Hague, 1967); Manfred Merkes, *Die deutsche Politik gegenüber dem spanischen Bürgerkrieg, 1936-1939* (Bonn, 1961); and Angel Viñas, *La Alemania nazi y el 18 de julio*, 2d ed. (Madrid, 1977).

Glenn T. Harper

BERRY, GORDON (1906?-). Berry, a pilot from the United States,* flew for the Spanish Republic in the autumn of 1936. He left the service of the Republic after accusing it of not paying him $1,200 for services. He managed to convince the U.S. Coast Guard to serve a writ on a Spanish ship, the *Mar Cantábrico*,* which was then in Long Island Sound. Nothing came of it, the ship sailed, and it was eventually attacked and captured by the Nationalists,* who confiscated it and executed the Spaniards on board. The entire episode received considerable press coverage in the United States at the time that the American government was implementing its policy of nonintervention in the Civil War, providing more reason for its position.

For further information, see Richard P. Traina, *American Diplomacy and the Spanish Civil War* (Bloomington, Ind., 1968).
See also Pilots.

James W. Cortada

BERTI, MARIO (? -1960). Berti was a career Italian army officer who commanded troops in Spain fighting for Franco.* He led soldiers in the Aragón* offensive and against Valencia,* thus offering one of the few positive contributions of Italian arms in Spain. This combat commander also served in Ethiopia during World War II.

For further information, see John F. Coverdale, *Italian Intervention in the Spanish Civil War* (Princeton, N.J., 1975).

James W. Cortada

BERZIN, JAN PAVLOVICH (? -1937). Berzin headed the Russian military mission in Spain assigned to help the Spanish Republic's armies. He arrived in Spain in September 1936 and left in the second half of 1937. While there, he managed a mission of nearly 500 Russians and often operated independently of the Republican Ministry of Defense. When he returned to the USSR,* Stalin* purged him, along with many Russians who had played prominent roles in Spain.

For further information, see David T. Cattell, *Communism and the Spanish Civil War* (Berkeley, Calif., 1955) and *Soviet Diplomacy and the Spanish Civil War* (Berkeley, Calif., ·1957).

James W. Cortada

BESTEIRO FERNÁNDEZ, JULIÁN (1870-1940).

Besteiro, born in Madrid,* was a professor of logic at the University of Madrid and a socialist theoretician of national stature. From 1914, he held various positions of leadership in the socialist movement, including the presidency of the *Unión General de Trabajadores* (UGT).* In 1931, 1933, and 1936, Besteiro was elected to the Cortes* as a socialist deputy from Madrid.* In 1931, he was voted president of the Constituent Cortes.

As president of the UGT, Besteiro decided on the UGT's policy position in the 1933 elections. Representing the extreme Right position of evolutionary reformism in the Socialist party,* he refused to support the October 1934 uprising and argued against the inclusion of the Communist party* in the Popular Front* government. However, by 1936, the revolutionary majority, led by Francisco Largo Caballero,* controlled the socialist movement and forced Besteiro from power. Besteiro withdrew even further from active participation in socialist activities, condemning the extremism of the revolution in the early months of the Civil War. He believed that the nation was not ready for a socialist government and was convinced that the cause of the Republic was doomed from the beginning. He held only a minor municipal post in Madrid throughout the war.

Because of his consistent opposition to the communists and his moderate political position, as well as because of his personal integrity and national reputation, many people thought Besteiro could provide the Republic with conciliatory leadership, acceptable both in Spain and abroad. In May 1937, he represented the Republic at the coronation of George VI of Great Britain.* While there, he explored the possibility of British mediation between the Republicans* and the Nationalists* with Sir Anthony Eden* of the British Foreign Office. In August 1938, Besteiro attempted unsuccessfully to persuade Premier Juan Negrín* to negotiate with the Francoists. As a result, he tried to convince President Manual Azaña* to remove Negrín and form a new government, which Azaña refused to do. Instead, the president asked Besteiro to contact the British consul in Madrid and request Britain's mediation, again apparently a fruitless effort. Finally convinced that neither General Franco* nor the British would negotiate with a Republican government

that included communists, Besteiro joined the coup d'etat led by Casado* in March 1939, which created a National Defense Council expressly to negotiate an honorable peace with the Nationalists. He served as a member of this council. Although these negotiations were aborted, Besteiro refused to leave Madrid.

Despite his moderate political convictions and his continuous efforts at peace, Besteiro was taken prisoner by the Falangists and sentenced to thirty years' imprisonment. He died of tuberculosis in Cormona Prison on September 27, 1940.

For further information, see Julián Besteiro, *Marxismo y antimarxismo* (Mexico City, 1966); Segismundo Casado, *The Last Days of Madrid* (London, 1939); Ricardo de la Cierva, *La historia se confiesa 1930-1977* (Barcelona, 1976); Stanley Payne, *The Spanish Revolution* (New York, 1970); Andrés Saborit, *Julián Besteiro Fernández* (Buenos Aires, 1967); and Georges Soría, *Guerra y revolución en España, 1936-1939* (Barcelona, 1978).

Shirley F. Fredricks

BILBAO.

Bilbao, the capital city of the province of Vizcaya* in the Basque country in northern Spain, had a population of about 160,000 in 1931, making it Spain's seventh largest urban center and a major industrial center. At the start of the Civil War, Basque nationalists insured that the Republican side controlled Bilbao and established defense *Juntas* throughout the three Basque provinces to protect them from Nationalist assaults. Soon after, Bilbao became the capital of the Basque government as well. In the months that followed, Bilbao was a port of entry for supplies and trade with other countries to the benefit of the Republic. Periodically, Nationalist bombers damaged portions of the city. However, the Nationalists* did not turn their serious attention to Bilbao until the spring of 1937. At that time, General Emilio Mola Vidal* decided to conquer the Basque country. He established a naval blockade around the nearby coast and assembled forces for the conquest of the province. Meanwhile, in anticipation of such an assault, Bilbao had established a defense perimeter known as the "Iron Ring."*

The Nationalist attack on the Basque country formally began on March 31, 1937. By June 6, most of Vizcaya was under Nationalist control with the exception of the area around Bilbao and to the northwest of the city. General Mola pressed forward toward Bilbao where General Mariano Gámir Ulíbarri* commanded troops defending the city. On June 1, Mola died in an airplane accident, and his command went to General Fidel Dávila Arrondo,* who at that time was known more as a bureaucrat than as a fighter. However, he intensified combat in the province, and by the middle of June, Bilbao experienced increased aerial bombardment. By June 17, Nationalist troops were in the suburbs of the city, and by June 19, Basque troops had evacuated the Basque capital. With the fall of Bilbao, the Basque Republic came to an end. Soon after, the entire Basque country came under Nationalist control. The casualties* on both sides were enormous: 4,500 dead Nationalists and possibly as many as 10,000 dead Republicans,* while each side had approximately 25,000 wounded.

The Nationalists did not execute large numbers of people in Bilbao as they had when they took Málaga* earlier, but they made every attempt to crush Basque nationalism.* Use of the local language or teaching Basque history and customs was forbidden, as was the practice of anti-Nationalist politics. The fall of Bilbao was a major Nationalist victory, reducing the Republican zone dramatically in size while freeing up military resources that could be used for the conquest of other Republican sectors. It also led to recognition of the Burgos* government by the Vatican* since the Church* no longer had to approve the activities of Basque priests in the Republican zone while acknowledging the Catholic nature of the Nationalist cause.

For further information, see José Manuel Martínez Bande, *Vizcaya* (Madrid, 1971); Stanley G. Payne, *Basque Nationalism* (Reno, Nev., 1975); and Hugh Thomas, *The Spanish Civil War* (New York, 1977).
See also Army, Nationalist; and Army, Republican.

James W. Cortada

BILBAO CRESCENCIANO, ANGEL. Bilbao was a little known vice-commissar-general in the Republican Army.* His job was to insure that the soldiers maintained a "correct" and enthusiastic attitude toward the Republic's political objectives. An Indalecio Preito* socialist, he rose to the rank of commissar-general in 1937 and, in effect, became an ombudsman for soldiers complaining about food* and living conditions; occasionally, he tended to political matters.

For further information, see Burnett Bolloten, *The Spanish Revolution: The Left and the Struggle for Power During the Civil War* (Chapel Hill, N.C., 1979).

James W. Cortada

BLACK ARROWS. The Black Arrows was a division of Italian troops that fought with the Nationalists*

during the Civil War. Their first major battle came at Guadalajara* (March 1937), the only campaign in which Mussolini's* forces fought on their own in the war. It was also a humiliating military defeat for them. After initial successful forward assaults on March 9, 10, and primarily on March 11, these forces pushed back Republican units among which was Lister's* 11th Division. The next day Republican aerial bombardment, artillery attacks, and heavy ground fire fights forced the Italians back. With their capture of Italian prisoners, the Republicans* had proof for the League of Nations* of Italian involvement in the Spanish war.

The battle of Guadalajara had a number of consequences for Italy.* First, Italy's involvement in the Spanish war was now made public. Second, all Italian forces may have lost up to 3,000 killed, about 4,000 wounded, and hundreds taken prisoners, making the event expensive. Third, Franco* never again allowed the Italians to initiate a military campaign on their own. Fourth, Mussolini's personal humiliation at Guadalajara contributed to Hitler's* growing conviction that the Duce was not as competent a leader as he had originally thought.

The Black Arrows played a less obvious combat support role in other campaigns later in 1937. This unit fought in the Viscaya* campaign (March-June 1937) and captured the port of Bermeo in the Basque country on April 30. The Black Arrows, numbering about 4,000 men, then advanced on Bilbao,* along with other Nationalist forces, helping to capture it in June. In the Santander* campaign in August 1937, some 25,000 Italians—including the Black Arrows— participated, fighting for the area approaching the Bay of Biscay. Some of the first Nationalist troops to occupy the city of Santander were members of the Black Arrows. These Italian troops were then moved to the Aragón* and the Levante* fronts where, in the spring of 1938, they encountered considerable opposition from Republican forces. On November 16, 1938, these men were withdrawn to Italy as part of the accord reached in the Anglo-Italian Mediterranean Pact* of April 1938.

For further information, see John Coverdale, *Italian Intervention in the Spanish Civil War* (Princeton, N.J., 1975); and Hugh Thomas, *The Spanish Civil War* (New York, 1977).
See also Black Shirts.

James W. Cortada

BLACK FLAMES. The Black Flames, an Italian division fighting for the Nationalists,* saw combat at the battle of Guadalajara* in March 1937, a battle which they and the Nationalists lost. The battle proved to the outside world that Italy* had obviously intervened in the Spanish Civil War with thousands of men.

For further information, see John F. Coverdale, *Italian Intervention in the Spanish Civil War* (Princeton, N.J., 1975).

James W. Cortada

BLACK SHIRTS. The Black Shirts were Italian fascists who fought with the Nationalists.* They first became prominent when a fanatical Italian fascist, Arconovaldo Bonaccorsi, occupied Majorca* in August 1936. These men, along with others who were not in the Black Shirts, ruled Majorca for several months until overthrown by pro-Republican units. Months later, the Black Shirts, along with other Italian contingents, were merged into a larger Italian force fighting in central Spain with regular army commanders. Additional members were shipped in from Italy,* bringing their total to some 3,000 men by late 1936. Thus, they became an early and visible proof of Mussolini's* intent to become involved in the Spanish Civil War.

Winston Churchill* called these Italian fascists "armed tourists" who quickly took part in the fighting around Madrid.* They participated in the fall of Málaga* in February 1937; nine batallions of Black Shirts, numbering over 10,000 men, joined in the march on Málaga. The fall of this city provided Franco* with an important victory. Just before the actual capture of Málaga, however, the Italians evacuated their combat positions outside the city, thinking that the fighting had ended. Therefore, it was finally the Nationalist forces that marched into the city. Total losses for the Italians in this campaign were about 130 dead and some 424 wounded. The Black Shirts next fought at Guadalajara* in March 1937. Together with the Black Arrows,* they were part of a humiliating defeat for Mussolini's forces and led Franco to prohibit the Italians from ever again operating as an independent unit in Nationalist Spain. Henceforth, the Black Shirts were submerged within the Nationalist Army* and its officers reported to Nationalist generals. The Black Shirts left Spain in November 1938.

For further information, see John Coverdale, *Italian Intervention in the Spanish Civil War* (Princeton, N.J., 1975); and Hugh Thomas, *The Spanish Civil War* (New York, 1977).

James W. Cortada

BLAKE, GEOFFREY (1882-1968). Blake, vice-admiral in the British Navy* and commander of naval forces off Bilbao* during the Civil War, provided protection to British commercial vessels attempting to trade with the Republic by way of Bilbao.* Although there were occasional incidents of Nationalist boardings of British ships and bombardments from the coast, he managed to prevent serious loss of life and property off the coast of Spain, thereby preventing any need for additional British involvement in the Civil War.

For further information, see Hugh Thomas, *The Spanish Civil War* (New York, 1977).

James W. Cortada

BLANCO, SEGUNDO. Blanco, an anarchist official in Asturias* at the start of the Civil War, entered the last cabinet of Juan Negrín* as minister of public instruction in April 1938. Blanco was a representative of those in the libertarian movement* who were willing to support the Republic in its final year as Soviet influence waned.

A protégé of the Asturian *Confederación Nacional des Trabajo* (CNT)* leader, José María Martínez, Blanco had been a public school teacher and active in syndicalist activities since 1918. He had been a member of the National Committee of the CNT since the early 1930s. The death of Martínez in the Asturias uprising of October 1934, and Blanco's own imprisonment following that revolt, made him a respected anarchist leader in the summer of 1936.

Blanco was a leader of the Gijón War Committee in the first days of the war. This provincial group set up commissions for war, transportation, food* supplies, and health in Asturias. In September 1936, he entered the Provincial Council of Asturias and León* as a member of the commission on industry. This was a key facet of the war effort because the munitions works were largely in Republican Spain for the first year of the war. When Asturias fell in the early autumn of 1937, Blanco fled to Madrid.* The following spring, he entered the government as minister of public instruction, but he did little in that capacity because of limited finances.

Blanco fled to Mexico* at the end of the war where he was active in the politics of the Republic-in-exile.

For further information, see Pierre Broué and Émile Témime, *The Revolution and the Civil War in Spain* (Cambridge, Mass., 1970).

See also Anarchists; and Gijon.

David V. Holtby

BLUE SHIRTS. *See* O' Duffy, Eoin.

BLUM, LÉON (1872-1950). Blum had consistently opposed the participation of his socialist party, the *Section Française de l'Internationale Ouvrière* (SFIO), in any government until it could be the dominant party. Since 1934, it had gained considerable support, and in 1935, when it took the leadership of the *Front Populaire*, it had become by far the largest party in France.* On June 4, 1936, Blum formed his first government (of socialists and radicals, supported from the outside by the communists) against a background of strikes and factory takeovers. He was already sixty-four years of age, and he had never before held a ministerial office.

On the evening of July 19, Blum received a telegram from José Giral* requesting immediate aid. Blum had visited Madrid* with other *Front Populaire* leaders in late February to participate in a Popular Front* demonstration, and his immediate reaction was a desire to help. On July 21, he instructed Air Minister Pierre Cot to send a certain number of aircraft and artillery pieces, and on the next day he left for London with Foreign Minister Yvon Delbos.* Primary sources disagree as to what caused Blum to reverse his policy, but it would seem to be a blend of several elements opposing him: Stanley Baldwin* and Anthony Eden,* together with the Admiralty in London, the conservative Senate and Quai d'Orsay, and the outcry in the French right-wing press initiated by Henri de Kérillis in *L'Echo de Paris*. In any event, on his return to Paris on the evening of July 24, Blum met with Delbos, Cot, Edouard Daladier,* Vincent Auriol, Jules Moch, and Fernando de los Ríos.* Although Delbos objected to French pilots* flying the planes to Spain, all agreed that France should honor the verbal commitment Blum had made to Giral. The supplies were ready to leave the next day, but the pandemonium in the press and the resignation of Spanish Ambassador Juan Cárdenas* delayed their dispatch until August 2. Three Cabinet meetings were held between July 25 and August 8, but no minutes have survived of any of the three. At the first, attended by President Albert Lebrun and the speaker of the Chamber of Deputies, Edouard Herriot, Blum could not hide his anguish. Only Lebrun, Herriot, and three ministers (Delbos, Camille Chautemps, and Paul Bastid) were opposed to open intervention, but the vote was nonetheless unanimous against such intervention. The solution was to be a compromise, in the form of a secret delivery of planes and arms over a period of eight to ten days (the Cot formula). Mexico* would be asked to act as intermediary in channeling this aid. France would not ban aid from French private industry, but otherwise it would declare its intention not to intervene unless Germany* and Italy* sent arms to the rebels. On July 30, evidence of Italian intervention was to be seen in the form of three planes forced to land in French North Africa. But by the same date Blum's policy was recognizably a failure. The Republicans* were unable to quell the rebellion, and Blum's ambivalent moves had provoked rumors that were enough for Germany and Italy to "condemn" French intervention and "justify" their own.

Up to now Blum could, and did, categorically deny that France had sent war matériel to the Republic, and his policy won the approval of the Chamber on August 1 by 379 votes to 200. On the same day, France proposed the policy of nonintervention to the other Mediterranean powers (Great Britain* and Italy) and on August 3 called on Rome, Berlin, London, and Moscow to join in an international nonintervention agreement. At the same time, Blum was following his other track, so that the first French arms left secretly for Spain on August 2. Fifty miscellaneous aircraft reached the Republic, but such aid could not pass unnoticed, and on August 7 the British government threatened to withdraw from the Treaty of Locarno. As a result, at the critical cabinet meeting held on August 8, Blum switched his policy to the Delbos-Daladier formula, suspending all aid shipments while urging the other states to follow suit. Blum had been on the verge of resigning, but the new Spanish ambassador, Álvaro de Albornoz,* begged him not to, and once he had decided on nonintervention he stuck to it in the face of all attacks. His policy switch was a heavy blow to the USSR,* which now found itself forced to assume the role of supplier to the Republic. The French Communist party and the left wing of the SFIO put constant pressure on Blum, notably in the demonstration of September 6 in Luna Park where the slogans were "Blum à l'action" and "Des avions pour l'Espagne." Nonintervention "weighed upon him like a coat of lead," as Cot put it, but he saw no alternative to it other than isolation and even a civil war in France which would have given Hitler* the mainland of Europe* without even a fight.

Blum held to his course despite the frantic pleas of the Republic, and in late August, when Madrid proposed to blockade all Spanish ports in rebel hands, he made it clear that French warships would not permit French merchantmen to be denied legitimate freedom of commerce. On the other hand, Blum held to his policy, shared by Baldwin, of refusing to confer belligerent rights* on the Nationalists* and was thus able to treat their attacks on French shipping as acts of piracy. On August 1, he had authorized Frenchmen and foreign volunteers* to cross the frontier, provided only that there was no organized recruitment and that they carried a valid passport and traveled singly and unarmed. Such regulations were considerably bent.

Against the overwhelming evidence of Axis duplicity, Blum survived, by 350 to 171, with the seventy-two communist deputies abstaining, a vote of confidence called on December 5. This time it was Álvarez del Vayo* who had to urge Blum to stay put, but with the abstention of the communists the unity of the Front Populaire was shattered. A worsening financial crisis finally forced Blum to resign on June 22, 1937, though he continued as vice-premier in the Chautemps cabinet that followed. At the annual SFIO congress held in Marseilles in July, Spain was the central theme in a vindictive debate. When, on January 18, 1938, Blum withdrew socialist support on the proposed budget, the government fell. Chautemps' second cabinet contained no socialists. But on March 13 this cabinet also fell, to be replaced by a second Blum government whose foreign minister, Joseph Paul-Boncour, was more to the Left than Delbos. Blum was now feeling regret for his earlier timidity, and following Negrín's* second visit to Paris to implore France to abandon non-intervention, Blum and Paul-Boncour were ready to comply. On March 15, Blum proposed sending Franco* an ultimatum, giving him twenty-four hours to renounce his Axis aid, failing which France would resume its freedom of action and adopt any measures it considered necessary. Two days later, Blum signed a confidential order authorizing the dispatch of French arms to the Republic. But any suggestion of open intervention faced the resolute opposition of Marshal Pétain* and General Maurice Gamelin (who allegedly threatened to resign), of Alexis Léger at the Quai d'Orsay, and of Daladier and others in the cabinet. The most Blum could do was to reopen the frontier to allow vast amounts of Soviet matériel that had been blocked in French ports and depots by the Chautemps cabinets to cross the border freely. But on April 10 this independent-minded cabinet fell victim to a new financial crisis and Blum was forced to resign.

Out of office, Blum vented his contempt on the appeaser Georges Bonnet,* Daladier's foreign minister, and as late as January 1939, he insisted that there was still time to save the Republic. Only now, in fact, did he give his unequivocal support, urging that the Catalan frontier be thrown open to the transit of arms, denouncing the recall of Ambassador Eirik Labonne and the unseemly haste of Léon Bérard's mission to conciliate Franco, pleading daily in *Le Populaire* against French recognition of Burgos,* and warning France and Britain that by facilitating Franco's victory they were hastening the day when they too would be confronted by the global ambition of Hitler and Musso-

lini.* But on February 13 Blum acknowledged that the Republic was beaten, and he now advised socialists not to incite the Republicans* to a Numantine suicide. His last act was to deplore the flattery shown to Franco by sending him Pétain.

Blum, according to his friend André Gide, was "the least poetic of men." But his heart beat to the rhythm of the "politique du juste," and to a politician like Pierre Cot his chief flaw lay instead in his excessive generosity and sensibility. How did so honest a man come to deal so dishonestly with the question of Spain? The answer lies in the particular nature of his faults: poor judgment, a passion for consensus, and an obstinate belief in the good faith of his fascist adversaries that led him into errors he could not recognize until after he had left office. He, more than anyone, set the course for the humiliating defeat of French policy. This policy was based upon a gamble that the Spanish Republic could win without French intervention, and the gamble failed, but the friends that Blum could turn to were few indeed. Under the onslaught of the Right, he was let down by a Left whose press failed to galvanize public opinion in his support. His own ambivalence was the determinant in the end. He was a socialist in the tradition of Jean Jaurès, whose horror of war he shared. His overriding purpose was therefore to preserve peace, not lead a crusade. Pacifism, the banner of socialism, was thus at odds with antifascism, the banner of the *Front Populaire*, and it was the latter that lost, for Blum lacked the raw will to deter an aggressor. It left him powerless to influence events, and as those bear witness who saw him in the late summer of 1936, it left him convulsed not only with agony and grief, but also with despair.

For further information, see Colette Audry, *Léon Blum ou la politique du juste* (Paris, 1955); Joel Colton, *Léon Blum: Humanist in Politics* (New York, 1966); Nathanael Greene, *Crisis and Decline: The French Socialist Party in the Popular Front Era* (Ithaca, N.Y., 1969); Georges Lefranc, *Histoire du front populaire* (Paris, 1965); *Léon Blum chef de gouvernement, 1936-1937. Actes d'un colloque* (Paris, 1967); Jules Moch, *Rencontres avec Léon Blum* (Paris, 1970); and David Wingeate Pike, *Les Français et la guerre d'Espagne* (Paris, 1975).

David Wingeate Pike

BOADILLA DEL MONTE, BATTLE OF. The battle of Boadilla del Monte (December 14, 1936) was part of the Nationalist offensive designed to seize Madrid* in the early months of the Civil War. The Nationalists* launched their offensive toward this small town, which was nearly 20 miles from Madrid, bombarding it and then engaging in bloody hand-to-hand combat with both the International Brigades* involved along with regular units of the Republican Army.* The Republicans* used Soviet tanks under the command of Russian officers, finally pushing the Nationalists out of the town. A counteroffensive resulted in severe casualties,* especially on the part of the International Brigades, allowing the Nationalists to retake the community and thus position themselves a few miles closer to Madrid. As another byproduct of the fierce fighting at Boadilla del Monte, the Nationalists decided to stop their advance on Madrid temporarily, thereby giving the Republicans an opportunity to regroup for the defense of the capital city.

Fighting in and around this community continued throughout 1936 and 1937 as Republican and Nationalist forces jockeyed for position in the area west of Madrid. During the battle of Brunete,* in July 1937, for example, heavy fighting took place here along one of the major roads to Madrid.

For further information, see José Manuel Martínez Bande, *La marcha sobre Madrid* (Madrid, 1968); and Esmond Romilly, *Boadilla* (London, 1971).

See also Appendix B.

James W. Cortada

BOLÍN BIDWELL, LUIS (1897-1969). Luis Bolín fulfilled two missions for the Nationalists* in July 1936 that were crucial to the successful launching of the uprising. He arranged for the airplane that transported Franco,* the military governor of the Canary Islands,* from Las Palmas to northern Africa on July 18, 1936. Three days later, Bolín arrived in Rome with a charge from Franco to convince the Italian government of Mussolini* to supply the Nationalists with bombers and fighter planes, without which the assault on the mainland from Melilla* begun on August 5 would have been jeopardized. During the war, Bolín served first as director of the press office accrediting correspondents and then, after February 1938, as the director-general of the Spanish State Tourist Department.

Bolín was born in Málaga* and was educated at the University of Granada. Having learned English from his British-born mother, Bolín began work in 1920 as the press attaché to the Spanish Embassy in London. Earlier, he served as a correspondent with the British forces in France* and Northern Europe* during the final year of World War I. He became the first Spaniard to work for the League of Nations* when he joined their information section in London in 1921. Later in the decade, he returned to Spain and served as a

regional delegate of the Spanish Tourist Board. When the Republic was proclaimed, he was dismissed from his post. He watched events leading up to the Civil War from London where he served as correspondent for the right-wing daily *ABC.**

The publisher of *ABC* was Juan Ignacio, the Marqués de Luca de Tena,* who on July 5, 1936, telephoned Bolín from Biarritz, in the extreme southwest of France, with plans to begin arrangements to secure a plane for Franco. Bolín was instructed to be in Casablanca by July 11 with a plane capable of flying from the Canary Islands to Ceuta,* in Spanish Morocco.* Once there he was to await further word from an unidentified agent. Bolín's mission was financed by Juan March,* the Majorcan entrepreneur, and drawn from an account with the London banking firm of Kleinwort.

Assisting Bolín in London with the arrangements was Juan de la Cierva, inventor of the autogiro which was manufactured at plants in England and the United States.* La Cierva arranged for Bolín to rent a de Havilland Dragon Rapide, which seated six plus the pilot. To avoid arousing suspicions about the intent of the flight, La Cierva suggested that two blondes and a second man accompany Bolín and the flight crew to give the impression of vacationing couples. Traveling companions were soon located—Major Hugh Pollard, a retired British army major, his daughter, and the daughter of a friend.

The group departed on July 11 and, after a delay in Portugal,* arrived in Casablanca on July 12. The next day, newspapers carried reports of the murder of Calvo Sotelo,* a prominent rightest deputy in the Cortes.* Bolín realized that the Republic would heighten security and that it would be difficult for an agent of the conspirators to reach him in Casablanca. He decided to proceed without delay, entrusting to Major Pollard the task of going on without Bolín to the Canaries and there making contact with an intermediary. This was done, and the plane arrived on Grand Canary on July 15. The next day Franco set into motion plans to secure the islands and fly to Spanish Morocco. Martial law was declared on Tenerife and then on Grand Canary, where fighting erupted, delaying Franco's departure until July 18.

Bolín rejoined the aircraft he had chartered when it carried Franco to Casablanca and then on to Tetuán* on July 19. Once Franco was with his troops, he authorized Bolín to negotiate for the purchase of airplanes and supplies, with the first stop being Italy.* These negotiations proved more difficult than Bolín had expected, but finally on July 30 he set out for Melilla in one of the twelve Savoia-81 bombers Mussolini made available. The bombers were laden with supplies, and when strong head winds were encountered three ran short of fuel and crashed. The remaining nine bombers and their pilots were enrolled in the Spanish Foreign Legion,* creating an instant air force in that unit, and pressed into service in the crossing of the Straits of Gibraltar* on August 5.

Bolín Italian fliers were first assigned to the forces of General Gonzalo Queipo de Llano,* and Bolín served as their liaison and set up a press office in Seville* to regulate and accredit correspondents. In late September, Bolín entered Toledo* with the victorious armies of Africa* and southern Spain commanded by Franco. There he recovered numerous art treasures that had been hidden or were being readied for evacuation. Among the pieces he recovered were El Greco's "The Burial of Count Orgaz."

Duty in Salamanca* at the headquarters set up by Franco followed beginning in October 1936. Bolín served as press director with the task of organizing war correspondents for tours of the battle areas. In this capacity, Bolín visited the various fronts with groups of correspondents.

The formation of Franco's first cabinet in mid-February 1938 occasioned Bolín's appointment as head of the Spanish State Tourist Department. Franco, an avid hunter and angler, encouraged Bolín to restore and reopen the national hunting preserves as well as the trout streams in the Nationalist zone. Bolín also set out to initiate motor coach tours of northern Spain beginning in July 1938. These tours, called *Rutas Nacionales de Guerra*, covered about 600 miles beginning at Oviedo,* with stops at San Sebastián, Bilbao,* Laredo, and Santander.* By the end of 1938, tours were running in Andalusia.* Twenty buses, each named after a battle, provided the transportation, and hotels and restaurants along the route soon were revitalized by the business. Bolín continued to run the tourist service during World War II as *Rutas Nacionales de España*, which encouraged Spaniards to visit and tour within their country.

For further information, see Luis Bolín, *Spain: The Vital Years* (London, 1967).

David V. Holtby

BONNET, GEORGES (1889-1973). Bonnet, born in France,* became a financial and diplomatic adviser in Spanish matters as early as 1920, when he attended the Madrid* conference of the Universal Postal Union. Although he avoided joining any French political party, he helped as an independent deputy to put together center-type coalition cabinets in the French parliament. Throughout the Popular Front era in Paris (1936-1938),

Bonnet's conservative attitude toward balanced budgets and fear of social revolution made him a constant enemy of the USSR* and the Popular Front* government in Spain. Just before the outbreak of the Spanish Civil War, he was sent as ambassador to the United States* to negotiate payment of France's World War I debts. From June 1937 to April 1938, he served as minister of finance in Paris.

As French foreign minister from April 1938 into World War II, Bonnet led the French parliamentary faction that advocated making concessions to Hitler's* Germany,* Mussolini's* Italy,* and Franco's* Spain. Bonnet secretly pressed the Czechoslovak government throughout the summer of 1938 to cede the Sudetenland to Hitler, while publicly he maintained that France's alliance with Czechoslovakia* remained in force. He endorsed the signing of the Munich Agreement,* and concluded a Non-Aggression Pact in Paris with Joachim von Ribbentrop in December 1938, in further appeasement of Hitler. These international moves helped strengthen the Nationalists* and weaken the Republicans* in Spain.

Regarding Juan Negrín* as an agent of Joseph Stalin* (whom Bonnet viewed as trying to provoke war between France and Germany), the French foreign minister made three crucial decisions that helped assure Franco's victory in the Civil War. First, he sealed the French border to Republican Spain on June 13, 1938. Second, he initiated steps to recognize the Franco regime on January 23, 1939, thus ending any hope that the Spanish Republic could continue receiving semiprivate military support from France. Third, he promised Nationalist Foreign Minister Francisco Gómez-Jordana* in February that Paris would return Republican gold and other valuables held in France to help the Burgos* government in its reconstruction efforts once the war had ended.

After Franco's victory, Bonnet pressed Britain* to lend the Nationalists* money in May and August 1939, and he tried to undermine the Chamberlain*-Halifax guarantee to Poland.* After the fall of the French Third Republic in June 1940, Bonnet sympathized with, but did not serve, the Vichy regime headed by Marshal Petain,* whom he had named first ambassador to Franco's Spain in 1939.

For further information, see Anthony Adamthwaite, *France and the Coming of the Second World War* (London, 1977); and Georges Bonnet, *Defense de la paix*, 2 vols. (Paris, 1946-1948), *Quai d'Orsay* (Isle of Man, 1965), and *Vingt Ans de Vie Politique, 1918-1938: De Clemenceau a Daladier* (Paris, 1970).

See also Blum, Léon.

Robert H. Whealey

BORBÓN-PARMA. *See* Bourbon-Parme, François Xavier de.

BORKENAU, FRANZ (1900-1957). Borkenau's *The Spanish Cockpit* (spring 1937) was the first account of the communists' resistance to social revolution in Spain. Borkenau concluded that the communists "have ceased to be a revolutionary party and become one of the mainstays of the anti-revolutionary forces."

Borkenau's criticism of communism was based on wide political exposure, most notably eight years spent as a member of the German Communist party and service for some time as an official of the Comintern, the Third International founded in 1919. He went to Spain on two six-week journeys—the first in August-September 1936 and then again in January-February 1937—to do field work as a sociologist on a country in revolution. His observations were confined to the Republican zone because the Nationalists* denied him access, but he did travel widely. The first journey to Barcelona,* Valencia,* Madrid,* and the western and southern fronts brought him into contact with troops of all political factions and even some rather intense military skirmishes. It was on the second journey, however, that his political commentary was sharply focused by events in Barcelona and Valencia.

His secretary, a communist, denounced him to the Valencia *Seguridad* because of his critical opinion toward the party. He was arrested without knowing the charges, interrogated, and finally released after several days. This experience as a political prisoner prompted him to denounce the repression being carried out by the communists.

George Orwell* hailed *The Spanish Cockpit* as "the best book yet written on the subject" of the Spanish Civil War in Orwell's review of it in July 1937. The theme of an antirevolutionary communism was one Orwell was about to write about in *Homage to Catalonia*. Together, the two books remain the best eyewitness accounts of the political machinations of the first year of the war.

For further information, see Franz G. Borkenau, *The Spanish Cockpit* (reprint; University of Michigan Press, 1963).

David V. Holtby

BOSCH GIMPERA, PEDRO (1892-1974). Bosch, a prominent archaeologist and rector of the University of Barcelona during the Civil War, worked steadfastly to apply principles of justice and compassion in the government posts he held. At the outbreak of the war, he used his office as rector to secure the safe passage to France* of a number of professors and clergymen in Barcelona.* In June 1937, he took up duties as a judge for the Generalitat,* and he immediately began to revise and reduce unjust and irregular sentences. He also succeeded in freeing political prisoners, including clergymen.

Prior to his work with the courts, Bosch served briefly with the Cultural Committee of the Generalitat and was rebuffed in Berlin when he attempted to present his credentials as ambassador in August 1936. He then went to Great Britain* to lecture at the leading universities and was offered a post as cultural attaché for the embassy of the Republic.

Bosch's work with the justice system brought him into inevitable conflict with the communist-run *Servício de Información Militar* (SIM),* which had set up its own tribunals and prisons and used torture. The death of several prisoners* prompted Bosch to crack down on agents of the SIM, a move that the government under Juan Negrín* countered in August 1938 by transferring more of the justice system to the SIM. One of his last attempts to apply principles of equal justice during times of war was to establish a tribunal of religion to provide priests for those in the army who sought a renewal of religious activity.

He left for England at the end of 1938 and soon went into exile, eventually settling in Mexico.*

For further information, see Pedro Bosch Gimpera, *Memòries* (Barcelona, 1980); and Carlos Rojas, *Retratos antifranquistas* (Barcelona, 1977).

See also Catalonia; and Police.

David V. Holtby

BOSCH Y ATIENZA, JOSÉ (1873-1936). Bosch was the military governor of Minorca* in July 1936. He attempted to turn over the island to the Nationalists,* only to be arrested by his troops who remained loyal to the Republic. In August he was tried and executed for treason and rebellion.

For further information, see Hugh Thomas, *The Spanish Civil War* (New York, 1977).

James W. Cortada

BOSCH Y BOSCH, CARLOS. Bosch, a career army officer, was the military governor of León* in July 1936 when a group of 2,000 miners demanded arms of him. He gave them 200 rifles and four machineguns on condition that they leave the city. They left León on July 19, and the next day, troops loyal to the Nationalists* rebelled under the command of General Bosch. The rebels were able to squash local resistance, bringing the entire province under Nationalist control quickly.

For further information, see Hugh Thomas, *The Spanish Civil War* (New York, 1977).

James W. Cortada

BOURBON-PARME, FRANÇOIS XAVIER OF (1889-1977). Bourbon-Parme was Carlist "regent" from 1936 to 1952, and pretender to the Spanish throne until 1975. Son of the last ruling duke of Parma, who had fought with the Carlists* in the 1870s, Bourbon-Parme played no part in Spanish affairs until the 1930s. He lived variously in Austria, Italy,* and France,* and fought during World War I in the Belgian Army. In 1931, the Carlist claim was inherited by his uncle, Don Alfonso Carlos, a childless octogenarian. Thereafter, he became increasingly involved with Carlism and consequently with Spain. During 1935 and 1936, he was kept informed of Carlist conspiratorial activities and worked unremittingly to arm the *Requetés*.* In April 1936, he was named regent in an attempt to resolve the problem of who should succeed Don Alfonso Carlos. It was in this capacity in July 1936 that he granted permission for the Navarrese Carlists to join the rising against the Popular Front.*

When Alfonso Carlos died in September 1936, Bourbon-Parme became titular head of Carlism, although he did not claim the throne until 1952. Throughout the Civil War and afterwards, he strove to uphold Carlism's independence vis-à-vis the Nationalist cause and the Franco* regime. As a result, he fell foul of Franco and lost the loyalties of those Carlists disposed to collaborate with Francoism. Bourbon-Parme's sincere dislike of fascism* inspired him, during World War II, to become linked with the French resistance, as a result of which he spent some time in Dachau. From the late 1950s onward, he presided, sometimes uncomfortably, over Carlism's evolution into a populist, and later socialist, opposition party. In 1972, he handed effective authority over to his son, Carlos Hugo, and in 1975, two years before his death, he officially "abdicated."

For further information, see Martin Blinkhorn, *Carlism and Crisis in Spain, 1931-1939* (Cambridge, England, 1975); Josep Carles Clemente, *Historia del Carlismo contemporáneo, 1935-1972* (Barcelona, 1977); and Javier Lavardin, *El último pretendiente* (Paris, 1976).

See also Alfonso XIII; and Navarre.

Martin Blinkhorn

BOWERS, CLAUDE GERNADE (1878-1958). Bowers, a Democratic diplomat and the American ambassador to the Republic of Spain from 1933 to 1939, was a journalist and biographer by profession. He strongly supported the cause of the Republic. During the Civil War, he implemented the American policy of neutrality within Spain and helped protect the lives of American citizens, while writing dispatches suggesting that nonintervention would not preserve the peace of Europe.*

Bowers had mixed relations with the Republic. During the years of the Republic before July 1936, he had to negotiate over matters of trade and international economics and found many of the government's commercial policies harmful to American interests. With the start of the war, he recognized that the Republic should be saved and helped if fascism was to be denied another victory in Europe. He quickly concluded that Germany* and Italy* wanted to expand authoritarian rule in Spain as part of a much larger scheme to destroy the republican tradition in Western Europe. He felt that if Spain fell to Franco* Europe would eventually be caught up in a general war, with the strong possibility of other republics falling by the wayside. The Spanish Republic perceived in Bowers a strong ally who could sway public opinion in the United States.* Unfortunately for the Republic, Bowers was not willing to do this, and he was unable to persuade the government of the United States* to strike out on a course of its own separate from the Anglo-French policy of nonintervention.

Upon his return to the United States in 1939, Bowers lectured on the war and its international implications. He eventually wrote his important memoirs on his years in Spain.

For further information, see Claude G. Bowers, *My Mission to Spain: Watching the Rehearsal for World War II* (New York, 1954); and Richard P. Traina, *American Diplomacy and the Spanish Civil War* (Bloomington, Ind., 1968).

See also Hull, Cordell.

James W. Cortada

BRAZIL. Brazil showed greater sympathy for the Nationalists* in the Spanish Civil War than perhaps any other country in the New World. Before 1936, Brazil, along with the United States,* had been significant suppliers of cotton to Catalonia.* After July 1936, this cotton no longer went to Spain, causing considerable hardship to the Catalan textile industry. The loss of business caused by the interference of war encouraged great interest in Brazil where hope for a rapid end to the war existed. Brazilians clearly favored Franco's* cause to the point where on September 19, 1936, for example, the Congress of Brazil observed a moment of silence in honor of dead Nationalists.* The Brazilian government maintained a running dialogue with the Nationalists throughout the war, although it was of a ceremonial nature. They were not willing to participate in the conflict in any formal diplomatic manner. Their enthusiasm for the Nationalists may be attributed to a growing indigenous fascist movement in Brazil. There was also strong sympathy for the religious clericals being persecuted in Republican Spain. At the same time, Brazil experienced difficult relations with Mexico* since Mexico enthusiastically sympathized with the Spanish Republic.

For further information, see Arnold J. Toynbee, *Survey of International Affairs, 1937,* vol. 2, *The International Repercussions of the War in Spain, 1936-1937* (Oxford, 1938).

See also Latin America.

James W. Cortada

BRENAN, GERALD (1894-1977). Brenan, a British writer and poet, wrote a brilliant study on the sociopolitical causes of the Spanish Civil War, *The Spanish Labyrinth* (Cambridge University Press, 1943). He argued that many of Spain's problems were caused by the tensions between local autonomist feelings and the pressures of political centralization, between the role of the Catholic Church* as a force in Spanish politics and society and the conflict among religious and anticlerical Spain, between countryside and city, between monarchist Spaniards and socialists, communists, and anarchists.* For nearly twenty years, his book remained the most important text on the causes of the war.

Brenan lived or visited in Spain on and off beginning in the 1920s, spending considerable time in Andalusia,* about which he often commented in his books. Throughout the 1940s and 1950s, he continued to write about Spanish society in a number of articles and books. During this period, his were the best English language works on contemporary Spain.

For further information, see Gerald Brenan, *Personal Record* (London, 1974), his memoirs; *South from Granada* (London, 1957); and *The Spanish Labyrinth: An Account of the Social and Political Background of the Civil War* (Cambridge, 1943).

James W. Cortada

BRITISH BATTALION. The British Battalion, made up of 2,000 volunteers* from Great Britain*—mostly working-class radicals, joined by a smattering of intellectuals*—fought for the Spanish Republic, and the overwhelming majority of them served in the ranks

of this battalion. The unit was incorporated into the 15th International Brigades (IB) in late January 1937, but long before that time Britons had been engaged in action. Some had appeared among the early *centuria* (company of approximately 100 men) on the Aragón front, others had helped to defend Madrid* in November, and a British company had already spent a month fighting with the 14th IB near Córdoba.*

In its very first battle, the battalion was almost devastated. Called to the Jarama* front in mid-February 1937 to help blunt the rebel drive on the Valencia Road, the 600-man unit suffered so much from the heavy firepower of the enemy that it was left with only 225 effectives after a single day in the lines. In the July 1937 Brunete* offensive, the British were at the leading edge of the Loyalists'* advance, and the following month in Aragón they were responsible for capturing Purburell Hill outside of Quinto. After extensive action in the winter campaign surrounding Teruel,* the spring retreats in Aragón, and the Ebro* offensive, the British ended the war with a record of heavy casualties,* with some 500 dead and another 1,200 wounded.

For further information, see Fred Copeman, *Reason in Revolt* (London, 1948); Esmond Romilly, *Boadilla* (London, 1937); William Rust, *Britons in Spain* (London, 1939); and Thomas Wintringham, *English Captain* (London, 1939).

See also Appendix B.

Robert A. Rosenstone

BRUNETE, BATTLE OF. In the early hours of July 6, 1937, the quiet, sparsely manned Nationalist front facing Madrid* erupted in a nightmare of bombardment from enemy artillery and aircraft. This was only a prelude to what was to become the most massive military offensive to date in the cruel history of the Spanish Civil War. For about three weeks, it drenched the thirsty soil of Castile* with the blood of thousands of Spaniards and hundreds of their foreign allies. The battle raged in over 100-degree heat from the blistering July sun. Men were not only to be blown to pieces, die from ghastly wounds, go mad from thirst, but also take their own lives when their cause was lost. Others mutinied and fled the field—only to be stopped by their own machineguns and tanks. This was all in the name of a small, seemingly unimportant *pueblo* in Castile only 15 miles west from Madrid. It was a *pueblo,* only a minor point in greater plans, which, because of the heroism and tragedy surrounding it, was to be projected into the pages of history. It was the battle of Brunete.

The planning for the battle might be considered brilliant, but its conduct was stupid. Its defense and reconquest might be considered heroic, but it was useless. It depends upon one's point of departure and return.

After its heroic defense of Madrid but reverses in the north, and now faced with the pending Nationalist assault on Santander,* the Popular Front* was in great need of an offensive victory. Its forces, well supplied and equipped by the Russians, were to grasp the initiative. It was to be, if not a deathblow to the enemy, a great tactical victory with the destruction of the Nationalist Army* besieging Madrid.

The master plan was devised by the Spanish Lieutenant Colonel Vicente Rojo,* but the details and conduct of the operation were in the hands of the Russians and communist advisers who were firmly in control of Madrid. All but one of the corps and division commanders were communists, and those brigade commanders who were not party members were carefully watched by their political commissars. Rojo's battle plan was a classical operation of double envelopment with destruction in detail of the Nationalist Army facing Madrid, cutting the enemy's vital lines of communications to the west, and completely disrupting the planned offensive against Santander.

The main attack zone in the west was south of Valdemorillo on a 10-kilometer front between the Perales and Aulencia rivers. The assembled force comprised two army corps (5th and 18th) consisting of fifteen brigades (including five International Brigades). They were equipped with seventy Russian T-26 tanks, twenty armored cars, and 130 field guns.

They were to seize the *pueblo* Quijorna (population 400) defended by a battalion (less one company) of Falangists and one anti-tank gun. The other company was deployed north of the village at the high ground of Los Llanos with two anti-tank guns. The advance was to storm Villanueva de la Cañada (population 800) defended by a militia battalion (less one company) equipped with two anti-tank guns and two field pieces. The remaining company was deployed across the Aulencia River at Villafranca del Castillo with five anti-tank guns and four field guns.

Brunete (district population 1,500) was to be surrounded and taken at dawn by a brigade of Lister's* 11th Division. His remaining brigades were to establish a bridgehead across the Guadarrama River to the west, and press on down to the Navalcarnero-Móstoles Road.

Brunete was the command post of a Nationalist sector. In the village, the Nationalists had only sixty combatants and twenty corpsmen who operated a casu-

alty clearing station. Also in this area was an army battalion, with two anti-tank guns, deployed around Villanueva del Pardillo between the Aulencia and Guadarrama rivers, as well as one company of volunteers* at the ruined medieval castle on the confluence of these two rivers. The area to be attacked by two army corps was defended by only 2,000 men. It seemed an easy offensive through terrain that was nearly perfect for both men and armor.

The Nationalists* learned of the pending offensive from deserters, but mistakenly underestimated its mass. The attack area was reinforced only by two *tabors* of Moors,* one at Quijorna and the other at Villanueva del Pardillo. This brought the defense strength to a mere 2,700 men.

The east wing of the Republican attack was from the southern suburbs of Madrid. This force consisted of one army corps of two divisions, plus five brigades, equipped with thirty tanks, ten armored cars, and twenty-four guns.

For reserves, the Republicans* had two divisions (of five brigades), three independent brigades, thirty tanks, ten armored cars, and twenty-four field guns. The combined Republic forces consisted of twenty-eight brigades, 130 T-26 tanks, forty armored cars, 188 guns (not including anti-aircraft), and support by over 200 aircraft. Their total strength was between 80,000 and 90,000 men, not including the 150,000 men who were to hold the line. No such massing of men and equipment had ever before been seen in Spain.

The east-wing attack force was to advance through Carabanchel* to near Móstoles and join with the main force driving south from Brunete. Trapped in the pocket would be the 54,000 men of the Nationalists' Army of the Center.* The latter had one division (Barrón's* 13th) in reserve which was well positioned near Navalcarnero.

In the early hours of July 6, Villanueva de la Cañada was pounded by artillery and aerial bombardment and then assaulted by tanks and infantry. Although outnumbered ten to one, the defenders threw back the assault. Two additional International Brigades* and the corps cavalry were committed, and General Miaja* issued his order that the village was to be taken "at all costs"—and if it was necessary—fire behind his forces with his own artillery. After a terrible fifteen-hour battle, the defenders were overrun.

A few miles to the west, the 5th Corps, in spite of heavy aerial and artillery support, failed to dislodge the few but determined defenders of Los Llanos and Quijorna. But Lister,* with one brigade, had surrounded Brunete with its eighty defenders. There is confusion in their own records as to how long it took to overrun the eighty men, but by 1100 hours the *pueblo* was in Republican hands. Lister's other brigades bypassed Brunete and continued down the open road towards Navalcarnero. But after exchanging a few shots with an enemy patrol, they turned back and established defensive positions south of Brunete.

The east-wing of the attack (from south of Madrid*), after the heaviest bombardment known in the city, with two divisions slightly dented General Yagüe's* tough 14th Division, but retreated in disorder. They tried again the next day and suffered heavy losses. Their effort through Carabanchel was a complete failure, and they were returned to the defense by the high command. All attention was now centered on the salient at Brunete.

The Nationalists' reaction was rapid and determined. It demonstrated fine staff work as well as full command over and in the field units. The single reserve division (13th) of the Nationalist Army of the Center was sent towards Brunete. A Lieutenant Colonel José Álvarez Entrena, on his own initiative, took command of the battalion at Villaviciosa, organized an additional 320 men as a rearguard, and then located his battalion on the high ground dominating Brunete as it fell. He was soon joined by a *tabor* of Moors. Repeated attempts to dislodge them with infantry and tanks failed. In addition, two *tabors* established themselves 1 kilometer from Brunete opposite Lister's 100th Brigade and, a legion *bandera* (battalion) moved up on the road south of Brunete. All night the Nationalists were bombarded, but their ranks held.

General Franco* suspended the offensive against Santander.* He ordered all Italian and Spanish air squadrons (some units placed under command of the German Condor Legion*) to deploy against the attack zone. Two divisions were pulled from Cáceres* and Galicia* and the 4th and 5th Navarre Brigades from the north. All units moved with amazing dispatch.

All day of July 7, the Republicans* hammered the small force holding Los Llanos and finally overran the position at nightfall. According to the 5th Corps commander (Modesto*), some of the Moors committed suicide by "shooting themselves in the belly." It was not until after Modesto had committed his reserve division (30th) that he was finally able to subdue the determined defense of Quijorna.

On July 8, Franco established his command post at the headquarters of the 13th Divison north of Sevilla la Nueva. By the next day, Franco had twenty-six battalions in direct contact, an additional twelve battalions in immediate reserve, and was supported by 100 pieces of artillery.

The enemy continued to widen his beachhead east of the Guadarrama River but was unable to carry the surrounded Villanueva del Pardillo until July 11. Here, the 13th International Brigade expended itself, and the Republicans in the attack zone were soon reduced to thirty-eight tanks and armored cars. The Nationalists broke the encirclement of Villafranca, and all further offensive efforts of the Republicans failed. The minister of defense, Indalecio Prieto,* on July 14 ordered the whole Madrid army on the defense. They had gained a pocket about 8 miles deep and 10 miles wide.

Franco deemed the enemy salient too dangerous and decided that the front, in part, would have to be restored. He committed his arriving forces against the bulge. In the west, there was the 4th Navarre Brigade under Alonso Vega,* from the east the 5th Navarre under Juan Bautista and a division under Asensio,* and from the south Barrón's 13th Division which was to drive directly north to Brunete. The Nationalist counterattack was more determined in its fury and was far better directed than the Republican offensive.

Still, the Republicans were equally determined to hold their gains. For days the battle raged through these few miles of Castile, and thousands of men were to die in the suffocating heat. El Campesino's* Republican 46th Division was shattered and had to be replaced. The 13th International Brigade mutinied and fled towards Madrid, only to be intercepted by the Assault Guards* in armored cars. Those not shot were "reeducated" and distributed through other units. The Nationalists disengaged full brigades (a dangerous maneuver that worked) and committed the same troops in different directions. At noon on July 24, Barrón forced Lister out of Brunete to the cemetery to the north. But the Nationalists themselves came under attack from a fresh Republican division. It was attack and counterattack through the night and the next day. Finally, in the late afternoon, Moorish and Spanish infantry charged into the Republican mass which broke and fled the field of battle. Barrón's tanks and cavalry pursued to a little more than 1.5 miles from Villanueva de la Cañada.

The Republican rout was stopped by execution of officers and men, and turning machineguns on their own men behind the lines. Franco decided that the threat had been eliminated and no further action in the sector was necessary. The battle of Brunete was over.

The Republic had gained a stretch of territory about 4 miles deep and 10 miles wide. Beyond that they failed in their objectives; the Nationalist Army of the Center was intact, its communications firmly held, and the Santander offensive only temporarily halted.

There is still argument as to the losses, but it seems that the Republicans lost over 23,000 men and the Nationalists 17,000. Republican losses in equipment were massive, and some of the units were so badly shattered that the survivors had to be merged with others. This was the case of the American battalions of the International Brigades. The German Me-109 had proven itself over Russian fighters. Use of tanks en masse as a shock force by the Nationalists proved far superior to use of tanks as infantry support, as was the case with the Republicans. The Spanish soldiers of both sides showed their worth, but the Nationalist leadership in all ranks, particularly field and company grade officers, was far superior. This was the only advantage that the Nationalists held. The communist leaders of the Republican forces were left heaping vituperations on each other.

For further information, see George Hills, *The Battle for Madrid* (New York, 1977); José Manuel Martínez Bande, *La ofensiva sobre Segovia y la batalla de Brunete* (Monografias de la guerra de España, No. 7) (Madrid, 1972); Ramón Salas Larrazábal, *Historia del ejército popular de la república*, vol. 4 (Madrid, 1974); and Vicente Rojo, *España heroica* (Buenos Aires, 1942).

See also Appendix B.

Raymond L. Proctor

BUIZA Y FERNÁNDEZ PALACIOS, MIGUEL (1898-1963). Buiza was a career naval officer in the service of the Republic. Born on January 25, 1898, in Seville,* he won distinction in the naval service before the Civil War. Appointed as commander of the Republican fleet in September 1936, Buiza led the naval expedition to northern Spanish ports in September-October. Subsequently, he followed Soviet desires to restrict the fleet to the protection of supply ships from the USSR* to Mediterranean ports. Buiza commanded the Republican fleet in the battle of Cherchell on September 7, 1937. Relieved by Ubieta* in November 1937, Buiza became naval chief of staff. Reappointed fleet commander in January 1939, on March 5 during the Cartagena* uprising Buiza ordered the fleet to sea and subsequently to internment in Bizerte. Buiza's permanent rank was lieutenant commander, although he exercised the duties of vice admiral, Spain's highest naval rank. He died in Hyères, France,* on June 23, 1963.

See also Navy, Spanish.

Willard C. Frank, Jr.

BULLFIGHTS. The *corrida de toros* had only limited appeal in the Republican zone, but was very popular in Nationalist Spain. The differing reception accorded bullfights reflected differences in both social attitude and conditions required for the event.

In August 1936, many bullfighters caught in the Republican zone performed a benefit *corrida de toros* to secure papers for safe passage to France,* where ostensibly their presence was required to fulfill a contract. In fact, however, most bullfighters preferred to leave Republican Spain for various reasons. Many bullfighters sumpathized with the Nationalists; leftists in the Republican zone condemned the bullfight as a vestige of the old, decadent Spain; the two centers of stockbreeding—Seville* and Salamanca*—were in Nationalist control; and bulls were not readily available in the Republican zone. Moreover, Franco* began to provide mass, popular entertainment by sponsoring bullfights, a move most likely prompted by his realization that entertainment was good for morale and kept people from thinking about the privations of war. The Nationalists,* in overtaking Republican towns, often used the bullring to hold prisoners* until the town was secured.

For further information, see Rafael Abella, *La vida cotidiana durante la guerra civil: La españa nacionalista* (Barcelona, 1973), and *La vida cotidiana durante la guerra civil: La españa republicana* (Barcelona, 1976).

See also Daily Life, Nationalist Zone; and Daily Life, Republican Zone.

David V. Holtby

BUÑUEL, LUIS (1900-   ). Buñuel, whose three films made between 1927 and 1932 established him as Spain's most gifted film maker, offered his services as a documentarist to the Republic in July 1936. He was already serving as a producer, but not director, of four commercial films for the Republic, and he was quickly assigned to gather material for a film on the Republic. The government sent him to Paris in 1936 where he pieced together *España 1936* or *España leal, en armas!*, a co-production with the French Communist party. In 1938, Buñuel was in Hollywood to supervise two commercial films, including *Cargo of Innocence*, about refugee children being shipped to the USSR,* a film eventually abandoned by MGM because of Franco's* imminent victory.

For further information, see Francisco Aranda, *Luis Buñuel: A Critical Biography*, trans. by David Robinson (New York, 1967).

David V. Holtby

BURGOS. Burgos was traditionally one of the more conservative regions of Spain, and after the July 1936 uprising, for political and strategic reasons, it served as a center for the Nationalists'* military and civilian administration.

Prior to 1936, Burgos was the center of a small group of Albinaña's* "Blue Shirts" as well as a small corps of Falangists. The 5th Army Division was stationed at Burgos, and in general most of the military officers in the area were opposed to the Republican government more because of questions of stability than any defined political ideology.

As the military conspiracy began to develop in the spring of 1936, Burgos leaders were involved, and it was determined that the rising of the Burgos units would be a major factor in the plans. On the night of July 17, as part of the general rebellion, military leaders took over the civil governor's offices, officers not supporting the uprising were arrested, and Burgos came into Nationalist hands almost without firing a shot. Fidel Dávila,* who later became a commander in the north, was largely responsible for the successful takeover in Burgos.

General Mola,* who was garrison commander at Pamplona* and a key figure in the northern area as the rebellion began, realized that complete control of Spain would not come quickly and that some sort of unified command or government was thereby necessary. He moved to Burgos on July 22 and the next day announced the creation of a seven-man military *Junta de Defensa Nacional* headed by Miguel Cabanellas* who was the ranking general at the time. Burgos was the obvious site chosen because it was a "safe" area, centrally located in relation to the rebel forces in the north and close to Madrid.*

Mola announced that Burgos was to be the new center of government, and on July 28 the *Junta* declared the rule of martial law for all of Spain. The intent was clearly to maintain an all-military government, and the primary concerns of the *Junta* were military affairs. On July 30, a member of the Spanish Navy* was added to the *Junta,* and on August 3 Franco* joined the group.

By September, particularly after the successes of the Army of Africa,* it became obvious to military leaders that a single command was necessary. A meeting of generals at Salamanca* on September 29 named Franco military chief and head of state. Franco in turn created a *Junta Técnica,* headed by General Dávila, to replace the original Burgos group. Because Salamanca remained the site of Franco's headquarters, power shifted to that area. Burgos retained the status of capital, and the *Junta* there was responsible for administrative matters relating to justice, labor and finance.

After August 1937, as Nationalist forces shifted to the northern offensive, Franco also moved his headquarters. In early November, Burgos once again became the real center of power and control in Nationalist Spain. In early 1938, when Franco announced his first formal government, it was located at Burgos, an area that remained the center of government until the end of the war. Negotiations for recognition by foreign powers, as well as those with the Republicans* for termination of the war, were carried out at Burgos.

For further information, see Stanley G. Payne, *Politics and the Military in Modern Spain* (Stanford, Calif., 1967); and Ruiz Vilaplana, *Burgos Justice: A Year's Experience of Nationalist Spain* (New York, 1938).

Jane Slaughter

BURILLO STOLLE, RICARDO (1891-1939). Burillo was a military commander in the Republican Army.* A career officer, he was an aristocrat with left-wing political views and strong sympathies for communism. He commanded troops at the battle of the Jarama* (February 1937). In June, Colonel Burillo became director-general of security in Catalonia* since he could be trusted by the Republic to be procommunist and antianarchist. His job was to suppress the anarchist militias* and prevent their taking over power again in Barcelona* as they had in the summer of 1936. In 1938, he commanded regular army units in Estremadura.* At the end of the war, Nationalist forces executed him.

For further information, see Hugh Thomas, *The Spanish Civil War* (New York, 1977).
See also May 1937 Riots.

James W. Cortada

C

CABALLERIST CURRENT. Caballerist Current, a movement within the Spanish Socialist party* between mid-1934 and the end of 1936, attempted a philosophical merger of the liberal middle class and intellectuals* with industrial and agricultural workers. The movement developed at a time when the salaries and living conditions of Spain's working classes had begun to deteriorate following two years of improvements during the early days of the Second Republic.* The Caballerist faction within the Socialist party, led by Largo Caballero,* believed the proletariat would eventually dominate Spanish political and economic social structures. They therefore concluded that the political system should serve the needs of the working classes. In this way, the Socialist party could expand its support and be the means to power for all workers.

While Largo Caballero was no messianic leader, he represented the unspecified feelings of many members of the Spanish working-class political movement on the eve of the Civil War. Many workers strongly believed that he and the other Caballerists would not compromise them and make bargains with the middle class to bring the Socialist party to power. The same could not be said about less radical socialist leaders, such as Julián Besteiro.* More conservative socialists did not share the Caballerist faction's belief that eventually collectives would be established in Spain much along the lines of those in the USSR.*

In the early days of the war, the Caballerist element within the Socialist party found much common ground intellectually with the anarchist political groups. Caballerist thinkers thus contributed to the kind of environment that would tolerate experimentation with collectives within the Republican zone during the war. Obviously, when Largo Caballero held political power, much of the Caballerist thinking at least had a sympathetic ear in the Republican government. In time, however, the movement melted away, and eventually Largo Caballero did too—a casualty of the Communist party's* successful bid for power.

For further information, see Gabriel Jackson, *The Spanish Republic and the Civil War, 1931-1939* (Princeton, N.J., 1965); and Hugh Thomas, *The Spanish Civil War* (New York, 1977).

See also Workers, Catalan.

James W. Cortada

CABANELLAS Y FERRER, MIGUEL (1872-1938). Cabanellas was born in Cartagena,* graduated from the General Military Academy in 1889, and served in the Cavalry in Cuba* and Morocco,* rising rapidly to division general. After quarreling with General Primo de Rivera in 1926, he was put on the reserve list. Because of his opposition to the dictatorship, the Republicans* appointed him military commander of Morocco in 1931 and director-general of the Civil Guard* in 1932. Reputedly a Mason, Cabanellas was elected to the Cortes* as a radical Republican deputy from Jaén* in 1933. Nevertheless, as head of the 5th Division in Saragossa* in 1936, he joined the military rebellion against the Popular Front* government. Reaffirming his republicanism in his declaration of martial law, Cabanellas appointed civilian radicals to administrative posts in the city and province. He opposed the policy of reprisals and the elevation of General Franco* to the rank of Generalíssimo. These policies soon earned him the distrust of the other members of the military *Junta de Defensa Nacional*,* of which he was the head because of his seniority. When Franco, as head of state, replaced the Burgos *Junta* with a *Junta Técnica* on October 1, he excluded Cabanellas. Franco appointed him inspector general of the army, an honorific position that deprived him of any real military or political power. Cabanellas died of natural causes in 1938 at Málaga.*

For further information, see Guillermo Cabanellas, *Cuatro generales*, 2 vols. (Barcelona, 1977); and Tomás Prieto, *Soldados de España: Datos para la historia* (Madrid, 1946).

Carolyn P. Boyd

CÁCERES. Cáceres, a province in western Spain along the Portuguese border in Estremadura,* quickly came under the control of the Nationalists* during the first days of the Civil War. An air base for use by the Nationalists, Italians, and Germans was soon established, and, for a short while during August and September 1936, Franco* made his headquarters in this province. From the earliest days of the fighting, German military advisers trained Nationalist soldiers here. One of the more famous groups to be trained were the Irish Blue Shirts under the command of General Eoin O'Duffy.* Other Nationalists chased down Republicans* who were attempting to cross the border into Portugal.*

For further information, see Manuel Aznar, *Historia militar de la guerra de España, 1936-1939* (Madrid, 1940).
    See also Air Force, Nationalist; and Army, Nationalist.

James W. Cortada

CÁDIZ. Cádiz, a province in Andalusia* in southernmost Spain across from Gibraltar* and facing the Atlantic Ocean, was an agricultural area dominated by its capital city of Cádiz, one of Spain's most important ports. The province was long a hotbed of liberal activities and, in the 1930s, anarchist politics. At the town of Casas Viejas in 1933, anarchists* revolted against the government, temporarily taking over the community. Assault Guards* (*Asaltos*) eventually retook the village, executing fourteen people. Because of this action, the Republic was criticized for operating as a government of "blood, mud, and tears." During the days of the Republic, conservatives in Cádiz had elected José Antonio Primo de Rivera* (founder of the *Falange** party) to the Cortes.* Yet, the area remained more anarchist and leftist in its political philosophy than conservative or monarchist.

In July 1936, some of the first Nationalist troops to arrive from North Africa in Spain landed at Cádiz, securing the city for Franco* and thereby making it one of the first areas to become insurgent territory. Within days, the entire province came under Nationalist control. Franco established a small naval base at Cádiz to support Nationalist operations in the western Mediterranean and as a port of call for foreign aid. The Germans brought supplies of aircraft and weapons into Spain by way of Cádiz throughout the war. Italy* landed troops here as well.

For further information, see Guillermo Cabanellas, *La guerra de los mil días* (Barcelona, 1973), Vol. 1; and Antonio Garrachón Cuesta, *De Africa a Cádiz a la España Imperial* (Cádiz, 1938).

See also Army, Nationalist; and Appendix B.

James W. Cortada

CALVET, JOSÉ. Calvet, a Catalan politician, entered the regional government as a councillor in the Generalitat* on December 16, 1936, representing the *Unió de Rabassaires*, a vine-growers' association with a solid political base throughout Catalonia.* He held the portfolio for agriculture throughout most of the Civil War, having responsibility for food* production. As part of his program, collectivization was allowed to continue in areas where it had already begun; where farmers generally owned land, private farming was preserved. Calvet enjoyed a mixed success in increasing food production, primarily because constant warfare in the region disrupted normal agricultural activity.

For further information, see Josep María Bricall, *Política económica de la Generalidad, 1936-1939* (Barcelona, 1970).
    See also Daily Life, Republican Zone; and Nutrition.

James W. Cortada

CALVO SOTELO, JOSÉ (1893-1936). Calvo Sotelo emerged during the Second Republic* as the most significant figure within that sector of the militant, authoritarian Right which stood apart from both the Carlists* and Falangists. His assassination on July 13, 1936, provided opponents of the Popular Front* with a convenient justification for a rising which in any case would have erupted at any moment.

Born into a devout, upper middle-class Galician family, Calvo Sotelo grew up in Tuy and in Saragossa.* He began his political life as a follower of the conservative statesman Antonio Maura and served a period as Maura's secretary. After attaining national prominence during the 1920s as Primo de Rivera's finance minister, Calvo Sotelo, was driven into exile with the advent of the Second Republic in 1931. While abroad, he fell under the intellectual influence of Charles Maurras and the *Action Française*, and of Portuguese Integralism, with the result that his already apparent authoritarian tendencies matured into wholehearted conviction. Amnestied in 1934, he returned to Spain and rapidly became the dominant personality in the monarchist organization *Renovación Española.**

By this time, however, Calvo Sotelo's support of the exiled Alfonso XIII* was subordinated to his advocacy of authoritarian or even "totalitarian" solutions to Spain's problems. His ideological stance was more "modern," centralizing and economically precise than that of most Carlists, while more frankly Catholic and less self-consciously "revolutionary" than that of José Antonio Primo de Rivera* and the Falange.* During 1934-1935, he attempted unsuccessfully to take over the Falange and then helped found and lead the *Bloque Nacional.* This openly counterrevolutionary organization was dominated by supporters of Alfonso XIII but also embraced some Carlists and independent rightists, and was closely linked with banking, industrial, and large landowning interests. Although the *Bloque Nacional* failed to attract mass support, its activities and Calvo Sotelo's own insistent authoritarian message helped bestow respectability upon counterrevolutionary ideas and attitudes under the Second Republic, as well as undermining the "legalist" tactics of Gil Robles* and the *Confederación Española de Derechas Antónias* (CEDA).* Before and especially after the elections of February 1936,* Calvo Sotelo's oratorical attacks on the Republic, both inside and outside the Cortes,* contributed to the general political deterioration in Spain. On July 13, 1936, he was shot dead by Assault Guards* in revenge for the killing of one of their number by a Falangist some days earlier.

Although Calvo Sotelo's death deprived the Nationalist cause of a political figure of major and rapidly increasing stature, perhaps it also spared Franco* the embarrassment arising out of Calvo Sotelo's undisguised ambition and prickly personality. Instead, Calvo Sotelo became one of the Franco regime's principal martyrs and one of its acknowledged ideological prophets.

For further information, see José Calvo Sotelo, *Mis servicios al Estado* (Madrid, 1931), *En defensa propia* (Madrid, 1932), and *La voz de un perseguido*, 2 vols. (Madrid, 1933); Aurelio Joaniquet, *Calvo Sotelo* (Santander, 1939); and Richard A.H. Robinson, "Calvo Sotelo's *Bloque Nacional* and Its Manifesto," *University of Birmingham Historical Journal* 10 (No. 2, 1966).
See also Origins of the Spanish Civil War.

Martin Blinkhorn

CAMACHO BENÍTEZ, ANTONIO (1892-   ).

Camacho served in the Republican Air Force* as a colonel. He became a subsecretary in the Ministry of Defense when, in May 1937, Indalecio Prieto* attempted to balance the influence of communists and Republicans* within the government while reducing the political importance of Largo Caballero's* Supreme War Council. Camacho had been a communist sympathizer, but his support for the movement waned as the war progressed. In 1937, his appointment to the Ministry of Defense insured that the Republican Air Force would have a voice at the subcabinet level.

For further information, see Jesús Salas Larrazábal, *La guerra de España desde el aire* (Barcelona, 1969); and Ramón Salas Larrazábal, *Historia del ejército popular de la república*, 4 vols. (Madrid, 1974).

James W. Cortada

CAMPBELL, ROY (1901-1957).

Campbell, a South African poet, supported the Nationalists* during the Spanish Civil War. He was in Toledo* at the start of the conflict but returned by the end of 1936 to Great Britain* where he wrote and lectured on the evils of communism and upon the need to support Franco.* Most English-speaking intellectuals* favored the Republic, thereby making Campbell part of a small minority of writers who found much to criticize in the Republic's ties to communism.

For further information, see Frederick R. Benson, *Writers in Arms: The Literary Impact of the Spanish Civil War* (New York, 1967).
See also Literature.

James W. Cortada

CAMPESINO, EL (VALENTÍN GONZÁLEZ) (? - 1965).

El Campesino ("The Peasant") was a communist activist and guerrilla leader before and during the Civil War, who sided with the Republicans.* Known by his strength, his beard, and his reputation as a violent and successful fighter, he was one of the better known communist commanders during the early months of the Civil War. He soon became a commander of one of the Mixed Brigades* and fought in all the major battles around Madrid.* His earliest important commands came at the battles of Boadilla* and Corunna Road* (December 1936) in which his men bore the brunt of the Nationalists'* attacks. At the battle of Guadalajara* (March 1937), El Campesino helped check Nationalist advances. At the battle of Brunete* (July 1937), his troops, reputed to be some of the best in the Republican Army,* went on the offensive to block Nationalist advances successfully. During this campaign, over 300 of his men were captured, their legs broken, and killed. In retaliation, he executed an entire Moroccan *tabor* (battalion) of some 400 men captured earlier.

El Campesino continued to lead troops in central Spain until the Republic reorganized its forces in Catalonia* into the Army of the East.* He then became part of that force that sought to reinforce the Aragón* front which the Nationalists wanted to assault. During the heavy fighting in the Aragón offensive (August-October 1937), he attempted to push back the Nationalists but with minimal success. At the battle of Teruel* (December 1937-February 1938), he and his men were surrounded in the city by Nationalist forces. They managed to fight their way out of this encirclement. For years after, he accused rival communist commanders of deserting him and his men to the Nationalists for political reasons. During the campaigns in Aragón and the Levante* (March-July 1938), when the Nationalists were pushing eastward, he held the city of Lérida* for a week before falling back. This communist general then continued fighting in the Catalan campaigns until the end of the Civil War.

After the war he went into exile in the USSR,* found life there unattractive and the discipline of the Communist party less so, and thus left by way of Persia, finally taking up residence in France.* He wrote a book detailing his criticisms of his party and died during 1965.

For further information, see Michael Alpert, *El ejército republicano en la guerra civil* (Barcelona, 1977); and Valentín González, *Comunista en España y anti-Stalinista en la URSS* (Mexico, 1952) and his *Listen, Comrades* (London, 1952).

See also Appendix B.

James W. Cortada

CAMPINS AURA, MIGUEL (1880-1936). Campins, a career army officer and a general in 1936, served as military governor in Granada* in July of that year. He sided with the Republic and called on his officers to do the same. On July 20, while visiting the army barracks under his control, he discovered that the entire officer corps there had decided to join Franco.* The officers promptly arrested him, and soon after Granada came under Nationalist control. The Nationalists* executed Campins in August, 1936.

For further information, see Joaquín Arrarás, *Historia de la cruzada española* (Madrid, 1940-1943), Vol. 11.

James W. Cortada

CAMPSA. *See Compañía Arrendataria del Monopolio de Petróleos, S.A.* (CAMPSA).

CANADA. The Canadian government, following the policies of Great Britain,* France,* and the United States,* declared its neutrality in the Spanish Civil War. Canada supported the efforts of the Non-Intervention Committee* and maintained correct and neutral relations with the Spanish Republic, until Franco* won the war, and gave no military aid to either side.

Public reaction to the conflict in Canada was mixed. In the English-speaking portions, public opinion favored neutrality and proved reluctant even to support a Spanish Popular Front* movement. In the French-speaking sections, particularly in the Province of Quebec where a growing fascist movement helped mold public opinion, greater emotional support for the Nationalist cause existed. At no time, however, did this pro-Nationalist feeling deter the Canadian government from its diplomatic neutrality.

Some Canadian citizens fought in the Mackenzie-Papineau Battalion,* which was part of the International Brigades* formed by the Spanish Republic in February 1937. One-third of its members were Canadians, while nearly all others were from the United States. Approximately 1,000 Canadian citizens fought for the Republic during the war, participating in each of the major campaigns in and around Madrid,* the Ebro,* and finally in eastern Catalonia.* Other forms of Canadian involvement included forty Gruman aircraft contributed to the Republic by France, and surplus food* shipped to Spain by the Canadian government as part of an international assistance program involving Norway* and Belgium.*

For further information, see Andreu Castells, *Las brigadas internacionales en la guerra de España* (Barcelona, 1974); John A. Munro, "Canada and the Civil War in Spain: Repatriation of the Mackenzie-Papineau Battalion," *External Affairs* 23, No. 2 (1971):52-58; and on diplomacy, Arnold J. Toynbee, *Survey of International Affairs, 1937,* Vol. 2, *The International Repercussions of the War in Spain (1936-37)* (Oxford, 1938).

See also League of Nations.

James W. Cortada

CANARIAS. The Nationalist cruiser *Canarias* (10,282 tons standard, 8-203mm [8in.] guns, 33 kts.) was in the final stage of construction in El Ferrol* in July 1936. Quickly made ready for war, she led a Nationalist squadron to victory in the decisive battle of Cape Espartel* on September 29, 1936, sinking the destroyer *Almirante Ferrándiz* and opening the Straits of Gibraltar* to Nationalist traffic. The *Canarias* spent most of the war in the Mediterranean, raiding the Republican coast and supply lines. She sank the Soviet freighter *Komsomol** in December 1936. The *Canarias* made a foray into the Bay of Biscay in March 1937, defeating a Basque convoy and capturing the Republican *Mar Cantábrico.* The *Canarias* participated in the battle of Cape Palos* on March 6, 1938, when her sistership, *Baleares,* was sunk. On August 17, 1938, the *Canarias* helped defeat the attempt of the Republican destroyer *José Luis Díez* to pass the Straits of Gibraltar. In March 1939, she participated in the abortive attempt to seize Cartagena* by amphibious assault.

See also Navy, Spanish.

Willard C. Frank, Jr.

CANARIS, WILHELM (1887-1945). Canaris, chief of German military intelligence from 1935 to 1944, was born in 1887 in Dortmund. He served on submarines and as an espionage agent in Spain in World War I. During the period 1925 to 1933, he helped carry out a contract (approved by King Alfonso XIII*) with the Echevarietta shipbuilders in Cádiz, aimed at constructing two U-boats for Germany* in circumvention of the Versailles Treaty. In this connection, he visited Spain at least a dozen times.

In 1933, as a superreactionary German nationalist, he supported Adolf Hitler* on the basis of anticommunism. Hitler appointed him vice admiral and Abwehr chief on January 1, 1935.

Admirals Eric Raeder and Canaris made contingency war plans in 1934 to fight the French Navy in Spanish waters. The Canary Islands* were to play a major role as supply port and intelligence post for German shipping. This strategy assumed that the British and the Americans, as well as the Spaniards, would remain neutral. Admiral Canaris worked toward better relations with Mussolini,* concluding an intelligence agreement with the fascist regime in September 1935.

Dozens of agents reported Spanish developments to Canaris. On July 17, 1936, he was the one German, with the possible exception of Ambassador Johannes von Welczeck, who was most informed on Spanish matters.

On the night of July 25, 1936, Hitler decided to send planes to Franco.* Whether Canaris played an active role in that decision may always remain speculative, since both Germans destroyed their records. On July 26, the intelligence chief helped organize the Special Staff "W" to carry out Hitler's "Operation Feuerzauber." On August 4, Canaris traveled to Italy to coordinate the joint Hitler-Mussolini aid to Franco. Throughout the Civil War, he visited Spain at least eight times. In late October 1936, he helped organize the 5,000-man Condor Legion.* In December 1936, Canaris encouraged Hitler's strategy of limiting German military aid to Franco to something less than that of Mussolini.

When, in April 1938, a Nationalist victory appeared imminent, Canaris visited Franco to encourage adherence to the draft Friendship Treaty and Anti-Comintern Pact. He made a similar trip, with more success, in April 1939. After the Condor Legion withdrew in May 1939, Canaris kept Abwehr agents in Spain for possible future wars with France* or Great Britain.*

In 1938, Canaris apparently developed private doubts about the feasibility and the morality of Hitler's foreign policy. He opposed any attack on Czechoslovakia* since it would risk a war with Great Britain, a war he thought Germany could not win. Nevertheless, Canaris cultivated Franco's Spain as a potential ally of the Reich during development of the plan to attack Poland.*

By September 1938, the Canary Islands had become one of Germany's four main Abwehr bases abroad. Dollars were deposited in the Canaries to purchase oil, food,* and information for submarine operations. The Abwehr stationed intelligence officers in Cádiz,* Barcelona,* Vigo,* Bilbao,* and other major ports, and maintained a radio station in Corunna* to aid *Luftwaffe* operations.

Despite his personal hesitancy about Hitler's war aims, Canaris carried out his duty as a "patriotic" German and served his nation. The possible complicity of some Abwehr officers in the attempt to assassinate Hitler on July 20, 1944, led to Canaris's arrest and execution by the Gestapo on April 9, 1945.

For further information, see Heinz Höhne, *Canaris Patriot im Zweilicht* (Munich, 1976); David Kahn, *Hitler's Spies: German Military Intelligence in World War II* (London, 1978); and Angel Viñas, *La Alemania Nazi y el 18 julio* (Madrid, 1974).

Robert H. Whealey

CANARY ISLANDS. The Canary Islands, located off the coast of Morocco,* played a crucial role in the early days of the Civil War. In early 1936, Manuel Azaña, fearing that General Franco* was plotting against the Republic, assigned him to command troops in the Canaries as a means of getting him out of Spain. If anything, the transfer made it easier for Franco to communicate with his major supporters within the army, those soldiers assigned to North Africa. When the rebels finally decided to revolt, Franco flew from Las Palmas on July 18 to Tetuán* where he assumed command of the insurgent forces perched near Gibraltar.*

After the rebellion began, troops loyal to Franco seized control of the Canaries, although resistance by Republicans* in Santa Cruz de la Palma continued until July 28. The occupation of the Canaries insured that the Nationalists* would not have a Republican zone to their backs threatening Franco as he moved northward through Spain to Madrid.* Moreover, the agricultural output of the islands contributed to the Nationalist war effort in the early days of the fighting. But the islands remained quiet for the rest of the Civil War. Republican forces were too far away to bother them, and within a few short months, Madrid's navy no longer posed a serious threat to them. The Canaries can claim one additional footnote to history: Juan Negrín,* the Republic's last prime minister, was born in 1889 in Las Palmas where his family owned considerable property.

For further information, see Luis Bolín, *The Vital Years* (London, 1967); and Ricardo de la Cierva, *Historia de la guerra civil española* (Madrid, 1969).

James W. Cortada

CAÑIZARES NAVARRO, EDUARDO. Cañizares, a colonel in the Nationalist Army,* had served with Franco* in Morocco.* At the start of the Civil War, he became Nationalist military governor of Badajoz,* the site of a well-publicized execution of prisoners by Franco's forces. For months he quarreled with the local military commander, General Gonzalo Queipo de Llano* over how much independence of action he should have. His significance to the Civil War continues to revolve around his actions in Badajoz. Historians are not certain whether he ordered the execution of hundreds of prisoners in the bullring at Badajoz, but he certainly, at least, acquiesced in the action, thereby following a Nationalist policy of exterminating their enemies. In 1938, he was transferred out of his position and was later arrested by Queipo de Llano who sentenced him to death. He was saved by a reprieve from Franco.

For further information, see Antonio Bahamonde y Sánchez de Castro, *Memoirs of a Nationalist* (London, 1939).
See also Seville.

James W. Cortada

CANTALUPO, RANDOLFO (1891-   ). Cantalupo was Italy's* ambassador to Nationalist Spain between 1936 and 1937. He was a professional journalist and had served as ambassador to Brazil* in 1932. While in Spain he concluded that Franco's* government was weak and executed too many of its enemies (especially after the conquest of Málaga*). He believed the Spanish general would develop a reactionary dictatorship should he win the war. He questioned Mussolini's*

policy of strongly supporting the Francoists, thereby alienating many Italian officials in Rome, particularly within the military and at the Foreign Office. He suggested that unless Italy was willing to give massive aid to Franco, the two sides in the war might otherwise be balanced sufficiently to continue fighting for years. He thought that Rome should not continue supporting the one-party rule of Franco without a major review of Italian policy. Cantalupo served in Spain while Italian troops were there, experiencing the aftermath of Italy's troubles following the battle of Guadalajara* in which Mussolini's troops did not perform well.

Cantalupo's relations with Franco were difficult. He complained about political shootings but was able to gain stays of execution for nineteen Masons and the removal from the bench of four harsh judges. He also criticized Franco's use and treatment of Italian soldiers, recommending that Rome reconsider their deployment in Spain. In March 1937, as a result of his poor relations with Franco and his lack of cooperation with and full support of Italian policies in Spain, he came back to Rome on consultation. Following a review of his ideas and suggestions, Mussolini relieved him of his responsibilities.

For further information, see Randolfo Cantalupo, *Fu la Spagna* (Milan, 1948); and John F. Coverdale, *Italian Intervention in the Spanish Civil War* (Princeton, N.J., 1975).
See also Terrorism.

James W. Cortada

CAPE ESPARTEL, BATTLE OF. The battle of Cape Espartel on September 29, 1936, was strategically the most significant naval engagement of the Civil War. Republican Navy Minister Indalecio Prieto* had sent the superior Republican fleet from the Straits of Gibraltar* where it had blockaded Nationalist forces in Morocco* to the Bay of Biscay to support beleaguered Republican cities. Encouraged by Franco,* Captain Francisco Moreno* took advantage of the opportunity and sortied from El Ferrol* with the only available Nationalist warships, the cruisers *Canarias** and *Almirante Cervera.** Moreno surprised the Republican destroyers guarding the Straits, sank the *Almirante Ferrándiz*, and damaged the *Gravina*. From that moment, Nationalist naval forces controlled the Straits, deployed into the Mediterranean, and retained the initiative at sea for the remainder of the war. Within a few days, 8,000 men of the Army of Africa* were safely convoyed to the Iberian Peninsula fresh for the assault on Madrid.*

For further information, see Hugh Thomas, *The Spanish Civil War* (New York, 1977).

See also Navy, Spanish.

Willard C. Frank, Jr.

CAPE PALOS, BATTLE OF. The battle of Cape Palos in the early hours of March 6, 1938, was a chance naval encounter 70 miles east of Cape Palos. The Nationalist cruisers *Baleares*,* *Canarias*,* and *Almirante Cervera** were escorting a convoy, while the Republican cruisers *Libertad** and *Méndez Núñez* with five destroyers were at sea to support an abortive raid by Soviet motor torpedo boats against the Nationalist naval anchorage at Palma de Majorca.* Republican torpedoes sank the *Baleares* with a loss of 782 men, including Rear Admiral Manuel de Vierna. In the confusion the two fleets separated, never to make contact again. Republican fleet commander González de Ubieta* received much criticism for not following up the initial success with a hard-pressed attack. The battle had no strategic consequences, although Republican morale received a brief boost.

For further information, see Hugh Thomas, *The Spanish Civil War* (New York, 1977).

See also Navy, Spanish.

Willard C. Frank, Jr.

"CARA AL SOL." "Cara al Sol" (Face to the Sun), the Falange* party's theme song, was used throughout the Civil War and for many years after during Franco's* rule. It was written by three followers of the party: Agustín de Foxá, Dionisio Ridruejo,* and José María Alfaro and composed by Juan Tilería. It was first performed in February 1936 and quickly thereafter became the most widely sung Falangist music. Some of the inspiration for this martial music may have come from a poem by the Cuban nationalist, José Martí, who used the theme of a dying face toward the sun in a poem entitled "The White Rose." "Cara al Sol" begins with this stanza:

> Face the sun, wearing the suit
> Which yesterday you decorated,
> Death shall seek me out; if it calls
> And I fail to see you again . . .
> Battalions go forth and conquer
> For Spain is rising from its sleep.
> Spain—United! Spain—Grand!
> Spain—Liberated! Spain—Arise!

Having a signature anthem was a common practice among all Spanish political parties and military organizations on both sides, following a generally widespread European tradition.

For further information, see Stanley G. Payne, *Falange: A History of Spanish Fascism* (Stanford, Calif., 1961); and Hugh Thomas, *The Spanish Civil War* (New York, 1977).

James W. Cortada

CARABANCHEL. Carabanchel, a suburb of Madrid,* was the site of a considerable amount of fighting for the city in the fall and winter of 1936. It was here that the Republicans'* line of defense was established and that Nationalist forces made a serious bid for entry into the city. Holding this location meant that Madrid did not fall to the Nationalists* and thus insured that the war would continue for a long time.

For further information, see Robert Colodny, *The Struggle for Madrid* (New York, 1958).

See also Army, Nationalist; International Brigades; and Militias.

James W. Cortada

CÁRDENAS Y RODRÍGUEZ DE RIVAS, JUAN FRANCISCO DE (1881-1966). Cárdenas was Spain's ambassador to Paris at the start of the Civil War, and during 1936-1939 he was the Nationalists'* representative in Washington, D.C. Cárdenas, a career diplomat, had a distinguished professional and conservative political background. Soon after the war began, he was replaced as ambassador to Paris by Álvaro de Albornoz,* a Left Republican whose political outlook was more in tune with that of the new French prime minister, Léon Blum,* a socialist. Prior to his departure from Paris, Cárdenas called on Blum to request that France* provide the Spanish Republic with twenty aircraft, an assortment of machineguns, rifles, shells, bullets, and bombs. Blum agreed to the request, although within days the British were able to force the French to cancel the requested arms.

Reflecting the behavior of nearly 90 percent of the Spanish diplomatic corp, Cárdenas switched to the Nationalist side, thus resigning his position as diplomat with the Republic. Franco's* government assigned this experienced diplomat to Washington, D.C., as its agent to plead the cause against the Republic. Although he had no official stature in the United States* (since the Republic was still the recognized government of Spain), Cárdenas was able to meet on occasion with members of the American government. During the next three years, he conducted a public relations campaign to help Franco's side, gathering support from conservative and Catholic elements in the United States. He was able to funnel some supplies and volunteers* into Nationalist Spain, and he attempted to help other pro-Franco sympathizers in the Caribbean assist the Nationalist cause. After the war ended, he was officially apppointed ambassador to the United States, serving until June 1947.

During the war, Cárdenas failed to gain any formal diplomatic or economic favors from the U.S. government. The fortunes of the Nationalist cause depended more on its ability to overthrow the Republic than on any diplomatic moves its representatives could make. For that reason, Cárdenas could do no more than plead the case for the Burgos* government and prepare for the day when the Nationalists won the Civil War.

For further information, see F. J. Taylor, *The United States and the Spanish Civil War* (New York, 1956); and Francisco Virgilio Sevillano Carbajal, *La diplomacia mundial ante la guerra española* (Madrid, 1969).
See also Diplomatic Corps, Spanish.

James W. Cortada

CARLISTS. Carlism, a Spanish political movement, generally accepted to be of the extreme Right, was born officially in 1833 and survived to oppose the Second Republic* between 1931 and 1936. During the Spanish Civil War, its militia, the *Requetés,** constituted an important element of the Nationalist forces.

Carlism takes its name from Don Carlos, the younger brother of King Ferdinand VII (1784-1833) and would-be King Carlos V. On Ferdinand's death in 1833, Don Carlos's claim to the throne of his niece, Isabella II, provided a rallying point for various elements of opposition to early nineteenth-century Spanish liberalism: opposition actually first manifested during the "royalist" and "malcontent" guerrilla activities of the 1820s. The Carlist cause was forged out of a complex combination of *apostólico* (ultra-Catholic) resistance to liberal secularism and both economic and political modernism, and a highly inchoate, popular revolt against numerous aspects of contemporary socioeconomic change. From 1833 to 1876, such forces gathered, intermittently and often uneasily, around four pretenders to the throne: Carlos V (1788-1855, pretender 1833-1845); Carlos VI, "Montemolín" (1818-1861, pretender 1845-1860); Juan III (1822-1887, pretender 1860-1868); and Carlos VII (1848-1909, pretender 1868-1909). The Carlist threat to the Spanish liberal system was greatest during the First Carlist War of 1833-1840 and almost as serious during the Third Carlist War of 1872-1876. The so-called Second

Carlist War of 1846-1849 was a regional struggle limited almost entirely to Catalonia* and is perhaps more aptly known by its alternative title, the War of the Early Riser (*matiners*—Cat.). In all of its nineteenth-century wars, Carlism's most characteristic form of combat was that of the guerrilla.

During this half-century of struggle, Carlism enjoyed considerable support within all levels of the Spanish Catholic Church* and on occasions at court: evidence of a tendency among the movement's elite to work within any broadly acceptable conservative system rather than seek to overthrow it, a tendency again apparent after 1876 and in relation to the Franco* regime of 1936-1975. On a more popular level Carlism's main bases lay in Navarre* and the Basque country, among a modestly prosperous, devoutly Catholic, and therefore politically conservative bourgeoisie and peasantry; and in Catalonia,* Valencia,* Aragón,* and parts of Old Castile,* where among other things it offered an outlet for protest to a variety of economically struggling sectors. This latter fact has encouraged recent Carlist historians and propagandists to argue that the true Carlism was an incipiently socialist movement with its roots in the *pueblo carlista* rather than in a clerical, reactionary elite. It is a doubtful claim, although it does not necessarily distort the truth of Carlism's complexity any more than those more conventional explanations which portray it as a uniformly, and consciously, conservative cause. What is undeniable is that with the defeat of 1876 Carlism was no longer a vehicle for genuine social protest. The cause now fell back upon its more unambiguously conservative strongholds in Navarre and the Basque country. In keeping with this retreat, during the late nineteenth and early twentieth centuries, Carlism gradually adopted an ideology and program, largely constructed by Juan Vázquez de Mella, of modern conservative, social-Catholic, corporatist character.

From 1876 to the fall of Alfonso XIII* in 1931, under Carlos VII and his son Don Jaime (1870-1931, pretender 1909-1931), Carlism labored to survive in the face of a monarchical regime, liberal in name but conservative enough to seduce much of Carlism's elite support, especially within the Church. Emergent left-wing movements now fulfilled its former protest role, while more up-to-date bourgeois forces—Catalan and Basque nationalism* and early Christian democracy—arose to appeal to conservative regionalists and middle-class Catholics, respectively. Carlism's possibilities of developing into a movement of the modern authoritarian right were inhibited by the more obvious claims of the Spanish Army, as exemplified by the Primo de Rivera coup d'état and dictatorship of 1923-1930.

Under these and other pressures, Carlism also proved subject to schisms: that of its most unyieldingly theocratic faction, the Integrists, in 1888 and that of Mella and his followers in 1919. ·Thanks mainly to the force of local and family tradition, especially in Navarre, Carlism did survive these difficulties, but as an ever-shrinking shadow of its former self. By 1931, it had become an insignificant element in national politics.

The fall of Alfonso XIII in April 1931 may well have saved Carlism from effective extinction by discrediting the rival liberal monarchy and creating an atmosphere in which a significant number of conservative Spaniards might seek the haven of an established right-wing movement. While Carlist leaders, from Don Jaime downward, welcomed the collapse of the despised Alfonsine monarchy, it would be going much too far to say that they were well disposed towards the Second Republic. Indeed, from the start, Carlism emerged as the first serious focus of right-wing opposition to the Republic and everything for which it stood. Any slight ambivalence in this regard revolved around the relative liberalism of the pretender himself and vanished when Don Jaime died in October 1931, to be succeeded by his ultraconservative, octogenarian uncle, Don Alfonso Carlos. Thenceforth, Carlism's hostility towards the Republic was wholehearted, even if doubts and disagreements persisted concerning the tactics the movement might adopt and the lengths to which it should go.

During the period 1931-1933, years of Left-of-Center, reforming, and anticlerical government, Carlism's popular support revived appreciably, chiefly in regions of longstanding Carlist tradition, residual strength, and surviving if sometimes rickety organization—for example, Navarre, the Basque country, Valencia, and to a lesser extent Catalonia and Aragón, but also, most notably Andalusia.* Popular support was drawn mainly from the Catholic bourgeoisie, the middling and lesser peasantry, and the artisan layer of the working class. The common factors linking these elements were a fervent Catholicism, inflamed by Republican anticlericalism, and a fear for the sanctity of private property, aroused above all by the regime's plans for agrarian reform. It appears that Carlism attracted such support initially because for all its weakness, in 1931-1932, it was the only movement of the extreme Right to combine a combative posture, a firm place in the Spanish political world, and something approaching a national organization. Moreover, it was untainted by association with the fallen regime and chanced to be blessed with a number of leaders displaying some flair for organization, propaganda, and populist politics. When other movements and parties

of the Right, in particular the *Confederación Española de Derechas Autónomas* (CEDA),* emerged to compete for the same ground during 1933-1934, the rate of Carlism's popular revival decelerated sharply, although it did not cease altogether.

During its 1931-1934 revival, Carlism, through its official organization, the Traditionalist Communion, pursued an essentially gradualist course of broadening its base; healing the schisms of 1888 and 1919—substantially achieved by mid-1932; increasing its mass support; disseminating its propaganda; and forging useful alliances: all with a view ultimately to overturning the Republic. An early regional alliance with the *Partido Nacionalista Vasco* (PNV)* in the Basque-Navarrese region, directed towards the achievement of autonomy, collapsed during 1932, primarily because the then Carlist leadership was less devoted to Basque autonomy per se and more to establishing regional control over religious affairs than were the Basque nationalists. Thereafter, the Carlists committed themselves unreservedly to a *national* campaign against the Republic. From 1931 onwards, the Carlists also cooperated with other right-wing Catholic elements in an attempt to win parliamentary seats and resist Republican legislation. At first, Carlists collaborated in *Acción Nacional* with Alfonsists and "accidentalist" Catholics, but gradually withdrew as their own numbers grew and as *Acción Nacional* itself evolved into the core of what in 1933 would become the CEDA. During this period, attempts were also made to arrive at a reconciliation between the Carlist and Alfonsine branches of the anarchist movement, but foundered on the rocks of insoluble differences. These differences were dynastic and personal rather than genuinely ideological.

Such tactics, namely, of cooperation with other Catholic and right-wing groups, of propaganda and persuasion, of electioneering and parliamentary obstruction of Republican policies, were associated with the legacy of Don Jaime and with the political leadership, between 1932 and 1934, of the Count of Rodezno* and a Navarrese faction of which he was de facto chief. The Traditionalist Communion's growth and its modest but real electoral successes (eight deputies elected in June 1931 in alliance with the Basque nationalists, and twenty-one in November 1933 in a broad right-wing alliance) were by no means insignificant. Nevertheless, by the start of 1934 there was arising within the movement a widespread sense of frustration at Carlism's failure to achieve more, its inability to shake the Republic, and the apparent lack of aggressiveness of its leaders. Such feelings were not wholly justified. The Rodezno leadership's commitment to the ultimate overthrow of the Republic was not in doubt, as evidenced by the joint monarchist mission to Rome in March 1934 which obtained Italian assurance of aid for a monarchist and military rising against the Republic at some future date. Few knew of this, however, and by the spring of 1934 the feeling of dissatisfaction, especially among younger Carlists and those in regions such as Andalusia where Carlist tradition was weakest, was irresistible. In May 1934, Rodezno resigned the political leadership of the Traditionalist Communion which Don Alfonso Carlos then conferred upon the leader of Andalusian Carlism, Manuel Fal Conde.*

The emphasis within the Carlist movement now changed to one of organizational and paramilitary efficiency in preparation for a rising against the Republic, which it was envisaged would be either exclusively Carlist or, more realistically and more probably, initiated and led by Carlists. Political cooperation, especially with Alfonsine monarchists, continued, above all in the mainly parliamentary *Bloque Nacional*, but with little show of enthusiasm from Fal Conde and other new figures such as the leader of the Carlist militia (*Requetés*), José Luis Zamanillo. The achievements of this new course were considerable. By the start of 1936, Carlism had been transformed from a loose, regionally based, quasi-confederal organization into a tightly controlled national hierarchy, with only the most important single region, Navarre, retaining some de facto autonomy. Special attention was now paid to the Carlist Youth and to the *Requetés*, which by early 1936 probably numbered some 30,000 throughout Spain as a whole, with perhaps 10,000 actually armed. While this force was hardly overwhelming, certainly it was the strongest right-wing paramilitary force at this stage. Arms began to be imported in significant quantities into Spain in late 1935 and continued to flow in throughout the early months of 1936.

Fal Conde's strategy depended, implicitly at least, upon the failure of the CEDA's "accidentalist" tactic in order to have any hope of success. With the Popular Front* victory in the February 1936 elections,* the CEDA's tactic did indeed collapse, and the CEDA with it. Carlist criticism now appeared vindicated, and the movement entered a new phase of growth, this time combined with an urgent preparation for rebellion.

Throughout the years of the Second Republic, Carlist political ideology, relentlessly articulated by the movement's press and political speakers, remained essentially that formulated earlier by Vázquez de Mella. The most distinguished ideological treatise of the 1930s, Víctor Pradera's *El Estado Nuevo* (1935), argued for a traditional, decentralized monarchy, supposedly inspired by that of the Catholic monarchs Ferdinand and Isabella. This monarchy would not be absolute but tempered by a network of corporate institutions. These, subject to the spiritual sovereignty of the Church, would protect the individual from all forms of exploitation and alienation, thereby guaranteeing social harmony and economic justice. Such ideas, strongly influenced by the neo-Thomism of the late nineteenth-century and early twentieth-century papacy and blessed anew by Pius XI's* 1931 Encyclical *Quadragesimo Anno*, had much in common with those of many non-Carlist Spanish Catholics, especially in the CEDA and the Alfonsine party, *Renovación Española*.* Theoretically, Carlists rejected the all-powerful, interventionist state of contemporary fascism which in Spain was accepted by the Falange* and, increasingly, by some Alfonsine monarchists such as Calvo Sotelo.* Some Carlists remained consistent in this rejection—Fal Conde, for example—but others fell prey during the 1930s to this and other voguish right-wing ideas, accepting the need for a temporarily strong state during the period of cleansing which they concluded must precede the installation of a decentralized Carlist utopia.

Despite much tactical disagreement and party rivalries between Carlists and other right-wing elements of broadly Catholic sentiment, and despite the fact that among Carlists there seethed little of the Falange's ostentatious and often superficial radicalism, in practice relations between Carlists and other rightists, especially at the local level, were more often than not amicable enough. What ensured this was a recognition of common enemies: republicanism and socialism. Carlist policies during the Republic, as distinct from abstract theories, reflected this common ground: a staunch defense of the Church and its role in Spanish life; a resolute defense of all forms of property against the real or imagined threat of socialism—a preoccupation that led to the crushing of Carlism's theoretical paternalism beneath the weight of Carlist property-owners' material conservatism; an ambivalence towards regional autonomy, favored in principle but opposed when in the wrong hands or seeming, as it increasingly did, to imperil national unity; and opposition to almost all the activities of the Left. In other words, the practical concerns binding Carlism to the rest of the Spanish Right far outweighed theoretical, dynastic, and other differences.

Although Carlism remained a minority movement within Spanish politics, and one with little or no serious chance of achieving its maximum goals, its role during the Republic was nevertheless significant in a number of ways. Until the sudden surge of Falangist support in the spring of 1936, Carlism was the best supported and most firmly established force of the Spanish extreme Right. The influence of its antiliberal critique and its traditionalist theories extended throughout much of the Catholic Right, including *Renovación Española*, the monarchist intellectual group *Acción Española*,* and the CEDA. While Carlism's own principles and program were not in any strict sense fascist, in providing a militant refuge for fearful, in this case Catholic, peasants and bourgeoisie, it played a part broadly comparable with that of fascism elsewhere. Indeed, its modest success between 1931 and 1936 probably helped inhibit the growth of the openly fascist Falange. In addition to helping to destabilize Spanish politics through its paramilitary and other activities, the Traditionalist Communion also made political coexistence between Left and Right more difficult by exerting constant pressure upon the CEDA to maintain extreme positions. Finally, Carlism's concentration of strength in certain areas, its reliable anti-Republican stance, and the relatively high level of military preparedness of the *Requetés* offered anti-Republican conspirators the certainty of substantial civilian, paramilitary support in the event of a rising.

After the victory of the Popular Front in the elections of February 1936,* Carlist preparation for rebellion intensified under the leadership of Fal Conde, Zamanillo, a newly created War *Junta* (committee), and the aging pretender's chosen regent and heir-presumptive, Don Javier de Borbón-Parma.* Hopes of a Carlist-led rising leading to the installation of the Carlist monarchy still burned in the movement's leading echelons and gave rise to a quixotic plan for a "march on Madrid" by the *Requetés* of several regions. This scheme came to nothing, but by March 1936 other, more practical conspiracies were afoot into which it was almost inevitable that Carlism would be drawn. When General Mola* became garrison commander in the Navarrese capital, Pamplona,* and shortly thereafter director of a large-scale military and civilian conspiracy against the Popular Front, he proved amenable to strengthening any rising's chances of success by ensuring the involvement of the *Requetés*—especially that of Navarre itself, which was still Carlism's principal bastion. Between March and July 1936, an intricate series of negotiations took place between Mola and the military plotters on the one hand and leading Carlists on the other. Carlism's national leaders—Fal Conde, Zamanillo, and Don Javier—were anxious that Carlism's identity, separate organization, and hopes of ultimate triumph should not be swamped within a wider, army-led right-wing rising. Throughout the negotiations, they therefore strove to extract from Mola,

in return for Carlist participation in a rising, firm guarantees of the movement's role in a future Spain. By early July 1936, negotiations appeared to have reached an impasse in the face of the combined stubbornness of Mola and Fal Conde, only for the deadlock to be broken through the intervention of Rodezno and the Navarrese Carlists. This group, more confident of their ability to survive alliances, less triumphalist concerning Carlism's hopes of going it alone, and unreservedly keen to join the planned rising, eventually prevailed upon Don Javier to permit the mobilization of the Navarrese *Requetés*. By now, in fact, the Navarrese *Requetés* were so ready for action that it is doubtful whether, in the event of a rising, anyone could have stopped their members from taking up arms. The negotiations and their outcome demonstrated the depth of the rivalries within the Carlist movement, the continued strength of the Navarrese, and the willingness of Rodezno and others to contemplate collaboration with the army and with other rightists even at the cost of Carlism's independence.

Once committed to the rising of July 17-18, 1936, Carlism threw in its forces with enthusiasm and played an important role, especially during the early months of the Civil War. Although figures are confused and contradictory, it may be reckoned that between 70,000 and 100,000 enrolled in the *tercios* (regiments) of the *Requetés* during 1936, though not all of these had been Carlists before the war. The *Requetés* played an especially significant role on the Basque front, notably in the capture of Irún* and the rest of Guipúzcoa* in autumn 1936; on the Aragón* front; in the battles of 1936-1937 in the Sierra de Guadarrama* north of Madrid*; and in several districts of Andalusia. In late 1936 and 1937 the *Requetés*, like the Falangist militia, were brought under increasingly close military control and gradually lost much of their distinct identity within the Nationalist forces. Nevertheless, Carlist claims that without the *Requetés* the rising might have foundered at the outset have some substance.

For most Carlists, the Civil War had a minimum purpose of destroying the Republic, the Popular Front, and the Spanish Left, and a maximum purpose of restoring, or more properly installing, the Carlist monarchy. During the early months of the war, Don Javier, Fal Conde, and the national hierarchy strove desperately to keep the maximum goal within view, if only by maintaining and asserting the individuality of Carlism within the Nationalist camp. In doing so, they fell increasingly foul of the military leadership, especially after the elevation of Franco* to the positions of Generalissimo and head of state in late September 1936. An attempt in December 1936 by Fal Conde to create a Royal Carlist Military Academy for the training, both military and political, of *Requeté* officers was interpreted by Franco as a challenge to his and the army's authority. The ensuing crisis ended with Fal Conde sent into exile in Portugal.* This further strengthened the hand of Rodezno and the more pliable Navarrese Carlists.

By early 1937, expectation reigned within Nationalist Spain that Franco would before long move to create some kind of single party embracing the Falange, Carlists, and other lesser organizations. For some weeks, sporadic negotiations took place involving leaders of both mass parties with a view to a spontaneous fusion that might forestall a forced one. Fal Conde and Don Javier, for the Carlists, resisted any merger that smacked of fascist totalitarianism, not unreasonably fearing the loss of Carlism's authentic corporatism and decentralization. The talks failed to bear fruit, and in April 1937 the Traditionalist Communion and the Falange were arbitrarily conjoined by Franco into the *Falange Española Tradicionalista y de las JONS*: the single party of Franco's Spain down to 1976.

Although Fal Conde and other prominent Carlists refused to acknowledge the fusion or to participate in the *Falange Española's* affairs, Rodezno and numerous collaborationists defied Don Javier's orders and accepted office in both party and state. Rodezno himself became minister of justice in January 1938, the first of a number of Carlists to hold that office under Franco. This effective schism in the Carlist ranks indicated a profound and sincere difference of outlook between the two factions headed by Fal Conde and Rodezno. The Fal Conde faction believed that the Carlist monarchy could and must be achieved and that a separate and powerful Carlist organization was indispensable to this end. Furthermore, it stated that too close a cooperation with fascists and army officers would mean Carlism's subjection to a modern, oppressive totalitarianism. The rival view was that Carlism would never be able to win power alone; that its maximum goals, however desirable in theory, were unattainable in practice; and that Carlism should therefore function as a vital current within a broadly acceptable right-wing regime, in particular by guaranteeing the spiritual, cultural, and educational role of Catholicism and resisting *from within* the more authoritarian and *étatiste* tendencies of others. If the second view proved over the years to be overoptimistic, the first, with its belief in the attainability of the Carlist monarchy, was for all its integrity nothing short of utopian.

After its revival in the early 1930s, Carlism never recovered from the convulsions of 1937. The majority of Carlists after the Civil War simply retired into private life, committed to the principle of the 1936 "Crusade"* while often, and increasingly, disillusioned with its outcome. Of those who remained politically active after 1939, some committed themselves wholeheartedly to the Franco regime; others sought an escape from Francoism through a reconciliation between Carlism and post-Alfonsine monarchism; yet others followed Fal Conde in his characteristically proud position of resolute "purism," a kind of rightist opposition to the regime; and eventually, during the 1960s and 1970s, a younger generation accompanied Don Javier's son, Don Carlos Hugo, in forming a Carlism of the Left, a *Partido Carlista* that based its posture upon the myth of the nineteenth-century *pueblo carlista's revolution manquée*. In view of Carlism's past history, it may perhaps be rash to suggest that Carlism is unlikely ever again to play a significant part in Spain's affairs, but at the time of writing (1981) this would certainly seem a reasonable assumption.

For further information, see Martin Blinkhorn, *Carlism and Crisis in Spain, 1931-1939* (Cambridge, England, 1975); Jaime del Burgo, *Conspiración y guerra civil* (Madrid and Barcelona, 1970); and Josep Carles Clemente, *Historia del Carlismo contemporáneo* (Barcelona, 1977).

Martin Blinkhorn

CARRILLO SOLARES, SANTIAGO (1915-   ). Carrillo, born on January 18, 1915, in Gijón,* was the longest serving secretary general of the Spanish Communist party* (the *Partido Comunista de España* —PCE). His father, Wenceslao, was a prominent socialist. In consequence, the young Santiago was drafted in to the *Federación de Juventudes Socialistas* (FJS), the *Partido Socialista Obrero Española* (PSOE)* youth movement, as a teenager. Already in November 1929, he published his first articles in *Aurora Social* of Oviedo,* calling for the creation of a student section of the FJS. Helped by the position of his father, Santiago had a meteoric rise within the FJS in the first years of the Second Republic.*

The socialist youth was closely associated with the radical positions adopted by Francisco Largo Caballero* in response to right-wing success in blocking the Republic's social reforms. Carrillo was a particularly vocal advocate of ultrarevolutionary positions. Accordingly, at the Fifth Congress of the FJS held in April 1934, he was elected its secretary-general and editor-in-chief of its newspaper, *Renovación*. He used his position to campaign for a broad working-class unity against fascism and for a more explicitly revolutionary stance by both the PSOE and the *Unión General de Trabajadores* (UGT).*

After the failure of the Asturian rising of October 1934, itself one of the fruits of the Socialist radicalization, Carrillo was imprisoned along with Caballero and many other PSOE leaders in the Model Prison of Madrid.* There, in collaboration with the FJS president, Carlos Hernández Zancajo, and Amaro del Rosal, Carrillo wrote the polemical pamphlet, *Octubre segunda etapa*. Denouncing the moderate and centrist sections of the PSOE, this widely distributed diatribe argued for them to be purged, called for the bolshevization of the party, and created bitter divisions within socialist ranks. The communists were not slow to exploit the schism in order to swell their own numbers at the expense of the PSOE.

When Carrillo was released from prison after the Popular Front* victory in the elections of February 1936,* he was invited to visit Moscow. This trip was to have crucial influence on his subsequent development. On his return, he worked with the Comintern agent Vittorio Codovilla* to bring about the unification of the FJS with the *Juventud Comunista Ibérica* (JCI). This was achieved in April 1936 with the formation of the *Juventudes Socialistas Unificadas* (JSU).* In effect, it constituted a massive advance of communist influence, and it is likely that by this time Carrillo was already a member of the PCE. In his book *Demain l'Espagne*, he claims to have attended central committee meetings of the Spanish Communist party at this time, a privilege not normally extended to outsiders. It was only after a further visit to Moscow in October that Carrillo announced, on November 6, 1936, his formal incorporation into the Communist party.

In January 1937, Carrillo completed the job begun nine months previously. He organized the first National Conference of the JSU and by packing it with communist militants ensured the entry of the majority of the united youth into the Spanish Communist party. Earlier, he was made delegate for public order in the *Junta de Defensa Nacional** left behind in Madrid when the government fled to Valencia.* During this time, a number of Francoist prisoners* being taken out of Madrid were killed by unknown elements at Paracuellos de Jarama. The incident is very obscure, and anticommunist propaganda has regularly tried to saddle Carrillo with the blame since the prisoners were technically under his jurisdiction.

The end of the Civil War found Carrillo in France* where he ingratiated himself further with the communist hierarchy by a public letter denouncing his father for his participation in the Casado* *Junta*. In September 1939, Santiago left France for Moscow where

he spent six months as secretary to the Communist Youth International, attending meetings of the Comintern executive. By now he had acquired considerable preeminence within the Spanish Communist party where he dominated the party's affairs during the next four decades. In 1977 the party was legally recognized and the Spanish parliamentary elections of June 15 were the first to have Communist party members elected to the Cortes.

For further information, see Carrillo's own reminiscences as recorded in *Demain l'Espagne* (Paris, 1974) and also by María Eugenia Yagüe, *Santiago Carrillo: perfil humano y político* (Madrid, 1977). Both works should be used with care since many crucial issues and dates are fudged. A more critical account of Carrillo in the post-1939 period can be found in Jorge Semprún, *Autobiografía de Federico Sánchez* (Barcelona, 1977) and Fernando Claudín, *Documentos de una divergencia comunista* (Barcelona, 1978). Carrillo's own writings are best found in the PCE doctrinal journal, *Nuestra Bandera*, and in a number of books, the most important of which are *Después de Franco, ¿qué?* (Paris, 1965), *Nuevos enfoques a problemas de hoy* (Paris, 1967) and *"Eurocomunismo" y Estado* (Barcelona, 1977).

Paul Preston

CARTAGENA. Cartagena, the port with the best natural harbor on the Mediterranean coast and in an excellent strategic position, was the main Republican naval base. The port was highly defensible and contained shipbuilding and repair facilities for smaller warships. Cartagena became the chief entry port for Soviet war material, October, 1936-October, 1937.

For further information, see Luis Romero, *Desastre en Cartagena* (Madrid, 1971).

See also Aid, Foreign Military; and Navy, Spanish.

Willard C. Frank, Jr.

CASADO LÓPEZ, SEGISMUNDO (1893-1968). Casado, a career army officer, supported the Republicans* during the Civil War. At the start of the conflict, he was a major in charge of President Manuel Azaña's* military household. He soon after joined the Republican general staff established in Madrid* and helped create the Mixed Brigades.* He subsequently received a combat command, served as the chief of staff for Republican forces at the battle of Brunete* in July 1937, and then helped to develop Republican Army* tactics in central Spain. By the end of 1938, now a colonel, he commanded troops in the central zone.

He is best remembered for his involvement in national Republican politics during the last several weeks of the war. Casado, an austere, hard-working officer, had concluded that further resistance against the Nationalists* was useless. Therefore, he attempted to convince Negrín to negotiate with Franco.* By February, Casado had started his own negotiations with the Nationalists and sought support for his efforts among the various political groups in Madrid. The communists objected to his efforts, while Negrín continued to urge resistance against Franco. Casado thought that if the communists were removed from Negrín's government, Franco might be willing to negotiate a compromise. He and his supporters believed Negrín was attempting to help friends get out of Spain while still publicly calling for resistance. Negrín tried to talk Casado out of his efforts but failed. Casado negotiated throughout February with the Nationalists, hoping to trade key Republican leaders in exchange for an end to the war and amnesty for the military. As late as February 24, 1939, Casado attempted to persuade Negrín to capitulate but he was rejected.

Yet, by the end of the month, most political and military factions in Madrid, with the exception of the communists, had allied themselves with Casado. Frustrated with Negrín, on March 5 they declared a revolt against the Republican government, and indirectly the communists, and established a national council with Casado taking the Ministry of Defense as his portfolio. Now he sought to arrest members of the old Republican government while Negrín could find no one to arrest Casado. The communists took matters into their own hands and started fighting Casado's allies in and around Madrid at the same time that the Nationalists were closing in on the Spanish capital. The communists, in control of Madrid, fought hard, but by March 11, they were contained sufficiently by Casado to agree to stop fighting. This mini-civil war had cost 230 lives and about 560 people were wounded.

With the communists eliminated as a threat and Negrín politically moribund, Casado attempted further negotiations with the Nationalists but was told on March 16 that Franco would accept only an unconditional surrender. By the end of the month, the war was over. Many historians have argued that Casado's machinations reduced Republican resistance against the Nationalists and that had he not struggled to end the war earlier, the Republicans might have found an entirely different international situation. For, on March 15, Germany* occupied Prague, just two weeks after the plots went into effect reducing the fighting in Spain. Hindsight is clearer than the realities at the time decisions were being made. Since he was isolated from much press coverage of European events, it is difficult to believe that he could be aware of broader international events. Furthermore, Casado was a military man, not a diplomat or a real politician. What was evident at the time, however, was that international tensions were rising to a point where the democracies might have tried to help the Republic, if the war had continued into the summer or fall of 1939. On a more positive side, Casado's activities allowed some Republican leaders time to get out of Spain without being captured and probably executed by the Nationalists.

Before Madrid fell, Casado went to Valencia,* where he tried to convince the British to evacuate refugees.* He finally left Spain on an English ship at the end of March. He lived in Great Britain* as an exile for a number of years and did not return to Spain until the 1960s.

For further information, see Segismundo Casado, *The Last Days of Madrid* (London, 1939); Ronald Fraser, *The Blood of Spain* (New York, 1979); José Manuel Martínez Bande, *Los cien últimos días de la república* (Barcelona, 1972), on Casado's ill-fated efforts; and Hugh Thomas, *The Spanish Civil War* (New York, 1977).

James W. Cortada

CASARES QUIROGA, SANTIAGO (1894-1950). Casares Quiroga, born in Corunna,* was a well-known Galician autonomist and Republican leader by the early 1900s. After more than twenty years' experience in Republican politics, he signed the Manifesto of the Revolutionary Committee as a representative of the Republican Organization of Galician Autonomists (ORGA) in 1930. The next year, he became a member of the provisional government. He was elected to each of the three legislatures during the Republic and was named to each cabinet in which the Left Republicans participated. Before becoming prime minister in April 1936, he had gained considerable cabinet experience, having served as minister of the marine, of the interior, and of public works.

During the first two years of the Republic, Casares Quiroga was most known for his militant anticlericalism rather than for contributing to the positive accomplishments of the Azaña government. As minister of the interior, responsible for maintaining order, he earned the enmity of the rightists for what they regarded as his partisan enforcement of the law. Shortly before becoming prime minister in 1936, he affirmed rightist perceptions of him by stating that he was concerned only with a potential revolution by the Right, and not with any excesses of the Left. He continued to confirm the Right's worst fears to the end: in the last week before the Civil War began, his government responded to the outrage among the rightists over Calvo Sotelo's* murder by suspending two rightist newspapers.

Although the prime minister stated his concern about the rumored military uprising, his actions as both prime minister and war minister suggested that he did not take the threat seriously. In order to upset the plans for an uprising, he changed the date of some summertime furloughs and transferred some of the lower ranking officers. These measures proved ineffective, however, largely because he left the generals in their places. He did not even move the chief conspirator, General Mola,* from Pamplona,* headquarters of the conservative Carlist Requetés.* Even after the revolt had begun, he refused the demand that the masses be armed; rather, on his last day in office, he threatened to execute anyone who opened the armories. Historians as diverse in their views as Hugh Thomas on the one side and Broué and Témine, on the other, consider this refusal a major cause of the early successes of the rebels.

Casares Quiroga was replaced as prime minister in the early hours of the war, and he played no important role in the war itself. He left political life to enlist as a private in the militia, and he also attended sporadic sessions of the Cortes.* After the war (except for the period of Nazi occupation), he lived in Paris until his death in 1950.

Both sides in the Civil War denounced Casares Quiroga for inept rule. Rightists often blamed him for making the rebellion "necessary," while leftists frequently accused him of enabling the revolution to be successful.

For further information, see Ricardo de la Cierva, *Historia de la guerra civil*, Vol. 1: *Perspectivas y antecedentes, 1898-1936* (Madrid, 1969); Gabriel Jackson, *The Spanish Republic and the Civil War, 1936-1939* (Princeton, N.J., 1965); and Domingo Quiroga Ríos, *Quien es y adonde va Santiago Casares* (Corunna, 1932), a hostile political biography on Casares Quiroga's early career.

See also Madrid; and Origins of the Spanish Civil War.

William J. Irwin

CASTEJÓN ESPINOSA, ANTONIO (1896-   ). Castejón sided with the Nationalists* during the Civil War. In July 1936, he was a major in the Spanish Foreign Legion* stationed at Tetuán* in North Africa. He rose in rebellion with Franco* and, within days,

commanded some of the first legionnaires who landed in Spain, seizing the town of Triana after heavy fighting near Seville.* Major Castejón went on to lead these combat-experienced *Moros* (known as the Army of Africa*) throughout southern Spain, marching northward during July and August to Badajoz,* Mérida,* Trujillo, upward toward Toledo,* and Madrid.* He thus participated in a highly successful 300-mile push northward in approximately one month, presenting Franco with a significant military and political victory. Castejón became a colonel and led troops on the advances toward Madrid in the fall of 1936, repeatedly defending himself against Republican attacks and launching successful counteroffensives. In early November, he again participated in fighting near Madrid, this time leading the assault forces on the city that fought at the University of Madrid. Ultimately, the Republicans* forced back the Nationalist penetration into the city but not without heavy loss of life. Subsequently, Castejón went on to command forces in most of the key campaigns of the war, for example, the battle of the Ebro* between July and November 1938.

For further information, see José Manuel Martínez Bande, *La lucha en torno a Madrid* (Madrid, 1968) and *La marcha sobre Madrid* (Madrid, 1968).

See also Andalusia; and Morocco, Spanish.

James W. Cortada

CASTELLÓ PANTOJA, LUIS (1881-1962). Castelló was commissioned as an infantry lieutenant in 1899 and spent part of his career in Morocco.* A Mason and a Republican, he was promoted to brigadier in 1932 and served as undersecretary of war with the Radical Republicans in 1934-1935. In July 1936, as commander of the 2d Brigade, he kept Badajoz* loyal to the Republic; on July 19, he was appointed war minister in the Giral* government. Fifteen days later, Castelló suffered a nervous breakdown, apparently in reaction to his brother's assassination by Estremaduran anarchists.* Taking refuge in the French Embassy, he subsequently escaped to France* but was returned by the Germans to the Franco* regime, which condemned him to death. He languished in jail until pardoned in 1946.

For further information, see Guillermo Cabanellas, *Cuatro generales*, 2 vols. (Barcelona, 1977); and Ramón Salas Larrazábal, *Historia del ejército popular de la República*, 4 vols. (Madrid, 1973).

Carolyn P. Boyd

CASTELLÓN. Castellón is a province located in the region of Aragón,* along the Mediterranean coastline below the province of Tarragona* and above Valencia.* For the majority of the Civil War, it remained in Republican hands. During this period, villages were divided in their loyalty between anarchists* and socialists. Both political movements held control over all villages within this province. Those communities that were under anarchist control usually entertained experiments in libertarian economics, communal living practices were common, and some experimentation with moneyless societies took place. Socialist-controlled neighborhoods—political rivals of the anarchists—were more conservative and retained traditional capitalist enterprises.

The war did not disturb local life materially until the spring of 1938 when the Nationalists* made their drive to the sea. Before then, the war had primarily meant the loss of local men to Republican recruiters. By June 1938, however, warfare erupted in various parts of the province. This agricultural area became a center of campaigning, which culminated on June 14 with the surrender of the capital (named after the province) to Nationalist forces under the command of General Antonio Aranda Mata,* one of Franco's* leading battlefield commanders. Fighting had been fierce in the days preceding the fall of this city, and reportedly the Republicans* executed some forty political prisoners* and sacked the town completely before the rebels moved in. Seizing this city and surrounding areas gave the Nationalists a major Mediterranean port—which they badly needed since the only other convenient ports of call were in the Balearic Islands* far to the north off Catalonia.* With the seizure of this province, and particularly its coastal communities, a strike southward toward Valencia* could be made from points as near as 50 miles away. The stage was thus set for the final Nationalist offensive to the south which began in July but took months to accomplish. Until Valencia fell, the Nationalists were unable to destroy what ultimately became the last Republican zone in southeastern Spain. It held out until the last days of March 1939.

For further information, see José Manuel Martínez Bande, *Los cien últimos días de la república* (Barcelona, 1972); and Hugh Thomas, *The Spanish Civil War* (New York, 1977).

See also Socialist Party, Spanish.

James W. Cortada

CASTILE. Castile, the area of northcentral Spain from Portugal* to Aragón* and Valencia* in the east and Andalusia* in the south, quickly fell to the Nationalists* in July 1936 with little bloodshed. Many of the urban centers of this Spanish land, such as Burgos* and Valladolid,* were staunchly conservative, while the two major Republican points were Toledo* and Madrid.* Toledo fell in September 1936, and Madrid resisted until almost the end of the Civil War. Franco* first made Salamanca* his headquarters and subsequently Burgos* in northern Spain. The entire area of Castile* was the scene of much battling in the years between 1936 and 1939 as Nationalist armies sought to capture Madrid and Republican forces to defend it. All the major battles for Madrid, including Boadilla,* Corunna Road,* Guadalajara,* and the siege of the Alcázar,* were fought in Castile.

Serious attempts at collectivization of this wheat-producing area had been undertaken during the Second Republic* but were halted when the Nationalists occupied the provinces of central Spain, diverting products to themselves while restoring lands to their original owners. The denial of wheat to the Republic led to bread shortages in Madrid. The Nationalists scoured their occupied zones for Loyalists,* labor activists, and Republican soldiers. This portion of Spain also provided Franco with thousands of soldiers who were recruited into his armies.

For further information, see Ricardo de la Cierva, *Historia ilustrada de la guerra civil española*, 2 vols. (Barcelona, 1970); Olao Conforti, *Guadalajara* (Milan, 1967); José Manuel Martínez Bande, *La lucha en torno a Madrid* (Madrid, 1968), *La marcha sobre Madrid* (Madrid, 1968), and his *La ofensiva sobre Segovia y la batalla de Brunete* (Madrid, 1972); Esmond Romilly, *Boadilla* (London, 1971); and Hugh Thomas, *The Spanish Civil War* (New York, 1977).

See also Daily Life, Nationalist Zone; and Daily Life, Republican Zone.

James W. Cortada

CASTILLA Y CAMPOS, CRISTOBAL DE (1892-   ). Castillo was a career diplomat who, in 1936, served as chancellor of the Spanish Embassy in Paris. When the Civil War started, he sided with the Nationalists,* as did more than 90 percent of the Spanish diplomatic corps.* During July 1936, just prior to his resignation, he did everything he could to block the sale of French arms to the Spanish Republic, successfully holding off such deliveries. Nothing is known about his activities during the war after July 1936.

For further information, see David Wingeate Pike, *Les Français et la guerre d'Espagne, 1936-1939* (Paris, 1975).

See also France.

James W. Cortada

CASTRO DELGADO, ENRIQUE (1907-1963). Castro was the first commander of the Communist Fifth Regiment* in the Republican Army,* in 1937 became director-general of the Institute for Agrarian Reform* which he used to recruit more members for the Communist party,* and was a member of the central committee of Spain's Communist party. He participated in the communist effort to discredit the government of Largo Caballero* in 1938 thereby breaking the political power of the Socialist party.

For further information, see Burnett Bolloten, *The Spanish Revolution: The Left and the Struggle for Power During the Civil War* (Chapel Hill, N.C., 1979), on Castro's political affairs; and Enrique Castro Delgado, *Hombres made in Moscú* (Barcelona, 1965), on his military activities.

James W. Cortada

CASTRO Y ALONSO, ARCHBISHOP MANUEL (1863-1944). Archbishop Castro of Burgos* (sometimes referred to as Manuel García de Castro y Alonso) was one of the Nationalists'* strongest supporters. Born in Valladolid* on April 10, 1863, he was consecrated bishop of Jaca in 1913, then bishop of Segovia* in 1918, and archbishop of Burgos in 1928. A conservative and traditionalist cleric, he opposed the Republic from the beginning. Cardinal Vidal* did not even try to obtain Castro's* support for the moderate policies he proposed for the rest of the Spanish episcopate.

When the military uprising began in 1936, Castro's see of Burgos was quickly established as a Nationalist stronghold, and he gave them complete support throughout the war, especially after Burgos became the seat of the Nationalist government. He was vehemently opposed to the Basque priests who supported the Basque separatist movement. On at least one occasion he sought to have them excommunicated by the pope, a proposal thwarted by Bishop Mateo Múgica,* exiled in Rome. Castro died in Burgos on September 3, 1944.

For further information, see Juan de Iturralde, *El catolicismo y la cruzada de Franco* (Vienna, 1955, 1960).

See also Basque Nationalism; Catholic Church, Spanish; and Vatican.

José M. Sánchez

CASUALTIES. An accurate count of the number of wounded or killed on either side during the Spanish Civil War is not possible, although serious attempts have been made to arrive at reasonable figures. Currently, it is believed that there were about 500,000 deaths from all causes (hunger, wounds, executions, combat mortality, and so on) in a country of 24.5 million inhabitants. Some historians still argue that it may have ranged upward to 800,000. Demographic analysis province by province has tended to push the number upward but far less than the 1 million figure believed in the first twenty years after the war. Of the half million dead, it is believed that about 200,000 died from combat-related causes. Of this group, about 110,000 were Republicans* and the rest Nationalists.* Hugh Thomas, from whom these figures were drawn, argues that some 10 percent of all soldiers perished. He has also tabulated the number of dead caused by executions within each zone at about 75,000 in the Nationalist sector and 55,000 in the Republican, or a total of 130,000. These deaths take into account executions at prisons, murders by various rival political groups, and the general repression of opposing sides. Malnutrition was a severe problem in the Republican zone, with some 25,000 believed to have died of this cause. Another 10,000 people, primarily in urban areas, were killed by bombs dropped from airplanes. The Francoist repression after the war may have caused another 100,000 deaths by execution throughout Spain in various prison yards. In addition to the loss of population* caused by deaths, one must add 300,000 Spaniards lost to Spain because they emigrated out of the country into exile. If one counts that last figure into the total loss of population to Spain, then the final count approximates about 800,000, or about 3.3 percent of the total population of Spain in 1936. About 25,000 of these Republicans died during World War II and possibly another 10,000 in concentration camps.*

Of the various foreign nations participating in the war, the best current figures suggest that on the Nationalist side about 5,300 died (300 Germans, 4,000 Italians, 1,000 others), while the Republicans lost approximately 4,900 (1,000 Frenchmen, 2,000 Germans and Austrians combined, 900 Americans, 500 British, and about 500 others) for a grand total of some 9,200 people.

Given the poor medical records for the period, it is virtually impossible to arrive at statistical conclusions about the number of wounded. Not limited to military personnel, casualties were suffered by all segments of society: women, men, children, rich and poor, old and young, and in all provinces. Thus, normal ratios of wounded to dead common at the time (say, as a result of experiences with World War I and the African campaigns) are not relevant. Indeed, the casualty rates for wounded were probably higher because of the injury done to civilians. But it would be safe to conclude that well over 7 or 8 percent of the Spanish population was hurt in addition to the 3.3 percent killed. This suggests that physical harm came to over 10 percent of the population as a whole; even this final total may be too conservative when wounds are taken into account.

Mortality and other casualty figures are the result of losses in almost every province in Spain. Since a great deal of the military loss of life occurred in the campaigns in central and northern Spain, it can be concluded that the higher percentages of population loss were also in these areas, both civilian and military. These areas were populated with cities which were bombed heavily thereby contributing to a higher rate of casualties when compared to more rural areas of southern Spain. Thus, one might expect to see lower casualty percentages in remote parts of the country that saw little combat and perhaps only limited repression by one side or the other. But until more detailed local demographic studies are completed, we will not be sure about the true distribution of deaths and injuries in Spain.

For further information, see Ricardo de la Cierva, *Historia ilustrada de la guerra civil española* (Barcelona, 1970); Ramón Salas Larrazábal, *Historia del ejército popular de la república*, 4 vols. (Madrid, 1974); Hugh Thomas, *The Spanish Civil War* (New York, 1977); and Jesús Villar Salinas, *Repercusiones demográficas de la última guerra civil española* (Madrid, 1942).

James W. Cortada

CATALAN ANTIFASCIST MILITIAS COMMITTEE. *See* Antifascist Militias Committee, Central.

CATALONIA. Catalonia was affected by the military uprising that occurred at dawn on July 19, 1936. The regiments in Barcelona,* which made up the forces of the 4th Division headquartered in the city, moved into the streets with the intention of occupying Barcelona and the key centers of power in Catalonia. These objectives failed because of opposition from the forces under the command of the Commissary of Public Order of the Generalitat,* an assault military group, the Civil Guard,* combined with the cooperation of the military air force stationed at El Prat de Llobregat and by reinforcements of syndicalist volunteers, especially from the *Confederación Nacional del Trabajo* (CNT).* The most violent clashes between forces loyal to the Generalitat and those in revolt took place in the center of the city: Diagonal Avenue at the corner of Paseo de Gracia, Plaza de Cataluña, Plaza de la

Universidad, Plaza de España, Paralelo, Avenida Sarriá, and at the end zone of the Ramblas. By dawn of July 20, the insurgents' fate was sealed, and their failure in Catalonia was completed with the surrender of General Manuel Goded,* the leader of the troops in mutiny.

In other Catalan urban centers with military contingents in their midst (Gerona,* Mataró, Lérida,* and Figueras), the revolutionary movement was quickly checked or the troops remained loyal to the legally constituted regime (in Tarragona,* Manresa, and at Seu d'Urgel). Nevertheless, the failure of the uprising did not permit a return to circumstances as they were before July 19. The revolutionary activity implied that certain economic realities would have to change to generate the same quantities of goods and services and support of the prewar institutions while converting to a new social revolution. This latter phase called for a period of experimentation and observation. In addition, Catalan public institutions—as others in Spain that remained faithful to the Constitution—were forced to deal with the lack of discipline and considerable disorder which affected working and civic conditions.

Possibly the most important problems affecting and conditioning the experiments of the new socioeconomic regime during 1936-1939 had to do with production. Therefore, the division of the Iberian Peninsula into two warring zones, as well as the problem of Catalan commercial development, presented the Catalan economy with two difficult requirements: on the one hand, the demands of production and consumption, and on the other, the contraction of demand in other sectors. Catalonia also had to face demands arising specifically from the Civil War, that is, with the transformation of Catalan peacetime economy into one geared for war. Obviously, the economic sector was not the only one feeling the impact of the war. The conflict affected Catalonia by virtue of its participation in the battlefronts, through the behind-the-lines attacks by the Burgos* government (primarily aerial bombardment), and because of the total occupation of the regime by Franco's* troops.

The Generalitat of Catalonia was restored in 1931, after having been abolished in 1714 by Philip V of Spain. The statute stated in precise terms the extent of Catalan self-government. Catalonia enjoyed not only administrative decentralization, but also an authentic political representation of its national personality within the structure of the Spanish Republic.

As of July 19, 1936, the Generalitat's powers were assumed by the executive branch, that is, its government, given the difficulty of convoking the Catalan parliament (which eventually was convoked in a limited fashion during the second half of 1937 and in 1938), and the urgency of identifying and finding solutions for ensuing problems.

The developments created by July 19 on the one hand confirmed the constitutional and statutory institutions. On the other hand, they introduced some new elements, such as active participation of labor in political life, particularly by anarchosyndicalists and orthodox Marxists, along the lines of the Third International (which founded the *Partit Socialista Unificat de Catalunya* [PSUC]* on July 21, 1936 through the fusion of several socialist and communist parties) and of the heterodox Marxism of the *Partido Obrero de Unificación Marxista* (POUM).* Events continued to give a dominant role to the *Esquerra Republicana de Catalunya*,* the majority party in Catalonia, sustained *Acció Catalana*, and totally eliminated the *Lliga Catalana*,* the party of the Catalan bourgeoisie which nevertheless supported the Republic and remained on the sidelines during the insurrectional preparations.

The Generalitat and its president, Luis Companys,* attempted to set up those organizations and councils required by the changed circumstances. At the same time, a new government was established which would include all political and syndical sectors. The new institutions would gradually languish until September 1936, when they disappeared or became merely consultative bodies. They adopted collegial organizational formulas, notably:

1. Central Committee of Antifascist Militia, which was the most important. Formed by representatives of all the Catalan political parties or movements (*Estat Català*, *Acció Català*, PSUC, *Federación Anarquista Ibérica* [FAI], and POUM) and the syndicates (*Unión General de Trabajadores* [UGT],* and *Unió de Rabassaires*). This committee organized all of the militia destined for service at the battlefronts and was organized by sections serving internal security, militias,* health, and transportation.
2. Council of New Unified School (CENU) with representation of all political interests. It organized education and the schools at all levels.
3. Economic Council, about which more will be said below.
4. Central Provisioning Committee, charged with providing food* for the population.*

On July 31, the government of Catalonia incorporated the labor organizations. Chaired by Juan Casanovas, it did not, however, achieve this goal. Nevertheless, the idea of unity eventually succeeded when President Companys ordered Juan Tarradellas* to form a new government with a cabinet made up of repre-

sentatives from the ERC, AC, *Unió de Rabassaires*, PSUC, CNT, and POUM. With the suppression of the original committees or reduction of their functions to an advisory status, it can be said that the Catalan government evolved into the only center of political power. The CNT leaders were to collaborate loyally with the Generalitat according to the decisions taken by its government. The regime forcefully reaffirmed its authority vis-à-vis the Republic's central government. It also attempted to control public order, which had been notoriously altered by the spontaneous and indiscriminate actions of groups that took to the streets in the stormy period following July 19. The Catalan government was unable to eliminate the security patrols created on August 9, 1936, which operated under the control of the Central Antifascist Militias Committee.*

The seriousness of the Catalan economic situation was apparent in November 1936 and certainly by February-March 1937. This malaise resulted in the formation of a new government on December 17, 1936 (which took advantage of the situation and surreptitiously eliminated the POUM from the government of the Generalitat) and in the ministerial crisis of April-June 1937 which pointed to the delicate problem of public security. Actions on public security and the grave problem of distributing consumer items led to the disturbances of May 3, 1937, which began with the occupation of the Barcelona telephone company's building by the Generalitat's security forces. During the following days, the CNT and POUM militants confronted the forces of the Generalitat, supported by the ERC and the PSUC in street fighting. Also in evidence was the grave schism between the base of the CNT and its leaders, the latter collaborating with the Generalitat and the Republic. As a result of these events, the administration consolidated control over public order but seriously compromised the broad autonomy of the war in Catalonia. Soon after, the central government assumed responsibility for military defense and public order throughout Catalonia.

Towards the end of June 1937, a new government of the Generalitat came into being, no longer presided over by Tarradellas but by President Companys (as permitted by the 1933 Constitution of Catalonia) without the presence of the CNT. The CNT was then in the process of gradual weakening. The new government (which lasted until the end of the Civil War) was forced to face the impact of the fighting. The hostilities placed unbearable burdens on the Catalan economy towards the end of 1937, a situation that worsened after the second quarter of 1938 when Catalan territory was occupied by Franco's* troops and the bombing of Barcelona and other Catalan cities intensified.

Likewise, the transfer of the Republican government to Barcelona on December 31, 1937, intensified the intervention of the central administration into Catalan public affairs, affecting inclusively the Generalitat.

The regional and local administration by the Generalitat also underwent changes during the war. The four provinces of Catalonia had been abolished by the Generalitat, the government charging a technical group in 1931 with responsibility for a study of a Catalan territorial division. The decrees of August 27 and December 23, 1936, established the division of Catalonia into nine regions (Barcelona, Gerona, Tarragona, Reus, Tortosa, Vic, Manresa, Lérida, and Tremp-Seu d'Urgell) which grouped thirty-eight basic units or districts together.

The events of July 19 gave rise to communal and revolutionary powers. Local committees exercised greater authority than the municipal governments had traditionally (such as defense, opposition to strikes, and help to refugees*). The Generalitat supported the existing municipal structures, filling vacancies through agreement with local political forces. Thus, at times two sources of local governmental power coexisted. This situation ended by decree of the Generalitat on October 9, 1936, when the local committees were dissolved. The government ordered the formation of new municipal structures according to the same proportion held in the government of the Generalitat by the different political and syndical forces. Either directly or indirectly, through the allocation of financial resources, the Generalitat reduced the powers of municipal governments to levels existing prior to July 19, establishing mechanisms for obtaining new municipal resources at the same time. By the end of 1937, a new municipal order had been established in which the authority of the Generalitat and of the municipalities was established juridically by the law governing Catalan communities.

Through expropriation, enterprises or centers of production were seized and run by a collective body of workers of the producing entity, syndicates, municipalities, Generalitat, or the Republic. Yet, the act of seizure did not presuppose the juridical future of such expropriated firms.

Collectivization denoted the economic power of the enterprise, factory, or establishment within the control of the workers laboring in them. Collectivization (also known as collectivism) was, therefore, equivalent to what is currently understood as workers' self-management. Logically, it implied contributing to the value of the enterprise and after subtracting taxes, interest payments, and rent, granting workers the difference in the form of wages and benefits.

When an organization different from the one exercising economic power in a particular enterprise interfered or was concerned with decision-making, it was said to control the firm. This control was exercised, for example, by the enterprises collectivized by delegates of the Generalitat. In those companies which continued in the hands of their former owners or managers—as will shortly be discussed—some of the decision-making authority rested with the workers who collectivized the plant.

The term "socialization" was applied in different ways depending on the party or political movement using it. Thus, from the anarchosocialist viewpoint, socialization was the expropriation effected by the vertical syndicate of all of the firms in a single industry. The socialists understood socialization to mean the attribution of political power of an industry to a people's government. There was no problem with the widely used terms "nationalization" and "municipalization" since they meant the same then as they do today.

There were differences between collectives in agriculture, industry, commerce, and credit institutions. Any generalizations with respect to the agricultural sector is risky because of the absence of global or systematic studies on the subject. Nevertheless, at the start of the Civil War, the CNT sent a questionnaire to collectives regarding their extent and functions, as was done with all agricultural syndicates adhering to the CNT. Starting on September 12, 1936, the information bulletin of the CNT-FAI published the responses obtained. On November 8, the Department of Agriculture of the Generalitat sent out a similar questionnaire devoted to livestock activities. Sixty-six Catalan localities responded and while some failed to answer the confederated questionnaire, sufficient data was collected to suggest that collectivism was centered mainly in the sectors of the ancient province of Tarragona* (as opposed to the then recently redistricted area of Tarragona).

The Generalitat did not consider the case of collectivism in the agrarian sector as a general norm, contrary to what occurred in industry. The decree of November 1, 1937, relieved agricultural partners, farmers, and *rabassaires* from real estate taxes, while an early decree, issued by the Generalitat on August 27, 1936, and implemented by regulations on December 19, established the Federation of Agricultural Syndicates of Catalonia. Therefore, the government could force independent producers to join cooperatives. These included farming operations that had been collectivized de facto into the commercial distribution area of the economy, acquisition of products, insurance, and credits. The FESAC was organized geographically according to the territorial division of Catalonia by the August 27, 1936, decree.

By August 5, 1936, labor activity in the main industrial centers, principally in Barcelona, had normalized. Frequently, when workers went to their jobs, they found a vacuum in management authority because former managers or proprietors were gone. In other instances, executives and managers offered no resistance to the demands of their former workers. Thus, the collectivization and socialization movements were the spontaneous result of the rebellion and not of government or syndicate intervention. The CNT, which encompassed the vast majority of Catalan workers in syndicates at the start of the war, spurred action from this base without waiting for orders from its directors, particularly from the Regional Committee of Catalonia.

When the former entrepreneurs remained with their businesses, the workers normally formed a committee that would watch and audit operations. This situation usually involved small industrialists and merchants. When the proprietors abandoned their enterprises or disappeared, the business was continued by the firm's own worker committee. On different occasions, the option was followed of respecting foreign enterprises, even though for all practical purposes these were affected in at least some fundamental way by the process of collectivization.

The transition to the new production order was often marked by the holding of a workers' meeting of the company or industrial sector, which then elected the control committee charged with responsibility for running the firm. Generally, this new arrangement resulted in operations as usual, although at times shops, installations, and branches were established separately. The new structures found themselves facing difficulties that stemmed as much from Spain's economic crisis of the 1930s as from the economic circumstances provoked by the war.

In view of this process, the Generalitat opted for a wait-and-see policy, a position that changed by the following August when it took two major actions. First, on August 8, 1936, it created the Commission of War Industries in order to coordinate the efforts of industrial enterprises (such as metallurgical, chemical, and mechanical) and adapt them to wartime necessities. This commission was made up of representatives of workers employed in those industries, by technicians (especially military ones), and by politicians representing the Catalan government. The commission provided guidance for a sector nationalized by the Generalitat and assured government intervention in other industries connected with the sector.

During the entire war, Juan Tarradellas chaired the commission.

Second, by decree of August 11, 1936, the Economic Council of Catalonia came into existence. This council was empowered to organize all aspects of Catalan industry and commerce, although from June 1937 on it functioned as a mediator and consultant. The council consisted of representatives of all the political parties and syndicates, although the POUMista representation was eliminated in August 1937. At the time, many noted that it was not easy to reconcile the different political positions of the popular power groups when facing the structuring of the new economy.

The Economic Council developed a transnational plan that earned unanimous approval. Called the Plan for the Socialist Transformation of the Nation, it consisted of eleven proposals for initiating the collectivization process: (1) regulation of production in accordance with consumer requirements, (2) foreign trade monopoly, (3) placement of large agricultural estates in collectives with obligatory syndicalization, (4) partial devalorization of urban property through changes in tax requirements and through lowering rents, (5) establishment of collectives in large industry, public services, and collective transportation, (6) seizure and collectivization of abandoned enterprises, (7) extension of cooperatives to the distribution industries, (8) workers' control of banks until their nationalization was completed, (9) workers' syndicate control over private enterprise, (10) rapid control of strikes, and (11) elimination of indirect taxation and establishment of a single tax.

The decrees of the Generalitat of August 6, 8, 21, and 24, the ordinance of August 28, the decree of September 2, and the ordinance of October 3 pointed towards the institutionalization of the revolution to assure the continuation of production, even if recognizing de facto seizures. Furthermore, the Generalitat reserved for itself a rather tenuous right of intervention into the enterprises through a "delegate" of the government in each establishment.

With the formation of a popular unity government presided over by Tarradellas, the Catalan authorities considered it necessary to regulate the process of the social revolution. Taking the Plan for the Socialist Transformation as a base, on October 24, 1936, the government published the Decree for Collectivization and control of industry and commerce by the workers. In its development, the ERC and PSUC shared common viewpoints in opposition to those of the CNT and POUM, with respect to the limits to be set for small enterprises (in which private ownership of means of production continued to be recognized), as well as in the matter of compensation for the former proprietors. The same situation also applied to the creation of the Industrial and Commercial Credit Bank.

According to the decree of collectivization and other complementary measures, Catalonia's formal structure of industry and commerce shaped up as follows. With regard to production units, some private firms continued to remain in the hands of their former proprietors whose ownership and management rights were recognized, but workers' control committees elected by the employees were formed in those enterprises. These firms corresponded to small and medium-sized owners and handicrafts. In practice, the norms established by the Generalitat, delineating the functions of the intervening control committee, were interpreted in various ways by the different committees.

Collectivized enterprises, also known as self-managed enterprises, employed more than 100 people or had been the property of owners who were declared collaborators of the rebels by judgment of the Tribunal of Public Security. Enterprises with less than 100 employees were also collectivized when the workers opted for collectivization or when the old owners and the workers came to an agreement. They were self-governing, and in this arrangement, the management end of the business depended on the will of the workers meeting in general assembly. The assembly appointed an enterprise council which functioned as top management, as well as a general manager responsible to the council and to the General Councils of Industry, respectively. The Generalitat assured its intervention by naming a representative from the Department of Economics. Other groups and concentrations were collectivized enterprises made up of all companies in a particular industrial sector in a specifically defined territory: local, regional, or Catalan. Such groups usually included larger units of production (such as big factories), all of which were subject to one management, and were characterized by the same arrangement that affected the collectivized industries. This formulation was intended to serve as a restructuring mechanism for the Catalan economy by means of regimenting large-scale industry. Nevertheless, this criterion, which the Generalitat and Economic Council maintained officially, was not the only criterion at the time a group was established. Primarily, the grouping was the legal expression of the syndicate's desire to control the production of each industrial syndicate by expanding their authority over the small firms and shops in a particular sector. This viewpoint reflected that of the CNT and naturally was opposed by the petit bourgeoisie, small merchants, and artisans. Through the "groupings," collectivization of small enterprises took place; the "totaling" of numbers of workers permitted the concentration of workers to rise making the unit or business eligible for collectivization. Thus, the "groupings" were one aspect most subject to polemics during the war.

Municipalization was introduced by urban governments and local committees from the early days of the revolution. The decrees of January 8, 1937 (from the series called S'Agaró) and the ordinance of March 3, 1937, determined the nature and limits of the municipalization. Nationalization of enterprises must be viewed from the vantage point of the Commission of Wartime Industries already discussed.

The various enterprises were classified into fourteen industrial clusters: fuel and lubricants; agricultural, mechanical and metallurgical; textiles; food; chemicals; construction; graphic arts; gas and electricity; transportation; communications; general irrigation services; hygiene and security; commerce; credit; and insurance. Subsequently, food* and agriculture were combined into one sector.

The general organization of production was entrusted to the General Councils of Industry established for each of the sectors. These councils were composed of technicians designated by the Catalan government, delegates from the collectivized enterprises, and syndical representatives. The presidency of the General Councils of Industry was held by a member of the Economic Council. Thus, the organization of the Catalan economy became structured. The general councils began functioning in March 1937. A Generalitat decree issued July 9, 1937, created the Economic Federations of Industry to organize industrial groups within each general council. Nevertheless, the federation never came into practical reality.

The branches of Catalan banks whose head offices were located outside the territory governed by the Generalitat were managed by one government delegate and two employee representatives. If the branches had no effective management, the Control Committee assumed the functions of a management committee directing operations. Catalan banks were integrated into a General Council for Catalan Banking formed by representatives of the Generalitat, employees, and depositors. In each bank employees formed a management committee. As an advisory body to the Department of Finances regarding banking matters, the government created the High Council for Credit and Banking which represented the credit sector as well as public administration. Similarly, the Catalan savings banks came under the General Council for Savings, composed of representatives of government, syndicates, and related groups. The basic regulations concerning the organization of the credit institutions grew out of the so-called *S'Agaró* decree of January 1937.

The Civil War, of course, also affected Catalan society militarily. The effects on the Catalan economy proper follow in a later discussion.

Catalonia initially fought the war beyond its frontiers. At the same time, the military barracks were occupied by the political and syndical organizations. (The Esquerra held the Montjuich Barracks, the POUM that of Lepanto, the PSUC that of Jaime I in the Ciudadela, and the rest by the CNT.) In order to defeat the rebellion in the rest of Spain, the political parties and syndicates enlisted volunteers* and militiamen who organized themselves into columns. The militiamen departed for the Aragón* front, beginning on July 23, 1936, during which the first group of 3,000 anarchosyndicalists under Buenaventura Durruti,* with Major Perez Farrás as adviser, marched on Saragossa.* Following this first expedition, Ortiz's Column (formed from various groups) also marched to the Aragón front. More men went under del Barrio* (of the PSUC) along with others under the command of Rovira i de Arquer (of the POUM), the Aguiluchos and Roja i Negra columns of the CNT, the Macià-Companys, and the column from the Esquerra, among others.

Even after these columns were placed under the control of the Central Antifascist Militias Committee and placed under the direct command of the Defense Commissariat, the various forces functioned in a dispersed fashion. An effort was made to create a unified command through the War Committee for the Aragón Front along the lines of a chief-of-staff concept, as well as a General Inspector of the Front.

After an initial penetration of the eastern front of Aragón, the Aragón became stabilized along a line that ran near Canfanc, very close to Huesca,* and that veered off by Tardienta, Osera, Fuendetodos, Vivel, Argente, and Teruel.* Thus, half of Aragón was beyond the rebels' control.

The subsequent stabilization of the front and the paralysis blocking any offensive were due to the dispersion of troops, their nonprofessional performance, and the difficulty in obtaining weapons. But this stabilization permitted a wave of agricultural collectives to develop in the eastern portion of Aragón, as well as the subsequent formation of a Council of Aragón.* The Republican government recognized the council on December 17, 1936, although it was disbanded in August 1937 by the Republican regime itself.

Felipe Díaz Sandino,* the new minister of defense for the Generalitat (a department created for the first time on July 31), organized a military expedition of volunteers under the command of Captain Alberto Bayo Girón* to conquer Majorca.* Although Cabrera and Ibiza* were occupied, the group had to return towards the beginning of September without securing its objective.

In order to unify the war effort in Catalonia, the Generalitat ordered the mobilization of the reserves from the classes of 1933, 1934, and 1935. An October 27 decree pointed to the elimination of the militia councils (which made evident militia misapprehension about professionalism and the professional military) and considered application of the military code. Thus, by the beginning of 1937 reference could be made to a Regular People's Army of Catalonia. Nevertheless, as a result of the events of May 1937, the Republic assumed all responsibility for matters of defense, at which time the Generalitat's Department of Defense ceased to exist.

From March 1938 onward, Catalonia gradually came under the control of General Franco's* rebel army. With the conclusion of the Francoist counteroffensive at Teruel—as a response to the Republican attack against Teruel the previous December—and the occupation of Belchite,* and with the further coincidence of a violent bombardment of Barcelona, the rebel forces entered Catalonia at Massalareig in March 1938 and captured Lérida* in April. Thus, by the end of the month, Catalonia had become virtually isolated from the rest of Republican Spain. Between July and November 1938, the bloody battle of the Ebro* raged. At Christmas, the rebel army commenced its movement against Catalonia, occupying Reus and Tarragona on January 15, 1939, Barcelona on January 26, Gerona on February 4, Seu d'Urgell on February 5, and Figueras on February 8, finally reaching the French frontier on February 10.

The conversion of the economy from a peacetime to a wartime one required a complex set of efforts. In the productive sector, industries had to adjust to the new situation; industrial imports from foreign countries and areas in Spain occupied by the rebels had to be replaced by domestic sources of clearly inferior quality. In effect, the events of July 19 resulted in a decrease in production because of the difficulty of obtaining raw materials, foodstuffs, and fuel—all of which had made Catalonia a tributary to the rest of Spain—rendering imports a significant problem. A similar problem developed with demand. All available resources went to industries that supplied the needs of war. Therefore, peacetime industries declined.

Most of the problems relating to the changeover to a new economic and social system in Catalonia centered on production and the allocation of economic resources. Hence, by the beginning of 1937, the division of the peninsula into two zones, coupled with the problems of foreign trade, produced agricultural and livestock shortages, scarcities that would subsequently increase. Meat and potatoes were particularly in short supply by the start of January 1937, oil during mid-year, and food for livestock by March 1937. By the end of 1936, there were shortages in phosphate fertilizers, jute, textiles, and chemical raw materials. Coal as an energy source was already scarce in October 1936, and a month later so were fuel oils. Electricity, Catalonia's most important energy resource, suffered an absolute loss in early 1938 when the hydraulic centers fell into the hands of General Franco.

Lack of balance between productive capacity and the allocation of resources required gave rise to price inflation. Inflation was the specific result of the problems generated in meeting the new demands of war and other essential obligations. Monthly wholesale prices increased an average of 5.5 percent. On the other hand, the monthly cost of living index increased by 6.6 percent.

Unemployment rose simultaneously because of the disorder produced by the revolutionary events of July 1936. A more serious cause was the strangulation of "inputs" for production and the abnormal development of certain enterprises which encountered difficulties in finding outlets for their production. As labor was not scarce, wages did not rise in proportion to the cost of living. The exception occurred on July 20 when the Generalitat could no longer resist the syndicate's pressures and increased wages while reducing the daily hourly work requirements. Despite this measure, which could be described as demogogic even though understandable, the nominal wage levels during the war period only doubled the July 1936 levels. Real savings were affected in the labor sector since, as explained, the cost of living increased spectacularly. However, wages were supplemented by fringe benefits, owing to the increased worth of labor based on merit and individual initiative.

The working class accepted the attendant conditions of diminished consumption and decline in real purchasing power, particularly in those sectors that were not connected to the war effort or to the production of basic consumer goods.

The total labor strike was no longer a recurring possibility towards the end of 1937 as a result of the progressive mobilization dictated by the war, the gradual restoration of order in public administration, and the conversion of the economy. In contrast, there was a tendency toward partial strikes, caused by specific problems in individual businesses and not necessarily due to the state of a particular industry.

Despite the inherent difficulties, the Generalitat attempted to implement an economic policy that would institutionalize the revolution by integrating it with government actions. On November 20, 1936, the Catalan government approved the Decree of Exceptional Powers which empowered the prime minister and the minister of finance, Tarradellas, to propose measures designed to unify Catalonia's financial and political life. In accordance with this decree, the Tarradellas Plan or the Decree of S'Agaro was elaborated, consisting of fifty-eight items of ordinances and decrees dated January 8, 9, and 12, 1937.

These measures related to municipal life and the restoration of the Generalitat's constitutional powers concerning local government and municipal life; to the system of seizures and political responsibilities; to the credit system, encompassing banks, savings banks, and insurance companies; to regulation of the formal processes regarding governmental expenditures and tax collection (for the first time in Spain, a general tax on expenditures under the name of tax on business volume came into existence); to the structure of the Generalitat's Department of Finances; and to the establishment of a legal system affecting housing, radio broadcasting, public employees, and foreign trade.

Through these measures, the government hoped to restore authority and adapt public power to the realities of wartime conditions. In this manner, a certain stability would be achieved indirectly in the Catalan economy and finances, while war industries would be supported. Nevertheless, with the drop in industrial production in August 1937, it was advisable to intensify the application of economic policy measures by augmenting controls. The institutionalization of the economic structure was completed through the establishment of the General Councils of Industry as a liaison mechanism, together with the Economic Council, between the public governmental organizations and the private and collectivized firms. The intent to intervene in the economy is shown most clearly in the decree of November 20, 1937, the so-called Special Interventions. In October of that year, the first attempt at this type of intervention was effected through the Unified Electrical Services of Catalonia.

For the first time in its modern history, Catalonia created a war industry that would be able to expand and contract. The basis for this development was the construction of new industries and the adaptation of existing ones, making them all dependent on the War Industries Commission. In September 1936, this commission controlled twenty-four factories; a month later it controlled 500, with more than 50,000 workers, plus 30,000 who labored in auxiliary industries.

With respect to the effects of this development on the rest of the industrial complex, from September 1936 to October 1937, the output of Catalan industry reached a volume of 60 to 75 percent of the January 1936 level. This decline as well as related tendencies—from November 1936 because of the exhaustion of stocks and as of February 1937—must be rationalized as effects of the situation described above.

From October 1937 to March 1938, the index of industrial production varied between 55 and 60 percent relative to January 1936. Finally, from April to December 1938, industrial production dropped acutely. The causes for this drop were not only general ones derived from the war environment, but also specific ones relating to the loss of electrical energy stemming from the enemy's occupation of the power plants in western Catalonia. Nevertheless, the average decline in industrial output hid a qualitative phenomenon: the growth of the metallurgical sector until April 1937 when it reached an index of 130 percent in comparison with January of the previous year. From that date on, the metallurgical sector did not escape the general decline, but this particular behavior in this sector—owing to the need for meeting the demands of the machinery industry—was related to the demands of war and would be prolonged until the sector could no longer stand up under the pressure of the economic disequilibrium existing in Catalonia.

From September 1936 to March 1937, the government attempted to develop a self-sufficient economy. Still, as 1937 wore on, the instruments of direct intervention were reinforced. But tension, heightened by the high rise in the cost of living, caused adamant resistance to the new measures. The crisis hit its high point in May 1937, with the result that a new drop in industrial production occurred which could not be normalized without a change in prevailing trends. Nevertheless, in October 1937, as already mentioned, the policy of state intervention was intensified.

The direct expenses of the war, the industrial conversion, and the transition to socialism (objectives of Catalan society in 1936-1939 officially implemented by the Catalan government) were extraordinary. The government, in order to avoid tensions arising from liquidity, flooded this liquidity of the banks and savings institutions without at the same time expanding credit. This phenomenon is understandable because demand as well as offers of financial funds were channeled by many means affected by war.

In contrast, new official credit institutions created by the Generalitat during the war were to play an important role. The Office for the Regulation of Wage Payment, in effect since July 1936, would advance payroll funds. This was difficult to do because of the economic collapse and strikes. The Official Bank for Discounts and Mortgages, created on July 28, 1936, in addition to helping the Office for Regulation in the advance of payrolls, focused on short-term credit. The Bank of Reparations and Assistance, formed on January 9, 1937, concerned itself with the circulation of funds derived from expropriations for use in reconstructing war-damaged property in the home areas. A more ambitious institution was the Central Bank for Agricultural Credit, which was transformed by decree of October 5, 1937, into the Bank of Agricultural and Cooperative Credit and adapted the structure of the FESAC. It financed syndicated agriculture. The Bank for Industrial and Commercial Credit, formed by decree on November 10, 1937, granted medium and long-term credit to collectivized enterprises. Funds were obtained from the enterprises themselves since 50 percent of their profits were required to be transferred to this bank.

The official credit institutions thus filled the void left by the banks and savings institutions. But these official organizations, which exceeded 200 million pesetas in extended credit during the entire period, required public funds for financing, given the low level of deposits and other assets obtained from both the collectivized and private sectors. The additional funds were added to budgetary and extrabudgetary credits which had to be met by the Generalitat's autonomous treasury. Hence, from July 19, 1936, to November 30, 1938 (remember that Barcelona was occupied on January 26, 1939, and that on February 10 the Francoist army reached the French frontier), the Generalitat spent slightly more than 1,500 million pesetas for extrabudgetary items. This sum was added to the 500 million budgeted figure, reaching a sum that had to be met by the Generalitat to meet war expenditures. In turn this created extra requirements for credit on the ministries. Direct war expenditures exceeded 1,000 million pesetas, followed by 350 million in extrabudgetary items of the departments (especially social assistance) and approximately 150 million assigned to official credit agencies.

The sums allocated to the prosecution of the war totaled 300 million pesetas. In justifying the figure before the Catalan parliament on March 1, 1938, Tarradellas, in a public hearing, advised that "The expenditures incurred in this regard by the Generalitat could be considered as a capital investment of a reproductive kind, since it can provide an important contribution to the future functioning of the Catalan industrial system." But the Generalitat could only provide 250 million pesetas from its own income, about half of which was of budgetary origin thanks to new taxes set by the *S'Agaró* decrees. The tax on business volume alone produced 110 million pesetas, despite its weakness as a tax. There was no other alternative but to seek relief from third parties, especially the Ministry of Treasury of the Republic.

By decree of August 27, 1936, the Generalitat "intervened" in the Catalan branches of the Bank of Spain* and of the Delegation of the Ministry of Treasury itself in reaction to the Madrid* authorities' silence on the Catalan petitions for means of financing. "Intervention" in foreign trade originating in Catalonia generated a total of 1,056 million, and an additional 182 million pesetas was contributed monthly by the Republic's treasury, through the Valencia agreements of February 15, 1937, between representatives of the Republic and the Generalitat. The complex negotiations between the Republic and the Generalitat from June 1937 to November 1938 on continuing sources of funds were ended only when Francoist forces invaded Catalonia.

For further information, see Rafael Abella, *La vida cotidiana durante la guerra civil: La España republicana* (Barcelona, 1975); Josep María Bricall, *Política económica de la Generalitat* (Barcelona, 1970); Manuel Cruells, *La societat catalana durant la guerra civil* (Barcelona, 1978); Ronald Fraser, *Blood of Spain* (New York, 1979); Frank Minz, *La collectivisation en Espagne, 1936-1939* (Paris, 1967) and *L'autogestion dans l'Espagne revolutionnaire* (Paris, 1970); Albert Pérez Baro, *30 mesos de collectivisme a Catalunya (1936-39)* (Barcelona, 1970); and Hugh Thomas, *The Spanish Civil War* (New York, 1977).

See also Anarchists; Daily Life, Republican Spain; Economy, Republican; May 1937 Riots; Nutrition; and Peseta, Nationalist and Republican.

Josep M. Bricall

CATHOLIC CHURCH, SPANISH. The Spanish Catholic Church, a major ingredient of Spanish society, has always exerted considerable influence upon the state. Although its power had been waning since the mid-nineteenth century, church-state tensions proved to be a major impediment to the success of the Second Republic* and helped account for the defeat of the Republicans* in the Civil War.

Part of the strength of the Church derived from its use by monarchs as a force for unity among the diverse peoples of the Iberian Peninsula, and much of its vitality came from the vigorous role played by clerics and laity motivated by religious ideals throughout the course of Spanish history. The *reconquista* against the Moslems, the colonization and christianization of America, and the leadership provided for the Roman Church as a whole by such orders as the Spanish-founded Jesuits are examples of this strength and vigor. On the other hand, Spain's economic and geographical decline in the seventeenth and eighteenth centuries can be attributed partly to religious fanaticism: witness the expulsion of the Jews* and the Moors,* the Inquisition, and the anticapitalistic disdain for secular values.

Expressions of opposition to this fanaticism were frequently supported by monarchs in the eighteenth century, and they began to restrict the clergy's growth, economic power, and landholdings, a process interrupted by the Napoleonic invasion of 1808. In perhaps their greatest moment of glory, the clergy rallied the people to a defense against the French invaders, but anticlericalism had already become a stable policy of progressive governments. The political struggles of the nineteenth century frequently were manifestations of the ideological conflicts of progressive, anticlerical, and liberal groups fighting clerical, traditionalist, and conservative groups, as in, for example, the Liberal-Carlist Wars.

During the course of the nineteenth-century conflict, the clergy suffered a great disaster—the *desamortización*, or nationalization of their landed property. This loss changed the course of development of the Spanish Church: previously oriented towards the masses, the clergy now came to defend and depend upon the financial support of the middle and upper classes. They therefore preached to the working class a doctrine of acceptance of the harsh realities of a developing capitalistic economy and miserable living and working conditions. The clergy also lost a degree of independence—although traditionally the crown had control of clerical appointments since the mid-eighteenth century: they were now paid salaries by the state as a form of compensation for the *desamortización* and became, in effect, civil servants.

The clergy responded to these events by developing a defensive mentality that became a professional approach precluding the essence of Christian charity. They lost the support of the masses, who in turn were converted to the secular doctrines of socialism and anarchism. The masses occasionally directed their pent-up frustrations against the clergy in violent anticlericalism—either assassination or, more frequently, incendiarism. Church burning and the sacking of *conventos* (residences of the regular clergy) became a common feature of changes of government or times of social unrest. By the early twentieth century, there was a clear decline in the number of practicing Catholics, particularly in the working-class areas. It was commonly stated that religion had become the preserve of the rich. This generalization was not completely true, but it was believed to be so, and the people and governments acted accordingly. The masses saw the Church as a force of oppression, while the upper classes and bourgeoisie viewed it as one of the main pillars of social stability.

Still, despite the loss of the masses—a Western European-wide phenomenon, it should be pointed out—there were signs of vitality. By the 1920s, there was a group of progressive clerics and laymen who recognized the Church's problem and tried to find a solution. Nor were all areas of Spain affected in the same way. In the Basque provinces there was little disaffection, and most of the Basques were practicing Catholics. Social Catholicism, the idea that Christians had a special responsibility to help the poor and the helpless, was an accepted notion to a growing number of people. Finally, the hidden vitality of the Church cannot be overlooked. In times of crisis and persecution, the Church seemed to be able to rally large numbers of otherwise unconcerned people to its support.

The history of the Church in the twentieth century centered upon church-state relations and upon coping with the hostility of moderate political and violently social anticlericals. Until 1931, church-state relations were governed by the 1851 Concordat. In this outmoded agreement between the Vatican* and the Spanish government, the Church was recognized as the official state religion and the clergy was given control of education* in all state schools. In return, the government was given the privilege of nominating all ecclesiastical appointees. An effort was made in the Concordat to regulate the growth of the regular clergy—the religious orders and communities—who had become special targets of anticlerical hostility.

There was little overt political anticlericalism until the fall of the monarchy in 1931. Before that, government viewed the Church as a force for stability, although attempts to regulate the influx of regular clergy from anticlerical persecution in neighboring France* and Portugal* were made in the early 1900s. More frightening to the clergy were the violent attacks of incendiary anticlericalism such as occurred in Barcelona* during the Tragic Week of 1909, a church-burning frenzy touched off by middle-class anticlericals who convinced the proletarian army reservists that they were being sent to Morocco* to save Jesuit-owned enterprises. Further isolated incidents of violent anticlericalism in the 1910s and 1920s, including the as-

sassination of Cardinal Archbishop Soldevila of Saragossa,* were a disturbing backdrop to the course of Spanish politics.

When the Second Republic was proclaimed in 1931, the Church, as a most visible prop of the old regime, met hostility on all three fronts: church-state tensions, political anticlericalism, and violent social anticlericalism. Immediately, the provisional government unilaterally abrogated the Concordat of 1851 with a proclamation of religious freedom and various decrees secularizing civil functions. The anticlerical government proposed a list of reforms to be enacted into a constitution, and these were placed before the deputies elected to a Constituent Cortes* in June 1931. Although all of the ecclesiastical hierarchy counseled moderation and acceptance of the new Republic, the archbishop of Toledo and primate of Spain, Cardinal Pedro Segura,* coupled his counsel of moderation with a eulogy to the departed King Alfonso XIII.* This provocation, along with renewed political maneuvering of the monarchists and the activity of some *agents provocateurs*, caused a wave of violent anticlericalism. Incendiaries burned or attacked over a hundred churches and *conventos* in Madrid and southern Spain in early May 1931. No clerics were harmed; most were conducted to safety by sympathetic onlookers. The incendiaries were careful to burn no buildings until all inhabitants were evacuated. The government took no action to arrest the incendiaries or to prevent their attacks at first, for fear of antagonizing the general populace, whom they mistakenly thought supported the violence. The result of these riots was to convince most clerics and lay Catholics that the government did not deserve their support. Even though the clergy continued to counsel moderation, many did so out of weakness rather than conviction.

The moderate faction in the Church, led by Cardinal Frances Vidal i Barraquer,* archbishop of Tarragona,* Angel Herrera Ória,* editor of *El Debate** and a leader of *Acción Católica*, and the papal *nuncio*, Monsignor Federico Tedeschini, tried to prevent the more extremist faction led by Cardinal Segura from directly attacking the Republic. Segura's supporters, most of them strong monarchists who viewed the Church and monarchy as consubstantial, were angered by the Vatican's moderate position. When the government expelled Segura from Spain and removed both him and Bishop Mateo Múgica* of Vitoria* from their sees for their overtly anti-Republican political activities, the moderates tacitly supported the government's position. They encouraged the pope, Pius XI,* to pressure Segura to resign his see as a gesture of conciliation in the hope that an anticlerical Constitution would not be passed.

Segura was pressured into resignation, but this did not prevent the passage of an anticlerical Constitution. After acrimonious debate, in October 1931, the Constituent Cortes approved a Constitution that provided for the disestablishment of the Church, the abolition of clerical salaries, the dissolution of the Jesuits and the nationalization of their property, and a prohibition against the religious orders teaching in any schools, public or private. The Cortes also implicitly confirmed the provisional government's earlier decrees of such ambiguities as prohibitions against "public displays of religion." This legislation further alienated many Catholics from the Republic.

In the two years from 1931 to 1933 that followed the passage of the Constitution, the anticlerical Republican-socialist coalition periodically enacted the provisions of the Constitution. The Jesuits were dissolved, their property was nationalized (bringing in about 200 million pesetas), and their schools were closed. Clerical salaries were scheduled to be phased out by 1934. Numerous petty anticlericalisms were permitted on the local level. For example, in some of the more anticlerical communities, the wearing of crucifixes as ornamental jewelry was prohibited as a "public display of religion." In May 1933, the Cortes passed the Law of Religious Denominations and Congregations which implemented the constitutional provision against the religious orders and forbade the regular clergy from teaching in Spain after December 31, 1933. By this time, it had become clear that the Republican-socialists were using the issue of anticlericalism as the cement of the coalition. While they were disunited on practically all other issues, anticlericalism was the one issue they could agree upon.

The pope condemned the Law of Religious Denominations and Congregations along with the other anticlerical legislation and the outbursts of incendiary violence in an encyclical, *Dilectissima nobis* (June 1933). By this time, however, the moderate Catholics had placed their hopes in a political party, *Acción Popular*,* the central party of the *Confederación Española de Derechas Autónomas* (CEDA),* as the best means of combatting anticlericalism. Under José María Gil Robles,* who united the rightists under the slogan of defending the interests of religion, the CEDA won a plurality in the elections of 1933. But, because the party depended so heavily on avowed monarchist support, the CEDA never governed. The leftists feared that the CEDA would restore the monarchy if the party were to occupy the main ministerial positions. From 1933 to 1936, Gil Robles supported Radical ministries. Committed to and supported by moderate Catholics, he demanded as the price of his support that the

anticlerical legislation be suspended. Thus, the prohibition against the regular clergy's teaching was suspended; clerical salaries continued to be paid, now under the guise of pensions; and internal security was strengthened so that there were far fewer incidents of church burning. (Still, some thirty-seven clerics were killed and fifty-eight churches were burned or destroyed during the 1934 uprising of the Left against the entry of three CEDAists [Catholic party members] into the ministry.) Negotiations were opened with the Vatican for a new Concordat; however, given the instability of the government, little progress could be expected.

In the elections of February 1936,* the Popular Front* came to power after a campaign in which it had promised "full implementation" of the Constitution and amnesty for all political prisoners.* This promise clearly indicated anticlerical violence because the prisons were filled with anarchists* and other violent anticlericals, most of them arrested during the 1934 uprising, and violence frightened the clergy even more than the implementation of anticlerical legislation. Some church schools were closed, in some places the regular clergy was forbidden to work in charitable institutions, and incidents of petty anticlericalism increased. But the anticlerical violence was truly terrifying. Churches were burned in increasing numbers. Gil Robles claimed on the floor of the Cortes* that between February and June 1936, 160 churches or *conventos* had been totally destroyed and 251 partially ruined. In Madrid,* a nun was attacked after the rumor was spread that she was distributing poison candy to working-class children. Under these circumstances, it is hardly surprising that the clergy and concerned Catholics were happy to see the military uprising of July 1936 as a solution to the disorder and anticlerical violence.

The military uprising, although not a conspiracy involving the clergy, was popularly thought to be so. In the first few days of fighting, there were rumors that the army had used churches as arms depots, and since the clergy had never given wholehearted support to the Republic, clerics were attacked and church buildings burned and sacked. For decades, revolutionary mobs had attacked the churches and clergy as the first act of any revolution. The clergy was easily identifiable and did not fight back. The year 1936 was different only in the scale of the attack. Practically every church and *convento* in Republican Spain was burned, sacked, or closed. Many were turned into offices or warehouses or hospitals. In Madrid* alone, fifty churches and *conventos* were burned on July 19 and 20, 1936. In some places, the anticlerical fury became macabre as long-buried corpses were disinterred from tombs and militiamen dressed in priests' robes danced in the streets with nuns' mummies. Statues were smashed, priceless works of art* ruined. Worst of all, clergy were killed, and some were tortured to death on a larger scale than during any anticlerical fury in history. During the first six months of the war, until the fury abated, 6,832 clerics were killed. This number included thirteen bishops, 4,171 priests and seminarians, 2,365 monks, brothers, and priests of religious orders, and 283 nuns. In some areas, the proportions of assassinated clergy were as high as 80 percent of the total clergy. Overall, about 13 percent of the priests and 23 percent of the regular clergy were killed. In addition to these deaths, laymen known or suspected of activity in Church organizations were imprisoned and killed.

Given these facts, it is easy to understand why the clergy generally supported the Nationalists,* who, although not particularly religious or even anxious to restore clerical privileges, could hardly turn down such a valuable ally. In some areas, the anticlerical fury was the decisive issue in turning support away from the Republic to the Nationalists. As the war took on an international character, the persecution of the clergy and Catholics became an issue in persuading Republican sympathizers abroad to support nonintervention instead. Only in the Basque provinces did Catholics and clergy support the Republic in large numbers.

There was little tradition of anticlericalism among the Basques, although some fifty priests were killed by leftists there during the first three months of the war. The Basques supported the Republic because they were offered regional autonomy, a goal of the separatist Basques since the nineteenth century. During the Second Republic, before 1936, the Basques had tried to negotiate their own Concordat with the Vatican, so little did they feel in accord with the rest of Spain on the religious issue. Their stance supporting the Republic after 1936 angered the Nationalists who saw the Catholic "front" breached by divisiveness. The Carlist Navarrese were most particularly offended because they were as strongly Catholic as their Basque neighbors, and in the fighting between the two, the Carlists* gave no quarter. The archbishop of Toledo, Cardinal Isidro Gomá,* concerned about Basque support for the violently anticlerical Republicans, wrote a pastoral letter condemning the Basques' position and pressured Bishops Mateo Múgica of Vitoria and Marcelino Olaechea* of Pamplona* into signing the letter. The letter was then broadcast by radio* to the Basques, but they refused to accept it, believing it to be Nationalist propaganda. Gomá then demanded that

Múgica order the letter read in the churches. Múgica refused on the grounds that he could not put the priests in his diocese in jeopardy of their lives, and he was forced into exile in Rome. By early fall 1936, it was learned that some fourteen priests had been executed by the Nationalists for their support of Basque separatism. The scandal of these executions caused repercussions in the Vatican and slowed the progress of attempts to get the Holy See to grant diplomatic recognition to the Nationalist government. It was some months before Cardinal Gomá was able to smooth things over. But the Basques remained true to their faith. After the initial anticlerical fury, theirs was the only area of Republican Spain where Catholicism could be openly practiced without fear of reprisal.

Shortly before the Basque provinces fell to the Nationalists in 1937, Cardinal Gomá felt the need to make the Church's position clear and to inform the world of the reasons why the clergy supported the Nationalists. He wrote a letter that was signed by all of Spain's bishops except the three exiles: Cardinal Segura, in Rome without a see since 1931 (but soon to be named archbishop of Seville*), Cardinal Vidal i Barraquer, who had fled Catalonia* at the beginning of the war after having been arrested and then given safe conduct to Italy,* and Bishop Múgica, also exiled in Rome. Segura was not asked, and both Vidal and Múgica refused to sign the letter. This document, the Bishops' Collective Letter, formally issued on July 1, 1937, immediately after the fall of Bilbao,* stated that the Church desired peace and had counseled acceptance of the Republic despite all of the provocations of the anticlerical legislation, but that after the military uprising and the violent persecution of the clergy, the war had taken on the character of a struggle between Bolshevism and Christian civilization. The bishops alleged that a Soviet Russian conspiracy was behind the hatred and persecution that had made the clergy and the Church the chief victims of the leftist revolution. The Nationalists' rebellion against the Republic, they argued, was justified by the norms of a just war, and recourse to violence was the only path open to those who wanted to establish order and justice in Spain. In the course of their argument, the bishops denied statements made in the foreign press that the Church was on the side of the rich, that the Church owned one-third of the national territory, and that the clergy was recruited only from the wealthy.

Whatever effect this document had abroad, by 1938 the Nationalists were clearly close to victory, and Franco* began issuing decrees abolishing the Republican anticlerical legislation. The Vatican granted his government diplomatic recognition in 1938, and by the end of the war in 1939, the Church had become one of the main props of the Franco regime.

Most historians accept the argument that the Republican government made a political mistake by attacking the Church, not only with its anticlerical legislation, but also by not taking action to protect the churches from violent attack. By their negative response to Spain's religious problem, they gave the conservatives and the Right a rallying point—defense of religious rights—that had an emotional appeal beyond calculation. The clergy and the Church had been a threat to the progressive state in the nineteenth century, and the liberals of that era had nationalized clerical property and thereby stripped the Church of its economic power and forced the clergy into dependence upon the middle and upper classes. In contrast, the liberals and proletarians of the twentieth century had the opportunity of at least maintaining the neutrality of the clergy and even the possibility of winning them over, and they rejected both. The clergy was not blameless either. Having withstood poorly the nineteenth-century shocks and having developed a defensive mentality, they thereby let their professional interests predominate over their primary Christian duty to comfort the poor and oppressed, thus making themselves the targets of violent anticlericalism. The resulting tragedy prolonged the Civil War and probably affected its outcome.

For further information, see Gerald Brenan, *The Spanish Labyrinth* (Cambridge, England, 1951); Juan de Iturralde, *El catolicismo y la cruzada de Franco* (Vienna, 1955, 1960); Antonio Montero Moreno, *Historia de la persecución religiosa en España, 1936-1939* (Madrid, 1961); and José M. Sánchez, *Reform and Reaction* (Chapel Hill, N.C., 1964).

José M. Sánchez

CAUDWELL, CHRISTOPHER (CHRISTOPHER SAINT JOHN SPRIGG) (1907-1937). Caudwell, born Christopher Saint John Sprigg, was a British poet and a communist who served on the Republican side during the Civil War in the International Brigades.* He wrote novels and books on philosophy, aviation, and Marxian economics. Like most British intellectuals,* he believed that Franco's triumph would symbolize the decline of European civilization, and he was hostile to all forms of fascism and dictatorship. He was killed at the battle of Jarama* in February 1937, along with nearly a third of the British Battalion.*

For further information, see Hugh Thomas, *The Spanish Civil War* (New York, 1977).

See also, Communist Party, Spanish.

James W. Cortada

CAUSES. *See* Origins of the Spanish Civil War.

CAZORLA, JOSE (?-1939). Cazorla was the communist youth leader in Madrid* responsible for maintaining public order during the Civil War. He has been blamed for authorizing the execution of political prisoners held in Madrid during the early days of the war. This activity led to a public protest in April 1937 by the anarchist newspaper, *Solidaridad Obrera,* after its editors feared some anarchists* were being held in a private communist jail. Largo Caballero* restricted communist control over Madrid as a result of Cazorla's activities by dissolving the local defense council and returning responsibility for running the city to the town council composed of representatives from various political parties. The Nationalists* executed Cazorla in 1939.

For further information, see Hugh Thomas, *The Spanish Civil War* (New York, 1977).
See also Communist Party, Spanish.

James W. Cortada

CEDA. *See Confederación Española de Derechas Autónomas* (CEDA).

CENTAÑO DE LA PAZ, JOSÉ. Colonel Centaño was a Nationalist spy during the Civil War. He ran a factory in the Republican zone which manufactured precision equipment at Aranjuez for the Republican Army.* From 1938 onward, he also ran a spy-ring nicknamed "Lucero Verde." At the direction of Nationalist intelligence officers in Burgos* (1938-1939), he negotiated with various Republicans* for the surrender of military forces, particularly the Republican Air Force.* However, nothing came of these negotiations.

For further information, see José Manuel Martínez Bande, *Los cien últimas días de la república* (Barcelona, 1972).
See also Espionage; *Servicio de Información Militar* (SIM); and *Servicio de Información y Policía Militar* (SIPM).

James W. Cortada

CERVERA Y VALDERRAMA, JUAN (1870-1952). Cervera, a career naval officer in Nationalist service, was born on October 8, 1870, in San Fernando (Cádiz)* of an old naval family and was the nephew and son-in-law of Admiral Pascual Cervera of the Spanish-American War. Entering the navy at sixteen, Cervera rose through the ranks demonstrating technical and organizational competence. With the advent of the Republic in 1931, Vice-Admiral Cervera, a monarchist, chose retirement, but Navy Minister Casares Quiroga* persuaded him to return to duty as chief of the Cartagena* maritime department. Cervera retired again following the elections of February 1936.* Quietly settling in Puerto Real (Cádiz), he successfully defended his home during the July 1936 uprising and immediately offered himself to the Nationalist cause.

On October 15, 1936, Franco* appointed Cervera chief of staff of the Nationalist Navy,* with responsibility for organizing and administering the naval war. Cervera rapidly appointed a staff and attached himself to Franco's headquarters in Salamanca.* Cervera's highest priority, and therefore the operations of the Nationalist fleet, focused on the battle of supply. He maintained a respect for the Republic's naval potential and did not unduly risk his limited naval force. Although never trusting Italian intentions, Cervera pleaded vigorously and constantly for Italy* and German* to cede warships for his navy, and pressed for Axis clandestine naval warfare as an alternative, especially in November 1936 and August 1937. Italian and German naval officers assigned to aid the Nationalist naval war thought Cervera to be overly cautious and of declining ability, but he continued to enjoy Franco's confidence.

In 1939, at the close of the war, Cervera was promoted to the reestablished rank of admiral and retired for the final time. He died at his home in Puerto Real on November 18, 1952.

For further information, see Juan Cervera Valderrama, *Memorias de guerra* (Madrid, 1968).

See also Navy, German; Navy, Italian; Navy, Spanish; and Submarines, Foreign.

Willard C. Frank, Jr.

CEUTA. Ceuta is a port city in northwestern Morocco* located on the narrow Almina Peninsula and situated directly across the Straits from Gibraltar.* Acquired from Portugal* in 1580, it was an isolated Spanish garrison in the Sharifian Empire until 1913 when it became military headquarters for the Spanish Protectorate's western zone. In 1936, its population was 51,044. During the Civil War, its importance rested on its strategic position at the mouth of the Mediterranean Sea and its use as an embarkation port for the Army of Africa.* Since Moroccan independence in

1956, Ceuta has endured as one of Spain's few remaining *dominions* in Morocco.

For further information, see Manuel Gordillo Osuna, *Geografía urbana de Ceuta* (Madrid, 1972).

Shannon E. Fleming

CHAMBERLAIN, NEVILLE (1869-1940). Chamberlain was prime minister of Great Britain* from the spring of 1937 to 1940. During his tenure in office, the British government pursued more vigorously than before a policy of appeasement toward Hitler* and Mussolini.* Chamberlain believed that both dictators would be satisfied with certain territorial acquisitions—Italy* in Abyssinia and Hitler in Austria and parts of Central Europe*—and that therefore a major confrontation between the governments of the democratic republics and those of Germany* and Italy could be avoided. Spain was simply a pawn in this larger game of international relations.

In September 1937, Chamberlain supported the effort of negotiating with Germany and Italy, via the Nyon Conference,* a termination of submarine attacks on neutral shipping in the Mediterranean. A year later at the Munich Conference,* he in effect gave Hitler British permission to take over parts of Czechoslovakia.* As a result, both Spanish factions feared he might want to negotiate an end to the Civil War which would leave a divided Spain. Thus, both sides hardened in their attitude toward fighting the war. Clearly, Chamberlain refused to block the growth of fascism in Western Europe. Nowhere was this more apparent than in Spain where his government continued to pursue the charade of nonintervention and neutrality which, in effect, gave the USSR,* Italy, and Germany the freedom to intervene. As the war came to an end, Chamberlain concluded that relations with the Nationalists* would not be detrimental to Britain's interests. He therefore became one of the first prime ministers in Western Europe to recognize Franco's* government.

For further information, see Jill Edwards, *The British Government and the Spanish Civil War, 1936-1939* (London, 1979); Keith Feiling, *The Life of Neville Chamberlain* (London, 1946); Keith Middlemas, *Diplomacy of Illusion* (London, 1972); and K. W. Watkins, *Britain Divided* (London, 1963).

See also League of Nations; and Non-Intervention Committee.

James W. Cortada

CHILTON, HENRY (1877-1954). Sir Henry Chilton, the British ambassador to the Spanish Republic from

1935 to the fall of 1938, was an unimaginative diplomat, ultraconservative, and extremely pro-Nationalist in his sympathies. He did little to hide his approval of Franco.* Other foreign diplomats in Spain agreed that he never did anything to help the cause of the Republic once the Civil War began. Chilton believed that Franco would bring order and peace to Spain and thereby protect the commercial interests of Great Britain.* Throughout the early years of the war, he therefore urged closer ties to the Burgos* government.

Chilton did not hesitate to communicate quietly with the Nationalist government at Burgos. He would often send information to Burgos regarding British diplomatic actions concerning Spain. He hoped that the war would end quickly, and at one point he told the American ambassador Claude Bowers* that he hoped Hitler's* government would "send in enough Germans to finish the war." During 1937 and 1938, when the British expressed considerable concern about the effectiveness of Franco's blockade of Republican ports, Chilton reported to London that it was effective, particularly around Bilbao* at a point in time when in fact it was not. His reporting, however, made the British government take the blockade more seriously and thus discourage its shipping from entering the port with badly needed supplies of food.* In 1938, he finally retired from the diplomatic service. For a short period of time, the Nationalists* perceived his retirement as a signal that Britain was reluctant to draw closer to Franco.

For further information, see Claude G. Bowers, *My Mission to Spain* (New York, 1954); Jill Edwards, *The British Government and the Spanish Civil War, 1936-1939* (London, 1979); Sir Robert Hodgson, *Spain Resurgent* (London, 1953); and Sir Geoffrey Thompson, *Front Line Diplomat* (London, 1959).
See also Chamberlain, Neville.

James W. Cortada

CHRONOLOGY. *See* Appendix A.

CHURCH, THE. *See* Catholic Church, Spanish.

CHURCHILL, WINSTON (1874-1965). At the start of the Civil War, Churchill was a Conservative critic of the British government, which he believed should remain neutral in the conflict. He also found much to criticize with the Spanish Republic, believing it to be too revolutionary. He condemned German and Italian intervention in Spain, calling Mussolini's* troops "armed tourists." He approved of the British government's efforts to hold the Nyon Conference* in Sep-

tember 1937, as a means of curtailing the destruction of Great Britain's* ships in the Mediterranean by Italiam submarines.* By April 1938, the growth of the German-Italian danger to the peace of Western Europe* led Churchill to favor the Republic in its fight against the Nationalists.* He proved extremely critical of London's appeasement of Italy* and Germany* in Spain. At the time he was quoted: "Franco has all the right on his side, because he loves his country. Also Franco is defending Europe against the communist danger," adding "but I prefer that the other side wins because Franco could be an upset to British interests."

For further information, see Winston Churchill, *The Gathering Storm* (London, 1948).

James W. Cortada

CIANO, GALEAZZO (1903-1944). Count Ciano was Mussolini's* foreign minister during the Spanish Civil War and thus a major architect of Italy's* policy of support for the Nationalist cause. He endorsed the idea of supporting Franco* in an attempt to check the power of the Spanish Republic which had close ties to democratic France* and Great Britain.* In the early months of the war, he also ostensibly endorsed the activities of the Non-Intervention Committee,* although at the same time he urged the supply of men and weapons to Franco from Italy within government circles in Rome. In the fall of 1936, Ciano worked out a closer relationship with the German government, using Spanish affairs as a vehicle for cementing the Berlin-Rome Axis. In the following months, Ciano helped forge Italian policies of continued and expanded military support for the Nationalists.* More men came to Spain, and submarines* were assigned to waters off the Iberian coast sinking Republican and neutral shipping. Ciano continued, however, to publicly entertain Anglo-French thoughts on containment and final reduction of the fighting in Spain.

In September 1937, after months of severe losses to British and other neutral shipping, the British and French called a conference at Nyon, Switzerland,* to develop a plan to stop the destruction of ships. Italy attended and agreed to participate in an international patrol to stop the submarine actions which everyone knew were Italian in origin. Throughout 1938, Ciano hardly hid his enthusiastic support for the Nationalists, dedicated to a policy of pushing for their total victory in Spain.

Ciano had risen quickly to power within Italian fascist circles, spending perhaps too much time on his active social life. Historians collectively feel that he was searching for an opportunity to exhibit his self-perceived abilities and that the appeal for intervention by Franco seemed to be that perfect opportunity. His interest in the Spanish Civil War was intense, and his support for Franco remained strong even during World War II. His primary diplomatic objectives in Spain were to see that a communist regime did not take power in the Iberian Peninsula and that international tensions in Western Europe* not grow as a result of the Civil War. That Mussolini wanted to see another fascist regime come to power was apparently of only secondary importance to Ciano.

For further information, see Count Galeazzo Ciano, *Ciano's Hidden Diary, 1937-1938* (New York, 1953), *The Ciano Diaries, 1939-1945* (New York, 1946), and *Ciano's Diplomatic Papers* (London, 1948); James W. Cortada, "Ships, Diplomacy and the Spanish Civil War: Nyon Conference, September, 1973," *Il Politico* 37 (1973): 673-89; and John Coverdale, *Italian Intervention in the Spanish Civil War* (Princeton, N.J., 1975).

See also Nyon Conference.

James W. Cortada

CIUDAD REAL. Ciudad Real, the province located immediately below Toledo* in New Castile,* became a part of the Nationalist zone later than most regions in southern Spain, falling to Franco* on March 29, 1939. Prior to its occupation by the Nationalists,* the local bishop became one of thirteen in Spain murdered by Republican sympathizers along with other priests and nuns. After the Nationalist occupation, churches were reopened, and property seized by organized groups of laborers was returned to their original owners. Yet, while under Republican control, this primarily agricultural district successfully experimented with various forms of collectivization.

For further information, see Rafael Abella, *La vida cotidiana durante la general civil: La España republicana* (Barcelona, 1975).

See also Economy, Republican; and Peasantry, Aragonese.

James W. Cortada

CIUTAT DE MIGUEL, FRANCISCO (1909-   ). Colonel Ciutat, a career army officer, remained loyal to the Republic. Colonel Ciutat was also an adherent of the Communist party.* He was chief of staff of the Army of the North*; in this capacity he participated in the heavy fighting in northcentral Spain in 1937. In October of that year, with the seizure of Asturias* by the Nationalists,* this able staff officer left Spain

on an English vessel. He remained in exile throughout the period of Franco's* rule, living first in Great Britain and then in Latin America.

For further information, see José Manuel Martínez Bande, *La guerra en el norte* (Madrid, 1969) and *Vizcaya* (Madrid, 1971).

See also Army, Republican.

James W. Cortada

CIVIL GUARD (*Guardia Civil*). The Civil Guard was a paramilitary police* force within the Ministry of the Interior established in 1844 to patrol in rural communities. At the start of the Civil War, this unit (along with its urban version, the Assault Guards*) numbered 69,000 men. Of these, approximately 42,000 chose to support the Nationalists,* while the remaining 27,000 remained loyal to the Republic. In those sectors of Spain where often the only disciplined military force was the *Guardia Civil*, their choice of sides usually determined which faction controlled the community. Thus, wherever they favored the Nationalists, Franco* often gained power. Western Andalusia* clearly illustrated this pattern. In Badajoz,* the Civil Guard supported Franco,* while in Cáceres* they helped hold the province for the Republic. In Barcelona* they played an important role in suppressing the Nationalist uprising, while at the Alcázar* in Toledo* in September 1936 they held out against the Republicans.*

The Civil Guard was always commanded by regular army officers, while its enlisted ranks often contained ex-soldiers with combat experience in Morocco.* These green-uniformed men were frequently considered a hostile force in the community since they usually did not establish close ties to local residents. They never served in the provinces in which they were born and raised. Often brutal—or perceived to be—they were targets of criticism, and, during the 1930s, attacks by anarchists* and other radical groups were common. Thus, by July 1936, tremendous hostility had grown between the guards and rural communities, while the men of the paramilitary police thought of themselves as a combat unit under siege. When the Civil War began, however, their loyalties split much like that in the army generally. Combat veterans or those with close ties to the Falange* sided with the Nationalists. Others, like many of their counterparts in the army, remained loyal to the Republic. These choices proved essential to the Republic in retaining control of Barcelona and Madrid* but made it easy for Franco in Valencia* and in many parts of southern Spain where the local radicalized agricultural population had a history of attacking these men. Once the fighting got underway, the Republican Civil Guard (renamed the National Republican Guard) played a minor role, being superseded by the much larger forces of worker militias.* On the Nationalist side, however, the Civil Guard blended in quickly with the rebel army, participated in many of the campaigns of the Civil War, and was especially useful in establishing control over territories south and west of Madrid.

For further information, see Michael Alpert, *El ejército republicano en la guerra civil* (Barcelona, 1977), on the Republican forces; Joaquín Arrarás, *Historia de la cruzada español*, 35 folios (Madrid, 1940-1943), on the Nationalist side; and Hugh Thomas, *The Spanish Civil War* (New York, 1977), on their size and distribution.

See also Andalusia; Army, Nationalist; Army, Republican; and Peasantry, Aragonese.

James W. Cortada

CLARIDAD (1935-1939). *Claridad* was a socialist newspaper established in Madrid* by Francisco Largo Caballero* in 1936 to publicize his views. By the summer of 1936, it had become a major Republican newspaper. Against the wishes of many officials of the Republic, especially in the Republican Army,* it often editorialized on the need to arm the young socialists and communists in 1936. Its editor was Carlos de Baráibar,* a close friend of Largo Caballero. As long as Largo Caballero was prime minister of the Republic (1936-1937), the paper enjoyed wide circulation. After the communists reduced his political power, the influence of the paper waned and eventually it came under the control of a communist editor.

For further information, see Burnett Bolloten, *The Spanish Revolution: The Left and the Struggle for Power During the Civil War* (Chapel Hill, N.C., 1979).
See also Socialist Party, Spanish.

James W. Cortada

CLINICAL HOSPITAL. The Clinical Hospital, located in Madrid* near the university, was in the center of the fighting in November 1936. As the point of deepest penetration by Nationalist forces attempting to seize the city of Madrid, considerable fighting took place there. The Nationalists* failed to occupy Madrid and soon after retreated to beyond the boundaries of the city. Failure to take Madrid prolonged the Civil War considerably beyond what either side had originally anticipated.

For further information, see Robert G. Colodny, *The Struggle for Madrid* (New York, 1958); and Dan Kurzman, *Miracle of November: Madrid's Epic Stand, 1936* (New York, 1980).

James W. Cortada

CODOVILLA, VITTORIO (1894-1972). Codovilla was the Comintern's representative in Spain throughout the Civil War. An Argentine citizen of Italian heritage, he had many years of experience organizing communist parties in Latin America* and came to Spain for the same purpose. Codovilla became particularly successful after the elections of February 1936* when the Spanish Communist Party* grew rapidly. Known in Spain as "Medina," he was enormously fat with a large appetite and middle-class habits. He helped establish the Popular Front* in prewar Spain. Santiago Carrillo,* then a socialist and in the 1960s and 1970s head of Spain's Communist party, admitted Codovilla's role in converting him to communism. As communism grew into a major political force in Republican Spain, the organizational skills of such men as Codovilla and others from the Comintern proved helpful. Stalin* employed Codovilla to execute Soviet policy in Spain, allowing him to help the Republic when it was advantageous to do so and withholding support as appropriate for Soviet interests. Codovilla helped organize the party's administrative structure, recruited communist volunteers* for the International Brigades,* and raised money for various activities in Spain.

When, in early 1937, the Spanish Communist party decided to work for the removal of Largo Caballero's* government and for its replacement with a friendlier one, Codovilla participated in the political planning sessions involved. After the end of the war, he returned to Buenos Aires, remaining there until his death in 1972.

For further information, see Burnett Bolloten, *The Spanish Revolution: The Left and the Struggle for Power During the Civil War* (Chapel Hill, N.C., 1979); and Manuel Tagüeña, *Testimonio de dos guerras* (Mexico, 1973).

James W. Cortada

COLLECTIVES. *See* Anarchists; Catalonia; Economy, Republican; Libertarian Movement: Peasantry, Aragonese; and Workers, Catalan.

COLLECTIVIZATION. *See* Aragón; Catalonia; Peasantry, Aragonese; and Workers, Catalan.

COMMERCE. *See* Economy, Nationalist; Economy, Republican; and Industry, Republican.

COMMISSION OF INQUIRY INTO ALLEGED BREACHES OF NON-INTERVENTION AGREEMENT IN SPAIN. The Commission of Inquiry into Alleged Breaches of Non-Intervention Agreement in Spain was established in September 1936 by the communist organization, Comintern, in London to bring pressure on the British government not to violate the neutrality agreement reached among the Western powers to stay out of the Spanish Civil War. It was part of a series of coordinated efforts by Communist parties in Western Europe* in the summer and fall of 1936 to create friendlier relations between France* and Great Britain* with the USSR,* which was then attempting to foster an alliance directed against Hitler's* Germany.* Moscow's concern was that Germany might expand its territorial holdings eastward in Europe at the expense of the Soviet Union. Thus, the commission was a public gesture of support to the British government and to the Labour party.

The commission had a prestigious membership, which included Philip Nöel Baker, Eleanor Rathbone, Geoffrey Bing, John Langdon-Davis, other intellectuals,* lawyers, journalists, and professors. Members were generally drawn from liberal and communist backgrounds, and the organization remained small. The commission did little to influence events in Great Britain and thus simply was a tactic on the part of the British communist movement. The Spanish Republic reacted to the formation of the commission by stating that it would accept nonintervention by the democracies, providing this did not mean a prohibition of arms sales to Madrid.* The Republic, however, received little help from the commission since most British citizens did not want arms sold to either side in the Civil War.

For further information, see Jill Edwards, *The British Government and the Spanish Civil War, 1936-1939* (London, 1979); Hugh Thomas, *The Spanish Civil War* (New York, 1977); and K. W. Watkins, *Britain Divided* (London, 1963).

See also League of Nations.

James W. Cortada

COMMUNE DE PARIS BATTALION. The Commune de Paris Battalion made up part of the ranks of the International Brigades* which contained more volunteers* from France* (9,000 to 10,000) than from any other nation. This battalion was the first and best known of the units in which the International Bri-

gades fought. Originally used for a *centuria* (large company) formed in Barcelona* in early September 1936, the name was carried on into the French-speaking battalion of the 11th IB when it marched into Madrid* on November 7. In the bitter and successful struggle to blunt the rebel attempt to capture the capital city, the French played an important role, first counterattacking against Moorish troops in West Park, then digging in to hold the lines in University City.

Despite heavy casualties,* the battalion was in combat for almost four straight months as the Loyalists* strove to hold Madrid. Mid-December saw the French at the forefront of the brutal fight over Boadilla del Monte,* west of the city. Early in January, they were rushed to the defense of the road from Corunna,* and the first week in February they were briefly sent southeast to the faroff Murcia* front. By this time, deaths and injuries had claimed so many volunteers that Spanish recruits composed fully half the battalion, a percentage that would continue to increase for the rest of the war. Recalled to the Madrid area, the battalion entered the battle of the Jarama River* Valley that helped to save the capital city's lifeline to Valencia.* In March, it played a role in the decisive defeat of Mussolini's* expeditionary force near Guadalajara.*

Late in the spring of 1937, the battalion, as part of a reshuffling of the Internationals along linguistic lines, was transferred to the 14th International Brigade, which included Belgian, Swiss, and Moroccan volunteers. Commanding the brigade was Jules Dumont, a former French Army colonel who had led both the original *centuria* and, until wounded in January 1937, the Commune de Paris Battalion. By this time, however, the great days of the unit were in the past. Too spent to take part in the summer 1937 government offensives, the French did help to block still another thrust at Madrid near Cuesta la Reina in October. After that, they played a minimal role in the war, although the battalion did cross the Ebro as part of the last-gasp Loyalist offensive in July 1938.

For further information, see Jacques Delperrie de Bayac, *Les brigades internationales* (Paris, 1968); and *Épopée d'espagne* (Paris, 1957).

See also Appendix B.

Robert A. Rosenstone

COMMUNIST PARTY, SPANISH. The Spanish Communist party (*Partido Comunista Española*—PCE) was founded in 1921 by several dissident groups within the socialist movement as well as by a faction of Leninist-inspired syndicalists* from the *Confederación Nacional del Trabajo* (CNT).* In April 1920, a certain number of militant, antiparliamentary members of the *Federación de Juventudes Socialistas* (FJS) seceded from the Spanish Socialist party or the *Partido Socialista Obrero Español* (PSOE),* when they created the Spanish Communist party. A year later, another splinter group from the PSOE formed the *Partido Comunista Obrero Español* (PCOE).* At a conference held on November 7-14, 1921, these two communist groups were finally amalgamated into the Spanish Communist party.

A minor factor in Spanish politics before the Civil War, with only sixteen seats in the Cortes* and an officially estimated membership of 40,000 on July 18, 1936, the Communist party was soon to mold decisively the course of events in the camp of the anti-Franco forces.

From its inception, the Spanish Communist party followed the directives of the Communist International so closely that their policies were identical. During the 1920s, it espoused a fiery brand of Marxism* that conformed to the Left extremism advocated by the Comintern during the period 1920-1934, calling for the establishment of soviets. Subsequently, after the Comintern adopted the moderate proposals adumbrated in the Popular Front* program at its Seventh World Congress in August 1935, aimed at improving Soviet relations with the Western democracies and offsetting the growing threat of Nazi Germany,* it modified its revolutionary stance. In the months before the Civil War, the fundamental dilemma facing the party was how to remain in touch with the revolutionary temper of the working class without contradicting the moderate Popular Front policies to which it was bound.

One of its main objectives was to absorb the left wing of the socialist movement led by Francisco Largo Caballero.* So cordial were their official relations before the outbreak of the conflict that the Left socialist leader had encouraged the fusion of the socialist and communist trade-union federations as well as the merging of the two parties' youth organizations. Moreover, in March 1936, the Caballero-controlled Madrid* section of the Socialist party had decided to propose the fusion of the Socialist and Communist parties at the next national congress. The communists themselves strongly advocated this merger. But, in spite of the smooth course of official relations, the communists were disturbed by the Left socialist leader's agitation in favor of an immediate social overturn and, in private, characterized his ultrarevolutionary tendencies as "infantile leftist."

With the advent in July 1936 of the Civil War and revolution, the underlying differences between the communists and the left-wing socialists were thrown into sharp focus, for whereas the Left socialists took the stand that the democratic Republic and no longer any *raison d'être*, the communists argued that the social overturn was not a proletarian, but rather a bourgeois, democratic revolution. According to Dolores Ibárruri (La Pasionaria),* a member of the Spanish politburo, the revolution that was taking place was a bourgeois democratic revolution such as was achieved earlier in other countries.

As a result, the Spanish communists ran afoul of the social revolution. This meant violating venerable Marxist principles, but Stalin* knew that as long as the Spanish government was recognized as the legally constituted authority by the democratic powers, it could insist on its right to purchase arms. He also knew that, if Great Britain* and France* were to abandon their policy of neutrality, the Civil War might develop into a European conflict from which he would emerge the arbiter of the Continent. It was therefore essential that democratic forms be preserved and that the president of the Republic, Manuel Azaña,* remain in office.

Although the left-wing opponents of the Spanish Communist party charged it with planning to reestablish the old regime, its goal was, in fact, far more subtle; for, under cover of a democratic superstructure, it aimed at controlling the principal elements of state power. This meant permeating the government, replacing the revolutionary police* squads and militia by a state police and a regular army, establishing state control over ports and frontiers, destroying the collective farms, dissolving the workers' committees in the collectivized enterprises, and, finally, nationalizing the basic industries. Nationalization, like decollectivization, would enable the government to undermine the left wing of the revolution at one of the principal sources of its power.

In pursuit of their objectives, the communists launched a campaign to win the support of the middle classes. By championing their interests—a stand few Republicans dared to assume in the prevailing revolutionary atmosphere—within a few months the Spanish Communist party became the refuge (according to its own figures) of 76,700 peasant proprietors and tenant farmers and of 15,485 members of the urban middle classes. The socialist historian Antonio Ramos Oliveira concluded that the middle class was surprised and pleased by the moderate tone of the Communist propaganda and the unity and realism of the party, and thus joined in large numbers.

That the Communist party's influence among the middle classes went far beyond the aforementioned figures is indubitable, for thousands of members of the intermediate classes in both town and country placed themselves under its wing without actually becoming adherents of the party. In the rich orange- and rice-growing province of Valencia,* for example, where the farmers were prosperous and had supported right-wing organizations before the Civil War, by March 1937 a total of 50,000 had joined the Peasant Federation, which the Communist party had set up for their protection in the first months of the revolution. In addition to providing its members with fertilizers and seed and securing credits from the Ministry of Agriculture—likewise controlled by the communists— the Peasant Federation served as a powerful instrument in checking the rural collectivization promoted by the agricultural workers of the province.

From the very outset of the revolution, the Spanish Communist party, like the PSUC, the *Partit Socialista Unificat de Catalunya** (the communist-controlled United Socialist party of Catalonia*), also took up the cause of the urban middle classes. To protect their interests in this region, the communists organized 18,000 tradesmen, handicraftsmen, and small manufacturers into the *Federación Catalana de Gremios y Entidades de Pequeños Comerciantes y Industriales* (GEPCI),* some of whose members were, in the phrase of *Solidaridad Obrera,** the CNT* organ, "intransigent employers, ferociously antilabor."

There is little doubt that the communists' support of the urban and rural middle classes was pragmatic rather than altruistic, for they were concerned above all with strengthening their position vis-à-vis their anarchosyndicalist and Left socialist opponents. The communists were thus acting in accordance with the Leninist dictum that the enemy can be conquered only by "taking advantage of every, even the smallest opportunity of gaining a mass ally, even though this ally be only temporary, vacillating, unstable, unreliable and unconditional."

The communists did what they could to preserve the Liberal Republican government of José Giral* formed on July 19. Together with the moderate socialists, they succeeded for a time in shoring up his shaky administration through their work within the ministries in unofficial but vital capacities, but by the end of August the government had lost most of its political credibility.

On September 4, Francisco Largo Caballero formed a new government. The fact that the Spanish Communist party held only two portfolios (Vicente Uribe* became minister of agriculture and Jesús Hernández Tomás* headed the Ministry of Education and Fine Arts) was no real index of its strength in the country. This was true either at the time the cabinet was con-

stituted, when the number of its adherents had swollen far beyond the prewar total of 40,000, or in March 1937, when, with an officially estimated membership of nearly a quarter of a million, it became the strongest political party in the Republican camp. According to José Díaz,* its general secretary, the precise figure was 249,140, of which 87,660 (35.2 percent) were industrial workers; 62,250 (25 percent) agricultural laborers; 76,700 (30.7 percent) peasants; 15,485 (6.2 percent) members of the urban middle classes; and 7,045 (2.9 percent) intellectuals* and members of the professional classes.

As we have already seen, the communists were able to attract new recruits among the middle classes largely because their party offered the hope of salvaging, as Louis Fischer observed, some of the remnants of the old system. An even greater number of sympathizers was swayed by the party's skillful propaganda, its organizing capacity, and the prestige and power it derived from Soviet arms.

Hardly inferior as a source of strength was the impotence of the Republican parties. From the inception of the conflict, the Liberal Republicans, lacking influence among the masses, had retired into the background— or, as Henry Buckley, a friend of the Spanish Republic, put it, they "remained in a comatose state throughout the war." They ceded to the communists the delicate work of opposing the left wing of the revolution and defending the interests of the middle classes. The political impotence of the Republican leaders is best reflected in the public pronouncement of the president of the Left Republican party: "The slight resistance we offered to the assaults of other organizations, our silence and our aloofness in face of the daring advances of the audacious led many persons to believe that we no longer existed."

Within the Left camp, the communists encountered few major obstacles in their drive to achieve political hegemony. The anarchosyndicalists, weakened by differences of principle and without centralized direction, were an unequal match for the communists with their monolithic organization, their cohesion, and, above all, their discipline. Thus, despite their numerical strength, the anarchosyndicalists could not compete with an organization such as the Spanish Communist party, which was guided and bolstered by some of the best brains from the communist cadres of other countries.

Early in the war, the socialists, despite anarchosyndicalist claims to the contrary, were probably still the strongest force in the capital and in Old and New Castile.* Nevertheless, their dominating position was soon undermined by open and secret defections to the

Spanish Communist party, for which their own passivity was in some degree responsible. The principal source of their political vulnerability lay in the factional strife within their party. In the hands of the centrists led by Indalecio Prieto,* the executive committee was in a state of irreconcilable belligerence, with local units sympathetic to Largo Caballero. The communists took full advantage of these divisions. Referring some years after the war to the dissensions among the leaders of the Socialist party, Jesús Hernández explained later that he benefited "from their suicidal antagonisms," playing one group against another, causing various elements to destroy each other.

In order fully to understand how the communists were able to deal so effectively with their political opponents, one must bear in mind the power that experienced Comintern representatives exercised over the Spanish politburo. According to the Peruvian communist, Eudocio Ravines, who worked on the staff of the Communist organ *Frente Rojo*, Boris Stefanov, a Bulgarian, one of Stalin's closest friends, was in Spain, and was in charge of many activities of the Communist party. He was considered the direct representative of Stalin. Equally important was the fact that Palmiro Togliatti,* the Italian communist and member of the Executive Committee of the Comintern, was also active in Spain, especially after the departure of the Argentinian representative, Vittorio Codovilla,* in 1937, when he became the virtual head of the party, directing strategy and writing many of the speeches of José Díaz and La Pasionaria. In the opinion of the American Communist John Gates, head commissar in 1938 of the 15th Brigade, Togliatti was the most powerful communist figure on the Spanish scene. He could take credit for much of the growth in size and power of the Spanish Communist party after the start of the Civil War. Togliatti was brilliant, and, in Gates' opinion, was one of the world's most able communists.

The communists were especially interested in gathering into their hands all the elements of state power that had been appropriated by the revolutionary committees at the outbreak of the Civil War and in reconstructing the shattered machinery of state. The communist view, shared by socialists and Republicans, was that the revolutionary committees, which in most cases were dominated by the more radical members of the CNT and *Union General de Trabajadores* (UGT)* and whose authority was practically unlimited in their respective localities, should give way to regular organs of administration, in which all the parties forming the government would be represented.

In November 1936, the anarchosyndicalists entered the Caballero government partly in the hope of preserving the revolutionary committees, which they regarded as the foundation stones of the new society. But once inside the cabinet, the CNT-FAI ministers yielded step by step to their opponents, who applied constant pressure to end the power of the committees on the ground of placating foreign opinion and enhancing the government's prospects of securing arms from the Western powers. As a result, the government, far from giving legal validity to the committees as the CNT had hoped on entering the cabinet, provided for their dissolution and replacement by regular provincial and municipal councils. All the parties adhering to the Popular Front* as well as the trade-union organizations were to be represented in the councils.

In addition to these measures, the communists believed that it was also necessary to break the power of the committees in the factories by bringing the collectivized enterprises, particularly in the basic industries, under government control. But they also knew that in order to impose the will of the government, it was first of all necessary to reconstruct the police corps and the regular army.

Shortly after taking office, Largo Caballero, at the urging of the communists, sought to bring the independent squads and police patrols of the working-class organizations under government control. Decrees were passed that soon proved to be but a preparatory step toward the dissolution of these groups and their incorporation into the armed forces of the state. Members of the Communist, Socialist, and Republican parties were quick to avail themselves of the opportunity to enter the official police corps. The communists, in particular, secured pivotal positions: Lieutenant Colonel Burillo* became Madrid's police chief; Justiniano García and Juan Galán were made chief and subchief, respectively, of the Interior Ministry's intelligence department; while two other communists were appointed to vital posts in the police administration. One became commissar-general in the Department of Security, the *Dirección General de Seguridad*, and the other became head of the training center of the Secret Police school, the *Escuela de Policía*, that formed the cadres of the new secret police corps. From the time of its creation, this corps became an arm of the Soviet secret police, which established itself in Spain quite early in the war.

While the communists were penetrating the police apparatus, they were calling for the militarization of the militias* and their fusion into a regular army. During the life of the Giral cabinet, the communists had refrained from calling for the merging of the militia into a government-controlled army because of the Caballero socialists' distrust of that cabinet's intentions. Once the Left socialist leader himself was at the helm and in charge of the War Ministry, they could do so without equivocation. Indeed, the two communist ministers and the Soviet military advisers, in urging their demands, made full use of the succession of defeats on the central front. They were thereby successful in getting measures passed for the militarization of the militia and the creation of a Popular Army, as it was called, on a conscripted basis and under the supreme command of the war minister.

To set an example, the Spanish Communist party progressively broke up its own militia, the Fifth Regiment,* which was the most efficiently organized and highly disciplined armed force on the Republican side. Enrique Líster,* the communist head of the regiment at the time, was made commander (with a Soviet officer at his side) of the 1st Brigade. Because they took the initiative in disbanding their own militia, the communists, according to the regiment's chief political commissar, Vittorio Vidali (known in Spain as Carlos Contreras), secured for themselves the control of five of the first six "Mixed Brigades"* of the embryonic army.

While they were thus gathering into their hands the control of the first units of the Popular Army, the communists were not neglecting its commanding summits. In fact, during the early weeks of Largo Caballero's taking office, they had already secured a promising foothold. This they were able to do largely because they possessed men of supposedly unquestioned loyalty to Largo Caballero in key positions in the War Ministry. These included such professional officers as Lieutenant Colonel Manuel Arredondo, his aide-de-camp, and Major Manuel Estrada,* the chief of the War Ministry general staff, who, unknown to Largo Caballero, were being drawn or had already been drawn into the communist orbit.

The communists also became firmly embedded in the General Commissariat of War, set up for the purpose of exercising political control over the armed forces through the medium of political commissars. This they achieved mainly because Julio Álvarez del Vayo,* one of Caballero's trusted advisers, who also served as foreign minister and commissar-general, secretly promoted the interests of the Spanish Communist party by appointing an inordinate number of communist commissars.

There can be little doubt that the communists' success in controlling critically important levers of the Popular Army was aided by their monopoly over the acquisition and distribution of Soviet supplies and

arms and by the pressure of Soviet representatives. Largo Caballero noted that the government frequently bowed to foreign pressures for fear of otherwise losing Russian assistance.

In their efforts to control the military apparatus, the communists found a formidable adversary in Largo Caballero. The socialist premier, after having been forced by the Soviet ambassador to remove General José Asensio,* his undersecretary of war, attempted to take action against communist influence by dismissing their votaries from important posts in the War Ministry and the General Commissariat of War. He also incurred the wrath of the communists when he refused Stalin's personal request to promote the fusion of the Socialist and Communist parties.

As Largo Caballero posed a threat to their designs, the communists launched a campaign to oust him from the premiership. A suitable opportunity came with the eruption of armed conflict in Barcelona,* the semiautonomous region of Catalonia* and stronghold of the anarchosyndicalists.

The May 1937 riots, known as the May events, were the culmination of social tensions that had been brewing in the region for several months. On the one side stood the revolutionary forces represented by the CNT and the Marxist *Partido Obrero de Unificación Marxista* (POUM).* On the other stood the Catalan communists of the PSUC and the Liberal Republicans of the Esquerra.* The resulting hostilities gave the communists sufficient pretext to press the Largo Caballero government to establish police and military authority in Catalonia.

At a cabinet meeting in Valencia, the communist ministers demanded the dissolution of the POUM, arguing that it was a gang serving international fascism. Although Largo Caballero made every effort to resist communist pressure, his hope of averting a government crisis was to no avail, and he was soon forced to resign from the government.

After the power of the anarchosyndicalists had been broken in Catalonia and the government of Largo Caballero had been replaced by that of Juan Negrín,* an ally of the communists, the offensive against the revolutionary conquests was stepped up. In August 1937, the communist-controlled 11th Division headed by Enrique Líster destroyed the collective farms in neighboring Aragón,* including those that had been formed voluntarily. The situation became so serious that José Silva, the communist general secretary of the Institute of Agrarian Reform,* confessed that this action was an error which disrupted the countryside. People took over the collectives on their own, seizing farm implements and harvests without respecting the collectives. Consequently, little work was done in the fields.

To redress the situation, the Communist party was forced to modify its policy, and some of the dismantled collectives were restored. But the hatreds and resentments generated by the breakup of the collectives and by the repression that followed were never wholly dispelled.

Under the second Negrín government, formed in April 1938, the economic gains in the urban centers came under increased assault. In keeping with its policy of attempting to gain the support of Great Britian and France, the government tried to conciliate foreign capital. It decreed that the foreign hydroelectric enterprises, operated in Catalonia by the CNT, be decollectivized and returned to their former owners, but, confident of General Franco's* ultimate victory, the companies involved ignored the gesture. Simultaneously, government comptrollers were appointed to decollectivize and nationalize certain Spanish enterprises, while others were returned to their original owners. Although comparatively few concerns were involved, because many of the owners had either been killed or had fled to Nationalist territory, the mere threat of rolling back the economic conquests of the revolution caused dismay in the libertarian movement.*

Although the communists held only the two seats in the first Negrín government, this was deceptive, for, in addition to retaining all the pivotal positions in the police administration they had held under Largo Caballero, Lieutenant Colonel Antonio Ortega,* a party member, was named director-general of security. As for the military apparatus, although Indalecio Prieto held the Defense Ministry, Álvarez del Vayo kept his key post as head of the General Commissariat of War. Furthermore, Colonel Antonio Cordón,* a Communist party member, whom Largo Caballero had removed from the technical secretariat of the undersecretaryship of war, was reappointed to that post. Captain Eleuterio Díaz Tendero of the Information and Control Department was also reinstated.

Within a few months of entering the Defense Ministry, Prieto, provoked by the proselytism and crescent power of the communists in the armed forces, removed Álvarez del Vayo from his post as well as Francisco Antón, the inspector-commissar on the Madrid front, who was secretary of the Madrid Communist party organization. He also ousted a number of other communist or procommunist political commissars and high-ranking officers, including Alejandro García Val, the director general of military transportation, Eleuterio Díaz Tendero, and Antonio Cordón, who was now chief of staff of the Army of the East.* The last two

officers, it will be recalled, had been removed by Largo Caballero before being reappointed by Prieto after the May crisis. Furthermore, defying Soviet threats, Prieto discharged Major Gustavo Durán,* the head of the Madrid section of the *Servicio de Investigación Militar* (SIM)*—the military investigation service he had formed on the advice of the Russians—for naming hundreds of communist agents.

Faced by Prieto's enmity towards them, the communists, backed by Negrín, ousted him from the Defense Ministry in April 1938. In the cabinet reshuffle that followed Prieto's resignation, the communists held only one portfolio. Once again, they appeared to be only a minor factor in the cabinet, whereas, in reality, they controlled more levers of command than before. Premier Negrín took over the Defense Ministry, pursuing what Prieto called an "insensate policy of assuring the predominance of one party." He elevated Antonio Cordón to the undersecretaryship of war, promoted Carlos Nuñez Maza to the undersecretaryship of air, and appointed Pedro Prados* to the post of Navy chief of staff; all three were Communist party members. Furthermore, Díaz Tendero, ousted by Prieto from the vital Information and Control Department, reappeared as head of the no less sensitive personnel section of the Defense Ministry. But more conspicuous than all these appointments was that of Jesús Hernández, who left the Ministry of Education to become chief political commissar of the Army of the Center,* which represented 80 percent of the land forces.

As for the Ministry of the Interior, although Paulino Gómez, a moderate socialist, headed this department, the communists retained all their pivotal positions in the police apparatus, including the post of director-general of security, now occupied by Eduardo Cuevas de la Peña, a party member.

The Finance Ministry went to Negrín's intimate, the Left Republican Francisco Méndez Aspe,* who had been involved in the shipment to Moscow of Spanish gold reserves. Méndez appointed Marcelino Fernández, a PSUC member, to head the *Carabineros* (Custom Guards), the most powerful force of public order. Álvarez del Vayo returned to the Foreign Ministry and, in addition to maintaining communist control in the foreign propaganda press agency, the *Agencia Española*, and in the foreign press bureau, gave Negrín's close collaborator, Manuel Sánchez Arcos, a party member, the important post of undersecretaryship of propaganda.

The following months saw a rapid decline in communist strength, largely because of the succession of military defeats and the communists' deteriorating popular image.

In this climate of dissolution, Negrín, at the behest of the politburo, which in turn obeyed the orders of Togliatti and Sergie Stefanov, decreed the promotion of two prominent communists, Antonio Cordón and Juan Modesto,* to the rank of general, and a number of other leading communist officers, including Enrique Lister and Francisco Galán,* to the rank of colonel. Fearing a communist coup, Colonel Segismundo Casado,* the commander of the Army of the Center, who had been conspiring with the socialist, Republican, and anarchosyndicalist leaders to overthrow Negrín, formed a National Council of Defense. The council included such prominent figures as General Miaja,* the socialists Julián Besteiro* and Wenceslao Carrillo, the Republicans Miguel San Andrés and José del Rio, and the anarchosyndicalists Eduardo Val and González Marín, in the hope of negotiating a surrender without reprisals.

Within hours, Negrín and his communist entourage, including Togliatti, Stefanov, and La Pasionaria, escaped by plane. So swift was their departure that no directives were given to the Madrid party organization, which, aided by communist military units, tried in vain to overthrow the Defense Council.

In the face of General Franco's insistence on unconditional surrender, the efforts of the council were aborted. On April 1, Franco declared that the war had ended.

For further information, see Burnett Bolloten, *The Spanish Revolution: The Left and the Struggle for Power During the Civil War* (Chapel Hill, N.C., 1979); Enrique Castro, *Hombres made in Moscú* (Mexico, 1960) for a picture of the Communist party from the viewpoint of some of the participants of the war; David Cattell, *Communism and the Spanish Civil War* (Berkeley, Calif., 1955), a general account; Cesare Colombo, *Storia del partito comunista spagnolo* (Milan, 1972), a general account; José Díaz, *Tres Años de lucha* (Paris, 1969), a war participant's viewpoint; Guy Hermet, *Los comunistas en España* (Paris, 1972), a general account; Jesús Hernández, *Yo fuí un ministro de Stalin* (Mexico, 1953); Dolores Ibárruri (La Pasionaria), *El único camino* (Paris, 1962), a war participant's viewpoint; Gerald Meaker, *The Revolutionary Left in Spain* (Stanford, Calif., 1974); and Pelai Pagès, *Historia del partido comunista de España* (Madrid, 1978), prewar histories of the Spanish Communist party.

Burnett Bolloten, in collaboration with George Esenwein

COMORERA, JUAN (1895-1960). The Civil War hastened the fusion of four small Catalan socialist parties into the *Partit Socialista Unificat de Catalunya* (PSUC)* with Juan Comorera as its secretary general. The PSUC was in reality the Communist party of Catalonia,* and Comorera diligently pursued the communists' attacks on anarchists* in the course of filling several positions in the Catalan parliament, the Generalitat.*

Comorera was the son of a blacksmith, but he followed first a literary and then a political career. He spent the years of the Primo de Rivera dictatorship in Argentina,* returning to Spain during the Republic. He was elected to the Cortes* and to the Generalitat, and he also set up successful collectives in agriculture, fishing, and industrial societies in the early 1930s. He served first as a councillor for agriculture and then for economy in the Generalitat in 1934 as a member of Esquerra,* a party of Republicans and leftists. He soon gravitated to the Spanish Communist party,* however, and was imprisoned following the Asturias* uprising of October 1934.

The portfolio of public services in the Generalitat was given to Comorera in late August 1936, but a reorganization of that body resulted in Comorera using his control of PSUC to gain a stronger position in mid-December. His selection as the minister of food* represented a transfer of the post from the anarchists to the communists. Comorera's actions in this capacity are the subject of much controversy. He abolished the bread committees set up by the anarchists, but when shortages of food occurred in Barcelona,* he responded to protests by calling in Assault Guards* on the crowds. The only relief he provided came from the arrival of Russian food shipments, which had been arranged for by the anarchists before Comorera took charge. Many observers claim that Comorera's actions were partisan and ill-conceived and created unnecessary hardship in Barcelona in the spring of 1937.

Comorera was a consistent opponent of the anarchists, having tried unsuccessfully to keep them out of the Generalitat in the fall of 1936 and having repeatedly called for the return to the Generalitat of the powers exercised by anarchists in the collectives that sprang up at the start of the war. Anarchist distrust of him was so great that a trip he took to Paris in late April 1937 was seen as part of the advance planning for the May revolution in Barcelona. Following that uprising, the PSUC emerged as a dominant political force in Catalonia, and in June 1937 Comorera was placed in charge of the economy in the Generalitat.

Comorera's political machinations are in sharp contrast to his literary efforts. Before the war, he edited the bilingual journal *Escuela de carácter republicano*, and at the beginning of the conflict he served as editor of the weekly *Justicia Social*.

Comorera went into exile in 1939, but he returned

secretly in 1954. He was arrested, tried, and convicted, and died in prison in Burgos* in 1960.

For further information, see Ricardo de la Cierva, *La historia se confiesa* (Barcelona, 1976), and Robert W. Kern, *Red Years/Black Years: A Political History of Spanish Fascism, 1911-1937* (Philadelphia, 1978).

See also Nutrition.

                                        David V. Holtby

COMPAÑÍA ARRENDATARIA DEL MONOPOLIO DE PETRÓLEOS, S.A. (CAMPSA). In June 1927, following the expropriation of all Standard and Shell properties in Spain, the Primo de Rivera government, largely at the instigation of José Calvo Sotelo,* established the *Compañia Arrendataria del Monopolio de Petróleos, S.A. (CAMPSA).* Granted a monopoly on all petroleum products, CAMPSA was initially capitalized at 195 million pesetas represented by 390,000 shares of 500 pesetas each. Of these shares, the state controlled 90,000, while the remainder were to be sold to the public. In 1929, a sister company, *Compañia Española de Petróleos* (CEPSA),* was granted a monopoly in the Canary Islands* and charged with supplying, through the refinery at Tenerife, petroleum products to CAMPSA.

With the outbreak of the Civil War, CAMPSA divided into two competing organizations: CAMPSA-Burgos and CAMPSA-Gentibus (Madrid*). The immediate advantage in petroleum supplies lay with the Republic, which possessed about 307,197 metric tons as compared with 84,983 in insurgent hands. From the outset of the conflict, both sides realized that a sustained war effort was dependent on a continuous flow of petroleum; therefore, both looked to foreign suppliers. During the course of the war, the Republicans* imported approximately 1.5 million metric tons, practically all from Odessa. The Nationalists* were far more successful and obtained from abroad nearly 3.5 million metric tons. Most of the Nationalists' petroleum was supplied by the Texas Oil Company whose chairman, Captain Thorkild Rieber, determined in September 1936 that his long-term contract with CAMPSA would be fulfilled by shipments to CAMPSA-Burgos.

For further information, see the official history, *Compañia Arrendataria del Monopolio de Petróleos, S.A., 1928-1958* (Madrid, 1959).

See also Foreign Trade, Nationalist.

                                        Glenn T. Harper

COMPAÑIA ESPAÑOLA DE PETRÓLEOS (CEPSA). The *Compañia Española de Petróleos, S.A.* (CEPSA) was founded in 1929 by Majorcan financier Juan March* together with Catalan bankers. The firm bought oil fields in Venezuela and in 1930 hired the Bethlehem Steel Company of Pennsylvania to construct a refinery at Santa Cruz de la Tenerife. This refinery in the Canary Islands* provided one-seventh of the oil used by the *Compañia Arrendataria del Monopolio de Petróleos, S.A.* (CAMPSA)* in Spain on the eve of the Civil War. Furthermore, CEPSA competed with British Shell, its large commercial rival at Las Palmas, for sales to international shipping.

Franco* commanded his troops in the Canaries at the outbreak of the war, thus assuring a major industrial asset for the Nationalist cause. CEPSA's "home-owned" source of refined petroleum products was an important supplement to the oil bought by CAMPSA (Burgos*). However, a major weakness of CEPSA was its dependence on chartered foreign tankers. Nonetheless, CEPSA expanded its facility in 1937-1938 into one of the largest refineries in Europe.* CAMPSA and CEPSA were for all intents and purposes the only Spanish companies to make increased profits during the Civil War.

The German Navy* was keenly interested in possible dollar purchases of bunker oil from the refinery from 1934 to 1941. This was to break an expected Anglo-French blockade and assist German submarine operations in case of war. Their plan was directed against France* alone in 1934, but the British were added as a potential enemy in June 1937. The Germans assumed the Canary Islands would be safe from possible British seizure. German support of the Nationalist cause in the Civil War expanded their contacts in the CEPSA organization.

In March 1938, the nationalization of Standard-Shell interests in Mexico* led the German Navy to suggest a three-way barter scheme between Mexico,* Germany,* and the Canary Islands. CEPSA needed German machinery and more dollars to buy additional crude oil. The scheme proved somewhat successful, and Juan March and CEPSA's managing director, Demetrio Carceller, both made money. In 1940, Franco named Carceller minister of industry and commerce.

For further information, see CEPSA, *Memoria* (1929 to 1939); Spain, *Estadística del Comercio Exterior de España* (1930-1935); and Robert H. Whealey, "La diplomacia española del petróleo: De junio de 1927 a abril de 1931," *Cuadernos Economicos de Información Comercial Española*, 10 (Madrid, 1979): 511-31.

See also Economy, Nationalist; and Peseta, Nationalist and Republican.

Robert H. Whealey

COMPAÑÍA HISPANO-MARROQUÍ DE TRANSPORTES (HISMA).

The *Compañía Hispano-Marroquí de Transportes* (HISMA) was formally organized in Tetuán* on July 31, 1936, by Johannes Bernhardt,* with Fernando de Carranza y Fernández-Reguera, a retired Spanish officer, as a nominal partner. It was built on the framework of an existing commercial firm with which Bernhardt was associated. Its initial purpose was to arrange the transport in German planes of Nationalist troops from Morocco* to the Iberian Peninsula. However, by early autumn its functions had greatly expanded. In conjunction with a Goering-backed sister organization in Berlin— *Rohstoffe-und-Waren-Einkaufsgesellschaft* (ROWAK) —it had secured a virtual monopoly of German commerce with the Nationalists,* handling not only German deliveries but also Spanish payments, chiefly in the form of raw materials.

During the course of the war, HISMA's economic influence in Spain increased dramatically, often at the expense of rival English and French firms. Finally, in November 1938, faced by the threatened withdrawal of all German support, Franco* yielded to Bernhardt's persistent demands and agreed not only to the continuation of HISMA's favored commercial position but also to its acquisition of extensive mining properties. Most of these were subsequently grouped within a new holding company called the *Sociedad Financiera Industrial, Ltda.* (SOFINDUS), which continued to dominate German economic interests in Spain until the collapse of the Third Reich.

For additional information, see Glenn T. Harper, *German Economic Policy in Spain During the Spanish Civil War, 1936-1939* (The Hague, 1967); Manfred Merkes, *Die deutsche Politik gegenüber dem spanischen Bürgerkrieg, 1936-1939* (Bonn, 1961); and Angel Viñas, *La Alemania nazi y el 18 de julio*, 2d ed. (Madrid, 1977).

See also Foreign trade, Nationalist; and Germany.

Glenn T. Harper

COMPANYS Y JOVER, LUIS (1883-1940).

Companys, a Catalan politician and president of the Generalitat* of Catalonia* during the Civil War, was executed after the conflict ended.

Born in El Torrós, province of Lérida,* on June 21, 1883, of middle-class rural proprietors, he studied law in Barcelona* where he became acquainted with Francesc Layret, later a Republican deputy to the Cortes.* Layret would become his mentor, and together they founded the *Asociación estudiantil republicana* (Republican Student Association). After Companys finished his legal studies, he frequently acted on behalf of prosecuted syndicalists,* which led to a close relationship with anarchist and anarchosyndicalist elements of the *Confederación Nacional de Trabajo* (CNT).* Companys participated in the various Republican Catalanist parties organized in Barcelona and because of his political activities was arrested on several occasions. He was a controversial newspaperman and editor-in-chief of *La Publicidad* and later, with Layret, founder of the daily *La Lucha*. In 1917, he was elected councilman in Barcelona. In 1920 he was arrested and together with syndicalist and Republican leaders was sent to the Castle of La Mola in Minorca.* While in prison he learned of the assassination of his great friend Layret by killers from Barcelona's *Confederación Patronal* (Employers Federation).

Freed in 1921, Companys was elected deputy for the district previously represented by Layret. That same year he founded the *Unió de Rabassaires*, an association or syndicate of farmers who worked leased lands (rental payment being half of the harvest reaped), and edited its weekly journal, *La Terra*. Companys thus created a rural Catalan syndicalism, giving it a Republican twist.

During the dictatorship of Primo de Rivera, Companys plotted with syndicalist elements. With the collapse of the dictatorship, he was arrested because of his membership in the coordinating committee of the Esquerra Catalana* (Catalan Left). He participated in the group headed by Francesc Macià, founder of the *Esquerra Republicana de Catalunya** (Republican Left of Catalonia), created hurriedly on April 12, 1931, which then won the municipal elections in Barcelona. Companys emerged as the elected councilman serving in the Catalan capital. On April 14, at the head of fellow activists, he occupied city hall and from it at 2:00 P.M. proclaimed the establishment of a republic. It was the first instance of such a proclamation in Spain during the 1930s. Immediately after, he assumed responsibility for the civil government of Barcelona.

Elected a deputy to the Spanish Cortes in June 1931, Companys participated in the defense of the Statute of Autonomy of Catalonia. After its approval, he was elected to the Catalan parliament and became its first speaker. He also became a minister in the government of Spain and founded and directed a daily, *La Humanitat*, the official organ of the Esquerra. Upon the death of Macià, the first president of the Generalitat (the autonomous government of Catalonia), Companys was elected as his successor on January 1, 1934.

During the summer of that year, a conflict developed between the government in Madrid* and that of the Generalitat. The Catalan government had enacted regulatory laws concerning the lease of lands against which the Madrid government took court action challenging the constitutionality of these Catalan laws. Declared unconstitutional by the Tribunal of Constitutional Guarantees, the Catalan government disregarded this ruling and passed the laws again.

In the interim, the parties of the Right, not Republican, were accepted in the government of Madrid. Concerned about Catalonia's autonomy, on October 6, 1934, Companys proclaimed the Statute of the Catalan State, known as the *Estado Catalan*, within the Spanish Federal Republic. This gesture of rebellion was squashed by the army and resulted in the arrest of Companys and the entire Catalan government. He was sentenced to serve thirty years in jail, but Companys remained locked up only until the elections of February 16, 1936,* when he was again elected a deputy and was amnestied, returning to his position as president of the Generalitat.

In May and June 1936, Companys sent various emissaries to the head of the Madrid government to inform him of clear evidence uncovered by the Catalan government's police* relating to preparations for a military coup. But in Madrid, the head of the government, Santiago Casares Quiroga,* remained convinced that there would be no army uprising and so Companys' warnings went unheeded. On July 19, 1936, when the troops in rebellion took to the streets of Barcelona, Companys ordered the police* to prepare to offer opposition. At the same time, poorly armed groups of militants belonging to the CNT, the *Partido Obrero de Unificación Marxista* (POUM),* and other leftist groups fought against the army. At one point the police appeared to weaken in its resolve to oppose the army, but Companys visited their barracks, strengthening their morale through the inflammatory and somewhat chaotic oratory that had always been his hallmark.

On July 20, after fighting ended in the streets of Barcelona with the army's defeat, Companys received the leadership of the anarchists.* He told them that since they had won the victory, if they so desired, governing authority would be transferred to them. Companys, knowing well how these leaders thought, knew their response would be negative. In this manner, he was able to persuade the CNT, when they were in control of the streets, to accept ipso facto the existence of the government of the Generalitat, and

forget that Companys, while president of this body in 1934, had permitted the most fanatical of Catalan extremists, then controlling the police force, to persecute the CNT.

The Civil War presented Companys with a grave dilemma. On the one hand, he was the leader of a middle-class party, reformist but not revolutionary, and with respect to tactics this position placed him close to the *Partit Socialista Unificat de Catalunya* (PSUC),* which at the time did not think it necessary to effect revolutionary changes in society. On the other hand, he was president of Catalonia, and it was precisely the revolutionary action of the workers that resulted in the broadening of the powers of the Generalitat beyond those specified in the Statute of Autonomy—control of banks and foreign commerce, presidential authority to cancel or change death penalties, and even now with regard to an army of militia volunteers* and a Ministry of War. Besides, the communists were now more dynamic and were less linked by tradition to the anarchosyndicalists than the Esquerra. Thus, the party attracted the traditional followers of the Esquerra, leaving the leadership of this group without a popular base.

Under these circumstances, Companys found it necessary to decide between the revolutionary posture (alliance of the middle and laboring classes) and the conservative approach (alliance with the PSUC). The first stance would consolidate the Catalan economy, and the second that of the middle class. The first alternative would allow a major portion of the middle class to go to the PSUC. The second would place the Generalitat in the position of coattailing Soviet diplomacy through the PSUC and Soviet blackmail because of arms supply.

Over a number of months, Companys attempted to conciliate both positions. He succeeded in persuading the anarchosyndicalists to participate in the government of the Generalitat and the city halls (as did also the POUM), while at the same time dissolving the town and city committees as well as the Antifascist Militias Committee.* But when the Soviet consul, Vladimir Antonov-Ovseenko,* threatened the suspension of Russian aid if Andrés Nin,* minister of justice and political secretary of the POUM, was not expelled from the Catalan government, Companys acquiesced and consequently provoked a governmental crisis. This happened within three months of having formed a cabinet with CNTists, POUMists, communists, and moderate Republicans (September-December 1936). This development aggravated the tension between revolutionary and conservative forces and in May 1937 led to armed conflict between the two in which

Companys and the Generalitat sided with the conservatives.

The May 1937 riots* (known as the May Days) resulted in the dissolution of the cabinet of the Spanish Republic of Largo Caballero* (into which the anarchists had entered in November) and its replacement by one headed with Dr. Juan Negrín.* In fact, Negrín was the instrument of the Communist party; thus, this change permitted Negrín to bring into broad play Soviet arms "blackmail." The Negrín government curtailed the powers the revolution had given the Generalitat, ultimately removing from Valencia* to Barcelona. The Generalitat became reduced simply to a bureaucratic and cultural institution without political functions or responsibilities and with its autonomy each day more limited and threatened.

The Communist party's persecution of the POUM and the CNT, both of which were particularly strong in Catalonia, led Companys to emerge discreetly in their defense in the hope of reestablishing some equilibrium between the CNT and the PSUC. Just as he did not want to see total control by the CNT, he did not wish similar power in the hands of the PSUC— hence his attempt to defend the CNT. He wrote letters and carried out efforts protesting· the PSUC's police methods and those of the Communist party, but all in vain.

Companys had lost his broad popular base—taken over by the PSUC—and had allowed the weakening of the CNT. He therefore was without political troops, remaining the mere president of an institution emptied of authority by virtue of the national government's measures. These included decollectivization of industry and seizure of collectivized war industries, and ultimately the separation of the Generalitat from the conduct of the war. Companys even complained to the president of the Republic that even though the Civil War was being fought in Catalonia, owing to the steady military losses of Negrín's government, he was forced to depend on the press for news of events.

Finally, the Esquerra removed from the Negrín government its cabinet minister, who was replaced by a PSUC member. When the definitive campaign against Catalonia started, at Christmas 1938, the Generalitat lacked the capacity or power to halt the assault. The Republican Army, demoralized by communist policy, could not even continue resistance. Barcelona fell to Franco's* troops on January 26, 1939. A month later, the president of the Generalitat crossed the frontier through the Pyrenees* taking refuge in France.* His previous status saved him from the concentration camps* to which a half million Republican refugees* were sent. But with the outbreak of World War II and the occupation of France by the army of the Third Reich, the Gestapo arrested him. He had remained in France so long because one of his children was ill in a French clinic.

Companys was turned over to Franco's police, who then transferred him secretly to Barcelona where he was imprisoned in the military citadel of Montjuich. He was court-martialed on October 14, 1940. During the proceedings, Companys at first wanted to address the court but in view of how the military tribunal functioned he shrugged his shoulders exclaiming, "What for?" He was condemned to death and on the next day (October 15) was killed by a firing squad in the castle's moat. His body lay buried in a nameless grave until after Franco's death when his memory was finally honored. Today streets and plazas in Catalonia bear his name, and he has become a legend because of his death—despite his mistakes and his indecisive nature.

Companys was a man of passion, an ardent but incoherent orator, a practical lawyer rather than a cultured man, an emotional politician rather than an astute statesman. He reflected that aspect of the Catalan character which passes so easily from common sense to emotionalism. He belonged to the latter type, and to him could be applied an Italian aphorism, "Un bel morir tutta una vita onora" (A glorious death honors an entire life).

Companys' execution de facto ignited the first sparks of resistance against Franco. Small groups began gathering together, forming nuclei of opposition, in order to divulge news which Franco's authorities had prohibited from being published, especially news of the execution. Following Companys' death and scarcely fifteen months after Franco's victory, at great risk the first clandestine anti-Franco pamphlets were published.

For further information, see Manuel Cruells, *El separatisme català durant la guerra civil* (Barcelona, 1975); Maximiano García Venero, *Historia del nacionalismo catalán*, 2 vols. (Madrid, 1967); Angel Ossorio y Gallardo, *Vida y sacrificio de Companys* (Buenos Aires, 1943), a dated biography; Josep M. Poblet, *Vida i mort de Lluis Companys* (Barcelona, 1976); Ferran Soldevila, *Historia de la proclamació de la República Catalana* (Barcelona, 1977); and Hugh Thomas, *The Spanish Civil War* (New York, 1977).

Victor Alba

CONCENTRATION CAMPS. Concentration camps were a feature of both Republican and Nationalist zones. They varied in number and size, and were established and dismantled rapidly throughout the Civil War primarily by the military and police. They were used to hold political and military prisoners, to house workers (as for example in Seville), and as centers for the execution of enemies. It is not known how many there were or their size. Some were established as temporary camps when one side or another occupied new territory, such as the Nationalists* did in Badajoz.* Others were more permanent; for example, the Unamuno camp for Republican prisoners run by the Nationalists. The convent of Saint Ursula, in the city of Barcelona,* served as a Republican concentration center mainly for political prisoners.

Another collection of concentration camps was established in southern France toward the end of the Civil War by the French government to collect the over 400,000 refugees fleeing Spain. These remained open until the end of World War II, had poor to horrible living conditions with little or no shelters or sanitary facilities, and sometimes were used to supply German concentration and work camps with "enemies" of fascism. The larger French camps were Barcerès* (population 70,000), Argelès* (40,000), and Saint Cyprien (30,000) by July 1939. Nearly 5,000 died in these French camps alone. An additional 10,000 Spanish refugees died in concentration camps during World War II as a result of fighting for France* against the Germans.

For further information, see Pilar Millán Astray, *Cautivas: 32 meses en las prisiones rojas* (Madrid, 1940); Antonio Bahamonde, *Memories of a Spanish Nationalist* (London, 1939); Melquesidez Rodríguez Chaos, *24 años de la cárcel* (Paris, 1968); Miguel García, *Franco's Prisoner* (London, 1972); and Guy Hermet, *Les Espagnols en France* (Paris, 1967).

See also Prisoners; and Refugees, Republican.

James W. Cortada

CONDOR LEGION. The German composite air unit, the Condor Legion, represented the peak of direct German military participation in the Spanish Civil War. The original German support of the Nationalists* was modest. On July 27, 1936, Hitler* sent Spain ten Ju-52 transport aircraft flown by crews drafted from *Lufthansa*. Ten additional Ju-52s were to be sent to the Spanish Nationalist Air Force* by ship, as well as six He-51 antiquated fighters, a section of light anti-aircraft cannon, and a small communications section for the defense and training of Spanish crews. More material support was to follow. General Wilberg of the Air Ministry, with a rapidly created Special Staff "W," was in charge of the operation known as "Magic Fire." In Spain, Major Alexander von Scheele

commanded the initial German force, which grew to a total of ninety-one officers, men and civilian technicians.

The first Ju-52 landed in Tetuán* on July 29, and that same evening airlifted a contingent of Moroccans to Spain. From that date until the operation was completed, on October 11, 1936, German aircraft and crews moved 13,000 men and 270,199 kilos of material across the Straits.* On August 15, the Germans realized their first losses in the Nationalist cause when airmen Helmut Schulze and Hebert Zeck died in the crash of their Ju-52 at Jerez de la Frontera.

The Germans first saw combat on August 13 when, against orders and with modified transports, they bombed the battleship *Jaime I*. This was followed on August 25 with German fighter pilots claiming two aerial victories. After repeated requests from von Scheele, Berlin permitted what the men had already made an accomplished fact—a German combat role.

From the beginning, it was obvious that the Nationalists did not have the technical skills to operate and maintain the German aircraft and equipment that began to arrive in Spain, and that additional German specialists were needed. This resulted in an almost weekly increase of German personnel. There was more direct control, as well as organization, of the German effort in early September 1936, when Lieutenant Colonel Walter Warlimont of the German General Staff arrived as the German commander and military adviser to General Franco.*

By early October, the Germans had grown to 600 officers and specialists. They assisted in the equipping and training of Spanish flights as well as manning the German flights that had been taking form. In addition, in a random way, they operated various types of aircraft from different bases. Included were German-manned flights of six reconnaissance He-46s, and fourteen fighter He-51s at Ávila,* a bomber flight of six Ju-52s at Cáceres* and Salamanca,* an experimental flight with two He-123s, three Bf-109s, with a single He-50 dive-bomber, and, finally, a seaplane flight with one He-59 and one He-60 at Cádiz.*

Late in October, at the suggestion of Colonel Warlimont, a German light *panzer* battalion of 600 men along with forty-one Krupp Mark I tanks and twenty 8.8cm anti-tank guns assembled at Cáceres. It was not intended as a German battleforce but as a training unit for Spanish crews.

At the same time, Berlin decided to increase its direct combat involvement and, unknown to either Franco or Warlimont, ordered General Wilberg to expand his "Operation Magic Fire" into a revolutionary air unit that was to become the German Condor Legion. The code name was "Operation Rügen."

The initial tactical force constituted a Bomber Group (K-88) of three squadrons of Ju-52 bombers; a Fighter Group (J/88) with three squadrons of He-51 fighters; a Reconnaissance Group (A/88) with two squadrons of He-99 and He-70 reconnaissance/bombers; and a Seaplane Squadron (AS/88) of He-59 and He-60 floatplanes. With the exception of the floatplanes, all tactical groups were to be expanded by an additional squadron as they absorbed the German flights already operating in Spain. For defense there was an Anti-aircraft Battalion (Flak) with batteries of 2cm, 3.7cm, and 8.8cm guns, along with a searchlight battery. The batteries were to be increased from guns already in operation in Spain.

In support, the legion had a Communications Battalion (Ln/88) with a radio company, telephone company, air warning company, flight security company, and several communications sections. In addition, there was an Air Maintenance Group (P/88), which also controlled the depots, and a Transportation Battalion. All came under the Legion General Headquarters Staff commanded by a general officer. All German flights and personnel already in Spain were absorbed into the legion structure. The German Army instructors (Imker) and personnel of the panzer battalion (Drone) were attached to the legion commander for administration. However, he exercised no operational control over these men. The legion itself was under the operational control of General Kindelán,* chief of the expanding Nationalist Air Force.

The legion was equipped with approximately 100 aircraft of various types and had a personnel strength (including Imker and Drone) of 5,136 men throughout its deployment. The personnel were rotated periodically. The first commander was General Hugo von Sperrle,* to be followed by General Hellmuth Volkmann, and finally General Wolfgang von Richthofen (who had originally been von Sperrle's chief of staff).

The personnel, the cream of the new Luftwaffe,* and equipment were gathered from units scattered all over Germany.* Most were to be shipped to Spain by sea, and not until the vessels were well on their way did the men know where they were going and why. The first ships arrived at Cádiz, in early November, almost at the very moment the Nationalists launched their abortive assault on Madrid.* The German aircraft which participated in this operation were flown mainly by those German flights already on hand or were flights from the hurriedly organized Spanish units. The legion aircraft had to be assembled and the squadrons organized, and this was not fully accomplished until after the issue of Madrid had been temporarily decided.

Even before the legion was organized, it had been proven that the German aircraft, of all types, were far inferior to the Russion aircraft on the other side. The open-cockpit He-51 was completely outclassed by Russian fighters, and the lumbering Ju-52 (although a dependable transport) as a bomber was an easy victim.

General von Sperrle adamantly demanded higher performance aircraft from Berlin, and by the spring of 1937 they began to appear in the legion squadrons. The Bf-109 replaced the He-51, which was diverted to a direct army ground support operation. The Ju-52s were turned over to the Spanish as they were replaced by the He-111. Before the war was over, there was hardly an aircraft in the growing Luftwaffe inventory (including Stuka dive-bombers) that at least, in some numbers, had not been used by the legion.

The legion's combat mission evolved into gaining air superiority and direct tactical support of ground armies. In the latter instance, the legion operated as a long-range artillery in direct support of Nationalist divisions. Effective operational procedures were developed, but, as expected, many tragedies did occur with the bombing of friendly forces. For example, a Nationalist division fighting across the Alfambra River, north of Teruel,* had suffered only scant casualties* in enemy action but lost over 500 men to a German bombing and strafing attack on their own ranks. The addition of the Bf-109, along with the fighter tactics developed by the brilliant Captain Wernher Mölders, eventually helped gain air superiority over the battlefields. Other than for the Seaplane Squadron, operating from Majorca* against the Levante* coast, only on very few occasions could one say that the legion was ever used as a strategic bombardment force.

The Germans learned many vital lessons in operations, maintenance, logistics, and communications. They would certainly have been remiss if they had not. Included was an appreciation of the very effective use of Flak cannon, specifically the deadly 8.8cm guns, as anti-tank and ground artillery.

From early 1937 to the end of the conflict, the Condor Legion participated in every single major engagement from the north through the battles for Bilbao,* Brunete,* Asturias,* Teruel, the massive offensive of the Aragón,* the battle of the Ebro,* and the sweep through Catalonia.* German aircraft were not committed to the Italian failure at Guadalajara,* but a German signal section was deployed for that engagement.

The legion records reveal that a total of 19,000 officers, men, and civilians served in Spain. Of these, 298 were lost, with 173 killed by the enemy. The bomber and reconnaissance squadrons lost 102 and the fighter squadrons twenty-seven. Some of these were killed on the ground. The anti-aircraft crews lost twenty-one dead, and the Communications Battalion had twelve killed. The *panzer* force lost seven, and the remaining dead were scattered through the command, including a naval officer attached to the legion staff. The other dead were largely killed in accidents (mostly vehicle accidents), but others were to die of sicknesses. A total of 139 Germans were wounded by enemy action, and an additional 459 were injured in various accidents (again mostly vehicular). The high ratio of deaths and injuries due to accidents was a matter of despair to the legion staff.

In aircraft the Germans lost to enemy action seventy-two bombers, fighters, or reconnaissance planes. Through accidents they lost an additional 160 planes for a combined total of 232. On the other hand, the Germans shot down (by fighters and Flak guns) 386 enemy aircraft. The number of enemy planes destroyed on the ground cannot be determined. In addition, six freighters attempting to run the blockade were sunk or damaged by the Seaplane Squadron. The same squadron also drove other vessels into the hands of the Nationalist Navy. An additional eight ships were destroyed by the dive-bombers.

The total kilos of bombs dropped (of all sizes) was 16,953,700, and the combined tactical air units expended 4,327,949 rounds of machinegun ammunition. The Flak batteries fired 75,899 rounds for the 2cm guns; 89,733 rounds for the 3.7cm guns; and 160,102 rounds for the 8.8cm guns.

The legion used over 1,500 transportation vehicles, and among these were over 100 different types, which created many maintenance problems. The legion was not able to perform the detailed depot maintenance of aircraft as required to keep the systems airworthy. As a result, many of the aircraft had to be sent back to Germany for the periodic inspections and overhaul. This involved disassembly in Spain, shipment to Germany by sea, reassembly and overhaul in Germany, disassembly again, and return to Spain where the aircraft had to be reassembled once more. It was a logistical nightmare.

The Condor Legion produced many outstanding airmen who where to become fighter and bomber-aces not only in Spain but also during World War II. Besides the brilliant Captain Mölders (with fourteen victories in Spain and 101 victories in World War II), a few of the other fighter-aces were Lieutenant Walter Oesau with seven and 117, Lieutenant Heinrich Sterr with seven and 123, Sergeant (became an officer) Herbert Ihelfeld with seven in Spain and 123 during World War II, and Lieutenant Hannes Trautloft with four

and fifty-three. Notable in the ranks of bomber-aces were Major Martin Harlinghausen and Captain Herbert Wittmann. Many of these, and others, were to become general officers of the *Luftwaffe*. The two legion commanders, von Sperrle and Richthofen, were to become *Luftwaffe* field marshals. Some of these same officers, after the war, were to build the new West German Air Force. Included in this list were Lieutenant General Harlinghausen, Major General Herman Plocher, General Hans Asmus, Colonels Douglas Pitcairn and Herbert Wittmann.

For further information, see W. Beumelburg, *Di Geschichte der Legion Condor* (Berlin, 1939); Captain R. Hidalgo Salazar, *La Ayuda Alemana a España 1936-1939* (Madrid, 1975); R. L. Proctor, "They Flew from Pollensa Bay," *Aerospace Historian* 24, No. 4 (December 1977): 196-202; Hannes Trautloft, *Als Jagdflieger in Spaien: aus dem Tagebuch eines deutschen Legionärs* (Berlin, 1940); and Angel Viñas, *La Alemania nazi y el 18 de julio* (Madrid, 1977).

Raymond L. Proctor

CONFEDERACIÓN ESPAÑOLA DE DERECHAS AUTÓNOMAS (CEDA). From its inception on February 28, 1933, the *Confederación Española de Derechas Autónomas* (CEDA) evoked a degree of controversy equaled by few political parties in history. It was viewed as fascist by many leftists and as too moderate by many rightists. Most contemporaries and historians have overlooked the key fact about the CEDA: it was, as it name states, a confederation of autonomist parties, each oriented in some way toward the Right. These parties were united by their opposition to the policies of the Azaña* government and by their determination *not* to make the nature of the regime (republic or monarchy) their major political concern. Although the party contained key members who favored the republican form of government and others (a majority) who would have preferred a monarchy, the accidentalist tactic proclaimed that policies of a government were more important than its form. Born in opposition to the Azaña government, *cedistas* were sharply divided over what they would do if they achieved power; this internal division caused much of the paralysis of the Center-Right governments of 1933-1935.

As the first broadly based rightist party, the CEDA achieved notable success in the 1933 elections, emerging with a plurality of seats. Because President Niceto Alcalá-Zamora was never sure of the party's loyalty to the Republic, he never appointed either the party's leader, José María Gil Robles,* or any other *cedista* as prime minister. Still, the CEDA came close to dominating the politics of the second *bienio*, for no Center or Center-Right government could survive without its support. Seven members of the CEDA (Gil Robles, Aizpún,* José Anguera de Sojo, Juan Casanueva, Manuel Giménez Fernández, Luis Lucía,* and José Salmón) served as ministers in the Lerroux and Chapaprieta governments. But despite the promise of the 1933 elections and of its power in the 1933-1935 period, the CEDA's tactic of taking power through elections failed in 1936. Instead of the 300 seats which the CEDA predicted, it won less than 100. Just as many socialists had refused to accept the Right's victory in 1933, many rightists refused to accept the Popular Front's* in 1936.

During the spring of 1936, the CEDA's parliamentary delegation opposed the victorious Left as best it could in the Cortes.* But many *cedistas*, by then regretting that Gil Robles had not attempted a coup in his last days as minister of war, deserted the party, or at least its political and legalist tactic. Carlist *Requetés** were filled with former members of the CEDA's youth organization, *Juventud de Acción Popular* (JAP). When the rising finally came, most members of the CEDA joined the movement, with only a few remaining neutral and almost none siding with the Republicans.* Party funds were apparently offered to General Mola* in June and again in July to finance the uprising. Gil Robles himself supported the Nationalist cause, but he was nevertheless exiled to Portugal* during the war. The CEDA, as a party, however, had no place in Nationalist Spain. In April 1937, scarcely four years after it formally came into existence, the CEDA was dissolved, for there could be no competition for the movement's new official party, the *Falange Española Tradicionalista y de las Juntas de Ofensiva Nacional-Sindicalista* (JONS).

For further information, see Gil Robles' memoirs, *No fue posible la paz* (Barcelona, 1968), indispensable for any study of the CEDA; William J. Irwin, *The CEDA in the 1933 Cortes Elections* (University Microfilms, 1975); José R. Montero, *La CEDA: El catolicismo social y política de la II^a República* (Madrid, 1977), a thorough study of the composition and ideology of the CEDA; Paul Preston, *The Coming of the Spanish Civil War* (New York, 1978), the most scholarly account attacking the CEDA's role in the Republic; Richard Robinson, *The Origins of Franco's Spain: The Right, The Republic and Revolution, 1931-1936* (Newton Abbot, 1970); and Javier Tusell Gomez, *Historia de la Democracia Cristiana en España*, Vol. 1: *Los antecedentes, La CEDA y la II^a República* (Madrid, 1974).

William J. Irwin

CONFEDERACIÓN NACIONAL DEL TRABAJO (CNT). The *Confederación Nacional del Trabajo*, the anarchosyndicalist organization organized in 1911, became the largest branch of the International Workingmen's Association during the Second Republic* and the Civil War. It was the biggest union of the Loyalists,* and as a political force it played a complicated role in the effort to establish a revolutionary society and to oppose the growth of communist power. At the same time, the weakness and confusion that sometimes surrounded it added to its complex history.

The formation of the CNT in 1911 was a response to the Tragic Week of July 1909 (mainly Catalan nationalist sentiment) and the execution of the prominent anarchist, Francisco Ferrer, in its aftermath. The CNT's birth marked the end of anarchist "propaganda of the deed" and the beginning of acceptance for French labor theories of large industrial unions and the concept of the general strike as a revolutionary tactic. This new labor orientation allowed anarchists* to end their isolation from the working classes caused by long involvement in illegal activities against the state. Faced with successful socialist labor activity, it became a means of survival at a time when organized labor was just emerging.

The collaboration of both anarchists and labor organizers within the CNT caused an almost constant state of tension within the organization. During World War I and the near-revolutionary period that lasted until 1923, this struggle was personified by the rivalry between Manuel Buenacasa and Salvador Seguí, the one a revolutionary and the other a labor leader. Unions sprouted everywhere, quickly transforming the CNT into a much larger union federation than the socialist *Unión General de Trabajadores* (UGT).* But the walkout of Eleuterio Quintanilla's Asturian Miners Syndicate during the CNT's First Congress in December 1919 over failure to develop a united front strategy with the UGT marked a loss of many skilled workers initially attracted to the CNT by its forcefulness. While this loss of numbers was made up by loose affiliation with the peasant *Federación Nacional de Agricultores de España*, the CNT subsequently suffered from a perpetual lack of cohesiveness that was perpetuated by the *cenetista* (of the CNT) concept of the *sindicato único*. According to this concept, the flexible industrial unions run by the CNT were opened permanently to peasants, anarchists, and workers of other skills who had no opportunity to affiliate with unions in their own area.

The confusion that this type of organization introduced made it difficult for the CNT to establish solid locals that could focus upon improvement of wages, hours, and conditions. However, it did promote a kind of mass revolutionary party in the midst of post-war economic difficulties and the flush of the Russian Revolution. Terrorist subgroups in the CNT like Buenaventura Durruti's* *Solidarios** faction (responsible for the assassination in June 1923 of Juan Soldevila Romero, archbishop of Saragossa*) proliferated in the climate of lockouts and wage cuts prevalent in the early 1920s. But such were the contradictions contained within the CNT that its euphoria with the Russian Revolution wore off as soon as CNT representatives heard the conditions laid down by Lenin at the Second Congress of the Comintern in July 1920 during its meeting in Moscow. A number of radical *cenetistas* did help to form the Spanish Communist party,* but the vast bulk of the CNT never followed them and thereafter remained generally Left of the communists.

The Primo de Rivera dictatorship banned the CNT after 1923, and legalization did not come until the creation of the Second Republic* in April 1931. One consequence of this ostracism was the appearance of the *Federación Anarquista Ibérica* (FAI)* in 1927 as a secret anarchist "inner core" of the CNT, a group reminiscent of the earlier Bakuninist "propaganda of the deed" phase with anarcho-Bolshevik overtones. The FAI hated the socialists for cooperating with the dictatorship in creating labor laws that made arbitration of industrial disputes mandatory, a practice carried over into the statutes of the Second Republic. *Faístas* argued that the law took all power away from strikers by denying them the right to strike, the most important weapon in a worker's arsenal. Orthodox *cenetistas*, however, reacted negatively to this point and moved closer to a labor party position that advocated abandonment of terrorism* in favor of prolonged organization activity in order to match the UGT. In 1931, the UGT was becoming more influential, though more from their political participation, which anarchists hated. Soon the FAI suspected the CNT of considering political party status. Indeed, some conservative *cenetistas* were interest in this possibility.

In the summer of 1931, the CNT thoroughly reorganized itself into a fully functional national labor movement. From the local syndicates through provincial, regional, and national committees and congresses, the organization established executive plenums at each level to facilitate recruitment and the bargaining power of its membership. Even though the FAI considered it as moderate or conservative, the CNT was actually very strike-prone, but in the eyes of the *faístas* these tactics merely duplicated those of the UGT. Their own violence, however, had the same effect upon the CNT leadership, and in September 1931 thirty of them wrote

the *Treintista* Declaration, a manifesto that advocated separation of the two groups. The FAI seized many of the CNT's agencies and syndicates and ousted moderates like Angel Pestaña and Juan Peiró* from their positions at the head of the CNT. Moderates retaliated by creating "syndicates of opposition" united in the *Federación Sindicalista Libertaria* or the *Alianza Obrera* that was formed with the help of the UGT and the International Workingmen's Association.

Under these circumstances, the CNT soon lost the organizational expertise it had begun to develop and temporarily collapsed into a series of warring factions, adding enormously to the political and social confusion of 1933. The Right's triumph in the elections of November 1933 was closely tied to the CNT-FAI difficulties, but the common hostility that Alejandro Lerroux, José María Gil Robles,* and José Antonio Primo de Rivera* had for all radicals and labor unions finally ended the factional schism, even though it was a gradual process without much formality and beneath the surface considerable antagonism continued to exist. But CNT moderates themselves moved to the Left as the UGT and Francisco Largo Caballero,* once the labor minister in both Primo de Rivera's and the Republican regimes and the official responsible for the continuation of labor arbitration laws, became markedly more radical. Now Largo Caballero was openly calling for revolution, and the development of the Popular Front* concept in August 1935 brought the CNT closer to the FAI. Both endorsed socialists and other radical candidates in the elections of February 1936* and of necessity cooperated more closely between February and July than in the previous four years. The cooperation was perhaps more apparent than real, since the victory of the Left in the election unleashed such chaos that both revolutionary and organizational activity coexisted without difficulty. More workers joined the CNT during this period than at any other except the summer of 1931, and the FAI was too busy fighting in the streets with fascist groups to interfere with CNT activity.

The outbreak of the Civil War found the CNT still the largest labor union in Spain, but confused and almost incoherent as to policy. Contact with international anarchism was seriously affected by the death in May 1936 of Valeriano Orobón Fernández, a leading CNT idealogue. Despite Largo Caballero's new radicalism, moderate CNT leaders were antagonized by the UGT in June and early July by a construction strike in Madrid* where the socialists went back to work under government pressure. In this turbulent situation, the new generation of moderate CNT leaders like Mariano Vázquez,* Horacio Prieto,* Juan

López,* and Juan Fábregas* had little choice but to reunite with the FAI. The two organizations became hyphenated, with the CNT acting as a union bureaucracy and the FAI as both its paramilitary and political arms.

During the first month of fighting, the CNT held a paramount position in Málaga* (which it later lost to the UGT), Valencia,* Barcelona,* Castellón, Gijón,* and Cuenca.* Its most solid bloc was the entire Catalan region which, with the exception of Sabadell and Lérida,* accepted CNT control from the start. The mining districts of the Basque provinces and Asturias* remained in UGT hands, as did Madrid, although the CNT showed some big gains in the capital. Perhaps the biggest loss to the movement was Saragossa, a city with old and strong ties to the CNT-FAI. Andalusia* was also severed from the movement's sphere of influence and with it the visceral anarchism of the southern peasants, although in fact neither the CNT nor the FAI had organized the area well.

The crucial focal point of the CNT-FAI was Barcelona and its Antifascist Militias Committee,* which replaced the Catalan separatist cabinet and legislature during the first three months of the Civil War. The Catalan politicians, suspicious of the anarchists and hostile because their own actions had always been dwarfed or overrun by the CNT-FAI, gave the movement the same number of seats as the UGT, which was much smaller in the northeast. David Antona, the general secretary of the CNT, was not even consulted in the process, although he did have more influence in Valencia on the Popular Executive Committee. Here the CNT played the biggest role of all groups, but the strength of this revolutionary government was weakened by its slowness in attacking the Valencia garrison and the city's proximity to the national government in Madrid.

Balancing these administrative positions was a sudden departure from the previous labor orientation of the CNT and its residual anarchism. To make matters worse, the organization was swamped by the wholesale syndicalization of Republican society. Union membership became mandatory because of *incautación* (direct workers' control) and *intervención* (control by workers and the Popular Front government). These forms of collectivization emphasized the new administrative tasks facing the CNT. The surge was so great that the CNT often had to operate in conjunction with the UGT or the government. In the process, the CNT bureaucrats grew more flexible and less dogmatic than the *faístas*, who largely dealt with more purely military and political concerns. This divorce from politics suited many of the conservative syndicalists* in the CNT, who guardedly talked of a "workers' state" without clear reference to ideology or sect, but in reality events were impossible to control. Workshops and factories differed enormously from one another in terms of success and purpose of their particular collectivizations. The CNT criticized syndical greediness in cases where assets were squandered or aid to other enterprises was refused, but it could not really engage in economic planning because banks, credit, and foreign trade were responsibilities assumed by Madrid. Economic councils of industry could advise but not remedy the problems of many collectivized firms, despite heroic efforts by some *cenetistas* to bring order and planning into daily economic life.

During the first six months of the Civil War, the CNT engaged in an amazing amount of activity. In the middle of shortages, financial hindrances, and the complete reorganization of the Spanish economy, the CNT managed to make some headway in its new role as an economic and administrative apparatus. National and regional conferences of peasants, communications workers, metal workers, teamsters, and railway employees established norms for collectivized industry, shared experiences of worker-managers, and attempted to put their organizations into a national perspective. In a labor federation that had once stressed spontaneity, the CNT surprisingly managed to develop at least a rudimentary planning ability. Critics, however, attributed this to the partial merger of the CNT and UGT on November 26, 1936, and to the role of the more sophisticated socialists in the development of the new revolutionary economy. It was certainly true that many companies went out of business altogether or experienced steeply declining productivity, but the dislocations of the Civil War clouded how much of this was circumstantial and how much was mismanagement, although the latter must surely have prevailed.

Closer ties with the UGT brought complications. Civil disruption, inaccessibility of supplies because of the Non-Intervention Committee,* and the sheer difficulty of mounting a war effort from scratch forced Largo Caballero to depend upon the USSR* during his premiership for increasing military aid. Since the Soviet Union lacked a strong party base in Spain, it relied upon socialists and the Republican middle class who were disturbed by the violence of the CNT-FAI revolution and worried about their own property. Socialists like Julian Besteiro,* Ramón González Peña,* and Indalecio Prieto* increasingly criticized the wasteful and inefficient aspects of CNT economic activity, just as the FAI complained of the CNT's moderation and indecisiveness.

The dilemma posed by the Right and Left was further complicated by sudden CNT membership in Largo Caballero's government. The Nationalist advance on Madrid in early November 1936 created such a crisis that the premier demanded an all-party government for the total mobilization of Republican Spain. Along with two *faístas*, Juan López and Juan Peiró became ministers of commerce and industry. These economic portfolios were proof of the important CNT economic role, but communist sympathizers controlled military and foreign relations, and as military needs increasingly became the most crucial policy determinant, the less control the CNT possessed in economic affairs.

The ebbing of CNT power came first in Valencia with the absorption of the Popular Executive on September 8; the Antifascist Militias Committee was replaced on September 26; and the beginning of national militarization came three days later. Economically, the CNT cabinet members saw fiscal resources almost entirely appropriated by the military authorities. When the CNT protested during the winter of 1937, their UGT allies played a part in blocking any changes. The CNT watched helplessly during the May 1937 riots* of Barcelona,* which drastically increased communist influence in the government. There were no more CNT cabinet members for almost a year, and while some extreme anarchists* hailed the opportunity for the movement to rid itself of political involvement, the majority were cut adrift to play a decreasing role, simply survive, or in some cases join the communists.

The last CNT defeat came with the disbandment in September 1937 of the Council of Aragón,* a CNT-FAI organized regional board with special powers in the Aragonese battle zone. Here communes had been organized throughout the countryside; anarchist power was almost total. But the socialists and communists who took over the FAI's militias* began to dismantle the council's power, much to the disgust of a few FAI leaders who had regretted the decision to accept a truce during the May crisis without guarantees that might have protected the council. It ceased operations on September 21, 1937, and was absorbed into the national government. Not long after, in December, the combined anarchist-socialist youth movement merged with the communists, an indication that the CNT was losing heart.

A similar decline took place in union and industrial affairs. The shop floor became a battleground as the procommunist cabinet of Juan Negrín* gradually prohibited strikes, altered existing labor agreements, and broke up industrial collectives. Plants were sometimes returned to their previous owners, a step that was an inducement to Catalan industrialists to support the new regime. Confiscated foreign industrial property was put under a new nationalization decree on August 11, 1938, which established a series of government-controlled basic industries, all hostile to CNT locals. CNT-FAI groups vigorously opposed this step by advocating noncooperation. This appeal skirted the limits of treason and led to the arrest of many anarchists. A full circle had been turned.

During the last year of the Civil War, the CNT looked to the future by setting out to reorganize the anarchosyndicalist movement. This resulted in the creation of the *Comité Ejecutivo del Movimiento Libertario* (CEML), an upper-level body incorporating all of the Spanish anarchist organizations. The spectrum of its values included federalism, collectivism, *and* political participation in the state. The last-named was an index of how far the CNT had traveled since 1911. Under the CEML scheme, the FAI designated itself as a revolutionary labor party with the CNT as its constituency. *Faístas*, in fact, did represent the CNT when Negrín belatedly reopened the parliament in 1938 and worked actively to depose him in favor of Manuel Azaña,* the inactive president of the Republic. But the Loyalist military collapse overcame these efforts, and *cenetistas* streamed out of Spain in February and March of 1939. The CNT operated in France* and Mexico* as an exile organization until its legalization again in the post-Franco period.

For further information, see Pierre Broué and Émile Témime, *The Revolution and the Civil War in Spain* (Boston, 1972); José Peirats, *La CNT en la revolución española* (Toulouse, 1951); and Robert Kern, *Red Years/Black Years: A Political History of Spanish Anarchism, 1911-1937* (Philadelphia, 1978).

See also Economy, Republican; Peasants, Aragonese; and Socialist Party, Spanish.

Robert W. Kern

CONSELL DE L'ESCOLA NOVA UNIFICADA (CENU). The *Consell de l'Escola Nova Unificada* (CENU) was established during the Civil War in Catalonia* to operate schools that would be devoid of any political tinge. The *Partit Socialista Unificat de Catalunya* (PSUC),* the *Partido Obrero de Unificación Marxista* (POUM),* and the *Confederación Nacional del Trabajo* (CNT)* actually honored an agreement to leave politics out of this educational system struck at the start of the Civil War by Barcelona's major political parties. This group of schools lasted for the duration of the Civil War in most Catalan urban centers but primarily in Barcelona.* Its significance lay in the fact that it provided quality education in an environment relatively free of politics—a rarity in Spanish affairs.

For further information, see Ronald Fraser, *The Blood of Spain* (New York, 1979).
See also Education; and Teachers.

James W. Cortada

ČOPIĆ, VLADIMIR (1891-1938). Čopić was a Yugoslavian volunteer in the International Brigades* fighting for the Spanish Republic. A communist deputy at home, he commanded the 15th International Brigade as shock troops at the battle of Brunete* in July 1937 and in other military campaigns. The 15th International Brigade played a significant role in the Republican offensive in the early stages of the battle by causing the Nationalists* to retreat at critical points.

For further information, see R. Casas de la Vega, *Brunete* (Madrid, 1967).
See also Army, Republican.

James W. Cortada

COPPI, GIOVANNI (1897-   ). General Coppi commanded an Italian fascist division, the Black Flames,* serving the Nationalists* in Spain in 1937. Under his command, the Black Flames joined with other Italian units in the battle of Guadalajara* in March 1937. While the Italians helped block a Nationalist advance on Madrid,* it was done at a heavy cost: many lives were lost, and the outside world clearly learned that Italy* was actively aiding Franco* with troops and supplies.

For further information, see John F. Coverdale, *Italian Intervention in the Spanish Civil War* (Princeton, N. J., 1975).
See also Army, Nationalist; and Italy.

James W. Cortada

CÓRDOBA. Córdoba, a province located in southern Spain in the region of Andalusia,* served as one of the oldest battle lines of the Spanish Civil War. The city of Córdoba fell to the Nationalists* after a short artillery bombardment and quickly became a source of support for Franco,* along with the southern portion of the province which could be used as a base of operations in the area. The northern and eastern sectors remained part of the southeastern Republican zone until March 1939. During the war, the Nationalists slowly gained ground in northern Córdoba after fighting members of the International Brigades,* the Republican Army,* and various local militias.* Most of the fighting in this area consisted of skirmishes rather than large pitched battles; even so, they were enough

of a deterrent to slow the Nationalist assault on central Spain. Much of the countryside had been pro-Republican and active in anarchist politics and collectivization long before the rebellion. Thus, when occupied by the Nationalists, it remained suspect.

The Nationalist occupation of southern Córdoba and the provincial capital led to a large number of executions, arrests, and some atrocities, possibly causing as many as 32,000 deaths. On August 20, 1936, a Republican force had marched into the province southward threatening the capital city. Although repulsed by the Nationalists, the rebels concluded that harsher control over Córdoba's population was necessary. By the end of 1936, Franco's armies had established communications between Córdoba and the major cities of Andalusia, thereby strengthening their control over the entire southern zone. Yet, sporadic fighting in the province continued throughout the war. Not until the last days of the Republic were Nationalist forces able to seize control of southeastern Spain, along with the remaining portions of Córdoba, finally sealing the fate of the Second Republic.*

For further information, see Ronald Fraser, *The Blood of Spain* (New York, 1979); and José Manuel Martínez Bande, *La Compaña de Andalucía* (Madrid, 1969).
See also Army, Nationalist; Peasants, Aragonese; and Appendix B.

James W. Cortada

CORDÓN GARCÍA, ANTONIO (1895-1965). Cordón was the Republic's chief of the technical secretariat, responsible for supplies within the Ministry of War. He had been an army officer prior to his resignation in 1932 and had returned to service, although as an avowed communist. By the end of 1936, Cordón, now a colonel, became chief of staff to General Sebastián Pozas Perea,* commander of the Republican Army of the East.* In March 1937, Cordón rose to the position of undersecretary of war, making him one of the highest ranking communist officials of the Republican government. Although there was talk in 1938 of making him minister of war, nothing came of it. He reached the rank of general officer before the end of the war.

For further information, see Antonio Cordón García, *Trayectoria (recuerdos de un artillero)* (Paris, 1971); and José Martín Blázquez, *I Helped Build an Army: Civil War Memoirs of a Spanish Staff Officer* (London, 1939).
See also Army, Republican.

James W. Cortada

CORNFORD, JOHN (1915-1936). Cornford was a British poet, a communist history student from Cambridge University, and one of the first volunteers* from Great Britain* to fight for the Spanish Republic. A grandson of Charles Darwin, he joined the *Partido Obrero de Unificación Marxista* (POUM)* on the battlefront in Aragón* during August 1936. In the following months, he fought in various battles in and around Madrid* where he was killed on December 29. Of his writings on Spain, the best remembered is *The Last Mile to Huesca*, which describes the fighting on the Aragón front.

For further information, see Peter Stansky and William Abrahams, *Journey to the Frontier* (London, 1966).
See also Intellectuals; and International Brigades.

James W. Cortada

CORTADA, ROLDÁN (1900[?])-1937). Cortada was a Catalan leader in the *Partit Socialista Unificat de Catalunya* (PSUC),* Catalonia's* communist party. At one time he had been a syndicalist and later a member of the *Federación Anarquista Ibérica* (FAI),* accepting the philosophies of anarchism. Ultimately, he joined the PSUC. He became a footnote to history when, on April 25, 1937, at Molins de Llobregat, he was assassinated. His death led the Catalan government to arrest large numbers of anarchists,* while communists all over the region battled in the streets with the anarchists. His funeral became a major display of communist strength and part of the party's effort to discredit anarchist groups. It was also the last important event before the May 1937 riots* in Barcelona* pitting anarchists against communists. It took only a small incident in early May to cause a civil war to break out in Barcelona between anarchists and communists, with the seizure of the telephone building by the police force.

For further information, see Robert W. Kern, *Red Years/Black Years: A Political History of Spanish Anarchism, 1911-1937* (Philadelphia, 1978).
See also Communist Party, Spanish.

James W. Cortada

CORTES. The Cortes, Spain's parliament, was diminished in membership and importance during the Civil War. While it was peripheral to the conduct of the war, it was of central importance to the Republic-in-exile after 1945. The history of the Cortes during the years 1936 to 1939 is one of a rump group isolated from decision-making. Its role after 1945 was more symbolic than substantive in maintaining the presence of the Republic-in-exile in Mexico* until the 1960s.

The bitter division between Left and Right in pre-Civil War Spain is nowhere better recorded than in the debates of the Cortes in the spring and early summer of 1936. The acrimonious debates degenerated to the level of verbal bloodletting by mid-June 1936. The session of June 16, 1936, typified the hostile atmosphere: the rightist leaders—José María Gil Robles* and José Calvo Sotelo*—accused the Popular Front* of leading Spain into a revolutionary state; the leftist leaders—Santiago Casares Quiroga* and Dolores Ibarruri (La Pasionaria)*—responded that it was the maneuvers of the Right that threatened the country. Casares Quiroga went on to say that he held Calvo Sotelo personally responsible for whatever came to pass in Spain. This warning looms large in the events that precipitated the Civil War. On the one hand, it was final proof to conservatives that their position was unheeded in the parliamentary process; on the other hand, it singled out Calvo Sotelo, who on the morning of July 13 was murdered by leftists in retaliation for a killing perpetrated by rightists. Two days later, the Cortes was suspended for eight days, but within seventy-two hours of that decision the Civil War erupted.

The Cortes was shunted aside along with the Constitution in the early months of the war. An agreement between communists and socialists to cooperate in the Cortes signaled efforts in August to reopen that body, but it was a Cortes decimated by the recent events of the summer of 1936. It is estimated that twenty-eight members of the Cortes were killed in the Republican zone at the outbreak of the war; nearly sixty deputies were believed murdered during the initial months of the war in the Nationalist zone; at least 100 deputies were loyal to the Nationalists* following the walkout of the Right on July 15; others were abroad as diplomats or in exile. The important decisions of the early months of the war were made without debate in the Cortes, or they were merely presented out of courtesy. An example of the former was the decision by Azaña* to place Spain's gold reserves in a secure place—the USSR*— a move he intended to submit to the Cortes for ratification when the opportunity arose. That the Cortes had become a rubberstamp was evident in the political negotiations of the coalition government to draft the Basque autonomy statute, which was voted upon in the Cortes only as a matter of formality.

The evacuation of the government from Madrid* to Valencia* in November 1936 initiated the Cortes's peripatetic period. Barely settled in Valencia, the Cortes was further reduced in importance when Juan Negrín* formed a government in mid-May 1937 and announced shortly thereafter that he would rule by decree. Six-monthly sessions of the Cortes were instituted to discuss carefully selected topics beginning with the sessions of October 1937 in the *ayuntamiento* (municipal government) of Valencia. The Cortes anticipated the move north to Catalonia* by seven months when it held its session of February 1938 at the monastery of Montserrat northwest of Barcelona.* At this session, Negrín confidently predicted the success of the Republic in the war, but events did not support his optimism. The next session of the Cortes, held at the monastery at San Cugat del Vallés in October 1938, was the occasion for a circumspect debate on Negrín's conduct of the military campaigns. Sentiment existed to challenge Negrín's leadership, but it never coalesced into a concerted effort to replace Negrín. By the meeting of February 1, 1939, at the old castle of Figueras, the last town in Catalonia short of the French border, the collapse of the Republic was evident: sixty-two members of the Cortes assembled to hear Negrín outline his three conditions for suing for peace. He sought a guarantee of Spanish independence, of the right of the Spanish people to choose their own government, and freedom from persecution after the war.

The next meeting of the Cortes was at a Paris restaurant on March 3, 1939, attended by seventeen deputies. Azaña's resignation as president of the Republic was accepted. His successor was Diego Martínez Barrio,* who had served as president of the Cortes during the war. Two days later, the Defense Committee, established in Madrid by Colonel Segismundo Casado* to supplant Negrín's government, issued its appeal to Spaniards to follow them in pursuing a course toward peace. The final session of the Cortes of the Republic was on March 31, 1939, one day before Franco's* victory. At this meeting, Negrín delivered a long defense of his actions and explained the takeover of the government by the Defense Committee, following which La Pasionaria pledged the support of the communists to Negrín, whom they considered the only legal government of the Republic. The session ended with a discussion of the refugee problem, with particular reference to representing their case to other governments in seeking aid in exile.

Following the end of the war, the Franco regime instituted a carefully controlled Cortes in 1942-1943, one whose membership reflected a corporatist basis and which acted only on legislation drafted by the executive branch. The Republic-in-exile opened its Cortes in Mexico,* where it maintained the pretext of a legitimate government for a number of years, finally fading in the late 1960s.

For further information, see Fernando Díaz-Plaja, *La España política del siglo XX*, 3d ed. (Barcelona, 1972), Vol. 3; and Hugh Thomas, *The Spanish Civil War* (New York, 1977).

David V. Holtby

CORTÉS GONZÁLEZ, SANTIAGO (1897-1937). Cortés was a captain in the Civil Guard* in the province of Córdoba.* He and a band of followers held out against the Republican forces by hiding in the mountains at the Monastery of Santa María de la Cabeza longer than any other rebel group in southern Spain, fighting local anarchist militias.* Eventually in March 1937, Republican military units overran his compound, mortally wounding the heroic captain. His last orders to his men were: "The Civil Guard and the Falange* die, but do not yield."

For further information, see Julio de Urrutia, *El cerro de los héroes* (Madrid, 1965).

James W. Cortada

CORUNNA. Corunna, a province located in the northwesternmost part of Spain in the region of Galicia* and facing onto the Atlantic, was the home province of General Francisco Franco,* who was born in El Ferrol.* The province was tied to the economy of ocean-borne trade and fishing. It also boasted the Spanish naval base in Franco's native city. Corunna and the rest of Galicia came under Nationalist control by the end of July 1936. Fighting in Corunna lasted only several hours on July 20, 1936. Manuel Hedilla,* one of the major national leaders of the Falange* party, then in the city of Corunna, aided rebel soldiers under the command of Colonel Enrique Cánovas Lacruz with local Falangists. They took the city over easily since the local workers were virtually unarmed. The civil governor of the province, Joaquín Pérez Carballo (then only twenty-seven years old), and his pregnant wife were executed, while local army officers loyal to the Republic were shot later. Some fighting continued throughout the province but ended within days.

After taking the province, supporters of the Nationalists* shot some 300 Republicans* in an attempt to "purify" the area. The province remained Nationalist territory for the duration of the war. The naval base served as a useful port of entry for foreign aid* and as a home for Nationalist ships.

For further information, see Joaquín Arrarás, *Historia de la cruzada española* (Madrid, 1940-1943), Vol. 14: 14-28; Alfonso Camín, *España a hierro y fuego* (Mexico, 1938); and Jean Flory, *La Galicie sous la botte de Franco* (Paris, 1938).

James W. Cortada

CORUNNA ROAD, BATTLE OF. Corunna Road was the scene of a battle in December 1936 connected with the Nationalists'* general campaign to surround Madrid* and thereby cut it off from outside help. Franco's* forces, under the command of General Luis Orgaz,* massed 18,000 troops for the push to Madrid. These soldiers were broken up into four units on the Corunna Road under the commands of Generals Francisco García Escámez,* Fernando Barrón,* Eduardo Sáenz de Buruaga,* and José Monasterio.* At first they took the town of Boadilla* but were pushed back with the help of international volunteers* and Russian tanks. Fighting had begun on December 13 with Nationalist offensives and Republican counteroffensives right through the Christmas season. A major battle took place at Boadilla after Christmas as the Nationalists attempted to cut this important communications link to Madrid. After taking about 7 miles of highway by January 10, 1937, members of the International Brigades* reinforced Republican forces and then inflicted heavy losses on Orgaz's troops. Soon after, fighting stalemated into inaction, broken only by sporadic fighting until the final months of the war. The fighting in this area, however, had seriously threatened Madrid and represented a major Nationalist attempt to capture the capital city and bring the war to a rapid close.

For further information, see Hugh Thomas, *The Spanish Civil War* (New York, 1977).
See also Appendix B.

James W. Cortada

COSTS. The Spanish government claimed, in 1944, that both sides spent a total of $9.375 million (30,000 million pesetas) to fight the Civil War. Property damage amounted to some 4,250 million pesetas. Only one-third of all bank deposits in existence in the Republican zone in July 1936 were recognized as legitimate in 1939, bringing the loss of accounts to some 6,000 million pesetas. In all, 150 churches were destroyed and nearly 5,000 others damaged, nearly half of which, for all intents and purposes, were considered ruined. Hundreds of towns were heavily damaged, while 250,000 houses could no longer be used.

An equal number were repairable. Costs in lost animals proved significant. One-third of all livestock vanished, and for certain types of animals, even greater losses were registered. The pig population, for example, dropped by 50.6 percent and cattle went down 34.3 percent. Productive farmland was not properly utilized, while farms lost considerable amounts of equipment. Statistics on agricultural productivity are only just now being collected; they indicate losses ranging from 11 million hectares of wheat in 1935 down to 8 million in 1939, an over 50-percent loss of wine production, and a nearly 100-percent loss of all agricultural output at battlefields. This last factor was important since many battles were fought near or on prime agricultural land, for example, along the Ebro River.* Nearly 42 percent of all train engines were destroyed, 40 percent of all rolling stock, and 70 percent of all passenger cars. A total of 220,000 tons of shipping, or 30 percent of the Spanish Merchant Marine,* also disappeared. Food* stocks virtually disappeared by early 1939. Roads, although generally in the same shape as in 1936, were not always convenient to use since bridges had been destroyed, especially those in towns and cities. In more general economic terms, by 1939 industrial production had dropped by 31 percent from 1936, agricultural production by 21 percent, national income by 26 percent, and per capita income by 28 percent.

Losses of a more intangible type, such as the death of García Lorca,* or the destruction of an old church, obviously cannot be measured. Surprisingly, many national treasures survived, despite stories of municipal records and private libraries being burned. In general, however, Spain suffered less damage as a result of the Civil War than, for example, France* did as a consequence of World War I or the USSR* in World War II. The effects of Spain's losses were visible longer because the Spanish themselves did not readily rebuild. They did not benefit from foreign aid significantly or from such massive programs as the Marshall Plan. When coupled to droughts throughout most of the planting seasons of the 1940s, recovery was slow and painful. Starvation was a real problem, especially in 1941-1942 and again to a lesser degree immediately following World War II when wheat supplies were far too low and had to be supplemented where possible by foreign sources. Lack of industrial equipment, capital, and adequate petroleum supplies during World War II also made the repair of communities and industries lethargic. It was not until the late 1950s that a more comprehensive economic recovery could be undertaken. In contrast, Western Europe* recovered from World War II by the early 1950s, obviously with significant amounts of American aid not available to Spain. The long-term psychological effects on the population* are not measurable, although health standards are. The average Spanish Army draftee, for example, did not grow in mean average height until the 1960s. Children were not receiving the kind of healthy diet required to foster growth until the late 1950s.

For further information, see Ramón Tamames, *La república; La era de Franco* (Madrid, 1973); and Hugh Thomas, *The Spanish Civil War* (New York, 1977).

See also Casualties; and Monetary Policy, Nationalist.

James W. Cortada

COUNCIL OF ARAGÓN. The Council of Aragón was the ruling body established by the anarchists* to run the region of Aragón* in the early months of the Civil War. Anarchists had entered the Catalan government in September 1936, along with other political groups such as the communists and the *Partido Obrero de Unificacíon Marxista* (POUM).* Yet, because the anarchist militia controlled Aragón, it became possible to establish there a libertarian form of government independent of the Generalitat* or the Republic. Local collectives defied the authority of both the Generalitat and the Republic by meeting that September at Bujaroloz where they formed a local Council of Defense, headquartering it in Fraga to run all of Aragón. Their thought was to establish a "Spanish Ukraine" in the rural sectors of Aragón and to manage the establishment with the Council of Aragón. In the spring of 1937, the Council of Aragón, now in Caspe, allowed representation from other political groups such as members of the *Union General de Trabajadores* (UGT),* Communist party,* and one Republican. Concurrently, anarchists joined the Republican government.

By this time, Aragón was virtually independent of the Republican government. The Council of Aragón negotiated trade with other countries (mainly France* and Belgium*), had a police* force, courts, and economic development program, and agencies to insure the development of a collectivist libertarian society. It did not have its own army, however. Collectives varied widely in structure within Aragón, but they did have some qualified successes in growing the 1937 crops. What ultimately destroyed the effectiveness of the semi-autonomous council was the hostility of the communists and the Republican government. Communists saw Aragón as a threat to their growing influence. The Republican government had the same concern, along with feelings of frustration at not being able to collect badly needed tax revenues or getting a great share of local resources for the war effort.

After the May 1937 riots* in Barcelona* were over and the power of the anarchists there was broken, it became easier to extend Republican control over Aragón. In August, an offensive directed by the Republicans* against the Nationalists* to the west was launched in Aragón. Republican leaders hoped that a byproduct of this offensive would be the demise of Aragonese independence and a return to the Republic of control over their affairs. In the same month, once that year's harvest was in, the government dissolved the Council of Aragón. Members of the council were arrested, along with some 600 other local anarchists. Collectives came under Republican and communist control, while some peasant farmers retrieved valuable equipment and food for their own use. Meanwhile, the military campaign in Aragón continued through September and into October. While the Nationalists suffered momentary reverses, the offensive failed to achieve any meaningful military victory, only political ones in Aragón.

The experience with the Council of Aragón clearly illustrates one of the fundamental causes of the Republic's failure to win the war. Various political groups in the Republican zone expanded much energy competing for power. Almost from the beginning of the war, anarchists and communists quarreled among themselves and even killed each other. The communists finally won the struggle in the spring of 1937 but not before a mini-civil war had taken place within the Republican zone. Rivalries constantly sapped the Republic's strength during the war years. In Aragón there existed the council, in Barelona* the Generalitat,* and in Valencia* the Republican government and throughout at least a half dozen major parties—all competing for power and resources. The Council of Aragón thus emerged as one example out of many of the conflicting and complex political matrix existing in the Republican zone.

For further information, see Robert W. Kern, *Red Years/Black Years: A Political History of Spanish Anarchism, 1911-1937* (Philadelphia, 1978); Gaston Leval, *L'Espagne libertaire* (Paris, 1971); César Lorenzo, *Les Anarchistes espagnols et le pouvoir* (Paris, 1969); Frank Mintz, *L'Autogestion dans l'Espagne révolutionnaire* (Paris, 1970); and José Peirats, *La CNT en la revolución española*, 3 vols. (Toulouse, 1951-1953).

See also Economy, Republican; and Peasantry, Aragonese.

James W. Cortada

COUNCIL OF ASTURIAS. The Council of Asturias was the local government of Asturias* on the Republican side during the first year of the Spanish Civil War, that is, until the entire north fell to the Nationalists* in 1937. This local government, dominated by members of the *Confederación Nacional del Trabajo* (CNT)* and the *Unión General de Trabajadores* (UGT),* attempted to establish independently of the Republican regime in Madrid* (which was separated from it by Nationalist-held territory in central and northern Spain) an economy characterized by collectivization of industry and agriculture. The Catholic Church* was banned, and its priests and nuns arrested. Workers' councils made decisions relevant to the community and were clearly represented in the local government.

For further information, see Hugh Thomas, *The Spanish Civil War* (New York, 1977).
See also Economy, Republican.

James W. Cortada

"CRUSADE, THE." *"La Crusada"* (the Crusade) was a widely used phrase employed by the Nationalists* to describe their "cause" in the Civil War. Born out of a combination of political and quasireligious rhetoric, and primarily generated by the Falange,* it suggested that Franco's* forces were those of order and justice, light, and traditional Spanish considerations. The Nationalists were "crusading" against the anticlerical pagan forces of anarchism, communism, socialism, and other non-Christian groups in order to reestablish a more conservative, even "true democracy." Thus, almost from the beginning, the term was used as a rallying point for political rhetoric and Nationalist propaganda.

For further information, see Stanley G. Payne, *Falange: A History of Spanish Fascism* (Stanford, Calif., 1961); and Hugh Thomas, *The Spanish Civil War* (New York, 1977).

James W. Cortada

CUBA. Cuba officially remained neutral in the Spanish Civil War. The government had the difficult problem of not offending large numbers of important Spaniards living in Cuba, some of whom favored the Nationalists* and others the Republicans.* Much of the business community in Havana, for example, was Spanish and became as emotionally involved in the issues of the Civil War as did Spaniards in Spain. A large, well-organized pro-Nationalist group in Cuba supported Falangist activities and raised money for Franco's* cause. For the Francoists Cuba became a listening post in Latin America* and a funnel for money, supplies, and information. Those on the political Left in Cuban politics, such as the local Communist party, favored the Republic. Communists who had combat experience from the Machado Revolution of 1933 fought for the Republic. About 100 Cubans fought in Spain, mainly in the North American brigades where they were viewed as a cultural link between Spain and the New World. Important Cuban political radicals fought in Spain, including Nicolas Guillen and the communist author Pablo de la Torriente Brau who died in the Civil War.

The government of Cuba, although mixed in its feelings toward the conflict, essentially followed the policies established by the United States* and the rest of Latin America, strongly favoring Franco only after he had won the war. Neutrality with support for a mediated end to the conflict in effect became the policy of the Cuban government. In conjunction with Washington, Havana supported efforts to stop the war short of its actual involvement and attempted to reduce the divisions caused by the fighting within Spanish communities in Cuba.

At the end of the war, a substantial number of Republican exiles came to Cuba where they became politically active during the 1940s and at a time when Havana enthusiastically approved of Franco's government. These exiles included academics, technocrats, and some members of the legal and medical professions.

For further information, see Norberto Fuentes, "Combatientes cubanas en España," *Areito* 5, Nos. 19-20 (1979):20-24; Raúl Roa, *Pablo de la Torriente Brau y la revolución española* (Havana, 1937); and Hugh Thomas, *Cuba: The Pursuit of Freedom* (New York, 1971).

James W. Cortada

CUENCA. Cuenca, a province located in central Spain just east of Madrid* in the region of New Castile,* was in the direct line of fighting for control of Madrid to the west and Valencia* to the east. These two cities served as capitals for the Republic during the Civil War. Although Cuenca remained in Republican control until the last days of the war, for many months, its northern border came close to the edge of Nationalist-controlled territory protruding from Catalonia* and Aragón.* Before the war, the province had been moderately liberal and supportive of the Republic. When hostilities began, the citizens of this province backed the Republic. In the provincial capital of Cuenca, crowds lashed out against the cathedral, burning its library of approximately 10,000 books, many of them rare, along with valuable art.* Local prejudice against the Catholic Church* extended to murdering the local bishop, one of twelve who died at the hands of Republican sympathizers during the war.

In the course of the fighting, normal law and order virtually ended in Cuenca as various anarchist militia columns wandered through the province. It had some of the poorest roads in Spain and hardly any telephone or telegraphic communications, making it difficult for the civil governor to manage the province. Thus, if anything, farmers continued to live as they had in past years, almost oblivious to revolutionary theories of collectivization and bothered only by marauding bands of anarchists* and periodically by warring elements from both sides. Yet, the fighting took a heavy toll in manpower drawn to the Republic's armies, making it possible for only 14 percent of the land usually sown with wheat to be in production during most of the war. Since Cuenca had contributed over 1 million hectares of land for raising wheat each year prior to 1936, the loss in productivity hit hard at the Republic's food* supply. The issue became a moot point in March 1939 when the Nationalist forces overran Cuenca on their way toward capturing Valencia and points south.

For further information, see José Manuel Martínez Bande, *Los cien últimos días de la república* (Barcelona, 1972); and Hugh Thomas, *The Spanish Civil War* (New York, 1977).

See also Daily Life, Republican zone; and Appendix B.

James W. Cortada

CUERVO RADIGALES, MÁXIMO (1893-   ). Cuervo, a career army officer, fought with the Nationalists.* By the end of the Civil War, he was director of prisons within the military legal corps. As such, he had responsibility for housing tens of thousands of Republican prisoners* and for carrying out the orders of execution imposed by Franco's* military courts after the war.

For further information, see Juan M. Molina, *Noche sobre España* (Mexico, 1958).

James W. Cortada

CUNARD, NANCY (1896-1965). Cunard epitomized the foreign writers and intellectuals* who, while stirred to defend the Republic passionately, knew nothing of the political machinations of the Civil War. Cunard enlisted her talents as poet and journalist in the international propaganda war on behalf of the Republic. Because she was primarily a propagandist, she is little remembered as an individual while the fruits of her efforts are well known.

In 1936, Cunard, granddaughter of the founder of the Cunard steamship line, was a minor British poet known more for her unconventional life-style, railings against racism, and fraternizing with writers than for her literary prowess. Her involvement in the Civil War was consistent with her past: her writing from the period is largely forgotten, but the support she secured from intellectuals was important for the Republican cause.

As a poet, her efforts to rally fellow writers to the defense of the Republic resulted in the series "Poets of the World Defend the Spanish People" and a *Left Review* pamphlet in which British authors took a stand on the war. The idea for the poetry series had been suggested to her by Pablo Neruda,* whom she had met in Madrid* during her four-month visit to Spain in the summer and autumn of 1936. In the spring of 1937, she initiated, solicited contributions, and published a series of six leaflets of poetry inspired by the war. The fifth leaflet contained W. H. Auden's* poem "Spain," perhaps there making its first appearance in print. That same spring she also drafted a questionnaire addressed to writers and poets in Great Britain,* asking them to take sides on the war. Joining her in issuing this circular were eleven other writers whom she had recruited, including Auden, Heinrich Mann, Neruda, and Steven Spender. Of the 148 replies, 127 were pro-Republic, five pro-Franco,* and sixteen neutral. The answers were published in November 1937 by *Left Review*. Sales of both the leaflets and the pamphlet were brisk, and portions of the revenue from both went to the Republic's benefit. These publications sponsored by Cunard began the now common practice of well-known writers and thinkers lending their support to manifestos on political causes.

Following her second trip to Spain from November 1937 to January 1938, Cunard began to work to help Republican refugees.* She continued aiding them through her journalistic pieces in the *Manchester Guardian* beginning in January 1939, which alerted the world to the privations of those placed in the refugee camps in southern France.* She also interceded, at considerable personal risk, to rescue some Spanish friends, an action that she recalled near the end of her life as the most meaningful of her wartime efforts.

For further information, see Anne Chisholm, *Nancy Cunard* (New York, 1979).

See also Literature.

David V. Holtby

CZECHOSLOVAKIA. In 1938, Hitler* was threatening to use force to gain control of the Sudeten, a portion of Czechoslovakia* which was inhabited primarily by people of German ancestry with strong ties to Germany.* The British, seeking to avert a general European war, asked Hitler to meet at Munich in September 1938. At the Munich Conference,* France* and Great Britain* agreed to allow Hitler to reclaim the contested area in Czechoslovakia by not supporting the Prague government on this issue and through public approval of the German move. In exchange, Hitler agreed that he would not attempt to acquire more property in Eastern Europe.* The crisis averted what each government perceived would be a general war in Europe.

Britain was particularly concerned that war not break out in Eastern Europe and, therefore, spent less time on the Spanish crisis and more on Czechoslovakia. At the time, Juan Negrín* believed that Spain would be drawn into a general war if the crisis in Czechoslovakia were not resolved, complicating the matters in the Iberian Peninsula to the point where current Spanish policies and expectations would have to be radically changed. Negrín hoped for such a crisis as a means of drawing France and Britain into the war against fascism and Franco.* The British thought that since the Czechoslovakian problem had been solved with a conference the Spanish war could perhaps be similarly terminated. The Spanish Republic objected, fearing Spain might also be divided into two, much like Czechoslovakia.

Both sides in the Spanish conflict sought to blunt the British move for another conference. On October 2, 1938, Negrín made a speech on the radio* calling on all Spaniards to settle their differences, thereby letting the world know for the first time that he would be willing to have a negotiated settlement. Franco hinted to Sir Robert Hodgson, the British diplomatic agent assigned to him, that the Munich formula would not meet with his approval. The Nationalists* told Germany that the war had to be pushed to its conclusion and that otherwise all efforts to that date would have been for naught. Franco now demanded more supplies and arms from Germany. Meanwhile, the USSR* concluded that France and Britain were not willing to stand up against Hitler. Stalin* therefore explored the possibility of a settlement with Berlin.

The result on Spain was clear: Stalin was prepared to withdraw from the Iberian Peninsula, deny the Republic its major source of help, and force the removal of the International Brigades* as well. The Germans had also concluded that, if France and Britain would not risk war for Czechoslovakia, then they might not fight for Spain. Hence, Berlin was now willing to help Franco push the conflict to a successful Nationalist victory. In fact, it was not until after Munich that German aid to Franco was decisive enough to help bring about his victory. Before Munich, significant aid might have brought on a general war in Europe, which Berlin did not want.

The great winner was Franco. He now had full German commitment to his cause. Had Germany lost its bid for Czechoslovakian territory, then a general conflagration might well have led to a French invasion of Spain in support of the Spanish Republic. Franco would have been one of the first casualties of the larger conflict.

Czechoslovakia played yet another role in the Civil War: it unofficially supported the Republic against all forms of fascism. Like France, Czechoslovakia wanted to restrict the fighting to Spain and hurt the Germans, and advocated an arms embargo to the Spanish Peninsula in 1936. Czechoslovakians helped the Republic in many ways as the war continued. They allowed Russians to pass through on their way to Spain. The Soviet Union established a bogus import-export company in the country to facilitate the shipment of supplies to the Republic, and allowed the sale of locally made arms quietly to go to Spain, which included anti-aircraft guns, cannons, and Chato fighters. More public was the contribution of Czechoslovakian citizens to the International Brigades. Approximately 1,500 fought in Spain, primarily in the Mazaryk Division of the 129th Brigade, which was also composed of Bulgarians, Yugoslavs, Hungarians, and Albanians. Their period of service was primarily during 1937 and the first half of 1938.

For further information, see Arthur London, *L'Aveu* (Paris, 1969); Frantisek Moravec (Czechoslovakian intelligence agent), *Master of Spies* (London, 1975); and K. G. Robbins, *Munich* (London, 1968).

James W. Cortada

D

DAILY LIFE, NATIONALIST ZONE. Daily life in the Nationalist zone became a subject of growing importance as Franco's* forces expanded their control over Spain. The area which from the beginning of the Civil War was called the Nationalist zone consisted of the entire region of Galicia,* the kingdom of Aragón,* the provinces of León,* all of Old Castile* (except Santander*), as well as Navarre.* In Estremadura,* the province of Caceres* was Nationalist, and in Andalusia,* the cities of Seville,* Córdoba,* Cádiz,* and Huelva. Broad areas in these sections did not initially submit to the rebels. The Nationalist zone was predominantly agricultural and had scarce industrialization; it represented what could be called conservative and traditional Spain. The success of the coup, initiated by part of the army, found an echo of favorable public opinion in the old cities of Castile and León, as well as in Navarre, given the right-wing nature of the rebellion's organization. In other parts, such as in Galicia, Aragón, and the cities of Andalusia, the victory can be attributed to the daring of the military uprising as well as to the need to overcome popular opposition through a violent oppression. A considerable mass of disaffected people lived in these zones, thereby leading to the imposition of a stern authoritarianism. At all costs it became necessary to avoid a rebellion in the rear that would have been a disaster for the uprising since the rebellion had triumphed in only one-third of the peninsula.

Daily life was affected by the fact that this was a fratricidal conflict, which was fought behind the lines as well as at the front.

Strict and severe order was introduced in the army-controlled zone. Military tribunals levied death sentences against leaders, militants, as well as Republicans,* socialists, anarchists,* and communists, that is, those convicted or suspected of belonging to a Popular Front* organization. In the early days of the war and throughout the summer of 1936, along the highways could be seen the bodies of those summarily executed without due process of law. Nightly seizures were made in the jails or arrests were made in workers' neighborhoods. In some places, such as Valladolid* or Pamplona,* the executions were converted into spectacles attended by large crowds, and eventually the military authorities were forced to prohibit the viewing of executions. The repression extended to include liberals and Masons. Just as the Republicans had imposed a "Red Terror," so among the Nationalists* there existed a "White Terror." In the Republican zone, the persecution affected property owners, industrialists, and, in general, members of the middle and upper classes. In the Nationalist zone, the objects of persecution were the working class and men in the liberal professions known to entertain leftist ideals. All of these persons were categorized as "reds," whereas in the Republican zone all opposed to the Republic were dubbed "fascists."

The newspapers, locales, and assets of such groups were seized, as were the assets of persons accused of having belonged to or having engaged in enemy propaganda. Repression and counterrevolutionary actions were imposed in the face of any opposition to what was later called the Glorious National Movement. Even listening to Republican radio* broadcasts that raised doubts about the success of the military coup led to charges of "defeatism," which was a serious crime.

If the atmosphere in the government zone was revolutionary, that in Nationalist-held areas was warlike. Troops and volunteers* marched to the front daily to the sound of martial music. For the leaders of the coup, who had been saved from failure by Italian and German air power, it was necessary to mobilize resources to the maximum.

Under the rigid order established, all inhabitants were required to have a document of identification, including a photograph which, through the cooperation of authorities, Civil Guard* chiefs and parish priests, stated whether the bearer favored, opposed, or was indifferent to the Nationalist cause. After this screening, many of those who were known to be dissaffected with the regime found themselves forced to modify their position. Not a few were forced to contribute money, gold, or jewelry to finance the war. Since the area that initially rebelled was so poor and there was a lack of gold reserves, private sources had to be tapped to pay off the expenses of the conflict.

The changes in usage and customs were those characteristic of the Falange.* People now saluted in the fascist manner, with an upraised arm. The term "comrade" came into vogue, while for a vocal salute a vigorous "Arriba España" was used. The informal "tu" (you) instead of the formal and customary "usted," "vosotros," and so on, was attempted but did not gain wide acceptance; it was limited mainly to official documents of the Falange party. In summary, the impulse of the Falange was to create new norms of behavior with respect to social relations. Such changes required toughness, precision, and energy, none of which were characteristic in a population* composed primarily of right-wing traditionalist conservatives and, therefore, somewhat retrograde. This was particularly so in the majority of the cities of Castile, León, and Galicia, all of them located in the Nationalist rearguard. Confronting the atmosphere of modernity advocated by the Falange were the legislative measures and actions of the military which tended towards a reactionary policy insistent on restoring certain religious, familial, and property values in accordance with those inherited from traditional Spain. The Republican zone was marked predominantly by an urban spirit, industry, and the democracy of a progressive community. As a result, the Nationalists viewed the Civil War as a clash between the countryside and the city, mysticism and science, faith and heresy. Facing variant modernizing currents, Nationalist Spain claimed it was returning the country to ascetism and to a military and religious spirit as a way of life.

The first organization created in the territory under military control was the *Junta de Defensa Nacional*,* which opposed all Republican measures aimed at liberalizing customs. Hence, the *Junta* forbade coeducation and annulled laws permitting divorce and civil marriages, specifying the religious matrimonial ceremony as the only valid one. Many children were hurriedly baptized, and quite a few couples opted for a church wedding rather than run the risk of having their union considered concubinage.

Also intensive were the efforts of the provincial governors in defense of "proper" behavior. With respect of bathing on beaches, regulations governed what kind of bathing suits were permitted, especially those for women. There were admonitions against lipstick, and specific rules for clothing, especially women's, with depth of necklines in front and length of dresses being spelled out.

The Catholic Church* threatened with biblical punishment those who in its judgment erred against modesty. The Church claimed that God had levied the war on the nation as punishment for its wantonness. Despite all these threats and admonitions, it was in the Nationalist zone during the war era that the modernization of habits for Spanish women began. Feminine mobilization and participation in hospitals, even in helping combatants, wrested the provincial woman from a protected home life. These changes and the vast mobility of the men brought the sexes closer together in a more direct and freer way.

For many young couples, the life of conventional morality was no longer possible. Husbands were absent from home at the front, and with so many battle deaths, widows were commonly seen. Small wonder, then, that military victories were celebrated with wild enthusiasm. On those occasions, repressed people threw themselves into merrymaking. Nine months after these emotional moments, an increase in the number of births would be recorded.

One unfortunate social byproduct of the Civil War was a considerable increase in prostitution. A great number of women—widows, daughters, or sisters of those who were killed, disappeared, or were incarcerated for long periods—found themselves alone and without preparation, let alone with the resources needed to face life. Many became prostitutes. The phenomenon became alarming with young women present in bars and places traditionally not frequented by Spanish women. In the Nationalist zone there were mandated rules prohibiting the "exhibition of women dedicated to carnal trade in public streets." The phenomenon of prostitution derived from circumstances of the times was one of the sad consequences of the war.

The Nationalist zone did not experience hunger and air attacks as systematically or acutely as the Republicans. At the beginning of the conflict, aerial bombardment certainly affected Granada, Seville, Valladolid, Saragossa* and other provincial capitals, but such attacks were not continuous as they were in the Republican zone. Hence, daily life in the Nationalist sector was a more normal one. The climate of victory was strong and was nurtured carefully from the top. The Nationalist leaders avoided confrontations between political groups supporting the military while promoting unity and patriotism.

While the children on the Republican side experienced separations and evacuation, were malnourished, and lived in fear, those in the Nationalist areas benefited from the calmness of their sector. Children were a favorite subject for Nationalist propaganda. From the earliest age, propagandists sought to impart to the children a reverence for symbols and ideas that were considered to belong to an "eternal" Spain. Children had toy arms as playthings, participated in parades, and played make-believe war in which those who took the part of the "Reds" would lose. Unfortunately, one of the "war games" played included the use of firing squads, with some players acting as "Reds" and the others as executioners. But children in the Republican zone faced the tragic realities of executions. The children of those who had been executed by real firing squads went to orphanages or were placed under the care of the Social Auxiliary Organization, the Falange agency which provided food* to families destroyed by the war. The "soto voce" commentary circulating at the time was that it would be better to decrease the number of those shot by firing squads in order not to find it necessary to "father" their children.

In October 1937, after conquest of the northern sector of the Republic—Vizcaya,* Santander,* and Asturias*—the Nationalist territory extended over almost 60 percent of the surface of Spain. With regard to the new population incorporated into the Nationalist area, purification criteria continued to be applied strictly. Military tribunals continued to apply the statutes of the code governing a state of war. This meant more firing squads, a larger penal population, and more Republican prisoners-of-war (unless they had someone to "guarantee" them) in concentration camps* and, after release, assignment to labor battalions.

Trials were significant for persons in the Republican zone owing to military defeats and loss of property, while in the Nationalist sector they were the consequence of the influx of fugitives and of people fleeing the terror reigning in the government-controlled areas. Those who sympathized with the Nationalist movement, who were persecuted by the Republic, or who had taken refuge in Madrid's* embassies and had managed to depart under the protection of a foreign flag in many cases reached the Nationalist zone by crossing the frontier at Irún.* In time, this stream of refugees became very great, and they were subjected to very tight control. Until the refugees could be guaranteed by someone in the Nationalist zone, they were detained. Their presence swelled the population of the cities in the rear lines of the Nationalists. Some cities such as San Sebastián acquired a brilliant and frivolous tone, much out of line with the gravity of the times. Shows were fully attended, and bullfights,* now vindicated as a national past-time in the Francoist zone, were held in the plazas of Burgos,* Salamanca,* Seville, and Saragossa. Each festivity was converted into a patriotic expression, replete with homage to the combatants and the militias.*

Speculators and opportunists were active in the Francoist zone, with both seeking to take advantage of the exceptional circumstances of war. Fear of devaluation led to the hoarding of silver coins almost from the beginning. Five peseta* coins, those with a face value of 2 and 1, also ceased to circulate by October 1936. Threats of severe punishment did not stop this phenomenon. Until paper money could be issued to replace the silver that had disappeared, existing paper was stamped in order to avoid as much as possible its transfer to the Republican zone. But many merchants, lacking confidence in the stamped paper currency, refused to accept it despite great personal danger. Their rationale was that "money should not be identified politically." The issuance of 1 peseta and 5 peseta notes solved the exchange problem, which together with the sound economic policy of the Nationalist side made it possible for this currency to maintain its purchasing power. As a consequence, the Nationalist peseta began to be priced advantageously in foreign markets against Republican pesetas whose decline accelerated as the war continued. Nevertheless, towards the end of the war, 5 and 10 centime coins also disappeared, with the result that postage stamps had to be used for change.

With respect to supplies, the Nationalist zone was in an advantageous position. Not only did it have fishing areas such as Galicia, cereals from Castile,* and livestock from Estremadura,* but it also did not have to feed large cities, which was the case with the Republic. Hence, an abundance of food prevailed in rebel areas. For the Republican zone, living conditions were more severe. Even though hoarding did take place in Nationalist areas, energetic measures taken by the authorities stopped speculation, sharply forcing markets to be supplied. As a result, surpluses were created with which inhabitants of those provinces that fell into Nationalist hands were eventually fed. On the other hand, controlled inflation resulted in modest price rises.

As a propaganda weapon, one of the Naionalist radio stations would read restaurant menus from Salamaca* or Burgos* quoting prices. Such broadcasts no doubt had effect on the starving populace in the Republican zone.

For those imprisoned or in hiding in the Republican sector, the Nationalist victory and the end of the war meant liberation at last, whereas the Republicans incarcerated in the Nationalist zone could only hope for general amnesty at the end of the war. Such hopes were in vain for with the Nationalist victory came severe repression and an enormous increase in the penal population. For those in Nationalist territory who had fled persecution and were in hiding, the end of the war brought no relief since Franco continued to jail and execute Republicans for over a decade.

"Lost" throughout the many towns of Spain were frightened men living subhuman existences in lofts or behind walls never seeing the light of day nor the sun. To these at the war's end were added those who remained in hiding to escape death or incarceration. Some did not emerge until 1976—twenty-eight years after the war's end—when a decree canceled all penalties associated with the war. One person did not emerge until the death of General Franco in 1975. The story of these men "buried alive" is terrifying evidence of the hate unleashed in a Spain divided by the Civil War.

For further information, see Rafael Abella, *La vida cotidiana durante la guerra civil: La España nacional* (Barcelona, 1973); Ronald Fraser, *Blood of Spain* (New York, 1979); Ramón Tamames, *La República: La era de Franco* (Madrid, 1979); and Hugh Thomas, *The Spanish Civil War* (New York, 1977).

See also Daily Life, Republican zone; Nutrition; and Workers, Catalan.

Rafael Abella

DAILY LIFE, REPUBLICAN ZONE. The Republican zone comprised all of New Castile,* including the capital Madrid,* the Basque provinces of Guipúzcoa* and Vizcaya,* Santander,* and Austurias.* The capital of Austurias, Oviedo,* remained surrounded by forces loyal to the Republic. Also in the Republican zone were the four Catalan provinces made up of the great urban center of Barcelona* and all of the Levante* provinces including Valencia,* Alicante,* and Castellón,* as well as Murcia* and Albacete.* In Andalusia,* Jaen* and a good portion of the provinces of Córdoba,* Granada,* Seville,* and Huelva* remained loyal, with the exception of their capitals. Finally, in the western region, Cáceres* and Badajoz* were divided, the first passing to the insurgents and the second remaining loyal to the Republic.

The Republican zone covered 61 percent of the total surface area of Spain and contained 16 million inhabitants, or 66.6 percent of the total population. From an economic point of view, it had the most highly industrialized zones, those whose standard of living was the highest and whose resources were the greatest, including the reserves of the Bank of Spain.* On the other hand, the Republicans* had no grain-growing and grazing lands or fisheries. Another disadvantage was that in the event of prolonged hostilities, the Republicans would face difficulties of food* distribution, for the zone contained major population* clusters— Madrid, Barcelona, Valencia, and Bilbao.*

Daily life in Republican Spain would be marked by the realities of war with a battle in the front and another one in the rear fought simultaneously. The revolution let loose a war of terroristic persecution against the enemies of the Republic. Sympathy for antirevolutionary ideas, as well as possession of religious goods or religious beliefs, could mean loss of life.

Daily life was filled with insecurity, with searches, lootings, arrests, and executions common. In some sections of Madrid, Barcelona, and the rest of the Republican capitals, victims would be exhibited publicly. Government, devoid of its coercive methods, was impotent to stop the disorder.

In the early days of the war, life changed radically, with a whole world of property values, hierarchies, and respect for others' beliefs destroyed after the July revolution. The general strike, decreed in response to the military pronouncement, had made workers evade discipline. Company and property takeovers had left ownership rights in a suspended state. "Bonds," or documents that substituted for money, shielded all expropriations. Shops and businesses were despoiled of articles and food in exchange for "documents" issued by the syndicates or by political organizations. Spoilage of property, goods, and vehicles belonging to those who were considered "enemies of the people" became a common event. Many of the appropriations were followed by arbitrary arrest of the owners, who were later executed so that they could not reclaim their seized property. With regard to the executions, the judicial system was powerless, merely providing official documentation of corpses found on highways, photographing the dead and cataloging their identification. Anonymous notes informing on others and personal vendettas became commonplace.

External aspects of the Republican zone changed the entire appearance of Spanish society. Hats and ties disappeared, people greeted each other with raised fists, while the traditional "goodbye" (*adiós*) was replaced by "health" (*salud*). Only being part of the proletariat protected an individual from suspicion. At first a union card was a guarantee of survival, and many people's lives were saved through a false union card.

The change in customs reflected the profound social revolution that had occurred in Republican Spain. The style of addressing people was changed, and the fraternal word "comrade" (*compañero*) was employed instead. The use of domestic servants was discouraged. Porters and janitors continued their respective functions but acted as the equals of the tenants. Waiters could not leave their jobs, but things that gave a servile quality to their labor, such as tips, were eliminated. Class distinctions disappeared. Generally, the people felt that the gigantic transformation in their lives was to their advantage, enabling their children to attend schools of the bourgeoisie and workers in the fields to own the land they worked. Other measure were geared toward protecting the poor, such as a decrease in rents and a reduction of the work week from forty-eight to forty hours.

The seizure of businesses, whose owners had been considered "enemies of the popular cause" (*enemigos de la causa popular*), made possible the socialization of property, principally of productive entities (such as factories and plants) which remained in the hands of committees representing their workers. Anarchists,* socialists, and communists mobilized their followers to demand the accomplishment of revolutionary precepts which were to embrace all aspects of society—political, economic, and social—and even the role of the individual.

One major social change wrought by the war was the participation of women as active militants in politics and in the war itself. Women were now assigned the role of helpmate to men, and marriage became an exclusively civil event while free unions proliferated. In this context, unwed mothers were rehabilitated, and their children were made legitimate. Another rehabilitative activity involved prostitutes. The anarchist organization "Free Women" (*Mujeres Libres*) instituted an extensive campaign to eradicate prostitution, encouraging women to develop their human values and to dedicate themselves to maternity or to the new society being created which would have no place for white slavery. To a certain extent, then, daily life in the Republican zone was influenced by the anarchists' utopian puritanism.

In the summer of 1936, internal disruptions provoked by the revolution had already combined with the external commotions caused by the war itself. Early difficulties centered on food and the Nationalist advances into Estremadura* and Castile. Large numbers of refugees* from these regions arrived in Madrid, fleeting from the Nationalist occupation of the south. The population of the capital increased, complicating the supply of food. When Franco's* troops reached the gates of Madrid in November 1936, there were artillery bombardments and air attacks on the capital. These threats to the civilian population posed the greatest problem to authorities: evacuation. This was only the beginning of a painful period for inhabitants of the Republican zone. After the evacuation of women and children from Madrid came the exodus of the population of Málaga,* occupied by the Nationalists* in March 1937 and later that of Asturias, Vizcaya, and Santander. Entire families found themselves uprooted from their land and homes. Shelters and hous-

ing had to be set up to accommodate them. The increase in aerial bombings forced the exodus of Spanish children to foreign countries, an exodus that was made even more necessary by the scarcity of food. Children were sent to France,* Great Britain,* Belgium,* Holland,* and even Mexico* and the USSR.* Later, when the Nationalist advance into Aragón* took place and again at the end of the Civil War, when Catalonia* fell, all the children who had been evacuated to these regions had to undertake a new exile. This time they turned toward France through snow-covered paths, suffering from cold and hunger, thus presenting the most pathetic image of the Republican defeat. The refugees became one of the Spanish Republic's greatest problems. The government was constantly faced with the loss of territories, which worsened the food situation. Many of the inhabitants of the conquered areas chose to flee from the forces of occupation. This gave way to family breakdowns, the disappearance of people, and all the grave problems associated with refugees.

Certainly, the two greatest problems that shaped the lives of those who lived through the war in the Republican zone were hunger and bombings. The first food scarcity began in the summer of 1936. The revolutionary upheaval disturbed the normal shipment of supplies, while the early symptoms of inflation led merchants to hide and hoard, a normal situation in such abnormal times. In this manner, the most expensive and necessary foodstuffs—meat, fish, and eggs—became scarce in normal quantities, only to reappear later in a black market that made these articles even more expensive.

Inflation caused the disappearance of silver money in legal use before the Civil War and, later, copper coins which constituted small denominations. This forced the issuance of an extraordinary amount of paper money, adding to the rise in public expenditures which degenerated into galloping inflation. The repercussions of this situation at the domestic level were enormous. People found themselves without small change for their daily purchases and for public services. The Madrid government authorized new coins to be made of copper and tin, but before they could appear housewives and the public in general faced the terrible problem of not being able to meet their most elementary needs. In view of these circumstances, companies had to be authorized to issue coupons with monetary value. This authorization was later extended to municipal governments, syndicates, cooperatives, and collectives. On the other hand, the geographic dispersion of the Republican territory and the autonomous governments which some of these zones enjoyed, such as those of

Euzkadi (Basque) and Catalonia, made governments in these regions, along with councils in Asturias and Santander, issue new bank notes.

This economic upheaval would bring in its wake the collapse of the peseta.* In 1937, it made the Republican zone a showplace for bills of the most varied origin and of coins manufactured with the strangest materials and given the most unusual shapes. Through this unprecedented issue of coins, the people were able to solve some of the problems of daily life because the new Republican peseta disappeared almost as soon as it was put into circulation. In May 1937, the Negrín* government stopped the crazy fiduciary circulations. But the harm had already been done, with the loss of confidence in the value of money producing irreparable consequences. It was difficult to attribute more value to official currencies that to that of the purely transactional such as plastic pieces, carton, leather, scrap metal, and aluminum. All "currencies" served solely to stop the general paralysis of the country or the return to prehistoric times in which barter was the only form of acquisition.

This economic turmoil brought with it the growth of speculation. Its most dramatic manifestation in daily life was with foodstuffs. The scarcity of provisions provoked by the loss of wheat-growing and grazing zones led to the substitutions practiced by merchants and their hiding of products (done also by farmers), so that they might sell them at higher prices than those established by the government. Although rationing was established, it posed no obstacle to the creation of great differences in the level of nutrition* in the Republican zones. As has already been noted, Madrid began to feel scarcities toward the end of the summer in 1936. In November, it was Barcelona's turn to suffer lack of supplies. When Madrid was attacked the same month, the capital was almost surrounded, making it necessary to supply the city of almost a million inhabitants through one road only. Municipal services and troops defending the city also had to use this highway.

With rationing, the bread allowance, for instance, dropped to 300 grams per person, while sugar was now sold for medicinal purposes only, meat and fish were exclusively for combatants. The nutrition of Madrid's million inhabitants, for example, rested primarily on greens and beans. At the beginning of 1937, the scarcity was extended to all Republican territories. Bread was reduced to 100 grams daily per person, and milk and meat disappeared; yet, it was possible to get them through the black market. The populace was limited to yams, tomatoes, lentils, and garden vegetables, a situation that did not change for the duration of the

war. In time, people had to eat the most varied of seeds, such as sunflower. Long lines formed for rationing where women, who had gotten up at dawn, would suffer through all kinds of weather and aerial bombardments by the Nationalists or from ships off coastal towns. Tobacco eventually disappeared completely, leading men to smoke the strangest herbs and weeds.

With the arrival of the second winter of the war, existence in the Republican zone became extremely difficult. By then, Republican territory had been reduced to 42 percent of Spain, but the losses in terms of inhabitants were not correlative because a good portion of the people living in overrun areas had fled to existing Republican zones, causing even greater scarcities of food. The daily struggle for food became obsessive. In Madrid, even cats and dogs were sacrificed. Life in the Republican rearguard thus had lost all traces of normalcy, while aerial alarms forced people into bomb shelters for long periods of time.

Scarcity forced some people to travel to nearby towns in search of food. Farmers did not turn over some supplies to rationing agencies and thus these commodities could be purchased. Rice and oil were usually obtained in this manner. Gardens and other available land were used to grow vegetables. The spectre of hunger forced many people to eat orange peels, peanut skins, beet stems, and burrs. Synthetic foodstuffs of dubious composition appeared: meatless broths, eggless scrambled eggs, sugarless custards. Foodstuffs that were formerly given to pigs were avidly consumed by people who, when the third winter of the war had arrived, were emaciated and ill clothed. In that third winter, lack of food and charcoal became critical. Shipments sent by foreign charitable organizations, such as the International Red Cross and the Quakers,* consisted of whale meat, roast beef, and condensed milk, all of which were reserved for infants and pregnant and lactating women. Without food or meat or warm clothing, and suffering from hunger and cold, the people were desperate. But more than that the Republic was losing the war, while the Nationalists stepped up their bombing of civilian targets.

Madrid was the first world capital to suffer the horrors of modern warfare. First, it endured the attacks by the aviation corps. Later, when the city was within range of cannon fire, artillery bombardments began. These attacks were even more insidious than those by aircraft since the impending arrival of aircraft was at least announced by the sound of airplane engines. The populace lived huddled in underground railroad stations and cellars. With time the city became used to the situation. Shows reopened and movies and theatres were filled with a public anxious to be entertained. The city was divided into two sectors: one sheltered from normal bombings and the other open to them. People strolled through the Gran Vía, occupied terraces in cafeterias, and entered into their favorite bars under the protecting shield of sandbags. The people of Madrid and other Republican cities became as accustomed to air raid warnings as to the thundering of cannon fire. Pedestrians scattered when bombs fell. Later, when the artillery stopped, the dead would be picked up and circulation renewed. When some event was suspended because of cannon fire, the public became indignant and asked for shows to go on, indifferent to all risks.

Madrid continued to be bombed intermittently throughout 1937, despite the fact that aerial bombardments were directed toward the northern campaign where the bombings of Durango* and Guernica* took place. Cities in the Levante also became targets for German and Italian planes, which constituted the base of General Franco's* aviation. In 1938, the aerial and maritime attacks (undertaken by warships) were intensified on the Mediterran coast at Valencia, Alicante, Cartegena,* Tarragona,* and Barcelona. This last city suffered a continuous attack every three hours, twenty-four hours a day in March 1938 staged by Italian pilots.* This attack caused great damage and many deaths. The psychosis made life unbearable. Lack of food and fear of bombings undermined the morale of the population. In the winter of 1938-1939, without warm clothing, food, or heat and ever fearful of bombings, the people yearned for peace, even at the cost of defeat.

For further information, see Rafael Abella, *La vida cotidiana durante la guerra civil: La España republicana* (Barcelona, 1975); Manuel Cruells, *La societat catalana durante la guerra civil* (Barcelona, 1978); Ronald Fraser, *Blood of Spain* (New York, 1979); Dan Kurzman, *Miracle of November: Madrid's Epic Stand, 1936* (New York, 1980); and Hugh Thomas, *The Spanish Civil War* (New York, 1977).

See also Daily Life, Nationalist zone; and Workers, Catalan.

Rafael Abella

DAJAKOVICH BATTALION.
The Dajakovich Battalion, consisting of Bulgarian members, was part of the International Brigades.* It served in numerous military campaigns, fighting in central Spain and around Madrid on Corruna Road, Boadilla, and in the Levante, throughout 1937.

For further information, see Andreu Castells, *Las brigades internacionales de la guerra de España* (Barcelona, 1974).

James W. Cortada

DALADIER, EDOUARD (1884-1970).
Daladier was the French minister of war from 1936 to 1938. He was a member of the Radical party which participated in the Popular Front government in France.* From 1938 to 1940 Daladier held the post of prime minister of his country and thus played a major role in carrying out the French policy of nonintervention in Spain. At the beginning of the Spanish Civil War, he favored selling arms to the Spanish Republic. He actually approved such transactions in 1936, only to change his mind within days under pressure from others within his government and the British.

He soon became an advocate of neutrality, supported decisions that denied either side French arms, and sought to support the policy of nonintervention out of fear that any other policy might drag France into a war with the Germans, Throughout his years in the cabinet, although he sympathized with the Republic, he steadfastly maintained that any intervention in Spain would result in a general European war. However, as prime minister, he allowed some supplies to slip quietly into Spain, and he permitted the Republican refugees* to come into France,* particularly when it became evident that the Spanish Republic would collapse. By 1938, he felt that if some assistance did not go to the Republicans,* the Nationalists* would win the war. Even so, he was reluctant to make the kind of commitment that was required to save the Republicans or to invest in the conflict as, for example, the Russians did. When he did allow tons of food* and matérial to move south, it was too little too late.

The British continually pressured him to reduce aid, succeeding in having him close the frontier on June 13, 1938. Finally, in February 1939, he extended recognition to the Nationalist government of General Franco* while authorizing acceptance of hundreds of thousands of refugees into specially established camps in southern France. Like many other Frenchmen, he had favored the Republic but was unwilling to support it in the way that Germany* and Italy* aided Franco. The Germans realized this and thus could play on his fears to keep France out of Spain while Berlin helped the Nationalists. Stalin,* hoping to form an alliance with Great Britain* and France directed against Hitler* in 1936 and 1937, learned by way of Daladier's Spanish policy that he could not count on Paris to help thwart the growth in German power.

This forced him to buy time by making an alliance with Hitler.

For further information, see Georges Bonnet, *De Washington au Quai d'Orsay* (Geneva, 1946); and David Wingeate Pike, *Les Français et la guerre d'Espagne, 1936-1939* (Paris, 1975).

See also Blum, Léon; and Chamberlain, Neville.

James W. Cortada

DÁVILA, SANCHO. Dávila, a little known Falangist from Andalusia,* was a member of a small delegation from the Falange* that attempted to negotiate a political alliance with the Carlists* in 1937. The goal was thus to provide a solid political block in Nationalist Spain. Since full agreement and trust could not be achieved, nothing came of the negotiations. He was a relative of José Antonio Primo de Rivera,* founder of Falange party, and headed up that organization in Andalusia. Dávila was a constant rival of another important leader of the Falange during the Civil War, Ramón Serrano Suñer,* an in-law of General Franco.*

For further information, see Stanley G. Payne, *Falange: A History of Spanish Fascism* (Stanford, Calif., 1961).

James W. Cortada

DÁVILA ARRONDO, FIDEL (1878-1962). Dávila, born on April 24, 1878, in Barcelona,* was an Infantry brigade general on the retired list at the outbreak of the Spanish Civil War. Even though he was already fifty-eight, he was destined to play a major role in the conflict and the Spanish political and military scene for many years. He was an infantry officer of the old school and was considered to be a highly trained staff officer. He has been described as pure, austere and Spanish. He was also the personification of an excellent bureaucratic general. He was unpolitical, and even nondenominational and unobtrusive. The Germans in the conflict commented that he brought direction, planning, and order to the Nationalists'* effort.

In stature, Dávila was even shorter than his Generalissimo. Being a quiet, dedicated officer, he hardly fit into the flamboyant roles played by such generals as Varela* and Yagüe.*

Politically, Dávila was considered an Alfonsist monarchist (but liberal in nature) who was one of the early key conspirators in the uprising against the Popular Front.* Shortly after the revolt, he was a member of the Burgos* *Junta de Defensa Nacional** created by General Mola.* This was followed by the important meeting when the generals gathered at the airfield outside of Salamanca.* There Dávila and the others elected Franco* as the Generalissimo. With the creation of the *Junta Técnica** (State Technical Committee), September 21, 1936, Dávila (because of his recognized management ability) was appointed its chairman. In this position he was charged with the finances, commerce, and labor, as well as the cultural matters, of Nationalist Spain. Along with these functions he was named army chief of staff. In December of the same year, he was promoted to division general. With the death of General Mola, Dávila was named commander of the Army of the North.* Dávila had to conduct the bitter Bilbao* operations that had been initiated shortly before. His ability as an army commander was now tested.

The enemy was secured in positions known as the "Iron Belt," consisting of a tight closing chain of fortified trenches around Bilbao thought to be impregnable. The offensive of Dávila's forces started on June 12, 1937. The enemy crumbled under the combined assault of artillery, aerial bombardment, and infantry. By 1530 hours on June 19, lead elements of the 5th Navarre Brigade entered the town. The city shortly surrendered to the colorful General García Valiño,* one of Dávila's division commanders. The Nationalists thus gained a very important port on the north coast and at the same time controlled a very rich industrial area.

Dávila now began to realign his forces for the Santander*/Asturias* offensive. This operation had to be suspended temporarily because of the enemy offensive against Brunete* (near Navalcarnero southwest of Madrid*). When the Nationalists blunted this costly offensive, Dávila's Army of the North was again committed to the Santander campaign.

Dávila started his attack on July 14, 1937. By July 26, his units were entering Santander, and the Popular Front* commander and his staff (along with many political leaders) were fleeing by sea. The Nationalists now held another major port on the Cantabrian Sea along with its rich resources of the hinterland. Still the rest of Asturias had to be gained, and along with this the port of Gijón.* The final offensive in the area began on September 1, 1937, and was fought through the difficult mountainous terrain in which the enemy held the high ground. After seven weeks of bitter fighting, Dávila's forces entered Gijón on October 21. But it was not until early spring of 1938 that the mountainous area would be cleared of the remaining enemy forces.

When the Popular Front launched it offensive against Teruel* (on December 15, 1937), Franco was determined not only that the enemy advance be halted, but also that Teruel be recaptured. Thus, he had to alter his plans for operations on the Madrid front. The Nationalists committed the realigned forces under the command of General Dávila. Their counteroffensive began in the bitter cold and snow of December 29, 1937. It was a cruel and costly campaign for both the attacking Nationalists and the defending government forces. Both suffered immensely from the terrible cold which is so typical of the region of Teruel. The difficult operation finally entered its concluding stage with Aranda's* forces, under General Yagüe, crossing the Alfambra River and cutting Teruel from the north. By February 22, 1938, after a long, bitter, and costly struggle, forces of the Army of the North liberated the city of Teruel. During this operation, General Dávila was appointed minister of defense of Nationalist Spain, but remained commander of the Army of the North.

After a short respite from battle, the Army of the North was directed to initiate the Aragón* offensive (in some works called the first battle of the Ebro*). The Nationalists decided to abandon any attempt to attack the Popular Front on the Madrid sector. Instead, the objective was an attack with a massive force through Aragón south of the Ebro River with a breakout on the Mediterranean coast. This would cut off the enemy forces in Catalonia* from Valencia* to the south. For this effort Dávila's Army of the North had three army corps. The attack started on the morning of March 9, 1938. The Popular Front divisions were shattered by the combined aerial and ground offensives.

The divisions belonging to the Corps Marroquí (under General Yagüe) recaptured the important town of Belchite* which had been lost to the Popular Front after a bitter struggle late the previous summer. Other Nationalist divisions pressed on the direction of Caspe at the confluence of the Guadalupe and Ebro Rivers. At the same time, others fought through the difficult craggy mountains toward the Levante* coast. On April 15, 1938, the division commanded by General Alonso Vega* broke out of the mountains on the narrow coastal plain and captured the village of Vinaroz. The enemy forces were now successfully divided.

The Nationalists realized a major reversal with the Popular Front offensive of the Ebro River which rolled back their lines and not only recaptured lost territory but made a decisive dent into their own front. Dávila's divisions expended much effort, manpower, and material to restrain the enemy offensive and at the same time recapture the areas lost. Once this was successfully accomplished, General Dávila's forces were in a position to launch the decisive campaign of Catalonia.

The Nationalists' offensive in Catalonia began December 23, 1938. The Army of the North numbered 300,000 men and was committed against a shattered Popular Front force divided within because of political cleavages. Barcelona* was taken, and by February 9, 1939 Dávila's forces reached the French border. Catalonia was in the hands of the Nationalists.

General Dávila went on to hold important positions within the ranks of the Nationalist government. In 1945 he became War Minister. In 1947 he was granted the title of *Marquis*. In addition he held the position of Army Minister. In 1949, when Franco left Spain to visit Portugal, Dávila acted as President of the Spanish Council of Ministers. When Franco celebrated his 25th anniversary as Chief of State in 1961, General Dávila attended the ceremony; he was the only still living member of the *Junta* that had elevated the little Galician to his position as Generalissimo back in the dim past of 1936.

General Dávila's military records reveal that he died five months later, March 22, 1962, in Madrid. The day after his death he was promoted to the position of *Capitán General del Ejército*.

For further information, see José Manual Martínez Bande, *La guerra en el norte* (Madrid, 1969); and Valentín Davila Jalon, *Una vida al servicio de España: el General Fidel Dávila Arrondo* (Madrid, 1978).

See also Appendix B.

Raymond L. Proctor

DAY, HEM (Marcel Dieu). Hem Day was the pseudonym of Marcel Dieu, a Belgian anarchist with close connections to the Spanish anarchist movement during the 1920s and 1930s. Dieu's friendship with Victor Serge, the well-known libertarian who participated in early revolutionary events in Catalonia* during 1917, brought him into early contact with the most violent Spanish anarchists.* A decade later, he was instrumental in organizing left-wing protests against the prosecution of Buenaventura Durruti* and several other exiled Spanish anarchists for plotting to assassinate King Alfonso XIII* during a state visit to Paris. The protests succeeded in embarrassing the French government, which expelled the prisoners* instead. Dieu managed to get them into Belgium* twice. The second time Durruti and his friend Francisco Ascaso* spent two quiet years there working with Day.

The Belgian made several trips to Spain in the period 1931-1937 and actively propagandized for the Spanish anarchist movement, making both the *Confederación Nacional del Trabajo* (CNT)* and the *Federación Anarquista Ibérica* (FAI) well known in French and Belgian political circles. He held many positions in the International Workingmen's Association and in these various capacities assisted in raising money and troops to support the anarchist military and revolutionary effort in Catalonia and Aragón.*

For further information, see Hem Day, *Histoire du Chant de L'Internationale* (Brussels, 1970), *L'Internationale de 1864* (Brussels, 1965), and *Michel Bakounine, Aspects de son Oeuvre* (Brussels, 1966); and Robert Kern, *Red Years/Black Years: A Political History of the Spanish Anarchists* (Philadelphia, 1978).

Robert W. Kern

DEATHS. *See* Casualties.

DEBATE, EL (1908-present). *El Debate* was the journalistic mouthpiece for liberal Catholic political views in Madrid.* During the days of the Republic, it advocated Christian Democratic party politics. On several occasions, the Republic suspended publication of *El Debate* which it considered to be right wing. This *Confederación Española de Derechas Autónomas* (CEDA)* newspaper declined during the Civil War and eventually ceased publication within the Nationalist zone in the early days of the war. It had failed to conform fully to the ideals then expressed by Franco's* government.

For further information, see Paul Preston, *The Coming of the Spanish Civil War: Reform, Reaction and Revolution in the Second Republic, 1931-1936* (London, 1978).

James W. Cortada

DELAGE GARCÍA, LUIS. Delage was a little-known communist army commissar on the Republican side. His first major command came in November 1936, when he was appointed commissar of the 6th Brigade, later for the 4th Division and the 5th Corps in the Army of the Ebro.* A long-time member of the Spanish Communist party* in Madrid,* after the Civil War he worked for the USSR* in Latin America* and toward the end of World War II (1944) in France* with Spanish exiles, probably as a political agent.

For further information, see Michael Alpert, *El ejército republicano en la guerra Civil* (Barcelona, 1977); and Ramón Salas Larrazábal, *Historia del ejército popular de la república*, 4 vols. (Madrid, 1947).
See also Ebro, Battle of.

James W. Cortada

DELBOS, YVON (1885-1956). Delbos, the French foreign minister from 1936 to 1937, was instrumental in creating his country's policy of nonintervention in the Spanish Civil War. During July 1936, he favored helping the Spanish Republicans* by sending them aircraft. He advocated such a move until British pressure led his government to abandon such a policy. Along with other members of the cabinet, he soon concluded that an Anglo-British policy of nonintervention made more sense. As German intervention in Spain became more obvious, he concluded that this policy would prevent France* from being drawn into a general European war that might erupt if the major powers took sides in the Spanish fighting.

By August 1936, the British and French were talking of a mutual policy of nonintervention, and soon after, he strongly supported the establishment of the Non-Intervention Committee.* He supported it within the League of Nations* as well. By the end of the year, he was asking various governments, including Germany* and Italy,* to agree to an arms embargo to both factions in Spain. He also initiated a proposal within the Non-Intervention Committee to offer mediation. Berlin and Rome rejected both proposals, although the British wanted to pursue them.

During 1937, the British and French failed to curb international intervention in Spain. Delbos again seriously considered opening the French border, thereby allowing the flow of supplies to the Republicans. When the destruction of neutral shipping increased sharply in 1937, Delbos suggested that all "interested powers" meet for a conference to resolve the problem. His suggestion led to the Nyon Conference* of September which resulted in an agreement to reinforce naval patrols in the Mediterranean. It did result in some Roman cooperation and eventually a decline in Italian submarine attacks against British and French shipping. Delbos also took the initiative in forcing the major powers to discuss withdrawing international volunteers* from Spain. He threatened to open the French frontier to the Republic if, for example, the Italians did not discuss the issue. His proposals came at a time when Italian intervention had served its purpose. Thus, he was able to gain agreement among the major powers and the Spanish Republic to remove the International Brigades* from the fighting in Spain. Of all the major French officials, he did more to help the Spanish Republicans while also initiating some useful diplomatic efforts during the war.

For further information, see John E. Dreifort, *Yvon Delbos at the Quai D'Orsay: French Foreign Policy During the Popular Front, 1936-1938* (Lawrence, Kans., 1973); and David Wingeate Pike, *Les Français et la guerre d'Espagne, 1936-1939* (Paris, 1975).

See also Chamberlain, Neville; Daladier, Edouard; and Great Britain.

James W. Cortada

DELGADO SERANNO, FRANCISCO. Delgado was a lieutenant colonel of infantry at Alhucemas in Morocco,* participated in the initial uprising in July 1936, and, in the major campaigns of the war, led the 82d Division, one of the Nationalists'* most successful combat divisions.

As a military professional, Delgado had led the Soría Regiment in Seville* where he was involved in the Sanjurjo* plot, after which he was transferred to Morocco. As one of the young *africanistas*,* he and his units took part in the July uprising and then moved to Spain with Yagüe's* African army. As they pushed north to Madrid,* he commanded on the left flank, aiding in the conquest of Talavera de la Reina* on September 3, and on to Maqueda by September 21. His units fought with those of Colonel José Asensio* at Valdeiglesias on October 8 and in the attack at Navalcarnero on October 21. In the first assault on Madrid on November 7, Delgado's forces were concentrated in the Casa del Campo and Ciudad Universitaria areas where fighting was extremely heavy.

With army reorganization in the spring of 1937, Delgado's units became the 82d Division, which was shifted to the Army of the North* where with Yagüe's* Marroquí Army Corps they fought successfully in the Teruel* sector in February 1938, concentrating in the area from Portalrubio to Perales de Alfambra. Between March and July 1938 in the Nationalist campaigns in the southern Ebro sector, Delgado's 82d Division, then with Aranda's* Galicia Corps, was involved in the attacks at Montalbán and Alcorisa, and in the push across the Maestrazgo Plain.*

As the Republicans* launched their attack along the Ebro from Mesquineza to Cherta in July 1938, Delgado was shifted north and in August led the first Nationalist counteroffensive in the Mesquineza-Fayon area. In September when General García Valiño* was transferred north to head the Army of the Maestrazgo,* Delgado and his 82d Division were incorporated into that army unit where they remained for the duration of the war. Under García Valiño, Delgado successfully commanded in the general attack along the Ebro* in October-November 1938. In the final attack in Catalonia* beginning on December 23, he moved with the Army of the Maestrazgo from Artesa to Manresa and then turned north to the French frontier in the last stage of the conflict in Catalonia. Because of his

record of military accomplishments, he was promoted to general in the last year of the war.

For further information, see Manuel Aznar, *Historia militar de la guerra de España*, 3 vols. (Madrid, 1969); and Luis María de Lojendio, *Operaciones militares de la guerra de España, 1936-39* (Barcelona, 1940).

See also Appendix B.

Jane Slaughter

DEUTSCHLAND. From July 1936 until February 1939 the German armored ship *Deutschland* made eight cruises to Spanish waters, alternating with other armored ships as flagship of the German squadron. On May 29, 1937, Soviet aircraft supporting the Republicans'* naval operation against Ibiza* discovered the *Deutschland* at anchor in Ibiza harbor and, mistaking her for a Nationalist warship, made a bombing attack, damaging the *Deutschland* and causing thirty-one deaths. On Hitler's* orders, her sister ship *Admiral Scheer* bombarded Almería* on May 31 in reprisal, and Germany* and Italy* withdrew from the Non-Intervention Committee's Sea Observation* patrols.

For further information, see Hugh Thomas, *The Spanish Civil War* (New York, 1977).

See also Germany; Navy, German; Navy, Spanish; and Appendix B.

Willard C. Frank, Jr.

DÍAZ BAZA, ANGEL. Díaz, a socialist, became the first head of the *Servicio de Información Militar* (SIM),* a consolidation of various intelligence agencies operating within the Spanish Republic. His duties were to develop a national intelligence service to generate data useful for military planning and security; control undesirable political elements; and reduce competition among the intelligence services within various military and civilian agencies. He failed in all three tasks, and was replaced by more ruthless administrators in 1937.

For further information, see Manuel Uribarri, *El SIM de la república* (Havana, 1942).

See also Espionage.

James W. Cortada

DÍAZ RAMOS, JOSÉ (1896-1942). Díaz was the secretary general of the Spanish Communist party* during the Civil War and was thus one of the Republicans'* most important political figures. He was born and raised in Seville* where he began as a baker. This energetic worker was an anarchist before becoming a communist. He quietly worked his way into a position of leadership within the party. Although he lacked great imagination, he was prepared to take guidance from Moscow on expanding the small Communist party in Spain. He took over leadership of the party in 1933, and, until the early months of 1936, his group remained a minor force in Spanish politics.

As Spanish politics became more polarized, the communists increased their membership in 1936 dramatically. Once the Civil War began, Soviet advisers provided Díaz with increased political consultation, guiding him toward a policy that appealed to law and order and the interests of the middle classes as both a means of canceling the influence of the anarchists* and as a form of moderation so as not to alarm the governments of Great Britain* and France* over increased Soviet activities in Spain. Díaz strongly supported the Republican cause, worked with the government, and sought to use his connections with other European communist parties to gain support and aid for the Republic. Yet, he could not institute any major programs without Moscow's help and approval. During 1937, he continued to expand party membership and to recruit soldiers for various communist units, the Fifth Regiment* perhaps being the most famous. He coordinated with the Soviets for the supply of advisers, arms, aircraft, and other matériel for the war effort.

The communists launched a major push to gain control of the Republican government in the spring and summer of 1937. Tensions had been building for months between communists and anarchists, finally erupting into fighting during May 1937 in the streets of Barcelona.* As early as March, Díaz had openly criticized the *Partido Obrero de Unificación Marxista* (POUM)* for not fully supporting the war effort, calling them protofascists. Tensions mounted in Barcelona among the POUM, anarchists, communists, and the *Partit Socialista Unificat de Catalunya* (PSUC)*. Meanwhile, the communists had concluded that Largo Caballero's* government should be replaced with one more friendly to themselves. The fighting in Barcelona finally destroyed the anarchists' power and allowed the Republic to regain full control of Catalonia.* Next, the communists sought to dominate the Republican government. Throughout 1937, a greater number of communists than ever before were put into higher positions within the government. The POUM was outlawed and its leaders arrested, thereby eliminating another major rival party within the Republican zone.

While Díaz believed that the Republic should expand its ownership of major industry, he was reluctant to support programs of collectivization, arguing that the primary need during the Civil War was to increase production and thus to experiment with socialization. Otherwise, different forms of management would simply disrupt manufacturing productivity. As long as the fighting went on, he did not want to make radical changes to the Republican economy. Yet, he argued that the material foundations of fascism had to be destroyed, and he suggested that the social order would eventually be altered. His specific targets were the large landowners, the Spanish Church,* and the career military officer corps as political forces in Spanish society.

Toward the end of the war, Díaz visited Moscow and remained in exile after the fighting ended. In exile, his control over the party was constantly challenged by other Spanish communists, most notably La Pasionaria* who in 1942 managed to become secretary general. In that year he "fell" to his death from a window in Tiflis. In all probability, he was assassinated by his rivals in the classic East European fashion by being pushed out of a window.

For further information, see Burnett Bolloten, *The Spanish Revolution: The Left and the Struggle for Power During the Civil War* (Chapel Hill, N.C., 1979); and José Díaz Ramos, *Por la unidad, hacia la victoria* (Barcelona, 1937).

See also May 1937 Riots.

James W. Cortada

DÍAZ SANDINO, FELIPE (1892?-   ). In 1936 Díaz was briefly the councillor of defense in the Catalan government, the Generalitat.* A career officer, Colonel Díaz had responsibility for recruiting troops and gathering supplies, primarily for the offensive in Aragón* that year. This little-known Catalanist proved an ineffectual leader and was replaced December 17, 1936. During his months in power, he was concerned that Catalans maintain control over local affairs in northeast Spain against any encroachments by the government in Madrid.* At one point he suggested to Azaña* that he declare himself a dictator in order to prosecute the war more forcefully.

For further information, see Hugh Thomas, *The Spanish Civil War* (New York, 1977).

James W. Cortada

DIMITROV BATTALION. The Dimitrov Battalion was part of the military forces of the International Brigades* that fought for the Spanish Republic. It formed part of the 15th Brigade and mainly comprised about 160 Greeks and some 800 Balkans of various nationalities. It saw combat at the battle of the Jarama* in February 1937, where it was part of the frontline chain of shock troops.

For further information, see Andreu Castells, *Las brigades internacionales de la guerra de España* (Barcelona, 1974).

James W. Cortada

DIO LO VUOLE DIVISION. The Dio lo Vuole Division was a division of Italian Fascist party members sent to Spain by Mussolini* at the end of 1936 to fight with the Nationalists.* It saw a considerable amount of combat during the battle of Guadalajara* in March 1937 and formed part of the only major Italian offensive in Spain where all of Mussolini's forces attempted to act in concert in a major military engagement.

For further information, see John F. Coverdale, *Italian Intervention in the Spanish Civil War* (Princeton, N.J., 1975).

James W. Cortada

DIPLOMATIC CORPS, SPANISH. At the start of the Civil War, the majority of the Spanish diplomatic corps favored the Nationalists.* Most of the career diplomats were conservative and monarchist and thus saw in Franco's* cause a return to the kind of Spain they wanted. About 90 precent of the diplomatic corps sided with Franco. However, a smaller percentage of ambassadors than of the entire corps eventually chose the Nationalists. A large number of these representatives had been appointees of the Republic, some had political but little diplomatic experience, while others (such as Salvador de Madariaga*) simply chose to support the Republicans.*

Within the first three months of the war, many diplomats resigned their appointments, leaving many embassies to be run by second- and third-level personnel, many of whom sympathized with the Nationalists. It took months for the Republic to refill all of these positions, and not always satisfactorily. The Nationalists used many diplomats as agents pleading Franco's cause in foreign capitals. In addition, neither side hesitated to use businessmen and military officers along with politicians for specific diplomatic missions. The Spanish Foreign Office, which had been staffed with personnel overwhelmingly in favor of the Nationalists, was restaffed during the war, but on a much smaller scale than before, by Foreign Minister Julio Álvarez del Vayo.* This staff moved from Madrid to Valencia* and then eventually to Barcelona* before finally evacuating with some of its files to France* in early 1939 after the Catalan city fell to Franco. The

Nationalists created an informal foreign ministry in Burgos* on a modest scale staffed with ex-Foreign Ministry personnel and others recruited for the task. Neither foreign office trained new diplomats from 1936 to 1939; rather, existing personnel were used.

For further information, see James W. Cortada, ed., *Spain in the Twentieth Century World: Essays on Spanish Diplomacy, 1898-1978* (Westport, Conn., 1979); and Julio Álvarez del Vayo, *Give Me Combat* (New York, 1973).

See also Great Britain; and United States.

James W. Cortada

DOMBROWSKI BATTALION. The Dombrowski Battalion was composed primarily of Polish miners of socialist or communist backgrounds who had recently lived in France* and had joined the Republicans* in the early days of the Civil War. They were quickly brought into the fight to defend Madrid.* In one portion of the campaign around Madrid, in late 1936, a whole company from this battalion was killed. Heavy fighting in and around Madrid, which included some hand-to-hand combat, resulted in large numbers of casualties.* The remaining survivors of the battalion who were not killed around Madrid in November-December 1936 were eventually reinforced by Hungarians and Yugoslavians and then transferred from the 11th Brigade to the 12th, 13th, and 150th.

For further information, see Andreu Castells, *Las brigades internacionales de la guerra de España* (Barcelona, 1974).

See also International Brigades.

James W. Cortada

DOMÉNECH, JUAN. Doménech, a leader of the *Confederación Nacional del Trabajo* (CNT)* in Barcelona* when the Civil War began, assumed responsibilities in the Central Antifascist Militias Committee.* When Luis Companys* abolished the committee in September in favor of an executive council of the Generalitat,* Doménech was appointed minister of supply to that council. He remained a member of the Economic Council. He planned for the socialist transformation of Catalonia* through collectivization of agriculture and industry. With Diego Abad de Santillán,* he was charged with drawing up plans to regularize and define this activity. The major obstacle to successful implementation of the plan was the Catalan republican parties and the *Partit Socialista Unificat de Catalunya* (PSUC).* This accounts for Doménech's strong objection to the inclusion of the communist-organized *Federación Catalana de Gremios y Entidades de Pequeños Comerciantes y Industriales* (GEPCF) into the communist-controlled *Unión General de Trabajadores* (UGT),* through which they could then exercise influence against collectivization.

For further information, see Diego Abad de Santillán, *Por que perdimos la guerra* (Madrid, 1975); Burnett Bolloten, *The Spanish Revolution: The Left and the Struggle for Power During the Civil War* (Chapel Hill, N.C., 1979); Gaston Leval, *Espagne libertaire, 1936-39: L'oeuvre constructive de la révolution espagnole* (Meuse, 1971); Edward Malefakis, *Agrarian Reform and Peasant Revolution in Spain: Origins of the Civil War* (New Haven, Conn., 1970); and Georges Soría, *Guerra y revolución en España 1936-1939* (Barcelona, 1978).

Shirley F. Fredricks

DOMÍNGUEZ, EDMUNDO. Domínguez was a vice-president of the *Unión General de Trabajadores* (UGT)* during the period 1936-1939, one of the largest politicized workers' unions in pre-Civil War Spain. Raised in Madrid,* he made his way up worker politics in the capital city's building workers' union in the 1920s. He was a socialist who, at the start of the war, became a member of the executive council of the UGT as vice-president and could thus be in a position to formulate the organization's basic policies. In this capacity, he swung his political support from Francisco Largo Caballero* to Juan Negrín.*

For further information, see José Peirats, *La CNT en la revolución española*, 3 vols. (Toulouse, 1951-1953), especially Vol. 1.

James W. Cortada

DOVAL BRAVO, LISARDO (1888-   ). Doval served with the Nationalists* as a police* officer. In 1934, as a police major, Doval brutally helped suppress the revolt of the Asturian miners. The actual military conquest of the area had been under the direction of a young general, Francisco Franco.* He next became police chief in Salamanca* where he successfully kept labor unrest at a minimum. At the start of the Civil War, he incompetently led Nationalist police units against the Republicans* near Ávila.* As commander of the Civil Guard* in Salamanca, he was instrumental in having Manuel Hedilla* arrested and condemned to death. Hedilla was a leading Falangist who questioned Franco's policies, particularly his attempt to mold the Falange party* into an organization under the general's control. (Hedilla's sentence was commuted.)

Doval arrested other dissidents and kept them in jail for months at a time.

For further information, see Hugh Thomas, *The Spanish Civil War* (New York, 1977).
See also Terrorism.

James W. Cortada

DULM, VAN DU. Vice-Admiral van Du Dulm of the Dutch Navy was the chairman of an international board established by the Non-Intervention Committee* in 1937 to prevent expansion of the Civil War into a broader conflict. His board was responsible for monitoring the waters around Spain and the border at the Pyrenees,* using a mixture of ships and personnel drawn from the member nations of the Non-Intervention Committee.

For further information, see Hugh Thomas, *The Spanish Civil War* (New York, 1977).

James W. Cortada

DUMOULIN, ECKHART (1884-   ). Dumoulin, a career German diplomat, served as the councillor of embassy in Lisbon during the Spanish Civil War (1936-1939). During these years, he would periodically communicate with Franco's* government at Burgos,* reporting to Berlin on the Nationalists'* activities. He was the German, for example, whom Hitler* sent to Burgos in October 1936 to congratulate Franco on assuming the title "head of state," thereby reconfirming Germany's* will to aid the Nationalist government and its leader.

For further information, see Manfred Merkes, *Die deutsche Politik gegenüber dem spanischen Bürgerkrieg 1936-1939* (Bonn, 1961).

James W. Cortada

DUNN, JAMES (1890-   ). Dunn, a career diplomat from the United States,* was chief of the Division of European Affairs in the U.S. State Department (1936-1939) and was one of the architects of American neutrality policies toward Spain during the Civil War. He was the American ambassador to Spain between 1953 and 1955, and negotiated the U.S.-Spanish Base Agreement of 1953.

For further information, see U.S. Department of State, *Biographical Register of the Department of State, September 1, 1944* (Washington, D.C., 1944).
See also Hull, Cordell.

James W. Cortada

DURÁN, GUSTAVO. Durán, a Republican Army* officer, led one of the Mixed Brigades* in the thick of the fighting in Madrid* in late 1936. Nationalist attacks on the city several times fell directly on his troops which held Franco's* back. Later, Durán became commander of the 39th Division of the Republican Army at the battle of Brunete* (July 1937). In July 1938, this skilled officer blocked the Nationalist advance in the Levante,* thus slowing down its attempt to march from central Spain to Valencia* and thereby reduce Republican territorial holdings even further. After the war, he moved to London, married an American in 1940, and eventually moved to the United States.*

For further information, see Michael Alpert, *El ejército repúblicano en la guerra civil* (Barcelona, 1977).

See also Appendix B.

James W. Cortada

DURANGO. Durango, a small village in the province of Vizcaya* in northern Spain, became the first unarmed community to be bombed from the air during the Civil War. This small community, hardly more than a rail crossing and small road on the way to Bilbao,* was bombed by German Junkers 52 flown by members of the Condor Legion* on March 31, 1937, as part of the Nationalists' campaign to seize all of Vizcaya. A total of 127 nonmilitary personnel died that day, and later an additional 121 died of wounds. Of the total dead, two were priests, thirteen nuns, and many communicants in two churches hit by bombs. World press attention momentarily focused on Durango as a symbol of the cruelties of war until soon after replaced by Guernica* further to the north. On April 28, the Nationalists occupied the town and the next day, Guernica, executing a few Republican soldiers found in the area.

For further information, see José Manuel Martínez Bande, *Vizcaya* (Madrid, 1971); and Stanley G. Payne, *Basque Nationalism* (Reno, Nev., 1975).

See also Air Force, Nationalist.

James W. Cortada

DURRUTI, BUENAVENTURA (1896-1936). Buenaventura Durruti, perhaps the most famous Spanish anarchist during the Spanish Civil War, was born in 1896 at León* and died while commanding a contingent of Aragonese militia on the Madrid* front at University City on November 20, 1936—a violent end to a violent life.

Durruti's notoriety came from many sources, but most notably from the creation of his *Solidarios* and *Nosotros* terrorist organizations, his adventures while a political exile in France* and South America, the series of revolutionary insurrections he led against the Second Republic* between 1931 and 1933, and the leadership he provided to the anarchist brigades that fought the Carlist *Requetés* and elements of General Mola's* army in Aragón* at the start of the war. Long after his death, Durruti has remained almost a cult figure of revolutionary idealism to Spaniard and non-Spaniard alike. He wrote nothing, and his anarchist philosophy still seems so visceral that he closely resembles the "primitive rebel" described by some historians as an archetype of Mediterranean political man.

The roots of Durruti's rebellion can be found in the general strike of August 1917, the first nationwide walkout in Spanish history, when he became a militant in his father's railway union. Sought by the police,* he joined other activists like Francisco Ascaso* and Juan García Oliver* and helped to establish the *Solidarios* group in 1919, an organization that prefigured the later and more important *Federación Anarquista Ibérica* (FAI),* the foremost purely anarchist movement of the twentieth century.

The *Solidarios* were responsible for the assassination of Juan Soldevila Romero, archbishop of Saragossa,* on June 4, 1923. Durruti fled to France* and was later joined by Ascaso, but their involvement in the Vera del Bidosa border raid on November 6, 1924, to protest the Primo de Rivera dictatorship in Spain, led to diplomatic pressure for their extradition. The two fugitives escaped to Cuba,* but further radical involvements and occasional bank robberies marked their line of flight through Cuba, Mexico,* Chile, and Argentina.* Upon return to France, Durruti's arrest and trial provoked a massive protest by the entire French Left in 1926. Governmental crisis finally permitted the Spanish anarchists to be deported rather than be returned to Spain, and Durruti settled in Brussels during 1928-1931, where he developed a lifelong companionship with a French woman, Emilene Morin, who bore him a daughter, Colette, in 1930.

The anarchist returned to Spain in April 1931 and settled in Barcelona,* where almost immediately he began to criticize the leadership of the fledgling Second Republic,* especially Labor Minister Francisco Largo Cabellero's* program of forced labor arbitration and the general failure of Republicans* to develop a revolutionary perspective. His personal expectations were millennarian. Not unexpectedly, Durruti's involvement in a violent Catalan labor dispute led to his arrest and deportation by Republican officials to Spanish Guinea in January 1932. He remained there until October, when a general pardon of political prisoners* followed an attempted military overthrow of the Republic. By January 1933, however, he again took the lead in protesting Casa Viejas, an incident centering upon a peasant land reform protest that had led to fighting with government troops and the death of a number of peasants in Andalusia.* Only the possibility of a right-wing electoral victory persuaded Republican officials to release Durruti from prison before the creation of Alejandro Lerroux's cabinet, but in December 1933 he was once again imprisoned for leading an uprising in Saragossa against the new conservative government of the *Bienio Negro*.

House arrest and ill health kept Durruti almost totally inactive for the next two and a half years, and he played no role at all in the 1934 Asturian insurrection popularly called "Red October." However, he did endorse the Popular Front* in the elections of February 1936* and urged anarchists to put aside their antiparliamentary principles in order to defeat the Right. Thus, he joined Diego Abad de Santillán,* Federica Montseny,* and Juan García Oliver in following a form of Peter Kropotkin's libertarian communism which stressed formation of communes, workers' committees, and the development of revolutionary federalism. It was a program designed to give anarchism a positive political tone and meet the challenge of anarchosyndicalists in the *Confederación Nacional del Trabajo* (CNT),* whose labor orientation disputed the revolutionary intentions of the FAI.

All of these sectarian internal dissensions disappeared briefly at the outbreak of the Civil War. Durruti played a major role in leading the defense of Barcelona against the Nationalist forces of General Manuel Goded.* He called together CNT and FAI forces to defeat the rebels at the university and the military installations of San Andres and Atarazanas, where his friend, Francisco Ascaso, was killed. A few days later, the new ad hoc Catalan government, the Antifascist Militias Committee,* appointed Durruti as commander of the militia it was putting into the field with anarchist help, and Durruti dedicated himself to avenging his friend's death. Later, his mother and a younger brother were also killed in the violence of the war. Another brother headed the revolutionary Council of Aragón.*

Durruti's success as commander-and-chief on the Aragonese front is controversial. His failure to take Saragossa and allegations concerning the excessive political orientation of the militia must be balanced by the lack of material support from Madrid and the extraordinary political climate that accompanied the war. Durruti, aware of his military inexperience, did delegate strategy-making to ex-officers, but he provided enormous charisma, rivaling La Pasionaria,* and he often led by example through raw courage and almost suicidal combat behavior. Sometimes political events seemed to overwhelm him, however, and violent acts were committed in his name that tarnished his reputation and intensified the difficulties being experienced in Aragón and Catalonia.* Foremost of these problems was Madrid's inability to supply the militia army. At one point in late September 1936, Durruti became involved in a political conspiracy to steal some of the Bank of Spain's* gold. But neither he nor the other anarchist leaders in Catalonia could keep Luis Companys* and the Esquerra* party from pushing the Antifascist Militias Committee from power. By mid-October, it seemed that the social revolution in the Northeast had run its course.

This bleak outlook caused Durruti to gamble his reputation in the siege of Madrid that began in early November. He and 5,000 militiamen, still ill-equipped and exhausted from two months of fighting, reached the capital on November 12 and almost immediately went into the center of the Republican line where the Manzanares River* passes through the university—the sector already targeted for attack by the Nationalists.* The major battle for possession of Madrid began early on November 15 and lasted until late on November 19. In the end the Nationalists, while managing to cross the river and advance as far as the University Hospital-Clinic, were contained: Madrid still remained a symbol of resistance against fascism to the international Left.

Among commanders on the front, however, there was considerable grumbling that Durruti's force had failed to keep the Nationalists south of the Manzanares. The charge was especially bitter since the militia had fought alongside the International Brigades,* a volunteer force which anarchists accused of forcing the will of Soviet communism over the libertarian Spanish social revolution. Durruti thus worked desperately to reinforce and rally his troops, but in the late afternoon of November 19, he was shot by a sniper from one of the upper stories of the Hospital-Clinic. Despite every effort, he died at 3:00 A.M. on November 20, 1936.

Controversy raged as to the identity of the assassin, with anarchists blaming communists and vice versa. If Nationalist troops had not been so exhausted, they might have been able to take Madrid rather easily, but the Republican Army* staff imposed severe discipline soon afterward and unified their command.

The shock of Durruti's assassination deeply affected Catalonia. More than 500,000 marched in his funeral procession, and a new ultra-Left organization, the

Amigos de Durruti, conducted a bitterly sectarian struggle with communists throughout the Northeast. This was one of the important factors in the May 1937 riots,* when communists and anarchists battled for four days for control of strategic points in Barcelona. This incident led to Juan Negrín's assumption of power after several communist cabinet ministers blamed Largo Caballero's Popular Front* cabinet for encouraging anarchist insurrectionism over antifascism. Even in death, Durruti's memory was capable of rousing Spaniards into political combat. He remains a symbol of the "pure" political revolutionary, the archetypical Spanish rebel.

For further information, see Hans Magnus Enzensberger, *Der kurze Sommer der Anarchie: Buenaventura Durrutis Leben und Tod* (Frankfort, 1972); Gilberto Gilabert, *Durruti, un héroe del pueblo* (Buenos Aires, 1937); Robert Kern, *Red Years/Black Years: A Political History of the Spanish Anarchists, 1911-1939* (Philadelphia, 1978); Joan Llarch, *La muerte de Durruti* (Barcelona, 1973); and Abel Paz, *Durruti, the People in Arms*, trans. Nancy MacDonald (New York, 1978).

See also Militias.

Robert W. Kern

E

EBRO, BATTLE OF THE. In the dead of night on July 24-25, 1938, rubber boats were launched in the dark waters of the Ebro River, and two full army corps of the Popular Front's* Army of the Ebro started their massive attack against the over-extended Nationalist lines along the river. This was the beginning of the great battle of the Ebro which was to prove the ugliest, bloodiest, and longest battle (three and a half months) of the Spanish Civil War.

In the spring of that year, during the battle of Aragón,* the Nationalists* had inflicted a crushing defeat on the Popular Front and had reached the Mediterranean Sea. With this victory, the two Popular Front forces of Catalonia* and the Levante* were successfully divided. It has been suggested repeatedly that, if the Nationalists had continued their offensive against the shattered forces of Catalonia, they would have been able to take Barcelona* and the war would have been shortened by several months. However, the decision was made to fight down the coast and through the rugged Maestrazgo Plain* to capture Valencia.* It is possible that General Franco* came to this decision because he feared the French might have acted on behalf of the Popular Front if he had succeeded in pushing his forces too near the French border. International tensions were very high in the summer of 1938. However, Franco's offensive to the south stalled in the face of a determined and well-conducted defensive action.

Without Nationalist pressure in the north, and within an amazingly short period of time, the forces of Catalonia were able to regroup, reorganize, and be resupplied with new equipment from across the French border. By June 24 they were ready for a determined offensive.

The attack was intended to disrupt the Nationalist communications along their front facing the Ebro River from Mequinenza* in the north to the Mediterranean Sea. At the same time, it was hoped to restore the land link between Catalonia and the rest of Popular Front Spain. For this purpose, a force of four army corps (5th, 12th, 15th, and 18th) consisting of twenty-seven brigades and constituting about 80,000 men was committed. They were supported by about 100 batteries of artillery and anti-aircraft cannon, tanks, and armored cars. From the air they were covered by the new high-performance Russian *Supermosca* and *Superchato* fighters flown by Russian and Spanish pilots* trained in the USSR.* All army corps and division commanders were communists, some of whom, such as Lister* and Modesto,* were not on the best of terms. The communist-led units had received the greater portion of the new and best arms and equipment.

Manuel Tagüeña's* 15th Corps carried the Ebro between Mequinenza and Fayón. Lister's 5th Corps crossed the river at many points between Flix, Ascó, the steep gorge at Mora la Nueva, and Miravet. The Nationalist front was 1,100 miles long and the Corps Morocco, under the tough and outspoken General Yagüe,* was to bear the brunt of the attack from Mequinenza to the sea. German aerial reconnaissance and other intelligence had indicated an attack was pending, but as in the case of Brunete* the leadership misjudged its scope and ferocity and was caught completely by surprise. Yagüe learned of the river crossings from his commander in the Mora la Nueva sector, who reported that he had lost contact with his flanks and the enemy was in his rear. His 50th Division was shattered.

Further downstream, near Amposta, the 14th International Brigade fought across the river but withdrew after some eighteen hours, leaving 600 dead and stores of equipment. Upstream, however, a general success was realized at daybreak. A massive bridgehead was established, and the attacking brigades thrust far from the river to overwhelm, isolate, and surround Nationalist units. By dawn at Mequinenza, the 15th Corps had advanced 3 miles from the river. In the center, the 5th Corps (Lister) continued to smash forward 25 miles and gain the high ground near Gandesa.* This town had witnessed much bloody fighting in March during the Aragón offensive.

General Franco was tempted to permit the enemy to penetrate deep into the Nationalist lines, but still to hold firmly on the ends of the pocket. At the right moment, he would close the wings in a massive trap and destroy the enemy in detail. Instead, he reacted in the pattern set by the battles of Brunete and Teruel*:

contain the enemy advance, rapidly reinforce the threatened area, and then, after a massive buildup, retake the lost ground, destroying as much of the enemy force as possible. To this end, air units were immediately committed against the breakthrough area. Included among these was the German Condor Legion,* which was pulled from its support of the Nationalist divisions stalled in the Sierra de Espadán. Quickly, all river crossings and enemy troop concentrations came under heavy aerial bombardment. The Germans committed their light, heavy, and dive-bomber forces against Corbera, Miravet, Mora de Ebro, and Ascó. In addition, both heavy and light anti-aircraft batteries of the legion were assigned as artillery to help the hard-pressed forces defending Gandesa. The gates of the Segre Reservoir were opened to raise the water level downstream, and very soon seven Nationalist divisions were headed to the Ebro front from other sectors. Some of these divisions Franco disengaged from action in the Sierra de Espadán far to the south.

Furious fighting raged at Gandesa, with the town repeatedly assaulted day and night. German aircraft were effectively concentrated against the attacking forces, reinforcements, and the bridge crossings behind them.

On July 30, the original Nationalist front at Mequinenza was reestablished with heavy losses inflicted on the enemy 15th Corps. German aircraft hourly pounded the bridgeheads from Cherta to Fayón with tons of bombs, but the Popular Front remained determined at Gandesa. On July 31, the Nationalists lost 300 men but counted 100 enemy dead and captured 160 prisoners.* The right wing of the Corps Morocco, however, regained about 2 miles in the direction of Benifallet.

By August 2, the Popular Front advance was halted on a front from Fayón to Cherta, but with Villalba de los Arcos and Gandesa still bitterly contested. At the same time, the Nationalists prepared their own counteroffensive, which was temporarily spoiled by enemy attacks in the Fayón to Mequinenza sector. The Army of the Ebro's offensive power was expended, and the Popular Front brigades were ordered to hold all that had been won. This order was carried out to the letter, with officers and men being shot for retreating, and sergeants being ordered to kill their officers if they attempted to withdraw their forces. Under threat of death, officers were ordered to retake lost ground in front of their own men.

The Nationalists' tactics were to select a small area in which they would concentrate artillery and air attacks. While the defenders were still stunned from bombardment, the Nationalists would attack with only

a few battalions. The Nationalists used 500 cannon on the Ebro. In a 114-day period, 13,593 rounds were fired daily from 336 guns. The first major Nationalist counterattack came on August 6, when the two tank companies and air cover they beat back to the Ebro an enemy attack between Fayón and Mequinenza. The Army of the Ebro lost 900 dead, 2,000 prisoners, and much material. The old front between Mequinenza and Fayón was reestablished. At other positions, the Popular Front continued to make an initial penetration but would be thrown back with heavy losses in men and material.

By August 11, Nationalist General Alonso Vega* and Colonel Alfredo Galera mounted their difficult offensive against the Sierra de Pandols on the southern wing of the front. Alonso Vega's division suffered very heavy casualties* in the face of bitter counterattacks. This was followed, on August 19, by General Yagüe's strong advance, supported by the Condor Legion. He struck from Villalba de los Arcos to Fatarella.* The aerial battle had been as bitterly contested as the battle on the ground. This day the Germans realized four aerial victories without losses, primarily through the tactics of Lieutenant Wernher Mölders, the brilliant German ace. Mölders laid the foundations for the German aerial fighter tactics which are still used by the U.S. and British air forces.

The German commander and crews were frustrated in that they expended thousands of tons of bombs attempting to destroy enemy bridgeheads and crossings, and if they did hit a small target such as a bridge, it would be rebuilt during the night. The entire operation then had to be repeated. Operational losses, as well as wear and tear on aircraft, were of great concern to the German commander, General Volkmann,* who was not properly supported by Berlin. He viewed the war of attrition along the Ebro as one in which his units were asked to perform beyond their capability. On September 17, he registered a strong protest to Berlin. He greatly criticized the Nationalist operations, and he noted that the quality of leadership at company and battalion level had been greatly diminished by the many months of war. Recounting the difficult aerial contest day after day, the legion records noted "Ground situation unchanged."

After much frustration, the Nationalists launched an offensive into the Sierra de Pandols on October 30. That same day the Germans celebrated six aerial victories, with an additional five probable. By November 3, the Nationalists had broken the front and had captured Pinell. This brought their frontlines to about 1.5 kilometers from the Ebro. The Popular Front defense began to crumble, along with a continued improvement and consolidation of the Nationalist advance. In the air, the Germans continued to realize one-sided victories, and each day the records reveal both the enemy losses and the positions captured. By November 10, only scattered Popular Front units remained west of the Ebro. On November 14, General Yagüe cleared the enemy from Fatarella, and, other than for a short line 2 kilometers south of Flix, the Popular Front successes of over three months before were wiped out. On November 18, Yagüe seized the last of the enemy bridgeheads across the Ebro. The battle of the Ebro was over.

There is controversy as to how many casualties each side suffered. The Popular Front deaths probably numbered almost 20,000, and an additional 55,000 were wounded and captured. The Nationalists' dead has been placed at over 4,000, with a total loss from all causes of near 57,000. In spite of their losses, the Nationalist forces, with the exception of certain units, had not suffered structural damage. On the other hand, the Popular Front forces were shattered. A few weeks later, the Nationalists launched their offensive into Catalonia and pressed to the border of France.*

As in all battles of the Spanish conflict, there was heroic determination and tragic sacrifice on each side. The Popular Front may be correctly criticized for launching a major offensive without the base to sustain it once the breakthrough was accomplished. Thus, it can be considered as a last effort in a lost cause. The Nationalists may be condemned for not pressing on into Catalonia after their successes of the Aragón, as well as faulty use of intelligence, and for then expending so much effort and lives to recapture lost ground— all of which might have been used elsewhere. On the other hand, it is suggested that the outcome of the civil conflict of Spain was finally determined along the west banks of the Ebro River, which was chosen as a battleground by the Popular Front.

For further information, see Julián Caubin, *La batalla del Ebro* (Mexico, 1944); General Alfredo Kindelán, *Mis cuadernos de guerra* (Madrid, 1945); Colonel Luis María de Lojendio, *Operaciones militares de la guerra de España 1936-1939* (Barcelona, 1940); Lieutenant General Carlos Martínez de Campos, *Dos batallas de la Guerra de Liberación de España* (Madrid, 1962); and Colonel Vicente Rojo, *España heroica* (Buenos Aires, 1942).
See also Appendix B.

Raymond L. Proctor

ECHEVARRÍA NOVOA, JOSÉ. Echevarría, a little-known police* official of the Spanish Republic, was named director of public security in the city of Barcelona* in May 1937, after the Republic reestablished control in the Catalan capital. Up to that point, anarchist militias* and their political apparatus ran local governments, often contrary to the wishes of the Republic. After the confirmation of the Republic's control over Barcelona with 4,000 militarized police in the city, the Loyalists* began to present a more united front to the Nationalists.* Echevarría's job was to restore normal juridical procedures in the courts that eliminated extralegal and capricious anarchist justice. A similar reordering of authority and control over the administration of local jails also became one of Echevarría's key priorities. With the support of the communists and the government of the Republic, Echevarría thus helped break the political back of the anarchists* in Barcelona.

For further information, see Burnett Bolloten, *The Spanish Revolution: The Left and the Struggle for Power During the Civil War* (Chapel Hill, N.C., 1979).
See also Catalonia.

James W. Cortada

ECONOMY, NATIONALIST. Supported by law and order, personal and financial security in business, and general confidence by international businessmen in Franco's* economy, the Nationalist zone enjoyed a higher standard of living than the Loyalists.* The Nationalists* controlled approximately two-thirds of Spain's wheat-producing sectors and almost all of its sherry production (important for export to Great Britain*), while having other substantial food-producing provinces (for wine, chick peas, olive oil, and vegetables). German and Italian aid amounted to some $570 million which allowed purchases of food,* medicine,* and military supplies, while other sterling transactions continued in other parts of Western Europe.* Business had extensive confidence in Franco's side. The Texas Oil Company sold on credit to the Nationalists some 2 million tons of oil over the period of 1936-1939, while in 1938 alone, $4 million in olives went to the United States. The British hardly protested the export of ore from their various Spanish mines to Germany* because they were confident that their properties would be fully restored at the end of the war. Exports to Western Europe were only approximately 20 percent less than that of all Spain two years before the Civil War. Sherry was sold to Britain and other countries in quantities nearly equal to prewar levels, while some banks extended credits to Franco despite his deferment of payments on the national debt.

The Nationalist peseta* retained twice the value of

the Republican version throughout 1937 and 1938. Credit lines were open, even though the Nationalists did not have any gold to back their currency (the Republicans* did). The Nationalists increased their cash supplies with added taxes on luxuries and high incomes, while debts owed to firms or people in Republican Spain were voided. Nationalist Spain comprised an area that before the war had generated about one-third of all Spanish taxes. During the conflict, tax receipts were lower, but government expenditures were covered by foreign aid,* credits, gifts of jewelry, and other valuables by citizens, as well as by the healthy international trade* in wine, olive oil, and minerals such as copper and tungsten.

Restaurants and bars remained open, less subject to control than in Republican zones, although libraries and bookstores often found their contents censured or destroyed. Taxes on meals were imposed early in the war; yet, private commerce in general was not suffocated by new duties or economic policies. The Nationalists introduced war bonds; therefore, private savings accounts continued to exist and those of the rich to grow.

For further information, see Ronald Fraser, *The Blood of Spain* (New York, 1979); Glenn T. Harper, *German Economic Policy in Spain* (The Hague, 1967); Ramón Tamames, *Estructura económica de España*, 3 vols. (Madrid, 1969) and *La república; La era de Franco* (Madrid, 1973); and Hugh Thomas, *The Spanish Civil War* (New York, 1977).

See also Bank of Spain; Economy, Republican; Foreign Trade, Nationalist; and Monetary Policy, Nationalist.

James W. Cortada

ECONOMY, REPUBLICAN. At the start of the Civil War, the Republican economy was subject to the rigors of the world economic crisis. Even though it affected Spain only tangentially, because of the country's limited industrial development, the Great Depression further complicated a situation made difficult by internal events. In 1934, the Bank of Spain* observed some sectors of the Spanish economy (such as shipping and steel and iron) had suffered the consequences of the world Depression. Generally, however, these effects were less visible than those affecting the world as a whole. The reasons had to do with the peseta's* devaluation prior to the crisis; the closed nature of the Spanish economy and of its financial system; and limited Spanish industrialization. In addition, special problems derived from the good crop years 1932, 1934, and 1935, which gave rise to some grain surpluses

such as wheat. There was also a crisis in the textile industry, a development evident throughout Europe.* Also important was the rise in unemployment resulting from Spanish emigrants returning to Spain in search of jobs that the world Depression eliminated elsewhere.

Accompanying the worldwide crisis was the financial shakeup that occurred when the Republic was proclaimed. The situation must be viewed in the light of the summer of 1936. The military uprising of July 17-19, 1936, divided Spain into two warring parts. During the most important period of the war, the area controlled by the Republican government could be considered stable. This area, encompassing Spain's largest cities (Barcelona,* Madrid,* Valencia,* and Bilbao*), had a larger population* than the rebel zone. On the other hand, the rebel sectors had the most productive agricultural land: Galicia,* León,* Burgos,* Ávila,* Salamanca,* Navarre,* and Estremadura.* Exceptions were citrus fruits, horticultural products, and rice which were produced in Republican territory.

Foreign trade in the Republican zone declined as a result of insuperable obstacles. In the first place, the peseta suffered a progressive devaluation which complicated commerce and made imports more expensive. In the Paris market, the cost of 100 pesetas was 86.25 francs in January 1937, 50.14 in July of the same year, 32.20 in January 1938, and 26.30 in the following July. Lack of support for the Republican regime by the liberal capitalist governments and by the USSR* on political grounds, as well as the blockade of its sea coasts by the Burgos* forces and its allies, also hurt the value of the peseta. On the other hand, the existence of two Spanish governments, both claiming identical responsibilities, as well as the unpredictability of the course of the war, all made it easier for foreign agencies to block demands by the Bank of Spain. Finally, interruptions in communications between agents of firms abroad and Spanish importers and exporters frequently occurred.

The basic regulations affecting foreign trade were set out in a decree of December 3, 1936, reinforced by another decree on August 13. According to these documents, the import and export of merchandise required prior authorization by the Ministry of the Treasury. Exports required approval by the Directory General of Commerce and were payable in foreign exchange. At the request of this agency, the ministry could authorize official organizations in autonomous regions to centralize and report on the export petitions in a liaison capacity between individuals and the ministry.

During the war, the Republican Ministry of Agriculture published statistics showing output in local zones and in the Republic in 1936 and 1937, as well as predictable crop forecasts. On the basis of this information, we can estimate comparisons with previous periods. Edible oil output increased, especially during 1937-1938, even though the 1936-1937 output was greater than in previous periods. Also showing notable increases was the production of roots and tuberous produce, with the exception of beets and turnips. In other sectors, production decreased. The wine industry declined because of commercial problems, adverse climatogical considerations, and sabotage. Grain production also suffered as a result of the lack of fertilizers and seeds, and the advent of drought. Yet, certain cereals, such as wheat and barley, increased. There was a decrease in the production of fruits and vegetables. The production of tomatoes and pimientos and related products for agricultural production were stable for the entire period.

There were two organizational approaches to agriculture. The first concerned direct development by the property owners (family farms) or by whoever cultivated the land free of the responsibility to the absentee owner. The Agrarian Reform Law* or specific regulations such as the Decree of the government of Catalonia,* dated January 1, 1937, covered liberation of responsibilities for sharecroppers and alike. The second approach involved exploitation by collectivized farm groups, among which can be mentioned those in Andalusia* and in the Republican zone of Aragón.* (The latter was created in October 1936 and was dissolved in August 1937.) The collectivization of lands in regions that had no industrial activity and whose economy was based on agricultural development made it easy for a system of bartering to develop. The anarchists* advocated bartering and its form took much of their thoughts. Decisions affecting the division of labor were easily controlled by communal councils established in a revolutionary atmosphere and centered in a geographical area.

Before the war, Spanish industry was centered in the Basque country and Catalonia. The nuclear basis and significance of industry lay in Catalonia. A number of changes occurred in industry in the Republican zone as it adapted itself to wartime conditions. The example of Catalonia is the most important because of the volume of output as well as the kind of organization developed for the purpose of modifying the structure of the economy and finally the speed of the decisions taken by the Generalitat* of Catalonia from the beginning of the war. The Generalitat created this industry in Catalonia, initially provoking a jealous reaction within the Republican government. At the start of 1937, the central government intervened directly in the Elizalde enterprise of Barcelona, which was al-

ready under the control of the Generalitat. Later, a decree of the Republican government, dated June 28, 1937, established three delegations of the Subsecretariat of Armaments within the Ministry of Defense with jurisdiction, respectively, over the center, north, and Catalonia. In the delegation for Catalonia, the Generalitat was represented, but this delegation was replaced by a mixed commission for war industries, formed with five representatives from the Republican government and three from the Generalitat.

The central government's intervention policy intensified on November 4, 1937, when it seized control over Siemens, Altos Hornos de Cataluña, and La Maquinista, all of which were dependent on the War Industries Commission of Catalonia. The government's efforts culminated in the decree of August 11, 1938, which provided for the Republic's expropriation of the war industries in Catalonia. This action provoked the partial crisis in the Negrín* government in which the Catalan Jaume Aguadé* and the Basque Manuel Irujo* resigned their cabinet positions.

No decrees were issued in the rest of Republican Spain regarding nationalizations and collectives. Apparently, in the Republican zone the workers themselves spontaneously began to occupy enterprises or establishments, particularly when the proprietor or manager had already fled. The same situation existed as in Catalonia until October 1936, when the Generalitat apparently anticipated revolutionary processes of an unpredictable nature were to take place. Yet, in the Republican zone (except in Catalonia) part of the industrial sector remained in private enterprise although with workers' committees in control and delegates of the central government allowed to intervene, in accordance with the Intervention Committee established by a decree dated July 25, 1936. In November of that year the decree of July 25 was cancelled. Subsequently, industry was governed by the Republic's February 23, 1937, decree and by the Ministry of Industry decree of March 2, 1937, as amended on September 16. These decrees authorized the Ministry of Industry to intervene in special cases. An August 10, 1937, order extended this authorization to commercial organizations. According to those regulations, there coexisted in the private sector the previous "controlers," the delegate of the central government, and the Workers' Control Committee.

An industry linked directly with foreign industry or with an enterprise whose proprietor was a collaborator of the rebels was subject to expropriation as decreed on February 23, 1937. In the case of a foreign enterprise, the decree was mandatory, including intervention. In the Republican zone, there also existed a collectivized organization which was tolerated by the central government, although, as the war progressed, attempts were made to reduce its extent, particularly after the Thirteen Points* enunciated by Juan Negrín,* president of the Council of Ministers.

Upon assuming his portfolio as minister, the former minister of industry, Juan Peiró,* stated his intention to extend to all of Spain the regulations regarding collectivization in effect in Catalonia. In January 1937 alone, his department had received more than 11,000 petitions of seizure and intervention in industries requesting governmental assistance. The then president of the Council of Ministers, Francisco Largo Caballero,* favored a less drastic policy than collectivization because of his concern about foreign reaction.

With regard to finances in the Republican economy, J. Sardá is at present making a systematic study of how the Republican government financed the Civil War. Some facts are already available. A distinction can be made between internal financing and meeting foreign trade needs. With respect to internal financing, it is important to indicate that expansion of monetary bills in circulation issued by the Bank of Spain was a result of the increase in its accounts arising from the extension of credit to the public sector. Thus, paper money in circulation increased from 5,399.37 million pesetas on June 30, 1936, to 9,212.13 million on April 30, 1938. By decree, the Republican government on April 29, 1938, made it possible for the law governing banking then in effect to permit exceeding the ceiling authorized by existing regulations. Once the Civil War was over, the Bank of Spain indicated that in the Republican zone paper money circulation amounted to 12,754.93 million pesetas. This expansion was achieved through increases of the accounts in the Ministry of Treasury and through decreases in metallic holdings.

The silver accounts for the treasury increased from 351.94 million pesetas at the start of the war to 9,181.54 million by April 30, 1938. The difference stemmed from the internal financing of the war caused by abuse in relation to 25 and 50 peseta notes and 5 and 10 peseta silver certificates placed in circulation. The decree of April 28, 1938, provided that the treasury account be credited with the receipts of war expenditures. This meant that 22,740 million was the total monetary supply in circulation in the Republican zone at the end of the war, as definitively established by the Bank of Spain.

In contrast, gold holdings and accounts of the Bank of Spain's foreign correspondents and agents diminished. With respect to operations related to foreign transactions, attention should be focused initially on the Republic's decree of September 13, 1936, whereby the Ministry of the Treasury was authorized to transfer the gold holdings of the Bank of Spain to the safest possible place. Accordingly, in November 1936, these metallic holdings were deposited with the Soviet Commissariat of Treasury with a value of 1,594.85 million pesetas of gold. Starting in February 1937, the minister of treasury signed twenty-one orders concerning the melting down of gold and its conversion into dollars until fully used up. On the other hand, the Ministry of Treasury authorized the Bank of Spain to proceed with the sale of gold, to facilitate its intervention, in international transactions for the account of the Bank of Spain and the treasury. Credits thus obtained amounted to 201 million pesetas. In this fashion, gold holdings on July 30, 1936, in the Bank of Spain amounted to 2,202 million pesetas, of which 1,592 million were destined for deposit in the USSR* and which in practice were fully drawn down and converted into dollars. They were used for financing foreign transactions. Another 321 million pesetas were distributed in credits to the treasury by virtue of the bank's intervention in international dealings (201 during the war and 120 for operations prior to July 18, 1936). Finally, 32 million went for the bank's account prior to July 18, 1936. There remained 257 million deposited in the Mont de Marsan which had been deposited in 1931 as a guaranty for credit extended by the Bank of France covering the cancellation of Spain's floating foreign debt. This was within the framework of orthodox monetary policy and also reflected the intangible nature of the reserves as determined by successive Republican governments. At the end of the Civil War, the Bank of France delivered this sum in the Mont de Marsan to the government of General Francisco Franco.* Therefore, the gold reserves of the Bank of Spain played a decisive role in financing foreign purchases of a country in which the war and internal security resulted in increased imports, a situation foreseen by the Republican government.

For further information, see Leandro Benavides, *Política económica en la II República española* (Madrid, 1972); Josep María Bricall, *Política económica de la Generalitat, 1936-1939* (Barcelona, 1970); Frank Minz, *La collectivisation en Espagne, 1936-39* (Paris, 1967); Angel Viñas, et al., *Política comercial exterior en España (1931-1975)*, 2 vols. (Madrid, 1979) and *El oro de Moscú* (Barcelona, 1979); and Pedro Voltes Bou, *Historia de la economía española en los siglos XIX y XX* (Madrid, 1974), Vol. 2.

See also Communist Party, Spanish; and Monetary policy, Nationalist.

Josep M. Bricall

EDEN, ANTHONY (1897-1977). Eden was British foreign secretary during the first two years of the Spanish Civil War and the leading architect of London's Spanish policy. During the early months of the war, he hammered out the policy of nonintervention with the French government and consequently became one of the authors of the Non-Intervention Agreement and founder of the Non-Intervention Committee,* which was headquartered in London and first met in September 1936. Eden wanted to restrict the Spanish war to the Iberian Peninsula, making it subservient to his general European policy of maintaining peace between the divided democracies of the West on the one hand and the growing threat of such leaders as Mussolini,* Hitler,* and Stalin* on the other. To this end he believed Spanish affairs had to serve the cause of European stability and peace. He developed Great Britain's* policy of neutrality and, in effect, exported this position to other foreign offices. When the Nationalists* announced in the fall of 1936 that they would attack any vessel carrying supplies to the Republic, Eden sought to block British shipping from supplying either side, although his government decided to protect ships carrying nonmilitary cargos but not arms. Eden privately favored the Republic but in public solidly defended the policy of neutrality and nonintervention as a means of preserving the peace of Europe.*

Throughout the war, Eden sought to mediate an end to the conflict, often with the help of the French. He launched such an effort in the early months of the fighting but with no success. He again attempted mediation in May 1937 at the request of the Spanish Republic, suggesting withdrawal of all foreign troops from Spain to be followed by the establishment of a settlement on both factions by the great powers. Both Franco and Mussolini rejected the plan outright since they thought the Nationalists had a better chance to win the war than the Republic. Thus, within weeks the plan had failed.

Throughout 1937, the Spanish conflict remained one of Eden's biggest problems. He sought to establish some understanding with the Germans that would satisfy Berlin's aspirations in Eastern Europe and thereby reduce international tensions closer to home. During 1937, damage to British shipping by Nationalist and Italian naval forces in the Mediterranean caused considerable concern in Britain. Eden proposed with the French that an international naval patrol be established to protect neutral shipping and that both the USSR* and Italy* participate. In September at Nyon, Switzerland,* an international conference was held which established such a patrol, and by the end of the month Italy had agreed to participate. This hardly stopped the sinking of British ships, although it did reduce the number destroyed during 1938. During this period, the Spanish Republic exerted pressure on Eden's government and that in Paris to stop Italian and German intervention on behalf of Franco, but in line with London's policy, the British refused to take action against Rome and Berlin.

As the years passed, Eden came to realize that the policy of appeasement was not really working. The regimes in Rome, Berlin, Moscow, and Paris violated the Non-Intervention Agreement in one fashion or another. The threat of international conflict kept increasing during the Civil War, while attempts to negotiate a reduction in tensions with Hitler and Mussolini never succeeded. It was a difficult period for this quiet, patient diplomat, an era when agreements were signed and then not honored, when blatant German imperialism became clearly obvious with hope for peace and stability shrinking. At times, he was at odds with his colleagues in the Foreign Office, many of whom sympathized with the Nationalists' cause. He found the British reluctant to take any hard stand against the threat to peace and saw little direction and determination in Paris either.

The prime minister during the last two years of the Spanish Civil War, Neville Chamberlain,* was a greater advocate of appeasement than Eden and so they quarreled often. Finally, the foreign secretary resigned from the cabinet in February 1938. Years later, in 1956, when he was prime minister himself, Eden sought to overthrow Nasser's Egyptian government rather than attempt a policy of appeasement which he had learned only encouraged authoritarian leaders to pursue more ambitious goals and policies.

For further information, see Anthony Eden, *Facing the Dictators* (London, 1962); Jill Edwards, *The British Government and the Spanish Civil War, 1936-1939* (London, 1979); Oliver Harvey, *The Diplomatic Diaries of Oliver Harvey* (London, 1972); and Keith Middlemas, *Diplomacy of Illusion* (London, 1972).

See also Blum, Léon; France; League of Nations; and Nyon Conference.

James W. Cortada

EDUCATION. Classroom lessons continued during the Civil War, but schooling became inseparable from ideology, with each side organizing education to fit its view of how future generations should be instructed. The Republicans* viewed education as an instrument of social change, and the pedagogic principles adopted were consistent with Progressive education practices in Europe* and the United States.* The Nationalists,* on the other hand, rejected all aspects of the educational innovation endorsed by the Republic and instead reintroduced the influence of the Spanish Church* into curriculum and administrative matters.

Cities, providences, and the government of the Republic itself all expanded their educational services in 1936 and 1937. At each level, the goal of social reform through educational change represented an acceleration of the school reforms introduced between 1931 and 1933, which had been attempts to secularize instruction, improve teacher salaries, and revise the curriculum. These reforms met with mixed success during the liberal biennium, but they were taken up with fervor in the summer of 1936 amidst widespread demands that new schools help forge a new society.

The privations of war, particularly the lack of trained personnel and adequate finances, imposed considerable constraints upon the educational initiatives of the Republic. Nevertheless, a number of important reforms were carried out. Ten thousand new teachers were employed the first year. Classrooms formerly controlled by the Church were turned over to municipalities to make available needed space for public-supported schools. Normal schools revamped their curriculum to give teacher trainees a thorough preparation in ideas of international peace, personal liberty, and social justice. Minimum salary for teachers was raised to 4,000 pesetas and in Catalonia* to 5,000 pesetas. Educational opportunity in the first two years of the war unquestionably was extended beyond what it had been, but it is impossible to give a precise measurement of improvement because statistics on construction, enrollment, and appropriations are either inaccurate or unavailable.

The most evident change in education during the Civil War related to the purposes of schooling. Schools were seen as integral to the social and economic transformation unleashed by the uprising. The goal of education was to train a new generation imbued with a secular, egalitarian spirit. The three Republican ministers of education who served during the Civil War represented leftist parties committed to using schools as agents to create a new social order. Francisco Barnés, a Left Republican who had served as minister in the summer of 1933, returned to the post from July 19 to September 5, 1936. He was succeeded by Jesús Hernández Tomás,* editor of the communist paper *Mundo Obrero*.* Tomás was one of two communists who entered the government in September 1936. He served until April 4, 1938, when he was replaced by Segundo Blanco,* an anarchist leader from Asturias,* who was the last Republican minister of instruction.

Education in the broadest sense of bringing people into contact with information and ideas was a special concern of Jesús Hernández Tomás. Numerous reforms were introduced that brought education to those who had not previously benefited from it. A decree of November 21, 1936 created *Institutos Obreros*, secondary schools open without cost to workers aged fifteen to thirty-five. The state paid students a stipend to attend a workers' institute if they had to quit a job in order to attend. Six such institutions eventually operated in Madrid,* Valencia,* Barcelona,* and Granollers. Compensation to families whose children went to school rather than to work enabled many lower class students to enter classrooms for the first time in their lives. A detailed system of scholarships was set up for that purpose in September 1937.

Perhaps the greatest obstacle to widespread educational opportunity in Spain was that, on a national average, nearly half the citizens were illiterate. Various programs were initiated to increase literacy on the Republican side. One of the most ambitious and successful was *Las Milicias de la Cultura* (the Cultural Militia) which was designed to teach reading and writing to the soldiers. Its slogan was "¡Fuera analfabetos!" A decree of January 30, 1937, initiated the Cultural Militia, and by the end of the year some 1,066 classes had been organized in the trenches by the Ministry of Public Instruction,. The Republic claimed that 75,000 soldiers became literate because of the Cultural Militia, which recruited its instructors from school teachers and the faculty of normal schools. Foreign observers often remarked in praise of the schools in the trenches that pen and books, together with rifles, were frequently carried by Republican soldiers. Literacy campaigns were conducted for noncombatants as well. An intensive, well-planned literacy program for rural areas began in November 1937 and lasted for five months.

In December 1931, the Republic had begun a program of *Misiones Pedagógicas* (Pedagogic Missions) which brought books, films, and lecturers to rural villages, along with assistance to public primary school teachers. The *Misiones Pedagógicas* were continued during the Civil War, but they were complemented by two other cultural missions: (1) *Cultura Popular*, which the communists were especially active with, sponsored propaganda for the war through books, magazines, and festivals. One of the most important activities came during the defense of Madrid* in November 1936 when, for days, *Cultura Popular* volunteers broadcast revolutionary hymns from loudspeakers. (2) *Altavoz del Frente*, organized by the 300 writers and artists in the Alliance of Intellectuals for the Defense of Culture, offered theatrical and literary programs for soldiers and civilians. Worker and popular education were also important concerns for anarchists.* In the hundreds of collectives and through the activities of *Mujeres Libres*, a libertarian feminist group formed in April 1936, anarchists worked to establish schools where instruction was secular, scientific and rational, coeducational, and dedicated to dignifying manual and mental work.

Curriculum innovations stemming from the work of various commissions were decreed in the fall of 1937 for primary and secondary schools in the Republican zone. Scientific and technical subjects were to be stressed henceforth, and a pedagogy that emphasized the active participation of the student through projects and direct observation was to be encouraged. Little came from these lofty decrees.

Education received less attention in Nationalist Spain than in the Republican zone, but although the pedagogic principles were few, their direction was unmistakably toward greater Church control of schooling. It was not until January 30, 1938, that Franco* appointed a minister of education, Pedro de Sáinz Rodríguez,* who had formerly served as a primary school inspector and monarchist deputy in the Cortes.* Prior to Sáinz Rodríguez's appointment, however, authority over the educational system in territory controlled by Franco had reverted to the Church, which in exchange for allying with Franco and giving the insurrection its blessing, had received tacit approval to reshape education to the Church's purposes. Among the Church's first changes were to require the display in each classroom of an image of the Virgin Mary and the crucifix and the saying of prayers when entering and exiting school. Sáinz Rodríguez issued a series of plans for reorganizing education in 1938 that further affirmed the re-Catholicizing of Spain as a principle of the new regime. The new primary school curriculum, for example, based instruction on religion, patriotism, and civic and physical education.

For further information, see Matilde Vazquez, "La reforma educativa en la zona republicana durante la guerra civil," *Revista de Educación* 240 (September-October 1975): 60-72.
See also Catholic Church, Spanish.

David V. Holtby

EHRENBURG, ILYA (1891-1967). Ehrenburg was a Russian writer and correspondent for *Izvestia* beginning in August 1936. He gathered intelligence and wrote some propaganda, and was a major source of information outside the Soviet government for Moscow and a useful tool. He was politically astute, for he survived Stalin's* purges which took the lives of many Russians who had worked in Civil War Spain. While his opinions did not always coincide with those of his government, he did not hesitate to cooperate with his nation's leaders by writing, for example, in *Pravda*, articles that enhanced Soviet policies in Spain.

For further information, see Ilya Ehrenburg, *Men, Years and Life*, 4 vols. *The Eve of War* (London, 1963), Vol.4.
See also USSR.

James W. Cortada

EIBAR. Eibar, in the province of Guipúzcoa,* had an arms factory which, in the early days of the Civil War, came under the management of Bilbao's* defense committee. The committee wanted to insure that the Basques would use its output. During the war, this plant was an important source of arms for the Republicans.* Ammunition and explosives were also made there.

For further information, see Hugh Thomas, *The Spanish Civil War* (New York, 1977).

James W. Cortada

EL CARMOLÍ. El Carmolí in Cartagana,* the site of a Russian Air Force base during the Civil War, became home for bombers, fighter planes, and military advisers assigned to the Republican Air Force.*

For further information, see Jesús Salas Larrazábal, *La guerra de España desde el aire* (Barcelona, 1969).
See also Pilots.

James W. Cortada

ELDA. Elda, a town located in the province of Alicante* in southeastern Spain, served as the Republican capital in February-March 1939. At that time the only remaining Republican zone was southeastern Spain since Catalonia* had just fallen to the Nationalists.* This town, a small manufacturing community and socialist stronghold nearly 20 miles from the provincial capital of Alicante, was conveniently close to the coast should Negrín's* government find it necessary to leave Spain quickly. Madrid* was constantly under attack and was always on the verge of occupation, while Barcelona* had already fallen to Franco.* For the moment then, Elda was safe. Finally, in early March, Negrín left Spain and the town again became a quiet, obscure community.

For further information, see Vicente Ramos, *La guerra civil en la provincia de Alicante*, 3 vols. (Alicante, 1974).

James W. Cortada

ELECTIONS OF FEBRUARY 1936. The elections held on February 16, 1936, were the last major ones to be conducted before the start of the Civil War. Following a tempestuous campaign by both the political Right and Left, the results reflected an unexpected victory for the Left. As a consequence, the political polarization of Spanish society, which had been developing throughout the years of the Second Republic,* continued, becoming yet another event along the road to war.

A number of political groups and parties competed for the voters' support. A cluster of liberal and radical parties formed the Popular Front,* advocating such programs as the restoration of Catalan autonomy, amnesty for political prisoners, agrarian reform, restoration of jobs to workers fired for political reasons, and damages for property owners who suffered during the revolt of 1934 to be paid for by the government. The Popular Front included a coalition of Lerroux's radicals, Zamora's progressives, Catalans of the Lliga,* socialists, and communists. The anarchists* remained aloof and actually discouraged voting.

The political Right clustered into a group called the National Front.* Composed primarily of the *Confederación Española de Derechas Autónomas* (CEDA),* Carlists,* Alfonsist monarchists, some Falangists, and other conservatives, it was hostile to the aims of the Republic. Officially, it should be noted, the Falange* was not a member of the alliance, although some of its members supported the aims of the National Front. Disagreements between the CEDA and the Falange in particular made the coalition less than a solid national front of conservatives hostile to the Popular Front. Briefly put, the Right proved critical primarily of the Republic, was antidemocratic and pro-Catholic, and supported the financial interests of the landed gentry.

Amid tensions that caused the Republic to station 17,000 Assault Guards* and some 34,000 Civil Guards* at the polls to insure the peace, Spaniards voted on Sunday, February 16. Of a possible 13.5 million voters, approximately 9,870,000 participated. In terms of seats gained in the Cortes* by the various parties making up the coalitions in the elections, the winners were on the political Left.

Several conclusions can be reached with regard to these hotly contested elections. First, the Spanish elec-

Elections of February 1936

Faction	Pct. of Votes Received	No. of Votes Received	No. of Deputies to Cortes Earned
Popular Front	34.3	4,654,116	263
National Front	33.2	4,503,505	133
Center parties	5.4	526,615	77

NOTE: Remaining percentages to come to 100 percent represented miscellaneous votes and absenteeism, with a second round of voting two weeks later to resolve disputed seats.

SOURCE: Hugh Thomas, *The Spanish Civil War* (New York, 1977).

Delegates to the Cortes by Party

CEDA	101
Socialists	88
Republican Left	79
Republican Union	34
Esquerra	22
Center party	21
Carlists	15
Communists	14
Monarchists	13
Lliga	12
Agrarians	11
Radicals	9
Basques	5
Falangists	0
TOTAL	424

torate was clearly divided politically between the Left and Right, with little compromise evident. The Center coalition had failed completely to draw support from either side. Second, as a result of the victory by the Left, the National Front coalition collapsed. Consequently, various elements on the Right now concluded that their interests would best be served by plotting the overthrow of the Republic. Thus, from February until July when the Civil War began, political intriguing on the Right increased sharply, while violent acts, murders, and heated propagandizing by both sides appeared in all provinces. As such, these elections contributed to the coming of the Civil War.

For further information, see Jean Bécarud, *La Deuxième République espagnole 1931-1936* (Paris, 1962); Hugh Thomas, *The Spanish Civil War* (New York, 1977); Javier Tusell, *Las elecciones del Frente Popular*, 2 vols. (Madrid, 1971); and José Venegas, *Las elecciones del Frente Popular* (Buenos Aires, 1942).

See also Communist Party, Spanish; and Socialist Party, Spanish.

James W. Cortada

EL FERROL. El Ferrol, a port with an excellent natural harbor on the coast of Galicia,* contained the best shipbuilding and repair facilities in Spain and was the Nationalists'* main naval base. Most of the major warships of the Nationalist fleet were captured here in July 1936.

See also Almirante Cervera; and Navy, Spanish.

Willard C. Frank, Jr.

EROLES, DIONISIO. Eroles was a Catalan anarchist from Barcelona* who, in the early months of the Civil War (July-December 1936), led an armed band in the city terrorizing members of the middle class. Such acts caused many urban property owners to support the local Communist party, the *Partit Socialista Unificat de Catalunya* (PSUC),* which promised to restore law and order. In May 1937, Eroles served as anarchist commissar (*Federación Anarquista Ibéria* police head) attempting to maintain some calm in the early stages of the May 1937 riots.* The Republic established its control over the city and broke the power of the anarchists,* along with Eroles' influence, by the end of that month.

For further information, see Burnett Bolloten, *The Spanish Revolution: The Left and the Struggle for Power During the Civil War* (Chapel Hill, N.C., 1979).
See also Terrorism.

James W. Cortada

ESCOBAR HUERTAS, ANTONIO (1879-1939). Escobar was a regular military officer who remained loyal to the Republic, spent most of the war in the central zone as commander of the Army of Estremadura,* and in the spring of 1939, opposed Negrín* and supported the Casado* coup and a quick end to the war.

In July 1936, Escobar was a colonel of the Civil Guard* and chief of the 19th *Tercio* (regiment) in Barcelona.* His actions were crucial in keeping the Civil Guard on the side of the Republic and preventing the rebels from taking over in Barcelona. Government confidence in his loyalty is demonstrated by the fact that in May 1937 he was named the delegate of the Azaña* government in Catalonia.*

Since most action in the first year of the war was centered in the south and in the central zone around Madrid,* Escobar was shifted from Barcelona and in

November commanded the defense in the sector of the highway from Madrid to Estremadura.* He remained in this area as head of the Army of Estremadura and consequently was not involved in the major campaigns of the war in 1937-1938 as they were concentrated in the north.

During January 5-13, 1939, he led a diversionary action on the borders of Estremadura, attempting to lessen pressure in the Catalonia sector. By that point, Escobar, like several other military leaders, had become convinced that further military resistance was impossible. At the meeting at Los Llanos Airport near Valencia* in February 1939, he argued with Negrín that it was madness to continue to fight because, as he said, in addition to spirit and zeal for one's cause, it was necessary to have arms and munitions.

In March 1939, Colonel Casado's plans to take over the government and end the war on the best terms possible essentially created a civil war among the Republicans.* In Ciudad Real,* loyal communist units resisted the Casado move, and Escobar used his troops to take control of that area, favoring plans for surrender. In that same month, Nationalist troops occupied Ciudad Real. Escobar was arrested and was executed with a number of other Republican military leaders at the end of the war.

For further information, see Guillermo Cabanellas, *La guerra de dos mil días*, 2 vols. (Buenos Aires, 1975); and Hugh Thomas, *The Spanish Civil War* (London, 1977).

Jane Slaughter

ESPAÑA. The Nationalist battleship *España* (ex-*Alfonso XIII*, launched 1912, 14,224 tons standard, 8-305mm [12 in] guns, 20 kts.) was in El Ferrol* in reduced commission during the uprising of July 1936. For two days, fighting raged in and around the immobilized battleship until victorious rebel forces ashore arranged her surrender. Minimally readied for sea, *España* bombarded coastal objectives in the Bay of Biscay. She later engaged in blockade operations until accidentally sunk by a German mine off Santander* on April 30, 1937.

See also Navy, German; and Navy, Spanish.

Willard C. Frank, Jr.

ESPIONAGE. Each side in the Civil War established large intelligence-gathering agencies such as the *Servicio de Información del Nordeste de España* (SIFNE)* (Nationalist), the *Servicio de Investigación Militar* (SIM)* (Republican), the *Servicio de Información y Policía*

Militar (SIPM)* (Nationalist), and the People's Commissariat for International Affairs (NKVD)* (Soviet). Each employed thousands of people, and communicated across battle zones and in other countries. They had the dual purpose of gathering military intelligence for their respective armies and identifying political enemies of the state.

The general performance of military intelligence-gathering organizations was excellent because they generated vast quantities of timely, relevant data. However, political intelligence often proved faulty and vengeful, and was used by one political faction or another to eliminate rivals. This was particularly the case in Republican Spain where political parties (such as the anarchists,* *Partido Obrero de Unificación Marxista* [POUM],* and communists) established their own intelligence networks to battle their enemies. In the Republican Army,* political commissars were appointed for a similar purpose. The Soviet NKVD became an insidious, cruel institution for expanding communist influence in Spain while assuring Soviet involvement in the highest levels of Republican politics. These intelligence agencies were often responsible for the torture, murder, and execution of prisoners* tried under military or civilian law.

Espionage is, of course, one of the least understood subjects connected with the Spanish Civil War. Each political party had its agents, as did every military organization, national, regional, and provincial government. Every town and city had spies, and in some parts of Spain, a significant portion of the population* was involved in some form of espionage (Andalusia* in 1937-1938, for example). Little is known of individual master spies or of how these organizations functioned.

For further information, see José Bertrán y Musitu, *Experiencias de los servicios de información del nordeste de España* (SIFNE) (Madrid, 1940); Ronald Fraser, *Blood of Spain* (New York, 1979); José Manuel Martínez Bande, *Los cien últimos días de la república* (Barcelona, 1972); Domingo Paster Petit, *Espionaje: España, 1936-1939* (Barcelona, 1977); and Hugh Thomas, *The Spanish Civil War* (New York, 1977).

See also Terrorism.

James W. Cortada

ESQUERRA REPUBLICANA DE CATALUNYA. The *Esquerra Republicana de Catalunya* (more commonly called just the Esquerra) was the Left Republican party of Catalonia.* Its members came primarily from the bourgeoisie, although a considerable number were also vine cultivators (*rabassaires*). It first came to prominence during the municipal elections of 1931, the year the Second Republic* was founded. Led by the aging romantic Francesc Macià, this party had its primary strength in the city of Barcelona* and other urban centers in Catalonia where it drew support from small businessmen, lower middle-class members, and the intellectual community. It had been formed from the membership of the *Partit Republicà Catalanista* (a left-wing lower bourgeoisie class group), the *Estat Català* (more extremist young separatists), and an assortment of socialists. Macià had been the founder and head of the *Estat Català*.* In the elections of 1931, the Esquerra came in first in Barcelona, thereby breaking the political hold of the party which, up to then, had been the strongest in Catalonia, the *Lliga Regionalista* (a more conservative Catalan party). The victory of the Esquerra in April 1931 indicated that the Catalan separatist issue would become a more serious political one than in the previous several years. Macià and another Catalan member of the Esquerra, Luis Companys,* called for the establishment of a Catalan republic, while the government in Madrid* hurriedly sought to make some concessions in order to fend off any attempt to create an independent government in Catalonia.

With the establishment of a local government for Catalonia, the Generalitat,* Macià became its president and was succeeded upon his death in 1933 by Companys, as new head of the Esquerra. The following year, the *Estat Català* and its military arm, the *escamots*, attempted to revolt against the wishes of Companys and the Second Republic, trying to establish an independent Catalan government on October 5, 1934. In order to prevent a split in the Esquerra as well as within the Catalan community, the next day Companys publicly advocated the creation of an autonomist government and urged all fighting to end. Following suppression of the revolt, Companys momentarily went to jail on the orders of Republican officials. In the elections of February 1936*—the last open elections before the start of the Civil War—the Esquerra won twenty-two seats in the national Cortes.* It eventually gained thirty-eight by the time the second round of elections was held and all disputed returns settled.

Once the Civil War started, Companys continued as head of both the Esquerra and the Generalitat, although he and his party constantly were challenged by the far Left, primarily by the *Federación Anarquista Ibérica* (FAI)* and the *Confederación Nacional del Trabajo* (CNT).* The party continued to staff heavily each of the Generalitat's cabinets and many of the posts within the Catalan government, even though the anarchists* and other labor parties formed an informal, not-so-hidden extra government of their own in 1936 which functioned until the May 1937 riots resulted in a sharp decline in the political power of the radicals. On July 31, Companys changed his title from president of the Generalitat to president of Catalonia. Thus, along with the Esquerra, he pushed his region one step further toward complete autonomy from the Republic while clinging to power. In the months that followed, the Esquerra competed continuously with the anarchists for control over the Catalan government and the local economy. Both advocated continued dismantling of the Catalan economy and its formation anew. Yet, the Esquerra was more inclined to protect the economic interests of small landholders and businessmen than were the anarchists. Madrid still recognized the power of this party because in its cabinet reshuffle in September, it included a member of the Esquerra, José Tomás y Piera, as the new minister of labor and health.

The Esquerra shared power in the Generalitat with other more radical groups throughout 1936. Finally, in May 1937, the anarchists, in an attempt to consolidate their control, pushed hard to squeeze out a number of their political enemies. Anarchist groups and their allies fought in the streets of Barcelona against their enemies (mostly communist) but within days had lost. Republican forces helped break the power of the anarchists, and Companys remained in office. The Republic now moved to curb the power of all political groups in Catalonia, especially separatists and anarchists. In the new Catalan government established in June, half the ministries (three) in the Generalitat went to the more conservative Esquerra. The best known of the three, Juan José Tarradelas,* minister of finance, went into exile after the war, only to return to Spain in the late 1970s as president of the reconstituted Generalitat.

The *Esquerra Republicana de Catalunya* had been the largest middle-class party in Catalonia during the days of the Second Republic. In the early months of the Civil War, it was swept along with events, allowing itself to participate in more radical actions than it might otherwise have approved. This course came about either out of individual fears of its members or as a means of continuing in power. During the war, its leaders hoped to eliminate the political divisions in Catalonia which invited both interference from the communists and the government in Madrid, either of which would set back any notion of local autonomy. Companys in particular hoped to manipulate and control the FAI and the CNT, although he failed. In the end, what he feared most happened: the communists

throughout Republican Spain were in the ascendancy by mid-1937, and the Republican government increased its control over affairs in Catalonia. Yet, down to the last months of the war, the Esquerra resisted (when it could) the encroachments of the Republican government, advocating local control over Catalan affairs.

For further information, see Burnett Bolloten, *The Spanish Revolution: The Left and the Struggle for Power During the Civil War* (Chapel Hill, N.C., 1979); and Jaume Colomer, et al., *Els grups politics a Catalunya, partits i programes*, 2 vols. (Barcelona, 1976).

James W. Cortada

ESTAT CATALÀ. The *Estat Català*, a Catalan separatist party formed in 1922 by middle-class youth, was active primarily within the city of Barcelona.* One of its earliest leaders was Francesc Macià, head of the larger, Esquerra* party. By the early 1930s, the small *Estat Català* was led by José Dencás, a medical doctor and councillor of the interior in the Catalan autonomist government, better known as the Generalitat.* This radical band of Catalan separatists, still consisting mostly of young men, was protofascist in demeanor. They dressed in green shirts, formed a militia called the *escamots* (under the command of Miguel Badía, a known terrorist), and advocated complete autonomy from Spain. During the days of the Second Republic,* the presence of the *Estat Català*, at a time when the Generalitat was governed by a left-wing coalition, insured divided Catalan political aspirations in the face of the hostile central government in Madrid.* Yet, the *Estat Català* was an offshoot of a much larger Catalan party, the Esquerra, whose members included a large number of Catalans advocating local home rule. As regards the quasi-fascist *escamots*, they drilled in Barcelona with some impunity, probably since at the time (around 1934) Dencás was serving as councillor of public order in the Catalan government.

In October 1934, Dencás thought that the time had come to establish an independent Catalan government. The *Union General de Trabajadores* (UGT)* had just declared a major strike against the admission of the *Confederación Española de Derechas Autónomas* (CEDA)* into the government, thereby insuring political instability. His *escamots* destroyed rail communications near Lérida* on October 5 and blocked the use of subway communications. Meanwhile, President Companys* of the Generalitat called on these conservatives to end their disruptive actions which came at a time when the Catalan Left was also critical of his rule. Anticipating that Dencás would establish a new government, Companys took the initiative by declaring the creation of a "Catalan state within the Spanish Federal Republic," on October 6, 1934. Soon after, Dencás's revolt collapsed.

At the start of the Civil War, most of the leaders of this movement were in exile in Paris as a result of their actions in October 1934. The majority expected Franco* and his Nationalists* to win a quick victory in central Spain and to occupy Madrid. Leaders of the *Estat Català* within Spain as well as in exile met in November 1936 to discuss the possibility of negotiating with Franco and recognizing his government as a means of obtaining an autonomous government for Catalonia.* When word of the discussions leaked out, members of the *Estat Català* reputed to be involved and working in the Generalitat (in the Repulican zone) in Barcelona were forced to leave their posts and go into exile. In the case of Andreu Reverter, chief of police for the Generalitat, he was publicly identified along with the president of the governmental body, Juan Casanovas. It is quite possible that Reverter was killed, although Casanovas quickly left for Paris. Soon after, the *Estat Català* declined as a political force and more radical political elements dominated Catalan politics, especially the *Confederación Nacional del Trabajo* (CNT)* and *Federación Anarquista Ibérica* (FAI).* The latter continued to limit and persecute the *Estat Català* until the May 1937 riots.

Although exact figures for membership are not available, it appears that the *escamots* alone numbered over 3,000 throughout Catalonia. Because they were so well organized, Companys had to bow to their demands for a more radical stand on Catalan autonomy, even at the price of alienating the more powerful anarchist parties in northeastern Spain. Yet, because the *Estat Català* was affiliated with the Esquerra, the largest political party in Catalonia, it meant that this group's influence would be extensive in regional Catalan political life.

For further information, see Jaume Colomer, et al., *Els grups politics a Catalunya, partits i programes*, 2 vols. (Barcelona, 1976); J. A. González Casanova, *Federalisme i autonomia a Catalunya (1868-1938)* (Barcelona, 1974); and Hugh Thomas, *The Spanish Civil War* (New York, 1977).

James W. Cortada

ESTREMADURA. Estremadura, a region located in southwestern Spain bordering on Portugal* and made up of the provinces of Cáceres* and Badajoz,* was one of the nation's major olive- and wine-producing areas and the home of large agricultural estates. Prior to the Civil War, this dry, mountainous, poor region was dominated by large agricultural holdings (*latifundia*), often run by absentee landowners who used their fields unproductively. One-eighth of all land in Cáceres, for example, was owned by the nobility. The mass of Estremadura's population* was landless, was paid wages that seldom covered the cost of food,* and worked between 180 and 250 days a year, although in the first three decades of the twentieth century closer to 150. This condition existed primarily because the labor supply exceeded the needs of the area by 50 percent as well as because weather conditions affected the rise of harvests.

These poor living conditions encouraged the growth of anarchism among landless agricultural laborers much as in Andalusia.* By the 1920s, the majority of the workers were avowed anarchists,* a more prosperous few flirted with socialism, and the landowners were associated with more conservative political movements such as monarchism or traditional Republican parties. For over 100 years, the nation had discussed agrarian reforms, yet little had happened, making the agricultural situation in Spain one of the fundamental causes of the Civil War. During the Second Republic,* the government attempted reforms that caused some workers to seize large estates, claiming land for themselves in anticipation of additional changes in this direction by Madrid.* In 1936, for example, 60,000 workers seized 3,000 farms in Estremadura alone, mainly in the province of Badajoz.

At the start of the war, therefore, the area was very unsettled. In July, Nationalist sympathizers seized Cáceres; yet, in the city of Badajoz, troops loyal to the Republic held on and thus had to be conquered. In those portions of Estremadura controlled by the Nationalists,* most of the lands seized by peasants were restored to their original owners, while others remained in the possession of workers for a year or more before being taken back. In the Republican zone to the south, Madrid's influence continued with peasants in greater control over the agricultural properties they worked until the Nationalists occupied all the region by late 1938. However, by March 1937, all of Cáceres and the western half of Badajoz were Nationalist, leaving the eastern portion as part of the central Republican zone. As the tensions of war increased in the Republican portions of Spain, so did the militancy of local farmers in Estremadura. Politicians from the *Unión General de Trabajadores* (UGT),* socialists, and communists competed for influence with the peasants, while the anarchists continued to push for collectivization projects. Expropriation of businesses in the towns also increased.

Major fighting took place in Estremadura. From

August through October, war came to Badajoz; the Nationalists seized the western portion bordering on Portugal, and the highly publicized repression in the city of Badajoz in August brought more tragedy. It was in Estremadura that Franco's* army made use of the Moors* and that the Moors developed a reputation for extreme brutality which thereafter preceded them wherever they went. Fighting continued on the north-south Badajoz front throughout 1937 in sporadic fashion and in most of 1938 as the Nationalists pushed northward and to the east in their drive to capture Madrid and later Valencia.* Those who sided with the Republicans* were purged in newly acquired areas, many of them being shot after brief trials. The last portions of Republican Estremadura fell to the Nationalists in March 1939 during the last days of the war.

For further information, see Manuel Aznar, *Historia militar de la guerra de España, 1936-1939* (Madrid, 1940); Robert W. Kern, *Red Years/Black Years: A Political History of Spanish Anarchism, 1911-1937* (Philadelphia, 1978); and Edward Malefakis, *Agrarian Reform and Peasant Revolution in Spain* (New Haven, Conn., 1970).

See also Agriculture, Nationalist Policy; and Appendix B.

James W. Cortada

EUROPE. Every country in Western and Eastern Europe recognized the international implications of the Spanish Civil War. While governments were establishing diplomatic policies, intellectuals* were deeply caught up in the Spanish issues. Manufacturers wanted to sell to contending factions, while individuals volunteered to serve in opposing armies. Religious beliefs influenced opinions, while charitable organizations sought to help both Republicans* and Nationalists.* Few events of the 1930s received more coverage via the press, novels, exposés, magazine articles, and discussions within governments, universities, and churches.

Governments in Western Europe, led by Great Britain* and France,* developed formal policies of neutrality toward the conflict and created the Non-Intervention Committee* to force noninvolvement in the war. They believed neutrality would keep the Spanish war from spreading to the rest of Europe. Their original fear of war grew out of an emerging rise in tensions between the democratic republics of the West and the rapidly expanding number of authoritarian (fascist or communist) regimes in other parts of Europe. The militant nationalism and fascist ideology

that strengthened and motivated Mussolini's* Italy* and Hitler's* Germany,* and communism in Stalin's* USSR* were rapidly leading to a confrontation over territory, national ambitions, and the rise of militarism. To combat the fear of another war, the Western powers sought an accommodation with Hitler and Mussolini, possibly with a counterbalance to the east in Russia, evolving into a policy of appeasement. While being allowed some latitude for national aspirations, Hitler and Mussolini were to be contained and not be allowed to use any international crisis such as the Spanish Civil War to upset the peace of Europe and start another world war. While much official sympathy for the Republic existed, particularly in France, neutrality and containment were the policies of the day in regard to Spain.

The exception to this rule was Russia which sought to find allies in the West to counter the growing threat of an expansionist-minded Germany to its west in Central Europe. Anything that could be done to curb the growth of fascist regimes, the natural allies of Hitler, would be carried out. This meant far more active support with arms and materiél for the Spanish Republic by Stalin, so long as this effort did not threaten relations with London and Paris.

Hitler and Mussolini saw the Spanish war as an opportunity to expand fascism at the expense of the democracies, while maintaining unsettled conditions in the West. A war in Spain would draw attention away from greater German aspirations in Eastern Europe, especially those sectors with large German-speaking populations. Italy sent arms and thousands of men in support of Franco's* cause, and Germany offered supplies and advisers while allowing its air force to acquire combat experience at the expense of the Spanish.

Intellectuals in Europe, communist and liberal, professors and writers, students and militants, all believed that the fate of Western civilization as they knew it hung in the balance. If the Spanish Republic fell, fascism and dictatorships in Europe would progress yet another step. Halting such a development was essential in preserving democracy, republicanism, intellectual activity, and freedom of expression and economic relations. To more conservative elements, including many Catholics and various right-wing and fascist organizations in each country, Franco's triumph meant the restoration of historical tradition in Spain, the victory of church and monarchism, of corporatist government and economic policies. For them Franco represented nationalism and stability, law and order.

Both sides in the conflict received massive aid from other European nations. Hugh Thomas estimates that both factions combined were given between $1.425 and $1.900 billion in aid. Thousands of Germans, Italians, and North Africans fought on the Nationalist side and between 35,000 and 40,000 volunteers* fought with the International Brigades* for the Republicans. According to Thomas, probably another 10,000 doctors, nurses, and other civilians served in the war. Hardly a writer in Europe did not comment in print on the conflict. Every major newspaper in Europe carried daily articles, while during 1936-1939 contributions in magazines and in the form of books ran into the thousands. Almost every leading producer and movie company made movies* on some aspect of the war.

Since the end of the war, Europeans have published over 10,000 books and thousands of articles. Two generations after the conflict, it is still seen as one of the most important events of the twentieth century. Many Europeans felt the wrong side won the war. The plight of thousands of Republican refugees* all over the world, particularly in France, presented visible evidence of the war's aftermath for decades, while Franco's close association with Hitler and Mussolini influenced international relations years after World War II. As recently as the early 1970s, the governments of France and Britain did not recommend Spanish membership in the Common Market because of Franco.

For further information, see Pierre Broué and Émile Témime, *La Révolution et la guerre d'Espagne* (Paris, 1961); Ricardo de la Cierva, *Historia ilustrada de la guerra civil española*, 2 vols. (Barcelona, 1970); Dante Puzzo, *Spain and the Great Powers, 1936-1941* (New York, 1962); Jesús Salas Larrazábal, *Intervención extranjera en la guerra de España* (Madrid, 1974); Fernando Schwartz, *La internacionalización de la guerra civil española* (Barcelona, 1971); Hugh Thomas, *The Spanish Civil War* (New York, 1977); and Julián Zugazagoitia, *Historia de la guerra en España* (Buenos Aires, 1940 and subsequent editions). For the role of specific countries, the bibliographic essay in Hugh Thomas's book is excellent.

See also Blum, Léon; Chamberlain, Neville; Delbos, Yvon; and League of Nations.

James W. Cortada

F

FABREGAS, JUAN. Fabregas, an anarchist leader from Catalonia,* joined the Generalitat* on September 27, 1936, as councillor for economics. Along with his fellow-anarchist colleagues in the Generalitat, the anarchists* now dominated the government at Barcelona.* Fabregas was responsible for maintaining the welfare of the Catalan economy, which he proved unable to do when the Civil War disrupted normal commercial affairs.

For further information, see Josep María Bricall, *Política económica de la Generalitat (1936-1939)* (Barcelona, 1970).

James W. Cortada

FAI. *See Federación Anarquista Ibérica.*

FALANGE ANTHEM. *See "Cara al Sol."*

FALANGE ESPAÑOLA. The *Falange Española*, an extreme nationalist movement of fascist inspiration, was organized in Madrid* in October 1933 by José Antonio Primo de Rivera* (eldest son of the former dictator Miguel Primo de Rivera) and a small group of collaborators. It soon merged with another small movement of revolutionary national syndicalism, the *Juntas de Ofensiva Nacional-Sindicalista* (JONS)* and its name was expanded to *Falange Española de las JONS*. An official program of twenty-seven points was adopted in 1934, standing for Spanish unity, strong government, a corporative state system of national syndicalism to embrace both capital and labor, the nationalization of banking and credit, military strength, cultural traditionalism, and imperial expansion.

Falangism declared for the "national revolution" instead of the Marxist or anarchist revolution, and at first willingly employed the label "fascist" imputed to it by its enemies. By the end of 1934, however, this definition was officially rejected, as José Antonio Primo de Rivera and other Falangist leaders resisted identification with foreign movements or regimes. They tended increasingly to reject Italian fascism as a model because of fascism's conservative compromises.

Under the Republic, the Falange remained little more than a fringe movement of the radical intelligentsia and nationalist students. At the time of the Popular Front* elections of February 1936* it probably had no more than 10,000 regular members, and considerably fewer if only adults were included. In March 1936, the movement was outlawed by the Popular Front regime, and many of its top leaders were arrested.

The Falange's first major expansion occurred amid the prerevolutionary climate of the spring of 1936. Thousands of Catholic and conservative youth who had previously supported the parliamentary Right flocked to Falangism as the "alternative revolution" to the rising power of the revolutionary and antinationalist Left. Together with socialists, communists, and anarchosyndicalists, Falangist militants played a major role in the political violence prevalent in the spring and early summer of 1936.

José Antonio Primo de Rivera and other Falangist leaders joined with the military conspirators who organized the rebellion of July 18 that precipitated the Civil War. The Falangists, however, played an altogether subordinate role and failed completely to win binding political concessions or guarantees from the organizers of the revolt. During the initial phase of the war, the Falangist militia nonetheless played a significant role as civilian and military auxiliaries of the rebel commanders.

The Civil War both created the great opportunity for the original Falange and precipitated their downfall. José Antonio Primo de Rivera and several other of the highest ranking leaders perished, most of them the victims of firing squads in Republican prisons. At the same time, membership of Falangist organizations in the Nationalist zone expanded ten times over. As Falangists became a major source of manpower and support for the Nationalists'* war effort, they would also have opportunity to participate in the development of a new Nationalist government and system.

That system was, however, completely controlled by the military command of General Francisco Franco.* He in turn was determined not to repeat the "Primo de Rivera error" of the dictatorship of 1923, which had largely failed to develop an explicit ideology or institutionalized system. Franco's was a new authoritarian nationalist state that inevitably must reproduce certain aspects of the other authoritarian regimes then existing in Central, Southern, and Eastern Europe.* This required a state party and a doctrine of social and economic organization. The best instrument at hand for the construction of such a party in Franco's new state was the Falange.

In April 1937, Franco directly seized command of the Falange, merging it with the Carlists* and the various right-wing political groups still tolerated in the Nationalist zone. It was elevated to the status of official state party of the new regime and, in recognition of its heterogeneous, syncretistic nature, renamed *Falange Española Tradicionalista*. In so doing, Franco did not give the state to the Falangists but placed the reorganized and reformed Falange at the service of the state. Although the Falangist doctrine was adopted as the official ideology of the new state, Franco made it clear that this constituted no rigorous philosophical self-limitation, declaring the Falangist program to be a mere point of departure. It would be modified or extended as seemed appropriate to the new system. Manuel Hedilla,* the last independent *Jefe Nacional* of the party, refused Franco's terms of political collaboration, was sentenced to death, and then served a commuted term in solitary confinement in the Canary Islands.* Several score other Falangist militants were arrested for failure to cooperate, but virtually all soon accepted Franco's terms. By that time, the Falange membership numbered at least a quarter of a million—twenty-five times the following of early 1936—but the mass of new adherents lacked leadership or indoctrination. They had joined to participate actively in the Nationalist cause, and even many of those who rejected the new political takeover continued to serve with dedication in Franco's military forces.

Their military contribution was undeniably large. From the beginning of 1937 until the end of the Civil War, more than 250,000 volunteers* served in Falangist and Carlist units, accounting for at least one-quarter the total manpower in Franco's forces. Membership in the civilian organizations of the *Falange Española Tradicionalista*, both political and social, grew even more rapidly. Total membership in the party, approximately 240,000 on the morrow of the Francoist takeover, increased to 362,000 in 1938 and approximately 650,000 by the end of the Civil War. Yet, the further growth in political membership after the Falange became the state party probably reflected bureaucracy and careerism more than political commitment.

A political secretariat and a supervisory *Junta Política* were immediately named for the state party as soon as Franco declared himself sole *Jefe Nacional*. In August 1937, the first new official party statutes were issued. They provided for the establishment of twelve sections of special services paralleling government administration. While an increasing number of old activists were lured into full collaboration, the tone of the organization was further clarified by the membership of the first official new National Council, appointed by Franco in October 1937. Of its fifty members, only twenty could be classified as more or less genuine Falangists; eight were Carlists, five were generals, and seventeen an assortment of monarchists, conservatives, or opportunists. Some degree of legitimacy was finally achieved for the new Falangist leadership when Raimundo Fernández Cuesta,* former close associate of José Antonio Primo de Rivera, was exchanged from captivity in the Republican zone and appointed the first official new secretary general of the party in December 1937.

Although lip-service was paid to the official Falangist program and the "totalitarian" goals of the state, Franco also made it clear that he considered the first Spanish-type totalitarian state to have been the unified monarchy of Ferdinand and Isabel. It was strongly emphasized that the new state of Spanish nationalism would be based on traditional and religious values rather than the revolutionary twentieth-century culture of radical fascism. Whereas some Falangists still used the label and banner of fascism as such, the government tried to avoid close mimetic political identification with Germany* and Italy.* Church commentators declared that they were not opposed to fascism if that meant traditionalism, religiosity, authority, and national unity, but rejected fascism that was an imitation of the political systems of Hitler or Mussolini.

The strict limitation of Falangist influence was revealed by the composition of Franco's first regular cabinet, appointed in January 1938. The only genuine Falangist minister was Fernández Cuesta, who became minister of agriculture. The effective head of Falangist affairs and of political administration in the Nationalist zone was in fact Ramón Serrano Suñer,* Franco's brother-in-law. He had played the leading role in negotiating the reorganization of the Falange after Franco's takeover and became minister of the interior in the new government.

Serrano Suñer endeavored to create a compromise in the political development of the new system. On the one hand, he intended to achieve an organized and institutionalized structure of law and administration under Franco's authoritarian aegis, but he also tried to include many of the Falangists willing to cooperate and hoped to realize as much of the Falangists' radical national syndicalist goals as was compatible with

Franco's semitraditionalist framework. Serrano became fast personal friends with the young Falangist poet and firebrand Dionisio Ridruejo,* whom he appointed director of propaganda under his administration.

A minor political crisis developed in June 1938, when a subcommittee of the Falangist National Council was asked to prepare a plan to reorganize the party structure. What Franco and his officials seem to have had in mind was simply a rationalization of the party's internal organization so as to make it a more effective bureaucratic tool. Ridruejo, one of the members of the subcommittee, proposed the elaboration of a totalitarian party-state scheme that would have given the Falangists effective control over the government. Franco was extremely displeased and quickly quashed the proposal, Ridruejo narrowly avoiding expulsion from office. Franco remained highly suspicious of some of the *camisas viejas* (veteran militants) of the party, whom he suspected (not altogether incorrectly) of plotting against him. Immediately after the Ridruejo incident, two other veteran Falangist members of the National Council were arrested and sent into internal exile.

One of the most important functions of the Falange as state party during the Civil War was to prepare the construction of a corporatist system of national syndicalist labor organizations to channel (and repress) working-class interests. The first minister of syndical organization was the neo-Falangist Pedro González Bueno, a conservative and something of a technocrat who had no sympathy with a radical form of national syndicalism. A new *Fuero de Trabajo* (labor charter) theoretically guaranteed the rights of labor but emphasized paternalist structure, and by April 1938 the organization of national syndicalist centers was decreed for each province. Comparatively little was accomplished, however, so long as the Civil War lasted, and the national syndicalist system was never fully developed until well after the war was over.

State or public social services throughout the Nationalist zone were eventually taken over by the Falange, the only notable exceptions being those administered by the Catholic Church.* Social assistance was especially the province of the Falange's *Sección Femenina*, the female auxiliary branch that had possibly numbered 4,000 members in early 1936. During the course of the war, the *Sección Femenina* grew proportionately even more than the central Falangist organization, numbering approximately 580,000 members by 1939. In fact, it became the chief organizational vehicle for the mobilization of women during the Civil War, far exceeding in size and scope any of the party-associated groups in the Republican zone. After the war ended, Pilar Primo de Rivera,* sister of the founder

of the original Falange, was named *Jefe Nacional* of the *Sección Femenina* (as it turned out, in virtual perpetuity).

Organization of children and teenagers in auxiliary and paramilitary organizations was also expanded in the latter part of the war, although the full development of the Falangist youth groups was not carried out until immediately afterward. By 1941, Falangist youth organizations claimed a membership of 564,399 boys and 371,538 girls, representing, respectively, 18.9 and 12.3 percent of their general age groups in Spain.

During the latter part of the Civil War and its immediate aftermath, Falangists were used to staff many common bureaucratic posts, and Falangist leaders were sometimes selected for local administrative posts. Some sectors of state employment and administration were made synonymous with the *Falange Española Tradicionalista* membership and rank, but more often than not this was done by appointing conservative non-Falangists to dual appointments and declaring non-Falangist state employees to be ipso facto party members, rather than by appointing the Falangist core membership to take over state positions.

The state party thus had become highly circumscribed and politically diluted within the structure of the Francoist state by the time the Civil War had come to an end. Rather than leading or taking over the state, it had become a mere tool of convenience for the state. Franco preferred to rely primarily on military officers, conservatives, and technocrats for nearly all key positions.

A phase of new opportunity and tension emerged in the early 1940s, as the threatened victory of the fascist powers in Europe temporarily encouraged several measures of renewed fascism within Spain. Even at the height of Hitler's* power, however, Franco maintained thorough subordination of the Falange within his syncretistic system. Plotting against the Caudillo on the part of dissident radical Falangists reached its high point in 1942-1943 as some of the latter entered into conspiracy with representatives of Nazi Germany,* but this moment of opportunity soon passed.

Of the original Falangists who survived the Civil War, some rejected politics altogether and returned to private life. The majority, however, resigned themselves to a bureaucratic and subordinate role within the new system, a status that only deteriorated further during the long evolution of the Francoist regime.

For further information, see Maximiano García Venero, *Falange en la guerra de Espana* (Paris, 1967), on Hedilla; Stanley G. Payne, *Falange: A History of Spanish Fascism* (Stanford, Calif., 1961); Ramón

Serrano Suñer, *Entre Hendaya y Gibraltar* (Madrid, 1947) and *Memorias* (Barcelona, 1977); Hugh Thomas, *The Spanish Civil War* (New York, 1977); and Felipe Ximénez de Sandoyal, *Biografía apasionada* (Barcelona, 1941), a biography of José Antonio.

See also Fascism, Spanish.

Stanley G. Payne

FAL CONDE, MANUEL (1894-   ). Fal Conde was born in the town of Higuera de la Sierra (Huelva) on August 10, 1894. He studied law at the University of Seville, and later earned a doctoral degree in Madrid,* before returning to Seville* to teach criminal law. While in Seville for this second time, he began to take part in traditionalist political life. He contributed articles to *La Unión*, the Carlist daily newspaper, and soon afterwards took control of *El Observador*, the Carlist weekly paper in Seville. In his only candidacy for the Republican legislature, he tried unsuccessfully to obtain a seat in the Constituent Cortes* by running in Cádiz* in June 1931. The next year, he joined a number of innocent rightists in jail after the Sanjurjo* fiasco.

Fal Conde began to play an important role in the national Carlist organization in 1934. After the Conde de Rodezno* resigned as general secretary, the pretender, Alfonso Carlos, appointed Fal Conde to that post. Almost immediately, Fal Conde reversed the general thrust of Carlist tactics. Rodezno, the parliamentarian, had been accustomed to cooperate with *Renovación Española*,* the Alfonsist political party; Fal Conde ended this cooperation and emphasized the dynastic struggle. He also placed greater emphasis on military preparations than had Rodezno. Therefore, he ordered the development of the *Requetés** and the recruitment of youths for the movement. In addition, shortly after taking office as general secretary, he reorganized the national Carlist organization, creating offices for the *Requetés*, for propaganda, and for youth (under José Luis Zamanillo, José María Lamamié de Clairac,* and Luis Arellano, respectively). This was designed, in part, to supplant the purely geographical division and thus reduce the Navarrese in the Carlist organization.

Although Fal Conde eagerly prepared for the overthrow of the Republic, he did not favor the type of uprising that ultimately occurred. Rather, he would have preferred an exclusively Carlist coup, designed to place Alfonso Carlos on the throne, ruling over a corporate, clerical state. Given these objectives, his reluctance to participate in a military revolt, which had intrinsically different objectives, can readily be understood. General Mola,* conspirator-in-chief in the spring of 1936, wished to reform, but not necessarily to abolish, the Republic. He intended to maintain military control of the country until a new Constituent Cortes could be convoked. In the interim, he would not restore the Catholic Church* to its former prominent place; nor would he install a corporate state. Fal Conde well understood that Mola's plan would mean defeat for the Carlist scheme: the Traditionalist Communion (Carlists) might conceivably execute a coup, but its ideas could not prevail in a freely elected Constituent Cortes.

Eventually, Fal Conde capitulated, but only two days before the uprising was to begin, and only after he found himself isolated within the Carlist organization. The Navarrese leadership (including Rodezno) was prepared to cooperate with the military, and General Mola directly negotiated with them, bypassing the recalcitrant Fal Conde. Although Fal Conde obtained new titles, "Delgate in Chief" and "President of the War Junta," in fact his influence diminished still further in the early days of the war. Navarrese support for the military was repaid, as promised, by Carlist civilian control of Navarre.* The Navarrese Carlists* proved that they were as interested in Navarrese local rights and in their own freedom to practice the Catholic religion as they were in any dynastic question. Andalusian *Requetés*, on the other hand, were assumed to be loyal to Fal Conde; they were discretely and efficiently absorbed into the army.

Fal Conde's difficulties with General Franco* came to a head in December 1936. Continuing his effort to retain independence for the Carlist *Requetés*, Fal Conde announced the creation of a separate military academy to train both commissioned and noncommissioned officers for the *Requetés*. Franco, who had not been consulted before the announcement, was not prepared to allow Fal Conde or anyone else to operate a military academy which he did not control. After considering the possibility of court-martialing Fal Conde, the Generalissimo first persuaded the Navarrese Carlists—never friends of Fal Conde—to repudiate the plan for a military academy. Then Fal Conde was sent to exile in Portugal.*

In 1937, after Franco decreed the creation of a single party, the *Falange Española* Tradicionalista y de las JONS*, he offered Fal Conde a token position on the powerless National Council of the new party. Fal Conde never assumed the position. His dream of a Carlist uprising and of a Carlist state shattered, he lived in Madrid* after the war, but he never accepted the Franco government.

For further information, see Martin Blinkhorn, *Carlism and the Crisis in Spain 1931-1939* (Cambridge, England, 1975), best scholarly account of the Carlist movement containing extensive information on Fal Conde; Jaime del Burgo, *Conspiración y guerra civil* (Madrid, 1970), Maximiano García Venero, *Historia de la Unificación (Falange y Requeté en 1937)* (Madrid, 1970); and Fernando Manuel Noriega, ed., *Fal Conde y el Requeté (juzgados por el extranjero)* (Burgos, 1937), all of which are partisan but informative. In addition, the various biographies of Generals Mola and Franco relate their relationships with Fal Conde.

William J. Irwin

FANJUL GOÑI, JOAQUÍN (1880-1936). Fanjul, born in Vitoria,* was the son of an infantry lieutenant colonel and studied at the Infantry Academy before attending the War College in 1898. In 1917, he completed a degree in law and combined law practice with service in the central general staff. He also served on several occasions in Morocco.* Fanjul acquired prominence as an outspoken defender of military interests in the Cortes,* first as a Maurist between 1919 and 1923 and then as an agrarian during the Republic. In May 1935, Gil Robles* made Fanjul his undersecretary in the War Ministry; after the fall of the government in December, Fanjul began to conspire actively against the Republic, making contact with the right-wing leadership of the *Unión Militar Española* (UME)* and with the military monarchists led by General Rodríguez del Barrio,* whose conspiracy collapsed in April 1936. Fanjul then joined the conspirators led by General Mola.* Slated to lead the revolt in the 1st Division in Madrid,* he found himself at the head of the movement in the capital after the intended leader, General Villegas,* proved indecisive. Unable to seize the War Ministry, Fanjul retired to the Montaña Barracks* with 2,000 troops on July 19. When the barracks fell to popular forces the next day, most of the defenders were killed and Fanjul was wounded. He was tried and executed for rebellion on August 18, 1936.

For further information, see Joaquín Fanjul Goñi, *Sociología militar: misión social del ejército* (Madrid, 1907); and Maximiano García Venero, *El general Fanjul: Madrid en el alzamiento nacional* (Madrid, 1967).

Carolyn P. Boyd

FASCISM, SPANISH. Spanish fascism was the attempt to apply to Spanish political life the formula invented by Benito Mussolini* in Italy,* and later applied to German politics by Adolf Hitler.* What was fascism? Fascism was that counterrevolutionary manifestation of capitalism which made its appearance within the geographical limits of Western and Central Europe* and within the temporal limits of the period that began with the Russian Revolution of 1917 and ended with the decolonization struggles that followed World War II. It was a modern and highly technically organized attempt to save the threatened (or seemingly threatened) capitalist structures in certain vulnerable countries. Specifically, these countries were to be saved by diverting the revolutionary passion of the workers into an opposing mass movement that channels this ardor away from the class struggle and toward an enterprise of class collaboration, in order to conquer the state. The establishment of this totalitarian state necessarily and ineluctably leads to an adventure of imperialist territorial expansion.

In order to be understood, the fascist era must be seen as another chapter in the centuries-long history of European territorial imperialism, a chapter that ended with all the European countries losing the major part of their extracontinental possessions.

The history of Spanish fascism can be divided into four stages. The first goes from February 1931 to February 16, 1936; during this time, five serious efforts to organize a fascist movement were undertaken, all without success. The second period was much shorter, running from February 17 to July 17, 1936, when the vestiges of the movement, forced into a clandestine existence, sought to destabilize the Popular Front* government and finally decided to take part in the military conspiracy. The third stage can be confined within the dates of July 18, 1936, and April 19, 1937; during this time, the movement grew by leaps and bounds, but was nevertheless finally absorbed by Franco* into the *Falange Española* Tradicionalista y de las JONS*. The fourth and final period of Spanish fascism began on April 19, 1937, and ended on November 8, 1942.

The first serious attempt to organize a fascist movement in Spain took place on an imprecise date in February 1931, but the roots of Spanish fascism, of course, go back much further in history, at least to the first quarter of the past century, when Spain lost the greater part of its ultramarine empire. The people of Spain began asking themselves about Spanish "decadence" and its causes. This tendency was greatly accelerated in 1898 when Spain was defeated by the upstart former English colony, the United States of America.* Spanish intellectual life was concentrated in the minds of the "generation of 1898." Spain was humiliated that while it was losing its colonies, other European countries (England, France,* Portugal,* Belgium,* and Holland*) were keeping theirs, or adding new ones.

The man who intellectually—and unwittingly—structured the cultural basis for Spanish fascism was the philosopher and writer José Ortega y Gasset,* the evangel of a dilletante nationalism, of an ambiguous imperialism. On March 23, 1914, at the Teatro de la Comedia in Madrid, he wept for the lost empire and cried out for "una España vertebrada y en pie." Significantly, Spain remained neutral in the imperialistic world war that broke out a few months later. In 1921, Ortega accepted Spanish reality and published *España invertebrada* (Spain invertebrate). This book was a lyrical lamentation for the lost glories of the empire, as well as for the disintegration of peninsular Spain, which he saw as almost the mechanical result of the loss of the extrapeninsular territories. Ortega did not seek to incite his readers to new imperial conquests. Some of the young Spaniards of the 1920s and 1930s who read his work, although they accepted his melancholy interpretation of Spain's past, refused his pessimistic view of the future and argued that Spain could and should reverse the trend of history and again become a great imperial power.

The inspiration for this new imperialist conception came first from fascist Italy and then from Nazi Germany.* Spanish fascism had no firm footing in Spanish reality. It was a mimetic movement, and its imperialist ambitions were at all times perceived as those of a very junior partner of Hitler and Mussolini. The first serious effort to organize a fascist movement in Spain came in February 1931, under the leadership of Ramiro Ledesma Ramos* and Ernesto Giménez Caballero, and in the form of a manifesto entitled "La Conquista del Estado" (Conquest of the State). Under this same title there followed a political movement and a weekly periodical (March 14-October 24, 1931). These two young Spaniards had previously taken profascist stands in *La Gaceta Literaria* (February 5-August 1, 1929). In June 1931, in Valladolid,* Onésimo Redondo, a young Catholic lawyer, founded a fascist group called the *Junta Castellana de Actuación Hispánica* (Castilian Junta for Hispanic Action), and began publishing a weekly entitled *Libertad.* The little anti-Semitism that can be found in Spanish fascism came from Redondo. It originated not, as one might suspect, from the time he had spent at the University of Mannheim, but from the counsels he was given by the Jesuit priest Enrique Herrera Oria, brother of Angel Herrera,* editor of Spain's most important Catholic daily *El Debate,* and, after the Civil War, bishop of Málaga.*

The programs can be summed up as follows: The employment of violence and direct action, of extreme nationalist propaganda, and of youth to forge a strong national unity in Spain. This unity was to be three-fold: territorial (no regional autonomy), political (no political parties, but a single movement), and socioeconomic (suppression of the class struggle and of worker-controlled unions). The movement based on this national unity was to conquer the state and set up a totalitarian structure that would then conquer the new empire.

Each of these two movements of 1931 failed. Then, late in 1931, Ledesma Ramos, in Madrid,* and Redondo Ortega, in Valladolid, combined their efforts and founded a new fascist movement, the *Juntas de Ofensiva Nacional-Sindicalista* (JONS).* This new movement had as part of its heritage the emblem of the Yoke and Arrows and the ideological expression of *Nacional-sindicalismo*, which owed more to Teutonic syntax than to that of Castile.* The JONS stagnated throughout 1932.

On January 30, 1933, Hitler took over the German state. This seizure of power by the German fascists inflamed hope in Ledesma and the JONS, and in other young Spaniards, particularly in the mind of José Antonio Primo de Rivera,* eldest son of the former dictator. There is no report that he had shown an interest in fascism at any previous time. Thus, the JONS which, like its two Spanish predecessors, had been largely influenced by the only successful fascism then known, the Italian example, now saw in the spread of fascism from Italy to Germany a confirmation of the possibility that other countries—even Spain—might follow Mussolini's and Hitler's precedent. This was to be a persistent myth of Spain's Orteguians, for the "Fascist Internationale" never existed, except in the minds of the antifascist propagandists. A fascist state, a highly nationalistic and aggressive state, could hardly desire the proliferation of other similar and competitive states.

Early in 1933, young Primo de Rivera founded a new group called the *Movimiento Español Sindicalista* (Spanish Syndicalist Movement) and subtitled *Fascismo Español.* This fascist attempt fared no better than the previous ones, and on October 29, 1933, Primo de Rivera, taking advantage of the electoral period for the new Cortes,* launched yet another movement. This was called the *Falange Española,* the initials of which recalled the word *fe* (faith) and probably also the two words previously used by the new leader, *fascismo español.* In the legislative elections that took place on November 19, 1933, Primo de Rivera presented himself as a candidate in Cádiz,* his family's fief, but not on the Falange ticket (which did not even exist electorally). He was duly elected in the right-wing victory. Neither in this election nor in that of February 1936* was any fascist, campaigning as such, elected a deputy in Republican Spain.

Thus, at the end of 1933 there were two groups competing for the privilege of representing fascism in Spanish politics: the JONS and the *Falange Española*. Neither had been able to make a significant breakthrough, and it was hardly surprising that in February 1934 the two unimportant movements joined forces, choosing the cumbersome title of *Falange Española de las JONS*. In reality, the two factions continued to function more or less autonomously during 1934. An event highly relevant to the history of Spanish fascism occurred in October 1934, when general strikes were called in several parts of Spain, regional autonomists proclaimed a Catalan republic in a federal Spain, and armed rebellion broke out in Asturias.* At this time, the *Falange Española* unhesitatingly declared itself on the side of the Center-Right government and the ensuing military repression. Later, in the Cortes, Primo de Rivera, despite his electoral origins, spoke out for Spain's fascist movement. He declared that for the Falangists the "separatist" demands of the Catalans presented a greater danger for Spanish unity that had the social claims of the Asturians. He thus sought to strike a balance between the "national" and the "syndicalist."*

However, the *Falange Española de las JONS* stagnated throughout most of 1934. A new program of twenty-seven articles was drawn up in November, and this charter remained (except for the amputation of the twenty-seventh article in April 1937) the Falangist declaration of faith throughout its existence. Primo de Rivera and Ledesma Ramos had never gotten along, and so in January 1935 Ledesma left the movement.

The year 1935 saw the Spanish fascist movement tightly controlled by Primo de Rivera. The dictator's son made frequent pronouncements, before audiences impressed by his name, but it is difficult to conclude that the movement grew greatly in numbers. Late in 1935, scandals caused by unscrupulous government actions brought down the government, and new elections were called for February 16, 1936.

Since the day Ledesma Ramos and Giménez Caballero launched the manifesto of "La Conquista del Estado" five years earlier, the *Falange Española* was the fifth attempt to organize a fascist movement in Spain. Its balance sheet, like those of its predecessors, was one of near failure. For one thing, neither Ledesma nor Primo de Rivera had ever been able to find adequate financial support within Spain. In an effort to bypass this obstacle, Primo de Rivera tried to obtain money from supposedly friendly foreign sources. First, he

put out feelers in the direction of the Nazis, but the first reactions were discouraging. When he went to Berlin in early May 1934, when he was received by Hitler, he did not press the matter. Earlier, before founding the *Falange Española*, he had visited Mussolini in Rome. Much later, in 1935, he began receiving a monthly subvention from the Italian fascists.

When the 1936 elections were announced, Primo de Rivera, realizing the weakness of the Phalanx, sought to negotiate with the Catholic leader Gil Robles* to obtain a certain number of sure places on the "counterrevolutionary" ticket for his followers. According to Gil Robles, this would ensure parliamentary immunity for the Falangist leaders. The little consideration in which the conservative Right held the Falange can be seen in its refusal to offer these seats to Primo de Rivera. Mathematically, the Right's calculations were proved exact, at least in this detail, for Primo de Rivera, who as a conservative candidate in Cádiz in 1933 garnered 41,720 votes, in 1936, as a Falangist candidate won 965 ballots.

Another indication of Falangist failure can be noted in the defections of two of Spanish fascism's outstanding theoreticians: Giménez Caballero and Ledesma Ramos. Giménez turned his coat and accepted the thirteenth and last place on the list for Madrid (capital) of the *Frente Nacional Contrarrevolucionario* (National Counterrevolutionary Front), headed by Gil Robles and Calvo Sotelo.* Late in 1935, Ledesma Ramos published a highly perceptive analysis of Spanish fascism under the interrogatory title *¿Fascism en España?*, which ended with this paragraph: "We can say, finally, that for Ledesma Ramos and his comrades the red shirt of Garibaldi fits them better than the black shirt of Mussolini."

The second stage of Spanish fascist development began with the electoral victory of the Popular Front* on February 16, 1936. This could have been the long-awaited moment for Spanish fascism: the moment when the conservative elements of Spanish society could be persuaded that their interests, which, up to that time, had been defended by the traditional, established parties of the Right, would henceforth be better protected by the more radicalized and demagogic fascist movement. Spanish fascism, like all other fascist movements, was based on the essential beliefs of a conservative society, but it differed from the other rightist groups in Spain in its insistence that the class struggle could be resolved only through a great national effort that would help upset the European empires and create a new imperial order, in which Spain would have its rightful place. The policy of the old traditional parties was not to transform the class struggle, but to win it through repression as had happened in 1934.

The great moment for fascist victory had arrived without too much difficulty for Mussolini in Italy and for Hitler in Germany, but when the moment arrived in Spain, the Phalanx was confronted with a state in the hands of the Left.

When the Popular Front won the 1936 elections, Gil Robles was blamed for the defeat and dethroned by the Right which showed a preference for the monarchist Calvo Sotelo. Those days of disarray, when the conservative elements were moving away from the Center-Right to a more extreme Right, constituted the moment when the Spanish fascists could have expected a call from the *Frente Nacional Contrarrevolucionario* and its allies. Such an appeal was never loudly formulated, and had it been, it could not have been heard for two reasons. The Spanish fascists in five years of endeavor had never been able to organize a national movement with mass support. In the spring of 1936, it was unable to assume the leadership of anything, except for an occasional assasination or a row in the streets. The Falangists' lack of a mass movement can be attributed in part to the sociological composition of the Spain of that epoch; the Spanish proletariat was more agricultural than industrial. But the real explanation for the Falange's lack of adherents came from Spain's deficiency in the source of the manpower that fed the ranks of the Italian and German fascist movements: the discontented ex-soldiers. Spain had not fought a major war for more than a hundred years and had long been weary of the imperial burden. The injustices of the peace treaties of World War I could hardly have aroused the Spanish people, for Spain had remained prudently neutral during that imperialist struggle.

The other factor that intervened in Spain in the spring of 1936 to block the Phalanx from playing a dominant role against the "menace" of the Left was precisely the unexpected victory of the Popular Front. The structural weaknesses of the Falange, caused by its sickly growth, were rendered weaker still by the energetic antifascist actions of the Popular Front government: the Falange centers were closed down; its press and propaganda were suppressed; and its leaders, including Primo de Rivera, were jailed.

It is frequently affirmed that the youthful followers of Gil Robles went over to the Phalanx in great numbers after the defeat in the February elections. That many such persons became Falangist sympathizers is highly probable, but after the arrest of Primo de Rivera on March 14, 1936, there remained but a skeletal structure of the Phalanx, and one can doubt that many new members were actually enrolled in the movement. Between February 16 and the outbreak of the Civil War, the Falangists distinguished themselves principally as rowdies and gunmen, seeking to disequilibrate the Popular Front through sporadic violence. Certainly, after March 14, the Falange led a clandestine existence. This antifascist activity of the Popular Front, however, formed part of an incomplete strategy. Spanish fascism, up to the outbreak of the Civil War, was never more than a violent intellectual game, with very few gamesters. Primo de Rivera was never during his lifetime the charismatic figure he was to become a few months after his death on November 19, 1936. The Spanish Socialist party* was beclouded by the tragic fate of the Austrian and German socialists, mistaking first Gil Robles and then Primo de Rivera for Hitler. The danger to Spanish democracy in 1936 came not from the second-rate intellectuals* of the Phalanx, not from Primo de Rivera, a would-be general without foot-soldiers, but from Franco, Mola, and the other military conspirators and their moneyed and monarchist backers.

Primo de Rivera gave his grudging consent to Falangist participation in the military rebellion. He feared that it would end, as it did, with Falangist support of a right-wing military dictatorship, disguised by the demagogic program of the fascist movement, with no real power of decision in fascist hands.

The third period of Spanish fascism lasted little more than the second, from July 18, 1936, to April 19, 1937. The rebellious generals had no political plan beyond the immediate seizure of power, and as the *pronunciamiento* lengthened into civil war, a political void was created. The prewar philosophies of the Right, the *cedista* program, Alfonsine or Carlist monarchism, meant little to the masses. On April 19, 1937, the military power adopted the Falange ideology (minus the last article which specifically forbade collaboration with other groups, unless the *Falange Española de las JONS* was in a position of power). Franco and his brother-in-law Serrano Suñer* took over control of the Falange, which had grown by leaps and bounds during the preceding months, and labeled the new movement *Falange Española Tradicionalista y de las JONS*. It was the only political formation allowed in the Nationalist zone, the others being merged in the new group.

There is no doubt that sincere believers in national syndicalism (who were not numerous), at the moment of this fusion, lost control of the Spanish fascist movement. Superficially, this did not appear to be so, since the blue shirt of the Phalanx became the proper dress for militants (plus the red beret of the Carlists*), and the Yoke and the Arrows the political emblem of the regime. In reality, when the Civil War was still in the early months, the Phalanx lost the war. No fascist movement, based on the national unity so necessary for the eventual imperialist war, had ever seized control of the state after a fratricidal, disunifying civil war.

One reason why the military took possession of the fascist movement so easily was the Falange's lack of leaders, after the deaths of Primo de Rivera, Ledesma Ramos, and Redondo. But this deficiency of *jefes* was the result of the failure of Spanish fascism to create a mass movement before the war.

We now come to the fourth and final stage of Spanish fascist history. The movement continued to grow in numbers after the general political merger of all Spanish political elements in the one organization, superficially dominated by the Falangist ideology. When the Civil War ended, on April 1, 1939, the savagery of the struggle had left the country divided by hatred. Tens of thousands of homes had been destroyed, the rail and road systems were out of running order, agricultural production was greatly diminished, and hundreds of thousands of Spaniards were on the verge of starvation.

Was Spain a fascist country when the Civil War ended? The touchstone for this problem lies in the definition of fascism. The purpose of a fascist movement was to build a totalitarian state whose sole *raison d'être* was to prepare the country for an imperial adventure. Although the Spanish fascists had not been able to seize control of the Spanish state, the construction of the state administration had been largely left in their hands. There were syndicates for the workers and the owners, the women, the ex-soldiers, the children, the farmers, the university students, and so on. (This vast organization gave well-paying jobs to the provincial Falangists, who were thus recompensed for permitting Franco to use their demagogic program, uniforms, and slogans.) A Spanish state set up in this manner could have entered the imperialist war that was forming on the horizon in 1939, had it not been ruined economically and been divided by class hatred, and had it not been in the hands of Francisco Franco, a conservative general, who was ready to play the fascist card if it suited his craving for power, or in other circumstances simply to sit out the game.

Spain needed at least two or three years to rebuild the economy and to assuage the wounds of the Civil War before participating, with fascist Italy and Nazi Germany, in the "coming struggle for power." In the summer of 1939, Count Ciano* reassured Serrano Suñer, then Franco's foreign minister, that Spain would

have this needed time. Then Hitler started World War II. Franco declared Spain to be neutral. When Mussolini attacked prostrate France* on June 11, 1940, Franco proclaimed Spain to be "nonbelligerent" and dispatched a messenger to the Führer declaring that El Caudillo was also ready to enter the war on condition that Hitler extend him (1) economic aid to rebuild his devastated economy, (2) military help, and (3) territorial compensations.

These conditions, with their imperialistic connotations, would have won the approval of the Phalanx. But Hitler equivocated, and as Britain* resisted Hitler's air attacks, Franco's initial eagerness lessened. Hitler feared Vichy's reaction if he promised lands to Franco that nominally belonged to France. After Franco's first talk with Hitler in Hendaye on October 23, 1940, Franco was furious at the Führer's reticence to promise in writing to give Spain its territorial demands. He said: "This new sacrifice of ours can be justified only by the counterpart of what is to be the base of our Empire." Spanish troops had already occupied Tangier on June 14.

At this moment Spanish fascism still had an opportunity to gain control of the Spanish state. Franco seems to have been disposed to take up the Falangist option, if Hitler would give him the economic and military help he so desperately needed and promise him his part of the booty. Would Franco have been able to enter the war even if Hitler had agreed to his economic, military, and territorial demands? Ever present in Franco's calculations was another factor, one on which Hitler could offer no aid: the deep antagonistic division of Spain into two blocs, separated by the violence of the war, by class hatred. But if this fact weighed on Franco's mind, he did nothing to bind up the wounds of the Civil War. Instead, throughout the 1940s, he continued to execute tens of thousands of Republican prisoners.*

Hitler never gave Franco what he asked for, and needed, and the negotiations dragged on. Franco sent troops to the war against the USSR,* but this was an action to increase Hitler's *Lebensraum* and not Franco's. Falangist hopes dwindled and finally died, on November 8, 1942, when American and British troops landed in North Africa, on the very soil that the Phalanx had claimed for the new *Imperio*, that Franco had requested from Hitler. The Spanish government made no protest and subsequently nobody thought seriously of the Falangist empire, although for years the word remained an essential part of Spain's political vocabulary.

The totalitarian state that the Falangists had set up as a springboard for the imperialist adventure continued in place for years and years. The Falangist functionaries, with no lesser breeds to exploit, turned their talents on their own people. No foreign armies came to liberate the Spaniards as they had come to the rescue of the Italians and the Germans. Finally, time—and the death of Franco—freed the Spanish people, although not completely. It is significant that the last of the delegations that the Falange had established to control the inhabitants of Spain, the organization for the working class, the "vertical syndicates," was the last to disappear.

For further information, see *La Gaceta literaria* (Vaduz, 1980); Maximiano García Venero, *Falange en la guerra de España: la unificación y Hedilla* (Paris, 1967); Ernesto Giménez Caballero, *Genio de España* (Madrid, 1932, 1939); Ramiro Ledesma Ramos, *Discurso a las juventudes de España* (Madrid, 1935) and *¿Fascismo en España?* (Madrid, 1935); José Ortega y Gasset, *España invertebrada* (Madrid, 1921, 1922, 1957); J. A. Primo de Rivera, *Obras completas* (Madrid, 1954); Ramón Serrano Suñer, *Memorias* (Barcelona, 1977); H. R. Southworth, *Antifalange* (Paris, 1967) and "The Falange: An Analysis of Spain's Fascist Heritage," in *Spain in Crisis* (London, 1976); and Stanley C. Payne, *Falange* (Stanford, Calif., 1961).

Herbert R. Southworth

FATARELLA. Fatarella, a town in the Catalan province of Tarragona,* resisted industrial and agricultural collectivization evident throughout the northern sectors of the Republican zone. During the early months of the Civil War, small business owners in the town successfully took up arms against the *Confederación Nacional del Trabajo* (CNT)* which wanted to collectivize local enterprises. Thus, the actions of this town served as proof that the collectivization did not exist uniformly throughout the Republican zone. In November 1938, Nationalist forces under the command of General Jaun Yagüe Blanco* occupied the town, signaling the anticipated fall of the province of Tarragona to Franco* and the return to capitalist economic practices.

For further information, see Albert Pérez Baró, *Trenta mesos de colectivisme a Catalunya* (Barcelona, 1974).

See also Catalonia; and Peasantry, Aragonese.

James W. Cortada

FAUPEL, WILHELM (1873-1945). Faupel was the first German diplomat assigned to General Franco's* government at Burgos.* He arrived in Spain in the fall of 1936, carrying instructions from Hitler* to keep the war going while Germany* pursued more important objectives in Eastern Europe.* Faupel was a career army officer with the rank of general when he came to Spain. He had commanded a corps in World War I and had helped organize *Frei Korps* units in the 1920s. This Nazi officer was completely fluent in Spanish and had served as head of the German Ibero-American Institute, a cultural exchange agency, since 1934. Faupel proved unpopular with Germany's foreign office and with Franco and his top officials, and irritated German officers serving in Spain in the Condor Legion.*

Faupel thought Franco was incapable of carrying the war to victory, disliked religion in general and Catholicism in particular, despised the Spanish upper classes, and consequently spent a great deal of time with the working-class extremist members of the Falange* whom he believed should staff a fascist movement. He encouraged their activities and gave them as much support as he dared. This support irritated Franco who was trying to balance the power of various political forces on the Nationalist side in order to consolidate his personal power over all of them. Faupel repeatedly urged Hitler to send divisions of German troops to end the war with a Nationalist victory without making Franco a part of his plans. His suggestions for introducing German ground forces in Spain were rejected in Berlin since the continuation of the war served a useful diversion for Western Europe away from Nazi concerns in the east. Franco found working with Faupel so difficult that in 1937 he even asked for his removal from Spain. However, at the same time, Faupel was able to negotiate with the Nationalists* a commercial agreement that would later pave the way for a formal economic trade treaty.

In 1938, Hitler recalled Faupel to Germany, replacing him with a professional diplomat, Baron Eberhard von Stohrer.* In 1945, when Berlin fell to the Allies, Faupel and his wife committed suicide. Historians have concluded that Faupel did little to help the German cause in Spain and, if anything, irritated personal relations among all concerned.

For further information, see Manfred Merkes, *Die deutsche Politik im Spanischen Bürgerkrieg* (Bonn, 1969); and Angel Viñas, *La alemanía nazi y el 18 de julio* (Madrid, 1974), on German policy from another perspective.

James W. Cortada

FAURE, SÉBASTIEN (1858-1942). Faure, one of the leading figures in the ranks of French anarchism, was instrumental in encouraging anarchist resistance to the Primo de Rivera dictatorship during the 1920s, which enabled the Spanish anarchist movement to return to Spain in 1931 with renewed vigor and violence.

Faure, a well-known libertarian author during the 1920s (*La douleur Universelle*, 1921, and *L'imposture religieuse*, 1923), worked in Paris publishing various broadsheets and presiding over an effort to publish an "anarchist" encyclopedia. Foreign anarchists* flocked to his office, and it was there that such exiles as Buenaventura Durruti* and Francisco Ascaso* came to meet Nestor Makhno, the Ukrainian anarchist of Russian Civil War fame. It was there too that the raid on the border at Vera del Bidosa was planned in 1924. Faure helped to free Spanish anarchists jailed in France* in the wake of this insurrectionary plot, and he continued to be a good friend to many Spaniards, including Juan García Oliver,* who later became the minister of justice in the Popular Front* cabinet of November 1936-May 1937. However, the lack of intellectual depth in the Spanish anarchist movement troubled him. His contacts with Spain tapered off until the Civil War, when he helped lead publicity efforts on behalf of the libertarian revolution in Catalonia,* which he visited. Upon the German invasion of France in 1940, he fled to Chile, where he died two years later.

For further information, see Sébastian Faure, *Temas subversivos* (Santiago, 1940).

Robert W. Kern

FE (1936-   ). *FE* was the official newspaper of the Falange* party. It was published in Seville* and reflected the political views of the movement. "Fe" became a symbolic word reflecting the faith of followers in God, movement, and Franco to provide the kind of society envisioned by the Falange and the Nationalists.*

For further information, see Stanley G. Payne, *Falange: A History of Spanish Fascism* (Stanford, Calif., 1961).
See also Falange Española; Hedilla, Manuel; and Primo de Rivera y Sáenz de Heredia, José Antonio.

James W. Cortada

FEDERACIÓN ANARQUISTA IBÉRICA (FAI). The *Federación Anarquista Ibérica* (FAI) was the ultra-Left faction of the Spanish anarchist and anarchosyndicalist movement. No group except the fascist Falange* played as controversial a role in Spanish politics and the Civil War. Some students of the war argue that FAI provocations did a great deal to unsettle Spanish politics during the Second Republic* and to set off the revolution within the civil war in Catalonia* and Aragón which complicated Republican politics in 1936 and 1937. Others maintain that the FAI under-

went a dramatic evolution from terrorism* to a more responsible collectivism that constituted the uniquely Spanish aspects of the Civil War's drastic social change.

The FAI grew out of anarcho-Bolshevik groups like Buenaventura Durruti's* *Solidarios* faction, one of the many post-World War I action bands that had practiced terrorism in a vain attempt to duplicate the Russian Revolution in Spain. Even after the flight of many anarchists* in 1923, when the Primo de Rivera dictatorship came to power, loosely organized groups in Catalonia and Aragón continued to operate and made several unsuccessful attempts to assassinate King Alfonso XIII.* In 1926, the Iberian political scene was complicated by the military coup d'etat in Portugal* by Generals Gomes da Costa and António Oscar de Fragoso Carmona, which seriously threatened the existence of the *Confederação Geral do Travalho*, the Portuguese anarchosyndicalist organization. Lusitanian radicals thus joined dissenters from the *Confederación Nacional del Trabajo* (CNT),* huge Spanish syndical federation, in opposing the two Iberian dictatorships by forming the FAI at Cabañal, on the Valencian coast, on July 24 and 25, 1927.

Despite the syndicalist origins of the FAI, *faístas* saw themselves founding an organization designed to fight "pure" unionism as well as militarism and early fascism with a libertarian program stressing workers' committees, agricultural communes, and active political formations of various kinds. Until 1927, however, little headway was made, particularly in Portugal, where the FAI failed to develop a foothold, despite creation of later groups like *Pro Agra*, a peasant union. Manuel Buenacasa popularized the FAI to a limited extent in Catalan radical circles, and several newspapers like ¡*Despertad*! in Vigo* and *Acción Social Obrera* in Barcelona* were founded, but political repression limited growth until the beginning of the Second Republic in April 1931.

The return of famous political exiles like Buenaventura Durruti, Francisco Ascaso,* Gregorio Jover,* and others attracted a much larger membership during the summer of 1931, including intellectual figures like Federica Montseny,* co-editor of *La Revista Blanca*, the only important opposition periodical during the previous era. Affinity groups of up to fifty people operated as semisecret chapters of the organization and formed a part of the regional federations. They were designed to become soviets in time of revolution, led by technical commissions to draw up the agendas for the regional bodies and to loosely set policy. The Peninsular Association, as the national congress of the FAI, was composed of regional representatives who acted as a permanent secretariat for the FAI. By

1936, probably 40,000 Spaniards formally belonged to the FAI, and many more thousands sympathized.

Long before the Civil War, the chief FAI problem was its objections to CNT moderation. *Faístas* all belonged to the CNT, but a schism between the two groups nevertheless appeared in the fall of 1931 over the moderate trade-union tactics used by CNT leaders. FAI-led wildcat strikes and revolutionary expectations clashed with CNT willingness to accept socialist-influenced labor arbitration provisions and in other ways to cooperate with the Republican government. Finally, on September 1, 1931, the *Treintista* Declaration, signed by such prominent CNT leaders as Juan Peiró* and Angel Pestaña, provoked the FAI to retaliate by seizing control of CNT institutions, although syndicates of opposition continued the CNT's activities through the next several years. The *faístas* aided continuation of moderate labor policies by embarking on a fanatic series of unsuccessful uprisings in January 1932, again during the Casas Viejas incident in January 1933, and finally in Saragossa* during December 1933. Their violence contributed to the confusion that brought the right to power in the elections of November 1933.

During the next two years of their rule, the FAI, while not proscribed, found it difficult to resume operations. The CNT, with its unions, suffered even more, since the FAI could always return to its underground tradition in times of crisis. Neither played much of a role in the Asturian insurrection of October 1934, and only the work of Diego Abad de Santillán* stood out. His mutualist orientation towards Peter Kropotkin, as developed in *El organismo económico de la revolución: como vivimos y como podrímos en España*, moved the FAI away from Michael Bakunin's more violent theories of spontaneous revolution to a new inclination of developing an economic base for libertarianism through creation of workers' councils and large agricultural communes.

The modernization of FAI doctrine came none too soon, since the radicalization of Western Europe* through the Popular Front* and the ineffectiveness of the right-wing regime led to new elections in February 1936* and the victory of the Popular Front coalition. The FAI, which had urged its constituency to vote for progressive candidates, immediately assumed that it was immune from government harassment (which in many ways it was) and began organizing factory workers and agitating for land confiscation and the creation of peasant communes all over the northeast. When the Right reacted violently to the radicalization which all Left and Center parties were going through, the FAI increasingly began to act as the Left's paramilitary

arm against the right-wing Falange. As many as 150 *faístas* died during this period, and their own assassinations and other fatalities probably exceeded this number. Efforts were made to train members to act as a militia for the Popular Front, but on the eve of the Civil War the group was only minimally prepared.

After July 18, 1936, the FAI found itself in military action in Catalonia, Valencia,* and Aragón. Its cadres were responsible for a great deal of indiscriminate violence, and the execution of priests and landowners in hasty trials frightened middle-class Republicans* deeply. While local animosities and fear of Nationalist rebellion prompted many of these atrocities, the FAI nevertheless paid off many old scores and in the process did a great deal to widen the gulf of fear between all Spaniards.

Barcelona became the FAI's most important center. Here it defeated General Goded's* efforts to seize the city within three days; *faístas* were particularly noticeable in the battles of San Andres and Atarazanas on Sunday, July 19. Identification of Durruti with the FAI and the death of Ascaso, his close friend, provided the party with both a hero and a martyr. Their control of the media also enabled them to obtain considerable notice in France,* Holland,* and Scandinavia, where they quickly became the very symbol of the Spanish revolution.

Not surprisingly, they received two seats on the Antifascist Militias Committee,* only one less than the CNT or the socialists. The committee itself was dictated by the need to use CNT-FAI strength against the Nationalists* without forcing anarchists into a regular government. The regional government of the Catalan state thus stood aside by assigning most of its powers to the committee, which styled itself a kind of revolutionary *Junta*, although the revolution had just begun and was destined, in fact, never to be completed.

Elsewhere the FAI's sphere of influence included Valencia (though it was dwarfed by the CNT), but it did not reach socialist and communist-dominated Madrid.* Even Valencia moved in this direction in September, and by early November when the national government moved, there was considerably less anarchist influence than before. Barcelona itself was not really a secure bastion of FAI power, mainly because of the Catalan separatists and their distrust of the *faístas*. This was a classic confrontation between middle-class and working-class revolutionaries, and one that remained unstable throughout the three-month period in which the Antifascist Militias Committee operated.

Leading *faístas* like Abad de Santillán, Federica Montseny, and Durruti held high positions on the committee, which extended their power into the running of the Army of Aragón,* which Durruti commanded; into the Catalan economic council, which Abad de Santillán dominated; and into the area of justice, where Aurelio Fernández,* José Asens,* Rafael Vidiella,* and Tomás Fábregas* and all played a role in the *patrullas de control* (police* squads) that administered justice in Catalonia and Aragón. Juan García Oliver,* who was later minister of justice for the Loyalist government in Madrid, first came to public attention in this way. The police squads soon adapted regular courts for their own purposes and remained controversial during the early period of the Civil War.

The FAI's most important institution was the Army of Aragón, Durruti's militia army, the means by which all *faístas* expected to bring the revolution to full climax. Many recruits were first introduced to the party in the army, and its contingents helped establish large communes in the territory it held. Socialists, Trotskyists, and other radicals may have outnumbered *faístas* in the Army of Aragón, but the FAI managed to dominate the militia by its control of the Council of Aragón, a creation of the Antifascist Militias Committee, which at one time was headed by Durruti's brother. The council worked harmoniously with the FAI, but with no one else at all, which forced all parties to go through the FAI where Aragón was concerned. Such power might not have been possible if Durruti had not headed the Army of Aragón. The legendary political bandit, now the charismatic military leader — a figure out of the grand Spanish guerrilla tradition—represented the FAI's libertarian tradition with every fiber of his being.

Despite Durruti and the power of the FAI in Aragón, the long-awaited revolution proved to be impossible to obtain. Sarogossa remained in Nationalist hands; Republican officials in Madrid could not, or would not, supply the militia army with adequate supplies; production problems in Catalan industry grew worse because of blockade, disruption of supplies, and inefficiency; and the communists, Catalan separatists, and socialists all challenged the FAI for leadership. As a measure of their desperation, FAI leaders briefly considered robbing Madrid's Bank of Spain* to obtain the gold needed to run the Aragón campaign. This pessimism was warranted after separatist resurgence dissolved the Antifascist Militias Committee on September 26 and began absorption of the militia into the regular Republican Army* (communist dominated) three days later.

During this period, the FAI was badly divided over whether to continue its social revolution or give in to the demands of its Republican partners to place antifascism first. This latter course convinced Federica

Montseny and Juan García Oliver to join the Popular Front cabinet of the socialist Francisco Largo Caballero* on November 4, 1936, as minister of health and justice, respectively, just at the height of the battle of Madrid. Shock waves stunned many anarchists, who felt that all anarchist values were being sacrificed to the antifascist cause. Schisms with the FAI dated from this moment. But even Durruti did not believe the anarchists' social revolution in the north could be saved if the Republic fell to the Nationalists. He and 5,000 of the best troops from the 26th Division joined the defense of the capital. Unfortunately, his death, by sniper or assassin, at the front on November 20 raised ugly stories of dissatisfied *faístas* who had resorted to the "propaganda of the deed" to show their opposition.

In the months after the Nationalists were stopped at Madrid, the fortunes of the FAI quickly crumbled in many parts of Spain. Anarchists in Málaga* were blamed unfairly for its fall in February 1937; militarization of the army placed more and more men under communist control; and anarchist power in the northeast rapidly disappeared under Republican and Catalan pressure. Ricardo Sanz, the new commander who replaced Durruti, failed in desperate campaigns to capture Saragossa and Huesca* to forestall further communist success. Fighting also had broken out along the northern border of Catalonia between anarchists and communists to keep volunteers* of the International Brigades* from entering Spain. Scattered conflicts also developed with Catalan patriotic groups and the communist *Partit Socialista Unificat de Catalunya* (PSUC).* The climax came on May 4, 1937, when elements of the CNT-FAI tightened control over the telephone building in Barcelona, only to face retaliation from the other groups. The siege of the building caused fighting to spread, with the FAI headquarters the focal point in the armed clashes. Gregorio Jover, one of the most militant *faístas*, finally led militiamen in a counterattack that led to a truce, but not before FAI members in many towns of the northeast were killed.

Even though Montseny and García Oliver had been active in the truce negotiations in Barcelona on May 8, both resigned when the communists threatened to cut off aid to Francisco Largo Caballero's* Popular Front cabinet a week later. Henceforth, the FAI was once again outside the organized structure of politics, much to the relief of some. It was now without military capability, however, since the militarization of all political groups fighting for the Republic took place rapidly after Largo Caballero's fall to Juan Negrín,* the new premier more sympathetic to the communists.

Enrique Lister* and the communist 11th Division moved into Aragón and eventually absorbed the 26th Division, although the communists never managed to capture either Saragossa or Huesca.

During the remainder of 1937, the FAI found itself dissenting strongly to growing Soviet power in Republican Spain. Both the underground newspaper *Libertad* and the secret *Grupo Ácrata* urged the FAI to use terrorism against Negrín, but the changes that the organization had undergone in 1936 and 1937 could not permit it to return to its old format. Ties with the CNT since the beginning of the Civil War had become strong. The *Treintista* schism had been healed by common need during the Civil War, and a terrorist campaign was not a strategy the FAI could follow without jeopardizing many of its gains. Thus, after Negrín announced the reopening of the parliament in order to make the regime more palatable, the FAI refashioned itself as the openly political arm of the CNT. FAI representatives carried the fight against Negrín and the communists to this forum so successfully that the government soon dropped the parliamentary idea. Nevertheless, in the short time left the Republic, the FAI continued as an open and political organization, an arm of the *Comité Ejecutivo del Movimiento Libertario*. This new concept of a revolutionary labor party set the tone for ultra-Left efforts in the postwar period, but the Republic fell before this radical transformation of the FAI had much impact in Spain.

For further information, see Murray Bookchin, *The Spanish Anarchists: The Heroic Years 1868-1936* (New York, 1977); Gaston Leval, *Espagne libertaire: 1936-1939* (Paris, 1971); and Vernon Richards, *Lessons of the Spanish Revolution* (London, 1953).

See also May 1937 Riots; and Peasantry, Aragonese.

Robert W. Kern

FEDERACIÓN CATALANA DE GREMIOS Y ENTIDADES DE PEQUEÑOS COMERCIANTES Y INDUSTRIALES (GEPCI).

The *Federación Catalana de Gremios y Entidades de Pequeños Comerciantes y Industriales* (GEPCI) was organized by members of the *Partit Socialista Unificat de Catalunya* (PSUC)* to protect the interests of petty bourgeois businessmen and artisans in Catalonia* during the second half of 1936. Its leaders wanted to make sure that this group would continue contributing to the welfare of the Republican economy* until a socialist society could take over and thereby eliminate the need for a petty bourgeois class. Although GEPCI comprised 18,000 Catalans, it appears that it never became a sizable

organization or a significant political force even though the anarchists* worried about its potential influence when it was first formed.

For further information, see Burnett Bolloten, *The Spanish Revolution: The Left and the Struggle for Power During the Civil War* (Chapel Hill, N.C., 1979); and Ronald Fraser, *The Blood of Spain* (New York, 1979).

James W. Cortada

FEDERACIÓN IBÉRICA DE JUVENTUDES LIBERTARIAS (FIJL).

The *Federación Ibérica de Juventudes Libertarias* (FIJL) was an anarchist youth organization dedicated to abolishing private property and government in general. During the Civil War, its membership approached 100,000. During the May 1937 riots* in Barcelona,* this group battled in the streets against the communists. Its leadership was not strong enough, however, to allow an alliance with other anarchists* to mount a coordinated campaign against the *Partit Socialista Unificat de Catalunya* (PSUC).* This kind of divisive independence ultimately enabled the Republic to break the power of the anarchists and to establish its control over Barcelona and Catalonia.*

For further information, see Burnett Bolloten, *The Spanish Revolution: The Left and the Struggle for Power During the Civil War* (Chapel Hill, N.C., 1979); and Robert W. Kern, *Red Years/Black Years: A Political History of Spanish Anarchism, 1911-1937* (Philadelphia, 1978).

James W. Cortada

FERNÁNDEZ, AURELIO. Fernández, an anarchist member of the *Confederación Nacional del Trabajo* (CNT),* joined the government of Barcelona* (Generalitat)* in July 1936. This Catalan became the powerful secretary general of the interior and thus had responsibility for police* in Barcelona. While in this post, anarchist bands exercised considerable freedom to deal out justice as they saw fit against their enemies and often terrorized members of the middle class during the fall and winter of 1936. On April 16, 1937, the Catalan government reorganized, and this time, Fernández became the minister responsible for health. In 1938, Republican authorities arrested Fernández along with many other anarchists* in an attempt to establish communist and Republican control over local political and economic affairs.

For further information, see Burnett Bolloten, *The Spanish Revolution: The Left and the Struggle for*

Power During the Civil War (Chapel Hill, N.C., 1979).

James W. Cortada

FERNÁNDEZ BURRIEL, ÁLVARO (1879-1936). General Fernández Burriel was a career army officer who, at the start of the Civil War, sided with the Nationalists.* In July 1936, he commanded the cavalry forces stationed in Barcelona* and plotted the uprising in this Catalan city with fellow officers. Along with others, he raised the cry of revolt in mid-July. Failing to insure the participation of various military units in the revolt, along with having to contend with extensive resistance from anarchists,* his revolt failed and with it went any hope for an immediate end to the Civil War in northern Spain. Now Franco* would have to conquer the Catalan sector slowly over a number of years. Fernández Burriel was tried and executed for rebellion by the Republic in August 1936.

For further information, see Hugh Thomas, *The Spanish Civil War* (New York, 1977).

James W. Cortada

FERNÁNDEZ CUESTA, RAIMUNDO (1897-   ). Fernández Cuesta was the secretary general of the Falange* party and nominal head when José Antonio Primo de Rivera* (founder of the party) went to jail in 1936. A lawyer and childhood friend of the party's chief, Fernández Cuesta proved unable to guide the party with strong leadership after the Republic arrested and executed Primo de Rivera. However, on December 2, 1936, Franco* did appoint Fernández Cuesta to his forty-eight member National Council while the Andalusian politician continued to act as secretary general of the Falange at Burgos.* On February 1, 1938, Franco established a cabinet and named Fernández Cuesta minister of agriculture. By this time, the true head of the Falange was a stronger willed man, Ramón Serrano Suñer,* brother-in-law to General Franco.

For further information, see Stanley G. Payne, *Falange: A History of Spanish Fascism* (Stanford, Calif., 1961).
See also Fascism, Spanish.

James W. Cortada

FIFTH REGIMENT. The Fifth Regiment was the most famous all-Spanish fighting unit in the Republican Army.* Formed and run by the Spanish Communist party,* it eventually had a membership of over 15,000 well-trained, disciplined men led by competent commanders. The Fifth Regiment had its own system of supplies and artillery, drawing much support from the political and military leadership of the Communist party. It evolved from a communist militia, the *Milicias Antifascistas Obreras y Compesinas* (MAOC),* and by the end of July 1936, had nearly 1,000 men in combat. Its first commander, Enrique Castro Delgado,* was a brilliant officer, while other important leaders were Enrique Lister* and Juan Modesto,* the regiment's second commander. These communists modeled their unit on the Red Army of the Russian Civil War, assigning political commissars at various levels of command to motivate the troops. In the first year of the war, it was one of their most disciplined units in the Republican Army. The Fifth Regiment fought primarily in the battles in and around Madrid* throughout the second half of 1936. As a result of a reorganization of the army, it was dissolved on January 21, 1937.

For further information, see E. Comín Colomer, *El quinto regimiento* (Madrid, 1973); Enrique Lister, *Nuestra guerra* (Paris, 1966); and Juan Modesto, *Soy el quinto regimiento* (Paris, 1969).
See also Appendix B.

James W. Cortada

FINANCE, NATIONALIST. With the outbreak of the Civil War, finances became a serious problem for the Nationalists,* as in other sectors of administration and economic activity. The first months of the conflict were marked by a rapid advance of the rebels towards the capital of the nation, allowing an expectation of imminent victory and a shelving of any question regarding the organization of the public finance sector. But with the failure of the attack on Madrid,* the perspective of a prolonged conflict forced the Nationalists to organize the financial sector of their economy, create an independent budget, and seek sufficient financial resources with which to attend to urgent necessities of the war.

When the *Junta Técnica* of the Nationalist state was formed in October 1936, public fiscal responsibility was assigned to the Finance Commission, which remained in function until the establishment of Franco's* first formal government (February 1938) in which Andrés Amado* was appointed to head the Ministry of Finance.

The first problem facing the Burgos* authorities in the area of fiscal issues was, of course, the rebuilding of the apparatus for collecting taxes. With Madrid under the Republicans'* control, the Nationalists were deprived of the administrative machinery, data, and instruments of implementation necessary for the normal collection of taxes, which without a doubt negatively influenced the volume of tax collection, at least in the beginning. Another adverse factor, easily understood, was the distortion in economic activity resulting from the war, which logically presupposed a decrease in the tax base, and therefore an important decline in revenues. To this must be added the fact that the nation's richest zones, and thus those contributing the most to the state's funds, such as the Basque country, Catalonia,* and Valencia,* remained under the control of the Republic.

All told, together with a sharp increase in expenditures, the result was a chronic budgetary deficit throughout the remainder of the war. A Ministry of Finance memorandum of June 1940 contained detailed figures for income and outflow of the treasury in the Nationalist zone, as shown in the table below.

Cash Inflow/Outflow for the Nationalist Government

Period	Income	Outflow	Deficit
Second Semester 1936	396[a]	819	423
First Semester 1937	552	1,291	739
Second Semester 1937	680	2,252	1,572
First Semester 1938	791	2,602	1,811
Second Semester 1938	847	3,258	2,411
First Trimester 1939	418	1,722	1,304
Total	3,684	11,944	8,260

[a]All figures in millions of pesetas.

Two aspects of this table invite comment. First, the low volume of income, particularly if compared with the total tax receipts for the year prior to the war (1935), which amounted to an estimated 4,127 million pesetas, should be noted. Second, and linked to the first observation, is the magnitude of the deficit which more than doubled the income levels.

In the outflow item, there were sharply increased levels of spending, deriving from constantly increasing military expenditures for soldiers and equipment, as well as greater assistance to the civilian population* (food* supply and distribution, for example). These levels increased as new territories were added. In order to curb the growth of public expenditures, the Nationalists resorted to various procedures. (1) By decree of August 1936, payment of interest on the public debt was postponed until May 1938, when payments were resumed but only for new coupons, the previous not being honored until 1940. (2) Payments were also postponed for 60 percent of war supplies. (3) Expenditures for public works were severely limited to essentials or to those that were war-related. (4) Wages of public employees and retirees were reduced

by the equivalent of one or two days' income, according to whether those wages were equal to or less than 4,000 pesetas annually.

The moratorium on the payment for interest derived from the public debt and for war-related supplies cannot really be considered a contraction in public expenditures. It was merely a postponement, which has led several authors to conclude that the true deficit in Nationalist public finances was greatly in excess of deficits officially declared. With regard to income, we have already mentioned that, in contrast to revenues of 4,217 million in 1935 (which in 1936 could have reached 5,000 million), the Nationalists could only collect in the first six months of the war no more than 396 million. It has been estimated that the share of the national budget prior to the war obtained in the areas which came under Nationalist control on or about July 19, 1936, could not exceed 30 percent. But even if this percentage represents a reduction, applying it to the total foreseeable for 1936 (previously cited), the returns would have been approximately 750 million pesetas. This figure, when compared to the sum actually collected, gives us an idea of the poor results obtained.

In order to fill the vaults of the treasury, the Burgos authorities at first depended on the taxes in effect at the start of the war. These taxes were collected through payment certificates made available by the delegations representing the Ministry of Finance for deposit to the account of the treasury in the Bank of Spain.* Because these proved insufficient, it soon became necessary to impose new taxes and assessments, as well as resort to a full gamut of seizures, requisitioning, and other extraordinary procedures.

With respect to taxation, the first extraordinary measure adopted (October 1936) was the so-called *plato único* (single plate) tax. The "single plate day" occurred on the first and fifteenth of each month and consisted of a 50-percent levy on the price of all food served in establishments open to the public. Subsequently, the practice was to occur on a weekly basis. Initially, the revenues obtained from this source were earmarked for "good works" (orphan asylums, dining facilities for the poor, kindergartens, and so on). Later, half of these revenues were used as subsidies for the families of combatants. A similar levy, imposed at a later date, was the *día semanal sin postre* (weekly day without dessert).

A second measure of a beneficent-social nature was the imposition (January 1937) of a 10-percent levy on several luxury items (furs, perfumes, jewelry, tobacco, public entertainment, consumption at bars, cafes, and the like), destined to be a subsidy fund for the families of combatants who, because of their obligatory military service, had no or insufficient funds. The subsidy paid varied between 3 and 8 pesetas per family, according to the size of each. This levy did not, however, yield appreciable results, as scarcely 40 million were actually collected out of 100 million originally estimated as necessary to meet the subsidy demands.

A third levy of a special character was an impost on extraordinary benefits (income), which because of its late enactment (January 1939) was never applied during the Civil War.

Together with tax measures, the Nationalists resorted profusely to requisitioning or seizures, a logical situation in time of war. Thus, in the same ordinance of July 1936, in which the *Junta de Defensa Nacional** declared the existence of a state of war, it provided for the seizure of all vehicles and means of communication. In August of the same year, the Nationalists authorized the seizure for purposes of the war effort of minerals, their derivatives, and products obtained from their industrial treatment. Similarly, it was decreed (March 1937) that Spanish subjects were obligated to cede to the state all foreign exchange and gold in their possession, regardless of rationale for their possession, and a decree affecting foreign stocks and bonds was also issued. Throughout the conflict, there were abundant calls to the population to contribute to the national cause jewelry and items of value, operations that were first performed in a rather disorganized fashion, but later in a more organized way by the central authorities. Use was also made of subscriptions and contributions of all kinds (Christmas gifts for the combatants, winter aid, and so on) with which the Nationalists intended at the same time to bring into play resources and to mobilize the emotional reactions of its population, exalting the social aspects of its regime.

As could be expected, the seizures and expropriations were fattened especially by the goods of the parties, syndicates, and organizations that opposed the national movement, as well as those persons regarded as hostile to the Nationalist cause. The legal basis for these actions was a decree of September 1936 by which the real estate and other goods and assets of the organizations forming part of the Popular Front* (such as offices) were dispossessed.

All the same, these resources were not sufficient to cover the treasury's expenditures, as is demonstrated in the table above. The deficit was so enormous (8.260 million pesetas) that the Nationalists were forced to exert constant pressure on the Bank of Spain* in Burgos for help. As a first measure, the credit balances of the delegations of the Ministry of Finance in

the Bank of Spain were negotiated and amounted to some 600 million pesetas, which permitted covering the deficit of the second six months of 1936 and part of that for the first half of 1937. Furthermore, once these means had been exhausted, advances were obtained directly from the Bank of Spain. This process began in April 1937 and continued systematically throughout the Civil War. It reached a total of 7,600 million pesetas, to which an additional 2,500 should be added, derived from the war, between April and September 1939.

The mechanisms for drawing on the Bank of Spain were the following. Upon the bank's granting an advance, its value was charged to the account of the treasury and credited to the delegation (representative office) of the Ministry of Finance. When the state had on hand new paper currency emissions (which during the war were issued in March 1937 and in May 1938), the new account was credited with the increase in the bills placed in circulation. Connecting the value of negotiated policies with the increase in monetary circulation, some authors have emphasized the inflationary effects of these measures. In effect, during the war the price index increased from 163 in July 1936 to 226 in February 1939.

In analyzing the evolution of Nationalist public finance during the war, finally it is necessary to refer to the mechanism concerning postponement of payments, for internal as well as for external obligations. Concerning the first, comment has already been made about the moratorium on the payment of interest on the public debt and for war supplies. With respect to international payments, the paucity of foreign exchange held by the Nationalist side, scarcely remedied by the cession of privately held currencies and income from exports, led to a solution through systematic reliance on foreign credit. The Nationalists requested foreign credit which was granted in various countries. Thus, for example, petroleum availabilities were assured Franco* from the beginning, thanks to the favorable attitude of North American suppliers and their agreement to wait for payment. In other financial circles in the United States* and Great Britain,* the Nationalists also obtained some help, although the truly important assistance from abroad came from the fascist powers. Italy,* as well as Germany,* constituted the outstanding source of support to the military-financial effort of the Franco regime. No study of the Nationalist finances during the Civil War would be complete without understanding what support Hitler* and Mussolini* gave in economic terms to the triumph of the Nationalists.

For further information, see Leandro Benavides, *La política económica en la Segunda República* (Madrid, 1972); Carlos Delclaux, "La financiación de la Cruzada" (Unpublished dissertation, University of Deusto, 1950); Enrique Fuentes Quintana and Cesar Albiñana, "Sistema fiscal español y comparado" (Unpublished dissertation, University of Madrid, 1961); and Angel Viñas, et al., *Política comercial exterior en España (1931-1975)*, 2 vols. (Madrid, 1979).

See also Economy, Nationalist; and Monetary Policy, Nationalist.

Fernando Eguidazu

FINANCE, REPUBLICAN. The finances of the Republicans* remain an almost complete mystery to historians as of this writing. Less research has been conducted on Republican finances than on Republican economic policies regarding such issues as agricultural reforms and collectivization. Yet, a few facts are known. At the beginning of the Civil War, the primary mechanism for generating and distributing money within the Republican government was the Bank of Spain* with the guiding policies of the treasury. The Bank of Spain was also the repository for the national reserves of silver and gold. In the early weeks of the war, various branches of this bank came under the control of the Nationalists* in southern Spain. Yet, these banks had few reserves of gold and silver and more of paper currency and coinage. Therefore, the Republican banking system at first continued to function much as before the war. Taxes were collected and over the next several years increased sharply in order to finance the costs of fighting. Funds passed through the government into the international and national banking networks, and pesetas were spent. Paper currency continued to be issued, while coinage disappeared (as it did in the Nationalist zone as well). As in the Nationalist zone, deficit financing became a way of life.

Two other developments characterized finances within the Republican zone: the selling of gold and silver and the emergence of local currencies and other lines of monetary instruments. The first came out of the need to pay large bills for war supplies outside of Spain. In order to do so, the Republican government had to sell off its silver and gold reserves. Most of the silver was used in France* and the United States* to pay for supplies, while gold was shipped to France and the USSR.* The most dramatic event in this regard was the shipment of almost all the Spanish gold reserves to Russia, both for safekeeping and as payment for war material as needed. The total estimated value of the gold sent to the Soviet Union alone was 1,581,642,000 pesetas out of a total reserve of 2,367,000,000. An additional 727 million pesetas' worth went to France throughout the war years. Put into American dollar terms, the Republic shipped about $500 million to the Soviet Union and $240 million to France out of a total national reserve of some $788 million. These funds included bullion, gold currency, and other items, some dating as far back as the reign of Charles V. Only some funds on deposit in France were ever returned to Spain; the Soviets claimed that everything that went to Russia was spent on supplies.

Despite the massive use of bullion, the Republic's credit in international financial circles declined as the war progressed in favor of the Nationalists. Thus, as Franco's* forces expanded their control over Spain, the value of their financial resources and credit increased, despite the fact that the Nationalists did not have any significant reserves of gold and silver. At best, they had the strong backing of Italy* and Germany* for war supplies, which meant that as long as their foreign aid* came in, the number of international bills to pay for materials would be proportionally smaller than those faced by the Republicans.* Hence, throughout the war, the value of the Republican peseta* remained consistently lower than that of the Nationalists. It was also symptomatic of the banks' and governments' lack of confidence in Republican prospects to win the war, which forced the Republic to spend gold rather than use credit to pay for its expenditures outside of Spain.

A second development came as a direct byproduct of the libertarian attitudes of many communities within the Republican zone. As communities took the initiative in establishing collectives, local governments, and autonomistic administrations, they also began printing local currencies, to deny the central government increasing proportions of tax revenues, and in some instances, to abolish the use of money altogether. Thus, in Aragón,* as an extreme example, certain communities toyed with a moneyless economy in 1937 with the result that tax revenues to the central government declined. The appearance of coinage made out of tin, wood, or plastic-like substances, along with certificates of credit, coupons, and eventually bartering, insured that the revenue base for the Republican treasury would recede. This development in turn weakened the financial posture of the treasury, thereby reducing its financial credibility within Spain and the international community as a whole. To what specific degree these developments existed has not yet been properly quantified, although historians are currently examining the problem.

Concurrent with the two developments described above—use of gold and silver and use of local currencies with a reduction in tax income—was a drop in national industrial production by nearly two-thirds. This decrease slowed economic activity throughout the Republican zone in general while fostering a sharp rise in inflation, making the use of whatever available money less significant.

The printing of paper money by the Republican government, tied to a decline in the availability of reserves to back up such currency, made inflation an inevitable process. Most obviously, then, deficit financing characterized the Republic's financial policies as it struggled to find the means to pay for the Civil War. Inflation had two consequences. First, it deteriorated international confidence in the Republic at the same time that the Nationalists were winning on the battlefield, making it that much more difficult for the Republicans to meet their foreign monetary obligations. Second, inflation made it increasingly difficult for the ordinary citizen to meet expenses for food,* shelter, clothing, and other necessities. This second consequence thus contributed to the decline in Republican enthusiasm for the war as it drew more closely to its end.

The Republic did not rely solely on the debasement of its currency with which to finance the war. It sought, as did the Nationalists, to squeeze more taxes out of its citizens. Constantly throughout the years of the war, both direct and indirect taxes were increased. It appears that indirect taxation (such as sales taxes and imposts on specific products as tobacco and foods) rose substantially, yet, at the moment no hard figures are available on these. Like the Nationalists, the Republic encouraged donations of gold rings and other valuables, and confiscated yet more for the use of the war effort. Confiscation of properties belonging to suspected Nationalist Sympathizers formed a particularly convenient source of funding, especially bank holdings. It is quite possible, however, that a substantial amount of the sources so confiscated were actually kept by local government agencies such as the Generalitat* in Barcelona* or by the municipal governments in other cities. Until there is a serious attempt to reconstruct financial affairs within the Republican zone, little will be known about the extent of these transactions.

For further information, see Leandro Benavides, *La política económica en la Segunda República* (Madrid, 1973); Ramón Tamames, *La República; La Era de Franco* (Madrid, 1976); and Angel Viñas, et al., *Política comercial exterior en España (1931-1975)*, 2 vols. (Madrid, 1979).

See also Bank of Spain; Economy, Republican; and Libertarian Movement.

James W. Cortada

FLECHAS. The *Flechas*, meaning arrows, were the Falange Youth, a paramilitary group within the Falange* party during the Civil War. Like other such youth groups within political parties (most notably the Communist* and Socialist* parties), these young members were both a political wing of the party and its muscle. Used in fights with competing political groups, they were also employed in militias* and other military units found in combat.

For further information, see Stanley G. Payne, *Falange: A History of Spanish Fascism* (Stanford, Calif., 1961).

James W. Cortada

FOOD. Food was a constant worry for both sides throughout the Civil War but particularly for the Republicans.* Its availability fluctuated with events of the war and continuously grew less available in central and northeastern Spain. Generally, the wheat-growing areas of Spain remained under the Nationalists'* control from the early months of the war, which insured that those Spaniards living in the Nationalist zone usually had more of it than the Republicans. In Loyalist sectors, especially in such urban centers as Madrid* and Barcelona,* residents experienced severe shortages of all classes of food. This resulted in an overall decline in nutrition and in an increase in diseases related to malnutrition, especially among children in Barcelona. During the last eighteen months of the war, this Catalan city suffered chronic shortages of almost all kinds of food and medicine,* leading people to eat cats, dogs, and even rodents. The Nationalist blockade of key Republican ports made the importation of food extremely difficult and nearly impossible by late 1938.

In the Republican zone, especially in Catalonia,* money was abolished, and a barter economy evolved whereby farmers in Aragón* would exchange wheat, chick peas, and meat with Barcelona for shoes, clothes, and tools. Yet, communications were constantly interrupted by battles and military movements. Wheat shortages remained a constant problem regardless of the fact that Aragón continued to produce wheat. Nationalist Spain controlled two-thirds of all wheat production. The worst shortages came in Catalonia which, before the war, had a population* density almost twice that of all Spain. During the conflict, thousands of refugees* poured into Barcelona and other Catalan communities, especially after Málaga* fell to the Nationalists in early February 1937. Local municipal and Republican agencies were established to insure quantities of food, but they failed to satisfy the demand. The continued lack of sufficient supplies contributed substantially to the general war-weariness evident in Catalonia by mid-1938.

In Vizcaya* (also Republican), similar problems existed. There by January 1937, food rationing had limited daily per capita consumption of rice, vegetables, or peas to 50 grams and olive oil to 250 grams. Wine was almost nonexistent, and fish and meat supplies infrequent. Ration lines existed all over Republican Spain and to a certain extent for many items in the Nationalist zone as well. By the winter of 1937-1938, the incidence of vitamin deficiencies had increased, along with skin problems and various bone diseases. In some Republican agricultural communities, farmers were able to hold back some food supplies, insuring that their families would at least enjoy greater quantities of bread and olive oil than in the cities.

Conditions were less severe in the Nationalist zone. There adequate supplies of wheat, along with wine, olive oil, and various chick peas, usually meant that the population had at least minimum levels of nutrients. The Nationalist radio station in Seville* would often broadcast into Republican Spain the menus of local restaurants, while at one point, late in the Civil War, it was reported that some Nationalist pilots* dropped bread into Madrid with notes saying there was more in Franco's* zone. But, as in Republican sectors, the demand for food required by the armies strained normal supplies and production systems, forcing the establishment of rationing laws, quotas for farmers, and government agencies to gather and distribute food while minimizing the prosperity of a black market.

The effects of severe food shortages remained evident in Spain for years after the war. Fertility rates remained low until the 1960s when a combination of economic prosperity and new generations of childbearing women began to establish their families. The height of the average Spanish soldier did not rise until the second half of the 1960s, when the generation born after the Civil War grew to military age. And, of course, it will never be known whether, and to what degree, insufficient nutrients in the first four years of life affected a whole generation of children.

For further information, see Rafael Abella, *La vida cotidiana durante la guerra civil: La España nacional* (Barcelona, 1973) and *La vida cotidiana durante la guerra civil: La España republicana* (Barcelona, 1975); and Ronald Fraser, *The Blood of Spain* (New York, 1979).

See also Andalusia; Daily life, Nationalist zone; Daily life, Republican zone; and Peasantry, Aragonese.

James W. Cortada

FOREIGN LEGION, SPANISH. The Spanish Foreign Legion was that unit of the Army of Africa* composed of volunteer shock troops. Originally designated the *Tercio de Extranjeros*, after Spain's sixteenth-century *tercios* (size of a regiment), the legion was the creation of Lieutenant Colonel José Millán Astray* who had studied the French Foreign Legion in Algeria. In a detailed report to the minister of war, Millán Astray recommended the establishment of a similar force in Spanish Morocco.* With King Alfonso XIII's* backing, the government authorized the legion in January 1920 and gave Millán Astray overall command of it. By September 1920, three batallions (*banderas*) had been created and housed at the legion headquarters of Dar Riffian, 22 kilometers south of Ceuta.*

In theory, the legion was to have been a foreign unit, but in fact it proved to be a mostly volunteer Spanish force. Men between the ages of eighteen and forty were enlisted and subjected to rigorous training and brutal discipline. This ascetic existence was tempered somewhat by higher wages and better rations than the average Spanish soldier received. To instill a sense of *esprit de corps*, Millán Astray composed a Legionnaires' Credo which stressed obedience, discipline, self-abnegation, and comradeship. "Death in combat," it announced, "is the greatest honor."

Led by such officers as Francisco Franco,* Rafael Valenzuela, and Amadeo Balmes, the legion witnessed ample combat during the pacification of Spanish Morocco (1920-1927). By the end of this colonial war, its casualties* amounted to some 2,000 dead and 7,000 wounded. Seven years later, a number of legion *banderas* were employed against the Asturian miners during the October 1934 uprising. In July 1936, the legion enthusiastically supported the military rebellion. Legion *banderas* led by Colonel Juan Yagüe* were among the first African units to be transported across the Straits of Gibraltar* to assist the Nationalists' conquest of south and western Spain, the relief of Toledo,* and the siege of Madrid.* After December 1936, many legion *banderas* were pulled away from the Madrid front and dispersed among the various divisions and corps. From late 1936 to 1939, the legion saw continuous service on most of the important battlefronts.

In July 1936, the legion was divided into two units of four *banderas* each for a total force of 3,758 men. In the course of the Civil War, it was amplified by twelve additional *banderas* which more than doubled its manpower. It has been estimated that from 1920 to 1939 the legion suffered 7,665 dead, 28,931 wounded, and 4,186 mutilated.

For further information, see John H. Galey, "Bridegrooms of Death: A Profile Study of the Spanish Foreign Legion," *Journal of Contemporary History* 4 (1969): 47-64; and Francisco Gómez de Travecedo, *La Legión Española* (Madrid, 1958).

See also Army, Nationalist; and Appendix B.

Shannon E. Fleming

FOREIGN TRADE, NATIONALIST. Before the Civil War, Spain had an adverse trade balance, with exports consisting mainly of agricultural products and minerals and imports primarily of finished goods and certain raw materials. This traditional trade imbalance, in conjunction with foreign exchange payments abroad, flight of capital, and other causes, forced Republican authorities to gradually stiffen foreign exchange control regulations and to submit this commerce to a rigorous licensing and control system.

The outbreak of the Civil War disrupted this traditional pattern. The war inevitably affected production, which simultaneously caused an initial decline in exports and an increase in imports. Heavily emphasized was the requirement for war matériel. With the division of territory into two zones, each with different production structures and demographic characteristics, import requirements and export possibilities changed. Finally, the need for alliances influenced who would be trading partners.

At the start of the war, particularly after the two respective zones consolidated, the Nationalists* assured themselves of a predominantly agricultural sector with a low population* density, while the Republicans* were able to retain the large cities and the industrial areas in Catalonia* and the Basque* country. Hence, the Nationalists assumed control over the olive oil exporting regions (Andalusia*) and cork production (Andalusia and Estremadura*), as well as the mining districts in Huelva* and Morocco,* without overlooking important export possibilities in the Canary Islands.* On the other hand, retention of the large grain-growing areas in Castile* assured bread supplies for the Nationalist population. Nevertheless, the Republicans retained other important sources of agricultural exports such as citrus and horticultural items from Valencia,* wine-producing

areas in general, and the Basque and Asturian mining districts.

With regard to import requirements, since the Nationalist territory encompassed areas marked by important agricultural output and low population density, there were no serious food problems. Yet, there were shortages of manufactured goods because the industrial areas had remained faithful to the Republic. The most pressing import needs were war matériel and petroleum. Because these products were essential for the war effort, and given the fact that gold and foreign exchange reserves of the Bank of Spain* had remained in Republican hands, the rebel authorities faced serious foreign payment problems.

The first Nationalist measures regarding exports were aimed at maintaining and increasing trade from Andalusian sources, a task in which General Queipo de Llano* played a crucial role. He rapidly organized exports from his fiefdom in Seville.* In another development, commercial and financial dealings with foreign markets, already intensely regulated by the government before the war, inevitably came under absolute regimentation by Nationalist authorities. Thus, the basic elements essential to a war economy—rigid administrative control, subordination of the economy to military efforts—were particularly evident in the field of foreign trade.

In order to increase state income, insufficient at best, the Burgos* government resorted to the seizure of gold, foreign exchange, and foreign assets held by private interests, and, like the Republicans, to campaigns designed to encourage the collection of jewels and other voluntary donations. But all of these efforts were not enough to provide the resources required to meet payments for war matériel, petroleum, and all kinds of war-related imports, and for meeting industrial requirements and those of the population at large. The situation on the rebel side would have been untenable had it not been for credits extended by the fascist powers. It, therefore, can be stated, albeit somewhat oversimplified, that while the Republic paid for its imports with gold from the Bank of Spain, the rebel bank did the same with credit facilities obtained from German and Italian sources and, to a much lesser extent, by some of the Western oil companies.

Throughout the war, the Nationalist advances affected the commercial picture. Particularly important in this sense was the campaign in the north which permitted the Nationalists to seize from the Republicans the important source for foreign exchange earnings which the Basque and Asturian mines represented. Still, despite increased exports, an adverse balance of trade continued to the end of the war.

Exports During the First Six Months of 1935-1938
(Nationalist Spain)

Country	1935		1936		1937	1938
	Spain	Nation-alists	Spain	Nation-alists		
Germany	37,484	9,198	52,169	9,411	34,394	38,798
Argentina	15,883	4,545	10,989	4,591	2,710	1,954
Belgium	14,675	3,369	18,530	5,979	3,484	2,588
United States	28,024	13,987	26,937	15,786	19,797	12,858
France	34,566	6,167	51,142	12,427	1,157	320
England	63,858	11,711	73,094	13,672	7,387	11,142
Holland	15,058	6,964	17,184	6,254	4,737	4,521
Italy	9,842	1,728	4,416	2,934	3,840	14,596
Norway	4,420	1,404	5,337	1,711	784	231
Portugal	4,774	2,337	5,660	4,269	3,955	351
Switzerland	4,332	231	5,610	225	163	39
Total	232,916	61,641	271,068	77,259	82,408	87,398

In millions of German Marks.
SOURCE: Angel Viñas, et al., *Política Comercial exterior en España (1931-1975)*, 2 vols. (Madrid, 1979).

Unfortunately, there are no complete statistics available concerning Spain's foreign trade during the war. Despite recent research, much remains to be studied. Yet, some statistics are available permitting a tentative listing of volumes for the period 1936-1938.

In summary, in terms of total figures for the years 1937 and 1938, the only available statistics are for the first six months of each of those two years. The table, although incomplete, establishes the fact that there was an important movement in favor of Nationalist trade with the fascist powers.

The information shown in this table can be made more meaningful by reference to the next table which shows total foreign trade for both zones for the same period (1935-1938), according to data obtained from Spain's principal trading partners.

In order to understand this second table, it should be noted that of the eight countries listed, three of them (Germany,* Italy,* and Portugal*) dealt almost solely with the Nationalist zone while France* traded with the Republican area. The remaining four countries carried on commerce with both sides. The trade data for the various countries (as published by their respective governments) were shown in their currencies, although in this table the amounts were converted into German marks for purposes of homogeneous presentation and comparison.

Four developments may be observed in these statistics: the rapid growth in trade between the Third Reich and the Nationalists; for practical purposes the near disappearance of all trade between the Nationalist area and France; the constancy of sales to the

Spanish Foreign Trade (both zones), 1935-1938, According to Principal Trading Partners

Imports	1935	1936	1937	1938
Germany	105.7	69.3	54.6	78.3
England	64.6	35.8	29.4	41.4
France	49.4	43.8	42.8	27.9
Italy	19.1	3.3	7.4	13.9
Holland	24.9	10.9	26.3	10.8
Portugal	4.7	3.0	6.4	6.1
United States	102.7	53.4	14.9	30.4
Argentina	10.8	7.7	2.6	4.7

Exports	1935	1936	1937	1938
Germany	118.3	97.7	101.1	92.4
England	135.3	129.7	104.7	69.4
France	55.6	71.9	32.0	13.8
Italy	22.8	8.0	15.8	23.2
Holland	15.3	16.5	11.1	5.5
Portugal	10.1	7.6	2.8	1.3
United States	49.5	46.7	35.4	23.7
Argentina	18.7	13.8	8.6	4.3

In millions of German Marks.
SOURCE: Angel Viñas, et al., *Política Comercial exterior en España (1931-1975)*, 2 vols. (Madrid, 1979).

United States* and to Great Britain*; and the considerable increase in Nationalist exports to Italy. From an analysis of the data for the last year for which information was available (1938), four of the trading partners—Nazi Germany, Fascist Italy, the United States, and Great Britain—accounted for 80 percent of all Nationalist exports. The Nationalists exported

Nationalist Exports by Product: First Six Months, 1935-1938

	1935		1936		1937	1938
	Spain	Nation-alists	Spain	Nation-alists		
Minerals and byproducts	21,225	8,551	23,116	9,314	7,929	11,240
Lumber	14,997	2,113	14,946	1,935	5,665	4,477
Animals and byproducts	11,054	19	11,528	17	12	180
Metals and metal products	14,197	4,553	15,342	8,549	363	6,921
Machinery and vehicles	1,821	88	1,608	42	44	41
Chemical products	18,432	1,595	14,607	554	3,209	3,185
Paper	3,943	194	4,116	118	—	—
Textiles	—	—	—	—	—	—
Vegetables, animal products	16,249	592	16,742	1,669	4,126	2,542
Food products	192,119	40,367	230,823	48,782	48,255	42,733
Various	645	74	754	49	43	169
Total	294,682	58,146	333,582	71,029	69,646	71,488

In thousands of gold pesetas.

SOURCE: Angel Viñas, et al., *Política Comercial exterior en España (1931-1975)*, 2 vols. (Madrid, 1979).

products typical of their zone: wine, olive oil, olives, and canned fish. Such products accounted for 75 percent of all exports from Nationalist territory.

With regard to imports, basic goods imported were related to the war effort to which would have to be added transportation goods such as trucks, all vital to the war economy, and petroleum. The first item came principally from the fascist powers, while the second from the very beginning of the war was supplied by American multinationals (primarily the Texas Oil Company) which appeared to have decided to play Franco's* card early in the war. Given the importance of the decisive role of the Germans and Italians as suppliers of war matériel to the rebels, it is necessary to review their contribution to Nationalist foreign trade during the Civil War.

In the case of Spanish-German foreign trade exchanges, the system established was that of compensation. Already towards the end of July 1936, a company called *Compañía Hispano-Marroquí de Transportes* (HISMA)* was formed in Tangier, with a German resident in Spain, Johannes Bernhardt,* playing a key role. HISMA's first responsibility was to transport, under covert conditions, the army that had risen in rebellion in Africa to the mainland and later to

implement delivery of Nazi war matériel to Franco. The Third Reich wanted to assure itself of deliveries of Spanish raw materials (especially minerals) necessary for the German economy. With this second objective in mind, starting in September 1936, Franco gave HISMA a free hand to organize Spanish-German exchanges on the basis of compensation for goods. The mechanism was completed a month later with the formation in Berlin of a German company called the *Rohstoffe-und-Waren-Einkaufsgesellschaft* (ROWAK). It would play in Germany the role HISMA had played in Spain as a commercial partner.

The HISMA-ROWAK combination operated throughout the Civil War. It functioned as a means of compensating Germany for the movement of merchandise between the two countries not requiring foreign exchange transactions. Spain's import possibilities were thus being governed by prospects of exports to Germany. If, indeed, in the first instance HISMA's objective was concern for the importation of military supplies, its subsequent evolution encompassed a wide range of products, as the military support for Franco (Condor Legion,* and so on) extended later to broader government-to-government relations. The activities of the HISMA-ROWAK combination did not escape wide criticism within Nationalist circles, many of which saw with complacency the marriage of the new regime with that of the Third Reich. Nor was there a lack of critics on technical grounds concerning the rigidity of the compensation system, as well as German pressures for a peseta*-mark exchange rate possibly favoring German interests. But Franco's support on the one hand and that of the Nazi party on the other assured the survival of the system.

Concerning trade with fascist Italy, in November 1936 a system of compensation was instituted within the framework of a clearinghouse. Both sides also sought to develop a system based on companies acting as interchange mechanisms. However, there was less interest in the case of Spanish-Italian trade than in the German case in securing access to Spanish raw materials, and even less interest regarding assurances for the control of sources. Hence, relations developed along less exacting lines, with equally less harm to the Spanish economy.

Spain also had commercial relations with the United Kingdom and with Portugal.* A *modus vivendi* was reached with Britain in December 1936 which permitted the development of stable commercial relations, a fact considered a triumph for the Nationalist government. Under this arrangement, the rebel zone was enabled to export iron, pyrites, and copper vital for British industry, and thus assured itself of the foreign exchange earnings necessary with which to pay obligations abroad. With Portugal, an agreement was reached in 1937 for payments within a clearinghouse arrangement, although not a satisfactory one. Commercial relations with Portugal were not significant because each country had a similarity of economies, while sources of traditional Spanish exports to Portugal (Catalan textiles in particular) remained in Republican hands.

Of all the items included in Nationalist exports, the categories covering trade with the United States are the least documented. Petroleum deliveries to Franco at the start of the Civil War were significant, as was the volume of trade between the two countries. They require further study.

For further information, see Glenn T. Harper, *German Economic Policy in Spain* (The Hague, 1967); Angel Viñas, et al., *Política comercial exterior en España (1931-1975)*, 2 vols. (Madrid, 1979); and Robert Whealey, "How Franco Financed His War—Reconsidered," *Journal of Contemporary History* 12 (January 1977):133-52.

See also Economy, Nationalist; Economy, Republican; Monetary Policy, Nationalist.

Fernando Eguidazu

FOREIGN TRADE, REPUBLICAN. Spain's foreign trade prior to the Civil War consisted of wine, cotton products, and olive oil along with minerals, in exchange primarily for other foodstuffs and industrial equipment. Imports of finished goods and raw materials (usually cotton) generally led to an imbalance of trade unfavorable to Spain. During the years of the Republic (1931-1936), this problem was compounded by a world depression, an increased demand for payment of goods abroad as opposed to their acquisition by credit, the flight of capital from Spain as the wealthy and large businesses became nervous over the Republicans' economic programs, and political unrest which upset the flow of normal business. The net result was that between 1931 and 1936 a series of restrictive programs of control and licensing by the government were imposed on foreign trade with Spain, primarily by the Spanish.

The outbreak of the Civil War disrupted normal trade patterns even more. First, ports that traditionally received or sent goods in and out of Spain were being bombed or otherwise occupied with affairs of war, making the flow of goods less secure. Second, the destruction of plants and transportation facilities also made the movement of goods more difficult while simultaneously decreasing demand, particularly for raw materials such as cotton. Third, money and credit ran in short supply in the Republican zone, restricting the possibility of imports being paid for while normal instruments of exchange could not be used. Fourth, areas that usually produced agricultural products for export became battlefields, and what few items were available for trade were in sporadic supply. A fifth problem involved the work force. Men who otherwise would be employed in industry, commerce, agriculture, or transportation joined armies and thus were pulled out of the economy and at a time when demand for goods and services dropped to meet the conditions of war. Finally, as the war continued, the value of the Republican peseta* declined, making foreign trade even more difficult.

With the need to acquire materials and goods necessary for combat, more traditional trade patterns shifted. Prewar trading partners did not necessarily continue to deal with the Republic after 1936. For example, Germany* traded heavily with Spain before the war but after 1936 traded only with the Nationalists. The same held true with Italy* and in reverse with France* and the USSR.*

Very early in the war, the Nationalists gained control over those portions of Spain that usually produced items of export for Spain such as wine and olives. The Republic still had the heavy industrial and mining

zones. While the mines of the north offered the potential of exports of minerals, the needs of the industrial sector could not be balanced against the export of such items as tungsten, coal, and iron. The establishment of a Nationalist blockade of various ports also restricted trade, and finally the rebels' occupation of the north in midwar denied the Republic even more export power.

Industrial production in Spain declined by over one-third during the war years, and almost all of this change took place in the Republican zone. An examination of several foreign trade figures suggests that trade also declined. Between 1936 and 1937, Spanish trade with France dropped eightfold, with Great Britain* by half, and with Argentina* by almost half. The Republic's primary trading partner during the Civil War was the Soviet Union which sold military supplies to the Republic in exchange for nearly a half billion dollars in gold pesetas from the national treasury. Similar financial transactions were employed using silver and were carried out with France and the United States.* As the Nationalist advances continued, the amount of territory from which the Republic could export goods and supplies in exchange for others diminished. By the end of 1937, the mining districts of the north, all the wheat-producing areas, and an increasing portion of the coastline were Nationalist. By the end of 1938, only a portion around Madrid* (whose economic activity had come to a virtual halt by then), a portion in southeastern Spain, and Catalonia* remained in Republican hands.

Thus, the Republic's foreign trade shrank sharply by late 1937, thereby contributing to its economy's general malaise. Unfortunately, historians have not yet pieced together meaningful statistics on the Republican zone's foreign trade. Available evidence makes clear, however, that the Nationalists had a growing foreign trade, first, because of the support it received from Italy and Germany, and second, because their control now extended to larger portions of Spain, along with its traditional sources of trade with other nations.

For further information, see Frank Minz, *La collectivisation en Espagne, 1936-39* (Paris, 1967); Ramón Tamames, *La República; La era de Franco* (Madrid, 1973); and Pedro Voltes Bou, *Historia de la economía española en los siglos XIX y XX* (Madrid, 1974), Vol. 2.

See also Economy, Republican; Industry, Republican; and Monetary Policy, Nationalist.

James W. Cortada

FRANCE. The outbreak of the Spanish Civil War was not responsible for the fatal division of French society that reached its logical end in June 1940, for that division dated back beyond February 1934 to the Dreyfus Affair, but the Spanish conflict certainly exacerbated the tensions that were tearing the Third Republic apart. After ten revolving-door ministries between 1930 and 1934, the *Front Populaire* was established in 1935 under the leadership of the socialist Léon Blum.* Having greeted Azaña's* victory of February 1936 as a prelude to its own, it defeated the rival Front National in the elections of April 26-May 5 by a vote of 57 to 43 percent.

Giral's* plea to Blum for aid on July 19 set off a chain of action and counteraction as Blum moved through three separate early phases: the Blum-Cot agreement of July 19 to send war matériel, without the decision being implemented; the discovery of Italian aid on July 30 and the dispatch of French aid from August 2; and the switch on August 8 from the Cot formula to the Delbos*-Daladier* formula as Blum found himself faced with massive opposition. Blum later gave four reasons for his backing down: the isolation of France,* the force of hostile press reaction, the divisions within parliament, and the need to safeguard the social legislation that had been enacted. As a result, the French government closed the Basque frontier on August 13, and the few hundred rifles and a small number of machineguns that had been dispatched from Barcelona* through France to protect Irún* were sequestered by the French gendarmerie at Hendaye. Some fifty French aircraft, however, were secretly dispatched to the Spanish Republic in August, at the same time that Blum was introducing a number of proposals to obtain an international nonintervention agreement. On August 15, while Léon Jouhaux, leader of the *Confédération Général du Travail*, was in Spain assuring Spanish workers that French workers did not share their government's desire to capitulate, France joined Great Britain* in a declaration prohibiting the direct or indirect exportation, reexportation, or transit to Spain or Spanish possessions of all war matériel. The underlying purpose was to force Germany* and Italy* to follow suit. Since the word "control" did not appear in the French proposal, the fascist states quickly understood that they could acquiesce and still continue their intervention. The result was the Non-Intervention Committee,* which opened its series of byzantine debates on September 9. The Delbos formula was now under increasing pressure from the French Communist party and the left wing of the French Socialist party. Paul Vaillant-Couturier, for the French Communist party, denounced the use against Republican Spain of sanctions that had not been applied against fascist Italy. On the other hand, the

Communist party was being asked why the Soviet people were not demanding "planes for Spain" from their own government. Moscow instructed the Communist party to insist that France abandon a policy that had been mocked by the fascist states and to brand as Trotskyist all those who would like the Soviet Union to take the lead in the defense of the Republic. Only when this tactic failed was the USSR* obliged, on October 28, to withdraw from the Non-Intervention Committee.

The one concession the Blum government made to the appeal to aid the Republic was to permit volunteers* to cross the border. The first group of these volunteers left Toulouse by car on July 29. These early volunteers met the conditions imposed by the Hague Convention, but after French Communist party leader Maurice Thorez visited Moscow on September 22, the Comintern began to organize regular recruitment agencies in French cities. The main center for all volunteers, French and foreign, was the Paris office of the party's Central Committee, at 128 rue La Fayette, but as a cover for the communist administration volunteers were received and dispatched at the Maison des Syndicats at 8 rue Mathurin-Moreau. Josep Broz Tito ("Tomanek"), responsible for recruitment from Central and Southeastern Europe,* operated from a small hotel on the Left Bank. The volunteers would then leave by train from the Gare d'Austerlitz for Perpignan, where they would spend the night in private barracks before being driven in trucks into Spain. Marseilles served as the principal center for dispatch by sea, the ships being provided by the Communist party-operated France-Navigation fleet. The casual indifference of the frontier guards under Raoul Didkowski, prefect of Pyrénées-Orientales, provoked outrage on the Right. Blum was accused of violating neutrality by permitting recruitment, and in January 1937, he was obliged to submit a bill prohibiting Frenchmen from volunteering for Spain. It passed by 591 to 0. But if foreign volunteers were subsequently prosecuted by the French authorities, the law made virtually no difference to French volunteers. The French contingent was by far the largest national group in the International Brigades.* All together over 9,000 served, mostly in the 14th and 15th Brigades, of whom some 3,000 were killed. Half of them went as communists, and a third of the rest became communist in Spain. But a considerable number deserted or otherwise returned in disgust at the behavior of André Marty* who, with two other French Communist party leaders (Lucien Geumann-Vidal and François Billoux), had been entrusted by the Comintern with the ideological discipline of the Brigades. French aid to the Nationalists,*

on the other hand, was insignificant, as Mola* admitted. Only some 200 fought in the "Jeanne d'Arc" *bandera* (subdivision of an infantry battalion) under Captain Bonneville de Marsangy, which consequently never become the *tercio* (regiment) which its French organizers (General Paul-Louis Lavigne-Delville, Charles Trochu, and Jacques Percheron) intended it to be. Jean Hérold-Paquis served the Nationalists by broadcasting anti-Republican propaganda in French on Radio Saragossa. For the Republicans,* the most prominent single volunteer was André Malraux,* who was in Madrid* within two days of the rebellion and in August began to organize an air squadron.

In a rare show of cooperation, the French parliament agreed at the start of the war to allocate 10 million francs for the protection and repatriation of Frenchmen living or caught unprepared in Spain. A number of humanitarian groups, mainly on the Left, provided aid to war victims, but their effectiveness suffered from a lack of coordination. Their committees generally included such familiar names as Victor Basch, Jean-Richard Bloch, Jean Cassou, André Chamson, Paul Langevin, Malraux, and Romain Rolland. Malraux's major contribution to the Republic was not in the air but in propaganda, and his novel *L'Espoir* (1937) was the most powerful of the war. It was followed in 1939 by Jean-Paul Sartre's *Le Mur* and by Pierre Drieu La Rochelle's *Gilles*, the latter a paean to the Nationalist crusade.

On November 27, 1936, Delbos proposed a moratorium on arms supplies to be followed by a mediation. The plan won the support of all the powers, but like the Non-Intervention Committee's resolution of February 16, 1937, to put an end to foreign intervention by introducing an international team of observers on land and sea, it did not inconvenience any of the purveyors. Cynicism went even deeper with the bombing of Guernica*: there was no French (or other) journalist present at the time of the raid, and the French correspondents arrived only with the Nationalists, four days later, but the cable Georges Botto sent to Agence Havas succeeded in discrediting the true reports that had already appeared in the British press. The destruction of Guernica produced intense anguish in Catholic circles, where Georges Bernanos, Georges Bidault, Francisque Gay, Gabriel Marcel, Jacques Maritain, François Mauriac, Victor Montserrat, and Emmanuel Mounier demolished the pretensions of Paul Claudel and Charles Maurras and the myth of the Franco* crusade.

The fall of Blum's government on June 22, 1937, brought a Radical-dominated cabinet under Camille Chautemps. To show its displeasure over the comedy of nonintervention, on July 12 the government suspended international control at the Pyrenees,* allowing contraband traffic to pass. It was on a French initiative, and with Delbos as chairman, that the nine states met at the Nyon Conference* on September 10 to put an end to the interference with Mediterranean commerce by Italian submarines.* Under British pressure, however, Chautemps reclosed the frontier in January 1938, thus losing whatever socialist support he still had. When he reopened the border, on March 12, it was too late: his government fell the next day, to be replaced by Blum's second cabinet. Blum now considered direct intervention in Catalonia,* but the opposition was again more resolute than his own will, and on April 10 Blum stepped down in favor of Edouard Daladier. Not least among the reasons for Blum's downfall was the schism within the French Socialist party itself. In 1937, the left-wing faction (*Gauche Révolutionnaire*) led by Marceau Pivert and Jean Zyromski had created a pressure group called the *Comité d'Action Socialiste pour l'Espagne* (CASPE). At the Socialist party's annual congress at Royan in June 1938, the *Gauche Révolutionnaire* was expelled from the party, whereupon Pivert formed the *Parti Socialiste Ouvrier et Paysan*, with its weekly *Juin 36*, which provided some aid to the Spanish Republicans. This left the French Socialist party under the undisputed control of its secretary general Paul Faure and Jean Longuet, whose pacifism Blum had opposed since 1914. The gap between Blum and Faure grew even wider with the Munich Conference* which Blum branded "cowardly relief."

After first reopening the frontier "as completely as possible," Daladier bowed in turn to British pressure and quietly reclosed the frontier on June 13. But despite the weakness shown at Munich, Daladier's foreign minister Georges Bonnet* informed Francisco Gómez Jordana (Franco's foreign minister) that if war broke out over Czechoslovakia,* the French General Staff planned to invade Catalonia, secure the Republic's harbors, and attack Spanish Morocco.* His reward, on September 27, was Franco's guarantee to France of Spain's "complete neutrality." The replacement, however, on December 31 of Ambassador Eirik Labonne* by the plenipotentiary Jules Henry was a signal to the Republic that the war was lost. In the last great debate on policy in the Chamber of Deputies, held in late January 1939, the vote was 360 to 234 in favor of denying aid to the beleaguered Republic. A huge influx of refugees* now moved toward France. At first they were refused entry, but on February 6 the frontier was thrown open to half a million. As the war ended, no fewer than 236,000 Spaniards found themselves living in hideous conditions in unprepared concentration camps,* mostly in the sand along the Roussillon Coast.

All that remained to France was to recognize Franco and to return the material that the Republicans had brought or sent into France. France had long hoped to make its recognition of Burgos* contingent upon the withdrawal of all foreign troops, but Daladier now felt that a neutral Spain, whatever its regime, was preferable to a third hostile frontier. On February 27, France conferred its recognition, naming Marshal Pétain* its ambassador. The art* treasures of Madrid and Barcelona that had been sent to France for safekeeping were now returned, together with the Republic's fleet, all it war matériel, and £8 million worth of the 174 tons of gold deposited in the Bank of France.

The end of hostilities left France more divided than ever, and on February 25 Blum denounced in the Chamber the rise of reaction and of class hatred. The vital center held by the Radical party had grown timid and defeatist. The Right, including Catholics, had chosen to overlook the use of Moorish troops and of pagan Nazis on the grounds that the struggle was a Christian, or at least anticommunist, crusade. The Left simply disintegrated, with the socialists refusing to commit France to the Republic's defense. France desperately needed to extend its defense alliance to redress the balance of power, but an opening to Italy was precluded by the Left and an opening to the Soviet Union was precluded by the Right. Although powerless to act, Blum saw the future clearly. If the democracies should fail to form a bloc, he wrote in November 1936, their days were surely numbered.

For further information, see Catherine Breen, *La Droite française et la Guerre d'Espagne, 1936-1937* (Geneva, 1973); David Wingeate Pike, *Les Français et la Guerre d'Espagne* (Paris, 1975) and *Vae Victis!* (Paris, 1969); Dante A. Puzzo, *Spain and the Great Powers, 1936-1941* (New York, 1962); Javier Rubio, "Las cifras del exilio," *Historia 16*, no. 30 (October 1978):19-32; Herbert Rutledge Southworth, *Guernica! Guernica!* (San Diego, 1978); and Angel Viñas, "Blum traicionó a la República," *Historia 16*, no. 24 (April 1978):41-54.

David Wingeate Pike

FRANÇOIS-PONCET, ANDRÉ (1887-   ).
François-Poncet, a distinguished French diplomat, was ambassador to Berlin during the Spanish Civil War (1936-1939). At the start of the conflict, he negotiated with the Germans on the possibility of their support-

ing the Anglo-French proposal for a nonintervention pact to contain the Civil War in Spain. Throughout July and August, all of his efforts were devoted to gaining German adherence to the principle of nonintervention. Finally, on August 17, Germany* agreed to participate in what eventually would be the Non-Intervention Committee.*

For further information, see John E. Dreifort, *Yvon Delbos at the Quai D'Orsay: French Foreign Policy During the Popular Front, 1936-1938* (Lawrence, Kans., 1973); and David Wingeate Pike, *Les Français et le guerre d'Espagne, 1936-1939* (Paris, 1975).

See also Europe; and France.

James W. Cortada

FRANCO, JOSÉ (1879-1937). Franco was a Republican Army* officer who ran an arms factory for the Republic at Trubía in Asturias.* He surrendered the town and this important arms factory to the Nationalists* in the fall of 1937. Before surrendering, he managed to help some 200 political prisoners* reach safety. The Nationalists* executed Franco in 1937.

For further information, see José Manuel Martínez Banda, *El final del frente norte* (Madrid, 1969).

James W. Cortada

FRANCO Y BAHAMONDE, FRANCISCO (1892-1975). Franco was born on December 4, 1892, to a family headed by a naval paymaster in El Ferrol.* Franco's boyhood ambition was to become a naval officer, but when he came of age the Navy was cutting back in the aftermath of the Spanish-American War and so Franco graduated from Toledo's* military academy instead, becoming an army second lieutenant in July 1910. Although physically short and ascetic in personal tastes, he proved to be a courageous officer in fighting in Morocco* and won rapid promotion. By August 1917, already a major, he engaged in strike-breaking in the Asturian coal fields. After his tour on the mainland, as a war hero, Franco was named second in command of the Spanish Foreign Legion* in 1921 and commander in 1923. In October 1923, he married Carmen Polo of Oviedo,* a member of a wealthy merchant family. The king thought his commander to be of sufficient prominence to send a representative to the wedding. After the fighting with the Riffs finally ended in 1926, Franco returned to the mainland.

In January 1928, ambitious Brigadier General Franco, the youngest general in Europe, was appointed commander of Spain's new military academy at Saragossa.* The post allowed him to observe maneuvers and to attend military schools in Berlin and in Paris from 1928 to 1930. Franco introduced textbook reforms to educate the young Spanish officers in the major lessons of World War I. He was convinced, for example, that artillery would have more importance in any future campaigns, while the infantry would have less.

Franco did not think seriously about entering politics until 1926-1927, although he had formed some basic conclusions. From his father and mother he learned to hate the Masons and the United States* which had stolen Cuba. The anarchist-Catholic confrontation which led to the Barcelona* strike of 1909 convinced Franco that only conservatives should head the government of Spain and that an imagined "international Masonic conspiracy" wanted to weaken the glory of Spain. Like most of the higher army officer corps during World War I, Franco sympathized with militaristic Germany* rather than with Spain's historic enemies, liberal Great Britain* and radical France.* The cold-blooded Franco emerged as a professional military man who elected to remain silent on political questions. Yet, by 1930, he could be considered well read as Spanish officers go. Other than Machiavelli's *Prince* and the life of Napoleon, historians know little about his reading except that it included history, politics, and French.

Franco presided over the court-martial of four Republican Army* officers who at Jaca in December 1930 had tried unsuccessfully to overthrow the monarchy. He handed down two death sentences in March 1931, only one month prior to the successful Republican referendum elections of April.

At the time of the proclamation of the Republic, this youngest brigadier in Spain entertained a very conservative-reactionary stance. He voted for no Republican party and never shouted "Viva la República." Even so, the accommodating Franco served various Republican ministers of war from 1931 until February 1936, believing that a counterrevolution to return the monarchy was not worth the spilling of blood. Meanwhile, his younger brother, aviator Ramón,* was a "red anarchist," while his brother-in-law Ramón Serrano Suñer,* educated in law in fascist Italy,* became a deputy in the Cortes* for the Catholic *Confederación Española de Dereches Antónomas* (CEDA)* in November 1933. The devious Franco kept his political opinions to himself.

Despite Franco's silence, the liberal-socialist ruling coalition demoted him from academy commander to a minor post in Corunna* in 1931. He was transferred to the Balearic Islands* in 1933. In the eventual repression of the Asturian miners' strike in October 1934, Major General Franco employed Moroccan mercenary troops, the first time in centuries that Moslems had fought in Spain. Although he aroused bitter opposition from the Left for the barbarian operation, the Asturian incident also illustrated Franco's caution. He demanded supplies and military facilities for an army several times the size of the one he had, which was a result of his long experience of campaigning in Africa under primitive conditions. This indicated his slow methods which he used in the future for his "reconquest" of Spain from the leftists.

One immediate result of his successful repression of the revolutionary strike was his promotion in May 1935 to chief of staff by the CEDA minister of war, José Gil Robles.* Their major ambition was to purge the army hierarchy of Republicans* and to promote reactionary monarchists. As chief of staff, Franco visited London in January 1936, representing Spain at the funeral of King George V. On the way back he stopped off in Paris for political visits, whose objectives are still unrevealed.

The leftist Popular Front* victory in the elections of February 1936 led many of the officers to plan a coup d'etat. The new liberal minister of war, suspicious of Franco, demoted him to the Canary Islands.* Although other army officers had been talking about a coup against leftist governments since May 1931, Franco had resisted committing himself. He had considered joining General Sanjurjo's* conspiracy in August 1932 but rejected the notion when he discovered that Sanjurjo was planning poorly. After the February 1936 elections, Franco toyed with the idea of hanging on to his post of chief of staff by encouraging other officers and the prime minister to lead a coup. But again the crafty major general found the prime minister and the army leadership unprepared. After the Popular Front took office, he backed off from all talk of conspiracy for the next four or five months. He even thought of seeking a seat in the Cortes* as a political Catholic, but chief of the Falange* José Antonio Primo de Rivera* and Gil Robles vetoed the bid.

Why did Franco finally decide to join the July 1936 conspiracy? As an opportunist, did he fear being left out by General Sanjurjo and others if they succeeded? Was he protecting the officer caste? Did he worry about the anarchist threat to property? The atheist threat to the Church*? Russian ties to the Communist party* of Spain? Or Jewish-Masonic ties to the liberals? What were his fundamental values as distinguished from the mere propaganda ploys announced for the benefit of his subjects and his allies? The general's motives still remain obscure.

What is clear is that in February 1936, Generals Mola* and Sanjurjo began talks with the Falange, the Carlists,* the Alfonsists, the political Catholics, the church hierarchy, and businessmen to plan a rebellion against the Popular Front government. Between February and the first week in July, various confusing plots and plans emerged. Mola nominated himself as chief coordinator, while the shrewd Franco, who said no by waiting until tomorrow, held back from any commitment.

As the Gallegan general came closer toward deciding to join the plotters, he gave the liberal minister of war a kind of last warning on June 23. He asked for the reinstatement of army officers court-martialed for the repression of the Catalan rebellion of 1934. During the spring and summer of 1936, Franco, speaking to his cousin and secretary, referred to the "hour of the communists." Whether by "the hour" he meant merely the Communist party of Spain or all the leftist proletariat is not known.

For Franco, the Spanish reds included communists, anarchists,* "Spanish Marxists" (Leninists or Trotskyites), both the revolutionary and the reform socialists,* plus the three liberal or republican parties, and the "separatists"—Basque and Catalan. He termed them "anti-Spanish." Franco's conception of Spain was actually an ideal abstraction like Phillip II's Spain. He was clearly a counterrevolutionary who longed for revival of Spain's past glories. The biggest "red" threat to the army came from Spanish socialist leader Largo Caballero* rather than from the small Spanish Communist party or from the USSR.* Liberal President Manuel Azaña,* although himself hostile to the anarchists and to Largo Caballero's revolutionary rhetoric, appeared in Franco's eyes to be synonymous with the rest of the reds. Azaña, a Mason, had already weakened the financial base of the army. The liberals had crushed the first Sanjurjo rebellion in August 1932 and had exiled Franco personally to the Canary Islands in March 1936. One of Franco's first acts of repression was to outlaw pro-British and pro-French Masons. Franco saw Paris, where Azaña had been educated, as the center of the problem, not Moscow. Paris had given birth to the French Revolution of 1789 and most recently to the Popular Front.

One of the civilian conspirators, Catholic historian and ideologue Sáinz Rodríguez,* sized Franco up in the period of April to July 17, 1936, as having no higher ambition than to become high commissioner for Spanish Morocco. In his view, Franco was weak in voice and insecure, and feared crowds and possible assassination (hence his Moroccan body guards), but he sustained absolutely no fear of death on the battlefield. Psychologically, his personality was secretive—more like Stalin* than like Hitler* or Mussolini.* Certainly, the soldiers' soldier was neither an ideologue nor a propagandist as were the two Axis dictators. After July 1936, Franco put on many publicized demonstrations of Catholic piety, but what precisely had he thought about the Catholic religion before? In the 1920s, he believed that priests and their metaphysics weakened the spirit of the fighting army. Now in July 1936 formal Catholicism could conceivably help re-erect a unitary state. The church's crusading tradition reinforced Franco's belief that the army was the savior of Spain.

Sáinz Rodríguez underestimated Franco's political sophistication somewhat. The general not only found Catholic symbolism useful, but he had also been in contact with Englishmen, Germans, and Frenchmen, particularly the French in Morocco and in Paris. He knew that anti-Russian, anticommunist views were widely held in Western Europe.* As one tactic in his war against the Popular Front from July 1936 on, Franco publicly labeled his Spanish enemies as "communists." In his first speech after the rebellion, Franco appealed for order and for the unity of the Spanish nation. Then, he specifically mentioned that the spirit of revolution was being exploited by Soviet agents. Whether he actually had evidence of Comintern activities remains to be shown. But denouncing alleged Soviet subversion without specific knowledge of their activities had long been a favorite technique of the Right. Only on October 10 when Franco learned that five Russian ships with fifty tanks were actually proceeding to Spain did the rebel general then say, "I not only face a red Spain, but also Russia."

Public order and counterrevolution were the key elements of Franco's ideas, not promoting Catholicism, or opposing Stalinism, and the Soviet Union. In Franco's own handwriting is his strong message of July 21, 1936, to a commander of the Civil Guards,* that the enemy—"the forces of revolution"—lacked discipline, while true Spaniards could win with confident troops. He signed it "Viva España."

Yet, General Franco, for tactical reasons, had to rely on foreign help. The Spanish general made his first appeal for aircraft to Hitler and Mussolini on the basis on anticommunism. Any reference to Moscow at this point was pure rhetoric. The main headquarters of the *Junta*'s foreign intelligence was in Biarritz. From there, they sent agents to London, The Hague, Rotterdam, Brussels, Antwerp, Paris, Lyons, Marseilles, Toulouse, Zurich, and Geneva—but no agents were ever sent to Moscow. The USSR* was too remote to threaten the military regime which was seeking to overturn the Loyalist government of Spain. The Spanish Republic would survive or die depending on French decisions, not on Russian.

Franco's early views on economics from the 1920s to 1935 remain more obscure than was his reserve on politics. He had met the agents of Juan March,* if not March himself, at least by June 1936. As chief of staff, Franco also had contacts with Spain's oilmen and manufacturers of weapons. His wife and brother-in-law Serrano had contacts with moneyed interests. Since childhood, the general had maintained friendly ties with naval engineer Juan Suanzes,* who in June 1936 worked for a Swiss company in Madrid.* Franco probably gained economic insights from his older brother Nicolás* who became a naval engineer and one of the directors of Union Naval de Levante, S.A., a shipyard in Valencia,* in 1925. By 1935, Nicolás had become state secretary for the Spanish Merchant Marine.* Shortly after the July uprising, Nicolás was put in charge of obtaining supplies from abroad through Portugal.* He became general secretary for economic and political affairs in the first months of the rebellion. Another aspect of Franco's early economic ideas is indicated by the fact that by 1938 his wife Carmen and possibly his sister Pilar were both becoming wealthy.

General Franco, commander of the Army of Africa* with German and Italian weapons and advisers, began to conquer southern Spain militarily in July 1936. By the end of September, nine other generals involved in the conspiracy came to the conclusion that Franco should be nominated Generalissimo. Elevating him to the status of chief of state on September 29 was a more controversial move, but the decision was not openly opposed after Franco's legal assistant made it a *fait accompli*.

Meanwhile, General Sanjurjo died in July, while José Antonio was shot by the Republicans in November. Although the Generalissimo did nothing to save the Falangist chief and was privately happy to see him eliminated politically, he made the dead man into a hero and mythological saint of the fascist movement, which was rapidly gaining in numbers throughout the Nationalist zone. The Generalissimo carried on slow military campaigns during the rest of the Civil War, and the Italians constantly and even the Germans occasionally complained of his many delays. These are clues that relate to the chief of state's political and diplomatic tactics. Next, Franco had the Carlist leader Manuel Fal Conde* exiled. Gil Robles had already fled to Portugal in July, and he was not welcomed back to Nationalist Spain.

In an April 19, 1937, decree, Franco forced the unification of the Carlists and the Falange into the one totalitarian party of Spain with himself appointed as Caudillo. The new administrative leader became Serrano, ex-CEDA leader and personal friend to Jose Antonio. His brother-in-law had escaped from Madrid* to Nationalist Salamanca* by February 1937. Unlike Hitler* and Mussolini,* the Caudillo had little experience with mass propaganda. Yet, the shrewd Machiavellian chose men and word-makers with care. Himself busy with military operations, Franco, in April 1937, turned his anticommunist propaganda and the new party organization over to lawyer Serrano. If fascism* were to consolidate in Spain, Serrano—who replaced Nicolás as general adviser and was appointed officially as minister of interior—would be the key to the future. From 1937 on, the Carlists gradually lost military and political power and were paid off with the ministries of education and justice. They restored the crucifix, the Jesuits, plus a paid state clergy, and also prohibited divorce. But real power remained in the hands of the two husbands of the Polo sisters.

Despite the superficial unification of the top, Spanish byzantine conflicts—as between radicals and reactionaries, as between the pro-German and pro-British factions inside Franco's entourage—persisted throughout World War II. Franco's position as Caudillo was an aspiration more than a reality. He never felt confident that some Falangist, Carlist, or army officer would not overthrow him, the same way General Primo de Rivera, King Alfonso,* and President Azaña had lost power.

It is significant then that the military *Junta* which Franco took over called themselves Nationalists,* not fascists, although fascists supported them. The *Junta* did not follow the Catholics, although Catholics supported them, and they were not monarchists, although the monarchists backed them. In short, Franco, with the aid of Serrano and the Catholic Church, won the war of propaganda among the Spaniards.

The revolutionary side could not afford to call itself the revolutionary side. In fact, they called themselves Loyalists.* The diverse coalition, also known as the Popular Front, which included only some revolutionary elements, allied themselves with what Franco called "the separatists"—the Catalans and the Basques. The Left missed the importance of long-term nationalism. They also lost the "silent majority," who in all countries are uninterested in politics, but who remain vague but firm patriots. In imitation of the fascists, giant photos of Franco and José Antonio were displayed along with this slogan, "One State! One Country! One Chief! Franco! Franco! Franco!" designed to deceive the illiterate. Catholicism confused with nationalism also appealed to many of the independent small farmers, the petty bourgeoisie, and salaried classes.

Stalin intervened on the side of the Popular Front and the Spanish Republic, but *not* on the side of revolution. The impact of Soviet advice, more interested in the reactions of the governments in Paris and in Berlin than in the future of Spain, was to crush the Spanish anarchists* and the *Partido Obrero de Unificación Marxista* (POUM).*

An International Brigade numbering some 35,000 to 59,000 men eventually lent some reality to Franco's exaggerated charges of worldwide communist, Masonic, Jewish imperialism intent to polluting the pure Spanish soul. The charges seemed ridiculous to any American or European democrat, but they were all too plausible to the average Spaniard brought up by the priests who ran the schools and the churches and by the reactionary journalists employed by the monarchist press of Alfonso's Spain.

A question then arises as to why the foreign Axis intervention did not destroy the credibility of the so-called Nationalists.* Aided by the power of the anticommunist conservatives in London, Paris, and Washington, Hitler's support of Franco remained one of the best kept secrets of the war. The Nazi dictator himself kept the deeds of his Condor Legion* a secret in order to flatter Mussolini. Because of the Italian military defeat at Guadalajara,* nobody, including generals in the Nationalist camp, took the Duce's "Imperium" very seriously. The clever Franco simply took over the code word "nationalist" from the assassinated Alfonsist Calvo Sotelo,* who had organized the National Bloc for the February 1936 elections.

Franco and his generals rose to power in part through their military conquest of Spain. They demanded unconditional surrender from 1937 to the end of the Civil War. Yet, without the $569 million worth of arms and troops (16,850 Germans and 80,000 Italians) that eventually came from the Axis dictators, Franco could not have won.

From the international perspective, the Caudillo won his war in eight decisive stages: (1) the bringing in of Italian and German air transport to cross the Straits of Gibraltar* in July 1936; (2) the capture of Badajoz* on August 15, joining his troops with those of General Mola's army from the north and thereby securing the borders with friendly Portugal; (3) Mola's victory at Irún* on September 4 sealing one unfriendly frontier with France; (4) Franco's capitalizing upon the self-imposed defeat of the Spanish Republican Navy in late September, which gave the Nationalists naval power in the Straits of Gibraltar and in the Balearic Islands; (5) the conquest of the Basque capital of Bilbao* in June 1937, providing the Caudillo with a major industrial base; (6) the French government's decision in June 1938 to close the Pyrenees* passes to further French leftist underground aid to the Spanish Republicans; (7) the decision of Republican Prime Minister Juan Negrín* and Joseph Stalin to withdraw the International Brigades in August and September 1938 on the eve of the Munich Conference;* and (8) then during the last six months, Franco took the final steps to winning his war by sheer military attrition. His decisive campaign in Catalonia* closed the last frontier to France in February 1939. The patient Franco now had only to wait for an isolated Madrid to surrender on March 31, 1939. Franco's victory, in part, resulted from a series of complex diplomatic maneuverings by the five great powers in which Hitler in Europe came out on top.

Militarily, Franco's strategy was flexible. When blocked at Madrid and Guadalajara in March 1937, he shifted his campaign to the Basque country. Tactically, he overvalued territory for the sake of mere territory, killing men unnecessarily at Teruel,* Brunete,* and the Ebro* in 1937-1938.

The human cost of Franco's vindictive victory included 43,000 to 70,000 battle deaths in the Nationalist zone and some 87,000 to 125,000 Republicans killed in combat. Cruel and unforgiving Franco was also responsible for the deaths of an estimated 40,000 to 200,000 political prisoners* through starvation, overwork, and disciplinary executions. This repression did not slacken until 1942 to 1944 when a number of amnesties and pardons were granted. The exact number of informal class and ideological executions carried out in both zones from 1936 to 1939 remains one of the most controversial of historical problems. Although patience and discipline were Franco's hallmarks, tolerance he lacked. On several occasions even Italian fascists and German Nazis appealed on the basis of common sense to Franco to slow down his executions.

As a diplomat, Franco demonstrated some independence from Hitler by demanding that the meddling Nazi Ambassador Faupel* leave Spain in August 1937. He declared his neutrality during the Munich Conference,* and he resisted German mining concessions by employing delaying tactics and by postponing repaying the Fuherer on Spain's war debt. He also delayed paying the Duce and rejected his military advice. The Caudillo prudently avoided Hitler's and Mussolini's invitations for personal meetings from June 1939 until October 1940 and until February 1941, respectively. When the Anti-Comintern Pact dictators did at last meet, the Spanish chief of state demanded that each of his Anti-Comintern partners come to the French frontiers for their conference.

Economically, Franco's choices were limited. He agreed with the Germans by treaty in July 1937 to postpone comprehensive economic negotiations but only until the end of the Civil War. Spain promised that the Third Reich, among all the great powers, would be given first option to conclude an economic treaty and that the two countries would meanwhile maximize their current trade. Believing that Italian and German principles of autarchy were the wave of the future, Franco was frankly anti-British in his economic policy. His first finance minister, Andrés Amado y Reygonbaud de Villebardet, and Juan Suanzes, his first minister of industry and commerce, both advocated rejection of all foreign loans, fearing that Spain would thereby sacrifice her independence.

As chief of state from April to September 1939, Franco managed, in view of his war-torn economy and growing Anglo-German rivalry, to hold both powers at bay. His autarchy brought economic poverty to the Spanish people but preserved Spanish political independence. His refusal to grant political concessions to either power meant his failure to obtain needed machinery on credit from either. Mussolini, too, was humored along with fascist speeches, but he obtained little payment covering his war credits.

On August 10, 1939, Franco shook up his cabinet. The move reflected his continued balancing of monarchist and fascist factions and his response to pro-British and pro-German pressures. His guess was that Britain, France, and Germany would fight over Poland* without involving Italy and the USSR. After cautiously rejecting economic offers from both London and Berlin for so many months, the Caudillo, after the cabinet realignment, called abruptly for deliveries of machinery on credit. But in light of the German-Polish crisis, Franco acted too late to provide much help to his ruined economy. The Anglo-French and the Anglo-American blockade put new pressures on a weak Spain down to 1945.

After the conclusion of the Nazi-Soviet Non-Aggression Pact on August 23, 1939, the Caudillo sent warm congratulations to Nazi Foreign Minister Ribbentrop* for the coup. He was greatly relieved by the pact, since it excused Spain from taking a hostile attitude toward France. If there must be a war. Franco preferred combat in the east rather than in western Mediterranean waters.

From Franco's point of view, the tragic aspect of the Polish crisis of September 1939 was not that Hitler invaded Poland, but that Britain and France were so ill-advised as to declare war on the Nazis. Franco thought that Danzig was not worth a fight. The much publicized sympathy for "Catholic" Poland and antipathy for "communism"—meaning the Soviet government—had little weight with the Spanish Generalissimo.

From 1939 to his death, Franco's major political problem was to hide from the Alfonsists, Carlists, and the Falange his numerous inconsistent promises. He intended to stay on as chief of state, whereas the assumption of the various factions of the radical Right that joined the "movement" in 1936 was that "Francito" was simply a temporary expedient. Eventually, the Caudillo saw himself as the successor of General Primo de Rivera's regime, in which the army was the embodiment of the state. The major threat to his power, as in Primo de Rivera's case, came from the monarchists infiltrated by Masons, once the working-class organizations had been crushed. Franco's thirty-year resistance to a restored monarchy under Don Juan began with advice given to him by Mussolini. The Duce called a dictatorship with a monarchy (such as ruled Italy when he was dictator from 1922 to 1943) "a two headed monster."

When Britain declared war on Germany in September 1939, Franco was forced to declare neutrality because of the economic legacy of the Civil War and British sea power, although his neutrality was interpreted in favor of Germany. Franco personally assumed that Germany would win, although his political advisers were deeply divided between pro-British and pro-German factions.

One of the major factors keeping Franco neutral during the days of Nazi military victories in 1940 and 1941 was Spain's dependence on the Anglo-American markets for oil, cotton, and rubber. Perhaps Franco's sphinx-like stance at his first and only meeting with Hitler—at Hendaye in October 1940—was forced upon him by economic circumstances. Or perhaps it was the fruit of a narrow nationalist vision. In any case, the Caudillo proved to be more shrewd as a diplomat and economist than was Mussolini, at least between 1936 and the end of World War II. By his constant delays Franco in effect said no to Hitler's request to take over Gibraltar.*

Nevertheless, during the European war Franco made three rash foreign policy decisions. The first was his abandoning neutrality for nonbellingerency on June 12, 1940—a public endorsement of the Axis. The second was his invasion of Tangier two days later, assuming that France was permanently defeated and that Britain would soon collapse. His third plunge into the world war was his decision of June 22, 1941, to send the Blue Division to assist Hitler's invasion of the Soviet Union. Franco, like Hitler, thought that it would be a short campaign, and then he would be in a better bargaining position for Mediterranean concessions. Second, his military participation encouraged Hitler to take German pressure off the Pyrenees.*

That he was motivated by revenge against Stalin for the Soviet dictator's intervention in the Civil War has been assumed by many, but not yet proven. Serrano's profascist press certainly thirsted for revenge. In any case, 47,000 Spaniards fought in the USSR, and some 4,500 of them died there.

Franco fired Serrano as foreign minister in September 1942, not because of allied pressure, but for domestic reasons. His replacement, General Francisco Gómez Jordana,* leaned toward the Anglo-American cause and wanted Spain to withdraw the Blue Division. The pro-Axis faction was still present in the government, even after Serrano's departure. Only the Soviet victory at Stalingrad and the Anglo-American victory in Tunisia silenced the most powerful pro-Axis voices in Spain. Franco pledged neutrality again in October 1943. Simultaneously, he told Hitler that he wanted gradually to withdraw the Blue Division. Officially, the last of the group left the Russian front in March 1944, but a Spanish SS batallion still fought for Hitler in Berlin to the very end in May 1945.

Following the Allied victory in Europe, sentiment was strong to ostracize Franco, who had come to power with the aid of the defeated Axis. He was saved economically by a quasi-fascist dictator, Juan Péron of Argentina,* who offered a timely commercial treaty. The foreign diplomatic boycott tended to strengthen Franco's cry for internal unity; hundreds of thousands demonstrated in favor of the Generalissimo shortly before the United Nations called for the withdrawal of all ambassadors from Madrid in December 1946.

Still under monarchist pressure for restoration, in 1947 Franco called for a referendum, which he won overwhelmingly, confirming himself as life-time regent. Prince Juan's son Juan Carlos, who became king after Franco's death, began his education in 1948 at age ten under Franco's supervision.

Franco more than ever appeared as a devoted son of the Church. The 1953 Concordat with the Vatican* confirmed the Church's recognition of Franco's power and granted the Generalissimo the right to final choice of a bishop from a list of several candidates proposed by the pope.

The remainder of the Falange put on demonstrations of patriotism and heroism. A favorite project of Franco's was the construction of the memorial, the Valley of the Fallen, with a 500-foot cross and huge underground basilica on a battleground of the Civil War, a concept inspired by an Egyptian pharoah's pyramid and which was completed over two decades after the end of the war.

To his dying day, Franco remained paranoid about Masons. Throughout his dozen cabinet shuffles, he could justify in his own mind the firing of any aide by suspecting him of Masonry.* Speaking to Western foreigners, Franco usually substituted "communists" for Masons. This stance stood him in good stead with the cooling of relations between the United States and the USSR. Franco thus undertook to rehabilitate himself with the West under the banner of anticommunism. The United States returned an ambassador to Madrid in 1950, and in 1953 an agreement was signed establishing four American air and naval bases. President Dwight Eisenhower in 1959 paid a courtesy call on Franco.

But Eisenhower was as much fooled by Franco as were Mussolini and Hitler. The three did not realize that in Franco's mind, "communists" were only the latest and most virulent international manifestation of a deeper problem of revolution. The subversion of Franco's united Spain could be traced back to the Dutch Calvinists who opposed Philip II, not just to the Russia of 1917 or the Cominform.

Franco's Mediterranean policy had two goals— recovery of Gilbraltar* and maintenance of African colonies—but Franco achieved neither. Spain's remaining territories were hit by the national independence sentiment epidemic throughout the world. When in 1956 the French suddenly caved in, Franco then had to come to terms with the sultan of Morocco by evacuating the protectorate.

The Spanish economy, hit first by the devastation of the Civil War and then by the dislocations of World War II, required more than a decade of recovery to get back to the standard of living of 1935. Autarchy came to a dead end by 1959 when private investment from abroad, previously held back, was welcomed. Behind the new course were ministers, also members of Opus Dei. These committed Catholic lay technocrats showed up among Franco's advisers particularly after 1957. In August 1969, the MATESA scandal tarnished the prestige of Opus Dei and exposed corruption in some of Franco's cabinets.

Franco's American connection ultimately led to the downfall of almost every idea he stood for as a counterrevolutionary. The fact that Eisenhower was a military man fooled Franco as much as Franco's brand of anticommunism had fooled the American president. On the one hand, the Generalissimo badly needed American military technology and money. Nor did he want French communists ruling in Paris, so that the National Atlantic Treaty Organization protected Franco's regime from international threats. Yet, the economic boom of U.S. capitalism spreading to the Common Market would mean that an expanding lower middle class in Spain would eventually Europeanize their cultural tastes. Pope John XXIII officially buried the Counter-Reformation at the same time that Franco's bankers opened up the country to foreign tourists and investors. From 1959 to his death, the aging Franco unknowingly became an increasingly lonely man in a strange country. Although preoccupied with the monarchists and the memory of Spain's constitutional crisis of the 1930s, the Caudillo paid little attention to the slow social and ideological changes brought about by Spain's increased production in the 1960s.

In conclusion, Franco retained power by following a careful policy of balance: he balanced a conservative General Jordana against a fascist Serrano; he balanced an anti-French Serrano with a pro-French Colonel José Ungría,* chief of military intelligence. His major value was a military discipline imposed on all Spanish society, even if that meant the cold-blooded execution of his class enemies. He also demanded unity for Spain and a balance of power abroad to preserve Spanish independence of action. Politically, he had a sharp sense of timing. His ideology and his economics were subordinate to his political tactics. Ideologically, he was stubbornly fixed on right-wing principles, yet he was flexible as between Alfonsists, Carlists, reactionaries, fascists, or conservatives (domestic or foreign). Although in the long run he proved to be economically flexible, he was much too slow, waiting until almost 1960 before moving away from militaristic autarchy to economic liberalism.

Strangely, his death on November 20, 1975, was mourned more by the working class of Spain—a class he had despised throughout his career—than by the European intellectuals* who thought he had clung to power too long. Surrounded by holy relics, kept "alive" the last month by all the miracles of modern medicine,* he expired on the thirty-ninth anniversary of the death of José Antonio. Characteristically, his last message included both a plea for Spanish unity and a warning against his opponents.

For further information, see Joaquín Arrarás, *Francisco Franco* (Burgos, 1938); Edouard de Blaye, *Franco ou la Monarchie Sans Roi* (Aubin, 1974); Raymond Carr and Aizpurúa Fusi, *Spain, Dictatorship and Democracy* (New York, 1980); Ricardo de la Cierva, *Francisco Franco: Un siglo de España*, 2 vols. (Madrid, 1973); S.F.A. Coles, *Franco of Spain* (London, 1955); Brian Crozier, *Franco* (Boston, 1967); Emilio Diez, *General Franco* (Seville, 1940); José Antonio Ferrer Benimeli, "Franco contra la Masoneria," *Historia 16*, No. 2 (July 1977): 37-51; Francisco Franco Salgado-Araujo, *Mi vida junto a Franco* (Barcelona, 1977) and his *Mis conversaciones privadas con Franco* (Barcelona, 1976); Luis de Galinsoga, *Centinela de Occidente* (Barcelona, 1956); Ramón Garriga, *La España de Franco*, Vol. 1: *La relaciones con Hitler*, 3d ed. (Madrid, 1976); Ernesto Giménez Caballero, *Memorias de un dictador* (Barcelona, 1979); Jóse M. Gironella and R. Borras, *100 Españoles y Franco* (Barcelona, 1979); Manuel Hedilla, *Testimonio. Obra escrita por Maximiano García Venero bajo la dirección de Manuel Hedilla* (Barcelona, 1972); George Hills, *Franco: The Man and His Nation* (London, 1967); Alan Lloyd, *Franco* (New York, 1969); Claude Martin, *Franco, soldado y estadista* (Madrid, 1965); José Millan Astray, *Franco el Caudillo* (Salamanca, 1939); Stanley G. Payne, *Politics and the Military in Modern Spain* (Stanford, Calif., 1967); Richard A.H. Robinson, "Genealogy and Function of the Monarchist Myth of the Franco Regime," *Iberian Studies* 2, No. 1 (Spring 1973):18-25; Luis Ramírez, *Francisco Franco: la obsesión de ser, la obsesión de poder* (Paris, 1976); George Rotvand, *Franco Means Business* (London, 1937); Pedro Sáinz Rodríguez, *Testimonio y recuerdos* (Barcelona, 1978); Francisco Salva and Juan Vincente, *Francisco Franco* (Barcelona, 1959); Jaime Sánchez-Blanco, *La importancía de llamarse Franco: El negocio imobilario de doña Pilar* (Madrid, 1978); Ramón Serrano Suñer, *Entre el silencio y la propaganda, La Historia tomo fue, Memorias* (Barcelona, 1977); Spain, Servicio Histórico Militar, *Partes oficiales de Guerra 1936-1939* (Madrid, 1977), Vol. 1; Herbert Southworth, *Le Mythe de la Croisade de Franco* (Paris, 1964); John W.D. Trythall, *El Caudillo: A Political Biography of Franco* (New York, 1970); Fernando de Valdesto, *Francisco Franco* (Madrid, 1943); *Vidas de soldados ilustres de la nueva España: Franco, Mola, Varela*, 2d ed. (Melilla, 1938); Angel Viñas, *Alemanía Nazi y el 18 de julio*, 2d ed. (Madrid, 1977); Robert Whealey, "Foreign Intervention in the Spanish Civil War," in *The Republic and the Civil War in Spain*, edited by Raymond Carr (New York, 1971): 213-38 and his "How Franco Financed His War, Reconsidered, " *Journal of Contemporary History* 12 (January 1977): 133-52; and Jesus Ynfante, "La fortuna de la familia Franco: Mas de cien mil millones," *Posible*, No. 157 (December 1977):14-18.

See also Appendix B.

Robert H. Whealey

FRANCO Y BAHAMONDE, NICOLÁS (1891-).

Nicolás Franco, General Francisco Franco's* eldest brother, served him in a number of ways during the Civil War. In July 1936, he obtained permission from the Portuguese government to establish an office in Lisbon for the purpose of purchasing arms for the Nationalists.* In August, he moved to Caceres* where he was a political advisor to his brother. Working with Generals Alfredo Kindelán* and Juan de Yagüe,* he was able to convince other Nationalist leaders in September that his brother should be the chief of state for the Nationalist government. On October 2, the *Junta Técnica** was announced as the government of the Nationalists with Nicolás Franco as secretary-general, a position he kept until 1937. In his new position Nicolás Franco expanded his role as political advisor to suggest governmental policies. He is credited with being the most influencial in drawing his brother's interest toward Germany* and in seeking out Hitler's* assistance in supplying General Franco's armies. In this same period, 1936-1937, he established the first Nationalist network of spies, expanded the purchase of arms through Portugal,* and advocated the establishment of a national political party to support the new state being created by his brother.

In 1937, Francisco Franco assigned his brother as ambassador to Portugal. Nicolás, an easy-going, unscheduled individual, had declined in power and influence in the eyes of his brother, displaced by more aggressive political advisors and especially by Ramón Serrano Suñer,* the Caudillo's (General Franco) brother-in-law. In August 1937, Nicolás made a quick trip to Rome hoping to persuade the Italians to make naval strikes against Russian and Republican* shipping in the Mediterranean which were bringing considerable amounts of supplies to the Republic. Nicolás Franco obtained little from the Italians that had not already been promised before and returned to Lisbon where he remained as ambassador for the duration of the war.

For further information, see Ricardo de la Cierva, *Historia ilustrada de la guerra civil española*, 2 vols. (Barcelona, 1970); Hugh Thomas, *The Spanish Civil War* (New York, 1977).

James W. Cortada

FRANCO Y BAHAMONDE, RAMÓN (1896-1937).

Ramón Franco, younger brother of Francisco Franco,* was born in El Ferrol* and served on the Nationalist side after a stormy career as a Republican. In sharp contrast to his more famous brother, Ramón Franco was impulsive, flamboyant, even reckless, and heavily involved in antimonarchical politics during the 1920s and 1930s. He first came to public attention in the late 1920s when, as a young air force pilot, he flew nonstop across the Atlantic to Buenos Aires. In 1930, he participated in an abortive coup against the government, dropping leaflets over the Royal Palace in Madrid* before flying to Portugal* and into exile. This politically unsophisticated air force officer also helped to establish the Republican Military Association in the waning days of Alfonso XIII's* reign for the purpose of introducing more politically radical innovations in Spanish life.

Following the elections of February 1936,* Major Franco was assigned to Washington, D.C., as military attaché. Two months following the start of the Civil War, he declared his support for his brother Francisco and the nationalists.* He then served as a commander of the Nationalist air base in Palma de Majorca.* On November 15, 1937, Ramón Franco was shot down and killed while flying a hydroplane in combat.

Best remembered for his flight across the Atlantic and for being the romantic, devil-may-care brother of Francisco Franco, Ramón had lent his name to a number of radical political activities during the last days of the monarchy and in the years preceding the Civil War. His role in the actual conflict, however, proved minimal and less important than that of other members of his family.

For further information, see Ramón Franco, *Deciamos ayer* (Madrid, 1931) and his *¡Villa Cisneros!* (Madrid, 1933); and Stanley G. Payne, *Politics and the Military in Modern Spain* (Stanford, Calif., 1967).

See also Air Force, Nationalist.

James W. Cortada

FRIENDS OF DURRUTI. The Friends of Durruti (*Amigos de Durruti*) was a group of extremists formed in 1937 within the Spanish anarchist movement during the Civil War. All had been members of the *Federación Anarquista Ibérica* (FAI)* and found much to fault with the policies and programs of the *Confederación Nacional del Trabajo* (CNT)* since November 1936. They advocated the use of political power rather than its elimination and flirted with Marxian views.

For further information, see Robert W. Kern, *Red Years/ Black Years: A Political History of Spanish Anarchism, 1911-1937* (Philadelphia, 1978).

See also Anarchists; and Durruti, Buenaventura.

James W. Cortada

FUENTES BARRIO, JOSÉ LUIS (1893-   ). Fuentes was the Republicans'* inspector-general of artillery from 1936 to 1939. He was a career army officer in the elite branch of the army and was responsible for de-

ploying artillery throughout all Republican armies. He did not work well with Russian artillery advisers and suffered from a lack of weaponry as the war progressed. However, he did use artillery in most of the major battles of the war. He remained in his post throughout the Civil War by staying politically neutral, an unusual accomplishment* for such a high-ranking officer in the Republican zone.

For further information, see Michael Alpert, *El ejército republicano en la guerra civil* (Barcelona, 1977); Ramón Salas Larrazábal, *Historia del ejército popular de la república*, 4 vols. (Madrid, 1974).

See also Army, Republican; and Appendix B.

James W. Cortada

FUERZAS REGULARES INDÍGENAS. The *Fuerzas Regulares Indígenas* were units in the Army of Africa* generally consisting of Spanish officers and Moroccan enlisted men. Patterned after France's* native Algerian forces, these troops were originally organized by Lieutenant Colonel Dámaso Berenguer in Melilla* in 1911. They grew from one group of three *tabores* (batallions) in 1914 to five groups of from five to seven *tabores* in late 1936 and ten *tabores* each in 1938. According to Republican figures, in 1934 the *Regulares* had 378 European and 124 indigenous officers, 196 senior noncommissioned officers, and 2,619 European and 8,539 indigenous enlisted for a total force of 11,856 men. More recent, and perhaps accurate, figures indicate that in July 1936 the *Regulares* numbered 10,639. In addition, this force also included five Moroccan *Mehal-las* (militia) of from three to six *tabores* each totaling 6,370 men. This produced an indigenous force of 17,009 men.

The *Regulares* saw considerable frontline combat during the pacification of Spain's Moroccan Protectorate (1912-1927). They were also used to crush the Asturian uprising of October 1934. When sections of the Spanish Army rose up against the Second Republic* in July 1936, *tabores* of the *Regulares* of Ceuta* were the first units of the African Army to be ferried across the Straits of Gibraltar.* As part of the Army of Africa, the *Regulares* participated in the Nationalists'* conquest of southern and western Spain, the relief of Toledo,* and the siege of Madrid.* In late 1936, some *tabores* of *Regulares* were taken from the Madrid front and apportioned among the various corps and divisions, serving on all the important battlefronts.

Between July 1936 and April 1939, some 62,271 Moroccans served in the peninsula. While these individuals acquired a reputation for rapaciousness and brutality—which was perhaps due to their primitive and rural origins—they were also hard-fighting and brave soldiers.

For further information, see Joaquín de Sotto Montes, "Notas para la historia de las fuerzas indígenas del antiguo Protectorado de España en Marruecos," *Revista de Historia Militar* 17 (1973):117-54; and Hugh Thomas, *The Spanish Civil War* (New York, 1977).

See also, Andalusia; Army, Nationalist; and Franco y Bahamonde, Francisco.

Shannon E. Fleming

G

GALÁN RODRÍGUEZ, FRANCISCO (-1971).
In July 1936, Galán was a lieutenant of the Civil Guard*
fighting the Nationalists.* A communist, he fought in
the Santander* campaign of August 1937, and later
as a colonel commanded the Republican Army's* 14th
Corps at the Aragón* offensive in the fall of 1937.
When the Nationalists conquered his sector, he escaped from Spain in a boat. He ended the war in 1939
as commander of the naval base at Cartagena.*

For further information, see Hugh Thomas, *The
Spanish Civil War* (New York, 1977).

James W. Cortada

GALÁN RODRÍGUEZ, JOSÉ MARÍA (1904-1939).
Galán, brother of Francisco Galán Rodríguez,* began
the Civil War as a lieutenant in the *Caribineros* (Customs Guards) and early led troops in combat against
the Nationalists.* Like his brother, Galán was a communist who sided with the Republicans.* By the end
of 1936, Galán had risen to the rank of colonel and
commanded troops at the battles of Boadilla* and the
Corunna Road,* both near Madrid.* Throughout the
Civil War, this officer proved a talented and resourceful opponent of the Nationalists. In 1939, he was tried
and executed by Franco's* forces.

For further information, see Hugh Thomas, *The
Spanish Civil War* (New York, 1977).

James W. Cortada

GALARZA GAGO, ANGEL (1892-1966). Galarza
Gago, a socialist politician, became minister of the
interior in the Republican government in September
1936. Until he was removed from the post in April
1938, he had responsibility for police* action within
the Republican zone, an authority he could hardly
control. He proved too weak to provide dynamic and
strong leadership in a war zone that had various armed
groups contending for power just within the Republicans'* sphere, not to mention the threat posed by the
Nationalists.*

For further information, see Burnett Bolloten, *The
Spanish Revolution: The Left and the Struggle for
Power During the Civil War* (Chapel Hill, N.C., 1979).
See also Socialist Party, Spanish.

James W. Cortada

GALARZA MORANTE, VALENTÍN (1882-1952).
Galarza Morante, born in Puerto de Santa María
(Cádiz*), was an army colonel who, in 1936, prior to
July conspired with other officers for the overthrow
of the Republic. Soon after the uprising, he was arrested by the Republicans.* After the Nationalists*
freed him toward the end of the war, he served Franco*
in various positions, including minister of the interior
from 1941 to 1942.

For further information, see Círculo de Amigos de
la Historia, *Diccionario biográfico español contemporaneo*
(Madrid, 1970), Vol. 2.

James W. Cortada

GALICIA. Galicia, the northwestern-most region of
Spain comprising the provinces of Lugo, Corunna,*
Pontevedra, and Orense, was the site of considerable
fighting in the early days of the Civil War and home
of a small regionalist movement. Francisco Franco*
also grew up in this region. In Corunna, heavy fighting took place during the first days of the revolt but
nonetheless came under Nationalist control. Pontevedra
also fell quickly after rebel army units fought local
civilians who were armed with sticks and stones. Vigo*
collapsed with hardly a struggle, bringing the entire
region into the Nationalist camp by the end of July
1936. The port of El Ferrol,* which had served as one
of Spain's principal naval centers, could now be used
to support Nationalist fighting for the nearby region
of Asturias.* The Nationalists* periodically experienced
difficulty during the Civil War, however, in governing Galicia* because of guerrilla activities encouraged by
the Republic. Continued repression of pro-Republicans*
contained the problem but did not completely eliminate it until after all of northern Spain had come
under Nationalist control.

For further information, see Ronald Fraser, *The Blood of Spain* (New York, 1979); José Manuel Martínez Bande, *La guerra en el norte* (Madrid, 1969); and Hugh Thomas, *The Spanish Civil War* (New York, 1977).

James W. Cortada

GALICZ ("GAL"), JANOS (-1938 or 1939?). Galicz, a Hungarian communist, was a commander in the International Brigades.* He led the 15th International Brigade in its first combat at the battle of the Jarama* in February 1937. Most of his men considered him incompetent and unpopular. He suffered many casualties* while failing to inflict heavy losses on the Nationalists* in several counteroffensives in this battle. As a general commanding the International Brigades, he also proved unable to maintain good relations among the various nationalities within his command. He continued to lead troops, however, fighting at the battle of Brunete* in July 1937, where his men were able to score a number of successes. After returning to Eastern Europe* in 1938, Stalin* purged him, along with many communists who had fought in Spain.

For further information, see Andreu Castells, *Las brigadas internacionales de la guerra de España* (Barcelona, 1974).

James W. Cortada

GALLAND, ADOLF (1912-   ). Galland, a German officer in the Reich's air force, served in Spain in the Condor Legion,* fighting for the Nationalists.* While in Spain, he and his fellow pilots* experimented with new bombing tactics. In the Asturias* campaign in September-October 1937, they practiced "carpet bombing," which involved dropping all bombs on the enemy from every aircraft at one time for maximum damage from low-flying aircraft. Earlier, on April 26, 1937, he had participated in the bombing of Guernica,* and years later he became one of the first Germans from the Condor Legion to admit to his government's participation in the event. In all, he flew approximately 300 sorties in Spain in his Messerschmitt 109. During World War II, this air ace flew additional missions in the battle of Britain and earlier in the conquest of France.*

For further information, see Adolf Galland, *The First and the Last* (London, 1957); and Jesús Salas Larrazábal, *La guerra de España desde el aire* (Barcelona, 1969).

See also Air Force, Nationalist.

James W. Cortada

GAMBARA, GASTONE (1895-1962). Gambara was an officer in the Italian forces sent to Spain by Benito Mussolini.* Gambara was promoted to general in Spain in 1936 and by 1938 commanded four Italian divisions fighting for the Nationalists* in Catalonia.* Along with Franco's* forces, they marched into the Catalan capital, his soldiers camping on Mount Tibidabo. During March 1939, Gambara led troops in the Nationalists' final push from Toledo.* On March 30, he occupied Alicante.* At the Nationalist victory parade on May 19 in Madrid,* Gambara's troops were given considerable attention. After the Civil War, Gambara continued his military career, fought in World War II, and eventually retired to Rome.

For further information, see John F. Coverdale, *The Italian Intervention in the Spanish Civil War* (Princeton, N.J., 1975).

See also Italy.

James W. Cortada

GÁMIR ULÍBARRI, MARIANO (1877-1959). Gámir, a Basque professional army officer of the old school, specialized in military theory. He served as director of the Infantry Academy during the 1920s and as director of the newly created Academy of the Infantry, Cavalry, and Quartermaster Corps in 1932. In 1933, he was promoted to brigadier general. As commander of the 5th Brigade in Valencia* in July 1936, he kept his troops loyal to the Republic; he remained in Valencia as head of the 5th and 6th Brigades until May 1937, when he was sent to coordinate the defense of the north. There Gámir, like his predecessor, General Llano de la Encomienda,* fell victim to the endemic factionalism within the Republican zone. Unable to establish a unified command and short of men and materiel, he failed to hold either Bilbao* or Santander* and was finally dismissed on August 28 by the autonomous Sovereign Council of Asturias* and León.* Subsequently, Gámir supervised the withdrawal of foreign volunteers.* In December 1938, he returned to Valencia, where he headed the General Inspection of Military Instruction. Exiled in France* after the war, he returned to Spain in the 1950s.

For further information, see Mariano Gámir Ulíbarri, *De mis memorias* (Paris, 1939); Ramón Salas Larrazábal, *Historia del ejército popular de la República*, 4 vols. (Madrid, 1973).

See also Army of the North (Republican).

Carolyn P. Boyd

GANDESA. Gandesa, in the province of Tarragona,* was the scene of heavy fighting during the battle of the Ebro* in July-November 1938. The center of the fighting during August developed at Gandesa, a town with a population of nearly 4,000. Thousands of men were killed or wounded in and just outside the town, while the community itself was subjected to considerable air and artillery bombardment by the Nationalists.* The community's economy was severely damaged by this heavy fighting. Of the 5.4 million grapevines in the area around Gandesa, nearly half had been destroyed by 1939, insuring the town the loss of its livelihood for years to come.

For further information, see Luis María Mezquida, *La batalla del Ebro*, 2 vols. (Tarragona, 1963).

James W. Cortada

GARCÉS, SANTIAGO. Garcés became the national director of the *Servicio de Investigación Militar* (SIM)* in February 1939. Under the control of this socialist, SIM maintained its ruthless pursuit of enemies of communism within the Republican zone. Numerous prisoners were tortured, murdered, and otherwise badly treated. Garcés was an unintelligent, often cruel leader. He earned a footnote in history by riding in the car with those who took José Calvo Sotelo* to the edge of Madrid* and murdered him on July 13, 1936.

For further information, see Hugh Thomas, *The Spanish Civil War* (New York, 1977).
See also Police; and Terrorism.

James W. Cortada

GARCÍA BENÍTEZ, ANGEL (1874-1944?). García Benítez, an army general, sided with the Nationalists* in 1936. He conquered the province of Álava* in the Basque country for the Nationalists, the only province in this area occupied by Franco's* forces during the summer of 1936.

For further information, see José Manuel Martínez Bande, *La guerra en el norte* (Madrid, 1969).

James W. Cortada

GARCÍA CONDE, PEDRO. García Conde was the Nationalists'* ambassador to Mussolini's* government during the Spanish Civil War (1937-1939). Rome and Berlin were the two key foreign sources of aid to Franco's* cause, and as his chief official representative in Italy,* García Conde had the important job of obtaining financial and military assistance for Burgos.* While decisions involving Spain were often made by the Italian government without consulting García Conde, he nonetheless was an important source of

data for Franco while the Nationalists were developing relations with Italy. The Italians also used him as a communications link to Burgos.

For further information, see John F. Coverdale, *Italian Intervention in the Spanish Civil War* (Princeton, N.J., 1975).

James W. Cortada

GARCÍA DE LA HERRÁN, MIGUEL (1880-1936). García de la Herrán commanded troops stationed in Madrid* in July 1936. He participated in the plot by other Spanish generals favoring Franco's* cause and sided with him at the start of the war. His officers executed him after the rebellion was squashed in Madrid on about July 25, 1936.

For further information, see Enrique Delgado, *Hombres made in Moscú* (Barcelona, 1965); Maximiniano García Venero, *Madrid, julio 1936* (Madrid, 1973); and Dan Kurtzman, *Miracle of November* (New York, 1980).

James W. Cortada

GARCÍA ESCÁMEZ Y INIESTA, FRANCISCO (1893-1951). General García Escámez, a Nationalist Army* officer, was born and raised in Andalusia,* served in Morocco,* and helped General Emilio Mola Vidal* plot the rebellion in 1936. He then commanded combat troops throughout 1936 and 1937 around Madrid.* He led soldiers at the battles of Boadilla del Monte* and Corunna Road* in December 1936, for example, and later at the battle of the Jarama* in February 1937. He participated in the Nationalist offensive into Aragón* and the Levante* between March and July 1938, and finally broke through to the Mediterranean before heading north for the final conquest of Catalonia* in 1939. In each campaign, he proved to be an effective officer and one of Franco's* most important commanders.

For further information, see Manuel Aznar, *Historia militar de la guerra de España* (Madrid, 1940); and Luis María de Lojendio, *Operaciones militares de la guerra de España* (Barcelona, 1940).
See also Appendix B.

James W. Cortada

GARCÍA LACALLE, ANDRÉS. García Lacalle, an engineer and a career officer in the Spanish Army, was in charge of the Republic's fighter aircraft during the Civil War. In March 1937, he commanded forces at the battle of Gaudalajara.* During 1938 and 1939,

García Lacalle controlled Republican Air Force* activities throughout Catalonia* where he advocated heavy use of his pilots.* His memoirs on the war is a good source on the Republican Air Force and on the role of Russian and French air support.

For further information, see Andrés García Lacalle, *Mitos y verdades: la aviación de caza en la guerra española* (Mexico, 1974); and Jesús Salas Larrazábal, *La guerra de España desde el aire* (Barcelona, 1969).

James W. Cortada

GARCÍA LORCA, FEDERICO (1898-1936). García Lorca, one of Spain's greatest writers of the twentieth century, was born in Fuente Vaqueros in the province of Granada.* He attended the University of Granada and soon after emerged as a major poet. He lived in Madrid* throughout most of the 1920s and early 1930s writing poems, lyrics for music, and articles, a total of over twenty volumes of writings. This giant of Spanish letters supported the Republic as did most intellectuals* in Spain. He was living in Granada in July 1936 when sympathizers of the Nationalists* began executing friends of the Republic. García Lorca was one of over 2,000 people executed in Granada. He was arrested because he had a socialist brother-in-law who was mayor of Granada (also executed) and had himself been closely associated with the literary Left. The local civil governor installed by the Nationalists, José Valdés Guzmán, was also head of the local chapter of the Falange,* and it was this man who made the decision to execute the poet sometime in mid-August. To this day García Lorca's burial place remains unknown. His death represented a major loss to the Spanish nation and Hispanic culture for which many criticized the Nationalists.

For further information, see Marcelle Auclair, *Enfance et mort de García Lorca* (Paris, 1968); Círculo de Amigos de la Historia, *Diccionario biográfico español contemporaneo* (Madrid, 1970), Vol. 2; Ian Gibson, *The Assassination of Federico García Lorca* (London, 1979).

See also Literature.

James W. Cortada

GARCÍA MORATO Y CASTAÑO, JOAQUÍN (1904-1939). García Morato, born in Melilla,* was a famous air ace in the Nationalist Air Force.* At the battle of the Jarama* in February 1937 he gained control over the air from Russian pilots* flying for the Republicans.* During the Aragón* offensive in August-October 1937, he commanded the Nationalist air fighters. His combat record was one of the greatest among those of the other Nationalist pilots: he shot down forty enemy planes and flew 511 sorties. He became a highly publicized officer in Franco's* sectors and rapidly rose in rank to become a general.

García Morato died as a result of an airplane accident at an air show. He had spent all his life in the army and had flown since 1926, including combat missions in North Africa and later for the government when it put down a rebellion in Asturias* in 1934. Eleven years after his death, Franco named him the Count of Jarama in recognition of his contributions to the Nationalist cause.

For further information, see Círculo de Amigos de la Historia, *Diccionario biográfico español contemporaneo* (Madrid, 1970), Vol. 2; and Jesús Salas Larrazábal, *La guerra de España desde el aire* (Barcelona, 1969).

James W. Cortada

GARCÍA OLIVER, JUAN (1901-　　). García Oliver became one of the four anarchist ministers of state in the Popular Front* cabinet of Francisco Largo Caballero* in November 1936 after a long career as a militant in the *Federación Anarquista Ibérica* (FAI)* and other anarchist groups. Unfortunately, his ministerial role put him under heavy attack by anarchists* in both Spain and abroad after the May 1937 riots* when communists destroyed Largo Caballero's cabinet and ended the anarchist social revolution in Aragón* and Catalonia*—disasters which some traditional anarchists blamed upon García Oliver and other *gubernativos*.

The career of García Oliver began in 1919 during the chaotic period of Catalan nationalism and social unrest after World War I. While working as a waiter, he met members of the anarchosyndicalist *Confederación Nacional del Trabajo* (CNT)* and soon gravitated towards its ultra-Left as represented by Buenaventura Durruti* and Francisco Ascaso,* both destined to become legendary figures of the Spanish Left. He joined their *Solidarios** group, formed to promote anarchobolshevism in celebration of the Russian Revolution, and played a part in the assassination of Juan Soldevila Romero, archbishop of Saragossa,* in June 1923. While others fled abroad, García Oliver remained in Barcelona,* secretly organizing support for the Vera del Bidosa raid by exiles in 1924 to protest Primo de Rivera's dictatorship, acting as a courier between anarchist exiles and the few remaining activists in Spain, and developing his own following. After six months' imprisonment in 1926, he, too, fled Spain for France* and remained there until 1931, making many friends throughout the European Left during these five years.

During the Second Republic,* García Oliver became an activist in *Nosotros*;* Durriti's new group, and in the FAI, created in 1927 as the main agency of a "purer" anarchist movement. He was adamant in opposing a labor orientation for the CNT and opposed plans to take advantage of the CNT's size to participate in politics by denouncing the laborites. After the Casa Viejas incident in January 1933 had led to FAI protests against the policies of the CNT and the Second Republic, he received a bad beating in prison and thus remained relatively inactive for the next three years.

The Civil War found García Oliver in Barcelona organizing resistance to the Nationalist uprising, sitting on the executive committee that directed the militia army, and leading the northern columns that besieged Huesca* in August 1936. There was some criticism of his conceit among those who worked with him in the Aragón campaign, and his work on the governing Antifascist Militias Committee* (which included chairmanship of the investigation and vigilance, food,* and transportation subcommittees) also led to later charges of brutality and ineffectiveness. But it was this experience which allowed him to join Largo Caballero's cabinet in early November 1936 when the siege of Madrid* forced anarchists to participate in a truly national government of all leftist parties.

García Oliver was minister of justice from November 4, 1936, to June 17, 1937. Because he was uneducated and not a lawyer, his tenure in office became extremely controversial. Communists claimed his actions stressed revolution rather than antifascism, while moderates decried his lack of expertise. Measures promulgated included stringent penalties for black marketeers, amnesty for many criminals convicted before July 1936, and the development of Popular Tribunals* as a part of a new legal code that permitted various social groups to develop their own concepts of justice and allowed lay judges and nonprofessional lawyers to take over the courtroom. Many of the reforms went so far that the Negrín* cabinet, embarrassed by such revolutionary zeal, abolished most of them by 1938.

García Oliver also sought to arbitrate the May 1937 crisis in Barcelona and finally obtained a truce after four days. This was at the expense of the anarchist cause, however, and became one of the factors leading to the collapse of Largo Caballero's government on May 17, 1937. Anarchists subsequently quarreled bitterly over this action, fragmenting the movement into rival groups and ending García Oliver's career. He has lived in Mexico* since 1939.

For futher information, see Robert Kern, *Red Years/Black Years: A Political History of Spanish Anarchism, 1911-1937* (Philadelphia, 1978); César Lorenzo, *Les anarchistes espagnols et le pouvoir 1868-1969* (Paris, 1969); and José Peirats, *Los anarquistas en la crisis política española* (Buenos Aires, 1964).

Robert W. Kern

GARCÍA VALIÑO, RAFAEL (1898-   ). García Valiño, a Navarrese brigade commander during the Civil War, fought for the Nationalists.* He was born in Toledo* and attended the Infantry Academy. He fought in North Africa and made the army his career. Throughout the war he commanded Navarrese soldiers, primarily in the 1st Brigade of Navarre,* and emerged from the war with the rank of general. He led troops during the campaigns in the north during 1936, and later in Bilbao* and Santander,* and he participated in the conquest of Asturias.* In 1938, he fought at Teruel* and in Catalonia.* García Valiño closed off the French border to escaping Republicans* at the end of the war. After 1939, he continued to serve in the army, and he wrote books on military history and strategy.

For further information, see Círculo de Amigos de la Historia, *Diccionario biográfico español contemporaneo* (Madrid, 1970), Vol. 2; and Rafael García Valiño, *Guerra de liberación española, Las compañas de Aragón y Maestrazgo* (Madrid, 1949).

James W. Cortada

GARIBALDI BRIGADE (BATTALION). Prior to the formal constitution of the International Brigades* by the Spanish government on October 22, 1936, exiled Italian leaders such as Pietro Nenni,* Randolfo Pacciardi, and Luigi Longo had advocated creation of an Italian volunteer force in Spain. By October, Italians were already fighting in such units as the Gastone Sozzi Centuria, and the Durruti and Lenin Columns; additional volunteers* were being recruited by the Italian *Comité de Paris*. In October, most of the Italians were grouped as the 3d Battalion of the 11th International Brigade, the first to be established. In early November, the battalion, consisting of 520 men in four companies plus an assault group, was shifted to form the basis of the 12th Brigade. After March 1937 (Guadalajara*) due to casualties,* additional Italian recruits (many of whom came from Carlo Rosselli's Matteotti Column in the north) were added to the battalion, along with Spanish soldiers who by then constituted some 30 percent of the brigade. With general army reorganization in April 1937, the Internationals were incorporated into regular army units, and the entire 12th Brigade became known as the Garibaldi. They served with the Kleber* and Luckacs Divisions until June 1937 when they became part of the 45th Division. The *garibaldini* were commanded by Randolfo Pacciardi until August 1937 and then primarily by Carlo Penchienati and M. Martini.

The first combat of the battalion was at Cerro de los Angeles, November 13, 1936. They also made significant contributions to the fighting at the Jarama* (February 1937), Guadalajara (March 1937), Brunete* (June-July 1937), Belchite* (August-September 1937), and the battle of the Ebro* until the Internationals were disbanded on September 25, 1938. Although about one-third of the Italians were members of the Italian Communist party, it is generally agreed that the Garibaldi maintained a greater degree of political autonomy and the spirit of the "Popular Front" than did any other international unit. For the Italians, the Spanish conflict was the initial phase of an all-out antifascist struggle, symbolized by their fighting slogan, "Today Spain, Tomorrow Italy." Many ex-*garibaldini* went on to serve in the Resistance in Italy, 1943-1945.

For additional information, see Sandro Attanasio, *Gli italiani e la guerra di Spagna* (Milan, 1974); Vincent Brome, *The International Brigades in Spain, 1936-39* (London, 1965); Andreu Castells, *Las brigadas internacionales de la guerra de España* (Barcelona, 1974); *Garibaldini in Ispagna* (Madrid 1937, Feltrinelli Reprint, Milan, 1966); Luigi Longo, *Le Brigate Internazionali* (Rome, 1956); Carlo Penchienati, *I giustiziati accusano: Brigate internazionali in Spagna* (Rome, 1965); and G. Pesce, *Un garibaldino in Spagna* (Rome, 1955).

Jane Slaughter

GAY, VICENTE. Gay, a little-known Nationalist, was Franco's* press officer. A writer and professor by profession, during the Civil War he published articles on the Nationalist cause. He eventually became head of the Press and Propaganda Department in the government at Burgos* where he developed a massive propaganda effort directed at both Spaniards within the Iberian Peninsula and other countries.

For further information, see Hugh Thomas, *The Spanish Civil War* (New York, 1977).

James W. Cortada

GENERALITAT. The Generalitat was the autonomous government of Catalonia* established by the Spanish Republic in 1932 to govern the local affairs of the four northeastern provinces. Catalan as a language was placed on an equal legal footing with Castilian; the local government shared control over education* and established regional authority over the courts, the police,* public administration, mines, museums, and some tax collection as a result of the law. The Generalitat could vote measures dealing with finances, radio* communications, all forms of local transportation, and harbors. Issues regarding national defense, foreign policy, and management of frontiers remained the responsibility of the Republic. Yet, the net result of its establishment was to bring the Republic increased support from Catalonia in 1932 and 1933. The first president of the Generalitat was Colonel Francesc Macià, a long-time Catalan activist. The second president of the Catalan government, Luis Companys y Jover,* came to power in 1933 and served to the end of the Civil War, continuing to press for additional local rights from the Republic.

At the start of the war, most Catalans supported the Republic, aware that if the Nationalists* won, Catalonia's hard-won local autonomy would die along with the Republican government. In mid-July, the Nationalist revolt in Barcelona* failed primarily because of the resistance put up by militiamen of the *Confederación Nacional del Trabajo* (CNT).* As a result, for all intents and purposes, the CNT now had political control over Barcelona. Members of the CNT at first refused to join the Generalitat and become members of the official government of Catalonia; they established their own councils and in reality ruled Barcelona. In the months that passed, various political factions were drawn into the Generalitat to broaden its base and to recapture some of its earlier political force. For example, the CNT finally joined the Generalitat in September 1936.

During the summer and fall of 1936, Catalan politics also became radicalized as anarchists* gained more influence in Barcelona over the affairs of state. The Generalitat, recognizing the current weakness of the Spanish Republic, assumed additional functions such as control over its border with France,* further responsibility for railways and harbors, the fort of Montjuich in Barcelona, local facilities of the Bank of Spain,* and management of hydroelectric plants. Each of these functions had belonged to the Republic and had not been fully a part of the law of 1932 defining the powers of the Generalitat. Republican leaders saw these moves as a direct threat to their authority, but there was little they could do at the moment. Catalonia could claim it had successfully defeated the Nationalists in its four provinces of Barcelona,* Lérida,* Gerona,* and Tarragona,* and was fielding anarchist militia units which were on the offensive against the rebels in Aragón.* The Republic could not claim such successes.

A big change came in September with the inclusion of various political factions within the Catalan government: Antonio García Birlán (anarchist) took over the Ministry of Health; Juan Domenech* (anarchist) Supply; Juan Fábregas* (anarchist) Economics; Andrés Nin* (*Partido Obrero de Unificación Marxista* leader) Justice; Juan Comorera* (*Partit Socialista Unificat de Catalunya* leader) Public Services; Buenaventura Gassol (Esquerra*) Education; Artemio Aiguadé* (Esquerra) Interior; Felipe Díaz Sandino* (Esquerra) Defense; and Juan José Tarradellas* (Esquerra) became prime minister. Companys continued as president. One of the first actions of this new Generalitat was to issue a decree of collectivization on October 22. The decree established the rules by which businesses and land could be collectivized while spelling out the role of the Generalitat in being present on various workers' councils.

Subsequently, unified political actions among the various groups in Catalonia became increasingly difficult to accomplish, while relations with the central government deteriorated. By May 1937, the communists were mortal enemies of the anarchists,* while the Republican government sought ways to destroy the power of the anarchists and curb that of the Generalitat. The mini-civil war in Barcelona between the anarchists and their enemies in May gave the Republic the opportunity it needed. The anarchists were defeated and the power of the communists increased, while the Republican government sent its own forces to Catalonia to reassert its own authority over Catalan affairs. Soon after, the Generalitat established a more conservative cabinet that proved more willing to work with the Republican government and that further helped deradicalize local politics. To further insure Republican control, the capital of the Spanish Republic moved from Valencia* to Barcelona that autumn.

The Catalan will to resist the Nationalists declined as they saw the Republic disregard their wish for autonomy and local regionalism. Nationalist military successes also made the will to continue increasingly difficult to justify. The conflicts between the Generalitat and the Republic continued to the end of the war, with declining cooperation between the two governments. Yet, like the Republicans,* members of the Generalitat attempted to function until late January 1939 when they quietly slipped out of Spain into France. The Generalitat was not reestablished until after Franco's* death in the mid-1970s. At that point, the Generalitat's president became Juan José Tarradellas.

For further information, see Josep María Bricall, *Política económica de la Generalitat* (Barcelona, 1970); Juame Miravitlles, *Episodis de la guerra civil espanyola* (Barcelona, 1972); Stanley G. Payne, *Basque Nationalism* (Reno, Nev., 1975); and Carlos Pi Sunyer, *La república y la guerra* (Mexico, 1975).

See also May 1937 Riots.

James W. Cortada

GEORGE WASHINGTON BATTALION. The George Washington Battalion consisted of American volunteers* in the International Brigades* fighting for the Republic in the major battles of 1937 under the command of a Yugoslavian-American, Mirko Marković. At the battle of Brunete* in July 1937, the George Washington Battalion and the Abraham Lincoln Battalion* sustained losses of over 50 percent, forcing the Republican command to merge the two units afterwards into one.

For further information, see Cecil Eby, *Between the Bullet and the Lie* (New York, 1969); and Robert A. Rosenstone, *Crusade of the Left: The Lincoln Battalion in the Spanish Civil War* (New York, 1969).

James W. Cortada

GEPCI. *See Federación Catalana de Gremios y Entidades de Pequeños Comerciantes y Industriales* (GEPCI).

GERMANY. On July 23, 1936, the German Foreign Ministry, through its consulate in Tetuán,* received an urgent request from Lieutenant Colonel Juan Beigbeder* that ten transport planes be sent to Spanish Morocco* to be used to ferry Nationalist troops to the peninsula. Foreign Minister Constantin von Neurath* bluntly rejected this request, expressing fear that any German involvement in Spanish affairs would provoke dangerous international complications. Neurath's decision was shortlived, however, for in the Germany of 1936 forces far more powerful and far less cautious than the Foreign Ministry determined national policy. It was to these forces that General Francisco Franco,* without waiting to learn the decision of the Foreign Ministry, proceeded to appeal.

On July 24, a *Lufthansa* plane commandeered two days earlier in Las Palmas arrived in Berlin. On board were Johannes Bernhardt,* prosperous merchant and ardent Nazi of Tetuán, and Adolf P. Langenheim, *Ortsgruppenleiter* of Spanish Morocco. They immediately established contact with Hermann Goering and with Ernst W. Bohle, both high government officials, and on the following evening were received by the

Fuehrer himself. Hitler* heard their plea and, after consultation with Goering, Bohle, Admiral Wilhelm Canaris,* and General Werner von Blomberg, agreed in principle to support the Franco rebellion. On the morning of July 26, he formally confirmed that the Third Reich had committed itself to the cause of Nationalist Spain. For Franco German support was to prove invaluable, but it was also to pose serious threats to his independence and ensure the lasting enmity of democratic elements in Western Europe* and the United States.*

Throughout the Civil War, Nazi spokesmen consistently claimed that their Spanish policy was simply an extension of their efforts to save the West from the perils of communist barbarism. Anticommunism was probably a factor in Hitler's decision to intervene, but there were other considerations of far greater significance. To intervene on behalf of Franco would provide a foundation for a closer relationship with Italy,* which was also supporting the rebellion, and would frustrate Anglo-French efforts to woo Mussolini.* A Franco victory owed at least in part to German support would weaken French security by creating a hostile frontier on the Pyrenees,* would threaten Anglo-French supremacy in the western Mediterranean, and would presumably provide Hitler with a grateful ally. Furthermore, a friendly Spain could be expected to maintain favorable commercial relations with Germany and supply the Reich's armaments industry with iron, copper, mercury, and pyrites. At least by 1937, Hitler had found yet another motive for his involvement in Spain. By carefully controlling the extent of aid given Franco, Germany could ensure a prolongation of the war. So long as the war continued, Anglo-French attention would be focused on the Mediterranean, and Hitler could expect greater freedom of action in the east. Finally, although it was hardly of major consideration in the initial decision to intervene, there did arise one additional motive for German involvement in Spain. Hermann Goering, Colonel Walter Warlimont, Colonel Ritter von Thoma, and other military leaders came to see the Spanish conflict as providing a proving ground for men, weapons, and tactics.

The Spanish Civil War was primarily a Spanish conflict: its battles were fought by Spaniards, and its outcome was largely determined by Spaniards. Yet, foreign intervention was significant, and none more so than that by Germany on behalf of Franco. Despite occasional lapses and Hitler's periodic threats of its termination, German support of Franco lasted from the earliest days of the rising until the Generalissimo's final conquest of Madrid.* Especially valuable to the Nationalists* was the aid provided during the initial

weeks of the war, during the fall of 1936, and during the fall and winter of 1938.

Hardly had the Nationalist generals proclaimed rebellion on July 18, 1936, than virtually all of Spanish Morocco came under their sway. In the peninsula, however, the Republic held firm, and those garrisons that did pronounce were threatened with isolation and defeat. The plight of the insurgents was desperate, for there appeared little chance of extending the rebellion unless Moorish units and the Foreign Legion* could be transported immediately to the peninsula. Because nearly all the Spanish Air Force and most of the fleet had remained loyal to the government, Franco was forced to seek outside aid in solving his transportation problems. Thus, the appeal was made to Berlin.

Hitler's decision to support the Nationalist cause resulted in the immediate dispatch of some thirty Junkers 52s from Berlin and Stuttgart to Tetuán and other Moroccan bases. By the end of July the Junkers, with some support from Italian aircraft, had transported about 2,000 Moors* and legionnaires to Seville,* and by the end of August the number had climbed to perhaps 15,000. German intervention thus permitted Franco to regain the initiative and to place a well-equipped and highly disciplined army in the heart of Andalusia.* The validity of Hitler's 1942 assertion that Franco owed his victory to the timely arrival of the Junkers 52s may be questioned; but there can be no doubt that German aid at this crucial period did enable the Nationalists to surmount a major crisis and to undertake their march toward Madrid.

During the late summer and early fall, while German diplomats discussed nonintervention with their British and French counterparts, Hitler continued his support of Franco. Headed by Lieutenant Colonel Walter Warlimont, the *Wehrmacht's* liaison officer with Franco, German officers worked closely with Nationalist military headquarters, conducted training schools for Spanish pilots* and tank crews, and occasionally even directed air strikes against Republican shipping and supply depots. In the meantime, a small but ever-growing stream of men, planes, tanks, and munitions flowed from Hamburg to El Ferrol* and Lisbon. From the Portuguese city they were guaranteed rapid transit to Spain by the pro-Nationalist Salazar government. Unlike the Italians, who made little effort to conceal their role in Spain, the Germans maintained a pretense of noninvolvement. Shipments of arms and munitions were camouflaged, and German soldiers sailed as tourists and, once arrived in Spain, continued to dress in civilian clothing.

By late October, Nationalist troops had reached

the gates of Madrid, and Franco boldly proclaimed the imminent fall of the Republican capital. This, however, was not to be. Russian planes and tanks, substantial in number and of far superior quality to those provided Franco by Germany, arrived to bolster the city's defenses, and on November 8 the first units of the International Brigades* marched along the Gran Vía toward the front. Madrid was saved; now both Nationalists and Republicans,* as well as their respective allies, geared for a long war.

For Hitler the possibility of a Republican victory was intolerable. Not only would it deprive the Reich of a potential ally, but it would also inevitably strengthen the Popular Front* forces in France. The Fuehrer, therefore, determined to honor Franco's plea for additional aid and, as a means of boosting Nationalist morale, to join with Italy in bestowing official recognition. Recognition was announced on November 18, and shortly thereafter the Condor Legion* was officially organized under the command of Lieutenant General Hugo von Sperrle.* Totaling nearly 8,000 men and authorized to act as an autonomous unit responsible only to Franco, the Condor Legion consisted of four bomber squadrons (Junkers 52s), four fighter squadrons (Heinkel 51s and Messerschmidt 109s), a reconnaissance squadron, a seaplane squadron, anti-aircraft and anti-tank units, and four tank companies commanded by Colonel von Thoma. The legion would eventually total nearly 12,000 men, and its obsolete Junkers 52s would be replaced by more modern Dornier 17s and Heinkel 111s. Although its initial efforts along the Madrid front brought no spectacular successes, its very presence offset the increased strength provided the Republic by Russian support and by the International Brigades.

Among Germany's motives in supporting Franco was a desire to gain a favorable economic position in Spain and particularly to obtain access to Spanish minerals needed by the Reich's armaments industry. From the earliest days of the conflict, the man primarily responsible for the implementation of German economic goals was Johannes Bernhardt, the Tetuán merchant who had delivered Franco's plea for aid to Hitler. On July 31, 1936, Bernhardt formally organized the *Compañía Hispano-Marroquí de Transportes* (HISMA).* Along with a sister organization, the *Rohstoffe-und-Waren-Einkaufsgesellschaft* (ROWAK), subsequently established in Berlin, HISMA secured a virtual monopoly on German-Spanish commerce, handling German deliveries of supplies as well as Spanish payments in the form of raw materials.

During the first year of the war, commerce between Germany and Nationalist Spain increased dramatically, despite the absence of any formal agreements. Wherever Nationalist armies were successful, HISMA agents followed to claim mineral resources for the Reich. Thus, by the end of 1936 the bulk of Moroccan iron ore production was being shipped to Germany, as was most of the copper output of the British-owned Río Tinto mines. HISMA's success, however, produced bitter protests, not only from outraged British capitalists, but also from influential Spaniards who objected to the prospect of their country's becoming an economic satellite of the Reich. Although Franco himself shared their objections and attempted to maintain economic independence, his continuing reliance on German arms forced him to yield, at least temporarily, to Bernhardt's demands. Therefore, in July 1937, he concluded with the Third Reich a series of protocols that not only preserved the HISMA-ROWAK trade monopoly but also provided, in vague terms, for German ownership of mining properties.

Bernhardt's victory was shortlived. Angered by HISMA's rapid and extensive acquisition of properties and its failure to keep his government informed, Franco, on October 12, 1937, issued a decree annulling all mining titles obtained since July 1936. Despite Nationalist denials, the decree was obviously directed toward HISMA, and Bernhardt fully realized that its enforcement would doom the Montaña Project*—the code name for the acquisition of mines. In an effort to overcome Spanish resistance to his goals, he sought and secured the full backing of the Reich. During the year that followed, Franco, under persistent German pressure, grudgingly granted concessions but still refused to agree to the major HISMA demands, and to the dismay of his German allies, he began negotiations with British firms. However, in the fall of 1938 he was again forced to yield. Threatened by a total withdrawal of German support and fearful that in the event of a war over the Czech question France would intervene on the side of the Republic, he determined to end the war quickly and to make whatever concessions were necessary. In December 1938, he recognized as valid the titles to all properties acquired by HISMA—five mining complexes in Spain and one in Morocco—and thus presented Bernhardt with what appeared to be a total triumph. At German insistence, he also agreed to begin negotiations on the whole question of his debts to the Reich. These negotiations continued sporadically until 1943 when they came to a virtual halt after Franco presented his own demand for payment for the services of the Blue Division.

Despite bickering over economic matters and despite controversy surrounding Faupel*—controversy that eventually resulted in the Nazi general's recall and replacement by Eberhard von Stohrer*—German-Nationalist relations remained close. German diplomats continued their successful tactics in frustrating feeble Anglo-French efforts to achieve genuine nonintervention; German military equipment continued to flow into Spanish harbors; and German soldiers, in marked contrast to their Italian counterparts, continued to fight in relative harmony alongside their Spanish allies. During the early months of 1937, the Condor Legion played a major role in the struggle for the Basque provinces, and on June 19 German tank companies were among the first Nationalist units to enter conquered Bilbao.* In the heavy fighting that erupted along the Madrid front in July, German air and tank units fought exceptionally well and, according to General Sperrle, saved the Nationalist Army* from total destruction. In August, the Condor Legion contributed significantly to Nationalist successes in Asturias.*

Notwithstanding fierce Republican resistance, by early 1938 the Nationalists appeared to be on the verge of victory. Nationalist forces reached the Mediterranean in April, and the Republic was cut in two. So confident was the Caudillo of imminent triumph that he suggested the withdrawal of all foreign "volunteers," hoping that the departure of his German and Italian allies would provide him greater independence and enable him to improve relations with Britain. However, stiffening Republican resistance, the opening of the Pyrenees frontier, and the subsequent arrival of more Soviet arms convinced him that triumph remained distant and even uncertain. He therefore reversed his stance and pleaded for a continuation of German support and specifically for a strengthening of the depleted Condor Legion. This plea Hitler honored, and by autumn, at a time when Soviet shipments to the Republic virtually ceased and the International Brigades prepared to withdraw, massive quantities of German aid were again on their way to Nationalist Spain. For Franco the price was high—acknowledgment of the acquisitions of Bernhardt's Montaña Project.*

In December, with overwhelming military superiority, Franco began his final offensive against Calatonia,* and in January Nationalist forces entered Barcelona.* In February, Great Britain* and France extended recognition to the Burgos* regime, and on April 1, following the surrender of Madrid, Franco officially proclaimed the end of the Civil War. Nationalist Spain had achieved its long-sought victory; sharing this victory was Hitler's Third Reich. The Condor Legion held a farewell parade on May 19, and a week later practically all German military forces sailed from Vigo* for Hamburg.

For Hitler, the success of the Spanish venture would soon sour. By war's end, Franco had concluded commercial agreements favorable to Germany, and more were to follow. On March 27, Spain adhered to the Anti-Comintern Pact, and on March 31, a German-Spanish Treaty of Friendship was signed at Burgos. In May, Spain withdrew from the League of Nations,* but in September, Franco proclaimed neutrality. For the next three years, he demonstrated his gratitude for German aid and his confidence in an Axis victory by permitting German use of Spanish harbors and airfields, by sending to the Reich vast quantities of raw materials, and, although at an exorbitant price, by dispatching the Blue Division to the Russian front. But he stubbornly refused Hitler's personal pleas that he enter the war as a full-fledged ally. By 1943, Franco began to sever his ties with the Third Reich and to demonstrate to his erstwhile ally that his own ability to follow the path of expediency was at least equal to that of the German Fuehrer.

For further information, see Clarence D. Beck, "A Study of German Involvement in Spain, 1936-1939" (Ph.D. dissertation, University of New Mexico, 1972); Marion Einhorn, *Die oekonomischen Hintergründe der faschistischen Intervention in Spanien, 1936-1939* (Berlin, 1962); Glenn T. Harper, *German Economic Policy in Spain During the Spanish Civil War, 1936-1939* (The Hague, 1967); Albert Cary Horton, "Germany and the Spanish Civil War" (Ph.D. dissertation, Columbia University, 1966); Manfred Merkes, *Die deutsche Politik gegenüber dem spanischen Bürgerkrieg, 1936-1939* (Bonn, 1961); and Angel Viñas, *La Alemania nazi y el 18 de julio*, 2d ed. (Madrid, 1977).

See also Appendix B.

Glenn T. Harper

GERONA. Gerona, one of the four Catalan provinces located in northeastern Spain on the French border facing the Mediterranean, was under Republican control until February 1939. The province had supported the Republic and participated in the collectivization of agriculture and some industry. Moreover, as in other Republican sectors, various political factions managed to repress the Catholic Church,* resulting in the persecution of clerical personnel and the destruction of some churches. Gerona's men fought for the Republican Army,* while its upper classes divided their loyalties between Catalan regionalism and the Republicans* on the one hand and the conservative monarchism* of the Nationalists* on the other.

The region came under military assault, totally disrupting life in the final months of the Civil War after Franco* had launched his campaign for the conquest of Catalonia* at Christmas 1938. As his forces marched eastward and finally into Barcelona,* hundreds of thousands of Republican refugees* passed through this province and Lérida* on their way to France,* blocking all major roads and overrunning villages and towns along the way. Nationalist occupation of Gerona followed the same pattern as in other parts of Catalonia. They repressed Republicans and destroyed Catalan nationalist activities. Many Catalans were arrested and subsequently executed for supporting the Republic. The use of the Catalan language, which had flourished during the previous seventy-five years more dramatically than at any time since the end of the Middle Ages, could not be used in public. Collectives were dismantled and properties returned to their original owners. Catalan regionalist politics ended. This series of Nationalist policies resulted in a dramatic change since, during the Civil War, anarchist and *Confederación Nacional del Trabajo* (CNT)* and *Unión General de Trabajadores* (UGT)* politicians had played a significant role in Gerona's affairs, despite the basically conservative attitudes of the province's population.*

For further information, see Josep María Bricall, *Política económica de la Generalitat* (Barcelona, 1970); José María Fontana, *Los catalanes en la guerra de España* (Madrid, 1951); José Manuel Martínez Bande, *La campaña de Cataluña* (Barcelona, 1979); and Carlos Pi Sunyer, *La república y la guerra* (Mexico, 1975).

See also Daily Life, Republican Zone; and Economy, Republican.

James W. Cortada

GETAFE AIR BASE. Getafe Air Base, located just outside of Madrid,* was the most important Republican home for its fighter aircraft in central Spain during the early months of the Civil War. Its capture by the Nationalists* on November 4, 1936, in effect temporarily denied the Republicans* the ability to wrestle control of air space in and around Madrid. Soon after its fall to Franco's* troops, the Republicans replaced it and established others nearby, particularly at Algete and at Alcalá de Henares,* primarily for use by Soviet pilots.*

For further information, see Jesús Salas Larrazábal, *La guerra de España desde el aire* (Barcelona, 1969).

See also Air Force, Nationalist; and Air Force, Republican.

James W. Cortada

GIBRALTAR. While Gibraltar followed the official British policy of diplomatic neutrality during the Civil

War, because of its critical location between Spain and North Africa, it did have a role in the hostilities. During the first days of General Franco's* revolt, General Alfredo Kindelán y Duany,* the highest ranking air force officer to side with Franco, used local telephone facilities to communicate with other rebellious units in southern Spain. He and others were also able to negotiate with the German and Italian governments during July within Gibraltar for initial aid to their cause.

In order to preserve the territorial integrity of Gibraltar, by August 1936 the British government realized that it could not offend whichever Spanish side won the war for fear that an enemy power might seize the colony and the important naval and air facilities that dominated the western entrance to the Mediterranean. Because of British neutrality, Gibraltar was not used as a center of operations blocking the flow of German and Italian supplies through its Straits* to the Nationalists'* cause, an important factor for Franco throughout the war. North African troops loyal to Franco also crossed over into Spain during July and August 1936 by way of the Straits of Gibraltar without any British interference. Several Spanish naval conflicts and shipboard rebellions took place in the area which insured that the seas would not be dominated by the Spanish Republic.

For further information, see Carlos Ibañez de Ibero, *Política Mediterranea de España, 1704-1951* (Madrid, 1952).

See also Army, Nationalist; and Great Britain.

James W. Cortada

GIBRALTAR, STRAITS OF. Gibraltar,* a British fortress and crown colony, early found its accommodation facilities strained beyond capacity as 2,000 Gibraltarians, who had been living on Spanish soil, took refuge on the Rock for the duration of the war. Thousands of additional British, Spanish, and other refugees, evacuated from Spanish ports, added to the crowding. The Spanish refugees were eventually returned to Republican or Nationalist territory. Gibraltar was a center for the activities of agents and spies of both sides and other interested states.

The Straits of Gibraltar were of major strategic significance for the Civil War. The rebel forces' failure in the uprising of July 1936 to secure the Straits for the Army of Africa* doomed General Mola's* strategy for the conquest of the peninsula. The Republican naval blockade in the Straits forced General Franco* to seek foreign aid* to break the blockade, if only by a two-month long German airlift and one furtive sea convoy protected by Italian aircraft, which introduced 16,000 troops from Morocco* into the peninsula by the end of September. The Nationalist Navy gained domination of the Straits in the battle of Cape Espartel* (September 29, 1936), and 8,000 further troops crossed in a few days with perhaps 50,000 soldiers and recruits to come. Nine-tenths of the Nationalist soldiers who engaged in the struggle for Madrid* had been shipped from Morocco across the contested waterway.

From late 1936 until the end of the war, Nationalist warships constantly patrolled the Straits, undisputed by the Republican Navy. Only a few Republican merchant ships and submarines* were able to slip through, effectively breaking Republican sea communications between zones and with sources of supply other than the USSR.*

Nationalist naval forces in the Straits enforced a blockade against any foreign trade with the Republic, detaining suspicious foreign merchant ships in Ceuta* for extensive examination and at times confiscating ships and cargos. British, French, and Dutch warships maintained a presence in the waterway to protect national shipping, producing frequent confrontations with Nationalist patrol boats.

Several times shells from naval engagements in the Straits fell on Gibraltar. From August to December 1938, the Republican destroyer *José Luis Díez*, damaged trying to pass the Straits from Le Havre to Cartagena,* took refuge in Gibraltar. On December 30, 1938, the ship again tried to elude Nationalist warships waiting just beyond British jurisdictional waters, only to undergo severe attack and be grounded at Catalan Bay, Gibraltar, producing shell damage and casualties* in that British community.

For further information, see Hugh Thomas, *The Spanish Civil War* (New York, 1977).

See also Navy, British; Navy, Spanish; and Uprising at Sea.

Willard C. Frank, Jr.

GIJÓN. At the beginning of the Civil War, Gijón, a coastal fishing town in Asturias,* witnessed a rebellion against the Republic but remained in Republican hands and under the control of the *Confederación Nacional del Trabajo* (CNT).* Gijón endured bombardment by Nationalist ships during the summer of 1936. After July 31, it was one of the few towns in northern Spain which still had pockets of Nationalists* resisting the Republic (primarily at the Simancas Barracks). Eventually, in August the Loyalists* stamped out the last vestiges of rebellion in the area. Thereafter, management of the town lay in the hands of local commit-

tees. Thus, for example, the fishermen formed a collective, as did the miners in surrounding towns. Nationalist pressure in Asturias brought the war constantly to the doorsteps of Gijón, particularly during the offensive in Asturias throughout September-October 1937. Finally, on October 21, 1937, the town fell to the Nationalists, a byproduct of the total occupation of northern Spain by the Nationalists. After October, Franco* controlled the entire coastline of northern Spain from the French border westward along the Bay of Biscay down to the northern shoreline of Portugal.* Throughout Asturias and in Gijón, Franco solidified his control by arresting and executing prominent Republicans.*

For further information, see José Manuel Martínez Bande, *La guerra en el norte* (Madrid, 1969); and Ramón Salas Larrazábal, *Historia del ejército popular de la república*, 4 vols. (Madrid, 1974).

James W. Cortada

GIL ROBLES QUIÑONES DE LEÓN, JOSÉ MARÍA (1898-1980). Gil Robles was the leader of the "legalist" Right, most notably the *Confederación Española de Derechas Autónomas* (CEDA),* during the Second Republic.* The son of a distinguished Carlist ideologue, he was born in Salamanca* and rejected a promising academic career during the early 1920s to become a journalist with the Catholic daily *El Debate.* After participating in the shortlived social-Catholic party, the *Partido Social Popular*, he passively accepted the dictatorship of Primo de Rivera and during 1930-1931 campaigned to save the monarchy. With the coming of the Republic in April 1931, however, he adopted the Vatican*-approved "accidentalist" line of accepting the new regime de facto without himself embracing republicanism. Associated first with *Acción Nacional* (renamed *Acción Popular*￼* in 1932), he was elected in June 1931 as agrarian deputy to the Constituent Cortes* for Salamanca and soon emerged as the "legalist" Right's almost effective politician in opposition to the reforming governments of 1931-1933.

As leader of the CEDA from March 1933, Gil Robles interpreted accidentalism as justifying the peaceful pursuit of power within the Republic in order to replace it with a regime based upon Catholic-corporatist principles. This tactic was attacked by the militant Right as implying acceptance of the Republic and by the Left as threatening fascism.* It enjoyed initial electoral and political success, crowned by the CEDA's entry into the government in October 1934—a development that precipitated the revolution of that month—

and Gil Robles' own appointment as minister of war in May 1935.

In the War Office Gil Robles, while strengthening right-wing elements in the army, shrank from directly encouraging a military coup. His confidence that the CEDA's political advance would continue and that its final electoral triumph would render military intervention unnecessary was nevertheless dashed with the Popular Front* victory in the elections of February 1936.* The CEDA, defeated, now began to disintegrate, leaving Gil Robles almost impotent politically. During the spring of 1936, he released CEDA funds to finance the civilian-military conspiracy that produced the rising of July 17-18. From the outset he embraced, and acted on behalf of, the Nationalist cause. With the Unification Decree of April 1937 he announced the official dissolution of the CEDA.

During the 1940s and 1950s, much of which time he spent in voluntary exile, Gil Robles was active in the cause of a monarchical restoration under Don Juan. From the early 1960s until the elections of 1977, he was one of the leaders of the Spanish Christian Democracy. He died in September 1980.

For further information, see José María Gil Robles, *Discursos politícos* (Madrid, 1971), *No fue posible la paz* (Barcelona, 1968), and *La monarquía por la que yo luche* (Madrid, 1976); Paul Preston, *The Coming of the Spanish Civil War* (London, 1978); and Richard A.H. Robinson, *The Origins of Franco's Spain* (Newton Abbot, 1970).

Martin Blinkhorn

GINER DE LOS RÍOS, BERNARDO (1888-1970). Giner was a professor of art history and of architectural history at the *Institución Libre de Enseñanza* at the start of the war. Prior to the Republic, he was probably best known for his role as municipal architect of Madrid.* He was elected to the Cortes* representing Málaga* in 1931 and Jaén* in 1936. In the Constituent Cortes he was a member of the intellectual Group in Service (an intellectual task force) to the Republic; he became a member of the Republican Union party* in 1934. First appointed to the cabinet in May 1936 as minister of commerce and the merchant marine,* he was the only person to hold cabinet office continually throughout the war. He deserves much of the credit for keeping the transportation network in Republican Spain in operational condition throughout the war.

After the war, Giner resumed his professional career as an architect, residing primarily in Mexico City. His major scholarly work, *50 Años de Arquitectura*

española (1955), was written during this time. As a prominent member of the exile community, he was also selected for a number of offices in the Republican government in exile. He died in Mexico City on August 24, 1970, at the age of eighty-two.

For further information, see José María García Escudero, *Historia política de las dos Españas*, 4 vols. (Madrid, 1976); Luis Romero, *El final de la guerra* (Barcelona, 1968); and Diego Sevilla Andres, *Historia politíca de la zona roja* (Madrid, 1954).

William J. Irwin

GIRAL Y PEREIRA, JOSÉ (1880-1962). Giral was prime minister of the Spanish Republic from July 19 to September 4, 1936. He started his adult life as a professor of chemistry, but like many other intellectuals* of his time, participated in the political life of the Second Republic.* A leading member of the Republican Left and close collaborator of President Manuel Azaña,* he had served in the cabinet as minister of the navy between 1931 and 1933, and again in 1936 before the rebellion. After the start of the Nationalist revolt, Azaña asked Giral to form a government of all-Republican party members. Giral did so, immediately agreed to arm the workers in Madrid* as a means of gaining rapid support for the fight against the Nationalists,* and telegraphed President Léon Blum* of France* for aid. Like Blum, Giral represented the ideals of the Popular Front* left-of center politics found in both Spain and France and thus hoped their bonds would result in assistance. Although initially willing to help Giral, the French changed their minds after the British persuaded Blum to be cautious.

Giral did not have the support of many socialists or anarchists,* for both groups thought him weak and not radical enough politically. Pressure mounted on Azaña to restructure the government. Finally, on September 4, Giral resigned, and Francisco Largo Caballero* formed a new cabinet in which Giral served merely as minister without portfolio. He in effect had been removed because he had not allowed more leftist politicians increased influence and because he attempted to discourage revolutionary terror and other extremist activities. He believed that militias* should not have the authority to do as they pleased; rather, he thought they should be part of an organized military program directed at resisting the rebellion. To make matters worse, he did not work well with Largo Caballero, often engaging in heated policy discussions with him.

On May 17, 1937, Juan Negrín,* socialist prime minister at that time and head of the Ministry of Finance, brought Giral into his cabinet as minister of foreign affairs. Now Giral hardly worried about attacks from either the anarchists or the socialists. The anarchists were destroyed as a political power in the May 1937 Riots,* while the communists were rapidly displacing the socialists as a key source of political power. While at times in conflict with the communists, Giral concentrated his efforts on obtaining aid from the USSR* and other countries hostile to the Nationalists. Toward the end of the Civil War, he also worked to protect the lives of escaping refugees* by asking the British and the French to carry off Republicans* from eastern Spain. While foreign minister, he reorganized the ministry which had deteriorated badly under the administration of Álvarez del Vayo.* Near the end of the fighting, Giral turned his attention to ending the war gracefully. By late January 1939, he knew the Republican population* had tired of battling and that the end was close at hand, despite Negrín's optimism. In the last few days of the Republic (March 1939), Negrín reorganized his cabinet, appointed Giral minister without portfolio, and soon after fled to France. He had made a similar appointment of Giral during 1938; yet, the minister continued his work in international affairs. By the end of March, this hard-working cabinet official had left Spain and had gone into exile.

For further information, see Manuel Azaña, *Obras completas*, 4 vols. (Mexico, 1966-1968); Burnett Bolloten, *The Spanish Revolution: The Left and the Struggle for Power During the Civil War* (Chapel Hill, N.C., 1979); and Hugh Thomas, *The Spanish Civil War* (New York, 1977).

James W. Cortada

GIRÓN DE VELASCO, JOSÉ ANTONIO (1911-   ). Girón de Velasco was a leader in the Falange* party throughout the Civil War. He was born in Herrera de Pisuerga in the province of Valencia* and before the war earned a living as a lawyer. He also had been active in the Falange. At the battle of the Guadarrama* in July-August 1936, Girón de Velasco participated as a member of a Falange military unit. On December 2, 1936, Franco* named him to his new National Council, an advisory group composed of representatives of various political factions on the Nationalist side. After 1939, he continued to serve Franco, most importantly as minister of labor from 1941 to 1957.

For further information, see Círculo de Amigos de la Historia, *Diccionario biográfico español contemporaneo* (Madrid, 1970), Vol. 2.

James W. Cortada

GODED LLOPIS, MANUEL (1882-1936). Goded was born in San Juan, Puerto Rico, and was educated at the Infantry Academy before graduating from the War College in 1902. Most of his career was spent in Morocco,* where his technical competence won him appointment as General Sanjurjo's* chief of staff during the Riff campaign. By 1927, he was a division general. In January 1930, he engaged in the constitutionalist conspiracy against the dictatorship that led to Primo de Rivera's resignation. Appointed undersecretary of war by General Damaso Berenguer, he continued to conspire with moderate Republicans* throughout 1930 and became the first Republican chief of the general staff in 1931. Nevertheless, by 1932 Goded was disenchanted with the Republic. A highly publicized confrontation with Colonel Julio Mangada* led to his dismissal in June, and shortly thereafter Goded joined the Sanjurjo conspiracy, although he did not actually revolt. In May 1935, Gil Robles* appointed Goded inspector general of the army, director-general of customs police,* and head of aviation. After the collapse of the government in December, Goded, a member of the Central *Junta* of the rightist *Unión Militar Española* (UME),* joined Mola's* conspiracy. As commander in Majorca,* Goded was slated to take charge of the forces marching on Madrid* from Valencia.* But at the last minute, he asked Mola to post him to Barcelona.* After securing Majorca for the Nationalists,* Goded flew on July 19 to Barcelona, where the uprising had already failed. After his surrender, Goded transmitted a controversial radio* message releasing his followers from their commitment. He was tried and executed there on August 12, 1936.

For further information, see Manuel Goded Llopis, *Un "faccioso" cien por cien* (Saragossa, 1938); and *Marruecos: las etapas de la pacificación* (Madrid, 1932). *See also* Catalonia.

Carolyn P. Boyd

GOICOECHEA Y COSCULLUELA, ANTONIO (1876-1953). Goicoechea was one of the supporters of the orthodox monarchy, first president of the *Acción Nacional* in 1931, and founder of *Renovación Española** in March 1933. Therefore, he was affiliated with a variety of right-wing groups in Spain for a long time.

Prior to World War I, Goicoechea was a follower of Antonio Maura, the old conservative leader who advocated regeneration and revolution from above, and in 1919 he served as conservative minister of the interior. Although always a supporter of Alfonso XIII,* Goicoechea (and those around him) often vascillated on the subject of the Spanish monarchy, support for parliamentary institutions, and use of force. As a result, he was able to develop liaisons with the whole spectrum of the political and military Right in Spain. In 1931, he became first president of *Acción Nacional*, a conservative constitutional Catholic movement with monarchist sympathies and, in 1932 he was involved in General José Sanjurjo's* plot against the government. In March 1933, Goicoechea broke with *Acción Nacional*, largely because he disagreed with their policy of "accidentalism" which implied obedience to the established government. He then founded *Renovación Española* which was described as Catholic, monarchist, legalist, and constitutionalist, but had as basic goals resistance to Manuel Azaña,* overthrow of the Republic, and reestablishment of the authoritarian monarchy. Never a mass party, *Renovación Española* had some middle-class support from Madrid* and from members of the aristocracy who remained loyal to the exiled Alfonso.

In 1934, Goicoechea led the monarchists in the Cortes* and consistently attempted to weaken and discredit the Azaña government. In March of that year, he and other leaders of the Right traveled to Italy* where they signed an agreement with Marshal Italo Balbo wherein Italy promised to provide money and arms to be divided among the leaders of the Spanish Right for the purpose of restoring the monarchy. At the same time, Goicoechea channeled some money to Ledesma Ramos* and the *Juntas de Ofensiva Nacional-Sindicalista* (JONS).* Though somewhat suspicious of the Falange* because it would not endorse the Bourbon monarchy, he also became a friend of José Antonio Primo de Rivera.* Their cooperation resulted in the signing of a seven-point pact on August 20, 1934, which established that the Falange would not attack in propaganda or hinder the activities of *Renovación Española* which in turn would provide financial aid to the Falange. Associated with Calvo Sotelo's* National Bloc in the Cortes, after Calvo Sotelo's death on July 13, 1936, Goicoechea swore revenge and shortly thereafter left Madrid for the safer environment of Burgos.*

In Burgos, Goicoechea worked with General Mola, encouraging him to create a *Junta de Defensa*,* and then on July 25 he again traveled to Italy to obtain support from Mussolini* for the Nationalists.* In the spring of 1937, in the midst of the controversies surrounding leadership of the Right, Goicoechea on March 8 announced the dissolution of the *Renovación Española*, and petitioned for unification of all parties. He ceased to be a major political force, but he always hoped to be appointed to Franco's* cabinets. He was named a commissioner of the *Banca Oficial*, and in 1943 a member of the *Comisión de Justicia*, but by

that point he had few followers and little impact on national affairs.

For further information, see William Askew, "Italian Intervention in Spain: Agreement with Monarchist Parties," *Journal of Modern History* 24 (June 1952): 181-88; Santiago Galindo Herrera, *Los partidos monarquicos bajo la segunda república* (Madrid, 1956); José Gutiérrez-Rave Montero, *Antonio Goicoechea* (n.p., 1965); and Richard Robinson, "La República y los partidos de la derecha," in R. Carr, ed., *Estudios sobre la Republica y la Guerra Civil española* (Barcelona, 1973).

Jane Slaughter

GOMÁ Y TOMÁS, CARDINAL ISIDRO (1869-1940). Gomá, archbishop of Toledo* and primate of Spain during the Civil War, was the leading spokesman for the Catholic Church* in its support of the Nationalists.* Born in La Riba, Tarragona,* on August 19, 1869, Gomá was the son of a middle-class paper manufacturer. He entered the seminary and was ordained a priest in 1895. He then earned doctorates in theology and philosophy from the universities of Valencia and Tarragona. He was appointed rector of the Seminary of the Archdiocese of Tarragona, a position he held more than twenty years.

In 1927, Gomá began his episcopal career when he was named bishop of Tarazona and was consecrated by his later opponent, Cardinal Francesc Vidal i Barraquer.* By this time, he had developed a florid preaching and writing style along with moderate political views, a discerning position considering that he was a Catalan in a Catalan diocese during Primo de Rivera's dictatorship. Presumably, this political moderation, together with his solidly academic theological abilities, prompted his nomination as archbishop of Toledo and primate of Spain in 1933 as successor to Cardinal Pedro Segura* who had resigned under both government and Vatican* pressure in 1931. In 1935, Gomá was made a cardinal.

Gomá suffered from a kidney ailment and was in Pamplona* taking the cure when the Nationalist uprising began in 1936. Although a political moderate when the war began, he quickly came to support the Nationalists. This position was prompted by the Republicans'* persecution of the clergy during the anticlerical fury of the early months of the war (over half of the priests in his archdiocese were killed), and by the Nationalists' guarantee of clerical rights and privileges. Gomá was also a realist who was aware of the strength of the Nationalist forces, and he saw that by supporting Franco* he could win concessions for the Church. His position became the Vatican's as well.

Gomá was appointed confidential and official representative of the Holy See to the Nationalist government in December 1936, a post he held until October 1937 when the Vatican sent a *chargé* to the Burgos* government. It was during this first year of the war that he faced the Church's most controversial problems: the Basques and the Bishops' Collective Letter.

The Basques, a solidly Catholic people, continued to support the Republic after the Nationalist uprising, chiefly because the Republic granted them their long-sought separatist goal. Gomá wanted to avoid divisiveness among Catholics, and perhaps he foresaw the great enmity which the Nationalists would feel for the Basques for not coming to their aid. He therefore urged the bishops of the Basque provinces to counsel their faithful to withdraw support from the Republicans, even to the extent of writing a pastoral letter for them and having it broadcast by radio.* The two bishops involved, Bishop Olaechea* of Pamplona* and Bishop Múgica* of Vitoria,* after some initial criticism of Gomá's method and views, supported him, but the Basque people and leaders refused, especially after the Nationalists executed some sixteen Basque priests. The Basque president, Jośe Antonio de Aguirre,* wrote an open letter to Gomá criticizing his support of the Nationalists, and Gomá then intervened with Franco to stop further executions. The Nationalists also put pressure on Bishop Múgica after he refused to order Gomá's pastoral letter read from the pulpits of his diocese, and Gomá arranged to have Múgica resign his see and go into exile in Rome.

By early 1937, Gomá felt it necessary for the Spanish bishops to make a collective demonstration of support for the Nationalist government, especially to counter what he considered the hostile views being spread abroad. He therefore wrote the Spanish Bishops' Collective Letter addressed to Catholic bishops throughout the world, detailing the reasons why the Nationalists deserved their support. The letter condemned Republican anticlerical legislation and the government's condoning of anticlerical violence during the prewar years, most particularly during the anticlerical fury of 1936. It alleged a Soviet plot to take over Spain and gratefully acknowledged Nationalist protection of the Church and clergy in the midst of continuing Republican persecution. Gomá arranged to have all of the bishops sign the letter: only Bishop Múgica and Cardinal Vidal, both in exile, refused.

For the remainder of the war, Gomá gave complete support to the Nationalists and worked with the Holy See on negotiations for a concordat with the Burgos government. He led the clergy in hailing Franco's victory. He died in Toledo on August 22, 1940. A year later an accord between the Vatican and the Spanish government was signed.

For further information, see Anastasio Granados, *El cardenal Gomá, primado de España* (Madrid, 1969); Juan de Iturralde, *El catolicismo y la cruzada de Franco* (Vienne, 1955, 1960); and María Luisa Rodríguez, *El cardenal Gomá y la guerra de España. Aspectos de la gestión pública del Primado 1936-1939* (Madrid, 1981).

See also Basque Nationalism.

José M. Sánchez

"GÓMEZ" (WILHELM ZAISSER) (1893-1958). Wilhelm Zaisser, better known as General "Gómez," was a German communist who commanded the 13th International Brigade fighting for the Spanish Republic. He had been a veteran of World War I and an exile in the USSR* from Nazi Germany* before volunteering to fight in Spain. He commanded troops in the campaigns in and around Madrid* in 1937. In 1938, he took charge of the military base at Albacete* which was the headquarters of the International Brigades.* He replaced Vital Gaymann who had been accused of embezzlement and who had run off to Paris under mysterious circumstances. Zaisser's appointment intensified disagreements between the Germans and the French at this base, resulting in increased disillusionment within the ranks at a time when the military was having difficulty recruiting more men for the Internationals. Zaisser later fought in World War II and served as minister of state security in the East German government for five years prior to his removal from office in 1953.

For further information, see Andreu Castells, *Las brigadas internacionales de la guerra de España* (Barcelona, 1974).

James W. Cortada

GÓMEZ CAMINERO, JUAN (GARCÍA) (1871-1937). Gómez Caminero was a career army officer. During the early days of the Republic, he reached the rank of general and served as the military governor of Málaga.* During the Civil War, he sided with the Nationalists,* commanding troops until his death in 1937 by natural causes.

For further information, see Hugh Thomas, *The Spanish Civil War* (New York, 1977).

James W. Cortada

GÓMEZ-JORDANA Y SOUZA, FRANCISCO (COUNT OF JORDANA) (1876-1944). Gómez-Jordana, the son of a high commissioner in Morocco,* was a staff officer who was promoted rapidly while serving in Africa. Promoted to brigadier general in 1922, he was named to the Military Directory in September 1923 by General Primo de Rivera, who also gave him his title and appointed him high commissioner in Morocco in 1928. An officer of the old school with ties to the Palace and the aristocracy, Gómez-Jordana was relieved of his post, arrested, and ultimately stripped of his political rights by the Republicans* as punishment for his collaboration with the dictatorship. He retired from the army and eventually joined the *Unión Militar Española* (UME),* a right-wing officers' group.

After the outbreak of the Civil War, Gómez-Jordana organized the High Court of Military Justice in the Nationalist zone. In June 1937, he was appointed president of General Franco's* provisional government, or *Junta Técnica,* in Burgos,* and in December he was named to the newly created National Council. In Franco's first regular government of January 30, 1938, he was vice-president and foreign minister. In this capacity, Gómez-Jordana's aristocratic bearing, diplomatic tact, and administrative ability were assets. But as an Anglophile and a monarchist, he did not suit the needs of the Franco regime on the eve of World War II. Although he successfully negotiated a five-year treaty with Germany* in March 1939, in August he was replaced by Colonel Juan Beigbeder* as foreign minister. In compensation, Franco appointed him president of the Council of State. In September 1942, Gómez-Jordana returned to the Foreign Ministry as part of a maneuver to reduce Falangist influence within the regime. He remained at his post until his death in a hunting accident in 1944 at San Sebastián.

For further information, see Stanley G. Payne, *Politics and the Military in Modern Spain* (Stanford, Calif., 1967); Tomás Prieto, *Soldados de España: datos para la historia* (Madrid, 1946); and Teresa Suero Roca, *Los generales de Franco* (Barcelona, 1975).

See also, Serrano Suñer, Ramón.

Carolyn P. Boyd

GONZÁLEZ, VALENTÍN. *See* Campesino, El (Valentín González).

GONZÁLEZ CARRASCO, MANUEL (1877-   ). González Carrasco, commissioned in the infantry in 1894, served nearly continuously in Morocco.* After 1919, he attracted national attention as the courageous leader of the *Regulares de Larache*. As a monarchist and prominent *africanista,* González Carrasco was distrusted by the Republicans,* who put him on the reserve list in 1931. In the spring of 1936, he joined General Mola's* conspiracy and was initially slated to lead the rebellion in Barcelona.* Replaced at the last minute by General Goded,* González Carrasco was sent instead to Valencia,* where he failed to act decisively, thus allowing forces loyal to the Republic to seize the initiative. González Carrasco was able to escape to North Africa and later returned to the Nationalist zone.

For further information, see Ricardo de la Cierva, *Historia ilustrada de la guerra civil española* (Barcelona, 1970); and Hugh Thomas, *The Spanish Civil War* (New York, 1977).

Carolyn P. Boyd

GONZÁLEZ DE LARA, GONZALO (1874-1940 [?]). González de Lara was a career army officer. At the start of the Civil War, the Republic suspected him of conspiring with the Nationalists* and thus relieved him of his command in Guadalajara.* He nonetheless unfurled the banner of revolt and resisted militia invasions of his province. The Republicans* won and arrested him, but soon after the Nationalists were able to release him. He played no other significant role in the war.

For further information, see Hugh Thomas, *The Spanish Civil War* (New York, 1977).

James W. Cortada

GONZÁLEZ PEÑA, RAMÓN (-1952). González Peña, a Basque socialist politician, became one of the principal leaders of the Asturian miners' revolution against the government in 1934. This moderate socialist was tried and condemned to death, although his sentence was commuted in 1935. He then joined the Cortes* as the representative from Asturias* where he identified with the Prieto faction within the Socialist party. At the outbreak of the Civil War in July 1936, he sided with the Republicans,* going back to Asturias to run a local defense committee. He soon after became the commissar-general in the Army of the North* which spent all of its time fighting Nationalists* in Asturias. He also became an influential socialist leader within the Republican government. By 1938, González Peña had become president of the executive committee the *Unión General de Trabajadores* (UGT),* worked to engineer Largo Caballero's* faction out of power, and became minister of justice with responsibility for law and order. The result was more like summary justice if a defendant was suspected of being politically untrustworthy. In February-March 1939, he expressed his disappointment with Negrín's* leadership and flirted for a few days with the possibility of joining Casado's* coup against the Republican government, but in the end, he decided not to participate. Throughout most of the war, this socialist owed his rise in political influence primarily to Negrín with whom he sided in ousting Largo Caballero. He was not a strong-willed man, which probably explains why Negrín brought him into the cabinet as minister of justice and the interior.

For further information, see Gabriel Jackson, *The Spanish Republic and the Civil War, 1931-1939* (Princeton, N.J., 1965); and Hugh Thomas, *The Spanish Civil War* (New York, 1977).

See also Prieto, Indalecio.

James W. Cortada

GORDÓN ORDÁS, FÉLIX (-1973). Gordón Ordás was the Spanish Republic's ambassador to Mexico* during 1936 and 1937 and acted as a purchasing agent for arms for his government. He began adult life as a professor of veterinary medicine, was a Mason, and during the 1930s, served in the Cortes* as a Republican member of the Radical party. During the Civil War, his primary activity was to purchase arms where he could, particularly in the United States.* While ambassador to Mexico, he developed strong official support for the cause of the Republic and prevented recognition of Franco's* Nationalist regime.

For further information, see Gordón Ordás's own memoirs, *Mi política fuera de España*, 2 vols. (Mexico, 1965-1967).

See also Latin America.

James W. Cortada

GORIEV, VLADIMIR YEFIMOVICH (-1937). Goriev was military attaché at the Russian Embassy to the Second Republic* during 1936-1937. This general served as a key military adviser to the Republicans* and was considered to be intelligent, reserved, yet also passionate. Many historians have credited him with giving the necessary military advice required by the Republic to defend Madrid* from the Nationalists'* attacks in the early days of the war. Later, he advised Republican forces around Bilbao* and in Asturias.* His lack of effectiveness in these two last areas resulted in his recall and execution by the Russian government.

For further information, see José Luis Alcofar Nassaes, *Los asesores Soviéticos en la guerra civil española* (Barcelona, 1971).

See also Army, Republican; and USSR.

James W. Cortada

GRANADA. Granada, a province located in Andalusia* in southeastern Spain on the Mediterranean next to Málaga,* became a hotly contested area during the Civil War. In the first days of the revolt in July 1936, the city of Granada and a small area surrounding it came under Nationalist control, while the rest of the province remained Republican. In the provincial capital, Republican officials were arrested. A bloody fight in the worker district lasted several days, but it fell to the Nationalists.* Sympathizers with the rebellion sought to rid the city of Republicans* and launched a bitter repression that reflected pre-Civil War political rivalries in the city. Thousands were arrested and killed; possibly as many as 26,000 throughout the province ultimately died in the process. Many of these deaths were the result of the Nationalists' belief that the working classes had to be terrorized into submission. Therefore, in such cities as Granada and Seville,* which had large populations of politically militant workers, the casualty figures were high. Among the dead during July alone were many academicians and intellectuals* associated with the University of Granada, including the famed poet Federico García Lorca* who edited a local newspaper, *El Defensor de Granada*, a politically leftist publication. Others included officials, the town council, the mayor, and some 2,000 or more people in the city alone.

In August, the Nationalists established communications between isolated Granada and other Andalusian cities held by Franco* such as Seville, Córdoba,* Cádiz,* and Algeciras. This effort caused some rural portions of southwestern Granada to fall to the Nationalists. By March 1937, nearly half the province was under the Nationalists along with the bulk of Andalusia. Thus, all of the province west of Granada city remained Nationalist, while the eastern portion did not fall to Franco until the last days of the war as a byproduct of liquidating the southern Republican zone in March 1939.

For further information, see Manuel Aznar, *Historia militar de la guerra de España, 1936-1939* (Madrid, 1940); Ian Gibson, *The Assassination of Federico García Lorca* (London, 1979); and José Manuel Martínez Bande, *La compaña en Andalucía* (Madrid, 1969).

See also Terrorism; and Appendix B.

James W. Cortada

GRANDI, DINO (1895-1960s [?]. Count Grandi was Italy's* ambassador to London during the Spanish Civil War. In this capacity, he represented Mussolini* in the Non-Intervention Committee* as well. Grandi constantly protected Rome's interests; he argued and manipulated within the committee to defend Italian actions in Spain and to compromise those of the Spanish Republic in international affairs. He supported the Italian policy of military intervention in Spain, hoping for the establishment of a Spanish government that would join with Italy in expanding Rome's influence in the western Mediterranean. By 1937, he was advocating granting belligerency status to both Spanish factions as a means of gaining partial diplomatic recognition by European governments of the Nationalists'* regime at Burgos.* After the war, Grandi continued to serve in the Italian government and in 1944 helped to undermine Mussolini's power. Thereafter, he went into business and lived out the rest of his life in Mexico.

For further information, see Dante Puzzo, *Spain and the Great Powers, 1936-1941* (New York, 1962); and Arnold J. Toynbee, *Survey of International Affairs, 1937*, Vol. 2: *The International Repercussions of the War in Spain, 1936-1937* (Oxford, 1938).

See also Belligerent Rights.

James W. Cortada

GREAT BRITAIN. Great Britain's fear that the Spanish Civil War might lead to a general European war initially led Britain to adopt a unilateral policy of nonintervention in Spain. While in retrospect Britain's adoption of nonintervention can also be rationalized on the grounds of tardy rearmament, pacifism of the electorate, and lack of strong support from either France* or the Dominions, in fact minimal discussion took place on the question of Spain before the parliamentary summer recess and the British government drifted into nonintervention without fully considering the issues involved. When it became necessary to adopt a definite attitude, nonintervention seemed the best way to prevent intervention in Spain by the French government which might have precipitated France, too, into civil war. This reflected the very real, almost obsessive fear of communism that prevailed in British government circles and that contributed to undisguised hopes that the rebel forces in Spain would win.

The first reaction of the British was therefore not to become involved, but this stance proved impossible once it became clear at the end of July that both Italy* and Germany* were assisting the military rebels. The French Popular Front government under Léon Blum,* always sympathetic to the Spanish Popular Front* government, wanted to and did from the start respond to the latter's call for aid. Knowledge that fascist arms were reaching the rebels made it almost impossible for Blum not to continue to do so unless an international agreement that would satisfy the French electorate as a whole could prevent all arms shipments to Spain. With this consideration in mind during the parliamentary recess the British Foreign Office came to support the idea of a multilateral nonintervention agreement proposed to them by the French. Without British support, this venture would have failed. Although details of the affair may never be fully revealed, some exchanges between the Foreign Office and the Quai d'Orsay in the first half of August do suggest that Britain played a more important role in steering the French government towards the final Non-Intervention Agreement than was admitted at the time.

The Non-Intervention Agreement was a collection of accords which twenty-seven countries eventually signed. To give it some semblance of authority, a committee was convened in London, staffed by a secretariat drawn from the Foreign Office and normally chaired by Lord Plymouth, parliamentary under secretary of state at the Foreign Office. The function of the Non-Intervention Committee was to hear evidence of infringements of the agreement, although it had no power to take any actions. The major work of the committee was performed by a chairman's subcommittee formed of representatives of major European powers, plus those of bordering or arms-producing countries. Eventually, other technical subcommittees were set up to work out a variety of schemes to control the entry of both arms and volunteers* into Spain. None had any degree of success. Britain, like most countries, used or tightened up existing legislation, for example, in the Merchant Shipping (Carriage of Munitions to Spain) Act, December 1936, and in an announcement of January 9, 1937, that the Foreign Enlistment Act of 1870 would be invoked to control the exodus of volunteers to Spain. Neither measure achieved its purpose.

Almost from the beginning it was clear that the Non-Intervention Committee* was no more than a public relations exercise. By the time Parliament reassembled in the autumn, the government was forced to face the pressing problems created by the Spanish conflict. The first was the necessity of finding some formula by which, acting within the limits of international law, it would be possible to continue to recognize the Republican government of Spain while not causing offense to the military rebels. This became official policy in line with a report made by the chiefs of staff at the end of August which suggested that Britain should maintain if possible: "i. the territorial integrity of Spain and her possessions; and ii. such relations with any Spanish Government which may emerge from this conflict as will ensure benovolent neutrality in the event of our being engaged in a European war." The British government performed this balancing act by retaining Sir Henry Chilton,* the ambassador to Spain, although he was moved to the safety of Hendaye just over the French border, and later at the end of 1937 by sending a commercial agent, Sir Robert Hodgson, to the Nationalists* at Burgos.* Although Hodgson carried neither official status nor diplomatic privileges, he was in fact accorded full diplomatic privileges by the Nationalist government and his appointment amounted to de facto recognition. The question of whether or not officially to recognize the Nationalists or to award some degree of official recognition such as belligerent rights* was constantly under review.

On the other hand, economic factors, while important, were less problematical than might be supposed. Naturally, British trade, representing 40 percent of all Spanish trade, was bound to suffer from the prevailing war conditions, but trade with Spain had already begun a comparative decline before the Civil War commenced. Even the disruption in the export of iron ores from Spain to Britain does not seem to have caused much governmental concern, mainly because large amounts of iron ore had been stockpiled so that there was never any danger of shortage. Slightly more serious was the question of imports of pyrites, an ore of special use in the chemical industries, but reassurances from Franco* as to the continued export to Britain of her quota of ores seems to have been accepted. Parliament expressed some concern over the supply of ore from the mercury mines at Almadén, but again no real difficulty appears to have occurred. Compared with the very grave international crisis which the war provoked, economic factors seem to have been of very little significance.

Far more grave for Britain were the almost intractable problems presented by the naval war being fought mainly in the form of blockades around the coast of Spain. Britain as a major sea power importing a high percentage of her basic needs via the Mediterranean could not afford any challenge to her long-established sea route whether from Spain, Italy, or Germany.* When the Spanish government issued its first blockade warning in September 1936, the British government was forced to examine, first, how best to deal with this challenge and, second, her own attitude to blockade as an instrument of war which she herself had used with sobering effect in World War I and

which she might well need to use again in the very near future. In fact, the Spanish government blockade was soon seen to present very little real threat, many of its officers having been imprisoned for mutiny and the ships themselves being in a very run-down condition. Franco's blockade was another matter, for although the Nationalists had at first secured very few of the navy's ships, with the aid of Italian submarines* and German surface support, Franco was able to mount a much more formidable blockade. On the whole, the British government, following strong pressure from the Admiralty, preferred not to challenge the blockade, although some attempt to do so was made in April 1937 as a sop to public opinion. This cautious attitude was prompted by the fact that ships flying the British flag, and therefore claiming British protection, were often only nominally British.

The image that this less than valiant attitude produced was temporarily lessened by the more vigorous stance Eden* was able to persuade the government to take in the late summer of 1937 following the extravagant attacks on shipping in the Mediterranean by the so-called unknown submarines generally recognized by all to be Italian. The Nyon Conference,* which was held in September to discuss this problem, was something of a success for Britain and France and resulted in the setting up of naval patrols to monitor shipping. Unfortunately, this effect was negated by Prime Minister Chamberlain's* increasing slighting of Eden, prompted by Chamberlain's sycophantic pursuit of rapprochement with Mussolini.* The deepening rift between the premier and his foreign secretary finally came to a head in February 1938 over the question of further concessions to be made to the Italians on the scheme for withdrawal of volunteers from Spain proposed by the Non-Intervention Committee. On the issue, Eden chose to resign, much to Mussolini's jubilation.

With the international tension caused by the Civil War still the most controversial and intractable problem facing him, Chamberlain promised the House of Commons that a settlement of the Spanish question was an essential feature of any agreement that might be arrived at with Italy. With the return to power of the Blum government in the spring of 1938, firmly opposed as it was to rapprochement with Italy, it appeared that Chamberlain's assurance would have to be fulfilled. The British government's worst fears were confirmed when it was learned that Blum had given serious consideration to a plan for direct military intervention in Spain, with the object of placing Catalonia* (at the Spanish government's invitation) under French protection. In fact, the French military opposed the scheme, but the incident caused sufficient alarm in Britain for the Foreign Office to contrive to bring about the fall of the Blum administration and to influence the selection of ministers in the new Daladier* government. Writing to the British Ambassador, Sir Eric Phipps, Sir Orme Sargent, assistant undersecretary of state, advised his colleague thus:

...you may very well properly be shocked at the suggestion that we, or rather you, should do anything which might embarrass or weaken a French Government, even if it be in the hopes that it will, as a result, be replaced by a government more adequate to the critical situation with which we are faced.

Considererable pressure did force Paul-Boncour, the strongly Italophobe minister of the Blum government, out of the Quai d'Orsay.

Meanwhile, the Nationalist bombardment of Spanish government ports and ships of many nationalities was intensified, and Chamberlain himself faced what he himself described as the most savage House he had ever encountered. Undeterred, he told his cabinet that he intended to inform Franco

that if he must bomb the Spanish Government ports he must use discretion and that otherwise he might arouse a feeling in this country which would force the Government to take action. Such a situation was by no means beyond the bounds of possibility if the sinkings were to reach, say, one ship a day.

Despite such opposition, the Republic held out. Field Marshal Sir Philip Chetwode, head of an international commission sent to Spain to arrange an exchange of prisoners,* paid the following tribute to the now starving Republicans*: "big men there are, really big men with brains and the fight they have put up against Franco, helped as he is by the Italians and Germans is little short of marvellous." Indeed, observers now thought that the Republic could hold the situation and that Franco's advance, much to the exasperation of his German and Italian allies, had lost much of its force. In September, in a desperate effort to consolidate its tenuous position and to impress the British and French, the Republic announced the withdrawal of volunteers, an exercise that continued over the next few months. With a contracting frontline, the need was for arms rather than for men who required to be fed. The Italians, too, not to be outdone, withdrew 10,000 troops. This was roughly one-quarter of their forces in Spain, but mostly those who were wounded or less technically able.

With the Munich crisis in September, it became very clear that, as one Foreign Office official put it: "The powers who did not fight over Czechoslovakia*

would be most unlikely to do so over Spain." In desperation, the Republic threatened to attack Italy, while Franco cannily secured Nationalist Spain's future position by assuring the British government of his intention to remain neutral in the event of a second world war. This made it easier for Chamberlain to push forward with the Anglo-Italian Mediterranean Pact* and to ignore an appeal in October from Negrín, the Republican president, for arms.

Oblivious of Mussolini's contemptuous attitude, Chamberlain ratified the Anglo-Italian Agreement. At the same time, the last major offensive of the Civil War was begun. Finally, military rebellion in Madrid* led by Colonel Casado* accelerated the end of the Republic. Casado falsely believed he could negotiate better terms with the Nationalists than the discredited government leaders, some of whom had fled to France. Rumor lingers that the abortive coup was supported or encouraged by the British secret service, but as all such information remains classified, this thesis is impossible to verify. It may have been mooted at one stage, but by the time the coup took place it would have been of little value to the British, who with the French had already recognized the Nationalists on February 27, 1939.

From January 1939, as criticism of Chamberlain's general foreign policy grew, the Foreign Office reexamined British policy towards Spain and acknowledged it to have been misconceived. By May 1939, with another European war looming, the strategic importance of Spain too late made an appropriate impression. The British government now found itself in a dilemma: having continually recognized the Republican government as the legitimate government of Spain throughout the war, while at the same time giving de facto recognition to Franco by appointing Sir Robert Hodgson as Agent, in the hope of remaining on good terms with whichever side would emerge victorious, Britain had in fact succeeded in alienating both parties. Moreover, the antagonism and distrust that British policy had engendered on the Nationalist side now became important, since Britain was left with no reliable ally in Spain. Since Franco's proclaimed aim had been to rid Spain of communism, if Britain opted for the USSR* as an ally, her chances of reconciliation with Franco would be very slim indeed. The strategic advantages of alliance with Spain as listed by the chiefs of staff were indeed formidable, although reluctantly it was agreed that Spain's warweariness meant that support of the Soviet Union was slightly preferable. It might be argued that a more positive and open policy in support of either one of the two parties in Spain would have left both Spain and Britain in a far stronger position in the testing time to come.

For further information, see Lord Avon, *The Eden Memoirs: Facing the Dictators* (London, 1954); Jill Edwards, *The British Government and the Spanish Civil War, 1936-1939* (London, 1979); Sir Robert Hodgson, *Spain Resurgent* (London, 1953); and K. W. Watkins, *Britain Divided, The Effect of the Spanish Civil War on British Public Opinion* (London, 1963).

See also Submarines, Foreign.

Jill Edwards

GREECE. The Spanish Civil War was a threat to Greece's maritime interests in the Mediterranean. Like most powers in Western Europe,* the Greek government sought to contain the fighting to the Iberian Peninsula and thus supported British and French efforts to form the Non-Intervention Committee* in 1936. The Greek merchant fleet soon began to suffer the same fate as other ships sailing in the western Mediterranean. Many vessels, bearing British names but registered in Greece, encountered difficulties when searched by the Nationalists.* When the Italian submarines* began their aggressive patrols of Spain during 1937, they did not hesitate to attack Greek ships. On August 7, 1937, for example, a Greek ship was attacked at a time when numerous assaults on foreign shipping were taking place. Greece participated in the Nyon Conference* held in September 1937 in order to reduce the danger to her fleet. Participation at Nyon was a continuation of earlier proposals made by Greece to the Non-Intervention Committee that the Mediterranean be patrolled for the safety of all international traffic.

For further information, see Peter Gretton, "The Nyon Conference—The Naval Aspect," *Economic Historical Review* 90 (January 1975): 103-12.

James W. Cortada

"GRIGOROVICH," (STERN?). Grigorovich, a Russian general, advised the army of the Spanish Republic. As chief Russian adviser, he influenced the development of the Republicans'* military strategy since he had supplies and pilots* under his control. He was heavily involved, for example, in the Republican military planning at the battle of Brunete* in July 1937 and later, between December 1937 and February 1938, at the battle of Teruel where he actively participated in commanding forces.

For further information, see David T. Cattell, *Communism and the Spanish Civil War* (Berkeley, Calif., 1955); and Ramón Salas Larrazábal, *Historia del ejército popular de la republica*, 4 vols. (Madrid, 1974).

See also Army, Republican; USSR; and Appendix B.

James W. Cortada

GUADALAJARA, BATTLE OF. The city of Guadalajara to the north and east of Madrid* on the highway to Saragossa,* though part of the uprising in July 1936, was retaken by militia units from Madrid shortly thereafter. It became one of the points of attack-defense in the continued fighting for Madrid and was the site of a major battle, March 8-23, 1937.

In mid-February 1937, while the Nationalists* were heavily engaged in an assault in the Jarama* area, Mussolini's* *Corpo di Truppe Volontarie* (CTV) had emerged successfully from their initial contest at Málaga.* The Italian commander Mario Roatta* proposed to Franco* that they carry out an attack toward Guadalajara, which together with the continued pressure in the Jarama would serve as a pincer movement resulting in the encirclement of Madrid. It had already been agreed that Italian forces were to operate independently and were to be involved only in quick offensive actions rather than in defensive measures. By February 17, the Nationalist troops were having trouble in the Jarama, and Franco agreed to the move on Guadalajara as a diversionary action. Although the Italian command assumed that the Nationalists would continue the offensive in other sectors of the Madrid front to correspond to their attack, this was not to be the case.

The attacking Nationalist Army* consisted of the 1st, 2d and 3d Italian Black Shirt* Divisions, and the Littorio Division,* with the Spanish Soría Division commanded by Moscardó.* In addition, there were two independent infantry regiments, several artillery corps, and a tank battalion, making up a force of some 50,000 men. The Italian units were well equipped and highly motorized compared with the Spanish units. The attack plan called for a three-pronged advance south from the area of Algora along the Saragossa road to Trijueque, Torija, and then Guadalajara. The 2d Division under General Giovanni Coppi* was in the center, Moscardó's Soría on the right, and Nuvolini's 3d Division on the left moving toward Brihuega. The 1st and Littorio Divisions were in reserve until the Republican counterattack.

At the time of the attack, the Republicans* had the 12th Division with 10,000 men in the area, but by

March 10 new forces were brought into the line. They consisted of Lister's* 11th Division accompanied by El Campesino's* Brigade and several international units, and Cipriano Mera's* 14th Division, along with the forces of the 12th International Brigade in which the Garibaldi Battalion* played a significant role. Total Republican forces numbered some 35,000.

The battle was characterized by a Nationalist advance to Trijueque and Brihuega, March 8-9, at which point the new Republican forces reached the area and took up defensive positions. The major fighting occurred in a small triangle of rough and wooded terrain marked by the points, Torija, Brihuega and 85 kilometers on the Saragossa highway. Extreme cold and heavy rain added to the difficulties both sides encountered.

The Republicans launched counterattacks on March 12-15 and again on March 18-22 in which they successfully broke through the left flank of the CTV and regained Brihuega and Trijueque. In several instances, particularly in the fighting around Brihuega, members of the CTV panicked and created disorder, and when General Silvio Rossi ordered the 1st Division's retreat, all other units were forced to do the same as their flanks would have been exposed. By March 23, the Italians had retreated to a line slightly to the south of their point of departure and were replaced by Spanish troops. The battle was over.

In a military sense, the Republicans could claim a minor victory, having eliminated another threat to Madrid, and the battle did mark the end of fighting in this area until Guadalajara fell to the Nationalists in March 1939. The Republicans lost 2,000 men, with 4,000 wounded in the battle. Nationalist losses were quite similar except that the CTV suffered major equipment losses as well (for example, twenty-five artillery pieces, ten mortars, and eighty-five machineguns).

More important were the psychological-moral effects and some long-range organizational changes. The victory over Mussolini's* "shock troops," particularly for international units such as the Garibaldi, was defeat of international fascism, and Guadalajara served as a major source of publicity and propaganda in the months that followed. The Italian command had completely underestimated Republican capabilities and motivations against their own relatively unmotivated troops. Franco had not pushed his offensive in the Jarama simultaneously with the CTV advance, and the result was a reevaluation of the relationship between Nationalist forces and those of the foreign power. After Guadalajara, the CTV was purged, and, on Franco's orders, the Italians did not operate independently again in the Civil War. For Mussolini the battle was an em-barrassment, as symbolized by the fact that he made no public statement about it until June 1937.

For further information, see Manuel Aznar, *Historia militar de la guerra de España* (Madrid, 1969), Vol. 2; Olao Conforti, *Guadalajara* (Milan, 1967); John Coverdale, *Italian Intervention in the Spanish Civil War* (Princeton, N.J., 1975); and *Guadalajara 1937 y otros* (Madrid, 1978).

Jane Slaughter

GUERNICA. The town of Guernica, with a wartime population* of 7,000 to 10,000 persons, situated some 30 kilometers east of Bilbao,* in the Basque province of Vizcaya,* was destroyed by fire on the afternoon of April 26, 1937, during the Spanish Civil War. The town held a deep mystical importance for the Basque people, who considered it to be the spiritual capital of their race. The inhabitants of the Basque provinces were generally believed to be the most Catholic people of Catholic Spain. The destruction of this town, primarily because of its military significance, but also because of several secondary circumstances (journalistic, religious and propagandistic, and artistic) remains one of the most discussed events of the war.

Militarily, the destruction of Guernica was important because the town was the first in the history of the world to have been entirely wiped out by aerial bombing. The importance of aircraft as a military weapon was underscored in a fearful manner, for the entire world to see. All of the journalistic writing that resulted, all of the propagandistic positions taken later, all of the religious polemics, and all of the artistic reactions came from the realization of the unspeakable menace of the weapon employed.

The military facts are as follows. Early on the afternoon of April 26, an Italian plane dropped bombs on the Rentería Bridge east of Guernica, causing little damage. Then, beginning around 4:30 P.M., the aerial bombardment of the town began. According to most accounts, Guernica was first struck by explosive bombs and then by incendiaries. As the population fled from the bombed houses, they were mercilessly machine-gunned by the fighter planes. The bombing ended with the night, leaving behind hundreds of dead and wounded.

The bombing was carried out by airplanes of the German Condor Legion,* a special force sent to Spain by Hitler* to help Franco* (probably with the secret hope of weakening France* in view of the coming struggle, and also to give battle experience to his aviators). The planes principally involved in the destruction were of three types: Heinkel 111s and Junkers 52s for bombing, and Heinkel 51s for pursuit and machine-gunning. Although from the first there was overwhelming proof that the raid had been carried out by aircraft on Franco's side, the Spanish Nationalists* denied this evidence for decades. Not until the 1970s did pro-Franco spokesmen begin grudgingly admitting that the raid had been carried out by the Condor Legion and adding at the same time that the Spanish military knew absolutely nothing of the planning or execution of the atrocity. However, in a 1970 book, the Spanish journalist Vicente Talón published the text of an official telegram from Franco's headquarters, dated May 7, 1937, which accepted full responsibility for having requested the attack. Although this telegram was hedged about with allegations of the accidental nature of the bombing of the town itself, and with claims of eventual "Red" incendiarism, the Franco military never disputed its authenticity. The military preferred to ignore its existence, and at the same time refused access to the archives of Franco's headquarters concerning what was done during the crucial dates of the Guernica bombing. Angel Viñas has done a masterful analysis of the combined responsibilities of the Franco (Mola*) command and the Condor Legion in the bombing of the town, using chiefly German sources.

Guernica was the most important news story of the Spanish Civil War, a war that in itself constituted the most significant journalistic event between World War I (and the Russian Revolution) and World War II. The Condor Legion and the Spanish Nationalist high command perpetrated the atrocity, but it can be affirmed with certainty that if there had not been four accredited foreign newsmen (three British, one Belgian) in Bilbao on the evening of April 26, there would never have been the Guernica story as we know it today, nor a Picasso* canvas called "Guernica." These four correspondents were George L. Steer, a South African, who was with *The Times*; Noel Monks, an Australian, who worked for the *Daily Express*; Christopher Holme, an Englishman, who reported for the English agency Reuters; and Mathieu Corman, a Belgian, who represented *Ce Soir*, a Parisian left-wing daily. These four men went to the burning town when they heard of the attack and cabled their messages in on the following day. The news broke in London in the afternoon newspapers of April 27, with texts based chiefly on the Reuters report. American news agency telegrams appeared on the front pages of American East Coast dailies on the same afternoon (even in late editions of some morning papers, for example, the *Chicago Tribune*). Steer's long message to *The Times* came out on the morning of April 28 (also in *The New York Times**), and the *Daily Express* printed Noel

Monks' version. All of the cablegrams from Bilbao said that the town had been set on fire by aerial bombs.

The importance given to the Guernica news story in the English and American press contrasted with the comparative silence of the French dailies. *Ce Soir* published Corman's telegram on the front page on April 27, but only one other afternoon daily mentioned the event. The official French news agency Havas waited until the morning of April 28 to send out a short, almost unintelligible, and badly edited report, ignored by the greater part of the newspapers. Many Parisian dailies were forced to repeat the news already printed in London. The result was that the newspaper coverage of the greatest journalistic story of the Spanish Civil War was never as complete in France as in Great Britain* and the United States,* nor were the reactions as swift and as emotional.

On Thursday, April 29, Franco's forces entered the still burning town of Guernica, and on Saturday the "Special Correspondent" of the Havas Agency with the Nationalist armies, Georges Botto, sent a long detailed account of the burning of the spiritual capital of the Basques: there was absolutely no sign of bombing in the town, but there were large craters caused by land mines; the town had been set on fire deliberately by the "Reds," and the smell of gasoline and kerosene persisted days after the acts of arson. However, this press telegram contained a few words in code which indicated to the Havas editors that the news in the message was false and had been sent under constraint. Despite this warning, the Havas Agency quickly forwarded the telegram to its subscribers throughout the world. This rapidity in transmission contrasted with the delay practiced by Havas in dealing with the first news of the bombing. A telegram of similar tenor was sent to *The New York Times* by its rabidly pro-Franco correspondent, William P. Carney, and the numerous Italian reporters with the Nationalist forces dispatched equally lying information to their editors. Why did the Havas editors use this false telegram? Apparently, the Quai d'Orsay, which through subventions controlled the news agency, feared that the truth about Guernica might offend Hitler and, through the force of public opinion, endanger the policy of nonintervention.

A counterforce in French public opinion was formed, through the same hazard that place the four foreign correspondents in Bilbao on April 26. The day of the bombardment, a Basque priest, Alberto de Onaindia, arrived at Guernica at the precise moment that the bombing began. He witnessed the air attack and, on returning to Bilbao the following morning, told the story of what he had seen to the Basque president,

José Antonio de Aguirre.* Onaindia had been acting as unofficial diplomatic agent in Paris of the Basque Republic for some months, and he was now sent back to Paris to give his testimony. His account appeared on April 30 in a slightly leftish, unofficial Catholic daily of limited readership, *L'Aube*. This newspaper, in presenting the recital of the Basque priest to the more liberal sectors of the French Catholic community, provoked a deep division in the ranks of Gallic Catholicism and ended by having a considerable influence on French thinking about the Spanish Civil War, despite the lying dispatches of the Havas Agency. The newspaper coverage of the destruction of Guernica is extremely complicated, but this short resumé contains the essential parts of the story.

It is impossible to separate the violent and seemingly never-ending polemic that has surrounded the destruction of Guernica—almost from the very hours of the bombing itself—from the propaganda work of the Roman Catholic Church concerning Guernica. The two actions—the polemical and Catholic actions—are therefore discussed together here. The polemic began around noon on April 27, when the first news of the English press reports was received in Salamanca.* The press chief of Franco's headquarters was a Spanish newspaperman named Luis Bolín Bidwell;* his mother was English, and he had spent a great deal of his life in England. During the years from 1931 to 1936, he reported from London for the Spanish monarchist daily *ABC*,* and he plotted with conservative English Catholics against the newly born Republic.

On learning of the English reaction to the news about Guernica, Bolín reacted, not as a military person indifferent to atrocities, but as an English Catholic, fearful of the reaction of English public opinion to the press reports from Bilbao. Bolín panicked and denied that an air raid had even taken place. If he had gruffly admitted that bombing and explained it away as a necessary military action (this would have been difficult, but perhaps it would have worked), he *might* have averted the political storm that followed all over the world. But Bolín denied a fact that had been witnessed by thousands of persons and thus provoked a propaganda battle that has not yet entirely died down.

To understand Bolín's decision to lie about the bombing in the face of so much evidence to the contrary, we must look at the position of the Church during the war in Spain. The Spanish Catholic Church* had adopted a stand favorable to the military rebellion from the beginning of the war, and almost immediately the Church all over the globe adopted this position. The revolt against the Spanish Republic was declared to be a "Christian Crusade," and the worldwide resources of the Catholic Church were used for pro-Franco propaganda. The pitiless violence employed by the Nationalist Army of Africa* in the massacre of the Spanish peasants during the march from Seville* to the gates of Madrid* was reflected in the daily newspaper reports of the nonfascist countries, and each day presented increasing difficulties for Church spokesmen. It was impossible to explain why the Church supported an attack against a legally elected government, or justified the murder of García Lorca,* the massacre of thousands of prisoners* in Badajoz,* and similar atrocities. Trapped by its longstanding tolerance for Italian fascism, the Church had reacted enthusiastically in favor of Franco, and, when confronted with the daily accounts of the bloody behavior of Franco's troops, it sought a way out by simply denying the newspaper reports. To put it baldly, Franco's clerical supporters all over the world had recourse to the lie.

When the news of the fire-bombing of Guernica hit the front pages of the nonfascist press of Western Europe* and the two American continents, the Church's spokesmen automatically followed Bolín's lead and denied the undeniable fact. In lying about an event witnessed by thousands of Basques, Spain's most fervent Catholics, the churchmen fell into the trap which they themselves had fabricated through their tolerance for fascism. They also unleashed the most fascinating propaganda battle of the century. The polemic was mainly one-sided and largely sustained by the defenders of the Nationalist military, who showed considerable ingenuity and imagination in inventing ever newer and more complicated explanations of the burning of the town. The accusations of the Basques and Spanish Republicans,* and their friends, against the Condor Legion and the Spanish generals were simpler, more coherent, and rarely varied.

The chief protagonists in the pro-Franco propaganda battle were English Catholic intellectuals,* retired military persons, and right-wing journalists; American Catholic priests and reactionary newspapermen; French journalists, intellectuals, retired diplomats, and military officers; Spanish American priests and conservative writers; and, in Spain itself, priests, military officers, and conservative journalists. The historian can make one general observation concerning their work: their ignorance of Spanish history and sociology were equaled only by the mediocrity of their language.

Only the artistic phase of the Guernica story is noncontroversial. Perhaps the masterpiece of twentieth-century painting is Picasso's "Guernica." The controversy concerning the bombing of the town was already deeply engaged before the exhibition of Picasso's painting. It was first shown on June 4, 1937, at the Spanish (Republican) pavillion of the Universal Exposition at Paris, accompanied with Paul Eluard's poem "La Victoire de Guernica." It is impossible to find in the tragic designs themselves material to feed the factual dispute. However, the picture and its title clearly suggested to its viewers that for Picasso the town had been set on fire and destroyed by aerial bombardment. The desolation of the scene and the fear evident in the faces of the men, women and children, and the animals, especially of the horse, leave an unspoken accusation in the thoughts of the millions who have meditated before the painting, in sober black and white and gray. When World War II broke out, Picasso left the picture in the hands of the Museum of Modern Art in New York City. Picasso's lawyer, Roland Dumas, now a French socialist deputy, announced in 1969 that the artist wanted the painting to be handed over to "the government of the Spanish Republic the day the Republic is restored in Spain." This condition has now been somewhat changed to become "the day democracy is restored in Spain." It was sent to the Prado Museum in Madrid in October 1981.

For further information, see Jean-Louis Ferrier, *Picasso's "Guernica"* (Paris, 1977); Klaus A. Maier, *Guernica, 26.4.1937. Die deutsche Intervention in Spanien und der "Fall Guernica"* (Freiburg, 1975); Herbert R. Southworth, *Guernica! Guernica! A Study of Journalism, Diplomacy, Propaganda and History* (Berkeley, Calif., 1977); Vicente Talóm, *Arde Guernica* (Madrid, 1970, 1973); Transcript of "Edward Lucie-Smith Talks to Dr. Herbert Southworth and Dominique Bozo on Picasso," in the program "Picasso—Creator or Destroyer," broadcast on BBC Radio 3, July 16, 1981; and Angel Viñas, "Guernica: Las responsabilidades," *Historia 16* (May 25, 1978): 127-43.

See also Basque Nationalism.

Herbert R. Southworth

GUIPÚZCOA. Guipúzcoa, one of the three Basque provinces located in northern Spain on the Bay of Biscay and the French frontier, sided with the Republic at the start of the Civil War. Like the other Basque provinces, Guipúzcoa supported efforts to establish a Basque republic which the government in Madrid* allowed, thereby gaining the support of this province for the war. The province was a strong Catholic* area and conservative. Basque nationalists were able to insure that the middle-class standard of living and political institutions would not be threatened, despite more radical forms of economic and political behavior evident in other Republican provinces. *Juntas de defensa* were established but were controlled by elements more conservative than the socialists and anarchists* who traditionally staffed such councils in other Republican zones. In July and August, the Nationalists* in northern Spain fought in the province in an attempt to seize the entire Basque country. Heavy fighting took place as they sought to cut off Basque communications with France.* They bombarded coastal towns, while pouring nearly 7,000 troops into the province. The Nationalists attacked Irún* on August 26, and it fell on September 3. Simultaneously, the rest of the province came under their control. As a result of this campaign, some 1,000 square miles of land became Nationalist territory with its rich farmlands, heavily populated districts, factories, and port towns. The capture of this province also cut off the Basques from france, depriving the Republic of a potential source of aid. The province never returned to Republican control.

For further information, see José Manuel Martínez Bande, *La guerra en el norte* (Madrid, 1969); M. Morales, *La guerra civil en Guipúzcoa, julio-agosto 1936* (Valladolid, 1937); and Stanley G. Payne, *Basque Nationalism* (Reno, Nev., 1975).

See also Basque Nationalism; and Appendix B.

James W. Cortada

H

HARO Y LUMBRERAS, GREGORIO DE. Haro, the civil governor of Huelva in 1936 and a career army officer, sided with the Nationalists.* In the seizure of Seville* in July 1936, this officer commanded the Civil Guards* helping the Nationalists to secure the area.

For further information, see Hugh Thomas, *The Spanish Civil War* (New York, 1977).

James W. Cortada

HAYA GONZÁLEZ, CARLOS DE (1902-1938). Haya González served in the Nationalist Air Force* flying fighter planes. The brilliant and effective pilot helped develop techniques for low flying air drops of supplies and flew dozens of combat missions against the Republicans.* Major Haya González also received considerable publicity during the Civil War as a Nationalist hero. He died in 1938 in an accident at an air show.

For further information, see Jesús Salas Larrazábal, *La guerra de España desde el aire* (Barcelona, 1969). *See also* Pilots.

James W. Cortada

HEDILLA, MANUEL (1902-1970). Hedilla was born in Santander* and became one of the key leaders of the Falange* party by the start of the Civil War. As the local head of the Falange in the province of Santander, he had proven to be an unimaginative leader. Nonetheless, he was an honest man who rejected acts of violence against political enemies. A one-time mechanic with little education,* he became, for all practical purposes, head of the party once José Antonio Primo de Rivera* was arrested by the Republicans* at the start of the war. He worked diligently to mold the Falange into a large national party once Franco* decided to use it as a vehicle to channel political activity within the Nationalist zone. The exigencies of war, however, made this task difficult, with the result that the party never gained sufficient strength to challenge the Caudillo's authority.

Hedilla had problems maintaining control over his party. In 1937, a considerable portion of the Falange leadership, feeling that he wanted to supplant Primo de Rivera's position, decided to remove him from power. Important leaders of this group included Agustín Aznar,* José Moreno,* and Sancho Dávila,* who concluded that Hedilla threatened their influence and was too "proletariat" in his views. Hedilla, for his part, commanded a large following within the rank and file, and most provincial chiefs in northern Spain still supported him. Although he allowed others to push him into the role of national leader, he often lacked tact and frequently sought intellectual inspiration for Falangism from the German fascist experience and less from internal Spanish needs and concerns. Most of his opponents favored a technocratic, authoritarian state without an elaborate political or philosophical base.

Citing an obscure party rule which stated that a triumvirate should rule in the absence of Primo de Rivera, opponents occupied the national offices of the party in Salamanca.* Hedilla himself only mildly protested this act, but pro-Hedilla elements began fighting with his enemies. On April 18, 1937, at a meeting of the Falange party's national council which he arranged for, Hedilla called for a vote of confidence. Of twenty-two possible voters, ten voted for him, four against, and the rest abstained. Franco* congratulated him on April 19 and declared that the Falange and the Carlists,* along with less important groups, would be united into one party called the *Falange Española Tradicionalista y de la JONS*, with Franco as its leader and serving as head of state and obvious commander of all the armed forces. This declaration, published without notifying Hedilla in advance, was clearly a surprise to him. Next, a new political secretariat was created in which Hedilla refused to serve. On April 25, officials arrested him, charging him, among other things, with having previously illegally arrested Dávila. Franco had other Falange leaders confined in an attempt to consolidate his control over the political movement. Soon after, Hedilla was charged with the murder of one of Dávila's bodyguards, found guilty, and condemned to death, but his sentence was commuted to a prison term which he served for four years. He had no further role in the Falange. Clearly, he had been removed by Franco who had felt Hedilla posed a threat to his total control over the affairs of state and over the political life of the Falange. Hedilla left prison in 1946 and spent the rest of his life in quiet privacy in Madrid.*

Hedilla was the symbolic leader of the "Old Shirts"* of the party and was remembered as such down through the years. As one of the earliest leaders of the Falange, he helped develop its early political philosophies. Pushed into national leadership by circumstance rather than by ambition, he was a victim of Franco's effort to consolidate control over all political parties in Nationalist Spain.

For further information, see Maximiniano García Venero, *Falange* (Paris, 1967), a biography; Manuel Hedilla, *Testimonio de Manuel Hedilla* (Barcelona, 1973); Stanley G. Payne, *Falange: A History of Spanish Fascism* (Stanford, Calif., 1961); and Herbert Southworth, *Antifalange* (Paris, 1967).

James W. Cortada

HEMINGWAY, ERNEST (1899-1961). Hemingway, an American novelist, grew up in the midwestern part of the United States.* During the 1920s and 1930s, he visited Spain often, learning its language, understanding Spanish society and politics, and writing about its culture. He remained aloof from political causes (although he despised fascism*) until the Civil War erupted, whereupon he sided with the Spanish Republicans.* He went to Spain in February 1937 as a journalist for the North American Newspaper Alliance reporting on the war, spending most of his time in or around Madrid* commenting on the local campaigns, and staying at the Hotel Florida which he made famous. Throughout the war he raised money for the Loyalists* while writing about their cause. Between April and May, he helped Dutch film maker Joris Ivens shoot *The Spanish Earth*, which depicted the cause of the Republic in and around Madrid and the fate of Spain's farmers, complete with actual scenes of combat. He also wrote a short play on the Civil War, *The Fifth Column*, which concentrated on the Republican cause. During 1937, he spent a great deal of time in the field, primarily with members of the International Brigades,* often writing about their activities. He returned briefly to the United States to deliver speeches on the war, visited President Roosevelt* to discuss Spain, and worked on the Ivens movie. He was soon back in Spain and finished his play in Madrid by December. The play portrayed living conditions in Madrid and thus complemented the work done on the movie and his articles. In March 1938 and again in September, he toured the Republican zone, concluding that the Nationalists* would soon win the Civil War.

From March 1939 to July 1940, he quietly wrote *For Whom the Bell Tolls* in the United States. This work, one of the major novels on the Civil War, deals with Republican partisans in the Sierra de Guadarrama* northwest of Madrid. The novel discusses the betrayal of the Spanish people by foreigners, their own lack of cohesive national politics, the forces of individualism, and the negative results of war. Robert Jordan, one of the major protagonists in the novel, is the vehicle for identifying multiple currents of thought and behavior in Spain during 1937 when the war, while going poorly for the Republicans, was not yet lost.

For further information, see Carlos Baker, *Hemingway: The Writer As an Artist* (Princeton, N.J., 1952); Frederick R. Benson, *Writers in Arms: The Literary Impact of the Spanish Civil War* (New York, 1967); and Ernest Hemingway, *For Whom the Bell Tolls* (New York, 1940), *The Fifth Column* (New York, 1938) and *The Spanish Earth* (Cleveland, 1938).

See also Intellectuals; and Literature.

James W. Cortada

HERNÁNDEZ, MIGUEL (1910-1942). Hernández, a communist poet, fought in the Fifth Regiment* during the Civil War. A representative of a large left-wing literary community that felt it was fighting for freedom in Spain, he wrote considerable amounts of poetry on this theme. Ironically, his father-in-law, a Civil Guard,* had been shot by anarchists* in 1936. This well-known poet was finally arrested by the Nationalists* and died in a jail in Alicante.*

For further information, see Claude Couffon, *Miguel Hernández et Orihuela* (Paris, 1963).
See also Intellectuals; and Literature.

James W. Cortada

HERNÁNDEZ SARAVIA, JUAN (1880-1974). Hernández Saravia, born at Ledesma (Salamanca),* was an artillerist. He was attracted to republicanism during the conflicts between his corps and General Primo de Rivera in the 1920s. In 1931, as head of Manuel Azaña's* military cabinet, he helped formulate the Republicans'* military policy. After the October 1934 revolution, Hernández Saravia retired from active service, returning only after the Popular Front* victory of 1936 to become the personal secretary of the prime minister, Casares Quiroga.* After July 18, he was the real power in the War Ministry and was appointed minister on August 6. In January, now a colonel, he was appointed to the committee in charge of the recruitment and training of volunteers.* In December 1937, he was promoted to general and given the command of the Army of the Levante* during the Teruel* offensive. In April 1938, he was made head of the Group of Armies in the Eastern Region, commanding 300,000 men in the battle of the Ebro.* Negrín* dismissed him for favoring a "defeatist" policy in February 1939. After the war, he lived in exile in France* and died in Mexico.*

For further information, see Manuel Azaña Díaz, *Memorias políticas y de guerra*, 2 vols. (Barcelona, 1978); Antonio Cordón, *Trayectoria: memorias de un militar republicano* (Barcelona, 1977); and Ramón Salas Larrazábal, *Historia del ejército popular de la República*, 4 vols. (Madrid, 1973).

See also Army, Republican.

Carolyn P. Boyd

HERNÁNDEZ TOMÁS, JESÚS (1906-1966?). Hernández Tomás, one of two communists to enter the government of Francisco Largo Caballero* in September 1936, served until April 1938 in the Ministry of Public Instruction. A reorganization of the military in the spring of 1938 resulted in the appointment of a number of communists, including Hernández Tomás as head of the war commissars in first the central and then the central-southern zone.

Hernández Tomás, a communist since his youth, had formed part of the Spanish Communist party* hierarchy during the Second Republic.* As a youth he had proven his loyalty to the party through such acts as plotting to assassinate the socialist leader Indalecio Prieto*—an attempt that failed. He served the party as editor of the communist newspaper *Mundo Obrero* at the outset of the Civil War, but soon after entered the government to work tirelessly for communist objectives. He was a strong advocate of a regular army to replace the anarchist militias,* a move that he knew would bring the military under the sway of communists. He also helped precipitate the collapse of the Largo Caballero government in mid-May 1937 by forcing Largo Caballero to resign in the face of threats of a cutoff of communist aid. Largo Caballero had balked at supporting Hernández Tomás's demand that the rival *Partido Obrero de Unificación Marxista* (POUM)* be outlawed following the May riots* in Barcelona.* One of the few actions that has not been subject to controversy was his interest in literacy campaigns while minister of education.

Hernández Tomás became disillusioned with communism while living in the USSR* after the Civil War

and was dismissed from his position as a member of the executive committee of the Comintern. He recounted the duplicity of Russian and communist participation in the Civil War in several books, including *Yo fui un ministro de Stalín*, which appeared in Spain twenty years after its release in Mexico* in 1953. He alleged that Spanish communists received all their orders from Moscow; that communists manipulated the Republican government to further their own sectarian ends, including forcing out Largo Caballero in favor of Negrín* and replacing Prieto as minister of war; and that Stalin* had little real interest in Spain but was merely playing it off against Germany* while he awaited developments in Europe.*

For further information, see Jesús Hernández Tomás, *Yo fui un ministro de Stalin* (Madrid, 1974).

David V. Holtby

HERRERA ÓRIA, ANGEL (1886-1968). Herrera, editor of *El Debate*,* was the chief formulator of the Catholic accidentalist position during the Second Republic.* Born in Santander* on December 19, 1886, into a middle-class, pious Catholic family (his three brothers became Jesuits), he took a law degree from Salamanca* and then went into journalism. In 1911, he became an editor of *El Debate*.

Herrera was imbued with the ideas of social Catholicism as propounded in the teachings of Pope Leo XIII. He believed that one reason for the de-Christianization of the masses, that phenomenon of nineteenth- and twentieth-century Europe,* was the lack of a proper response by the clergy and Catholic leaders to workers' needs. He believed that Catholics should organize to combat increasing secularization and anti-Catholicism. Thus, Herrera supported efforts to establish a major publishing house, *La Editorial Católica*, and to organize *Acción Católica* (a clerically dominated organization of the laity), and he helped found an organization for newspapermen, the *Asociación Católica Nacional de Propagandistas*. In 1922, he helped establish a political party, the *Partido Social Popular*, a moderate Left Catholic party on the model of Luigi Sturzo's Italian *Partito Popolare*, but the explosive political situation that resulted in Primo de Rivera's coup of 1923 ended these political efforts.

With the proclamation of the Republic in 1931, Herrera became a major political power among Catholics. By that time, *El Debate* had become one of the largest Madrid* dailies with a modern printing plant and news-gathering service. With Herrera as editor, it became the voice of Catholic accommodation with the anticlerical Republic. In a number of editorials before and after the April 1931 municipal elections and the June 1931 Constituent Cortes* elections, Herrera supported the accidentalist position. He argued that the form of government was not important as the substance, direction, or actions of government. Therefore, Catholics should accept the Republic and work within the framework of legality to ensure that the Church's rights were respected. He rejected the monarchist contention that church and monarchy were consubstantial.

This accidentalist position was also that counseled by the Vatican* and supported by the progressives within the Church, especially Cardinal Francesc Vidal i Barraquer* and the papal *nuncio*, Monsignor Federico Tedeschini, with whom Herrera worked closely. Shortly after the Republic was proclaimed, Herrera announced the formation of a new political party, *Acción Nacional* (later changed to *Acción Popular**), which would appeal to Catholics and which would endorse accidentalism so that Catholics could put aside their differences and work together in defense of "Religion, Country, Order, Family and Property." He purposely avoided any mention of form of government so that Republicans* as well as monarchists could support the party.

From the beginning, Herrera's position was attacked by the monarchists, and when he ran for a seat in the Constituent Cortes in June 1931, he was defeated. Thereafter he worked at organizing *Acción Popular* for the next two years, while the party's leadership was taken over by José María Gil Robles.* In November 1933, the *Confederación Española de Derechas Autónomas* (CEDA),* a confederation dominated by *Acción Popular*, won a plurality in the Cortes elections. Herrera resigned his position on *El Debate*, took over the presidency of *Acción Católica*, and reportedly became the *éminence grise* behind Gil Robles and the CEDA. Little is known of his political activity during this period, but there seems to be no doubt that he was one of Gil Robles' most important advisers, as well as an effective supporter of the Vatican's policy of moderation.

After the Popular Front's* victory in the elections of February 1936,* Herrera decided to give up political activity, and he entered the seminary in Fribourg, Switzerland. He spent the Civil War years there, was ordained a priest in 1940, and returned to Spain. He founded the *Instituto Social de León XIII* in Madrid to promote the cause of social Catholicism and worked actively among the poor of southern Spain. He was consecrated bishop of Málaga* in 1947, was named a cardinal in 1965, and died in Madrid on July 28, 1968.

For further information, see Ángel Herrera Ória, *Obras selectas* (Madrid, 1963); Javier Tusell Gómez, *Historia de la democracia cristiana en España* (Madrid, 1974); and Richard A. H. Robinson, *The Origins of Franco's Spain* (Pittsburgh, 1970).

See also Catholic Church, Spanish; and Monarchism.

José M. Sánchez

HIDALGO DE CISNEROS Y LÓPEZ-MONTE-NEGRO, IGNACIO (1896–1966). Hidalgo de Cisneros, born in Vitoria* into an aristocratic Carlist family, was commissioned in the quartermaster corps but in 1920 entered the aviation service. He flew in the Riff campaign, for which he received a merit promotion to major in 1926. In December 1931, he joined his fellow aviator, Ramón Franco,* in the Republican uprising at Cuatro Vientos Airfield in Madrid,* but his Republican convictions developed only in exile in Paris where he first met Indalecio Prieto* and Marcelino Domingo. In 1932, shortly after his marriage to Constancia de la Mora, a granddaughter of Antonio Maura, he was appointed air attaché in Rome and Berlin, a position he held until May 1935, when he was dismissed by Gil Robles.*

In 1936, Hidalgo de Cisneros became an aide to the prime minister, Casares Quiroga,* and during the first weeks of the Civil War he was one of a group of Republican officers led by Juan Hernández Saravia* that was the real power in the War Ministry. When Largo Caballero* formed his government in September 1936, Hidalgo de Cisneros was appointed head of the Republican Air Force* by Prieto, the new minister of aviation and the navy. At the same time, he continued to fly bombing missions out of Alcalá de Henares.* In October 1936, he joined the Spanish Communist party,* whose efficiency and discipline seemed to him to offer the best chance of winning the war. The arrival of Soviet airplanes, pilots, and technicians shortly thereafter further strengthened his commitment to the party, although it soured his hitherto good relations with Prieto. In May 1937, after participating in the battle of Guadalajara* and in the suppression of the *Confederación Nacional del Trabajo* (CNT)* and the *Partido Obrero de Unificación Marxista* (POUM)* revolt in Catalonia,* he transferred his headquarters to Valencia;* then in October, he followed the government to Barcelona.* Suffering a heart attack a month later, he went to Moscow to recuperate, but he returned to direct the Republican Air Force in the battle of the Ebro* in 1938.

At the start of the Nationalists'* offensive against

Catalonia, Prime Minister Negrín* sent Hidalgo de Cisneros back to Moscow to solicit $100 million in foreign military aid* personally from Stalin.* Although his mission was successful, the matériel did not arrive in time, and Hidalgo de Cisneros was forced to order the removal of air force personnel and equipment across the French border. Unable to secure French permission to transfer this equipment to Spain, he returned to Madrid in March 1939. He rebuffed the overtures of Colonel Casado,* choosing to remain loyal to Negrín and his communist advisers.

After the Civil War, Hidalgo de Cisneros lived in exile in France,* Mexico,* and a number of Eastern European countries. In 1954, he became a member of the Central Committee of the Spanish Communist party. He died at Bucharest in 1966.

For further information, see Antonio Cordón, *Trayectoria: memorias de un militar republicano* (Barcelona, 1977); Ignacio Hidalgo de Cisneros, *Cambio de rumbo (memorias)*, 2 vols. (Barcelona, 1977); Constancia de la Mora, *In Place of Splendor: The Autobiography of a Spanish Woman* (New York, 1939); and Ramón Salas Larrazábal, *Historia del ejército popular de la República*, 4 vols. (Madrid, 1973).

Carolyn P. Boyd

HISMA. *See Compañía Hispano-Marroquí de Transportes (HISMA)*.

HITLER, ADOLF (1889-1945). Hitler, chancellor of Germany* from 1933 to 1945, determined on July 26, 1936, to support the Nationalist rebellion. In doing so, he overruled cautious Foreign Ministry officials, who feared dangerous international repercussions, and yielded instead to the personal pleas of Johannes Bernhardt,* Nazi merchant of Tetuán,* and Ernst W. Bohle, chief of the *Auslandsorganisation*. Two days later, a Junkers 52 ferried twenty-two Moroccan soldiers from Tetuán to Seville,* and within two weeks nearly 15,000 troops had crossed the Straits* in German transports. German intervention in Spain had begun in earnest, and Franco* had acquired a valuable but dangerous ally.

Throughout the Civil War, Hitler and other Nazi spokesmen sought to justify intervention as a means of halting the spread of communism. But certainly there were other factors of far greater import. A Franco victory would complete the encirclement of France* by hostile powers and would presumably gain for the Reich a grateful ally in the West—one that, in the event of a major European war, would pose a direct

threat to France and perhaps even to the British presence in Gibraltar.* Furthermore, a Spanish government indebted to Germany could be expected to maintain favorable commercial relations with the Reich and provide Hitler's hungry armaments industry with much needed iron, copper, and pyrites. Within the early weeks of the war, an additional motive for intervention became apparent. Since Italy,* too, was supporting Franco, a similar course by Germany would permit close cooperation with Mussolini,* thwart Anglo-French efforts to improve relations with Rome, and at the same time prevent Italy's gaining undue influence in Spain. By late 1937, Hitler had found yet another reason for his Spanish policy. By providing enough support to ensure an ultimate Nationalist victory but not enough to produce an immediate victory, he could prolong the war and in doing so divert Anglo-French attention from the east.

In helping bring about a Nationalist victory, Hitler secured the immediate goals of his Spanish venture. But Franco's proclamation of neutrality in 1939 and the stubborn evasiveness displayed at Hendaye in 1940 convinced the angry Fuehrer that his dream of an active Spanish ally was ended.

For further information, see Albert C. Horton, "Germany and the Spanish Civil War" (Ph.D. dissertation, Columbia University, 1966); Manfred Merkes, *Die deutsche Politik gegenüber dem spanischen Bürgerkrieg, 1936-1939* (Bonn, 1961); and Angel Viñas, *La Alemania nazi y el 18 de julio*, 2d ed. (Madrid, 1977).

See also Great Britain; and Stalin.

Glenn T. Harper

HOLLAND. Holland exhibited considerable sympathy for the Spanish Republic, although some conservative elements expressed support for the Nationalists.* The Dutch government took an official position of neutrality and like many of its neighbors, followed the guidelines established by France* and Great Britain.* In August 1936, Holland adhered to the principles of the Non-Intervention Committee* and encouraged its citizens not to sell arms to the Spanish. During 1937, the number of Dutch ships that were damaged by Italian or Nationalist forces patrolling off Spain led the government to support stringent procedures to make the Mediterranean safe. The democracies established a naval board to monitor the sea which was headed by a Dutchman, Vice-admiral van Dulm.* It was hoped that this naval patrol would be able to prevent the recurrence of losses (eighteen cargos between November 1936 and April 1937 for the Dutch alone). The destruction of Dutch ships continued, the most publicized incident being that of the merchant-man *Hannah* sunk on January 11, 1938.

For further information, see Arnold J. Toynbee, *Survey of International Affairs, 1937* (Oxford, 1938). *See also* Europe; and Nyon Conference.

James W. Cortada

HUESCA. Huesca province, located in the northern part of Spain between Basque Navarre* to the west and Catalan Lérida* in the east, was the Aragón* region that quickly fell to the Nationalists* in July 1936. However, the province was the scene of much fighting that summer since it was the locale of the Aragón front. Republican militias* invaded the area in July and August. Members of the *Partido Obrero de Unificación Marxista* (POUM)* primarily marched and fought near the provincial capital. On August 28, 1936, Italian anarchists attacked the provincial capital, although they failed to take it. Despite all the fighting, the province remained under the Nationalist's control throughout most of the Civil War. Franco's* forces, especially local Falangists, were energetic in purging suspected Republicans* in Huesca. In May 1937, the Republicans again attacked Huesca in order to draw the Nationalists away from Bilbao* which they were then attacking, but the effort failed to save the Basque city. The major Nationalist offensive against Catalonia* in 1938 and 1939 took Franco's forces through the province of Huesca where fighting continued until the last days of the war.

For further information, see Franz Borkenau, *The Spanish Cockpit* (London, 1937); and José Manuel Martínez Bande, *La gran ofensiva sobre Zaragoza* (Madrid, 1973).

James W. Cortada

HULL, CORDELL (1871-1955). Hull was secretary of state of the United States* (1933-1945) under President Franklin D. Roosevelt.* As the chief architect of American foreign policy, Hull was responsible for de-veloping the policy of neutrality followed by his government and for establishing a series of neutrality regulations and laws designed to keep the United States out of the Spanish Civil War. He also supported the Anglo-French policy of nonintervention in the conflict. While his personal sympathies lay with the Republic, he fashioned an American policy that was designed to forbid the sale of arms to either side and to discourage Americans from serving in the International Brigades.* He was unable to reduce the emotional and intellectual interest in the war, but he did slow the flow of supplies (except medical) to either side.

For further information, see Richard P. Traina, *American Diplomacy and the Spanish Civil War* (Bloomington, Ind., 1968). *See also* Neutrality Acts (USA).

James W. Cortada

HUNGARY. Hungary provided important leaders to the Comintern and to the highest levels of Communist party* leadership in Spain. In addition, 1,000 Hungarians served in the International Brigades,* particularly in the Rakosi Battalion (formed in June or July 1937). The head of the Communist party in Catalonia* was a Hungarian, Ernö Gerö. Gerö was one of the first Communist leaders in Spain to break with Largo Caballero* in 1937 and has been accused of instigating the May 1937 riots* in Barcelona* in the same year. Taking orders directly from Moscow, Gerö ran the *Partit Socialista Unificat de Catalunya* (PSUC)* skillfully. He spoke fluent Catalan and with his understanding of local politics was able to make the PSUC conform to the Communist party's plans for Spain. After World War II, he served in the Hungarian government.

For further information, see Burnett Bolloten, *The Spanish Revolution: The Left and the Struggle for Power During the Civil War* (Chapel Hill, N.C., 1979); and José Esteban Vilaro, *El ocaso de los dioses rojos* (Barcelona, 1939).

James W. Cortada

I

IBARRURI GÓMEZ, DOLORES. *See* Pasionaria, La (Dolores Ibarruri Gómez).

IBIZA. Ibiza's residents rose in rebellion against the Republic in July 1936 and successfully turned the island into a Nationalist position. In August, a small group of Republicans* retook the island in the Balearics and released from jail Luis Araquistáin,* a friend and adviser to Francisco Largo Caballero,* along with Rafael Alberti, a communist poet. Soon after, Ibiza fell to the Nationalists.* Within a very short period of time there had thus been great loss of life on the island: fifty-five as a result of Nationalist air raids, 239 killed by the *Federación Anarquista Ibérica* (FAI),* and another 400 by Franco's* men. For the rest of the war, Ibiza remained a Nationalist stronghold and a port of call for German and Italian warships.

For further information, see José Manuel Martínez Bande, *La invasión de Aragón y el desembarco en Mallorca* (Madrid, 1970); and Elliot Paul, *The Life and Death of a Spanish Town* (New York, 1937).

James W. Cortada

ILUNDÁIN Y ESTÉBAN, CARDINAL EUSTAQUIO (1862-1937). Cardinal Ilundáin, archibishop of Seville,* was the first high-ranking cleric whose see came under the Nationalists'* control in the early days of the Civil War. Born in Pamplona* on September 20, 1862, he was consecrated bishop of Oviedo* in 1904, became archbishop of Seville in 1920, and was named a cardinal in 1925. Along with Cardinals Segura* and Vidal,* he was an important leader of the Spanish Catholic Church.*

Ilundáin followed a moderate policy during the years of the Republic, generally supporting the leadership of Vidal in trying to get along with the leadership of the Republicans.* When the military uprising began in 1936, his see of Seville was captured quickly by the Nationalists. Thereafter, Ilundáin was frequently seen in public with Generals Quiepo de Llano* and Franco* when they visited Seville. Some historians have argued that this support was crucial to the Nationalist victory in Seville, but this hardly seems likely in view of his past history of moderation and lack of public statements, along with the traditionally high incidence of anticlericalism in the city and the quick success of the military uprising there. Ilundáin signed the Bishops' Collective Letter in 1937 and died shortly thereafter in Seville on August 10, 1937.

For further information, see L. Tovar González, *Ensayo biográfico del Exmo. Sr. Cardenal Ilundáin y Esteban* (Pamplona, 1942).

José M. Sánchez

INDUSTRY, REPUBLICAN. Industry and commerce in the Republican zone were characterized most by expropriation, a process that evolved very rapidly. According to Souchy and Folgare in *Colectivizaciones* (Barcelona, 1937), "There were no bosses. The workers not only had to resume their work in the furnaces, locomotives, trolley cars and as deliverymen, but they also had to manage factories, shops and transportation industries." In other words, the workers and employees took over the administration of industries. But the socialization or collectivization was not premeditated, for no preparations had been made. As in all revolutions, practice preceded theory. The anarchists* and syndicalists* of Spain had a well-defined doctrine. The Marxists, with respect to socialization, defended the concept that the state should have control over the economy, that industries should be nationalized. In Spain, especially in Catalonia,* the socialization process started as collectivization. After July 19, 1936, the syndicates of the *Confederación Nacional del Trabajo* (CNT)* took charge of distributing food* supplies. Eating centers for the people were opened in all neighborhoods in syndicalist locales. The supplies came from wholesale warehouses and from the countryside. Payment was made by notes guaranteed by the syndicates. All those affiliated with the syndicates, wives and children of the militiamen, as well as the population* in general, received their meals free.

The moneyless economy lasted two weeks, when work was resumed and economic life renewed. After a few weeks, even automobile fuel had to be purchased with cash, but the syndicates continued to control the supply of fuel as before.

The first phase of collectivization started with labor taking charge of enterprises. In each shop, factory, office, warehouse, and store, syndicate delegates were appointed to manage affairs. In many instances, these managers had no theoretical preparation whatsoever. The owners were brushed aside if they opposed the direction of events; if they accepted the change, they were absorbed into the operation. The owners then worked as technical or commercial administrators, and at times as wage-earning laborers or technicians. This process and the changes it caused were relatively simple.

While the workers simply replaced the previous proprietors, the system was neither capitalist nor socialist. Rather, it was a kind of collective capitalism, with the employees now becoming collective proprietors. Those who worked in a prosperous business gained greater income than those in less fortunately situated ones.

In the Republican zone, socialization did not mean nationalization, the transfer of ownership to the state. The funds of all the syndicates went into a central deposit point; the concentration within the framework of the local federation would transform the latter into a collective economic enterprise. It would be socialization from the bottom up, that is, from the workers' enterprises to the entire collective. Without labor organizations there would be no socialization.

In the first weeks of the Civil War, the government in Madrid* went against the syndicalists' collectivization policy. Its first revolutionary economic measure, decreed on August 1, 1936, required a 50 percent reduction in the housing rents paid by labor. A more important decree was that issued on August 2, which provided for the confiscation of industries abandoned by owners or managers. By virtue of other measures passed by the Giral* government, holders of checking accounts could withdraw from banks only about 1,000 pesetas monthly.

On August 3, the State confiscated the Transatlantica Company and assets in other railroad industry companies. An ordinance of July 31, confirmed by decree on August 30, established a system whereby the workers' committees which had taken charge of enterprises could effect certain operations in their name, including the use of funds with which to pay wages. By an August 30 decree, the government removed many advisers of the Industrial Credit Bank, replacing them with members of the Popular Front.* On the same day, the minister of finance suspended all members of the administration council of the Exterior Bank of Spain and appointed an administration committee for the bank made up of Popular Front representatives. By decrees of August 14, August 30, and September 1, 1936, the government named a number of advisers of state in different electric utility companies and formed the General Electrical Council, which then "intervened" in those companies. The executive committee of this council also consisted of members of the Popular Front.

The government's actions were initiated basically to punish those who opposed the Republican regime by confiscating their goods and jobs and by placing persons faithful to the regime in key positions. At the time, the government had no systematic program for taking over property. The Madrid ministers had reservations about a revolutionary restructuring of the economy, for they were concerned about international public opinion, especially if confiscatory measures were to affect foreign-owned property.

The most important economic changes developed in Catalonia, eastern Aragón,* and Asturias* before coming to the central zone. In Asturias, early in the war the syndicalist councils seized control of most of the mines and industries, causing considerable friction between the *Confederación Nacional del Trabajo* (CNT)* and the *Unión General de Trabajadores* (UGT).* Nonetheless, the syndicates did not intend collectivization and total reorganization of Asturian production. The only industry fully collectivized were the Gijón* factories. Syndicalist actions may have been so fragmentary because a great deal of foreign capital was invested in Asturian enterprises. Stanley G. Payne argues that the socialists were aware of both the diplomatic and military implications of confiscating foreign-owned properties. He indicates that the apogee of the social and economic revolution of 1936 was reached in Catalonia and eastern Aragón. The anarchist Council of Aragón* functioned in Aragón, and the situation there was overshadowed by the CNT and *Federación Anarquista Ibérica* (FAI) which had come from Catalonia. These two organizations imposed the same collectivist regime in Aragón as existed in Catalonia.

The CNT sponsored several assemblies in Madrid and Barcelona* which were designed to promote collectivization, while the UGT published a manifesto to that effect. Curiously, the same CNT which in Madrid had advocated socialization only for large industry, big business, and transportation, workers' control of enterprises that remained in the hands of their owners, as well as imposing planning controls on industry, in Catalonia pressed for drastic collectivization of all enterprises without distinction and deposit of their assets and income into a common fund managed by the Economic Council of the Generalitat.*

For its part, the UGT advocated the organization of industries marked by absentee ownership into cooperatives; the control of other industries within the framework of private property; and the protection of small middle-class businesses and manufacturing operations. The Madrid government took advantage of these differences to justify taking a definitive stand. Thus, 1936 ended without any final decision on these matters.

In contrast, in autonomous Catalonia, events occurred more rapidly and resulted in the collectivization experiment. Collectivization emerged from the Economic Council of the Generalitat, created in 1932 and revitalized by decree of this body on August 11, 1936, in which it assumed responsibility for the "structuring and convenient normalization of the Catalan economy." The most prominent member of this council was its president, Dr. Don Manuel Serra Moret, a distinguished economist with degrees from Harvard and the University of Chicago. The council was controlled by the CNT, and as a result its directives, orders, and ordinances all dealt with collectivization.

The new order of things was encompassed in the decree of the Generalitat* dated October 24, 1936. Units of production could be private enterprises managed by the owner or administrator, with the cooperation of and auditing by the workers' control committee—collectivized entities often administered under the responsibility of the workers' councils and the collectivized groupings, which included all the enterprises of the same economic sector (industry type). The mechanisms for administering the collectivized enterprises were a general workers' assembly, council of enterprises, and director and delegate or comptroller of the Generalitat. In private businesses, decision-making authority was divided between the boss and the workers represented in a control committee. Interestingly, the idea of grouping enterprises would be reiterated persistently in later theory. No less interesting was the proposal (never carried out) to establish an Industrial and Commercial Credit Bank in which half of the benefits (assets) would be deposited and also to create a number of general industrial councils, fourteen of which were to be created in order to coordinate the programs of the new entities.

Among the many conflicts and problems stemming from the implementation of this decree were those involving foreign capital investments. The consuls of the respective countries made vigorous protests on behalf of the owners of affected enterprises. Albert Pérez Baró observes that the position of the consular corp in Barcelona relative to the provisions of the collectivization decree which affected the nationals of the various countries echo, no more nor less, the general tone of the atmosphere prevailing beyond Spain's frontiers against the collectivist regime established in Catalonia.

Other developments occurred in the rest of Republican Spain with respect to private ownership of enterprises. Outside of Catalonia, the contrast between the syndicalist dogma of collectivization and the Marxist call for nationalization can be seen clearly. The Marxists observed with glee and criticized without restraint the disorder which the collectives introduced into the economy. A Marxist study of Spain published in Moscow in 1966, called *Guerra y revolución en España*, stated that placed at the heads of two ministries of decisive economic importance—that of Industry and Commerce—were the anarchosyndicalist Juan Peiró* and Juan López* who then tried by all means to legalize and consolidate CNT control over the major part of economic life. They drew on State funds for financing syndicalized enterprises then in bankruptcy. In January 1937, the ministry of industry had already received 11,000 petitions from enterprises requesting economic assistance from the State. Peiró prepared a decree collectivizing Spanish industry. This proposal caused an acute struggle within the government.

The socialists did not have a unanimous opinion on the subject. But opposed to Peiró's plans was the minister of finance, Juan Negrín,* who, with the support of the Federation of Banks and Exchanges of the UGT, had been able to keep banking and monetary systems essentially under the government's direction and authority. Negrín's plan consisted of forcing enterprises, to the extent that they required credit or subsidies from the state, to accept a certain degree of government control or intervention.

The result of these economic discussions was the compromise decree of February 23, 1937, signed by Manuel Azaña* and Peiró, the preamble of which stated:

The reality of the situation which has placed the economy of diverse industries at the edge of bankruptcy, which weakness in many instances has to be remedied by the State, forces the latter to extend its titular function with a view to intervene and channel the administrative and directive factors of the economic industry in danger.

The principal stipulations of the decree were the following:

Article Two: Industries. . . may be the object of intervention or confiscation by the State. Companies intervened are understood to be those which while continuing under the management and economic responsibility of the entrepreneur will be sufficient supervision by the State of the activities of an enterprise in accordance with the requirements set forth in the present decree. Confiscated industries are those in which the management and economic responsibility is transferred to the authority of the entities representing the State.

Article Three: The Ministry of Industry will arrange through representatives appointed for the purpose to deal with all the interventions in industry, factories, shops, laboratories and commercial establishments or those with an industrial character, as well as raw materials or products manufactured which are considered to be of national interest.

Article Four: The Ministry of Industry is authorized to propose to the council of ministers the confiscation of establishments, materials or related products when such action is considered necessary for the achievement of the objectives of the regulations promulgated.

The decree offered a legal framework permitting government control over the nation's basic industries and the exercise of effective intervention in industrial activity. Nevertheless, this decree was nullified by the implementation regulations developed by Peiró on March 2 which, for practical purposes, left industry in the hands of the so-called industrial councils or central committees concerned with the manufacture of articles that did not meet the army's most urgent needs. In time, Peiró's efforts were recognized as disastrous.

In the March assembly, the Communist party* again set the creation of a powerful war industry as one of the highest priorities. To achieve this end, it considered it absolutely necessary to "nationalize the large industries and shops which had been abandoned by their owners or directed by troubled elements, as a precautionary measure to reach the effective coordination of production and the creation of a powerful war industry." For this purpose, the assembly proposed the creation of a Ministry for Armaments.

Taking into account the importance of the heavy industry of Euzkadi (Basque Country) and of Catalonia, the Communist party demanded an end to the de facto division within the economic system of Euzkadi and the rest of the Republican territory. Another urgent matter was the nationalization of all land, sea, and air transport. As a basic measure, the Communist party emphasized the nationalization of banks and mines inasmuch as they represented essential productive elements of the economy.

The failure of collectivization itself, as well as the growing communist influence in the power structure, explains why the original syndicalist thesis was thrust aside and why there was increasing reference to socialization and nationalization of production. On July 19, 1937, the adviser of the council on the economy of the Generalitat, Juan Tarradellas, made available to the public sixty-five decisions that formed the S'Agaró Plan (named after the site where the authors had gathered). The first decision referred to the municipalization of urban public services. Number 38 involved the interesting and novel measure of establishing a tax on the total volume of business; other dispositions regulated insurance, credit, and banking institutions, and created delegations of the Generalitat in various banks and in the *Mercado Libre de Valores* (Free Stock Exchange). Number 48 ordered a stop for the moment on all rental payments pending the establishment of a new way of dealing with housing.

In August 1937, the UGT and the *Partit Socialista Unificat de Catalunya* (PSUC)* started to agitate for the nationalization of gas and electrical utilities in Catalonia. In the same month, Doctor Serra Moret was named head of the Economic Council of the Generalitat. Elsewhere, it should be noted that in the statute granted the Basque provinces on October 16, 1936, there was attributed to the new Euzkadi government the power to socialize "the natural resources and the economic entities" (Article 2, c), which meant that in that region collectivization solutions were also brushed aside. In this manner, the autonomous Basque government was responsible for the matters of supply, savings, credit and loans, cooperatives, and mutuals.

The changing fortunes of the Civil War led to increasing centralization in Republican Spain. On the one hand, the Nationalists' capture of the Basque provinces canceled this politico-economic experiment in that region. On the other, the transfer of the government from Madrid to Valencia* ended the organizations created in Valencia in 1936. Later, when the government was installed in Barcelona, the central government itself took over most of the functions and activities of the Generalitat.

In short, industrial production in the Republican zone during the Civil War evolved in four distinct phases: (1) July and August 1936: The impact of disorganization stemming from the war was manifested. (2) September 1936 to October 1937: The area began to adapt to lost markets and sources of supply for raw material. Output declined to 60 to 75 percent of that of January 1936. Significant events occurred in November 1936 when there was a total depletion of inventories and in February 1937, when the crisis became evident, owing to the conversion of the Catalan economy to a wartime economy. Starting in March 1937, there was a rise in prices. (3) October 1937 to March 1938: Difficulties for the Catalan economy so increased that the production index fluctuated between 55 and 60, based on an index of 100 for January 1936. The stage was set for a directed war economy. (4) April to December 1938: A general decline in industrial production took place, and Catalonia became a theater of war. All economic activity began to disintegrate.

For further information, see Frank Minz, *La collectivisation en Espagne, 1936-39* (Paris, 1967); Albert Pérez Baró, *30 mesos de collectivisme a Catalunya (1936-39)* (Barcelona, 1970); Ramón Tamames, *La República. La era de Franco* (Madrid, 1973); and Pedro Voltes Bou, *Historia de la economía española en los siglos XIX y XX* (Madrid, 1974), Vol. 2.

See also Libertarian movement.

Pedro Voltes Bou

INSTITUTE OF AGRARIAN REFORM. The Institute of Agrarian Reform, established in 1932 to carry out the agricultural programs of the Second Republic,* was important to Spain's agricultural economics and politics in the years just before the Civil War, and, to some degree, it contributed to the start of the conflict. The need for agricultural reform was a fundamental one in Spanish society throughout the nineteenth and early twentieth centuries. In 1932, the Republic, recognizing the seriousness of this need, passed a law outlining a complex set of reforms that in effect called for landless agricultural workers to acquire farms confiscated from large landholders. Complex formulas for compensation were established, along with guidelines defining who would be eligible for land grants and the establishment of collectives. The law also called for the use of new technology in planting, irrigation, and harvesting. The Institute of Agrarian Reform, within the Ministry of Agriculture, became the agency most responsible for implementing the law.

The law failed to produce fundamental land reform or even significant redistribution of property prior to the Civil War. Through loopholes in the law, large landowners could retain their properties; critics on the political Left accused the law of failing to bring about reforms. The lack of quick results dashed the hopes of thousands of agricultural workers and contributed to their general alienation from existing governmental institutions. Their political radicalization was the inevitable byproduct of the institute's failure to improve their quality of life.

Yet, during its existence, the institute did attempt to carry out the terms of the law of 1932. Land was expropriated and turned over to agricultural workers, particularly in Andalusia* and in Estremadura,* areas characterized by large landholdings and massive numbers of poor peasants. But landless workers thought the institute moved too slowly, and in some instances they seized land on their own. A dramatic example came in March 1933 when 60,000 peasants in Estremadura seized 3,000 farms—a number of people and properties that were far in excess of those which the institute had thus far acted upon. The government did not make these 60,000 farmers return the land to the previous owners; instead, it felt compelled to speed up resettlement totaling nearly 190,000 people by the start of the Civil War. From 1932 through 1939, the institute resettled about 300,000 peasants on 1.5 million acres. During the Civil War, the establishment of collectives (often independent of the institute) accounted for another 500,000 people on almost 9 million acres of land.

As more land came under Nationalist control, the institute's influence diminished. Land granted to peasants now in Nationalist territory reverted back to the original owners. When the Civil War ended, the institute died along with the government of the Republic. During its existence, it had influenced the change in ownership of early 13 million acres (approximately 25 percent of all cultivable land in Republican zones).

Although land redistribution had been the institute's primary activity, it also attempted to make available information on modern farming techniques, and it established programs for financing irrigation and the acquisition of machines. Yet, the collectives had greater success in acquiring farming equipment on their own, and the Nationalists* did more to introduce irrigation schemes during the Civil War.

For further information, see Ronald Fraser, *The Blood of Spain* (New York, 1979); and Edward Malefakis, *Agrarian Reform and Peasant Revolution in Spain* (New Haven, Conn., 1970).

See also Aragón; and Workers, Catalan.

James W. Cortada

INTELLECTUALS. Intellectuals in Spain were profoundly moved by the fratricidal conflict that divided their country and were soon joined in this concern by many others around the world. Spain rapidly became a center of irresistible attraction. For many, the future of humanity hung in the balance in Spain where the "last great cause" for those who opposed fascism* could be found. Until the Spanish Civil War, the Spanish intellectual was usually a pacifist. If he did take up arms, it was out of pure obligation such as in the Cuban war in 1898, or in Morocco* in the 1900s, or in World War I. The Spanish drama cracked the secular tradition of the ivory tower intellectual, and now men who in earlier years would never have thought of fighting were carrying a gun, particularly those with leftist political sentiments supporting the Republic.

Many perceived the tragedy of Spain as shaking the foundations of society and as touching something basic to human existence. It was the greatest crisis affecting European civilization, and thus they believed that all human beings were obliged to take a definitive stand. They had to "obligate" themselves as Jean-Paul Sartre would state some years later.

Previously, intellectuals had not only recognized their neutrality in national affairs but also widely broadcast it. One of the most ardent defenders of neutrality was the Frenchman Julian Benda in *La trahison des clercs* (Paris, 1927). Benda attended the Congress of the International Association of Antifascist Writers, held in the Republican zone in July 1937, and in his opening speech he explained how the Civil War had turned him completely around. He concluded his address with these words: "I am certain that this is the moment when I am the interpreter of all intellectuals worthy of the name in declaring with what sentiment of solidarity, as well as from the heart, and with what interest we sympathize with the temporary trials undergone by Republican Spain and call for its victory."

This meeting, mostly of leftist and communist persuasions, took place in Madrid* and Valencia,* and had the greatest implications because it gathered intellectuals from many countries. This group was affiliated with the revolutionary writers who had met for the first time in Paris in July 1935 and whose international committee was formed by André Gide, Thomas Mann, André Malraux,* Romain Rolland, Aldous Huxley, and Waldo Franc. Republican Spain was represented by Antonio Machado, José Bergamin, Rafael Alberti, Julio Álvarez del Vayo,* and younger writers such as Miguel Hernández,* José Herrera Petere, Arturo Serrano Plaja, and Antonio Aparicio. From France* came André Malraux, Louis Aragon, Tristan Tzara, Julian Benda, André Chamson, and Clause Aveline; from Great Britain* Stephen Spender; from Germany* Ludwig Renn, Gustav Regler,* Anna Seghers, and Willi Bredel; from the USSR* Alexis Tolstoi, Ilya Ehrenburg,* and Fedor Kelyin; from Yugoslavia* Theodor Balk; from Denmark Andersen Nexo; from Holland* Jef Last; from Belgium Dario Marion; from Portugal* Jaime Cortaçoa; from Mexico* José Mancisidor and Octavo Paz; from Chile Pablo Neruda; from Peru César Vallejo; from Argentina* Raúl González Tuñón; from Cuba* Nicolás Guillén and Juan Marinello; and from the United States* Malcolm Cowley, Ernest Hemingway,* and John Dos Passos. During the Civil War, all of these figures worked to develop sympathies in their home countries for Republican Spain. As is evident from this lengthy list, most intellectuals favored the Republic. Their immense number of works on the

Spanish Civil War demonstrates the extent of their interest as well as the depth of their passions on the matter.

The best known and most prestigious forum for such writing was without question *Hora de España*, a periodical published in the Republican zone between February 1937 and October 1938. Among its contributors were Antonio Machado, León Felipe, José Moreno Villa, José Bergamín, Tomás Navarro Tomás, Damaso Alonso, Joaquín Xirau, José F. Montesino, Pedro Bosch Gimpere, José Goas, Emilio Prados, Luis Cernuda, and Corpus Barga. Its editorial board consisted of highly capable men who were completely dedicated to their work, men such as Manuel Altolaguirre, Rafael Dieste, Antonio Sánchez Barbudo, Juan Gil-Albert, Juan Antonio Gáya Nuno, María Zambrano, and Arturo Serrano Plaja.

Parallel to the *Hora de España*, but an older publication, was *El Mono Azul*, put out by the *Alianza de Intelectuales Antifascistas* (Alliance of Antifastist Intellectuals). This periodical, inspired by Rafael Alberti and José Bergamín, purported to be a flyer that would take views to the front, bringing a clear and stern message of antifascism. Its principal importance lies in the fact that its pages carried "romances" of the war.

On the Nationalist side, towards the end of 1936, a review called *Jerarquía*, issued by the *Delegación Nacional de Prensa y Propaganda* (Delegation of Press and Propaganda), was published for the first time in Pamplona.* It was directed by a priest, Fermín Yzurdiaga, and the editorial board consisted of a group of friends— Eugenio d'Ors, Pedro Laín Entralgo, Luis Rosales, and Luis Felipe Vivanco—together with Gonzalo Torrente Ballester, Rafael García Serrano, and Manuel Díez Crespo. The first issue included contributions by Eugenio Montes, José-María Pemán,* Adriano del Valle, Fray Justo Pérez de Urbel, and Angel María Pascual. It aspired to be a "national syndicalist guide for the Empire, wisdom, and offices," but only four editorials were ever published. Another publication, *Vértice*, of the *Falange Española Tradicionalista** and the *Junta de Ofensiva Nacionalista-Sindicalista** lasted longer, from April 1937 until 1946, but also sought to exalt imperial heroism while glorifying the cultivation of culture and art as propounded in the Nationalist zone. *Vértice* featured Ernesto Giménez Caballero, Agustín de Foxá, Mourlane Michelena, Víctor de la Serna, Samuel Ros (its first director), Manuel Halcón (its second director), José María Alfaro (its last director), Dionisio Ridruejo,* Edgar Neville, Jacinto Miquelarena, Eugenio Montes, Alvaro Cunqueiro, and José María Castroviejo.

Participation in one or another of the publications of the Spanish intellectuals clearly revealed their ideology: there were also publications by groups in many countries in effect doing the same thing. In addition to writing, some foreign intellectuals actually fought in the Spanish Civil War—Malraux, George Orwell,* and Roy Campbell*—while others, such as Ludwig Renn, Gustav Regler, Willi Bredel, Luigi Longo,* and Ralph Fox, joined the International Brigades.* There were so many intellectuals in the International Brigades that they have been described as the most intellectual military units in history.

For further information, see Frederick R. Benson, *Writers in Arms* (New York, 1967); Rafael Calvo Serer, *La literatura universal sobre la guerra de España* (Madrid, 1962); Fernando Díaz-Plaja, *Si mi pluma valiera tu pistola. Los escritores españoles en la guerra civil* (Barcelona, 1979); *Les escrivains et la guerre d'Espagne. Les Dossiers H* (Paris, 1975); Aldo Garosci, *Gli intellettuali e la guerra di Spagna* (Milan, 1959); Vicente Marrero, *La guerra española y el trust de los cerebros* (Madrid, 1961); Herbert R. Southworth, *El mito de la Cruzada de Franco* (Paris, 1963); and María Zambrano, *Los intelectuales en la drama de España* (Santiago de Chile, 1939; Madrid, 1977).

See also Literature.

Maryse Bertrand de Muñoz

INTERNATIONAL BRIGADES. More than 35,000 men—and a handful of women—from some fifty countries served in the International Brigades (IB), the vast bulk of them coming from eleven national groups. These included approximately 10,000 French, 5,000 Germans and Austrians, 5,000 Poles, 3,400 Italians, 3,000 Americans, 2,000 British, 1,500 Yugoslavs, 1,500 Czechs, 1,200 Canadians, and 1,000 Hungarians. Between 5 and 10 percent of them, largely those who arrived in the first two months of the war, got to Spain on their own, but beginning in the fall of 1936 virtually all volunteers* came through an underground railroad provided by Communist parties, which recruited, organized, and directed brigades.

This does not mean that all the volunteers were communists, although in fact a high percentage were. What it does indicate is that the Spanish war became a serious test of the antifascist Popular Front,* a policy enunciated by the Comintern in mid-1935. The rebel uprising in Spain tapped a deep-seated fear among a wide variety of leftists, liberals, and republicans over the growing strength of right-wing dictatorships and fascist regimes in Central and Eastern Europe.* For exiles from countries like Germany,* Italy,* and Poland*—and these included union leaders, students, anarchists,* and socialists as well as communists— enlisting in the brigades was, they hoped, the first step on a road that would lead to a change of government at home. For Frenchmen, Belgians, Britons, Scandinavians, or Americans, the aim was to stop the spread of the Right before it came to power in their own lands or plunged Europe into another world war.

While the motives of the leaders of the USSR* in both supporting the Spanish Republic and directing the brigades are still the subject of historical debate, it is clear that the decision to do so allowed the Russians to capitalize on the widespread enthusiasm for the Loyalists* which had sent volunteers across the border since the first days of the war. By September 1936, the Republic's need for some kind of military assistance was glaringly obvious. Much of the regular army was involved in the rebellion, and the untrained militias* formed by labor unions and political parties— brave enough to crush the initial uprising in major cities like Barcelona* and Madrid*—proved for the most part useless in open-field warfare. As rebel forces marched from the south towards Madrid, Randolfo Pacciardi, an Italian republican, made an offer in early September to organize a legion of his countrymen, but it was declined by Prime Minister Largo Caballero.* A month later, Largo Caballero reluctantly accepted a similar proposal to form foreign military units from a delegation of communists headed by Luigi Longo.* In truth, he was presented with a virtual *fait accompli*. An international recruiting center had been set up in Paris, where such figures as the Yugoslav Joseph Broz (later known as Tito) were already funneling volunteers into Spain.

As headquarters and central training base, the brigades in mid-October took over the former depot of the communist Fifth Regiment* in Albacete.* Hundreds of volunteers were already on hand, and in the next few months they continued to arrive at a rate of 600 to 700 a week. On November 1,900, men formed into four battalions—French, Italian, German, and Slavic— were formally organized into the 11th International Brigade, under the command of Lieutenant Colonel Jules Dumont, former head of the Commune de Paris *Centuria*. Four days later the ill-equipped unit was on its way to Madrid. It was followed on November 7 by the 1,550 volunteers of the 12th IB, consisting of German, Italian, and Franco-Belgian battalions and led by the Hungarian-born General Lukacs* (real name, Mata Zalka Kemeny). These first two brigades soon received worldwide attention for their role in "saving" Madrid. Although this judgment was an exaggeration, certainly the Internationals were an important factor in blunting the rebel thrusts into and around the capital city between early November and mid-January. First, they helped battle the enemy to a standstill in the Casa de Campo and University City; later, in November, they stymied attacks northwest of Madrid; and in December they made the rebels pay dearly in the capture of Boadilla del Monte.* Casualties* in all of these actions were high. By early December, each of the brigades had suffered close to 50 percent fatalities, and they remained in the lines only because new volunteers were continually rushed up to refill depleted ranks.

While the battle of Madrid raged, several foreign artillery batteries and three more IBs were organized at Albacete. Although at one point two other brigades with international troops—the 129th and the 150th— were briefly in the field, for most of the war only five IBs existed.) The 13th, originally one of the most heterogeneous of the brigades, with twenty-one nationalities represented in a single battalion, saw action on many winter fronts and then spent the spring and part of the summer isolated near Pozoblanco, in Estramadura.* The 14th and 15th Brigades, the latter including the British and Abraham Lincoln Battalions,* joined the 11th and 12th in the all-important battle of Jarama,* which in February 1937 saved Madrid's lifeline, the Valencia Road. The next month the overworked 11th and 12th IBs were hurled into action again, this time in the battle of Guadalajara,* where the Italian Internationals had the special pleasure of helping to completely rout two of Mussolini's* divisions near Brihuega.

A three-month lull in military activity that began in mid-March 1937 allowed for reorganization of the IBs and their incorporation, under government orders, as units into the slowly developing Republican Army.* A brigade was now to consist of four battalions of approximately 700 men each. Supporting machinegun, mortar, and transportation units were to raise the number of effectives to about 3,500 (although this was always more true on paper than in the field). The brigades were, in turn, grouped into two international divisions: the 35th, commanded by General "Gal"* (the Hungarian, Janos Galicz), made up of the 11th, 13, and 15th Brigades; and the 45th, led first by Lukacz and then General Kleber* (a Rumanian whose name was either Lazar or Manfred Stern), consisting of the 12th and 14th.

At the same time, battalions were shifted about to make for some sort of linguistic consistency. After June 1937, the 11th IB consisted of North Europeans (Germans, Austrians, Scandinavians, Dutch); the 12th of Italians; the 13th of Slavs; the 14th of French and

Belgians; and the 15th of English-speaking volunteers. Later, when enlistments began to divide and casualties continued to run high, the IBs were brought up to strength with Spanish replacements. This began with the incorporation of Spanish battalions into the brigades and continued with companies in the battalions and, eventually, with squads in the companies. So, although five IBs were always in the field, late in the war they were international units more in name than in fact.

Overseeing the changes from brigade headquarters was a triumvirate of veteran foreign communists. The commander was André Marty,* the French hero of the 1919 Black Sea Mutiny. He was assisted by two Italians, Longo (known as "Gallo") and Giuseppe di Vittorio* ("Nicoletti"). Marty, who saw Trotskyists and spies (the two terms being equal in his mind) everywhere, was largely responsible for an atmosphere of suspicion and fear that hung over Albacete. The extent to which his paranoia was carried beyond threats into action in the form of executions tied into the larger issue of an alleged "terror" in the IBs. This, in turn, led to the role of the commissars, which originated in the Communist Fifth Regiment and spread to most units of the Republican Army.

Assigned to each level of the IBs (brigade, battalion, and company), commissars were not only responsible for the continuing political "education" and general morale of the troops, but they also had the specific function of weeding out spies, defeatists, and provocateurs. That they were virtually all communists is true, the extent to which the anti-Trotskyist fervor then raging in Moscow infected their activities is less clear. As volunteers and believers in the Popular Front, the Internationals were not likely to oppose communist direction of the brigades. Certainly, there was dissent in the ranks, certainly there were desertions during major battles and instances of cowardice shown in the face of the enemy, and certainly, as in any army, Internationals were on occasion either imprisoned or executed for such offenses. But a review of the available evidence (by French historian Jacques Delperrie de Bayac) leads to an estimate of no more than fifty executions of Internationals. Since some were for frontline offenses, this suggests that "terror," however lamentable, was hardly widespread and makes Marty's nickname the "Butcher of Albacete" more dependent upon words than deeds.

After the reorganization, the Internationals tended to be used as shock troops in government offensives. The first came in July 1937, in a drive on the plains west of Madrid that was aimed at Brunete.* Here all the brigades except the 14th were engaged. The first days of action saw the 12th being cited for the capture of Villanueva del Pardillo, while the 15th marched on the Mesquite Ridge, reaching the limits of the Loyalist advance. Quick counterattacks, supported by German and Italian Air Force units, caught and heavily punished Republican units in the open countryside. The 11th IB suffered 600 casualities, the British Battalion* was left with forty-two out of 300 effectives, and the Lincoln and Washington Battalions lost 50 percent of their men and were then merged together. Late in August, the same four brigades helped to spearhead the Aragón* offensive, the 11th capturing Codo, the 15th first taking Quinto, then being called to help in the assault on Belchite,* which fell after several days of house to house fighting. A continuation of the thrust towards Saragossa* in October by the 12th and 15th Brigades failed to capture Fuentes de Ebro. Meanwhile, the 14th was thrown into a costly (1,000 casualties in ten days) but successful defense of Aranjuez.

While for propaganda purposes at home and abroad the December capture of the important provincial capital of Teruel* was undertaken without any Internationals, both the 11th and 15th IBs were called upon in January 1938, as part of a vain attempt to prevent the city from being retaken. A few weeks later disaster struck. Early in March, a major Nationalist thrust caused the entire Aragón front to collapse, and all five brigades were caught up in the immense confusion of the ensuing retreats. Six weeks of makeshift, hopeless rearguard stands only ended when the bridges across the Ebro River were blown and the rebels reached the Mediterranean, cutting Loyalist Spain in two. With enlistment from abroad now at an end, the brigades were rebuilt that summer almost entirely with Spanish personnel. They were strong enough to re-cross the Ebro in late July as part of the last Republican offensive, but now no more than 30 percent of the troops were foreigners.

By the summer of 1938, it was obvious that the small number of remaining volunteers, many of them in hospitals anyway, could no longer play an important military role in the conflict. Hoping for some propaganda advantage—perhaps an end to the Non-Intervention Agreement, or international pressure on Italy* and Germany* to withdraw their military units from the rebel side—the government of Prime Minister Juan Negrín* decided unilaterally to remove the volunteers. Late in September, the foreigners in the IBs were pulled back across the Ebro. A League of Nations* commission arrived to count them (they numbered 12,763) and to help either repatriate the volunteers or to make arrangements with other governments, primarily Latin American, to accept those who could not return to their native lands.

Towards the end of the year, the foreigners began to leave Spain, but in a Catalonia* now being overrun by the enemy, the process was slow. The final groups reached the border at Le Perthus in early February 1939, as part of the half million refugees fleeing to France just ahead of the Nationalist Army.* If they left defeated in their purpose, the Internationals in the coming years would ultimately experience feelings of triumph. Large numbers of them fought in various armies and resistance movements against Germany and Italy during World War II. Unable to make Spain "the tomb of fascism," they ever after took pride in their early actions against the malign force with which all of Europe soon had to deal.

For further information, see Jacques Delperrie de Bayac, *Les brigades internacionales* (Paris, 1968); Vincent Brome, *The International Brigades* (London, 1965); *International Solidarity with the Spanish Republic* (Moscow, 1975); Verle B. Johnston, *Legions of Babel: The International Brigades in the Spanish Civil War* (University Park, Penn,, 1967); and Luigi Longo, *La Brigate internazionale in Spagna* (Milano, 1956).

Robert A. Rosenstone

IRELAND. Ireland participated in the Spanish Civil War mainly by contributing volunteer soldiers to both sides. Officially, Ireland remained aloof from the war. However, Irishmen fought in the International Brigades* in most of the major battles and campaigns of 1937. Members of the Irish Republican Army (IRA), with combat experience fighting the British, were especially useful and provided important military leaders such as Frank Ryan, who had over fifteen years' experience in the IRA. During the campaign of the Jarama* (March 1937), Irishmen also fought with the Nationalists.* General Eoin O'Duffy* led 600 Blue Shirts (Irish fascists) in this campaign.

For further information, see J. Bowyer Bell, *The Secret Army* (London, 1970); Fred Copeman, *Reason in Revolt* (London, 1948); and Eoin O'Duffy, *Crusade in Spain* (London, 1938).
See also Europe; and Great Britain.

James W. Cortada

IRON BATTALION. The Iron Battalion was made up primarily of criminals from Valencian prisons who served under the command of *Confederación Nacional del Trabajo* (CNT)* officers on the Republican side. It initially operated in the region around Valencia* terrorizing communities and attacking members of the middle class. This militia unit, also known as the Iron Column, operated autonomously from the Republican Army* during 1936. The regime finally put pressure on this unit and on the CNT to conform to military ways. Eventually, in March 1937, it was integrated into the regular army as the 83d Brigade.

For further information, see Burnett Bolloten, *The Spanish Revolution: The Left and the Struggle for Power During the Civil War* (Chapel Hill, N.C., 1979).

James W. Cortada

IRON COLUMN. *See* Iron Battalion.

IRON RING. The Iron Ring refers to a belt of fortifications built to protect the city of Bilbao* in 1937 from Nationalist attacks. They were constructed by Asturian miners and Basque workers, and consisted mainly of two rows of trenches outside the city with some concrete bunkers. They were clear targets for German aircraft throughout the siege of Bilbao (1937). The Nationalists* first broke through the Iron Ring on June 12, 1937, and soon after it no longer provided any defense for the city.

For further information, see José Manuel Martínez Bande, *La guerra en el norte* (Madrid, 1969).

James W. Cortada

IRUJO Y OLLO, MANUEL DE. Irujo, a leading Basque nationalist, joined the Republican cabinet as minister without portfolio on September 25, 1936. In the days just before the Civil War, he identified the sympathizers of the would-be rebels and did the necessary planning to establish local defense committees. When the revolt broke out, he was thus able to have pro-Nationalist sympathizers arrested and defense preparations made. His efforts, for example, permitted the Republicans* to hold on to Bilbao* at the start of the revolution. In order to insure continued support from the Basques, therefore, the Republic brought him into the cabinet. In May 1937, he protested Largo Caballero's* actions and policies, especially the prime minister's criticism of the communists, thereby helping force his removal from office and his replacement by Negrín.* That same month Irujo became minister of justice. He resigned his post in January 1938 as a protest against the establishment of military tribunals for the purpose of prosecuting spies and other criminals. However, he continued in the cabinet as minister without portfolio. Negrín, who found that Irujo did not always support him, dropped the Basque from

the cabinet in the fall of 1938. Irujo had criticized Negrín for trampling on Catalan rights which he suspected might next happen to the Basques. Soon after, the Civil War ended along with Irujo's career as a politician.

For further information, see Burnett Bolloten, *The Spanish Revolution: The Left and the Struggle for Power During the Civil War* (Chapel Hill, N.C., 1979); Hubertus von Loewenstein, *A Catholic in Republican Spain* (London, 1937); and Stanley G. Payne, *Basque Nationalism* (Reno, Nev., 1975).

See also Basque Nationalism.

James W. Cortada

IRÚN. Irún is a town close to the border between France* and Spain near the Bay of Biscay. As part of the overall Nationalist offensive in the north during August 1936, Franco's* forces invaded Irún and bombed it in late summer. The battle for Irún began on August 26 and ended on Sptember 3 with its capture by the Nationalists,* thus cutting off one of the Republicans'* avenues of escape into France. During the battle, most of the town's residents fled into France. With Irún's capture Basque communications to France were cut off. The Nationalists also captured valuable factories located in the area which could now be used to support their military efforts. Irún remained in Franco's hands for the remainder of the war.

For further information, see Hugh Thomas, *The Spanish Civil War* (New York, 1977).

James W. Cortada

IRURETAGOYENA SOLCHAGA, JOSÉ (1879-1952?). José Iruretagoyena was a career army officer who had reached the rank of general by the start of the Civil War. He fought with the Nationalists,* commanding troops throughout the war. In June 1938, his forces captured sizable numbers of Republican soldiers in the Valle del Alto Cinca near Valencia.* This was the only significant Nationalist victory in an area where a military stalemate had set in for the summer. Later that month, Iruretagoyena participated in the capture of the town of Bielsa in the Pyrenees,* thus reducing the region through which Republicans* could escape to France* or through which supplies could come into Spain.

For further information, see José Manuel Martínez Bande, *El final del frente norte* (Madrid, 1972).

James W. Cortada

ISGLEAS, FRANCISCO. Isgleas served as a councillor in the Catalan governing body, the Generalitat,* during 1936.' He represented the interests of the *Confederación Nacional del Trabajo* (CNT).* On April 16, 1937, President Companys* of the Catalan government formed a new cabinet, naming Isgleas to the position of minister of defense. While minister, considerable pressure came to bear on him to consolidate the militias* of various anarchist and Catalan groups into the Republican Army,* which is what eventually happened. He was constantly the target of communist criticism as the war progressed, and eventually they pushed him out of power.

For further information, see Burnett Bolloten, *The Spanish Revolution: The Left and the Struggle for Power During the Civil War* (Chapel Hill, N.C., 1979).
See also Catalonia.

James W. Cortada

ITALY. Italy, like most of Europe,* maintained correct but not particularly close relations with Spain during the first two decades of the twentieth century. In the 1920s, ideological affinities between Mussolini* and the Spanish dictator, General Miguel Primo de Rivera, led to somewhat more frequent contacts between Rome and Madrid,* but did not give rise to any effective collaboration between them. By contrast, Spain's proclamation of the Second Republic* in April 1931 aroused Mussolini's hostility.

Fascist Italy soon began to work for the Republic's downfall by aiding and encouraging anti-Republic conspirators. Italian ambassadors maintained contacts with leaders of the Falange* and other philofascist groups, but they placed most of their hope in monarchist and military conspirators. In March 1934 in Rome, Mussolini met a group composed of three monarchist politicians and one general. He promised them 10,000 rifles, 10,000 hand grenades, 200 machineguns, and 1 million pesetas in cash, with further aid to follow when conditions justified it. The Republicans* turned up a copy of this document in a police raid in May 1937 and presented it as proof of Mussolini's complicity in the preparation for the Civil War.

In fact, however, after March 1934, Rome lost interest in Spanish affairs. It had very little, if any, contact with the military groups that actually planned and carried out the July 1936 uprising against the Republic. In the month immediately preceding the outbreak of the Civil War, Italian observers formed a very pessimistic view of the probable outcome of any attempt to overthrow the Popular Front* government established early in 1936. A careful review of the evidence suggests that Italy played no part at all in the actual planning and preparation of the uprising that initiated the Civil War.

During the first week of the war, Mussolini refused three requests from Franco* for aircraft and other aid. Only after the French right-wing press revealed that the French government intended to support the Republic did Mussolini agree to sell the rebels twelve Savoia S81 bombers for slightly over a million pounds sterling. The crash of one of these bombers in French Morocco, on its way to Spanish Morocco,* gave the world its first news of direct Italian intervention in the incipient Spanish Civil War.

During the following three and one-half months, Italy gradually became more and more involved in the Spanish conflict. Throughout these early months of the war, officials in Rome believed that the Nationalists* were on the verge of victory. Each new shipment of arms was justified in terms of being the last aid the Nationalists would need to win the war. In late August 1936, Italy accepted the Franco-British proposal for a Non-Intervention Agreement, but this did not prevent Rome from continuing to support the Nationalists on a growing scale. Italian adhesion to the Non-Intervention Agreement was from the beginning an empty gesture. During October, Italian shipyards fitted the cruiser *Canaris*, the largest ship in the Nationalists' fleet, with the guns it was lacking when the Civil War broke out. During the first 100 days of the war, almost ninety Italian aircraft reached Spain.

During the early months of the war, the most spectacular Italian activities took place not on the Spanish mainland but in the Balearic Islands.* An Italian adventurer, Arconovaldo Bonaccorsi, using the pseudonym "Conte Rossi," collaborated with the commander of the Italian heavy cruiser *Fiume*, at anchor in the Bay of Palma, to stimulate the discouraged Nationalists on the island of Majorca* and to organize their defense of the island against an invasion launched from Barcelona* by the Republic. Bonaccorsi played a leading role in the political repression that followed the Nationalists' success in rejecting the Republican invasion of the island. He was a leading figure in the political and military life of the island until his withdrawal in December 1936.

Franco's failure to capture Madrid in November 1936 led to Italo-German diplomatic recognition of Franco and closed the first period in the story of Italian intervention in Spain. During the first period, the level of Italian intervention had been slight. Italy had provided arms and small numbers of men to act as instructors or to use complex equipment in battle, but had not committed any large body of combat troops.

In keeping with this modest level of support, Rome had generally been careful during this period to avoid interference in the internal politics of the Nationalist zone. Bonaccorsi's activist role in Majorca constitutes the only significant exception to this rule.

Diplomatic recognition of Franco brought with it a change in the character of Italy's presence in Spain. This was most evident in the military field. Not only were supply shipments vastly stepped up, but Italy now decided to send large numbers of combat troops as well. These decisions were preceded by the signing on November 28 of a secret treaty between the Spanish Nationalists and the Italian government. The text of the treaty gave Rome a sweeping series of rights that would, at least in theory, make it possible for Italy to establish bases on Spanish territory in the case of a conflict with France.* Many of the clauses were vaguely worded, and Franco would subsequently take advantage of their vagueness to avoid fulfilling his obligations to Italy. For the moment, however, the Italians were convinced they had won sweeping concessions.

In December 1936, Italy began sending large numbers of Black Shirts* to Spain. The first 3,000 sailed for Spain on the old transatlantic *Lombardia* on December 18. By the end of the month, some 10,000 Italian troops had departed for Spain. By mid-February 1937, this number had grown close to 50,000, of whom roughly 30,000 were from the Black Shirt militia and 20,000 from the regular army. Hand-in-hand with troop shipments went a vast increase in Italian supplies. In the two and one-half months from December 1, 1936, to February 10, 1937, Italy sent to Spain some 130 aircraft, 2,500 tons of bombs, 500 cannons, 700 mortars, 12,000 machineguns, 50 whippet tanks, and 3,800 motor vehicles. By February 16, the Italians in Spain had been organized into four purely Italian divisions that formed the *Corpo Truppe Volontarie* (CTV) under the command of General Mario Roatta.*

As Italy's military aid* to Franco multiplied, her political presence in Nationalist Spain also became more active. Propaganda efforts increased, and a regular press and propaganda office began to work in Salamanca.* In January, Mussolini named Randolfo Cantalupo* his first regular ambassador to Franco. In addition, he sent Robert Farinacci, ex-secretary general of the Fascist party and member of the Fascist Grand Council, on a special personal mission to Franco. Both in his contacts with Franco and in his dealings with leaders of the Falange,* Farinacci attempted, albeit unsuccessfully, to promote the development of fascism in Spain.

Italian troops saw action in Spain for the first time in the battle of Málaga* in early February. One Black Shirt Division, supported by tanks, armored cars, and some fifty aircraft as well as by five Spanish Nationalist columns, began its assault on Málaga on February 5. The Italian commander, General Roatta, was wounded during the attack, but the Italians met little resistance and occupied the city on February 8. Italian losses included nine officers and eighty-five men killed, twenty-six officers and 250 men wounded, and two men missing in action.

At Málaga, the Italians deployed their recently developed *guerra celebre* tactics, a sort of *blitzkrieg* in which motorized columns moved ahead very rapidly, spearheaded by armored cars. Little effort was made to protect the flanks of the advancing columns whose security was entrusted almost exclusively to the rapidity of their advance. If the tactic was successful, it was largely due to the weakness of Málaga's defenses.

The occupation of Málaga shortened the front by about 150 miles and gave the Nationalists control of a Mediterranean port. Some 10,000 prisoners* were taken, many of whom were eventually incorporated into the ranks of the Nationalist Army.* The victory also did much to boost the morale of Franco's forces, who were depressed by their failure to take Madrid.

After their victory at Málaga, the Italians became overconfident. They devised a plan for an offensive from Siguenza toward Guadalajara* in which the Italians would be the northern half of a pincers whose southern half would be formed by Spanish forces moving up from the Jarama River.* The two would meet near Alcalá de Henares,* thereby sealing off Madrid. Franco would have preferred to have dispersed Italian troops among his own Spanish units, but Mussolini was anxious for the glory which he hoped to derive from stunning victories. He insisted on using the CTV as a single unit.

For the attack on Guadalajara, the CTV had on paper the most powerful striking forces assembled by either side during the first nine months of the Civil War, totaling about 35,000 men: 1st, 2d, and 3d Black Shirt divisions, and the army Littorio Division, as well as two groups of 75 millimeter guns, four of 100 millimeter, two of 105 millimeter, and two of 149 millimeter. Their forces were completed by a tank battalion with eighty-one whippet tanks, a company of eight armored cars, a company of motorized machine-gunners, and a corps motor pool. Although it did not enjoy the overwhelming advantage in armament which many authors have credited it, the CTV was extremely well armed by the standards of the Civil War. The CTV was to be supported by the Nationalist Soría Division, operating on its right flank under the command of General Moscardó.*

From its very inception on March 8, the Italian offensive encountered unexpected problems. Despite relatively weak resistance, the Italians failed to break the enemy front during the first day of the offensive. On the second day, the Italians advanced more rapidly and succeeded in disorganizing the remaining Republican defenses. For a moment, it seemed that the Guadalajara offenses might become the glorious success its planners had envisioned. The Republic, however, soon rushed reserves to the Guadalajara sector. The failure of the Spanish Nationalists on the Jarama south of Madrid to launch any significant attack allowed the Republic to concentrate most of its best forces against the Italians, including almost all of the International Brigades.* These forces succeeded in stopping the Italian offensive on March 10 and 11, and a stalemate soon developed. On March 18, the Italians were caught off guard by a powerful Republican counteroffensive, which soon drove them out of their positions and forced them to begin to retreat.

Fortunately for the Italians, on the evening of March 18 the Republicans broke off all contact with the retreating Italian units. This enabled them to establish new positions some 8 to 10 miles behind their point of furthest advance, but still close to 10 miles from their original jumping-off points. A few days later, Spanish Nationalist troops replaced the Italians in the lines north of Guadalajara, signaling the end of the battle.

In strategic and tactical terms, Guadalajara was a relatively minor success for the Republicans. The CTV, which had broken a weak and poorly organized defensive line, had been stopped before it reached any vital objectives. Thus, the Republicans successfully parried another threat to Madrid as they had done in the fall at the University City and in February on the Jarama, but they were unable to make any significant gain or even to recover all of the ground they had lost in the initial stages of the fighting. Republican losses amounted to 2,000 killed and 4,000 wounded at Guadalajara. Italian casualties were 400 killed, 1,800 wounded, and some 500 prisoners or missing in action. The Italians also lost significant quantities of arms and supplies, including at least twenty-five artillery pieces, ten mortars, eighty-five machineguns, and sixty-seven trucks.

From a moral and psychological point of view, Guadalajara represented a great victory for the Republic and a stinging defeat for the fascists. Fascism had massed its forces against the Republic and had been turned back. This success greatly raised the morale of Madrid's defenders and of their supporters throughout the world.

The Italian defeat at Guadalajara was due in large part to the strength and rapidity of the Republic's reaction. The inactivity of Franco's troops to the south of Madrid enabled the Republic to throw almost all its tanks and airplanes against the Italians at Guadalajara. The 20,000 to 25,000 Republican troops brought into the sector between March 8 and March 21 included many of the Republic's best units, including the International Brigades.

The weakness and defects of the CTV, in both troops and commanders, also contributed importantly to the Italian defeat. Many of the Italian soldiers were seriously wanting in physical fitness, training, and motivation. General Roatta and his staff clearly underestimated their adversary, even after the experiences of the first few days demonstrated that the Republican defenses in this sector were much more serious than those at Málaga. Italian planning for the attack was hasty, incomplete, and based on inadequate information.

Guadalajara and Málaga were the only two battles of the Civil War in which Franco allowed the Italians to play a central role independently. In the future, he would insist on their operating as part of larger units made up primarily of Spanish troops and commanded by Spanish generals.

Italian fighting units were reorganized by the end of April, but except for the air force which played an important role at Brunete,* Italian soldiers saw little action until the second phase of the northern offensive in August 1937. Italian units played a significant military role in the Nationalist attack on Santander,* but even more important was their political role in negotiating the surrender of Basque units in and around Santoña. Although the Italians promised not to turn Basque prisoners over to Franco, they reneged on these promises.

The months immediately following the battle of Guadalajara were characterized by a high degree of international tension over Italian intervention in Spain. Republican air attacks on Italian and German ships participating in the international patrol of the sea lanes leading to Spain by the Non-Intervention Committee* led to a series of international crises in May and June 1937. Rome and Berlin temporarily suspended their participation in the meetings of the Non-Intervention Committee and permanently withdrew their ships from the patrol's scheme. This forced the committee to turn its attention to questions of belligerent rights* and the withdrawal of volunteers,* but negotiations over these issues soon led to a complete deadlock.

A more serious crisis arose in August 1937 when Italian submarines,* at Franco's request, began torpedoing ships bound for Spanish Republican ports. In the face of strong Franco-British protest, Italy suspended its attacks on shipping early in September, but refused to attend the Nyon Conference* (in Switzerland*)to discuss the problem. Despite the Italian boycott, Great Britain,* France, and the USSR* agreed to a set of vigorous measures to prevent "piracy" in the Mediterranean. Italy did not renew its attacks on merchant shipping, and the level of international tension over Spanish affairs quickly decreased. The Nyon Conference thus marked the end of serious international tension over Spain. After Nyon the Spanish Civil War, though still important, became a secondary factor both in Italy's foreign relations and in the diplomacy of Western Europe.*

During the final eighteen months of the war, Italian units in Spain contributed on several occasions to Franco's offensives, but their activities were generally of secondary importance. More than once, Mussolini became so frustrated with the slow pace of Franco's advance that he threatened to withdraw his support altogether, but his political commitment was already so great that these were in fact mere idle threats. Down to the very end of the war, Mussolini not only maintained his forces in Spain, but also continued to provide Franco with vital arms and equipment.

During this final part of the war, Franco began to institutionalize his regime. He created a National Council of the Falange, established a civilian government, and issued a labor charter. Particularly in the National Council of the Falange and in the labor charter, it is easy to find similarities with Italian fascist institutions. These similarities, however, were not due in any significant degree to direct Italian pressure or even to specific Italian attempts to influence the internal politics of Nationalist Spain. Italy's direct intervention in the internal political development of the Nationalist zone was all but negligible, although Franco's dependence on her for arms and for diplomatic support would surely have permitted her to exercise much more influence had she so desired. After Guadalajara, Mussolini returned to the policy he had briefly abandoned during the Farinacci mission of allowing the Nationalists to organize their political life as they saw fit, without Italian interference. His passive "hands-off" policy confirms that his aims in Spain were more strategic and political in the classical sense than ideological. He was much more interested in preventing the victory of the antifascist Republic than in promoting fascist institutions in Spain.

A similarly passive attitude characterized most of Italy's economic dealings with Spain. The Italians did make some efforts to guarantee that they would at least be paid for the supplies they provided. Compared to those of the Germans, however, their efforts were weak and half-hearted. They made almost no attempt to guarantee favorable positions for themselves in the economy of postwar Spain.

Italian support was an essential element in the Nationalist victory. Franco needed Italian diplomatic support. France had many solid reasons for wishing to see a Republican victory. It is highly probable that the French government would have provided the Republic the aid it needed to overcome the Nationalist uprising, if it had not been for Italian and German diplomatic support of the rebels.

Franco also needed the arms and material supplied by Italy. During the course of the conflict, Italy shipped to Spain some 1,800 cannon, 1,400 mortars, 3,400 machineguns, 6,800 motor vehicles, 157 tanks, 213 bombers, forty-four assault planes, 414 fighters, eight million artillery shells, and 320 million rounds of small arms ammunition. The total value of Italian supplies was some 6 billion lire, or about 64 million pounds sterling at 1939 exchange rates. In addition, Italy sent to Spain roughly 80,000 men, of whom almost 6,000 belonged to the Italian Air Force, 45,000 to the army, and 29,000 to the fascist militia. Italy also provided important naval support to the Nationalists by arming the *Canarias*, by providing submarines and other vessels to the Nationalists, and by using her own navy to impede shipments to Republican Spain.

Considering both the quantity of aid and the quality of the material provided, Italian weapons, equipment, and supplies probably contributed as much as the German to Franco's victory. Italian pilots* and other air force personnel played a vital role in Franco's triumph, both in direct combat and in training Spanish pilots. At no time during the war did Italian—or German—officers play a central role as Franco's advisers in the planning of operations. In this field, Italo-German influence on the Nationalists was less direct and less significant than Soviet influence on the Republicans. Most Italian attempts to influence Franco involved the pace of the war. Mussolini was anxious to end his commitment in Spain and was convinced that Franco could win the war more quickly if he really tried. Franco, however, continued to carry out the war in his own way and at his own pace, despite Rome's vigorous protests and threats to discontinue its aid. Italian infantry troops, despite their numbers, were not a significant factor in Franco's victory. They never fulfilled the function of an elite shock force, as did the International Brigades for the Republic. They made valid contributions at Málaga, Santander, and elsewhere, but with over a million men under arms by the end of the war, Franco did not vitally need 70,000 foreign infantry soldiers.

For further information, see Galeazzo Ciano, *Ciano's Hidden Diary, 1937-38* (New York, 1953), *Ciano's Diplomatic Papers* (London, 1948), and *The Ciano Dia-*ries, *1939-1945* (London, 1946); John F. Coverdale, *Italian Intervention in the Spanish Civil War* (Princeton, N.J., 1975); Dante Puzzo, *Spain and the Great Powers, 1936-1941* (New York, 1962); and Robert H. Whealey, "Foreign Intervention in the Spanish Civil War," in Raymond Carr, ed., *The Republic and the Civil War in Spain* (London, 1971), pp. 213-38.

John F. Coverdale

J

JAÉN. Jaén was one of the provinces in southern Spain to come under Nationalist control. Its bishop was killed by a militia woman in front of a crowd of nearly 2,000, and other prelates were persecuted before Franco's* forces occupied the region. Throughout the war, the province remained under the control of militia units of the *Unión General de Trabajadores* (UGT).* It was not until the very end of the war that the Nationalists* fully occupied the area.

For further information, see Luis Garrido González, *Collectividades agrarias en Andalucia: Jaén (1931-1939)* (Madrid, 1979); and Edward E. Malefakis, *Agrarian Reform and Peasant Revolution in Spain: Origins of the Civil War* (New Haven, Conn., 1970).
See also Andalusia.

James W. Cortada

JAIME I. The Republican battleship *Jaime I* (ex *Alfonso XIII*, launched in 1914, 14,224 tons standard, 8-305mm [12 in] guns, 20 kts.) was ordered from Santander* to the Straits of Gibraltar* on July 17, 1936. On the way, Republican crewmen captured the ship from the officers after an armed struggle. *Jaime I* joined the blockading squadron in the Straits and used her heavy guns to bombard rebel port installations. In a German air raid on August 13, a bomb damaged the battleship's bow. *Jaime I* helped evacuate Catalan forces from Majorca* in September and joined the Republican fleet's cruise to threatened northern ports in September-October 1936. The ship spent much of the spring of 1937 as a floating battery in Almería.* She was in Cartagena* preparing for an overhaul on June 17, 1937, when destroyed by an internal explosion which killed eighty-seven.

See also Navy, Spanish.

Willard C. Frank, Jr.

JARAMA, BATTLE OF. Following the failure in January 1937 to envelop Madrid* by an attack across the Corunna* highway, the Nationalist command decided upon a similar effort from the south, in a three-phase operation along an 11 mile front, 4 to 8 miles west of the Jarama River. The plan was to seize Ciempozuelos (in the south) and the heights above Vaciamadrid, near the junction of the Manzanares* and Jarama rivers (in the north), then cross the Jarama and take Arganda, and, finally, swing northeast to Alcalá de Henares* while pressing on to Morata (and Perales) de Tajuña, south of Arganda. Scheduled for January 24 but postponed because of heavy rains, the insurgents' plans were known to but discounted by the Republican authorities in Valencia,* who were planning an offensive of their own westward from the Jarama to sever the Nationalists'* communications between Toledo* and Madrid. At the time, the Republicans* had only two brigades in the immediate area (the 28th at La Maranosa and the 18th at Ciempozuelos), plus a group of Assault Guards* at San Martín de la Vega.

The Nationalist assault was launched by General Varela* on February 6, with five brigades initially totaling 18,500 effectives in twenty-eight infantry battalions, twelve cavalry squadrons, twenty-eight artillery batteries, and three companies of tanks. The 5th Brigade (García Escámez*) quickly overran Ciempozuelos, while the 1st (Rada) and 3d (Barron*) Brigades smashed through the heights overlooking Vaciamadrid on February 7-8. The 2d (Sáenz de Buruaga*) and 4th (Asensio*) Brigades reached the crest overlooking the Jarama and San Martín de la Vega on February 9, by which time some Republican reinforcements were brought in, including the 3,000-man 12th International Brigade, and mainly deployed east of the Jarama between Vaciamadrid and Pajares, north of San Martín de la Vega.

On February 11, Barron's Brigade led the assault across the Pindoque Bridge and pushed towards Arganda against strong resistance from the 12th International Brigade, while to the south, Asensio's group took San Martín de la Vega, crossed the Jarama, and seized the 693-meter Pingarron Hill west of Morata de Tajuña. Bolstered by 12,500 replacements and reinforcements, Varela, in an effort to straighten his front, on February 12 shifted the main attack from Arganda towards Morata de Tajuña, whose approaches were now defended by the 11th and 15th International Brigades,* joined by Lister's* Division on February 13 and by the 14th International Brigade the following day. By now, the Republicans had achieved complete domination of the air, and Varela committed his last reserves to Sáenz de Buruaga in the fierce fighting that centered between the Jarama and Tajuña rivers, about 5 kilometers west of Morata. Sáenz de Buruaga's and Asensio's troops pushed the defenders back towards Morata, while Barron's Brigades swung south in an effort to split the 11th and 12th International Brigades and compress the front between Arganda and Morata. They were stopped by fifty Russian tanks which, with strong air cover, then helped repulse Sáenz de Buruaga's Moroccans.

On February 15, General Miaja* replaced General Pozas* as commander of the Republican forces, which were reorganized into four divisions of twelve brigades (approximately fifty battalions), plus a brigade at Aranjuez. Approximating 35,000 effectives, they now faced forty Nationalist battalions and fifteen cavalry squadrons, several of which counted less than 60 percent of their original strength. On the same day Sáenz de Buruaga's Brigade succeeded in advancing slightly to a point about 4 kilometers from Morata, but neither side made any significant gain over the next several days. Asensio's troops lost and retook Pingarron Hill three times, and the Nationalists suffered 650 casualties* on February 23 alone. On February 27, Americans of the recently arrived Lincoln Battalion* of the 15th Brigade suffered 300 casualties in an attack on Pingarron Hill, and the Republicans give up the attempt to push the Nationalists back across the Jarama. The lines then stabilized and remained virtually unchanged until the end of the war.

Nationalist sources variously place Nationalist casualties from 6,360 to about 10,500, and cite Republican documents placing Loyalist casualties at 7,963, including 2,800 Internationals, between February 6 and February 23. However, losses of at least 10,000 (25 percent) on each side seem more likely. On balance, the battle represented a defensive victory for the Republicans.

For further information, see Robert G. Colodny, *The Struggle for Madrid* (New York, 1958); Cecil Eby, *Between the Bullet and the Lie* (New York, 1969); Editorial Codex, "Los Sangrientos Olivares de Jarama," *Crónica de la Guerra Española*, No. 52 (Buenos Aires, 1967); José Manuel Martínez Bande, *La lucha en torna a Madrid* (Madrid, 1968); López Muñiz, *La batalla de Madrid* (Madrid, 1943); and Robert A. Rosenstone, *Crusade of the Left* (New York, 1969).

See also Appendix B.

Verle B. Johnston

JERÉZ. Jeréz, located in the province of Cádiz* in southern Spain, continued to serve as a traditional producer of wines and sherries during the Civil War. In July 1936, rebellion against the Republic broke out in the region, parts of which remained under anarchist control for some time. Eventually, the Nationalists* occupied Jeréz.

For further information, see Hugh Thomas, *The Spanish Civil War* (New York, 1977).

James W. Cortada

JEWS. Jews in twentieth-century Spain were a numerically insignificant part of the population* (probably less than 5,000 out of 30 million in 1930), but they played a larger role because of the historical memory of their expulsion in 1492, the existence of some half a million Sephardim in Europe,* along with 25,000 Jews in Spain's Moroccan Protectorate, and the propagation of the idea by anti-Semites that there was an international Jewish conspiracy, usually in alliance with "international Masonry,"* intent upon destroying the Catholic Church* and traditional Spanish values.

In fact, Spanish Jews had achieved a relatively high degree of toleration under the reign of Alfonso XIII* who was viewed as a special friend of the Spanish Jewish community. In 1910, the first Jew was elected to the Cortes,* in 1915 a chair of Hebrew Studies was established at the University of Madrid, in 1917 Alfonso offered his services to protect the Palestinian Jews in World War I, and in 1924 Spanish citizenship was offered to the Sephardim who had lost their Turkish protection under the Treaty of Lausanne. During the Second Republic,* the Jewish community welcomed official religious toleration, but there were few tangible benefits which the Jews had not already won, and the various republican governments never acceded to a Jewish request to officially revoke the 1492 edict of expulsion.

After the Civil War broke out, the theme of a Jewish international conspiracy supporting the Republic became a staple item of Nationalist propaganda, but there are no facts to bolster such a contention, General Gonzalo Quiepo de Llano* emphasized anti-Semitism in his broadcasts from Seville* and levied fines on the Jewish communities in Seville and Morocco.* Franco* generally disapproved these actions, although the Nationalist regime required Jews to lower rents and confiscated some Jewish-owned property during the war. On the Republican side, the government confiscated and/or nationalized some Jewish property, along with that of other middle-class owners. As a result, many Jews emigrated from Spain.

After 1939, Franco's government, while paying lip-service to German anti-Semitism, opened Spain's frontiers to Jewish refugees and took special care to protect the Sephardim of France* and Greece* from transportation to German death camps.

For further information, see Caesar C. Aronsfeld, *The Ghosts of 1492* (New York, 1979).

José M. Sánchez

JIMÉNEZ DE ASÚA, LUIS (1889-1970). Jiménez, born and educated in Madrid,* became professor of penal law at the national university in 1918, quickly branched out into advocacy of social reform, joined the Socialist party,* and by the 1930s was one of its leading functionaries—one of the men closest to Francisco Largo Caballero,* premier from September 1936 to May 1937.

Jiménez's many works included *El estado de necesidad. El hombre ante las leyes penales* (1922), his controversial *Libertad de amar y derecho a morir* (1928), and his political credo, *Al servicio de la nueva generación* (1930), a book that is essential in understanding the mentality of the Second Republic's* makers and of Spanish socialist intellectuals* in general.

Jiménez's political career spanned the years from Primo de Rivera's dictatorship to the end of the Civil War. He led demonstrations for intellectual freedom against Primo de Rivera, which resulted in his temporary deportation. He was a prominent drafter of the San Sebastián manifesto in 1930, which outlined a pact among socialists, radical liberals, and regionalists to overthrow the monarchy, and he chaired the committee that drafted the outlines of the Constitution of 1931. Some said he was responsible for the high degree of socialist ideas that it contained. After ratification of the constitution, he served as a deputy in 1932-1933 and was returned to the Cortes* in February 1936. He served as an adviser to the premier from September 4, 1936, through the first half of 1937, acting as minister of justice on several occasions, although he was passed over in November 1936 in the Popular Front* coalition put together by Largo Caballero. Nevertheless, he represented the Second Republic as ambassador to Czechoslovakia,* Poland,* and the League of Nations.* After the fall of the Republic in 1939, Jiménez moved to Argentina,* where he taught and wrote until his death.

For further information, see Luis Jiménez de Asúa, *Memorias 1897-1936*(Buenos Aires, 1977).

Robert W. Kern

JOURNALISTS, FRENCH. The peculiar mix of journalism and politics in France* in the 1930s makes it hard to distinguish between journalists with political ambitions and politicians using the press, but several in both categories made the most of the Spanish conflict. Among the writers of signed editorials, the leading figures on the Right were Charles Maurras of *L'Action Française* and Léon Bailby of *Le Jour*, who gave their support to the Nationalists*without reservation, as did Gaston Guèze of *L'Express du Midi*. On the Left, the Republicans* had equal support from Paul Vaillant-Couturier and Gabriel Péri in *L'Humanité*, Jean Zyromski in *Le Populaire*, and Léon Hudelle and André Leroux in *Le Midi Socialiste*. Between these two positions of total support, other writers expressed nuances. In *Le Figaro*, even if Wladimir d'Ormesson consistently sided with the Nationalists, Lucien Romier was more concerned with the implications of Spain to world peace. War crimes and peace were also the major concern of Georges Bidault in *L'Aube* and of Georges Boris in *La Lumière*. In *La Dépêche*, which quickly moved from impartial to pro-Republican, the jurist Georges Scelle concentrated on points of international law, while Manuel Chaves Nogales, the former director of *Ahora* of Madrid,* set the war in the context of Spanish history and accurately predicted its trajectory. In the radical press, Geneviève Tabouis of *L'Oeuvre* had close family connections with the diplomatic world, especially in Rome, but her articles on foreign policy were of uneven worth. Pierre Dominique in *La République*, and Emile Buré in *L'Ordre*, showed a sympathy for the Spanish Popular Front* that they never did for the French *Front Populaire*. And it was Buré, with Henri de Kérillis, who emerged as the only journalists on the Right to take an uncompromising stand against Axis intervention and against appeasement. Like his colleague "Pertinax" (André Géraud), who opposed the Popular Front and French intervention but who opposed Axis intervention even more, Kérillis abandoned *L'Echo de Paris* in mid-May 1937 out of distaste for its editorial policy of total support for the Nationalist cause. Kérillis emerged as the most celebrated editor of the war. It was he who in July 1936 fired the outrage on the Right over Blum's* plan to aid the Republic, and it was on his initiative in mid-October that *L'Echo de Paris* opened a subscription to offer a sword of honor to a Nationalist general, Franco* later being selected to receive the award. In the new daily *L'Epoque*, Kérillis did not abandon his conservative views but began to present Hitler* as the gravest threat to French security. By January 1939, he had come to see the victory of Franco as "a veritable catastrophe for France."

Crossing into Catalonia* was difficult during the

first two weeks of the war, and those journals with correspondents already in Spain thus had an advantage, but François Andrieu, in Valencia* for *La Dépêche*, complained in early August of the sorry state of the telephone service and preferred to phone his dispatches from the frontier. Other journals exaggerated the difficulties of access to excuse the weakness of their news coverage. Several right-wing journalists entered Spain only after the fall of Irún;* *Le Jour*'s correspondent crossed the international bridge giving the fascist salute. Pro-Republican journalists on the Basque border were thereafter denied access, and even one-right wing reporter (Pierre Plessis of *Combat*) was severely beaten in September just for being French. Andrieu, who spent three weeks in Nationalist-held Morocco, reported that every Frenchman was suspected of spying. Indeed, the Nationalists decreed that any foreign journalist who had worked on their side and who was afterwards captured with Republican troops would be sentenced to death. Journalists were expelled even for calling the Nationalists rebels, and some were forced to disguise themselves as tourists. They were regularly prevented from entering towns captured by the Nationalists while the executions were in progress, but some witnessed the scene nonetheless. At Badajoz* the press was not allowed to enter until August 16, and Jean Esmé (*L'Intransigeant* and *Le Petit Journal*) was arrested. When permitted to fly back to France he was in a piteous condition. Several French correspondents were killed. Guy de Traversay (*L'Intransigeant*) was shot by the Nationalists in Majorca* during the Republican débâcle of August 1936 for carrying a letter of introduction to Captain Bayo* signed by the Generalitat.* Louis Delaprée, whose dispatches from Madrid *Paris-Soir* refused to publish, was killed in December 1936 when his plane, flying from Madrid to Toulouse, was attacked by unidentified aircraft. Serge Ala (*L'Humanité*) and Renée Lafont (*Le Populaire*) were also killed in the opening months. Andrée Viollis (*Le Petit Parisien*), whose dispatches from Madrid were either rejected or bowdlerized, sent telegrams of protest to other journals but to no effect. She resigned and joined *Vendredi*. Aubin Rieu-Vernet, chief correspondent for *La Dépêche*, was in the Nationalist camp in July, then switched to Madrid, and shared the stigma laid on the government when he followed it in its panicky flight to Valencia. Among others, Antoine de Saint-Exupéry (*L'Intransigeant*) covered the Republican front and Bertrand de Jouvenel (*Paris-Soir*) the Nationalist. Pierre Héricourt (*L'Action Française*) entered Guernica* on May 1, 1937, and set out to "demolish the myth of the German planes." His report of finding the town "still smelling of the gasoline used by the Red arsonists" was a major contribution to the obfuscation that followed. Against this, the Generalitat's invitation, in November 1936, to a team of French journalists to travel at random in Republican Spain illustrated the far more open policy of the Republic.

For further information, see Hugh Thomas, *The Spanish Civil War* (New York, 1977).
    See also France; and Newspapers.

David Wingeate Pike

JOVER, GREGORIO (-1937). Jover was a long-time anarchist politician who, during the Civil War, commanded militia units fighting for the Republicans.* As a dedicated violent anarchist, he did not hesitate to threaten to march on Barcelona,* for example, when the interests of his political followers were threatened. He eventually died under unusual circumstances, possibly killed by communist rivals, who had him arrested. Communists had marked him for punishment since the May Days* during which he actively fought against the government and its communist supporters in Barcelona.

For further information, see Robert W. Kern, *Red Years/Black Years: A Political History of Spanish Anarchism, 1911-1937* (Philadelphia, 1978).

James W. Cortada

JUNOD, MARCEL (1904-1961). Junod was a Swiss Red Cross official who, during the Civil War, continuously sought to exchange prisoners* among the Republicans* and Nationalists.* He enjoyed remarkable success, despite the general lack of interest on the part of either side for exchanges. In Bilbao* in September 1936, for example, he managed to evacuate 130 women, while on another occasion he exchanged a Republican mayor for other prisoners. He traveled all over Spain exchanging prisoners and facilitating evacuations of small groups of individuals. For many writers on the Spanish Civil War, Dr. Junod remains one of the rare humanitarians to emerge from this struggle.

For further information, see Marcel Junod, *Warrior Without Weapons* (London, 1951).

James W. Cortada

JUNTA DE DEFENSA NACIONAL. The *Junta de Defensa Nacional*, formed in September 1936, was the first military governing body formed by the Nationalists,* which evolved into the broader group known as the *Junta Técnica*,* which in turn became the Nationalist government of General Franco.* Its initial membership consisted of generals leading the revolt against the Second Republic* in July 1936.

James W. Cortada

JUNTAS DE OFENSIVA NACIONAL-SINDICAL-ISTA (JONS). The *Juntas de Ofensiva Nacional-Sindicalista* (JONS) was a conservative political organization formed in October 1931 by Ramiro Ledesma Ramos,* a young political radical, and by Onésimo Redondo, a conservative Catholic academician. They advocated the acquisition of Gibraltar* and such portions of North Africa as Tangier and French Morocco; rejected regional separatism, class warfare, exploitation of the ignorant and the poor; and proposed the control of profits and support for the Catholic Church* as the preserver of traditional Spanish values. JONS remained miniscule in 1931 and throughout all of 1932. Yet, this group increasingly allied itself with those who eventually made up the Falange* party, founded in October 1933. The JONS and the Falange united their forces in that year following the death of a JONSista selling a Falangist newspaper. The union, officially effective on February 11, 1934, increased the size of the Falange by several hundred members. The two groups continued to question the Republic's policies throughout 1934 and 1935. It was also the JONS which contributed its symbol—the yoke and arrows—to the Falange for its own. By the time the Civil War came in 1936, leaders in the JONS had been fully integrated into the Falange, the latter absorbing and even contributing its own conservative philosophies to the entire union of forces. Ledesma became one of the intellectual pillars of the Falange; both he and Redondo, however, died in the early days of the war, thereby insuring that the Falange would win full control over JONS.

For further information, see Stanley G. Payne, *Falange: A History of Spanish Fascism* (Stanford, Calif., 1961).

See also Primo de Rivera, José Antonio.

James W. Cortada

JUNTA TÉCNICA. The *Junta Técnica* was the first Nationalist government. Formed on July 23, 1936, by General Emilio Mola* and called the *Junta de Defensa Nacional** after consultation with such key conspirators within the monarchist camp as Goicoechea* and the Count of Vallellano,* it was nominally run in the beginning by General Miguel Cabanellas,* then the senior officer of the rebellion. Its initial membership was all military and included Mola, Miguel Ponte, Fidel Dávila,* Andrés Saliquet,* Fernando Moreno Calderón, and Federico Montaner.* Only in August did General Francisco Franco* finally become a member. It was first headquartered in Burgos,* and its initial task was the reorganization of the two rebel armies into one north of Madrid* then surrounding

the area of Pamplona* under the command of General Mola, and another to the south belonging to General Franco's command. Colonels Moreno Calderón and Montaner became the nucleus of an administrative support staff. For all intents and purposes, public officials in the Nationalist zones operated as always, although gradually adhering to the authority of the *Junta* which in turn functioned with the principles of military law in its early days. In the first months of the war, the three major Nationalist leaders who actually ran their respective zones were Mola in the north, Franco in southernmost Spain, and Queipo de Llano* in Andalusia* proper.

At a meeting of the *Junta,* held on September 21, it was decided that Franco should be head of a unified Nationalist command. Franco dominated the leadership, having already won a considerable number of victories to the south; entertained monarchist sympathies and thus could be counted upon by many of the generals to restore the monarchy; and had proven military abilities not tainted by an active political past. On September 29, he was publicly declared Generalissimo and head of state for the duration of the war, acquiring as the decree on the occasion read, "all the powers of the Spanish state." After October 1, he was called the Caudillo.

Proposing a policy of national regeneration that called for the destruction of the Republican state, Franco also advocated supporting the Church,* a monarchy, and the program of the Falange,* sought support from the Carlists,* and wooed the help and blessings of the middle and upper classes of traditional Spanish society. Toward these ends, a reorganized *Junta* was formed on October 2 which became a provisional government charged with the full responsibilities of operating the Nationalist state. General Dávila became its head, Franco's brother Nicolás* secretary general, José Antonio Sangroniz* took charge of foreign affairs, and Juan Pujol* propaganda. The military organization was left untouched for the time being, yet directly under Franco's personal control.

Government functions moved to Salamanca* where Franco and a small staff were the governing force in Nationalist Spain. In addition to the few people already mentioned, by late fall the staff had grown to include a lawyer, Colonel Lorenzo Martínez Fusset,* and two staff officers, Juan Vigón* and Antonio Barroso.* Juan Cervera,* a career naval officer and an admiral, took charge of the Nationalist Navy, while additional offices were established to run the Falange, the Bank of Spain,* and the ministries of the treasury, justice, and labor. The last three remained in Burgos during the early months of the new government. By this time, the group was being called the *Junta Técnica*. German and Italian diplomats also called on the *Junta Técnica* in Salamanca. Finally, generals commanding various military forces periodically called on Franco and the *Junta* in Salamanca, the nominal first capital of the Franco regime.

In addition to running the war, the *Junta* in the winter of 1936 was responsible for reestablishing the Nationalist zone's economy, conducting relations with Germany* and Italy,* which were strongly supporting their war effort, purifying Nationalist zones of potential political and civilian enemies, and consolidating political power from rival organizations and groups (such as the Carlists,* monarchists, Falange, and other conservative forces). The political crisis ended in April 1937, which led to the further development and consolidation of the Nationalist government under the control of General Franco.

It was clear that a considerable amount of power would be in Franco's hands as the various political forces came under his personal control. By mid-1937, the Nationalists* occupied and controlled nearly two-thirds of Spain. The *Junta*, now ostensibly under the control of General Gómez-Jordana,* and headquartered by this time at Burgos, expanded its services. On December 2, 1936, Franco had created a forty-eight member advisory council representing all major elements within Nationalist Spain, leaving to the *Junta* daily administrative matters. Hugh Thomas likens this advisory council to the Italian Grand Council. It had members from the Carlists, Falangists, military, and other groups, including three women. Yet, it had little power.

During the second winter of the Civil War, both the council and the *Junta* evolved into a cabinet-type government. For example, on February 1, Franco took the title of president of the council, Gómez-Jordana that of vice-president and minister of foreign affairs, Dávila minister of defense, and the aging Martínez Anido* minister of public order. A Finance Ministry was created under the direction of Andrés Amado,* while Juan Antonio Suanzes* headed the Ministry of Industry and Commerce. Rodenzno* took charge of justice, while Sáinz Rodríguez* the portfolio for education.* Franco's brother-in-law, Serrano Suñer,* headed the Ministry of the Interior which at the time had the greatest amount of power. A Ministry of Agriculture, under the control of Fernández Cuesta,* added depth to the cabinet. Two other ministries were added, one for labor under the control of a technocratic member of the Falange, Pedro González Bueno, and a Ministry of Public Works, taken by Alfonso Peña Boeuf.* Thus, Spain under the Nationalists had a government

that could and did replace the *Junta Técnica*, absorbing Republican agencies as the war progressed and those normal functions of a Spanish government, all sworn to obey Franco.

For further information, see Martin Blinkhorn, *Carlism and Crisis in Spain, 1931–1939* (Cambridge, England, 1975); Jaime del Burgo, *Conspiración y guerra civil* (Madrid, 1970); Stanley G. Payne, *Falange: A History of Spanish Fascism* (Stanford, Calif., 1961); and Hugh Thomas, *The Spanish Civil War* (New York, 1977).

James W. Cortada

JURADO BARRIO, ENRIQUE (1883-1954?). Jurado was a career army officer in the artillery. At the start of the Civil War, he held the rank of colonel and eventually rose to general in the Republican Army.* In March 1937, at the battle of Guadalajara,* where the Republicans* blocked a Nationalist attempt to encircle Madrid,* he commanded the 4th Army Corps. This skillful officer continued to lead combat troops at the battle of Brunete* in July. In February 1939, he became commander-in-chief of all Republican Army units in Catalonia.* After the war, he crossed over into France* and eventually died in exile.

For further information, see Michael Alpert, *El ejército republicano en la guerra civil* (Barcelona, 1977).

James W. Cortada

JUST GIMENO, JULIO. Just, as a member of the Left Republican Radical party of Valencia,* the town of his birth, was elected to the Cortes* in 1931 and in 1933. In 1936, he returned to the Cortes as a supporter of the Popular Front.* This man of pacifist temperament became minister of public works in Francisco Largo Caballero's* government between September 1936 and May 1937. His appointment was to give the government a degree of credibility in the minds of the bourgeoisie and foreign governments such as France* and Great Britain.* Just was also a member of the *Consejo Superior Interministerial de Guerra* (Superior Interministerial Council of War), a kind of inner cabinet devised to monitor the influence of the communists upon Largo Caballero's policies and his prosecution of the war. During the last days of the war, in March 1939, Just negotiated the settlement between the communists and Casado's* followers in Madrid.*

With the end of the war days off, Just fled from Madrid to France and then to Latin America.* He held posts in the Republican governments-in-exile and wrote for *España Libre*, published in Toulouse.

For further information, see Burnett Bolloten, *The Spanish Revolution: The Left and the Struggle for Power During the Civil War* (Chapel Hill, N.C., 1979); Segismundo Casado, *The Last Days of Madrid* (London, 1939); César M. Lorenzo, *Les anarchistes espagnols et le pouvoir 1868-1969* (Paris, 1969); and Cipriano Mera, *Guerra, exilio y cárcel de un anarcosindicalista* (Paris, 1976).

Shirley F. Fredricks

JUVENTUD COMUNISTA IBÉRICA (JCI). The *Juventud Comunista Ibérica* (JCI) was a radical youth group within *Partido Obrero de Unificación Marxista* (POUM)* which, in the summer of 1936 in Barcelona,* advocated the establishment of soviets and the execution of nonconformists to communist doctrine. They were armed and militant in carrying out their programs. As late as April 1937, this group continued to defy the Republic and at times represented a splinter group within the otherwise well-disciplined Spanish Communist party.*

For further information, see Joaquin Maurín, *Revolución y counterrevolución en España* (Paris, 1966); and Andrés Suárez, *Un Episodio de la revolución española: El proceso contra el POUM* (Paris, 1974).
See also May 1937 Riots.

James W. Cortada

JUVENTUDES SOCIALISTAS UNIFICADAS (JSU). The *Juventudes Socialistas Unificadas* (JSU) was formed in 1934 by young socialists and communists. Among its members were Santiago Carrillo* who, after the Spanish Civil War, became head of Spain's Communist party.* The majority of the membership was socialist, although most of its views and control were communist. In the early months of the war, members of the JSU executed numerous individuals in major cities, especially in Madrid* and Barcelona,* who were middle class or whom they perceived to be a threat to the Republic. There was heavy communist influence under Carrillo's leadership. During the course of the Civil War, the JSU fought in various military units, while providing an armed wing of the Communist party to reduce opposition to communism within the Republican zone. It should be added, however, that the JSU leadership was always more committed to communism than its members were.

For further information, see Burnett Bolloten, *The Spanish Revolution: The Left and the Struggle for Power During the Civil War* (Chapel Hill, N.C., 1979); and Ramón Casterás, *Las JSUC ante la guerra y revolución, 1936-1939* (Barcelona, 1977).

James W. Cortada

K

KAHLE, HANS (-1952). Kahle, a communist German in the International Brigades,* fought for the Second Republic* during the Civil War. He had spent most of his adult life as an officer in the German Army after being raised in Prussia. He came to Spain with some of the first volunteers* and quickly gained command of the International Brigade that was soon after renamed the Edgar André Battalion. Under his control, this unit fought in some of the earliest battles around Madrid* during the fall of 1936. He commanded Republican forces throughout 1936 and 1937, finally leaving Spain with the rank of colonel in late 1937 after the international volunteers were withdrawn from service in the Iberian Peninsula. He served with distinction in the various battles for Madrid, especially during the fall of 1936 when most foreign volunteers were under his command. In 1952, he became a police chief in Mecklenburg where he died.

For further information, see Andreu Castells, *Las brigadas internacionales en la guerra de España* (Barcelona, 1974); and Jacques Delperrie de Bayac, *Les Brigades internationales* (Paris, 1968).

James W. Cortada

KINDELÁN Y DUANY, ALFREDO (1879–1962). Kindelán was the chief of the Nationalist Air Force* during the Civil War. He was born in Santiago, Cuba,* and was commissioned in the Engineers. In the early days of aviation, he was one of the founders of the Spanish Air Force. As a captain in Morocco,* in 1913, he commanded a squadron of aircraft which was one of the earliest applications of aviation in military history. In 1929, he was promoted to brigade general. He was close to King Alfonso XIII* and a devout monarchist. He remained attached to the monarchy and attempted to restore it until his death in Madrid in December 1962.

At the time of the rising in 1936, Kindelán was on the retired list and one of the key members of the conspiracy. He was greatly concerned that a unified command be created, and he was the driving force behind calling together late in September 1936 the *Junta* of generals to resolve this issue. He proposed that Franco* be appointed Generalissimo and act as "chief of state" as long as the "war" should last. With the end of the conflict, he believed the monarchy would be restored. With arguments among some of the generals, and dissent from others, on October 1 the decree was issued which named Franco head of government and stated he should assume powers of the new state.

As an important figure in the Nationalist High Command, Kindelán influenced the course of events. Sometimes his efforts were not successful, as when he warned Franco that if he insisted on saving the garrison of the Alcázar* of Toledo* the Nationalists* might not be able to capture Madrid.*

Kindelán built the Nationalist Air Force into an effective force, considering this time in history, with the assistance of Italian and German material and training. The air units of these countries were ostensibly under his command, but at times they acted on their own initiative or on orders from Berlin or Rome. These actions caused problems for Kindelán. In May 1937, he was promoted to division general. With the end of the war, his insistence on the immediate restoration of the monarchy continually brought him political problems with members of the regime. Still, in 1940 he was promoted to lieutenant general, and in 1942, he was named captain general of Catalonia.* Then he was temporarily exiled to the Canary Islands.* Back in Madrid in 1944, he was made head of the Superior War School, but he was again to be relieved of command, In spite of his political problems, shortly after his death he was named a marquis.

For further information, see General Alfredo Kindelán, *Mis cuadernos de guerra* (Madrid, 1945); and Jesús Salas Larrazábal, *Air War Over Spain* (Surrey, England, 1974).

See also Pilots; and Appendix B.

Raymond L. Proctor

KING, NORMAN (1880–1963). King was the British consul general in Barcelona* during the Civil War (1936–1939). An astute observer and a career diplomat, he found little to praise in the revolutionary activity in that city. Throughout most of the war, his principal responsibilities were to protect British lives and report political events to London.

For further information, see William L. Kleine-Ahlbrandt, *The Policy of Simmering: A Study of British Policy During the Spanish Civil War, 1936–1939* (The Hague, 1962).

See also Great Britain.

James W. Cortada

KLÉBER, EMILIO (LAZAR OR MANFRED STERN) (1895–1938). Kléber, whose real name was Lazar or Manfred Stern, was one of the most colorful members of the International Brigades* to fight for the Republic in Spain. Born in Bucovina, Rumania, which then was part of the Austro-Hungarian Empire, he fought in World War I for the Austrians, rising to the rank of captain. The Russians captured him, but he escaped, joined the Bolsheviks, fought in the Russian Civil War, and participated in a variety of secret military operations during the 1920s. His exploits were well known in communist circles, and, when the first of the International Brigades was being formed for Spain (heavily manned with communists), he became one of its first commanders. An experienced officer, he worked to discipline and train his men for combat around Madrid.*

This short, grey-haired commander led his men fighting in central Spain, commanding what by late fall 1936 was called the 11th Brigade. During the battle for Madrid in November, his brigade held the Casa del Campo against repeated assaults by the Nationalists.* Kléber was a popular and able commander who managed to gain the loyalty of his troops and thus marshaled them to fight well. Throughout the fall of 1936, he fought around Madrid. Kléber urged the Republicans* at the end of 1936 to go on the offensive rather than wait for Nationalist attacks on Madrid, and he even suggested that the International Brigades spearhead the operation. Officials of the Republic, jealous of his popularity and concerned that he might use his position to stage a communist coup over the government, mistrusted his motives. Following disagreements with the Republic, Kléber gave up his command in January (some say he was relieved of his duties) and moved to Valencia.* However, he resumed his military career as commander of the 45th Division just before the battle of Brunete* (July 1937), fighting in central Spain and in the campaign in Santander* (August 1937). He returned to the USSR* in late 1937 with other volunteers* from the Russian state. Like many who went back to the Soviet Union, Kéber was "liquidated" in one of Stalin's* purges during 1938.

For further information, see Dan Kurzman, *Miracle of November: Madrid's Epic Stand, 1936* (New York, 1980); and Ramón Salas Larrazábal, *Historia del ejército popular de la república*, 4 vols. (Madrid, 1974).

James W. Cortada

KOESTLER, ARTHUR (1905-   ). Koestler was born and raised in Budapest, began his career as a journalist, spent a number of years in Germany* prior to the Civil War, and wrote fiction. He also had close connections with the Communist party dating from 1931. At the start of the Civil War, he went to Spain for the party to gather evidence of Italo-German intervention in the conflict. He passed through southern Spain, which was then under Nationalist control, acting as a right-wing Hungarian journalist. He eventually left by way of Gibraltar.* Soon afterward, he returned, again gathering data for the communists. At the end of 1936, he began writing a book on Spain, published in 1937, under the title of *L'Espagne ensanglantee.* The Nationalists* arrested him in Seville* in February 1937, but in 1938, after his release, he published his account of life in a Nationalist prison (along with some other material), under the title of *Spanish Testament.*

A byproduct of Koestler's experiences in Spain was his disillusionment with communism. He found both sides were wasting lives and perverting goals and ideals. Moreover, like many other intellectuals* of his time, he felt that the Spanish conflict represented a true battle between the enlightened forces of Western civilization and those who would pervert them. Yet, in the 1940s he concluded that his own personal beliefs no longer coincided with those of the Communist party. Like some other writers, such as Hemingway* and Regler,* Koestler's books on Spain had wide circulation. Today, as then, they are considered some of the better pieces of literature* to emerge from the conflict.

For further information, see Frederick R. Benson, *Writers in Arms: The Literary Impact of the Civil War* (New York, 1967); and Koestler's books mentioned above and his *The Invisible Writing* (London, 1954).

See also Communist party, Spanish; and Europe.

James W. Cortada

KOMSOMOL. The Soviet motorship *Komsomol* (launched in 1932, 5,109 gross tons), the first and most famous ship bringing Soviet arms to the Republic, was sunk by gunfire from the Nationalist cruiser *Canarias*,* on December 14, 1936. *Komsomol*'s crew was later exchanged. The Republic launched an unsuccessful effort to raise funds for a new *Komsomol*.

Willard C. Frank, Jr.

KUZNETSOV, NIKOLAI GERASIMOVICH (1902-1974). Kuznetsov was chief Soviet naval adviser to the Republican Navy. Born in the Arkhangelsk district in 1902, Kuznetsov rose in the Soviet Navy* to become a promising cruiser captain when he was ordered to Spain in August 1936. Captain 1st Rank Kuznetsov, stationed in Cartagena,* directed the Soviet-originated strategy of reserving the Republican fleet for the escort of Soviet and Spanish arms transports from Odessa to Cartagena and other Republican ports. In 1937, he attempted to strengthen the Republican Navy with naval aircraft, submarines, and fast motorboats, all directly commanded by Soviet naval personnel. These efforts hardly aided the Republican war at sea. Recalled in August 1937, Kuznetsov became chief of the Soviet Navy in 1939. He died in December 1974.

For further information, see N. G. Kuznetsov, *Na dalekom meridiane* (Moscow, 1966).

Willard C. Frank, Jr.

L

LABONNE, EILRICK (1888-   ). Labonne was the French ambassador to the Spanish Republic from 1938 to 1939, serving at a time when Paris joined with London in a policy of nonintervention in the conflict in the face of known and massive intervention by Italy* and Germany.* While he sympathized with the Spanish Republic, as did his government, he witnessed the decline of the Loyalists'* prospects during 1938. By the end of the year, he was clearly indicating to Paris that the Republic was being defeated. He even offered Juan Negrín's* cabinet refuge in his embassy and passage to France.* His views and reports on Republican Spain were a significant source of information on Spanish affairs for the government in Paris; thus, his perspective was important. The half-hearted attempts by the French to provide partial support for the Republic quickly receded as 1938 wore on and more pessimistic reports arrived from Labonne on the military situation. Because of his position, he frequently called on the Spanish Republic's top leaders who considered him a major contact for help from Paris.

For further information, see David Wingeate Pike, *Les Français et la guerre d'Espagne, 1936-1939* (Paris, 1975).
See also Blum, Léon; and Daladier, Edouard.

James W. Cortada

LABOUR PARTY, BRITISH. The Labour party, one of Great Britain's* major political organizations, represented a large segment of British thinking when it encouraged London's policy of neutrality toward the Spanish Civil War. It believed that no arms should be sold to either faction and strongly supported the rapid establishment of the Non-Intervention Committee.* When, by late 1936, it became clear that Germany* and Italy* were actively intervening in Spain on behalf of the Nationalists,* many members of the Labour party urged the sale of arms to the Republicans* but not military involvement. Throughout the war, however, the Labour party officially maintained a policy of nonintervention in the conflict, although a large number of its members actively sought aid for the Republic. Through newspapers influenced by the Labour party, there was considerable discussion of the Spanish situation, and numerous political confrontations took place with the Conservative party between 1936 and 1939.

For further information, see K. W. Watkins, *Britain Divided* (London, 1963).
See also Chamberlain, Neville; and Eden, Anthony.

James W. Cortada

LA GRANJA OFFENSIVE. The Republican offensive at La Granja on May 30, 1937, was one of two simultaneous actions (the other, an attack on Huesca*) designed to relieve the mounting pressure on Bilbao* by diverting the Nationalist forces from the north. Initially intended to take Segovia* by surprise through a hard strike, the operation (which provided the backdrop for Hemingway's *For Whom the Bell Tolls*) represented the first offensive action ordered by Indalecio Prieto* as minister of war.

The immediate objectives of the attack were the villages of Cabeza Grande and Matabuye, assigned to the 69th Brigade; Valsain, assigned to the 14th International Brigade; and La Granja, assigned to the 31st Brigade, all in the 35th Division under the command of General "Walter" (pseud. Karol Swierczewski). On the night of May 29-30, a sergeant with plans of the attack deserted to the Nationalists,* who also spotted the Republican convoys—using headlights—moving into position. The attack began on the dawn of May 30, but only the 69th Brigade temporarily succeeded in taking its objective. The 31st Brigade reached the outskirts of La Granja and temporarily cut off the road to Segovia (8 kilometers distant), but the 14th Brigade was unable to take Valsain and help secure La Granja. Under the command of General Varela,* legionnaires from Barron's* 13th Division were brought from the Madrid* front to bolster the defending units of the 75th Division and retook Cabeza Grande on June 2. Although reinforced by the 21st Brigade, the Republicans* were steadily pushed back, and after suffering over 1,500 casualties,* suspended the operation on June 3. Poor preparation, the repeated use of troops in frontal attacks on easily defensible positions, and ineffective tank and aerial support in conjunction with the Nationalists' tenacity and effective air power, assured its failure.

For further information, see Jacques Delperrie de Bayac, *Les Brigades internacionales* (Paris, 1968); and José Manuel Martínez Bande, *La ofensiva sobre Segovia y la batalla de Brunete* (Madrid, 1972).

Verle B. Johnston

LAMAMIÉ DE CLAIRAC Y DE LA COLINA, JOSÉ MARÍA (1887-1956).

Lamamié de Clairac was born in Salamanca.* He reached his greatest prominence in the period 1934-1937, when he served in a number of crucial leadership positions in the Carlist political organization. Although he represented Salamanca in the 1931 and 1933 legislatures, he vehemently rejected the Republic. Yet, his Cortes* membership allowed him to play the parliamentary tactician, delaying legislation which he opposed. Moreover, his parliamentary immunity permitted him to travel around the country speaking against the government's actions without being arrested. In 1936, his apparent reelection was voided by the leftist majority in the Cortes. He was deemed ineligible because a union in which he was an official had purchased agricultural products for the state in 1935.

Within the Carlist organization itself, he headed the Propaganda Section from May 1934 to December 1935, and he represented the Carlists* on the Executive Committee of the National Bloc. In 1936 and 1937, he served on the council of the *Communión Tradicionalista* (Traditionalist Communion) and as general secretary of the Carlists' National War *Junta*. Although he would have preferred a purely Carlist uprising in 1936, he quickly acquiesced to the Carlists' supportive role in the military uprising. From 1937, when the *Communión Tradicionalista* was merged into *Falange Española* *Tradicionalista y de las JONS*,* until his death, Lamamié remained out of political life. He died in Salamanca in 1956.

For further information, see Martin Blinkhorn, *Carlism and the Crisis in Spain, 1931-1939* (Cambridge, 1975); Richard Robinson, *The Origins of Franco's Spain: The Right, the Republic and Revolution, 1931-1936* (Newton Abbot, 1970); and Javier Tusell Gómez, *Las elecciones del frente popular*, 2 vols. (Madrid, 1971), on the 1936 elections.

William J. Irwin

LA MANCHA.

La Mancha, the area in central Spain made famous by Cervantes in *Don Quixote*, was a stronghold of Republican support both before and during the Civil War. The large agricultural estates were collectivized and controlled by the *Unión General de Trabajadores* (UGT).* In the early days of the war, the Nationalists* could not capture the area and bring it under their control. This olive-growing area, known also for the manufacture of knives, was spared heavy fighting when the Nationalists moved northwest toward Madrid,* thereby avoiding much of La Mancha. The area did see some military activity, however, because the International Brigades* set up their headquarters in Albacete* and stayed there through most of 1937. The Nationalists were not able to occupy this region fully until the spring of 1939, whereupon they arrested and prosecuted many Republican sympathizers.

For further information, see Hugh Thomas, *The Spanish Civil War* (New York, 1977).

James W. Cortada

LAMONEDA FERNÁNDEZ, RAMÓN (1892-   ).

Lamoneda Fernández was the secretary of the Socialist party's* executive committee from 1922 to 1939 and during the Civil War was a moderate Prieto* socialist. During the war, he slowly moved toward an alignment with the communists. Thus, by mid-1937, he concluded that Largo Caballero had to be replaced by Negrín.*

For further information, see Hugh Thomas, *The Spanish Civil War* (New York, 1977).

James W. Cortada

LARGO CABALLERO, FRANCISCO (1869-1946).

Largo Caballero was a Spanish socialist trade-union leader who rose to prominence during the Second Republic.* He served as prime minister and minister of war between September 1936 and May 1937. A former stucco worker by trade, a reformist for more than forty years, except for an occasional spurt of revolutionary activity, and a member of the Council of State during General Primo de Rivera's dictatorship, Largo Caballero, after two years of disillusionment as minister of labor during the Republican-socialist coalition, had been fired in 1933 by revolutionary ideas and had become metamorphosed—at the age of sixty-four—into the exponent of the left wing of Spanish socialism.

During the first years of the Republic, Largo Caballero's power and influence within the socialist movement derived primarily from the widespread rank-and-file support he enjoyed as head of the socialist *Unión General de Trabajadores* (UGT),* from the vigorous socialist youth movement, from most of the local sections of the party—particularly the *Agrupación Socialista Madrileña* (Socialist Group of Madrid)—and from his mouthpiece, the *Claridad*.* By 1934, Largo Caballero and his supporters had become so dissatisfied with the results of collaboration with the liberal Republicans that they pressed increasingly for the radicalization or Bolshevization of the Socialist party.* Within two years, this tendency had become fully articulated within the socialist movement. In March 1936, for example, four months before the Civil War, the influential Madrid* socialist organization, over which Largo Caballero presided, had drafted a new program for the Socialist party to be submitted to its next national congress, affirming that its "immediate aim" was "the conquest of political power by the working class by whatever means possible" and "the dictatorship of the proletariat organized as a working-class democracy." "The illusion that the proletarian socialist revolution. . .can be achieved by reforming the existing state must be eliminated," ran the preamble.

There is no course but to destroy its roots. . . . Imperceptibly, the dictatorship of the proletariat or workers' democracy will be converted into a full democracy, without classes from which the coercive state will gradually disappear. The instrument of the dictatorship will be the Socialist party, which will exercise this dictatorship during the period of transition from one society to another and as long as the surrounding capitalist states make a strong proletarian state necessary.

Clearly, some of the language of the new program was borrowed from the standard works of Lenin and Stalin,* whose teachings the aging Largo Caballero had studied and embraced only in recent years. In the succeeding months, aglow with his newfound faith, Largo Caballero toured the provincial capitals, proclaiming before rapt audiences that the Popular Front* program could not solve Spain's problems and that a working-class dictatorship was necessary.

Largo Caballero's revolutionary stance deepened the already irreconcilable divisions within the Socialist party. Julián Besteiro,* the dignified and once influential "academic" Marxist, representing the right wing of the party, had urged his socialist colleagues in 1933 to accept democracy and had declared himself an enemy of the dictatorship of the proletariat. He had retired into the background, and the struggle for control of the socialist movement between the revolutionary Largo Caballero and the evolutionary Indalecio Prieto*—at once political and highly personal—had moved to center stage. To Prieto, Largo Caballero was irresponsible: "He is a fool who wants to appear clever. He is a frigid bureaucrat who plays the role of

a mad fanatic." To Largo Caballero, Prieto's reformism was anathema. "For me," he wrote some years later, "Prieto was never a socialist. . .either in his ideas or his action." "[He] was envious, arrogant, and disdainful; he believed he was superior to everyone; he would tolerate no one who cast the slightest shadow in his path."

It was the bitter feuding between the two factions on the crucial issue of revolution or evolution that led Salvador de Madariaga,* independent Republican and historian, to assert:

What made the Spanish Civil War inevitable was the civil war within the Socialist party. . . . No wonder Fascism grew. Let no one argue that it was fascist violence that developed socialist violence. . .; it was not at the Fascists that Largo Caballero's gunmen shot but at their brother socialists. . . . It was [Largo Caballero's] avowed, nay, his proclaimed policy to rush Spain on to the dictatorship of the proletariat. Thus pushed on the road to violence, the nation, always prone to it, became more violent than ever. This suited the fascists admirably, for they are nothing if not lovers and adepts of violence.

Immediately following the outbreak of the Civil War and revolution in July 1936, Largo Caballero, through the UGT and *Claridad*, reaffirmed his ultrarevolutionary posture. On August 22, in an editorial in *Claridad*, he asserted: "The war and the Revolution are one and the same thing. Not only do they not exclude or hinder each other but they complement and support each other." By identifying the revolution as a corollary of the July uprising, Largo Caballero had set himself against the liberal Republican government of José Giral* and its supporters, namely, the "Prietista" faction of moderate socialists and the Spanish Communist party.* In particular, the communists—a small if rapidly growing political force—did what they could to shore up Giral's almost powerless administration. But Largo Caballero railed against its "complete ineptitude," and, according to the *Pravda* correspondent, Mikhail Koltzov, he accused Giral's ministers of not possessing "the slightest conception of responsibility or of the gravity of the situation."

By the end of August 1936, the Giral government lost all of its political credibility except with the communists. Even Indalecio Prieto, who for weeks worked assiduously behind the scenes to bolster the government, scorned its impotence. It was in these circumstances that Prieto supported the formation of a new government headed by his old rival, Largo Caballero. In an interview with Koltzov on August 26, Prieto described Largo Caballero's political significance in the following way: "He is a man capable of ruining everything and everybody. Our political differences during the past few years lie at the heart of the struggle within the Socialist party. But, at least today, he is the only man or, better still, his is the only name that can appropriately head a new government."

Largo Caballero, who sensed his own political worth, demanded for himself at the beginning of September 1936 the premiership and War Ministry. Despite his inflexible attitude of demanding "all or nothing," he was asked to form a new government. On September 4, he assumed power, combining the functions of premier with those of minister of war. Two of his close associates, both left-wing socialists, held key posts: Angel Galarza,* who became minister of the interior, and Álvarez del Vayo,* at the time Largo Caballero's trusted adviser but a secret communist sympathizer, who became minister of foreign affairs. Three other socialists, belonging to the center faction of the party, Anastasio de Garcia,* Juan Negrín,* and Indalecio Prieto, became ministers of industry and commerce, finance, and navy and air, respectively. The communists, after having initially refused to take part in the cabinet, ultimately yielded to Largo Caballero's insistence that they join the government: Vicente Uribe,* who became minister of agriculture, and Jesús Hernández,* who became minister of education and fine arts. The remaining cabinet positions were taken by Republicans,* José Giral becoming minister without portfolio. The *Confederación Nacional del Trabajo* (CNT),* the anarchosyndicalist labor federation, was the only major organization not represented in the government. When forming his cabinet, Largo Caballero had tried to secure the anarchosyndicalists' participation in the belief, as his paper *Claridad* later put it, that they "would feel themselves bound by its measures and its authority." But much as he needed them to share the responsibilities of office in order to forestall any criticism of his government's decrees, he offered them only a single seat without portfolio, a meager reward for what would have entailed a flagrant breach of principle. That offer, commented their Madrid organ, CNT, some weeks later, was "neither generous or enticing" and was "absolutely disproportionate to the strength and influence of the CNT in the country."

On assuming the premiership, Largo Caballero clearly committed himself to a policy directed at winning the war effort and not to a policy of social revolution. In fact, from the day his government was formed, he adopted the communist viewpoint that it should impress the outside world with its moderation. He had tempered his prewar revolutionary stance, because he believed that it was essential for foreign opinion that legal forms be observed. During a private con-

versation shortly after taking office, Largo Caballero proclaimed that it was necessary "to sacrifice revolutionary language to win the friendship of the democratic Powers." In this respect he was not remiss. "The Spanish Government is not fighting for socialism but for democracy and constitutional rule," he stated to a delegation of British members of parliament. And in a communique to the foreign press he said: "The Government of the Spanish Republic is not aiming at setting up a Soviet regime in Spain in spite of what has been alleged in some quarters abroad. The Government's essential aim is to maintain the parliamentary regime of the Republic as it was set up by the Constitution, which the Spanish people freely assumed." By playing down the profound revolutionary changes that had taken place, Largo Caballero and his cabinet hoped to secure foreign military aid* from Great Britain* and France,* aid that was critically needed to counter Italian and German support of the Nationalists.*

The first measures taken by Largo Caballero toward winning the war were directed at reorganizing the military. The problems were undoubtedly the defects of the militia system, for, in spite of *Claridad*'s claim that the militia's efficiency could not be greater, these defects were indubitably among the principal reasons for General Franco's* swift advance up the Tagus Valley toward the Spanish capital.

Although he had long resisted the idea of a regular army, Largo Caballero, at the urging of the communists, gradually came around to accepting the idea of militarization during the first months of his administration. Indeed, the insistence of the two communist ministers and the Soviet military advisers who, in urging their demands, made full use of the succession of defeats on the central front, caused measures to be promulgated providing for the militarization of the militia and the creation of a military force, or Popular Army, on a conscripted basis and under the supreme command of the war minister. These plans, however, met with stiff opposition from the anarchosyndicalists, who initially refused to accept militarization because it threatened their independently organized militia. But backed by the socialists and communists, Largo Caballero set into motion his military reorganization program. Within a short while, workers' and soldiers' councils were abolished, columns became regiments or battalions, and ranks and insignia that had disappeared in the anarchist militias* were reintroduced.

Another important step taken by Largo Caballero towards consolidating government authority was to reform the police.* Under his government, thousands of new members were recruited for the Civil Guard,* reorganized into the National Republican Guard. The same was true of the Assault Guard,* whose numbers increased by 28,000 at the beginning of December, according to Angel Galarza, the left-wing socialist minister of the interior. No less important was the growth of the *Carabineros*, or carabineers, a corps composed of customs and excise officials and guards dependent on the Ministry of Finance.

Parallel with the reconstruction of the government police corps, important changes took place in the field of justice. The revolutionary Popular Tribunals* set up by the left-wing organizations in the early days of the war were gradually displaced by a legalized form of tribunal composed of three members of the judiciary and fourteen members of the Popular Front parties and trade-union federations, two representing each organization. Although the Giral government decrees promulgated at the end of August 1936 provided for the creation of the new courts, they did not begin to function in all the provinces of the Left camp until several weeks after the CNT had entered the Largo Caballero government in November.

The restoration of the state and its institutions through these reforms were, in the main, executed under the direction of Largo Caballero, who, acting as both premier and minister of war, was able to exert some measure of personal control over their development. Largo Caballero, to be sure, was incessantly preoccupied with the question of governmental authority. When he offered the anarchosyndicalists four ministries at the beginning of November 1936, for example, there is evidence that he was motivated partly by his desire to invest his government with greater authority—at a time when he was planning to transfer his government to Valencia*—in the belief that at any moment Franco's forces might seize the capital. He also feared, whether or not with grounds, that if the cabinet should leave Madrid without first admitting representatives of the anarchosyndicalist movement, the CNT and the *Federación Anarquista Ibérica* (FAI)* might set up an independent administration. But in spite of his attempts to exercise influence over the direction of policies within his government, Largo Caballero's authority was increasingly challenged by the communists.

In the months before the Civil War, the official relations between Largo Caballero and the communists were so friendly that the Left socialist leader had encouraged the fusion of the socialist and communist trade-union federations as well as the merging of the parties' youth organizations. Since the uprising in July, however, Largo Caballero's experiences with the communists had stamped out the last spark of enthusiasm for amalgamating the Socialist and Communist parties, and no enticement laid before him by the Spanish Politburo and the Comintern, not even a promise that he could head the united party, could induce him to yield to their importunity. Perhaps the first major sign that his relations with the communists were rapidly deteriorating was the dispute that arose between them after Largo Caballero appointed General José Asensio* to the undersecretaryship of war on October 22, 1936.

As a commander during the first weeks of the war of the militia forces in the Sierra de Guadarrama,* defending the northwestern approaches to Madrid, Asensio, at the time a colonel, had so inspired Largo Caballero's confidence that when he became premier and war minister in September, he made Asensio a general and placed him in charge of the threatened central front in command of the Army of the Center.* The communists, who had already been striving to win Asensio's adherence to their party, acclaimed his promotion and new assignment, and made him an honorary commander of their Fifth Regiment.* All of these attentions, a prominent communist acknowledged later, were designed to wean Asensio away from Largo Caballero. In the succeeding weeks, when Asensio showed no inclination to follow the trajectory of other professional military men who had yielded to the courtship of the communists, and even evinced for the latter a profound antipathy, they demanded his removal from the command of the central front.

Although for a time Largo Caballero refused to remove Asensio, he finally yielded. But while propitiating the communists with one hand, he diminished their victory with the other by elevating him to the undersecretaryship of war. The communists were undaunted by Largo Caballero's obstinacy. Asensio had become such an impediment to their plans for hegemony within the armed forces that the Russian ambassador, Marcel Rosenberg,* personally demanded his dismissal. To this demand, Largo Caballero, afire with indignation, replied by expelling the Soviet diplomat from his office.

This signal event, confirmed by several colleagues of the premier and by Largo Caballero himself, threw into sharper relief the dimensions of the conflict now developing between the premier and the communists. In fact, by March 1937, Moscow's primary short-range objective was to remove Largo Caballero from the War Ministry and premiership. An opportunity presented itself only two months later at the turning point in the Spanish Revolution, the May 1937 riots,* known as the May days or May events.

The May events centered around the issue of the revolutionary gains that had taken place in Catalonia* since the outbreak of hostilities in July 1936. It was specifically in Barcelona,* where the gains of the revolution and the armed power of the workers still survived in the spring of 1937, that the stage was set for a contest between the prorevolutionary forces, as represented by the CNT-FAI and the radical Marxists of the *Partido Obrero de Unificación Marxista* (POUM),* on the one side, and those determined to roll back the revolution, namely, the communists, and President Luis Companys'* liberal Republican Esquerra,* on the other. The issue came to a head during the first days of May when the forces of the two opposing groups engaged in street fighting that lasted for four days. By May 7 the will of the revolutionaries had been broken, marking the political defeat of the revolution that had begun ten months earlier.

Although the origin of the May events has been a source of many hotly disputed discussions, their undeniable effect was to hasten the end of Largo Caballero's political career.

The communists, eager to exploit the upheaval, demanded that the government suppress the POUM, which they held responsible for the bloodshed, and whose leaders they had long been denouncing as Trotskyists and fascist agents. They clearly viewed the episode as one that posed a crisis for Largo Caballero's government, for they publicly announced that if his government did not impose order in the rear another would have to do so. In reply to the communists' demands, Largo Caballero told their ministers in the government that he did not believe that the POUM was a fascist organization, that he would not dissolve their party, that he had not entered the government to serve the political interests of any of the factions represented in it, and that the courts of law would decide whether or not a particular organization should be dissolved. Largo Caballero's declaration allowed the communist ministers to withdraw from the cabinet, signaling an end to the government coalition. When Largo Caballero attempted to form a new cabinet, he found the communists, Republicans, and Prietistas unanimous in their demand that he relinquish the War Ministry. Largo Caballero refused, declaring that he had "the firm intention of fighting it out with the Communist party and all its accomplices." As Largo Caballero would not budge, President Azaña* asked Juan Negrín to form a new cabinet.

Largo Caballero had now been defeated, and the communists had triumphed. Not only had the communists deprived him of his authority in the socialist youth movement, in the Catalan UGT, and in the Catalan federation of the Socialist party—as a result of the creation of the *Partit Socialista Unificat de Catalunya* (PSUC)*—and taken over *Claridad*, not only had he been betrayed or forsaken by some of his closest collaborators, but he had now been ousted from the government.

In October 1937, the communists, fearing that their opponents on the Left might rally around Largo Caballero, who as secretary of the UGT executive had just negotiated a provisional alliance with the CNT, delivered the coup de grace in their campaign against the leftist socialist leader. Acting in agreement with former supporters of Largo Caballero and with moderate socialists—who, after the fall of his government, had seized *Adelante*, his mouthpiece in Valencia—they formed a new UGT executive on October 1, with González Peña,* a former Prietista but now a Negrinista, as president. On October 19, Largo Caballero denounced the Communist party at a mass meeting, but was prevented from further activity by both his socialist and communist opponents. On November 30, he was divested of his newspaper *La Correspondencia de Valencia*, his last daily medium of communication. The conflict over the two rival executives boiled on until January 1938, when it was settled by Léon Jouhaux, the French trade-union leader, who was then partial to the communists, at the expense of Largo Caballero, whose political career had now ended.

In February 1939, after the fall of Catalonia, Largo Caballero went into exile in France. During the German occupation, he was interned in Dachau concentration camp, but he survived the war and returned to Paris, where he died in 1946.

For further information, see Burnett Bolloten, *The Spanish Revolution: The Left and the Struggle for Power During the Civil War* (Chapel Hill, N.C., 1979), source of all biographical data used here; and Largo Caballero, *Mis recuerdos* (Mexico City, 1954), *Qué se puede hacer?* (Paris, 1940), and *La UGT y la guerra* (Valencia, 1937). Although these works provide valuable information, new material should come to light when his personal memoirs are published.

Burnett Bolloten in collaboration with George Esenwein

LATIN AMERICA. Latin American responses to the Civil War developed out of conditions peculiar to each of the New World republics, but a few common denominators are discernible. Throughout Latin America, regenerationist hopes surged in the 1930s as the international capitalist order appeared to collapse. Often, the hopes for a new order resulted from the discontents produced by the initial incursions of capitalist modernization into undeveloped lands. Confronting discomfiting dislocations, many intellectuals* envisioned a new life-style more congenial to the full scope of human aspirations. To them it appeared that similar circumstances had motivated the various ideological and political factions which, unable to find consensus on the proper approach to innovation, had plunged Spain into armed struggle.

Confronting Latin America's social critics were elites who had benefited from incipient modernization and looked forward to further incorporation of their national economies into the international capitalist system. Lacking substantial economic ties to Spain and finding nothing in common with that country's ideologues, they looked forward to stronger ties with the United States,* in whose economic recovery they trusted. This helps explain part of Latin America's indifference toward events in Spain. Historically, the area's intellectuals have been least concerned with Spain, or with Europe,* during periods of rapprochement with the United States. As for the masses, they cared little and in many cases did not even know about the war.

Never have Latin American republics presented a united front in assessing foreign political events and ideologies, and lack of cohesiveness was seldom more evidenced than by the differing responses to the Civil War. Even when countries shared the same sympathies and prejudices, they arrived at them altogether in their own way. In this complex maze, Brazil* is a special case. With their Portuguese-African origins, Brazilians have tended to look on Spain with indifference not lacking a measure of hostility. The rule of Getulio Vargas (1930-1945), at the outset of which the "unofficial alliance" with the United States grew all the firmer, provided no exception to this pattern.

Emerging from a period of gradual reforms which had expanded the political base to include more middle sectors, Argentina* weathered a brief threat of fundamental restructuring touched off by the world depression. By 1932, the country settled into traditional patterns of rule by urban and agrarian elites set upon muddling through without sweeping renovation and aided in their intentions by strengthened economic ties with Great Britain.* While the 1932-1938 concordancía government inclined definitely toward the Nationalists,* domestic political considerations prevented it from recognizing the Burgos* regime until almost the final days of the Civil War. In neighboring Uruguay, only the shooting of three sisters of the vice-consul in Madrid* led to the severing of relations with the Republic in September 1936. Less grave problems of treatment of their nationals soured the relations of most Latin American countries with the Republic.

An elected rightist government headed by Arturo Alessandri assumed power in Chile at the end of 1932. Despite its anticlericalism and dislike of military incursions into politics, Alessandri's government favored the Nationalists. The president found it convenient to justify his use of extraordinary powers against domestic radicals as necessary to avoid following Spain into chaos. When a Popular Front government came to power in 1938, its caution and moderation reflected in part the desire to avoid the extremes of its earlier namesake administration in Spain.

Oscar Benavides came to the Peruvian presidency in 1933 during a violent struggle against militants clamoring for the revolutionary restructuring of the old order. Viewing their soon vanquished adversaries as Marxist and communist fanatics akin to the Republican extremists blamed for having convulsed Spain, Benavides and the ruling classes remained even cooler to the Republic than their counterparts in Argentina and Chile. Furthermore, movements in behalf of the large Indian population had assumed a Marxist orientation, a development that further soured the predominantly white privileged sectors on the ideology they associated with the Republic. Similar considerations influenced military corporatist movements in Bolivia and Ecuador, each containing large indigenous populations, in the mid-to-late 1930s.

Jorge Ubico in Guatemala, Anastasio Somoza in Nicaragua, and Maximiliano Hernádez Martínez in El Salvador, all beginning lengthy dictatorships in the early-to-mid 1930s, equated Spanish Loyalists* with dangerous social levelers. Martínez was especially sensitive to the communist menace, having repressed in 1932 the first major uprising in America in which communists played a major role. In sharp contrast, Fulgencio Batista, coming to power in Cuba* in 1933, collaborated openly with the island's formidable Communist party. Inheriting the revolution that had recently overthrown the tyrant Gerardo Machado, Batista posed as the liberator of his country from all forms of oppression. To enhance his image as the forger of a new Cuba, he found it expedient to identify with the Spanish Republic. Along with Argentina and Mexico,* Cuba had a sizable Spanish colony, and the majority of these immigrants approved Batista's stance.

In Colombia, 1930 marked the return of the Liberals to power, and they liked to compare the end of protracted Conservative rule to the collapse of the monarchy in Spain one year later. Colombia remained the Republic's most persistent supporter, after Mexico, among Latin American governments. Opposition Conservatives, however, and the Catholic Church provided an increasingly vocal opposition, extolling the

Nationalists as saviours of Christian civilization. Meanwhile, neighboring Venezuela emerged in 1935 from the crushing dictatorship of Juan Vicente Gómez. While new administrations were too preoccupied with maintaining order to pay serious attention to Spain, their spokesmen did find that lip-service to the Loyalist cause met with general approval.

In an ebullient self-congratulatory mood over the announced successes of the 1910 revolution, Mexican leaders in the 1930s saw themselves as having devised a unique synthesis of modernity and traditionalism, one that the entire Hispanic world would profit by following. A favorite rhetorical device was to depict Spanish Republicans* as engaging in the sort of revolution that Mexicans had made some twenty years earlier. As the revolution in actual practice moved rightward, President Lázaro Cárdenas (1934-1940) and his colleagues maintained their radical credentials by unstintingly praising the Loyalists while damning the Nationalists. Overt partisanship for the Republic created a favorable climate for a large and distinguished group of Loyalist exiles.

On the whole, Latin American leaders seldom went beyond political self-service in the attention they paid the Civil War. Among intellectuals a bourgeoning spirit of nationalism curbed attentiveness to Spain. One manifestation of nationalism was pride, especially evident among Argentines, Chileans, Uruguayans, and Mexicans, in having advanced beyond wayward Spaniards in adjusting to contemporary problems. By sinking into anarchy in their quest for solutions, Spaniards had proved their long-suspected inferiority.

For further information, see Mark Falcoff and Fredrick B. Pike, eds., *The Spanish Civil War: American Hemisphere Perspectives* (Lincoln, Nebr., 1982).

Fredrick B. Pike

LAW, OLIVER (-1937). Law was a commander in the International Brigades.* He was one of the few black Americans to serve in Spain and the only one to become a brigade commander, leading the Lincoln Brigade* in 1937. He was killed in Spain.

For further information, see Cecil Eby, *Between the Bullet and the Lie* (New York, 1969), a better study than Arthur Landis, *The Abraham Lincoln Brigade* (New York, 1967).

James W. Cortada

LEAGUE OF NATIONS. The League of Nations served as an international forum of discussion on the Spanish Civil War. The Spanish Republic sought to mar-

shal foreign and diplomatic support for its cause through the league; however, this international body provided little assistance to the Republic. No Spanish representatives of the Nationalists* sat in the league during the war. Following its previous history of weakness and inability to foster world peace and stop military aggression, the league was unable to mediate an end to the fighting in Spain or to serve as the vehicle for assisting the government of the Republic. Yet, throughout the war, Republican diplomats appealed to the nations of the world to sell and supply arms, support the government of Madrid,* and put pressure on Italy* and Germany* to withdraw their support for Franco.*

On September 24, 1936, the League of Nations held a major open debate on the war. Julio Álvarez del Vayo,* speaking for the Republic as its minister of foreign affairs, protested that the Non-Intervention Agreement (supported by the league) had equated his government with that of the rebels in that both were to be denied the sale of arms. In fact, he argued, it should be Franco who should be denied military supplies. Great Britain* and France* were able to influence league members to extend little support to the Republic, and the international body desired to contain the fighting to Spain at no cost of multinational involvement. On December 10, Álvarez del Vayo again spoke in Geneva, defending the cause of the Republic. He wanted the league to condemn the intervention of Germany and Italy into the war and their recent recognition of Franco's government. He argued that world peace was in danger due to the international involvement of fascist regimes in Spain. Collective action on the part of the league resulted in nothing more than approval of the Non-Intervention Committee's* efforts.

In 1937, Spanish diplomats continued to press for international assistance to the Republic and for condemnation of foreign support and assistance to Franco's cause, but to no avail. On March 13, the Republic sent captured Italian documents to the league to prove that regular military units from Italy were serving on Franco's side, thereby violating Article 10 of the League of Nations Covenant. No action was taken to censure the Italians. By September 1937, heated debate about Italian submarines,* attacking neutral shipping in the Mediterranean on their way to Republic ports, led to the Nyon Conference* near Geneva. During these discussions, public debate on the war in Spain took place within the League of Nations. Juan Negrín,* Republican prime minister, spoke to the assembly requesting an examination of the Spanish situation, hoping to move the league to condemn Italian and German intervention in Spain. The USSR* and Mexico* supported his effort, and other governments did not. Members of the League of Nations did approve of the efforts at the Nyon Conference which resulted in a general agreement to reduce naval attacks in the Mediterranean through a system of sea and air patrols. At the end of September, the league passed a resolution which in essence formally approved the agreements of the Nyon Conference. The vote was two against, fourteen abstaining, and thirty-two in favor.

Discussions and presentations initiated by Republican diplomats continued throughout the winter and spring of 1937-1938. On May 13, for instance, Álvarez del Vayo asked that debate again be opened on the question of international intervention in Spain. He argued that Italy and Germany had continued to intervene in direct violation of the nonintervention policy, and therefore, the members of the league should examine the problem. A vote was taken on the Spanish resolution, with only Spain and the Soviet Union supporting it. The British, more concerned with the growing crisis in German-Czech relations, preferred not to encourage governments to concentrate their attention on Spain. Yet, Negrín and Álvarez del Vayo continued to demand league action against both Italy and Germany until the very end of the war. They made their last major effort in September 1938, just before the culmination of the Munich crisis, but with the same results as before. Afterwards, little attention was paid to the problem of intervention in Spain.

When, after Munich, Stalin* came to the conclusion that an Anglo-Franco-Soviet alliance directed against Germany was impossible to form, he decided to ally with Berlin as a means of reducing tensions in Eastern Europe* while buying time to develop a strong Russian Army to protect the Soviet Union. Part of his change in policy meant withdrawing support for the International Brigades* and causing them to be sent back to their respective nations. Soon after, Negrín asked the League of Nations to administer the withdrawal of these troops. The secretary general of the league, Joseph Louis Anne Avenole, supported the measure. On October 1, the necessary resolution passed, and a commission made up of fifteen members led by a general was assigned the task of evacuating the troops from Republican Spain.

Throughout the duration of the war, the league formally encouraged humanitarian assistance to both sides in the conflict. Through a series of resolutions, debates, and informal discussions, this international organization encouraged a variety of aid, particularly for noncombatants. Specifically, international organizations (such as the Red Cross and churches) were assisted in providing medical supplies, doctors, and ambulances for Spain; the care and movement of refugees* (particularly in the Republican zone); and the collection and shipment of food* and clothing to civilians. Private organizations and government agencies did most of this work. A great deal of the administrative coordination, however, came from technical agencies of the League of Nations. The league took care never to provide such assistance if it meant departing from its neutral position on the Civil War. Thus, it encouraged other governments and groups to perform the actual humanitarian relief work.

For further information see Julio Álvarez del Vayo, *Give Me Combat: The Memoirs of Julio Álvarez del Vayo* (Boston, 1973); Salvador de Madariaga, *Morning Without Noon: Memoirs* (New York, 1974); and Arnold J. Toynbee, *Survey of International Affairs, 1937* (Oxford, 1938). There is no history of the League of Nations in the Civil War as of this writing.

James W. Cortada

LECHE, JOHN (1889-1960). Leche, a professional British diplomat, served as London's charge d'affaires to the Spanish Republic in 1936 and was named minister to the Spanish government in 1937. Throughout the war, he followed the Republican Foreign Ministry as it moved from city to city, reporting on its activities to London. At several points during the war, it was Leche who negotiated with the Republican government on the possibility of a mediated peace sponsored by the British but to no avail. He also had responsibility for repeatedly defending the British policy of nonintervention to the Spanish Republican leadership.

For further information, see Jill Edwards, *The British Government and the Spanish Civil War, 1936-1939* (London, 1979); and K. W. Watkins, *Britain Divided* (London, 1963).

See also Chamberlain, Neville; Eden, Anthony; and Great Britain.

James W. Cortada

LEDESMA RAMOS, RAMIRO (1905-1936). Ledesma was leader of the *Juntas de Ofensiva Nacional-Sindicalista* (JONS),* and perhaps the best Spanish representative of the revolutionary Right in the pre-1936 period. Son of a schoolmaster in Zamora, Ledesma went to Madrid* in 1920 and pursued a degree in philosophy at the university. In the 1920s, he worked as a minor bureaucrat and wrote several essays on German philosophy, but he became increasingly interested in applying his political philosophy to practical affairs. An opponent of both Liberalism and Marxism,* he conceived of a nationalist proletarian movement that favored Spanish expansion and the glory of empire, national syndication of labor, land expropriation, the legitimacy of violence, but nevertheless retained a place for traditional Catholicism.

By March 1931, Ledesma had gathered a small group around him and began publishing the weekly *La Conquista del Estado* which lasted until October of that year. At this time, he became acquainted with Onésimo Redondo who was the leader of a small right-wing group in Valladolid,* and in October 1931 the two joined to form the JONS, although for the next year the group was without funds or really cohesive organization. By 1933, the JONS still had only several hundred members, but Ledesma had met with José Antonio Primo de Rivera,* and preliminary discussions occurred about joining forces. In the next year, the influence of the JONS expanded as they created a syndicate of university students with some 400 members, and organized militant squads for street fighting. On February 11, 1934, Ledesma and José Antonio met in Madrid and agreed to fuse their groups into the *Falange Española** *de las Juntas de Ofensiva-Sindicalista* headed by a triumvirate of the three previous leaders. Ledesma favored the merger because he felt it would provide a wider political forum. His influence on the movement was more theoretical than practical as he attempted to push Primo de Rivera to a more revolutionary position, and frequently criticized him for maintaining contacts with the Church* and upper class.

Although not pleased when Primo de Rivera was elected sole head of the party in October 1934, Ledesma did serve as president of the *Junta Política* and really authored the party's twenty-seven point program. Most of his energy at this time was put into organizing a never very successful workers' syndicate called the *Confederación de Obreros Sindicalistas* (CONS). Conflicting personal ambitions and contradictory philosophical issues made Ledesma's position in the party increasingly difficult. By early 1935, he had decided the Falange was no longer effective, and he attempted to split the JONS from the larger group to build broader syndicalist organizations. His older partner Redondo and most JONS members did not agree, and the result was that in January 1935 Ledesma was expelled from the party. Thereafter he attempted unsuccessfully to build another splinter group. Still in Madrid in October 1936, on the basis of his fascist politics he was ordered shot by the Republican government and died on October 29. His theoretical imprint on the Spanish Right remained. In fact, after the war, more radical youth groups in the Falange often hearkened back to Ledesma as the real leader of Spanish national syndicalism.

For further information, see Emiliano Aguado, *Ramiro Ledesma en la crisis de España* (Madrid, 1943); Juan Aparicio, *Ramiro Ledesma, Fundador de las JONS* (Madrid, 1942); Ramiro Ledesma Ramos, *Los escritos filosóficos de Ramiro Ledesma* (Madrid, 1941); Stanley Payne, *Falange: A History of Spanish Fascism* (Stanford, Calif., 1961); and José María Sanchez-Diana, *Ramiro Ledesma Ramos: biografía política* (Madrid, 1975).

Jane Slaughter

LEIZAOLA, JESÚS MARÍA. Leizaola, a Basque nationalist and politician, was the minister of justice in the Euzkadi Republic (Basque regional government) from 1936 to 1937 and on the defense council of Bilbao* before its fall to the Nationalists* toward the end of the Civil War. Leizaola attempted to negotiate a separate peace with the Nationalists when he felt that the Republic was not prepared to give the Basques political concessions in 1937. He escaped from Spain and in 1960 became the president of the exiled Basque government in France.

For further information, see Stanley G. Payne, *Basque Nationalism* (Reno, Nev., 1975).
See also Basque Nationalism.

James W. Cortada

LEÓN. León, a province located in northwestern Spain below Asturias* and north of Portugal,* quickly reacted to news of the revolt in July 1936. Some 2,000 miners asked the military governor of the province, General José Bosch,* for arms which he gave them (200 rifles and four machineguns). These miners then left to fight in Madrid,* making it easier for local rebels to seize control of the provincial capital. Other workers resisted the rebels but lost. Fighting took place in other parts of the province with similar results. At the town of Ponferrada a small battle took place, causing the deaths of many workers. Thus, by about July 21, the entire province had come under Nationalist control. In the mountains of northern León, guerrillas still operated against the Nationalists* until all of northern Spain had fallen to the rebels. Pitched battles took place here. In October, a few mountain tops remained under Republican control following fighting in the area, irritating the Nationalists who were intensely involved in the conquest of Asturias directly to the north. Although Asturias fell to the Nationalists in October, several thousand guerrillas remained in the mountains of León until about March 1937 when they finally were eliminated. Their presence, however, prevented the Nationalists from diverting troops from the area for campaigning near Madrid. After March 1937, when Franco* had full control over the province, he completely purged it of enemies and used its mineral wealth for his cause.

For further information, see Joaquín Arrarás, *Historia de la cruzada española*, 35 folios (Madrid, 1940-1943), 15:134-37; and José Manuel Martínez Bande, *La guerra en el norte* (Madrid, 1969).

See also Appendix B.

James W. Cortada

LÉRIDA. Lérida, one of the four Catalan provinces located in northern Spain on the French border, supported the Republic throughout the Civil War. It constituted part of the autonomous Catalan government, the Generalitat,* and experienced agricultural and industrial collectivization, anarchist, socialist, and communist politics, a severe purge of the Catholic Church,* and, eventually, military invasion by Franco's* Nationalists* in 1938. In January and February 1939, thousands of Republican refugees* passed through the province on their way to France.* Throughout the war, Lérida remained primarily under the political control of the *Partido Obrero de Unificación Marxista* (POUM),* who were anti-Stalinist communists and launched an intensive campaign to persecute the Catholic Church. Lérida's bishop was executed along with a large number of priests, nuns, and monks. Churches were burned as was the cathedral. Monasteries and libraries were destroyed, religious statues broken up, and church property either burned or confiscated. The city of Lérida was run by a *Junta* dominated by the POUM but also represented by the *Partit Socialista Unificat de Catalunya* (PSUC)*-*Unión General de Trabajadores* (UGT)* and the *Confederación Nacional del Trabajo* (CNT)*-*Federación Anarquista Ibérica* (FAI)* factions. The process of agricultural and industrial collectivization in the province disrupted economic life in many cases which, with the decline in foreign trade* and sources of raw materials, resulted in a steady decline in productivity throughout the province during each year of the war. Other economic groups did not suffer as much. The shoemakers' collective in the provincial capital, for example, noticed little difference from prewar conditions. Communities often functioned autonomously of the Republic, running their businesses as they had prior to the war. Manpower in the province dropped, thereby contributing to the economic decline evident throughout Lérida primarily due to the Republican Army* draft.

Serious fighting broke out in Lérida in March 1938 when Nationalist forces penetrated the province battling against the 15th International Brigade. By Christmas, the Nationalists occupied the provincial capital, splitting the province in half with the eastern portion still under Republican control. Some 300,000 Republican troops stationed in the area faced a large Nationalist Army.* Throughout January 1939, the rebels advanced through the province bringing it entirely under their control by February 1939. They liberated the Republican prison camp at Omells de Nagaya, while continuing to hunt down pro-Republicans* throughout the province. They purged Lérida, arresting and executing thousands between 1938 and 1942, with additional arrests taking place even later. Franco outlawed use of the Catalan language in public along with regionalist politics. He replaced officials with others loyal to the Nationalists, while properties collectivized during the Republic or the Civil War were returned to their original owners.

For further information, see José María Bricall, *Política económica de la Generalitat* (Barcelona, 1970); Robert W. Kern, *Red Years/Black Years: A Political History of Spanish Anarchism, 1911-1937* (Philadelphia, 1978); José Manuel Martínez Bande, *La compaña en Cataluña* (Barcelona, 1979); Antonio Montero, *La persecución religiosa en España, 1936-39* (Madrid, 1961); and Carlos Pi Sunyer, *La república y la guerra* (Mexico, 1975).

See also Barcelona; Catalonia; and Gerona.

James W. Cortada

LEVANTE. The Levante, an area with rich and prosperous farmland, produced large quantities of foodstuffs in the 1930s, primarily for the Spanish economy. The phrase "Levante" generally refers to the wheat-producing provinces of Valencia* and Murcia,* that is to say, the southeastern area of Spain. Besides wheat, farmers also grew oranges, rice, and truck vegetables, often in three to five crops per year. Anarchism thrived in the western portions of the Levante. It supported a healthy anarchist movement in the 1930s, while the greener, rain-soaked areas to the east remained primarily conservative and even Catholic* in political views. The city of Valencia had a particularly active political life, as did most Spanish urban centers, supporting a strong anarchist and anticlerical movement. In other communities, the anarchists* and socialists competed for political control over villages. Collectivization was practiced in wide sections of the area in 1936 and 1937, following a similar pattern evident to the north in Aragón* and in parts of Catalonia.* The Levante remained in the hands of the

Republicans* until the final weeks of the Civil War when it became an area that was evacuated before the invading Nationalist armies.

For further information, see Gerald Brenan, *The Spanish Labyrinth* (Cambridge, England, 1943); and Hugh Thomas, *The Spanish Civil War* (New York, 1977).

See also Economy, Republican; Libertarian Movement; and Peasantry, Aragonese.

James W. Cortada

LIBERTAD. The Republican cruiser *Libertad* (ex *Príncipe Alfonso*, launched in 1925, 7,475 tons standard, 8-152mm [6 in] guns, 33 kts.) was ordered from El Ferrol* on July 18, 1936, to prevent rebel troops in Morocco* from crossing the Straits of Gibraltar* to the peninsula. On the way, Republican crewmen wrested control from unprepared officers, and the *Libertad* joined the blockading squadron in the Straits and soon became its flagship. She participated in the evacuation of Catalan forces from Majorca* in September 1936 and led the Republican fleet to support threatened northern Republican ports in September-October. The *Libertad* spent the rest of the war as the flagship of the Republican fleet operating out of Cartagena,* mostly in protection of incoming supply ships, but also in the naval engagements of Cherchell (September 7, 1937) and Cape Palos* (March 6, 1938). The *Libertad* interned in Bizerte on March 7, 1939.

See also Navy, Spanish.

Willard C. Frank, Jr.

LIBERTARIAN MOVEMENT. Two months after the Republic's inauguration, the libertarian movement's mass organization, the *Confederación Nacional del Trabajo* (CNT)* declared that it remained in "open war" with the state. It was a victory for the ultra-Left "purists" organized around the *Federación Anarquista Ibérica* (FAI),* and reflected a division that had marked the movement for the previous half century.

All libertarians could agree on the ultimate revolutionary objectives: the abolition of private property, of government and state, and the administration of production by free associations of producers. They were divided on how this was to be achieved, and the structure to be given to it once it had been achieved. One side argued that revolution could be attained by violent actions which would set the masses in spontaneous movement. The other believed that revolution required the prior organization and education, within a coherent revolutionary strategy, of the masses. The first was, in essence, a rural vision of libertarian communism based on village uprisings that would establish the free municipality or commune. The second was based on the premise that to overthrow the capitalist industrial order and to manage the means of production after the revolution, a strong proletarian organization—the *sindicato*—was needed.

Two months after its declaration of continued war on the state, the CNT—undoubtedly the European working class's most revolutionary mass union organization—split along the line of its major tension. Thirty leading CNT militants signed a manifesto maintaining their allegiance to the second of these positions. The ultra-leftists immediately attacked the *Treintistas* (as the thirty signers and, by extension, their supporters were known) as counterrevolutionary. In the following year, some 70,000 of the half million members were expelled from the CNT, which was just recovering from seven years of a clandestine existense under the dictatorship. Many militants who agreed with neither side in the dispute became inactive.

Between January 1932 and December 1933, the ultra-Left staged three revolutionary insurrections, the major foci of which were outside the large conurbations. While each mobilized more participants than its predecessor, none of them was the spark that fired the countryside. But each more seriously than the last contributed to destabilizing the Republican regime.

The Republican-socialist coalition of 1931-1933 responded to the CNT's declaration of war by virtually outlawing the anarchosyndicalist m "ement. In consequence, the historic division between socialists and anarchosyndicalists was reinforced, and the working class found itself irremediably divided at the start of a new revolutionary period.

In the 1933 general elections, the CNT called on its members to abstain. This overtly political move in the name of a hallowed apoliticism represented the libertarians' profound disillusionment with the Republic which had solved few, if any, of the problems faced by the working class. Allied with other factors, among them the women's vote for the first time, the CNT abstention contributed to the Right's electoral victory.

In October 1934, the Asturian libertarian movement participated alongside socialists, Trotskyists, and orthodox and dissident communists in a proletarian insurrection against the government. But the Catalan libertarians took no part in the simultaneous but short-lived Barcelona* rising. The Asturian CNT had a long history of common action with the socialists in the struggle against the class enemy, and the Asturian FAI did not share its Catalan counterpart's enthusiasm for "revolutionary gymnastics."

The FAI was created secretly in 1927 as a federation of individual anarchist groups, its founding objective being to propagate revolutionary anarchist ideals among the working class. There was no general FAI "line" which all groups had to adhere to; such would have run counter to the very nature of anarchism. Thus, some groups, notably in Catalonia,* could interpret their objective as that of preventing the CNT's deviation to reformism or pure syndicalism, or permitting communist infiltration of the union. Yet, it is erroneous to conceive of the FAI as a force exterior to, and manipulating, the CNT. It was part of the CNT and represented a tendency which, to one degree or another, had existed in the movement virtually since its inception.

In the general elections of February 1936,* the CNT did not repeat its call to abstain. Three months later, in May, at the CNT's extraordinary congress in Saragossa,* a large number of *Treintista* unions rejoined the confederation. Nonetheless, the congress reaffirmed the anarchist tendency within the movement. The free commune was to be the keystone of the future libertarian society. Industrial federations and economic plans, while recognized, were to be created only if the communes considered them necessary.

It was with this "rural" vision of libertarian communism that on the outbreak of the Civil War the CNT found itself confronted with the task of establishing a new revolutionary order in industrialized Catalonia. Many of the ambiguities and contradictions of the libertarian movement were now revealed in the harshness of the new reality.

On the one hand, the CNT became the de facto power in Barcelona; on the other, hostility to "power," distrust of "politics," led the libertarian leadership to reject taking and organizing power politically. The local CNT federation opted to collaborate with the Popular Front* parties in an Antifascist Militias Committee* to put down the military rising. The libertarian revolution, it was argued, could not take place yet, for to do so would necessitate libertarian dictatorship—a contradiction in terms. Yet, the revolution in Barcelona was daily taking root in CNT collectives and union-run industries, often at the expense of the petty bourgeoisie who were the libertarians' allies in the struggle against the military. For weeks, the libertarians dominated the Antifascist Militias Committee, exercising power through it but refusing to make it the real instrument of their power.

Meanwhile, thousands of libertarian militants joined the militia columns that advanced from Catalonia into Aragón.* Although they failed to capture Saragossa, the capital, the underarmed and poorly equipped columns occupied about three-quarters of Aragón. Libertarian collectivization began to spread in the rearguard, but at the front, as though their initial momentum were spent, the columns dug in for a war of position. The opportunity to develop an alternative, perforce revolutionary, strategy relying on mobility, harassment, erosion—the irregular warfare well suited to libertarian concepts—was lost. As a result, the libertarian movement did not prove itself in the only manner that would have guaranteed its *revolutionary* success: by defeating the enemy, by sweeping him back.

In Barcelona, even the CNT could no longer doubt that some form of organization was needed. At the end of August, a secret meeting of Catalan libertarians (for they alone could decide a matter that affected their region) accepted President Companys'* repeated enjoinder for the CNT to take part in the Generalitat* government. The decision was kept secret. A few days later in Madrid,* Largo Caballero,* the socialist leader, formed the first Popular Front government. This the CNT was not yet ready to join. Instead, it proposed for Madrid what it failed to propose for Catalonia—a working-class government (called a National Defense Council to avoid the word "government" which was anathema to the libertarians) of the *Unión General de Trabajadores* (UGT)* and CNT with Republican participation. In what was to become a persistent pattern, the libertarian movement reacted to, rather than acted on, political events. But the reaction came too late, for a new Madrid government already existed.

While heated discussions continued in Madrid, the Catalan CNT sprang its surprise: three CNT members were joining the Generalitat council, alongside five Republicans, two *Partit Socialista Unificat de Catalunya* (PSUC)* representatives, and one from the *Partido Obrero de Unificación Marxista* (POUM). The next step was decided three weeks later, in mid-October, and announced at the beginning of November: four CNT ministers were joining the central government.

These decisions, which ran counter to anarchist principles, caused a certain dismay among rank-and-file militants. But even greater dismay was caused in some libertarian militia columns by militarization, their conversion into units of the Republic's Popular Army.* Antimilitarism was a basic tenet of libertarian ideology. But here again, by accepting militarization tardily, the libertarians lost a chance of seriously influencing the shape of the Popular Army, a chance the Spanish Communist party* seized and capitalized on.

Libertarian participation in the national and Catalan governments lasted six and nine months, respectively. At the national level, the CNT ministers were able to achieve little: in particular, the attempt by Juan Peiró* as industry minister to put through a collectivization decree was blocked by Juan Negrín,* then socialist finance minister.

Libertarian ministerial responsibility was effectively brought to an end by the May 1937 riots* in Barcelona. The street fighting in the Catalan capital—a civil war within the Civil War—was a desperate attempt by libertarian rank-and-file militants to protect their revolution from the communists, right-wing socialists, and Republicans* who saw it as jeopardizing the war effort. The attempt was disavowed by the libertarian organizations, indicating the distance that had grown between them and their Catalan base during the war. In fact, the failure of the revolution to create a proletarian power capable of winning the war, which was the prime revolutionary task, had sealed the revolution's fate many months earlier.

With the formation of Juan Negrín's government after the May events, the Republican state, fully backed by the Spanish Communist party, gained control. The Council of Aragón,* the only libertarian-dominated government in the Popular Front zone, was now dissolved on government orders, and many Aragonese libertarians were killed, imprisoned, or otherwise persecuted. The pitiless, sectarian, and often bloody struggle waged by the Spanish Communist party against its political adversaries in its own camp, and the senseless individual assassinations by which some libertarian groups pursued their ends, was a bitter reflection of the disunity in the Republican zone.

The ambiguities of the libertarian movement in relation to the dual objectives of waging war and making the revolution were now tardily resolved. In June 1937, the CNT agreed on a political program which included the creation of a single, strictly hierarchical military command, the setting up of a national council of war industries and of an economics council that would plan economic development and whose decisions would be rigorously applied.

In January 1938, libertarian revisionism was carried still further. The CNT agreed to the administrative centralization of all industries and agrarian collectives controlled by the confederation, the establishment of differential salaries, and the creation of a corps of factory inspectors who could sanction workers and workers' councils. Meanwhile, the FAI became a legal mass organization which agreed to collaborate officially in various political and administrative organisms. A move to convert it into a socialist libertarian political party was rejected, however.

In March 1938, the CNT formally joined the Popular Front. The following month, when Negrín formed a new government, a CNT representative, chosen by the prime minister, became education minister, a post he held until the end of the war.

Fear that Negrín's premiership would lead to a communist takeover continued to haunt the libertarian movement. It took its revenge for past defeats by joining Casado's* *Junta de Defensa Nacional* in Madrid and beating off a communist-led offensive against the *Junta* in the capital's streets. It was a Pyrrhic victory which, fatally weakening the already weak Republican will to resist, led to unconditional surrender to Franco's* forces and the end of the war.

For further information, see Antonio Elorza, *La utopía anarquista bajo la segunda república española* (Madrid, 1973); César M. Lorenzo, *Los anarquistas españoles y el poder* (Paris, 1972); José Peirats, *La CNT en la revolución española*, 3 vols. (Paris, 1971); and Vernon Richards, *Lessons of the Spanish Revolution, 1936-1939* (London, 1972).

See also Socialist Party, Spanish.

Ronald Fraser

LISTER FORJAN, ENRIQUE (1907-   ). Lister was a communist who became one of the most famous militia and army commanders in the Republic during the Civil War. A one-time quarryman, in July 1936, he helped La Pasionaria* persuade the army units in Madrid* to support the Republic. He then participated in the defense of Toledo.* Lister soon after became one of the commanders in the famed Fifth Regiment* which was composed primarily of communist militiamen, defending Madrid throughout 1936 until it was disbanded in January 1937. However, he became commander of the Mixed Brigades* on October 10, 1936. He led Republican troops in each of the major battles in and around Madrid, performing brilliantly, especially at the battle of the Jarama* in February 1937. The following month, Lister led soldiers at the battle of Guadalajara,* where he inflicted considerable damage on the Nationalists.* General Lister headed the offensive against Brunete* in July. At the Aragón* front that fall, Lister commanded the 11th Division of the Army of the East* which also fought at the battle of the Teruel* between December 1937 and February 1938. Between March and July, he continued to command troops in the campaigns of Aragón and the Levánte* where he had difficulty achieving any major successes with his weary men. He was also at the battle of the Ebro* between July and November, pushing the Nationalists back and inflicting large numbers of casualties.*

Lister was one of the key commanders of Republican forces in the Catalan campaign which began on December 23, 1938, concluding in late January 1939.

The Nationalists attacked his forces, pushing them northward toward the French border. This communist general then slipped into France* and came back into remaining Republican territory southeast of Madrid during March. He subsequently moved to Moscow before organizing guerrilla operations in Spain against Franco* in 1946 and 1947. Lister spent the decades of the 1950s through the 1970s involved in Spanish Communist party* politics outside of Spain, although with decreasing importance.

General Lister was one of the most important combat commanders of the Spanish Republican Army.* He held positions of field command at most of the major battles during the war. A resourceful, skilled, and energetic officer, he often commanded troops that were poorly disciplined and hardly provisioned; yet, he proved successful in launching offensives against the Nationalist armies on several occasions.

For further information, see Michael Alpert, *El ejército republicano en la guerra civil* (Barcelona, 1977); Enrique Lister, *Nuesta guerra* (Paris, 1966); and Ramón Salas Larrazábal, *Historia del ejército popular de la república*, 4 vols. (Madrid, 1974).

See also Appendix B.

James W. Cortada

LITERATURE. More literature is available regarding the Spanish Civil War than any other twentieth-century war. Intellectuals* throughout the world were profoundly moved by the Spanish events, and it was, therefore, natural that they started writing early about these developments and continued to do so for a long period of time. Nevertheless, this literature is not widely known and has hardly been studied for various reasons: scarcity of information, documentation, thorough bibliographies; great difficulty in locating writings produced since 1936 in so many countries in Europe,* North and South America, and in some African nations; and the near impossibility of obtaining access to books published in Spain during the war years.

This output covers the entire range of fictional literature, from poetry, the theatre, full-length and short novels to stories and essays. All of these writings share two broad characteristics. First, during the Civil War writers felt obliged to produce convincing texts, to flag their ideals as loudly as possible. Thus, their works have an "urgent" aspect and a lack of objectivity. Second, this bias, almost a necessity in times of intense agitation, has been maintained over many years, almost down to today. All of this does not mean, however, that a few very valuable works were not produced dealing with the Civil War theme.

Chronologically, poetry appeared first and, in terms of a value scale, has remained in first place. It flourished extraordinarily among combatants on both sides, but particularly among the Republicans.* Simple couplets circulated rapidly, reminiscent of ancient traditional folklore of this type: "Sing, militiaman, sing// and sing everyday, // because with your songs I want to // live (our) joys //as well as (our) sadness." The periodical *El Mono Azul* [The Blue Monkey] served as a channel for this output. Known poets such as Rafael Alberti, Antonio Machado, and Miguel Hernández* spurred budding poets and formed a new collection of "romances." The romance (tale of chivalry) so cultivated in Spain from the time of the Middle Ages returned to inspire poets to tell and sing about tragedies of the moment. This collection of romances was published twice before the final edition, *Romancero general de la guerra de España* [General Romance of the War in Spain] (Madrid and Valencia, 1937) appeared. Besides this work, there were more than fifty collections of poems dealing with the theme of the national fratricide published under the title of "romancero" (romancer) or "cancionero" (songbook), not only in Spain but elsewhere too. The best known include *Cancionero de la guerra de España (Aportación de los mejores poetas españoles)* [Songbook of the War in Spain With Contributions by the Finest Poets of Spain] (Madrid, 1937), Georges Pillement, *Le Romancero de la guerre civile* [Romancer of the Civil War] (Paris, 1937), Esteban Calle Iturrino, *Romancero de la guerra* [Romancer of the War] (Bilbao, 1938), *Romancero de los voluntarios de la libertad* [Romancer of the Volunteers for Liberty] (Madrid, 1937), and H. L. Tweeleit, *"No pasarán" Romancero aus den Freiheitskampf des Spanischen Volkes, 1936* (Berlin, 1959).

In addition to these poetical collections, many books of poems written when the revolution started were published. Some writers were most prolific. Rafael Alberti left memorable reminders in the fourth section of his *De un momento á otro: Poesía e historia, 1932-1937* [From One Moment to Another, Poetry and History, 1932-1937] and "Madrid, capital de la gloria" (Madrid, 1937). Those which have retained public attention are "Galope" [Gallop] and particularly "A las Brigadas Internacionales." Antonio Machado, always a defender of liberty, dedicated his first poem written during the conflict to the death of García Lorca.* This poem was followed by several others such as one on the defense of Madrid* and, perhaps the loveliest of all, the sonnet "Todo Vendido" [Everything Sold], all of which are included in his *Poesías de guerra* [Poetry of War] (San Juan de Puerto Rico, 1961). Machado was among those in the exodus to

France* at the beginning of 1939; he died in a town near the Spanish frontier on February 22 of the same year.

A greater tragic end perhaps was that of another great poet, Miguel Hernández, who died in a Francoist jail in 1942, as did many other intellectuals. He had enlisted in the Republican Army* and had fought valiantly. His splendid book, *Viento del pueblo* [Winds of the People] (Valencia, 1937), overflows with references to factory and farm workers, praise of labor, and hatred of social injustice. His emotional "Canción del esposo soldado" [Song of the Soldier Husband] figures among the finest amatory poems of Spanish literature. Before hostilities ended, he also wrote *El hombre acecha* [Man in Ambush] (Valencia, 1939).

Worthy of mention among other Republican poets are Vicente Aleixandre (winner of the Nobel Prize), León Felipe, Emilio Prados, José Herrera Petere, Pedro Garfias, Rafael Dieste, Luis Cernuda, José Moreno Villa, and José Bergamín.

The best known poet among the Nationalists* was José María Pemán* because of his interminable *Poema de la Bestia y del Angel* [Poem of the Beast and the Angel] (Madrid, 1939), which was both grandiose and epic in tone. Enthusiasm for eternal Spain, Nationalist fervor, Christianity, violent opposition to Marxism,* atheism, and Masonry* are the main themes of this work. Its anti-Semitic tone is notorious. Because of its grandiloquence and manichaeism in overpowering doses, this work remained outside current trends in contemporary post-Civil War literature and even stood in sharp contrast to that produced during the conflict. Yet, violence and manichaeism are very frequent in Pemán's poetry, and not only in Nationalist poetry but in that of many Republicans as well. In the Nationalist Zone, recourse was made to dramatic imagery invoking strong emotions and sentimentalism. Moralism, traditionalism, acceptance of death, as well as the idea of an indivisible, imperial Spain usually characterize the poetry of fascist tendencies. The personality cult is very evident in both zones: Antonio Machado composed a sonnet to Líster* and Lister's brother Manuel one to Moscardó,* while Pedro Laín Entralgo wrote his only wartime poem in honor of José Antonio Primo de Rivera.* Manuel Machado, opposite to his brother in both ideology and style, can almost be considered the prototype of the traditionalist. In *Horas de Oro* [Hours of Gold] (Valladolid, 1938) he sings the glories of Franco* and of the leading Nationalist figures of the Civil War.

Eduardo Marquina and Dionisio Ridruejo* share the same inclination to eulogize and exalt the heroes, particularly Franco and José Antonio. Agustín de Foxá

collected most of his wartime output in *El almendro y la espada* [The Almond and the Sword] (San Sebastián, 1940). Perhaps the most important work published in the Nationalist zone was an anthology of imperial poetry collected by Luis Rosales and Luis Felipe Vivanco in *Poesía heroica del Imperio* [Heroic Poetry of the Empire] (Barcelona, 1940). These two thick volumes included the works of José Camón Aznar, Gerardo Diego, Luys Santa Marina, José María Castroviejo, Felipe Sassone, Ridruejo, Rafael de Balbín Lucas, Francisco Javier Martín Abril, and Manuel Machado. Despite the considerable quantity of poems produced in the Nationalist Spain, its quality cannot be compared with that of the Republican zone. Franco lost the war of verses.

Some of the literature from abroad has already been mentioned. Many men also wrote individual works with extraordinary repercussions. In 1937, the Hispanic Americans, Pablo Neruda, César Vallejo, and Nicolás Guillén all published poems with titles beginning with the word Spain: *España en el corazón* [Spain in the Heart], *España aparta de mí este cáliz* [Spain Keep This Chalice from Me], and *España, Poema en cuatro angustias y una esperanza* [Spain, Poem Reflecting Four Afflictions and One Hope]. All three stressed the theme of fraternity with their Spanish brothers, anguish in view of the martyred nation, and satisfaction that the International Brigades* came to Spain to help the Spaniards, singing praises to the valor of these soldiers as well as that of the Spanish people who fought fiercely against oppression and obscurantism. A better known and more influential work was the poem written by Paul Claudel, *Aux martyrs espanols* [To the Martyred Spanish]. In this poem the French poet resolutely adopted the defense of the Catholic Church* and its party. The poem served as prologue to the book authored by the former Catalan deputy to the Cortes,* Joan Estelrich, *La persécution religieuse en Espagne* [The Religious Persecution in Spain] (Paris, 1937), a poem that was also published in the periodical *Sept* in the July 4, 1937, issue. Roy Campbell,* an Englishman, a pro-Nationalist and a partisan in Spain, wrote *The Flowering Rifle* (London, 1939) in which he chastised all ideologies opposed to the Nationalists.

Poetry in Great Britain* during the period between the two world wars was marked by a political character and the "Oxford Group" formed by leftists W. H. Auden,* Louis MacNeice, Stephen Spender, and Cecil Day Lewis, all of whom went to Spain except Lewis. Others, such as Ralph Fox, Julian Bell, and John Cornford,* participated in the International Brigades and died in Spain. All left a written record of their experiences. The best known was Spender, a convinced communist. He visited both zones, took an active part in the *Congreso de la Alianza de Escritores Antifascistas* (Congress of the Union of Antifascist Writers), published in *Hora de España* [Hour of Spain], and in *The Still Center* (London, 1946) gave his impressions of the war. This view was more of an emphasis on the suffering of an injured people than a focus on Lenin's doctrines, because already at this time he was questioning the validity of his own ideology.

Of all the literary genres drama reflected the least bellicose themes, but from the start it became a basic means of propaganda. Scarcely any theatres closed in Madrid,* Barcelona,* and Valencia,* except for a few days after July 18, 1936. New activities organized by the labor syndicates received official support in September of that year. There also developed the "Guerrillas de Teatro" (Guerrillas of the Theatre). These actors visited all the fronts, political organizations, and syndicates offering quality performances. A great number and variety of representations were offered in the large cities, ranging from classical Greek and Spanish, the traditional Don Juan, French and Russian, to Cervantes' *Numancia* by Alberti, and *Fuenteovejuna*, in addition to the very important works of García Lorca and new shows belonging to the "teatro de urgencia" (theatre of urgency).

Many works were produced in the Republican zone. One of these, the outstanding *Pastor de la muerte* [Shepherd of Death], was based on the heroic figure of Pedro, a brave farm laborer, who reflected the virtues of the common people. The piece incites to action and struggle. Other interesting works were *Tiempo a vista de pajaro* by Manuel Altolaguirre (1937), *La fam* by Joan Oliver (one of the most important productions of the Catalan revolutionary theatre, awarded a prize by the Generalitat* in 1937, and shown for the first time in Barcelona*), *Al amanecer* by Rafael Dieste (1938), and *Pedro López García* by Max Aub (1938).

Alberti, who was active in the Republican zone, wrote many pieces for the theatre, but his best work dates from 1956: *Noche de la guerra en el museo del Prado* [Night of War in the Prado Museum] (Buenos Aires, 1956). In this play the educational aspect, excess of populism, and lyricism characteristic of his wartime output disappeared, and a close parallel between the events of 1808 and 1937 is highlighted. Two more pieces produced in the Republican sector warrant attention because of their success in the following decades: *Morir por cerrar los ojos* [Death by Closing Eyes] written by Max Aub (Mexico, 1944) and *¡Viva la muerte!* [Hail to Death] by Salvador de Madariaga* (Buenos Aires, 1962).

In the Nationalist zone, the theatre did not achieve the importance it acquired in the Republican sector, and there were no noteworthy productions during the wartime period. For the postwar era, mention can be made of *El tragaluz* [Light Swallower] by Antonio Buero-Vallejo (Madrid, 1972) and *La casa de las Chivas* [House of Goats] by Jaime Salom (Madrid, 1970).

Abroad, only three works reached a not too numerous public: Berthold Brecht's *Los fusiles de la madre Carrar* [Mother Carrar's Rifles] (Frankfurt am Main, n.d.), Ernest Hemingway's* *The Fifth Column* (New York, 1938), and Arman Gatti's *La passion du général Franco* [General Franco's Passion] (Paris, 1969).

Another literary genre—narratives—was broadly in evidence during the Civil War and afterwards. The short novel and stories proliferated in the one period as in the other, while the full-length novel abounded in the postwar years, as would be natural because of the length of the texts, almost impossible to write during times of emergency. The same strengths and weaknesses are found in the short stories as in the longer narratives. Therefore, we shall focus on the latter as they offer greater variety and are more numerous.

The first novel dealing with the Civil War appeared in 1936 in Madrid by Elías Palma, *Gavroche en el parapeto* [Gavroche on the Parapet] and co-authored with Antonio Otero Seco. As in the case of all other works that appeared during the conflict or later, this short work abounds in subjectivity and is very close to vivid experiences. Ramón Sender's *Contraataque* [Counterattack] (Barcelona, 1938) and *Unitats de Xoc* [Shock Units] by Pere Calders (Barcelona, 1938) are outstanding among the novels published in the Republican zone, while on the other side there appeared *Madrid, de corte a checa* [Madrid, From Court to Checa] by Agustín de Foxá (San Sebastián, 1938), and *Retaguardía* [Rearguard] by Concha Espina (Cordoba, 1937).

During the past forty years, no year has passed without the appearance of a new novel inspired by the Civil War. Thus, the bibliography of such books includes nearly 900 titles. In the period close to the Civil War, young soldiers such as Rafael García Serrano, Cecilio Benítez de Castro, and Pedro García Suárez wrote enthusiastic anti-defeatist novels in favor of the Nationalist cause. Among the writers well known before 1936, only Foxá, Concha Espin, Tomás Borrás, *Checas de Madrid* (Checas of Madrid [Madrid, 1940]) Wenceslao Fernández-Flórez, *Una isla en el mar rojo* (One Island in the Red Sea [Madrid, 1956]), and Pío Baroja, *El cantor vagabundo* (The Vagabond Singer [Madrid, 1950]), wrote novels concerning the tragedy. The reasons may be that the majority of the intellectuals identified with the parties of the Left later went into exile, and that the output of those in exile was the product of writers only recently concerned with literature.

José María Gironella is the contemporary novelist best known for works dealing with the Civil War. His trilogy, *Los cipreses creen en Dios* [The Cypresses Believe in God], *Un millón de muertos* [One Million Dead], and *Ha estallado la paz* [Peace Broke Out] (Barcelona, 1953, 1961, 1966), has caused immense interest and controversy. Each book was published through subsequent editions and in several languages. These lengthy novels remain classics on the Civil War.

In the 1950s, *Las lomas tienen espinos* [The Hills Have Thorns] (Barcelona, 1955) by Domingo Manfredi and *Cuerpo a tierra* [Body to Earth] (Barcelona, 1955) by Ricardo Fernández de la Reguera were typical of frontline novels. *Las dos barajas* [The Two Cards] by Angel Ruiz-Ayúcar (Barcelona, 1956) is a great tale of espionage;* *La montaña rebelde* [The Rebellious Mountain] by Juan Antonio Cabeza (Madrid, 1960), a fine novel of love; and *El vengador* [The Avenger] by José Luis Castillo-Puche (Barcelona, 1956), a psychological work that deals with a man full of rancor against those who had killed his own family.

More recently, *Las últimas banderas* [The Last Flags] (Barcelona, 1967), by Angel María de Lera, reflects a new direction for novels in that it is told from the viewpoint of a Republican soldier. This was the first time censorship was relaxed enough to treat the subject (as a result of the greater freedom allowed writers in the Press Law of 1966). After this book appeared, numerous others were published with left-wing sympathizers as leading subjects: *Memorias de un intelectual anti-franquista* [Memoirs of an Anti-Franco Intellectual] (Madrid, 1972) by Angel Palomino, *El miliciano Borrás* [Militiaman Borras] (Barcelona, 1970) by Luis Perpiñá Castilló, and *Los niños que perdimos la guerra* [We, The Children Who Lost the War] (Madrid, 1971) by Luis Garrido. Other books reflecting new techniques and written by the new wave of writers who emerged in the 1960s include *San Camilo, 1936* (Madrid, 1969) by José Cela, *Volverás a región* (Barcelona, 1967) by Juan Benet, and *Azaña* (Barcelona, 1973) by Carlos Rojas. These no longer followed the realistic approach of earlier novels.

Among the publications by exiles, *La forja de un rebelde (La forja, La ruta, La llama)* [The Making of a Rebel—The Making, the Route, the Flame] (Buenos Aires, 1954) by Arturo Barea, enjoyed the same popularity as Gironella's trilogy did among the Nationalists. Despite their unquestionable merits, those works were devoid of subjectivity. If Gironella tended to-ward a reportorial technique, Barea sought self-justification, particularly in the third volume. Max Aub composed numerous narratives and theatrical works at the start of the revolution, and his series "El laberinto mágico" [The Magic Labyrinth] is the most brilliant: *Campo cerrado, Campo abierto, Campo de sangre* [Closed Country, Open Country, Country of Blood] (Mexico, 1943, 1951, 1955) and his *Campo del moro* [Country of Death], and *Campo de los almendros* [Country of the Almond Trees] (Mexico, 1963, 1968). Also noteworthy were *El rey y la reina* [King and Queen] (Buenos Aires, 1949), *Los cinco libros de Ariadna* [Adriadna's Five Books] (New York, 1956), and *Mosén Millán* (Mexico, 1953) republished under the title *Requiem por un campesino español* [Requiem for a Spanish Farm Laborer] (New York, 1960) by Ramón Sender, as are *El cura de Almuniaced* [The Priest of Almuniaced] (Mexico, 1950) by José Ramón Arana; *Diario de Hamlet García* [Diary of Hamlet Garcia] (Mexico, 1944) by Pauline Masip; and *Juan Caballero* (Mexico, 1956) by Luisa Carnés.

Two of Juan Goytisolo's last novels were published in Mexico: *Señas de identidad* (1967) and *Reivindicación del conde Don Julián* (1970), and Juan Marsé's *Si te dicen que caí* was also published in Mexico (1973). Both writers were residents of Spain (Goytisolo was also in France). Interestingly, Manuel Andújar, an exile who returned to Spain at the end of the 1960s, produced his best novel after coming back to his native country: *Historias de una historia* [History of a History] (Madrid, 1973). Thus, all of these works belonged to a new type of novel on the Civil War.

Apart from Spaniards, the French expressed the greatest interest in Spanish events. Already as early as 1937, André Malraux* had drawn on his experiences as chief of the Spanish Squadron to describe the Civil War, in *L'Espoir* (Paris, 1937), a novel reflecting the influence of motion pictures and Hemingway.* In this book, despite the turmoil of a revolution, Malraux still held out hope for a better life. Jean-Paul Sartre, Albert Camus, Drieu la Rochelle, Henry de Montherlant, and Claude Simon were in the first wave of French writers dealing with the Spanish theme. Jeanne-Pierre Simon, Georges Conchon, Christian Murciaux, and Joseph Peyré were among some sixty French novelists who also wrote on the war. To these must be added the names of three Spaniards who wrote and published their novels in France: Michel del Castillo, José Luis de Vilallonga, and Jorge Semprún.

The Fair Bride (London, 1953) by Bruce Marshall and *The Spirit and the Clay of Shevawn* (Boston, 1954) are the best known British books on the Spanish Civil War. But there is no doubt that the North Americans have had the best success. *For Whom the Bell Tolls* by Ernest Hemingway (New York, 1940) rapidly went around the world, and the motion picture based on the book featuring Gary Cooper and Ingrid Bergman added fame to the work. Upton Sinclair's ¡*No pasarán!* [They Shall Not Pass] (Pasadena, 1937), and John Dos Passos's *Adventures of a Young Man* (New York, 1939-1940) were published soon after. It is noteworthy that even in the last decade weighty tomes based on the Civil War were still being produced in the United States.* Recent examples include *Hermanos* [Brothers] (New York, 1969) by William Herrick and *La Guerra: A Spanish Saga* (New York, 1970) by Stephen Frances. In addition, the English-Canadian Hugh MacLennan also produced an excellent book based on the life of Dr. Norman Bethune, a Canadian physician, called *The Watch That Ends the Night* (Toronto, 1959).

In German, the most outstanding works were *The Great Crusade* (New York, 1940) by Gustav Regler,* *Wir sind Utopia* (Munchen, 1942) by Stefan Andres, *Die Kinder von Gernika* (Amsterdam, 1938) by Hermann Kesten, *Fünf Patronenhülsen* (Berlin, 1960) by Walter Gorrisch, and *Grüne Olive und nackte Berge* (Zurich, 1945) by Cladius Eduard; in Sweden, *Den Femte existensen* (Stockholm, 1939); in Holland, *De Woende Christus* (Antwerp, 1965) by Aster Berkhof; in Russian, Ilya Ehrenburg* wrote ¿*Qué más quereis?* (Barcelona, 1938). Among the Italians, only Indro Montanelli and Alba de Céspedes favored the Republic, while other Italians produced books praising fascism and the Nationalists.

The numerous titles listed above represent only a small portion of the Spanish and foreign writers who wrote on the Spanish Civil War.

For further information, see Maryse Bertrand de Muñoz, "Fuentes bibliográficas de la creación de la guerra civil española," and "La guerre civile et la littérature"; Fernando Díaz-Plaja, *Si mi pluma valiera tu pistola. Los escritores españoles en la guerra civil* (Barcelona, 1979); *Les écrivains et la guerre d'Espagne. Les Dossiers H* (Paris, 1975); Corrales Egea, et al., *Los escritores y la guerra de España* (Barcelona, 1977); *Hispanía*, 56, No. 3 (September, 1973): 55-56; María-José Montes, *La guerra española en la creación literaria* (Madrid, 1970); and *Mosaic* 3, No. 1 (Fall, 1969): 62-80. On poetry, see Fernando Díaz-Plaja, *Los poetas en la guerra civil española* (Barcelona, 1975); Hugh Ford, *A Poet's War: British Poets and the Spanish Civil War* (Philadelphia, 1965); Marilyn Rosenthal, *Poetry of the Spanish Civil War* (New York, 1975); and William Shand, *Poesía inglesa de la guerra española*

(Buenos Aires, 1947). On the theatre, see Robert Marrast, *El Teatre durant la guerra civil espanyola* (Barcelona, 1978). On novels, see Maryse Bertrand de Muñoz, *La guerra civil española y la novela. Bibliografía comentada* (Madrid, 1971) and her *La guerra civile espagnole et la littérature française* (Paris, 1972); Michael D. McGaha, *The Theatre in Madrid During the Second Republic* (London, 1979); José R. Marra-López, *Narrativa española fuera de España, 1936-1961* (Madrid, 1962); José Luis Ponce de León, *La novel española de la guerra civil, 1936-1939* (Madrid, 1971); and Birgitta Vance, *A Harvest Sown by Death. The Novel of the Spanish Civil War* (New York, 1975).

Maryse Bertrand de Muñoz

LITTORIO DIVISION. The Littorio Division, a unit of the regular Italian Army, fought in the Spanish Civil War for the Nationalists.* The division saw its first major combat at the battle of Guadalajara* in March 1937. Although this fight did not result in a victory for the Nationalists, it demonstrated to the rest of the world that Italy* had sent regular army units to Spain to fight for Franco.* This division fought again in the more successful Nationalist campaign in Santander* in August. The 12,000 men of this division stayed in Spain after November, when the bulk of all foreign troops left under an international agreement reached affecting both sides in the conflict. The remaining men were the best of the Italian units which had been in Spain, and they stayed until the end of the war.

For further information, see John F. Coverdale, *Italian Intervention in the Spanish Civil War* (Princeton, N.J., 1975).

James W. Cortada

LITVINOV, MAXIMO (1876-1951). Litvinov was foreign minister of the USSR* throughout the Civil War period and was thus one of the architects of the Russian policy toward the Iberian war. Throughout the 1930s, Litvinov had advocated a policy of "collective security" directed against Germany,* calling for an alliance among Great Britain,* France,* and Russia directed against Berlin. Within this view, Litvinov judged the course of the war in Spain. In the League of Nations* he urged mediated intervention to bring peace. By 1937, he recognized that German influence in Spain had to be blocked. Hence, for the last two years of the war, he carried out Moscow's policy of using the Iberian war as a means of weakening and diverting German attention while trying to contain the Nazi threat in Eastern Europe.*

For further information, see David T. Cattell, *Soviet Diplomacy and the Spanish Civil War* (Berkeley, Calif., 1957).

James W. Cortada

LLANO DE LA ENCOMIENDA, FRANCISCO (1879-1963). Llano de la Encomienda gained battlefield promotions in Morocco* and won the Military Medal. He was promoted to general in 1931, and on February 22, 1936, he was appointed by the Popular Front* government to head the 4th Division with headquarters in Barcelona.* He repeatedly assured the government of his loyalty and refused to join the rebellion. Nevertheless, he was dismissed from his command, probably at the insistence of the Anti-fascist Militias Committee* which was dominant in Barcelona after July 19, 1936. He gave evidence at the trial of rebel officers, one of whom, General Goded,* had arrested him when he had refused to declare a state of war.

Llano de la Encomienda had no appointment until the state of the army in the Basque country demanded the presence of a man of high rank. He was appointed commander of the newly created Army of the North* on November 15, 1936. The appointment was communicated to him by Asensio,* the undersecretary for war. In the chaos of reorganizing the government, Llano de la Encomienda did not see the prime minister and minister for war, Largo Caballero,* and seems not to have received clear orders.

The three regions in northern Spain which were still in Republican hands, Asturias,* Santander,* and the Basque provinces, maintained autonomous military organizations. The Basque provinces, which had recently received their statute of autonomy, had created under President Aguirre* an independent army. The Army of the North was a ghost army whose components were not subordinated to its commander. Llano de la Encomienda was thus not responsible for the failed offensive carried out by the Basques on November 13, 1936, and he soon clashed with Aguirre over the autonomy of the Basque troops. On January 9, 1937, Llano de la Encomienda asked Largo Caballero a series of fundamental questions, designed to clarify his role and the position of Basque forces. In order not to precipitate a crisis, Largo Caballero did not press Aguirre, who bluntly told Llano on January 20 that the latter had no authority. Consequently, Llano moved his headquarters to Santander and asked the government to confirm whether or not the army which he had been appointed to command really existed.

Aquirre's view of Llano de la Encomienda is illustrated by his communication to Indalecio Prieto,* the defense minister, dated May 24, 1937: "General Llano de la Encomienda is the personification of incompetence...he is influenced by pernicious elements who are politically mistaken." In Santander and Asturias, however, Llano de la Encomienda organized the army efficiently. But the separatist nature of the northern provinces made proper military operations difficult.

Llano de la Encomienda still found himself in this position of doubtful authority when the Nationalists* began their campaign in the north on March 30, 1937. As the Nationalists advanced, he struggled with the insubordinate Basque army and made anguished pleas to the air force for aid. After Juan Negrín* became prime minister, the Basque Army was separated from the other forces in the north and entrusted to General Gámir,* while Llano de la Encomienda remained in command of the forces in Santander and Asturias until June 29, 1937, when Gámir took over and Llano de la Encomienda returned to Valencia.* He was appointed inspector-general of infantry and held this post until almost the end of the Civil War. Having crossed into France,* he returned to the central zone, escaping when Nationalist forces overran the region. He lived the rest of his life in Mexico.*

For further information, see José Manuel Martínez Bande, *La guerra en el norte* (Madrid, 1969); and Ramón Salas Larrazábal, *Historia del ejército popular de la república*, 4 vols. (Madrid, 1974).

See also Army, Republican; and Basque Nationalism.

Michael Alpert

LLOBREGAT RIVER. The Llobregat River flows through Catalonia* north to south just west of Barcelona.* Battles were fought on both its banks between December 1938 and February 1939, when the Nationalists* pushed through Catalonia to the French border. Fighting had also taken place here in the first few months of the Civil War. The river thus served as a strategic barrier between east and west and as a line of defense or a military obstacle. Farms on both sides of the river were collectivized and remained under the Republicans'* domination until the final months of the war, despite all the local fighting.

For further information, see José Manuel Martínez Bande, *Los cien últimos días de la república* (Barcelona, 1972).

James W. Cortada

LONGO, LUIGI (EL GALLO) (1900-   ). Longo was an Italian communist volunteer in the International Brigades.* In the early months of the Civil War, he represented the Comintern in Spain, raising money, finding supplies, and recruiting volunteers* for the Spanish Republic. He then commanded troops in the many battles around Madrid,* probably having his greatest influence on the fighting at the battle of Guadalajara* in March 1937, where his troops inflicted considerable damage on Mussolini's* soldiers fighting for Franco.* He finally left Spain by way of Catalonia* in 1939. From 1943 through 1944, he commanded Italian partisans at home, and from 1964 to 1969, he served as secretary-general of Italy's Communist party. After 1969 he became president of the party.

For further information, see Luigi Longo, *Le Brigate Internazionale in Spagna* (Rome, 1956).

James W. Cortada

LÓPEZ AMOR Y JIMÉNEZ, JOSÉ (-1936). López Amor was a career army officer who, in July 1936, rose in rebellion against the Republic along with other Nationalists* in Barcelona.* Major López Amor commanded troops in the shortlived revolt, managing to capture the telephone building in the Plaza de Cataluña, one of the centers of local fighting. He and his soldiers were overcome and López Amor killed.

For further information, see Frederic Escofet, *Al servei de Catalunya i de la república*, 2 vols. (Paris, 1973).

James W. Cortada

LÓPEZ OLIVÁN, JULIO (1891-1964). López Oliván was Spain's ambassador to London at the start of the Civil War. He resigned his position in August 1936 to join the Nationalists.* A conservative monarchist, López Oliván served the Republic in the early days of the war urging the sale of arms to Madrid.* He later discouraged such aid when he switched to Franco's* Nationalists after August.

For further information, see Pablo de Azcarate, *Mi embajada en Londres durante la guerra civil española* (Madrid, 1976).
See also Great Britain.

James W. Cortada

LÓPEZ PINTO, JOSÉ (1876-1942). López Pinto was a career army officer and a general with the Nationalists.* In 1936, he served as the military governor of Cádiz* where he successfully rose in revolt against the Republic. His victory was important because Cádiz, a major port in southern Spain, became a convenient point at which Franco* could land troops from Morocco* in the early weeks of the Civil War.

For further information, see Antonio Garrachón Cuesta, *De Africa a Cádiz y de Cádiz a la España Imperial* (Cádiz, 1938).

James W. Cortada

LÓPEZ SÁNCHEZ, JUAN (1900-1972). López Sánchez, though born in Bullas, Murcia,* was raised in the radical labor ferment that characterized Barcelona* prior to World War I. He became a syndicalist,* secretary of the *Sociedad de Moldistas y Piedra Artificial* (a section of the construction syndicate in Barcelona) and was jailed for his radicalism by the time he was twenty. During the 1920s, he emerged as a leader of the *Confederación Nacional del Trabajo* (CNT).* With Angel Pestaña, López attempted to establish an acceptable relationship between the CNT and the Primo de Rivera dictatorship. This compromising temperament led to his expulsion from the CNT as a *Treintisa*.

When the Civil War started, López Sánchez founded a newspaper, *Fraga Social*, as a platform for spreading the ideas of the social revolution. Although he had no political experience and despite his anarchist* principles to the contrary, López Sánchez became minister of commerce in the Largo Caballero* government in November 1936. While the position was more symbolic than powerful, he attempted to insure the continuation of the anarchist revolution in the face of communist opposition. To this end, he and Juan Peiro,* minister of industry, drew up the decree of February 23, 1937, which defined and regularized the operation of factories, businesses, and commerce. The decree was a much needed statement to allay the uncertainty and insecurity in the minds of owners and managers which had been created by nationalization, collectivization, loss of workers to the military front, and worker involvement in the management of businesses, foreign and domestic.

Despite López Sánchez's anarchist belief that all means of production were the patrimony of the Spanish worker, and despite his active promotion of nationalization and collectivization, he went to Paris to sign commercial accords with the French government, becoming the first of the anarchist ministers to appear in the international political arena. At the end of the war, he went to England where he remained until 1954, when he moved to Mexico City. In

1966, he returned to Spain, dying in Madrid in August 1972.

For further information, see S. John Brademas, *Anarchosindicalismo y revolución en España (1930-1937)* (Barcelona, 1974); Ricardo de la Cierva, *La Historia se confiesa 1930-1977* (Barcelona, 1976); Robert W. Kern, *Red Years/Black Years: A Political History of Spanish Anarchism, 1911-1937* (Philadelphia, 1978); César M. Lorenzo, *Les anarchistes espagnols et le pouvoir 1868-1969* (Paris, 1969); and Georges Soría, *Guerra y revolución en España 1936-1939* (Barcelona, 1978).

See also Libertarian Movement.

Shirley F. Fredricks

LOYALISTS. The Loyalists were those Spaniards who remained loyal to the Second Republic* after the outbreak of the Civil War. They believed that the Republic was the legal government of Spain and Franco's* uprising a rebellion against it. The Loyalists opted for more democratic institutions and opposed the reestablishment of a monarchy.

For further information, see Hugh Thomas, *The Spanish Civil War* (New York, 1977).

James W. Cortada

LUCA DE TENA Y GARCÍA DE TORRES, MARQUIS OF (JUAN IGNACIO) (1897-). Luca de Tena, born and raised in Madrid,* was the son of a wealthy journalist and founder of the newspaper *ABC*.* He entered politics in 1923 as a member of the Cortes* from Seville,* and in 1929, he became editor of his father's newspaper which he ran until the start of the Civil War when the Republicans* seized it. He sided with the Nationalists* in July 1936, instructing one of his employees, Luis Bolín,* to fly Franco* to Spain. Luca de Tena had been plotting against the Republic since its inception and, after the fighting started, aided Franco by raising money and serving as a military aide-de-camp to a Nationalist general. Following the Civil War, he served as ambassador to Chile (1940-1944) and then to Greece (1962), and did a considerable amount of writing, primarily on the theatre and on contemporary Spanish affairs.

For further information, see Círculo de Amigos de la Historia, *Diccionario biográfico español contemporaneo* (Madrid, 1970), Vol. 2.; and Juan Ignacio Luca de Tena, *Mis amigos muertos* (Barcelona, 1971).

James W. Cortada

LUCÍA LUCÍA, LUIS (-1941). Lucía's role in the Civil War is unclear. A former Carlist, he had founded and led the *Derecha Regional Valenciana*, the Valencian component of the *Confederación Española de Derechas Autónomas* (CEDA).* Elected to the Cortes* in 1933 and 1936, he also served as minister of commerce and of public works from May to December 1935 under Prime Ministers Lerroux and Chapaprieta. During the spring of 1936, he took part in negotiations for a coalition government which would have ranged from Prietist socialists to liberal members of the CEDA. According to some reports, he was slated to become minister of communications in such a government.

In the first hours of the Civil War, Lucía sent a telegram to President Azaña,* announcing his support of the Republic. Both sides have questioned his motives for sending this message, but the telegram seems to have helped the government to hold Valencia.* Not trusted by either side, he was imprisoned by both. He was freed during the the Fifth Anniversary celebration of the uprising, on July 18, 1941, and he died shortly afterwards.

For further information, see Jaime del Burgo, *Conspiración y guerra civil* (Madrid, 1970); José María García Escudero, *Historia política de las dos Españas*, 4 vols.(Madrid, 1976); and Richard Robinson, *The Origins of Franco's Spain: The Right, the Republic and the Revolution, 1931-1936* (Newton Abbot, 1970).

William J. Irwin

LUFTWAFFE, GERMAN. *See* Condor Legion.

"LUKÁCS," GENERAL (MATA ZALKA KEMENY) (-1937). General "Lukács" (born Mata Zalka Kemeny) was a Hungarian commander in the International Brigades* who fought for the Spanish Republic in 1936 and 1937. This communist and novelist was a veteran of World War I and of the Russian Army and came to Spain where he played a useful role commanding Republican volunteers.* He commanded the 12th International Brigade, for example, in November when it defended the area in and around the University of Madrid, thereby helping to prevent the Nationalists* from seizing Madrid.* He fought in the region around the capital during the rest of the year. In March 1937, he led troops at the battle of Guadalajara,* and soon after, Ernest Hemingway* visited his 12th International Brigade. That May, the Republicans* undertook an offensive at Huesca* where Lukács died from a shell.

For further information, see Gustav Regler, *The Owl of Minerva* (London, 1959).

James W. Cortada

M

MACKENZIE-PAPINEAU BATTALION. The Mackenzie-Papineau Battalion was mustered into the 15th International Brigade in early July 1937, the last foreign unit to be incorporated into the Loyalist Army. Despite a name derived from two nineteenth-century leaders in Canada's* independence movement, more than half of its personnel and virtually all of its officers and commissars were from the United States.* Clearly, the designation was a way of honoring the more than 1,200 Canadians—half of them immigrants, and these largely Ukrainians and Finns—serving in Spain.

Earlier, Canadians had been incorporated into the Lincoln Battalion* and had fought in every engagement since the battle of Jarama* in February 1937. The battalion's first action on October 13, 1937, was part of a badly planned, ill-coordinated assault upon Fuentes de Ebro, near Saragossa,* which left sixty dead and 200 wounded. The battalion also took part in the winter war around Teruel* and in the final Loyalist offensive across the Ebro River in July 1938. In the course of these actions, almost half of the Canadian volunteers* lost their lives.

For further information, see Victor Hoar, *The Mackenzie-Papineau Battalion* (n.p., 1969).

Robert A. Rosenstone

MADARIAGA Y ROJO, SALVADOR DE (1886-1980). Madariaga was born in Corunna* and obtained his formal education in Madrid.* He became a journalist and writer, and spent the 1920s producing novels and essays. In 1921, he became an employee of the League of Nations* and in 1922 its director of the Section for Disarmament. Between 1928 and 1931, he taught at Oxford University. Then during the Republic's first days he received the appointment as ambassador to the United States.* Several months later, he was transferred to the embassy at Paris and returned to the League of Nations as Spain's envoy. During the Civil War, he was engaged in academic pursuits at Oxford. Between 1936 and 1939, he defended the Spanish Republic, and, after 1939, he refused to support the Franco* regime. He never took up residence in Franco's

Spain. He lived in other parts of Europe, developing an international reputation through his writings on literature, society, and history.

For further information, see Círculo de Amigos de la Historia, *Diccionario biográfico español contemporaneo* (Madrid, 1970), Vol. 2; and Salvador de Madariaga, *Memorias, 1921-1936* (Madrid, 1974).

James W. Cortada

MADRID. Madrid, the capital of the Spanish Republic, was an enormous metropolis of 900,000 inhabitants in 1936. It did not even have an industrial suburb, and for the traveler arriving by road, it rose directly out of the dry fields surrounding it.

Madrid had few industries in 1936. The only workers' organization of any importance was that of the building union which consisted of almost 60,000 members. The others were dispersed among dozens of small trades and hundreds of small businesses, of which tapestry and porcelain production were the oldest and most prestigious. However, the development of capitalism and business activities, as well as the administrative and centralizing role that the capital city still played during the twentieth century, helped to concentrate in Madrid offices and banks, agencies and social seats, publishing houses and newspapers. With them came administrators, corporate heads, bankers, and their "followers," more than 300,000 servants, five times more than the number of Masons and a mass of civil servants and white collar workers. Finally, the lights of the city attracted thousands of poor people from the countryside. Many became beggars, people living on the fringes of society, small thieves, jack-of-all trades, and building workers. In the 1930s, only one out of every two inhabitants was born in Madrid.

On March 1, 1936, 10,000 workers marched with raised fists in the capital, stressing the key phrase "workers' government." They were preceded by well-ordered ranks of quasi-military who were young socialists in uniform. Although Madrid was not a revolutionary center, for a long time it had been bound to the socialist tradition of Pablo Iglesias. The Socialist party* had gained the majority of all votes in each election since the beginning of the Republic. Indeed, the reformist and humanist tradition embodied by Julían Besteiro,* one of Iglesias's traditional supporters in the Cortes,* put Iglesias's principles into question by forming the leftist *Agrupación* of Madrid (5,200 members). The group was guided by Largo Caballero* and by his shattering declaration of rallying to the "dictatorship of the proletariat." The majority of Madrid's workers, beginning with the white collar members, were organized into the *Unión General de Trabajadores* (UGT)* which had ties to the Spanish Socialist party—*Partido Socialista Obrero Español* (PSOE). After the electoral victory of the Popular Front,* its unions showed considerable aggressiveness, which their leaders generally disapproved of.

The division of the socialist ranks among the followers of Largo Caballero and Indalecio Prieto* on each side at the beginning of 1936, along with the influx into the capital of young rural people, could only help expand the *Confederación Nacional del Trabajo* (CNT).* At this time it began to constitute an authentic militant force in the capital and, in particular, within the construction union. Led by brave, aggressive young militants, the anarchist union furnished the organizational structure for the most advanced elements of the proletariat and the poorest workers.

Madrid's role was quite important during the period that led to the Civil War and during the conflict itself. First, because Madrid was the capital, nothing went unnoticed there. Because the government of the Popular Front thought it could get rid of the restless building strikers at the beginning of July, it thus set off, quite involuntarily, a civil war causing *pistoleros* (armed gunmen) to gain power. Next, Madrid stayed in the hands of the Loyalists* after the defeat of the military insurrectionists of General Fanjul.* This last event led the Republican camp to initiate campaigns for reconquering power by a loyalist and constitutional government against all the revolutionary authorities. In another significant development, powerful feelings and international interests concentrated from October 1936 on what has become known as the "siege of Madrid." Finally, it was the center of the Civil War which in 1939 finally rang the death knell of the Republican Army's* resistance against materially superior forces.

Like all cities, since February 1936 Madrid had experienced strikes in all trades, even in the most unexpected ones such as the union for waiters and for subway workers who launched a slowdown program to insure transportation without collecting fees. In many well-known cases, salaries were rejected and interest was expressed in other issues.

Beginning on June 1, 1936, an atmosphere of violence permeated Madrid. There were two general strikes, the first in the construction union and the second in the electrical trade (which included elevator operators) resulting from the efforts of the combined leadership of these two major unions. The strikers demanded up to 20 percent salary increases, a thirty-six-hour week, a one-month paid vacation, and recognition of work-related illnesses such as rheumatism. But the employers decided to resist. The CNT then ordered its followers to initiate "libertarian communism" with "self-helping." The employers wanted to starve the strikers, while the workers marched in groups into restaurants to have themselves served without paying as they also did in grocery stores. Socialists and communists protested, and spoke of "provocations" on the part of workers. Brawls increased, and merchants called in the police* who in turn were overrun. On June 20, the unions within the UGT accepted the mediation proposals that were made, which included wage raises of 1 to 10 percent and a forty-hour week, but the CNT continued to strike. UGT leaders did not give orders to resume work, which they did not decide to do until July 4, while invoking a dangerous exposure for the Republican regime by continuing the strike. Revolutionary union members of the CNT replied by labeling the leaders cowards and by calling for "revolutionary unity" over their heads. As a result, brawls erupted between strikers and nonstrikers on all working sites.

The small fascist band thought its hour had arrived with this strike. Several times during June, it started punitive expeditions against isolated strikers. With the attacks increasing, the strike committee of the CNT called on its "defense committee," a paramilitary force, to become involved. When the leader of the Falange,* Fernández Cuesta,* was freed from prison on July 4, Falange attacks increased under his leadership. He thought that the new conditions made it possible to crush a strike that had become a minor event and thereby eliminate a portion of the CNT leadership that had been isolating itself. The Falange sent *pistoleros* against the strikers, while the strikers answered with their commandos, shooting down, as an example, people in the cafe used as the general headquarters for the commandos. Work at construction sites commenced only very slowly; elevators remained on the ground floor. The government closed the local chapters of the CNT and thwarted the strike committee's activities, especially the leaders of the construction union affiliated with the anarchosindicalists.

On July 12, Captain Faraudo, the socialist militia instructor, and José Castíllo, the lieutenant of the *asaltos* (Assault Guards),* were found assassinated in

Madrid. A few days later, José Calvo Sotelo,* leader of the right-wing parliamentary group, was taken from his home by Assault Guards and socialist Civil Guards and also assassinated. In Madrid's streets, there was a repetition of the events of the Civil War. And who could oppose it? The Republican authorities refused to pay attention to the activities of several restless generals. For the generals the most urgent priority was to disarm and break the resistance of the anarchist Masons who seemed to be the *avant-garde* of a revolution that the government had to prevent.

On Friday, July 17, troops linked to the conspiracy of General Francisco Franco,* who would come from Tenerife by plane, announced the revolt in Morocco,* occupied public buildings, and took by force the official government structures at Tetuán* and Melilla,* overcoming momentary resistance. At Madrid, the president-councillor of the Popular Front government, Santiago Casares Quiroga,* was informed of these activities, but no related issues were brought before the government that convened at 6:00 P.M. that same day. Casares Quiroga thought the revolt was a matter of local concern only. This feeling was confirmed by a memorandum published by the government on the morning of Saturday, July 20: the commotion was over, nothing was happening on Spanish soil, and the government was master of the situation that would quickly be returned to normal. A joint message of two major parties—the Socialist and Communist*—indicated a less perfect situation: "The government commands and the Popular Front obeys."

The popular movement did not encompass the entire working class of Madrid. The CNT, under the direction of its Committee of Defense and of Eduardo Val, had already been on the brink of war for several days. Its shock groups proceeded to reopen local offices by force on Luna Street and found and distributed arms. On the morning of July 19, its principal leader in Madrid, David Antona, was freed. He immediately went to the Ministry of the Interior to demand the release of imprisoned militants, threatening, in case of refusal, to have his men attack Madrid's prisons.

Casares Quiroga instructed the governors of the provinces that they were to prepare themselves for the eventuality of a coup by local garrisons, but he told them to refuse all distribution of arms to the people. He declared this policy before a socialist delegation, stating that he did not want to be a Kerensky who opened the way to the Bolsheviks and that he did not want to make Spain of 1936 what the Asturias of October 1934 had been.

Others, however, prepared themselves. On July 18, the telegram from Franco at Santa Cruz de Tenerife had reached all the plotters at the various garrisons. In Madrid, General Fanjul was held up at the Montaña Barracks, biding his time. Garrisons in the surrounding area to Madrid waited for a signal to start a repression against the enemy on a scale infinitely larger than that of 1934 directed toward suppressing the working class, its organizations, and its allies. In prisons and barracks, men, simple soldiers, junior officers, Republicans,* and socialist military personnel had been arrested, while others had begun passing out arms before the beginning of any fighting. Socialist youths, their militia and those of the party, organized a preliminary distribution of arms already buried in advance for such an occasion (October 1934). Several officers contacted by socialist friends promised to give arms to the militias* which were then grouping around local union offices and party headquarters. Lieutenant Colonel Carratalá promised 1,000 rifles, although he was soon defeated by officers loyal to the insurrection. Lieutenant Colonel Rodrigo, a Mason, turned over 5,000 rifles to the socialists who organized at Carranza street. Everywhere people took the initiative. At a local UGT headquarters, Carlos Baráibar* organized a telephone network of information that would permit Madrid to follow minute-by-minute the situation in the country from one telephone operator to the next. At the Ministry of the Navy, Benjamin Balboa, the communications officer and also a Mason, had made known the existence of Franco's telegram and continued his work by alerting warships by telegraphers who knew him and by organizing a counter-uprising of sailors against officers. Already, others were setting up barricades against the barracks. One group from Getafe Air Base* left for the north, improvising a militia that congregated before the Montaña Barracks. For the time being, General Fanjul renounced any attempt to escape this situation.

On the afternoon of July 18, the president of the Republic, Manuel Azaña,* proposed the creation of a government of "national concentration," combining the Right and the Popular Front while proposing the "moderation" of Spain "in order." The socialists refused to cooperate. During the night, Casares Quiroga resigned. It was not obvious to Casares Quiroga to arm the people since his objective was to convince the generals that under his care a compromise was possible. On July 19, he was out of office after a brief and deceiving talk over the telephone with General Mola.* The man who replaced him, Professor Giral,* also a Republican, had no choice with regard to "arming of the people"; they had already armed themselves.

The sailors, who were triumphing over their officers, impeded the plan laid out by the rebels, reducing the barracks that were not yet attacked. It was a similar situation in the capital: General José García of the Herran jails, in his attempt to take control of the military camp of Carabanchel,* fell into the hands of the enemies of the uprising. The supporters of the generals were placed in Getafe, and, after several hours of fighting, the Nationalists* were wiped out at the military airport. In Madrid, where loudspeakers were on every street corner, the latest news about the stunning victory in Barcelona* and of the surrender of the head of the insurrectionists there, General Goded,* was reported, along with details about the rapport between the forces in both cities. Three cannons, two 75 mm and then one 155 mm, were brought up and were used to bombard the barracks. Planes from the Cuatro Vientos also came and bombarded the Montaña. A white flag was raised around 10:00 A.M. within the barracks. The crowd outside immediately rushed into the buildings and was shot at without pity. Was it a trap or a misunderstanding? This scene was repeated two times, indicating that the defenders of the barracks were divided between those who wished to surrender and those who did not. At about noon militants of the CNT instigated another assault against the recommendation of officers present outside the barracks and with the socialist youth supporting the more aggressive action. After the assault was made, the barracks were invaded and all within were massacred within minutes. The only survivors were the military men who were held in the prison and had not yet been executed. In the barracks, the Loyalists found 50,000 rifles and breaches for 60,000 others stored at the Artillery Park (they had been taken away as a precaution by a friend of the insurrectionists), machineguns, and hand grenades. These weapons from the Madrid garrison were then distributed to the military members of the parties and unions. This "taking of the Bastille" signaled the start of the Civil War.

From July 21 on, as long as small detachments assured the "cleansing" of the capital of isolated snipers, the first makeshift troops of workers and military men rushed around Madrid, also in the direction of Guadalajara,* Toledo,* Alcalá de Henares,* and Cuenca,* with a Mason, Cipriano Mera,* operating with 800 militia armed with bricks and stones and one machinegun.

Dr. F. Borkenau,* visiting Madrid in August 1936 after Barcelona and Valencia,* was struck by the differences between the two centers which he recalled in his book on the Civil War.

Certainly there are fewer well-dressed people than in ordinary times, but there are still lots of them especially women, who display their good clothes in the streets and cafes without hesitation or fear, in complete contrast to thoroughly proletarian Barcelona. Because of the bright colors of the better-dressed female element, Madrid has a much less lugubrious aspect than even the Ramblas in Barcelona. Cafes are full, in Madrid as in Barcelona, but here they are filled by a different type of people, journalists, State employees, all sorts of intelligentsia; the working class element is still in a minority. One of the most striking features is the strong militarization of the armed forces. Workers with rifles, but in their ordinary civilian clothes, are quite exceptional here. The streets and cafes are full of militia, all of them dressed in their *monos*, the new dark blue uniforms; most of them do not wear any party initials on their caps. We are under the sway of the liberal Madrid government, which favors the army system as against the militia system favored by Barcelona and the anarchists. Churches are closed but not burned here. Most of the requisitioned cars are being used by Government institutions, not political parties or trade unions. Here the governmental element is much more in evidence. There does not even exist, in Madrid, a central political committee. Very little expropriation seems to have taken place. Most shops carry on without even control, let alone expropriation. To sum up, Madrid gives, much more than Barcelona, the impression of a town in social revolution.

Because Madrid was the capital, the political parties that made up the Popular Front believed it would be impossible for any authority other than the government to dominate the city. Yet, it was increasingly being run by a government lacking in authority. Was it the authority of the PSOE, or that of the UGT, or that of the Communist party whose influence was rapidly increasing that which prevailed during these summer months in the capital? In any case, the authority was that of a moderate element. No revolutionary measures were taken. Banks were controlled by the government. There was money for debts, a 50-percent reduction in the cost of rents, and even where the goods of agitators were being seized, the only "external sign" that marked the passage of a social revolution was the multiplication of community restaurants where militia and workers could eat in exchange for tickets issued by a union.

In fact, members of the UGT and of the PSOE (soon also of the Communist party and mostly of the *Juventudes Socialistas Unificadas*—JSU*) were cautious in their enthusiasm when dealing with state institutions. The chief of police hired socialist militants, while other government officials saw that the *laissez-passer* could be substituted for that of the UGT. Special police units were dispatched after the faithful Assault Guards along with socialist militia reinforcements considered reliable by public officials. Thus, the "Dawn Patrol," or the "Band of Criminal Research," which was run by the old socialist typographer A. García Atadell, quickly won Atadell a reputation for pillaging and torturing. But every political party and union sought to have its own specialized units, called *tchékas*, or private police, with their own prisons, executioners, and policemen.

On July 31, a government decree provided that the militia be paid salaries if members had a certificate of membership issued by a union or party. This represented a timid first step towards reestablishing a traditional army starting from the militia. At the Ministry of War, a handful of career officers, old military attachés, and staff officers, also members of the presidential guard, organized what was the beginning of a headquarters function for the new military service. Under the influence of the communists and the political organization that constituted their principal channel of influence, the Communist party and other labor groups helped in the rehabilitation of militarism. The JSU formed battalions, such as the October Battalion and the Largo Caballero Battalion. The Communist party formed its famous Fifth Regiment* through which men learned how to salute, march, and parade as well as how to use weapons. The iron fist of the Italian Vittorio Vidali, who called himself Carlos Contreras and was linked to the Soviet secret service, imposed a never-failing discipline on all his men. Such units received arms and munitions, and "military technicians" (mostly officers) voluntarily enlisted to serve in them.

Thus, "the order," recognized daily by communist speakers and journalists, allowed them to focus on winning the war. Yet, the communists had their own *tchékas*, just like the anarchists* who quickly developed their own policy on the matter. The government did not have the necessary strength to prevent a repression not of its own design, while still informing the public about atrocities being inflicted on towns and villages conquered by the Nationalists. On August 23, about 200 political prisoners* and an additional 1,500 inmates of the Model Prison attempted to escape. A few dozen escaped in the confusion caused by a fire they had set. The crowd outside moved toward the prison en masse, screaming "Death to the Fascists!" Militia guards—ordinary men crazed by the event, or simply determined anarchists—executed a number of the better known prisoners such as the political moderate Melquiades Alvárez and two Falangists, Ruíz de Alda and Fernando Primo de Rivera. Special tribunals and quickly executed sentences were promised to the crowd to persuade them to retreat. The crowd knew that along with the four columns marching on Madrid there was, as Zola proclaimed, a "fifth" one within the capital itself.

On September 28, after the fall of the last Republican stronghold in Toledo, all observers agreed that Madrid would fall into the hands of the Nationalists in a few weeks. The capital had no means by which it could withstand a siege. Madrid had neither provisions of food* nor anti-aircraft defenses, nor even a fortified position, let alone trenches. The militias defending Madrid were poorly equipped, poorly armed, and very poorly led. Avoiding the working-class sections, the Nationalists' strategists decided to enter the capital by way of the University of Madrid campus. Getafe fell on November 4 and Carabanchel on November 6. On November 7, Franco announced that he would attend Mass in Madrid the next day. Largo Caballero, the left-wing socialist chief of government since September 4, finally convinced the communist and anarchist ministers that the government should leave Madrid to run the country without running the risk of falling into the hands of the enemy.

"Hail Madrid without a government" (Viva Madrid sin gobierno), shouted the most resolute of the anarchists. In fact, the government of Largo Caballero, by leaving Madrid to go to Valencia, left the capital in the hands of a provisional government that revealed itself to be an iron regime—the *Junta de Defensa** of Madrid, over which presided General Miaja.* Key positions of this regime were in the army and police, which were in the hands of the communists and their most recent recruits, the young socialist-communist leaders of the JSU.

Madrid did not fall—at least not right away—for it held on for more than two years. It was only on March 28, 1939, that General Franco could come and attend a Mass there.

Madrid resisted because the population of the city certainly did not want domination by the Nationalists. Madrid resisted because the Madrileños knew that the forces attacking them were not only those of Spanish reaction and of obscurantism but also the barbarous Nazis and fascists who were ready to transform Europe* into a concentration camp. Madrid held on because it was necessary to hold on. And the will to hold on was bolstered by Stalin's* decision to give Madrid the means by which it could hold on.

Stalin was looking for an alliance against Hitler's* Germany* with the French and the British democracies. He wanted to assure them that they had nothing to fear from his Spanish policy. Stalin agreed to the policy of nonintervention. But the fall of Madrid would spell the end of the Spanish war and be a major victory for Hitler, his alliance with Mussolini* sealed on the battlefields. This development would have been caused by defeatists in France* and Britain* who allowed the bright victory of the "totalitarian" forces. On the other hand, the continuation of the Spanish war offered the best opportunity to build a military alliance between the USSR* and the Western democracies. The Soviets could thus act in Spain as an antifascist force. And so Stalin helped Madrid hold fast, consenting to an effort that would not be equaled during the remainder of the Civil War elsewhere.

In October 1936 and then massively in November and in December, badly needed arms arrived either directly or indirectly through the Russians. Henceforth, Madrid's defenders had guns, ammunition, grenades, automatic weapons, artillery, including antiaircraft weaponry, tanks, and planes, both fighter craft and bombers. These arms enabled the city to hold on but were not sufficient to win the war. A small group of military advisers arrived in September with a new Soviet ambassador, Marcel Rosenberg.* A more important group came around October 20. From then on, every Spanish unit at the Madrid front had its own adviser, a Stern or a Berzine, Malinovski, Rodimitsev, Joukov, and others less well known.

On November 8, 8,500 men of the 1st International Brigade arrived and were stationed at the University of Madrid front. Coming from all over the world, recruited from the toughest militants, the most courageous, and the most indestructible Italian and German communists, but also French and English, North African and East European fighters, they brought with them a spirit of sacrifice. Their sense of discipline would constitute an irreplaceable force, and their example was worth at least as much as their direct involvement in the fighting.

In September, only 2,000 of the 20,000 who had volunteered for the construction of fortification had been used. Yet, all courage was soon galvanized by the arrival of Russian aid. Madrid was cast in the tradition of the October Revolution, and its defense followed the defense of Petrograd. Its movie theatres showed such big Soviet films as *Tchapaiev, Cuirassé Potemkine*, and *Les Marins de Cronstadt*. La Pasionaria,* clothed in black as if she were the widow of all the fighters who died daily, led demonstrations of women, stressing the heroic words of order: "It is better to die standing than to live kneeling."

Finally, to insure the defense of the capital, the *Junta de Defensa* and the organizations of the Popular Front were surprised by the threat, and thus used the same means by which they before had fought when they were praised by the extremists of the CNT or by the *Partido Obrero de Unificación Marxista*

(POUM).* On November 9, columns of unarmed workers were finally organized and replaced those who fell in battle. Barricades were erected in the streets, and, as Robert Colodny wrote:

In the Casas del Pueblo, the socialist, communist and anarchist trade union leaders began to gather not soldiers but men and women, and in the streets leading to the western suburbs, the crude barricades continued to arise as men, women and children formed a living conveyor belt and passed the stones of Madrid to the masons who raised the symbolic walls, militarily useless, but psychologically invincible, that awaited the belated offensive.

Communists and socialists did not denounce each other in the beginning of November, but rather turned to various other organizations to help in the struggle, calling on block committees and women's organizations for communal meals and laundry services. After a large number of the regular police forces departed for Valencia, the remaining members were severely purged. Security guards from the Fifth Regiment, led by Pedro Checa, and "special services" of the Ministry of War, which was led by the *cenetista*, Manuel Salgado (a key Anarchist figure), had to fight against the Fifth Regiment, using searches and arrests, and did not retreat in the face of summary executions. On November 6, the representative of *Pravda*, the Russian Mikhail Koltsov, who was little more than a journalist, talked with the men in charge of public order—leaders of the JSU such as Santiago Carrillo,* Serrano Poncela, and José Cazoría—who had 600 prisoners considered particularly dangerous evacuated from the Model Prison. Two days later, these men and, according to Jesús Galindez, 400 others, were beaten about the head while being evacuated. There was no retreat before diplomatic "prejudices" either; Serrano Poncela led an attack on the Embassy of Finland where 1,100 "fascists" had sought refuge. Meanwhile, the *Junta's* agent Pablo Verardini from the "special services" had organized a trap at the Embassy of Siam destined to capture fugitives.

Between November 15 and 20, the Nationalist troops got closer to Madrid than at any other time during the war. The fighting was house by house, stone by stone. On November 21, the anarchist leader Durruti,* having come from the Aragón* front with his famous column of troops, was killed and, on the same day, the 11th International Brigade had its first victorious counterattack on the campus of the University of Madrid. Madrid had not fallen. This ferocious resistance led Franco to try to break the city's residents through fear of aerial bombardments. Through this method several thousand civilians died each night. A Catholic

Basque and an excellent observer, Jesús Galindez concluded: "The enemy has not entered. He was only successful in provoking the hatred of those who were still indifferent, he has only succeeded in surpassing the massacres of the *tchékes*, making them seem good in comparison."

By now, Madrid was no longer the frivolous and gay capital it had been, nor the city in "heroic disorder" that a visitor, Louis Delaprée, had seen in September. It was a dark city, living without lights at night, with the noise of firing and the rumbling of cannon or the explosion of bombs twenty-four hours a day:

Death is the constant companion of a population of which the nerves are stretched to the extreme, of people who constantly look towards the sky in anguish, hurrying into shelters at the first signal, buries its victims without warning them, stays ready all the time, people guarding for the call of the block or house committee to chase spies, to go to the front where one went by subway.

But the battle of Madrid, the turning point of the war, in turn became the turning point in the politics of war and in the history of Madrid. Stalin's men were in power within the *Junta* and quickly refused entry to any members of the POUM whom they called "fascists" and wanted to exterminate. In November, they had tolerated and even revived the soviet type of organization, like the committees on housing, on the condition they were composed of representatives of parties and unions of the Popular Front and were not elected by the population. (As good followers of Stalin, they distrusted elections.) The *Junta* worked to prevent these organizations from becoming rival authorities. The new question that had arisen was how to get rid of them and take away their power. On December 12, all militia units were militarized along with, on December 24, the functions of retired policemen from the ranks of the militia, while various headquarters were turned over to the Assault Guards controlled henceforth by the leaders of the Communist party. The cries of protest started between the new "forces of order" and the militia of the CNT which on December 26 even fired weapons during a muster-role, seriously wounding a communist member of the *Junta*.

Forced to be prudent when faced by the CNT, which had a considerable force, the *Junta* did not have the same scruples as the POUM, a minority group in Madrid, even though it had furnished several thousand fighters, especially the heroic defenders of the cathedral of Sigüenza. The defenders of "democracy" stopped the advance of the POUM, closed its radio trans-mitters and its headquarters, and forbade help. The *Junta* also forbade militants from chasing Trotskyists as announced on December 16 by *Pravda* in Moscow.

The *Junta de Defensa* of Madrid perished because of its political excesses. In April 1937, the newspaper of the CNT, confident of certain socialist movements, publicly attacked the leader of the JSU, José Cazorla,* councillor for the *Junta*, and confirmed the existence of communist *tchékas* and of private prisons where people arrested without reason by communist police were interrogated and tortured within Madrid. Socialist police conducted an investigation and discovered that among Cazorla's followers was a gang that would free guilty prisoners in return for gold. The scandal was enormous. It made it possible for Largo Caballero, at the time enmeshed in a bloody battle with the Communist party, to dissolve the *Junta* on April 23, 1937.

Madrid, now no longer the capital anyway, ceased to be the enemy's number one objective, and it continued to be run by a *Junta*. Madrid lived in obscurity until the last weeks of the Civil War.

Far from the essential military operations, but within earshot of enemy lines, Madrid spent the rest of the Civil War suffering from hunger and cold. At the beginning of 1939, the city's material situation was shockingly poor. There were no means of heating, no hot water, medications, or dressings, while 400 to 500 people died daily from starvation. Lack of nutrition* caused the Quakers* to point out that the continuation of very low levels of rationing over several months would not be sufficient to prevent starvation. Hunger, cold, and runaway inflation gnawed away at the morale of a population that only distantly remembered the heroic fighting crowds of 1937. Merchants openly refused bank notes which the Franco radio* stations said would not be recognized after the victory of "the Crusade."* Workers and socialists in Madrid and middle-class and moderate Republicans had rejected and fought fascism, enthusiastically accepting the unified front with the communists. But, as wrote Gabriel Jackson, "at the end of 1937, the population were no longer 'fellow travelers.' " The mysterious reactionaries who inhabited embassies and secret caves had renewed hope of once again seeing the light and of taking revenge. Franco's personal representative was simply a colonel in the Republican Army, head of an artillery park in the capital.

In March 1939, with the loss of Catalonia* and the fall of Barcelona without a shot, everyone know that the war was over. With the surrender of hundreds of thousands of men interned in France, the departure of President Azaña, and the recognition of the Burgos* regime by the French government, no hope survived. Negrín's* government hoped to negotiate an honorable surrender but did not succeed. The *Junta* at Madrid along with the help of Colonel Casado* rose in revolt and, as in 1936, placed government leadership in the hands of General Miaja, hoping to have a better chance to resolve a negotiated peace.

It was at Madrid that the ultimate tragic scene unfolded. The *Junta* of Madrid, perhaps convinced by the last series of military promotions handed out by Negrín (which gave the communists control of the ports and the means for evacuation), decided to form a coalition generally of all who within Republican Spain were not linked to the Communist party. This coalition included career army officers, all types of socialists, various shades of Republican political views, the most famous anarchist military chiefs such as Cipriano Mera, and the old reformist Julián Besteiro (deputy for the city for decades) who had refused to leave it during the siege, as he would refuse to do after its fall. (This caused Besteiro to languish in a Madrid prison after Franco occupied the city.)

The *Junta* was formed at midnight on March 4, 1939. On March 7, Colonel Barceló,* a member of the Spanish Communist party, put his troops into motion to block the entry points into the capital, occupying several ministries and the headquarters of the Central Army, and rejecting Casado's men in the southeast corner of the capital. But soon after, the 4th Corps, under the command of Cipriano Mera, began a counterattack in order to help Casado. Fighting took place in the capital on March 8. At first, it seemed that the communists were winning; Pedro Chaca was arrested by order of Casado and Jesús Hernández,* at the head of the 22nd Army, cut through the supply lines of Madrid to capture enemy soldiers and free his comrade. But on March 9, the balance leaned in Mera's favor; on March 11 a cease-fire was drawn up. The *Junta* demanded the return of all the positions occupied on March 2 and also ordered Colonel Barceló and his commissioner shot—two more deaths added to the 2,000 victims of the internal fighting of the past few days.

On March 28, Casado's attempts to negotiate with Madrid were not fruitful; for Madrid it was the end. The "fifth column" left its hiding places within the city. The first Nationalist units arrived at noon and began their occupation of official buildings. They were immediately followed by 200 judicial officials escorted by truckloads of soldiers. Those men and women who had just come out of the embassies and who had always cheered the Nationalist victors saluted enthusiastically the passage of Franco's soldiers through the

streets while shouting that they "had passed!" (han pasado!). Julián Besteiro went to jail along with thousands of civilian combatants.

The victory parade was held in Madrid on May 19, 1939. In July, Count Ciano,* Mussolini's son-in-law, visited Madrid, noting in his diary that in the capital proper 200 to 500 people were being shot daily.

For further information, see Manuel Aznar, *Historia militar de la Guerra de España* (Madrid, 1940), a Nationalist perspective; Franz Borkenau, *The Spanish Cockpit* (London, 1937); Sigismundo Casado, *The Last Days of Madrid* (London, 1939); Robert G. Colodny, *The Struggle for Madrid* (New York, 1958); CNT, *De Julio a Julio* (Barcelona, 1937); Jesús de Galíndez, *Los Vascos en Madrid sitiado* (Buenos Aires, 1945); José García Pradas, *Cómo terminó la Guerra de España* (Buenos Aires, 1940); Dan Kurzman, *Miracle of November: Madrid's Epic Stand, 1936* (New York, 1980); Antonio Lopez Fernández, *Defensa de Madrid* (Mexico, 1945); Juan-Simeon Vidarte, *Todos fuimos culpables* (Barcelona, 1978); and Julián Zugazagoitia, *Historia de la Guerra de España* (Buenos Aires, 1940).

See also appendix B.

Pierre Broué

MAESTRAZGO PLAIN. Maestrazgo Plain, located in the region of Aragón,* became one of the last battlegrounds of the Civil War in southern Spain. Throughout the second half of 1938, the Nationalists* cut across this plain in southern Aragón in their drive to the Mediterranean, splitting the Republic in two. As late as April 18, 1938, the Republicans* attacked the Nationalists as the Loyalists* attempted to slow Franco's* advance northward. However, the Nationalists were able to push north and eastward, ultimately occupying the port city of El Grao de Castellón on the Mediterranean in June.

For further information, see Hugh Thomas, *The Spanish Civil War* (New York, 1977).

James W. Cortada

MAISKY, IVAN MIKHAILOVICH (1884-   ). Maisky was the Soviet ambassador to London during the Spanish Civil War. He also represented the USSR* in the Non-Intervention Committee* which sat in London. Throughout the war, he strongly supported the international position of the Spanish Republic, proved critical of Italian and German intervention on behalf of the Nationalists,* and insured that Moscow played an active role in all major diplomatic consultations on the war. He was particularly active within the Non-

Intervention Committee where he aggressively sought to force the Germans and the Italians out of Spain. Thus, for example, throughout 1937 and 1938, he asked Italian and German diplomats if they would consider withdrawal of their forces. Maisky constantly proposed various formulas for naval blockades that would help curtail the influence of Rome and Berlin within Spain. Maisky was a hard-working, realistic (even cynical) diplomat who executed Soviet policy in London effectively. Although unable to limit fascist influence in Spain until it became convenient for Rome and Berlin, he constantly brought international notice to the problem of the Spanish Civil War as a general European crisis.

For further information, see Ivan M. Maisky, *Spanish Notebooks* (London, 1966).

See also France; Great Britain; and League of Nations.

James W. Cortada

MAJORCA. Majorca, the largest of the Balearic Islands,* fell to the Nationalists* on July 19, 1936, after General Manuel Goded,* acting with decisive speed, occupied Palma de Majorca* with Falangist and Carlist units. At first, neither the Republicans* nor the Nationalists considered Majorca a significant element in the Civil War.

A Catalan expedition under the command of Captain Alberto Bayo,* in an effort more political and regionalistic than strategic, attempted to retake the island in a landing at Point Amer on August 16, 1936. Despite a primitive organization and lack of equipment, Bayo's invasion was on the verge of success when General Franco* replaced the hesitant Nationalist leadership in Majorca, as much to prevent Italian as Republican control of Majorca. Mussolini* ordered military forces into Majorca on August 26, and Italian aircraft quickly appeared over the front. Colonel Luis García Ruiz launched a counteroffensive on September 3. That same day, the Republican Navy minister, Indalecio Prieto,* and the Central Committee of the fleet ordered Bayo to evacuate the island. Prieto did not think Majorca worth the effort, and Bayo was forced to comply.

With the removal of enemy forces, Majorca progressively became a major Italo-Spanish naval and air base, the only strategically favorable position available to the Nationalists in the Mediterranean. For months, it was uncertain whether Nationalist leaders or Italian agents headed by the fascist organizer Arconovaldo Bonaccorsi ("Conte Rossi") exercised the real authority in Majorca. Spaniards slowly awoke to the island's strategic significance, and Franco's atten-

tion to the area ensured Spanish control while accepting an increased Italian military presence. Italian naval Commander Carlo Margottini organized a naval base at Palma, which by December 1936 supported Italian warships and became the major Nationalist naval operating base. From the Italian-outfitted base at concealed Sóller, ceded Italian submarines began operating in May 1937, and Italian submarines* from September 1937 to February 1938. Six squadrons of Italian bombers and two of fighters, almost half of the Italian Air Force in Spain, operated from Majorcan airfields against maritime and coastal targets. Italian seaplanes were based at Alcudia, and German seaplanes in Pollensa Bay. In October 1937, Admiral Francisco Moreno* established blockade headquarters at Palma. For the rest of the war the entire Spanish, Italian, and German naval and air campaign against Republican and foreign shipping and against the Republic's ports and coastal transportation network operated from Majorca, a hub of the Nationalist war effort.

For further information, see José Manuel Martínez Bande, *La invasión de Aragón y el desembarco en Mallorca* (Madrid, 1970); and Josep Massot i Muntaner, *La guerra civil a Mallorca* (Montserrat, 1976).

See also Air Force, Nationalist; Air Force, Republican; Navy, German; Navy, Italian; and Navy, Spanish.

Willard C. Frank, Jr.

MAKHNO, NESTOR (1889-1935). The Russian anarchist leader, Nestor Makhno, was best known in Spain for his association with Buenaventura Durruti,* Francisco Ascaso,* and Juan García Oliver* while they were in exile during the 1920s. Makhno provided a model for the idealized anarchist revolutionary, and when Durruti formed the militia army of Aragón* in 1936, he consciously tried to use Makhno's ideas.

Makhno rose to greatest prominence during 1918-1919 in the Ukraine, leading guerrilla attacks against the Germans and then both the Red and White sides in the Russian Civil War. He was the de facto ruler of the area, much as the Spanish anarchists* were later in Catalonia,* and like Durruti, his anarchism was more a personal charismatic style than a theory. The *Makhnovshchinas*, however, were defeated by the Bolsheviks in the summer of 1920. Makhno fled abroad and lived the rest of his life in Paris, though he twice journeyed to Spain to consult with the *Federación Anarquista Ibérica* (FAI).*

For further information, see Paul Avrich, *The Anarchists in the Russian Revolution* (Ithaca, N.Y., 1973); James Joll, *The Anarchists* (New York, 1964); and Rob-

ert Kern, *Red Years/Black Years: A Political History of Spanish Anarchism 1911-1937* (Philadelphia, 1978).
See also Libertarian Movement.

Robert W. Kern

MÁLAGA. Málaga, a province located in southern Spain fronting on the Mediterranean near Gibraltar* in the region of Andalusia,* was the scene of much activity during the Civil War. Before 1936, the province was heavily anarchist and pro-Republican. The city of Málaga was primarily controlled by the *Confederación Nacional del Trabajo* (CNT)* and the *Federación Anarquista Ibérica* (FAI),* especially during the early days of the war. Pro-Nationalists were arrested and executed throughout the province as various anarchist groups competed for political and military control over the area. The province was cut off from the rest of Republican Spain in the first few weeks of the war and was subjected to periodic aerial attacks, thereby increasing tensions, particularly in the port city of Málaga. The city came under the control of a militia *Junta*, while various other towns nearby were run by other rival anarchist elements.

Málaga avoided attack by the Nationalists* in the early months of the war primarily because of the mountains surrounding the province but also because Franco* wanted to head directly north from Cádiz* and Seville* for Madrid.* Málaga was too far east. War came to Málaga in full force, however, in 1937. On January 17, Nationalists under the command of General Gonzalo Queipo de Llano* began a campaign to capture the provincial capital of 100,000. A three-pronged attack from the east, north, and south led to Nationalist occupation of land near Málaga in January and February. On February 3, the Nationalists* began their attack on the poorly defended and equally miserably managed city. Finally, on February 8, it fell to the Nationalists. The victors then executed perhaps as many as 4,000 individuals, primarily as retribution for the Republicans'* earlier killings of nearly 2,500 people. With the conquest of Málaga, the Nationalists now had a Mediterranean port while reducing the length of their battle front in Andalusia.* It now became possible for the Nationalists to concentrate on their advance toward Madrid.* The area remained under Nationalist control for the rest of the war.

For further information, see Ronald Fraser, *In Hiding: The Life of Manuel Cortes* (London, 1972) and *The Blood of Spain* (New York, 1979); José Manuel Martínez Bande, *La compaña de Andalucía* (Madrid, 1969); and Antonio Nadal, *La Guerra civil en Málaga* (Málaga, 1980).

See also Italy; Terrorism; and Appendix B.

James W. Cortada

MALRAUX, ANDRÉ (1901-1976). Malraux, perhaps the most famous French writer of the 1930s, supported the cause of the Spanish Republic. Although not a Communist party member, he agreed with many of its policies and programs and inspired many to advocate its involvement in Spanish affairs. From the earliest days of the Civil War, he believed air superiority would determine the outcome of the war and thus acted as a go-between for Paris and Madrid* in negotiations (during July and August 1936) on the purchase of airplanes. Later, he organized a squadron of French flyers to fight for the Republic. Malraux helped establish the *Comité International de l'Aide au Peuple Espagnol* to recruit volunteers* for the Republic and to gather supplies. His air unit proved the most famous in the Republican Air Force* and was composed of some twenty aircraft, one dozen pilots, and an assortment of support personnel. The unit primarily used Potez 54 bombers. Malraux's men operated out of Madrid. The famous writer actually did some flying himself and perhaps even participated in some combat flights. His unit flew missions as early as August-September 1936 in Guipúzcoa* and in other battles and campaigns in central and northern Spain. Many of its aircraft, men, and supplies were destroyed or killed by the end of February 1937, however, causing the remaining portion to be integrated into other units of the Republican Air Force.

Malraux is also remembered for his public relations campaign on behalf of the Spanish Republic, particularly after February 1937, when he spent more time writing than flying. He wrote a book on the Spanish Civil War, *L'Espoir* (Paris, 1937), and made a movie by the same title in 1939. This widely publicized novel summarized the feelings of most Frenchmen who fought on the side of the Republic and provided many details on their experiences.

For further information, see Frederick Benson, *Writers in Arms: The Literary Impact of the Spanish Civil War* (New York, 1967); Jean Lacouture, *Andre Malraux* (Paris, 1973); and David Wingeate Pike, *Les Français et la guerre d'Espagne* (Paris, 1975).
See also France; and Intellectuals.

James W. Cortada

MANGADA, JULIO (1877-1946). Mangada, a career army officer, supported the Republicans* at the start of the Civil War and soon became a brigadier general. He staunchly supported the Republic prior to the war at a time when many of his fellow officers did not, even to the point of being jailed for insubordination. After the war began, he commanded troops marching on Ávila* against the Nationalists.* Mangada was a vegetarian, theosophist, poet, and sometime nudist who proved unable to inflict any serious injury on the Nationalists. His march involved some military personnel but also devotés of the cafe society of Madrid,* giving his short campaign a farcical character for which his men elected him general. More seriously, however, at the start of the war he presided over trials of suspected Nationalists at the Casa de Campo in Madrid, primarily to try officers who had rebelled.

For further information, see Antonio Cordón, *Trayectoria* (Paris, 1971); and Hugh Thomas, *The Spanish Civil War* (London, 1977).
See also Popular Tribunals.

James W. Cortada

MANTECÓN, JOSÉ IGNACIO. Mantecón was born and raised in Saragossa* where he first became involved in radical politics in the early 1930s. He was a member of the Left Republican party and served as the Republican governor general of Aragón* during 1937. He ruled over a predominantly anarchist area and was, in 1937, transferred out to become councillor of justice. During his tenure in Aragón, the local government operated virtually apart from the Republic, using its own police,* courts, and commercial and educational institutions. This communist sympathizer dissolved the Council of Aragón* which had, in effect, broken ties with the Republic, dismantling its beaureaucracy by decree on August 11, 1937. From then on, Republican rule in the area increased. Mantecón next received orders to produce large quantities of food* for the Republic in this region which he did during his tenure.

For further information, see Burnett Bolloten, *The Spanish Revolution: The Left and the Struggle for Power During the Civil War* (Chapel Hill, N.C., 1979).
See also Federación Anarquista Ibérica (FAI); Huesca; and Libertarian Movement.

James W. Cortada

MANZANARES RIVER. The Manzanares River flows through the city of Madrid.* During the battle of Madrid in November 1936, it served as a natural barrier, temporarily blocking the advance of the Nationalists* into the city. Eventually, the invading troops crossed the Manzanares and fought the Republicans*

at the University of Madrid, although the Nationalists were later pushed back across the river. For the rest of the Civil War, the river played no major role. When Madrid fell in 1939, it served as a convenient means of transporting some Nationalists into the city.

For further information, see Robert Colodny, *The Struggle for Madrid* (New York, 1958).

James W. Cortada

MAR CANTÁBRICO. The Republican merchant ship *Mar Cantábrico* (launched 1930, 6,632 gross tons, 15 kts.), carrying war material from the United States* and Mexico* to the Republic, was captured by the Nationalist cruiser *Canarias* in the Bay of Biscay on March 8, 1937. Converted into an auxiliary cruiser (4-152mm [6in], 4-88mm guns), she raided Republican shipping and eventually served as flagship for Admiral Moreno's* blockade forces in the Mediterranean.

See also Navy, Spanish.

Willard C. Frank, Jr.

MARCH ORDINAS, JUAN (1880-1961). March, born in Majorca* in 1880, was the richest man in Spain on the eve of the Spanish Civil War. His newspapers denounced the Popular Front,* and he had deposited abroad much of his money from investments in tobacco, shipping, oil, banks, real estate, and electric power. From February 1936, March personally traveled between Biarritz and Rome, encouraging a military conspiracy against the Republican government. He helped finance Franco's* famous July flight from the Canary Islands* to Morocco.* March encouraged Mussolini* to send aid, and he paid for the first dozen Italian Savoia 81 bombers which flew from Italy* to Franco's Moroccan air base on July 29-30, 1936. He may have financed the purchase of as much as a tenth of the Nationalists'* war material throughout the war. From 1936 to the end of the war, March remained in Rome, negotiating sales of Italian equipment on a daily basis and coordinating his activities with the Nationalist embassy in Rome.

Juan March's prime motivation was neither ideology, politics, nor patriotism, but rather accumulating money. Involved in scandals before World War I, he was condemned by idealistic Republicans* in 1931-1932 in the Cortes* for his connections with smugglers and illegal tobacco sales. The guilty verdict led March to finance various conspiratorial parties on the Right, so that the successes which Franco won on the battlefields from 1936 to 1939 from March's viewpoint only provided new opportunities to make money in Spain under a capitalist regime.

In the spring and summer of 1939, March traveled to London, Paris, Berlin, Brussels, and Zurich looking for reconstruction possibilities outside the official policy of strict pro-Axis autarchy. From September 1939 to 1940, March pressured the Franco regime toward neutrality rather than toward the Axis. But he also dealt with Admiral Canaris,* selling oil to the German Navy* from the *Compañia Española de Petróleos* (CEPSA)* refinery in the Canary Islands for hard currency. March dealt with Great Britain* as well as with Germany* (as he had done in World War I), convincing each side that he was helping it the more.

The secret of March's lifetime success was his maintenance of bank accounts throughout Europe* and the United States* and his consequent ability to convert quickly into a new currency or a new commodity whenever he sensed political trouble. From 1941 to 1944, he found Franco's brand of fascist-regulated capitalism so burdensome that he moved to Lisbon. March was neither a friend nor a foe of anyone. "March was for March." He died of old age in 1961.

For further information, see John Brooks, "Annals of Finance," *New Yorker* (May 21, 1979, May 28, 1979): 42ff, 42ff; Bernardo Díaz Nosty, *La irresistible ascensión de Juan March: Notas previas para una investigación biográfica* (Madrid, 1977); Ramón Garriga, *Juan March y su tiempo* (Barcelona, 1976); and Robert H. Whealey, "La diplomacía española del petróleo: De junio de 1927 a abril de 1931," *Cuadernos Económicos de Información Comercial Española* 10 (Madrid, 1979):511-31.

Robert H. Whealey

MARIANO VÁZQUEZ, RAMÓN. When the Civil War began, Mariano Vázquez was the secretary of the Catalan Regional Federation of the *Confederación Nacional del Trabajo* (CNT).* This intelligent, politically astute man worked closely with Horacio M. Prieto,* the national secretary of the CNT, and consequently was an important labor leader.

In September 1936, in the face of a desperate need for revolutionary unity, Mariano Vázquez eased the doctrinaire conscience of anarchist leadership by arguing that concession was better than losing the war, that anarchist participation in the government of Barcelona* was working, and that if the anarchists* did not assume responsibility in the government they would lose the revolution by default to the communists. This argument led to Indalecio Prieto's* appointment of four anarchists to the Largo Caballero* cabinet in November 1936. When Prieto's departure from Madrid* two weeks later led to his resignation as national secretary, Mariano Vázquez assumed the position.

Until June 1937, Mariano Vázquez worked diligently to promote a unified Popular Front* government and a strong centralized army. He supported a continuation of anarchist efforts to collectivize agriculture and industry. He accused the communists of trying to subvert the social revolution, while at the same time, he explained CNT objectives to foreign powers in conciliatory terms. Mariano Vázquez sought to calm their fears of the Largo Caballero government, so that the government might obtain credit to buy abroad much needed raw materials.

Mariano Vázquez went to Barcelona to help mediate the May 1937 uprising,* barely escaping assassination on the road back to Valencia.* As the leader of the CNT, he refused membership in Negrín's* government formed in the wake of the Barcelona uprising. He insisted that unless the number of anarchists equaled *Unión General de Trabajadores* (UGT)* and Spanish Communist party* representation, the anarchists could not participate. As this was not agreed to, the CNT-*Federación Anarquista Ibérica* (FAI)* refused further support of or participation in the national government until the spring of 1938.

For further information, see Diego Abad de Santillán, *Por que perdimos la guerra* (Madrid, 1975); John Brademas, *Anarcosindicalismo y revolución en España (1930-1937)* (Barcelona, 1974); Burnett Bolloten, *The Spanish Revolution: The Left and the Struggle for Power During the Civil War* (Chapel Hill, N.C., 1979); César M. Lorenzo, *Les anarchistes espagnols et le pouvoir 1868-1968* (Paris, 1969); and Georges Soría, *Guerra y revolución en España, 1936-1939* (Barcelona, 1978).

Shirley F. Fredricks

MARSEILLAISE BATTALION. The Marseillaise Battalion was part of the International Brigades* and was one of the first units of foreign volunteers* to fight in Spain. It saw its first major action at the battles of Boadilla* and the Corunna Road* in December 1936 as part of the 14th International Brigade. It fought in Spain throughout 1937, primarily in and around Madrid.*

For further information, see Andreu Castells, *Las brigadas internacionales en la guerra de España* (Barcelona, 1974).

James W. Cortada

MARTÍN ALONSO, PABLO (1896-1964). Martín Alonso was a career army officer who served with the Nationalists* during the Civil War. He began the war as a major and eventually rose to the rank of general. In July 1936, he successfully headed the rebellion in Corunna* and then went on to command combat troops throughout the war. This effective commander, born in El Ferrol,* was one of Franco's* most useful generals, serving in Asturias,* at the battle of Belchite,* and in the reconquest of Teruel.* He also occupied Sagunto and Valencia* for the Nationalists towards the end of the war. After 1939, Martín Alonso continued his military career, and during the last two years of his life he served as the minister of the army.

For further information, see Círculo de Amigos de la Historia, *Diccionario biográfico español contemporaneo* (Madrid, 1970), Vol. 2.
See also Appendix B.

James W. Cortada

MARTÍN MORENO, FRANCISCO (1879-1941). Martín Moreno, a career army officer, was General Franco's* chief of staff during the Civil War. He was thus a member of a very small group of Spaniards who daily influenced Franco's thinking on many matters dealing with the war. Towards the end of the conflict, Franco promoted him to general and put him in charge of the entire staff that served at his headquarters. Martín Moreno continued to serve Franco in various personal capacities within the military and in Madrid* after the war, and in 1947 he was named a count posthumously.

For further information, see Hugh Thomas, *The Spanish Civil War* (New York, 1977); and José Manuel Martínez Bande, *Los cien últimos días de la república* (Barcelona, 1972).

James W. Cortada

MARTÍNEZ ANIDO, SEVERIANO (1862-1938). Martínez Anido was the oldest general fighting on the side of the Nationalists.* Born in El Ferrol,* he graduated from the Infantry Academy in 1884, fought in the Philippines in the 1890s, participated in the repression of riots in Barcelona* in 1902, served in Morocco,* and was commandant of his alma matter. In 1917, he became the military governor of San Sebastián, and between 1920 and 1922, he served as the ruthless, heavy-handed civil governor of Barcelona. During the dictatorship of Primo de Rivera in the 1920s, he commanded troops in Melilla* in Morocco and then became minister of the interior.

After the Civil War began, he joined the Nationalists, serving as chief of internal security, and in 1938 he became Franco's* minister of public order, a position he occupied until his death later that year. Franco appointed him to a post that would throw fear into the hearts of Republicans* who remembered Martínez Anido's policies of repression in past decades. However, the old general proved to be humane, insisting on military trials, thereby reducing the indiscriminate killings in the Nationalist zone. Like other generals close to Franco, he did not like the Falange* particularly and simply wanted the restoration of a more conservative government without the trappings of fascism.*

For further information, see Círculo de Amigos de la Historia, *Diccionario biográfico español contemporaneo* (Madrid, 1970), Vol. 2.
See also Police; and Terrorism.

James W. Cortada

MARTÍNEZ BARRIO, DIEGO (1883-1962). Martínez Barrio was born in Seville* where he engaged in radical politics, ultimately heading the Republican Union party (RUP)* as speaker of the Cortes* at the start of the Spanish Civil War. This experienced and astute politician had a long career in Spanish politics, serving as a member of the Cortes in the early days of the Republic, heading a caretaker government in 1933, and serving as a minister of the interior, before forming his opposition party in 1933. In the elections of February 1936,* his party gained the third largest number of seats in the Cortes, and soon after he became speaker. During the confusion of July 18-19, he attempted to form a government for the Republic but failed. He thereupon left for Valencia* where he established rule over the provinces of the Levante.* Local *Confederación Nacional del Trabajo* (CNT)* and *Unión General de Trabajadores* (UGT)* leaders, however, forced him out of power, even making him live outside Valencia. He soon after headed a Republican committee established to reorganize the army. By 1938, he had concluded that without a negotiated peace, the Nationalists* would win and kill thousands of Spaniards. In this thought he reflected the opinions of many top Republican leaders.

Martínez Barrio continued to head the Cortes during the Civil War, attending its famous meeting on February 1, 1939, in Figueras in northern Catalonia,* where Negrín* talked of conditions for peace before the Cortes adjourned and its members fled to France.* On February 5, Martínez Barrio finally crossed over into France. On February 28, Manuel Azaña* resigned as president of the Republic, and Martínez Barrio assumed the title as provided for in the Constitution of the Republic, retaining the position until his death in 1962.

For further information, see Burnett Bolloten, *The Spanish Revolution: The Left and the Struggle for Power During the Civil War* (Chapel Hill, N.C., 1979); and Patricia W. Fagen, *Exiles and Citizens: Spanish Republicans in Mexico* (Austin, Texas, 1973).

James W. Cortada

MARTÍNEZ CABRERA, TORIBIO (1874-1939). Martínez Cabrera, a graduate of the War College in 1892, was a strongly republican staff officer and a Mason. He returned to the War College as chief of studies in 1932 and was promoted to brigadier general in 1933. The Popular Front* government gave him the command of the naval base at Cartagena,* which he kept loyal to the Republic in July 1936. Subsequently, he was named inspector general of the Army of the North.* In December 1936, he became chief of the general staff in Valencia.* In this position, he found his autonomy and functions considerably reduced by General Asensio Torrado,* the undersecretary of land forces, who was close to the prime minister, Largo Caballero.* After the fall of Málaga* in February 1937, the communists blamed both Asensio and Martínez Cabrera for the defeat. Martínez Cabrera was replaced by Vicente Rojo,* who was more willing to cooperate with the communists. Early in 1938, Martínez Cabrera was arrested and tried for treason along with several other officers held to be responsible for the disaster at Málaga. Found innocent and released, Martínez Cabrera was appointed military governor of Madrid,* a position of little military significance. A supporter of Colonel Casado* (a staff officer like himself), Martínez Cabrera became undersecretary in Casado's National Council of Defense. At the end of the war, he was executed by the Nationalists* in Madrid.

For further information, see Antonio Cordón, *Trayectoria: memorias de un militar republicano* (Barcelona, 1977); Ramón Salas Larrazábal, *Historia del ejército popular de la República*, 4 vols. (Madrid, 1973); and Hugh Thomas, *The Spanish Civil War* (New York, 1977).
See also Army, Republican; and Communist Party, Spanish.

Carolyn P. Boyd

MARTÍNEZ DE CAMPOS, CARLOS (1887-1975). Martínez de Campos was a career army officer who fought on the side of the Nationalists.* Born in Paris,

he served with Franco* in Morocco* during 1913 and later held various posts within the artillery. During the Civil War, he commanded troops in the campaigns in Guipúzcoa,* Vizcaya,* Santander,* Asturias,* Aragón,* and Catalonia.* He commanded Franco's artillery at the battles of Teruel* and the Ebro,* and around Madrid.* He is best remembered for the predominance of artillery at the battle of Ebro, July-November 1938, during which much of the heavy fighting was an artillery duel. After the war, General Martínez de Campos served in numerous capacities in Franco's government.

For further information, see Carlos Martínez de Campos, *Ayer, 1931-1953* (Madrid, 1970).
See also Army, Nationalist.

James W. Cortada

MARTÍNEZ FUSET, LORENZO (1899-   ). Martínez Fuset was General Franco's* chief legal adviser throughout the Civil War. As part of Franco's inner circle, he exercised considerable influence and carried out the general's wishes in regards to the law. Thus, for example, as head of the juridical corps, he was responsible for prosecuting enemies of the Nationalists* and for minimizing the influence of various political groups when their impact threatened Franco's power. He was thus one of the chief legal architects of Franco's program of suppression and trials during the war and had a heavy hand in drafting the laws that established his government.

For further information, see Hugh Thomas, *The Spanish Civil War* (New York, 1977).
See also Police; Popular Tribunals; and Terrorism.

James W. Cortada

MARTÍNEZ MONJE RESTORY, FERNANDO. Martínez Monje, a career army officer, began the Civil War as military governor of Valencia.* After some hesitation, he decided to remain on the side of the Republic. Within months, he formed the Republican Army of the South* which included elements of the International Brigades* fighting in central Spain. His career did not reflect any major achievements, and he spent much of the war occupying administrative positions. After the war, he retired to Latin America* but not before the Republicans,* in 1938, then under the influence of the communists, questioned his loyalty and caused him to be arrested for a short period of time.

For further information, see Michael Alpert, *El ejército republicano en la guerra civil* (Barcelona, 1977); and Ramón Salas Larrazábal, *Historia del ejército popular de la republica*, 4 vols. (Madrid, 1974).

James W. Cortada

MARTY, ANDRÉ (1886-1955). Marty, a French delegate to the Chamber of Deputies and a member of the Comintern's central committee, was a leading European communist and took a strong interest in the Spanish Civil War. He became the first chief of the communist military volunteers* fighting for the Republic in Spain to come out of France.* Appointed by Stalin* to lead the communist soldiers, Marty proved to be a suspicious and malicious leader. He had been born in Perpignan and spoke Catalan. With his connections in France, he obtained considerable support from the French Communist party in clothing and feeding the volunteers in the early days of the Civil War. Marty participated in the highest councils of the Spanish Communist party* and actively worked to increase the influence of that organization in Republican affairs during 1936 and 1937, the crucial period during which his colleagues struggled for control over the government. He tried to prevent the disintegration of the International Brigades* during the campaigns in Aragón* and in the Levante,* March-July 1938, when the Nationalists* scored successes against communist soldiers. He commanded with an iron hand, not hesitating to execute his own men if he suspected them of wavering in their communist faith or in the face of the enemy.

For further information, see Henri Dupré, *La 'Légion Tricolore' en Espagne* (Paris, 1942) and *L'Épopée d'Espagne* (Paris, 1957).

See also Army, Republican.

James W. Cortada

MARXISM. Spain was not fertile soil for Marxism. The *Partido Socialista Obrero Español* (PSOE)* was organized in 1878, but none of its theoreticians could be considered Marxists, even though the party declared itself Marxist in its statutes. Dr. Jaime Vera and Julián Bestere (the latter a professor of logic) were the only socialists who drew on Marxism in their analysis of Spanish society.

Until the start of the Civil War, the bulk of the labor movement leaned towards anarchosyndicalism. As in Italy* or Argentina,* Spain's proletariat was of recent rural origin and felt attracted to anarchistic and anti-authoritarian ideas rather than to the com-

plexities of Marxist socialism. While membership in the *Unión General de Trabajadores* (UGT),* the socialist syndical center, did not exceed 125,000 in 1919, the *Confederación Nacional del Trabajo* (CNT),* founded in 1910 by a series of scattered anarchosyndicalist organizations, reached a membership of 700,000 in the same year.

It was also in 1919 that the CNT decided to adhere provisionally to the Third International and that youth groups split, one part founding the Spanish Communist party* in 1920. A further division occurred in 1921 leading to the formation of the PSOE. Under pressure from the Communist International, both parties fused and became the Communist party of Spain. But this party, even if it described itself as Marxist, as in the case of all communist parties, never had within its ranks a single theoretician of note, nor did it contribute anything to Marxist doctrine.

It was from the dissident groups that Marxist analysis of the Spanish reality made its appearance as well as the effort to develop Marxist policy and doctrine. The most important of these groups was the Workers and Farmers Bloc (*Bloque Obrero y Campesino*—BOC) organized in 1930 through the fusion of the Catalan Communist Federation of the Communist party, which had split from the latter in 1928 when it refused to accept the so-called ideological colonialism of Moscow, and the small Communist party of Catalonia* founded in 1928. The secretary of the BOC was Joaquín Maurín* of anarchosyndicalist persuasion and the author of some of the most important books concerned with Marxist analysis: *The Men of the Dictatorship (Los hombres de la dictadura)* (1930); *The Spanish Revolution (La revolución española)* (1932); and *Towards the Second Revolution (Hacía la segunda revolución)* (1935), reedited in Paris and released in 1966 as *Revolution and Counterrevolution in Spain (Revolución y contrarevolución en España)*.

Another dissident group, much smaller in number, was the Communist Opposition (Trotskyist) which in 1933-1934 abandoned Trotsky and became left-wing communist. Its secretary general was Andrés Nin,* also an anarchosyndicalist, who had worked in the Comintern from 1921 to 1928 (also known as the Profintern) and upon his return from Russia was expelled because of his pro-Trotsky* sympathies. He was the author of several books, including *The Dictatorship of Today (Las dictaduras de nuestros dias)* and *The Movements of National Emancipation (Los Movimientos de emancipación nacional)*, as well as many translations from the Russian.

The BOC took the initiative in 1933 in calling for the formation of a workers' alliance, to which a number of smaller organizations did adhere, but not the CNT or the PSOE. Subsequently, Nin and Maurín initiated conversations for the purpose of unifying all the Catalan groups that called themselves Marxist into a *Unión Socialista de Cataluña*, but it was soon apparent that outside of the left-wing communist group and the BOC no other elements followed the inclinations of the Communist party. Thus, these and the BOC fused in 1935 into the *Partido Obrero de Unificación Marxista* (POUM).* Meanwhile, the other groups continued their negotiations, which, three days after the outbreak of the Civil War, without consultations with the majority of its following, became the *Partit Socialista Unificat de Catalunya* (PSUC).* While the PSUC became affiliated with the Communist International, the POUM was a member of the so-called London Bureau, which included the faction led by Marceau Pivert of the French Socialist party, the Independent Labor party, the faction of Angelica Barabano of the Italian Socialist party, and splinters from the German Communist party, among whose members was Willy Brandt.

At the beginning of 1936, the leaders of the *Juventudes Socialistas* (JS) traveled to Moscow and upon their return combined their organization with the *Juventudes Comunista Ibérica* (JCI)* and created the *Juventudes Socialistas Unificadas* (JSU)* which, while nominally connected to the *Internacional Juvenil Socialista*, was really a branch of the Communist party as was the PSUC. The Spanish Communist party could therefore draw on the JSU and the PSUC but still lacked syndical support. Its syndicates, organized within the *Confederación General del Trabajo Unitario* (CGTU) had joined the socialist UGT in 1935, as a result of the Popular Front* initiated that year by the Communist International.

Parallel to these tentative efforts towards unification, there was in the core of the PSOE a deep ideological division. During the Republican era of 1931-1936, that party had formed part of the government in the first two years and in the opposition for the remainder, and in 1936 joined the Popular Front. The PSOE had always consisted of three tendencies: the republicanism of Indalecio Prieto,* the moderate Marxism of Julián Besteiro,* and the syndicalism of Largo Caballero.* In 1933-1934, Largo Caballero, already sixty years old, moved sharply to the Left, discovered Marxism (that is, the communist version of Marxism), and, encouraged by the youth of the party, adopted postures close to those of the Communist party. But the party's capture of the JS and its desire that the Popular Front continue after a triumph at the polls in February 1936, in order to lend support to the moderate republicans, led to his divorce from the commu-

nist group without any weakening of his neophyte enthusiasm for Marxism. Largo Caballero did not control the PSOE, but he did rule the UGT-which had more than 500,000 members (the CNT claimed 1 million), and he had a substantial minority within the PSOE.

The Civil War resulted in the polarization of all those organizations that called themselves Marxist within the Republican zone. From the first weeks of the war there were two opposing sides within the same political zones. Those who for the purpose of winning the war felt it was necessary to fight only to defend the Republic and democracy believed it should not be the occasion to carry out social revolution. The Republican parties (somewhat lukewarm at the beginning), the Right and Center of the PSOE and, in a persistent and active fashion, the official communists adopted this position. They argued that revolutionary activities would adversely affect military efficiency, fracture antifascist unity, and impede assistance from the democracies to the Republic (help which in any event was not rendered). Those who supported this viewpoint proposed the establishment of an army (referred to as the popular people's army) to replace the voluntary militias,* the nationalization of enterprises abandoned by their owners, and even the promise of eventual compensation to these owners.

That the Republicans and right-wing socialists would hold such a position was logical. That the communists would also take this stand can be explained only by examining the international situation of the USSR.* This country, allied to France* and developing closer relations with conservative Great Britain* and Roosevelt's* United States,* did not wish to see its diplomacy weakened by awakening the suspicion that, by underhanded means, or through the Communist party of Spain, it attempted to spark a social revolution. For this reason, the Spanish communists were very persistent in explaining that they were only defending democracy. Besides, the revolutionary measures adopted in the Republican zone did not tend to strengthen the state and did not follow the Soviet model. Moscow, therefore, could not look with sympathy on a revolution that offered an alternative to the Russian example. These revolutionary measures did not stem from communist initiative, nor did the communists play a role in their implementation. Thus, a revolution would develop if non-Communist measures were to continue, over which Moscow would have no ideological influence.

In effect, those who supported the other posture were organizations remote from Moscow, such as the anarchosyndicalist CNT, the left wing of the PSOE (in a vacillating manner), and the POUM, whose existence was a problem for the Spanish communists and Moscow, even if it carried weight only in Catalonia.* This situation had developed because it was a dissident group from Moscow's position and because if it succeeded with its policies the London Bureau would benefit by growth, which even if still weak was nevertheless an alternative to the Third International. It must not be forgotten that for the communists a group's small size did not mean that it was not a future menace, for they themselves stemmed from a miniscule Bolshevik group that had nonetheless seized power. Official communism regarded any adversary, no matter how small, as a threat. And the POUM was anything but miniscule (100,000 members in 1936, more than the Communist party before the elections of February 1936* and bigger than the PSUC).

These organizations maintained that in order to win the war it was necessary to carry out the revolution, because only with the enthusiasm, voluntary discipline, and spirit of sacrifice engendered by the revolution could deficiencies in arms, experience, and military organization be overcome. Besides, this second element maintained, the Republic's only help came from the USSR (they forgot, as did everyone else, about the assistance secretly obtained from French socialists), and it would not, they believed, withhold aid if a revolution was undertaken. As can be seen, even in these groups an understanding of the Stalinist phenomenon was far from perceived. If the militias become transformed into an army and the collectives into nationalized entities, enthusiasm would be lost, and with that development Franco* would obtain an advantage that would lead him to victory.

These were the organizations which in the first days of the war, especially in Catalonia, collectivized abandoned industries, distributed farmlands to the rural proletariat organizing them into cooperatives (socialists and POUMistas) or collectives (by the CNT), and defeated the military in all of those cities where the Republican authorities furnished the labor organization militants with arms. To continue the war, they organized the voluntary militia which stabilized the first fronts, stopped the Franco advance, and saved Madrid.*

Over a period of ten months, an effort was made to reconcile the two positions within Republican Spain. Without dissolving the militias, the government began to organize an army. On the other hand in Catalonia, where the CNT and the POUM participated in the autonomous government, the collectives were institutionalized and extended to include all enterprises with a hundred workers or more, even if they had not been abandoned by their owners, at the same time that worker control committees were organized in the smaller entities.

From December 1936 onward, when it had become clear that the democracies would not assist the Republic and that the democracies could depend only on military supplies from the Soviet Union (paid for in advance in gold, inasmuch as the Central Bank's gold and currency reserves had been transferred to Moscow in October), the communists initiated an attack against the revolutionary forces. By threatening to stop the flow of supplies from Russia, they were able to force the POUM out of the Catalan government. In May 1937, after a series of violent incidents between CNT and PSUC militants, open conflict between the two organizations broke out in the streets of Barcelona* (which George Orwell* described in a now classic book, *Homage to Catalonia*). The violence terminated without victory for anyone, but the communists requested the Republican government, headed by Largo Caballero,* to suppress the POUM, an action that he declined to take, whereupon the communist ministers walked out. The government had no other alternative than to resign as a result of pressure from the Republican and right-wing socialist ministers. Only the CNT ministers who had become part of the government in November supported Largo Caballero.

Largo Caballero was replaced by Dr. Juan Negrín* of the PSOE right wing, supported by Prieto, the Republicans, and the communists. The government started to declare as nationalized all war industries that until then had been collectivized—and that had been organized especially by the Catalan government and the CNT. The army definitively replaced the militias which disappeared as such through absorption by the army. The Council of Aragón,* which had administered captured areas, was dissolved. In addition, the government permitted communist elements in the police* under the direction of a number of NKVD* agents to initiate persecution of POUM members. The political secretary of the NKVD, Andrés Nin, was arrested, tortured, and then assassinated. At the same time, the communist press started a campaign against the POUM accusing it of being an agent for Franco, but in October 1938 in the trial against the Executive Committee of the POUM, the judges recognized that the POUM, while supporting the workers in the streets of Barcelona in the May 1937 riots,* was neither fascist nor Francoist. Moscow therefore did not obtain what it wanted, that is, "proof" that apart from the USSR—where there had been a series of trials against old Bolsheviks—Moscow dissidents were "traitors" and "fascist agents."

Many POUMistas were arrested, and their organizations had to go underground; many CNT members were also incarcerated. Under communist pressure, Prieto had to leave the government because he refused to follow indications from "advisers" sent by Moscow. Dr. Negrín and his government, from which important and prestigious figures had left, was reduced to being a subservient instrument of Moscow.

During this period, with popular enthusiasm lost, productivity dropped by half within the economy and the Republic lost successively the north, part of the Levante,* and Catalonia. Finally, the Republican Army* initiated an attack along the Ebro* on orders of the "Russian advisers." The battle was lost, and Franco's forces occupied Catalonia in January-February 1939. Part of Negrín's government moved to the center-south zone where he appointed communists to all of the high command posts. In view of this development, the Republicans, socialists, and anarchists* combined into a Council of Defense presided over by Colonel Segismundo Casado* who refused to obey Negrín. At any rate, Negrín soon left for France by plane accompanied by the communist leaders. On April 1, 1939, Franco's forces occupied Madrid and all of the center-south zone, and thereby ended the war.

As can be seen, alongside the battle between Francophiles and antifascists was another involving two different interpretations of strategy: the one communist, of an opportunistic character adhering to the Stalinist line, and the other relating to the socialist left wing of the POUM and CNT which could be called Leninist. While the Leninist held the upper hand the Franco onslaught continued; when control passed to the Stalinist line the war was lost.

With the end of the Civil War, no Marxist analysis of the fighting emerged from the Spanish exiles. There was a great deal of anecdotal and polemical literature but no solid serious analysis. Not even Trotsky* tried his hand at the task, as he devoted all of his output during that era to attacks on the POUM, even when the POUM was under official communist censure. It proved necessary to wait for foreign authors to start the task, which is still in its beginnings.

It can be said that Marxism as a doctrine did not influence positions and developments in the Civil War. The communists and their adversaries followed strategies determined not by principle (except the POUM inspired in Lenin), but by the exigencies of the moment and the requirements to benefit Moscow's interests (in the case of the CNT). Franco's charge (which found expression only at the end of 1936) that he fought against communism and Marxism was simply a propaganda ruse.

For further information, see Victor Alba, *El Partido Comunista en España* (Barcelona, 1979) and his *Histoire du POUM* (Paris, 1975); Burnett Bolloten, *The Spanish Revolution: The Left and the Struggle for Power During the Civil War* (Chapel Hill, N.C., 1979); Ronald Fraser, *The Blood of Spain* (New York, 1979); Jesús Hernández, *Yo fui un ministro de Stalín* (Mexico, 1952); and George Orwell, *Homage to Catalonia* (Boston, 1952).

See also Libertarian Movement.

Victor Alba

MASONRY. Freemasonic lodges originated in Spain in the eighteenth century, appealing largely to enlightened deists. In the first half of the nineteenth century, progressive army officers used the lodges as convenient, secret meeting places to conspire against traditionalist and reactionary regimes. By the twentieth century, the lodges had acquired a distinctly anticlerical cast; Masonic membership was drawn chiefly from middle-class republicans and some army officers, seldom from proletarians.

Because the aims of the middle-class political anticlericals—separation of church and state, restrictions on religious education, abolition of all special clerical privileges—coincided with historic Masonic aims and because a large proportion (in relation to the rest of the population) of the Republican leaders were Masons, many Catholics tended to view the Masons as a conspiratorial international organization directed against both the Catholic Church* and the traditionalist concept of Spain. Thus, freemasonry became identified as the propelling agent of the anticlerical Republican revolution, sometimes in conjunction with "international Judaism" or "international communism," and as such it became a convenient scapegoat. In fact, freemasonry was a convenient vehicle, and just as the Jesuits were viewed by anticlericals as conspirators of the Right, so freemasons were seen by clericals as conspirators of the Left. In both cases, organizational secrecy simply added to rumor and exaggeration.

Among important Masons in the 1930s were Diego Martínez Barrio,* Manuel Portela Valladares, and Manuel Azaña* (although Azaña did not join the lodges until 1931). Many Masonic politicians were members of the Radical party and reflected its conservative, mildly anticlerical views. There were also lodges among the military to which Generals Eduardo López Ochoa, Sebastián Pozas,* and Miguel Cabanellas,* among others, belonged, although those who supported the military uprising of July 1936 dropped their membership. During the Civil War, the ideologically extreme Nationalists* viewed membership in a Masonic lodge as an offense punishable by death. In 1939, Masonic membership after 1934 was made a statutory offense.

For further information, see Eduardo Comín Colomer, *Lo que España debe a la masonería* (Barcelona, 1956); and Gabriel Jackson, *The Spanish Republic and the Civil War, 1931-1939* (Princeton, N.J., 1965).

José M. Sánchez

MASQUELET LACACI, CARLOS (1871-). Masquelet Lacaci was a general at the start of the Spanish Civil War. He was a close friend of Manuel Azaña* and was acting-minister of war in the Popular Front* government of 1936. During the years just preceding the war, he developed plans for fortifications established by the government around Madrid.* He did not play an active role in the war. Eclipsed by other generals, he retired to France* in 1939.

For further information, see Michael Alpert, *El ejército republicano en la guerra civil* (Barcelona, 1977).

James W. Cortada

MATALLANA GÓMEZ, MANUEL (1894-1952). Matallana was an infantryman and *diplomado* of the War College. Only a major at the beginning of the Civil War, he remained loyal to the Republic and won rapid promotion thereafter, rising to brigadier general in August 1938. Matallana served as head of information services at the beginning of the war and in November 1936 became General Rojo's* chief of staff in Madrid.* As General Miaja's* chief of staff in 1937, he planned the Brunete* offensive; subsequently, he commanded the Army of the Levante* and the Army of the Center.* His role at the end of the war has been surrounded by controversy. Like many professional officers, Matallana was initially sympathetic to the communists because of their organizational ability, efficiency, and opposition to the social revolution. But by early 1939, he had come to believe that further resistance was useless, and thus shared Colonel Casado's* belief that army officers could negotiate a fairer peace than Negrín's* communist-dominated government. From February on, Matallana was in contact with Nationalist headquarters and at the end of the war, he delivered information concerning the Republicans'* military positions to Franco's* side. After the war, he was imprisoned and deprived of his commission for several years.

For further information, see José Manuel Martínez Bande, *Los cien últimos días de la República* (Barce-

lona, 1973); Luis Romero, *El final de la guerra* (Barcelona, 1976); Ramón Salas Larrazábal, *Historia del ejército popular de la República*, 4 vols. (Madrid, 1973); and Hugh Thomas, *The Spanish Civil War* (New York, 1977).

Carolyn P. Boyd

MATTHEWS, HERBERT (1906-). Matthews was an American correspondent in Spain during the Civil War and chief writer on Spanish Republican affairs for *The New York Times.** Matthews had a great deal of influence on the American public's interpretation of events in Republican Spain because his articles were widely read. He was, and continued to be, extremely pro-Republican in his newspaper articles and later in his books on the Spanish war. During the 1930s, and through the 1970s, he remained a staunch apologist for Negrín,* arguing that Spain's best interests lay in having a free, republican government.

For further information, see Herbert L. Matthews, *The Education of a Correspondent* (New York, 1946), *Half of Spain Died: A Reappraisal of the Spanish Civil War* (New York, 1973), *Two Wars and More to Come* (New York, 1938), and *The Yoke and the Arrows* (New York, 1942, rev. ed. 1961).
See also United States.

James W. Cortada

MAURIAC, FRANÇOIS (1885-1970). Mauriac was a leading French Catholic writer during the 1930s who supported the Republicans.* Like other French Catholic writers, Mauriac criticized Franco's* cause and at the same time did not hesitate to object in print to the Republicans' violations of civil rights. He wrote numerous articles defending the Basques and the Spanish Republic and worked for the exchange of prisoners.* His greatest influence was in the press which he used to sway French public opinion in favor of the Republic.

For further information, see David Wingeate Pike, *Les Français et la guerre d'Espagne, 1936-1939* (Paris, 1975) and *Propaganda and Deceit and the Spanish Civil War* (Stanford, Calif., 1970).
See also France; and Journalists, French.

James W. Cortada

MAURÍN JULIÁ, JOAQUÍN (1897-1973). Maurín, a prominent theoretician and activist on the Spanish Left during the 1920s and 1930s, is perhaps best known for having co-founded with Andrés Nin* the *Partido Obrero de Unificación Marxista* (POUM).* Born in

Bonansa (Huesca),* Spain on January 12, 1897, Maurín developed an interest in politics between 1914 and 1918, while teaching history and geography at the *Liceo Escolar* in Lérida.* There he joined the *Juventud Republicana* and contributed regularly to its daily organ, *El Ideal*. During the winter of 1917-1918, Maurín established his first links with the organized labor movement, which soon led to his conversion to a fiery brand of Sorelian syndicalism.

Upon leaving the military in 1920, Maurín returned to Lérida and joined the *Confederación Nacional del Trabajo* (CNT),* becoming in quick succession the secretary of its provincial committee, editor of *La Lucha Social*, and director of the *Centro Obrero*'s school.

Maurín belonged to a group of young militants in the CNT whose Marxist-Leninist outlook set them apart from the majority of *cenetistas*. He was typical of this tendency, being a middle-class intellectual with political ideas drawn from both the socialist and syndicalist traditions.

As a CNT delegate sent to Moscow in 1921 to attend the Third Congress of the Comintern and the founding congress of the Red International of Trade Unions (Profintern), Maurín supported the Leninist-backed resolution calling for an "organic-link" between these two bodies. After returning to Spain, his views met stiff opposition within the CNT. Throughout 1922, he struggled to keep his ideas alive, first by organizing a tiny group inside the CNT called the *Comités Sindicalistas Revolucionarios*, and then by founding a Marxist trade-union weekly, *La Batalla*.* But his efforts proved fruitless, and he thereupon left the CNT.

Between 1923 and 1930, Maurín was arrested on several occasions, imprisoned for nearly three years, and finally forced into exile. At all times, however, he strove to maintain his contacts with the revolutionary movement, joining the *Federación Comunista Catalano-Balear* (FCCB) in 1924, and attending the Fifth Congress of the Comintern and the Third Congress of the Profintern that same year.

After the collapse of Primo de Rivera's dictatorship in 1930, Maurín returned to Spain, where he created the basis for a communist movement that reflected his political aims. He resurrected *La Batalla*, of which he was director until 1936, he resumed his leadership of the FCCB, and he founded a Marxist theoretical journal, *La Nueva Era*. That summer, his longstanding differences with the Spanish Communist party* over Comintern policy finally erupted, resulting in his faction's expulsion from the party. He then forged an alliance between the FCCB and the *Partit Comunista Català* (PCC). In March 1931, these two groups merged

to become the *Bloque obrero y Campesino* (BOC), with Maurín as its secretary general.

The creation of the BOC marked a new phase in Maurín's intellectual development. He now espoused a sophisticated kind of Marxism,* one in which an understanding of the historical process formed an indispensable part of his revolutionary strategy. Two of his works published at about this time, *Los hombres de la dictadura* (1930) and *La revolución española* (1932), manifested this theoretical shift in that both were models of Marxian historical analysis.

In 1933, Maurín and the BOC launched an ambitious program aimed at uniting workers' groups throughout Spain. Their plans crystallized with the formation of the *Alianza Obrera* (AO) which, according to Maurín, transcended ideological barriers and thus made possible "the miracle of uniting workers without destroying existing organizations." During the *bienio negro* (1933-1935), the revolutionary strategy of the Left as a whole embodied Maurín's idea of a workers' alliance.

For all his organizing efforts during the 1930s, Maurín never attracted a mass following. The organizational framework and influence of the BOC were limited to Catalonia,* and its membership never exceeded a few thousand. Above all, Maurín achieved notoriety at this time as a polemicist and unorthodox Marxist.* Under his direction, the BOC, by refusing to conform to the tactics imposed by the Comintern and the Fourth International, incurred the wrath of Stalinists and Trotskyists alike. For promoting political alliances between the BOC and the Republican Left (Esquerra),* Maurín was indicted as a "charlatan" and pro-Stalinist by the Trotskyist-oriented communist Left (*Izquierda Comunista*) (IC), whereas the Stalinist-dominated Spanish Communist party branded him a Trotskyist.

In 1934, the IC, which was founded in 1932 by Maurín's close friend and sometime critic Andrés Nin, broke with Trotsky* and his followers and subsequently decided to join forces with the much larger BOC. The two groups amalgamated in September 1935 to form the POUM, with Maurín serving as secretary general.

At first, the POUM pursued a course of action that clearly echoed the dominating influence of the Maurín-BOC tendency. At a congress held in January 1936, the party adopted a platform that agreed in form and substance with the revolutionary program which Maurín had only recently adumbrated in his major theoretical work, *Hacia la segunda revolución* (1935). Among other things, the POUM's strategy reiterated Maurín's urgent call for a united electoral front (*Frente Unico*) to counter fascist influence and also emphasized the importance of the *Alianza Obrera* as an agent in bringing about the democratic-socialist revolution.

The POUM formed part of the Popular Front* alliance in the elections of February 1936,* and, although the Left emerged triumphant, Maurín was the only POUM member to win a seat.

Given the POUM's unpopular Marxist stance, Maurín had little hope of implementing his party's policies in the Cortes.* It should be borne in mind that Maurín attached significance to the POUM's parliamentary role only insofar as it could serve as a step toward the dictatorship of the proletariat. Failing this, he and his party believed that the dictatorship would have to be achieved by means of an armed insurrection.

Maurín was attending a POUM meeting in Galicia* when the military uprising began in July 1936. Trapped in Nationalist territory, he assumed several false identities as he attempted to make his way to the Republican zone. Upon reaching his native province of Huesca, Maurín was arrested under the name Joaquín Julió Ferrer. In September 1937, he was released from Jaca Prison, only to be reincarcerated a few days later when he was recognized at the French border.

During the first months of the Civil War, no one on the Republican side knew exactly what had befallen Maurín. Andrés Nin assumed the leadership of the POUM, and he was supported in his new role by such talented activists as Julián Gorkin (born Gómez) and Juan Andrade. Meanwhile, Maurín had become the Left's first important martyr: he was eulogized in *La Batalla*,* a street in Badalona and a militia were named after him, and the Independent Labor Party (ILP) of Great Britain* formed a *Joaquín Maurín* ambulance unit.

Later, when it was discovered that Maurín was alive, his wife Jeanne worked indefatigably to effect his release, soliciting the aid of such diverse organizations as the British and French Foreign Offices, the International Red Cross, and the ILP. Following the notorious May 1937 riots,* the communists under the Negrín* government waged a campaign of persecution against the POUM which ultimately decimated the party. Maurín's brother, Manuel, was one of the POUMists who fell a victim to this witch-hunt, for despite the fact that he was absolved of any crimes, he was kept in a Republican prison until he died in September 1937. In view of all this, Jeanne grew increasingly skeptical of any prospect of ever freeing her husband. Maurín, in fact, was not released from Francoist prisons until October 1946, when he joined his wife and son in New York.

Although Maurín himself never participated in the war, his legacy as the chief theoretical architect and organizer of the POUM undeniably left its stamp on the party's policies. While one cannot assess precisely the impact of his absence, there can be no doubt that it created profound problems for the POUM during the war. This is illustrated by the fact that when Nin took over the leadership, he lacked the ascendancy which Maurín had enjoyed. For as Ignacio Iglesias, a good friend of Nin's and a POUMist, later wrote Victor Alba: "Maurín was, for the majority of the POUM, something more than the *máximo* leader (*dirigente máximo*): He was for them, purely and simply, the leader, the only leader."

For further information see Victor Alba, *Dos Revolucionarios: Andreu Nin/Joaquín Maurín* (Madrid, 1975); Victor Alba, *El Marxismo en España (1919-1939)*, 2 vols. (Mexico, 1973), on Maurín's political career; Gerald Meaker, *The Revolutionary Left in Spain: 1914-1923* (Stanford, Calif., 1974), on Maurín's political career; and Joaquín Maurín Archives, Hoover Institution, Stanford, California.

George Esenwein

MAY 1937 RIOTS. One of the most famous political incidents of the Spanish Civil War, the May crisis of Barcelona* (May 3-8, 1937), involved fighting between anarchists,* communists,* and Catalan separatists for strategic spots, beginning with the telephone exchange, throughout the city. While the fighting ended before any great military victory had been won, the political ramifications of the crisis signaled the rise of communist dominance among Loyalists* and the end of Popular Front* solidarity among parties on the Left. Hereafter, the revolutionary side of Republican activity came to be subordinated to communist insistence upon strict antifascist behavior.

The cause of the crisis went back to the anarchist revolution of July-October 1936 and the reassertion of Catalan separatist gubernatorial power by Luis Companys* and the separatist Esquerra* party, assisted by the *Partit Socialista Unificat de Catalunya* (PSUC),* a latecomer to Catalan politics and a vehicle of socialist and communist influence into an area once solidly anarchist. Military crises on the Aragón* front and the siege of Madrid* forced Premier Francisco Largo Caballero* to accept a closer alliance with the USSR* in order to obtain military goods embargoed by the Non-Intervention Committee.*

Initially, the point of conflict in Catalan politics was the Trotskyist *Partido Obrero de Unificación Marxista* (POUM)*, identified with the *Confederación Nacional del Trabajo* (CNT)* by its earlier efforts to penetrate the anarchist CNT. In fact, the exclusion of the POUM from participation in Catalan affairs was a trial run for the later effort to exclude other noncommunist groups. Both the PSUC and the Esquerra increased their power at the expense of the POUM in December 1936. President Companys and Premier José Tarradellas,* weakened by middle-class impatience for a rapid end to anarchist power in order that they might avoid economic ruin, did not move fast enough to suit the PSUC. The PSUC exploited Companys' and Tarradellas' prudent tactics by linking itself with bourgeois groups and the sharecroppers and tenant farmers of the *Unió de Rabassaires* (ardent supporters of Catalan separatism). Juan Comorera,* the PSUC secretary, used this support to appoint a fellow party member, Eusebio Rodríguez Salas,* and the procommunist Artemio Aiguadé* as Barcelona police* commissioners to end control of police powers by the anarchist "patrullas de control" (police squads). In fact, the CNT fought so vigorously that dual power existed in Barcelona throughout the winter, a frustration that the PSUC met by demanding compulsory military service and the final merger of the militia into the regular Republican Army.* These demands incensed the libertarians, whose mood of uneasiness was compounded by continual communist gains at both the national and regional levels, and the unceasing propaganda of the POUM against "Stalinism," the PSUC, and the separatists.

Support from the central government in Valencia* helped the PSUC and the *Unión General de Trabajadores* (UGT) agitate for militarization, nationalization of the basic war industries, creation of a single internal security organization, and government control of arms. Companys reshuffled the Catalan regional cabinet on April 16 to create a façade of normalcy, but a combined POUM-*Federación Anarquista Ibérica* (FAI,* the anarchist heart of the CNT) group called the *Amigos de Durruti* took up arms and attempted to assassinate Rodríguez Salas. The effort failed, but the next day, on April 25, 1937, the murder of Roldán Cortada,* a PSUC member and secretary of the UGT Municipal Workers' Federation, led to a giant PSUC parade two days later at his funeral, and an even larger POUM-FAI-CNT demonstration in the streets of Barcelona on May Day. Many armed libertarians warned onlookers that the day of reckoning was not far off.

Retaliation from the PSUC came three days later, when at 3:00 P.M. on May 3 Rodríguez Salas ordered Assault Guards* to occupy the central telephone exchange in Barcelona, an enterprise that when collectivized from International Telephone and Telegraph had been awarded jointly to the CNT and UGT. The most recent study of this act argues that, while the instigator, Rodríguez Salas, operated on behalf of the PSUC and had communist support, he also got tacit support of all members of the Catalan cabinet except the CNT ministers.

The CNT immediately called for the resignation of Rodríguez Salas and Aiguadé, which Companys rejected, much to the surprise of Tarradellas, who seems to have known nothing about the plan to crush the libertarians—evidence of the plan's hasty formulation. When the rejection became known, CNT workers barricaded the streets, so overwhelming PSUC and Assault Guard forces that it was Manuel Azaña,* president of the Second Republic* and hitherto only a bystander to the sectarian conflict raging in the city to which he had fled at the outbreak of the Civil War, who demanded of Tarradellas that Premier Francisco Largo Caballero* (an ally of the CNT) send loyal troops to complete the seizure of the telephone building. The forces he requested could not be dispatched immediately, and May 4 initially saw little violence, although as night fell shooting increased. Emissaries from Valencia (including the anarchist ministers Federica Montseny* and Juan García Oliver*) arrived in Barcelona, but when on May 5 Companys surrendered control of the police to Largo Caballero without any noticeable effect upon anarchist and Trotskyist militancy, Largo Caballero's opponents in Valencia, most importantly Indalecio Prieto* and Juan Negrín,* pushed hard for a government takeover of the city, particularly in light of the anarchist representatives' inability to control the most violent libertarians.

On the barricades, political debate grew more bitter and sectarian with each passing hour. Communists attacked anarchists, while the Trotskyists blamed the CNT for being so involved with official government business that it never could bring itself to order the Barcelona workers to counterattack, proof, the POUM concluded, of *cenetista* fear that a "real" workers' revolution was brewing. This overexaggerated millennarianism seized the hearts and minds of participants and led to serious fighting on May 5, when the CNT-FAI headquarters almost fell to elements of the Catalan police and communist troops. Companys, bitter at the loss of police power which he felt breached Catalan autonomy, sought unsuccessfully to regain this right from the Republican government in Valencia, a move the CNT could only interpret as hostile. Morever, Azaña was now furious with Largo Caballero's delay in sending troops, which alarmed Prieto into sending further reinforcements to Barcelona. Thus, the arrival of military forces was staggered in such a way that every attempt to call a ceasefire met frustration as new outbreaks of violence occurred through May 5 and 6.

Control of Barcelona by the CNT/FAI soon received

a serious challenge as all of the antianarchist forces exerted a maximum effort to overthrow the CNT/FAI. This startling reality emerged in the early morning hours of May 6 when death squads assassinated a number of prominent anarchists in their houses and apartments. The most important victim was Camillo Berneri, an antifascist, anti-Stalinist Italian exiled writer. In the afternoon, following another hasty truce, Companys, now desperate to regain Barcelona in order to protect Catalan autonomy, arranged an evacuation of the telephone exchange but allowed PSUC and UGT members to occupy it and put the system back in working order. Although militia soldiers of the CNT began to arrive back from the Aragonese front on orders of Gregorio Jover,* the anarchist military leader in the city, more Assault Guards than militia filled the Plaza de Cataluña and in the area around the Generalitat* palace. By May 7, it fell to Mariano Vázquez,* the CNT secretary, and Federica Montseny, the national minister of health and welfare, to begin negotiating a truce. Disarmament continued warily throughout that day, and by the next morning Barcelona was finally quiet again.

The consequences, however, wrecked the Popular Front coalition. All of the non-Soviet forces harbored suspicions of their former allies, thus pitting the CNT against separatist and socialist alike. Azaña's anger at Largo Caballero turned into hatred, and Prieto also became increasingly critical of the premier. Matters came to a head on May 13, when the communist ministers Jesús Hernández, Tómas* and Vicente Uribe* criticized Republican failure to maintain public order and demanded the POUM's banishment. The debate raged in Valencia for several days and saw not only communist ministers but also moderate socialists resign from the government. On May 17, Largo Caballero's new cabinet, which omitted both groups, was rejected by Azaña, and Juan Negrín, a close friend of Prieto's but, more importantly, a communist sympathizer, became the new premier. Soviet control of the Spanish Civil War expanded with the demise of the revolution, and the internal affairs of Loyalist Spain soon became marked by the trial and execution of Trotskyists, dismemberment of anarchist institutions like the Council of Aragón,* full militarization of the Republican Army* under the control of Soviet commissars, and a growing estrangement of the Spanish people themselves from the war.

For further information, see Burnett Bolloten, *The Spanish Révolution: The Left and the Struggle for Power During the Civil War* (Chapel Hill, N.C., 1979); Raymond Carr, *Spain 1808-1939* (Oxford, 1967); Felix Morrow, *Revolution and Counter-Revolution in Spain* (New York, 1938); and George Orwell, *Homage to Catalonia* (London, 1938).

See also Catalonia; and Libertarian Movement.

Robert W. Kern

MEDICINE. As one of the important byproducts of its involvement in the Spanish Civil War, the medical profession experienced a number of achievements. As a result of their part in World War I and especially the Spanish war in North Africa, both sides in the Civil War had medical units in their armies familiar with combat-related wounds. Initially, each side had medical units made up of army doctors, medical assistants, and nurses and, as the war expanded, civilian medical personnel and volunteer aides were incorporated to staff field hospitals and rearguard recovery facilities. Ambulance corps were also established on both sides, often with civilian volunteers* wearing military uniforms. There were two groups of medical personnel. First, there were doctors and medical stations attached to recruitment and training facilities who examined new recruits and took care of their medical needs during training. Invariably, civilian doctors cursorily handled recruitment exams in such places of military induction as Barcelona,* Madrid,* and Seville.*

A second group consisted of field hospital doctors and aides. These people set up medical facilities in houses and tents near or on battlefields to care for the wounded as they were brought in from combat zones, performing surgery and other lifesaving procedures as needed before sending them to rearguard hospitals for further treatment and convalescence. Often working under unsanitary and dangerous combat conditions, doctors provided interim care until the wounded could be sent to the rear. As the war progressed, the amount of medical supplies available to doctors in the field and in rearguard hospitals within the Republican zone decreased. Thus, soldiers were frequently operated on with little or no pain killers. The Nationalists,* with medical supplies from Germany* and Italy,* generally had more abundant supplies than the Republicans,* but their medical skills generally remained below those of the Republicans.

Wounded men who were initially treated at a field hospital and unable to return to their units were sent to rearguard hospitals. On each side, these hospitals were often staffed with civilian doctors, nurses, and volunteers who used both existing facilities and others converted from barracks, schools, university buildings, and other public facilities. These hospitals were never completely sanitary and were always crowded with the combat wounded and the sick. As the war progressed, hospitals in the Republican zone experienced the same lack of supplies as field units and occasionally were bombed. This was particularly the case in Barcelona which experienced severe bombing attacks by the Italians in 1938. Enemy troops overrunning a community would periodically break into a hospital killing the wounded enemy. The most widely reported case was at Toledo* where Nationalist troops killed the wounded in a hospital near the Alcázar* in the fall of 1936.

While historians have not produced an accurate ratio of wounded to dead in the Civil War, and thus calculate the survival rate as a result of medical treatment, progress in carrying for the wounded did take place, particularly on the Republican side. The most important advances were made at the General Hospital of Barcelona, under the direction of its chief surgeon, Josep Trueta.* He and his staff developed procedures for immediate surgery on wounds. These procedures involved stitching the peripheries of wounds, various methods for protecting injuries, new uses for plaster of Paris, and convalescence. Most welcome to the patient was Trueta's policy of not changing dressings on wounds every day, a practice which the wounded had feared for centuries as a painful experience. He found that daily change was unnecessary and that it actually inhibited healing. Using plaster of Paris in treating broken limbs was essentially a byproduct of the Civil War, although some doctors had worked with the procedure before 1936.

Trueta and other Republican doctors tried to make available as many facilities in the field as possible, believing that immediate action would save lives. These facilities included operating facilities and blood banks in the field. They also developed methods for using blood transfusions. The blood bank was the special contribution of Dr. Francisco Durán-Jordá, also of Barcelona. The first blood transfusion under combat conditions in the Western world was made on December 23, 1936, by a Canadian doctor on the Republican side, Dr. Norman Bethune, during the fighting for Madrid* at University City. Other advances came in the treatment of frostbite, while sulphoanamides were better used. In addition, better techniques in neurosurgery were developed. As a result of these advances, the death rate of Republican soldiers from wounds fell below that of the French in World War I.

Another outgrowth of the Spanish Civil War was the virtual conquest of gangrene which historically took many lives during wars. Fortunately, these innovations came early in the war. Transfusions were done in late 1936, Trueta's innovative work was standard practice by the end of 1937, and gangrene was eradicated by early 1938.

A further word needs to be said about supplies. Throughout the war, both sides received medical supplies from supporting groups outside of Spain. International organizations, such as the International Red Cross and the Quakers,* sent doctors and supplies to Spain, while various private groups in dozens of countries supplied the side they favored. Thus, for example, French groups usually supported Republican needs, while other private groups, primarily Catholic, in the United States* and Western Europe* frequently helped the Nationalists. Governments such as Germany and Italy sent supplies to the Nationalists while the Russians helped the Republicans. Support consisted not only of medical supplies but also of doctors, nurses, and ambulances.

For further information, see Ted Allan and Sydney Gordon, *The Scalpel, Not the Sword* (London, 1954); Hector Colmegna, *Diario de un médico argentino en la guerra de España* (Madrid, 1941); Hugh Thomas, *The Spanish Civil War* (New York, 1977); Josep Trueta, *The Atlas of Traumatic Surgery* (Oxford, 1947), *Principles and Practice of War Surgery* (London, 1943), and *Treatment of War Wounds and Fractures* (London, 1939).

James W. Cortada

MELILLA. Melilla is a port city in extreme northeastern Morocco.* Conquered by the Spanish in 1497, it remained an isolated *presidio* (outpost) and penal colony until the early years of the twentieth century when it became the embarkation port for the iron ore and lead mined in its hinterland. In 1913, it was designated the military-administrative capital of the Spanish Protectorate's eastern zone. By 1935, it had a population of 71,202. Since 1913, Melilla's significance in Spanish affairs has derived from its proximity to the infamous colonial debacle at Annual in July 1921, and the fact that it was the location for the initial military rising against the Second Republic* on July 17, 1936. Since Moroccan independence in 1956, Melilla has endured as one of Spain's few remaining *plazas de soberanía* (colonies) in North Africa.

For further information, see Ronald Fraser, *The Blood of Spain* (New York, 1979); Charles R. Halstead, "A 'Somewhat Machiavellian' Face: Colonel Juan Beigbeder as High Commissioner in Spanish Morocco, 1937-1939," *The Historian* 37 (November 1974):46-66;

and Robert Rézette, *Les enclaves espagnoles au Maroc* (Paris, 1976).

See also Franco, Francisco.

Shannon E. Fleming

MÉNDEZ ASPE, FRANCISCO. Méndez was the Republic's minister of finance from April 5, 1938, until the end of the Civil War. This nervous Left-Republican had been a career civil servant and a confidant of Juan Negrín,* working directly for him in charge of delivering gold to the USSR.* Equally important, while subsecretary of the treasury, he concluded with the cabinet that the safest place to deposit the gold reserves of the Spanish Republic would be the Soviet Union. Méndez personally managed the physical transfer of the gold from Madrid* via truck convoy to the north and eventually its loading onto ships bound for the Soviet Union. He also helped develop the Republic's policies on gold and silver deposits, drawing up the plans that resulted in the use of these metals for purchases of supplies throughout Western Europe* and with the Soviet Union for the war effort.

For further information, see Angel Viñas, *El oro de Moscú* (Barcelona, 1979).

See also Bank of Spain; Economy, Republican; and Monetary Policy, Nationalist.

James W. Cortada

MENÉNDEZ LÓPEZ, ARTURO (1893-1936). Menéndez López was director of public security in 1932 during the Casas Viejas incident in which the government brutally suppressed an anarchist revolt in the province of Cádiz,* an event that received considerable press coverage at the time. At the start of the Civil War, supporters of the Republic, remembering him because of the episode, executed him after removing him from a train in their zone.

For further information, see Hugh Thomas, *The Spanish Civil War* (New York, 1977).

James W. Cortada

MENÉNDEZ LÓPEZ, LEOPOLDO (1891-1965). Menéndez López, a career army officer, was one of the principal commanders of the Republican Army.* In August 1936, he became subsecretary of war in the Republican government and later commander of troops in the area in and around Córdoba.* He next commanded the 20th Corps and during 1937 the combined armies of Maniobra and of the Levante.* In 1938, he reached the rank of full general. He next commanded

troops at the battle of Teruel* (December 1937-February 1938). Later in 1938, he battled the Nationalists* along the Mediterranean coast, successfully preventing the Levante from falling to Franco's* forces. In February 1939, he joined with other Republican officers in the Casado* peace effort designed to bring a negotiated end to the war; however, the effort failed. Therefore, he continued to resist the Nationalists in the Levante in southeastern Spain until the end of the war. After March 1939, he moved to Great Britain* and ultimately to Mexico.*

For further information, see Ramón Salas Larrazábal, *Historia del ejército popular de la república*, 4 vols. (Madrid, 1974).

James W. Cortada

MEQUINENZA. Mequinenza, in the province of Saragossa,* became a key point in the fighting that took place along the Ebro River* between July and November 1938. During that battle, Mequinenza was one of the points over which Republican forces crossed in their attempt to defeat substantial numbers of Nationalist troops but which ultimately resulted in a Loyalist defeat caused by Franco* launching a counterattack. Before the campaign ended, both the Republicans* and Nationalists* came through the town and fought outside its limits. Thousands of men were killed or wounded on both sides. On December 23, the Nationalists launched their own offensive at this point near where the Segre and Ebro rivers connect. This event signaled the start of the last major campaign of the Civil War—Franco's successful effort to conquer Catalonia* between December 1938 and January 1939.

For further information, see Luis María Mezquida, *La batalla del Ebro*, 2 vols. (Tarragona, 1963-1967) and *La batalla del Segre* (Tarragona, 1972).

James W. Cortada

MERA, CIPRIANO (1879-1975). Mera, born in Madrid,* became the outstanding anarchist commander of the Spanish Civil War. As a construction worker by trade and as founder and leader of the *Único de la Construcción* in Madrid, Mera had long been committed to social revolution when he joined with Buenaventura Durruti* and Isaac Puente in forming the Revolutionary Committee of Saragossa* in December 1933. Dedicated to the overthrow of the Second Republic,* they directed the revolutionary strike that same month in Saragossa which resulted in Mera's incarceration in Burgos* Prison on sabotage charges.

Recognizing the need for anarchist strength and solidarity, Mera promoted reconciliation with the *Treintistas* at the national meeting of the *Confederación Nacional del Trabajo* (CNT)* held in Saragossa in 1936. Against the formation of militias* to protect the Popular Front* government elected in February of that year, Mera instead directed the CNT- *Unión General de Trabajadores* (UGT)* strike of construction workers, electricians, and elevator operators in June, a strike that lasted to the eve of the Civil War. The prominence he gained in this strike and his presence in Madrid when the war broke out insured a leadership role for Mera. On the central front throughout the war, he first led the 14th Division and then the 4th Army Corps, which included columns of the International Brigades.*

A man of strong conviction and popular support, Mera vehemently protested the departure of the national government and of Horacio M. Prieto,* national secretary of the CNT from Madrid in November 1936. Mera insisted that their shameful flight broke faith with the people of Madrid, who were valiantly defending the city. This precipitated Prieto's resignation as secretary of the CNT.

Mera participated in all the major battles on the central front, especially in the military and moral victory over the Italian forces at the battle of Guadalajara* in March 1937. This victory reinforced Mera's earlier, and not entirely popular, commitment to the need for a strong army based on discipline, an established chain of command, and a central authority responsible for organizing and coordinating the war effort. Before most other anarchists* would consider this idea, he had insisted that only if this commitment was made would the revolution prevail.

By 1939, Mera was convinced that the war was lost, and he hoped, with Casado's* adherents, that an honorable peace could be made with General Franco* if the communists were eliminated from power on the Republican side. Mera therefore joined the Casado revolt. With their revolt, Negrín's* government immediately went into exile. However, in Madrid, the communists continued to fight, confident that there could be no such peace with Franco. It was Mera's troops that broke this last communist resistance and that opened the way for negotiations between Franco and the Defense Council created by Casado's followers.

Mera's role in the Casado revolt earned him the lasting enmity of the communists and not a few anarchists, who state that he saved himself, securing safe conduct from Spain, while his less fortunate comrades were imprisoned or executed. In fact, Mera fled Spain for Algeria where he was arrested and jailed for seven years. Upon leaving prison, he went to France* where he was a bricklayer until his death in Paris in 1975.

For further information, see Segismundo Casado, *The Last Days of Madrid* (London, 1939); Robert G. Colodny, *The Struggle for Madrid* (New York, 1958); Joan Llarch, *Cipriano Mera, un anarquista en la guerra de España* (Barcelona, 1976); and Cipriano Mera, *Guerra, exilio y cárcel de un anarcosindicalista* (Paris, 1976).

Shirley F. Fredricks

MERCHANT MARINE, SPANISH. In 1936, the Spanish merchant marine was the ninth largest in Europe,* totaling 1,180,000 registered gross tons. There were 683 vessels over 100 tons, of which about 600 were active in commerce in July 1936, and 800 smaller merchant vessels. The Spanish fishing fleet was the fourth in Europe, with 1,800 vessels over 10 tons, 80 percent of which operated in the Atlantic and the Bay of Biscay. The merchant and fishing fleets employed 44,500 seafaring men. As a result of the uprising, the Nationalists* gained only 176,000 tons of merchant shipping, but captures and expropriations had raised the total to 400,000 tons by the end of 1937. Throughout the Civil War, the Nationalists captured 238 Republican vessels and added twenty-seven captured foreign merchant ships to their maritime service. The Republican losses totaled approximately 600 vessels, and Nationalist losses about forty. Of the fifty Republican merchant vessels extensively utilized for military purposes, twenty-seven became war losses. Of the thirty-eight Nationalist and nineteen captured foreign vessels so employed, two were lost. The Spanish merchant marine was an indispensable element in the supply of both the civilian populations and the opposing armies as well as the commercial trade vital for the foreign credit necessary to the war effort of both sides. The fishing fleet progressively fed the Nationalist zone far better than the Republican zone.

For further information, see Rafael González Echegaray, *La marina mercante y el tráfico marítimo* (Madrid, 1977).

See also Navy, Spanish.

Willard C. Frank, Jr.

MÉRIDA. Mérida, a town located in the province of Badajoz* in the dry southwestern part of Spain, was the scene of a battle during the Civil War. Nationalist forces under the command of Juan de Yagüe Blanco* marched northward toward Madrid* when on August 10 the town was captured. Yagüe, soon to become one of Franco's* most important combat officers, fought his first battle of the war 4 miles south of the town at the River Guadina. There the committee of defense for Mérida put up a fight but was quickly defeated and many of its members executed. The capture of Mérida allowed the Nationalists* in southern Spain to establish communications and later actual contact with the rebels in northern Spain. Morevover, the important nearby town of Badajoz could now be attacked by the Nationalists. While Yagüe marched onward for this purpose, the local militia of Mérida, many of whom had run away when the Nationalists approached their town, now returned from Madrid with some 2,000 Assault* and Civil Guards.* On August 11, they attacked the Nationalists who were able to prevent these Republicans* from rescuing Badajoz. Badajoz was taken and Mérida remained in Franco's hands.

For further information, see José Manuel Martínez Bande, *La compaña de Andalucía* (Madrid, 1969).
See also Andalusia.

James W. Cortada

MERRY DEL VAL Y ALZOLA, ALFONSO

(1903-   ). Merry del Val, a diplomat on the Nationalist side, was born in Bilbao.* Before the Civil War, he had a career as a lawyer and diplomat, serving in London, Washington, D.C., Chicago, Asunción, and Bucharest. From the earliest days of the Falange,* he had been a member and even participated in beating up opponents, and possibly killing at least one individual prior to the war. During the conflict, he conducted some minor diplomatic negotiations with the Italians on behalf of Franco.* After the war, he remained in Spain's diplomatic service as ambassador to Brusells, Lima, Ciudad Trujillo, Copenhagen, and Washington, D.C.

For further information, see Círculo de Amigos de la Historia, *Diccionario biográfico español contemporaneo* (Madrid, 1970), Vol. 2.
See also Diplomatic Corps, Spanish.

James W. Cortada

MESSERSCHMIDT, EBERHARD (-1972).

Lieutenant Eberhard Messerschmidt, a career engineer in the German Navy,* served as a vital link to Spain from 1925 to 1933. The German Navy, then seeking to circumvent the Versailles Treaty, had a contract through King Alfonso XIII* to build two U-boats in Cádiz.* Messerschmidt made several trips to Spain on this business with his commander Captain Canaris.* Prime Minister Azaña and the Horacio Echevarietta Shipbuilders extended the German con-

tract, after the advent of the Republic, but the completed submarines* were eventually sold to Turkey.

When the Civil War broke out, General Mola's* agent conferred on August 2-8, 1936, in Berlin with Messerschmidt as a representative of now Admiral Canaris, chief of German military intelligence. Messerschmidt then toured the Nationalist zone from August 29 to September 27, and afterwards sent a detailed report to Canaris. This mission annoyed other Germans who were directing Nazi foreign policy in Spain, namely, Johannes Bernhardt,* director of the *Compañia Hispano-Marroquí de Transportes* (HISMA),* and General Helmuth Wilberg, commander of Special Staff "W."

Messerschmidt escorted Admirals Moreno* and Cervera* when they visited German military installations in November 1937. As liaison between the Spanish Navy* and German industry, Messerschmidt returned to Spain from May to November 1938 in a vain attempt to oust Britain's* Vickers-Armstrong Shipyard (*Constructora Naval*) from Spain. He sought to replace British arms contractors and technical advisers with German advisers, but failed.

Messerschmidt returned to Spain in April 1939 to do intelligence work against Britain. After World War II, he stayed in Spain, dying in Madrid in 1972.

For further information, see José Escobar, *Así empezó* (Madrid, 1974); and Angel Viñas, *La Alemania Nazi y el 18 de julio* (Madrid, 1972).
See also Germany.

Robert H. Whealey

MEXICO.

Mexico consistently supported the Republic throughout the Civil War and after 1939, refused to recognize the government of General Franco.* It continued to maintain relations with the Republican government for decades while offering asylum to its exiled leaders. The Mexican government also sent arms and ammunition to the Republic during the first summer of the war—the only major nation to do so—and in September, it admitted that some 20,000 rifles and nearly 20 million rounds of ammunition had already been sent to Spain. After the United States* announced in 1936 that arms should not be sold to either side, the Republic's ambassador to Mexico, Félix Gordón Ordás,* had to work more quietly behind the scenes to obtain supplies. Mexican diplomats refused to participate in or cooperate with the policy of nonintervention or to join the Non-Intervention Committee* proposed by France* and Great Britain* during August 1936. In March 1937, the Mexicans argued in the League of Nations* that nonintervention was a disguised form of support for the Nationalists* against the legally established Spanish Republican government and was contrary to the Covenant of the League. During the negotiations resulting in the Nyon Agreements in September 1937, Mexico and the USSR* were the only two nations which supported the interests of the Spanish Republic within the league. In short, unlike her neighbors whose policies were noncommittal, Mexico took a distinct stand on the question of the Civil War. Her policy directly contradicted that of the United States, thereby increasing tensions in the New World.

In assessing the amount of assistance Mexico gave Spain, it appears that approximately 330 Mexicans volunteered to fight in the war while over 20,000 rifles, nearly 30 million shells, and a miscellaneous assortment of trucks, planes, and artillery went to the Republic. More significantly, Mexico provided full diplomatic support in international councils and after the conflict, allowed thousands of exiles to live within her borders.

For further information, see Patricia W. Fagan, *Exiles and Citizens: Spanish Republicans in Mexico* (Austin, Tex., 1973); Félix Gordón Ordás, *Mi política fuera de España*, 2 vols. (Mexico, 1965-1967), memoirs of the Republican ambassador to Mexico City; T.G. Powell, *Mexico and the Spanish Civil War* (Albuquerque, N.M., 1980); and Lois Elwyn Smith, *Mexico and the Spanish Republicans* (Berkeley, Calif., 1955), for a general overview.

See also Latin America.

James W. Cortada

MIAJA MENANT, JOSÉ (1878-1958). Miaja, born in Asturias* in 1878, obtained a bachelor's degree in Oviedo* prior to attending the Military Academy. Like most of his contemporaries, he served in Morocco.* He attained the rank of general prior to the outbreak of the Civil War. Following the victory of the Popular Front,* he was transferred from Estremedura* to command of the 1st Division in Madrid* and, shortly before the rising, refused to distribute arms to the workers. The ambivalence in his attitude and subsequent career was underscored by his acceptance of the position of minister of war in Martínez Barrio's* government on the night of July 18-19, in the apparent expectation that it would capitulate to the insurgent generals. He then refused to retain the post in the Giral* government on the grounds that an insurgent victory was inevitable because the government had neither an army nor a police* force to combat the rebellion. Subsequently (1937), he endeavored to elim-

inate evidence of membership in the *Unión Militar Española* (UME).

Shortly following the rebellion, Miaja-was transferred to command of the 3rd Division in Valencia,* and on August 20 he directed a column of 10,000 militia in an unsuccessful attempt to take Córdoba,* where he was beaten back by Moroccans under General Varela.* Relieved of command, he returned under some suspicion to Valencia but was reappointed commander of the 1st Division (Madrid*) on October 24. When the government abandoned the capital on November 6, Miaja and General Pozas* were given instructions by General Asensio* in misaddressed envelopes (quickly rectified) in which Miaja was ordered to organize a *Junta de Defensa*,* with representatives of all Popular Front parties to defend the capital "at all costs." Nearly weeping with rage at what he considered a deliberate attempt to sacrifice him in a probably hopeless effort to save the capital, Miaja was quickly advised by the communist Fifth Regiment* that its entire facilities were at his disposal. Thus began the marriage of convenience that was to catapult the communists into positions of increasing power and elevate Miaja to the legendary hero of Madrid. Miaja's decision to join the Communist party* was described by President Azaña* as "laughable" and prompted the comment of the American Louis Fischer that Miaja "probably knows as much about Communism as Francisco Franco."*

Miaja's military abilities have also been the subject of dispute. Like his biographer (Somoza-Silva, in 1944), the Nationalist military historian Salas Larrazábal* credits Miaja with considerable intelligence and ability. However, Soviet participants claim that Miaja knew "very little" about operational details, and the evidence strongly supports the view that his chief of staff, Vicente Rojo,* working (in Rojo's words) "in close contact" with General Goriev* and other Soviet advisers, planned the defense of Madrid.

During the battle of the Jarama* in February 1937, Miaja replaced General Pozas as chief of the Army of the Center.* He subsequently supported the communists' rejection of Largo Caballero's* plans for an offensive in Estremedura, in favor of an offensive at Brunete* in July. In April 1938, he was made supreme commander of all military forces in central and southern Spain. Following the collapse of Catalonia,* he urged continued resistance, but early in March agreed to accept the position of president of the anti-Negrín* and anticommunist National Council of Defense proposed by Colonel Casado.* Following the failure of Casado's attempted negotiations with the Nationalists,* Miaja left Madrid for Valencia on March 27 and subsequently emigrated to Mexico.* Escoriated in 1940 by the Spanish communist Antonio Mije* as a "dull witted general" and denounced as a "traitor," Miaja has received virtually no mention in the chronicles of other Spanish communist contemporaries. He died in 1958 and, during his last days, reportedly commented that "if we had been able to turn the enemy's left wing at Brunete, I would now be in El Pardo dictating my memoirs."

For further information, see Burnett Bolloten, *The Spanish Revolution: The Left and the Struggle for Power During the Civil War* (Chapel Hill, N.C., 1979); Editorial Codex, *Crónica de la guerra de España*, various issues, including No. 52 (Buenos Aires, 1967); Mijail Koltsov, *Diario de la guerra de España* (Paris, 1963); Ramón Salas Larrazábal, *Historia del ejército popular de la República* (Madrid, 1973), Vol. 1; Lazaro Somozo-Silva, *El General Miaja: Biografía du un héroe* (Mexico City, 1944); and Julián Zugazagoitia, *Historia de la guerra de España* (Buenos Aires, 1940), reprint, *Guerra y vicisitudes de los españoles* (Paris, 1968).

Verle B. Johnston

MICKIEWICZ (PALAFOX) BATTALION. The Mickiewicz (Palafox) Battalion fought on the side of the Republic as a unit in the International Brigades.* It was the 4th Battalion of the 13th Brigade, formed in December 1936 primarily with Polish volunteers.* It fought most of the war in and around the city of Madrid* and proved particularly important at the fighting in the University of Madrid in December 1936. It continued to be at the forefront of much combat throughout 1937 as well. The 13th Brigade had three other battalions made up almost entirely of French and Belgian volunteers and some Balkans.

For further information, see Andreu Castells, *Las brigadas internacionales de la guerra de España* (Barcelona, 1974).

James W. Cortada

MIGUEL DE CERVANTES. The Republican cruiser *Miguel de Cervantes* (launched 1928, 7,475 tons standard, 8-152mm [6 in] guns, 33 kts.) was ordered from El Ferrol* on July 18, 1936, to prevent rebel troops in Morocco* from crossing the Straits of Gibraltar* to the Iberian Peninsula. On the way, Republican crewmen wrested control from Rear Admiral Miguel de Mier and the ship's officers, and the *Miguel de Cervantes* joined the blockading squadron in the Straits. In September-October, she participated in the cruise of the Republican fleet to threatened northern ports.

At anchor off Cartagena* on November 22, 1936, the *Miguel de Cervantes* was severely damaged by two torpedoes from the Italian submarine *Torricelli*. After lengthy and incomplete repairs, the *Miguel de Cervantes* rejoined the fleet in March 1938, but she was subsequently twice damaged by bombs in air raids on Cartagena, and the cruiser never participated in a major engagement. She interned in Bizerte on March 7, 1939.

See also Navy, Italian; Navy, Spanish; and Uprising at Sea.

Willard C. Frank, Jr.

MIJE GARCÍA, ANTONIO. Mije served as a leading member of the Spanish Communist party.* Born in Andalusia,* he had at one time been an anarchist, and before the Civil War was secretary to the small Communist party. During the early days of the conflict, he directed the party's propaganda efforts which portrayed communists as a moderating influence in society, calling upon Spaniards to resist the Nationalists* much as they had fought against Napoleon's armies in the early 1800s. During the war, he also became a political commissar within the Republican Army* for the purposes of recruiting more members to the Communist party and of reducing criticism against communist and Republican* policies.

For further information, see Burnett Bolloten, *The Spanish Revolution: The Left and the Struggle for Power During the Civil War* (Chapel Hill, N.C., 1979).

James W. Cortada

MILICIAS ANTIFASCISTAS OBRERAS Y CAMPESINAS (MAOC). The *Milicias Antifascistas Obreras y Campesinas* (MAOC), a paramilitary communist group formed in 1933, was led by Juan Modesto,* an ex-regular army veteran of the Moroccan wars. During the early days of the Civil War, the MAOC was one of the first Republican militia units equipped and ready to fight the Nationalists.* The famed Fifth Regiment,* made up primarily of communists, evolved out of the MAOC units.

For further information, see E. Comín Colomer, *El quinto regimento* (Madrid, 1973); and Dolores Ibarruri, *They Shall Not Pass: The Autobiography of La Pasionaria* (London, 1967).

See also Army, Republican; and Communist Party, Spanish.

James W. Cortada

MILITARY TRIBUNALS, REPUBLICAN. Republican military tribunals existed throughout the Civil War for the purpose of trying violators of military law within the Republican Army* and prosecuting prisoners* and suspected enemies of the Republic. The tribunals often operated with the minimal of evidence. While the exact number of prisoners sentenced to death (execution was the primary form of punishment) will never be known, a reasonable total of Republican executions would approach about 55,000, of which over half could be attributed to tribunals. An estimate of deaths caused by the Nationalists* would be around 75,000 for the years 1936-1939 and perhaps an additional 100,000 by Franco's* government after the war. Thus, the tribunals contributed greatly to the ferocity of the war. The Republican military tribunals competed with those of various political groups and local governments in sentencing men and women to death, although many prisoners were killed without trial. As various political factions rose and declined in power within the Republican zone (for example, the anarchists*), additional deaths occurred, although many resulted from vendettas and were not byproducts of formal trials. In short, the excesses typical of wars were clearly evident in the behavior of these tribunals. These judicial structures were often handled by judges with no legal and little military background who prejudged most of the accused as enemies of the state to be eradicated.

For further information, see Gabriel Avilés, *Tribunales rojos* (Barcelona, 1939); and Hugh Thomas, *The Spanish Civil War* (New York, 1977).

See also Police; and Terrorism.

James W. Cortada

MILITIAS. Each of the major radical Republican political groups prior to the Civil War had various paramilitary organizations which, in the early months of the war, were militia units operating in the field. Eventually, on both sides, these armed wings were incorporated, respectively, into either the Nationalist or Republican armies as companies, divisions, or brigades. The largest number of fragmented militias were serving on the Republican side drawn first from the anarchists* and later the communists. Units were put together quickly by various anarchist organizations, the Socialist party,* the Communist party,* and regional and trade-union groups before being consolidated into regular army commands by the end of 1936. The Fifth Regiment,* made up of communists, for example, grew out of this militia tradition, as did those units formed by anarchists in Catalonia* and Aragón.*

The Durruti Column was perhaps the best known of these units. The Nationalists experienced a similar phenomenon, although not as diversified. Most paramilitary wings came from the Falange* party and the *Requetés* of the Carlists.* As with the Popular Army* (Republican), these units were eventually merged into the regular army, certainly by early 1937.

For further information, see Michael Alpert, *El ejército republicano en la guerra civil* (Barcelona, 1977); and Ramón Salas Larrazábal, *Historia del ejército popular de la república*, 4 vols. (Madrid, 1974). There is no comprehensive study of the Nationalist forces, but see Stanley G. Payne, *Politics and the Military in Modern Spain* (Stanford, Calif., 1967).

See also Army, Nationalist; Army, Republican; and Mixed Brigades.

James W. Cortada

MILLÁN ASTRAY Y TERREROS, JOSÉ (1879-1954). Millán Astray was the son of a lawyer and writer from Corunna.* He became one of Spain's most colorful and dedicated professional officers in the Moroccan wars. Because of his multiple grave wounds, he held no active combat command during the Spanish Civil War, but with his close association with Generalissimo Franco* he did influence the conduct of this conflict.

In the Philippine Islands (1896-1897), Millán Astray gained a reputation as an infantry officer infected with great heroism. He studied for several years in the Spanish War College and taught at the Toledo* Military Academy. In Morocco,* he created and commanded the native police* force of Larache and was assigned to the Moorish *Regulares*. He was an adviser to the Tactical Commission which had been directed to rewrite the antiquated military texts.

Millán Astray viewed the Spanish military efforts in Morocco as a disaster. What was needed, he said, was an elite force of highly skilled and disciplined men patterned on some aspects of the French Foreign Legion. In 1920, he was promoted to lieutenant colonel and was directed to create and command a Spanish Foreign Legion* known as the *Tercio de Extranjeros*. The term *Tercio* dates to the formations of the Spanish Army in its great days of the sixteenth and seventeenth centuries. Neither Millán Astray, his officers, nor his men, however, ever accepted the term, which to them was simply *La Legión*! The legion did accept men from many lands and of many nationalities, but Spain herself furnished most of the legionnaires.

The legion was popularly said to be made up of the dregs, castoffs, and misfits of not only Spain's but also the world's society, and that Millán Astray offered them redemption for their past misconduct and the opportunity to reestablish (or create) a new identity. Millán Astray was a man who grasped the strange mystique of the legionary and at the same time had the qualities of leadership and the understanding of men that could instill unusual emotion and attachment in others. He demanded heroic bravery which expressed a disdain and contempt of death. This is mirrored in his seemingly illogical motto and the battlecry of the legion "¡Viva la muerte!" ("Long Live Death!" is the usual translation, but it could be translated as "Hail Death!") In his music the legionnaire became "El Novio de la muerte" ("One Betrothed to Death"). There was a strong sense of brotherhood in the legion; in moments of stress and danger, even in death, the cry of "¡A mí la Legión!" ("Legion to my aid!") brought immediate response.

Leading his legion in battle, Millán Astray was hit in the chest by a bullet while standing alongside his second in command, Major Francisco Franco.* Shortly thereafter, he was promoted to colonel of infantry. At Djebala he lost an arm. It is not unusual that in some circles such a soldier would be viewed as a heroic figure, but in others he would be looked upon with scorn as being too primitive or uncultured.

Those who resented Millán Astray were in the so-called *Juntas de Defensa.** Even though these officers had many legitimate grievances, objections centered on their low pay and lack of opportunity for promotion as opposed to those officers who were willing to take the risks of war in Africa. Millán Astray became one of the main objects of their scorn and attack. In the storm surrounding the actions of the *Juntas*, he submitted his resignation. However, he was reinstated with the legion when Franco was promoted to brigade general. In 1926, Millán Astray lost his right eye. His enemies in Madrid* circulated the rumor that this wound (and possibly others) had been self-inflicted to bring attention and glory to himself. To others he was known as "El glorioso Mutilado."

In 1927, he was promoted to brigade general. During the Republic, he was given an assignment by Alejandro Lerroux. At the time of the military rising he was in Argentina;* he made his way back to Spain and gave his support to the Nationalists.* In the early days of the Franco government, Millán Astray held the position of chief of the press and propaganda department. His major contribution to the Nationalist cause was the military force, *La Legión*, which he created. In the Spanish Civil War, as in Morocco, it was the vanguard of the Army of Africa.*

Historians have variously described Millán Astray as austere, dedicated, possessing a strong sense of honor, reckless to the point of folly, infected with evangelical medievalism, appealing to chivalrous Christianity, a legend of military fanaticism, quick, full of histrionic flair, having a morbid cast of mind, brutal, picturesque, eccentric, a fantastic condottiere, fiery, a rigid disciplinarian, a mystic, a genius in leadership, cadaverous with wild eyes, a rare bird, and having a vocation for constant danger.

Today his portraits overlook the conference rooms of the Spanish Legion. One eye is covered with a black patch, one sleeve is empty, and a riding crop is held in the fingers of what is left of his other hand. To the legionnaires he is still "El Glorioso Mutilado." Millán Astray died a division general on January 1, 1954, in Madrid. He held the titles of chief general of the legion and director general of the corps of mutilated gentlemen.

For further information, see Millán Astray, *La Legión* (Madrid, 1923); and General Carlos de Silva, *General Millán Ástray* (Barcelona, 1956).
See also Army, Nationalist.

Raymond L. Proctor

MINORCA. Minorca was the only one of the Balearic Islands* to remain in Republican control. The port of Mahón contained a small naval base, its strategic potential for the Republican Navy never exploited. In February 1939, the British cruiser *Devonshire* aided the transfer of the island from Republican to Nationalist authority, thus excluding Italian occupation.

Willard C. Frank, Jr.

MIRALCAMPO AGRICULTURAL COLLECTIVE. The Miralcampo Agricultural Collective, a farm located in the province of Guadalajara,* experienced a growth in agricultural production while under the Republic's control. It had once been the property of the Count of Romanones, one of the dominant political figures in Spanish politics during the 1920s. At Miralcampo, wheat, barley, wine, melon, and alfalfa production increased between one-third and over 100 percent from the 1935-1936 through the 1936-1937 seasons. New organizational techniques, together with more efficient labor and land usage, brought Miralcampo a success that was not typical of the region.

For further information, see Hugh Thomas, *The Spanish Civil War* (New York, 1977).
See also Economy, Republican.

James W. Cortada

MIRAVITLLES, JAUME (1901?-   ). Miravitlles was born in Barcelona* and became a leading Catalan politician during the 1930s. As a leader in the Catalan Left party, the Esquerra,* he represented this faction in the Generalitat,* Catalonia's* governing body. His primary role during the Civil War was as general secretary of the Antifascist Militias Committee,* formed by the Catalan government in mid-1936 to link official authority to the actual power of militant groups in Barcelona. Miravitlles supervised 600 employees, many of whom worked with subcommittees responsible for administering various militias* and supplies. After Franco's* death in 1975, he resumed his role as a Catalan politician in local government.

For further information, see Jaume Miravitlles, *Episodis de la guerra civil espanyola* (Barcelona, 1972).

James W. Cortada

MIRET, JOSÉ. Miret represented the *Partido Obrero de Unificación Marxista* (POUM)* on the Antifascist Militias Committee,* which was set up in 1936 to help govern the four provinces of Catalonia,* primarily in military matters. This Catalan communist next became minister of food* in the Catalan government in April 1937. He was responsible for controlling food supplies in Catalonia and feeding the troops and refugees,* particularly in and around Barcelona.*

For further information, see Andrés Suarez, *Un Episodio de la revolución española: El proceso contra el POUM* (Paris, 1974).

James W. Cortada

MIXED BRIGADES. The term "Mixed Brigades" refers to the basic unit of military organization in the Republican Army.* It grew out of the government's decision to merge various militias* into the regular army and consisted of three battalions of militia and another from the regular army. A battalion comprised one machine-gunners company and three companies of infantrymen. Later, other companies which joined the Mixed Brigades included artillery and other branches of the army. While the mixture of the Republican forces officially began after October 16, 1936, it took months of work to make it a reality. Political commissars were added to the Mixed Brigades to insure that none of the soldiers would waiver in their political enthusiasm for the Republican cause. Moreover, these commissars were charged with reducing animosities between members of the regular army and the various militias.

By the end of 1936, there were fifteen Mixed Brigades, including now volunteers* in the International Brigades* from other countries. Four of these had militia commanders, while the remainder were led by regular army officers. The total size of the Republican Army in the first winter of the war approximated 350,000, although as a result of faulty records and some corruption in payroll files the exact number cannot be determined. By the spring of 1937, each brigade had a population* of some 3,800 men. Forty brigades were at full strength, fifteen were in training, and another sixty were being organized.

The Mixed Brigades fought in all the battles of the Spanish Civil War, from the fall of 1936 to the spring of 1939. As the war progressed, the term "Mixed Brigade" was used less frequently, particularly after May 1937 when the Republican government and the Spanish Communist party* were able to expand their control over most segments of life in their zones to the exclusion of more narrowly based or regional political groups.

For further information, see Michael Alpert, *El ejército republicano en la guerra civil* (Barcelona, 1977); and Eduardo Comín Colomer, *El comisariado político* (Madrid, 1973), on the political commissars.

James W. Cortada

MODESTO GUILLOTO, JUAN (1906-1969). Modesto served in the army in Morocco* as a noncommissioned officer and from 1933 onward commanded the Communist party's* paramilitary group, the *Milicias Antifascistas Obreras y Campesinas* (MAOC).* When the Civil War began, the MAOC and other communist units were integrated into the famous 5th Army Corps which fought in and around Madrid* throughout 1936. He soon became its commander (October 1936) and later fought in the battle of the Jarama* in February 1937, with his first major combat command, managing to blunt the Nationalist offensive on Madrid. He continued to command Republican troops in central and northern Spain throughout 1937, fighting in every major campaign of the year. Modesto also participated in the battle of the Ebro* between July and November 1938. This despotic Andalusian officer was a realistic and effective commander with no political ambitions, unlike many other communist leaders. He subsequently was given command of the Army of the Ebro* and continued to lead combat forces until the end of the war. This brilliant officer spent the rest of his life in exile (reportedly in Latin America) from Spain.

For further information, see Luis María Mezquida, *La batalla del Ebro*, 2 vols. (Tarragona, 1963); and Juan Modesto, *Soy del quinto regimiento* (Paris, 1969).
See also Fifth Regiment; and Appendix B.

James W. Cortada

MOIX, JOSÉ. Moix was a Catalan communist who served in Juan Negrín's* last cabinet from August 16, 1938 to March 1939 when the government left Spain. He hardly had the opportunity to serve as minister of labor and social welfare since the government in these last days of the Civil War was more concerned with the military situation and deciding whether to stay in Spain, surrender, or leave without a fight.

For further information, see Hugh Thomas, *The Spanish Civil War* (New York, 1977)

James W. Cortada

MOLA VIDAL, EMILIO (1887-1937). Mola organized the conspiracy in 1936 against the Popular Front* government of Spain. He commanded the Army of the North* and was the field commander for the futile assault on Madrid.*

Mola was born on a military post in Cuba* (June 9, 1887) into an old military family. Following the family tradition, he was commissioned in the infantry in 1907. He was six feet tall, but in his thick glasses was not the picture of a dashing military figure. Some regarded him as homely. He was very studious and intelligent, a man of detail and decision, but very nervous and outspoken. Some called him "Prussian" because of his ascetic dedication to duty. He was very literate and wrote extensively and pointedly on military affairs. He was good-natured and had a charm that made him very popular with his men.

In 1910, Mola was assigned to the Moorish *Regulares*. There he became known as an Arabist for his understanding of the Moors.* His constant contempt for danger won their admiration, but also resulted in his being badly wounded. By 1927, he was promoted to brigade general.

Politically, Mola was considered to have little attachment to the monarchy and was Republican in his leanings. In 1930, General Damaso Berenguer appointed him to the thankless task of director of general security, at a time when plots were the rule of the day. Upholding the law of the land, he incurred the wrath of the factions that wanted to overthrow the monarchy. As a result, with the advent of the Republic he was without a position. During this period, he acquired a violent dislike for Manuel Azaña* and his concepts of liberal republicanism, but still he was not involved in plots against the government.

Under the Gil Robles* ministry, Mola was assigned as military commander in Melilla,* Morocco.* But, with the victory of the Popular Front he was recalled to Spain and posted as garrison commander in Pamplona.* He believed that the political situation in Spain was heading for a disaster that could be averted only by the military. Soon he became involved in a plot with young officers of the *Unión Militar Española* (UME),* and he hoped to interest other generals.

His plan involved a coup against the Popular Front in which no political factions would be allowed to interfere. It would be under the flag of the Republic, and it would not be an attempt to restore the monarchy in any form, nor would it be a struggle to establish a state such as that proposed by the Falange.* A military directorate would be set up which would eventually surrender power to an elected president. But a military veto would be in the hands of two military ministers. He felt that for the coup to succeed, it had to have support from civilian moderates and the Falange, as well as Alfonso* monarchists and Carlists.* It all seemed hopeless; still his plans progressed. Sanjurjo,* in exile, agreed to act as the commanding general of the revolt, and Mola was recognized as the director. It appeared that it would all come to naught because of the intransigent positions of the Falange and Carlists. However, with the murder of Calvo Sotelo,* the opposing factions threw their support behind the conspiracy without gaining any promise from Mola for their ultimate political aims. At dawn on July 19, 1936, General Mola issued his proclamation of revolt in Navarre.* The next day General Sanjurjo died in a plane crash, and the revolt was without its commanding general.

Whereas the uprising was a disaster in many parts of Spain, there were successes in the Canary Islands,* Morocco, Seville,* and in Mola's region of responsibility with the leading towns of Old Castile* and Aragón,* at least tentatively, under his control. His forces were limited, but some were to drive toward Madrid and in heavy fighting control the important invasion passes through the mountains. But, by July 29, Mola was frantic because he only had 26,000 rounds of ammunition left for his entire army. As he considered desperate alternatives including killing himself, 600,000 rounds arrived from the Army of Africa* in the south.

Mola was instrumental in creating the Burgos* *Junta de Defensa Nacional* in the summer of 1936, and in getting Franco* approved as Generalissimo, but he balked at Franco being named head of government.

His argument was that the two positions were too much for one man. It is suggested that Mola would have liked to have been head of government himself.

After a bitter struggle, a column of Mola's army captured Irún,* on September 4, and cut the Basque region off from the French border. His main effort was now to hold his positions in the north and Aragón,* but still, to converge on Madrid. It was during the preparations for the Madrid offensive that he was asked which of his four columns would take Madrid, and he responded that it would be the fifth column of supporters in the city. The term "Fifth Column" is now a part of all languages, but unfortunately the remark was to bring about the deaths of many people in Madrid.

With the failure to capture the capital, Mola returned to the Army of the North.* In December 1936, he was promoted to division general. After the disaster of the battle of Guadalajara* in March 1937, the Nationalist command decided to concentrate its efforts on clearing the enemy from Vizcaya* and strategically important Bilbao.* For this endeavor Mola had a force of some 25,000 men, 200 guns, Spanish and Italian aircraft, as well as the now fully committed German Condor Legion.* The attack began on March 31, 1937. The offensive was painfully slow and frustrating to the German command. It took thirty days to advance 10 miles on a 30-mile front in heavy rains and though high mountains. In May 1937, the Army of the North was increased to about 50,000 men, but it still took several weeks to advance 5 miles from Guernica.* On June 3, as Mola flew to Burgos to confer with Franco, his plane crashed in the fog. German records note that Mola was the spiritual leader of the fighting in the north and that he was knowledgeable of the conditions of the land and a believing fighter. The Germans considered his death a great loss, despite his bitter disagreements with some of the German leaders. Mola was promoted to lieutenant-general the day he died.

General Mola is buried in the Cathedral of Pamplona near his old commander General Sanjurjo.

For further information, see General Alfredo Kindelán, *Mis cuadernos de guerra 1936-1939* (Madrid, 1945); Félix Maiz, *Mola, aquel hombre, diario de la conspiración de 1936* (Barcelona, 1976); Emilio Mola Vidal, *Obras Completas* (Valladolid, 1940) and his *Memorias* (Barcelona, 1976); and Jorge Vigón, *General Mola, el Conspirador* (Barcelona, 1957).

Raymond L. Proctor

MOLERO LOBO, NICOLÁS (1871-1947). Molero was minister of war prior to the Civil War and at the start of the conflict commanded the military forces stationed at Valladolid.* Asked by officers whether he would side with the Republicans* or the Nationalists,* he declared himself a Loyalist.* He was promptly arrested and spent the rest of the war years in jail.

For further details, see Hugh Thomas, *The Spanish Civil War* (New York, 1977).

James W. Cortada

MONARCHISM. Monarchism in Spain represented both a type of government and a quasi-political movement. The Spanish government continued to be a monarchy until April 1931 when the Second Republic* was formed. Except for a brief intermission, with the establishment of the First Republic in the late 1860s, the government in the modern period was a monarchy. By the early decades of the twentieth century, Spain had a parliamentary political system. Prime ministers ruled over daily political and administrative affairs in conjunction with a two-house parliament (Cortes).* The king officially appointed the prime ministers, who, in practice, were heads of the parliamentary party in power. Typically, in the early 1900s, the monarchist element included members of the nobility, the wealthy, high government officials, political conservatives, and philosophers and political sages who believed the monarchy symbolized the unity that was Spain.

During the days of the Republic, supporters of the monarchist state, and specifically of Alfonso XIII,* encouraged efforts to restore the throne and eliminate the new state. After the municipal elections of 1931, Alfonso XIII left Spain without officially abdicating. Thus, supporters of the throne were left without a viable leader. After he left Spain, a republic was formed. From 1931 to mid-1936, the two Spains so frequently conjured up by contemporary writers and later historians became quite evident. In the one Spain were traditionalists, political conservatives, and those who advocated little or no change in the political structure and the country's social and economic institutions. In the other Spain were those who wanted a change in politics and society. They advocated a stronger parliamentary system that could come with the creation of a republic. Never speaking with a united single voice, they were liberals, communists, anarchists,* or simply reformist in views. The image of those who stood for tradition—the monarchists—and those who wanted change—liberals—helped polarize political behavior during the pre-Civil War days of the Republic as, in effect, amorphous groups clustered either to the Right or the Left in national and local politics. Monarchism, while not a formally defined movement or political party, nonetheless reflected an identifiable perspective on national affairs and contributed to a country-wide image.

Clustered within the monarchist camp in what clearly was not a well-defined group were rivals for the throne. Traditional monarchist rivals for the crown were the Carlists* with their pretenders since the 1830s. One hundred years later, and after two civil wars in the nineteenth century, their rivalry continued with Alfonso's supporters. The Carlists were staunchly conservative, often even supposedly reactionary, and militant in their support of the Catholic Church.* The Church itself abhorred the anticlerical stance of many leaders within the Republic and worked to enjoy the support of both monarchist rival camps. Thus, a block of supporters within the monarchist side emerged during the days of the Republic made up loosely of Alfonsoists, Carlists, the Catholic Church, aristocrats, the wealthy in many cases and especially in agriculture, and conservative politicians and thinkers.

With the outbreak of the Civil War, the Nationalists* had the support of the more conservative political sectors, including each element within the monarchist camp along with large portions of the armed services. General Francisco Franco* catered to their prejudices by endorsing the concept of restoring the monarchy at some future date, along with the political institutions necessary to make it function. He suggested that the restoration of the monarchy would include a strong central government managed by a ruling elite, solid support for the army and, in return, its endorsement of the government, and a reduction or elimination of the political influence of radical groups such as the communists, Marxist splinter groups, anarchists, other libertarian elements, and the socialists. The monarchist element advocated nearly totalitarian or centralist reforms in government, a sense of unity with tradition, and a major role for the army, Church, and aristocracy in running the regime.

Opinions on both sides polarized by the end of the summer of 1936. Such monarchist supporters as the Carlists, Navarrese, and Falange* frequently fielded whole divisions within the Nationalist camp. As before the war, there were differences of opinion within this group, and yet there was also less defined commonality of specific thought. Rivalries persisted throughout the war years much as they had in the past. Competition for influence and control within the Nationalist camp represented one of the single most important (though still unstudied) aspects of Spanish politics during the war. This was particularly the case with regard to the rivalries of the Falange with the Carlists and the Alfonsoists. Franco managed to play one group off against another, thereby maintaining control over the entire Nationalist cause, never allowing one element to dominate more over another. Ultimately, by the end of 1939, he was the most important member of the victorious side and held enormous personal power.

For further information, see Martin Blinkhorn, *Carlism and the Crisis in Spain, 1931-1939* (Cambridge, 1975), on the Carlists; Vicente Pilapil, *Alfonso XIII* (New York, 1969), on the Alfonsoists; Hugh Thomas, *The Spanish Civil War* (New York, 1977); and John W. D. Trythall, *El Caudillo: A Political Biography of Franco* (New York, 1970), on Franco.

James W. Cortada

MONASTERIO ITUARTE, JOSÉ (1882-1952). Monasterio, from Palma (Baleares), was an outstanding Nationalist horse cavalry commanding general. Politically, he was a devoted monarchist. He served under General Franco* when Franco commanded the Military Academy at Saragossa.*

With the revolt of 1936, Monasterio was a colonel and one of the key figures in the rising in Saragossa. He commanded a horse cavalry force in a drive south to join with the Army of Africa.* On September 3, 1936, the junction was accomplished at Arenas de San Pedro in the rugged Sierra de los Gredos. He then commanded a Nationalist column for the advance against Madrid.* His horsemen drove to Illescas, 30 kilometers south of Madrid, but on October 29, 1936, they came under attack of Russian aircraft and nine-ton tanks with revolving cannon turrets. This was one of the first uneven battles between cavalry and armor. The cavalrymen, in part, solved the problem with an innovative weapon consisting of petrol and tar-filled bottles with grenades attached. They were able to put some Russian tanks out of action and capture others in a usable condition.

In 1937, Monasterio was promoted to brigade general and was given the added task of commander of the militia and auxiliary forces attached to the Nationalists.* These forces were to a large part to be led by his cavalry officers.

During the battle for Teruel* (December 1936-February 1937), Monasterio commanded a cavalry division in the assault on the Alfambra River. Here was one of the most striking cavalry charges of the Civil War, and it was probably the last such spectacular event in Western Europe.*

He commanded a cavalry corps in the Aragón* offensive in March 1938. There the horsemen rode through very difficult terrain with surprising speed—

so much so that for a time the Nationalist command lost all contact with two cavalry brigades. During this operation, Monasterio's forces were supported by the German Condor Legion.*

In 1943, Monasterio was one of the eight lieutenant generals who wrote a letter to Generalissimo Franco, in a futile appeal, to have the monarchy restored. He died in Valencia on December 4, 1952.

For further information, see Manuel Aznar, *Historia militar de la guerra de España* (Madrid, 1958-1963); and R. Casas de la Vega, *Brunete* (Madrid, 1967), and *Teruel* (Madrid, 1975).

Raymond L. Proctor

MONETARY POLICY, NATIONALIST. The division of Spain into two zones provoked monetary and fiscal confusion. These areas, while independent of each other politically and militarily, were linked by a common economic and financial structure (one currency, a single network of banking facilities, and a unified monetary, credit, and financial system) which forced the Nationalists* to restructure immediately an independent monetary system within the territory they controlled.

When the war erupted, the branches of the Bank of Spain* located in the rebel areas had to adopt emergency measures, for their links with the administrative center of the Bank of Spain in Madrid* had been interrupted. There were weeks of great confusion as each local administration attempted to deal with the situation in the best manner possible. Nevertheless, those responsible for Nationalist finances had to coordinate the situation of the various branches, take stock of their assets, and adopt a minimum plan of action for monetary affairs. In August 1936, they created a National Commission for Private Banking for the purpose of directing and unifying banking and credit policy. A little later (on September 24), the Council of the Bank of Spain met in Burgos* under the presidency of the first subgovernor, Pedro Pan, attended by all the council members connected with the bank within the Nationalist zone.

One of the most difficult problems which the council had to face was that of money circulation: an attempt was made to "isolate" the bills in use in rebel-held territory, differentiating them from those in circulation within the Republican zone. A second problem was to make sure that sufficient bills were in circulation to meet commercial demands. At the beginning of the war, the second problem was the most pressing because the money supply in the Bank of Spain's branches in the Nationalist zone did not exceed 393 million pesetas in paper currency and 123 million in silver.

The first few months of the war were marked by a sense of "interim" status for the financial community within the Nationalist zone. The rebel forces' rapid advance towards Madrid and the consequent hope of a quick end to the uprising seemed to make it unnecessary to reorganize in a more complete form the managerial cadres of the Bank of Spain. However, the failure of the attack on the capital in November 1936 and the prospect of a prolonged conflict made it necessary to think of an institutional and legal structure in the full sense of these terms. Beginning in December, personnel sympathetic to the Republic felt the impact of dismissal. The situation remained transitory until March 1938 when a new governor was appointed for the Bank of Spain, the well-known financier and monarchist leader Antonio Goicoechea,* as well as a new group of government representatives in the bank, of whom the most outstanding was José Larraz, future minister of finance. In December 1938, at a special meeting of the general stockholders of the bank, held in Santander,* the main concern was to develop an approach to be made before international courts to reclaim the assets (gold and deposits) of the bank abroad.

The two basic concerns of the bank of Spain in Burgos were, logically, the separation of the monetary system in its zone from that of the Republican area, and the interior and exterior financing of the Nationalists' war expenditures. In terms of monetary policy, the first important measure was taken in September 1936 which, in addition to limiting credit levels, consisted of rediscounting rates available in the Bank of Spain and establishing 1,500 pesetas as the maximum sum that could be withdrawn from checking and credit accounts by private individuals. This was done in order to avoid a massive run on bank deposits.

With regard to paper currency, the bank attempted to separate entirely the one from the other in the two zones so that the Nationalist authorities would have full control of the monetary circulation in their territory. Undoubtedly, the most pressing need was to expand the money supply. Later, as Franco's troops incorporated additional territories into Nationalist Spain, the key problem was to isolate the monetary circulation in the two zones from each other in order to avoid massive and destabilizing movements of currency from one zone to the other.

In order to resolve both problems—availability of money and its isolation from Republican currency—it proved necessary to identify the money circulating as legal tender in both zones—hence, the issuance of

Nationalist paper money to replace Republican bills. In order to achieve this objective, in October 1936 the bank began discussions with the normal suppliers of bills to the Bank of Spain in London. These talks proved fruitless as the British firms preferred to maintain their relations with the Republic. Consequently, the Burgos government turned to Germany,* specifically to the firm of Gieseke and Devrient of Leipzig, which agreed to print the new issues. This money, dated November 21, 1936, was ready for distribution by March 1937.

Inasmuch as a delay of several months would be inevitable before the new bills could circulate, emergency measures had to be taken to separate the old bills circulating in the Nationalist zone from those in the Republican sector. Hence, in November 1936, the Nationalist Bank of Spain and the Finance Commission required that all paper money in circulation in Nationalist territory bear an imprint (designed for the purpose) of the Burgos government superimposed on the old bills in order to be legal tender. This stamping was limited to bills issued prior to July 18, for Republican issues after that date were declared valueless as currency of exchange. Starting in March 1937, the Burgos government placed new bills in circulation, and at the same time the Nationalist Bank of Spain issued a decree requiring that paper money with the superimposed stamp be exchanged for the new paper currency.

The Nationalist government placed in circulation two important issues of new bills, one dated November 1936 and another, increased in May 1936. A still more important and final issuance came in July 1938. Two issuances were printed in Germany, while the third was ordered in Italy* and eventually canceled. Apart from these issues and in order to provide currency for payments of small amounts, in view of the scarcity of coin, six emissions were effected consisting of the so-called fractioned paper in amounts of 1, 2, 5, and 10 pesetas.

An urgent concern of the Bank of Spain in Burgos was rapidly to increase its treasury holdings with a parallel augmentation of checking and savings accounts. With these objectives in mind, the same decree of November 1936 which required the stamping of paper money in circulation also permitted holders in the Nationalist zone to choose between having their paper money stamped or depositing them in a checking account. In the latter case, accounts could be drawn on freely with no limitation on the amounts that could be withdrawn at any given moment. As Professor Juan Sardá has pointed out, this allowed the bank to channel an important part of funds in circulation into bank accounts, thus avoiding excessive expansion of funds in circulation outside banks. The measure resulted in a total increase of some 900 million pesetas in the Bank of Spain's holdings.

While at the start of the war total accounts in the Bank of Spain for the entire nation amounted to 1,128 million pesetas, on December 31, 1937 (the date of the first balance sheet of the Bank of Spain in Burgos), the sum for the Nationalist sector was considerably greater, amounting to 1,715 million pesetas. Paper money in circulation (outside of banks) totaled only 3,405 million, while those exchanged amounted to 3,223 million. These figures reflect the Nationalist authorities' initial effort to limit the volume of currency circulation and to rebuild a healthier structure in the money market, one based on bank deposits with preference to legal tender in the public's hands. It should not be concluded, however, that the Nationalists succeeded in maintaining monetary stability. From 1937 onward, the policy of covering deficit financing by the Ministry of Finance through advances by the Bank of Spain no doubt contributed to the excessive rise in monetary circulation (5,580 million pesetas in December 1938 and 8,707 million by the end of the war), which, obviously, by affecting the limited offer of goods and services translated into a substantial increase in prices. This development has led some historians to conclude that the basic cost of the Civil War was financed mainly by inflation.

Later in the war as the Nationalists occupied additional areas, the Burgos government faced the problem of dealing with the paper currency in circulation and the bank balances in the conquered zones. Both of the latter were very substantial as a result of inflation in the Republican zone and could provoke excessive increases in monetary availabilities in the Nationalist zone. For the paper currency, the same procedure previously described was followed for bills issued before July 18, 1936, as well as cancellation of those released after that date. But for the bank balances the matter of conversion was undoubtedly more complicated. This situation acquired considerable urgency after the Nationalist authorities issued a decree on October 13, 1938, blocking the balances of all checking and savings accounts opened after July 18, 1936. For accounts established prior to that date, the blockage affected only those exceeding balances in effect on July 18.

The volume of paper money in circulation in the Republican zone was always a constant worry to the Nationalist authorities. A memorandum of the Ministry of Treasury (Finance) dated July 1940 estimated this volume to be in excess of 13,000 million pesetas during the war, to which had to be added as the sources of additional problems frozen obligations in banks. The same memorandum indicated that the total of balances frozen by virtue of the law of 1938 amounted to 9,000 million pesetas.

Of course, the freezing of the balances was only a temporary solution, for after the war the matter needed to be resolved either by recognizing their value to the holders or through cancellation. In order to solve the problem definitely, a law dealing with the unfreezing issue was promulgated in December 1939. The law recognized the worth of the bank balances accumulated in the Republican zone during the war in accordance with a scale of values.

With respect to financing the war in the Nationalist zone, the Burgos Bank of Spain effected substantial advances to the Ministry of Finance in order to cover the deficit between receipts and expenditures. Such advances, according to the Ministry of Finance's 1940 memorandum, amounted to 7,600 million pesetas, to which must be added another 2,500 million extended between April and September 1939, which, even if made after the Civil War, must be included in the latter's cost.

With regard to meeting foreign obligations, it should be pointed out that almost from the beginning of the conflict (August 1936) the Nationalist government prohibited the sale and export of gold, foreign exchange, and foreign assets, as well as the hoarding of precious metals. Some time later (March 1937), Burgos required that all Spanish subjects convey to the state gold and foreign exchange in their possession, as well as placing at the pleasure of the government foreign assets or Spanish assets marketable in foreign countries within their ownership. A series of subsequent measures regulated these obligations, completing the cycle through the freezing of peseta balances owned by foreigners or foreign interests, and additional measures tended to center in the state all foreign exchange and foreign assets that could be used to pay the regime's foreign debts. In order to center decisions affecting foreign exchange matters, already in November 1936, the Nationalists had created the Committee for Foreign Exchange, which in Nationalist areas replaced the defunct Committee for Foreign Exchange. The Nationalist committee assumed the task of publishing foreign exchange rates requiring private parties to convey to it within a period of eight days foreign exchange in their possession for whatever reason. Toward the end of 1938, Burgos promulgated a severe law concerning monetary violations which penalized by threats of fines and pressures designed to reduce illegal holding of foreign exchange and foreign assets, as well as unauthorized

transactions with foreign markets. With these measures and those previously cited regarding monetary policy, the new Nationalist regime developed a rigorous system for monetary and financial control. This system continued for many years after the Civil War ended.

For further information, see Bank of Spain, *Los billetes del Banco de España* (Madrid, 1979); Fernando Eguidazu, *Intervención monetaria y control de cambios 1900-1977* (Madrid, 1978); Enrique Fuentes Quintana and Cesar Albiñana, *Sistema fiscal español y comparado*, 2 vols. (Madrid, 1961); Juan Sardá, "El Banco de España 1931-1962," in *El Banco de España, una historia económica* (Madrid, 1970); Robert Whealey, "How Franco Financed His War—Reconsidered," *Journal of Contemporary History* 12 (January 1977): 133-52.

See also Economy, Nationalist; Economy, Republican; and Peseta, Nationalist and Republican.

Fernando Eguidazu

MONTALBÁN. Montalbán, in the province of Teruel,* was the site of a great deal of fighting during the Civil War. The town is located near the Ebro* in an area that became a frontline location for both the Republicans* and Nationalists* trying either to retain control over Aragón* and Catalonia,* or to capture them. Heavy fighting took place at the end of the summer of 1936 and again during the campaigns in Aragón and the Levante* during March-July 1938. From March 13, 1938 onward, the town remained in Nationalist hands.

For further information, see José Manuel Martínez Bande, *La batalla de Teruel* (Madrid, 1974).

James W. Cortada

MONTAÑA BARRACKS. The Montaña Barracks were army barracks in Madrid* near the Plaza de España at the high end of the Gran Vía. Workers in Madrid attacked the building in July 1936 demanding arms from the soldiers inside. They overran the barracks, executed many officers, and seized nearly 50,000 rifles and large quantities of ammunition. For the rest of the Civil War, Republican military units used the facilities.

For further information, see Robert Colodny, *The Struggle for Madrid* (New York, 1958).

James W. Cortada

MONTAÑA PROJECT. The Montaña Project refers to a German plan in 1938 to acquire mining interests in Spain. By this means, Berlin hoped to insure a steady supply of iron ore to Germany* from Spain. The Nationalists,* reluctant to become too dependent on the Germans, issued a decree on October 9 canceling any titles to mines not owned by Spaniards acquired since July 1936. Over the protests of the Germans, Franco* remained adamant in not allowing Hitler* to control a major natural resource of Spain.

For further information, see Glenn T. Harper, *German Economic Policy in Spain* (The Hague, 1967).
See also Bernhardt, Johannes.

James W. Cortada

MONTANER CANET, FEDERICO. Montaner, a career army officer, sided with the Nationalists.* For much of the war, Colonel Montaner served as the aide-de-camp to General Fidel Dávila Arrondo,* one of Franco's* most important commanders. In this capacity, Montaner was assigned to the Army of the North* which fought throughout the Basque area and in Catalonia.*

For further information, see José Manuel Martínez Bande, *La guerra en el norte* (Madrid, 1969).

James W. Cortada

MONT DE MARSAN. At Mont de Marsan, located in France,* gold belonging to the Spanish Republic remained on deposit during the Civil War. Approximately $48 million was deposited there, representing roughly 7 percent of the Republic's gold reserves.

For further information, see Angel Viñas, *El oro de Moscú* (Madrid, 1979) and his earlier study, *El oro español en la guerra civil* (Madrid, 1976).
See also Bank of Spain; Economy, Republican; and Monetary Policy, Nationalist.

James W. Cortada

MONTEIRO, ARMINDO. Monteiro was the Portuguese foreign minister during the Spanish Civil War. He developed Lisbon's policy of support for the Nationalists,* while actively pursuing a diplomacy of nonintervention within the League of Nations* and the Non-Intervention Committee.* His primary interest lay in maintaining close contacts with the side that won the Civil War, yet favoring Franco's* cause at the instruction of Antonio Salazar,* head of the Portuguese government.

For further information, see Hugh Kay, *Salazar and Modern Portugal* (New York, 1970); and Portugal, *Dez años de política externa (1936-1947)* (Lisbon, 1965), Vol. 3.
See also Portugal.

James W. Cortada

MONTSENY, FEDERICA. Montseny, born in Catalonia,* was a leading anarchist during the 1930s and one of the more important female politicians of the Spanish Civil War. In the 1920s, she became interested in left-wing politics and in 1928, after her father had been arrested on suspicion of being a subversive, she joined the year-old *Federación Anarquista Ibérica* (FAI),* which was then a small anarchist organization. She quickly lent her writing skills as journalist and orator to anarchism and the FAI. Intellectually better prepared than many other anarchist thinkers, she articulated a strong case for the movement years before the Civil War began. By 1931, for example, she had concluded that anarchism was the only vehicle open to labor for improving their lot in life. Concurrently, Montseny found much to criticize in the Second Republic,* which she felt was not doing enough for workers.

Montseny frequently argued that if a society failed to permit individuals to develop their own plans as part of a general contribution to a country, then that person or group of people had the right to overthrow the existing political system. However, she did not believe that an organization should provide an elite to accomplish this mission, feeling instead that reform has to emanate from below, not from the top. Thus, she found the syndicalists,* the Leninists, and other more institutionalized movements too rigorous for her taste. Instead she sought a more unstructured movement, such as libertarian communism, which focused more closely on the role of the individual in a position of great freedom intent on accomplishing personal objectives.

As the FAI grew in importance, primarily in Barcelona* but also in other cities during the 1930s, so did Montseny's significance within the anarchist movement. When the Civil War began, she helped recruit one of the first anarchist militia columns, known as the *Tierra y Libertad* (Land and Liberty), while convincing other anarchist leaders that they should join the Catalan regional government in Barcelona. In November 1936, her arguments won over other anarchists,* and so she was able to join the Catalan government as its minister of health. The first woman in Spanish history to be a member of a cabinet, she proved to be an active and competent politician working to develop good relations among the government, the *Confederación Nacional del Trabajo* (CNT),* the *Unión General de Trabajadores* (UGT),* and the FAI in order to prosecute the war. She proved instrumental in convincing the anarchist militia columns under the command of Buenaventura Durruti* to leave the Aragón* front to help defend Madrid* at its most critical moment of crisis with Franco's* armies poised at its gates. Later, she joined the Republican cabinet as minister of health, retaining this post until the anarchists fell from power in mid-1937, helping to expand medical services and child care centers and to improve standards of hygiene. She was a competent administrator, able to attend to her ministry's affairs while continuing to play an active role in national politics.

The political crisis which spelled the death of anarchist power in Republican Spain came in the spring of 1937. Locked in a political struggle with its enemies, and primarily the more disciplined communists, the FAI and other anarchist organizations were soon involved in a mini-civil war against their foes in the streets of Barcelona in May 1937. Throughout the few days of fighting and the weeks of crisis before, Montseny urged some accommodation to the anarchist position by the Republic. Once this effort failed, she tried to end the street fighting but to no avail. By May 8, the fighting was ending as the anarchists lost power. Now the Republican government sought to expand its direct control over the affairs of Catalonia and decrease the influence of the local government. Communist influence expanded rapidly as well. From then on, anarchism had no control over its affairs and could only conform to the will of others. Although she urged the firing of Juan Negrín,* the prime minister who had done so much to reduce the power of the anarchists, she could do little to affect the course of events in Spain. After the war, she went into exile in Toulouse, France,* and did not return to Spain until after Franco's death.

For further information, see Shirley Fredricks, "Federica Montseny," in Jane Slaughter and Robert Kern, eds., *European Women on the Left: Feminism, Socialism and the Problems Faced by Political Women, 1880 to the Present* (Westport, Conn., 1981); Robert W. Kern, *Red Years/Black Years: A Political History of Spanish Anarchism, 1911-1937* (Philadelphia, 1978); Federica Montseny, *Cent días de la vida d'una dona* (Barcelona, 1976); and Hugh Thomas, *The Spanish Civil War* (New York, 1977).

See also May 1937 Riots.

James W. Cortada

MOORS. Derived from the Greek word *Mauros* to designate the peoples of ancient Mauritania, Moor is an archaic and general term applied to the mixed Arab and Berber populace of northwest Africa. Through the centuries, the Spanish used the term to refer to almost anyone of the Islamic faith. By the twentieth century, however, they had limited its use primarily to the inhabitants of their Moroccan Protectorate and, in particular, to those Moroccans who fought with the Nationalists* during the Spanish Civil War. These Moroccans were drawn mainly from the protectorate's sixty-nine rural *kabyles* (tribes) and were known for their military prowess and their fierce independence. Through eighteen years of bloody colonial war, they both opposed the Spanish occupation of northern Morocco* and, as members of the Army of Africa's* indigenous forces, helped to subjugate it.

Participating on both sides of this conflict, they perpetuated an already well-established reputation for brutality. According to reliable Spanish accounts, during the Riff Rebellion of 1921-1926, Abd-el-Krim's fighters showed little inclination to take prisoners,* preferring instead to kill them and then mutilate their bodies. (Admittedly, many of these actions were the consequence of wartime exigencies as well as retribution for equally appalling Spanish atrocities.) This reputation was further enhanced during the Asturian "Revolution" of October 1934. To crush the workers' uprising, the Republican government brought in units of Moorish *Regulares* and legionnaires from the protectorate. In some instances, these troops were loosened upon recalcitrant mining villages and committed random acts of murder, rape, and pillage.

When segments of the Spanish Army rose up against the Second Republic* in July 1936, the protectorate's indigenous population rallied to their cause. In fact, the Moorish *Regulares* were a particularly notable element of this rebellion, and for the Nationalist rebels they constituted a doubly potent force: first because of their location, numerical strength, and military preparedness; and second, because of the psychological fear they generated among the Spanish people.

At the beginning of the war, the first factor was of paramount importance. In July 1936, Moorish *Regulares* and *Mehal-las* (militia) constituted approximately one-half of the Army of Africa,* or 17,009 men out of a total force of 34,047 men. They were organized into five groups of *Fuerzas Regulares Indígenas* and five groups of *Mehal-las*—each group based in one of the protectorate's five administrative-military regions. The *Fuerzas Regulares Indígenas* were composed of three infantry *tabores* (batallions), one cavalry *tabor*, and one supply company. The *Mehal-las* contained from two to six infantry *tabores* and, depending on the unit, one cavalry *tabor*.

Once these men were airlifted (with German and Italian help) across the Straits of Gibraltar* in August-November 1936, they gave the Nationalists* crucial military superiority in southern Spain. During the Civil War, their numbers doubled. At any one time there were approximately 34,800 Moroccans serving in the Iberian Peninsula, and it has been estimated that between July 1936 and April 1939 a total of 62,271 Moroccans fought in Spain.

The second factor became increasingly important during the course of the Civil War. As rumors spread concerning real or fabricated atrocities, the very presence of Moroccan troops at a front gave the Nationalists a psychological edge. In a few instances, whole Republican units were known to have deserted their posts at the suggestion that they would be facing Moorish troops. And numerous Spanish villages were abandoned in a panic at the least rumor of advancing Moors.

The Moroccans were willing to serve in the Nationalist ranks for a variety of reasons, including (1) the close and personal relationship that Spanish Army personnel, particularly the tribal *interventores*, had developed with rural Berber notables; (2) the army's importance as the employer of substantial numbers of Moroccans; (3) the Nationalist recognition of the Moroccan independence movement, and, in turn, its approval of the Nationalist Crusade;* and (4) the Moroccans' acceptance of Nationalist propaganda which portrayed the Republic as a godless, secular state.

As part of the Army of Africa, the Moors participated in the Nationalist uprising in the protectorate in July 1936, the quick subjugation of southwestern Spain in August-September 1936, the relief of Toledo* in late September 1936, and the sanguine siege of Madrid* in the winter of 1936-1937. As the Madrid front lost its transcendent importance in 1937, Moorish units were apportioned among the various corps and divisions. Between 1937 and 1939, they served on all the significant battlefronts.

Following the Nationalist victory in April 1939, all the Moroccans who were still in the peninsula were returned to the protectorate. The only exception was Francisco Franco's* personal Moorish guard which was not disbanded until late 1957, a year after Morocco* achieved its independence.

For further information, see Angel Domenech Lafuente, *Un oficial entre moros* (Larache, 1948); José María Gárate Córdoba, *La Guerra de las dos Españas* (Madrid, 1976); and Hugh Thomas, *The Spanish Civil War* (New York, 1977).

See also Army, Nationalist.

Shannon E. Fleming

MORAYTA NÚÑEZ, RAFAEL. Morayta was secretary general of the Institute of Agrarian Reform.* Thus, this communist had part of the responsibility, within the Republican Ministry of Agriculture, to expand the program of agricultural collectives, a process that led many farmers to believe that the government was less interested in their welfare than in that of the state.

For further information, see Enrique Castro Delgado, *Hombres made in Moscú* (Barcelona, 1965).

James W. Cortada

MOREAU, RUDOLPH V. Moreau was a German Air Force officer who transported thousands of Franco's* soldiers from North Africa to Spain in July and August 1936. This made it possible for the Nationalists* to launch their successful campaign to occupy large portions of southern Spain during the early months of the Civil War. This skillful pilot also gained some fame during the war by dropping supplies into the Alcázar* at Toledo* during September 1936 while it was being besieged by Republican forces. He also helped bomb Guernica* on April 26, 1937, as a member of the Condor Legion.*

For further information, see Max von Hoyos, *Pedros y Pablos* (Munich, 1941).

James W. Cortada

MORENO, JOSÉ. Moreno was born in Navarre* and early in the life of the Falange* party became a regional leader. By the time of the Civil War, he was serving as a member of the party's top *Junta*. He also continued to run the local party in Pamplona* throughout the 1930s.

For further information, see Stanley G. Payne, *Falange: A History of Spanish Fascism* (Stanford, Calif., 1961).

James W. Cortada

MORENO Y FERNÁNDEZ, FRANCISCO (1883-1945). Moreno was a career naval officer in the Nationalist service. He was born to a naval family in San Fernando (Cádiz)* on November 7, 1883, and entered the navy in 1898. Captain Moreno was a leader in the uprising in El Ferrol* in July 1936, and was named to the *Junta de Defensa Nacional* as its naval representative on July 30. He quickly prepared Nationalist warships in El Ferrol for combat and led the Nationalist squadron to victory in the battle of Cape Espartel* (September 29, 1936). Moreno continued as operational commander of the Nationalist fleet after Vice-Admiral Juan Cervera* took over administrative and strategic responsibilities as naval chief of staff in October 1936. Moreno remained in Cádiz-Mediterranean waters with his flagships *Canarias** or *Baleares** and personally commanded in several naval engagements. On July 29, 1937, Moreno was formally promoted to rear admiral, responsibilities he had already been exercising. On October 10, 1937, he was promoted to vice-admiral and was given charge of the fleet reorganized as the Blockade Forces of the Mediterranean, which he usually commanded from Palma de Majorca,* maintaining this post until the end of the war. Moreno died in El Ferrol on January 21, 1945.

For further information, see Francisco Moreno, *La guerra en el mar* (Barcelona, 1959).
See also Navy, Spanish.

Willard C. Frank, Jr.

MORIONES LARRAGA, DOMINGO (1883-1964).
Moriones, one of the few noblemen to remain loyal to the Republic, was born in 1883 and succeeded his father as Marqués de Oroquieta in 1894. He made the army his career and had risen to the rank of lieutenant colonel by the start of the military uprising. During the first days of the Civil War, he fought in the hills north of Madrid.* He later took part in the battles of Segovia* and Guadalajara* before he was transferred to the Army of Andalusia.* He remained there until Colonel Casado* removed him in the last weeks of the war. He went into exile after the war, remaining in Latin America until his death in 1964.

For further information, see Luis Romero, *El final de la guerra* (Barcelona, 1976); Ramón Salas Larrazábal, *Historia del ejército popular*, 4 vols. (Madrid, 1973); and Cristobal Zaragoza, *Los generales del pueblo* (Barcelona, 1977), on his wartime activities.

William J. Irwin

MOROCCO, SPANISH.
Spanish Morocco was a 20,693 square kilometer protectorate officially established by a French-Spanish agreement in November 1912. Constituting approximately 20 percent of Morocco, it included a small northern littoral along the Atlantic and Mediterranean coasts.

Administratively, the Moroccan sultan was represented by a caliph who in fact was subordinate to the Spanish high commissioner. Except for a short period in 1923 and again during the Second Republic* when the military and the civilian functions were legally separated, the various high commissioners were army major generals and much of the protectorate's bureaucracy was staffed by army officers. After its complete pacification in 1927, the protectorate was divided into five administrative/military territories centering on the cities of Tetuán,* Larache, Xauen, Villa Sanjurjo, and Melilla-Nador. In 1935, the total population* was estimated to be 795,300.

From 1912 to 1927, the protectorate witnessed a period of fierce indigenous resistance to the Spanish occupation which culminated in Abd-el-Krim's rebellion of 1921-1926. At that time the Army of Africa,* as it was called, grew to over 100,000 men, adding important units of indigenous and foreign troops. Despite efforts during the Second Republic to civilianize the protectorate, it endured as a military enclave and provided both the physical location and the personnel for the military uprising of July 17-18, 1936. During the course of the Civil War, the protectorate continued to furnish the Nationalists* with large numbers of indigenous troops, a safe haven to train its personnel, and substantial amounts of iron ore and lead for foreign exchange. Following the war, the protectorate remained a Spanish possession until its incorporation into independent Morocco in April 1956.

For further information, see Tomás García Figueras and Juan L. Fernández-Llebrez, *La zona española del Protectorado de Marruecos* (Madrid, 1955); Víctor Morales Lezcano, *El colonialismo hispanofrancés en Marruecos (1898-1927)* (Madrid, 1976); and Miguel Martín, *El colonialismo español en Marruecos (1860-1957)* (Paris, 1973).
See also Melilla.

Shannon E. Fleming

MOSCARDÓ ITUARTE, JOSÉ (1878-1956).
Moscardó, a career army officer, served as the commander of Franco's* forces at the famous siege of the Alcázar* in September 1936. This colonel of infantry, stationed in Toledo* at the start of the Civil War, rose in rebellion against the Republic. Very quickly, he moved into the Alcázar, the school of infantry for the Spanish officer corps, with about 1,300 people. The Republicans* laid siege to the Alcázar until late September when Franco's forces relieved Moscardó. He repeatedly refused to surrender, despite lack of food* and water, and the constant assault on his fortress. This famous siege,

which received wide attention all over Spain and quickly became a symbol of Nationalist resistance to the Republicans, was made even more dramatic by a telephone call. On July 23, the Republicans captured Moscardó's twenty-four-year old son, Luis, called the colonel, and threatened to shoot the hostage if the Alcázar did not surrender. The colonel told his son, "commend your soul to God, shout *Viva España*, and die like a hero," hanging up the telephone. The son was executed the following month but in reprisal for an air raid and not because of his father's actions. Nevertheless, the episode made the officer a hero.

This quiet officer of perhaps average ability had been destined for an uneventful military career until the siege of the Alcázar. He soon took command of troops at the battle of Guadalajara* (March 1937), a corps during the Nationalist campaign in Aragón* between March and July 1938, and led the Army of the Aragón* during the final campaign in Catalonia (December 1938-February 1939). His men closed the border with France* to fleeing Republicans on February 9, 1939, ending the war in the north for all intents and purposes.

Moscardó was born in Madrid* and first served in the Philippines in 1897. He fought in North Africa just before World War I and during the 1920s had tours of duty in Toledo. After the Civil War, he was promoted to lieutenant general (1943) and became captain general of Catalonia (1943-1945). In 1946, he served in the same capacity in Andalusia.* In 1948, he became the Conde del Alcázar de Toledo.

For further information, see Círculo de Amigos de la Historia, *Diccionario biográfico español contemporaneo* (Madrid, 1970), Vol. 2; Cecil Eby, *The Siege of the Alcázar* (London, 1966); and Antonio Vilanova, *La defensa del Alcázar de Toledo* (Mexico, 1963), on the Alcázar.

James W. Cortada

MOVIES. Movies were important in the propaganda campaigns of both the Nationalists* and Republicans* during the Civil War. Between 1936 and 1939, forty-seven films were made in Nationalist Spain, and 255 in the Republican zone; forty-eight partisan films on the Civil War were produced in other countries. Commercial films from Hollywood also remained a popular diversion in both zones, but to many Madrileños enemy shelling seemed to coincide with the time the cinema let out.

Most of the films produced during the Civil War were short documentaries. On the Republican side, virtually every political group and several ministries brought out films, but the most prolific were the communists and anarchists,* each of which sponsored nearly seventy movies. The communists and anarchists used their films to advance their own ideology as well as to urge an all-out commitment to victory. Most of the Republican documentaries were characterized by moral fervor, political advocacy, and appeals for civic cooperation in the war effort. Only about a third of the films made in Republican Spain survived a fire of suspicious origin in August 1945, and these are today preserved in the *Filmoteca* in Madrid.

Perhaps the best known films sympathetic to the Republican cause were made by foreigners, including *Sierra de Teruel (L'Espoir)* directed by André Malraux* and *Spanish Earth* directed by Joris Ivens and narrated by Ernest Hemingway.* Malraux worked in Spain with a subsidy provided by the Republic, but events overtook the release of the film—which was hurriedly finished in early 1939—and it was not effective propaganda. *Spanish Earth*, on the other hand, was completed in 1937 and was frequently shown in the United States* at Republican fund-raising rallies. In England, Ivor Montagu produced four documentaries, one of which, *Spanish ABC*, about literacy campaigns, caused a furor when screened in Geneva during a League of Nations* debate on Spain. Hollywood supported the Republic in various ways: some eight actors, writers, and directors signed an open letter to President Roosevelt* in February 1937 protesting the Nationalist bombing of Barcelona;* a rally in the summer of 1937 raised $1.5 million for the Republic; and three full-length feature films were made in defense of the Republican cause—*Last Train from Madrid* (1937), *Love Under Fire* (1937), and *Blockade* (1938). In *Blockade*, produced by Walter Wanger, Henry Fonda played a member of the International Brigades* who at the end of the film delivers an impassioned soliloquy praising the Republic and denouncing the Non-Intervention Agreement.

Nationalist films were sponsored by the *Falange Española*,* the *Requetes*,* and the *Departamento Nacional de Cinematografía*. The last-named was established in April 1938 to coordinate the political content of films with the emerging ideology of Franco.* A year earlier, in March 1937, Franco had established the *Junta nacional de censura cinematográfica* to control the film industry. Censorship was heavyhanded in the early years of the regime, and among the many stars whose films were banned were Bing Crosby, Bette Davis, and Douglas Fairbanks, Jr. Italy,* Germany,* and Portugal* supplied movies favorable to the Nationalists, with Italy producing the most numerous pro-Franco films (fifteen). Two full-length movies were made by the Nationalists, including *Romancero Marroqui*, an homage to the Moors* who fought in the Civil War.

For further information, see Anthony Aldgate, *Cinema and History: British Newsreels and the Spanish Civil War* (London, 1979); José María Caparrós Lera, *El cine republicano español, 1931-1939* (Barcelona, 1977); Carlos Fernández Cuenca, *La guerra de España y el cine* (Madrid, 1972); and José Enrique Monterde and Esteve Riambau, "La guerra civil en el cine," *Nueva Historia* 2 (September 1978): 30-39.

See also Literature.

David V. Holtby

MUEDRA MIÑÓN, FÉLIX (1895-   ). Muedra was a colonel in the Republican Army.* He became chief of staff to General Manuel Matallana Gómez,* who commanded four armies in central Spain toward the end of the Civil War. Historians suspect that Muedra contemplated surrendering some of these troops to the Nationalists* on his own initiative near the end of the war because he did talk to representatives of General Franco.* However, the Nationalist leader would not entertain any proposals for a compromised peace and so the talks broke off.

For further information, see José Manuel Martínez Bande, *Los cien últimos días de la república* (Barcelona, 1972).

James W. Cortada

MÚGICA Y URRESTARAZU, BISHOP MATEO (1870-1968). Múgica, bishop of Vitoria,* one of the most controversial of Spain's bishops during the Second Republic* and Civil War, was a Basque, born in Idiazabal, Guipúzcoa* on September 21, 1870. He was named bishop of Osma in 1918, bishop of Pamplona* in 1924, and bishop of Vitoria in 1928.

Múgica's first prominent political role came in 1931 when, before the municipal elections that led to the overthrow of the monarchy, he issued a pastoral letter to his faithful clearly forbidding them to vote for any but monarchist candidates under penalty of mortal sin. This was the most extreme statement made by any churchman during the campaign, and after the Republicans* came to power he was expelled from Spain.

By 1933, Múgica had returned to his diocese and had become an ardent supporter of the Basque separatist movement. When the war began in July 1936, he once again became the focus of controversy. Because the Catholic Basques continued to support the anticlerical and Catholic-persecuting Republic, the pri-

mate, Cardinal Isidro Gomá,* wrote a pastoral letter condemning such support, and he asked Múgica and Bishop Marcelino Olaechea* of Pamplona* to sign it. Múgica sent his vicar-general to Pamplona to meet with Gomá and to return with a copy of the letter. Múgica then agreed to sign it, and Gomá had the contents broadcast by radio* in August 1936. The Basques refused to accept the authenticity of a pastoral letter released in such a fashion, so Gomá told Múgica to order his priests to read the letter from their pulpits. Múgica refused, arguing that such action would place his priests' lives in jeopardy, although he claimed that he himself supported the Nationalists.*

The Nationalist military *Junta* asked Múgica to come to Burgos.* He refused, fearing that Falangists would use his visit as a pretext to assassinate him for his support of Basque separatism. The military then demanded his expulsion from Spain, and Gomá was called in to intercede. He was able to persuade Múgica to go to Rome in October 1936, and a year later Múgica resigned his see.

Múgica remained in Rome for the remainder of the Civil War. He refused to sign the Bishops' Collective Letter in 1937. After the war, he justified the apparent contradictions in his actions by claiming that he did not have full knowledge of the facts at the time. Some years later, he returned to Spain and lived in retirement at Zarauz, Guipúzcoa, where he died on October 27, 1968.

For further information, see Juan de Iturralde, *El catolicismo y la cruzada de Franco* (Vienna, 1955, 1960); and Mateo Múgica, *Imperativos de mi conciencia* (Buenos Aires, 1945).

See also Basque Nationalism; and Catholic Church, Spanish.

José M. Sánchez

***MUNDO OBRERO* (1936-1939).** *Mundo Obrero* was the official newspaper of the Spanish Communist party* throughout the Civil War. Its editor, Jesús Hernández Tomás,* made it one of the major newspapers in the Republican zone as the influence of the Communist party grew between 1937 and 1938.

For further information, see Burnett Bolloten, *The Spanish Revolution: The Left and the Struggle for Power During the Civil War* (Chapel Hill, N.C., 1979).

James W. Cortada

MUNICH CONFERENCE. The Munich Conference was held in September 1938 to decide the fate of the German-populated portions of Czechoslovakia.* In effect, the British and French governments allowed Hitler* to divide Czechoslovakia, taking over the German-speaking portion. The conference had the following consequences for Spain. (1) Germany* realized it could now commit enough resources to insure a Nationalist victory, knowing France* and Great Britain* would not fight Hitler over Spain, (2) the Republic acknowledged its willingness to negotiate a mediated peace, yet feared a partitioned Spain, (3) Franco* determined to fight until he won the war, concerned that a mediated settlement might result in two Spanish governments, and (4) Munich encouraged the British to offer mediation in Spain, which was rejected by all parties concerned.

For further information, see Jesús Salas Larrazábal, *Intervención extranjera en la guerra de España* (Madrid, 1974), and Dante Puzzo, *Spain and the Great Powers, 1936-1941* (New York, 1962).

See also Germany; League of Nations; and Non-Intervention Committee.

James W. Cortada

MUÑOZ, MANUEL. Muñoz was the director of security in 1936 for Madrid.* While in this position, he did little to stop the late-night executions of the Republic's supposed enemies by young militiamen in Madrid. He was soon replaced and played no other significant role in the Civil War.

For further information, see Robert Colodny, *The Struggle for Madrid* (New York, 1958).

James W. Cortada

MUÑOZ GRANDES, AGUSTÍN (1896-1970). Muñoz Grandes was a Castilian from Carabanchel* (Madrid)* who was a Nationalist Army* Corps commander during the Civil War. He was to hold far more important positions in Nationalist Spain from the end of the war until his death in Madrid on July 11, 1970.

Muñoz Grandes was a tough, battle-scarred veteran of the Moroccan wars. Much of his service in Africa was with the *Regulares* where he gained the reputation of being a strict, dedicated professional soldier. He held a monk-like devotion to duty and had a simple austere nature, coupled with an unapproachable honesty that endeared him to his fellow officers and men. His many wounds stood as evidence that he disdained danger, and, in many respects, he seemed fatalistic. In politics, he was considered moderate and an officer who attempted to avoid being involved or attached to any political ideology. As it happened,

however, he was to become involved, begrudgingly, in political affairs until his death.

With the advent of the Republican provisional government, he was given the task (as a lieutenant colonel) of creating the Republican police force, the Assault Guards.* He recruited many of its members from the ranks of former Spanish legionnaires. In 1935, as a colonel of infantry, he returned to the *Regulares* in Africa hoping to escape political entanglements. He became aware of a possible conspiracy against the government, and hoping to avoid being compromised, he asked to be placed on the inactive list, even though the government offered to reappoint him to the Assault Guards. His decision may have been influenced by his chronic poor health. He did become associated with the *Unión Militar Española* (UME),* but was not apparently involved with any conspiracy.

With the uprising, Muñoz Grandes was seized in Madrid and was tried by a Republican tribunal for his connection with the UME. He was sentenced to nine years in prison. Almost a year later, he was released in return for what was expected to be services for the Popular Front.* He immediately made his way to the Nationalists* and offered his services to General Franco.* He was given command of the 2d Navarre Brigade and then a division which he commanded in the Aragón* offensive. He was promoted to brigade general and commanded an army corps.

Following the war, Muñoz Grandes was made secretary general of the Falange,* but he asked for relief and was made commander of the 22d Division in the Gibraltar* region. With the German attack on the USSR,* and the formation of the Spanish Blue Division to fight with the *Wehrmacht*, he was named its first commander. The Germans in both Russia and Berlin recognized him as an outstanding frontline commander. He returned to Madrid in December 1942 and was promoted to lieutenant general; shortly thereafter, he was made chief of Franco's military household. In 1951, he was appointed minister of war. He was very influential in concluding the American/Spanish agreements of 1954, and he was promoted to captain general in 1957 (the only one besides Franco to hold the title). In 1962, he was named vice-president of the Spanish Council of Ministers (and thereby Franco's successor). He held this position until 1967 when he resigned because of his poor health. However, he continued to hold his post as chief of the high general staff. After a prolonged kidney illness, he died in Madrid on July 11, 1970, still as honest and unpretentious as he had been as a company grade officer in Morocco.*

For further information, see Joaquín Arrarás, *Historia de la Cruzada Española* (Madrid, 1940), Vol. 2; Stanley G. Payne, *Politics and the Military in Modern Spain* (Stanford, Calif., 1967); and Raymond L. Proctor, *Agony of a Neutral* (Moscow, Idaho, 1974).

See also Appendix B.

Raymond L. Proctor

MURCIA. Murcia, a province located in southeastern Spain along the Mediterranean coast and surrounded by Alicante,* Albacete,* part of Granada,* and bordering Almería,* remained under Republican control until the last several days of the Civil War. This generally rich agricultural area, generously irrigated in the years before the war, frequently produced between three and five crops of vegetables yearly—one of the highest levels of agricultural productivity in Europe.* Farms were small, however, often ranging in size between 1 and 2 acres, with 10 considered a large holding. The western portions of the province were typically too dry, and so male residents of the area frequently migrated to such cities as Valencia* and Barcelona* searching for work. They brought with them a strong commitment to anarchism, helping expand this particular brand of political thinking in both cities.

During the Civil War, the provincial capital city of Murcia had a population* of over 100,000—one of the largest urban centers in Spain. The city remained under the control of Republicans* for the duration of the war and in the final days became a point of debarkation for Republican refugees* fleeing Franco's* armies. In the final days of the war, a conflict occurred in Murcia similar to the one being fought between Casado's* forces and his opponents in Madrid* but on a smaller scale. Socialists fought the communists for control of the area, only to be snuffed out by the advance of the Nationalists.* Finally, on March 31, 1939, Nationalist troops entered the provincial capital marking the final and complete occupation of the province. In these final days, thousands of Republican refugees were also captured by the Nationalists.

For further information, see José Antonio Ayala Pérez, *Murcia y su Huerta en la II República, 1931-1939* (Murcia, 1978).

See also Anarchists; and Levante.

James W. Cortada

MURO, JESÚS. Muro was the Falange* party's territorial chief in Catalonia,* headquartered at Saragossa,* during the early days of the Civil War. He also com-

manded the local unit of *Requetés** and served on the national Falangist *Junta* throughout the war.

For further information, see Stanley G. Payne, *Falange: A History of Spanish Fascism* (Stanford, Calif., 1961).

James W. Cortada

MUSIC. Unique musical compositions emerged during the Spanish Civil War as lasting echoes of the conflict. Old songs with new lyrics were written as were ballads concerning specific episodes. Military music from all over Europe* was heard in Spain while the communists sang the *International* in a dozen languages. In addition, foreign troops brought their own military and popular music to Spain. Some of the more famous Republican tunes included *Canciones de las Brigadas Internacionales* (1938), sung originally by militia workers in Barcelona,* while *Die Thaelmannkolonne* (1936) was used by German volunteers* in the Republican Army.* A popular change to an old Spanish folk song was *Los cuatro generales*, a derivation of *Los cuatro mileros*, and refers to Franco,* Mola,* Varela,* and Queipo de Llano* (1936). The Lincoln Brigade,* made up of American volunteers, took an old folk song, *Red River Valley*, and added new words, *Jarama Valley* (1937). This was perhaps the most famous song to emerge from the Civil War.

The Nationalists* had an equally rich collection of music to draw upon. Most common were many of the same military marching pieces used by the Republican armies, old Carlist tunes, but primarily military ones such as *Himno de la academia de infantería* (song of the Alcázar*), *Legionarios y regulares*, a favorite of the veterans of Morocco,* and *Himno nacional*. The Falangists generated a large number of musical contributions, including their own signature song and other patriotic tunes.

For further information, see Rafael Abella, *La vida cotidiana durante la guerra civil: La España Nacional* (Barcelona, 1973) and his *La vida cotidiana durante la guerra civil: La España republicana* (Barcelona, 1975).

James W. Cortada

MUSSOLINI, BENITO (1883-1944). Mussolini, head of the Italian state and chief of Italy's Fascist party from the 1920s to late in World War II, took considerable interest in Spanish affairs. He believed that the societies of Italy and Spain had a common cultural base fruitful for the growth of similar authoritarian systems of government. During the Civil War, he supported Franco's* Nationalists* in the belief that the rebels would establish a form of government more similar to his than to those of France* and Great Britain,* countries that the Duce considered his rivals, especially France. Before the Civil War, Mussolini served as partial model for the regime of yet another dictator, General Primo de Rivera, who ruled in Spain during the 1920s. Fascists in Spain during the 1930s looked to Mussolini's Italy for roles and identification as well as for moral and political support. The Italian leader philosophically and politically found much to fault with the Spanish Republic from 1931 to 1936, thus explaining to a considerable extent why he embraced the cause of the Spanish generals after July 1936. His prior support for monarchist plotters in the early 1930s, especially in 1934, had clearly established his views on the Republic in the minds of many conservative Spaniards long before the Civil War. Mussolini's support for the Nationalists proved significant, especially in the first half of the war since it consisted of manpower, supplies, financial assistance, and political acceptance.

Mussolini dominated Italian foreign policy formulation, with little influence from professional diplomats in his country. Thus, his views on international affairs are important in understanding Italy's role in the Spanish Civil War. He entertained an expansionist foreign policy aimed at increasing Italy's world stature and power, particularly in the Mediterranean. The Duce also had an enormous need for recognition, ego gratification, and hence prestige. He believed Spain's Civil War would feed each of these desires by presenting an opportunity to support his personal requirements while supporting fundamental Italian foreign policy objectives. The threat of a communist regime in Spain (the Republic) presented the possibility of a "contagion" of unacceptable political thinking coming into Italian society. The fear of left-wing political views threatening the stability of his government and the view of what European civilization should look like was a compelling force in his thinking. In his mind, providing a counterrevolutionary force in the form of support for Franco would thwart the danger to Italy posed by an alternative political system.

Thus, from the earliest days of the Civil War, the fear of communism triumphing in Spain provided ideological and political motives for helping Franco. This belief in the danger of communism was clearly in place even before significant Soviet assistance to the Republic began in the late fall of 1936. In short, aid to Franco was generally an extended form of defense of fascism and specifically of Italy's particular form of government. However, while the primary impulse was

the protection of Italian fascism, the establishment of a Spanish fascist state was not a primary motivating factor for Mussolini. At best, such a development was only a potential added benefit of his assistance to Franco. One should recall that in 1936, the Nationalists were primarily conservatives and generals, not fascists, and yet the Duce chose to support them, especially before the Falange* had great political power within Franco's camp.

Another facet of Mussolini's attitude toward the Spanish Civil War involved his relations with Germany.* Hitler* had also agreed to support the Nationalists, and so both Germany and Italy negotiated among themselves on what aid to provide and when. On the one hand, the Duce wanted Germany to support the Nationalists with more aid than Hitler was offering; on the other hand, he did not want German influence in the Mediterranean to grow at the expense of Italy's own influence there. And yet Mussolini wanted closer bonds with Germany in general. It is quite possible, therefore, that Mussolini sought Franco's ultimate victory to come more quickly than Hitler as a means not only of expanding Italian influence in the Mediterranean but also of slowing continued German interest there. The Germans, interested in upsetting the stability of the democracies in the West, wanted to expand their influence in the Mediterranean and thus, for a combination of reasons, were not as enthusiastic about bringing the Civil War to a close as was Italy.

While Mussolini periodically reviewed the need to support Franco during the early months of the conflict, after the defeat of Italian forces at the battle of Guadalajara* (March 1937), he became irreversibly committed to the Nationalist cause as a means of expiation. While he periodically complained that Franco's prosecution of the war was not vigorous enough, he was firm in the need to support Franco until the end. Thus, international assistance, aid, and propaganda continued to uphold the Nationalist cause throughout 1937-1939. Even at the Nyon Conference* in September 1937, while paying lip-service to British and French complaints of "pirate" (Italian) submarines* sinking their shipping, naval support for the Nationalists continued. Throughout this period, Mussolini did not express any serious desire to influence the nature of the Nationalist state. This fact provides additional proof that his interest lay in preventing the establishment of an antifascist Spanish republic which would likely be communist in character.

Throughout the 1922-1939 era, Mussolini had sought to block all French attempts to establish closer ties to Spain and thereby expand its influence into the Mediterranean, which obviously would have to be at Rome's expense. Therefore, it was in Italy's interest to support the Nationalists and prevent the establishment of a Republic that would be more receptive to a French alliance. Moreover, a fascist movement in Spain clearly stimulated Mussolini's thinking regarding the future character of the Iberian Peninsula and the long-term implications of the Civil War. By helping Franco, Mussolini had an opportunity to work more closely with Hitler's Germany, which he saw as the rising power in Europe.* Finally, a Nationalist victory with the help of Italian arms would enhance Italy's international prestige.

That Italy helped Franco to win the Civil War is not in doubt, nor can it be denied that Italy and Germany developed closer links on the eve of World War II. Yet, Italian military intervention was far from a political and international success and, if anything, created tremendous personal embarrassment for Mussolini. While his attempt to put a wedge between closer Franco-Spanish ties became a moot point with the start of World War II, his thinking at least followed a traditional one in Italian foreign policy.

For further information, see Richard Collier, *Duce: A Biography of Benito Mussolini* (New York, 1971); John F. Coverdale, *Italian Intervention in Spain* (Princeton, N.J., 1975); and Mario Donosti, *Mussolini e l'Europa. La politica estera fascista* (Rome, 1945).

James W. Cortada

N

NANETTI, NINO (-1937). Nanetti, an Italian volunteer in the International Brigades,* fought almost from the beginning of the Civil War, participating in many of the battles in central Spain. He arrived in Barcelona* on July 20, 1936, and soon fought on the Tardienta-Huesca line (Aragón).* At the battle of Guadalajara* (March 1937), he distinguished himself as an officer in the 12th Division. In June, he became a divisional commander. This skilled commander was killed in an aerial attack during the fighting for the defense of Bilbao.* Nanetti was not the only Italian who fought with the Republicans;* yet other Italians formed military units for the Republic. Nanetti had been a communist leader for many years in Italy.*

For further information, see Verle B. Johnston, *Legions of Babel: The International Brigades in the Spanish Civil War* (University Park, Pa., 1967); and Luigi Longo, *Le brigade internazionale in Spagna* (Rome, 1956).

James W. Cortada

NANGLE, GILBERT (1902-1944). Nangle was an able British volunteer who fought on the side of the Nationalists,* a rarity since as few as one dozen English citizens joined Franco's* side. He enlisted in the Nationalist Army* on September 9, 1936, with the rank of captain. Nangle became one of two individuals to receive an officer's commission in the Spanish Foreign Legion* without having come up through the ranks, probably because of his previous military experience in the Indian Army.

For further information, see Peter Kemp, *Mine Were of Trouble* (London, 1957).

James W. Cortada

NÁRDIZ, GONZALO DE. Nárdiz was a Basque politician from Vizcaya* who, like most Basque politicos, sided with the Republic during the Civil War. He had helped to establish the *Acción Nacional Vasca* (ANV) which had participated in the Popular Front* alliance during the election of February 1936,* unlike the major Basque party, the *Partido Nacionalista Vasco*

(PNV).* At the start of the war, he was instrumental in getting local militia to the front to fight the Nationalists* as well. He participated in the Basque government as its minister of agriculture until Franco* finally overran the Basque country.

For further information, see Ronald Fraser, *The Blood of Spain* (New York, 1979).
See also Basque Nationalism.

James W. Cortada

NATIONAL FRONT. The National Front consisted of a coalition of all the major conservative political parties bound together for the purpose of winning the elections of February 1936* against another alliance of more Republican and radical political groups known as the Popular Front.* The National Front comprised the *Confederación Española de Derechas Autónomas* (CEDA),* monarchists, and other conservatives. Members were also drawn from the large landed aristocracy and upper middle class, many officers of the armed forces, and those supporting the Catholic Church.* In the February elections, this coalition failed to win a majority of the seats in the Cortes,* thereby heightening the ever-increasing perception that Spain was dividing into the Left and the Right, with little compromise between the two possible.

Considerable support for this coalition came from both the Alfonsoist monarchists and the Carlists* who had been extremely active during the days of the Republic in attempting to contain the growing influence of more radical political parties, their economic programs, and anticlericalism, but to no avail. Finally, in the elections held in February, the results became clearer. That National Front's candidates won 133 seats in the Cortes, the Popular Front 263, and various center groups seventy-seven. Two weeks later, additional elections were held for twenty seats, but by then the National Front had totally fallen apart and was no longer a political force in Spanish affairs. From then until the start of the Civil War in July, each party acted on its own and at the time when conspirators plotting against the Republic had realized that the Right could no longer use legitimate constitutional means either to have their programs seriously considered or to gain a majority power. With the assassination of Calvo Sotelo,* a leading CEDA politician and thus a member of the National Front, the army officers plotting against the government concluded that the time had come to act.

For further information, see José María Gil Robles, *No fue posible la paz* (Barcelona, 1968); Hugh Thomas, *The Spanish Civil War* (New York, 1977); and Javier Tusell, *Las elecciones del Frente Popular*, 2 vols. (Madrid, 1971).
See also Origins of the Spanish Civil War.

James W. Cortada

NATIONALISTS. The term "Nationalists" was coined early in the Civil War to describe those who fought on Franco's* side. It implied that those favoring Franco were advocates of the nation's "best" interests, her culture, and traditional form of government—the monarchy. In general, the Nationalist cause was supported by political conservatives, many older middle-class professionals, the military to a large extent, and a substantial number of government personnel.

For further information, see Hugh Thomas, *The Spanish Civil War* (New York, 1977).
See also Army, Nationalist; and *Falange Española*.

James W. Cortada

NATIONAL REPUBLICAN GUARD. The National Republican Guard was the name which the Republic gave to the Civil Guard* units of pre-Civil War Spain. They played a minor military role during the war since many of their duties were taken over either by the regular army or by militias.*

For further information, see Ramón Salas Larrazábal, *Historia del ejército popular de la república*, 4 vols. (Madrid, 1974).

James W. Cortada

NATIONAL YOUTH CONGRESS. The National Youth Congress was a convention held in January 1937 in Valencia* by socialist-communist youth groups under the direction of Santiago Carrillo* to rally support for the Republicans.* At this congress, many political observers became aware that the leadership of socialist youth organizations was being taken over by the communists as part of their overall objective of gaining control of the Republican zone.

For further information, see Burnett Bolloten, *The Spanish Revolution: The Left and the Struggle for Power During the Civil War* (Chapel Hill, N.C., 1979).
See also Communist Party, Spanish.

James W. Cortada

NAVAL PRESENCE, FOREIGN. Throughout the Civil War, a foreign naval presence was maintained in the harbors and off the coasts of Spain to evacuate refugees* and to protect commercial and strategic interests. There was a total of about 150 foreign warships in 1936 and somewhat diminished numbers in 1938. The British Navy* was most in evidence, followed by the navies of Italy,* France,* and Germany.* Only the Italian and German navies engaged in hostilities. The United States* maintained a squadron for the Spanish war, usually one cruiser and two destroyers. Portugal* retained a few destroyers or sloops in the Straits of Gibraltar* and underwent a naval rebellion on Spanish lines on September 9, 1936. Argentina* sent one cruiser and one destroyer, mostly to rescue those seeking political asylum. A Mexican gunboat aided evacuations. A Dutch warship was maintained in the Straits to protect national shipping.

Willard C. Frank, Jr.

NAVARRE. Navarre, a province in northern Spain, was the principal stronghold of Carlism during the 1930s. Incorporating an area of 4,055 square miles, it is bounded to the northeast by the Pyrenean frontier with France,* to the southeast by the Aragonese province of Huesca,* to the southwest by the River Ebro, and to the northwest by the Basque *sierra* and heartland. The region is heir to the medieval kingdom of Navarre, joined to the crowns of Castile* and Aragón* in 1512, and down to the nineteenth century it enjoyed a measure of autonomy based upon its historic *fueros* (local rights).

Before the Civil War, Navarre, with a population* (1930) of 345,883, was still an overwhelmingly rural province despite the existence of small industrialized pockets devoted mainly to the manufacture of paper and cement. Northern Navarre possessed a smallholding rural economy concentrating upon dairy, livestock, and mixed arable farming, while south of the capital, Pamplona* (population 42,259), larger landed estates produced chiefly grain and vines. This rough north/south division was cultural, linguistic, and to some extent political as well as economic, for while in the northern districts Basque survived as a minority tongue and Basque consciousness was fairly vigorous, the south was wholly non-Basque.

Although during the Second Republic* Navarre did possess a lively socialist movement, its relatively stable and modestly prosperous rural society and its high level of religious devotion made it one of Spain's most politically conservative regions. Dominated politically by Carlism and its fellow-travelers, it returned large right-wing majorities at every election between 1931 and 1936. During 1931-1932, Navarrese politics were monopolized by the Basque (or Basque-Navarrese) autonomy issue. Common antagonism to Republican leftism and anticlericalism initially made possible collaboration among Carlists,* Basque nationalists, and other Catholics. This collapsed during 1932 as the Basque nationalists moved towards pragmatic acceptance of the Republic, while most Navarrese Carlists effectively embraced a militant *españolismo* and antirepublicanism. The division thus exposed between Basque and Spanish nationalism in Navarre is still plainly visible. From 1932 onwards, Carlist and general conservative hostility towards the Republic turned to systematic preparation for rebellion. After 1934, arms were continuously being smuggled across the Pyrenees* into Navarre, and the Carlist militia, the *Requetés,* trained for combat. During 1936, Pamplona became the chief focus of civilian-military conspiracy, principally involving the local Carlists led by the Conde de Rodezno* and the military commandant, Mola.* Similarly, when the rising began in July 1936, Navarre was one of the rebels' main initial bases of operation for attacks against the Basque country, Aragón and Madrid.*

From the outset, Navarre's commitment to the insurgent cause was unequaled in numbers and fervor. Especially in the *tercios* (regiments) of the *Requetés*, thousands of Navarrese volunteered for service, entire villages being emptied of their active male population. During the war, those Carlists under Rodezno who proved willing to cooperate with Franco* were permitted to exercise effective control over the province. A practice was thereby inaugurated which was to be maintained throughout the life of the Franco regime, when Navarre became a virtual fief of "collaborationist" Carlists.

For further information, see José Antonio Aguirre y Lecube, *Entre la libertad y la revolución* (Bilbao, 1976); Martin Blinkhorn, *Carlism and Crisis in Spain, 1931-1939* (Cambridge, England, 1975); Jaime del Burgo, *Conspiración y Guerra Civil* (Madrid and Barcelona, 1970); and Antonio Lizarza Iribarren, *Memorias de la conspiración. Como se preparó en Navarra la Cruzada, 1931-1936* (Pamplona, 1957).

Martin Blinkhorn

NAVARRO LÓPEZ, JOSÉ (-1937). Navarro López, chief of staff of the Republican Navy, evacuated Vizcaya's* naval forces in June 1937 as the Nationalists* closed in on the area. He was criticized for his action. He later returned to the Republican zone where he was arrested by communists and executed. It is not clear whether his death was caused by his actions at Vizcaya or by other circumstances.

For further information, see José Manuel Martínez Bande, *Vizcaya* (Madrid, 1971).

James W. Cortada

NAVY, BRITISH. The British Navy operated in Spanish waters from the first days of the Civil War to evacuate refugees* and to safeguard British strategic and economic interests. By the end of 1936, seventy British warships had evacuated 17,000 foreigners, after which ships rotated on station at Spanish ports. The Admiralty rejected repeated French pleas for a strong demonstration of Anglo-French naval power to counter the Axis in the Mediterranean, for Great Britain* was desperate to reduce the number of potential enemies, and especially to calm Mussolini.* British nonrecognition of a legal state of belligerency led the Royal Navy actively to escort British merchant ships with nonmilitary cargos to Republican harbors in the Bay of Biscay in the face of the Nationalists'* attempts at blockade. The British had dominant power on the scene and won a series of tense naval confrontations with Nationalist warships. British warships were frequently endangered by war action. German mines heavily damaged the destroyer *Hunter* on May 13, 1937. The destroyer *Havock* barely escaped being torpedoed by the Italian submarine *Iride* on August 31, 1937. British warships were often the subject of air attack. In September-October 1937, under the provisions of the Nyon Conference,* the Royal Navy was heavily engaged in patrolling against "pirate" submarines.* In 1938, warships unsuccessfully tried to protect British shipping in Spanish waters from German and Italian air attacks. In February 1939, the Royal Navy helped ensure the peaceful transfer of Menorca* from Republican to Nationalist control.

For further information, see Hugh Thomas, *The Spanish Civil War* (New York, 1977).

Willard C. Frank, Jr.

NAVY, GERMAN. The German Navy constantly maintained a squadron in Spanish waters, usually six surface vessels and two submarines, which proportionally was the largest contingent of any foreign navy involved in the Civil War. It gained experience and asserted German influence as opportunities arose. After evacuating 15,000 refugees,* warships escorted German supply ships to Spain, maintained a reconnaissance of Republican ports and ship movements, engaged in clandestine submarine warfare in November-December 1936, and participated in nonintervention patrols in April-June 1937. The German Navy established a liaison office with the Nationalist Navy, operated a training establishment and a communications system, ceded five fast motorboats, and developed a specialty in mine warfare. German mines scored hits on five merchant vessels, but also accidentally sank the Nationalist battleship *España* and severely damaged the British destroyer *Hunter*.

For further information, see Ramón Hidalgo Salazar, *Ayuda Alemana a España, 1936-1939* (Barcelona, 1975).

Willard C. Frank, Jr.

NAVY, ITALIAN. The Italian Navy was involved in operations connected with the Spanish war throughout the conflict. Mussolini* intervened deeply in the war and coveted bases in the Balearic Islands,* from which he could threaten French strategic communications. The duties of the Italian Navy included evacuating 9,000 refugees,* organizing and protecting the shipment of Italian forces and supplies to Spain, building and maintaining naval bases in Cádiz* and Palma de Majorca,* maintaining a constant naval presence in Palma and Tangier, providing communications between Spain and Italy,* providing reconnaissance of Republican military shipping, and engaging in clandestine naval warfare as well as nonintervention and Nyon patrols as ordered. An Italian naval mission was maintained at Nationalist headquarters. The Italian Navy ceded two submarines,* four destroyers, and four fast motorboats to the Nationalist Navy. Italian submarines engaged in clandestine operations against shipping from November 8, 1936, to February 5, 1938, sinking six vessels and damaging nine others. Italian destroyers in nocturnal torpedo attacks sank four merchant ships, and Italian auxiliary cruisers captured two others in August 1937, also the period of greatest submarine activity. Victims included Soviet, British, and Panamanian, as well as Spanish, vessels. Italian cruisers and surfaced submarines shelled Republican ports on seven occasions in early 1937. As a result of the Nyon Conference* in September 1937, Mussolini severely curtailed clandestine naval operations. Italy never received the naval bases Mussolini had coveted.

For further information, see John F. Coverdale, *Italian Intervention in the Spanish Civil War* (Princeton, N.J., 1975).

See also Navy, Spanish; and Non-Intervention Committee.

Willard C. Frank, Jr.

NAVY, SOVIET. The Soviet Navy contributed seventy-eight naval officers to the Republican fleet, but no more than thirty served at one time. These officers advised Republican counterparts, conducted the strategy of defense of Soviet supply shipments from the Black Sea, and directly commanded Republican submarines and motor torpedo boats. Four torpedo boats were donated by the Soviet Navy.

For further information, see N. G. Kuznetsov, *Na dalekom meridiane* (Moscow, 1966).

Willard C. Frank, Jr.

NAVY, SPANISH. The Spanish Navy in 1936 was the most powerful in the world aside from those of the seven powers that fought the world wars. It was a balanced fleet on contemporary lines and was based at El Ferrol,* Cartagena,* Cádiz,* and Mahón on Minorca.* Republican leaders had alienated the officer corps more through a general spirit of mistrust than by specific reforms. Discipline among crews cracked with the advent of the Republic, and sailors grew bitter over a perceived arrogance among officers. Naval personnel became polarized, the most militant leaders for political action coming, respectively, from socialist or anarchist junior petty officers and from rightist officers of middle rank. In July 1936, the navy contained 104 vessels displacing 124,252 tons. Personnel included 658 general corps officers, 590 specialist officers, 3,034 senior petty officers (*Auxiliares*), and 1,600 junior petty officers (*cabos*), with 12,000 inducted seamen.

As a result of the uprising of July 1936, the Republicans* retained fifty-six warships: one battleship (*Jaime I*),* three cruisers (*Libertad,* Miguel de Cervantes,* Méndez Núñez*), ten destroyers, nine torpedo boats, twelve submarines, one gunboat, six patrol boats, and fourteen landing craft, displacing a total of 60,816 tons. The Republic kept eleven naval auxiliaries, totaling 9,383 tons. The Nationalists* gained control of twenty-six warships: one battleship (*España**), one active cruiser (*Almirante Cervera**) and one under extensive repair (*República*, later *Navarra*), one destroyer (*Velasco*), five torpedo boats, four gunboats, and thirteen patrol boats, a total of 36,544 tons. The

Nationalists won eleven auxiliaries, totaling 17,504 tons. About 400 general corps officers and at least 250 specialist officers fell into Republican hands, and 6,500 petty officers and seamen were caught in the Nationalist zone. Many were purged. The Republicans eventually executed 241 officers, and the Nationalists perhaps 1,400 petty officers and seamen.

Through the war, the Republican Navy added six destroyers, seventy-one patrol boats, four fast motorboats, and one minelayer, a total of 81,467 tons. A separate Basque Navy was formed with twelve patrol boats, thirty-one minesweepers, and seven auxiliaries, for 14,565 tons. The Nationalists added two cruisers (*Canarias** and *Baleares**), four destroyers, two submarines, three minelayers, one gunboat, fourteen auxiliary cruisers, one torpedo boat, seventy-four patrol boats, nine fast motorboats, thirty-two minesweepers, and two landing craft, totaling 99,869 tons. Twenty-five additional Nationalist auxiliaries came to 9,034 tons.

The Republican Navy established a blockade in the Straits of Gibraltar* in July-September 1936, effectively isolating the bulk of Nationalist forces in Spanish Morocco.* An attempted blockade of Cádiz and other Nationalist ports against foreign military aid* failed. The navy supported the Catalan invasion of Ibiza* and Majorca* in August. Outnumbered Nationalist naval forces were capable of only one convoy across the Straits (August 5, 1936), and bombardment raids were made against the Biscay coast.

In September, the Republican Navy minister, Indalecio Prieto,* and the Central Committee of the fleet forced the abandonment of the Majorcan expedition and then sent the main fleet to the Bay of Biscay in support of harassed northern ports. Nationalist Admirals Cervera* and Moreno* took advantage of the absence of the Republican fleet to send a naval force into the Straits and win the Battle of Cape Espartel* (September 29, 1936), thus opening a passage for the Army of Africa* to the Iberian Peninsula, relieving a slow and inefficient airlift. Nationalist warships now entered the Mediterranean, raiding the Republican coast and shipping lanes, and, with Italian help, establishing a naval base at Palma de Majorca.* In October 1936, the Republican fleet returned from the Bay of Biscay to Cartagena, where, with Soviet help, it organized and defended supply lines from the USSR.* Unlike the aggressive Nationalist Navy, the Republican fleet seldom attempted to carry the war to the enemy and never attacked Nationalist supply routes.

In January-February 1937, the Nationalist Navy supported the Málaga* campaign, and in March-October it blockaded the Republican ports of northern Spain.

Republican naval opposition was slight. With the collapse of the northern front in October 1937, a strengthened Nationalist Navy concentrated blockade forces in the Mediterranean. By this time, Nationalist and Italian naval operations had forced the curtailment of the Soviet logistic route through the Mediterranean. Thenceforth, the blockade focused on the prevention of nonmilitary commerce with the Republic. Republican response was meager, the Republican victory in the battle of Cape Palos* (March 6, 1938) being the only exception. Republican morale soon waned. A pro-Nationalist revolt erupted in Cartagena in March 1939, followed by the internment of the surviving units of the Republican fleet in Bizerte.

Republican naval losses throughout the war included one battleship, three destroyers, six torpedo boats, eleven submarines, one gunboat, forty-four patrol boats, two landing craft, one fast motorboat, one minelayer, and six naval auxiliaries, a total of 43,169 tons. In addition, one cruiser and five destroyers were badly damaged. The entire Basque Navy was lost. Nationalist losses were one battleship, one cruiser, one torpedo boat, nine patrol boats, one landing craft, two fast motorboats, one minesweeper, and one auxiliary, a total of 27,399 tons. Reported Nationalist navy personnel killed in action were 825, and the Republicans probably 500.

For further information, see Bruno Alonso, *La flota republicana y la guerra civil de España* (Mexico City, 1944); Manuel D. Benavides, *La escuadra la mandan los cabos* (Mexico, 1944); Juan Cervera Valderrama, *Memorias de guerra* (Madrid, 1968); Francisco Moreno, *La guerra en el mar* (Barcelona, 1959); and Servicio Histórico del Estado Mayor de la Armada, "La Marina en la guerra de España (1936-1939)" (Madrid, 1977-   ).

See also Merchant Marine, Spanish; Navy, British; Navy, German; Navy, Italian; Navy, Soviet; Non-Intervention Committee Sea Observation Scheme; and Uprising at Sea.

Willard C. Frank, Jr.

NEGRÍN, JUAN (1892?-1956). Negrín was a Spanish professor of physiology and moderate socialist who became Spain's last prime minister during the Second Republic.* The son of a wealthy Canary Islands* businessman, he was educated largely on the Continent where he studied medicine* at several German universities. He later served as one of the youngest professors of physiology at the Medical Faculty of Madrid University between 1923 and 1931. Turning to politics in 1929 as a moderate socialist, Negrín was elected to the Cortes* on three occasions: 1931, 1933, and 1936. At the outbreak of the Civil War, he was an adherent of Indalecio Prieto's* anticommunist center faction of the Socialist party.* He became in turn minister of finance in Largo Caballero's* government from September 1936 to May 1937; prime minister from May 1937 to April 1938; and premier and defense minister from April 1938 until the end of the war in March 1939.

In his capacity as finance minister in September 1936, Negrín was one of the central figures in the highly controversial episode of the war that involved the transfer of the Spanish gold reserves to the USSR.* Because of the military threat to Madrid,* the question of moving the reserves to safer keeping had been considered even by José Giral's* cabinet, although the idea was not acted upon until Largo Caballero formed his administration on September 4 with Negrín as finance minister. On September 13, by a *decreto reservado* (a confidential decree) countersigned by President Manuel Azaña,* Negrín obtained authority from the cabinet to transfer the gold and silver stocks as well as paper currency held by the Bank of Spain* to a place which, in his opinion, offered the maximum security. Within a few days, 10,000 cases of gold coins and ingots were transferred to a large cave at Cartagena.*

Soon after the reserves had been moved, the Nationalists* began waging a highly emotional campaign to prevent the Republicans* from selling gold in France.* Largely because of this campaign, both Largo Caballero and Negrín, acting in agreement with the Soviet trade envoy Arthur Stashevsky, decided to ship the bulk of the gold reserves to the Soviet Union to be used for the purchase not only of Soviet arms, but also of foreign exchange necessary for the acquisition of arms and supplies in other countries. For the role he played in this incident, Negrín became the focus of criticism, because this important transfer, worth at the time over $500 million, was to make the cabinet dependent in large measure on Moscow's good-will.

While serving as finance minister, Negrín also achieved notoriety among his opponents for having considerably strengthened the *Carabineros*—or carabineers, a corps composed of customs excise officials and guards—to the extent that they became the most powerful force of public order. Shortly before the May 1937 riots* in Barcelona,* for example, his *Carabineros* (later characterized by his opponents as "Negrín's 100,000 sons") were to play a crucial role in seizing the frontier posts along the Franco-Spanish border, hitherto controlled by the revolutionaries of the *Confederación Nacional del Trabajo* (CNT)* and the *Partido Obrero de Unificación Marxista* (POUM).*

The May events provoked a government crisis that brought down Largo Caballero's cabinet. President Azaña asked Negrín to form a new cabinet, and on May 18, 1937, a government headed by Negrín was installed. Negrín became prime minister at a time when the power and influence of the communists were ascending rapidly. In fact, he more than any other Spaniard was responsible for the success of communist policy during the last year of the Civil War. When he took over the Ministry of Defense from Prieto in April 1938, Negrín (who retained his post as premier) helped the communists extend their influence over the operations of the state machinery by appointing party members or sympathizers to military and civilian posts of great importance. He elevated Antonio Cordón,* whom Prieto had removed as chief of staff of the Eastern Army, to the undersecretaryship of war; promoted Carlos Nuñez Maza to the undersecretaryship of air; and appointed Pedros Prados* to the post of navy chief of staff. Furthermore, the Finance Ministry went to Negrín's intimate, the Left Republican Francisco Méndez Aspe,* who had been involved in the shipment to Moscow of the Spanish gold reserves, and who appointed Marcelino Fernández, a communist, to head the *Carabineros*, the most powerful force of public order. Álvarez del Vayo,* who had long been a supporter of the Communist party,* returned to the Foreign Ministry and gave Negrín's close collaborator, Manuel Sánchez Arcos, a party member, the key portfolio of the undersecretaryship of propaganda. Equally important was the fact that the communists retained all their key positions in the police* apparatus, including the post of director-general of security, occupied by Eduardo Cuevas de la Peña, a party member. From then onwards, Negrín, backed by communist propaganda and Russian supplies, pursued a course of government action that was in accordance with the policies advocated by the Soviet Union.

That Negrín followed the communist line is illustrated not only by his appointment of communists to key positions but also by the fact that he adhered religiously to Stalin's* policy of resistance, which was predicated on the belief that Great Britain* and France* would eventually be forced to intervene in defense of their own interests. In keeping with this policy, the Negrín government attempted to conciliate foreign capital. On April 27, it decreed that the foreign hydroelectric enterprises, operated in Catalonia* by the CNT under the name of *Serveis Electrics Unificats de Catalunya*, be dissolved. Simultaneously, government comptrollers were appointed to decollectivize and nationalize certain Spanish enterprises. Although comparatively few concerns were involved because many owners had been killed or had fled to Nationalist territory at the outbreak of the war, the communist-controlled foreign press censorship, which in the past had attempted to conceal the revolution, allowed foreign correspondents to make great play with the restitution.

On May 1, 1938, Negrín took a further step to influence the Western democracies, when he enunciated his thirteen-point program. Among other things, it included the promise of a Spain free of all foreign interference, with full civil and political rights together with freedom of religion, but the Thirteen Points* made no impression on the democratic powers.

On February 27, 1939, after the fall of Catalonia, Great Britain and France officially recognized the Franco* regime as the legal government of Spain. Despite this critically important diplomatic setback, and despite the fact that only the central and southeastern parts of Spain remained to the Republic, Negrín and the communist leaders decided to continue the war, but when they arrived in the central zone accompanied by members of the government, they found that the factions of the Left had coalesced against them. Embittered by political injury and oppression, demoralized by the attacks on the revolution, as were the Left socialists and the anarchosyndicalists, and exhausted by a protracted war that offered no hope of victory, they execrated the Negrín government—which the socialist Luis Araquistain* described as the "most cynical and despotic" in Spanish history—as much as they detested its resistance policy.

In this climate of dissolution, Negrín decreed the promotion of two prominent communists, Antonio Cordón* and Juan Modesto,* to the rank of general, and a number of other leading communists officers, including Enrique Líster,* to the rank of colonel. Fearing a communist coup, Colonel Segismundo Casado,* the commander of the Army of the Center* who had been conspiring with socialist, Republican, and anarchosyndicalist leaders to overthrow Negrín, formed a National Council of Defense in the hope of negotiating a surrender without reprisals.

Within hours, Negrín and his communist entourage escaped by plane. So swift was their departure that no directives were given to the Madrid party organization, which, aided by communist military units, tried unsuccessfully to overthrow the Defense Council.

In the face of General Franco's insistence on unconditional surrender, Casado's efforts to negotiate a settlement without reprisals were aborted. By the end of March, the forces of the Left were in full retreat and the war was over.

Following the war, Negrín and other Republican leaders resided in France, where they attempted to maintain a government in exile. Negrín went to live in England in 1940, where he actively campaigned for the restoration of the Republic. He later returned to France, where he died on November 12, 1956.

Negrín has been regarded by some observers as politically naive, while others have labeled him an accomplice of Soviet designs. However Negrín's political career may be characterized, it is apparent that his close ties with the communists had a profound effect on the course of events.

For further information, see Julio Álvarez del Vayo, *Freedom's Battle* (New York, 1940), pro-Negrín; Mariano Ansó, *Yo fui ministro de Negrín* (Barcelona, 1976), pro-Negrín; and Epistolario, *Prieto y Negrín* (Paris, 1939) and *Cómo y porque salí del ministerio de defensa nacional* (Mexico City, 1940), an appreciation of the strife between Negrín and Prieto.   All biographical data used here covering the Civil War period can be found in Burnett Bolloten's *The Spanish Revolution: The Left and the Struggle for Power During the Civil War* (Chapel Hill, N.C., 1979).

See also Socialist Party, Spanish.

Burnett Bolloten
in collaboration with George Esenwein

NELKEN, MARGARITA (1897-1968). Nelken, perhaps the best known woman member of the Spanish Socialist party* before 1931, agitated for women's rights throughout the period and was actively involved in land reform movements in Estremadura* and Andalusia.* Born in Málaga* to German Jewish parents, she was educated in France* as an artist. Conflict with the Catholic Church* over an orphanage she had started led to involvement with socialists and the writing of *La condición social de la mujer en España* in 1922. She campaigned for reform throughout the 1920s, but friendship with Ricardo Zabalez, an activist in the *Federación Nacional de Trabajadors de la Tierra*, broadened Nelken's politics and enabled her to be elected as a deputy to the Constituent Cortes* from Badajoz* —but only after she was hurriedly made a naturalized citizen.

Nelken's activity in the Cortes was less noticeable than her continued agitation for land reform and her participation in the Castilblanco riot on December 31, 1931, near Badajoz, when four Civil Guards* were killed. Her impatience with the parliamentary process led to friendship with Francisco Largo Caballero* in 1933 and 1934. She was soon among the most radical of the Spanish Socialist party in denouncing Manuel Azaña and the Republican coalition. It was her thesis, for example, that Spanish women had been responsible for the right-wing vote in November 1933, and so she turned her back upon feminism in favor of collaboration with the USSR.* She visited there in late 1934 and supported Soviet policies throughout the Civil War, although she was eclipsed as a leader by La Pasionaria.*

Nelken fled Spain for France* in 1939 but ended up in Mexico,* where she tried with indifferent success to resume her career as an art educator and journalist.

For further information, see Robert Kern, "Margarita Nelken," in Jane Slaughter and Robert Kern, *European Women on the Left: Feminism, Socialism, and the Problems Faced by Political Women, 1880 to the Present* (Westport, Conn., 1981).

Robert W. Kern

NENNI, PIETRO (1891-1980). Nenni, one of the international volunteers* and a major organizer of antifascist activities, came from a peasant family in Romagna. Initially a Republican, he was a sergeant in World War I; after the war, he joined the Italian Socialist party and became editor of *Avanti!*, the party newspaper. Like other major figures of the Left, he was forced into exile in France* in 1926 where he became a consistent supporter of an antifascist Popular Front, as well as leader of the Italian Socialist party.

Nenni traveled to Spain on August 5, 1936, to contact Spanish socialist leaders and visit the socialist Octubre Battalion commanded by Fernando de Rosa. Advocating the creation of an Italian unit to fight in Spain, he was a member of the Italian *Comité de Paris* designed to recruit volunteers in September 1936. When the Garibaldi Battalion* was formed in October, he served briefly as commander of the 3d Company. Although he fought with the Garibaldi at the Jarama* and at Guadalajara,* he functioned mainly as the Italian Socialist party representative to the Republican government and devoted most of his energy to building support for the Republic in Europe.* After dissolution of the International Brigades* in September 1938, he continued to work for a united antifascist front from centers in southern France. He was arrested by the Gestapo in March 1943 but released in August after the fall of Mussolini.* Thereafter, he served as the Italian Socialist party representative to the Italian Committee of National Liberation in Rome and resumed leadership of the Italian socialists. After 1945, he held a variety of government posts (vice-president, foreign minister) in three of Aldo Moro's cabinets in the 1960s and continued to lead the Italian Socialist party.

For further information, see Gaetano Arfe, ed., *Storia dell'Avanti!* (Milan, 1958); Ezio Bartalini, *Pietro Nenni* (Rome, 1946); and Pietro Nenni, *Vent'anni di fascismo* (Milan, 1965), *Pagine di diario* (n.p., 1947), and *Spagna* (Milan, 1958).

Jane Slaughter

NERUDA, PABLO (1904-1973). Neruda was the Chilean consul in Madrid* during the Civil War. He is best remembered as a poet; he wrote numerous poems defending the Spanish Republic and glorifying the role of the International Brigades.*

For further information, see Pablo Neruda, *Tercera residencia* (Buenos Aires, 1961).

See also Europe; Intellectuals; and Literature.

James W. Cortada

NEURATH, FREIHERR CONSTANTIN VON (1873-1956). Baron von Neurath was German minister of foreign affairs throughout the Civil War period. He was a career diplomat who had served as ambassador to several European capitals before becoming foreign minister in 1932. He proved to be an unimaginative, weak individual. Diplomatic issues concerning Spain were primarily handled out of Hitler's* offices and not from the Ministry of Foreign Affairs. During the Spanish war, Neurath was thus left with only the responsibility of implementing Hitler's foreign policy in Spain and not its formulation. Throughout the period, his ministry competed for influence in Spanish affairs with Hitler's aides, the military, and other agencies. On several occasions, however, Neurath urged moderation in German involvement in Spain, fearing that war might be expanded to other parts of Europe.*

For further information, see Gordon A. Craig, et al., *The Diplomats, 1919-1939*, Vol. 2: *The Thirties* (Princeton, N.J., 1953); and Manfred Merkes, *Die deutsche Politik im Spanischen Bürgerkrieg* (Bonn, 1969).

See also Germany.

James W. Cortada

NEUTRALITY ACTS (USA). The Congress of the United States* passed two neutrality acts to restrict the sale of arms to belligerents in countries at war. The first, approved in May 1935, was intended to block the sale of weapons to either side in the Abyssinian crisis. When the Spanish Civil War erupted, the Roosevelt Administration applied this act to Spain, although the legislation did not specifically mention civil wars. Simultaneously, the government declared a "moral embargo" on American involvement in the conflict. In 1937, when the original neutrality act was scheduled to expire, a new version was passed that specifically addressed the problems of civil wars.

For further information, see Richard A. Traina, *American Diplomacy and the Spanish Civil War* (Bloomington, Ind., 1968).

See also Hull, Cordell; and Roosevelt, Franklin D.

James W. Cortada

NEWSPAPERS, FRENCH. Even if the French press had passed its golden age, it still consisted (in 1937) of no fewer than 253 dailies, with a daily run of 11.5 million copies, including almost 6 million in Paris. The provincial press, which was growing in importance, included (in 1938) 177 dailies and 860 weeklies, of which total nineteen (in 1939) were printing more than 100,000 copies.

The "Big Five" of the Paris press, which had operated since World War I as a consortium holding practically a monopoly of the advertising market, consisted of *Le Petit Parisien* (with a run of 1.3 million in 1936), *Le Journal* (650,000), *Le Matin* (500,000), *Le Petit Journal* (220,000) and *L'Echo de Paris* (100,000). All but *Le Petit Journal*, like most of the rest of the Paris press, belonged to the Center-Right or the Right. A distinction should be made here between the conservative dailies, such as *L'Echo de Paris* and the evening *L'Intransigeant* (200,000), and the reactionary dailies such as *Le Matin* and *Le Jour* (250,000), which openly expressed sympathy with fascism. All five newspapers were in decline, but this phenomenon is true, especially from 1937, of the right-wing press in general, and indeed of the entire French press, even when controlled by financial or industrial interests.

In terms of circulation, *Le Petit Parisien* had been overtaken by the front-running *Paris-Soir* (1.7 million). Both considered themselves politically impartial, but in fact their conservative editors were at odds with their liberal correspondents who found their dispatches frequently rejected or truncated. *Le Petit Journal*, under the Franco-American millionaire Raymond Patenôtre, himself a successful Front Populaire candidate in the elections of May 1936, appealed to the middle-class supporters of Léon Blum* but was sold on July 8, 1937, to François de La Rocque. From that time on, it served his reactionary *Parti Social Français*. *L'Echo de Paris* also experienced a change when on May 13, 1937, Deputy Henri de Kérillis resigned with others to form a maverick daily, *L'Epoque*, which

more than any other conservative organ represented a patriotic independence. Meanwhile, on March 28, 1938, Léon Bailby merged *L'Epoque* with his Axis-leaning *Le Jour*.

Other dailies of the Right included two moderates: *Excelsior* and *Le Figaro* (both 100,000); and three extremists: *L'Ami du Peuple* (150,000), *L'Action Française* (80,000), and *La Liberté* (80,000). *L'Ami du Peuple* was the organ of Deputy Pierre Taittinger, leader of the extreme Right *Jeunesses Patriotes*, but in late September 1936 his journal passed to Georges Mandel who reversed its policy by appealing for friendship with the USSR.* A new editorial team in January 1937 adopted an anodyne policy, and *L'Ami* disappeared at the end of October. *L'Action Française*, the organ of Charles Maurras, merged Church and monarchy with fascism, supporting Mussolini* but not Hitler,* and receiving no encouragement from pope or pretender. *La Liberté*, launched on May 24, 1937, by Jacques Doriot, was the organ of his fascist *Parti Populaire Français*. Equally rabid were the weeklies *Gringoire* (640,000), *Candide* (465,000), and *Je Suis Partout* (100,000).

In a special category was the evening *Le Temps* (70,000 to 90,000), considered the most serious of Paris newspapers and the semi-official organ of the Quai d'Orsay. While its news coverage was generally fuller than that of any of its rivals, the Left considered it to be governed by conservative bankers and industrialists.

The left-wing press consisted mainly of *L'Humanité* (320,000), the organ of the French Communist party, with thirty-nine regional editions; *Le Populaire* (300,000), the organ of the *Section Française de l'Internationale Ouvrière* (the French Socialist party); *L'Oeuvre* (230,000), the organ of the left wing of the radical socialists; and *Le Peuple* (30,000), the organ of the socialist *Confédération Générale du Travail*, the largest of the French labor unions. On March 1, 1937, the Communist party launched *Ce Soir* (200,000), with the help of Patenôtre and money sent from Barcelona* by Juan Negrín.* Even though it was directed by the communists Louis Aragon and Jean-Richard Bloch, it attracted leftists of all factions. These dailies were supported by several leftist weeklies, of which the most important were *Marianne* (120,000) and *Vendredi* (100,000). To the Left-of-Center press should be added certain liberal Catholic periodicals, notably *Esprit*, *Sept*, *Temps Présent*, *La Vie Intellectuelle*, and (more to the Center) the Catholic daily *L'Aube* (12,000) of Georges Bidault, which appealed to all parties to join in a "Front Français" against Nazi Germany.*

Among the Radical dailies, the most important was *L'Ordre*, alone among the press on the Right to support the Republican cause in Spain, even while it continued to oppose Blum's Front Populaire. Its small circulation (12,000) was challenged by two radical socialist dailies: *L'Ere Nouvelle* (10,000), the organ of Edouard Herriot's right-wing faction, and *La République*, the organ of Edouard Daladier's* centrist faction, which was sinking from 140,000 in 1936 to 6,000 by 1939. But all three dailies had an influence far beyond their modest circulation, as did the independent weekly *L'Europe Nouvelle*.

Of the provincial press, by far the most important was that of Toulouse, consisting of the dailies *La Dépêche* (radical socialist), *Le Midi Socialiste* (an auxiliary of *Le Populaire*), *L'Express du Midi* (Catholic and monarchist, replaced in 1938 by *La Garonne*), and the weekly *Le Journal de Toulouse*, which shared the sympathies of *L'Express du Midi*. Of these, *La Dépêche* (260,000) had national and even international stature.

As for the press agencies, Havas controlled more than 99 percent of the news inflow. The Spanish Republicans* had the services of *Agence Espagne*, an official information and press bureau inaugurated in Paris in October 1936 by Jaume Miravitlles*; it was placed under the direction of the Yugoslav Otto Katz ("André Simone"—"O.K. Simon"). Other such offices were subsequently opened in the capitals of the major European democracies, notably the Spanish News Agency in London under the direction of Geoffrey Bing. The Spanish Nationalists* especially used the services of Juan Estelrich and his Franco-Spanish propaganda fortnightly *Occident*, published in Paris between October 25, 1937, and May 30, 1939. Among such Spanish papers published in Paris must be added the Republicans' weekly *Voz de Madrid* (from July 1938 to April 1939) and the Basque exiles' *Euzko Deya* (appearing monthly, then weekly, in French, Spanish, and Basque).

For further information, see Claude Bellanger, et al., *Histoire générale de la presse française* (Paris, 1972), Vol. 3; and David Wingeate Pike, *La Presse française à la veille de la Seconde Guerre mondiale* (Paris, 1973).

David Wingeate Pike

NEW YORK TIMES, THE (1851-PRESENT). *The New York Times* provided some of the most extensive coverage of the Civil War available in North America. Two important and highly influential correspondents wrote for it: W. P. Carney (pro-Nationalist covering Franco's* cause) and Herbert L. Matthews* (pro-Republican assigned to the Republican side).

For further information, see Gabriel Jackson, *A Concise History of the Spanish Civil War* (New York, 1974).

James W. Cortada

NIN, ANDRÉS (1892-1937). In the 1920s, Nin was a communist as well as an ex-socialist journalist, and he also served as general secretary of the *Confederación Nacional del Trabajo* (CNT).* After his break with Stalin* by 1931, he became a Trotskyist of sorts and soon after a founding member of the *Partído Obrero de Unificación Marxista* (POUM),* made up almost entirely of ex-communist Catalans rejecting allegiance to Moscow. This controversial politician joined the Generalitat* as councillor of justice in September 1936 and remained in office until December 1937 when the Spanish Communist party managed to force a rapid decline in the POUM's political power. While councillor, Nin antagonized many people in Barcelona* by such acts as appointing a prosecutor who conducted justice with a pistol rather than by due process of law.

During the summer of 1937, the Communist party* concentrated a great deal of effort on destroying the POUM, its arch-rival within the Republican zone. In June, the government was persuaded to arrest members of POUM and to declare the organization illegal. Nin was arrested along with most of the leadership in POUM. Because he was one of the better known Spanish revolutionaries, questions were asked in the Spanish and international press concerning Nin's whereabouts and if he were still alive. In fact, he had been arrested and sent to a Soviet camp at Alcalá de Henares,* near Madrid,* for interrogation and on June 20, 1937, was killed. His treatment of both Nin and the POUM made Stalin the object of considerable international criticism. Many observers now realized that the Spanish Republic was profoundly under the control of communists and probably by Moscow.

For further information, see Burnett Bolloten, *The Spanish Revolution: The Left and the Struggle for Power During the Civil War* (Chapel Hill, N.C., 1979); Andrés Nin, *Los problemas de la revolución española* (Paris, 1971); Pelai Pagés, *Andreu Nin. Su evolución política, 1930-1937* (Barcelona, 1975); and Andrés Suarez, *El proceso contra el POUM* (Paris, 1974).

James W. Cortada

NIZAN, PAUL (1905-1940). Nizan, a novelist, journalist, essayist, and polemicist, was a leading spokesman of French communism until the signing of the Nazi-Soviet Non-aggression Pact in August 1939, at which time he severed all ties with the party. The following year he was killed at Dunkirk (May 23). His major works include *Aden Arabie* (1932), *Antoine Bloyé* (1933), *Le Cheval de Troie* (1935), and *La Conspiration* (1938); the last-named work was awarded the Prix Interallié. A projected novel, *La Soirée à Somosierra*, a continuation of *La Conspiration*, was to contain scenes set during the Spanish Civil War.

Nizan's writings on Spain, an eleven-part reportage entitled "Secrets de l'Espagne" published in the communist weekly *La Correspondance Internationale* (Nos. 27-33, June-July 1936), were inspired by his travels to Madrid,* Oviedo,* Cuenca,* Toledo,* Valencia,* Albacete,* and other cities, towns, and villages in May 1936. His articles, based on direct observations and thorough investigation, and written in simple lucid prose, vividly capture the political tensions of Republican Spain in the months preceding the insurrection of July 17. As the collective title clearly indicates, one of Nizan's major objectives was to reveal to his communist readership several aspects of Spain that were little known in France* at that time.

Nizan's earliest article on the Spanish Popular Front* had appeared only six days after the triumphs in the elections of February 1936.* While celebrating the people's victory, he alluded to the many dangers that lay ahead and forewarned of a possible fascist coup d'état, two concerns that are frequently voiced in "Secrets de l'Espagne." As a communist, Nizan supported the Popular Front coalition, and several of his articles emphasize the communists' contribution to the working-class revolution, for example, the establishment of a *kolkhoz* at Tarancon. Recognizing that the teachings of Bakunin were also deeply rooted in the Spanish working class, Nizan shows a sensitive understanding of anarchism, even though he stressed its limitations as a political philosophy and dismissed the policies of the *Confederación Nacional del Trabajo* (CNT)* as "infantile."

In emphasizing the continuing power and influence of the Right—he gave particular attention to the army and the Civil Guard*—Nizan had perceived the precariousness of the Popular Front. The government's failure to dismantle the monarchist infrastructure, its ineffectual response to Falangist provocation against workers, its hesitation in securing key positions in the administration and in the armed forces, its delay in implementing radical agrarian reforms, and its inability or refusal to forestall imminent fascist rebellion are among the major criticisms that are formulated incisively in his reportage.

In one exceptionally perspicacious piece penned in the immediate aftermath of the *pronunciamiento*, Nizan denounced the duplicity of nonintervention and warned that Blum's* vacillation in rescuing the Spanish Republic would ultimately result in France's being entirely encircled by right-wing regimes.

Although not entirely free from error, Nizan's writings on Spain, particularly "Secrets de l'Espagne," provide a useful, though partial, corrective to many misconceptions prevalent in the French press during the summer of 1936. They constitute an unusually clear-sighted evaluation of the period immediately preceding the fascist coup d'état, as seen by a sympathetic and not entirely orthodox communist.

For further information, see *Paul Nizan, intellectuel communiste 1926-1940* (2 volumes), Présentation de J-J. Brochier (Paris, 1970). See in particular Vol. 2, pp. 40-86.

See also Europe; Journalists, French; and Newspapers, French.

Robert S. Thornberry

NKVD. The NKVD (People's Commissariat for International Affairs) was the USSR's* secret police* and espionage* agency which, during the Civil War, had considerable influence in the Republican zone. Stalin* gave it responsibility for coordinating all Soviet aid to the Spanish Republic and for providing necessary manpower in Spain. The Spanish activities of the NKVD were directed by Alexander Orlov.* The NKVD established a network of front companies to buy arms for Republican Spain. It participated in the transfer of Republican gold to Soviet vaults. NKVD police arrested Spaniards hostile to communist policies, especially after May 1937, and in general supported the expansion of influence by the Spanish Communist party.* The NKVD even investigated the backgrounds of volunteers* in the International Brigades* to make sure they posed no threat to Spanish communism.

The NKVD was responsible for over 2,000 Russians coming into Spain and perhaps as many as 3,000 during the Civil War. It is unknown how many were NKVD police or secret agents, but Manuel Azaña estimated that the number was around 700. Other authorities claim thousands. Some 1,000 airplanes, over 700 cannon, nearly 30 anti-aircraft guns, 700 tanks, almost 1,400 vehicles, 30,000 tons of ammunition, and 70,000 tons of other supplies came from the Soviet Union, most under the NKVD's administration. It also became one of the most powerful police forces within the Republic in silencing opposition to the communists. The net result was that the NKVD enhanced Moscow's capability to influence politics and events in the Republican zone in the last eighteen months of the war.

For further information, see Burnett Bolloten, *The Spanish Revolution: The Left and the Struggle for Power During the Civil War* (Chapel Hill, N.C., 1979); Walter Krivitsky, *I Was Stalin's Agent* (London, 1963); and Hugh Thomas, *The Spanish Civil War* (New York, 1977).

See also Germany.

James W. Cortada

NON-INTERVENTION COMMITTEE. The Non-Intervention Committee was formed in September 1936 at the suggestion of the Italians but with Great Britain* taking the lead, particularly Anthony Eden.* Its purpose was to give the appearance that the nations of Western Europe* were willing to confine the fighting to Spain and to block the sale of arms to either side. Throughout its life, until its dissolution in 1939, the role of the committee was to provide a united international policy for the governments of Europe to follow in restricting the spread of war from Spain. It failed since the committee had no power to block Italian, German, and Russian intervention into Spain or the sale and delivery of military supplies by almost every major nation at one time or another.

The British Foreign Office provided the necessary administrative support for the committee, headquartered in London. W. S. Morrison of the British Treasury led the English delegation, the British Foreign Office provided staffing, and each major European government's ambassador to London served on the committee. The sole exception was Switzerland* which never joined. The committee had a distinguished membership, its leading personalities including Charles Corbin for France,* Count Dino Grandi* for Italy,* Ivan Mikhailovich Maisky* for the USSR,* and Joachim von Ribbentrop (1893-1946) for Germany.* Subcommittees to handle various aspects of the Civil War were staffed by diplomats of the lesser powers.

Throughout the war, the committee served as a public forum for diplomatic complaints and discussions on the Spanish question. Violations of neutrality by Italy and Germany were often aired in its meetings, while British and French concerns for at least the appearance of nonintervention influenced its actions. The democracies' primary concern was to avoid the expansion of the fighting outside of Spain. The Italians, Germans, and Russians used the forum for open debate when it proved useful to them. In 1937, and again in 1938, the committee was called upon to provide the administrative support for developing a naval and air patrol of the Mediterranean to stop the destruction of neutral shipping by those favoring the Nationalists.* It failed in this task, as it did to prevent intervention in Spain, although ships flying its flag of two black balls on a field of white did appear for a while in the Mediterranean. Many of its watchdog responsibilities had also come about when the League of Nations* in effect shifted specific responsibility for international reactions to the Civil War to this committee. Hence, many of the heated diplomatic debates on the war that might otherwise have taken place within the League of Nations were instead held within the committee.

The British and the French were careful not to threaten the Germans and Italians when the latter two intervened in Spain with troops for fear that Rome and Berlin would withdraw from the committee and thus close off an avenue of debate. Struggles over monitoring naval affairs in the Mediterranean resulted in the Italians and Germans resigning from the neutrality patrols in 1937, although Rome agreed to participate again as a result of post-Nyon Conference* negotiations that fall.

The last meeting of the Non-Intervention Committee, prior to the end of the war, was held in July 1938. Between then and the end of the fighting, no additional meetings of the full membership were held, although subcommittees occasionally met. On April 20, 1939, the thirtieth and last full meeting was held for the purpose of dissolving the committee. Historians of the Civil War generally agree that the Non-Intervention Committee was an integral part of the diplomatic story of the war, a highly visible element, but one that hardly influenced the course of events. Hugh Thomas labels the group "hypocritical" since it called for neutrality when its members were anything but unbiased. For intellectuals* and diplomats in the democracies, it was a hoped-for avenue of curtailing fascist and communist interference in Spain's Civil War.

For further information, see John Bowyer Bell, "The Non-Intervention Committee and the Spanish Civil War, 1936-1939" (Ph.D. dissertation, Duke University, 1958); David Carlton, "Eden, Blum, and the Origins of Non-Intervention," *Journal of Contemporary History* 6 (Fall 1971):40-55; Patricia A.M. van der Esch, *Prelude to War: The International Repercussions of the Spanish Civil War, 1936-1939* (The Hague, 1951); and Arnold J. Toynbee, *Survey of International Affairs, 1937* (Oxford, 1938).

James W. Cortada

NON-INTERVENTION COMMITTEE SEA OBSERVATION SCHEME. Beginning on April 20, 1937, the Non-Intervention Committee Sea Observation Scheme provided for patrols by British, French, Italian, and German warships and observing officers on non-Spanish European merchant ships to ensure that violations of the Non-Intervention Agreement would be reported for corrective action. No violations were proved, for German arms ships flew the flag of exempt Panama, Italian forces and supplies arrived in exempt Spanish vessels or in escorted Italian "naval auxiliaries," and Soviet arms were largely shipped in exempt Spanish ships. Germany* and Italy* abandoned participation after the bombing of the *Deutschland** and definitively on June 23, 1937, following an alleged attack on the cruiser *Leipzig*. With British and French naval participation, the Sea Observation Scheme officially remained until the end of the war.

For further information, see Patricia A.M. van der Esch, *Prelude to War: The International Repercussions of the Spanish Civil War, 1936-1939* (The Hague, 1951).

Willard C. Frank, Jr.

NORWAY. Norway followed the British and French policies of neutrality in the Spanish Civil War. As a member of the League of Nations* and the Non-Intervention Committee,* Norway sought to minimize its involvement in Spain. Like Great Britain* and France,* Norway wanted to prevent a general European war, particularly in the face of potential German expansion into Western Europe* and British appeasement of Hitler.* In 1937, Norway participated in the naval patrol board established by the Non-Intervention Committee to protect neutral shipping in the Mediterranean. In the early part of 1939, Norway joined a number of other nations in sending surplus food* supplies to northern Spain to feed refugees.*

For further information, see the memoirs of the Norwegian chargé d'affaires in Spain at the start of the war, Felix Schlayer, *Diplomat im roten Madrid* (Berlin, 1938).

James W. Cortada

NOSOTROS (1936-1937). *Nosotros* was a key anarchist newspaper published in Valencia* during the Civil War, until the Republic closed its operations as a byproduct of the May 1937 riots.* During its existence, it gave its readers the *Federación Anarquista Ibérica* (FAI)* interpretation of events, expounded its anarchist philosophy, and became the main organ of the Iron Column. It was always critical of the Republican War Ministry of Francisco Largo Caballero,* constantly criticizing his dislike of anarchist politicians

and his removal of army officers from high command who sympathized with the FAI or the communists. Its attacks on him were very vehement; for example: "Largo Caballero is old, too old, and does not possess the mental agility necessary for solving certain problems." *Nosotros's* attacks on Largo Caballero were a major factor in his fall from power.

For further information, see Burnett Bolloten, *The Spanish Revolution: The Left and the Struggle for Power During the Civil War* (Chapel Hill, N.C., 1979).

James W. Cortada

NÚÑEZ DE PRADO SUSBIELAS, MIGUEL (1882-1936). Núñez de Prado was commissioned as a cavalry lieutenant in 1898 and later entered the Aviation Service. From 1920 on, he served in the regulars of Melilla,* earning in Africa several decorations and his promotion to general. Converted to republicanism after the fall of the dictatorship, he was involved in the abortive military conspiracy of 1931. The Republicans* made him an inspector-general of the army and in 1936, director-general of aviation. A Mason and a member of the leftist *Unión Militar Republicanas Antifascista* (UMRA),* Núñez de Prado placed politically reliable officers in key air force commands. On July 18, he was sent to Saragossa* to persuade General Cabanellas* not to revolt. He was arrested and later executed by the Nationalists* at Saragossa.

For further information, see Guillermo Cabanellas, *Cuatro generales*, 2 vols. (Barcelona, 1977); and Hugh Thomas, *The Spanish Civil War* (New York, 1977).

Carolyn P. Boyd

NUTRITION. *See* Food.

NUVOLINI, LUIGI. Nuvolini, a career Italian Army officer, commanded troops fighting in Spain on Franco's* side. On February 16, 1937, Mussolini* named him commander of the 3d Black Shirt* Division, one of four units sent to Spain. He commanded these soldiers at the battle of Guadalajara* in March 1937. As a result of this Italian military failure, Nuvolini and other generals were recalled to Rome and replaced with new commanders.

For further information, see John F. Coverdale, *Italian Intervention in the Spanish Civil War* (Princeton, N.J., 1975).
See also Italy.

James W. Cortada

NYON CONFERENCE. The Nyon Conference was a diplomatic gathering held near Geneva in mid-September 1937 for the purpose of finding a way to stop the destruction of commercial shipping (primarily Russian and British) in the Mediterranean and usually by Italian submarines.* The hosts were Great Britain* and France.* Italy* and Germany* did not attend. The Russians accused Italy of destroying two ships, the *Tuniyaev* and the *Blagaev*, while the British expressed concern over their own vessels. The results were the Nyon Agreements which stated that the Mediterranean would be patrolled by various nations to protect shipping. Italy subsequently agreed to participate in this police action, although she continued to sink ships. As Count Galeazzo Ciano,* the Italian foreign minister, put it, it would be the pirates patrolling themselves. The conference, however, indicated that the British were at least willing to stand up to Italy and Germany, although the agreements reached and the patrols established did not prevent continued destruction of neutral commercial shipping.

For further information, see James W. Cortada, "Ships, Diplomacy, and the Spanish Civil War: Nyon Conference, September, 1937," *Il Politico* 37 (1972): 673-89; and Peter Gretton, "The Nyon Conference—The Naval Aspect," *Economic Historical Review* 90 (January 1975):103-12.

James W. Cortada

O

O'DUFFY, EOIN (1892-1944). O'Duffy organized Irish volunteers* to fight for the Nationalists.* He had been a fascist in Ireland* and now led a group called the Blue Shirts. In Spain he commanded 600 soldiers who fought at the battle of Jarama* in February 1937; they sustained a high level of casualties with minimal effect on the outcome of the battle.

For further information, see Eoin O'Duffy, *Crusade in Spain* (London, 1938); and Seumas McKee, *I Was a Franco Soldier* (London, 1938).

James W. Cortada

OLAECHEA LOIZAGA, BISHOP MARCELINO (1889-1972). Bishop Marcelino Olaechea Loizaga of Pamplona* played a controversial role in the first months of the Civil War. Born on January 9, 1889, in Baracaldo, Vitoria,* to working-class parents, he was ordained a Salesian priest and named bishop of Pamplona in 1935. He signed the pastoral letter written by Cardinal Isidro Gomá* calling upon the Basque separatists to break off their support of the Republican government after the Civil War began, although he apparently did not entirely agree with the statement. He was a vocal counselor of moderation to his Carlist faithful in their fury against the Republicans.* He became archbishop of Valencia* in 1946 and died there on October 21, 1972.

For further information, see Juan de Iturralde, *El catolicismo y la cruzada de Franco* (Vienne, 1955, 1960).
See also Basque Nationalism; and Catholic Church, Spanish.

José M. Sánchez

OLD SHIRTS. The "Old Shirts" refers to the original members of the Falange* party prior to the Civil War. Most of these individuals supported Manuel Hedilla's* faction within the party during the war. By the spring of 1938, their political power had been broken by other groups within the Falange and in Franco's* government, resulting in some of the "Old Shirts" even

being arrested. From then on, they had no influence on Spanish politics.

For further information, see Stanley G. Payne, *Falange: A History of Spanish Fascism* (Stanford, Calif., 1961).

James W. Cortada

ORGAZ YOLDI, LUIS (1881-1946). Orgaz, born at Vitoria,* was commissioned in the infantry in 1898. Most of his career was spent in North Africa, where he won several merit promotions, rising to brigadier general in 1926. An ardent monarchist and an unconditional supporter of the dictatorship of General Primo de Rivera, he helped subdue the artillery revolt in Ciudad Real* in 1929 and the revolt at Cuatro Vientos in 1931. After the creation of the Republic, he plotted tirelessly to restore the monarchy. Exiled to the Canary Islands* in December 1931 for conspiracy, he was sent back in August 1932 for his participation in the abortive coup of General Sanjurjo.* In late 1935, he made contact with the right-wing leadership of the *Unión Militar Española* (UME)* and with various military conspirators. In April 1936, he was once again exiled to the Canaries for his part in the military plot led by General Angel Rodríguez del Barrio.*

In the Canaries, Orgaz organized the revolt that began on July 17 and assumed command there when his superior, General Francisco Franco,* departed for Morocco.* Five days later, Orgaz himself flew to Tetuán,* where he recruited battalions of Moroccan soldiers and organized their transfer to the peninsula. Appointed to the *Junta de Defensa Nacional** in August, he was a strong supporter of General Kindelán's* proposal to unify the Nationalists* under the single command of General Franco who, on October 1, appointed Orgaz high commissioner in Morocco. In December, Orgaz replaced General Mola* as supreme commander of the forces attacking Madrid.* By mid-January, having gained only 7 miles at the cost of 15,000 casualties,* Orgaz called off his attack on the capital and turned his forces to the Jarama River in an attempt to sever the Madrid-Valencia* road. Criticized for failing to provide a diversionary offensive to aid the Italian forces at Guadalajara* in March

1937, Orgaz was made head of Mobilization, Instruction, and Recuperation, where he won acclaim for the successful organization of a training academy for sergeants and provisional officers. In December, he was appointed to the newly created National Council, a largely honorific advisory body. A year later, he was given the command of the Army of the Levante.*

After the war, Orgaz served in a number of high-ranking military and political posts, including captain general of Barcelona,* high commissioner in Morocco, chief of the central general staff, councillor of state, vice-president of the National Economic Council, and *procurador* in the Cortes.* In these positions, he represented the anti-Falangist interests in the army. In 1943, he and seven other generals petitioned Franco to restore the monarchy. He died in Madrid in 1946.

For further information, see Felipe Bertrán Güell, *Caudillo, profetas, y soldados* (Madrid, 1939); Teresa Suero Roca, *Los generales de Franco* (Barcelona, 1975); and Hugh Thomas, *The Spanish Civil War* (New York, 1977).

See also Nationalist Army.

Carolyn P. Boyd

ORIGINS OF THE SPANISH CIVIL WAR. The Spanish Civil War started as a military uprising, but became a class war, a social revolution, a religious struggle, a crusade for national unity, and an assertion of regional separatism. Its origins are correspondingly complex but in the broadest sense lie in the revolutionary tensions generated by the delayed process of modernization in a relatively isolated, traditional, stratified, church-dominated society. The danger in such a context was that the political system would prove inadequate to the strains of modernization and would break down, permitting a polarization of society between groups determined to perpetuate the old order and those seeking radical change. This danger was made greater by the relative weakness and political immaturity of the middle classes—usually the bulwark of the moderate, parliamentary center against the extremes—which in turn was largely the result of the sluggish development of Spanish capitalism after 1870.

In retrospect, Spain's best chance to pass safely through the shoals of modernization without either a repressive dictatorship or a shattering social struggle apparently lay in the continuation for a while of a regime much like that established by Antonio Cánovas del Castillo in 1876: monarchical, semi-authoritarian, conservatively liberal, and quasi-parliamentary, with the masses quiescent but gradually awakening. Based on the alliance of the old agrarian elites with the rising commercial, financial, and industrial groups, this oligarchical regime was committed to what Barrington Moore has called conservative modernization, compatible in the short run with the perpetuation of existing political and social structures. Spain made progress under such a regime, though not as much as would have been desirable. While the breakdown of the two Canovite parties beginning early in this century, along with traumatic episodes such as the Tragic Week of 1909 and the General Strike of 1917, pointed toward a growing polarization of society, there were also signs, especially in the period 1918-1923, that the system was ceasing to be an artificial one, that it was beginning to involve the people and to permit the growth of an authentic parliamentary regime responding to authentic forces.

At some point, modernization inevitably meant the politicization of the masses and their involvement in running the country. But it was also clear that if the people ever awakened en masse from the apolitical slumber induced by the Canovite system, this would bring both promise and great peril. On the one hand, a genuinely mass-based, democratic political order might emerge. On the other hand, the sudden awakening of an impoverished, illiterate, and politically inexperienced people could only exert extreme pressures on any parliamentary system, whether monarchical or republican, and increase the likelihood of breakdown. The hazard at that point in Spain's evolution would be that the fervor of the newly politicized masses could not be contained within a liberal-constitutional framework and would be channeled into a popular revolutionary movement which, by a familiar dialectic, would inevitably rouse the forces of counterrevolution.

Since the prevention of this kind of polarization, latent in most societies, is the main function of a political system, the central causal thread that must be followed through the Spanish "labyrinth" toward an understanding of the origins of the Civil War is the struggle of the political Center—the moderate, proparliamentary Left and Right—to maintain a precarious unity against the antiparliamentary extremes in an increasingly revolutionary context. In fact, the history of the origins of the Civil War is essentially the history of a political debacle: the failure of the relatively moderate centrist forces of the Second Republic* in the years 1931-1936 to preserve that minimum of political cohesion upon which parliamentary government, progress, and social peace depended.

The overthrow of the faltering Canovite system by General Primo de Rivera in September 1923 paved the way for civil war in at least two ways. First, since the king was known to have connived in the subversion of the constitution, the coup politicized him, gravely weakened his support among the people, and thereby undermined the monarchy as a bridge between the several Spains, making impossible a return to the semiconstitutional restoration system of Cánovas which, of course, depended on the monarchy for its proper functioning. Second, it was mainly the authoritarianism of the dictatorship which marked the real beginning of the political awakening of the masses, a process greatly accelerated by Primo's fall in 1930 and by the dramatic collapse of the monarchy in 1931.

The fall of the monarchy brought to the fore with a vengeance all the dangerous and divisive problems of an invertebrate and underdeveloped society—issues that had been contained or submerged by the collusive Canovite polity and by the dictatorship: class conflict, regionalism and separatism, clericalism, economic and educational policy, the agrarian question, the role of the military. All of these problems, while they gravely overloaded the agenda of the new Republic, might have been dealt with successfully had it not been for the most divisive force of all: the rising revolutionary mood of the urban and rural masses, which was a natural consequence of their politicization and which was aroused more by the arbitrary methods of the dictatorship and by the hope engendered by its fall than by the Great Depression, which did not greatly affect Spain until 1932. The importance of this unexpected but powerful upsurge of mass emotion can hardly be exaggerated, for in the final analysis this mood forced the departure of the king, which made the establishment of the Republic possible, which encouraged the hubris of the Left-Republicans, and which, in the end, rendered the Republic unworkable, condemned either to paralysis and collapse or to dictatorial transformation. Above all, it was this mood which most served to divide the country and to rouse the spirit of counterrevolution in threatened groups and classes. It would not be too much to say that the wave of popular revolutionary feeling in the early 1930s was the single most important cause of the Civil War. No other factor contributed so directly and in so many ways to the reciprocal process of political breakdown and polarization which made the war virtually inevitable.

The Second Republic, inaugurated in 1931, went through three major phases, each of which left the nation more divided into extremes than before and the political system closer to collapse: a Left phase, 1931-1933; a Right phase, 1933-1935; and another Left phase, 1935-1936. The cumulative effect of these alternating phases, in which first one "Spain" and then the other believed itself mortally threatened, was an accelerated erosion of an already fragile consensus and the steady crumbling of the political center. This process began with the founding of the Republic, which was accompanied by an outbreak of quasi-revolutionary disturbances on a large scale in both the southern latifundia provinces and in the major cities, and by the rapid growth of the revolutionary Left (anarchosyndicalists, socialists, and communists) and of the extremist Right (Carlists,* clericalists, and fascists). Nevertheless, throughout the 1931-1936 period the forces of the moderate Left and the moderate Right could easily have controlled large majorities in the Cortes* and saved the country from civil war had they ever found the will and the flexibility to compromise and to work together.

The first phase of the Republic (1931-1933), after a very brief liberal Catholic interval under Alcalá-Zamora, was dominated by a coalition of Left-Republicans and socialists who had triumphed in the elections to the Constituent Cortes in June 1931. The prime minister and dominant personality of this period was the middle-class radical Manuel Azaña,* in many ways the prototype of the French-influenced Spanish intellectual. Obsessed with ideological and anticlerical issues and determined that Spain should at last have a revolution on the French model, he was less vitally interested in social and economic questions. Never popular as a writer, he found his metier as a revolutionary ideologue and parliamentary tribune. No one articulated better than he the long-thwarted anticlerical aspirations of Spanish republicanism as well as its relatively newfound hostility toward the military. Nor did anyone reveal more clearly the hubris to which the intellectual who attains power is so susceptible.

With his intellectual brilliance, his austere, intimidating manner, and his monotonal but overpowering and often sarcastic rhetoric, Azaña dominated the Constituent Cortes and carried through it a number of enactments which, though not truly revolutionary, succeeded in arousing the conservative and counterrevolutionary forces without really satisfying the more radical groups. Many of these enactments were valuable and necessary; some were merely provocative; and all were to a degree marred by an ill-concealed spirit of vindictiveness against the Republicans'* old enemies. Despite the fact that the country was divided nearly equally between Republicans and monarchists, Azaña and his followers acted and talked as though their somewhat artificial parliamentary majority reflected a massive popular mandate. Often arrogant and always sectarian, Azaña's greatest flaw was his lack of magnanimity; his greatest mistake was his persistent failure to grasp the vital need to strengthen a broad Center coalition, encompassing Left-Center and Right-Center, upon which alone the Republic could be securely founded. Thus when forced, late in 1931, to choose between continued cooperation with the Right-centrist followers of Lerroux or increased dependence upon the more revolutionary socialists, Azaña chose the latter course, thereby creating the first major division within the centrist coalition that had launched the Republic earlier that year.

The most controversial enactments of the Azaña regime had to do with the Church.* This was the sphere in which the emotions of the zealously anticlerical Left-Republican intellectuals* were most involved and where they most relished their newfound power to act. This was a natural response to the centuries-old cultural hegemony of the Church, but it is nevertheless clear that a more gradualist approach to the religious question could have won over to the Republic many moderate Catholics who were instead alienated. The divorce law was the least objectionable of Azaña's enactments, but the terms of the law secularizing cemeteries was clearly punitive. Separation of church and state was doubtless desirable, but the decision to sever all state financial aid in only two years was unwise, driving away from the Republic thousands of poor priests who could have been recruited to its defense. Thus, Azaña's clerical measures did little to create a broad base of support for the Republic and instead gave to extreme clericalists a banner by which to rally large numbers of moderate Catholics to their side. The failure of the Left-Republicans earlier (before Azaña became premier) to act decisively against the burning of churches and convents in Madrid* was a serious political mistake, aborting the hopeful possibility of a fusion of republicanism and liberal Catholicism, which could have put the new Republic on a solid foundation from its inception.

Second only to the Church as an object of the Left-Republicans' rancor was the Spanish Army. Azaña carried through a number of measures, some well conceived and some not, but all of them advanced in a spirit of antipathy and bound to antagonize the military establishment: elimination of the law of jurisdictions, integration of the military with civil justice, retirement of surplus generals—albeit on full pay—and the rescinding of all merit (that is, combat-based) promotions won under the dictatorship. In addition, the Azaña government made a large number of command assignments designed to displace conservative monarchist officers by their more politically reliable colleagues. Finally, although logistics and training were improved, the army budget was cut slightly. In the grip of a doctrinaire animosity, Azaña made little or no effort to win the officer corps over to the Republic, despite the fact that a large majority of the officers in 1931 were either apolitical or pro-Republican. The result was a growing antigovernment hostility on the part of the military only a little less marked than that of the clergy.

This hostility was worsened by a reform carried out by the government in another area, that of Catalan regionalism. The willingness of the Left-Republicans to make a rather liberal grant of autonomy to the Catalans was in many ways statesmanlike, but it further irritated army leaders, for whom the army was the self-consecrated guardian of national unity. Many conservatives and moderates, including many intellectuals, also believed the Catalan Statute went too far. Indeed, however well-intentioned, the autonomy statute had many adverse political effects, alienating many and giving a decisive and even fatal impetus to the polarization process. Many prominent persons who had initially supported the Republic now ceased to do so, including Ortega* and Unamuno.*

The Republic's agrarian legislation was aimed at the single most serious national problem, but it too helped erode the political Center. The situation in the southern latifundia provinces, where nearly a million landless, impoverished peasants had been roused to a condition of militant expectancy by the fall of the monarchy, was virtually revolutionary. Not only did Azaña's Left-Republicans feel the urgent need to defuse this social time bomb, but they were also pushed toward action by intense pressure from their main political ally, the Socialist party* (over half of whose members were now peasants), which saw the solution of the agrarian problem as the highest priority and chief justification for the party's unprecedented participation in the government. The socialist leader Largo Caballero* became minister of labor and immediately took crash measures to aid the peasants' desperate situation and thereby forestall their recruitment by the anarchosyndicalists. Arbitral committees were staffed in favor of the land workers, employers were forbidden to hire workers from outside the local area, and the eight-hour day was imposed. These measures resulted in an immediate improvement in the peasants' condition and won them for the Republic, but in the process the government incurred the hostility of the landed classes who felt that their ability to farm profitably was being seriously impaired.

The major agrarian reform which Azaña pushed through the Cortes was a law calling for the expropriation of landholdings over a certain size (which varied widely from one area to another) or of a particular type (for example, poorly cultivated). Under pressure from the socialists, the Left-Republicans unwisely and excessively broadened the application of the law so that nearly 85 percent of the owners affected by expropriation were medium or even small holders rather than latifundists. Left to their own instincts, the Azaña Republicans, not really eager to launch a social revolution, would probably have attacked only the great landowners, thereby holding the support of moderates both in the Cortes and in the country. But their dependence on the socialists precluded such a course, and it is essential to recognize that the dependence was necessary primarily because they resolutely scorned any accommodation with the more conservative Republicans to their right, that is, with the Radicals led by Alejandro Lerroux.

With the exception of some features of the clerical legislation, the reform program of the first phase of the Republic cannot be described as truly radical, and it was clear that the Left-Republicans did not intend a social revolution. Nor with the exception of the agrarian law did their socialist allies push as hard as they might have for a radical social transformation. Had the Azaña legislative program been the only threat posed by the Left to the possessing classes, it would have been traumatic but not necessarily devastating. Hence, it should be noted that the polarizing effect of these reforms was exacerbated by the violent actions and rhetoric of the extreme Left, that is, of the anarchosyndicalists and communists whose impact in this period must be borne in mind if the increasing radicalism and obduracy of the Right is to be made comprehensible.

The anarchosyndicalists in particular had for many years made clear that a republic held no mystique for them and that they would regard it only as a transitional thing, to be quickly trod underfoot on the march toward a total reconstruction of society on the basis of libertarian communism. They therefore gave the Republic very little respite but immediately launched a wave of strike actions, shootings, bombings, and church burnings whose purpose was simply to undermine the new regime. The left wing of the Socialist party also grew rapidly in this period, with its leaders using the harshest kind of class-war rhetoric. In this early period, the communist party,* though still extremely small (about 25,000 in 1932), also adopted an extremely revolutionary position that furthered the polarizing process.

Inevitably, the pendulum of public opinion began to swing back to the Right, as was revealed in the municipal elections of 1933, in which the more conservative Republicans of the Radical party and the still more right-wing (but on the whole proparliamentary) *Confederación Española de Derechas Autónomas* (CEDA) of Gil Robles* made impressive gains. The realistic next step ought to have been a shift to the Right by the Azaña Republicans, who would end their alliance with the socialists and seek a rapprochement with the Radicals, the largest single Republican party. Such a move toward the Center, however painful for the Left-Republicans, would not only have demonstrated political capacity but would also have strengthened the Center forces at the expense of the antiparliamentary extremes and provided a stronger political structure for the young Republic.

But Azaña and his fellow intellectuals-in-politics felt a fatal aversion to the Radicals which was partly temperamental, having to do with the elitist antipathy of university-trained, doctrinaire, sincerely anticlerical Republicans toward the not very intellectual and no longer truly anticlerical republicanism of Lerroux and his followers who were, in addition, regrettably pettybourgeois and opportunistic in character. But it was also true—and this may have been the heart of the matter—that a rapprochement with the more numerous Radicals would almost certainly have made Lerroux prime minister in place of Azaña. Whatever the reasons, by rejecting an alliance with the Radicals, Azaña and his Left-Republicans were condemning themselves to an alliance with the socialists, whose commitment to republicanism had always been very conditional and who, moreover, were in this period being radicalized and divided by an influx of rural masses more interested in social gains than in forms of government.

The revolutionary upsurge among the masses, along with Azaña's agrarian and especially his clerical reforms, naturally ignited a growing reaction among the conservative classes. The anticlerical vehemence and unrestrained class-war rhetoric of the Left was taken seriously by those on the Right, who believed that their extinction, as well as that of the Church, was being contemplated. Indeed, clericalism and anticlericalism were symbolic surrogates, standing for the clash of the two Spains on a whole range of social issues. A major consequence of the arousal of the conservative elements was the emergence, in 1932, of the pro-Catholic CEDA, formed by the lawyer-politician Gil Robles to defend the Church's interests. Although the rhetoric of Gil Robles and especially of his youthful followers in the *Juventud de Acción Popular* (JAP) often had—in reaction to the rhetoric of the Left—a shrill and pseudofascist tonality, the fact is that Gil Robles, though preferring a monarchy, was a parliamentarist and, by Spanish standards, a moderate who was trying to lead his followers into collaboration with the Republic.

This ought to have been perceived and applauded by the Left-Republicans. But not only did they not applaud, but they, along with the socialists, greatly exaggerated the rightist and sinister propensities of the *cedistas*. They did this largely under the spell of a European analogy of dubious applicability. Shocked by the crushing of the Left by the Nazi regime in Germany* and by the Dolfuss regime in Austria, they stubbornly identified the CEDA with "fascism" and were almost hysterical in their resolve that the German-Austrian scenario not be played out in Spain. This feeling led them, in turn, seriously to overreact to the prospect that the CEDA, which was growing rapidly, might come to power as part of a Right-of-Center coalition governing a republic which the partisans of the Left had come to regard as their special creature. Thus, the polarization process that was undermining the unity of the political Center in Spain in the early 1930s was aggravated by a factor extraneous to the Spanish scene—an ideological intervention by Europe* that portended the military intervention that lay ahead.

The second of the three political phases that marked Spain's path toward civil war was launched by the decisive victory of the Right-Center and rightist parties in the elections of November 1933, a victory partly caused by the refusal of the Left-Republicans and socialists to join in electoral coalitions. The result was that, though the popular vote totals of the Left did not decline significantly, its strength in the Parliament dropped markedly.

Hence, the Left lost control of the Republic, and a new governing coalition was created in December 1933 by the Radical leader Lerroux. Lerroux, a far more pragmatic, albeit less intellectually gifted, leader than Azaña, made statesmanlike efforts to build a strong Center coalition. He did this mainly by trying to win Gil Robles and the proclerical *cedistas* over to the Republic and bring them into the government. These efforts, entirely justified by the CEDA's electoral gains, were exaggeratedly viewed by the socialists as the gravest possible threat to themselves, and it now became clear that their loyalty to the Republic and to the democratic process was as provisional and opportunistic as that of many monarchists. When it finally became evident to them that the Republic was something more than merely their instrumentality and that it might be used not to promote but to oppose their revolutionary social aspirations, they quickly turned against it and began to contemplate revolt.

The improbable leader of this newfound revolutionary impulse in Spanish socialism was the long-time reformist leader Francisco Largo Caballero. "Bourgeois" parliamentarism had never had a high priority for him; he had always preferred to rely on trade-union organizational power. In the period 1932-1933, he felt compelled to make a sharp turn to the Left and to stress the rhetorical themes of class war and proletarian dictatorship in order to prevent the capture of the increasingly aroused socialist trade-union masses by the more radical anarchosyndicalists. His decision effectively split the Socialist party and thereby further weakened the Center forces upon which parliamentary democracy and the viability of the Republic depended. But it must be repeated that the process at work here was not the caprice of Largo Caballero but rather the force of the popular revolutionary mood of which Largo Caballero and the *Unión General de Trabajadores* (UGT)* chiefs had to take leadership, lest it leave them behind.

Inevitably, the rising revolutionary spirit of the working classes—with its attendant disorders—and the shock of the anticlerical and agrarian legislation passed since 1931 had a galvanizing effect on conservative opinion, stimulating the growth of a variety of right-wing groups and parties. These ran the gamut from ultramonarchists, Carlists, authoritarian nationalists, and fascists (who were not, of course, precisely conservative) to more moderate proclerical groups of which the CEDA of José María Gil Robles was the largest and most prominent. The policy of Lerroux, the new prime minister, was to come to terms with this right-wing upsurge, particularly with the growing electoral power of the pro-Catholic CEDA. Thus, his government rescinded or nullified in practice much that the Azaña regime had done. Salaries of Spanish priests were extended through 1934, thus delaying the separation of church and state; and the educational functions of the Spanish Catholic Church were not curtailed as the Left-Republicans had wished. The Catalan statute was suspended, though not nullified. In the countryside, Lerroux swung the balance of power away from the land workers and back to the landowners by the appointments he made to the "mixed juries" deciding wage and other disputes, thus liquidating most of the gains made during the Azaña era and building up an anger among the workers that would erupt with revolutionary force in 1936. In general, between 1933 and 1935 both the urban and rural working classes felt themselves to be under sustained attack.

Lerroux also attempted to placate the army and halt its growing alienation from the Republic. He pardoned General Sanjurjo,* who had rebelled in 1932, and he endeavored to improve morale in the officer corps by restoring merit promotions and improving training. Most crucial, perhaps, was his determination to bring Gil Robles and the CEDA into his cabinet, whereby he hoped to make that pro-Catholic party a pillar of the Republic rather than its nemesis. Unfortunately, the socialists had developed an almost pathological dread of CEDA participation, having convinced themselves that such a step would inevitably lead to the destruction of Spanish socialism. Certainly, it was regrettable that Gil Robles would not explicitly accept the Republic for fear of losing his more monarchist supporters. Still, it was evident that he accepted the Republic de facto and was prepared to work within its framework, even as he changed its "content" with respect to the clerical laws. But in a Spain where the masses were increasingly aroused and politicized, the process of polarization had by now acquired a dynamic of its own, and Lerroux's attempts at conciliation proved as divisive as Azaña's intransigence. The announcement in October 1934 that a new Lerroux ministry would include three CEDA members, though not Gil Robles, touched off a workers' revolt against the Republic.

There were, in reality, three attacks against the Lerroux-dominated Republic in the period 1933-1934. The first of these had been launched by the anarchosyndicalists late in 1933 and involved bombings, assassination attempts, attacks on the Civil Guards,* and revolutionary strikes, the most serious of which was the nearly two-month strike at Saragossa.* A revolutionary committee of anarchists* was set up here, headed by Durruti,* and pitched battles were fought against the authorities, who needed tanks to put the strikers down. The second attack came in October 1934, shortly after the three *Cedistas* were added to Lerroux's cabinet. Convinced that the "fascist" CEDA was going to overthrow the Republic, the socialists were determined to move first. This they did in Madrid, where the UGT declared a general strike and armed assaults were made on public buildings. Some communists adhered to this movement, but the peasants in the countryside, having risen earlier in the year, did not join the revolutionary effort which, under the uninspired leadership of Largo Caballero, was quickly extinguished in the capital and in the few other cities where it had gained support. Simultaneous with this was the proclamation in Barcelona* of a Catalan state by the Republican leader Luis Companys* amid a wave of nationalist feeling aroused in part by Lerroux's suspension of the autonomy statute. The anarchosyndicalist masses did not join this movement, and it was easily suppressed by the army with a minimum of bloodshed.

The third phase of the attack on the Lerroux-dominated Republic was, for a time, far more successful, being spearheaded by the socialist miners in Asturias.* It is

to this movement that the term "October Revolution" properly belongs. Only in this part of Spain were the working-class factions—socialists, communists, and anarchosyndicalists—relatively united. The tough Asturian workers were well armed and were filled with a fanatical conviction that they were fighting for their very survival against the forces of fascism. Their intent was clearly revolutionary: they formed a "Red Army" and proclaimed the total overthrow of the old society as well as of the new republic, which would be replaced by socialism and the dictatorship of the proletariat. They soon conquered by force of arms nearly the whole of Asturias and gave the country a foretaste of the future by executing a number of their class enemies, including businessmen, priests, and some thirty Civil Guards. They also burned a number of churches and convents.

When the Lerroux government proved determined to put down the revolt with all the force necessary, the fighting developed into a brief, bitterly fought, and destructive civil war. Generals Goded* and Franco* were called in to direct the Republican Army* forces, and they in turn brought in Moorish and Foreign Legion* troops from North Africa. There was heavy fighting especially in Oviedo* and Gijon,* and in the end the workers' revolt was suppressed after numerous casualties were suffered on both sides. Perhaps as many as 30,000 workers were arrested following the socialists' defeat, and some summary executions were carried out by army commanders at the scene. But it was also true that the Lerroux government did not order the execution of a single leader of this rebellion and refused to allow the generals to carry out more massive reprisals. It also refused, in the aftermath of the uprising, to make any attempt to set up a dictatorship. Even the taking over of the War Ministry by Gil Robles in 1935 did not lead to any effort on his part to subvert the Constitution. Nevertheless, despite this essential moderation, the conviction became rooted among the men of the Left that the Asturian uprising had been repressed with the utmost barbarity, and this created a profound sense of alienation from middle-class Spain.

The October Revolution was therefore the fatal turning point, and the single most polarizing event, in the whole process that led to the Civil War, making that conflict all but inevitable. It completed the politicizing and revolutionizing of the working classes all over Spain, engendering a class hatred and militancy that would flare up violently in the summer of 1936. But the conservative classes were scarcely less stirred and angered than the workers. In the revolt's aftermath, under the mantle of the Lerroux ministry, they reasserted themselves, often with excess and unwisdom, in the cities (where wages were pushed down and working hours extended) and in the countryside (where most of the gains won earlier by the land workers were annulled). On the other hand, the Lerroux government did not attempt to take back any of the land that had already been distributed to poor peasants.

The third and final phase leading to the Civil War began with the fall of the Lerroux government late in 1935 as the result of the Straperlo scandal, which involved corruption and nepotism. Even though the Right-Center Cortes still had two years remaining in its mandate and had the support of the army, the president of the Republic, Alcalá-Zamora, feeling that the pendulum of politics had swung too far to the Right, decided, after much urging by Azaña and the Left, to dissolve the Cortes and call for new elections. This was a crucial contingency in the drift toward civil war, setting the stage for a leftist victory that was almost bound to push the army into revolt against the Republic.

The election of February 1936* was a bitterly waged contest between the National Front,* which was a coalition of right-wing, anti-Marxist parties, and the Popular Front,* which was made up of Left-Republicans, socialists, and communists. Largely because of the Asturian repression, the tide of public opinion now turned sufficiently back to the Left to give victory at the polls to the Popular Front parties. But again it should be noted that the swing in the popular vote was not very great. Indeed, most Spaniards once again voted for either the Center-Right or the Center-Left parties and not for the antiparliamentary extremes. One of the most important results of this election was that Azaña, wearing the aura of a martyr by virtue of his unjust arrest in Barcelona during the 1934 uprising, was now the man of the hour among the partisans of the Left. Unfortunately, he was also the single most unpopular figure in the country as far as the army and most clericals were concerned. His victory in this election was a red flag to the generals, and his elevation to the presidency in May 1936 was positively provocative.

Crucial also was the division within the ranks of the socialists between Indalecio Prieto* and his moderate, proparliamentary followers and Largo Caballero who, having for the first time read Marx and Lenin in his cell following the abortive general strike, now moved still more sharply to the Left and put himself at the head of the revolutionary current which, in the spring of 1936, was sweeping the UGT masses along. As a result, the socialists did not enter the new Azaña ministry, which was thereby deprived of the support which

a united and relatively moderate Socialist party could have supplied. Thus, the radicalization of the socialists contributed both to the paralysis of the Azaña government and to the quasi-revolutionary uproar that finally motivated the military rebellion in July. Madariaga* wrote that the Spanish Civil War was made "inevitable" by the civil war within the Socialist party, but it is equally true to say that the rupture in the Socialist party was made inevitable by the growing revolutionary mood of the urban and rural workers, who, it must be reiterated, would have moved to the Left and toward revolution whether or not Largo Caballero led them.

This revolutionary mood was, in turn, an aspect of the impressive revitalization—social, cultural, political, and to a lesser degree economic—that Spaniards had experienced since 1898. The country, emerging from a long period of somnolence, was bursting with energy in nearly every field of endeavor, and nearly every social class was affected. The vitality of the working class was especially revealed in the rising numbers, vigor, and self-confidence of the socialist and anarchosyndicalist movements and in the revolutionary spirit that increasingly dominated them. Had Spanish capitalism been more vigorous and productive, this revolutionary mood might have been dissipated by the wider spread of material well-being. But the uncertain process of modernization in Spain had created a fatal tension between a sluggishly developing capitalism and a numerically expanding and ideologically precocious proletariat influenced by European ideas but also prone to antimodernist outbursts. Demography also became a revolutionary force, first because rural population* grew more rapidly than industrial cities could absorb it, and second because the labor movement was, in essence, a youth movement. The driving force behind the extremism of both Right and Left was youth. Even within the army it was the young officers, on the whole, who were the most activist. In a sense, then, the Civil War was the obverse and destructive side of the Spanish Renaissance—the price Spaniards paid for an excess of national energy that could not in the end be constructively channeled either by the monarchy or by the Republic that followed it.

The spring of 1936, following the victory of the Popular Front, was a time of unprecedented revolutionary excitement and exaltation among both urban and rural masses. Socialists and anarchosyndicalists vied with each other in launching hundreds of strikes in which obviously excessive wage and other demands were made on employers with the purpose not of bargaining but of bringing down the capitalist system.

These strikes were accompanied by a great deal of violence, much of it directed by workers against other workers. In the countryside, thousands of workers simply moved in and occupied farmlands while terrorizing the rural middle classes with assaults, false arrests, and murder. These expropriations were essentially revolutionary but were nevertheless sanctioned by the Azaña-Casares Quirogas* government which made virtually no attempt to preserve order in the countryside, or even in the cities where tumult grew day by day. The major precipitating cause of the Civil War was the strange paralysis of the Left-Republican government over a period of several months in the face of the revolutionary or prerevolutionary turbulence sweeping the country. Although this regime was now a minority government based only on a fragment of the crumbling Center, there was little organized opposition to it in the Cortes. The business community had in effect capitulated to the economic demands of the Popular Front, asking only that the government take steps to restore order in the cities and in the countryside. The failure to take such steps was due in part to the fact that in this quasi-revolutionary situation much of the ministers' power and authority had slipped away and into the hands of labor organizations—the UGT and the *Confederación Nacional del Trabajo* (CNT)*—outside the political framework.

But the government's inertia also reflected in part a paralysis of the will of Azaña, the man who could have done the most either to carry Spain into a full-fledged revolution or to restore order. Either one of these courses would probably have prevented civil war, but the prolonged drift between them was fatal and called out for some outside force to step in and restore tranquility. The source of Azaña's curious withdrawal and apathy in these months probably lay in the fact that, like many intellectuals in politics, he was sentimentally disposed toward the extreme Left and "revolution" without being a revolutionary. Although he did not lack the means with which to act to restore order, he was reluctant to sanction the use of force against a working-class movement which, however turbulent or even misguided it might be, he regarded as historically progressive and with which he felt himself allied in a struggle against groups that he, along with most Left-Republicans and workers, increasingly regarded as "fascist." And yet at the same time he lacked the resoluteness to take control of the diffuse revolutionary movement enveloping the country, give it leadership, and put it on a constructive course. Failing to do that, he ought to have accepted Martínez Barrio's* urgent call for the establishment of a national government, a government that would have encompassed all the proparliamentary parties from Left to Right and been so broadly based that it could have brought the country under control. A more politically gifted and less doctrinaire leader, one suspects, could have found a way out of the impasse. But Azaña, whose talents were more rhetorical than political, could only withdraw increasingly within the presidential palace and leave his exalted, confused, and divided nation to its fate.

Although various monarchist figures had been plotting revolt since 1931, the great majority of army officers had held aloof from such conspiracies. What swung them over to rebellion was primarily the steady disintegration of both the economy and of law and order under the Popular Front government. They were gravely concerned by the growing revolutionary current in the country, even though it continued to be diffuse, disjointed, and slow to mature, and by attacks made on the army by the ultra-Left which urged its dissolution and replacement by people's militias.* The army revolt developed very slowly in the months after the Popular Front victory. The military plotters, led by General Mola,* were not particularly right-wing and had no clear ideology beyond the patriotic preservation of social order and authority and the prevention of the proletarianization of either the army or of Spain. Increasingly, they, like so many on the Right, came to feel that they had only two choices: passivity, which, they believed, would lead to their extinction; or revolt, which would mean the effective end of the Republic.

Still, the army revolt very nearly did not materialize. The majority of generals were not eager to rebel, and the support of other social groups was problematical. The main thrust toward revolt came from the midlevel and junior officers. The crucial event that made the uprising possible was the Carlist militia's decision on July 12 to go against their own national leadership and support a military uprising. The murder by police* agents on July 13 of the prominent conservative Calvo Sotelo,* leader of the monarchist opposition in the Cortes, was the final factor that pushed the army into rebellion, giving a certain urgency to the conspirators' belief that their was a defensive move against an immediately impending left-wing takeover. Even so, the revolt—whose details cannot be discussed here—was a tour de force carried off by a minority of resolute officers against enormous odds and without the support of the majority of the middle class who, though fearful of impending revolution, were not initially in favor of a military coup. Above all, the military revolt was the spark, the catalyst, which, injected into the charged and by now extremely polarized Spanish milieu, produced the explosion of civil war.

The final contingencies needed to turn a *pronunciamiento* into a civil war were, first, the failure of the Azaña regime to move promptly to put down the revolt which began on July 17 and which could almost certainly have been crushed by resolute action by the government, and, second, the converse failure of the revolt to triumph quickly over all of Spain. This failure to be crushed or to prevail quickly was extremely grave in that it meant a period of uncertainty during which the various social groups and regions lined up— or were perforce lined up—either on the side of the rebellion or against it. Hence, what started as one more *pronunciamiento* rapidly escalated into a full-scale Civil War in which the "two Spains"—one revolutionary and the other counterrevolutionary—achieved the ultimate polarization of armed combat with no quarter given.

For further information, see Joaquín Arrarás, *Historia de la segunda republica española*, 4 vols. (Madrid, 1956-1964), for a pro-Franco interpretation; Manuel Azaña, *Memorias íntimad de Azaña* (Madrid, 1939) and his *Obras completas* (Mexico, 1966), by a president of the Republic; Alberto Balcells, *Crisis económica y agitación social en Cataluña, 1930-1936* (Barcelona, 1971), on the impact; John Brademas, *Anarcosindicalismo y revolución en España, 1930-1937* (Barcelona, 1974), on the far Left; Gerald Brenan, *The Spanish Labyrinth* (Cambridge, England, 1943), on social origins; Pierre Broué and Emile Témime, *La révolution et la guerre d'Espagne* (Paris, 1970), for a view favorable to the Republican cause; Raymond Carr, *The Republic and the Civil War in Spain* (London, 1971), for a collection of essays by various authors and his earlier *Spain, 1808-1939* for a general history; Ricardo de la Cierva, *Los documentos de la Primavera Trágica* (Madrid, 1967), for contemporary material; José María García Escudero, *Historia política de las dos Españas*, 3 vols. (Madrid, 1976), for massive data on political life; José María Gil Robles, *No fué posible la paz* (Barcelona, 1968), by a conservative Republican who later supported the post-1939 regime for a while; Gabriel Jackson, *Costa, Azaña, el Frente Popular y otros ensayos* (Madrid, 1976), by an historian sympathetic to the Republic; Edward Malefakis, *Agrarian Reform and Peasant Revolution in Spain* (New Haven, Conn., 1970), on one of the key causes of the Civil War; Stanley G. Payne, *Falange: A History of Spanish Fascism* (Stanford, Calif., 1961), *La Revolución y la guerra civil española* (Madrid, 1977), and his *Politics and the Military in Modern Spain* (Stanford, Calif., 1967), all

dealing with major political affairs; Paul Preston, *The Coming of the Spanish Civil War* (London, 1978), also on political life during the Republic; Richard Robinson, *The Origins of Franco's Spain* (Newton Abbot, 1970), on the political Right; Hugh Thomas, *The Spanish Civil War* (New York, 1977), for a general one-volume history; Manuel Tuñon de Lara, *La España del siglo XX* (Paris, 1966), for an interpretive overview; and Javier Tusell, *Las elecciones del Frente Popular*, 2 vols. (Madrid, 1971), on some immediate events before the Civil War.

See also Basque Nationalism; Catalonia; and Workers, Catalan.

Gerald H. Meaker

ORLOV, ALEXANDER (1890s?-1970). Orlov was the head of Soviet NKVD* (People's Commissariat for International Affairs) operations in Spain during the Civil War. His real name may have been Nikolsky, and he was an ethnic Russian, probably born in the late 1890s. Orlov fought in the Red Army during the Russian Civil War. With some specialization in intelligence, he was early recruited for the OGPU (Soviet Secret Police), which later became the NKVD and subsequently the KGB (Soviet Commissariat for State Security). During the 1920s, he was trained in Soviet police and security law, working in the legal section of the OGPU, but was later moved to intelligence operations.

According to a twenty-seven-page questionnaire which he prepared for Stanley G. Payne in 1967, Orlov was appointed by the Soviet Politburo as adviser to the Spanish Republican government on matters pertaining to intelligence, counterintelligence, and guerrilla warfare behind enemy lines. This appointment, made in Moscow on August 26, 1936, was combined with that of head of NKVD operations in Spain, where Orlov arrived in mid-September.

The staff of NKVD experts directed by Orlov was given wide authority in the main Republican zone (especially the triangle of Madrid*-Valencia*-Albacete*) for intelligence and counterintelligence. Orlov later claimed that within a few months these were effectively organized and that Franco's order of battle in major operations was usually known in advance. However that may be, the NKVD counterintelligence operation did not succeed in apprehending many of the spies and potential spies sympathetic to the Nationalists* in the Republican zone.

Orlov supervised a rather large-scale guerrilla operation behind Nationalist lines. He has claimed that by March 1937 six schools for guerrilla fighters had trained 1,600 operatives, and that by the latter part of that year a total of 14,000 pro-Republican guerrilla fighters were active in the Nationalist zone. They were effective only in the areas of the Tinto River and the Asturian hills.

The most sensitive aspect of Orlov's activities was the development of a special NKVD and communist police system that was employed not merely for purposes of military counterintelligence but as a political weapon in the Republican zone. The most active period of NKVD activity was 1937, when hundreds of anti- and non-Communist political activists and military volunteers* were imprisoned and many executed. The most famous operation was the purge of leadership of the *Partido Obrero de Unificación Marxista* (POUM),* climaxed by the arrest and torture-execution of Andrés Nin.*

Orlov himself was ordered back to the USSR* in July 1938, at the height of Stalin's* great purge of Soviet operatives. Orlov was fully aware of what had happened to many other senior NKVD officials in the USSR and expected to be liquidated. Therefore, instead of returning, he, together with his wife and daughter, disappeared into France* and later made their way to the United States.* He remained in hiding for years and only emerged publicly when he testified in 1950 before a subcommittee of the U.S. Senate on Stalin's crimes, about which he subsequently sold a series of articles to *Life* magazine.

In later years, Orlov was employed as a research specialist in Russian law at the Law School of the University of Michigan. He died in 1970.

For further information, see Burnett Bolloten, *The Spanish Revolution: The Left and the Struggle for Power During the Civil War* (Chapel Hill, N.C., 1979); Alexander Orlov, *Evidence at Senate Internal Security Sub-committee* (Washington, D.C., February 14, 1957); and Stanley G. Payne, *The Spanish Revolution* (New York, 1970).

See also Espionage; and Police.

Stanley G. Payne

ORTEGA, ANTONIO (-1939). Ortega, a career officer in the *Carabineros* (Customs Guards) became Republican director of security in 1937. During his tenure, his department arrested Andrés Nin,* the internationally famous Spanish revolutionary. Prior to his appointment as director-general of security, Ortega had been governor of San Sebastián. Several months after Nin's arrest, this communist was transferred to field command with the rank of colonel. In 1939, he unilaterally tried to mediate a settlement of the war between the Nationalists* and the Repub-

licans.* Franco's* government eventually executed him.

For further information, see Burnett Bolloten, *The Spanish Revolution: The Left and the Struggle for Power During the Civil War* (Chapel Hill, N.C., 1979).

James W. Cortada

ORWELL, GEORGE (ERIC BLAIR) (1903-1950). In late December 1936, Eric Blair, better known as George Orwell, went to Barcelona* to write newspaper articles about the Civil War. Orwell was astounded, yet agreeably impressed, by the revolutionary zeal of the working class which then controlled most of the Catalan capital. He joined the militia, as he later said, "because at that time and in that atmosphere it seemed the only conceivable thing to do." Since he was carrying letters of introduction from the British Independent Labour party, which had connections with the *Partido Obrero de Unificación Marxista* (POUM),* he was assigned to the Lenin Division at the Lenin Barracks in Barcelona. Motivated mainly by a desire to combat fascism and fight for common decency, Orwell, a democratic socialist in the fullest sense of the word, was unaware of the internecine struggles dividing pro-Republican parties and was equally aware that the Lenin Division (which became the 29th when the militias* were incorporated into the Popular Army*) consisted almost entirely of members of the POUM.

After only a brief period of instruction in modern warfare and with no weapons training whatsoever, Orwell was sent to the Aragón* front in January. Except for one short period of leave, he stayed there until May 1937. He was ranked corporal (or *cabo*) and placed in command of a guard of twelve men. He had his first taste of trench warfare, with its attendant waiting and boredom, at Alcubierre, behind the line fronting Saragossa.* In mid-February, after three weeks of inactivity, Orwell was transferred to a mainly English contingent supporting the army besieging Huesca.* Shortly thereafter, he participated in a holding attack when the anarchists* tried to take Jaca. For most of this time, Orwell recalled later that the real enemies were "mud, lice, hunger and cold," and it was only after two months of intermittent sniping that he had his first taste of actual fighting. At Torre Fabian, fifteen volunteers* from Orwell's militia (by then half English and half Spanish) stormed a fascist redoubt as a diversionary measure designed to aid the anarchists in their assault on Huesca. Unfortunately, unknown to the volunteers, headquarters canceled the assault, and the diversion ended with the deaths of two militiamen. On April 25 after 115 days on the line, Orwell was granted a leave of absence and returned to Barcelona.

During the long periods of waiting on the Aragón front, Orwell had, of course, become more aware of the different social and political aims and objectives of the *Partit Socialista Unificat de Catalunya* (PSUC),* the *Federación Anarquista Ibérica* (FAI),* the *Confederación Nacional del Trabajo* (CNT),* the POUM, and other organizations fighting on the Republican side. Surprised that the word "socialist" could be used to designate members of a particular political party, he apprised himself of the radical differences separating the major parties that were organizing the resistance to Franco.* After four months of privation at the front, Orwell had expected to find in Barcelona the same explosive vitality, sense of hope, and egalitarianism that had moved him so deeply the previous December. Disillusioned by the rapid return to bourgeois democracy, he was appalled by the complacency of the reconstituted middle class and its basic indifference to the outcome of the war.

As a pragmatist, Orwell considered his mere presence on the relatively peaceful front somewhat ineffectual and felt his modest skills could be better employed in a sector like Madrid,* where the fate of the Republic was hanging in the balance. His sympathy for the revolutionary gains made by the CNT in Catalonia* made him contemplate joining an anarchist militia, but as this would probably have entailed a transfer to Teruel* rather than Madrid, he declined. A move to Madrid would have involved joining the International Brigades,* which would have required a recommendation from a member of the Communist party.* As late as April 1937, Orwell was prepared to leave the POUM for a communist-organized brigade. The events of May changed all that.

It was Orwell's lot to witness and actively participate in what has been described *inter alia* as the "street-fighting in Barcelona." This minor civil war within the Republican camp was waged by the Negrín * government, with strong backing from the PSUC and Soviet advisers, to wrest from the CNT-FAI the remaining gains it had made in the weeks after the military rebellion. The fighting began on May 3 when the Barcelona Telephone Exchange, operated by CNT workers, was attacked by Civil Guards,* apparently acting without orders. The POUM supported the CNT, and Orwell, as a member of the POUM militia (though not of its political organization), helped guard party headquarters by doing sentry duty.

Orwell returned to the front at Huesca three days after the Barcelona fighting ended, before the many political repercussions of the struggle became known.

Promoted to *teniente* (second lieutenant), he commanded about thirty men (half English, half Spanish) for a brief period. His experience of warfare was abruptly terminated when he was hit by a sniper's bullet, which passed through his neck. Orwell was first shunted from hospital to hospital (Sietamo, Barbastro, Lérida), finally recuperating in the Sanatorium Maurin just outside Barcelona. As a result of his wound, Orwell's left side was paralyzed, and he temporarily lost his voice because a vocal chord had been damaged.

Orwell's convalescence was aggravated by the news that the POUM had been declared an illegal organization and that many of its leaders had been imprisoned without being charged. Almost overnight Orwell was transformed from an idealist antifascist volunteer into a criminal on the run by the very Republican government he had sought to defend. After a picaresque existence in Barcelona, with the help of the British consul, he managed to obtain the discharge papers that would enable him to cross into France,* which he did, with the police only one step behind him. These experiences are recounted in *Homage to Catalonia*, published in London on April 25, 1938.

Homage to Catalonia was one of the many books to appear during the Civil War which attempted to dispel general misconceptions prevalent among English-speaking readers. It is a personal *témoignage*, and one can idly speculate as to how different it might have been had Orwell's diaries, press clippings, and book collection not been confiscated by the police* during an anti-POUM raid in May 1937. Be that as it may, Orwell's account of his experiences as a militiaman in the Huesca sector is one of the most intriguing to have emerged from the Spanish Civil War. It provides a vivid description, written by an accomplished novelist, of the vicissitudes of war as lived by a lucid idealist. The emphasis is less on military matters, which are, of course, carefully examined, than on the seemingly interminable waiting and discomforts of trench warfare. Orwell's account and his tone are decidedly antiheroic, even when he is acknowledging examples of genuine heroism.

Homage to Catalonia is more than a personal narrative of one man's reactions; it is at the same time an attempt to explain and clarify the political situation for a readership unaccustomed to working-class political parties such as the CNT/FAI and the POUM, which had no English equivalents. Two balanced, yet controversial, chapters (5 and 11) supplement and provide a coherent corrective to interpretations of events in Spain advanced in both the capitalist and communist presses. In these chapters, Orwell makes no attempt to hide his partiality, but at the same time manages to remain largely objective. Orwell's book exposes the sham and errors of much counterrevolutionary propaganda disseminated in such communist newspapers as *The Daily Worker* and *Inprecor*. It also shows how the liberal and capital presses had unquestioningly accepted the Popular Front* strategy that the war must be won at all costs, ignoring the CNT-POUM thesis that war and revolution are inseparable. He defends the POUM, which had no voice in the foreign press, against absurd yet widespread accusations of its being a counterrevolutionary movement in the pay of Franco.

In spite of its literary interest and its avowed intent as counterpropaganda, *Homage to Catalonia* had sold only 900 to 1,500 copies at the time of Orwell's death in January 1950. Its first American printing did not appear until 1952. Figures alone, however, cannot explain a book's impact or influence. *Homage to Catalonia* was undoubtedly a key work in Orwell's political development; furthermore, it is generally agreed that the unrelenting antitotalitarianism of *Animal Farm* and *1984* can be better understood in the light of the author's experience in Spain during the Civil War. As Orwell himself has concisely stated: "Every line of serious work that I have written since 1936 has been written, directly or indirectly, *against* totalitarianism and *for* democratic socialism, as I understand it." This tersely worded political credo is evidence of Orwell's determination not to let his fundamental belief in "common decency" and the forging of a more equitable society be undermined by his undoubted disillusion over the betrayal of the Second Spanish Republic.*

For further information, see Frederick R. Benson, *Writers in Arms* (New York, 1967); George Orwell, *Homage to Catalonia* (London, 1938); "Looking Back on the Spanish War" (1943), in *Such, Such Were the Joys* (New York, 1953); and "Notes on the Spanish Militias," in *The Collected Essays, Journalism and Letters of George Orwell, Vol. 1. An Age Like This 1920-1940* (London, 1970).

See also Literature; and May 1937 Riots.

Robert S. Thornberry

OSSORIO Y GALLARDO, ANGEL (1873-1946). Ossorio was the monarchist governor of Barcelona* in 1909 who, at the start of the Civil War, was responsible for convincing his friend Manuel Azaña* not to resign the presidency of the Republic. He served as Republican ambassador to Brussels from 1936 until 1937 when he took the same position in Paris. The Republic hoped his appointment would mollify the French Catholic attitude toward the Loyalists.*

For further information, see Angel Ossorio y Gallardo, *La España de mi vida, Autobiografía* (Buenos Aires, 1941); and David W. Pike, *Les Français et la guerre d'Espagne, 1936-1939* (Paris, 1975).

See also France.

James W. Cortada

OTERO FERNÁNDEZ, ALEXANDRO (1888-1953). At the beginning of the Civil War, Otero was a socialist deputy in the Cortes* from Granada.* The Republicans* appointed him an arms buyer in Europe,* headquartered in Paris. Dr. Otero returned to Spain in 1937 to become undersecretary in the Ministry of Defense responsible for armaments. In December, Indalecio Prieto,* minister of defense, dismissed him, whereupon he returned to Paris to continue trading in arms. In April 1938, he was back in Spain, this time as subsecretary of defense. Many considered this gynecologist a simple profiteer; yet, he managed to obtain large amounts of arms for Spain and ran the Republic's arms factory while in Madrid.*

For further information, see Hugh Thomas, *The Spanish Civil War* (New York, 1977).

James W. Cortada

OVIEDO. Oviedo, a province located in the region of Asturias* in northwestern Spain, was the scene of much fighting during the first half of the Spanish Civil War. In 1934, Oviedo became the center of a major revolt by the miners of Asturias against the "conservative" Republican government in Madrid.* The revolt was brutally squashed by the government's forces (many of whom were North African) led by General Francisco Franco.* During the short revolt, the miners had established numerous soviets and local *Juntas* in direct competition with established governments. Thus, a militant tradition of radical politics in the area combined with an intense dislike of Franco insured that Oviedo as a province would support the Republic during the war.

Fighting broke out in the early days of the war throughout Asturias, making it the only sector in northcentral Spain not to fall quickly to the Nationalists.* Since most of central and southern Spain remained in Nationalist or Republican hands with no Loyalist territory contiguous to Asturias, throughout 1936 Oviedo and the rest of the region governed itself autonomously of either Nationalist or Republican authority. The miners in this province relentlessly sought after the pockets of Nationalist resistance in the entire area, particularly in their provincial capital of Oviedo in August. In the city, pro-Nationalist troops were fighting Republicans,* with the rebels dominating the community for all intents and purposes. The Republicans outside the city prevented these Nationalists from expanding their control over the province until the middle of 1937 when additional rebel forces poured into Asturias. During September and October 1937, Nationalist forces finally overcame Republican pressures in Oviedo, conquered it, and persecuted their enemies throughout Asturias. The conquest of this region brought northern Spain (with the exception of Catalonia*) under Franco's control.

For further information, see José Manuel Martínez Bande, *El final del frente norte* (Madrid, 1972), and *La guerra en el norte* (Madrid, 1969).

See also Appendix B.

James W. Cortada

P

PACCIARDI, RANDOLFO (1899-   ). Pacciardi commanded the 12th International Brigade (Garibaldi) from October 1936 to August 1937. He came from a poor family in Tuscany, was a battalion commander in World War I, and was decorated several times. As a leading member of the Italian Republican party, Pacciardi was personally threatened by fascist policy and left Italy* in 1926 for exile in France* where he engaged in a variety of antifascist activities. In August 1936, he traveled to Spain and became a strong advocate of the antifascist volunteer units; in September he offered (to Largo Caballero*) to create an Italian legion. When the International Brigades* were formally constituted in October 1936, Pacciardi was named commander of the Garibaldi Battalion* of the 12th Brigade and effectively led his unit in its first engagement in the Madrid* sector in November 1936. He was promoted to lieutenant colonel on November 30, 1936, and was wounded at the battle of Jarama* in February 1937. After a brief rest, he returned to the front in the midst of the battle of Guadalajara* in March.

After the army reorganization of April 1937, Pacciardi remained commander of the Garibaldi (now the 12th Brigade). During the May riots* in Barcelona,* he refused to use the Garibaldi in any sort of police* action and subsequently lost favor with the Republican leadership. After heavy losses at Brunete* in the summer of 1937, he went on leave during which time Carlo Penchienati replaced him as brigade commander. Returning to Spain in August, Pacciardi was offered a division command and the rank of general. He preferred to remain with the 12th, had increasing doubts about internal Republican tactics, and therefore refused the offer, leaving Spain immediately thereafter. From there he traveled in the western countries to try to gain support for the Republicans.* After 1940, he increased his overall antifascist activity, publishing *Giovane Italia* and *La Legione dell'Italia del Popolo*. Pacciardi commanded a unit of Italian volunteers* with the British in North Africa and returned to Italy with the allies in 1943. In postwar Italy, he headed the Italian Republican party, served continually in Alcide De Gasperi's coalition governments until 1953, and was the founder of the Movement for a New Republic.

For further information, see Andreu Castells, *Las Brigadas Internacionales de la guerra de España* (Barcelona, 1974); *Epopée d'Espagne: Brigadas Internacionales, 1936-39* (Paris, 1957); *Garibaldini in Ispagna* (Madrid, 1937; Feltrinelli Reprint, Milan, 1966); and Randolfo Pacciardi, *Il Battaglione Garibaldi* (Lugano, 1938).

See also Army, Republican; and May 1937 Riots.

Jane Slaughter

PALENCIA, ISABEL DE. Palencia, a socialist, was the Republican ambassador to Stockholm during the Civil War and worked in Barcelona* toward the end of the war. She wrote two books describing life in the Republican zone which have served as widely read defenses of the Republic's cause and the plight of Barcelona in the final months of the war. After 1939 she frequently spoke out against the regime of Francisco Franco in both Europe and the Americas.

For further information, see Isabel de Palencia, *I Must Have Liberty* (New York, 1940) and her *Smouldering Freedom* (New York, 1945).

James W. Cortada

PALMA DE MAJORCA. Early in the Civil War, Palma de Majorca, the largest town on the island of Majorca,* became a Nationalist stronghold and a base for Italian air raids on Catalonia.* A naval base here also supplied both Nationalist and Italian military ships. The Republicans* repeatedly bombed this port, periodically damaging Italian and German ships and thereby creating international crises. This included the damaging of the Italian ship *Barletta* on May 24, 1937, and the German battleship *Deutschland** two days later near Ibiza.* Italy* hoped to make Palma a permanent base for its forces after the Civil War but Franco* refused to cooperate.

For further information, see José Manuel Martínez Bande, *La invasión de Aragón y el desembarco en Mallorca* (Madrid, 1970).

See also Navy, German; and Navy, Italian.

James W. Cortada

PAMPLONA. Pamplona, the home of many Basque and Carlist political groups, enthusiastically rose up in rebellion in July 1936 to support Franco.* Within days 6,000 Carlist *Requetés** were armed and prepared to help the Nationalists.* This uprising made the entire province a stronghold in the north for Franco's cause. The province experienced a severe reign of terror as Republican sympathizers were rooted out and executed to insure Nationalist control. Pamplona served for a time as a major military headquarters where General Emilio Mola* gathered thousands of troops and sent them into central Spain for the campaigns around Madrid* and for operations in the northwest. The Nationalist appeal in Pamplona grew primarily out of the intense Catholicism and antirepublicanism of the region with which Franco's supporters identified.

For further information, see José Manuel Martínez Bande, *La guerra en el norte* (Madrid, 1969); and Stanley G. Payne, *Basque Nationalism* (Reno, Nev., 1975).

See also Army, Nationalist; Army of the North; Carlists; and Appendix B.

James W. Cortada

***PARTIDO COMUNISTA DE ESPAÑA* (PCE).** *See* Communist Party, Spanish.

***PARTIDO NACIONALISTA VASCO*(PNV).** The *Partido Nacionalista Vasco* (PNV), the Catholic nationalist party of the Basques, was led by José Antonio de Aguirre* during the 1930s. Its objective was to gain autonomy for the Basque country. It supported the Republic during the Civil War because the Republicans* granted Vizcaya* and Guipúzcoa* autonomy in October 1936. It also advocated the support of the Catholic Church* within the Basque country—the only Republican zone to do so.

For further information, see Stanley G. Payne, *Basque Nationalism* (Reno, Nev., 1975).

See also Basque Nationalism.

James W. Cortada

***PARTIDO OBRERO DE UNIFICACIÓN MARXISTA* (POUM).** With the establishment of the Second Re-

public,* a group of exiled Marxists returned to Spain. These opponents of Stalin,* led by Joaquín Maurín* and Andrés Nin,* formed small working-class groups, the most important of which became the Workers and Peasants Revolutionary Alliance which had evolved into the *Partido Obrero de Unificación Marxista* (POUM) by the eve of the Civil War. The POUM supported collectivization of the means of production and Trotsky's* concept of permanent revolution, both of which they promoted as essential to the social revolutionary phase of the Civil War.

Though small in numbers, the POUM was a power on the Left to be recognized, in part because of its always considerable propaganda ability, notably in *La Batalla,** and in part because of the organization's close connections with the anarchists.* The party supported the 1934 October Revolution and castigated the governmental repression that followed. It promoted the Popular Front* in the elections of February 1936,* and received representation on the Antifascist Militias Committee* which governed Catalonia* in the early weeks of the war. In September 1936, Andrés Nin became the minister of justice in the Generalitat.* Important foreigners, such as George Orwell,* the prominent English communist John Cornford,* and Camillo Berneri,* the Italian syndicalist, supported the POUM. The revolutionary zeal and romantic utopianism of the POUM attracted many more. The group represented a clearly revolutionary position absent in three common political trends of the 1930s: in anarchist partisanism and lack of discipline, in the strict authoritarian centralism of the Spanish communists (the *Partit Socialista Unificat de Catalunya*) (PSUC)* and in the evolutionary, bourgeois attitude of the socialists. Thus, POUM's power, prestige, and membership increased rapidly during the early months of the Civil War. This increase in power and the rising antideviationist attitude in Moscow made the group the first casualty in the PSUC's efforts to capture control of the Republican government.

The PSUC excluded the POUM militia from equipment supplied by the USSR* in order to discredit its fighting ability. By December 1936, the communists had maneuvered Nin out of the Generalitat. Then at the Popular Front meeting in Valencia,* on March 5-8, 1937, the PSUC vilified POUM for the attacks it made against the Moscow purges, for its efforts to bring Trotsky to Spain to promote the revolutionary aspects of the Civil War, and for its charges that the Popular Front was bourgeois and capitalistic and much more concerned about defeating Franco* than about securing the revolution for the Spanish people. The PSUC called the POUM an agent of both Trotsky and fascism; neither charge was true. Stating that POUM's propaganda was harmful to the war effort, the PSUC insisted on the seizure of POUM's newspapers and radio* stations everywhere, except in Catalonia where the POUM remained too strong and popular for such a communist move. The destruction of the POUM so ardently sought by the communists came because of its participation in the Barcelona* riots during the first week of May 1937.

Beginning in March of that year, tensions within Republican ranks intensified, particularly in Catalonia where the POUM and the anarchists were losing their traditional predominance over the socialists and the PSUC as illustrated by the removal of POUM representation in the government on April 16. By April 26, the POUM had allied with radical anarchists who agreed with them that the revolution was surely lost if the PSUC policies continued to gain acceptance with the governmental leadership. These tensions peaked with the Barcelona uprising on May 3.

While moderate anarchists in the city and the anarchist ministers in the national cabinet tried to restore peace through negotiation with the Generalitat, POUM, joined by the Friends of Durruti,* a radical anarchist group, urged the workers to continue the revolt to save the revolution from betrayal by the PSUC, the Generalitat, and the national government. However, by May 5 negotiations had secured the dissolution of the government in Barcelona and a promise of POUM representation in the new one to be formed. A truce had been achieved and peace restored to the city three days later. It soon became clear that POUM's efforts to continue the social revolution of 1936 had failed when the communists immediately began a massive propaganda campaign charging that the POUM, filled with agents of the Falange,* caused the Barcelona uprising in order to destroy the Republican government and the revolution. They demanded that the Largo Caballero* government dissolve the POUM and arrest its leadership.

Largo Caballero and the anarchist ministers refused, and the government collapsed. Juan Negrín* was called upon to form a new cabinet which excluded the anarchists and, of course, POUM. Controlled by the PSUC, the government accused the POUM of treason and espionage.* By mid-June, the POUM had been declared illegal and forty leaders were arrested, including Andrés Nin who disappeared. While communist newspapers screamed propaganda against the POUM, PSUC ministers claimed no knowledge of what had happened to Nin, although he was being held by the communists in Alcalá de Henares* Prison.

Despite terrible pressure and torture, Nin refused to confess to treason, nor would he name any of his friends as agents of the Falange. In a mock raid, publicized as a Falangist attack to free Nin, Nin was killed by German members of the International Brigades* in order to cover up the fact that he had in reality been tortured to death. The communists' apparent aim had been to stage purge trials in Spain such as those that were occurring in Moscow at that time, a desire thwarted by the courage of Nin and of other POUM leaders who had not confessed either.

The rest of the POUM's leadership was finally brought to trial in October 1938, at which time they were absolved of the charges of treason and espionage, although they did receive sentences of various lengths for their part in the May uprising. Finally freed by their jailers just before the fall of Barcelona to the Nationalists* in 1939, remnants of the POUM escaped across the border into France.*

Immediately following the POUM trials in October, at which they had given conclusive witness in support of the POUM, Largo Caballero and the anarchists who had been ministers in his cabinet went to the president of the Republic, Manuel Azaña,* and denounced Negrín as a dictator because of his role in the trials and called for his dismissal as premier, but to no avail. The May uprising had given the PSUC the opportunity it had needed not only to destroy its ideological enemy, the POUM, but also to discredit the Largo Caballero government and gain control of the national government, which it retained until the end of the war.

While the POUM was small in numbers, shortlived in its participation in the Civil War, and limited thereby in its specific contributions to the social revolution, its influence was considerable, both in Spain and abroad. The death of Nin and Berneri as a direct result of their participation in the May uprising in Barcelona produced sympathy and publicity for POUM's cause. The enmity that arose between POUM and PSUC because of their ideological differences and POUM's role in the uprising provided the PSUC with a vehicle for capturing the national government. But the PSUC's action against the POUM bred a lasting distrust between the communists and other Republican factions which hampered both war and revolutionary efforts. Foreigners going home from the Spanish conflict reported on the destruction of POUM by the communists. This did much to stem the flow of foreign recruits for the International Brigades and to create disillusionment among the supporters of the Republic abroad. At the same time, the communist intrigue surrounding the demise of the POUM and their dominance of the Republican government gave credence to the conservative condemnation of the Republic as a puppet of the Bolsheviks.

For further information, see Burnett Bolloten, *The Spanish Revolution: The Left and the Struggle for Power During the Civil War* (Chapel Hill, N.C., 1979); Franz Borkeneau, *The Spanish Cockpit* (Ann Arbor, Mich., 1963); Pierre Broue and Émile Témime, *The Revolution and the Civil War in Spain* (Cambridge, 1972); Arthur H. Landis, *Spain! The Unfinished Revolution* (Baldwin Park, Calif., 1972); Cesare Lorenz, *Les Anarchistes Espanols et le Pouvoir, 1868-1969* (Paris, 1970); George Orwell, *Homage to Catalonia* (New York, 1952); Stanley Payne, *The Spanish Revolution* (New York, 1970); and Leon Trotsky, *The Spanish Revolution (1931-1939)* (New York, 1973).

See also Libertarian Movement; and May 1937 Riots.

Shirley F. Fredricks

PARTIDO SOCIALISTA OBRERO ESPAÑOL (PSOE). *See* Socialist Party, Spanish.

PARTIT CATALÀ PROLETARI. The *Partit Català Proletari* was a pre-Civil War Catalan left-wing party with socialist views which, in 1936, joined with other small groups to form the *Partit Socialista Unificat de Catalunya* (PSUC).* The PSUC quickly became a communist-dominated Catalan party and would play a significant role in Republican wartime politics until the Spanish Communist party* eliminated it as an influence on national affairs in 1937-1938.

For further information, see Manuel Benavides, *Guerra y revolución en Cataluña* (Mexico, 1946); and Carlos Pi Sunyer, *La república y la guerra* (Mexico, 1975).

James W. Cortada

PARTIT SOCIALISTA UNIFICAT DE CATALUNYA (PSUC). The *Partit Socialista Unifacat de Catalunya* (PSUC) was formed in July 1936 primarily from the Catalan branch of the Spanish Socialist party* (*Partido Socialista Obrero Español*—PSOE) and the Catalan portion of the Communist party.* In addition to the PSOE and the Catalan communists, members were drawn from the *Unió Socialista* and the *Partit Català Proletari.** Additional support came from members of the Spanish Socialist party which had connections with local *Unión General de Trabajadores* (UGT)* groups. The PSUC also affiliated itself with the Third International from almost the beginning. Thus, the PSUC represented a wide spectrum of left-wing politics in Barcelona* and nearby Catalan communities. Because of this broad representation at the outbreak of the

Civil War, when the local government established the Antifascist Militias Committee,* which in effect ran the city, the PSUC participated heavily in its activities. Almost from its inception, local communist elements dominated the PSUC leadership, coordinating its activities with those of the Spanish Communist party. The general secretary of the PSUC, Juan Comorera,* although a socialist before the war, became a communist and by the end of 1936, a member of the communist central committee. By the middle of 1937, the PSUC claimed a membership of 50,000 made up of farmers, members of the UGT, government employees, lower middle-class tradesmen, policemen, teachers,* sharecroppers, and a few shopkeepers. In short, as time passed many of its members came from the Catalan lower middle classes, with increasing representation of factory workers.

The PSUC represented a fairly conservative element in what had become a highly radicalized political environment in Catalonia. To its Left were still the anarchists*; yet linked to the PSUC were the communists. Like them, the PSUC cooperated with the Generalitat* and worked to make improvements within the existing social order, subscribing to economic and social reforms and leaving to the future any concern about a new society. The Civil War had to be won first. Like the communists, the PSUC defended the rights and interests of the Catalan middle classes, while executing a strategy that would more closely integrate the PSUC members into the Republican government. Thus, for example, the PSUC supported the idea of a national Republican Army* rather than an assortment of militia forces. More conservative Catalans flocked to the PSUC as a hedge against the growth of the anarchists and their affiliated organizations. By the early part of 1937, Republican officials were following the same strategy of winning over those groups critical of the anarchists. Tensions mounted between the PSUC and the government on the one hand against the anarchists on the other. Friction over government policies, integration of militias,* and membership in Catalan and Republican cabinets eventually led to fighting in the streets of Barcelona in the spring of 1937.

The May 1937 riots* caused the demise of the anarchist movement. Republican forces and the Communist party won in Barcelona, while the power of the anarchists was broken. The PSUC emerged from the mini-civil war with its leadership intact and with greater influence in the political affairs of the Republican zone. A newly reorganized Catalan government now only had members from the Esquerra* party and the PSUC. The PSUC held the cabinet posts of labor, supply, and economy—three critical portfolios. By the start of 1938, the PSUC's political power was so great that its allies could murder or arrest critics with little fear of restriction by Catalan or Republican police* forces. Yet, in the second half of 1937 and throughout 1938, the Communist party controlled the PSUC, also dominating all major aspects of Republican politics. Catalan autonomy disappeared. The centralization of economic programs, war production, police and military forces, and social policies took place, with an inevitable submersion of splinter and regional political groups into the larger movement of the communists and the Republican government by the end of 1938.

The PSUC played a leading role in integrating Catalan affairs into those of the Republic during the second half of the war. In 1937, for example, local currencies were abolished, while collectivization of the farms slowed and, in many instances, stopped out of fear that without incentives farmers would lower production. The PSUC took an early stand favoring the integration of militias into the Republican Army, while coordinating the acquisition of military supplies with other Republican sectors of Spain. Its leaders relied more on capitalist methods of managing food* supplies than on either pure libertarian theories or the policies desired by many anarchists (the *Federación Anarquista Ibérica* —FAI).* Such policies ultimately and inevitably led the PSUC into conflict with the FAI in the first half of the war and caused the conflict that destroyed Spain's anarchist movement. The PSUC's relations with the communists and cooperation with the Republican government made it clear that when the Nationalists* overran Catalonia members of the PSUC would be treated as harshly as those of the FAI, UGT, *Confederación Nacional del Trabajo* (CNT),* *Partido Obrero de Unificación Marxista* (POUM),* and Communist party.

For further information, see Manuel Benavides, *Guerra y revolución en Cataluña* (Mexico, 1946), which gives a PSUC perspective on the war; and Burnett Bolloten, *The Spanish Revolution: The Left and the Struggle for Power During the Civil War* (Chapel Hill, N.C., 1979), which takes the story of Republican politics to the middle of 1937.

James W. Cortada

PASCUA, MARCELINO. Pascua was the Republican ambassador to Moscow from September 1936 to March 1938, at which time he moved to the Republic's embassy in Paris, serving until the end of the Civil War. He negotiated with Stalin's* government on the transfer of Spanish gold to the USSR.* Prior to his diplo-

matic missions, he had held the position of director-general of health. He was a medical doctor by training, a member of the Socialist party,* and, before 1936, a member of the Cortes* in the lower house.

For further information, see Angel Viñas, *El oro español en la guerra civil* (Madrid, 1976); and David Wingeate Pike, *Les Français et la guerre d'Espagne, 1936-1939* (Paris, 1975).
    See also France.

James W. Cortada

PASIONARIA, LA (DOLORES IBARRURI GÓMEZ) (1895-1981). Ibarruri, one of the most famous and controversial figures of the Spanish Civil War years, was the only communist to gain national prestige outside of the party. This powerful orator, tireless politician, and party organizer is a Spanish folk hero.

Born in 1895 in the small Vizcayan village of Gallarta, her family was in mining for generations. (Her husband also would be a miner.) Although raised and educated as a devout Catholic, the grinding poverty of her youth, her disillusionment when she could not afford to become a teacher, and the reading of Marxist classics led Ibarruri to communism. The death of her children convinced her of its necessity. Only two of her six children survived to adulthood for want of food* and medical attention. Their father spent months in jail as a striker and communist organizer, and Ibarruri alone could not earn enough as a seamstress to support the family. As a result of these circumstances, Ibarruri ardently and continuously demanded the right and necessity of equality for women.

Elected to the first Provincial Committee of the Basque Communist party in 1920, Ibarruri worked throughout the decade organizing strikes, negotiating with the mine owners, and recruiting members for the Communist party. These activities led to her election to the Central Committee of the Spanish Communist party* in 1930. The following year she became editor of the communist newspaper *Mundo Obrero* and the director of the party in charge of women's affairs. In this capacity, she sought to improve women's conditions in Spain, working closely with other individuals and organizations such as *Mujeres Libres* and the Women's Aid Committee.

Ibarruri helped to organize Spanish participation in the World Committee of Women Against War and Fascism. She was a delegate to the international meeting of the organization in Paris in August 1934. She achieved national attention for her intimate involvement in the October 1934 uprising, including her work with the Committee to Aid Workers' Children.

With the swing to conservatism in the Republican government in 1933, Ibarruri worked diligently to form Antifascist Workers' and Peasants' Militias as a protection for the Spanish Communist party.

In 1933, Ibarruri was a member of the Spanish delegation to the Thirteenth Plenary Session of the Communist International which met in Moscow. She attended the Comintern meeting in Paris in 1935, where the Popular Front* plan was formulated. She returned to Spain to campaign for this concept and in 1936 was elected communist deputy and vice-president of the Cortés.*

During her first months as deputy, Ibarruri secured the release of political prisoners.* She sought legislation to improve working, housing, and health conditions for the people. She called for land reform and helped avert a general miners' strike by negotiating a settlement with mine owners that was favorable to the workers. Acutely sensitive to rightist activities, she made impassioned and demogogic speeches attempting to expose plots to overthrow the Republic.

On July 18, 1936, while the president and premier vascillated about arming the citizens, Ibarruri made her now famous radio* speech rallying Madrid* and the nation to the defense of the government against the fascist revolt. Ending with "No Pasarán!" she gave the defenders of the Republic their battle cry for the war. From this point on, Ibarruri was the chief propagandist for the Republicans,* stressing national pride against international intrusion, democratic principles against fascist dogma, and the needs of the people against militaristic, aristocratic, and capitalistic exploitation. She called on the women of the Republic to fight with kitchen knives and boiling oil if necessary to protect their homes from fascist invaders.

During the war years, Ibarruri organized antifascist committees throughout the Republic and aid for the soldiers at the fronts. In September 1936, she was sent to Paris and Brussels to rally support for the Republic and to get much needed supplies and equipment. She was a member of the committee designated to administer funds sent to Spain by the Comintern. She was influential in all the political machinations of government throughout the war, including the May 1937 riots* in Barcelona,* the destruction of the *Partido Obrero de Unificación Marxista* (POUM),* and the dismissal of Francisco Largo Caballero* as premier and of Indalecio Prieto* as defense minister. She supported Juan Negrín* for prime minister and his Thirteen Points* as a basis for peace negotiations with the Nationalists.*

In March 1939, hours before the fall of the Republic, Ibarruri flew up to the USSR* by way of Paris and became president of the Spanish Communist party in exile. Her son Rubén died defending Leningrad in World War II. In 1964, she received the Lenin Peace Prize and in 1965 the Order of Lenin.

At the age of eighty-one, after thirty-eight years in exile, Dolores Ibarruri returned to Spain on May 13, 1977 as the elected deputy of the Asturian Communist party to the Cortes. On May 22, in Bilbao,* Ibarruri, with her legendary powers of oration little dimmed by age, brought 10,000 cheering, weeping listeners to their feet. La Pasionaria had returned to Spain where she died in 1981.

For further information, see Franz Borkenau, *European Communism* (New York, 1953); David C. Cattell, *Communism and the Spanish Civil War* (Berkeley, Calif., 1955); Ricardo de la Cierva, *La historia se confiesa 1930-1977* (Barcelona, 1976); Dolores Ibarruri, *They Shall Not Pass* (New York, 1966); Carlos Rojas, *La guerra civil vista por los exiliados* (Barcelona, 1975); Georges Soría, *Guerra y revolución en España, 1936-1939* (Barcelona, 1978); and Hugh Thomas, *The Spanish Civil War* (New York, 1977).

Shirley F. Fredricks

PAVLOV, DIMITRI (-1941). Pavlov was a Russian tank commander who fought with the Republicans* in the Civil War. General Pavlov saw combat at the battles of Boadilla* and the Corunna Road* in December 1936 with his tanks near Madrid* and again at the battle of the Jarama* in February 1937. At the battle of Guadalajara* in March, Pavlov's tanks seriously crippled Italian forces fighting for the Nationalists,* thus playing a major role in blunting Franco's* efforts in the area. Stalin* had Pavlov executed in 1941 when the general failed to stop advancing German armies from penetrating Soviet territory in World War II.

For further information, see Ramón Salas Larrazábal, *Historia del ejército popular de la república*, 4 vols. (Madrid, 1974).

James W. Cortada

PAXTOT MADOZ, FRANCISCO (1876-1936). Paxtot was a career army officer and a general in 1936. In July 1936, he commanded troops in Málaga* where he hesitated to raise the cry of rebellion. Republicans* had threatened a naval bombardment of Málaga if he did. Pro-Nationalists,* however, did take over the city and lynched the general.

For further information, see Ronald Fraser, *In Hiding, The Life of Manuel Cortes* (London, 1972).
See also Andalusia.

                                        James W. Cortada

PEASANTRY, ARAGONESE. In the 1930s, the Aragonese peasantry consisted predominantly of small-holders farming less than 10 hectares of land. Their scattered plots covered about one-half of the region's land but made up over 95 percent of all landholdings, a proportion higher than the national average. At the other end of the scale, large estates of over 100 hectares covered about one-fifth of the land, a percentage smaller than the Spanish average. Medium-sized holdings of between 10 and 100 hectares accounted for some 25 percent of the land.

Cereals, vines, and olives provided the mainstays of peasant production, with some important market garden and forage-growing areas. Cereal yields, especially in the steppe lands of Huesca,* were notorious for their tremendous fluctuations depending on rainfall. Almost everywhere crop failures were frequent in drought years. Teruel,* the southernmost of the region's three provinces, was one of Spain's most sparsely populated and poor areas.

In the previous two decades, Saragossa,* the region's capital, had become a leading anarchosyndicalist stronghold. However, the influence of anarchosyndicalism among the peasantry was much more diffuse. When in December 1933 there was an anarchist uprising, some twenty villages participated. In these villages, peasants, workers, and artisans burned land registries, abolished money, fought off the paramilitary Civil Guard,* and established libertarian communism for a few days before the movement was crushed. The majority of Aragonese villages, however, remained unaffected.

At the outbreak of the Civil War, Catalan militia columns swept into eastern Aragón, advancing to the gates of Saragossa and Huesca. Behind them lay about three-quarters of Aragón and somewhat under half the region's population* of 1 million. Within two months, nineteen rural collectives were recorded as having been created, seven of which were in villages that had risen in 1933. Of the remainder, collectivization was initiated in seven in the presence of *Confederación Nacional del Trabajo* (CNT)* militia forces.

These figures, though too small a sample to be considered representative of the collectivization movement as a whole, nonetheless reveal a certain truth. In some villages where anarchosyndicalists had strength before the war, local CNT militants seized the moment, even where the militia columns were not CNT-led, to carry out their long-awaited revolution. In others, villagers found themselves under considerable pressure to collectivize: the coercive climate created by the CNT militias'* armed strength, in which fascists were being shot, sufficed. Thus, "spontaneous" and "forced" collectives coexisted, as did willing and unwilling collectivists within them. Indeed, the dual origins of the rural collectives corresponded to dual objectives: on the one hand, the need to organize supplies to feed the militia columns at the front; and on the other, the anarchosyndicalist commitment to social equality. The collectives represented forms of both libertarian and war communism.

Although for the first seven months there was no overall plan, the collectives from the start shared certain features. They controlled both production—extending to artisans (carpenters, barbers, bakers, and so on) and middle-class professionals (doctors, school teachers, veterinarians, and the like)—and consumption. The national money was abolished; collectivists were paid a family wage in newly created village currency or in rations.

Land, tools, livestock (with the exception of the pig or two which each family fattened yearly), stocks of wheat, and other produce had to be handed over to the collective. These formed its founding capital. The collectivized land was divided into work sectors and was assigned to groups of men, often neighbors, who elected their own delegate or leader. All produce went to "the pile" (the collective) for communal consumption. Surpluses (their value expressed in prewar prices) were bartered for other products, one of the most prized being agricultural machinery—usually a threshing machine—where there had been none before.

Village assemblies elected a committee to run the collective; major decisions would be referred back to the assembly. Bars were closed, or at least no longer served alcohol, in accord with libertarian principles, and great attention was paid to improving the villages' cultural facilities and the children's education. The poor peasantry generally ate better than before, and the more prosperous no worse.

In principle, membership in the collectives was voluntary. Republicans* and socialists were usually free to choose, but if they remained outside the collective they were not permitted to employ labor (or in some cases even to call on relatives and neighbors) to help them work their land. Nor did they as a rule receive any assistance from the collective which controlled most agricultural supplies. Right-wingers, on the other hand, usually joined to protect themselves or were coerced into doing so.

The Aragón collectives appear to have maintained, and even increased, productivity. In the first and only year, 1937, maximum collectivization in the region saw a 20-percent increase in wheat harvested, though it would be foolhardy to judge success on the basis of a single year's crop. The many drawbacks suffered by the collectives are undeniable. Localisms ran counter to egalitarianism, permitting rich and poor collectives to coexist. There was a lack of trained administrators, which was hardly surprising in a region where 40 percent of the population was illiterate. The possibility of arbitrary conduct by committee members was not forestalled by a built-in democratic procedure making them subject to immediate recall if they failed to carry out the majority will. And last, but not least, the CNT-dominated Council of Aragón* signally failed to provide a coherent structure for the collective movement.

For a revolutionary minority, which here and there included socialists, a new world was dawning. But what of the majority of peasants? It is impossible to give a conclusive answer about their attitudes, but testimony forty years later from survivors of the experience suggests a number of different elements.

There can be little doubt that there was a generalized acceptance that war inevitably entailed controls and restrictions. In this sense, the collectives were seen as an extreme war measure. If survivors so rarely complained directly about the loss of their land, it was for two reasons. First, there was always hope that a war measure would not outlast the war, whichever side won. During the war, this hope was given reality by the hostility of the Communist party, and later of the Negrín* government, to anarchosyndicalist domination of Aragón. Second, and more significantly, for it overshadowed the loss of their land, was the repression in the rearguard. Land was less of a loss than lives. It was the arbitrary coercive climate that surrounded the experience, more than collectivization itself, which occasioned terror and hostility to libertarian domination. In some instances, villages collectivized in order to prevent reprisals.

In this climate, it was not surprising that by May 1937, ten months after the start of the war, 450 rural collectives (more than half those in the Popular Front* zone) were operating in Aragón. Three months later, the Negrín government sent in Lister's* division to dissolve the Council of Aragón and to end forced collectivization. The peasantry was given the choice to withdraw. Great numbers did. Coercing peasants into collectives not only ran counter to libertarian ideology, but also was no way to ensure their loyalty in the struggle against Franco.*

The collectivist movement, however, did not collapse. It reflected a commitment that was seen throughout the Popular Front zone where the number of rural collectives was steadily increasing (even if the number of collectivists was on the decline). As many Aragonese libertarians came to recognize, the collectives functioned better when membership was voluntary. This was yet another lesson which the libertarian movement* learned very late in the bitter crucible of war.

For further information, see Eloy Fernández Clemente, *Aragón contemporaneo (1833-1936)* (Madrid, 1975); Gaston Leval, *Collectives in the Spanish Revolution* (London, 1975); Frank Mintz, *L'autogestion dans l'Espagne révolutionnaire* (Paris, 1970); José Peirats, *La CNT en la revolución española*, 3 vols. (Paris, 1971); and Agustín Souchy y Bauer, *Entre los campesinos de Aragón* (Valencia, 1937).
See also Economy, Republican.

Ronald Fraser

PEDRERO GARCÍA, ANGEL (-1940). Pedrero was a socialist involved in police* activities in Madrid.* In 1937, he became director of the *Servicio de Investigación Militar* (SIM)* in Madrid. Before assuming that responsibility, he had participated in the murders of suspected Nationalist sympathizers in Madrid and also in minor counterespionage activities. As head of Madrid's SIM, he was responsible for eliminating similar free-lance activities. When in March 1939, Segismundo Casado* attempted to plot a coup against Negrín's* government, Pedrero pledged the SIM's support, thereby giving encouragement to the effort.

For further information, see Diego Sevilla Andrés, *Historia política de la zona roja* (Madrid, 1954).

James W. Cortada

PEIRATS, JOSÉ. Peirats was a Catalan anarchist, probably from Lérida,* who edited a newspaper, the *Acracia,** published in his home province during the 1930s. His paper was particularly radical in its editorial policy, rejecting any call for national regimentation for the war effort. He also served as a lieutenant in the Republican Army.* In the twenty-five years following the war, he became an historian commenting prolifically on the subject and on Spanish anarchism in general.

For further information, see Robert W. Kern, *Red Years/Black Years: A Political History of Spanish Anarchism, 1911-1937* (Philadelphia, 1978); and José Peirats, *La CNT y la revolución española*, 3 vols. (Toulouse,

1951-1953) and his *Los anarquista en la crisis política española* (Buenos Aires, 1964).

See also Anarchists; Aragón; *Federación Anarquista Ibérica* (FAI); Libertarian Movement; and Peasantry, Aragonese.

James W. Cortada

PEIRÓ BELIS, JUAN (1887-1942). Peiro, born in Catalonia,* became a steel worker in Barcelona.* By 1911, he was a confirmed syndicalist. Although he associated with Buenaventura Durruti* and Francisco Ascaso* during the 1920s, increasingly Peiro thought that collaboration with the government was more effective than terrorism in achieving social reforms.

In 1924, Peiró became secretary of the National Committee of the *Confederación Nacional del Trabajo* (CNT).* He organized the Catalan Regional CNT to promote the decentralization of the anarchist labor movement. By 1927, he had been labeled a moderate, compromising labor politician by militant anarchists.* When the CNT was legalized in 1930, Peiró called a meeting of the national executive committee, where he proposed a program of extensive social reform. He strongly opposed anarchist violence, characteristic of the methods of the *Federación Anarquista Ibérica* (FAI),* recommending instead a moderate response to the new political freedom that had come with official recognition. This attitude antagonized the FAI, which led to a break between the *faístas* and the moderate CNT leadership. Peiro signed the *Treintista* Declaration that denounced the FAI and precipitated the break. Having captured the CNT, the *faísta* leadership also forced Peiró from his position as editor of the *Solidaridad Obrero,* the major newspaper of the CNT.

From 1934 to 1936, Peiró supported all actions aimed at reversing the growing power of the conservatives, including the strikes in Catalonia* and Asturias.* In 1936, he promoted the idea of the Popular Front.* At the national CNT meeting that year, the *Treintistas,* including Peiró, were readmitted to the organization. In November 1936, Peiró was appointed minister of industry in Francisco Largo Caballero's* cabinet.

Believing that the industrial complex of the state, and all other means of production, should belong to the people, Peiró promoted the collectivization of industry and agriculture. But, if necessary, he insisted on governmental intervention in industrial management to insure continuous production. This led to progressive centralization of principal industries in the hands of the state. Peiró also attempted to establish workers' banks as a way to insure the success of collectivization. However, the communist and socialist members of the cabinet refused to vote the necessary funds. In May 1937, he ordered the collectivization of all mines, a decree not implemented by the new communist-dominated cabinet that replaced the Largo Caballero government that same month.

When the government fell, Peiró left the ministry. At the end of the war, he fled into France,* where he lived in a concentration camp until 1940, when the Germans sent him back to Spain. In 1942, he was executed.

For further information, see Stephen John Brademas, *Anarcho-sindicalismo y revolución en España 1930-1937* (Madrid, 1974); Robert W. Kern, *Red Years/Black Years: A Political History of Spanish Anarchism, 1911-1937* (Philadelphia, 1978); Cesar Lorenz, *Les anarchistes Espagnols et le pouvoir 1868-1969* (Paris, 1969); Ricardo Sanz, *El sindicalismo y la política* (Toulouse, 1966); and Georges Soría, *La revolución y guerra, 1936-1939* (Barcelona, 1978).

Shirley F. Fredricks

PEMÁN Y PEMARTÍN, JOSÉ MARÍA (1898-   ). Pemán was a conservative political thinker and a poet. He had been an active member of the *Unión Patriótica* (nationalistic party supporting the regime of General Miguel Primo de Rivera) in the 1920s and was considered a monarchist in political circles. In the 1930s, he identified with the Falange* and wrote extensively on its ideas. He argued that the Nationalists'* rebellion was a modern version of the *Reconquista* for the elimination of the heathen "Republicans."* He constantly used Spanish history to draw analogies with contemporary events, especially for those Nationalist actions that seemed to be logical extensions of national historical experience.

On October 2, 1936, Franco* named a provisional government, with Pemán in charge of cultural activities. On October 12, at the University of Salamanca, in celebration of the *Día del raza,* Miguel Unamuno,* rector of the university, delivered a lecture critical of some earlier comments made by one of Franco's generals attending the session, José Millán Astray.* Millán Astray, the founder of the Foreign Legion,* earlier that day had exclaimed: "Long live death!", a statement Unamuno found empty of any positive meaning. At this famous confrontation, which General Franco's wife had to interrupt to protect Unamuno's life, Pemán made a speech critical of intellectuals* who found fault with the Nationalists.

For further information, see Stanley G. Payne, *Falange: A History of Spanish Fascism* (Stanford, Calif., 1961);

and José María Pemán y Pemartín, *Mis almuerzos con gente importante* (Madrid, 1970) and his *Seis conferencias pronunciadas en Hispano América* (Madrid, 1941).

James W. Cortada

PEÑA BOEUF, ALFONSO (1888-1966). Peña was an engineer by training who in 1938 became minister of public works in Franco's* government. This wealthy engineer had previously established an embassy for Paraguay which sheltered some 300 refugees* in Madrid.* The Republicans* arrested Peña and eventually exchanged him for a prisoner held by the Nationalists.*

For further information, see Alfonso Peña Boeuf, *Memorias de un ingeniero político* (Madrid, 1954).

James W. Cortada

PÉREZ DE AYALA, RAMÓN (1880-1962). Pérez de Ayala, born in Oviedo,* was a prominent novelist and a diplomat before the Civil War. He declared his support for the Loyalists* in July 1936 while in Republican territory. As soon as he left Spain, however, he denounced the Republic because of increased communist influence within the government and because he was outraged at the atrocities committed in the Republican zone. During most the war, he lived in Argentina;* he returned to Spain after 1939.

For further information, see Círculo de Amigos de la Historia, *Diccionario biográfico español contemporaneo* (Madrid, 1970), Vol. 2.

James W. Cortada

PÉREZ FARRAS, ENRIQUE. Pérez Farras, a major in Barcelona's* police* force in July 1936, commanded armed forces which helped to suppress the Nationalist revolt there. Later that month, he led forces outside of Barcelona fighting various groups of armed Nationalists.* He also served as a military adviser to Buenaventura Durruti* who commanded large numbers of anarchist militia.

For further information, see Robert W. Kern, *Red Years/Black Years: A Political History of Spanish Anarchism, 1911-1937* (Philadelphia, 1978).

James W. Cortada

PÉREZ MADRIGAL, JOAQUÍN. Pérez Madrigal was an ex-radical socialist who, during the Civil War, was a radio* announcer in Nationalist Salamanca.* He was best known for his program "La Flota Republicana,"

an amusing program in the otherwise dreary stream of wartime propaganda.

For further information, see Rafael Abella, *La vida cotidiana durante la guerra civil: La España nacional* (Barcelona, 1973); and Joaquín Pérez Madrigal, *Aqui es la emisora de la flota republicana* (Madrid, 1939), *Augurios, estallido y episodios de la guerra civil* (Avila, 1937), and *Memorias de un converso*, 9 vols. (Madrid, 1943).

James W. Cortada

PERPIGNAN. Perpignan, a port city located on the Catalan side of France* near the Spanish border, became a refuge for Republican exiles during the Civil War. Spies for both sides, the Germans, French, and other nations often used the town as temporary headquarters. Supplies from France for Republican Spain, such as aircraft in 1936, came through Perpignan, and the first French volunteers* to help the Republic came by way of this city in October 1936. When Negrín's* government left Spain in 1939, it passed through Perpignan.

For further information, see Hugh Thomas, *The Spanish Civil War* (New York, 1977).

See also Espionage: and Refugees, Republican.

James W. Cortada

PESETA, NATIONALIST AND REPUBLICAN. In the years immediately preceding the outbreak of the Civil War, the rate of exchange of the peseta to the pound sterling was between 36 and 40 pesetas to 1 pound, and between 7.30 and 8.40 pesetas to the U.S. dollar. These favorable levels were reached as a result of an orthodox monetary policy and official strategy designed to strengthen the monetary unit. By the end of 1934, the peseta had reached a level that many thought to be overvalued. However, these rate levels must be interpreted with caution because during the Republic the authorities gradually established a central exchange system that was very troublesome and rigid in order to discourage the flight of capital, and thus be in a position to meet all potential difficulties in meeting foreign payments. In 1930, the *Centro Oficial de Contración de Moneda* (COCM) was created for the purpose of exercising foreign exchange control implementation.

After the Popular Front's* victory in the elections of February 1936,* the flight of capital intensified, as a result of which the new government tightened exchange control operations. Thus, on July 18, the nation was subject to a rigid exchange control system which, in effect, rendered the peseta nonconvertible.

During the first few months of the war, the Nationalist authorities did not adopt any general measures affecting rates of exchange. Certainly, the military authorities imposed regulations in the various regions. Thus, in August 1936 in Andalusia* Queipo de Llano* had already established a rate of exchange of 37.50 pesetas to the pound sterling. Shortly thereafter, on August 23, exports payable in Spanish currency were prohibited, and payment in foreign exchange was required. In addition, within three days after receiving any payment exporters had to surrender to the military authorities any foreign exchange obtained, at a rate of 40 pesetas to the pound.

Between July and November 1936, the Nationalist authorities did not promulgate any general foreign exchange control measures, possibly because they felt that the rapid military advance on Madrid* could have resulted in an early capture of the capital and a quick end to the conflict. However, the failure of the attack on the city in November 1936 and the growing feeling that the conflict might be prolonged led the Nationalist officials to develop institutional measures leading to the creation of a new state resting on bases different from those within the Republican zone.

With respect to exchange control, a decree dated November 18 abolished the COCM, creating in its place for the Nationalist zone the so-called Committee for Foreign Exchange (CME). The CME was given broad authority in matters relating to foreign exchange operations. Among its attributes was the specific authority to publish daily foreign exchange rates. In meeting this obligation, the CME started publishing the exchange rates as of December 1936 every fifteen days. There were fourteen foreign currencies with regularly announced rates to the peseta: the French franc, pound sterling, U.S. dollar, Swedish and Norwegian crowns, Italian lira, Swiss franc, German mark, Belgian franc, Dutch florin, Danish crown, Portuguese escudo, Czechoslovak crown, Argentine peso, and, on an irregular basis, the Moroccan franc.

From the beginning there were two kinds of rates. One was applicable to currencies derived from exports, and another, a more favorable one, was applicable to foreign currencies "voluntarily and definitively" transferred to the government by its owners. This second list represented an advantage of 20 percent over the first and was used in all relinquishments by Spanish residents who were under no obligation "to surrender them" (liquidation of real estate abroad), although in time the advantage was extended to encompass items of a most varied nature.

The two most important characteristics of the official rate publications by the CME were their marked regularity and a notable difference with rates prevailing in the international markets. The first foreign exchange rates list published (December 31, 1936) was based on 42 pesetas to the pound sterling—derived from exports—and 52.50 pesetas to the pound sterling—from British currency voluntarily turned over to the exchange control authorities. For the U.S. dollar, the rates were 8.55 and 10.70, respectively. These rates, with minor modification, were maintained until the end of the conflict. With respect to the pound, the only change took place at the end of July 1937 in a very small amount. Two small changes also affected the U.S. dollar. Only with respect to the franc, among the major currencies, were there frequent changes, and this was because of the weakness of the French currency. The table below shows the official CMF rates that prevailed throughout the war.

The official exchange rates for the Nationalist peseta throughout the conflict were very different from those prevailing in the international markets. In London and Paris, as well as in Tangier (a traditional market for the peseta), the published rates were less favorable for the Nationalist currency. For example, during the first part of 1938, while the official rates were maintained at 42.45 and 53.05 for the peseta against the pound sterling, the free market rates varied between 90 and 100 pesetas, indicating an overvaluation of the official rate in excess of 100 percent. With respect to other important currencies, the differences were equally substantial. However, neither the official nor the free market rates can be considered to be absolutely significant: the first because it concerned a rate imposed arbitrarily by the CME through which transfer of foreign exchange to the state was compulsory; the second because in a situation in which Spain was at war, the rates could not respond readily to economic considerations. Rather, these rates were the result of assessment by the international community stemming from wartime developments and the prospect of victory by one side or the other. Nevertheless, while both rate systems were greatly influenced by other than economic factors, the Nationalist government maintained a constant policy of foreign exchange rate overvaluation. In its insistence on a strong peseta, the government was concerned about the economic impact of higher import prices related to cheapening the peseta abroad.

Unquestionably, such a distorted rate of exchange would have an adverse effect on the balance of trade, raising the price of exports and cheapening imports. The Commercial Services of the Nationalist Adminis-

Official Rates of Exchange of the Committee for Foreign Exchange

Currencies	12/31/36		3/31/39	
	A	B	A	B
1. French franc	39.95	49.95	23.80	29.75
2. British pound	42.00	52.50	42.45	53.05
3. U.S. dollar	8.55	10.70	9.10	11.37
4. Italian lira	45.00	—	45.15	—
5. Swiss franc	196.50	245.50	207.00	258.75
6. German mark	3.44	—	3.45	—
7. Belgian franc	144.30	180.25	154.00	—
8. Dutch florin	4.66	5.82	4.95	—
9. Portuguese escudo	38.10	47.65	38.60	48.25
10. Argentine peso	2.50	3.12	2.07	2.58
11. Czech crown	30.00	—	31.10	—
12. Swedish crown	2.17	—	2.19	—
13. Norwegian crown	2.11	—	2.14	—
14. Danish crown	1.87	—	1.90	—
15. Morrocan franc	39.00	49.00	—	—

List A - Exchange derived from exports
List B - Exchange voluntarily and definitively surrendered
(Foreign Exchange Rates)

SOURCE: *Boletín Oficial del Estado de Burgos*.

tration deliberated over this problem without success. On more than one occasion, the agency called the attention of higher officials to the thorny problem of currency values. Such observations were without effect, for except for minor readjustments, the CME rates were practically unchanged from the end of 1936 to the end of the war.

In order to diagnose the true dimension of the exchange rates fixed by the CME, it should be remembered that almost from the start of the war the Nationalist authorities established a very strict exchange mechanism. Various decrees and orders required that all Spanish subjects yield to the Burgos* government their foreign currency, gold, and foreign stocks and bonds. All operations concerned with payment and collection in foreign transactions were subjected to a rigid control. By a March 1937 decree, all foreign-owned peseta balances and foreign-owned property were blocked. These measures peaked in a law concerning monetary violations promulgated in November 1938. The measure established severe monetary fines and imprisonment for anyone engaging in foreign economic operations without CME authorization. In this manner, the Nationalist authorities assured themselves of the control as well as the management of foreign collections and payments (ipso facto the balance of payments) and a

rigid defense of the official exchange rates, albeit at the cost of making the Burgos peseta a nonconvertible currency.

With respect to the Republican peseta, its value in the international market progressively deteriorated throughout the conflict, as a logical consequence of the war's adverse course for the Republic. As could be expected, the Burgos authorities frequently cited the different evolution of the Republican and Nationalist peseta as evidence of the poor state of the Republican economy* compared to the effectiveness of the Nationalist government. The comparison may also have influenced the CME which insisted on maintaining official rates at an artificially high level. The table below shows a comparison of the values of the peseta in Tangier versus the pound sterling for both sides.

As can be observed, the difference between the two rates of exchange, already notable in 1937, reached extremes in mid-1938, when the operations of the Nationalists* in Catalonia* indicated the beginning of the end for the Republicans.*

As much for the Republican peseta as for the Nationalist, as previously indicated, an interpretation of the rate of exchange must be established in light of an important consideration. Even before the outbreak of hostilities, the Republic had established a rigid for-

Tangier Free Market Peseta/Sterling Exchange Rates

Date	Nationalist Peseta	Republican Peseta
July 1936	36	36
December 1936	—	116
July 1937	81	217
December 1937	87	226
July 1938	113[a]	291[b] (635)[c]
December 1938	132	450 (1,462)
March 1939	129	386 (13,538)

Notes: [a] From 1938 on, the Nationalist government issued new bills.
[b] From 1938 on the Republican government also issued new bills.
[c] For 1938 and 1939, the free exchange rate peseta/sterling for the new Valencia* bills is shown in parentheses.

SOURCE: C. Delclaux, *La financiación de la Cruzada* (Deusto, 1950); and H. Thomas, *The Spanish Civil War* (New York, 1977).

eign exchange control, which among other aspects included prohibiting Spanish banks from crediting foreign accounts with the proceeds from Bank of Spain* currency received from abroad, unless it could be proven that remittance from Spain had been previously authorized. With this measure, adopted in March 1936, it was hoped that the convertibility of pesetas taken abroad could be prevented. This flight of capital, already quite intense in the months before the war, presumably intensified further during the conflict. Inasmuch as the Republican government barely used the peseta in satisfying its international payments, it can be assumed that the greater part of pesetas held abroad, be they in currency or in bank accounts, proceeded from illegal capital flight operations. Under those circumstances, for a foreign bank to be willing to exchange Spanish currency for other monies at a reasonable rate of exchange, it would be necessary to be assured of exchange within the Spanish banking system, either against other currencies or in a convertible foreign account. Such an assumption would logically suppose that as the possibility of a Republican victory diminished, the value of the Republican peseta would worsen. In effect, given the assumption of a Nationalist victory, it was not realistic to foresee the redeeming of Republican currency or funds held abroad. Even supposing the remote possibility of a Republican triumph, it would not be reasonable to believe that the Republic would redeem currency or funds which in the final analysis stemmed from capi-

tal control evasion. Therefore, it is apparent why the Republican peseta worsened as the conflict continued.

The Republican government exerted no effort to maintain the value of its currency, since its foreign obligations were paid for mainly from the sale of gold held in the Bank of Spain. It could have supported the rates of exchange for reasons of prestige, but that would have entailed obligating scarce currency needed for the war effort, a priority under any circumstances. It may, therefore, be concluded that since the Republican peseta as well as the Nationalist currency was nonconvertible, their rates of exchange abroad would have very limited economic significance and would reflect no more than foreign judgments as to the final result of the conflict. Nevertheless, the Franco* regime always pointed to the difference in rates abroad as one more argument against the Republic's efforts.

For further information, see Fernando Eguidazu, *Intervención monetaria y control de cambios en España, 1900-1977* (Madrid, 1978); and A. Viñas, J. Viñuela, F. Eguidazu, C. F. Pulgar, and S. Florensa, *Política comercial exterior de España, 1931-1975*, 2 vols. (Madrid, 1979).

See also Economy, Nationalist; and Monetary Policy, Nationalist.

Fernando Eguidazu

PÉTAIN, HENRI-PHILIPPE (1856-1951). Pétain was a French career army officer, a field marshal during World War I, and one of the great heroes of that war. He served as the French commander in Morocco in 1925 and thus gained some familiarity with the Spanish colony and understood the aspirations of the military which rose in rebellion against the Republic in Madrid* in July 1936. At the end of the Civil War, Pétain became the French ambassador to Franco's* government. During the war, he expressed few opinions about the Nationalists.* Yet, Pétain had been of some use to his own government during these years by describing Franco the man since he had known him briefly in North Africa. Moreover, he knew that if Franco won the war, the Spanish could be as much of a threat to French holdings in North Africa as could either the British or the Germans. Franco apparently did not like Petain, or he expressed no positive opinions about him. Franco gave him a cold reception when he came to Spain as French ambassador since the government in Paris had at first refused to turn over Republican naval vessels and other Spanish assets to Madrid. Although Pétain had been of little help to Franco's government as ambassador, during World War II, as head of the Vichy government, he avoided actions that would have caused the Germans to invade Spain and thus augment their hammer-hold over France.* and Western Europe.*

For further information, see Maître Isorni, *Philippe Pétain* (Paris, 1972); and Jacques Szaluta, "Marshal Pétain's Ambassadorship to Spain: Conspiratorial or Providential Rise toward Power?," *French Historical Studies* 8, No. 4 (1974):511-34.

James W. Cortada

PHILIPPINES. The Philippines, under the administration of the United States* at the time of the Civil War, ostensibly followed Washington's diplomatic policy of neutrality. However, the vast majority of its Spanish inhabitants favored the Nationalists.* They raised thousands of pesetas for Franco,* published literature and newspapers supporting him, and maintained an active branch of the Falange* party. Throughout the war, the Spanish Republican Consulate protested the outwardly pro-Nationalist position of most Spaniards in the Philippines.

For further information, see Theodore Friend, *Between Two Empires: The Ordeal of the Philippines, 1929-1946* (New Haven, Conn., 1965).

James W. Cortada

PICASSO, PABLO (1883-1973). Picasso came from Barcelona.* This great artist spent most of the Civil War years in France.* His sympathies were with the Republicans,* and he reflected his anti-Nationalist viewpoint in his work. In 1936, for example, he etched a series of pictures called "The Dream and the Lie of General Franco,"* continuing an old Spanish tradition of satirical art. In 1937, he painted "Guernica"* in which he symbolized the horrors of war. He immediately sent the painting to the Metropolitan Museum in New York where it received international attention for decades. It was not returned to Spain until October 1981 after Franco's death.

For further information, see Círculo de Amigos de la Historia, *Diccionario biográfico español contemporaneo* (Madrid, 1970), Vol. 3; and Patrick O'Brian, *Picasso. A Biography* (New York, 1976).

See also Art; Europe; Guernica; and Intellectuals.

James W. Cortada

PILOTS. A significant role in the Spanish Civil War was played by pilots and air warfare—their most vital warfare role prior to World War II. Many of the battles and the nature of some campaigns were fundamentally influenced by bombing, and pilots were employed as integral parts of campaigns by both sides in the conflict. Pilots from France,* Great Britain,* the United States,* and the USSR,* among others, flew for the Republicans,* while Germans in the Condor Legion* and Italians in their own units flew for the Nationalists.* Each side had an air force and drew many of its pilots and supplies from non-Spanish sources. Some of the more famous groups included the German Condor Legion which was credited with bombing Guernica* in April 1937 and Andre Malraux's* *Escuadrilla España* which was made up of French, British, and some American and Spanish crewmen.

Individual ace pilots emerged from this war. The German Rudolph Von Moreau dropped supplies into the Alcázar's* center for its Nationalist defenders in September 1936 and in April 1937, he bombed Guernica. During the campaign in Asturias* in September-October 1937, such pilots also developed a technique for bombing called "carpet bombing" whereby an entire area would be simultaneously bombed by a number of airplanes. (This method was used on Germany* during World War II by the Allies.) The leading Italian air aces flew under Nationalist command alongside such Spaniards as Angel Salas Larrazábal* and Joaquín García Morato.* The Italian government later claimed their pilots flew 5,318 air raids and participated in 266 aerial flights and that 6,000 Italians served the Nationalist air corps.

The Russians supplied the Republicans with several hundred pilots during the course of the war. Within the first eighteen months of the war, Russian pilots dominated the Republican Air Force,* after which Soviet-trained Spanish pilots began to replace them. On the Nationalist side, Spanish, German, and Italian pilots flew primarily under Spanish command, and, by the second half of the war, most of the crews were in the Spanish, many trained by the Germans. At the start of the conflict, the Republicans had approximately 175 available pilots (150 of whom were on active service at the time), while the Nationalists had closer to ninety. Republican air superiority was reversed by the end of 1937 as the Nationalist forces grew in strength and size.

Air heroes abounded by midwar since fighting in the air still called attention to the exploits of individuals as opposed to the operations of large armies on the ground. Carlos de Haya* flew over 300 sorties for the Nationalists, while Salas Larrazábal clocked in 618 with forty-nine aerial fights, holding the record on his side for the greatest amount of combat time in the air. The best known Nationalist was García Morato who flew 511 sorties and shot down forty enemy aircraft. Republican pilots recorded similar achievements.

German pilots brought Franco's* North African troops into southern Spain in July and August 1936 in numbers as high as 500 a day, making it possible for the Nationalists to gain a quick foothold in the south. Franco flew to North Africa and later to Spain. Republican and Nationalist pilots participated actively in the campaigns in and around Madrid* throughout the war, while others bombed such cities as Málaga,* Seville,* and Barcelona,* introducing the world to the bombing of civilian targets. Italian pilots helped capture Majorca,* while Republican pilots participated in every major Republican offensive in central and eastern Spain.

For further information, see Juan Antonio Ansaldo, *¿Para Que?* (Buenos Aires, 1951), a Nationalist account; José Goma, *La guerra en el aire* (Barcelona, 1958); Andrés García Lacalle, *Mitos y verdades* (Mexico, 1974), a Republican pilot; Joaquín García Morato, *Guerra en el aire* (Madrid, 1940), a Nationalist account; José Larios, *Combat over Spain* (London, 1966), a Nationalist account; Salvador Rello, *La aviación en la guerra de España*, 4 vols. (Madrid, 1969-1971); Jesús Salas Larrazábal, *La guerra de España desde el aire* (Barcelona, 1969); Miguel Sanchís, *Alas rojas sobre España* (Madrid, 1956); Oloff de Wet, *Cardboard Crucifix* (Edinburgh and London, 1938), a Republican pilot; and F. G. Tinker, *Some Still Live* (New York, 1938), a Republican pilot.

James W. Cortada

PINA. Pina, in the province of Saragossa,* was headquarters for anarchist militia pitted against the Nationalists* during the Catalan invasion of Aragón* during July and August 1936. The anarchists* executed numerous individuals in the village, nearly provoking a revolt against them. In March 1938, the Nationalists, under the command of General Juan de Yagüe Blanco,* captured the town as part of an effort to invade Aragón.

For further information, see Hugh Thomas, *The Spanish Civil War* (New York, 1977).

James W. Cortada

PIUS XI, POPE (1857-1939). Pius XI, born Achille Ratti in Desio (Milan) on May 31, 1857, was elected pope in 1922 after a long career as a librarian and professor of theology and a short stint as *nuncio* to Warsaw and archbishop of Milan. The Spanish situation proved to be one of his most difficult problems.

Pius had to face the worldwide political, physical, and moral chaos arising out of World War I. He continued his predecessor's (Benedict XV) policy of strengthening the international role of the Holy See, and in attempting to safeguard the Church in the unsettled conditions of the 1920s and 1930s, he negotiated concordats with the new governments and regimes, most significantly the Lateran Accords with Mussolini* and the Reich Concordat with Hitler.*

By 1931, when the anticlerical Republic in Spain had been proclaimed, Pius had already appointed Cardinal Eugenio Pacelli (later Pope Pius XII) as his secretary of state. His *nuncio* to Spain, Monsignor Federico Tedeschini, had been in Madrid* for almost a decade. All three agreed upon a policy of moderate conciliation and accommodation with the new Republic. Thus, Pius urged Spanish bishops to accept the government and he himself tacitly accepted Cardinal Pedro Segura's* expulsion from Spain, all in a vain attempt to prevent the enactment of an anticlerical Constitution.

This policy of conciliation foundered on the government's implementation of anticlerical legislation, including the dissolution of the Jesuits in 1932 and the passage of further legislation prohibiting the clergy from teaching. Pius became less accommodating and protested these actions in an encyclical letter, *Dilectissima nobis*, in June 1933. Although the Catholic *Confederación Española de Derechas Autónomas* (CEDA)* made its strong presence felt in the Cortes* after 1933, the pope felt that the political situation was too unstable to conclude negotiations for a concordat.

After the Civil War touched off the massacre of the Spanish clergy in Republican-controlled territory, Pius's sympathies were with the Nationalists.* He made this position clear to a group of Spanish pilgrims in September 1936. However, problems with the Basques and the execution of Basque priests by the Nationalists disappointed him in his relations with Franco's* government, and the ferocity of the war dashed any hope he may have had of mediating the Spanish conflict. It was not until October 1938 that he granted full diplomatic recognition to the Burgos* government. Pius died in Rome on February 10, 1939.

For further information, see Carlo Falconi, *The Popes in the Twentieth Century* (Boston, 1967); and José M. Sánchez, "The Second Spanish Republic and the Holy See: 1931-1936," *Catholic Historical Review* 49 (April 1963):47-68.

See also Catholic Church, Spanish.

José M. Sánchez

PI Y SUÑER, CARLOS (1888-1971). Pi was a Catalan politician and a member of the Esquerra* party. He was an old friend of President Luis Companys* of the Catalan government and a political moderate. Pi joined the regional government in the spring of 1937 as councillor of culture where he also had responsibility for education.* He made a serious attempt to restore sound educational policies and programs in war-torn Catalonia* that represented a balance between Catalan nationalism and the normal needs of basic education. Like most of his Catalan colleagues, he found the Republic more interested in itself than in Catalonia. He did not hesitate, for example, to demand payment for services rendered by the Generalitat* for the Republic. Like his colleagues, he wanted to insure that, after the war ended (should the Republic win), regional autonomy would be restored to Catalonia by the Republican government, with rule by the traditional, middle, and upper class Catalan politicians.

For further information, see Maximiano García Venero *Historia del nacionalismo catalan*, 2 vols. (Madrid, 1967); and Angel Ossorio y Gallardo, *Vida y sacrificio de Companys* (Buenos Aires, 1943).

James W. Cortada

PLA Y DENIEL, BISHOP ENRIQUE (1876-1968). Pla, bishop of Salamanca* during the Civil War, was a firm supporter of the Nationalists.* Born in Barcelona* on December 19, 1876, he was ordained in 1900 after being educated at the Gregorian Pontifical University in Rome. He was named bishop of Ávila* in 1918 and became bishop of Salamanca in 1935.

When the military uprising began in 1936, Pla quickly became one of its strongest supporters. On the occasion of General Franco's* nomination as chief of state in October 1936, Pla wrote a pastoral letter, *Las dos ciudades*, in which the term *cruzada* (crusade)* was first used in a religious sense to apply to the Nationalist movement in Spain.

After the war, Pla was named to succeed Cardinal Isidro Gomá* in 1941 as archbishop of Toledo* and primate of Spain. He was made a cardinal in 1946 and died in Madrid on July 5, 1968.

For further information, see Juan de Iturralde, *El catolicismo y la cruzada de Franco* (Vienna, 1955, 1960).

See also Catholic Church, Spanish.

José M. Sánchez

PLYMOUTH, IVOR MILES WINDSOR-CLIVE, EARL OF (1889-1943). The earl of Plymouth was a British representative to the Non-Intervention Committee* during the Spanish Civil War. He proposed international patrols around Spain to reduce damage to shipping while containing the fighting; obtained international approval for placing observers on the French and Portuguese borders and at Spanish ports in 1936; and continued to negotiate on naval patrols throughout 1937.

For further information, see Dante Puzzo, *Spain and the Great Powers, 1936-1941* (New York, 1962).

James W. Cortada

POBLET MONASTERY. The Poblet Monastery, located in the Catalan province of Tarragona,* managed to escape destruction at the hands of anarchists* and communists who burned and destroyed a large percentage of Catalan religious centers. It was at Poblet, however, that anarchists arrested the cardinal-archbishop of Tarragona who was later saved by President Companys* of the Catalan government.

For further information, see Antonio Montero, *La persecución religiosa en España* (Madrid, 1961).

See also Catholic Church, Spanish; and Religious Orders and Communities.

James W. Cortada

POLAND. During the 1930s, Poland found herself threatened by her traditional enemy the USSR* on the one side and an ambitious Germany* on the other. Therefore, she avoided irritating either side as much as possible while developing close relations with France* and Great Britain* as a protection against Berlin. During the Civil War, Poland thus tried to remain neutral, even to the point of discouraging discussions of the Spanish question in the League of Nations.* As early as August 11, 1936, Poland forbade the shipment of arms to Spain, although later bogus Russian companies in Poland would transmit supplies to the Spanish Republic. Several thousand volunteers* from Poland (mainly intellectuals,* leftist activists, and university students) also fought in the International Brigades.* In March 1939, Paris and London announced their alliance with Warsaw, a clear signal to Berlin that the German division of Czechoslovakia* would not be allowed in Poland. Historians have speculated that if the Spanish war had continued into the summer of 1939, the invasion of Poland in September and the onset of World War II might have been delayed or averted.

For further information, see Seweryn Ajzner, *Polska*

a wojna domowa w Hispanii, 1936-1939 (Warsaw, 1968).

James W. Cortada

POLICE. Police activities became increasingly complex during the Civil War as two Spanish governments attempted to maintain law and order in their sectors while hunting down enemies of the state. This process took place in a country that had multiple police forces prior to the war, numerous local militias* and political vigilante groups, along with various military agencies established between 1936 and 1939 by both sides.

The Republican zone had four police forces operating throughout the war. First, there was the Civil Guard* (known as the Republican Guard during the 1930s) with responsibility for general law and order in the countryside. Second were the Assault Guards* which were used in urban centers to prevent riots and to help maintain order in the streets and guard public buildings. A third group, the Customs Guards or Carabineers (*Carabineros*), under the control of the minister of finance, served as border guards and customs inspectors. Another, much smaller group, called the corps of "investigation and vigilance," had charge of civilian intelligence activities. Besides these four were military police, militia units of the *Federación Anarquista Ibérica* (FAI),* the *Confederación Nacional del Trabajo* (CNT),* the *Unión General de Trabajadores* (UGT),* and a half dozen other organizations, regional guards, and a variety of quasi-secret police and intelligence groups, such as the *Servicio de Investigación Militar* (SIM), most of which were under the control of the military. The Assault Guards played a minor role after the first few weeks of the Civil War since they were badly divided in their loyalties towards one side or the other. All other police groups were to have major effects on their respective areas throughout the Civil War. The *Carabineros*, for example, were expanded to approximately 40,000 by the middle of 1937 to protect frontiers.

The Nationalists* inherited a portion of each of the various police groups found in Republican Spain. They also had specially created vigilante groups, although primarily drawn from the Falange,* while the military established various units. Of the approximately 32,000 Civil Guards in 1936, 14,000 sided with Franco* and 18,000 with the Republic; 5,000 Assault Guards joined the Nationalists while the other 12,000 remained loyal; 4,000 *Carabineros* remained in Republican areas, another 10,000 stayed with Franco, but the Republicans* augmented their own *Carabineros* with over 30,000 additional recruits. As in the Republican zone, each city had regular police forces for routine criminal investigations and others to direct traffic. However, there are no accurate statistics on the number of individuals in any Republican or Nationalist police force.

Between the army, navy, and police, in July 1936 Spain had approximately 200,000 men (on paper) under arms, of whom a third were probably on vacation or leave that summer. Yet, just using the paper statistics, about 65,000 of these men were police (a little over one-third). They were stationed all over Spain, often at critical points, and influenced the flow of events in the early days of the Civil War. Thus, for example, in Barcelona,* the rebel army units were unable to seize that city primarily because local police sided with the Republicans. Since they were the only disciplined and trained military contingents that could be pitted against the army rebels, they saved the Catalan city for the Republic. The same story could have been told for every major city that remained in Republican hands or fell to the Nationalists in the first two months of the Civil War. Moreover, many of the large number of murders committed during the first several months depended in large part on the support or active participation of local police chiefs such as Manuel Díaz Criado in Seville,* Lisardo Doval in Salamanca,* José Valdés Guzmán in Granada,* or Joaquín del Moral in Burgos.* It was only after each side began to restrain extremist police, and subsequently the vigilante-style militias,* that the more normal functions of law and order could be carried out. Yet, until the very end of the Civil War, police forces throughout Spain were actively involved in prosecuting the war as extensions of the military campaigns.

For further information, see Ronald Fraser, *The Blood of Spain* (New York, 1979); and Hugh Thomas, *The Spanish Civil War* (New York, 1977). There is no general history on the role of police services or judicial systems in the Spanish Civil War.

See also Espionage; NKVD; and each of the major political groups.

James W. Cortada

PONFERRADA, MASSACRE OF. Ponferrada, in the province of León,* was the site of a massacre of pro-Republican miners by Nationalist troops in July 1936. Thinking the area secure for the Republicans,* these miners resisted the Nationalists* in the region. Ponferrada was the only point in the entire province at which a pitched battle took place during the Civil War.

For further information, see Joaquín Arrarás, *Historia de la cruzada española*, 35 folios (Madrid, 1940-1943).

James W. Cortada

PONTE Y MANSO DE ZÚÑIGA, MIGUEL (MARQUIS OF BÓVEDA DE LIMIA) (1882-1952). Ponte, born at Vitoria,* was a cavalry officer who won rapid promotion to general in Morocco.* He retired from active service in 1931 and in April 1932 sought support in Italy* for a monarchist coup. He was expelled from the army for his role in the Sanjurjo* revolt in August 1932. An active conspirator throughout 1936, Ponte negotiated with the Salazar* regime and in July seized the 7th Division in Valladolid,* along with General Andrés Saliquet.* Both later became members of the *Junta de Defensa Nacional* in Burgos.* During the war, Ponte was head of the 5th Division; in November 1937, he became commander of the 1st Army Corps at the Madrid* front. Promoted to lieutenant general in 1940, he held several high-ranking military posts after the war.

For further information, see Felipe Bertrán Güell, *Caudillo, profetas, y soldados* (Madrid, 1939); Stanley G. Payne, *Politics and the Military in Modern Spain* (Stanford, Calif., 1967); and Teresa Suero Roca, *Los generales de Franco* (Barcelona, 1975).

Carolyn P. Boyd

POPULAR ARMY. Popular Army was a phrase used to describe the Republican Army* in general, particularly after the various militia units were incorporated into regular army units.

See also Army of the North (Republican); and Militias.

James W. Cortada

POPULAR FRONT (FRENCH). The French Popular Front refers to a coalition of parties on the political Left which resulted in Léon Blum* becoming the prime minister on June 5, 1936. He headed a government composed of radicals, republicans, and socialists with the blessings of the communists. The formula essentially repeated the Spanish experience. The Popular Front wanted to institute domestic reforms and initially acted as an alliance to eliminate the conservatives from national government. The Popular Front government of Léon Blum took a great deal of interest in the fate of the Spanish Republic with which it sympathized. Blum assumed that a Nationalist Spain would not be friendly toward France.* Moreover, right- and left-wing elements in France were clashing in the streets, thereby giving Blum the impression that Spain's Civil War would increase tensions in France. Thus, when the Spanish Republic requested help on July 20, Yvon Delbos,* the French foreign minister, and Edouard Daladier,* the minister of war, both members of the Radical party, agreed with Blum that some assistance was appropriate. Members of the Popular Front, however, hardly deviated from the nonintervention policy developed by their own government with that of Great Britain.*

For further information, see John E. Dreifort, *Yvon Delbos at the Quai D'Orsay: French Foreign Policy during the Popular Front, 1936-1938* (Lawrence, Kans., 1973); David W. Pike, *Les Français et la guerre d'Espagne, 1936-1939* (Paris, 1975); and Pierre Renouvin, *Léon Blum, chef de Gouvernement* (Paris, 1967).

James W. Cortada

POPULAR FRONT (SPANISH). The Spanish Popular Front was a coalition of parties on the political Left that agreed to work together in January 1936 to win the national elections of February* against conservative incumbents. Their program called for the further republicanization of legal and economic institutions to which the socialists and communists also subscribed as members of the Popular Front. In the February elections, 34.3 percent of the vote went to the Popular Front, 33.2 percent to the Right, and the rest to regional and center parties. Because of the way the vote was distributed, the Popular Front won a large majority of seats in the Cortes,* while virtually eliminating moderate Center groups from political power. As a result of the election, a new Republican government reflecting Popular Front views was set up within days, leftist extremists released political prisoners* from jail and caused some street disturbances, and the Cortes had 271 members of the Popular Front, 137 from the Right, and forty from the Center.

From February onward, the architects of the July 1936 rebellion against the Republic became increasingly concerned that they would have to take Spanish affairs into their own hands. Thus, the election brought the Civil War even closer. The new government released leftist political prisoners from jail, without due process of law in many cases, which irritated conservatives; Catalonia* regained her political and administrative autonomy; and more initiative was taken on agrarian reforms that were disadvantageous to the large landed aristocracy. Leftist groups did not maintain a united alliance after the elections, however, often taking matters into their own hands. Members of the

Unión General de Trabajadores (UGT),* for example, occupied land in Badajoz;* serious strikes by workers all over Spain threatened normal economic activity; and banks and the wealthy took vast sums of capital out of the country. The Popular Front government was unable to repress street violence or improve the value of the peseta,* which damaged export/import trade and tourism, caused the cost of living to rise, and thereby encouraged more pressure by labor for higher wages. The Communist party* grew enormously in size, with tens of thousands of new members that spring. By April, the party had taken over all major socialist and communist youth organizations—the basis of the militias* in post-July Republican Spain.

The emasculation of the political power of the Right became a major objective of the Popular Front. The moderately conservative President Niceto Alcalá-Zamora was removed and replaced with Manuel Azaña,* which meant that the last moderate influence disappeared from the Spanish government. Azaña had worked more to form the Popular Front alliance than any other Spaniard; thus, his elevation to the presidency insured that the Left had extensive power. By May, therefore, Spanish Army officers began their serious plotting to restore a more conservative Spanish government which could count on the support of the Church, the middle class, and the aristocracy. Meanwhile, Azaña promoted officers who had liberal views on politics and who, in many cases, had not served in the wars in North Africa. The more conservative Moroccan veterans banded together to form the source of much plotting that spring. The last event demonstrating the Popular Front government's inability to provide leadership and stability came on July 12, when police* officers and communist militia murdered José Calvo Sotelo* who, at that time, led the opposition in the Cortes. This one event more than any other finally led to the start of the Civil War which came within five days.

For further information, see Ricardo de la Cierva, *Historia de la Guerra Civil Española,* Vol. 1, *Antecedentes: monarquía y república, 1898-1936* (Madrid, 1969); Gabriel Jackson, *Costa, Azaña, El Frente Popular y ostros ensayos* (Madrid, 1976) and *The Spanish Republic and the Civil War, 1931-1939* (Princeton, N.J., 1965); and Stanley G. Payne, *Spanish Revolution* (New York, 1970).

See also Anarchists; and Socialist Party, Spanish.

James W. Cortada

POPULAR TRIBUNALS. Both the Nationalists* and the Republicans* made use of popular tribunals, primarily to try prisoners* accused of being enemies of the state. These courts usually executed those found guilty. Typically, the formal judicial process found in Spanish courts before 1936 did not exist in these tribunals. In many cases, accusation was evidence enough to find a person guilty and subsequently be shot. Judges had little, if any, legal training and were on the bench as representatives of key political groups. Tribunals were usually established in the early days of the Civil War to help purge an area of enemies, and often their greatest amount of work came soon after a new region had been occupied by one side or the other. There are no valid statistics as to how many prisoners were tried in such courts, sentenced, executed, or released. However, the number is believed to be tens of thousands for each side.

The majority of such courts were established in the Republican zone where apparently a greater number of executions took place, particularly in the first two months of the war. The Republican Ministry of Justice established such courts to replace existing ones whose judges and lawyers had deserted to the Nationalists. These newly established popular tribunals were staffed with fourteen delegates representing such political groups as the *Confederación Nacional del Trabajo* (CNT),* the *Unión General de Trabajadores* (UGT),* or the *Federación Anarquista Ibérica* (FAI).* Each of these factions established its own tribunal to which its strongmen brought prisoners as well. The FAI in Barcelona* was especially guilty of this practice until May 1937, when the Republic regained control over governmental affairs throughout Catalonia.* In competition with the government were many communities which also established tribunals when they deemed it necessary (as, for example, throughout Asturias* in 1936).

While Nationalists had fewer systems of popular tribunals, they did exist. Cities and towns created courts, often with heavy representation by the Falange.* During the first two years of the Civil War, however, military courts served the same function as the Republican popular tribunals and often with the same casual respect for judicial procedure. As the Nationalists established a larger civilian government, a Ministry of Justice evolved and slowly a system of courts. But as in the Republican zone, justice was swift. The accused were often found guilty after a short trial, and execution was a common sentence carried out the same day or the next morning. On both sides, therefore, appeals were almost unheard of. While the number of prisoners handled by the Nationalist courts grew as Franco* occupied more territory, by mid-1939 this prisoner population apparently exceeded 100,000. Again, as with the Republicans, no reliable figures are known.

The types of prisoners taken by both sides varied. The Republicans sought deserters, members of the Falange and other right-wing or conservative political groups, enemies of the state (including soldiers fighting for the Nationalists), and criminals. Sometimes there were members of political factions within the Republican zone who had fallen out of favor, such as anarchists* after the communists gained the upper hand in the Republic. Priests, nuns, and other clerical personnel were also subject to prosecution in Republican popular tribunals. On the Nationalist side, the arrest of Republican enemies was a more rational process. The Nationalists sought to prosecute Republican mayors, key public officials, leaders and members of left-wing political and labor groups, other supporters of the Republic accused of taking up arms against the Nationalists, and military personnel.

For further information, see Ronald Fraser, *The Blood of Spain* (New York, 1979); Robert W. Kern, *Red Years/Black Years: A Political History of Spanish Anarchism, 1911-1937* (Philadelphia, 1978); and Hugh Thomas, *The Spanish Civil War* (New York, 1977).

See also Police; and Terrorism.

James W. Cortada

POPULATION. As of December 1930, Spain's population was 25,563,867. The population density was 46.7 per square kilometer, far less than the nearly 100 for most of Western Europe.* In some cases, such as in Great Britain* and in Germany,* density statistics were closer to 200 per square kilometer. Spain experienced far less dramatic growth than the rest of Western Europe, probably because the Industrial Revolution did not affect the Spanish economy as positively because in 1797 Spain's head count was 10.5 million, in 1900 it reached 18.6 million, and by 1930 25.5 million. Between 1900 and 1930, the period of the Second Republic,* 975,350 people left Spain to live in other countries but 106,243 persons returned, primarily because of the world Depression. Thus, Spain's population continued to grow on the eve of the Civil War.

Some additional data on the war years suggest a few demographic trends:

Demographic Issues: 1936-1939
(population in millions, trends per thousand)

Year	Population as of Jan. 1	Marriages	Births	Deaths
1936	24,693	5.59	24.74	16.67
1937	24,926	5.72	22.59	18.85
1938	25,160	4.47	20.02	19.18
1939	25,397	5.63	16.45	18.42

As is obvious from the table, births declined while deaths went up. The exact number of deaths is still an object of considerable controversy, although statistics suggest over 3.3 percent of the population. Furthermore, the data in the above table are a best guess in severe need of further clarification. The distribution of Spain's population across urban and rural areas, although not precise, confirms what economists have argued, namely, that Spain was still an agricultural economy in the 1930s. Political historians can point to the same data to show why worker politics was so intense and why internal migration to the cities in the 1930s was quite extreme. If the populations of the largest cities in Spain are totaled (Madrid,* Barcelona,* Valencia,* Seville,* Saragossa,* Málaga,* and Bilbao*), they equal 13.5 per cent of the population. If those for provincial capitals and other towns are added, probably about 25 percent of all Spaniards lived in urban centers. Madrid and Barcelona had populations of about 1 million, while an additional ten cities claimed populations of over 100,000 each.

An examination of where people worked gives a better view of population:

Work Distribution
(in % of population)

Year	Agriculture	Industry	Services
1931	45.51	25.51	27.98
1941	50.52	22.13	27.35

Of the total population, 35.51 percent was working as of 1931, the only year close to the Civil War for which we have reasonably accurate data. The information in the work distribution table suggests where the work force found jobs. Clearly, Spain was still a nearly preindustrial society. Perhaps because of war deaths, only 34.61 percent of the population was employed in 1941, a drop of over 1 percent in ten years.

For further information, see Jordi Nadal, *La población española (siglos XVI a XX)* (Barcelona, 1971); Spain, Instituto Nacional de Estadística, *Cincuenta años de vida española, 1900-1950* (Madrid, 1952); and Ramón Tamames, *La República; La era de Franco* (Madrid, 1979).

See also Casualties; Costs; and individual provinces by name.

James W. Cortada

PORTAGO, MARQUIS OF. The Marquis of Portago was a Spanish Nationalist agent sent to Berlin in the

Spain: Population Dynamics

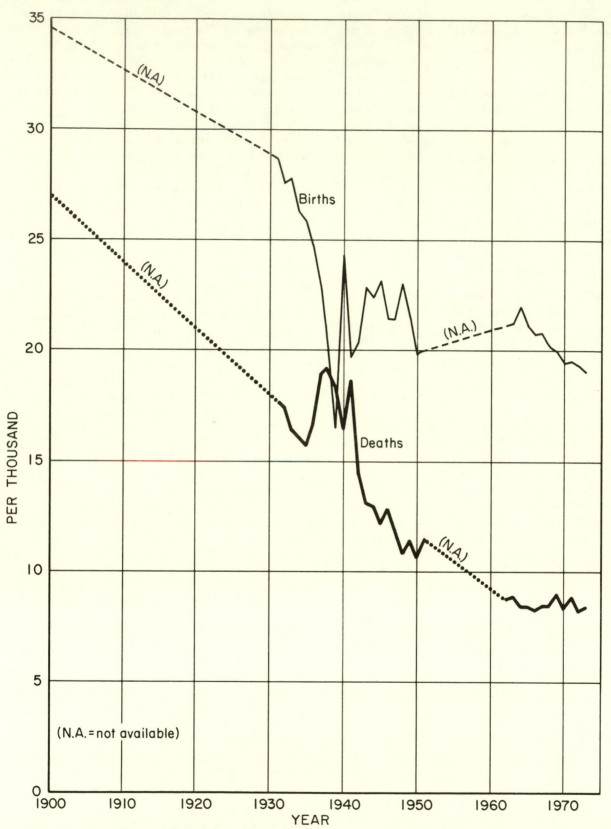

Source: Eugene K. Keefe et al., *Area Handbook for Spain* (Washington, D.C.: U.S. Government Printing Office, 1976),
p. 77.

early days of the Civil War to negotiate aid from the Germans. He later lived in London gathering information and help for the Nationalists.*

For further information, see José Ignacio Escobar, *Así empezó* (Madrid, 1974).

James W. Cortada

PORTUGAL. From the very beginning of the Spanish Civil War, the Portuguese government of Antonio de Oliveira Salazar* strongly favored the Nationalists,* which was perceived to be a conservative, stable, and traditional force. From the first days of the fighting, Salazar concluded that if radically Left factions (that is, anarchists* or communists) in Spain should win the conflict, his authoritarian government in Portugal might be invaded by the Spaniards, bent on overthrowing it. Thus, from the onset of the war, Salazar had to take sides, and he did what he could to aid Franco.* Nationalist leaders were allowed to meet on Portuguese soil and to negotiate with Germany,* for example, for the procurement of supplies. As early as August 1936, the Salazar regime made it clear to the Germans that Portugal could be used as a funnel for supplies to the Nationalists. Portugal served as a place of refuge when necessary and as a communications link during the early days of the fighting when the Nationalist zone was in two distinct geographical pieces. From the summer of 1936 beyond the spring of 1939, Salazar returned to Spain Republicans* who had crossed his borders seeking to escape the Nationalists. On occasion, this policy meant the execution of returned Republicans by Franco's forces. Along with the support at the border came propaganda from Lisbon defending the Nationalists, and in the nearly three years of fighting, Portuguese volunteers* served in Franco's armies.

On the diplomatic front, Portugal was at first reluctant to join the majority of Western Europe* in early August 1936 in opting for a policy of nonintervention in the Spanish War. However, on August 13, Salazar accepted the policy in principle, providing his borders were not threatened. Otherwise, Portugal reserved the right to intervene to protect its national interests. On September 24, after considerable British efforts to persuade Salazar's government, Portugal formally joined the Non-Intervention Committee.* In October, the Portuguese broke off diplomatic relations with the Spanish Republic because of Russian accusations that Lisbon was not honoring the objectives of the Non-Intervention Agreement. After October, Portugal became more open in its support of Franco's cause. In early December, Anglo-French proposals for mediating a conclusion to the war led nowhere. However, during the course of these negotiations, Portugal, like most other nations, including Germany and Italy,* agreed in principle to participate in such talks, although the feeling in Lisbon was that neither Spanish side would compromise with the other.

The leading members of the Non-Intervention Committee (particularly Great Britain* and France*) devoted considerable diplomatic effort during the course of 1937 in establishing various international patrols and observation groups to monitor the traffic of supplies into Spain for either side. The sought to block the flow of military aid. Germany and Italy were willing to participate if they could continue to aid Franco, while the USSR* felt the same way about the Republic. The Portuguese objected to international observers being stationed on her mutual border with Spain, using the excuse of violations of sovereignty. In fact, she wanted to maintain maximum flexibility to help the Nationalists. Again, the Portuguese agreed reluctantly to allow a few naval observers and half-heartedly participated in some patrolling. Portugal's policy of no longer patrolling its frontier with Spain under the guise of international nonintervention in 1937 almost provided the French with an excuse not to do the same on their border with Republican Spain. British pressure brought France back into line but not the Portuguese who continued to aid Franco.

Throughout 1938, Franco's government negotiated with the Portuguese, hoping to sign a formal treaty of alliance as a means of stabilizing relations, especially on their mutual frontier. Franco may well have also wanted to maintain indirect links to London by way of Portugal's ancient alliance with the British, particularly access to economic trade via Lisbon and as a counterbalance to German influence in Spain. From the Munich crisis of September 1938, his government at Burgos* had learned that the possibility of a general European war existed. A major objective was to mitigate the impact of such a conflict on a new government with no allies in the West. In early 1939, negotiations were renewed on a possible treaty which, by March, resulted in a Non-Aggression Pact. This treaty brought assurance of peace on the Spanish border if a new war should erupt, while giving the Franco regime some international prestige. The treaty was clearly another example of the Portuguese government's warm support of the Nationalist cause.

Portugal aided the Nationalists during the Civil War, if not in actually military terms, certainly in public support, in the use of Portuguese territory, and in the capture and return of Republicans. Portugal's quiet international resistance to measures that might negatively affect Franco were useful, as were the facilities made available (especially in Lisbon) for the Germans and Italians to negotiate the shipment of supplies to the Nationalists. Furthermore, several thousand Portuguese fought for Franco with the blessings of the Salazar regime.

For further information, see Hugh Kay, *Salazar and Modern Portugal* (London, 1970); Portugal, *Portugal ante la guerra civil de España* (London, 1939), on diplomacy, and *Diez años de política externa (1936-1947)* (Lisbon, 1965), Vol. 3; and José Sepúlveda Vellos, *Páginas do diario de un aviador na guerra de España* (Lisbon, 1972), on military help.

See also League of Nations.

James W. Cortada

POSTAL SERVICES, INTERNATIONAL. During the Spanish Civil War, foreign correspondents continually complained about the difficulties of mailing their dispatches. In the early months of the war, many preferred to take their dispatches to the frontier themselves and telephone them from the French side of the border. After Irún* fell to the Nationalists* on September 5, 1936, all mail for Spain traveling by land was routed from Toulouse to Cerbère, regardless of the zone of destination. Thus, all mail addressed to Pamplona* or San Sebastián (after its fall on September 13) never reached the addressee, since it had to pass through Barcelona* and Madrid.* Nationalist supporters in France,* for their part, overcame this problem by delivering their mail by hand at the Irún frontier post. The situation changed in mid-November when the French postal service invited the public to indicate the appropriate route whenever this was known: Bayonne, for the Basque zone in Republican hands; Cerbère, for the rest of Republican Spain; and Hendaye, for the Nationalist zone.

For further information, see Rafael Abella, *La vida cotidiana durante la guerra civil: La España nacional* (Barcelona, 1973); and *La vida cotidiana durante la guerra civil: La España republicana* (Barcelona, 1975).

David Wingeate Pike

POZAS PEREA, GABRIEL (1880-1937). Pozas served as the aide-de-camp to General Emilio Mola,* the chief Nationalist commander in northern Spain and one of the principal architects of the July 1936 rebellion. Colonel Pozas was a career army officer whose brother, General Sebastián Pozas Perea,* was the Republicans'* minister of the interior in the early days of the conflict. Pozas died with General Mola on June 3, 1937, when their plane crashed into a mountain near Burgos.*

For further information, see José María Iribarren, *El general Mola* (Madrid, 1945).

James W. Cortada

POZAS PEREA, SEBASTIÁN (1876-1946). Sebastián Pozas was born in 1876 into a family of strong monarchist convictions. He entered the cavalry academy at sixteen, served brilliantly during the Moroccan Wars, and was promoted to general at the age of fifty during the dictatorship of Primo de Rivera. Notwithstanding his conservative background, Pozas enthusiastically supported the Republic upon its advent in 1931. Shortly after the advent of the Popular Front* in February 1936, he was made inspector general of the Civil Guard* and, according to his son-in-law, was approached by General Franco,* through an intermediary, who offered Pozas funds in a Swiss bank in return for his support of a national government. Given the post of minister of the interior in the Giral* government on July 18, Pozas favored arming the people and was successful in retaining the loyalty of the Civil Guards in several urban centers, including Madrid,* where the Civil Guards stayed in their barracks and thereby contributed to the failure of the rising.

In a famous episode involving misaddressed instructions (rectified by the recipients, General Miaja* and himself), Pozas was given command of a new Army of the Center* with headquarters at Tarancon, when the government left Madrid for Valencia* on November 6. At about this time, he joined the Communist party,* and the Soviet General Gregori Ivan Kulik and his aide (later Marshal) Roden Malinovsky served as his advisers during the battles of Jarama* and Guadalajara.* According to Malinovsky, Pozas was absolutely loyal to the Republic but casual in the performance of his duties, and his dependence upon the Soviet advisers was apparently substantial.

In May 1937, following the disturbances in Barcelona,* Pozas was appointed chief of staff of the Army of the East* and with the aid of 5,000 Assault Guards supervised the restoration of order. Under threat of bombing, he turned back anarchosyndicalist and *Partido Obrero de Unificación Marxista* (POUM)* elements moving on Barcelona from the Aragón* front. Subsequently, Pozas helped plan the abortive Republican attack on Huesca* late in May, and, with his chief of staff, the Spanish communist Antonio Cordon,* and Soviet advisers was in at least nominal charge of the planning and execution of the Aragón offensive in August, which culminated in the taking of Belchite.*

At this time, he also supervised the dissolution of the powerful anarchist Council of Aragón.*

Following the Nationalist breakthrough in their Aragón offensive in March-April 1938, Pozas was relieved of command of the Army of the East and thereafter did not hold any position of importance. At the war's end, he emigrated to Mexico,* where he died in 1946.

For further information, see Burnett Bolloten, *The Spanish Revolution: The Left and the Struggle for Power During the Civil War* (Chapel Hill, N.C., 1979); Editorial Codex, *Crónica de la Guerra Española*, various issues, including No. 64 (Buenos Aires, 1967); and Hugh Thomas, *The Spanish Civil War* (New York, 1977).

See also Army, Republican; May 1937 Riots; and Appendix B.

Verle B. Johnston

PRADA VAQUERO, ADOLFO (-1962). Prada fought with the Republicans* during the Civil War. He commanded troops that were repeatedly attacked by the Nationalists* outside of Madrid* in the fall and winter of 1936-1937 and later the 14th Republican Army Corps in the Santander* campaign in August 1937. This combat officer also led troops in the Aragón* offensive during August-October and in Asturias.* He reorganized various divisions and a corps for the Republican Army,* and in 1938 he commanded the Army of Estremadura* before becoming a sub-inspector general and fought in the final campaign in and around Madrid. This able commander was the Republic's last chief of the Army of the North,* and eventually the Nationalists arrested Prada after he surrendered his forces to them. Like many combat officers on the Republican side, he held left-wing political views and may have sympathized considerably with communism.

For further information, see Manuel Azaña, *Obras completas*, 4 vols. (Mexico, 1966-1968); and José Manuel Martínez Bande, *Los cien últimos días de la república* (Barcelona, 1972).

James W. Cortada

PRADOS, PEDRO. Prados was a career naval officer who, briefly in 1938, was the naval chief of staff for the Republican Navy. He was a communist and received his appointment as part of an effort by the Communist party* to increase its penetration into the highest levels of Negrín's* government.

For further information, see Burnett Bolloten, *The Spanish Revolution: The Left and the Power for Struggle During the Civil War* (Chapel Hill, N.C., 1979).
See also Navy, Spanish.

James W. Cortada

PRETEL, FELIPE. Felipe Pretel was a socialist and a political commissar who sided with the Republicans.* He also held the second highest position of authority in the *Unión General de Trabajadores* (UGT).* His primary role was to build enthusiasm for communism within the military and to have political enemies removed. He also continued to be the treasurer of the UGT in Madrid.* By 1938, like many other UGT members he fully supported Negrín* and the programs of the Communist party.*

For further information, see Burnett Bolloten, *The Spanish Revolution: The Left and the Struggle for Power During the Civil War* (Chapel Hill, N.C., 1979).

James W. Cortada

PRIETO, HORACIO. Prieto was a little-known anarchist leader during the Civil War who, just before the conflict, had been secretary of the *Confederación Nacional del Trabajo* (CNT).* After the fighting started, he became secretary general of the CNT. He was considered a political realist who advocated cooperation among labor and political leaders in the national and regional governments. Criticized by opponents, Prieto resigned in 1937 rather than have his pride offended. He remained in the CNT, however, and persuaded many anarchists* to accept nationalization of industries in exchange for collectivization of agriculture and small companies for the good of the Republican war effort.

For further information, see Cesarm Lorenzo (son of Horacio Prieto), *Les Anarchistes espagnols et le pouvoir* (Paris, 1969).
See also Libertarian Movement; Peasantry, Aragonese; and Workers, Catalan.

James W. Cortada

PRIETO Y TUERO, INDALECIO (1883-1962). Prieto was raised in abject poverty in Bilbao* after his father's death in 1889. He joined the Socialist party when he was only sixteen and soon began a meteoric rise within its regional hierarchy. Instrumental in founding Spain's first Young Socialist League in 1903, he also became one of the first two socialists in Spanish history to be elected to a provincial council in 1911.

In 1914 and 1915, after a fierce struggle with Facundo Perezagua, Vizcayan Socialist party leader since the 1890s, Prieto emerged as the dominant figure of Basque socialism.

A person of extraordinary vitality, Prieto simultaneously carved out a successful business career as journalist, newspaper editor, and general *homme des affaires*. The August 1917 general strike and Prieto's election to Parliament in February 1918 finally tipped the balance. From that time on, Prieto devoted himself almost exclusively to politics, increasingly on a national level.

Prieto's mixed past permanently marked his political outlook. Never an ideological Marxist or deeply involved with the trade-union side of socialism, Prieto sought rather to link the Spanish Socialist party with middle-class reformists so as to create an interclass, progressive force capable of transforming Spanish politics. The struggle with Perezagua had been over the question of collaboration with Republican groups. In Parliament, Prieto's opposition to the Moroccan War was far more impassioned than his defense of purely working-class interests. The Primo de Rivera dictatorship presented him with his first major political crisis, as he resigned from the Socialist party executive committee in 1924 rather than accept its policy of flirtation with the nondemocratic regime.

Prieto reached his political acme in the early 1930s. He played the leading role in bringing a repentant Spanish Socialist party into the Republican coalition that would overthrow the monarchy in 1931. His administrative skills made him a key contributor to the Republic's early achievements, first as minister of finance and then especially as minister of public works in a Depression-ravaged economy. Many of the great irrigation and urban revitalization projects completed under Franco* were inaugurated by Prieto during his tour in office.

This fruitful period of balance between Prieto's socialism and liberalism was destroyed by the disintegration of the progressive Azaña* coalition and the radicalization of the Spanish Socialist party in the autumn of 1933. After fighting ineffectually against the revolutionary orientation which Largo Caballero* was giving to the Socialist party, Prieto unenthusiastically went along with the new party line and even supervised clandestine arms shipments to Socialist party groups in northern Spain. But following the crushing of the October 1934 revolution, Prieto returned to his old course, and he sought to defeat the radicals and restore the Socialist party to its earlier reformist policies. He enjoyed some success, especially in getting the party to join the Popular Front* electoral coali-

tion with the Left Republicans in early 1936 and in frustrating Caballerista efforts to regain control of the official party mechanism thereafter. But a price had to be paid: Prieto's position within the party was seriously eroded, and he seemed destined inexorably to lose his struggle against the more popular Caballeristas after the spring of 1936.

Too controversial and too closely tied to the waning star of Left republicanism, Prieto had little real chance of becoming prime minister during the Civil War itself, although he was frequently mentioned for this post. Instead, he served as naval and air minister in the Largo Caballero government of September 1936 to May 1937, and became head of a United Ministry of National Defense, which also encompassed the army, from May 1937 to March 1938 under Juan Negrín.*

Prieto was never as effective in either of these critical positions as he had been in his peacetime ministries. In the first, there was continuous conflict with Largo Caballero, who served as army minister as well as premier. Prieto, initially confident that the Republic would win the war because of its early superiority of resources, increasingly attributed the Republican reverses to the incompetent leadership of his old rival and supported the communist drive to oust Largo Caballero after the May 1937 riots* in Barcelona.* Yet, the leadership change to his former protege Negrín and Prieto's own expanded functions brought no permanent improvement in his or the Republic's fortunes. Prieto soon found himself in serious conflict with the communists, as he tried to reduce their influence in the army. But more important, like his predecessors, he was unable to put together a successful major army offensive. This was proven when the surprise Republican attack that conquered Teruel* in December 1937 was reversed in January and February 1938 by Franco's forces, which followed it up in March by their spectacular breakthrough on the Aragón front.

Teruel's loss and Prieto's increasingly obvious pessimism as to the possibility of winning the war triggered a communist propaganda offensive against him reminiscent of the one waged earlier with Prieto's support against Largo Caballero. Negrín also became convinced that Prieto should no longer serve because he had become defeatist as well as too controversial. Thus, on March 30, midst the collapse on the Aragón front, a highly embittered Prieto was removed from office.

Prieto would never again exercise power on Spanish soil. A new career awaited him in exile, however. With the early deaths of his older party rivals, Besteiro* and Largo Caballero, and with the postwar ostracism of Negrín as crypto-communist, Prieto finally emerged as the Spanish Socialist party's principal leader and therefore as one of the chief figures of the Republican government-in-exile until his death in Mexico* in 1962. His last major public act, the public reconciliation with the Catholic leader Gil Robles* in Munich, was consistent with the policy that had dominated his entire political career: a social democratic rapprochement between Marxian socialism and middle-class progressivism.

For further information, see Burnett Bolloten, *The Spanish Revolution: The Left and the Struggle for Power During the Civil War* (Chapel Hill, N.C., 1979), for a broader treatment of socialist-communist relations; Edward Malefakis, ed., *Indalecio Prieto: Discursos fundamentales* (Madrid, 1975); and Indalecio Prieto, *De mi vida*, 2 vols. (Mexico, 1965-1970), *Cómo y porqué salí del Ministerio de Defensa Nacional, intrigas de los rusos en España* (Mexico, 1940), *Convulsiones de España*, 3 vols. (Mexico, 1967-1969), *Epistolario Prieto y Negrín* (Paris, 1939), *Palabras al viento* (Mexico, 1942), and *Yo y Moscú* (Madrid, 1955).

Edward Malefakis

PRIMO DE RIVERA, PILAR (1913-   ). Pilar Primo de Rivera was a Falangist supporter of the Nationalists* and politically active as the head of the *Auxilio Social* from 1937 onward. The *Auxilio Social* was one of many charitable organizations that took care of orphans and provided other social services. General Franco* appointed her to an advisory council on December 2, 1937, established as the first formal government under his control. She was born in Madrid* and was the sister of José Antonio Primo de Rivera,* one of the founders of the *Falange Española.**

For further information, see Círculo de Amigos de la Historia, *Diccionario biográfico español contemporaneo* (Madrid, 1970), Vol. 3.

James W. Cortada

PRIMO DE RIVERA Y SAENZ DE HEREDÍA, JOSÉ ANTONIO (1903-1936). Primo de Rivera established the *Falange Española,** and he later became the subject of a political cult worship during the years of the Franco* regime. Son of General Miguel Primo de Rivera, Spain's military dictator during the 1920s, José Antonio was born in Madrid* where he eventually practiced law. His earliest political activities began at the end of the 1920s with speeches and writings defending his father's policies and programs. In 1930, he became a member of the newly formed *Unión Monárquica Nacional* established to defend the politi-

cal viability of the Spanish monarchy. After the formation of the Second Republic* in 1931, he concluded that more conservative political remedies were needed for the nation's ills than a republic. In 1933, he edited a conservative political periodical, *El Fascio*, which the Republic soon shut down. He continued to write on conservative political themes in such periodicals as *ABC** and *La Nación*. On October 29, 1933, he established the *Falange Española*. Along with Ramiro Ledesma Ramos* and Onésimo Redondo, he expanded the influence and membership of the Falange throughout southern and central Spain. That year he entered the Cortes* as delegate from Jerez de la Frontera. He soon after founded two newspapers, both of which the Republic closed down: *Fe* in 1934 and *Arriba* in 1935. These were the first two newspapers of the Falange. For the remaining period before the Civil War, José Antonio Primo de Rivera participated in opposition politics in the Republic.

Although a product of upper class Andalusian society with a paternalistic attitude toward workers and the poor, José Antonio early developed a social conscience which attracted other young men to the Falange. He was an enemy of socialism which he feared would destroy the country, and he favored a strong government, possibly a monarchy but certainly not a republic. He did not admire the Nazi movement but found much of interest in Italian fascism. He advocated a strong nationalist state, integration of the Catholic Church* and army in national political and governmental life, and yet, until the days just before the Civil War, he was reluctant to advocate revolution against the Republic. As the weeks crept toward July 1936, members of his party increasingly became eager for plots and violence, all sensing that the day for action was rapidly approaching. In the months after the elections of February 1936* and before July, membership in the Falange exceeded 25,000. *Falangistas* more often appeared in public with their uniforms and frequently with arms, drawing considerable public attention. By July, membership in the Falange, consisting primarily of young right-wing conservatives, had jumped to over 40,000, threatening to discolor the nature of Primo de Rivera's party and more important, his control over it.

At the start of the war, the Falange overwhelmingly supported the Nationalist revolt. The Republicans* immediately arrested *Falangistas*, including José Antonio. Jailed at Alicante* on July 6, he still attempted to run the party from his cell as the war approached. But as the months passed, this became increasingly difficult while the Republicans discussed having a trial. Finally, they decided to prosecute this popular leader, found him guilty of crimes against the state, and sentenced him to death. Despite some attempts to have the sentence commuted, on November 20, 1936, José Antonio died before a firing squad. His death gave the Nationalists* a well-known martyr. As the influence of the Falange party grew in the Nationalist zone, so too did the views and image of José Antonio as a national hero. In the years following the Civil War, the Falange extolled his virtues and reprinted all his writings. Dozens of books appeared on the man and on the movement he founded.

Briefly stated, he believed that man was the repository of some eternal values and the nation a unity of destiny with a purpose. He advocated a nation based on its historical and economic traditions, as represented by the principles of private property, God and church, army, and the existing social classes. He postulated a theory of organic organization that borrowed heavily from the fascist thinking of the 1930s. Byproducts of such thinking included the concept of vertical syndicates to take care of the economic and social interests of workers, managers, and the best needs of the state and economy.

For further information, see Stanley G. Payne, *Falange: A History of Spanish Fascism* (Stanford, Calif., 1961); José Antonio Primo de Rivera, *Obras completas* (many editions, mostly in 4 vols.) (Madrid, 1942 and since); Hugh Thomas, *Selected Writings of José Antonio Primo de Rivera* (London, 1972); and Felipe Ximénez de Sandoval, *Biografía apasionada* (Barcelona, 1941).

James W. Cortada

PRISONERS. The Spanish prison population increased during the Civil War to include military and political inmates along with more traditional criminals. Both the Republicans* and Nationalists* arrested those they considered political liabilities, while executing tens of thousands in preference to detention. Arrests were made by police* forces, the military, civilian intelligence, and political parties, especially in the Republican zone which experienced more violent rivalry among political groups than did the Nationalists. Each time a new area was occupied by either side, arrests inevitably increased. The Nationalists methodically arrested the leading members of the local political and economic establishment and of the labor unions, often executing them. The Republicans arrested similar individuals, adding priests, monks, and nuns to their lists. Both took military prisoners and often shot them.

Prisons were run by provinces, national governments, the military, political parties (especially in Barcelona*), and foreign participants (the Russians, for example).

There are no accurate statistics on the prison population of Spain for the years 1936-1939. However, it is estimated that each side arrested hundreds of thousands, particularly after major military actions. The Nationalists, for example, stated in September 1938 that they had taken 210,000 military prisoners up to that time, and yet extensive political arrests were made by the Francoists as well. Life in prison was often arbitrarily primitive, improvised, and cruel. With massive arrests being made, old penal institutions were strained to the limits, while many were pens and improvised facilities (bullrings were popular). Political and military prisoners outnumbered criminal inmates, thereby making life unsafe for all. Local residents sometimes broke into prisons, seeking to take vengeance over a war-related event, causing the deaths of both criminal and political inmates. Since the process of law had broken down during the Civil War along with many juridical institutions, the military, political groups, or self-styled vigilantes arbitrarily conducted trials. Execution was the most common form of punishment inflicted on prisoners, and death could come for the slightest provocation as, for example, in the Nationalist zone, simply yelling out "Viva la República!" It is conservatively estimated that an average of over 1,500 people were executed each month on either side. More is known about the pattern of executions. In the early months of the war, executions were random in the Nationalist zone, but as the months passed, trials and a more organized approach to eliminating Nationalist enemies took place. On the Republican side, those executed included Nationalist supporters, clerical personnel, rivals among political groups (for example, anarchists* versus members of the *Partit Socialista Unificat de Catalunya* [PSUC]*) and those with private grudges throughout the war, along with prisoners of war and those violating even minor laws.

With regard to prisoner exchanges, neither side expressed much interest in them since each was committed to the total elimination of their enemies. However, on rare occasions, exchanges did take place. Most responsible for such events were the Red Cross and the Quakers.* They continuously attempted to negotiate small exchanges, often experiencing successes when few individuals were involved. Dr. Marcel Junod* of the Red Cross managed, for example, to exchange the socialist mayor of Bilbao* for a Carlist deputy in 1936. The Nationalist commander in the north, General Emilio Mola Vidal,* explained the problems commanders faced on both sides when dealing with the issue of prisoner exchanges. He argued that any exchange would draw criticisms from fellow supporters and cries of "traitor." On one occasion, however, Dr. Junod did manage the exchange of several hundred military prisoners, but that was the exception. It was easier to execute them.

Another group of "captives" about which little is known were the pro-Nationalist sympathizers who hid in various embassies in the Republic zone. Their population* has been estimated at some 2,500, of which 500 were in the French Embassy alone. Many embassies, especially those of Latin American countries (Chile and Paraguay, for instance) rented additional buildings in which to shelter these people who would probably have been executed if seized by their enemies. As the embassies moved from Madrid* to Valencia* and then northward again, these Spaniards traveled under the protection of foreign diplomats. Both sides in the Spanish Civil War formally respected the right of diplomats to protect people. While the embassies were still in Madrid, the Republicans infiltrated some chanceries secretly and convinced individuals to try and escape, only to be captured outside their compounds in "tunnels of death" and be executed.

For further information, see Antonio Bahamonde, *Memories of a Spanish Nationalist* (London, 1939) and *El clero vasco frente a la cruzada franquista* (Bayonne, 1966), on the Nationalist repression; Pierre Broué and Émile Témine, *La Révolution et la guerre d'Espagne* (Paris, 1961); Pilar Millan Astray, *Cautivas: 32 meses en las prisones rojas* (Madrid, 1940); Antonio Montero, *La persecución religiosa en España* (Madrid, 1961), on the Republican zone; and Hugh Thomas, *The Spanish Civil War* (New York, 1977).
    See also Espionage; and Terrorism.

James W. Cortada

PUJOL, JUAN (1890s?-   ). Pujol was a Catalan journalist with monarchist political views. In October 1936, Franco* made Pujol head of propaganda and press relations for the Nationalists,* a position he held for only a short while before being replaced by General José Millán Astray.* While it is not clear why Pujol was replaced, General Millán Astray was ambitious and Pujol did not speak German well. He spent the rest of the Civil War as a journalist in the Nationalist zone. All of his articles were in defense of the Nationalist cause. As German assistance to Franco increased, so too did his articles on anti-Semitism, racist theories, and extremely conservative political views.

For further information, see Hugh Thomas, *The Spanish Civil War* (New York, 1977).

James W. Cortada

PYRENEES. The Pyrenees Mountains separate Spain from France.* They served as a conduit for volunteers* from France fighting in Republican armies and as an avenue for their supplies. As the Civil War came to a close, thousands of refugees* poured into these mountains on their way to France. The towns nestled at the foothills of the Pyrenees became military targets for the Nationalists* in their attempt to close off avenues of retreat and escape. From Irún* on the west to the little Catalan fishing communities on the Costa Brava, military battles and skirmishes took place throughout the war. After 1939, enemies of the Nationalist state continued to fight in these mountains until the early 1950s.

For further information, see Burnett Bolloten, *The Spanish Revolution: The Left and the Struggle for Power During the Civil War* (Chapel Hill, N.C., 1979); and Hugh Thomas, *The Spanish Civil War* (New York, 1977).

James W. Cortada

QUAKERS. The Quakers provided charitable services to both the Republicans* and the Nationalists* during the Civil War. In Barcelona,* for example, they fed children and found homes for orphans using staffs often made up of refugee women under their guidance. In Murcía,* Quakers fed children bread and cocoa, while in Barcelona they had milk as well. The Nationalists suspected the Quakers of being Masons, and certainly many Quakers sympathized with the Republic's cause. Even so, Franco's* government allowed the Quakers to feed people in Oviedo* and Gijón* in 1937, and in Saragossa,* Teruel,* and Lérida* during the spring of 1938. They managed to provide food* to approximately 10 percent of all the Spaniards whom they felt needed their services. They did feed about 40,000 child refugees* out of a total population* of 600,000 homeless children. The Quakers also provided some medical attention. Over one dozen countries contributed money to the Quaker International Commission for the Assistance of Child Refugees, most of which was spent in Spain.

For further information, see Howard Kershner, *Quaker Service in Modern War* (New York, 1950).

See also Junod, Marcel.

James W. Cortada

QUEIPO DE LLANO Y SERRA, GONZALO (1875-1951). Queipo de Llano was one of the key conspirators in the military rising in Spain and became one of its triumvirate, along with Generals Mola* and Franco.* He commanded the Nationalist Army of the South* and administered most of Andalusia* and southern Estremadura.* He was not only a unique but also an outstanding character among the Nationalist leaders.

Queipo de Llano was born on February 5, 1875, in historic Tordesillas. He spent many years in a seminary, destined for the priesthood. But as a youth, as well as later, he was a rebel, and he deserted his school, joining the army as a gunner and bugler. He became a cadet in the Royal Cavalry Academy and was a dashing cavalry officer. He fought in Cuba* and extensively in Morocco.* In appearance, Queipo de Llano was an arrogant, imposing figure. He was tall, lean, stiff-backed, and immaculate in uniform and mufti. He was handsome, with sharp, penetrating eyes, and sported a dapper mustache that was often waxed with ends twisted to sharp points. His blustering, colorful, passionate, and ambitious personality, enhanced by his talkative excesses and notorious escapades in Africa, not only in heroism but complete arrogance, gave him the air of the lead of an incompetent Hispanic general in a comic opera. He was, however, a very capable soldier who scorned the enemy as well as those he considered his own incompetent superiors at the highest level.

In Morocco,* Queipo de Llano was noted for his swashbuckling cavalry charges such as at Alcazarquivir and Al-Ksar-el-Kebir which earned him rapid promotions. By the time of the government of General Primo de Rivera, he was a brigade general. He was highly critical of the structure and conduct of the Spanish Army and founded the journal *La Revista de las Tropas Coloniales* to give voice to these views. It was suspended after a few issues by Primo de Rivera who also relieved Queipo de Llano of active command and assigned him to garrison duty in Tetuán.* His response was to write Primo de Rivera that he should be relieved from Morocco if he were not given an active command. He was returned to Spain and for a short time languished in prison. In 1926, he was restored to new duties which he almost lost for his continued slashing attacks against Primo de Rivera. He described the dictator's UP movement meaning "public urinals" as well as *Unión Patriótica*.

In 1928, he was in line for promotion to division general; however, he was transferred to that rank on the reserve list which ended his active career. By now, he was an outspoken supporter of a republic for Spain. In 1930, his seniority gave him the nominal leadership of the Republican Military Association. During the government of General Damaso Berenguer, he associated himself with the National Revolutionary Committee in a plot to overthrow the monarchy. This group was made up of Republican officers and politicians which extended to the far radical Left. One of his associates was Ramón Franco* (brother of General Franco). For a short time during the attempted coup d'état, they did hold the air field of Cuatro Vientos near Madrid,* and Franco dropped leaflets on the Royal Palace. However, the entire affair was poorly handled, and both the general and Franco fled to Portugal.*

When the Second Republic* came into being, Queipo de Llano returned to Madrid to the important post as commander of the 1st Division in Madrid. The fact that one of his daughters was married to the son of Alcalá-Zamora (president of the Republic) is figured to have contributed to the assignment. Later, he became head of the president's military staff.

In April 1936, the Popular Front* government posted him as director-general of the *Carabineros* (Customs Guards). He now seems to have become greatly alarmed as to the direction in which the Republic was heading, and he was also outraged that Alcalá-Zamora was deposed by the political Left. It was not long before he was involved in the conspiracy with General Mola, who although initially suspicious of him because of his Republican past and alleged Masonic connections, accepted him into their ranks. He was given the task of securing southern Spain for the rising.

Queipo de Llano's takeover of Seville* was a storybook *coup de main*, carried out with the aid of three officers, gall, bluff, imagination, and seemingly impossible good luck. The commanding general and his staff were arrested one by one, and the local regiment swung behind Queipo de Llano. He was distressed to find that the unit was composed of less than 200 men; with this he was to try to take a city of hundreds of thousands. Time and again he had the same soldiers drive through the streets to give the impression of a massive force. He seized the Seville radio* and broadcast that the city was in his hands and shouted "¡*Viva la República!*" A detachment of the legion arrived at the air field and was added to the charade. There was some fighting but the bluff worked and the city was in the hands of the Nationalists.*

Queipo de Llano was a member of the Burgos* *Junta* that elevated Francisco Franco (junior in rank to himself) to the position of Generalissimo. But in Seville he continued to operate in an independent manner except when it met with his pleasure to listen to orders first from Burgos and then Salamanca.* His rule in the south has been described as one of a viceregal authority, that of a bad baron of a paternal fief, an autonomous proconsulate, or a sultanate.

Nightly, he took to the airways, and all of Spain listened to his caustic, taunting blasts at the "reds" and his vivid boasting of Nationalist victories. These were coupled with gross descriptions of the ruthlessness of the legion and the appetites of the Moors*

which could only be satisfied by the women of the "reds." He knew how to use mass communications and propaganda and thereby contributed to the demoralization of the enemy militias.* In some instances, his excessive descriptions may have kept enemy units fighting to the end rather than surrendering.

His nightly broadcasts infuriated his foes and amused his friends although, at times, his directness and excessive language distressed his friends as well. He was not above repeating with relish stories of the extramarital love affairs of the leadership of the opposition. His accounts of Nationalist victories were frequently overstated, but his friends liked to be reassured and his enemies were thrown into terrifying doubt. By both friend and foe he was called the "Radio General."

The military ventures of his Army of the South were limited. His major contribution was the offensive against Málaga,* which because of Italian involvement and the propaganda concerning subsequent excesses of the victors did much to degrade Queipo de Llano in the eyes of history.

It must be recognized that the region of Spain he controlled contributed much to the eventual Nationalist success. This was not only in logistical support but also by providing the Nationalists with about 150,000 soldiers. It is difficult to evaluate the role of his bombastic, witty, and caustic broadcasts. The key might be found in the hatred reaped upon him in the writings of the Popular Front's supporters.

In addition to his title as "Radio General," Queipo de Llano was known as the "Social General" for the institutions he introduced in the areas of his almost autonomous command. He established committees to oversee the production and distribution of stable goods. He introduced rice production in the Guadalquivir River Delta and reclaimed 240,000 acres from marsh lands. Laws were promulgated to punish merchants guilty of hoarding and overpricing. He boasted that the rich and poor alike were subject to the same laws. He distributed lands of Republican supporters and was aided by grants of lands from others such as the Duke of Alba.* In addition, through collections, he instituted construction of housing for the poor of Seville. Absolute limitations were established on maximum interest on agricultural loans. To help the farmers, seeds were distributed free.

Queipo de Llano had no use for the Falange,* and when it pressed itself into the political picture he cut off his nightly broadcasts. By the end of 1938, his administrative authority had been taken over, and he was left only as commander of the Army of the South. But he remained outspoken. At the end of the war, he was promoted to lieutenant general and sent into semi-exile by being given an honorary position as head of a Spanish mission to Italy* where he remained for over two years. In 1942, he returned to Spain but was never again to hold a position of importance. In 1947, he was made a marquis. He died on March 9, 1951, at a country estate near Seville that had been given to him by the people of Seville.

For further information, see General José Cuesta Monereo and Antonio Olmedo Delgado, *General Queipo de Llano* (Barcelona, 1957); and Julio de Ramón-Laca, *Bajo la férula de Queipo de Llano* (Seville, 1939).

Raymond L. Proctor

QUINTANILLA, LUIS. Quintanilla was an artist who commanded Republican forces at their siege of the Alcázar* in 1936. This socialist proved to be an ineffective military commander, however, and the Alcázar was held by the Nationalists.* Quintanilla played no other significant role in the War.

For further information, see Cecil Eby, *The Seige of the Alcázar* (London, 1966).

James W. Cortada

R

RADIO, SPANISH. The Spanish Civil War was the first conflict in which radio played a role, but the paucity of receiving sets and the weakness of the broadcasting stations reduced its effectiveness. At the beginning of 1936, there were about 300,000 licensed sets. To these must be added the much larger number of crystal sets which were mainly unlicensed. When the war began, Spain had no stations powerful enough to cover the entire country. There were only six stations of any respectable power: Madrid* (7 kilowatts), Barcelona* (5 kilowatts), San Sebastián (3 kilowatts), Valencia,* Seville,* and Oviedo* (1.5 kilowatts). Thus, all were below 10 kilowatts in power, while that of Budapest, for example, had 120 kilowatts. Consequently, the range of the Spanish stations was limited to 300 to 600 kilometers, and often only powerful receiving sets could pick up the broadcasts. The balance was thus in favor of the Republicans.*

Clandestine radio stations were set up from the outbreak of hostilities. In July 1936, Radio Seville was sending messages from Madrid, and Radio Madrid from Seville, by using the other station's wave-length and signal. From September 1936, messages were transmitted by "Radio Fantasma," and by late November, there were no fewer than six rebel radio stations operating in Madrid. In Barcelona, the anarchists* took the radio station for themselves, and in due course both the Republicans and the Nationalists* established their own stations. The National Radio of Salamanca,* which was built with German material and inaugurated on January 19, 1937, had a power of 20 kilowatts. Directed by Antonio Tovar and controlled by Ramón Serrano Suñer,* this radio was well adapted to the needs of the war by being mounted on trucks. Its range was more or less nationwide. To this was added Radio Saragossa, of 30 kilowatt power; hence, it was by far the most powerful station in Spain. The advantage had thus passed to the Nationalists within six months of the uprising. The Nationalists also had the benefit of the Lisbon and Tangier radios which supported their cause, and of the stations in the region of Seo de Urgel (in the province of Lérida*) which transmitted useful information. The French Agence Radio at the beginning of the war was in the hands of the Blum* government. It was sold in 1937 to Agence Havas and provided that agency with an important listening post on the Pyrenees* frontier.

For further information, see Aníbal Arias Ruiz, *50 años de radiodifusión en España* (Madrid, 1973).

See also Queipo de Llano y Serra, Gonzalo.

David Wingeate Pike

REFUGEES, REPUBLICAN. Since the Spanish Civil War is in large part the story of the Nationalists* expanding their control over the entire nation of Spain, the majority of all refugees were people living in Republican zones who moved from the countryside to cities, from towns and cities being invaded to other communities, or, as was particularly the case in 1939, out of Spain into France.* The two major centers that experienced large influxes of refugees during the war were Madrid* and Barcelona.* As the Nationalists moved northward through central Spain and simultaneously seized territory in the north, refugees by the tens of thousands poured into Madrid, straining local services and food* supplies. A similar migration took place in eastern Spain in 1937-1939 as the Nationalists moved toward Catalonia, causing thousands of refugees to move into crowded Barcelona and points north.

There are no accurate statistics available on the number of displaced persons during the Civil War, but some estimates have been calculated. The number of refugees who crossed into France from January to March 1939 ranges from a total of 400,000 to 527,800, of which approximately 220,000 were members of the military. Of this approximately half million refugees, 10,000 to 13,000 were wounded—both military and civilian. The French government established camps to house these people, eventually supporting a population* of some 400,000 men, women, and children in poor condition. Thousands of refugees made their way to Mexico* and Argentina* (about 50,000), while a smaller number found homes in Great Britain* and the USSR* (7,000). About 150,000 people eventually returned to live in Nationalist Spain.

For further information, see José Luis Abellán, ed. *El exilio español de 1939*, 6 vols. (Madrid, 1976); José María Aroca Sardagna, *Los republicanos que no se exilaron* (Barcelona, 1969); Patricia W. Fagen, *Exiles and Citizens* (Austin, Texas, 1973), for Mexico; Guy Hermet, *Les Espagnols en France* (Paris, 1967); Eugene Kutischer, *The Displacement of Population in Europe*, Studies and Reports Series D, No. 8 (Montreal, 1944); David Wingeate Pike, *Vae Victis!* (Paris, 1969); Javier Rubio, *La emigración de la guerra civil de 1936-1939*, 3 vols. (Madrid, 1977); Javier Rubio, *La emigración española a Francia* (Barcelona, 1974); and Louis Stein, *Beyond Death and Exile: The Spanish Republicans in France, 1939-1955* (Cambridge, Mass., 1979).

James W. Cortada

REGIONALISM. *See* Andalusia; Aragón; Catalonia; Galicia.

REGLER, GUSTAV (1898-   ). Regler was a German intellectual and member of the Communist party* prior to the Spanish Civil War. This novelist, although disillusioned with the party (he left it in 1935), came to Spain when the Civil War began and fought in the International Brigades,* becoming a commissar in the army. He fought effectively in most of the campaigns in and around Madrid* during the fall and winter of 1936-1937 and was wounded at the battle of Huesca* on June 11, 1937. He spent many months in a hospital before leaving Spain and returning to his writing. He is best remembered for his literary comments on the war. His important memoirs, *The Owl of Minerva* (New York, 1960), and his earlier work, *The Great Crusade* (London, 1940), are two of the more widely read pieces on the conflict and the attitudes of Europeans in the 1930s. In his writings, Regler condemned the Republic for the many political factions that divided and twisted the efforts against Franco's* Nationalists.* He also felt that the democracies' lack of support hampered the work of the International Brigades and the ideals for which the Republicans* fought.

For further information, see Frederick R. Benson, *Writers in Arms: The Literary Impact of the Spanish Civil War* (New York, 1967).

See also Intellectuals; and Literature.

James W. Cortada

RELIGIOUS ORDERS AND COMMUNITIES. Religious orders and communities (sometimes called "regular" clergy) made up a large proportion of the clerical establishment of the Catholic Church* in Spain in the 1930s. While only 7,000 of the 39,000 Spanish priests were members of religious orders, there were some 5,000 monks and brothers and 53,000 nuns. Among the largest of these orders were the Jesuits, Franciscans, Dominicans, Augustinians, Christian Brothers, and Brothers of Mary; and of the nuns, the Daughters of Charity of Saint Vincent de Paul. Most were engaged in teaching, hospital work, or other charitable enterprises. The orders were traditional targets of anticlerical animosity. They were viewed as business competitors (this attack was directed against the fabled but mythical wealth of the Jesuits); the urban workers were angered by some regulars who dispensed charity only to those who attended Mass; and intellectuals* saw the regulars as perpetuating antihumanistic values with their control over the nation's secondary schools.

As a result, the *conventos* (residences of the regular clergy) were the targets of incendiary anticlerical attacks, and the anticlerical Constitution of 1931 provided for the dissolution of the Jesuits and the regulation of the remainder of the regular clergy. The law dissolving the Jesuits was put into effect in February 1932: some 3,600 Jesuits were no longer recognized as such by the state, their educational establishment (7,000 students) had to close, and all Jesuit-owned property was nationalized (bringing in some 200 million pesetas by 1935). In May 1933, the Cortes* passed the Law of Religious Denominations and Congregations to implement the other constitutional provisions. The law required the regular clergy to list all of their property with the government and ensure that two-thirds of their members be Spanish citizens, and it forbade them to engage in political activity, commerce, or industry, and to teach in any school, public or private, after December 1933.

The law was not put into effect by the specified date. In the November 1933 elections, the Catholic *Confederación Española de Derechas Autónomas* (CEDA)* won a plurality and made its support of ministries dependent on the suspension of the law. After the Popular Front* victory in 1936, the prohibition against the orders' teaching was put into effect in some areas until the military uprising occurred. In the anticlerical fury of the first few months of the war, some 2,600 regulars were killed and most of the *conventos* in Republican Spain were destroyed. The Burgos* government rescinded all of the anticlerical legislation in 1938 and 1939.

For further information, see José Manuel Castells, *Las asociaciones religiosas en la España contemporánea*

(1767-1965) (Madrid, 1973); and Antonio Montero Moreno, *La persecución religiosa en España, 1936-1939* (Madrid, 1961).

José M. Sánchez

RENOVACIÓN ESPAÑOLA. *Renovación Española* was a small right-wing party formed in March 1933 by Antonio Goicoechea,* and it consisted of a loose alliance of Carlists,* orthodox monarchists, and Catholic rightists. They came into national prominence after the elections of 1933 in which they gained thirty-five seats in the Cortes.* For a short while, José Calvo Sotelo* was a leading member before forming his own party, the *Bloque Nacional.* The party had grown as a result of the expulsion of Alfonsine monarchists from the *Acción Popular.** They believed in a strong authoritarian government to counter the revolutionary mood of the political Left. During the Civil War, most members of the *Renovación Española* supported the Nationalists.* Many of its politicians served in important positions in Franco's* government, while Calvo Sotelo's death was the final event that triggered the war. This party dissolved itself formally in March 1937 since parliamentary politics no longer existed. But because it never had a mass following, its members were considered politically harmless by such groups as the Falange* and the Carlists. This it was that its members survived the political infighting that took place in the Nationalist zone.

For further information, see José Gutiérrez Ravé, *Antonio Goicoechea* (Madrid, 1965); Paul Preston, "Alfonsist Monarchism and the Coming of the Spanish Civil War," *Journal of Contemporary History* 7, Nos. 3 & 4 (July and October 1972); and Richard Robinson, *The Origins of Franco Spain* (Newton Abbot, 1970).
    See also Confederación Española de Derechos Autónomas (CEDA).

James W. Cortada

REPUBLICANS. The Republicans, those who fought on the side of the Republic during the Civil War, were also called Loyalists.* Typically, the Republicans had liberal or leftist political views, ranging from a traditional middle class liberalism to an extreme of anarchism. Many supporters of the Republic were intellectuals, middle-class professionals, and workers both rural and urban. They were most frequently concentrated in urban and middle-class communities.

For further information, see Hugh Thomas, *The Spanish Civil War* (New York, 1977).

James W. Cortada

REPUBLICAN UNION PARTY (RUP). The Republican Union party (RUP) was a small organization formed and dominated by Diego Martínez Barrio,* a little-known politician from Seville.* In the elections of February 1936,* the RUP joined the Popular Front* and gained thirty-seven seats in the Cortes.* Martínez Barrio became the speaker of the Cortes and thus an important Republican official at the start of the Civil War. His party also took over the monarchist newspaper *ABC** in Madrid* and operated it after July 1936 under the title of *ABC de Madrid.*

For further information, see Gabriel Jackson, *The Spanish Republic and the Civil War, 1931-1939* (Princeton, N.J., 1965).

James W. Cortada

REQUETÉS. The *Requetés* were Carlist paramilitary units made up of men from all classes of Basque society and others from sections of western Catalonia.* They were politically monarchist, extremely Catholic, and advocated local autonomy. In past civil wars, they had defended the rights of Carlist pretenders to the Spanish throne. In July 1936, the *Requetés* enthusiastically rose in rebellion against the Republic. Through their efforts, vast tracks of the Basque country quickly became Nationalist. In the early months of the Civil War, thousands of these fighters aided Mola's* Army of the North* and poured into central Spain for the battles in and around Madrid,* and later at Guadalajara.* While the number of *Requetés* during the war is not known, it seems reasonable to suppose that there were over 100,000 members at one time or another between 1936 and 1939. By the end of 1936, General Franco* began consolidating these units into a broader military organization, in order to use them more effectively and to prevent them from becoming an independent political block that could threaten his control over all Nationalists.* He achieved his objectives while effectively employing these troops.

For further information, see Martin Blinkhorn, *Carlism and Crisis in Spain* (Cambridge, 1978); and Luis Redondo and Juan de Zavala, *El requeté; la tradición no muere* (Barcelona, 1957).
    See also Army, Nationalist; Carlists; Mola Vidal, Emilio; Navarre; and Pamplona.

James W. Cortada

RICHTHOFEN, WOLFRAM VON (1893-1945). Richthofen was born in Barzdorf, Kreis.Striegau/Schlesin, Germany.* He was a cousin of the legendary "Red Baron" of the Great War. Richthofen served with the

German Condor Legion* in the Spanish Civil War as chief of staff from November 1936 to October 1937, and then as legion commander from November 1938 until its withdrawal in March 1939.

As a young ensign, Richthofen was assigned (1913) to the German 4th *Husaren* Regiment, but in 1917 he was transferred to the flying service. Following World War I, he returned to his regiment but left the service until 1923 when he returned as a second lieutenant of cavalry. In 1924, he obtained a doctorate in engineering. He held many positions in the *Reichswehr* such as service in the artillery, infantry, cavalry, and War Ministry. In 1933, he was moved to the *Luftwaffe*, and as a major in 1934 he was made head of the *Luftwaffe* Testing Department and a member of the general staff. In 1936, he was promoted to lieutenant colonel and assigned as the first chief of staff of the Condor Legion, under command of General von Sperrle.*

Sperrle left the operation of the legion largely to the discretion of his chief of staff. Even though he commented in his writings about the hard work and responsibilities, Richthofen appears not to have attempted to avoid them. He deplored the poor performance of German aircraft against the Russian planes and was able to obtain new and experimental aircraft from Germany. He was instrumental in developing the required new operational procedures and became a strong advocate of the close tactical air support for ground armies which the legion followed in Spain and the *Luftwaffe* was to employ later with such success in France* and the USSR.*

Richthofen's relations with the Italians and Spanish commands were sometimes strained, and he frequently felt most frustrated in obtaining what he viewed as the desired military cooperation. He was highly respected by the Spaniards for his unselfish devotion to duty and professionalism, although at times they felt him to be somewhat insensitive to their problems. As chief of staff of the legion, he shared in the condemnation and propaganda for the destruction of Guernica.* He was very demanding of others, but even more so of himself.

When Richthofen returned to Spain in 1938 to command the legion, he held the rank of major general. In 1940, he was a general of flyers, and then in 1943 he was promoted to field marshal. Because of illness he was placed on the reserve list in October 1944. He died of a brain tumor as a prisoner of the Americans on July 12, 1945, at Bad Ischl.

For further information, see Werner Beumelburg, *Kampf um Spanien, Die Geschichte der Legion Condor* (Berlin, 1939); Manfred Merkes, *Die deutsche Politik gegenüber dem spanischen Bürgerkrieg, 1936-1939* (Bonn, 1961); and R. Hidalgo Salazar, *La Ayuda Alemana a España 1936-1939* (Madrid, 1975).

See also Air Force, Nationalist.

Raymond L. Proctor

RIDRUEJO JIMÉNEZ, DIONISIO (1912-1975). Ridruejo was born in Burgos de Osma in the province of Soria, and later became a Falangist chief and journalist. In 1937, he headed the party first in Segovia* and then in Valladolid.* Subsequently, he became director-general of propaganda and served on Franco's* National Council and in the Political *Junta*. During the Civil War, he wrote considerably on the Nationalist cause while being heavily involved in Falangist politics. He often sided with Ramón Serrano Suñer* in political debates, which suggested his clear identification with Franco's faction within the Nationalist zone.

For further information, see Círculo de Amigos de la Historia, *Diccionario biográfico español contemporaneo* (Madrid, 1970), vol. 3; and Dionisio Ridruejo Jiménez, *Casi unas memorias* (Barcelona, 1978), and *Escrito en España* (Buenos Aries, 1962, Madrid, 1976).

James W. Cortada

RÍOS URRUTI, FERNANDO DE LOS (1879-1949). Fernando de los Ríos Urruti was a socialist politician and diplomat active in Republican affairs. This Andalusian-born politician from Granada* served as minister of justice in the first cabinet of the Second Republic* in 1931. This appointment came after he had served many years in the Cortes* and as a professor at the University of Granada. During his early tenure in the Republican cabinet, he negotiated with the Catalans to prevent them from declaring a separate government of their own while Madrid* prepared a Statute of Autonomy. By 1933, he had become minister of education* participating in the great reforms of the Republic in this area. He helped push through the construction of 7,000 schools, providing elementary education to more than three times as many students as had been in school before 1931. This gentle humanist also advocated political freedoms and reforms to help raise the peasant's standard of living.

At the start of the Civil War, de los Ríos became involved in diplomacy, first as a Republican representative at the League of Nations* where he attempted to negotiate arms sales for his government with Great Britain* and France* and second, as a temporary envoy to France. His primary objective there was to obtain French support for the Republic and to acquire arms. In the early days of the Civil War, private French citizens supplied some weapons, planes, and pilots* to the Spanish. However, the majority of the supplies and pilots he negotiated over with the French government did not come to Spain. In the fall of 1936, he became the Republican ambassador to the United States,* serving until 1939. In Washington, he defended the Republic's international rights to buy arms and argued the cause of his government in the war. Although he had little success in persuading the American government to help his side in the war, de los Ríos did manage to wage a public relations campaign against Franco* that won his side much unofficial support. After the war he remained in exile.

For further information, see David Wingeate Pike, *Les Français et la guerre d'espagne, 1936-39* (Paris, 1975); and Richard P. Traina, *American Diplomacy and the Spanish Civil War* (Bloomington, Ind., 1968).

James W. Cortada

RÍO TINTO COMPANY. The Río Tinto Company, located in Andalusia,* mined copper at a site that had been a source of supply since Roman times. During the Civil War, it was a major source of copper for the Nationalists.* Although British owned, the Nationalists established the production schedules for the company. They sent much of its output to Germany* as partial payment for supplies sent to Franco's* armies. The British protested, but there was little they could do since, at the end of 1936, the Nationalists had virtually taken over control of these facilities following a protracted period of labor unrest at the mines.

For further information, see Glenn T. Harper, *German Economic Policy in Spain* (The Hague, 1967).

See also Economy, Nationalist; Great Britain; and Trade, International.

James W. Cortada

ROATTA, MARIO ("MANCINI") (1887-1968). Roatta was a career officer in the Italian Army who commanded some of Mussolini's* troops in Spain fighting for Franco.* In the early days of the Civil War, he also became Italy's* principal contact with the Nationalist rebels in determining what aid to provide. Much of Mussolini's information on Franco in the first few days of the Civil War also came from General Roatta. During 1937, he commanded Italians fighting throughout central Spain, particularly at the battle of Guadalajara* in March 1937. After the war, he was Mussolini's chief of staff, fell out of favor, and

escaped to Spain as an exile. In the 1960s he returned to Italy where he died.

For further information, see John F. Coverdale, *Italian Intervention in the Spanish Civil War* (Princeton, N.J., 1975).

James W. Cortada

RODEZNO, COUNT OF (TOMÁS DOMÍNGUEZ ARÉVALO) (1883-1952). Rodezno was a leading Carlist politician during the Second Republic* and the Civil War. An aristocrat of long Navarrese pedigree and the owner of extensive landholdings in several Spanish regions, he served as a senator under Alfonso XIII,* despite being a personal confidant of two Carlist pretenders, "Carlos VII" and "Jamie III." By 1931, Rodezno was the most influential Carlist in Navarre.* Elected to the Constituent Cortes* in June 1931, he was appointed to the ruling National *Junta* of Carlism's political organization, the *Comunión Tradicionalista*, in January 1932. Between May 1932 and April 1934, as president of the National *Junta*, he was Carlism's de facto political chief. His policies of accommodation with Alfonsists and other rightists, however, aroused growing discontent within Carlist ranks, and in April 1934 he was replaced by Manuel Fal Conde.* Rodezno nevertheless remained an important figure and in 1936 committed Carlism to the military rising in the face of the misgivings of Fal Conde and others.

During the war, Rodezno emerged as leader of those Carlists* who were willing to cooperate closely with Franco* and, in April 1937, accepted absorption into the *Falange Española Tradicionalista* y de las JONS (FET). He held office in the FET, and, when Franco formed his first full cabinet in January 1938, he became minister of justice. Throughout the 1940s and until his death in 1952, Rodezno labored for the restoration of Don Juan de Borbon as the best means of effecting Spain's escape from Francoism and, in the process, of healing the century-old dynastic schism that had given birth to Carlism in the first place.

For further information, see Martin Blinkhorn, *Carlism and Crisis in Spain, 1931-1939* (Cambridge, England, 1975); Jaime del Burgo, *Conspiración y Guerra Civil* (Madrid and Barcelona, 1970); and Antonio Lizarza Iribarren, *Memorias de la conspiración. Como se preparó en Navarra la Cruzada, 1931-1936* (Pamplona, 1957).

Martin Blinkhorn

RODRÍGUEZ, FRANCISCO. Rodríguez was the socialist civil governor of Málaga* between 1936 and 1937. Before 1936, he had been a teacher and principal who, at the start of the war, became the president of the local committee of public safety and then, soon after, civil governor. Málaga, although Republican, was constantly under threat of Nationalist attack from Franco's* stronghold to the Northeast at Granada,* making daily life in the Republican zone* one of tension and danger.

For further information, see Hugh Thomas, *The Spanish Civil War* (New York, 1977).

James W. Cortada

RODRÍGUEZ, MELCHOR. Rodríguez was an anarchist living in Madrid* who, in August 1936, became director of local prisons. He eventually acquired responsibility for a large number of jails within the Republican zone. Unlike many other anarchists* with power over life and death, Rodríguez proved to be a humane administrator. In March 1939, he became the last Republican mayor of Madrid.

For further information, see Robert Colodny, *The Struggle for Madrid* (New York, 1958).
See also Police; and Prisoners.

James W. Cortada

RODRÍGUEZ DEL BARRIO, ANGEL (1876-1936). Rodríguez del Barrio was an infantryman and *diplomado* of the War College. He served in Morocco* on several occasions and was promoted to division general in 1925. Perhaps because he had not been closely associated with the leading *africanistas*,* the Republicans* relied on him. In 1931, he became an inspector-general of the army, vice-president of the Supreme Military Council, and president of the Promotion Review Board. Nevertheless, by 1936 Rodríguez del Barrio was disillusioned with the Republic, and in April 1936 he committed himself to lead a military coup against the Popular Front* government. At the last minute, he failed to act, partly because of poor health, partly because of lack of support in the officer corps. He died of stomach cancer in November 1936.

For further information, see Stanley G. Payne, *Politics and the Military in Modern Spain* (Stanford, Calif., 1967); and Hugh Thomas, *The Spanish Civil War* (New York, 1977).

Carolyn P. Boyd

RODRÍGUEZ SALAS, EUSEBIO. Rodríguez Salas became the chief of police* in Barcelona* in 1937 after scandal forced the removal of his predecessor. Rodríguez was a native son and a communist. On May 3, 1937, he sought to gain control of the Telefónica building in Barcelona, thereby causing the anarchists* who were in the structure to fire weapons on his men. This episode escalated the rivalry between the anarchists and the communists into open civil war in Barcelona known as the May Days. Ultimately, this fighting caused the reinstatement of the Republican government as master over Catalan affairs and the decline of all political factions except for the victorious communists.

For further information, see Burnett Bolloten, *The Spanish Revolution: The Left and the Struggle for Power During the Civil War* (Chapel Hill, N.C., 1979).
See also Communist Party, Spanish; *Federación Anarquista Ibérica* (FAI); May 1937 Riots; *Partido Obrero de Unificación Marxista* (POUM); and *Partit Socialista Unificat de Catalunya* (PSUC).

James W. Cortada

RODRÍGUEZ VEGA, JOSÉ (1902-   ). Rodríguez Vega was secretary of the *Unión General de Trabajadores* (UGT)* in 1937 and thus was an important labor leader in the Republican zone. This socialist worked actively to form a political alliance between the UGT and the *Confederación Nacional del Trabajo* (CNT)* throughout the war to harness more effectively Republicans'* capabilities to combat the Nationalists.* He managed to leave Spain late in 1939, thereby avoiding imprisonment by the Nationalists.

For further information, see Hugh Thomas, *The Spanish Civil War* (New York, 1977).

James W. Cortada

ROIG, ELEUTERIO. Roig was a Catalan radical member of the *Federación Anarquista Ibérica* (FAI)* who broke with the main organization to help found the Friends of Durruti,* a Trotskyist group formed in 1937. He participated in the operation of a newspaper in Barcelona,* *El Amigo del Pueblo*, writing editorials from April until the paper's demise in November 1937. It was critical of the *Partit Socialista Unificat de Catalunya* (PSUC)*, the Catalan government, and the *Confederación Nacional del Trabajo* (CNT)* for sacrificing romantic libertarian principals in exchange for cooperation and regimentation in support of the Republican war effort.

For further information, see Robert W. Kern, *Red Years/Black Years: A Political History of Spanish Anarchism, 1911-1937* (Philadelphia, 1978).
See also Libertarian Movement.

James W. Cortada

ROJO LLUCH, VICENTE (1894-1966). Rojo was one of the Republicans'* most important military commanders. At the start of the Civil War, he held the rank of major and taught tactics at the Infantry Academy in the Alcázar* of Toledo.* During the siege of that facility in 1936, he negotiated with the Nationalists* for their surrender but without success. Soon after, the government in Madrid* appointed him chief of staff of the newly created general staff of the army in Madrid. This well-educated, exceptionally capable officer soon developed the strategy for defending Madrid against Nationalist attacks. Now a colonel, Rojo became chief of staff for the Republican Army* which fought at the battle of Guadalajara* in March 1937, effectively developing the plan to punish the Nationalist forces. He also continued in his post as chief of staff of the army defending Madrid. In November, he became a general, albeit a pessimistic one since he believed the Republican forces would suffer greatly at the hands of the better organized and supplied Nationalist forces in central Spain. In 1938, Rojo planned the Republican actions in the campaigns of Aragón* and the Levante* and became the author of the Republican offensive that led to the battle of the Ebro* between July and November 1938. He miscalculated the aggressive capability of the Nationalists to invade Catalonia* in the winter of 1938-1939, making it difficult for him to plan properly an effective Republican defense of the north, a defense that he rapidly concluded was perhaps impossible because of the public's weariness with the war.

After the war, Rojo lived in exile in Latin America.* He returned to Spain in 1958 and died in 1966 a respected foe of the Nationalists. Throughout the Civil War, he had remained politically neutral, working with whatever faction had the upper hand in military policy, avoiding controversy. He concentrated his efforts primarily on the technical aspects of each major Republican campaign and battle throughout the war. He also attempted to provide some organization to a military establishment riddled by politics, staffed with inexperienced officers and soldiers, and mixed with international volunteers,* foreign advisers, and revolutionary worker militias.*

For further information, see Michael Alpert, *El ejército republicano en la guerra civil* (Barcelona, 1977), for comments on administration; Vicente Rojo, *Así fue la defensa de Madrid* (Mexico, 1967), the general's memoirs; and Ramón Salas Larrazábal, *Historia del ejército popular de la república*, 4 vols. (Madrid, 1974), for campaigns and politics.

See also Appendix B.

James W. Cortada

ROMERALES QUINTO, MANUEL (1875-1936). career army officer, gained his combat experience in Morocco.* Although in North Africa, he did not become a party to the plotting that took place there among many officers in the weeks before the Civil War. As an outsider to these machinations, Romerales was an exception among the officers in North Africa. He was a naïve man and clearly the fattest general in the Spanish Army. Since he favored the Republicans,* his officers forced him to resign his command at gun point. Soon after, the rebels executed him, making him one of the earliest casualties* of the war.

For further information, see Joaquín Arrarás, *Historia de la cruzada española*, 35 folios (Madrid, 1940-1943); and Stanley G. Payne, *Politics and the Military in Modern Spain* (Stanford, Calif., 1967).

James W. Cortada

ROMERO BASSART, PEDRO (1881-   ). Romero, a colonel in the Civil Guard* who sided with the Nationalists,* was at the siege of the Alcázar* in July 1936. The Nationalists, in the compound, were besieged by the Republican forces, and much of the defense of the Alcázar came under his control. This siege quickly became one of the heroic episodes of the Civil War, and in large part the credit had to go to Romero who prevented the Alcázar from falling to the Republicans.*

For further information, see Cecil B. Eby, *The Siege of the Alcázar* (London, 1966).

James W. Cortada

ROOSEVELT, FRANKLIN D. (1882-1945). Roosevelt was president of the United States* (1933-1945) during the Spanish Civil War. While his personal sympathies were with the Republic, his foreign policy was designed to keep the United States out of the conflict. Through his orders, an embargo of arms sales to Spain reduced the shipment of weaponry to a trickle, while his efforts resulted in legislation to preserve his neutrality. During the closing days of the Civil War, Roosevelt admitted he should have aided the Republic, especially through the sale of arms which may have greatly aided the Republicans* against the better armed Nationalists.*

For further information, see Richard Traina, *American Diplomacy and the Spanish Civil War* (Bloomington, Ind., 1968).

See also Bowers, Claude G.; Hull, Cordell; and Neutrality Acts (USA).

James W. Cortada

ROSENBERG, MARCEL (-1937). Rosenberg, the Soviet ambassador to the Spanish Republic between 1936 and 1937, was deputy secretary of the

League of Nations* several years earlier. Stalin* sent him to Spain in August 1936 to determine what Soviet aid was needed to expand the influence of the local Communist party and to direct the course of Russian activities there. This experienced diplomat discharged his responsibilities effectively, expanding Soviet influence so greatly with the help of the other Russians that many Republican leaders considered him one of the most powerful men in Spain. By late 1936, the communists had decided that Francisco Largo Caballero* should be replaced as prime minister by someone they could better control—this decision took several months to implement, however, and in late January 1937, Largo Caballero called Ambassador Rosenberg into his office to criticize him for trying to dictate appointments and policies to the Republicans.* Later that year, Stalin recalled Rosenberg and purged him, along with a large percentage of the Soviet diplomatic corps.

For further information, see Burnett Bolloten, *The Spanish Revolution: The Left and the Struggle for Power During the Civil War* (Chapel Hill, 1979).
See also Communist Party, Spanish; and USSR.

James W. Cortada

ROURET CALLOI, MARTÍ. Rouret briefly served as chief of police* in the Generalitat* (the Catalan autonomist government) at the start of the Civil War. He owed his appointment to his friendship with President Luis Companys.*

For further information, see Stanley G. Payne, *The Spanish Revolution* (New York, 1970).

James W. Cortada

ROVIRA CANALES, JOSÉ. Rovira was a commander in the *Partido Obrero de Unificación Marxista* (POUM)* during the Civil War. Born and raised in Lérida,* he had the rank of major, leading a militia unit called the 29th Division in the Republican Army.* His unit fought in Catalonia* and in Aragón* during 1936 and 1937. In June 1937, the communists expanded their control over Republican affairs at the cost of dissident Marxist groups being pushed out of positions of authority (such as the POUMists) by convincing the government to arrest leaders of the POUM and to outlaw its existence. Among the leaders arrested was Rovira; thereafter, he played no role in the war.

For further information, see Ramón Salas Larrazábal, *Historia del ejército popular de la república*, 4 vols. (Madrid, 1974).

James W. Cortada

RUIZ ALONSO, RAMÓN (1900-   ). History will remember Ramón Ruiz Alonso primarily for his association with the execution of the great Spanish poet, Federico García Lorca.* The nature of his involvement will perhaps remain the subject of debate, for it may never be known whether Ruiz Alonso was merely involved in the arrest, or whether he was the prime mover behind the poet's execution.

Ruiz Alonso was born in the Salamancan village of Villaflores in 1900. After studying in Valladolid,* he moved to Madrid* and then to Granada* as an organizer for Catholic trade unions.* He was elected to the Cortes* in 1933, as a member of the *Confederación Española de Derechas Autónomas* (CEDA);* he appeared to have been reelected in 1936, until the balloting in Granada was overturned because of alleged irregularities.

In the first weeks of the war, Ruiz Alonso helped organize *Españoles Patriotas*, a local militia that aided in holding Granada for the rebel cause. During this time, he cooperated with other rightists in eliminating suspected enemies of the uprising from the city; García Lorca was but one victim of this purge. Once Granada was secure, Ruiz Alonso headed the ineffective Pérez de Pulgar Batallion, which was intended to give those who were suspected of leftist tendencies a chance to prove their loyalty. After most of that batallion deserted, Ruiz Alonso went to Burgos,* where he worked under Vicente Gay* in the Propaganda Department. During the Franco* regime, he lived in Madrid, without ever achieving prominence or a position of high responsibility.

For further information, see Ian Gibson, *The Death of Lorca* (Chicago, 1973), for the terror in Granada; Ramón Ruiz Alonso, *¡Corporativismo!* (Salamanca, 1937); and Javier Tusell Gómez, *Las elecciones del frente popular*, 2 vols. (Madrid, 1971), on the 1936 election.
See also Terrorism.

William J. Irwin

RUIZ FORNELLS RUIZ, RAMÓN (1901-   ). Ruiz Fornells was a Republican colonel in the Civil War. By early 1939, he had become chief of staff of the Army of Estremadura.* In early March 1939, he conspired with other Republican officers to see if a surrender could be negotiated with the Nationalists,* an effort that failed.

For further information, see José Manuel Martínez Bande, *Los cien últimos días de la república* (Barcelona, 1972).

James W. Cortada

S

SÁENZ DE BURUAGA Y POLANCO, EDUARDO

(1893-1964). Sáenz de Buruaga commanded a legion and regulars at Tetuán* in July 1936, and as a Nationalist military commander saw most of his action under the command of General Varela* in the southern campaigns and at Madrid.*

Born in Cuba,* Sáenz de Buruaga entered the Spanish Academy of Infantry in 1910, was promoted to lieutenant colonel in 1926, and was stationed at Tetuan where he participated in the uprising in July 1936. With other African units he was transferred to Spain in August 1936 and fought under Varela in the southern campaigns in the Córdoba*-Málaga* sector. In December 1936, he commanded four mobile brigades in the Madrid sector where he was involved in the attack on the Corunna Road.* In the continued assault on Madrid in January 1937, Sáenz de Buruaga led his troops at Pozuelo where after a gain of 7 miles with heavy losses the front was stabilized. In February 1937, in the Nationalist attack at the Jarama,* his unit, now the 150th Brigade, was to cross the river at San Martín. Beginning the attack on February 12, the unit occupied defensive positions across the river on February 16. In the Nationalist attack at Brunete* in July 1937, Sáenz de Buruaga commanded the left flank of the attack at Los Llanos and broke through the Republican lines on July 24 suffering heavy casualties* in the process.

Franco* then shifted his focus to the northern area, and Sáenz de Buruaga and the 150th were sent to Aragón* to relieve Belchite* in August 1937. He arrived in that sector on August 26 and took up positions in the area of Fuente de Ebro-Medina. He remained in the northern sector until the liberation of Teruel* in February 1938, serving as part of the Army of the North* under General Dávila.* With army reorganization after Teruel, the 150th was put under the command of Agustín Muñoz Grandes* in the Army of Galicia,* and later (October 1938) became part of the Army of Urgel.* In the meantime, Sáenz de Buruaga was shifted back to Madrid where he became commander of the 3d Brigade of the *Ejército del Aire*. He was promoted to general in February 1939. Later that year, he was named military governor of Madrid and continued to function in regular military capacities.

For additional information, see Manuel Aznar, *Historia militar de la guerra de España*, 3 vols. (Madrid, 1969); Luis María de Lojendio, *Operaciones militares de la guerra de España, 1936-39* (Barcelona, 1940); and Hugh Thomas, *The Spanish Civil War* (London, 1977). *See also* Appendix B.

Jane Slaughter

SAINT JEAN DE LUZ.

Saint Jean de Luz is a small town in France* just opposite the Spanish border where the diplomatic corps set up their de facto embassies during the Civil War, leaving junior diplomats to operate the official chanceries in Madrid.* Most ambassadors began operating out of Saint Jean de Luz from the first days of the war since, in July, most had been at nearby San Sebastián, the Spanish summer capital. In the early days of the war, the town became the working headquarters of the International Red Cross which was negotiating prisoner exchanges and from which it distributed food* and medical supplies to Spain.

For further information, see Hugh Thomas, *The Spanish Civil War* (New York, 1977).

James W. Cortada

SÁINZ RODRÍGUEZ, PEDRO DE

(1897-   ). Sáinz Rodríguez was a Nationalist intellectual. Born in Burgos,* this very fat monarchist participated in numerous right-wing plots and political movements during the 1930s. In July 1936, he became part of a small delegation sent by the Nationalists* to Rome to request aid from Mussolini.* When, on February 1, 1938, Franco* established his first formal cabinet, he appointed Sáinz Rodríguez as minister of education.* Sáinz Rodríguez soon developed "Plan 38," which called for elementary education* to be under the control of the Catholic Church* and the universities to be dealt with later. He was soon removed from the cabinet, however, as a result of numerous personal indiscretions which offended various political groups and individuals within the cabinet.

For further information, see Rafael Abella, *La vida cotidiana durante la guerra española: La España Nacional* (Barcelona, 1973).

James W. Cortada

SALAMANCA. Salamanca, a province located northwest of Madrid* bordering on Portugal,* quickly fell to the rebels in the early days of the fighting as a result of strong pro-Nationalist support by local police.* By September, Franco* had established his headquarters in Salamanca from where he directed the military campaign for the capture of Madrid. It was at the provincial capital city of Salamanca, on October 12, 1936, that the famous incident with Miguel de Unamuno,* rector of the local university, took place in which Unamuno criticized the Nationalists* and the war in general. Franco's small staff served the general nearby where he lived in the episcopal palace. Nationalist headquarters remained in Salamanca deep into 1937, although portions of its functions were moved to Burgos* in the fall of 1936. At Salamanca, the Nationalist staff remained small and informal, while such functions as civilian government, diplomatic relations, and military administration were created for the first time. Salamanca was also a major stronghold of the Falange.* Manuel Hedilla,* one of the founding members of the *Movimiento* (the Spanish Falange) lived in Salamanca where he established a base of operations for expanding the party during 1936 and 1937. The Nationalists also had a radio* station in the city of Salamanca which beamed its programs into Republican Spain, discussing such things as the menus in local restaurants for hungry Republicans* to hear along with editorials critical of the Loyalists.*

For further information, see Brian Crozier, *Franco* (London, 1967), on Franco's life in the city; Jacinto Miquelarena (the radio announcer in Salamanca), *Memorias de un converso*, 11 vols. (Madrid, 1943); Luis Ramírez, *Francisco Franco* (Paris, 1964); and Emilio Salcedo, *Vida de don Miguel* (Madrid, 1964), on the incident with Unamuno.

See also Army, Nationalist.

James W. Cortada

SALAS LARRAZÁBAL, ANGEL. Salas Larrazábal was a Nationalist combat pilot and air ace during the Civil War. He flew over 600 missions mainly in the battles around Madrid* and later in Aragón* and in Catalonia,* more than any other Nationalist pilot. He received considerable press coverage at the time as a genuine Nationalist hero.

For further information, see Jesús Salas Larrazábal, *La guerra de España desde el aire* (Barcelona, 1969). *See also* Air Force, Nationalist; and Pilots.

James W. Cortada

SALAZAR, ANTONIO DE OLIVEIRA (1889-1970). Salazar was the prime minister of Portugal* during the Spanish Civil War. Before becoming chief of state in Portugal, he was an economics professor and a minister of finance. He created a politically conservative, authoritarian, corporatist state. Salazar's first major international crisis came with the Spanish Civil War. Before 1936, relations between his government and the Spanish Republic had been correct, although not without controversy since left-wing radicals in Spain had encouraged revolutionary activities by their Portuguese counterparts. With the Civil War, Salazar immediately recognized that a victory by the Left in Spain could pose a direct and serious threat to his more conservative government. Thus, before the end of July 1936, he decided to follow a two-point policy: to provide quiet yet effective aid to the Nationalists* and to support publicly the policy of nonintervention. This dual strategy allowed him to help Franco* with troops and supplies. His police quietly arrested Republicans* while he maintained an official foreign policy that drew minimum criticism from such governments as Great Britain* and France* on whom Salazar depended to keep the peace in Europe.*

Salazar, very concerned about the effect the Civil War would have on his domestic programs, quickly sought to develop appropriate policies. In order to strengthen his control over Portuguese affairs, he organized a new militia that could serve as an auxiliary police, arrested dissidents, removed politically "unreliable" people from educational and governmental institutions, and established his first Ministry of Culture to expound the philosophy of the new state. He simultaneously rejected the creation of fascist or Nazi-styled groups within his country in order to keep his control over political affairs uniquely Portuguese, and not tied to broader international currents.

Thus, Salazar reacted to the Civil War by further consolidating his control over Portugal, while making it clear that he favored Franco's cause. As early as 1937, he sent an unofficial representative of his government to Franco's headquarters and expanded assistance to the Nationalists. He also sealed off the Portuguese frontier to Republicans and periodically turned over to the Nationalists some Republicans who had eluded his border guards.

After the war, Salazar maintained close ties to

Franco's government. Both followed similar foreign policies during World War II and constantly talked of an historical and economic Iberian bloc.

For further information, see Hugh Kay, *Salazar and Modern Portugal* (New York, 1960); Christian Rudel, *Salazar* (Paris, 1969); and Pedro Teotónio Pareira, *Memorias*, 2 vols. (Lisbon, 1972-1973).

James W. Cortada

SALIQUET ZUMETA, ANDRÉS (1877-1959). Saliquet Zumeta, born at Barcelona,* was an infantryman and *diplomado* of the War College and served in Cuba* and in Morocco.* By 1929, he was a division general. As an *africanista** who had supported the dictatorship, he was regarded with suspicion by the Republicans,* who left him without a command. In July 1936, he led the military rebellion in Valladolid* and became a member of the *Junta de Defensa Nacional** in Burgos.* During the Civil War, he commanded the Army of the Center* in Estremadura;* in March 1939, at the head of the 1st Division, he occupied Madrid.* After the war he was given the title of marquis, promoted to lieutenant general, and appointed captain general in Seville.* Until his death at Madrid* in 1959, he was president of the Tribunal for the Repression of Communism and Masonry.

For further information, see Felipe Bertrán Güell, *Caudillo, profetas, y soldados* (Madrid, 1939); Teresa Suero Roca, *Los generales de Franco* (Barcelona, 1975); and Hugh Thomas, *The Spanish Civil War* (New York, 1977).

Carolyn P. Boyd

SÁNCHEZ ALBORNOZ, CLAUDIO (1893-   ). Sánchez Albornoz, one of Spain's most prolific and brilliant historians of the twentieth century, like most Spanish intellectuals* of the 1930s, supported the Republicans.* During the Civil War, he was ambassador to Lisbon. Earlier he had been a foreign minister. During the war, Salazar's* government conducted more negotiations with agents of the Nationalist government than with Republican representatives in Lisbon. After the war, Sánchez Albornoz refused to return to Spain until after Franco's* death, spending his exile in Latin America* writing on Iberian history.

For further information, see Hugh Kay, *Salazar and Modern Portugal* (New York, 1960); and Claudio Sánchez Albornoz, *De mi anecdotario político* (Buenos Aires, 1972).

See also Portugal.

James W. Cortada

SÁNCHEZ GONZÁLEZ, JUAN BAUTISTA (1893-1957). Sánchez Gonzalez was a colonel in the Nationalist Army* commanding a Navarrese brigade. He had considerable combat experience, leading troops effectively during the campaigns around Madrid,* at Brunete,* and later in the Nationalist offensive in the north.

For further information, see José Manuel Martínez Bande, *La guerra en el norte* (Madrid, 1969) and *La ofensive sobre Segovia y la batalla de Brunete* (Madrid, 1972).

James W. Cortada

SANGRÓNIZ Y CASTRO, JOSÉ ANTONIO (1895-   ). Sangróniz, born in 1895 in Santiago, Chile, chose a career in the diplomatic corps.* Before the advent of the Republic, he served in London, Tangier, and his native city. As early as 1933, he discussed the possibility of an uprising, and he aided the conspiracy in July 1936 by carrying messages to General Franco* and by lending him his diplomatic passport.

Shortly after Franco assumed complete control, he appointed Sangróniz head of the civilian cabinet; his duties resembled those of a foreign minister. After losing a power struggle to Serrano Suñer* in 1937, Sangróniz was appointed to an ambassadorial post in Caracas, Venezuela. He continued his diplomatic service until he reached the mandatory retirement age. His noble title, Marqués de Desio, is of Italian origin; it was granted in 1946, and he was authorized to use it in Spain in 1951.

For further information, see Brian Crozier, *Franco* (London, 1967); and Maximiano García Venero, *Historia de la Unificación (Falange y Requeté en 1937)* (Madrid, 1970).

William J. Irwin

SANJURJO SACANELL, JOSÉ (1872-1936). Sanjurjo, in exile in Portugal* at the time of the military rising of 1936, was the designated general-in-chief of the forces in rebellion. However, on July 20, 1936, he was killed in an airplane crash. This left the forces of insurrection, for a time, without a supreme commander.

Sanjurjo was a man of vast prestige, but was not an impressive military figure, being only slightly over five feet tall. But he had fantastic endurance and determination, and was admired for his cool bravery and for being a tough, hard soldier. At the same time, he was humane. Because of his pleasant, open, and general good nature, he was very popular with his fellow officers and common soldiers.

During the wars in Morocco,* he was repeatedly promoted for meritorious service. In a fifteen-year period, he rose from lieutenant to lieutenant general. To all Spaniards he was known as the heroic "Lion of the Riff." When he returned to Spain, he was named director of the Civil Guard,* a position he held at the time of the pronouncement of the Republic. He made the important judgment to stand his force behind the new provisional government. Furthermore, he advised the minister of war that the monarchy could not depend upon support from the majority of the Spanish military—whom he knew so well. Not long after this decision, several of his men were brutally murdered by radical elements in Estremadura.* The Civil Guard's reaction to these killings resulted in his being reduced to the post of chief of the *Carabineros* (Customs Guards). Sanjurjo was now alarmed as to the general direction Manuel Azaña's* Republic was taking.

General Sanjurjo was politically naïve and soon found himself standing among Republican associates (who wanted to depose Azaña) and monarchist conspirators against the Republic. He lent both factions his name and support in an ill-conceived abortive coup in 1932. He was taken captive, tried, and sentenced to death. The death sentence was commuted to life in prison in the garb of a common criminal. After the success of the "moderates" in the election of 1934, Sanjurjo was granted amnesty and sent into exile. However, when the Popular Front* assumed power he became involved in the plot against that government. Eventually, he was able to bring together the Carlists* and their antagonist (the genius of conspiracy) General Mola.* The depth of Sanjurjo's attachment to Carlism is still difficult to determine.

On July 20, 1936, Sanjurjo took off to fly to Spain and assume command of insurrection on his native soil, but his small plane lost power on takeoff and crashed. The general died in the flaming wreckage; the pilot managed to escape with grave injuries. Some months later, after General Mola also died in a plane crash, General Franco's* detractors suggested that Franco was responsible for the deaths of his fellow officers. No such connection has ever been found.

For further information, see Juan Antonio Ansaldo, *¿Para que?* (Buenos Aires, 1951); General Emilio Esteban-Infantes, *General Sanjurjo* (Barcelona, 1957); and Stanley G. Payne, *Politics and the Military in Modern Spain* (Stanford, Calif., 1967).

Raymond L. Proctor

SANTANDER. Santander, a province located on the coast of the Bay of Biscay in northern Spain, was the scene of major fighting during the Civil War. In July 1936, the province remained under the Republicans'* control along with the rest of Asturias;* all other northern sectors quickly fell to the Nationalists.* Members of the *Confederación Nacional del Trabajo* (CNT)* then began executing suspected Nationalist sympathizers and established defense committees throughout the area in anticipation of a Nationalist offensive. Nationalist armies cut off Santander from both Madrid* and Barcelona*; thus, the *Unión General de Trabajadores* (UGT)* ran the province independently of the Republican government throughout 1936 and early 1937. Isolated from other provinces by military circumstances and rough terrain, the province even established its own currency. Coal mines were managed by local miners independent of companies or municipal authorities, while fishermen in some cases organized themselves into collectives. The city of Santander had various forms of administration. The socialists, for example, operated all port facilities while the UGT attempted to run other services. Over 10,000 Republican soldiers and militia were already in the province by December 1936 nominally as part of the Republican Army of the North.* Within months this number grew manifold.

After the Basque country fell to Franco,* the Nationalists began their campaign to conquer Asturias (1937). The main fighting came in August. Defending Santander were the 14th and 15th Republican Army Corps, and attacking them was the Nationalist Army of the North commanded by General Fidel Dávila,* with experienced Navarrese and Italian troops as well. Heavy fighting took place beginning on August 14 and continued until the city of Santander came under Nationalist control on August 24. It was a major victory for the Nationalists, with over 60,000 prisoners,* and now an important port in the north.

After reprisals, executions, and the establishment of Nationalist military control, Santander remained in Franco's hands for the rest of the war.

For further information, see José Manuel Martínez Bande, *La guerra en el norte* (Madrid, 1969); and José Ramón Saiz Viadero, et al., *Crónicas sobre la Guerra Civil en Santander* (Santander, 1979).

See also Appendix B.

James W. Cortada

SARAGOSSA. Both the city and the province of Saragossa are located in northern Spain in Aragón* next to Catalonia.* The area saw considerable combat during the war as each side attempted to gain or maintain control of the northeast. In July 1936, troops loyal to the Nationalists* managed to occupy quickly the majority of the province, including its capital before worker militias* could extend their authority. Afterwards, numerous people suspected or known to support the Republic were executed. Jesús Muro,* the local Falangist leader, was especially ruthless in searching out and executing suspected enemies of the Nationalists. Some estimates of the killed in Saragossa place the number at 2,000. Meanwhile, Republican militia commanders, especially in Barcelona,* sought to organize a campaign to regain Saragossa. Their campaign in July and August 1936 halted in front of Saragossa for eighteen months. From March through July 1938, the Nationalists launched an offensive in Aragón and in the Levante,* successfully cutting the Republican zone in half with a march to the Mediterranean. Saragossa became one of several staging areas for the offensive and in the process periodically was bombed by the Republicans.*

For further information, see José Manuel Martínez Bande, *El final del frente norte* (Madrid, 1972) and *La invasión de Aragón y el desembarco en Mallorca* (Madrid, 1970).

James W. Cortada

SAYAGÜES, PRUDENCIO. In 1938, Sayagüez became director of the *Servicio de Investigación Militar* (SIM),* a Republican intelligence agency whose mission was to monitor the activities of the state's political enemies and to eliminate them. The organization was a tool of the communists, particularly of the Soviet advisers in Spain. Prior to his appointment, Sayagüez had served as the deputy director of the agency. In the first few months of the Civil War, he also ran a counterintelligence operation out of the Ministry of War.

For further information, see Manuel Uribarri, *El SIM de la República* (Havana, 1942).
See also Communist Party, Spanish; Espionage; NKVD; and USSR.

James W. Cortada

SBERT, ANTONIO MARÍA. Sbert was a Catalan politician and member of the Esquerra* party. In December 1936, he entered the Catalan government in a cabinet reshuffle that saw an increase in the power of the *Confederación Nacional del Trabajo* (CNT).* As councillor for education,* Sbert attempted to reform the educational system to provide for more education in basic skills and less regional and political training in the schools. On April 16, 1937, in another cabinet reshuffle, he became councillor of culture. In June, as part of the Republic's effort to reimpose con-

trol over Catalonia,* another Catalan cabinet came into existence, this time with Sbert as councillor of the interior responsible for police* functions. This position allowed him to restore public order in the following months. He remained in the government until the end of the Civil War.

For further information, see Burnett Bolloten, *The Spanish Revolution: The Left and the Struggle for Power During the Civil War* (Chapel Hill, N.C., 1979).
See also Generalitat; and Appendix C.

James W. Cortada

SECONDARY EDUCATION LAW. The Secondary Education Law, decreed on September 20, 1938 by Franco's* minister of national education, Pedro de Sainz Rodríguez,* was the first step in creating a secondary school system based on pedagogic principles of a classical, humanistic education* that sustained religious and patriotic ideals. The Nationalists* claimed that this law would enable them to establish a new direction for both education and the social formation of Spaniards. Seven fundamental instructional areas were mandated; religion and philosophy; classical languages; Spanish language and literature; geography and history; mathematics; two modern languages; and cosmology. To these were added lessons in drawing, physical education, and patriotism. The state supervised and inspected the teaching of this curriculum and awarded the degree of *bachillerato* to students passing a comprehensive exam at the end of their seven years of study. This law was not altered for ten years.

For further information, see Manuel Utande, "Treinta años de enseñanza media," *Revista de Educación* 240 (September-October 1975): 73-86.

David V. Holtby

SECOND REPUBLIC. The Second Republic came into existence in April 1931 and officially lasted until the end of the Civil War in 1939. However, its effective life concluded at the outbreak of war in July 1936, after which "Republic" became a label for antifascist forces rather than a continuing reality.

The Republic was born on April 14, 1931, as a result of local elections held by the monarchy as a belated first step in a return to representative government following the Primo de Rivera dictatorship of 1923-1930. The contest became a virtual plebiscite on the future of the monarchy itself, and in most Spanish cities and large towns produced a victory for Republican and socialist opponents of the regime. This represented the climax of an upsurge in Republican feeling among the middle classes, and a growth of socialist support within the working class, evident since the mid-1920s and especially since the dictatorship's collapse in January 1930. Faced with these results, fearful of civil strife, and all but abandoned by his supporters and by both army and Civil Guard, * King Alfonso XIII* went into exile. The Republic was declared in many parts of Spain, and power was assumed by a Republican Revolutionary Committee, several members of which had until recently been imprisoned for their political activities.

The change of regime was neither the product nor the harbinger of any major shift in the essential power structure in Spain. Despite the views of some socialists such as Besteiro,* it was not a bourgeois revolution or even the dawn of one. While the republicanism of much of the intelligentsia and the professional middle class may have been sincere enough, most of the landholding, banking, and industrial oligarchy accepted the Republic as little more than a tactical maneuver necessary to forestall social convulsion. The bourgeois intellectuals* and professional politicians who now took office thus possessed no economic power base of their own. Those among them who were anxious to transform Spain were confronted by an entrenched ruling class whose republicanism was either nonexistent or, more insidiously, contingent upon the Republic's proving to be a monarchy in disguise under which little of importance would change. The chameleonism whereby countless locally influential monarchists adopted Republican colors without Republican conviction was a pronounced feature of the new regime's early weeks and boded ill for hopes of serious reform.

The diversity of the political forces actively committed to one or other notion of republicanism dated from the pact of San Sebastián of August 1930 between Republicans and socialists, and was amply illustrated by the personnel of the provisional government formed on April 14. Left republicanism, epitomized by the minister of war and future Republican strongman, Manuel Azaña,* was represented by his own party, *Acción Republicana*; by the virulently anticlerical Radical-socialists; by the *Organización Republicana de Galicia Autonomía* (ORGA) (Galician Republicans); and by the Esquerra* (Catalan Left). These "Jacobins" wanted to transform the mentality of Spain by tackling its institutions rather than its socioeconomic infrastructure. Above all, they sought to curb drastically the role and power of the Catholic Church;* to laicize, extend, and improve the educational system; and to prune, modernize and depoliticize the officer corps of the army. Commanding real mass support only among the lower middle class and peasantry of Catalonia,*

Left republicanism was and remained dependent for votes and for political force on an alliance with the Socialist party.* Most of the socialists were at first enthusiastic about the Republic and eager to participate in government. They hoped the new regime would attack Spain's social and economic fabric, most urgently be effecting a thoroughgoing land reform in the latifundist regions of the south and west.

The relationship of the Left Republicans with the socialists created a gulf between them and their more conservative colleagues: the Radical Republican party of Alejandro Lerroux, and the Catholic Republicans led by the prime minister, Alcalá-Zamora, and the minister of the interior, Miguel Maura. Both groups were essentially concerned with socioeconomic continuity, financial and fiscal conservatism, the maintenance of public order, and the containment of the Left. Both looked to secure the Republic by broadening its base in a rightward direction: the Radicals through an appeal to all antisocialists, and the Catholics through the creation of a mass Catholic-Republican party, the Liberal Republican Right.

The conservative Maura believed that the Spanish ruling class was for a time so paralyzed by the monarchy's fall as to be vulnerable to a revolution by decree which might have destroyed its position forever. If this was so, and it is highly doubtful, then its paralysis was shortlived. What is more significant is that, apart from some Radical-socialist murmurs, the provisional government showed itself to be unanimously unwilling to attempt any such thing, preferring a course of the utmost constitutional propriety: the election of a Constituent Cortes* and the elaboration of a new Spanish Constitution.

The San Sebastian parties received an impressive mandate when elections were held in June and July, winning some 361 out of 470 seats (the Socialist party 116, the Radicals 90, the Radical-socialists 56, the Esquerra 36, the *Acción Republicana* 26, the Liberal Republican Right 22, and ORGA 15). The non-Republican Right was seriously underrepresented in the Constituent Cortes owing to the general disorientation of its potential supporters, large-scale abstentions, and its poor organization in the context of an electoral system favoring broad and cohesive alliances. Most of its fifty or so deputies were divided between the Basque-Navarrese bloc of Carlists* and Basque nationalists and a loose agrarian bloc representing Catholic and landowning interests.

During the summer and autumn of 1931, the Constituent Cortes debated and eventually passed the Republican Constitution, a document embodying the principles and prejudices of the Republican Left and the socialists. Its most significant and controversial areas were those dealing with property, which was declared subject to social imperatives and therefore liable to socialization, and with religious affairs. It was the latter, especially Article 26, which announced an attack upon the property and activities of religious orders, that provoked the resignation from the government of Alcalá-Zamora and Maura. Although Alcalá-Zamora shortly afterwards became president of the Republic, Maura entered a political wilderness from which he was never to emerge. Their projected mass party soon disappeared without a trace from the Republican scene.

This first breach in the San Sebastián coalition was quickly followed by another. When Azaña, appointed premier in October succeeding Alcalá-Zamora, reshuffled his cabinet in December, he was obliged by Lerroux to choose, in effect, between a broad Republican alliance excluding the socialists, and one with the socialists in which the Radicals would not participate. Azaña chose to ally with the socialists. The Radicals, their ranks now swollen with ex-monarchist chameleons, began a steady move into opposition and towards the Right. Azaña's alliance of the Left Republicans and socialists, armed with a Constitution tailored to their needs and a draconian Law for the Defense of the Republic for use against troublesome opponents, was to govern Spain until September 1933.

Between 1931 and 1933, the provisional government and then successive Azaña administrations pursued the reforms desired by Left Republicans and socialists, discovering in the process the difficulty of achieving, in the face of conservative resistance, peaceful yet substantial and rapid change. Azaña's army reforms aimed to reduce the gross surplus of officers. Almost half accepted retirement on full pension, but the bitterness with which the measures were applied, and the intrusion of party prejudices into the promotion system, alienated many officers, both serving and newly retired. The rising of General Sanjurjo* in August 1932, though premature and unsuccessful, gave early warning of growing military disillusionment with a Republic towards which few officers had been truly hostile at the outset.

Catalan autonomy, enshrined in the Statute of 1932, was another stimulus to discontent within the traditionally anti-Catalan army, as well as arousing irritation in other regions of Spain, especially Castile.* A matter of conviction for the Esquerra and its leaders Macià and Companys,* Catalan autonomy was a simple political debt for most non-Catalan Republicans and for the strongly centralist socialists. The statue itself satisfied most Catalans but contained dangerous areas of constitutional ambiguity.

Anticlericalism, the burning passion of Left Republicans, did the Republic itself more harm than good. In particular the 1933 Law of Confessions and Congregations, which sought to end the educational activities, among others, of religious orders, served only to reduce total educational provision at the secondary level and thus vitiate the very positive accomplishments of Marcelino Domingo and his successors at the Education Ministry. The assault on the religious orders, especially the Jesuits, together with the promised phasing out of state support for clerical salaries and other anticlerical measures, deeply offended Catholic feelings. Despite Azaña's claim, Spain had not ceased to be Catholic. The uneasiness of many Catholics at the mere existence of a Republic had been fueled in May 1931 by the provisional government's apparent impassiveness in the face of mob anticlerical incendiarism. Now, during 1932 and 1933, disgruntled Catholic opinion provided welcome material for the organizers of right-wing opposition to the Republic as defined by the 1931 Constitution.

Middle-class Republican zeal for military, religious, educational, and regional reform did not extend to the social questions that preoccupied socialists. Discussion of agrarian reform was allowed to drag on for a year before the passage of the Agrarian Reform Act of September 1932. Officially intended to destroy latifundism, it was marred by technical ignorance, confused drafting aggravated by piecemeal parliamentary revision, and inadequate financial backing. By the end of 1933, only about 4,400 landless peasants had received land; perhaps 70,000 lesser proprietors found their property threatened; while most large landowners escaped unscathed.

Catholic peasants and the bourgeoisie constituted the popular base of a powerful right-wing response to the Republic which emerged between 1931 and 1933. The germ of this revival was *Acción Nacional*, founded during April-May 1931 with considerable Church support in order to defend conservative interests during the Republic's honeymoon period. Initially bringing together monarchists, Carlists, and other Catholics unwilling to embrace the Republic, *Acción Nacional*, renamed *Acción Popular** in 1932, gradually adopted an officially accidentalist policy of working within the Republic without accepting it as permanent. Under the leadership of José María Gil Robles,* *Acción Popular* became in turn the core of the *Confederación Española de Derechas Autónomas* (CEDA),* founded in March 1933 as a confederation of numerous regional Catholic parties and interest groups. Drawing its mass support from Catholics offended by anticlericalism and fearful of communism, and its leadership from a Catholic landholding and professional elite skillful at exploiting such susceptibilities, the CEDA, at its birth the largest political party in Spanish history with approximately 750,000 members, stood for the peaceful conquest of power and the transformation of the Republic into a corporate state.

As accidentalism came to dominate *Acción Popular*, most open monarchists left. Alfonsine monarchists formed their own party in 1933, the authoritarian, monarchofascist *Renovación Española*.* Carlism also reemerged as a significant minority force, especially in its stronghold of Navarre.* Neither monarchist party made any attempt to conceal its wish to overthrow the Republic by any means available.

The nature of the resurgent Right indicated the Republic's failure to broaden its base in one direction; the development of the Left appeared to signal its actual contraction in another. In 1931, socialist commitment to the Republic was enthusiastic, and the party held posts in every government between April 1931 and September 1933. Indalecio Prieto,* minister of finance and later of public works, remained devoted to cooperation with the Republican Left, but Francisco Largo Caballero,* minister of labor from 1931 to 1933, gradually adopted an anticollaborationist and quasi-revolutionary posture. This was due both to disillusionment with the achievements and potentialities of Spanish bourgeois democracy and to changes within the body of Spanish socialism itself. Although Largo Caballero's labor policies improved the position of workers and raised real wage levels during 1931-1932, he and other socialists soon grew frustrated at the Republic's failure to achieve more in the social, especially agrarian, spheres. Bourgeois-Republican lack of true social commitment, plus the oligarchy's continuing power to resist the passage and application of reform, persuaded them of the limitations of democracy itself. This tendency was reinforced by changes between 1927 and 1933 in the composition and character of the socialist union, the *Unión General de Trabajadores* (UGT).* From a union of the urban working-class elite, it was becoming one dominated by its fast-growing rural branch, the *Federación Nacional de Trabajadores de la Tierra* (FNTT). Socialist militancy thus reflected the thwarted expectations of a new, rural rank-and-file. The result, during the spring and summer of 1933, was a drawing away from the Left Republicans and an eventual refusal to renew the electoral alliance of 1931 which was to have dire results in the November 1933 elections.

The socialists' change of strategy was also influenced by the constant competition for working-class allegiance offered by the anarchosyndicalist *Con-federación Nacional del Trabajo* (CNT).* After initially displaying a degree of acceptance towards the Republic, the CNT quickly reverted to a more combative line when the authorities, both national and local, showed themselves to be no less repressive than those of the monarchy. Largo Caballero's hopes of undermining the CNT's position through the demonstrable fruits of socialist participation in government were soon dashed, and the CNT, increasingly influenced by the revolutionary anarchists* of the *Federación Anarquista Ibérica* (FAI),* continued to claim a million members. Bitter and harshly repressed CNT-led strikes during the summer of 1931 were a foretaste of successive waves of syndical and, more sporadically, insurrectionary activity. A symbolic climax to the latter insurrectionary activity came in January 1933 with the massacre of anarchist peasants at Casas Viejas (Cádiz): an incident embarrassing enough to the Azaña government but especially so to the socialists.

By 1933, the political situation had thus greatly altered, with the Catholic Right immeasurably stronger and more confident, the socialists increasingly alienated from the Republican Left, and the ever more conservative Radicals in opposition and lusting after power. Local elections in April 1933 exposed the Azaña government's new weakness, which thereafter increased until Azaña finally fell from office in September. The premiership now passed to the Radicals: Lerroux, briefly, and then his lieutenant Martínez Barrio* pending a general election. The election was held in November and December and took a very different form from the 1931 contest. This time the Republican Left and the socialists ran separately in most provinces, while in many provinces an alliance developed, in the second round if not the first, between the Radicals and the CEDA. The acrimonious election, in which both CEDA and socialist campaigners uttered words apparently threatening to the Republic in its existing form, resulted in a serious defeat for the dominant parties of 1931-1933. While the socialists won only fifty-nine seats and the combined Republican Left forty, the CEDA—nonexistent in 1931—obtained 115 and the Radicals 102. The apparent shift in public opinion was not, perhaps, as great as it might seem. Apart from the unverifiable possibility that the women's vote, operating for the first time, may have somewhat favored the more conservative parties, much of the difference between 1931 and 1933 can be explained in terms of changing alliances—the collapse of the San Sebastián coalition, especially that of the Left Republican-socialist alliance—and differential abstention—that of Catholics in 1931 and that of CNT members in 1933.

However distorted, the result remained an unfavorable verdict on two and a half years of reformism. Having decided against any attempt at revolution by decree in early 1931, the Republican governments of the next two years learned that gradual reform was very problematical. The Azaña governments, especially their Left Republican members, unquestionably placed undue emphasis upon doctrinaire policies, in the religious and related spheres, which created unnecessary enemies for the Republic itself without any commensurate gains. For all that, matters elsewhere were simply not under governmental control. In the honeymoon period of 1931, anything may have seemed possible; the reality, however, was that neither the time, the expertise, not financial means existed for the kind of social program to which the Azaña Republic was committed. These were, after all, years of general economic Depression from which Spain was certainly not immune. The Spanish state, saddled with an archaic taxation system which the Republic would have done well to revise, but did not, remained underfinanced throughout the early 1930s. As the fate of agrarian reform demonstrated, the resources were simply not there to support costly agrarian, military, educational, and other reforms. The depression forced sound financial policies on Republican finance ministers, savaged Spanish exports, slashed profit and rent margins, and, admittedly very selectively, created unemployment and exacerbated land-hunger. In these circumstances, two-and-a-half years may not have been long enough to change the face the Spain, but they were certainly long enough to stimulate unsatisfied appetites on the political Left and create assorted fears on the Right. Between 1931 and 1933, the Republic had ushered Spain into an age of mass politics, a phenomenon that in itself made the containment of economic and social conflicts within the framework of a democratic regime all the more difficult.

From September 1933 until September 1935, Spain was governed by Radical-led coalition governments, the balance of which shifted steadily rightwards. The Radical party, having since 1931 opened its doors to so many ex-monarchists, including numerous provincial *caciques* (political bosses), had by now lost what traces of true radicalism had survived into the Republic. In order to govern, it was bound to other conservative parties, principally the Agrarian party, the Lliga (Catalan conservatives), and, most important, the CEDA. The CEDA was now the largest parliamentary party was barred from the premiership by its refusal to accept the permanence of the 1931 Constitution and the Republic itself, a stance that ensured the hostility of President Alcalá-Zamora and of the entire Republi-

can and socialist Left. The CEDA possessed its own tactic for the conquest of power: first, as from November 1933, to make its support essential for the conduct of government; then to insist on participation in government; and, finally, to assume power itself and preside over, at the very least, the drastic revision of the Constitution in a corporatist direction.

Lerroux's tactic was a different one: to attract the CEDA *into* the Republic, which he hoped would thereby be stabilized. This course, rendered relevant by the alienating effects of Republican anticlericalism and other policies, and by the political failure of Alcalá-Zamora and Maura, necessitated a markedly more conservative governmental line: something in any case acceptable to most, though not quite all, of the Radical party. This commenced before the 1933 election, when in the first Radical-led government the socialist-sponsored system of rural wage-maintenance began to be dismantled. During 1934, the process continued. Much of the work of the Azaña governments was either reversed or allowed to lapse, both in the religious and in the social realms; those involved or implicated in the Sanjurjo rising were amnestied; and with a right-wing Radical, Salazar Alonso, at the Interior Ministry, an ostentatiously tough attitude was adopted towards all brands of left-wing militancy.

The dethroned Spanish Left interpreted the drift of events during 1934 as the advance of fascism. The prospect most feared, especially by the socialists, was the entry of the CEDA into the government. For the socialists, any such development promised a Spanish version of February 1934 in Vienna, when their Austrian comrades were crushed by Dollfuss, a CEDA hero; for the Republican Left, the prospect seemed rather one of the unacceptable revision of a Constitution which for them was the very essence of the Republic. From February 1934, Largo Caballero attempted to create a Workers' Alliance, which would embrace all labor movements, anarchosyndicalist and communist as well as socialist, and would be capable of contesting in the streets any CEDA assumption of office. The spring and summer of 1934 were months of acute conflict. Government economic and public order policies, and more significantly the revived confidence and even vengefulness of landlords and employers, helped provoke widespread working-class protest. Examples were the month-long, CNT-inspired Saragossa* general strike of April and the Andalusian peasants' strike of the early summer, both of which were heroic defeats that left their protagonists greatly weakened. Tension also arose between Madrid* and Catalonia,* when the central government attempted to block the Generalitat* from enacting a rural leases law favoring tenant cultivators (*rabassaires*). When in October three CEDA ministers were at last appointed to another Radical-led cabinet, revolution erupted in Catalonia and in Asturias,* the only region where the Workers' Alliance proved a reality. The Catalonian revolt was a fiasco; it was swiftly crushed and its reluctant leader, Prime Minister Companys, arrested. The Asturian rising, however, lasted for two weeks, was bloody, and succumbed only to overwhelming military intervention and repression.

Given the international climate of 1934, the CEDA's studied ambivalence towards democracy, and the behavior of its supporters at the local level, the Left's apprehensiveness in October 1934 is easy to understand. The response was nevertheless as excessive as it was ill prepared. The rising of two former mainstays of the Republic—the socialists and the Esquerra—against an uncongenial but duly elected and appointed government, out of fear of what it might do in the future, seriously weakened the standing of the Republic itself and undermined its own moral right to speak on its behalf.

In the wake of the October Revolution, the governmental move to the Right accelerated. With between 30,000 and 40,000 alleged rebels in jail and Catalan autonomy suspended, the extreme Right and most of the CEDA demanded an even more thorough repression, executions included, which if pursued and successful would have crushed not only the working-class movements but the Republican Left as well. The CEDA reached its apogee in May 1935 when it obtained five portfolios in yet another Lerroux government. Although Gil Robles,* as minister of war, labored to strengthen rightist tendencies within the army, he appears to have resisted any temptation to engineer a coup. He did so not so much out of constitutional propriety as out of an awareness that military intervention would in all probability produce military and not CEDA rule, and a confidence that the CEDA would in any case soon obtain total power via the ballot box. Meanwhile, the party's *conservadurismo* and legislative barrenness were starkly exposed when attempts at modest social reforms by its social Catholic minority were swept aside by the majority of its deputies and the reactionary interests they represented.

The tide began to turn against the CEDA and the Right during the summer of 1935. The Radicals, sensitive to their position as the would-be center party, began to retreat from the divisive politics of repression, while the Right attempts to ruin Azaña by holding him guilty of plotting revolution in October 1934 collapsed ignominiously. Azaña now reemerged as the focus of a reformed, broadened version of the 1931-1933 coalition: the Popular Front.* Political polarization was apparently irresistible as the Radical party disintegrated under the strains of the CEDA alliance and a rash of financial scandals, taking the political Center with it. The CEDA, from its peak of five ministries in May, sank back to three in the Chapaprieta government of September, and lost office months later with the appointment of a preelection government under the moderate independent Portela Valladares. The success of the CEDA tactic now depended entirely upon election victory.

Just as the socialists were tugged leftwards by the revolutionary competition of the CNT, so throughout the *bienio negro* of 1934-1935 any possibility of the CEDA's actually embracing the Republic was lessened by the pressure of the monarchist and fascist extreme Right. The Alfonsine *Renovación Española* remained numerically weak—a general staff without an army—but disproportionately influential thanks to its members' contact in the banking and business world, the landowning elite, and the armed forces. The Carlists possessed the numbers and the popular touch which the Alfonsines lacked, and a growing paramilitary force, the *Requetés*. When, in 1934, Calvo Sotelo* assumed the Alfonsine leadership and Fal Conde* that of the Carlists, both movements stepped up their aggressiveness and their criticism of CEDA gradualism. A more modern competitor appeared in October 1933 with the foundation of *Falange Española*,* led by Jośe Antonio Primo de Rivera.* This, Spain's first significant fascist movement, remained relatively weak numerically until 1936, but like the monarchist parties presented the CEDA with a constant threat of the loss of mass support to the extreme Right should its tactic fail.

Meanwhile, on the Left the CNT/FAI remained consistent in its revolutionism, while the so-called bolshevization of the Socialist party continued. Despite the electoral miscalculation of 1933, when he had claimed to expect a socialist victory, and the poorly prepared October Revolution, Largo Caballero and his followers not only retained but actually tightened their control of the Socialist party and UGT, systematically removing from influential positions both Besteiro and Prieto. Although unable to refuse participation in the Popular Front, Largo Caballero remained convinced that governmental partnership with the Republican Left was no longer desirable. Instead, the Republic would become a socialist republic through a combination of political and popular pressure: in effect, a tactical position not unlike the accidentalism of the CEDA. Though dubbed the Spanish Lenin by his entourage, Largo Caballero had neither the intellect, the tactical instinct, not the sheer revolutionary will of a Lenin.

Like Gil Robles on the Right, he found his own relatively moderate inclinations diverted by the pressures of a militant youth movement and an aggressive rural rank and file. Also like Gil Robles, he was constantly aware of competition from, and the danger of losing support to, more extreme forces—in his case the CNT and the fast-growing Communist party.* The result, by the start of 1936, was an acute tactical and ideological confusion within the Socialist party, which was electorally committed to the Popular Front but unprepared, despite the continued collaborationism of Prieto and others, to assume office in the event of victory.

The election of February 1936* was a direct confrontation between the Popular Front, an alliance ranging from the communists to the breakaway radicals of Martínez Barrio's Republican Union party, now part of a consolidated Republican Left led by Azaña; and a rather looser National Front* consisting principally of the CEDA and the two monarchist parties. The absence of a credible Center offered a graphic demonstration of the political polarization that had taken place over the preceding five years. Understanding of this process is best sought in the relationship between the sociopolitical effects of the change of regime and the particular political forms into which these were channeled. Obviously, the intensity of class conflict in Spain during the 1930s was great, being the product of yawning economic gaps between rich and poor, gross insensitivity on the part of the rich, and the short-term aggravating effects of the Depression. The *political* conflicts and ultimate absence of coexistence to which all this gave rise were especially sharp owing to the sheer pace of mass politicization after 1931. Whether any democratic regime could ever expect to contain the pressures and conflicts released in Spain by the coming of the Republic is doubtful. What made the possibility still less likely was the channeling of socioeconomic and political conflict into mass parties— the CEDA and the Socialist party—whose attachment to the Republic was conditional upon its developing along lines unacceptable to the other, and in either case unacceptable to the Republican Left whose mark on the Constitution was perhaps excessively pronounced. To speak of the greater responsibility of either party for the Republic's difficulties raises problems that are out of place here. Suffice it to say that the survival of the Republic became the more difficult as the Catholic masses of Spain turned their backs upon Catholic Republicanism and embraced a party to which the label *fascist* could with some degree of credibility be attached.

The election of February 1936 produced a Popular Front victory, narrow in votes but substantial in terms of seats thanks to the electoral system's eccentricities. In order to avoid a dangerous power vacuum into which it was feared the army might step, Azaña was allowed to resume office without delay at the head of an entirely Republican cabinet.

The polarization evident before and during the election campaign now intensified. The Socialist Left under Largo Caballero considered the Popular Front to be an antifascist electoral device with no long-term future. The 1931-1933 program would be reenacted by a Left Republican government with socialist support, and at some point thereafter power would pass inexorably into the hands of the working class and its socialist leaders. The timing and details of this process were vague, deliberate violence by the Left being envisaged only in the wholly foreseeable event of rightist obstruction or attempted takeover. This was no revolutionary plan or plot but an openly admitted vision, comprehensible in the light of the sustained rivalry of the CNT, the bolshevization of the socialist youth, and an explosion of grass-roots militancy. The CNT, having survived socialist competition during 1931-1933 and the repression of 1934-1935, was now more numerous and assertive than ever, as manifested at the triumphalist Saragossa congress of May 1936. The communists, too, continued to advance, and an unpredictable future was created for the Socialist party when its youth movement and that of the communists fused to form the *Juventudes Socialistas Unificadas* (JSU)* in April. All the while, the spate of strikes and land occupations that followed the election, partly in anticipation of meaningful agrarian and labor reform, helped convince Largo Caballero that this was no time for reformism.

If anarchosyndicalists and many socialists and communists believed the future of Spain to be a revolutionary, socialist one, there was, it is worth repeating, no left-wing plan, coordinated or otherwise, to launch revolution in the short run. Ironically, the development most likely to unleash a revolutionary process was the kind of right-wing rising that very definitely *was* being schemed. With the CEDA tactic in shreds, the party's mass base deserted it in the direction of the monarchist and fascist extreme Right. The Carlists were now preparing the *Requetés* for an imminent rising, in which they optimistically hoped they would lead and the rest of the Right, army included, meekly follow. The Falange, while also planning rebellion, concentrated its efforts on destabilizing the Republic through the use of *pistolerismo* (shootings) against the left. Despite the banning of the Falange and the imprisonment of several of its leaders, including José Antonio Primo de Rivera, the movement's expansion, voguishness, and militancy managed to survive its disorganized and almost leaderless state. Viewed as a whole, the activities, however hampered, of the Falange, the paramilitary preparations of the Carlists, and the stirrings of what might be termed *squadrismo* among ex-*cedistas* in, for example, Valencia,* suggest at least the beginnings of the kind of right-wing civilian mobilization embodied in fascism in Italy* some fifteen years before. What prevented such a process from maturing was perhaps not so much the government's decisiveness, which was uneven, as the expectation of so many Spanish rightist that when it came to striking at the Republic in the name of preventing left-wing revolution, the army could be relied upon to carry out the task.

Such beliefs were well founded. Although the conservatism of the governments of 1935 had dampened conspiratorial tendencies in the army, right-wing feeling had been on the increase in the middle ranks especially of the officer corps, notably in the clandestine *Unión Militar Española* (UME).* There could be little doubt that a Popular Front victory would be followed by serious conspiratorial activity. And so it proved. After a number of false starts a plot developed, centered around General Mola* in Pamplona* and gradually drawing in other important officers (Franco* in the Canary Islands* being one of the last) and civilian militia organizations such as the *Requetés* and the Falange. By late spring, a major right-wing blow against the Popular Front government was all but certain, even if doubts lingered as to its timing, precise character and goals, and likely degree of success.

Amid this fraught atmosphere, the Republican government struggled to maintain political viability and with it the very Republic. The premiership of Azaña lasted only until May, when he was elected president of the Republic by the Cortes* in place of Alcalá-Zamora, deposed by the left-wing majority, in effect (though not officially) for having admitted the CEDA into the government in 1934-1935. The removal of Azaña from day-to-day politics was damaging, especially when combined with the socialist party's refusal to permit Prieto to replace him as premier or even serve in a broad-based government. This deprived the Republic at a crucial time of the political services of the two figures with sufficient personal will and wide acceptance to be able to rally support to the regime. Talk of a national government, constant between February and July 1936, came to nothing.

Under Azaña's successor as premier, Casares Quiroga,* an explosion was only a matter of time. Although there were promising signs of a reduction in rural ferment and even of a possible *Prietista* revival within the

Socialist party, the military-rightist conspiracy was now advanced. The assassination by left-wing police,* on July 13, of the monarchist leader Calvo Sotelo was merely a convenient pretext and trigger for a rising already poised to take place. It commenced on July 17-18, 1936, first in Morocco* and then in several parts of the Iberian Peninsula. Faced with the crisis, the Republican government possessed two alternative courses of action, either of which would transform the Republic into something entirely different: to reach an accommodation with the rebels or to resist by the only means apparently available, namely, the arming of the CNT and UGT trade-union militia. After Casares Quiroga resigned, Martínez Barrio, the most conservative personality within the Popular Front, served for a day as premier while he tried vainly to reach an accommodation with the rebels. His successor, the Left Republican José Giral,* adopted the latter course on July 19, 1936.

As Azaña, now president of the Republic, later noted, from the installation of the Giral government the Second Republic, as born in April 1931 and enshrined in the 1931 Constitution, effectively ceased to exist. Legally speaking, it continued—Constitution, presidency, appointed governments, Cortes, and all. Among other things this was necessary in order to persuade those abroad who might provide help that the Republican cause was indeed that of a democratically elected government embodying the principles and values of Western liberalism. It was ironic, however, that a return to Republican democracy was from the very start of the war the least likely outcome. The division of Spain into two zones, the government's surrender of practical authority to the working class in July 1936, and the unwillingness of the Western democracies to assist the Republican cause, implied the demise of the representative democracy for which Republican Spain was supposed to stand. In the event of an insurgent victory, this was in no doubt; in that of a rebel defeat, the alternatives for Spain were those of a social-revolutionary order as pursued by the forces unleashed in July 1936, or the authoritarianism of the Soviet-backed communists upon whom the government became dependent during 1936-1937 for the supply of arms, the creation of an efficient army, and the gradual restoration of state authority. For most of the Civil War, therefore, the Republic was not a constitutional or institutional reality but a thin label for a cause united, if at all, only by a generalized antifascism. Dead in all but name from July 1936, the Second Republic died in name also when the Civil War ended in 1939. In 1945, a Republican government-in-exile was formed under Giral, but it and its successors were little more than nostalgic and impotent symbols of a Spain that disappeared nine years before.

For further information, see Gabriel Jackson, *The Spanish Republic and the Civil War, 1931-1939* (Princeton, N.J., 1965); Edward E. Malefakis, *Agrarian Reform and Peasant Revolution in Spain* (New Haven, Conn. and London, 1970); Paul Preston, *The Coming of the Spanish Civil War: Reform, Reaction and Revolution in the Second Republic* (London, 1978); and Richard Robinson, *The Origins of Franco's Spain: The Right, the Republic and Revolution 1931-1936* (Newton Abbot, 1970).

Martin Blinkhorn

SEGOVIA. Segovia, a province located directly northwest of Madrid,* supported the Nationalists* from the beginning of the Civil War. The ancient city of Segovia fell to the rebels without a fight. However, warfare between Republican and Nationalist forces continued on Segovian soil throughout the war. A major battle took place in May-June 1937 in the province. The Republicans* launched an offensive there under the command of General Domingo Moriones Larraga* with three Republican divisions, attacking Nationalist forces at San Ildefonso and pushing them back as far as La Granja* before additional rebel forces under the command of General José Enrique Varela Iglesias* stopped the advance and ultimately forced the Loyalists* back. As a result of this Nationalist victory, the rebels were soon after able to seize Bilbao* by concentrating large numbers of forces in the north without fear of attack from central Spain.

For further information, see José Manuel Martínez Bande, *La ofensive sobre Segovia y la batalla de Bruenete* (Madrid, 1972).

James W. Cortada

SEGURA Y SÁENZ, CARDINAL PEDRO (1880-1957). Cardinal Segura, archbishop of Toledo* and later archbishop of Seville,* was Spain's most controversial cleric during the Second Republic* and Civil War. Born in Carazo (Burgos)* on December 4, 1880, he was ordained in 1906, consecrated bishop of Valladolid* in 1916, made bishop of Coria-Cáceres in 1920 and archbishop of Burgos in February 1927, named a cardinal in the same year, and in December 1927, was appointed archbishop of Toledo and primate of Spain.

Part of the reason for Segura's rapid rise in the ecclesiastical hierarchy was the patronage of King Alfonso XIII* who was impressed with his piety and humanitarian labors among the poor. Notwithstanding these traits, Segura was an uncompromising monarchist and puritan traditionalist who remained obstinate in the face of all challenges to his authority as head of the Spanish Church.* He demonstrated his loyalty to the monarchy shortly after Alfonso left Spain in April 1931, following the proclamation of the Second Republic. On May 6, 1931, he issued a pastoral letter outlining the duties of Catholics towards the new government, counseling them to follow the attitude of the Holy See in giving respect and obedience to the constituted political power. He urged Catholics to exercise their political rights. But he also lauded the departed monarch in unmistakable tones of approval and gratitude. This letter was viewed by the anticlerical Left as a provocation, and the government called Segura's letter "interference by the Church in politics." The letter, along with unsubstantiated rumors that Segura had "invoked God's wrath upon the Republic" in a sermon, also inflamed popular opinion. These, together with renewed monarchist activity for the upcoming Constituent Cortes* elections, led to the incendiary anticlerical riots of May 11-13, 1931, in Madrid* and southern Spain.

Segura went to Rome for consultations with the pope following the riots. As Spain's ranking churchman, he sent a note to the government protesting the incendiarism and some of the government's anticlerical activities. When he returned to Spain in June 1931, he was arrested and expelled from the country on the grounds that his presence in Spain was "dangerous to the public spirit" and that he was "counseling unrest to a badly disturbed people." Two months later, in August, after Segura continued his campaign of public protest from exile in France* against both his expulsion and the government's anticlericalism, the government issued a formal notice that Segura and Bishop Mateo Múgica* of Vitoria* were removed from their sees and stripped of episcopal rank. The reason for this action, the government said, was that Segura had sent instructions to the Spanish bishops to sell church property and send the money out of Spain for fear of confiscation and/or nationalization. As proof, the government cited documents found on the vicar-general of Vitoria who was arrested in a border search at San Sebastián following a visit to Segura.

Segura protested, and government consultations with the papal *nuncio* followed. In October 1931, the Vatican* announced that Segura had resigned the see of Toledo. This resignation was undoubtedly forced upon Segura, partly to demonstrate the Vatican's avowed policy of moderation and partly as a concession of hope that the Constituent Cortes would reject the anticlerical provisions of the proposed Constitution. Segura settled into forced exile in Rome.

In 1937, following the death of Cardinal Ilundáin,* Segura was appointed archbishop of Seville, which had been in Nationalist hands since the early days of the Civil War. Segura had not signed the Bishops' Collective Letter supporting the military uprising (he was not occupying a see at the time, and it is uncertain anyway if he would have agreed with all of the letter's points), nor was he in particular a supporter of Franco.* He wanted a restoration of the monarchy; perhaps Franco's tacit approval of Segura's appointment may be seen as sop to the monarchists.

Segura soon showed himself to be a foe of the Falange* as well. When Falangists began a campaign after the war to paint the name of José Antonio Primo de Rivera* on the walls of every large church in Spain, Segura, alone among the episcopate, refused the use of the Seville Cathedral for this purpose: he had no more use for fascist ideas than for Republican ones. He also objected to the American bases agreement of 1953, by which U.S. armed forces were stationed in Spain; as an ideological opponent of religious toleration, he feared that American materialism and Protestantism would weaken the fabric of traditional Spanish society. He died in Madrid on April 8, 1957.

For further information, see Juan de Iturralde, *El catolicismo y la cruzada de Franco* (Vienna, 1955, 1960); Jesús Requejo San Román, *El cardenal Segura* (Toledo, 1932); and José M. Sánchez, *Reform and Reaction* (Chapel Hill, N.C., 1964).

José M. Sánchez

SERNA ESPINA, VICTOR DE LA (1896-1958). Serna, a journalist, was born in Valparaiso, Chile, although he was raised in Madrid.* Before the Civil War, he became a Falangist, wrote articles on the movement, and directed the publication of various periodicals such as *El Imparcial* and *La Libertad*. He gained a certain reputation within the Nationalist zone during war for publishing a laudatory piece entitled *Caminos del frente sobre las tierras de España y por la Fe*. After the war, he continued his career in journalism in Madrid.

For further information, see Círculo de Amigos de la Historia, *Diccionario biográfico español contemporaneo*, 3 vols. (Madrid, 1970), Vol. 3.

James W. Cortada

SERRA BARTOLOMÉ, MOISÉS (1878-1936). Serra, a colonel in the army, sided with the Nationalists.* He

commanded the Montaña Barracks* in Madrid* in July 1936 and refused to hand out weapons to the militias* of the *Unión General de Trabajadores* (UGT)* and the *Confederación Nacional del Trabajo* (CNT),* disobeying his instructions from the Ministry of War. His refusal initiated the rebellion in Madrid. Pro-Republicans* stormed the barracks during the night of July 19-20 and eventually overran it, killing many of the soldiers within, including Colonel Serra who had already been wounded earlier in the fighting.

For further information, see Maximiano García Venero, *Madrid, julio 1936* (Madrid, 1973).

James W. Cortada

SERRANO SUÑER, RAMÓN (1901-   ). Serrano Suñer had a wide range of contacts with various civilian right-wing leaders in Spain prior to 1936, and as Franco's* brother-in-law helped create a centralized, unified government in which he held several posts. Among these posts, the most important were minister of the interior (February 1938), minister of public order (1939), and foreign minister (October 1940 to September 1942).

As a law student at the Universidad Central where he received his degree in 1923, Serrano Suñer became friends with José Antonio Primo de Rivera,* and both worked with Catholic student associations. By 1933, Serrano Suñer was the leader of the *Juventud de Acción Popular* (JAP), the militant youth party of the *Confederación Española de Derechas Autónomas* (CEDA),* and part of the conservative *Acción Popular*.* As such, he associated not only with Gil Robles* but also with other right-wing leaders such as Antonio Goicoechea* and José Calvo Sotelo.* Elected to the Cortes* as a CEDA candidate from Saragossa* in 1933, he often represented right-wing coalition views and served as Franco's contact with many of these groups. His own political views made it difficult for him to affiliate completely with any established organization, for he felt that revolutionary syndicalism was superficial. He was not a monarchist, and he did not feel that military government could serve a lasting function in Spain. Instead, he advocated an authoritarian civilian regime constructed on a solid legal and juridical base, resting on organized popular corporatism to insure unity and stability. Often emotional and subjective, Serrano Suñer was also a clever politician and a shrewd manipulator of others.

Reelected to the Cortes in February 1936, Serrano Suñer was not intimately involved in the plans for the military uprising in July 1936. As a result, he was trapped in Madrid where he was arrested and imprisoned. Once again it was his contacts with influential leaders, both Spanish and foreign, that aided in arranging his "escape" from Madrid, and he eventually joined Franco in Salamanca* in February 1937.

During the confusing events in the months that followed, Serrano Suñer was extremely influential in Franco's development of a unified nationalist government, utilizing all of his old contacts with the Right to encourage a fusion of their forces with the new military authority. He helped draw up the April 19, 1937, decree which formally unified the parties of the Nationalist area. During the remainder of that year, as part of the directorate of the *Falange Española*,* Serrano Suñer spent most of his time negotiating with recalcitrant Falangists and disappointed monarchists in order to consolidate Franco's control. In January 1938, when a new national government was created to replace the *Junta Técnica*, Serrano Suñer was named minister of the interior, serving as vice-president of the *Junta Política*; he was also the vice-president of the National Council of the party. In both capacities, he continued to pursue his goals of centralization and his cooperation with his brother-in-law. Serrano Suñer never had a personal following. In fact, he was disliked and distrusted by many of the leaders of Nationalist Spain.

He was particularly criticized for his apparent pro-German sentiments. He traveled to both Germany* and Italy* in September 1940 and was named foreign minister on October 18 of that year. His policy was essentially that of cooperation with the fascist powers because he felt they would be victorious. In his famous *Entre Hendaya y Gibraltar* (published in 1947) and later in his *Memorias*, he insisted that his policy was one of expediency and that he was always a true Spanish nationalist and had simply followed Franco's lead. Nevertheless, he became an increasingly controversial figure, thus leading to Franco's decision to dismiss him from the government on September 2, 1942.

Serrano Suñer returned to private legal practice and thereafter had no formal political role in the state. He did, however, continue to express his concern for the development of a stable regime based on law as evidenced in his testimony in the Cortes relating to the Law of Succession (1947) and the Law on Reform of Local Administration (1955). Most of his later writings were attempts to dispel the image of personal opportunism, and pro-Axis, prowar sentiments with which he was associated.

For further information, see Angel Alcázar de Velasco, *Serrano Suñer en la Falange* (Madrid, 1941); Maximiano García Venero, *La Falange en la guerre de España: La unificación y Hedilla* (Paris, 1967); and

Serrano Suñer, *Entre Hendaya y Gibraltar* (Mexico City, 1947) and *Entre el silencio y la propaganda, la Historia como fue* (Paris, 1967).

Jane Slaughter

SERVICIO DE INFORMACIÓN DEL NORDESTE DE ESPAÑA (SIFNE).

The *Servicio de Información del Nordeste de España* (SIFNE), the major information-gathering unit for the Nationalists,* focused primarily on the northern Republican zone and events in foreign areas. When the Civil War began, General Mola* and the Conde de los Andes, a leading monarchist who helped create SIFNE, discussed the need for information on varied activities in the Republican zone. José Bertrán y Musitú, as head of the *Somatén* (militia police) in Barcelona,* already had extensive contacts in Catalonia* and was providing some information from that sector. In November 1936, a regular organization, the SIFNE, under Bertrán y Musitú was set up in the Grand Hotel in Biarritz. Its purpose was to provide information on any activity, internal or external, which might harm the state.

The agents collected reports on military, political, and economic affairs and had a network of contacts in Great Britain,* Holland,* Belgium,* France,* and the Republican zone, as well as cooperation with other information centers in Spain and the activities of frontline military intelligence. The SIFNE consisted of map, decoding, press, radio,* and statistical sections. Once information was received and clarified, it was forwarded to the Second Section of the *Estado Mayor del Cuartel General*. Included in the range of information reports were communications relating to troop movements, planned attacks, sabotage, effects of Nationalist bombardments and assaults, foreign aid to the Republicans,* nature of foreign investments in Spain, and transmission of gold from the Bank of Spain* to outside centers. In particular, the SIFNE provided rather detailed reports on the Republican plans for offensives at Belchite* (August-September 1937) and Teruel* in December of that year. Eventually, the SIFNE moved to Irún,* and with the establishment of a more rationalized Nationalist government, on February 28, 1938, a decree from Burgos* fused the SIFNE with the *Servicio de Información y Policía Militar* (SIPM)* established in November 1937, and thereafter the unit was headed by Colonel José Ungría.*

For further information, see José Bertrán y Musitú, *Experiencias de los servicios de información del nordeste de España durante la guerra* (Madrid, 1940);

and Hugh Thomas, *The Spanish Civil War* (London, 1977).

See also Espionage.

Jane Slaughter

SERVICIO DE INFORMACIÓN Y POLICÍA MILITAR (SIPM). The *Servicio de Información y Policía Militar* (SIPM) was the largest and most important intelligence agency of the Nationalists.* It was created in November 1937 by Colonel Jośe Ungría* to consolidate numerous other intelligence agencies, especially the *Servicio de Investigación Militar* (SIM).* Its mission was to gather political and military intelligence and to carry out counterintelligence activities. Spying in the Spanish Civil War was a major activity about which historians know very little. The SIPM, for example, employed nearly 30,000 people by the middle of 1938, while operating spy rings in major sectors of the Nationalist and Republican zones. Historians believe that over 100 people daily passed between Spain and France* gathering or delivering data to the SIPM.

For further information, see José Bertrán y Musitú, *Experiencias de los servicios de información del noreste de España durante la guerra* (Madrid, 1940); and J. M. Fontana, *Los Catalanes en la guerra de España* (Madrid, 1951).

See also Espionage; and *Servicio de Información del Nordeste de España* (SIFNE).

James W. Cortada

SERVICIO DE INVESTIGACIÓN MILITAR (SIM). The *Servicio de Investigación Militar* (SIM) was a Nationalist intelligence agency. At the outset of the Civil War, Nationalist leaders were interested in developing networks of political and military intelligence. For this purpose, sections of special services were created, using regimental, divisional, and National Army* structures, as well as the important *Servicio de Información del Nordeste de España* (SIFNE) located at Biarritz under José Bertrán y Musitú, an old minister of Alfonso XIII* and a friend of the Conde de los Andes.

The geographical center for information was in Burgos* at the *Oficina Central de los Servicios de Información*, staffed mostly by professional military who were too old for frontline duty. At this early stage, each army corps had a second section responsible for gathering military and political information. By the spring of 1937, as Franco* increasingly centralized the military and governmental structures for

Spain and unified the various right-wing political groups, he also felt it necessary to centralize the intelligence sections. He recognized that since events of the war were clearly affected by international affairs, it was necessary to expand the sort of information gathering done by the SIFNE.

Colonel Jose Ungría,* an old friend of Mola's* who had received training at the School of War in Paris and served as military attaché there before 1936, was named to head the unified SIM. A special counterespionage section had been added to the information services in January 1937, and Ungría's SIM, though continuing to use military categories and personnel for its information structure, was placed outside military jurisdiction. In November 1937, the more centralized and expanded service became known as the *Servicio de Información y Policía Militar* (SIPM),* and in February 1938 Bertrán y Musitú's SIFNE was merged with the central unit. By then, the service had some 30,000 people working for it and was involved in espionage,* counterespionage, as well as military intelligence.

For further information, see Armando Paz, *Los servicios de espionaje en la guerra civil española* (Madrid, 1976).

Jane Slaughter

SERVICIO NACIONAL DE REFORMA ECONÓMICO SOCIAL DE LA TIERRA (SNRET). The *Servicio Nacional de Reforma Económico Social de la Tierra* (SNRET) was established by the Nationalist government in April 1938 to control the growing and distribution of agricultural products. It issued regulations regarding the quantities to be produced, how it was to be sold, by whom, and at what prices. Its primary mission, however, was to introduce modern methods of production and to expand the use of irrigation to increase the amount of food* grown. The SNRET also had responsibility for determining who were the real owners of agricultural land, supposedly title-holders who had them expropriated by the Republic or agricultural collectives.

For further information, see Rafael Abella, *La vida cotidiana durante la guerra civil: La España Nacional* (Barcelona, 1973).

See also Agricultural Reform, Institute of.

James W. Cortada

SEVILLE. Seville, a province located in southern Spain in Andalusia,* quickly became a Nationalist stronghold. The provincial capital, also named Seville, became the most important Nationalist center in southern Spain. By the 1920s, this old city, once the gateway to the New World, had developed an active circle of anarchists* and by the mid-1930s, an equally energetic cell of Falangists. Seville, Spain's fourth largest city (population* 229,000 in 1931), thus had a dual tradition of conservative and leftist politics in modern Spanish affairs. On July 18, General Gonzalo Queipo de Llano* led the uprising in Seville against the Republic. With one small artillery barrage, he gained control of the inner city and soon after, larger portions after some fighting with workers loyal to the Republic. The general then got on the local radio* station, giving an enthusiastic speech to Andalusia on the Nationalist cause. Many historians believe that this presentation helped bring large sections of the south to Franco's side. In the months that followed, the general continually appeared on the radio giving speeches on the war, extolling the virtues of the Nationalists,* and criticizing the Republicans.* Meanwhile, he continued to expand his control over the entire province. First, he seized the suburbs of the capital city, which had remained in the hands of the working class. Next, he persecuted workers and others throughout the province perceived to be enemies of the Nationalists. The repression in Seville led to some 9,000 deaths, while other sources place the number as high 47,000 for the entire province. As late as 1939, an average of eighty individuals a day were being executed.

In the months that followed, the Nationalists extended their control over other portions of Andalusia. General Queipo de Llano daily spoke on Seville's radio, making him famous all over Spain. His speeches were harsh and biting, and boastful; yet, they were listened to at a time when he extended his personal control over large portions of Andalusia. Repression of the working classes proved extensive under his command, death becoming the common means of suppressing resistance to the Nationalists. The general used his newly acquired base of operations to receive and then transmit north Nationalist troops fighting toward Madrid.* Between July 29 and August 5, 1936, the German flew approximately 1,500 Nationalist soldiers into Seville from North Africa and subsequently an average of 500 daily. This force became Franco's Army of Africa* which marched northward to Madrid. The air field also became a base for airplanes bombing Republican areas in central Spain. On August 6, Franco arrived in Seville to take charge of the growing armed forces in the area. For the rest of the war, Seville simply supported the military ventures further north. Periodically, war came to the province when, for ex-

ample, Republican aircraft bombed Seville on October 29, 1936. Falangists and army officers dominated local politics, while all vestiges of Republican institutions vanished. By the middle of 1938, Queipo de Llano had to give up some of his absolute power in Seville, even stopping his daily 10:00 P.M. broadcasts.

For further information, see Antonio Bahamonde, *Un año con Queipo de Llano* (Barcelona, 1938); Guillermo Cabanellas, *La guerra de los mil días*, 2 vols. (Barcelona, 1973); Lawrence Dundas, *Behind the Spanish Mask* (London 1943), on Seville's radio and propaganda; and Luis Romero, *Tres días de julio* (Barcelona, 1972), on the first few days of the war.

James W. Cortada

SIERRA DE GUADARRAMA, BATTLE OF. The mountain complex known as the Sierra de Guadarrama, running from the northeast to the west of Madrid,* was strategic to the defense of the city as well as of the northern provinces held by the Nationalists* at the outset of the war. As a result, both sides rushed troops to the area in the first weeks of the war where a variety of conflicts occurred between July 22 and early August when the front was stabilized.

Of particular importance in the mountain range are the two passes, Somosierra (1454 metres) and Alto de León* (1511 metres). The first of these commands the Madrid-Burgos* highway, while the Madrid-Segovia-*Medina railway and the road to Valladolid* run through the second. The third major pass, Navacerrada, was considered of only subsidiary interest and thus was the site of only minor skirmishes, through Republicans* did dominate in this central zone.

It was at Somosierra and Alto de León between July 20 and July 22 that the first real conflicts of the Civil War occurred. Immediately after the uprising, militia units from Madrid were sent to secure the two passes, while from the north Falangist militia and *Requetés** volunteers* were sent from Burgos and Valladolid for the same purpose. As of July 19, a small Nationalist force held the Somosierra; Republican forces under the brothers Galán moved to the area, attacking on July 22. On July 23 Mola* sent, as reinforcements to the area, the column under Colonel García Escámez.* They counterattacked on July 25, taking Somosierra, and would have advanced on Madrid, but Mola called a halt as munitions and supplies were limited. Nationalist troops then took up defensive positions at the pass which, with the exception of a few minor encounters, could remain unchanged for the next two and a half years.

In the south and west at Alto de León, troops from

Madrid occupied the area, and on July 22 Falange* units from Valladolid and Segovia were sent to the sector where under the leadership of Colonel Ricardo Serrador Santés they attacked. Additional forces were sent to both sides as fighting intensified. On July 26, Mola sent General Miguel Ponte y Manso de Zúñiga to take command, with the result that he launched an offensive on August 5 that secured the area. The Republicans in the meantime had sent in a column under Julio Mangada* directed to move toward Ávila,* but which only reached Navalperal. In early August, defensive positions were also set up in this sector as the first phase of the conflict around Madrid came to a halt, overshadowed at that point by the advance from the south of the Nationalist Army of Africa.*

The opposing forces in the Guadarrama were about equal, although the Nationalist units were better organized and their actions more coordinated, while the Republicans had the advantage in artillery and air support. In the Guadarrama, certain leaders emerged who would continue to play important roles in the war, for example, Valetín González (El Campesino)* on the Republican side. The battle resulted in the creation of a line to the north and west of Madrid that would remain fairly stable for the duration of the war.

For further information, see Manuel Aznar, *Historia militar de la guerra de España* (Madrid, 1969), Vol. 1; and Rafael Cases de la Vega, *Las milicias nacionales en la guerra de España* (Madrid, 1974).

See also Appendix B.

Jane Slaughter

SOCIALISTA, EL (1885-1939). *El Socialista* was the official newspaper of the Spanish Socialist party* during the days of the Second Republic* and throughout the Civil War. It reflected the views of Indalecio Prieto,* head of the Socialist party, and thus remains a major source of information on Spanish socialism. In the early months of the war, this Madrid-based paper ran articles demanding that the Republic arm young socialists for the defense of the capital, bringing enormous pressure on the government to give up its monopoly on arms.

For further information, see Indalecio Prieto y Tuero, *De mi vida*, 2 vols. (Mexico, 1965-1970).

James W. Cortada

SOCIALIST PARTY, SPANISH. The Socialist party of Spain (*Partido Socialista Obrero Español*—PSUE) was the largest political grouping in Iberian politics just prior to the Civil War. This party, founded in 1879 as a reaction to the growth of anarchism and in support of Marxism,* remained a minor political movement in the years before World War I. The same observation could be made of its sister organization, the *Unión General de Trabajadores* (UGT).* The anarchists* dominated the large working-class politics of Barcelona,* while the UGT and the socialists cultivated followers and support primarily in Madrid,* the mining districts of Asturias,* and the industrial sectors of Bilbao.* A major figure of the Spanish Civil War, Francisco Largo Caballero,* took charge of the socialist union when, in 1925, its head, Pablo Iglesias, died. Largo Caballero was willing to work with existing political institutions in order to maintain control over the working-class politics of his party and union and always as a means of blocking the advance of anarchism among the Spanish proletariat. He was never a good speaker, an equally bad theoretician, but a stern practitioner of practical politics designed to help the lot of his workers and of the Socialist party when it represented them.

In April 1931, when the Second Republic* was established, his party had about 20,000 members while the UGT claimed nearly 300,000. Largo Caballero joined the first Republican cabinet along with his greatest rival within the Socialist party, Indalecio Prieto.* In contrast to Largo Caballero, Prieto spoke well, served in the Cortes,* and had a concern for theoretical issues. Throughout the 1930s, these two men competed for control over the socialists and dominance of their ideas. Prieto had a reputation of supporting the middle class and its intellectuals* while Largo Caballero supported the workers of his union. In 1931, Largo Caballero was sixty-two and Prieto forty-eight; thus, both men were of prime age at the start of the Civil War and in their period of greatest influence on Spanish history.

As minister of labor in the Republican government, Largo Caballero played a major role in formulating the Republic's agrarian policies and programs which called for the distribution of landownership to agricultural landless laborers. As a result of these and other efforts, the UGT and the Socialist party gained enormous support from agricultural laborers. By 1932, for instance, some 450,000 landless workers supported the socialists, far exceeding the support they gave to the anarchists. The net result was that the socialist movement no longer was simply an urban-based workers' movement since half its membership came from the agricultural sector. This enormous expansion of support caused the Socialist party to become the political giant of Spanish politics during most of the years immediately preceding the Civil War. Yet, the large influx of new members did not make political action necessarily easy.

The political Right resisted reforms and used the Republican political institutions (as established by the Constitution) to thwart socialist programs in 1933-1934, causing many of the new socialists (particularly the less disciplined agrarian sector) to shy away from the party's earlier enthusiastic support for constitutional efforts at reform. This situation made it possible, for example, for Largo Caballero to argue that if the legal tools available were of no use, then revolution would be necessary. Prieto, on the other hand, still sought to work within the existing political system. The divergence of views caused by these two leaders split the Socialist party significantly on all major issues by the start of the Civil War. Hence, the party contained reformists, Fabians, procommunists, revolutionaries, and parliamentarians united by only one fundamental issue: defeat of the political Right. And yet the party was no small institution because even with such splits within its ranks, it claimed to have 75,000 members on the eve of the Civil War which, when combined with the vast membership of the UGT, was significant.

A strong case could be argued that one of the reasons for the failure of the Second Republic to survive and avoid the conflict of civil war was the lack of support for its institutions by rival political groups from both the Left and Right. This charge of negative politics can also be leveled against the socialists as much as toward other parties. The splits within the socialist movement on how to resolve problems and establish policies, the rivalries among its leaders, and ultimately its rejection of existing institutions contributed to a growing national attitude of revolutionary change. Like groups on the right—such as the Carlists* and the Falangists—it even armed and trained paramilitary units in the months before the start of the war. At the same time, Largo Caballero injected such words as "revolution" and "change" into his speeches. The inability to provide a united front at most levels and to support existing institutions robbed the socialists of the discipline that subsequently made it possible for the better organized Communist party* to gain control over Republican affairs while signaling the decline in power and size of the socialist movement. Indeed, the political history of the Republic during the Civil War is a cantation of the decline of the socialists and the rise of the communists, with the resulting demise of the anarchists which neither group tolerated.

As a spot check on strengths on the eve of the Civil War, the elections of February 1936* offer evidence.

The socialists supported the Popular Front* which gained 34.3 percent of the vote, while the Right won 33.2 percent—a near split of the nation along two halves. Within the Cortes the political Left dominated with 263 seats to the National Front's* 133. On the Left the socialists had eighty-eight deputies, the Republican Left seventy-nine, the Republican Union thirty-four, and the communists only fourteen. Thus, one of the remarkable stories of the Civil War was the rapid rise of the Communist party which would dominate political affairs in Spain in the second half of 1937—hardly eighteen months later. From the elections in February to July, support for the Republic waned within the socialist camp much as it already had on the political Right. Largo Caballero, then infatuated with thoughts of being a "Spanish Lenin," talked about fundamental changes which Prieto countered with words of caution. Their growing split within the Socialist party now became clearly visible to the public, pushing forward a polarization within the party to the extent that by the time the Civil War came, politics could and did veer sharply to the Left in the heat of war. Such a development carried with it a significant portion of the socialist movement. Therefore, by May 1936, one could already read of various socialists using such phrases as "conquest of power by any means," "collective social and common property," and the "triumph of the proletariat." And the war had not even started yet!

The first step toward communist infiltration into the socialist camp came in June, just before the start of the war, when the youth movements of both parties were merged into one called the *Juventudes Socialistas Unificadas* (JSU)* which was ostensibly socialist but whose leaders were either communists or communist sympathizers. Prieto fumed, while Largo Caballero took less interest in this development. There was also talk of fusing both parties together in Madrid—all of which upset the political Right more, making an impending revolution from one side or the other increasingly probable.

With the outbreak of fighting in July, events exploded with a speed surprising to many politicians in all camps. The UGT quickly gained dominance over affairs in Madrid, while workers, primarily anarchist, did the same in Barcelona. The communists, better organized and led, expanded their influence within the UGT while propagandizing a moderate policy of cooperation within the Republican government and protection of property rights. The socialists, divided on all issues, hardly presented a unified front, let alone leadership, as a means of expanding their influence over events. Communist-socialist youth organizations spread their control over towns in central Spain while simultaneously executing suspected enemies. A similar effort was under way to marshal sufficient strength with which to curb the influence of the anarchists in Barcelona. This effort paid off in the spring of 1937 with the destruction of the anarchists' political power in street fighting.

In September, Largo Caballero became prime minister of the Republican government, with Prieto's support as the only option available at the moment. The communists were also brought into the government for the first time, clearly a recognition of their growing power and influence within socialist circles. Six socialists also entered the cabinet along with Prieto who now headed the Ministry of Navy and Air. Other socialists were given positions as subsecretaries and ambassadors. The objective was to form a coalition government to prosecute effectively the war against the rebel Nationalists.* This task proved difficult for both military and political reasons. The rivalry between Prieto and Largo Caballero was only momentarily sublimated, while the communists continued to expand their influence within the Republican zone. The anarchists sought their own power and proved difficult to work with at both the national and local levels. If anything, the Socialist party was now moving to the Left (indeed, it was being pushed leftward by its members and circumstance), while its leadership remained moderate, if not conservative. Worker or "proletarian" programs (such as libertarianism and collectivization in the economy) became popular. Anarchist and communist military units (such as the Fifth Regiment*) brought publicity and glory to more radical views than those expostulated by the leaders of the Socialist party. The political theme for Republican Spain from the summer of 1936 through the spring of 1937 was consequently political fragmentation at all levels. This situation stood in sharp contrast to the political actions within the enlarging Nationalist zone which tended toward centralization and unification. The communists, who at the moment were proponents of property and order, grew in strength during the fall and winter at the expense of all other Republican groups as they sapped the middle-class support of more traditional political parties. Even leading military officers, for instance, Hidalgo de Cisneros* and Pozas,* became communists. Socialists and other Republicans also lent their support or joined what appeared to be an efficient and moderate Communist party. The socialists thus "lost" their previous position of strength through their vague approach to problems and through internal splits on ideology, programs, and tactics. The result was easily evident, for communist strength grew sharply. By June 1937, its party (*Partido Comunista Española*, known as the PCE) claimed a membership of nearly 400,000, with some 64,000 in Catalonia,* the stronghold of the anarchists. In contrast, the Socialist party had a membership of only 160,000 and was outnumbered by the anarchists. Communist influence within the Republican Army* also grew; the party claimed a membership of some 130,000, or about one-third of all the men in arms. At the expense of the Republicans,* the communists tried to staff as many jobs within the Republican government as possible. This was yet another means of expanding their power to appoint other communists to positions of influence within both military and civilian organizations. Then came communist effort to purge from its movement those who did not fully support the party. Next the communists' political opponents in local governments were attacked. In Catalonia, this campaign resulted in the demise of the anarchists in the May 1937 riots* and the rapid expansion of communist power in northeastern Spain in the weeks that followed.

Concurrent with these developments were rivalries within the Socialist party. Prieto and such followers as Juan Negrín* sought to ally themselves with the communists in order to compromise Largo Caballero's power and ultimately either force him out of office or modify his views on how to conduct the war and reshape the economy. Hugh Thomas correctly charges that they disliked Largo Caballero's "policy of immoderate revolution" which was either confusing or ineffective. The communists had allies with liberals and seemed far more disciplined in their policies toward the war and politics in general. As a result of Prieto's cooperation with the communists, Largo Caballero's faction within the socialist party lost its influence over events.

By spring 1937, Largo Caballero had lost his control over the UGT, was being pushed out of the cabinet, and earlier had seen the youth movement become communist. With his decline came the decline of the Socialist party. In October 1937, as insurance that he would be completely crippled, the communists formed a new executive committee to run the UGT, finally denying Largo Caballero the support of old allies and the base of power that he had controlled for so many years. With that final act, his political career came to an end. Yet, his achievements and those of the socialists should not be overlooked. They managed to channel the energy of the revolution within Republican Spain into the institutions of the state, particularly in the confusing months immediately following the start of the Civil War. The power of the central government over local administrative bodies and worker committees, which did not exist for practical purposes during the summer of 1936, was reestablished by the following summer. But because Largo Caballero refused to work with the communists and finally resisted them, all his support drifted away until finally he was left alone with the anarchists who also resisted the Communist party—ironically, long the arch enemy of the Socialist party. After his fall from power in the summer of 1937, the political history of Republican Spain became that of communist rule.

That summer, the Communist party began to unify the Socialist party to itself. Negotiations continued as the Largo Caballero wing of the Socialist party was demolished. Nothing came of these talks, and so the communists began to win over members of the Prieto wing in the communists began to win over members of the Prieto wing in the fall and winter of 1938. Meanwhile, in early 1938, Prieto became overwhelmed with a pessimistic outlook on the prospects of winning the war. The Nationalists had continued to expand their control over central and northern Spain and were next trying to push eastward into Aragón* and would later march into Catalonia. Support for Prieto from within his own party eroded during the winter and came to a point of crisis during a meeting of the executive committee of the Socialist party in March 1938. The Communists were also working to squeeze him out of power, which he had indirectly inherited from Largo Caballero in 1937 as head of the Socialist party. He was then serving as minister of defense. In May 1937, Negrín, also a socialist and hostile to Largo Caballero, had become prime minister and by early 1938 had the support necessary to remove Prieto from a position of authority. With the reorganization of the Republican cabinet in April 1938, Prieto was left out of the government. Negrín, a moderate socialist, had worked well with the communists. He therefore retained the job of prime minister and acquired the portfolio of defense (Prieto's old job), positions he kept until the end of the Civil War.

In examining the causes of Republican failure to win the Civil War, historians have cited many factors. These have included the military prowess of the Nationalists, their political unity, the role of foreign governments on both sides, and the impact of economic institutions and conditions, as well as politics in general. In looking at the Republican zone, high on most historians' lists of causes of Republican failures has always been the political disunity which sapped the energy of so many people in political infighting. Besides leading to the deaths of many talented rivals, it caused administrative inefficiency, and confusion in plans and programs, and contributed to a sense of defeatism because of the appearance of confusion and the lack of leadership required in war. Discordant voices among too many political groups could hardly give direction to or confidence in the Republic's cause. Socialists fought among themselves and against anarchists and communists in the political arena along with the Nationalists on the battlefield. The Communist party, disciplined and supported by the USSR,* inevitably could not lose in its bid for political mastery over Republican affairs. The anarchists, by definition too split and eclectic, simply contributed to a patchwork of political intrigues that could hardly be expected to provide efficient leadership to a wartime government. Leaving aside political errors of judgment on the part of specific individuals, such as by Largo Caballero, some additional comments can be made about the socialists in general.

For one thing, too many diverse groups made up the party's membership, making it difficult for it to have unity in a nation not known for compromising. For too many years there were those who supported Largo Caballero and others Prieto. Radical and large groups of youth, intent on more revolutionary and activist politics than they felt the socialist leadership would provide, concluded that their future lay more with the communists who offered action. Others saw an equally bright future with the anarchists. In addition, as always personalities played too great a role in Spanish politics. Largo Caballero was an old trade unionist, Prieto was a Socialist Democrat, Julián Besteiro* flirted with Marxism and was too genteel, and Negrín was an administrator willing to work with the communists. It seemed that loyalties were given as much to a specific leader as to a particular party. The divergence of perspectives within the Socialist party, therefore, was too great for any one individual to overcome. No one person could provide the cohesive leadership and programs that all socialists could live with the support against the attacks of other political parties. In the end, the "might have beens" became speculations for historians as the reality of Nationalist victories on the battlefield made the role of the Socialist party in Spain a moot point for the next thirty-six years.

For further information, see Burnett Bolloten, *The Spanish Revolution: The Left and the Struggle for Power During the Civil War* (Chapel Hill, N.C., 1979); Edward Malefakis, *Indalecio Prieto: Discursos fundamentales* (Madrid, 1975); and Hugh Thomas, *The Spanish Civil War* (New York, 1977).

James W. Cortada

SOCORRO BLANCO. *Socorro Blanco* (White Aid) was an underground movement in the Republican zone formed to help those who felt their lives were in danger get out of Loyalist-held territory. It grew spontaneously with that purpose in mind, but by the middle of the Civil War it had also established a network of espionage* and participated in sabotage. It facilitated the movement of people into France,* issued false medical certificates to help other people avoid the Republican Army* draft, and even made it possible for some citizens to attend Mass.

For further information, see Rafael Abella, *La vida cotidiana durante la guerra civil: La España republicana* (Barcelona, 1975).

James W. Cortada

SOCORRO ROJO. *Soccoro Rojo* (Red Aid) was an underground, communist-dominated organization in the Nationalist zone that helped pro-Republicans* escape to Loyalist Spain. It undertook some espionage* activities, but often its members were caught and shot by the Nationalists.* Little else is known about its size or other activities.

For further information, see Rafael Abella, *La vida cotidiana durante la guerra civil: La España nacional* (Barcelona, 1973).

James W. Cortada

SOL, EL (1916-1937). *El Sol*, the major independent daily newspaper in Madrid,* continued publication in the early part of the Civil War. Founded in 1916, it quickly became the premier Madrid daily, without, however, achieving financial success. Although the paper had not championed the Republican cause before 1931, during the Republic, it usually supported Center to Left Republican politicians. During the early part of the war, *El Sol* lost readers to the more radical newspapers, and it ceased publication in 1937.

For further information, see Francisco Javier Fernández Lalcona, *El Sol: Diario Independente* (Madrid, 1968). Microfilmed copies of *El Sol* are available from the U.S. Library of Congress.

William J. Irwin

SOLANO PALACIO, FERNANDO. Solano was an anarchist leader in Asturias* during the early days of the Civil War before the Nationalists* conquered the area. His book on Asturias while in Republican hands is virtually the only contemporary account of life in a region cut off from the rest of Republican Spain.

For further information, see Fernando Solano Palacio, *La tragedia del norte* (Barcelona, 1938).

See also Santander.

James W. Cortada

SOLCHAGA ZALA, JOSÉ (1881-1953). Solchaga was a career army officer who served with the Nationalists* during the Civil War. This Navarrese began the war as a colonel, having once served in North Africa, and entertained conservative political views. In August 1936, he became a leading commander of Navarrese troops in the northern campaign. He commanded troops in the area throughout 1936 and 1937, and led the Nationalist forces that occupied Guernica* in the late spring of 1937. General Solchaga participated in the campaign for the capture of Vizcaya* and successfully went on to campaign in Asturias* in September-October 1937. He next took his Navarrese troops into battles in the Aragón* and the Levante.* His men recaptured Belchite* in March 1938, attacked Huesca,* and fought as far north as the Segre River near France.* This combat commander spent the bulk of 1937 with his Army of Navarre* fighting in the Pyrenees* and subsequently taking part in the Nationalist campaign in Catalonia* (December 1938-January 1939). He fought to the Llobregat River,* marching toward Barcelona,* and his troops were some of the first of the Nationalists to occupy the Catalan capital on January 26, 1939. He continued to push northward through Catalonia, seizing Gerona* on February 5, Figueras on February 8, and the next day the Spanish side of the French frontier. Franco* immediately sent this able general to the central zone where the last Republican units were fighting east of Toledo* to the Mediterranean. By the end of March, this Republican zone had ceased to exist, bringing the Spanish Civil War to an end.

For further information, see José Manuel Martínez Bande, *La campaña en Cataluña* (Barcelona, 1979), *El final del frente norte* (Madrid, 1972), *La guerra en el norte* (Madrid, 1969), and *Vizcaya* (Madrid, 1971).

James W. Cortada

SOLIDARIDAD OBRERA (1929-1939). *Solidaridad Obrera* was a leading newspaper of the anarchist movement of the 1930s. Under the direction of Angel Pestaña, it was outspoken in presenting libertarian views and enjoyed a wide circulation among the Left. Founded in 1907, by the time of the Civil War it was the most important anarchist publication in Spain, serving a constituency of over 200,000. During the first year of the war, expounded the political and economic philosophies of the anarchist movement and did not hesitate to be critical of either the socialists or the communists. After the decline of the anarchist movement, as a result of the May 1937 riots* in Barcelona, the paper's influence declined sharply. Eventually it was suppressed, the victim first of its stronger enemies— the communists and the socialists—and later of Franco's* armies.

For further information, see Robert Kern, *Red Years/Black Years: A Political History of the Spanish Anarchists, 1911-1937* (Philadelphia, 1978); and Hugh Thomas, *The Spanish Civil War* (New York, 1977).

See also Aragón; Barcelona; Catalonia; Communist Party, Spanish; Durruti, Buenaventura; and *Federación Anarquista Ibérica* (FAI).

James W. Cortada

SOLIDARIOS. The *Solidarios* terrorist group, best known as an anticipation of the *Federación Anarquista Ibérica* (FAI),* saw such young men as Buenaventura Durruti,* Francisco Ascaso,* and Juan García Oliver* join its ranks during its brief existence from 1920 to 1923. Its philosophy might loosely be called anarcho-Bolshevik, since the *Solidarios* celebrated the Russian Revolution and called for a centralized and permanent revolutionary cadre to provide leadership for a social revolution in Spain. Its newspaper, *Cristol*, bitterly attacked King Alfonso XIII,* calling him *el rey felon* and *el africano*, both of which were slurs on his involvement in the Moroccan war. The group assassinated eight or ten public figures, the most important being Juan Soldevila Romero, archbishop of Saragossa,* in 1923. The Primo de Rivera dictatorship jailed many of its members, while others fled to France.* In subsequent years, its membership became extremely important in the FAI.

For further information, see Robert Kern, *Red Years/Black Years: A Political History of the Spanish Anarchists, 1911-1937* (Philadelphia, 1978).

Robert W. Kern

SPERRLE, HUGO VON (1885-1953). Von Sperrle, born in Ludwigsburg, Germany,* was the first commander (November 1936-October 1937) of the German Condor Legion* in Spain. He entered the German military in 1903 as an ensign in the infantry. In 1914, he transferred to the air arm as an observer where he served throughout the Great War. He remained in the *Reichswehr* in the ground forces, but was also involved with the secret flying service. In 1934, he entered the Air Ministry, and in 1935 he was promoted to major general.

In Spain, von Sperrle was promoted to lieutenant general in April 1937. There he was frustrated with the poor and obsolete German equipment and operational procedures. He was also at great odds with the German ambassador and, at times, with both the Spanish and Italian commands. He was able to obtain some new and experimental equipment from Germany, which eventually helped shift air superiority to the Nationalists,* but he remained frustrated with the Spanish war. Both he and the Spaniards were relieved when he and the German ambassador were recalled to Berlin.

During World War II, he became one of the four *Luftwaffe* field marshals. He was placed on the reserve list in August 1944. He died in Munich in 1953.

For further information, see Werner Beumelburg, *Kampf um Spanien, Die Geschichte der Legion Condor* (Berlin, 1939); Manfred Merkes, *Die deutsche Politik gegenüber dem spanischen Bürgerkrieg, 1936-1939* (Bonn, 1961); and R. Hidalgo Salazar, *La Ayuda Alemana a España 1936-1939* (Madrid, 1975).

Raymond L. Proctor

STALIN, JOSEPH (1879-1953). Stalin took an active interest in the Spanish Civil War. In the early years of the conflict, he personally believed it was in Moscow's best interest not to allow the Spanish Communist party* to grow too quickly or too powerfully for fear of offending France* and Great Britain.* At that time Stalin was attempting to establish an alliance with London and Paris directed against Hitler's* Germany,* which he perceived to be the USSR's* primary enemy. As it became clearer that the British and the French would not stand up to Hitler, Stalin determined that he would have a freer hand in Spain with the Germans as his only major adversary there. Hence, in the early years of the conflict, he instructed the Communist party to appeal to the middle classes of Republican Spain. He sent advisers and military supplies, yet not in the quantities that Germany and Italy* did to Franco.* He wanted to keep the Civil War continuing so that he could use the instability of the area to pressure Western Europe* in one direction or in another. Thus, he believed in helping the Spanish Republic sufficiently so as not to see it defeated but not so much that the Nationa ists* would lose. When by mid-1937 it appeared that the Nationalists were doing well, he escalated Soviet influence in Spain.

At the same time, Stalin wanted to make the most of his help. He charged the Republic for supplies shipped. His government convinced the Republic to deposit the national gold reserves on account in the Soviet Union for purchases of supplies. He sent advisers to Spain to expand the influence of the Communist party within the Republic. Stalin personally did not want to see the Republic end the war too quickly because that would have meant an ongoing commitment of military supplies which he needed in Eastern Europe for the day when Hitler would turn on the Soviet Union. By the time the Civil War ended, Hitler was already moving eastward and in September attacked Poland,* a major step toward a direct hit at the Soviet Union.

For further information, see Burnett Bolloten, *The Spanish Revolution: The Left and the Struggle for Power During the Civil War* (Chapel Hill, N.C., 1979); and Angel Viñas, *El oro de Moscú* (Madrid, 1979).

See also Bank of Spain.

James W. Cortada

STEVENSON, RALPH (1895-   ). Stevenson, the British consul in Barcelona* during the Civil War, reported to London on Republican politics and conditions, and evacuated British citizens when necessary. In the last days of the war, in early February 1939, the Negrín* government came to Stevenson to explore the possibility of a negotiated peace with the Nationalists.* Before any work could be done on the proposal, however, the war had ended.

For further information, see Jill Edwards, *The British Government and the Spanish Civil War, 1936-1939* (London, 1979); and K. W. Watkins, *Britain Divided* (London, 1963).

See also Great Britain.

James W. Cortada

STOHRER, EBERHARD VON (1883-1944). Baron von Stohrer was the German ambassador to Franco* from 1938 to 1942. A career diplomat, he had served in Madrid* at the German Embassy during World War I, working against the Allies in the Iberian Peninsula. He knew Spain well, spoke Spanish, and proved partially effective in dealing with Spanish officials. He believed in increasing German influence in Nationalist Spain by a program of expanded German financial interests in Spain agriculture and mining properties. Franco resisted these efforts with considerable success. Simultaneously, he argued with Berlin that additional German aid would be necessary for him to win the war. Periodically throughout 1937 and 1938, the German ambassador had small quarrels with the Spanish government as he sought concessions in the local economy and protected the interests of the Condor Legion.* After the Munich Conference*

in September 1938, he suggested that Franco consider a mediated peace settlement in Spain. Franco rejected the idea.

Toward the end of the Civil War, von Stohrer negotiated a five-year treaty of peace and friendship with Nationalist Spain, signed on March 31, 1939. This treaty became the basis for a great deal of German-Spanish diplomacy and trade during World War II.

For further information, see Charles W. Burdick, *Germany's Military Strategy and Spain in World War II* (Syracuse, N.Y., 1968); Ramón Hidalgo Salazar, *Ayuda Alemana a España, 1936-1939* (Barcelona, 1975); and Manfred Merkes, *Die deutsche Politik gegenüber dem spanischen Bürgerkrieg, 1936-1939* (Bonn, 1961).

See also Germany.

James W. Cortada

SUANZES, JUAN ANTONIO (1891-   ). Suanzes, born in El Ferrol* in 1891, joined the army in 1912. In 1917, he became a naval engineer for Great Britain's* Vickers Armstrong at its Spanish branch, *Constructora Naval*, with the shipyards in El Ferrol. He quit the firm in 1934 over a dispute with the British management and began to work for a Swiss elevator firm in Madrid,* where he lived at the outbreak of the Civil War.

Despite the fact that the British Embassy saved his life and helped smuggle him to Nationalist territory in March 1937, Suanzes remained hostile to British interests and became a proponent of an autarkic economic policy. He visited Italy* in 1937 to inspect naval facilities and was made Franco's first minister of industry and commerce in January 1938. Naval Captain Suanzes, a personal friend of Franco* since childhood, became more interested in building a great Spanish Navy* than in reconstructing his war-torn country. In September 1938, he proposed an ambitious project to construct four battleships, twelve cruisers, and sixty destroyers, in a ten-year program that would require mostly Italian, but also some German, aid. At this time, throughout 1938 Suanzes resisted the demands of Bernhardt* of the *Compañía Hispano-Marroquí de Transportes* (HISMA)* for acquiring more mineral rights in Spain to pay for increased German economic and military aid.

In March 1939, Suanzes invited a German economic delegation to come to Spain for comprehensive postwar negotiations. Meanwhile, through Juan March* he he sought credits from Belgium,* France,* Great Britain,* and the United States.* Although Suanzes wanted Bernhardt's monopoly rights in foreign trade* (the (the HISMA-*Rohstoffe-und-Waren-Einkaufsgesellschaft*

[ROWAK] system) curtailed, other Germans involved in the Four-Year Plan regarded him as a man of talent.

To Britain's joy, Franco relieved Suanzes of his post in August 1939. He nevertheless returned as director of a government-sponsored corporation, the *Instituto Nacional de Industria* (INI) in 1941.

For further information, see Arthur P. Whitaker, *Spain and the Defense of the West* (New York, 1961).

See also Economy, Nationalist; and Trade, International.

Robert H. Whealey

SUBMARINES, FOREIGN. Foreign submarines waged clandestine war on behalf of the Nationalists.* With none of the twelve Spanish submarines in their hands, Nationalist naval officers solicited the cession of services of foreign submarines. From November 8, 1936, pairs of Italian submarines under severe restrictions stalked Republican and Soviet ships, the *Torricelli* damaging the cruiser *Miguel de Cervantes** on November 22. Two German submarines similarly patrolled from November 30 to December 12, the *U-34* sinking the submarine *C-3* on December 12. Germany* withdrew from clandestine submarine warfare, leaving Italy* to furnish submarine patrols from December 13, 1936, accounting for only two freighters by March 1937. On April 17, Italy ceded the submarines *Torricelli* and *Archimede* (*General Sanjurjo* and *General Mola* under the Nationalist flag), which sank four merchantmen by the end of July. Submarines had yet to stop a Soviet arms shipment, and on August 7, Mussolini* agreed to wage large-scale submarine warfare under looser instructions, employing fifty-two submarines. Four merchant ships were sunk: two Spanish vessels with military cargos, one loaded British tanker, and one Soviet freighter with an undetermined cargo. One Republican destroyer was damaged. Strong international reaction (the Nyon Conference)* forced Mussolini* to require stringent restrictions once more. Italian submarines continued to patrol from September 17, 1937, with minimal success until February 5, 1938, when clandestine submarine operations finally terminated. In all, fifty-eight Italian submarines completed ninety-one missions, launched seventy-one torpedoes, obtained hits on fifteen vessels, and sank six.

For further information, see John F. Coverdale, *Italian Intervention in the Spanish Civil War* (Princeton, N.J., 1975).

See also Navy, Italian.

Willard C. Frank, Jr.

SWITZERLAND. Switzerland maintained strict neutrality* on the question of the Spanish Civil War. It was the only European country that did not belong to the Non-Intervention Committee* because membership would have violated Swiss laws on international commitments. Switzerland, however, was the home of the League of Nations,* where some of the most heated international debates on the Civil War were held. It was also at Nyon, Switzerland, in September 1937 that the major powers in the West discussed the destruction of ships in the Mediterranean.

For further information, see Dante Puzzo, *Spain and the Great Powers, 1936-1941* (New York, 1962); and Max Wullschleger, *Schweizer Kämpfen in Spanien* (Zurich, 1939).

See also Nyon Conference.

James W. Cortada

SYNDICALISTS. The syndicalists subscribed to a political philosophy which called for the means of production to be in the hands of the labor unions. This philosophy was popular among trade unionists in Spain and in other parts of Europe.* Syndicalists rejected conventional political behavior, preferring industrial action such as shop floor strikes to make their points known. In Spain, a strong strain of Bakuninist anarchism prevailed in the Republican zone among all the labor and anarchist groups. Anarchism and its variety, syndical-anarchism, were byproducts of the syndicalist tradition of nineteenth-century European labor unionism, especially that of France,* Italy,* and Spain. Manifestations of this philosophy included such diverse groups as the *Federación Anarquista Ibérica* (FAI),* the *Confederación Nacional del Trabajo* (CNT),* the *Unión General de Trabajadores* (UGT),* and the various anarchist splinter groups. Barcelona* remained the stronghold for syndicalists throughout the Civil War. Most of its leaders, politics, militias,* and programs came from this city.

For further information, see Burnett Bolloten, *The Spanish Revolution: The Left and the Struggle for Power During the Civil War* (Chapel Hill N.C., 1979); James Joll, *The Anarchists* (London, 1964); Robert W. Kern, *Red Years/Black Years: A Political History of Spanish Anarchism, 1911-1937* (Philadelphia, 1978); José Peirats, *La CNT en la revolución española*, 3 vols. (Toulouse, 1951-1953); and Josep Termes, *Anarquismo y sindicalismo en España* (Barcelona, 1972).

See also Libertarian Movement.

James W. Cortada

T

TAGÜEÑA LACORTE, MANUEL (1913-1971).
Tagüeña was a communist who became a corps commander before the age of thirty. Before the Civil War he was a socialist, becoming a communist only in November 1936. He had no prior military experience before 1936, but after the war started, he fought in the Sierra de Guadarrama* in July, at the Tagus River* in September, in and around Madrid,* the next month and commanded a Mixed Brigade* during the winter. In mid-1938, he received command of the 15th Corps in the newly created Army of the Ebro,* which sought to divert Nationalist attention away from Valencia* and thereby save it. He performed his duties well at the battle of the Ebro* during July-November 1938, which resulted in some Republican successes. After the war, Tagüeña went to Mexico* where he remained until his death in 1971.

For further information, see Luis María Mezquida, *La batalla del Ebro*, 2 vols. (Tarragona, 1963); and Manuel Tagüeña, *Testimonio de dos guerras* (Mexico, 1973).

James W. Cortada

TAGUS RIVER. The Tagus River runs horizontally between Portugal* to the eastern half of Spain through Toledo.* Throughout the Civil War, it became a mode of transportation and the scene of much fighting. An important battle named after the river took place at the town of Talavera de la Reina,* west of Madrid,* in mid-September 1936. Nationalist forces drove away Republican military units, thereby placing western Spain under Franco's* control. The siege of the Alcázar* also took place on the banks of the Tagus River that same month. The Tagus Valley became a battleground that fall and again the Nationalists* were able to drive off the Republican militia units sent out to protect Madrid. Toledo fell to the Nationalists on September 28, 1936, while the Republicans* bought time to regroup for a stronger defense of Madrid.

For further information, see Robert Colodny, *The Struggle for Madrid* (New York, 1958); Cecil Eby, *The Siege of the Alcázar* (London, 1966); and José

Manuel Martínez Bande, *La lucha en torno a Madrid* (Madrid, 1968) and his *La marcha sobre Madrid* (Madrid, 1968).

James W. Cortada

TALAVERA DE LA REINA. Talavera de la Reina, a town on the Tagus River* in the province of Toledo,* was the scene of several battles during the Civil War. The Nationalist offensives toward Madrid* several times brought Franco's* troops into contact with Republican units in the area. The most important of these clashes came in September 1936 and on September 3, the Nationalists* occupied it. Talavera was the last important town between Franco's army and Madrid. Later that month, Franco occupied Toledo.

For further information, see José Manuel Martínez Bande, *La Lucha en torno a Madrid* (Madrid, 1968).

James W. Cortada

TARRADELLAS, JUAN JOSÉ (1900?-). Tarradellas was a Catalan politician and one of the principal leaders of the Esquerra* party. On September 27, 1936, he joined the Generalitat* as the prime minister of the Catalan government. He maintained strained relations with the government in Madrid* which he accused of not helping the Catalans in the war effort. He also chaired the Catalan War Industries Committee which worked throughout 1936 and 1937 to mobilize local industrial power for the production of military supplies. For instance, by mid-1937, Catalan factories were producing a half million rifle bullets daily. After the May 1937 riots,* the Generalitat* reorganized itself under the direction of the Republican government, and again Tarradellas became prime minister and councillor of finance. This time, however, the cabinet was more conservative with no anarchists* in it. After 1939 he went into exile. He did not return to Spain until 1977, becoming the first president of the Generalitat to serve after Franco's death. During his long years in exile, he acted as the head of the defunct Generalitat.

Throughout the Civil War, Tarradellas strove to

maintain a working relationship with the various political factions in the Catalan government in order not to allow the Spanish Republic to encroach on Catalonia's* autonomy. He always sought to manipulate the politically less sophisticated *Confederación Nacional del Trabajo* (CNT)* and the *Federación Anarquista Ibérica* (FAI),* always distrusting the anarchists. Tarradellas thought that the anarchists' political immaturity would eventually lead to their collapse as a force in Catalan politics. He defended them from the communists in order to retain their support, since he believed they would ultimately fade away while the communists would not. Both he and President Companys* fought to prevent local authority from being given up to the Spanish Republic. In dealing with both the anarchists and Madrid, he enjoyed successes and failures. The anarchists destroyed themselves as a result of the riots in May. The communists, however, expanded their control over Republican politics. As a result of the internal civil war between leftists in Barcelona* in May 1937, Catalan autonomy declined rapidly in the remaining period of the Spanish Civil War. Hence, by the time Tarradellas left Spain, Catalan autonomy had become a fiction.

For further information, see Burnett Bolloten, *The Spanish Revolution: The Left and the Struggle for Power During the Civil War* (Chapel Hill, N.C., 1979); Josep María Bricall, *Política económica de la Generalidad* (Barcelona, 1970); and Carlos Pi Sunyer, *La república y la guerra* (Mexico, 1975).

James W. Cortada

TARRAGONA. Tarragona, one of the four Catalan provinces in northeastern Spain situated below Barcelona* along the Mediterranean coast, remained under Republican control for the majority of the Civil War. Anarchists* were responsible for burning many churches in the province, although they spared the cathedral in the city of Tarragona. Hundreds of priests, monks, and nuns, as well as the local bishop, were killed. The archibishop-cardinal of Tarragona was saved from a similar fate only by the intervention of President Companys.*

Many of the political activities evident in Barcelona could be seen in Tarragona. For instance, in May 1937, anarchists fought in the streets much as they did in Barcelona, and over forty were killed before Republican forces restored order. It also became the scene of considerable fighting, especially toward the end of the Civil War. The Nationalists* decided, in December 1938, to push from central Spain directly to the sea, thereby cutting the Republican zone into

two pieces—the area around Madrid* and Catalonia.* Franco's* forces initiated their successful campaign in December and moved eastward from a line running north from Tortosa up through Lérida* onward to the French border in a three-pronged march by way of Gerona,* Barcelona, and Tarragona. Tarragona was captured on January 17, Barcelona on January 26, and Gerona on February 7, 1939. In Tarragona, the Nationalists reestablished the Catholic Church* and arrested or executed Republican officials and sympathizers.

For further information, see José Peirats, *Los anarquistas en la crisis política española* (Buenos Aires, 1964); and José Manuel Martínez Bande, *Los cien últimos días de la república* (Barcelona, 1972).

James W. Cortada

TAXES. *See* Bank of Spain; Economy, Nationalist; Economy, Republican; Finance, Nationalist; and Finance, Republican.

TEACHERS. The 51,000 public primary school teachers in Spain in 1936 were inexorably drawn into the Civil War. The conflict gave full vent to the animosities and tensions that had been building up over public education* since the late nineteenth century. As a result, many teachers suffered the effects of violence and reprisals. As individuals, teachers fought on both sides as militiamen, but the professional teachers' associations gave more direct support to the Republicans* than to the Nationalists.*

The majority of Spain's primary school teachers served in villages and small towns. There, as salaried employees of the state, they were one of the few government officials people knew. All too often in these rural areas, teachers became the focus of local discontent with government actions, especially the secularization of education carried out by the Republic. In the opening months of the war, teachers of both conservative and liberal views suffered for their beliefs.

Primary school teachers found representation for their professional and political concerns in five associations. Of these five, only the two leftist unions organized militia units that fought for the Republic. The 4,500-member *La Federación Española de Trabajadores de la Enseñanza* (Spanish Federation of Workers in Education, FETE), which was affiliated with *Union General de Trabajadores* (UGT),* had an especially active military contingent. They had a separate company in the Levante* and proved to be energetic and trainable as soldiers. The Union of Educators and Liberal Professions, the other leftist association, represented teachers with anarchist sympathies and was affiliated with the anarchist union, the *Confederación Nacional del Trabajo* (CNT).* Its membership rose to about 1,000 during the war. Most of its teacher recruits were from private schools in Catalonia,* which had long experience with anarchist education.

The educational reform carried out by these two teacher unions was a notable contribution to the Republic in the first year of the war. Typical of the actions taken was the reorganization of public primary education in Catalonia. The governing body of the province, the Generalitat,* issued a decree on July 27, 1936, establishing *El Comité de la Escuela Nueva Unificada* (Committee of the New Unified School) (CENU); its twelve members represented the FETE, the Union of Educators and Liberal Professions, and the Generalitat. Their goal was ambitious and reflected the social reformism that swept Barcelona* in the first ten months of the Civil War: they were to provide classrooms for 70,000 children in Barcelona who lacked schools and to prepare each child for the trade, career, or profession best suited to his or her ability.

The two largest associations—*La Asociación Nacional de Maestros* (National Association of Teachers) (ANM) and *La Confederación Nacional de Maestros* (National Confederation of Teachers) (CNM)—took no formal and organized part in the war. However, the sympathies of the leadership were clearly with the Republic. The only pro-Nationalist teacher group was the smallest one—*La Federación Católica de Maestros* (Federation of Catholic Teachers) (FCM). It allied with Franco's* movement, and two of its leaders became important in the field of education during the Franco period: Alfonso Iniesta Corredor, the educational historian, and Víctor García Hoz, director for over twenty-five years of the pedagogic institute that is part of the state-sponsored system of the *Consejo Superior de Investigaciones Científicas* (Superior Council of Scientific Investigation) (CSIC).

The Nationalists' intention to reorganize totally the teaching profession was first expressed in an order in November 1936. The principal agent of the restructuring of the personnel in the primary schools was the Purifier Commissions (*Las Comisiones Depuradoras*), set up in the areas which Franco's forces captured during the war. These commissions began a systematic and ruthless purging of teachers that lasted until 1943. An elaborate screening for religious orthodoxy and patriotism was applied to teachers to remove anyone who had belonged to FETE, a Popular Front* party, or had abetted the Republicans* during the war. As a consequence of this ideological dragnet, numerous teacher were dismissed and a great many

others were imprisoned. Thousands of teachers also went into exile.

The primary schools were initially staffed under Franco by those former students who, undergoing their teacher training during the Republic, received the endorsement of military, civil, and ecclesiastical leaders in 1939. Many more teachers, however, were recruited from the ranks of former soldiers in the Nationalist Army.* In many cases, their professional training was limited to a series of brief courses on pedagogy and the role of religion and patriotism in the curricula. The teacher associations were suppressed and replaced in 1942 by the *Servicio Español del Magisterio* (SEM) in the course of the creation of the corporatist political order instituted by Franco.

For further information, see David V. Holtby, "Society and Primary Schools in Spain, 1898-1936," Ph.D. diss. (University Microfilms, 1978).

David V. Holtby

TECHNOLOGY. As in all wars, Spain's peacetime innovations were applied to wartime needs. Through the radio,* the uprising was announced to the entire peninsula in mid-July 1936. The Republicans* attempted to play down the seriousness of the fighting, while the Nationalists* broadcast their exploits from different points in Spain, thereby helping to spark revolt in sectors of the peninsula that might not otherwise have participated. Throughout the war the radio station in Seville* was a propaganda tool for the Nationalists, while putting fear into the hearts of those Spaniards living in central Spain's Republican zone. The radio made a hero out of General Gonzalo Queipo de Llano* and allowed the Catalans to force the Nationalists to concede defeat in Barcelona.* Without the radio it would have been difficult, if not impossible, for generals to coordinate the activities of large armies in short periods of time.

Telephone service also influenced the outcome of the war. For example, the Republicans used the telephone to try and convince the Nationalists in the Alcázar* to surrender in September 1936. It was used to link the rebellion in the north to that in the south. The communist occupation of the telephone building in May 1937 became the spark that set off the May 1937 riots* in Barcelona, resulting in the collapse of the Spanish anarchist movement and the assertion of communist and Republican control over Catalonia.* Telephone service, along with telegraphic communications, allowed foreign reporters to tell the world quickly about events in Spain, making the conflict a central event in European affairs.

In no European war was the use of trucks and automobiles so important. Taxis became a popular way of taking political adversaries to certain execution at the edge of many towns. García Lorca* went to his death in a Buick, while thousands of others died under similar circumstances. Trucks carried the Republic's gold reserves for shipment to the USSR,* while others took supplies and troops quickly from one battle zone to another.

The greatest application of advanced technology was in armament. Germany* in particular, but also the Soviet Union, tested out new aircraft and military tactics in Spain while training their pilots* under combat conditions. New forms of machineguns and hand grenades were tested and used alongside every form of existing weaponry available in Europe. Some dated back to the mid-nineteenth century. Units in the Republican Army* often fought side by side with different rifles and varying calibre ammunition. Various aircraft bombers and fighters were employed, and some air units were outfitted with a variety of different planes and brands of bombs.

Manufacturing facilities were converted to wartime needs. In Barcelona, a factory that once made lipstick containers now produced bullets, and plants that had manufactured trams built tanks. Sewing factories that used to make clothes now made covers for cannon and uniforms. Thus, the manufacturing capabilities of Catalonia and the Basque country were almost entirely converted over to producing supplies to outfit armies. They often employed women for the first time since most men were already under arms. Managers who had run factories in peacetime were required to use these same skills for war manufacturing, regardless of whether the factories in question were nationalized or collectivized, privately owned or partially destroyed.

With regard to medical technology, doctors developed new methods for dealing with broken limbs, thereby reducing the number of amputations and mortalities. The introduction of new pain killers and medication that forecast the role of antibiotics in later decades was common. X-ray machines for the first time became a widely used tool of combat doctors. Hospitals appeared in unusual places as, for example, in the subway tunnels of Barcelona and Madrid, and in factories.

Both events and political views were communicated through the use of movies. Newsreels graphically told the story of Spain to the world, while both sides prepared movies that explained their points of view. Propaganda therefore took on a new dimension which, with the radio, no longer limited itself to the medium of the printed word or the spoken speech. Typewriters,

which had been so rare during World War I, had become a vital tool for most reporters.

For further information, see Ronald Fraser, *The Blood of Spain* (New York, 1979); Salvador Rello, *La aviación en la guerra de España*, 4 vols. (Madrid, 1969-1971); Hugh Thomas, *The Spanish Civil War* (New York, 1977); and José Trueta, *Treatment of War Wounds and Fractures* (London, 1939).

James W. Cortada

TELECOMMUNICATIONS, SPANISH. At the beginning of the war, telephone and telegraph communications, like radio,* favored the Republicans,* but throughout Spain they were extremely unreliable. General Miguel Cabanellas,* as head of the provisional Nationalist government, complained in mid-September 1936 to the *Commission Internationale des Postes, Télégraphes et Téléphones* in Berne that communications had not yet been reestablished to connect Nationalist territory with the rest of Europe.* From June 1937, the Nationalists* controlled the three principal Spanish centers; in Vigo,* Málaga* (Italcable), and Bilbao* (Eastern Cable). The complaint of Luis Bolín,* the Nationalist press chief, that correspondents on the Nationalist side could rarely transmit their dispatches to their home office in time to appear in the next edition or to compete in the race to press with journalists on the Republican side therefore has no substance. Besides, Bolín made the situation worse by expelling a large number of journalists. Telecommunications throughout Spain did not recover their prewar service levels until the Civil War had been over for more than a year.

For further information, see Hugh Thomas, *The Spanish Civil War* (New York, 1977).

David Wingeate Pike

TELLA, HELI ROLANDO (1888-). Tella was a Nationalist Army* officer with combat experience in North Africa. In the early days of the Civil War, Colonel Tella commanded troops in Nationalist operations in southern Spain and led some of the troops that crossed over from North Africa in July 1936. He occupied land and towns in Andalusia* throughout that summer, fighting nearly daily with Republican militias.* He next fought in the battles around Madrid* in the fall and winter of 1936. He continued to command troops at Madrid throughout 1937 and 1938.

For further information, see José Manuel Martínez Bande, *La marcha sobre Madrid* (Madrid, 1968).

James W. Cortada

TERRORISM. Terrorism affected every town, city, and province in Spain, touching all political parties and all social classes. It sprang from almost every armed group in the nation and became a weapon for the elimination of enemies on either side. Terrorism sometimes led Spanish society to the edge of complete anarchy and indiscriminate violence. In the first few months of the Civil War, for example, it reigned in Barcelona* and Madrid* as various Republican factions rooted out Nationalist sympathizers and suspected enemies. Throughout the war, it intimidated large groups of people, settled old personal quarrels, and expanded authoritarian control over an area. Its effects were particularly felt in civilian zones where the fear of war, sabotage, and conflicting political forces threatened to burst into violence.

Several conditions made terror an ongoing concern of all Spaniards. First, no one really knew the facts about any situation. People worried about the results of local military campaigns, the policy of their police* forces, the date of a person's execution after trial, the fate of relatives and friends, the activities of political rivals. Second, denouncing people was often sufficient to insure arrest and execution. Thus, people never knew if they were in trouble. They would attempt to lead normal lives in the hopes of not arousing any suspicion, or they turned in someone, expecting to be left alone by the powers they helped. Everyone saw the bodies of people murdered in the night and knew of atrocities. The pornography of war was becoming the normalcy of routine. Each village experienced a range of terror, from minor vendettas all the way to mass executions as, for example, in Badajoz.* Stories of women raped, children killed, priests crucified, prisoners* burned to death, of people mutilated or tortured—all created a sense of terror which repetition never dulled.

Third, acts of violence throughout the war continued a pattern that had developed during the days of the Republic. For example, anarchists* in Barcelona (often members of the *Federación Anarquista Ibérica* [FAI]*) fought communists, and they blew each others' headquarters up, killing members. In the early months of the war, Republican officials were especially concerned about proletariat militias* which would pick up suspected enemies and take them for "rides" at night into the countryside where they would be executed and their bodies be left on the side of roads.

Later, the courts on both sides summarily supported their respective government's policies of repression, adding to the profound sense of insecurity. In one extreme case, fear of arrest and execution led Manuel Cortes to remain hidden in a closet in his home until the twilight years of the Franco* regime.

Historians have recognized that, along with the dangers of actual warfare and the frustrations caused by long periods of inadequate food* supplies, terrorism bore heavily on Spain's wartime population.* The hatred associated with it was visible decades after the war ended.

For further information, see Rafael Abella, *La vida cotidiana durante la guerra civil: La España nacional* (Barcelona, 1973) and *La vida cotidiana durante la guerra civil: La España republicana* (Barcelona, 1975); Ronald Fraser, *The Blood of Spain* (New York, 1979) and *In Hiding, The Life of Manuel Cortes* (London, 1972); and Antonio Montero, *La persecución religiosa en España* (Madrid, 1961).

See also Daily Life, Nationalist Zone; and Daily Life, Republican Zone.

James W. Cortada

TERUEL. Teruel, an area located in southern Aragón,* was the site of one of the major battles of the Spanish Civil War. It was fought between December 1937 and February 1938, and was another victory for the Nationalists.* The province of Teruel was a poor agricultural area before the war, with a smaller population than that in many of its surrounding provinces. Yet, it quickly became a major point of contention between both sides because it was a buffer between central Spain and the eastern portion of the Republican zones of the Levante* and Catalonia.* By the end of July 1936, the northwestern portion of the province, including the city of Teruel, was in Nationalist hands, while the eastern and southern portions remained loyal to the Republicans* or at least was under their control. The provincial capital was won by a Nationalist officer and seven men without a fight in the first days of the rebellion. But the division of the province early in the war insured that it would have one of the main battlefronts as the Nationalists worked their way northward through central Spain and later toward Catalonia and southward to the Mediterranean coast. Behind the lines, each side arrested and usually executed people suspected of being disloyal to their cause as each side attempted to solidify its control over the area. This was much the same pattern of behavior evident in such divided areas as Córdoba* and Badajoz.*

Once the Nationalists captured Asturias,* they again

turned southward toward Madrid* in late 1937. The Republicans, hoping to draw Franco's* attention elsewhere, launched an offensive on the city of Teruel with an army of about 100,000 men on December 15, 1937. Seizing areas in and around the city would have shortened communication lines between central Spain and Aragón while forcing the Nationalists away from northeastern Republican territory and, of course, away from Madrid. Teruel was reputed to be the coldest spot in Spain. The battle began with snow falling and lasted two months with subzero weather on many days and invariably with snow deep on the ground. By Christmas, however, the Republicans had penetrated the city of 20,000 inhabitants. Franco launched a counterattack on December 29. Temperatures were well below zero causing widespread frostbite among the Nationalist troops. Still the Nationalists advanced toward the city, bombarding it with artillery by January 1, 1938. Meanwhile, fighting in the city between Republicans and pro-Nationalists proved bloody and extremely damaging to the buildings in the town. In-town fighting took place during blizzards which prevented much movement on the part of either army poised outside Teruel. The pro-Nationalists in the city were soon overrun, now leaving the Republicans besieged, and the Nationalist forces continued to shell the town.

Troops under the command of Generals Antonio Aranda* and José Enrique Varela* had fought in southern Spain over the preceding eighteen months. They now pushed forward while on January 19, the International Brigades* joined in the fighting on the side of the Republicans. By February 7, combat in and around Teruel cost the Republic some 500 square miles of land, the loss of about 7,000 men as prisoners,* and an additional 15,000 in dead and wounded, not to mention substantial amounts of war material. Yet, the fighting continued. Nationalist forces encircled the town, and by February 20, Franco's men were entering portions of Teruel. The Republicans were by now in a full retreat, and losing more men; some 14,500 Republicans became prisoners of the Nationalists at Teruel.

The number of casualties* remains in dispute. It appears that Franco's losses were about 14,000 dead, another 16,000 wounded, and an additional 17,000 ill. Republican casualties, for which we have less accurate figures, appear to have been at least 50 percent greater in each category.

As a Nationalist victory, the battle of Teruel gave yet another moral boost to Franco's side which quickly began their campaigns in Aragón and the Levante in March. General Franco went eastward toward the Mediterranean, cutting Catalonia off from central Spain. The battle also gained additional Italian support for the Nationalists as confidence in Franco's ability to win the war increased. Finally, the battle further eroded the Republican will to fight and caused many outside of Spain to question the Republic's ability to win the war.

The battle of Teruel followed an all too familiar pattern evident at Brunete* and Belchite* in which the Republicans launched the offensive, won some early victories, were pushed back by the Nationalists, and finally suffered major defeats. As was true of other Republican losses in the spring of 1938, the Nationalists were able to expand their control over additional portions of central and eastern Spain.

For further information, see R. Casas de la Vega, *Teruel* (Madrid, 1975); Carlos Llorens Castillo, *La Guerra en Valencia y en el frente de Teruel* (Valencia, 1978); José Manual Martínez Bande, *La batalla de Teruel* (Madrid, 1974); and Hugh Thomas, *The Spanish Civil War* (New York, 1977).

James W. Cortada

TETUÁN. Tetuán, a city in northwestern Morocco,* is situated in the valley of the Martín River, 10 kilometers west of the Mediterranean coast and 35 kilometers south of the Straits of Gibraltar.* Occupied by the Spanish Army in February 1913, it became the capital of Spain's Moroccan Protectorate and the residence of both the high commissioner—the supreme Spanish authority in the protectorate—and the caliph, the representative of the Moroccan sultan. In 1930, the population* was estimated to be 34,700. At the beginning of the Civil War, Tetuán was Franco's* temporary headquarters until he followed the Army of Africa* to the peninsula on August 6, 1936.

For further information, see Mohammed Daud, *Síntesis de la historia de Tetuán* (Tetuán, 1955).
See also Melilla; and Morocco, Spanish.

Shannon E. Fleming

THAELMANN BATTALION. The Thaelmann Battalion was part of the International Brigades* and fought with the Republicans* in the Civil War. The unit consisted mainly of German and some British communists and was formed by Ernst Thaelmann in 1936. It first saw combat in the battles of Madrid* in November 1936 and was in the center of the fighting at the University of Madrid, Boadilla,* and other engagements in and around the capital. The battalion experienced hand-to-hand combat at various points and suffered enormous casualties* in each action. The Nationalists* virtually destroyed this unit on January 6, 1937, in fighting near the town of Las Rozas northeast of Madrid. In March, however, the battalion scored an important victory against Italian troops in the battle of Guadalajara.* By the early part of 1938, the work of all the International Brigades was over, and later that year the Thaelmann Battalion was disbanded.

For further information, see Gustave Regler, *The Owl of Minerva* (London, 1959); and Ludwig Renn, *Der Spanische Krieg* (Berlin, 1955).

James W. Cortada

THIRTEEN POINTS. The Thirteen Points were enunciated by Prime Minister Juan Negrín* on May 1, 1938, as a statement of the Republicans'* goals. Negrín intended to counter recent laws passed by the Nationalists,* canceling reforms made by the Republic in 1931 and in 1936, to rally support for a specific program, and to persuade the Western powers that his views were similar to theirs and thus define their stake in his government's fate. Some of the points included freedom of foreign domination, freedom of religion, civil rights, political liberty, protection of Spanish and foreign property, and general amnesty. However, international support for Negrín did not materialize, the Thirteen Points having little effect on any nation's attitudes.

For further information, see Burnett Bolloten, *The Spanish Revolution: The Left and the Struggle for Power During the Civil War* (Chapel Hill, N.C., 1979).

James W. Cortada

TOGLIATTI, PALMIRO (1893-1964). Togliatti, a leading Italian communist before the Spanish Civil War, was an important figure in the Comintern by July 1936. When the fighting broke out in Spain, he was in Moscow and advised Stalin* to support the Spanish Republic with arms and foreign aid.* He immediately went to the West after discussing the Spanish situation with Stalin. He worked out of Paris rallying support for the government in Madrid* within European communist circles. Using his influence and power, he raised money for the Republic from Comintern and trade-union sources, and established a mechanism for funneling men and supplies to the Republican zone.

Togliatti may have visited Spain during the winter of 1936-1937 and clearly was the Comintern's representative in Spain by June 1937. As a major international communist leader, he advised and persuaded the Spanish Communist party* to support Soviet aims in Spain, and he increased his influence over Republican affairs as the fortunes of the Spanish Communist party improved. In May 1937, the *Partido Obrero de Unificación Marxista* (POUM)* and other elements hostile to the Communist party suffered a setback as a result of the May riots* in Barcelona.* Togliatti pushed to eliminate from government those who were critical of the communists, including Indalecio Prieto,* minister of defense, after a series of Republican military defeats threatened the Republic's cause. He pushed for the promotion of communist officers into the general ranks and by the spring of 1938 was urging Juan Negrín* to assume nearly dictatorial powers in his zone. He continued to urge resistance to Franco* until the final days of the Civil War, despite momentary negotiations, and then fought against Colonel Casado* in Madrid. He finally left Spain in March 1939, urging other communists to do the same before the Nationalists killed them. By that point he was, for all practical purposes, head of the Spanish Communist party. After World War II, he served in the same capacity in Italy.*

For further information, see Burnett Bolloten, *The Spanish Revolution: The Left and the Struggle for Power During the Civil War* (Chapel Hill, N.C., 1979); and Hugh Thomas, *The Spanish Civil War* (New York, 1977).

James W. Cortada

TOLEDO. Toledo, a city and province located just south of Madrid,* was the scene of heavy fighting during the early days of the Civil War. The Nationalists,* seeking to take Madrid from the south, battled northward through the province of Toledo, ultimately occupying the city in September 1936. After arresting or executing pro-Republicans,* the city became a Nationalist stronghold and base of operations for the lengthy assault on Madrid. This effort continued until nearly the end of the war. It was at Toledo also that the Alcázar* was located, the scene of a heroic defense by pro-Nationalists against the Republican Army,* Civil Guard,* and militia units in the early fall of 1936. Its defense and relief by the Nationalists made for one of the great heroic episodes of the war. However, military historians believe that the capture of Toledo and the relief of the Alcázar cost Franco* the opportunity to seize Madrid since his campaigns in Toledo bought the Republicans time to regroup for the defense of the capital.

For further information, see Cecil D. Eby, *The Siege of the Alcázar* (London, 1966); and José Manuel Martínez

Bande, *La lucha en torno a Madrid* (Madrid, 1968) and *La marcha sobre Madrid* (Madrid, 1968).

See also Army, Nationalist.

James W. Cortada

TOMÁS ÁLVAREZ, BELARMINO (1887-1950). Tomás was born and raised in Asturias* and became a socialist in the years preceding the Civil War, active politically in his region and a leader in the Asturian revolt of October 1934. At the same time, he was a deputy in the Cortes* but nonetheless went to jail for his role in the revolt. In July 1936, he sided with the Republicans* against the Nationalists* and became the governor of Asturias. Under his rule, based primarily on the support of the local miners, Tomás proved vain and a poor administrator. In October 1937, when the entire area came under Nationalist control, Tomás fled Spain by ship. He had meanwhile become a member of the executive committee of the *Unión General de Trabajadores* (UGT)* as a pro-Largo Caballero* politician and thus came back into the Republican government. This anticommunist next became the commissar of air in the government in 1938, one of the few noncommunist members of the war apparatus.

For further information, see José Manuel Martínez Bande, *La guerra en el norte* (Madrid, 1969); and Fernando Solano Palacio, *La tragedia del norte* (Barcelona, 1938).

James W. Cortada

TRADE, INTERNATIONAL. From World War I to the Spanish Civil War, Spain generally had an unfavorable balance of trade. Machinery, tin, petroleum, rubber, jute, cotton, and palm oil were among the necessary imports. The price of practically everything which Spain imported or exported was controlled in New York, London, and Paris. These included even such particularly Spanish exports as cork and mercury.

In 1935, Great Britain* bought over one-fifth of Spain's total exports, being the number one market for Spanish pyrites (imported by the chemical industry), iron ore, wine, and produce. Until 1934, France* was the second largest market for Spanish exports, especially wine, lead, pyrites, and Canary Islands* bananas. Germany* surpassed France in 1935 as a market for Spanish exports as the Nazis' financial policies brought an early recovery from the Depression.

Spain bought more from the United States* than from any other country—mostly wheat, cotton, and oil. Germany was the second largest source of Spain's imports, accounting especially for chemicals and electric appliance purchases.

The prolonged Civil War split Spain's productive base into two parts. Exports provided an important supplement of foreign exchange to both sides for cash purchases abroad of war-related goods. Tight controls regulated foreign trade* on both sides as they sought to maximize cash for needed purchases.

The Left held Spain's major orange- and rice-producing regions. Catalan textile mills were converted to war production, and surplus textiles were exported to the USSR.* By 1938, the Republicans* had little else to sell except mercury and oranges. Food* had to be imported to feed Republicans and city dwellers.

The coal fields of Austrias* and the iron mines of Vizcaya* perhaps were decisive in the struggle for economic control of Spain. During the first year of war, they were under Republican control, but after their conquest by Franco* in mid-1937, the ores and heavy machine industries of Vizcaya contributed to his cause.

The Right, deprived of city markets, had a surplus of wheat, olive oil, pyrites, bananas, and tomatoes to export. Moroccan iron ore and plywood, and chocolate from the African colonies, were also sources of foreign exchange for the Nationalists.* The ship that transported the first German aviation unit to Spain in August 1936 returned with copper ore from Huelva province. Johannes Bernhardt,* who pursuaded Hitler* to provide German aid to Franco, developed the *Compañía Hispano-Marroquí de Transportes* (HISMA)* (later *Sociedad Financiera Industrial, Ltd.* and better known as SOFINDUS) into fourteen companies monopolizing German trade with Spain. The state company, *Rohstaffe-und-Waran-Einkaufsgesellschaft* (ROWAK) increased Germany's share of Spanish exports from iron ore, pyrites, wool, and skins from 35 percent in 1935 to 80 percent in 1939.

The Nationalist Army* sacrificed everything for the war effort. The strictly regulated exports provided foreign exchange for Nicolás Franco's procurement office at the vice-presidency in Burgos* in the first half of the war. After the formal organization of the Nationalist cabinet in February 1938, the rationing of foreign purchases was placed in the hands of the *Jefetura Nacional de Adquisisiones* (JNA) headed by Colonel Francisco Moreno Calderón.

Oil, essential to operating modern war machines, had to be imported by both sides. The approximately $20 million worth of petroleum sold by Texaco, Shell, Standard, and Atlantic companies on credit was of great importance to the Nationalist victory because Germany and Italy,* from whom the rebels obtained most of their military supplies, produced no oil. The Republicans bought Soviet oil with gold.

The oil monopoly sales company, *Compañia Arrendataria del Monopolio de Petróleos, S.A.* (CAMPSA),* founded in 1927, was split in two by the Civil War. The Loyalist company expanded into a general state-operated export-import company, CAMPSA-Gentibus. Eventually, it employed 2,000 people and had offices in Barcelona* and Paris, operating a state purchasing office somewhat parallel to the HISMA-JNA system of the Nationalists. CAMPSA-Gentibus worked closely with Mid-Atlantic Shipping Company of London, the Hanover Sales Company in New York, and the Soviet-controlled *Banque Commercial pour l'Europe du Nord* in Paris. Although the Republicans were viewed with suspicion by the U.S. National Foreign Trade Council, which wanted payment for goods seized early in the Civil War by workers' committees, arrangements were made for purchases of goods such as U.S. trucks through Hanover in 1938.

A prime factor contributing to Franco's victory was that he won the foreign exchange war. The military forced exports into German, Italian, British, and American channels. But the Republicans supplied their army on gold and silver deposited in Moscow and Paris, while cannibalizing prewar machinery built up in Barcelona, Madrid,* and Valencia.* Franco's capitalist friends also received more international credit and support than the Popular Front.*

After the Nationalist victory in April 1939, a key question for Spanish foreign trade was how to pay off sizable war and prewar commercial debts. Before this question could be resolved, World War II intervened. Nationalist politics added to Spain's slow recovery because in June 1939, thinking that fascism was the wave of the future, Franco adopted Hitler's and Mussolini's* principle of "autarky," or national self-sufficiency in economics, a policy that prevailed for the next twenty years in one form or another.

For further information, see Jill Edwards, *The British Government and the Spanish Civil War, 1936-1939* (London, 1979); Glenn T. Harper, *German Economic Policy in Spain* (The Hague, 1967); Angel Viñas, *El Oro de Moscú* (Barcelona, 1979); and Robert H. Whealey, "How Franco Financed His War, Reconsidered," *Journal of Contemporary History* 12 (January 1977):133-52.

See also Bank of Spain; Economy, Nationalist; Monetary Policy, Nationalist; and Peseta, Nationalist and Republican.

Robert H. Whealey

TRADE UNIONS. Trade unions emerged as a result of the growth of the proletariat class in Spain during the late nineteenth and early twentieth centuries. By World War I, two major organizations dominated working-class unionism in Spain: the *Unión General de Trabajadores* (UGT),* which was conservatively Marxist, and the *Confederación Nacional del Trabajo* (CNT),* which was Bakuninist in philosophy. These two groups represented the largest labor organizations in Spain with membership in the tens of thousands. Most of them came from the industrial sections of the Basque country and Catalonia,* although considerable numbers of followers lived in other parts of Spain. During the early to mid-1930s, these unions fought hard for workers' rights and became involved in politics, often supporting socialist or anarchist political movements. At the start of the Civil War, the majority of the trade unions overwhelmingly defended the Republic. Members of trade unions in Nationalist zones were subjected to arrest and often execution.

Trade unions were extremely active in the Republican zones. Member of the CNT and UGT, for example, participated in local governments and in the various cabinets of the Generalitat* in Catalonia.* In Barcelona,* during the first several months of the war, they were in fact the government of the city, despite the existence of legally constituted authorities. They took the initiative in collectivizing industries and individual factories, all governed by committees made up of workers. They established Popular Tribunals* to prosecute their class and political enemies. Trade unions recruited militias* and later raised volunteers* for Republican armies. They became intertwined in more traditional political groups such as the anarchists* and socialists, thereby participating in national politics. These unions were often powerful enough to act almost independently of the Republic as, for example, in Asturias* and for a while in Barcelona.

State control over union activities, production, and plant management increasingly came under the control of state agencies. A similar process took place in the Nationalist zone as Franco* developed a more efficient form of government by 1938 to manage the economy. In the Nationalist zone, following theories of syndicalist economics, vertical syndicates were established by industry groups under the control of the government in which workers could not strike and where working conditions and compensation were established, in effect, by the state and not by workers or factory owners. A series of syndicates were established by industry types such as the *Servicio Nacional del Trigo* (SNT) for wheat, the *Servicio Nacional de Reforma Económica Social de la Tierra* (SNRET), others for textiles, clothing, food,* consumer goods, and mining.

For further information, see Diego Abad de Santillan, *Contribución a la historia del movimineto obrero español,* 2 vols. (Mexico, 1962); Robert W. Kern, *Red Years/Black Years: A Political History of Spanish Anarchism, 1911-1937* (Philadelphia, 1978); José Peirats, *La CNT—la revolución española,* 3 vols. (Toulouse, 1951-1953); and Albert Pérez Baró, *Trenta mesos de colectivisme a Catalunya* (Barcelona, 1974).

See also Libertarian Movement; and Workers, Catalan.

James W. Cortada

TRONCOSO, JULIÁN. Troncoso was the Nationalist military governor of Irún* during the Civil War. As the chief military official in the area, he was responsible for preventing Republicans* from escaping into France,* particularly during 1937 when the Nationalists* were expanding their control throughout the North. He was also a point of contact between Franco's* unrecognized government at Burgos* and the diplomats of France* and Great Britain* on the other side of the Franco-Spanish border.

For further information, see Hugh Thomas, *The Spanish Civil War* (New York, 1977).

See also Refugees, Republican.

James W. Cortada

TROTSKY, LEON (1879-1940). Trotsky's analysis of the Spanish conflict may be viewed as an extension of his theory of the permanent revolution. The class struggle knows no national frontiers, although its manifestations vary from one country to another. The revolutionary élan of the working class to overthrow bourgeois capitalism and replace it with the dictatorship of the proletariat is international in character. Trotsky viewed the Stalinist doctrine of "socialism in one country" as a betrayal of the revolution, and the crushing defeats of the communist parties in China, Germany,* and Austria confirmed his interpretation. The creation of the Fourth International (Bolshevik-Leninist) in the 1930s was intended to provide a truly revolutionary alternative to the Stalinist directives, to counteract the rapid advance of reactionary forces in Europe,* and to further the conquest of power by the proletariat.

Trotsky's hostility to Stalin's* divergence from the principles of Lenin was intensified when, at the Seventh Congress in 1935, the Comintern approved and advocated the coalition of working-class and bourgeois parties against fascism. In Trotsky's view, this attempt to reconcile deep-seated (and basically irreconcilable) class antagonisms was misguided, opportunist, and dangerous. The electoral triumphs of Popular Front* governments in both Spain and France* the following year did nothing to make him change his mind. Frequently drawing an analogy with the mistaken Menchevik theory of two independent revolutions, the one democratic, the other communist, Trotsky denounced the Popular Front strategy as a cowardly capitulation before the forces of reaction. Power-sharing by leaders of working-class parties with their hereditary enemies was predicated upon compromises and half-measures that merely bolstered the bourgeois state, and often weakened the resolve of revolutionary movements. Furthermore, Trotsky argued, by frustrating the upper bourgeoisie, it served to provoke the fascist coup d'état. Maintaining that both democracy and fascism were forms of bourgeois capitalism, he concluded that in the event of a Popular Front victory in Spain, neither the proletariat nor the peasantry would make substantial gains. The defense of democracy deluded the Spanish workers into thinking that their sacrifices would result in tangible gains. In actual fact, it served and strengthened the interests of Franco.*

In addition to condemning the Spanish Popular Front for its policy of class collaboration, Trotsky proposed a revolutionary program that provided a real alternative. Rather than advocating military victory, followed by social reform, as Stalin had done, he urged the immediate expropriation of the landowners, the abolition of private property, and collectivization of the land, as a means of obtaining military victory. The liquidation of semifeudal ownership would transform the peasantry into a bulwark against Franco's forces. The immediate implementation of radical agrarian reform was crucial to Trotsky's policy of involving the peasantry, as well as the proletariat, in a united struggle against both liberal democracy and fascism. According to Trotsky's analysis, had such a program been realized during the early days of the Civil War, it would have consolidated those gains won by the masses, particularly in and around Barcelona,* where factories had been occupied and collectives established. The gradual return to middle-class normalcy in a matter of months was the inevitable result of an unpardonable error of judgment and tactics for which Trotsky held the working-class leadership responsible. Though equally critical of anarchist participation in the Popular Front alliance, Trotsky was particularly forthright in his condemnation of the one party that was, in his eyes, most guilty of betrayal, the *Partido Obrero de Unificación Marxista* (POUM).* In that the POUM, a fusion of the *Izquierda Comunista,* an oppositionist party supportive of Trotsky, and Maurín's*

Bloque Obrero y Campesino represented the far Left of the political spectrum, it had the greatest potential for bringing about revolutionary change, and it also bore the greatest responsibility for failure to do so.

The POUM had in fact signed the Popular Front pact, and Maurín, its only deputy, had voted for Prime Minister Azaña.* It had also joined the Catalan Generalitat,* until ousted from it in December 1936. Trotsky approved of POUM participation in the militias* and in the military struggle against fascism, but he denounced its conciliatory policy of cooperating with a capitalist government instead of taking arms against it. He condemned the POUM leaders, especially Andrés Nin* (a former personal secretary), for their inability to express the revolutionary aspirations of the workers, and he accused them of being a step behind those whom they were supposed to lead. Trotsky's writings on the Spanish conflict offer further evidence of his conviction that, without effective leadership, revolutionary action could not be productive.

Trotsky's persistently sharp attacks upon POUM policies are proof that he did not consider it to be a truly revolutionary party, let alone a Trotskyist organization. Such a distinction was irrelevant to Stalin who lumped together all unorthodox left-wing groups into a monolithic opposition. This was indiscriminately labeled Trotskyist, an epithet that was rapidly amalgamated with fascist. The Moscow trials, which had begun in the summer of 1936, shortly after the outbreak of the Civil War in Spain, dramatized Stalin's determination to annihilate his political foes, the most dangerous of whom was undoubtedly Trotsky. These trials must also be seen as an attempt to stifle the voice of the nascent Fourth International, the Trotskyist counteroffensive to the Third International.

When the Non-Intervention Agreement deprived the Spanish Republic of the possibility of legitimately acquiring a means of self-defense in France and Great Britain,* it became increasingly dependent upon the USSR* as the principal provider of military support. An inevitable consequence of this was the increase in Soviet influence and interference in Spanish affairs. The most blatant example of Stalinist sway was what has been euphemistically labeled the "street-fighting" of May 1937* in Barcelona, in which the POUM, the *Federación Anarquista Ibérica* (FAI),* and the remnants of the Trotskyist movement were virtually eliminated. The suppression of the noncommunist opposition of the Left was followed by a change of government, with socialist Largo Caballero* replaced by Negrín* as prime minister. That change provided Trotsky with further evidence of the essentially counterrevolutionary character of the Popular Front alliance.

Trotsky's unrelenting and well-documented indictment of the Popular Front and Stalin's policies in Spain, his prophecy that such an alliance would inevitably culminate in a disaster, and his proposal that an agrarian revolution during the war would guarantee victory must be carefully considered by historians attempting to explain the collapse of the Second Republic.* His interpretation provides a challenging alternative to the views of those who have regarded the Spanish conflict from either an international or a military/technical point of view.

For further information, see Leon Trotsky, *La Révolution espagnole (1930-1940)*, Textes recueillis, présentés et annotés par Pierre Broué (Paris, 1975); and *The Spanish Revolution (1931-39)*, Introduction by Les Evans (New York, 1973).

See also Communist Party, Spanish; and Marxism.

Robert S. Thornberry

TRUBIA ARMS FACTORY. The Trubia Arms Factory was located in the province of Oviedo.* During the early days of the Civil War, Republican labor militias* seized the plant which they operated twenty-four hours a day to supply the Republic. It was one of three arms factories remaining in the Republican zone. In the fall of 1937, the Nationalists* occupied the province and seized this arms plant.

For further information, see José Manuel Martínez Bande, *El final del frente norte* (Madrid, 1972).

James W. Cortada

TRUETA, JOSEP (1897-). Trueta was a medical doctor who developed a number of procedures to treat combat-related wounds. At the start of the Civil War, he was the chief surgeon at the General Hospital of Barcelona.* This Catalan doctor developed new methods for treating fractures through immediate surgery, as well as alternative techniques for stitching wounds, and he advanced the use of plaster of Paris to protect wounds and broken bones. He advocated the use of combat doctors who worked in the field rather than back at the hospitals. With this change alone, he was able to provide more immediate medical attention to wounded soldiers. In order to support such medical care, he also developed better methods for the transportation, preservation, and use of blood in the field, working closely with Dr. Juan Duràn-Jordà and others. Trueta also gave up changing dressings on wounds daily (the common practice up to that time), thereby saving the lives of numerous patients who now avoided slipping into shock, experiencing additional pain, or developing infections. Although other Republican doctors initially opposed his procedures, most Republican armies eventually made use of them.

After the Civil War, Trueta accepted the position of professor of orthopaedic surgery and traumatology at Oxford University. Many of his methods were adopted by all the armies of Western Europe* and by the United States* during World War II.

For further information, see Josep Trueta, *The Atlas of Traumatic Surgery* (Oxford, 1947); *The Principles and Practice of War Surgery* (London, 1943); *Treatment of War Wounds and Fractures* (London, 1939); and *Trueta: Surgeon in War and Peace* (London, 1980).

See also Medicine.

James W. Cortada

23 MARCH DIVISION. The 23 March Division, an Italian army unit, fought in Spain on Franco's* side. It was named for the date on which the Italian fascist movement was founded in 1919. This divison fought in several of the campaigns of 1937, notably in Santander* in August.

For further information, see John F. Coverdale, *Italian Intervention in the Spanish Civil War* (Princeton, N. J., 1975)

James W. Cortada

U

UBIETA, LUIS GONZÁLEZ DE (1899-1961?). Ubieta, born on November 18, 1899 in León,* was a career naval office in the service of the Republic. He commanded the survey ship *Artabro* in Cartagena* in July 1936. In early weeks of the war, Ubieta commanded the destroyer *Sánchez Barcaíztegui* and the cruiser *Miguel de Cervantes** when torpedoed in November 1936. He was the Republican naval chief of staff from December 1936 until he relieved Miguel Buiza* as fleet commander in November 1937. He led the Republican fleet in the battle of Cape Palos* in March 1938. Ubieta did much to reestablish discipline in the navy, but his Soviet advisers criticized him for unaggressive leadership. Relieved by Buiza in January 1939, Ubieta became commander of Minorca* and negotiated its surrender in February. Throughout the war, he retained his permanent rank of lieutenant commander, although he exercised the duties of a vice-admiral, Spain's highest naval rank. Ubieta was killed in a shipwreck at Barranquilla, Colombia, in 1961(?).

See also Navy, Spanish.

Willard C. Frank, Jr.

UGT. *See Unión General de Trabajadores (UGT).*

UNAMUNO JUGO, MIGUEL DE (1864-1936). Unamuno, a philosopher and one of Spain's greatest modern writers, was born in Bilbao.* He was also a member of the "Generation of '98," a professor, and, at the start of the Civil War, rector of the University of Salamanca. At first, he favored the Nationalists,* for he found much fault in the Republicans'* cause. He questioned their anticlerical positions and the benefits of agrarian and economic reforms; he felt the Republic was as inefficient as its predecessors. Almost from the beginning of the war, his university was located in Nationalist territory. By October 1936, however, Unamuno became concerned about both the spiritual and physical effects of the fighting on the national well-being. On October 12, the holiday "Day of the Race," which celebrated the discovery of the New World by Columbus, a ceremony was held at the university. Among the attending dignitaries was General Millán Astray,* the one-eyed, one-armed founder of the Spanish Foreign Legion.* After several excited speeches in favor of the Nationalist cause, followed by the general who inspired cheers from the crowd in support of Nationalist Spain, Unamuno, who disliked the officer, delivered a speech in which he said, "A cripple who lacks the spiritual greatness of a Cervantes is wont to seek ominous relief in causing mutilation around him." Millán Astray jumped up and shouted, "Death to Intellectuals" and "Long Live Death," causing an uproar in the audience. Unamuno chastised the general and his followers, and for a moment it appeared that some of the legionnaires might kill him. General Franco's* wife, who was present at the session, went up to the rector and graciously escorted him out of the hall and thereby probably saved his life. He never spoke in public again, remaining under house arrest, and he died only two months later, on December 31, 1936.

For further information, see Cyril Connolly, *The Golden Horizon* (London, 1953); Emilio Salcedo, *Vida de don Miguel* (Madrid, 1964); and Hugh Thomas, *The Spanish Civil War* (New York, 1977). (Salcedo and Thomas contain the best accounts of the October 1936 incident.)

See also Intellectuals.

James W. Cortada

UNGRÍA JIMÉNEZ, JOSÉ (1890-1968). Ungría was Franco's* chief of intelligence activities from 1937 onward. In November 1937, he merged the *Servicio de Investigación Militar* (SIM)* and all other military and civilian intelligence and counterintelligence investigative bodies into one coordinated unit called the *Servicio de Información y Policía Militar* (SIPM)* which by early 1938 employed around 30,000 individuals. He managed SIPM efficiently, providing the Nationalists* with a considerable amount of information on the Republicans'* activities. SIPM became the basis of Franco's* post-Civil War national intelligence apparatus.

For further information, see Hugh Thomas, *The Spanish Civil War* (New York, 1977).

See also Espionage.

James W. Cortada

UNIÓN GENERAL DE TRABAJADORES (UGT).

As the second largest union federation in Spain and the main expression of socialist activity, the *Unión General de Trabajadores* (UGT) played a major but controversial role throughout the Spanish Civil War, with different factions becoming allies of the anarcho-syndicalist *Confederación Nacional del Trabajo* (CNT)* or the communist-dominated Negrín* cabinet of 1937 and 1938. The feuds and factions developed by the UGT leaders such as Francisco Largo Caballero* and Indalecio Prieto* cast a cloud over Loyalist politics and complicated the Republic's defense against Franco.* Yet, the socialists and their unions provided the manpower for industrial and military opposition to the Nationalist challenge, and without the UGT the war would have been settled in favor of Franco much earlier.

The origins of the UGT stemmed from the foundation in 1879 of a new Socialist party* that split off from the Bakuninist radicals of the day. The UGT itself first appeared in 1882, largely an organization of the Madrid* printers led by Pablo Iglesias, the earliest major figure of Spanish socialism. The newspaper *El Socialista** spread Iglesias's program of trade unionism, republicanism, and evolutionary socialism. So muted were parts of this platform, however, that the UGT failed to appeal very strongly to the more revolutionary Catalans or the rebellious southern workers and peasants in Andalusia.* UGT strength came mainly from the mining district of Asturias,* Madrid, and some railway unions that later followed the miners into the union.

Growth proved difficult. Until 1931, the *caciquismo* (bossism) of governments created a hostile climate, and the appearance in 1911 of the CNT eventually led to the eclipse of the UGT as Spain's largest union. Nonetheless, campaigns for municipal reform, support from a rapidly growing Republican movement, and the appearance in 1917 of a social crisis created by inflation and military unrest brought the UGT into the streets. The General Strike of August 1917, Spain's first, led to tentative cooperation with the CNT, while the Russian Revolution spurred later strike activity, especially in Asturias. But the UGT rejected a united front with the CNT and refused to enter Lenin's comintern. While UGT locals struck long and often between 1919 and 1923 when General Primo de Rivera created a military dictatorship in September 1923,

the UGT made its peace with the regime and was rewarded by a cabinet seat and freedom to organize, unlike the now illegal CNT.

The UGT's leadership matured during this period. Largo Caballero succeeded Iglesias as UGT labor leader, while Indalecio Prieto, a Bilbao* newspaperman, increasingly represented a more middle-class, moderate, Republican faction. Intellectuals* like Julián Besteiro,* Luis Araquistáin,* and Luis Jiménez de Asúa* flocked to the party and were soon lecturing to workers in the socialist *Casas de Pueblo* (party headquarters) which operated in many cities and towns. The UGT thus entered the Republican period with its ranks enlarged and its leadership relatively united.

Between the start of the Second Republic* in April 1931 and the victory of the Right in the parliamentary elections in November 1933, the UGT grew more slowly, now that the CNT was again legal, but its prestige expanded enormously through its alliance with the Republicans* in the Cortes.* Unfortunately, the strains of this period soon eroded these gains. Largo Caballero's labor arbitration policy, acceptable to the UGT because it trusted the government to mediate neutrally between labor and management, alienated the anarchists,* who made no such assumption and so attacked the Republic. Problems concerning land reform also drastically decreased the popularity of the socialist and Republican coalition, while the economic difficulties inflicted by worldwide Depression caused many UGT locals, anarchist-like, to lose faith in the government. Strikes multiplied throughout 1932 and 1933 as the UGT rank-and-file became perceptibly more radical.

Radicalism turned towards revolution after the Right's victory in late 1933. Mild labor laws like the creation of socialist-controlled labor exchanges and laws prohibiting strike-breaking, or the more radical extension of social security to agricultural labor, now struck down by the Right, soon were not enough. Largo Caballero's evolution is a case-in-point. His strictly unionist position disappeared, to be replaced by a new revolutionary stance—an alleged "discovery" of Marxism* —which in fact represented a new appreciation of the anarchists' militancy and a feeling of desperation at seeing old Spanish traditionalism buttressed by the rise of European fascism. This shift eventually led to "Red October," a bloody insurrection of Asturian miners in the fall of 1934 that was put down by General Francisco Franco and the Spanish Legion.* The UGT felt the sting of repression throughout the country, and among Madrid construction workers, railworkers of Valencia,* and rural militants of the UGT-affiliated *Federación Nacional de Agricultores de España* a mutinous mood spread. The rapidity of this change, frightening in its intensity, caused moderates like Prieto to question Largo Caballero's leadership.

The events of 1935 and early 1936 seemed to plunge the UGT even further to the Left. UGT membership in the Popular Front* brought it closer to the communists, and the formation of groups like the *Partit Socialista Unificat de Catalunya* (PSUC)* realized joint efforts in areas not formerly penetrated by the socialists—though it was questionable whether they or the communists benefited more. This volume of new activity, however, boosted the UGT's electoral profile, and in the elections of February 1936* the union elected a majority of the Popular Front's deputies. But unlike 1931 this election now brought a bitter personal feud between Prieto and Largo Caballero over whether socialists should join a bourgeois government, one again dominated by the Republican Manuel Azaña.* Prieto, a believer in a planned economy, either pushed or forced Azaña out of the premiership and into the less powerful presidency, largely out of fear of the social revolution that was daily becoming more possible. Largo Caballero's faction, however, prevented Prieto from succeeding Azaña, and the UGT's failure to conclude an alliance with the CNT against military, right-wing, and fascist forces left the socialists floundering just when the *Unión Militar* conspiracy began the Civil War. The UGT's disunity had never been greater.

Socialist initiatives in the early weeks of the war were so uncoordinated that any idea of a "Red plot," as Raymond Carr has pointed out, was simply the propaganda of the generals. While the UGT rank-and-file joined the Republican Army,* moderates like Besteiro or Prieto openly opposed any revolutionary action. Even Largo Caballero, so revolutionary in the spring, found himself, as premier of the Republican government after September 4, 1936, a captive of the kind of antifascist moderation preached by the Spanish Communist party.* Unable to obtain arms from the Western European democracies, he had only the USSR* to rely upon for arms while Germany* and Italy* liberally stocked Nationalist armories. The irony was, of course, that the larger a role the Soviet Union played in Republican military affairs, the more socialists found themselves outpoliticked by communists on the issue that to give the social revolution primacy over the war would mean utter defeat.

On this crucial point, Largo Caballero tried to counter by bringing the UGT and CNT closer together. His new cabinet, created in early November 1936 on the eve of the battle for Madrid, included four anarchists. The significance of this was not lost on moderate socialists like Prieto, or upon the communists, for that matter, who were soon wooing the Prieto wing of the UGT for support. Under these pressures, relations between anarchists and many socialists grew cool in the army with the aid of a growing number of Soviet advisers. The UGT itself stood divided by January 1937 into *Prietista* and *Caballerista* sections, whose Byzantine political differences aided the communist conquest of military and police power. Largo Caballero ultimately resigned in May 1937 after the near-destruction of the Popular Front during the May riots* in Barcelona* between anarchists, socialists, communists, and separatists.

The presumed triumph of moderate socialism in the cabinet of Juan Negrín, a doctor who counted himself as a Prieto socialist, seemingly received confirmation in Prieto's assumption of the Ministry of Defense, hitherto a bastion of communist influence. Prieto longed to bring victory on the Aragón* front and thus expropriate the charisma of the fallen Buenaventura Durruti,* an anarchist leader and organizer of the Army of Aragón.* But heavy-handed communist pressure against other Left groups ultimately alienated Prieto and many other UGT leaders, who grew bitter in their condemnation of "middle-class" communism and destruction of what some trade-union militants now recognized as the traditional Spanish labor movement.

By this time, unfortunately, the UGT was, as a union movement, almost dwarfed by its political apparatus. And yet union membership had been mandatory for most workers since early 1936, so that the rolls of the UGT, which had stood at about a million in 1933, now greatly enlarged were swollen by thousands of new members. UGT councils operated nationalized industries in war production areas as managers, and many rose to the level of government experts within the Valencia bureaucracy. Perhaps one of the most unusual aspects of all this confusion, however, concerned the lack of difference between trade and industrial unionism. The UGT organized along the most efficient lines regardless of organization philosophy. This fact unintentionally brought the UGT and CNT closer together. UGT officials sometimes acted in place of municipal bureaucrats and frequently operated labor placement services on a large scale. This was particularly true in 1937 and 1938 when the communists depended upon moderate socialists to do many of the lesser jobs in running the Republic. But no amount of official responsibility could disguise the frustration many UGT members felt, and Prieto's inability to control the military or achieve success finally led to his resignation. The UGT and CNT subsequently plotted against Negrín, but by war's end these efforts had achieved little.

For further information, see Burnett Bolloten, *The Spanish Revolution: The Left and the Struggle for Power During the Civil War* (Chapel Hill, N.C., 1979); Raymond Carr, ed., *The Republic and the Spanish Civil War* (London, 1971); Amaro del Rosal, *Historia de la UGT*, 2 vols. (Barcelona, 1977); Andrés Diego Sevilla, *Historia política de la zona roja* (Madrid, 1963); and Stanley G. Payne, *The Spanish Revolution* (New York, 1970).

Robert W. Kern

UNIÓN MILITAR ESPAÑOLA (UME). The *Unión Militar Española* (UME) was a conservative organization of army officers founded in 1933. Like most such organizations, this one advocated better working conditions, more pay, and faster promotions. It advocated favoritism toward politically leftist officers by the Republic and worked to protect the benefits it enjoyed as a group in Spanish society. The UME flirted with the political Right and had many monarchist members. Individuals within the UME participated in a variety of plots against the Republican government in the three years prior to the Civil War and in 1936, when the conflict began. Yet, it always remained a small, insignificant military association whose importance has repeatedly been exaggerated by historians. Its true relevance will not be fully understood until a detailed study is made of the entire army officer corps during the Republic that identifies the aspirations and achievements of the entire military leadership. All that is known with certainty is that the UME was small, many of its members were more interested in politics than in soldiering, and it coordinated poorly with the conspirators who launched the war in July 1936.

For further information, see Stanley G. Payne, *Politics and the Military in Modern Spain* (Stanford, Calif., 1967).

See also Army, Nationalist; and Origins of the Spanish Civil War.

James W. Cortada

UNIÓN MILITAR REPUBLICANA ANTIFASCISTA (UMRA). The *Unión Militar Republicana Antifascista* (UMRA) was an organization of Spanish Army officers formed in 1935 to support the Republic against promonarchist, conservative elements within the army. It had chapters throughout Spain, the largest perhaps in Madrid* with approximately 200 members, at least two of whom were generals. Its organization grew out of two groups that merged to form the UMRA—the *Unión Militar Antifascista* (UMA) founded by the Span-

ish Communist party* in 1934, and the *Asociación Militar Republicana* (AMR). The formation of the UMRA was also a reaction against the creation of the more conservative and possibly more popular *Unión Militar Española* (UME).* In Barcelona,* the UMRA had excellent relations with the local government (Generalitat),* and in both the Catalan capital and in Madrid, it recruited many members who eventually became top commanders in the Republican Army* during the Civil War.

For further information, see Michael Alpert, *El ejército republicano en la guerra civil* (Barcelona, 1977).

James W. Cortada

USSR (UNION OF SOVIET SOCIALIST REPUBLICS). The USSR had an important role in the Spanish Civil War from the earliest months of the fighting until nearly the end. Before 1936, relations with the Spanish Republic had not always been friendly. These contacts had usually been sympathetic after the creation of the Republic, and both worked to expand commercial ties through foreign trade.* The Spanish communist party* remained a small political force before the war, although its leaders maintained ties to colleagues in the Soviet Communist party and within the Comintern. Once the war began, however, radical changes took place both in Soviet foreign policy toward Spain and in the role of the Spanish Communist party.

Stalin's* government was faced with a possible alliance between Hitler's* Germany* and the democracies of the West. While such a coalition remained a possibility, Stalin feared that some sort of an arrangement might be worked out with France* and Great Britain.* At the same time, Germany feared an Anglo-French-Russian alliance directed against Germany and consequently strove to drive a wedge between East and West. One way of doing so was by encouraging the establishment of other fascist states, as for example, in Spain. During the early and mid-1930s, Moscow's policy was to counteract the possibility of a German alliance system through available methods. One of its tactics included an attempt to change the image of the Soviet Union from one bent on the destruction of democratic governments and the middle class to a supporter of such values. Various national communist parties were instructed to participate in national political life (as, for example, in the Popular Front* in France), all for the purpose of allaying any fears in Western Europe* that the Soviet Union was a threat to the democracies. It was hoped that such a step would create an environment that would be more conducive to an antifascist alliance directed against Germany. Therefore, almost from the first days of the Civil War, the Soviet Union attempted to appear and act as a stabilizing force in Spain and in Southern Europe, with far less radical social or political objectives than might otherwise be assumed. The Communist party in Spain was encouraged and instructed to support the interests of the middle class in the Republican zone, to plead the case for political moderation, and to support the political process within the Republic. Soviet policy-makers hoped that these efforts would induce the democracies of Great Britain and France to look more favorably on the Soviet Union, while helping London and Paris to keep the fighting in the Iberian Peninsula from spreading into a broader European war.

The desire to support the Republicans* against the insurgent forces of Franco* and his supporters stemmed primarily from an immediate concern in August 1936 that the Spanish rebels would establish a fascist regime in Spain and thus be a natural ally of Germany and, secondarily, of Italy.* The establishment of yet another fascist regime, this time in the western Mediterranean, posed a growing threat to the security of the Soviet Union and came precisely at a time when Stalin keenly felt German expansionism was being directed against his nation. Politically and philosophically, there were fundamental differences which can quickly be highlighted by simply recalling that fascist and communist political ideologies and policies were frequently in sharp contrast to each other. This perception of differences was evident in Spain where the Nationalists* saw the Soviet Union as a moral enemy, the harbinger of "Red" society, and anti-Catholic. On the other hand, the Republican zone saw the Soviets as allies in a fight to the finish against a more backward, primitive Spanish society as represented by the "fascist" Nationalists.

By the fall of 1936, Soviet policy evolved into a two-pronged effort. On the one hand, the Soviet Union did not want to offend the middle-class sensibilities of the democracies and thus preached moderation and worked within established international institutions to contain the Spanish conflict within the Iberian Peninsula. Second, Stalin committed his government to provide support to the Republic to counter the efforts of the Germans and Italians on behalf of the Nationalists. The Communist party within Spain was therefore instructed to work within the framework of Republican politics, while the Soviet Union used the Comintern, other front organizations, and governmental agencies to provide the Republican side with men, military supplies, and military advisers. Stalin sought

to continue the war until international events had created a more favorable atmosphere for checkmating growing German threats to his country's security and sphere of influence in Eastern Europe. To this end, Stalin's government also participated in the Non-Intervention Committee* and in discussions at the League of Nations* critical of German and Italian intervention in Spain. It also continued feeding arms and supplies to the Republicans in sufficient amounts to keep the Nationalists from winning the war.

Within Spain, the influence of the Spanish Communist party grew sharply during the first year and a half of fighting. By mid-1937, the party was able to challenge the authority of all other major political groups for dominance within the Republican government. Following the destruction of anarchist power in May 1937, the Communist party consolidated its political hold on the Republican government and staffed key cabinet and subcabinet positions with members, not to mention a large number of senior military and civilian posts. Throughout the war years, the Soviet Union furnished the Spanish Communist party with considerable political expertise and suggested specific policies, including when to start the campaign to eliminate Largo Caballero* from power, switching support to Dr. Juan Negrín.* The Soviet Embassy became a focal point for much discussion and planning, so much so that the president of the Republic at one point had to remind a cabinet official that the Soviet ambassador was not part of the government and that Spain came first in political considerations. In the second half of the war, communist influence was augmented further with police* action from NKVD* personnel who took a direct part in liquidating enemies of the Soviet Union and the Communist party within Spain.

One of the most famous transactions of the Spanish Civil War involved the Soviet Union. The Republican government agreed to deposit with the Soviets Spanish gold reserves for payment of supplies. To cover the costs of these stocks of matériel, Spain, with the world's fourth largest reserves of gold, finalized the arrangement for shipping gold to the Soviet Union in September 1936. Spanish officials believed this gold would be safe from both the Nationalists and others within Republican Spain who wanted control over it by moving it to Russia. Approximately $500 million, or two-thirds of Spain's reserves, were shipped to the Soviet Union. It was never returned because ostensibly it was applied against bills owed to the Russians. It left Spain on October 25, under direct orders of then finance minister Juan Negrín, with approval of the prime minister and the cabinet. While there has been considerable controversy among historians and members of the Republican government regarding this episode, including the quantity shipped and the wisdom of this move, the decision nonetheless followed a pattern already established of shipping bullion out of the country to cover the costs of supplies as, for example, to France.

With regard to what supplies and help the Soviet Union extended to the Republic, some specific data are available. Soviet aircraft totaled about 1,000—a combination of fighter craft and bombers, or approximately 80 percent of all aircraft brought into the Republican zone from all foreign sources. Exact amounts of other types of equipment, while various and numerous, are not precise. It is known, however, that between September 1936, when supplies first began arriving in Spain, and March 1938, nearly 1,000 cannon came to Spain along with over 700 tanks, nearly 1,400 trucks, 30,000 tons of ammunition, and about 69,000 tons of other matériel—all by sea. During this period, the Soviets also provided some 920 military advisers, an undetermined number of special police (mostly NKVD personnel), and political advisers. In addition, there were 28,000 tons of gasoline, 32,000 tons of crude oil, thousands of tons of lubricants, tractors, howitzers, clothing, and rifles. Hugh Thomas, from whom the above figures were extracted, reports that the Nationalists put together estimates of Soviet aid to the Republicans, which placed the shipment of tanks closer to 200, 3,247 machineguns, about 4,000 trucks with additional tons of ammunition, fuel, and other supplies. Other aid continued arriving until the final weeks of the Civil War. Comintern's purchases on behalf of the Republic made the final Soviet figures much higher. Thomas has concluded that the useful tanks totaled about 900 for the entire period along with some 1,550 artillery pieces, 300 armored cars, 15,000 machineguns, 30,000 automatic firearms, 30,000 mortars, and 500,000 rifles (perhaps too high a figure) —all of various types drawn from a number of countries. Trucks amounted to some 8,000, along with 4 million shells, 1 billion cartridges, and about 1,500 tons of gunpowder. Regardless of whose figures are used, the total amount of supplies from Soviet sources was impressive. In addition, between 2,000 and 3,000 Russians operated in the Republican zone, which was far less than the 17,000 Germans or the 75,000 Italians assigned to Nationalist Spain.

Soviet aid enabled the Republic to fight on longer against the better organized Nationalists, and so the intent of Stalin's government to extend aid to the Republic as a means of prolonging the war was achieved. The expansion of communist participation in the Re-

publican government, while it allowed for greater Soviet influence in the Republic's affairs, apparently was not without controversy. Historians are mixed in their final judgments about the communists' effective contribution and impact in Spain during the Civil War. On the one hand, they argue that the Communist party was better disciplined than the anarchists* and other groups, and thus brought the promise of control which the Republicans so badly needed. On the other hand, they stiffened the resolve of the Nationalists not to compromise and settle for a negotiated settlement of the Civil War. Regardless of which view is taken, it is clear that the Soviet Union used the local Communist party as yet another instrument of its foreign policy. It treated the Spanish war as an international pawn in the larger chess game of national security against the rising threat of Hitler's Germany.

The use of military advisers and matériel was not as efficient as the implementation of German and Italian assistance by the Nationalists. The Russian tanks, for example, were better built and heavier than those supplied by Germany but as a rule were not effectively used in central Spain, especially in the various Republican offensives in 1937 and 1938 designed to protect Madrid.* The Republican predominance in aircraft during the first half of the war, made possible to a considerable extent by the availability of Soviet aircraft and pilots,* did not lead to a dominance of the air. In effect, then, the Republicans ineffectively used this particular weapon against the Nationalists. Lack of proper control over the air eventually made it possible for the Nationalist forces to bomb cities like Madrid and Barcelona* almost with impunity. In addition, Soviet advisers did not always get along well with their Spanish counterparts, while communist commissars assigned to various military units were known to be there more for political than for military reasons to improve the soldier's general lot in the field.

The Soviets had an enormous influence in Republican Spain primarily because no other major power was willing to aid the cause of the Spanish Republic so directly. France vaccilated too much between allowing some aid to come through and remaining neutral, while Great Britain avoided any active involvement on behalf of the Republic. If anything, many British officials in London favored the Nationalists. The United States,* while sympathetic, was bent on maintaining a strict neutrality. Thus, no other major power was willing to help the Republic. The Republican government had little choice but to rely increasingly on the Soviet Union for help while continually pleading its cause of legitimacy in the face of Nationalist revolt before the international community and to no avail.

Consequently, Stalin could do a great deal to influence events in Republican Spain in order to support his broader international objectives than might otherwise have been the case. For their part, the Germans and Italians had far less influence in Nationalist Spain than the Soviet Union in Republican zones. Franco could always play one side off against the other to minimize the influence of any particular country. That flexibility did not exist in the Republic.

Whether Soviet policy in Spain staved off a confrontation with Germany is not known since war between Berlin and Moscow eventually came along with British and American support for the Soviets. That Stalin's policy in Spain might have helped would be difficult to deny as a minimum judgment. Until historians can study Soviet diplomatic documentation for the period, it might be difficult to come to a more precise assessment of the Soviet Union's role in the Spanish Civil War.

For further information, see Burnett Bolloten, *The Spanish Revolution: The Left and the Struggle for Power During the Civil War* (Chapel Hill, N.C., 1979); David T. Cattell, *Communism and the Spanish Civil War* (Berkeley, Calif., 1955) and his *Soviet Diplomacy and the Spanish Civil War* (Berkeley, Calif., 1957); Hugh Thomas, *The Spanish Civil War* (New York, 1977); Angel Viñas, "Gold, the Soviet Union, and the Spanish Civil War," *European Studies Review* 9 (1979): 105-28 and his more detailed treatment in *El oro de Moscú* (Barcelona, 1979).

See also Orlov, Alexander; and *Partido Obrero de Unificación Marxista* (POUM).

James W. Cortada

UNITED STATES OF AMERICA. From the first days of the Spanish Civil War, the U.S. government declared its neutrality and followed the Anglo-French lead in preventing its citizens from selling arms to either side. The government sought to restrict American supplies to either faction through the enforcement of the Neutrality Acts* of 1935 and 1937, which gave the president the authority to keep the United States out of foreign wars. The government approved of the work being done by the Non-Intervention Committee* and by the League of Nations* in containing the fighting to the Iberian Peninsula. The American government also used its influence to reduce Latin American involvement in the Civil War.

American citizens, however, did take part in the war. About 2,800 Americans fought in the International Brigades,* mainly in the Lincoln* and Washington* battalions while a few joined the Nationalist

side. Liberal opinion in the United States favored the Republicans* and a much smaller minority, the Nationalists.* Public debate on the question of the Spanish Civil War was so great that historians have dubbed this conflict the most important international topic to concern American opinion-makers during the 1930s. Actually, polls taken throughout the fighting indicated that American interest in the war did not increase substantially until near the end of the conflict. By then, most Americans had concluded that Franco* was an intimate ally of Hitler* and Mussolini* and thus an enemy of the democratic, free West.

Leading American officials sympathized with the Republic privately but were neutral publicly. Claude Bowers* was the U.S. ambassador to the Republic. Cordell Hull,* the U.S. secretary of state, was the primary architect of American neutrality and worked closely with the British in its implementation. As the Spanish ambassador to Washington, D.C., Fernando de los Ríos* argued the case for the Republic, but without any success. With the victory of the Spanish Nationalists, the American government extended recognition to Franco's regime on April 1, 1939.

For further information, see Claude Bowers, *My Mission to Spain* (New York, 1954); Cecil Eby, *Between the Bullet and the Lie* (New York, 1969), on the International Brigades; F. J. Taylor, *The United States and the Spanish Civil War* (New York, 1960); and Richard Traina, *American Diplomacy and the Spanish Civil War* (Bloomington, Ind., 1968).

See also France; and Great Britain.

James W. Cortada

UNIVERSITIES. At the outbreak of the Civil War, Spain had twelve universities. Four were in the Republican zone—Barcelona,* Madrid,* Murcía,* and Valencia*—while the Nationalist zone had universities in Granada,* Oviedo,* Salamanca,* Santiago, Seville,* Valladolid,* Saragossa,* and La Laguña. Instruction continued at these centers, although each was diminished in enrollment and a few, especially Madrid, suffered the ravages of war. The intellectual ambience in the Republican zone favored education,* while an anti-intellectualism that would remain an undercurrent of the Franco* regime became apparent in Nationalist Spain.

In the fall of 1935, a total of 29,249 students were enrolled in Spanish universities, 91 percent of whom were male. No reliable statistics exist for matriculation during the Civil War, but several trends are known. Enrollment declined dramatically because the youth of Spain were recruited as soldiers. Yet, the percentage of women attending increased in both zones, particularly in the Republican-held areas. School faculties were often greatly reduced through flight, execution, or voluntary retirement. At the University of Barcelona, for example, the rector, Pedro Bosch Gimpera,* assisted many of the faculty in fleeing to France* in the early days of the war, while in Seville and elsewhere professors were targets of terrorist mobs unleashed in the summer of 1936.

The contrasting intellectual atmosphere of the two zones affected higher education, as can be illustrated in two vignettes of university life in the fall of 1936. The encouragement given education in Republican Spain is seen in the founding of the Basque university in the fall of 1936. One part of the Autonomy Statute approved in October 1936 granted the Basques a university, which they had long sought. *El euzkera*, the language of the region, was to be a part of the curriculum. The first faculty—that of medicine*—opened in November 1936, but when the tide of war turned, the school closed during the summer of 1937. A poignant struggle for the survival of the university as a center of learning was also enacted at Salamanca during the opening of the university in October 1936. The rector, Miguel de Unamuno,* defended intellectual pursuits and civilized values in a bitter confrontation with General Millán Astray,* a crippled soldier who had organized and led the Spanish Foreign Legion.* Millán Astray was a nihilist and demagogue whose battlecry had been "Long live Death!" Unamuno attacked that slogan as a "necrophilous and senseless cry." When the remarks were reported to Franco,* he ordered Unamuno's execution. Since such an action would have caused an international furor, however, Unamuno was instead placed under house arrest. He died suddenly on the last day of 1936, a casualty of the anti-intellectualism of the Franco regime.

The University of Madrid was another major casualty of the war. The faculty and students fled to Valencia* with the government in November 1936. The campus at University City was under siege and suffered the brunt of the battle for Madrid. The buildings housing the faculties of philosophy, science, and medicine were held by the Loyalists,* while the faculties of architecture, agriculture, and the clinical hospital were controlled by Nationalist soldiers. By the end of the war, only the shells of buildings remained at University City.

Franco began to reorganize the universities as soon as the war ended. A decree of April 1939 reorganized universities under the inspection of the state and the Catholic Church,* controlled their finance, and imposed loyalty requirements for the appointment of professors. The emphasis on theology and Scholastic philosophy and mandatory instruction in religion indicated the tenor of the revised curriculum. Almost a completely new professorate had to be recruited because literally thousands of former professors had fled Spain.

For further information, see Hugh Thomas, *The Spanish Civil War* (New York, 1977).

David V. Holtby

UPRISING AT SEA. The uprising at sea of July 1936 developed without planning or coordination and thus failed. By June, General Mola* had developed a strategy that depended on the reliable 24,000-man Army of Africa* to secure the Iberian Peninsula. Mola called for naval intervention to ensure the success of the uprising in port cities and to convoy troops across the narrow waters, respectively, from Melilla* and Ceuta* to Málaga* and Algeciras and thence to Madrid.* Mola did not involve naval officers in planning, and so they were unprepared to aid the uprising.

On July 16-17, the suspicious Republican Navy Minister, José Giral,* ordered naval forces to the Straits of Gibraltar* and to Melilla to prevent any crossing of insurgent forces to the peninsula. They included the battleship *Jaime I*, the cruisers *Miguel de Cervantes** and *Libertad,** the destroyers *Churruca, Lepanto, Sánchez Barcaíztegui,* and *Almirante Valdés*, the gunboats *Dato* and *Laya*, and several smaller warships. Beginning on July 17, the officers of most of these ships attempted to take their vessels into the rebellion, and the *Churruca* and *Dato* on July 18 and 19 succeeded in escorting ships with several hundred troops from Ceuta, to control Cádiz* and Algeciras, respectively. Crewmen in these warships, except *Dato* and one torpedo boat, seized control from the officers after being alerted by Republican radio officer Benjamín Balboa from Radio Central in Madrid. This revolutionary Republican fleet gathered in the Straits to isolate Franco's* Army of Africa in Morocco.*

In all four naval bases, El Ferrol,* Cartagena,* Cádiz,* and Mahón, revolutionary sailors struggled with officers for control, failing in El Ferrol* and Cádiz only because of the intervention of local army units.

By July 22, the uprising at sea was over. Violence had been sharp but brief, and the massacres of later weeks had not yet taken form in the victors' minds. During the uprising in the navy on July 17-22, only seventeen officers and nine petty officers and seamen had been killed.

For further information, see José Cervera Pery, *Alzamiento y revolución en la marina* (Madrid, 1978).

See also Merchant Marine, Spanish; and Navy, Spanish.

Willard C. Frank, Jr.

URIBARRI BARRUTELL, MANUEL. Uribarri was a Republican captain of the Civil Guard* in the city of Valencia* at the start of the Civil War. He took the initiative in releasing arms to the public to counter the Nationalist revolt. In August, he landed at Ibiza* with a small group of armed men and helped to restore the island to Republican control. He went on to command troops at the Sierra de Gredos in October and at Toledo.* He established networks of spies to help in his operations and supported the Indalecio Prieto* faction in the government while working within the Ministry of War. In 1938, he became chief of Republican intelligence services. Uribarri was unable to keep the communists from infiltrating his operations which they ultimately came to dominate, turning them into an extension of the Russian NKVD.* The *Servicio de Investigación Militar* (SIM)* now became a center for torture as well as an intelligence-gathering organization. Eventually, Uribarri escaped into France* taking with him substantial sums of government funds.

For further information, see José Peirats, *Los anarquistas en la crisis política española* (Buenos Aries, 1964); and Manuel Uribarri, *La quinta colomna española* (Havana, 1943).

See also Espionage.

James W. Cortada

URIBE, VICENTE. Uribe served as the Republican minister of agriculture from September 4, 1936 to 1939. Before the Civil War, this Basque communist politician edited the party's newspaper, *Mundo Obrero*,* and served as the theoretician on Spanish communism. His political influence increased with the size of the party's membership in early 1936. Uribe came into the government when it became necessary to include communists as part of the coalition gathered for the war against Franco.* As minister of agriculture, he attempted to use the state's power to confiscate lands held by Nationalists,* and he signed them over to collectives, thereby confirming what peasants throughout the Republican zone had already done. Yet, he opposed confiscation of land belonging to Republicans* for fear of alienating the middle-class landowner from the communist movement. He worked closely with Russian advisers and in fact had been one of the few Spanish communists even to visit Moscow in the years before the Civil War. As a member of the Spanish politburo, he wielded considerable influence in Republican politics. He spared no opportunity to expand his party's political influence and legal authority in the Republican zone. For example, he participated in ousting Largo Caballero* and backing Negrín.

For further information, see Burnett Bolloten, *The Spanish Revolution: The Left and the Struggle for Power During the Civil War* (Chapel Hill, N.C., 1979).

See also Communist Party, Spanish; Largo Caballero, Francisco; and Negrín, Juan.

James W. Cortada

URRACA PASTOR, MARÍA ROSA. Urraca was a Carlist nurse who organized medical services for the Nationalists.* Franco* appointed her to his first national council on December 2, 1936. Known as La Coronela, she was one of three women in this council of forty-eight.

For further information, see María Rosa Urraca Pastor, *Asi empezamos* (Bilbao, 1940).

James W. Cortada

URRUTIA GONZÁLEZ, GUSTAVO (1890-   ). Urrutia, a general who sided with the Nationalists,* commanded combat troops throughout the Civil War. His most notable efforts were in the Aragón* campaign during the Republican offensive between August and October 1937. His soldiers successfully resisted repeated Republican attacks.

For further information, see José Manuel Martínez Bande, *El final del frente norte* (Madrid, 1972).

See also Appendix B.

James W. Cortada

V

VALENCIA. Valencia, a province located in eastern Spain facing the Mediterranean, was the target of considerable Nationalist military action inasmuch as it was a capital of the Republic. The provincial capital (the population* in 1931 was 320,000, making it the third largest city in Spain) had an active political life. In 1927, militant anarchists* formed the *Federación Anarquista Ibérica* (FAI),* others flirted with the *Confederación Nacional del Trabajo* (CNT)* and with communism, while more conservative elements toyed with the idea of rebellion against the Republic. Still others were regional nationalists. Tensions rose throughout the province in the weeks before the revolt of July 1936. On the first day of the revolution, supporters of the Nationalists* hesitated to follow after hearing that the revolt was in trouble in Barcelona.* Workers in the city of Valencia united in the streets to prevent an uprising, received arms from army officers loyal to the Republic, and burned several churches. By July 20, workers had attacked army barracks, while officers waivered in their loyalty to the rebellion. The chief conspirator in the city, General Manuel González Carrasco,* decided the situation was hopeless and escaped by sea. This turn of events made it possible for the Republic to secure the entire province for its side with the help of politically active workers.

Soon after, Diego Martínez Barrio,* speaker of the Cortes,* attempted to form a *Junta* governing five provinces from the city of Valencia. Because he was a poor administrator, power remained in the hands of a committee made up of the CNT-*Unión General de Trabajadores* (UGT).* Political life became more stable, with bourgeois attitudes prevailing in local government, even in the provincial capital. Collectivization of industry and agriculture was at a slow pace in comparison with other Republican zones. Communists discouraged radical changes in the local economy, as did the UGT, the *Confederación Española de Derechas Autónomas* (CEDA),* and various Republican parties.

In November 1936, the Republican government decided to leave Madrid* and move to Valencia, leaving the threatened capital in central Spain with truckloads of files, officials, and diplomats. Collectivization of the local Valencian economy increased, as did the stra-

tegic value of the province to both sides. Most factories were operating under the control of worker committees by early 1937, allowing them more power over the political life of the Levante* than the old bourgeois had ever allowed. Moving the government to Valencia also forced centralization of authority in the province. Meanwhile, the Communist party* increased its political power in Valencia and elsewhere by supporting the rights of small farmers and businessmen who wanted to retain control over their parties. In May 1937, the Republic destroyed the political power of the anarchists in the Republican zone, and soon after the communists became the dominant political force in the Republican zone.

The war finally came to Valencia in 1938. On July 5, the Nationalists began their campaign to capture Valencia. In the months that followed, some of the heaviest fighting took place in eastern Spain. The battle of the Ebro* (July-November) temporarily saved Valencia from capture but at a cost of combined deaths for both sides of about 21,000 and an additional 40,000 in wounded. Valencia finally fell to the Nationalists on March 30, 1939, after the Republican government had left the city.

For further information, see Burnett Bolloten, *The Spanish Revolution: The Left and the Struggle for Power During the Civil War* (Chapel Hill, N.C., 1979); Aurora Bosch Martínez, *Colectividades anarquistas y guerra civil en el Pais Valenciano* (Valencia, 1980); Raymond Carr, *The Spanish Tragedy: The Civil War in Perspective* (London, 1977); Carlos Llorens Castillo, *La guerra en Valencia y en el frente de Teruel* (Valencia, 1978); José Manuel Martínez Bande, *Los cien últimos días de la república* (Barcelona, 1972) and *La ofensiva sobre Valencia* (Madrid, 1977); Luis María Mezquida, *La batalla del Ebro*, 2 vols. (Tarragona, 1963); and Hugh Thomas, *The Spanish Civil War* (New York, 1977).

See also various political parties; and Appendix B.

James W. Cortada

VALERA APARICIO, FERNANDO (1899-1982). Valera was a Left Republican, born and raised in Valencia,* who served as the Republican subsecretary of communications and a member of the lower house of the Cortes* from 1936 to 1939. As subsecretary of communications, he had responsibility for radio* programming from the Republican zone and periodically made speeches on the air to stir the spirits of those living in Madrid.* After the Civil War he lived in exile in France and was active in exile Republican politics. From 1946 to 1971 he served in the cabinet-in-exile, and from 1971 until his death was the president of the Republic-in-exile. During his presidency—after Franco's death—he returned the archives of the Republic to Spain although he never returned himself.

For further information, see Gabriel Jackson, *The Spanish Republic and the Civil War, 1931-1939* (Princeton, N.J., 1965).

James W. Cortada

VALLADOLID. Valladolid, a province located in Old Castile* in north-central Spain, was politically conservative. On March 14, 1934, the first national gathering of the Falange* party with the *Juntas de Ofensiva Nacional-Sindicalista* (JONS),* for example, took place in the ancient capital city of Valladolid. Throughout the 1930s, plotters against the Republic believed Valladolid could be counted upon to rise in rebellion against the government in Madrid* if given an opportunity. Certainly by 1936, one of the best organized cells of the Falange existed in Valladolid. At the start of the Civil War, the province supported the Nationalists.* Falangists gained control over the city and later the province as a whole, conducting a severe purge of leftists. Each night for many weeks, truckloads of their enemies would be taken out of Valladolid into the countryside to be executed, as happened in other nearby cities. The Nationalists purged approximately 9,000 individuals in this manner during the war. Other violence took place at the very start of the conflict. In the capital city alone in July 1936, workers and some soldiers bitterly resisted the Falangists, rebel troops, and pro-Nationalist civilians in the streets, causing the *casa del pueblo* to be destroyed and many people to be injured. After one day, the generals commanding the rebellion in Valladolid, Andrés Saliquet Zumeta* and Miguel Ponte y Manso de Zúñiga,* gained full control of the city.

Subsequently, Onésimo Redondo, founder of Valladolid's JONS, led Falangists and other volunteers* to Madrid to fight during late July 1936. This provincial capital also served as the ad hoc national headquarters for the Falange in the early months of the war. National political strategy meetings were held here,

and it was in Valladolid that Mercedes Sanz Bachiller, widow of Onésimo Redondo (killed on July 24, 1936), established within the Falange the *Auxilio de Invierno* (Winter Help), a charity organization to take care of orphans. In October 1937, it had 711 branches throughout Spain and by October 1939, 2,847, serving as one of the major positive forces to emerge from the war.

The province was not totally isolated from the fighting, however. On occasion, Republican bombers attacked communities in Valladolid. On January 26, 1938, Republican aircraft bombed Valladolid and Seville* in retaliation for Nationalist air raids on Barcelona.* The damage was minimal compared to that inflicted on Barcelona. Men from Valladolid were subjected to the Nationalist Army* draft, and thus many served in battles throughout Spain from the fall of 1936 to the end of the war.

For further information, see Rafael Abella, *La vida cotidiana durante la guerra civil: La España Nacional* (Barcelona, 1973); Juan De Iturralde, *El catolicismo y la cruzada de Franco*, 2 vols. (Bayonne, N.J., 1955); and Stanley G. Payne, *Falange: A History of Spanish Fascism* (Stanford, Calif., 1961).

James W. Cortada

VALLELLANO, COUNT OF (FERNANDO SUÁREZ DE TANGIL Y ANGULO) (1886-1964). The Count of Vallellano was a leading monarchist politician at the start of the Civil War. In the early days of the conflict, when the monarchists represented a significant political faction within Nationalist Spain (particularly in the north), the rebels consulted with the Count of Vallellano regarding political matters. As the Falange* increased its power and Franco* his authority, the influence of the monarchists declined, along with the count's.

For further information, see Ramón Serrano Suñer, *Entre Hendaya y Gibraltar* (Madrid, 1947) and his *Memorias* (Barcelona, 1977).

James W. Cortada

VANGUARDIA, LA (1881-present). A Castilian language newspaper, *La Vanguardia* was founded in 1881. It grew steadily throughout the reign of Alfonso XIII,* and in 1927, it had the largest circulation of any Barcelona* daily newspaper. Although it supported the Conservative party during the monarchy and Center Republicans during the Republic, it never became a party organ. It supported the rebel cause in its issues of July 18 and 19, 1936, but it quickly came under Republican control. The occasional appearances of a comic strip, "Aventuras del ratón Miguelín," added some levity to its thorough, well-written, reasonably objective coverage of the war. Its name was changed to *La Vanguardia Española* when the Nationalists* captured Barcelona in January 1939. It remains one of the finest European papers.

For further information, see Augustín Calvet, *Historia de La Vanguardia (1884-1936)* (Paris, 1971); María Campillo, *La prensa a Barcelona, 1936-39* (Barcelona, 1979); and Arturo Mori, *La prensa española en nuestro tiempo* (Mexico City, 1943).

William J. Irwin

VARELA IGLESIAS, JOSÉ ENRIQUE (1891-1951). Varela was one of Franco's* leading generals during the Spanish Civil War. Born in San Fernando, in the province of Cádiz,* Varela joined the army as an enlisted soldier and rose through the ranks to become a general. He fought in the African campaigns during the 1920s and became a decorated hero. Varela emerged from the Moroccan wars having worked with General Franco and with the rank of lieutenant colonel. He then held a variety of military appointments during the Second Republic,* even though he did not support its political views. In fact, during 1934, this brave and ambitious officer trained *Requetes** (Carlist militia), traveling from one town in the Pyrenees* to another dressed as a priest, establishing camps and recruiting groups for rebellion against the Republic.

Varela next became one of the principal conspirators with Franco and others in the days before the Civil War, and even planned the rising as it should take place in Madrid.* The Republic, suspecting him of such activity, arrested him in Cádiz on July 6, 1936. On July 18, General Varela was out of jail and helped seize Cádiz for the Nationalists.* He soon after led North African troops campaigning in southern Spain, captured Granada,* moved on to Córdoba,* and in September relieved the besieged Nationalists at the Alcázar* in Toledo.* He subsequently went on to command troops fighting around Madrid. He initiated each of the major Nationalist assaults on the city, most of which were frustrated by the Republican Army.*

Varela's troops attacked the University City in Madrid in November 1936, and he led the Nationalist efforts at the battles of Boadilla* and the Corunna Road* in December. In February, the Nationalists initiated the battle of the Jarama* in an attempt to further encircle the city of Madrid. This field commander continued to push aggressively against Republican forces in an attempt to seize Madrid. In July, the Republicans* mounted an attack against General Varela's positions, now known as the battle of Brunete,* where he was supreme field commander of the Nationalist forces. Both sides claimed victory in this battle, although the Republicans sustained heavier losses of veteran soldiers and important military equipment. Varela turned his attention next to the Maestrazgo* campaign which had as its objective to push from Teruel* to the Mediterranean in the early months of 1938. By June, he had achieved the majority of his objective. Varela spent the rest of the war fighting in southeastern Spain, finally pushing the last of the Republicans into the sea.

Varela participated in national affairs following the war, becoming minister of war in 1942. By this time, he had become one of the most decorated Spanish officers of the twentieth century. Twice during the Moroccan wars he had received Spain's highest military decoration, the *Cruz Laureada de San Fernando*, once personally from King Alfonso XIII.* He received sixteen other military decorations as well. Poor health plagued the general following the war, forcing him to step down from his position as minister of war in 1944. He died of leukemia in 1951.

For further information, see José Manuel Martínez Bande, *La lucha en torno a Madrid* (Madrid, 1968), *La marcha sobre Madrid* (Madrid, 1968), and *La ofensiva sobre Segovia y la batalla de Brunete* (Madrid, 1972); and José María Pemán, *Un soldado en la historia* (Cádiz, 1954).

See also Andalusia; and Appendix B.

James W. Cortada

VATICAN. The Vatican is the popular name for the Holy See, the government of the papacy. Its policies do not always coincide with those of the leaders of the national churches because the Vatican represents the interests of the Catholic Church* as an international institution. This fact is nowhere more evident than in the Spain of the 1930s. The reigning pope, Pius XI,* had as his secretary of state and adviser on foreign relations Cardinal Eugenio Pacelli (later Pope Pius XII, 1939-1958), and his *nuncio* to Spain was Monsignor Federico Tedeschini. As a general rule, the Vatican wanted security for the Church in each country, along with guarantees of religious education.* The bishops in Spain supported these goals, but they also wanted to retain the historic privileges which the clergy had managed to secure over the centuries.

The Vatican's relations with monarchist Spain were governed by the 1851 Concordat which recognized Catholicism as the official religion of the state and gave the clergy control over public education along with state-paid salaries. In return, the state was given a weighty influence over ecclesiastical appointments. When the anticlerical Republic was proclaimed in 1931, the Vatican was prepared to relinquish some of the clergy's privileges in return for security, and it counseled the Spanish bishops to accept the Republic in the hope that Republican anticlericalism would be moderated. While most of the bishops went along with the Vatican's policy, the primate of Spain, Cardinal Pedro Segura,* did not, and the anticlerical government expelled him from Spain. The Vatican accepted his expulsion; its only retaliation was the refusal to accept Luís de Zulueta as the Republic's ambassador to the Holy See. But the policy of moderation was not successful: the Cortes* legislated the disestablishment of the Church and the dissolution of the Jesuits, and not only provided for secular public education but also prohibited the regular clergy from teaching, even in the Church's own schools.

The Vatican still counseled moderation, but it also encouraged the formation of a Catholic party to secure concessions for the Church. This party, the *Confederación Española de Derechas Autónomas* (CEDA),* won a plurality in the elections of 1933. While it could not itself rule, it could and did prevent the enactment of the anticlerical legislation. Negotiations were opened for a new concordat with the Vatican's acceptance of Leandro Pita Romero as ambassador to the Holy See in 1934.

Actually, a concordat was impossible in 1934-1935 because of the lack of governmental stability, a fact demonstrated in 1936 when the Popular Front* came to power. The anticlerical legislation was again enforced, and the Vatican was now willing to make the best of a bad situation. Zulueta was accepted as the new ambassador. Tedeschini was recalled to Rome, and a new *nuncio*, Monsignor Felipe Cortesi, was named. Before Cortesi arrived in Madrid, however, the military arose and the Civil War began.

The anticlerical fury of the first few months of the war was clearly decisive in ensuring that the Vatican's sympathies would be with the Nationalists.* As Cortesi was not at the Nunciature in Madrid,* relations between the Holy See and the Republic were broken, de facto, even though Zulueta remained in Rome. By 1937, the only practicing Catholic in the Republican government, Manuel de Irujo* (representing the Basque separatists), tried to convince the cabinet to renew relations with the Vatican so that Franco's* Burgos* government would be undermined on this important issue. This proved too difficult, however, and by 1938 Irujo had left the cabinet.

By that time, the Vatican had already established diplomatic relations with the Burgos government. In December 1936, Cardinal Isidro Gomá,* primate of Spain, was called to Rome and named the Holy See's "official and confidential representative" to the Burgos government, an appointment Franco made public immediately. In October 1937, Monsignor Ildebrando Antoniutti was named chargé d'affaires to the Burgos government, following the difficulties the pope had with Franco over the execution of Basque priests. Franco pressed for the naming of a *nuncio* and full diplomatic relations, but this was not done until his government actually began to revoke the Republic's anticlerical legislation. In October 1938, Monsignor Gaetano Cicognani was named *nuncio* to the Burgos government. After the Civil War, a *modus vivendi* was signed in 1941, and a new concordat was negotiated in 1953.

For further information, see Juan José Ruiz Rico, *El papel político de la iglesia católica en la España de Franco* (Madrid, 1977); and José M. Sánchez, "The Second Spanish Republic and the Holy See: 1931-1936," *Catholic Historical Review* 49 (April 1963):47-68.

José M. Sánchez

VÁZQUEZ CAMARASA, ENRIQUE (-1946). Vázquez was a priest who administered a general absolution for sins to the defenders of the Alcázar* at Toledo* while it was besieged by Republican forces in September 1936. At the time he performed this ceremony, many believed that the Alcázar would soon be overrun by the Republicans.* As it turned out, the Nationalists* outside of Toledo were able to come to the aid of those in the Alcázar, turning the rescue into a triumph. By the end of 1936, Vazquez left Spain for Paris, having decided to have nothing more to do with the Spanish Civil War.

For further information, see Luis Quintanilla, *Los rehenes del Alcázar de Toledo* (Paris, 1967).

James W. Cortada

VEGAS LATALPIÉ, EUGENIO. Vegas was a monarchist journalist in Burgos* who, in 1931, founded a magazine called *Acción Española.* He advocated the demise of the Second Republic,* was promonarchist, and believed that the political Right had the responsibility to rise up against the Republic. When Franco* did so in July 1936, however, Vegas felt concerned that insufficient attention had been paid to building an ideological base for a new form of government. He continued to publish his journal in the Nationalist zone once the Civil War began. He became one of the few Nationalists* who personally protested to Franco the number of indiscriminate assassinations that took place in their zone in the early months of the Civil War, but to no avail. He also managed to have the heir to the Spanish throne, Don Juan, visit the Nationalist zone, which threatened to upset the delicate political alliance established between Franco and the Carlists.* The Carlists resented the claims of the Alfonsist branch of the family to the throne. Vegas was also present at the famous confrontation between Miguel de Unamuno* and General José Millán Astray* in October 1936 at the University of Salamanca.

By early 1937, Vegas no longer edited *Acción Española*. Although he had irritated the Francoists with his activities, Franco nonetheless appointed him to his first government at the end of 1936 as a representative of the monarchist faction in the Nationalist zone. Soon after, Vegas became the Nationalist secretary general of press and propaganda. In 1938, however, he gave up that responsibility and enlisted in a Falange* military unit (*bandera*) as a private. Before the end of the war, he transferred to the Spanish Foreign Legion.*

For further information, see Ronald Fraser, *Blood of Spain* (New York, 1979); and Richard Robinson, *The Origins of Franco Spain* (Newton Abbot, 1970).
    See also Terrorism.

James W. Cortada

VIANA, MARQUÍS OF (FAUSTO DE SAAVEDRA)
The Marquis of Viana was a monarchist politician before the Civil War. On July 22, 1936, he traveled from Vienna (where King Alfonso* lived in exile) to Rome to urge the Italians to help the Nationalists.* He arranged for a representative of Franco's,* Luis Antonio Bolín,* to meet with Count Galeazzo Ciano,* the foreign minister, to plead the case for aid. This was the first contact between the Italians and the Spanish Nationalists. In the weeks that followed, Italy* decided to extend assistance to Franco.

For further information, see John F. Coverdale, *Italian Intervention in the Spanish Civil War* (Princeton, N.J., 1975).
    See also Mussolini, Benito.

James W. Cortada

VICH. Vich, located in the Catalan province of Barcelona,* was the home of a cathedral, a seminary, and a bishop. In the early days of the Civil War, anarchists* burned the cathedral and over the course of time killed various religious officials from this city. Vich became one of the final points of retreat for the Republican government as it fled into exile during

February 1939. Vich also became a refugee center for many days just before the Nationalists* closed the border with France.*

For further information, see Antonio Montero, *La persecución religiosa en España* (Madrid, 1961).
    See also Barcelona (Province); Catholic Church, Spanish; and Vatican.

James W. Cortada

VIDAL I BARRAQUER, CARDINAL FRANCESC (1868-1943). Cardinal Francesc Vidal i Barraquer, archbishop of Tarragona,* was Spain's leading progressive churchman during the 1920s and 1930s. Born on October 3, 1868, in Cambrils, Tarragona, into an upper middle-class professional family, he was trained as a lawyer and practiced law until he entered the seminary at age twenty-eight to study for the priesthood. Ordained in 1898, he made rapid progress through the ecclesiastical ranks under the patronage of Bishop Torras i Bages of Vich.* He was consecrated bishop of Solsona in 1913 and became archbishop of Tarragona in 1919. He was made a cardinal in 1921. From this position as the leading churchman of Catalonia,* Vidal supported Catalan separatist aspirations, although he was not an ardent separatist himself. Because of this position, Primo de Rivera singled Vidal out as one of his main opponents and sought Vatican* pressure against him. Vidal's stand took on symbolic importance and gained him a great deal of popular support.

A humble but shrewd cleric, Vidal publicly disdained the clergy's political role, but of necessity he was involved in a great deal of political activity. With the advent of the Republic in 1931, he became one of the leaders of the progressive faction in the Church, along with the papal *nuncio*, Monsignor Federico Tedeschini. Despite the Republican-socialist coalition's anticlerical legislation and the terrorist incendiarism of the anarchists,* Vidal used his personal friendship with leaders of the Republic, the Church, and the working classes to urge policies of moderation on all. When Cardinal Pedro Segura* was expelled in 1931, Vidal became, in effect, acting primate and the leader of the Spanish bishops until the appointment of Isidro Gomá* in 1933 as archbishop of Toledo.* Vidal consistently urged moderation on the Vatican as well, arguing that a harsh and condemnatory policy would do little to protect Spain's Catholics and might cause them harm. At the same time, he had to take leadership in such important internal issues as devising fiscal reforms to provide for clerical needs, as the clerical budget was pared and due to be phased out by successive Republican governments. His role was most effective in Catalonia where his personal popular support prevented many of the anticlerical excesses that occurred in the rest of Spain.

When the Civil War began in July 1936, even Vidal's popularity could not prevent the anticlerical fury from engulfing Catalonia, and like many churchmen in Republican Spain, he was arrested and imprisoned. The moderate leaders of the Catalan Generalitat* secured his release and then, fearing for his safety, arranged with the Italian consul in Barcelona to have Vidal escorted to Italy.* Vidal went into exile in Lucca in August 1936.

Vidal's exile was as stormy as his pastoral career. When Cardinal Gomá drafted the Bishops' Collective Letter in 1937 supporting the Nationalist cause and urging Catholics throughout the world to lend their support as well, he asked all of Spain's bishops to sign the letter. Vidal (along with Bishop Mateo Múgica* of Victoria*) refused. He wrote to Gomá that, while foreigners should be informed about the extent of the persecution of Catholics, he did not feel that a pastoral letter was the best way to do so and would, in fact, be counterproductive. The bishops, he said, should stay out of politics as an example to the other clergy. He feared the repercussions that would affect the clergy in Republican Spain, particularly those in his own diocese. After the letter was published, Vidal offered himself to the Republican government as a hostage in return for the release of all imprisoned priests. This offer was refused, and when the Republican government later offered to safeguard a visit to his see, Vidal refused to make the trip as long as priests in his diocese remained in prison. He spent the remainder of the war years unsuccessfully trying to mediate peace through the offices of the Vatican.

After the fall of Catalonia to the Nationalists* in early 1939, Vidal made plans to return to his see, but the Nationalist government refused to allow it, apparently because he had not signed the 1937 Bishops' Letter. Pope Pius XI* was ready to support Vidal in his effort to return to Spain, but the pope died in February 1939, and his successor, Pius XII, was unwilling to push the matter. In effect, Vidal was condemned to permanent exile. He died in Fribourg, Switzerland, on September 12, 1943.

For further information, see M. Batllori and V. M. Arbolea, eds., *Arxiu Vidal i Barraquer: Esglesia i estat durant la Segonya República Espanyola, 1931-1936* (Monestir de Montserrat, 1971-); and Ramón Muntanyola, *Vidal i Barraquer: el cardenal de la paz* (Barcelona, 1971).

See also Catholic Church, Spanish.

José M. Sánchez

VIDIELLA, RAFAEL. Vidiella was an anarchist, a member of the Catalan *Confederación Nacional del Trabajo* (CNT)* since the 1920s, and a politician in the Generalitat* during the Civil War. He had become a socialist and leader in the *Partit Socialista Unificat de Catalunya* (PSUC)* in the mid-1930s and by the early days of the Civil War, a member of the Communist party.* In 1936, he was appointed councillor of justice and in April 1937, councillor of labor in the Catalan government with the additional portfolio for public works.

For further information, see Burnett Bolloten, *The Spanish Revolution: The Left and the Struggle for Power During the Civil War* (Chapel Hill, N.C., 1979).

James W. Cortada

VIGO. Vigo, a port in southern Spain, fell to the Nationalists* early in the Civil War and became important to Franco* for debarking troops from North Africa. Later, this city linked the Nationalists with the outside world and was a port of entry for supplies. In addition, a large transmitter, the strongest in the Iberian Peninsula, was set up at Vigo in order to broadcast Nationalist programs all over the country.

For further information, see Hugh Thomas, *The Spanish Civil War* (New York, 1977).

See also Andalusia; Army, Nationalist; and Germany.

James W. Cortada

VIGÓN SUERODIAZ, JUAN (1880-1959). As a colonel in 1936, Vigón served as a staff officer to General Franco* when Franco established his headquarters as Generalissimo in Salamanca.* Vigón was a small, slim man whose thick glasses and mustache masked a sharp mind and a determined nature. He was a dynamic individual devoted to his assigned tasks, which he met with great intellectual ability. Some officers considered him overdemanding, but others had great respect for his thorough staff work and grasp of broad military problems, as well as his understanding of political realities. He was known to relieve incompetent commanders on the spot and to assume direct command of units. In matters of politics he was a strong monarchist.

Vigón was assigned as General Mola's* chief of staff for the Vizcaya* offensive, and it is assumed that Vigón was the one who proposed that the Nationalists* concentrate their effort in the north after the failure of the assault on Madrid.* In this position, he did much to soothe the ruffled tempers of the Spanish, Italian, and German commanders. He was highly respected by the Germans who considered him one of the outstanding Spanish staff officers; many Germans developed a warm personal feeling toward him that lasted through World War II.

After General Mola's death, Vigón served as chief of staff to General Dávila.* As a general officer, Vigón played an important role in the counteroffensive against Teruel.* Later, he was second in command of the Nationalist Army* for the Aragón* offensive. Here he again worked closely with the Germans and Italians.

In July 1938, Vigón was chief of staff to Generalissimo Franco. In 1940, he was minister of air and chief of the high general staff. During World War II, Franco entrusted him with many delicate assignments dealing with the Germans, and he acquired a reputation as being "pro-German." After the war, Vigón continued to hold important positions in the Spanish government, such as minister of war.

In 1954, General Vigón was one of the Spanish ministers who concluded the American-Spanish military and economic agreements which permitted the stationing of American military forces in Spain.

For further information, see Manuel Aznar, *Historia militar de la guerra de España* (Madrid, 1940); and General Alfredo Kindelán, *Mis cuadernos de guerra, 1936-1939* (Madrid, 1945).

See also Army, Nationalist.

Raymond L. Proctor

VILLALBA RUBIO, JOSÉ (1889-   ). Villalba was a Republican Army* officer who led the troops at Málaga* when the Nationalists* attacked in February 1937. He commanded approximately 12,000 men, of whom only 8,000 were armed. Heavy Nationalist assaults led to the fall of Málaga on February 7, 1937. The Nationalists then initiated a harsh retribution on the city, executing possibly thousands and certainly a minimum of about 1,000 people. Nothing more is known of Colonel Villalba after 1937.

For further information, see José Martínez Bande, *La compaña de Andalucia* (Madrid, 1969).

James W. Cortada

VILLEGAS MONTESINOS, RAFAEL (1875-1936). Villegas was one of the key rebel plotters in Madrid* of the July 1936 uprising. When the revolt broke out, the Republicans* quickly arrested him. In August, local militiamen broke into his prison and executed approximately seventy individuals, many of whom were important residents of Madrid. Among them was General Villegas.

For further information, see Hugh Thomas, *The Spanish Civil War* (New York, 1977).

James W. Cortada

VITORIA. Vitoria is the capital of the province of Avila* in the Basque country. It quickly fell to the Nationalists* in the early days of the Civil War and became one of the first cities to be fully controlled by Franco* for any extended period of time.

For further information, see Stanley G. Payne, *Basque Nationalism* (Reno, Nev., 1975).

See also Army of the North; and Basque Nationalism.

James W. Cortada

VITTORIO, GIUSEPPI DI ("NICOLETTI") (1892-1948). Vittorio was an Italian commander of troops fighting for the Republic in Spain. Most of his compatriots in the Iberian Peninsula helped Franco* under orders from Mussolini.* Vittorio had been secretary of the General Workers' Confederation (CGT) in Italy,* and while in Spain he led volunteers* in the 12th Brigade, known also as the 2d Garibaldi Battalion,* one of the International Brigades,* formed in November 1936. He fought throughout 1937, especially at the battle of Guadalajara* in March, where his unit was pitted against fellow-Italians fighting for Franco.

For further information, see John F. Coverdale, *Italian Intervention in the Spanish Civil War* (Princeton, N.J., 1975).

James W. Cortada

VIZCAYA. Vizcaya, one of the three Basque provinces in northern Spain, was the scene of heavy fighting during the first year of the Civil War as the Nationalists* campaigned to consolidate their control over all of northern Spain. One of the major campaigns of the war took place there between March and June 1937 and involved nearly 200,000 men. The Nationalists wanted to occupy Bilbao,* a major port and industrial center in Vizcaya that had both factories and facilities for shipping iron ore for export trade. The Nationalist Army* was commanded by General Emilio Mola* and the Republican Army* by General Francisco Llano de la Encomienda.* It was during this campaign, in April, that the small town of Guernica* was bombed, creating an international furor over Nationalist tactics.

For further information, see José Manuel Martínez Bande, *La guerra en el norte* (Madrid, 1969), and

Vizcaya (Madrid, 1971); Herbert R. Southworth, *Guernica! Guernica! Diplomacy, Propaganda, and the Press* (Berkeley, Calif., 1977); and Gordon Thomas and Max Morgan, *Guernica* (New York, 1975).

See also Appendix B.

James W. Cortada

VOLKMANN, HELMUTH (1889-1940). Volkmann was from Diedenhofen, Germany.* As a lieutenant general (in November 1937), he became the second commander of the German Condor Legion* in Spain (replacing General Sperrle*). He entered German service as an ensign of pioneers in 1908. In 1914, he became a flyer and served as a fighter pilot in World War I. He remained in the *Reichswehr*, but served in the infantry, artillery, and cavalry. In 1934, as a colonel, he was a department chief of the *Luftwaffe*. In October 1936, he was a major general and chief of the *Luftwaffe* Service Department.

In the Condor Legion, Volkmann had more modern and experimental aircraft than his predecessor, but he continued to be plagued with operational and maintenance problems, as well as coordination with the Spanish and Italian commands. He was bitter over the stalemate on the Ebro River* and complained to Berlin not only about the conduct of the war, but also about Germany's lack of support for the legion. He was recalled in October 1938.

For a while Volkmann commanded the *Luftwaffe* Flight School, but with the outbreak of World War II, he asked to be returned to the army. As a general of infantry, he commanded an infantry division in France* in 1940. En route to Berlin for a staff visit, he died in an automobile accident on August 21, 1940.

For further information, see Werner Beumelburg, *Kampf um Spanien, Die Geschichte der Legion Condor* (Berlin, 1939); R. Hidalgo Salazar, *La Ayuda Alemana a España 1936-39* (Madrid, 1975); and Manfred Merkes, *Die deutsche Politik gegenüber dem spanischen Bürgerkrieg, 1936-1939* (Bonn, 1961).

See also Air Force, Nationalist.

Raymond R. Proctor

VOLUNTEERS. Volunteers, primarily foreign, served on both sides in the Spanish Civil War, with the large majority of them enlisting in the Loyalist cause. (Excluded here are all those who arrived as members of German, Italian, or Soviet Russian military units.) The original movement to support the Republic was spontaneous and ill coordinated, a matter of individual or small group decisions made by two kinds of people: political refugees* from right-wing regimes of Central and Eastern Europe,* and leftists (largely working class) from the democracies of the West. What joined them was a Popular Front* mentality, a belief that the rebel generals were front-men for Adolf Hitler* and Benito Mussolini,* and that Spain was the place to stop the spread of European fascism.

When the military uprising began, hundreds and perhaps thousands of left-wing foreigners were in Catalonia* for a "People's Olympiad" being held to protest the official games scheduled for Germany.* A number of them took part in the street fighting that crushed the initial rebellion in Barcelona* on July 19. Then they joined various militia groups that set out for the Aragón* front. At the same time, exiles living in Paris and native Frenchmen began pouring across the border until, within a few weeks, some 1,000 to 1,500 were fighting on Spanish soil. By late August, military units called *Centuria*, comprising almost entirely foreign nationals and divided along linguistic lines, were in the field alongside the native militia.

The first of the foreign units was evidently the French Paris Battalion, which took part in the unsuccessful defense of Irún.* Italians, joined by a few Swiss, fought in Aragón under two banners, *Gastone Sozzi* and *Giustizia e Libertà*, the latter group made up largely of anarchists.* The Polish also had two units, the Wroblewsky and the Dombrowsky,* while Hungarians fought under the name of Rakosi. Perhaps the most disciplined and respected of these fighting groups was the Ernst Thaelmann* *Centuri* (named for a communist who was then in a Gestapo prison), formed by Hans Beimler and the Central Committee of the German Communist party in exile. The nucleus of the unit was some eighty exiles who had been living in Barcelona. Early English volunteers attached themselves to other nationalities until the Tom Mann *Centuria* was organized by Sam Masters and Nat Cohen, two East London garment workers who cut off a cycling vacation in France* to join the conflict. Distance prevented many Americans from seeing early action in Spain, but a few like Trotskyist Rosario Negrete were scattered into either Spanish or foreign military units. When the center of action shifted to the Madrid* area in October, the *centuria* were incorporated into the newly formed International Brigades,* which were then in training around Albacete.* There they were joined by fresh volunteers—eventually some 35,000 from more than fifty nations—and their story blends into that of the International Brigades.

Also serving the Loyalists* in various capacities were volunteers prominent in the world of letters. The two most famous were French writer André Malraux* and

English author George Orwell.* Malraux, flashy and histrionic, formed and commanded an air squadron of foreigners—the *Escuadrilla España*—based first in Barcelona and then in Barajas, outside Madrid. Orwell served in a more humble capacity as a footsoldier in a *Partido Obrero de Unificación Marxista* (POUM)* column in Aragón, beginning in December 1936. Wounded in the spring, after the suppression of the POUM, he was forced to go underground and flee the country in June 1937. German writer Gustav Regler* was commissar of the 12th International Brigade in the fall of 1936 during the battle of Madrid, while his countryman Ludwig Renn, celebrated for a pacifist novel based on World War I experiences, commanded a battalion in the same brigade. When the siege of the capital city began, American correspondent Louis Fischer took the position of International Brigades quartermaster for a few weeks, until a quarrel with brigade chief André Marty* sent him back into the ranks of the journalists.

In contrast to the Republican experience, the bulk of the volunteers on the Nationalist side (with a couple of notable exceptions) did not form separate, distinctive military units. Motivated by the same pro-Catholic, antiliberal, and antileftist ideology professed by rebel leaders, they joined regular military organizations like the Spanish Army, the Foreign Legion* and the Carlist *Requetés.** The largest contingent, totaling several thousand, came from Portugal,* while right-wing Frenchmen (500 of them fighting in a battalion at Jarama* under the name "Jeanne d'Arc"), Latin Americans, and White Russian exiles numbered perhaps 1,000 more. Few northern Europeans entered Nationalist ranks, although a handful of Englishmen did serve and four American pilots* flew missions for the air force. A battalion of 650 Irishmen, whose faith was made up of equal parts of anti-British and anticommunist sentiments, arrived in November 1936. Led by General Eoin O'Duffy,* the Irish played a negligible military role, spending most of their six months in training for a few brief skirmishes in which casualties* were not heavy. In May they voted 654 to 9 to return to Ireland.*

For further information on Republican foreign volunteers, see Vincent Brome, *The International Brigades* (London, 1965); Jacques Delperrie de Bayac, *Les brigades internationales* (Paris, 1968); Verle B. Johnston, *Legions of Babel: The International Brigades in the Spanish Civil War* (University Park, Penn., 1967); André Malraux, *L'Espoir* (Paris, 1937); Pietro Nenni, *La guerre d'Espagne* (Paris, 1960); George Orwell, *Homage to Catalonia* (London, 1938); Randolfo Pacciardi, *Il battaglione garibaldi: Voluntari italiani nella Spagna republicana* (Rome, 1945); Gustav Regler, *The Great Crusade* (New York, 1940); Esmond Romilly, *Boadilla* (London, 1937); and Peter Stansky and William Abrahams, *Journey to the Frontier* (London, 1966).

For further information on Nationalist foreign volunteers, see Peter Kemp, *Mine Were of Trouble* (London, 1957); General Eoin O'Duffy, *Crusade in Spain* (London, 1938); and José Sepúlveda Velloso, *Páginas do diario de un aviador na guerra de España* (Lisbon, 1972).

Robert A. Rosenstone

W

WEIZSÄCKER, ERNST VON (1882-   ). Baron von Weizsäcker served in the German Foreign Ministry before Hitler* came to power. When the Spanish Civil War broke out, he was deputy to the political director and fourth in command to the passive foreign minister Neurath.* Weizsäcker did not favor German military aid in July 1936 when Franco* appealed for German planes.

In November and December 1936, both the German Army and the Foreign Ministry pressed Hitler to decelerate military intervention in Spain. Weizsäcker supported ambassador to Italy Ulrich von Hassell's advice to limit German military aid to the rebels and allow Mussolini* to take the lead. The results were partly unforeseen, but profitable for Hitler. The Spanish conflict diverted the attention of the other great powers, thus facilitating Hitler's later expansion in Eastern Europe.* In his famous Reich Chancellery speech of November 5, 1937, Hitler announced his strategy for taking Czechoslovakia,* while the British, French, and Italians worried about the future of Spain. In part, the Führer was merely quoting Weizsäcker's prior memos. A conservative rather than a Nazi, Weizsäcker claimed his advice was motivated by a desire to avoid another 1914 and to facilitate peace with Great Britain,* France,* and the USSR.* Hitler cleverly exploited French and Italian differences in Spain by giving Mussolini first priority with Franco. This meant Hitler asked Franco for little politically.

Yet, throughout 1937, Weizsäcker urged the Nationalists* to pay promptly on their war debt to Germany.* In April 1938, new Foreign Minister Ribbentrop* promoted Weizsäcker to the position of state secretary and second in command. Weizsäcker then had considerable influence on the making of Nazi foreign policy, since Ribbentrop was basically lazy and unintelligent. From early 1938, Weizsäcker sponsored in Berlin Ambassador von Stohrer's* idea of tying Nationalist Spain directly to the Third Reich through a Friendship Treaty and Anti-Comintern Pact. Ribbentrop supported the idea until April 1938, but the Fuehrer, for the sake of Mussolini's sensibilities, delayed signing any treaty with Spain until the conclusion of the Civil War. Stohrer and Weizsäcker revived both projects in January 1939, however, for Hitler's approval and Franco's adhesion.

Weizsäcker privately opposed the Chamberlain*-Hitler confrontation over Poland* in 1939 but did nothing, other than to offer Hitler mild cautionary advice. The state secretary thought of himself as a Talleyrand trying to check Napoleon. But his hopes were not put into action; he turned out to be more like a weak Hamlet faced with a determined Hitler.

For further information, see Leonardis Hill, ed., *Die Weizsäcker Papiers, 1933-1950* (Berlin, 1975); and Ernst Weizsäcker, *Memoirs of Ernst von Weizsäcker*, trans. John Andrews (Chicago, 1951).

Robert H. Whealey

WISNIEWSKI, STEPHAN. Wisniewski was a Polish communist who fought in Spain as a member of the International Brigades* between 1936 and the end of 1937. He was a communist official who helped recruit East Europeans for the war in Spain. He was part of a large group of Communists appointed to help the Spanish by various communist parties in Eastern Europe.

For further information, see Andreu Castells, *Las Brigadas internacionales de la guerra de España* (Barcelona, 1974).

James W. Cortada

WORKERS, CATALAN. Industrial workers made up just over half of Catalonia's* total working population of 1 million in the 1930s, while agriculture employed only 26 percent. This was a dramatic reversal of the all-Spanish ratios in which agriculture still accounted for 45 percent and industry only 26 percent of the working population.* Catalonia's 180,000 textile workers formed the largest sector—twice as numerous as the next category, metal workers. Building workers (73,000) were a close third. The chemical, wool, and clothing industries were the only other significant sectors, each employing about 35,000 workers. These figures show that, while Catalonia was highly industrialized in comparison to Spain as a whole, prewar Catalan industry was still largely in the primary phase of industrialization—textiles.

As is well known, the *Confederación Nacional del Trabajo* (CNT)* was the dominant trade union* in Catalonia. In August 1931, the Catalan Regional CNT claimed 400,000 members; 58 percent of the workers of both sexes in Barcelona* were affiliated. By May 1936, largely as a result of the *Treintista* split in the union, the figure had dropped to 142,000, but this still represented 30 percent of the industrial working class. The *Federación Obrera de Unidad Sindical* (FOUS), organized by the *Partido Obrero de Unificación Marxista* (POUM),* was the second largest union, although a long way behind the CNT. The socialist-led *Unión General de Trabajadores* (UGT)* had only a small foothold, and in areas where it enjoyed some strength (as in the port of Barcelona) serious clashes occurred with the CNT.

It should also be noted that by 1936, 25 percent of Catalonia's (and over one-third of Barcelona city's) inhabitants came from Spain's poorer agrarian regions. The percentages among the working class as a whole were inevitably much higher, the immigrants providing the bulk of the unskilled labor.

After the military uprising in Barcelona on July 19, 1936, had been crushed in the streets by loyal Republican police* and working-class militants, the city came increasingly under proletarian (effectively CNT) control. Although the leading CNT committees issued no instructions to the effect, within days public transport, telephone, gas, and water supplies were functioning, most factories had reopened, food* supplies were arriving, and shops, cinemas, theaters and greyhound tracks were open—all to one extent or another organized and run by their respective workers.

The initiative was taken by individual CNT unions impelled by revolutionary syndicalist militants, who discovered that large numbers of employers and managers had fled, not before ensuring as a rule that their enterprises' financial resources had preceded them.

On October 24, 1936, the workers' takeover was officially recognized and regulated by the Generalitat's* Collectivization and Workers' Control Decree. This was a unique (and, in the central government's eyes, an unconstitutional) law, for nowhere else in the Popular Front* zone were industrial collectives given legal status. Under the decree, industrial and commercial firms employing more than 100 workers, or whose owners had fled or been declared insurgent, were automatically collectivized. Firms with fewer workers could choose to collectivize if the majority of the workers and the owner(s) agreed. Workers councils, elected by an assembly of the workers, administered the en-

terprise. Each collective (or private firm under workers' control) in a particular sector of an industry was to be represented in an Economic Federation, which in turn was to be topped by a General Industrial Council that would closely control the whole industry.

In all, some 2,000 industrial and commercial collectives were registered under the decree. But it would be a mistake to believe that all of them conformed to the letter of the law, which was approved three months after the initial wave of worker takeovers had created situations which in many cases were never reversed. Thus, a great number of small businesses, artisan in the main, were taken over and not returned to their owners, a move that alienated the numerically and politically important Catalan petty bourgeoisie. At the other end of the scale, some industries—including transport, woodworking, and public entertainment—were immediately socialized, which meant that the CNT union took over and ran the whole industry rather than collectivized the individual plants within it as required by the decree. In the textile industry, where factories were collectivized individually, the organic structure necessary to eliminate competition and rationalize the industry was not rapidly created. Intermediate experiments also existed: individual collectives were formed under the tutelage of a CNT union or, as in the armaments industry, under state control.

The absence of overall planning and the failure to create the proposed Industrial and Commercial Credit Fund led to the coexistence of rich and poor—often deficitary—collectives. As the CNT textile workers' union openly acknowledged, the market economy was not abolished. Meanwhile, in the rest of Catalonia, the Collectivization Decree was not always observed, and enterprises that should have been collectivized remained under the workers' control.

As the CNT lost its numerical superiority, by November 1936, UGT membership, thanks largely to an influx of petty bourgeois members, slightly outnumbered the anarchosyndicalists. But, more importantly, as the CNT lost its power, the collectives came increasingly to be controlled, albeit indirectly, by the resurgent Catalan government. Here Juan Comorera,* the *Partit Socialista Unificat de Catalunya* (PSUC)* secretary general and economics minister, played an important role, attempting to centralize the collectives under Generalitat (or PSUC) control. Unlike the Spanish Communist party,* the PSUC did not propose to abolish industrial collectivization, nor did the Catalan UGT, whose members established a number of collectives. But both were resolutely opposed to trade-union (or autonomous working-class) power as envisaged by the anarchosyndicalists.

The collectives faced many difficulties, both economic and political. No party or organization supported them (or at least the October decree) wholeheartedly. The structures that might have created a coherent collectivized economy were not set up rapidly enough; the central government displayed an unremitting hostility to the experiment. Moreover, there was a constant shortage of raw materials.

Indeed, it is estimated that, overall, Catalan production fell in the first year of the war by 30 percent, and by another 40 percent in the second year. The one notable success appears to have been the engineering sector in which, largely through the creation of an armaments industry where none had existed before, production increased by 22 percent in the first year.

Inevitably, the working class bore the brunt of the war. Overall unemployment rose by nearly a quarter in the first year, the cost of living quadrupled in just over two years, while wages only doubled. And yet, through every difficulty, including bitter internecine political struggle, the Catalan workers kept collectivized production going for thirty months.

The question that must be asked is not whether the collectives were a revolutionary success, but whether they were the correct revolutionary response to the needs of the moment: winning the war. Did the Catalan working class best serve its own revolutionary interests and the war effort by a multifaceted collectivization which, among other things, failed to ensure the redistribution of labor and the rapid rationalization of its main industry, textiles? By maintaining large numbers of deficitary collectives? By the failure, in short, to plan a collectivized economy?

For further information, see Albert Barcells, *Cataluña contemporanea,* II *1900-1936* (Madrid, 1974); Josep María Bricall, *Política económica de la Generalitat, 1936-1939,* 2 vols. (Barcelona, 1970-1979); José Peirats, *La CNT en la revolución española,* 3 vols. (Paris, 1971); and Albert Pérez-Baró, *Trenta mesos de collectivisme a Catalunya* (Barcelona, 1970).

See also Economy, Republican; and Libertarian Movement.

Ronald Fraser

Y

YAGÜE BLANCO, JUAN DE (1891-1952). Yagüe was a capable Nationalist field commander in the Civil War. The son of a rural doctor, he was born in the pueblo of San Leonardo de Yagüe (Soria), which was noted for its picturesque sixteenth-century castle. He entered the Infantry Academy of Toledo* with Francisco Franco,* and the two were commissioned at the same time. They met again in Africa where Yagüe commanded a unit of the *Regulares*.

Yagüe's stature was powerful. He had broad features disrupted by his glasses, when he wore them, and a handsome shock of premature grey hair. He was brisk, direct, and blunt, which at times brought him problems. He was a tough, professionally ambitious soldier who represented this characteristic flair of the legion* officers. He was a good organizer and a field commander who was popular and respected by the Nationalists* and feared by the enemy. At the same time, Yagüe had a desire for social justice which led him into political fields, and he was one of the few Nationalist officers of note who associated himself with the Falange* and its concepts of national syndicalism. In time, this gained him the title "Falange General."

In the early years of his career, although a competent officer, his promotions came routinely. In 1932, Yagüe was a lieutenant colonel and was posted to an independent mountain infantry battalion in Spain. But in 1934 Franco appointed him to lead the African troops to put down the violent leftist revolt in Asturias* against the Republic. Because of the brutality of this venture, the Left called him the "Hyena of Asturias." At the same time, he was involved in a monarchist plot concerning General Sanjurjo,* but it never materialized.

In 1936, Yagüe was again in Africa and commanded the 2d Legion. From here he became deeply involved in the conspiracy against the Popular Front* government. He was the guiding force for the revolt in the Army of Africa.* With the uprising, he seized Ceuta* and then assumed command of the legion. He went quickly to the mainland and on August 2 left Seville* with a *bandera* (military unit) headed for Mérida* which he captured by August 10. He then turned his column west to attack strongly held and fortified Badajoz* on the frontier of Portugal.* This was necessary to protect the Nationalist rear for their offensive against Madrid* and to open communications with Portugal. With inferior numbers, Yagüe carried Badajoz by storm in a very bloody battle. Descriptions of the later massacre vary, and by his own admission there were excesses. He thereby acquired another label, "The Butcher of Badajoz."

Yagüe then turned his forces in the direction of Madrid, capturing Cáceres* (which for a time was to be the Nationalist headquarters), Trujillo, Navalmoral de la Mata, and Talavera de la Reina.* Because of exhaustion and the effects of a respiratory infection, he surrendered his command to General Varela.* Some writers claim the change of command was made because Yagüe was opposed to the diversion of the Nationalist forces from the Madrid offensive to save the garrison holding the Alcázar* in Toledo. But it was at this time that he was outspoken in his support of Franco being named Generalissimo and chief of state of Nationalist Spain.

Yagüe returned to field command of African forces in a futile effort to take Madrid in November 1936. He was promoted to colonel of infantry, and then in 1937 was given command of the Madrid front. When the Republic launched the Teruel* offensive, Yagüe was rushed into the threatened area and led the forces that breached the Alfambra River. Now a brigade general, he was given command of the Corps *Marroquí* which was to spearhead the brilliant Aragón* offensive carrying Belchite* and Caspe and capturing Lérida* on April 3, 1938.

Shortly thereafter Yagüe went to Burgos,* where he gave a speech in his usual blunt and brisk manner. He praised the valor of the enemy forces his troops fought against, and at the same time denounced his German and Italian allies as beasts of prey. He went on to attack the imprisonment of some of the "old shirts"* of the Falange as a miscarriage of justice. This was a challenge to his old friend Franco which resulted in Yagüe's being relieved of command and restricted to the Burgos area, possibly to face court martial charges. However, before long he was returned to his command. The enemy launched the offensive of the Ebro River* and badly mauled some of Yagüe's divisions, but he threw in his reserve division and was able to hold the strategic Gandesa.* Eventually, he was able to launch a counteroffensive, and along with the rest of the Nationalist Army of the North* was to carry on into the battle for Catalonia.* Barcelona* was taken without a fight January 26, and the remnants of the Republican forces were fleeing to France.*

In the reorganized postwar Nationalist government, Yagüe was appointed the minister of air. With the outbreak of World War II, he was considered very pro-Axis in sentiment. In 1941, he became involved in the anti-Franco *Junta Política* led by Falangist Colonel Emilio Tarduchy. However, this contact with Yagüe was reported to Franco who took him privately to task. Franco chose not to make an issue of the matter and promoted Yagüe, which nullified his position in any conspiracy. In the twilight of World War II, Yagüe was given command of the troops to resist those forces made up of Spaniards and foreigners who crossed from France under the misguided thought that they would be able to liberate Spain from Franco's rule. He died a lieutenant general of the army in Burgos on October 29, 1952, and was posthumously made a marquis.

For further information, see Juan José Calleja, *Yagüe, un corazón al rojo* (Barcelona, 1963); and Stanley G. Payne, *Politics and the Military in Modern Spain* (Stanford, Calif., 1967).

See also Army, Nationalist; and Appendix B.

Raymond L. Proctor

YUGOSLAVIA. Yugoslavia, like much of Eastern Europe,* sought to maintain strict neutrality in the Spanish Civil War. Liberal elements hostile to the government, however, favored the Republic and sought to aid it. Approximately 1,500 Yugoslavian citizens fought in the International Brigades,* recruited from the universities, radical Left parties (especially from among the communists), and groups otherwise hostile to the regime. For instance, elements supporting Josep Broz Tito volunteered for the International Brigades. The experience they gained there helped them in the late 1940s when establishing a communist regime at home. After the war, many officers who had served in Spain became generals in the Yugoslavian Army.

For further information, see Vladimir Dedijer, *Tito Speaks* (London, 1953).

James W. Cortada

Z

ZABALZA, RICARDO (-1939). Zabalza was a Spanish socialist and a leader in the *Unión General de Trabajadores* (UGT).* In 1937, he became the civil governor of Valencia,* the site of the Republican government. He supported the expansion of Republican control in Valencia and in the Levante* against the interests of local autonomists. He also expanded his authority to the point of even selecting who would serve as mayors in his province. In 1938, he became a member of the executive committee of the UGT, representing the minority politics of the Largo Caballero* faction.

For further information, see Burnett Bolloten, *The Spanish Revolution: The Left and the Struggle for Power During the Civil War* (Chapel Hill, N.C., 1979).
See also Communist Party, Spanish; and Socialist Party, Spanish.

James W. Cortada

ZAISSER, WILHELM. *See* "Gómez" (Wilhelm Zaisser).

ZUGAZAGOITIA, JULIÁN (-1940). Zugazagoitia was a socialist and minister of the interior in the Re-public from 1937 to 1938. Before the Civil War, he was the editor of *El Socialista*,* Indalecio Prieto's* mouthpiece. Zugazagoitia joined the cabinet in May 1937 as minister of the interior, in charge of Republican police* activities. While in this position he resisted attempts by the communists, and especially by Russian advisers, to encroach in his area of responsibility but with declining success as the war moved nearer to conclusion. In 1938, he became secretary general of defense which involved less responsibility; he had been pushed out of the cabinet for not supporting the communists. Between May and July 1937, the communists gained considerable influence within the government. This Basque politician was eventually arrested by the Nationalists* and executed.

For further information, see Burnett Bolloten, *The Spanish Revolution: The Left and the Struggle for Power During the Civil War* (Chapel Hill, N.C., 1979); and Julián Zugazagoitia, *Historia de la guerra en España* (Buenos Aires, 1940).

James W. Cortada

APPENDIX A

A Chronology of the Spanish Civil War: 1930-1939

DOUGLAS W. FOARD

1930

January 28   General Miguel Primo de Rivera is dismissed after, according to his own words, "2,326 days of continuous uneasiness, responsibility, and labor."

August 17   As King Alfonso XIII struggles to constitute a new basis for his regime, antimonarchical forces coalesce in the Pact of San Sebastián, insisting upon a Republican future for the nation.

December 12   An abortive Republican uprising by civil and military forces at Jaca. Captains Fermín Galán and García Hernández are subsequently executed for the act.

1931

April 12   Municipal elections are conducted in Spain's urban centers, with the results running heavily against the monarchy.

April 13   King Alfonso is advised to leave the country by the commander of the *Guardia Civil* (Civil Guard), General José Sanjurjo. Gregorio Marañón and the Conde de Romanones negotiate a transfer of power with the "shadow cabinet" created by the Pact of San Sebastián.

April 14   At 8:45 P.M., King Alfonso departs from the royal palace in Madrid for the port of Cartagena. There he sails for Marseilles and exile. Before midnight the provisional government has occupied its posts in Madrid and issued its first decrees, among which is one amnestying all political prisoners. In Barcelona, Francesc Maciá proclaims the Catalan State in a radio broadcast.

April 16   The president of the provisional government, Niceto Alcalá-Zamora, is obliged to declare martial law to quell disturbances in Seville. The new minister of war, Manuel Azaña Díaz, dismisses the commanders of five of the nation's military districts.

April 17   *ABC* publishes King Alfonso's parting manifesto, claiming that he had left the nation in order to avoid a civil war.

April 18   Hurried negotiations in Barcelona convince Maciá to revise his declaration of a Catalan State to an announcement of the creation of the Generalitat of Catalonia.

April 23   The "Azaña law," requiring officers and men of the armed forces to swear loyalty to the Republic, is proclaimed. Officers who refused the oath are to be allowed to retire from the services with full pay.

April 27   The Republican tricolor and the "Himno de Riego" are officially adopted by the state.

April 28   The first of the agrarian reform laws is decreed. This law of *términos municipales* seeks to protect local agricultural workers from losing jobs to those brought in from outside their communities.

May 1   While government ministers and leading socialists parade together for the *fiesta de trabajo* in Madrid, Cardinal Pedro Segura, archbishop of Toledo, publishes a pastoral letter hostile to the Republic.

May 6   Marcelino Domingo Sanjuán, minister of public instruction, proclaims an end to compulsory religious instruction in state-operated schools.

May 7   The socialist minister of labor, Francisco Largo Caballero, decrees the creation of *jurados mixtos agrarios*, arbitration panels for rural Spain to mediate labor grievances.

May 8   The electoral law is revised to permit women and priests to vote. Still another decree formalizes relationships between the Republic and Generalitat.

May 10   The organization of the *Círculo Monarquico* in Madrid touches off street clashes and the threat of a *Confederación Nacional del Trabajo* (CNT) strike in the capital. Minister Miguel Maura (*Gobernación*) pleads with the cabinet to be permitted a show of force. He is denied.

May 11	Seven church-owned structures are burned in Madrid with similar episodes in Seville, Málaga,and Cádiz.
May 12	Martial law is decreed throughout the nation.
May 14	Cardinal Segura becomes *persona non grata* to the Republic and leaves for exile, obstensibly explained as consultations in Rome.
May 19	Martial law is suspended.
May 22	Freedom of religion is decreed for the nation as well as the removal of religious images from the classrooms of state-operated schools.
May 24	The Vatican refuses to accept the credentials of the Republic's diplomatic representative, Luis Zulueta.
May 25	Azaña announces the first of his sweeping reforms of the military, reducing the number of active army divisions from 16 to 8. The number of serving officers is to be slashed from 26,000 to less than 10,000. Those retired by this reorganization are to receive full pay.
June 3	Spain's bishops address a joint letter to the government protesting its religious policies and arguing that they violate the Concordat of 1851.
June 4	National elections for a Constituent Cortes are announced for June 28, with that body to be convened on July 14.
June 9	Cardinal Segura is detained in an attempt to return to the nation incognito. Four days later he is ordered into exile.
June 12	Marcelino Domingo pledges the government to the construction of 27,000 new elementary schools. At the same time, the Cabinet extends the benefits of Spain's industrial accident insurance to rural laborers.
June 14	In Estella, representatives of 480 Basque and Navarrese municipalities assemble to consider a proposal for the creation of an autonomous Basque State, while at Pamplona there is a rally protesting the government's treatment of Cardinal Segura.
June 19	The Bank of France agrees to extend the Republic a 300 million franc credit after the minister of finance, Indalecio Prieto, leaves a deposit of $20 million worth of Spanish gold with the French institution. This agreement is urgent since a Morgan bank credit to Spain has been canceled.
June 28	National elections for the Constituent Cortes attract more than 4 million of the nation's 6 million eligible voters. Although the Socialist party gains the largest number of seats (115), the assembly is to be dominated by the various middle-class factions.
July 4	The CNT launches a strike against the nation's telephone company, controlled by AT&T. The strike successfully interrupts services in Barcelona and Seville, but the socialist labor union (the *Unión General de Trabajadores* [UGT]) refuses to honor the work stoppage. Clashes result.
July 14	The Constituent Cortes convenes in Madrid, while the telephone strike continues.
July 22	After four days of strike-connected conflict in Seville, Miguel Maura declares a state of martial law in the province.
July 23	Disturbances throughout the nation as a result of conflict between the UGT and CNT prompt Maura to order the closing of all CNT headquarters in Spain and the arrest of its leaders.
July 28	The provisional government resigns only to be reconfirmed in office three days later by the Constituent Cortes. Order has been restored in Seville at the cost of thirty dead.
July 29	A parliamentary commission is constituted to draft a Constitution under the presidency of the socialist jurist, Luis Jiménez de Asúa.
August 2	A plebiscite in Catalonia approves the proposed Catalan Statute of Autonomy by a vote of 592,691 to 3,276.
August 18	The Constituent Cortes is presented with the proposed Catalan Statute and its own commission's draft of a national Constitution.
August 20	The government issues a decree forbidding the Church from transferring or mortgaging its properties in Spain.
September 2	The Commission on Responsibilities, established by the Cortes to investigate those culpable in the creation of the dictatorship in 1923, orders the detention of those persons who served the former regime as ministers.
September 30	Pope Pius XI accepts the resignation of Cardinal Segura (which the Vatican had been urging upon the Spanish primate).

October 2	D. Jaime de Borbón, Carlist pretender to the Spanish throne, dies less than a month after having reached a minimal accord with the exiled king, Alfonso XIII.
	Intense debate begins in the Constituent Cortes over the proposed Article 26 of the Constitution concerning the role of the religious orders within the nation.
October 13	After Azaña's "Spain has ceased to be Catholic" address, the Constituent Cortes approves Article 26 in spite of the Radical-Socialist abstention.
October 14	The adoption of Article 26 triggers the first cabinet crisis of the Republican era. Alcalá-Zamora and Miguel Maura resign their posts in protest. Azaña keeps his post as minister of war and steps in to replace Alcalá-Zamora as head of the government. Maura's post at *Gobernación* is taken by Santiago Casares Quiroga.
October 17	The Constituent Cortes approves Article 43 of the proposed Constitution legalizing divorce.
October 20	The Law for the Defense of the Republic is approved by the Cortes. This legislation grants the minister of the interior (*Gobernación*) sweeping powers to suspend civil liberties in the maintenance of public order.
November 14	*Mundo Obrero*, the Communist party newspaper, publishes its first edition.
November 17	José María Gil Robles becomes president of the Catholic conservative party, *Acción Nacional*.
November 26	Since the proposed Constitution would establish a unicameral legislature, the Constituent Cortes agrees to create a Tribunal of Constitutional Guarantees to monitor the legality of the acts of the Parliament.
	Alfonso XIII is indicted and perpetually banished by the Constituent Cortes.
December 9	After months of debate, the Cortes approves the new constitutional instrument by a vote of 368 to 38.
December 11	Alcalá-Zamora is elected overwhelmingly by the members of the Constituent Cortes to serve as the president of the Republic. According to a carefully prepared agreement, Azaña then resigns.
December 15	The first edition of the right-wing journal *Acción Española* appears.
December 17	With Alcalá-Zamora as president, a new cabinet is organized, which excludes the Radical party and yields the premiership and the Ministry of War to Manuel Azaña.
December 19	The Constituent Cortes suspends its sessions until January 5.
December 31	Four members of the Civil Guard are slain and their bodies mutilated in the Badajoz village of Castilblanco. The violence originated when the mayor refused agricultural workers a permit to stage a peaceful demonstration and the Civil Guard was summoned to clear the streets.

1932

January	In the midst of this sometimes tumultuous month, the Constituent Cortes passes laws legalizing divorce and secularizing cemeteries.
January 5	Unemployed factory workers in Arnedo (Logroño) demonstrate. The Civil Guard, called in to restore order, fires into the crowd, killing six persons and wounding thirty. There are angry calls in the Cortes for the removal of the Guard's commander, General Sanjurjo.
January 17	A serious clash occurs in Bilbao between socialists and traditionalists in which three socialists are killed.
January 19	The *Federación Anarquista Ibérica* (FAI) initiates a workers' revolt in the Llobregat Valley.
January 21	The army is used to suppress the Llobregat revolt, while the government closes anarchist and communist headquarters in Barcelona.
January 23	The Constituent Cortes acts to dissolve the Jesuit order in Spain by prohibiting their communal life and the free disposition of their property.
January 29	The papal *nuncio* Monsignor Tedeschini officially protests the government's actions toward the Jesuits.
February 5	General Sanjurjo is replaced as commander of the Civil Guard and is assigned the directorship of the frontier guards, the *Carabineros*.
February 20	A schism occurs in the Radical-Socialist party, leading Botella Asensi to create the Left Radical-Socialists.
March	During this month, the value of the peseta reaches its weakest point during the Great Depression. Subsequently, it steadily becomes stronger.
March 14	The Agrarian Reform Bill is introduced in the Cortes and is quickly approved. The law envisions govern-

mental confiscation of untilled lands in southern Spain and their distribution to individual peasant families or to peasant cooperatives.

April	The Vatican selects Isidro Gomá y Tomás to succeed Segura as Spain's cardinal-archbishop.
April 5	President Alcalá-Zamora, visiting Valencia, decrees that province's autonomy over its *Tribunal de las aguas*.
April 6	Violent encounters occur on the campus of the University of Madrid as rightist factions attempt to challenge the dominant student organization, the *Federación Universitaria Escolar*.
April 9	The proposed Catalan Statute gets its first reading in the Constituent Cortes.
April 12	Government concern over impending peasant strikes and threatened crop burnings leads it to authorize the importation of 300,000 tons of wheat.
April 29	Gil Robles' *Acción Nacional* is obliged by the effect of a decree to alter its name to *Acción Popular*.
May 1	The *fiesta de trabajo* produces an absolute work stoppage in Madrid.
May 11	The founder of the Spanish Nationalist party, José María Albiñana, is arrested for sedition and is later imprisoned at Las Hurdes.
May 13	Spain establishes commercial relations with the Soviet Union.
June 2	During debate in the Constituent Cortes, José Ortega y Gasset and Melquiades Álvarez express their opposition to the proposed Catalan Statute.
June 8	Indictments are issued against Calvo Sotelo and Juan March for corruption in the handling of the Moroccan tobacco monopoly. March is Jailed in Madrid the following day.
June 15	The first article of the Catalan Statute is approved by the Constituent Cortes. On the same day, Juan March is convicted, fined 6 million pesetas, and confined to prison in Alcalá de Henares.
June 19	An assembly of representatives of the Basque and Navarrese municipalities gathers in Pamplona to consider a proposed Basque Statute. The Navarres refuse to endorse the regional autonomy plan.
June 27	A verbal incident following a military review at Carabanchel leads to the trial of Colonel Julio Mangada for insubordination, the eventual resignation of General Manuel Goded, and change in command of the 1st Army division.
July 8	Some struggles occur in connection with the harvest of 1932. At Villa de Don Fadrique (Toledo), the Civil Guard clashes with demonstrating peasants, and four are killed.
July 28	The Constituent Cortes passes a Law of Public Order, augmenting the previous Law for the Defense of the Republic. This legislation defines the powers granted the government under a state of prevention, state of alarm and state of war (martial law).
August 9	In the initial move of a planned armed uprising against the "anticlerical dictatorship of Azaña," General Sanjurjo leaves Madrid in the afternoon for a trip to Seville.
August 10	Upon reaching Seville, Sanjurjo declares martial law and dispatches troops to occupy key points in the city. The workers in the region retaliate with a general strike. In Madrid, rebel troops under the command of General Emilio Barrera are foiled in their efforts to seize the centers of power. Learning of the debacle, General Sanjurjo attempts to reach the Portuguese border only to be arrested at Huelva.
August 11	Several conservative newspapers are forced to suspend publication as Sanjurjo arrives in the capital for questioning.
August 13	The government dissolves the third *cuarto* of the Civil Guard, which had supported Sanjurjo.
August 17	The Cortes hears a bill that would expropriate the estates of those landowners involved in the August 10 uprising. It is approved the following day by a vote of 262 to 14.
August 24	The Supreme Court considers the case against General Sanjurjo and his co-conspirators. The general is eventually sentenced to life in prison, and 145 of his followers are sent to the penal colony at Villa Cisneros.
September 6	In legislation revising the penal code of 1870, the Constituent Cortes abolishes capital punishment.
September 8	Speaking in support of the proposed Agrarian Reform Bill, Prime Minister Azaña proclaims that the Republic is "revolutionary" in nature.
September 9	The Agrarian Reform Bill gains the approval of the Constituent Cortes. Through its provisions the property of 80,000 landowners is confiscated.

	In the same session, the Cortes approves the Catalan Statute by a vote of 334 to 24. The assembly had revised the wording of the document to delete any reference to federalism.
September 10	President Alcalá-Zamora journeys to San Sebastián to sign the Catalan Statute, while the Cortes suspends its sessions until October 1.
September 23	In accordance with the Agrarian Reform Bill, the Institute of Agrarian Reform is established. In two years it manages to transfer land to only 12,000 families.
October 1	The Constituent Cortes reconvenes.
October 3	Operating under the new Catalan Statute, Maciá reorganizes the cabinet of the Generalitat.
October 11	The monarchist intellectual, Antonio Goicoechea, is arrested on charges of sedition.
October 18	The minister of finance, Jaime Carner Romeu, introduces his 1933 budget in the Cortes, providing for a progressive taxation on rental income. That item is approved in less than an hour.
October 30	The French prime minister, Eduard Herriot, pays an official state visit to Spain.
November 1	A Law for the Intensification of Cultivation passes the Cortes. This act settles landless peasants on untilled portions of estates in several provinces. More than 40,000 farmers take advantage of its provisions within six months.
	In Valencia, a gathering of regional mayors convenes to consider the possibility of a Statute of Autonomy.
November 9	A coalition of Cortes factions, including some Radical-Socialists, agrees to form the *Federación de Izquierdas Republicanas*.
November 14	In response to serious unemployment in the mines of Asturias, the government proposes to purchase 350,000 tons of coal in order to prevent a general strike in the region. Within five days, the strike leaders accept the settlement.
November 20	General elections are held in Catalonia with a coalition of socialists and Left Republicans prevailing.
December 1	Fernando de los Ríos, minister of public instruction, decrees that educational institutions must begin offering evening courses for adults. By year's end he can claim that the Republic created 9,600 elementary schools, constructing them at a rate ten times faster than that established under the monarchy.
December 6	The Catalan Parliament inaugurates its sessions.
December 17	Autonomists in Galicia assemble to consider a statute for their region.
December 31	Twenty-nine prisoners at Villa Cisneros escape in a French schooner.

1933

January 1	Police in Barcelona uncover a considerable munitions deposit. Meanwhile, terrorist bombs explode at La Felguera.
January 8	An explosion wrecks the entrance to police headquarters in Barcelona, and anarchist attacks on barracks are reported in Saragossa, Seville, Bilbao, and Madrid.
January 11	Anarchists in Casas Viejas (Cádiz) rebel in the name of libertarian communism, and a pitched battle with the Civil Guard ensues. Reinforcements, *Guardias de Asalto* (Assault Guards), quickly arrive for the police, but fighting continues throughout the day. A siege develops at the hut of the anarchist, "Seisdedos," and is concluded only when the building and its six occupants are incinerated. A Captain Rojas of the *Asaltos* orders the execution of fourteen prisoners in reprisal for casualties suffered by his subordinates.
January 12	The government's handling of the Casas Viejas incident is roundly denounced in the Cortes by such diverse speakers as Martínez Barrio and Ortega.
January 30	Adolph Hitler becomes chancellor of Germany.
February 8	After a heated debate, the Constituent Cortes appoints an eight-man commission to investigate the events at Casas Viejas.
February 28	The national congress of *Acción Popular* announces the creation of the *Confederación Española de Derechas Autónomas* (CEDA).
March 1	Antonio Goicoechea, released from prison, announces the program of *Renovación Española* at a meeting of the monarchist organization in Madrid.

March 4	While five of his fellow officers in command at Casas Viejas are released, Captain Rojas continues in detention.
March 5	The director-general of security, Arturo Menéndez, is dismissed in connection with the Casas Viejas incident.
	Students at the University of Madrid form a syndicate affiliated with Onésimo Redondo's *Juntas de Ofensiva Nacional-Sindicalista* (JONS).
March 9	General Queipo de Llano is removed from the *Jefetura de la Casa Militar*.
March 11	Arturo Menéndez, former director-general of security, is jailed for his role in the Casas Viejas incident.
March 16	The Cortes concludes its debate on Casas Viejas with a vote of confidence in the government.
	The weekly journal *El Fascio* makes its debut with contributions from José Antonio Primo de Rivera, Ramiro Ledesma, and Gimenez Caballero.
April 8	The Constituent Cortes suspends sessions until April 25.
April 13	Catalonia's *rabassaires*, sharecroppers in the viniculture industry, stage a massive protest demonstration in Barcelona.
April 19	The communist-dominated *Asociación de amigos de Rusia* is formed.
April 23	Municipal elections for councilmen reveal a strong antigovernmental shift of opinion.
May 8	Two days of fighting between FUE and JONS students at the University of Madrid requires the summoning of the police to campus.
May 17	The Constituent Cortes approves the Law of Religious Congregations. This bill, emphatically opposed by the Catholic parties, excludes the monastic orders from commerce, industry, and teaching (threatening the existence of some 259 secondary schools). The legislation envisions the nationalization of stipulated church properties and the regular government inspection of church-operated hospitals and seminaries.
May 20	After a previous, unsuccessful effort, assassins kill Pedro Caravaca, the leading member of the landowners' *Federación Económica de Andalusia*.
June 1	Students, drawn primarily from the University of Madrid, embark upon the first of the *misiones pedagógicas* cultural missions to the hamlets of rural Spain.
June 2	From Rome the Spanish bishops once again address a letter to the government protesting its religious policies.
June 3	Pope Pius XI condemns the Law of Religious Congregations in the encyclical *Dilectissima nobis*.
June 7	The Constituent Cortes establishes the Tribunal of Constitutional Guarantees, defining its membership and function.
June 8	President Alcalá-Zamora hesitates to approve a Cabinet reorganization proposed by Prime Minister Azaña. The prime minister resigns, and a four-day crisis begins.
June 12	After coaxing Alejandro Lerroux and Indalecio Prieto to attempt to form a government, Alcalá-Zamora once again calls upon Azaña to accept the premiership.
June 14	The presentation of the new Azaña cabinet to the Constituent Cortes prompts Miguel Maura and his Conservative Republicans to walk out of the assembly.
June 16	Widespread peasant seizures of uncultivated lands occur in Catalonia.
July 2	Warning against the increasing radicalization of the Socialist party, Julián Besteiro proclaims in a speech at the Mieres mines that Spain is not yet ready for socialism.
July 3	Catalonia imposes a two-year residency requirement on those seeking jobs in the region.
July 13	The minister of justice, Álvaro de Albornoz, is elected president of the Tribunal of Constitutional Guarantees.
July 27	The electoral law of 1907 is formally revised by the Constituent Cortes, enfranchising millions of women voters. On the same day, the government for the first time extends diplomatic recognition to the Soviet Union.
August	Throughout Estremadura frustrated peasants set fire to crops standing in the fields ready for harvest.
August 6	The representatives of the *Comisiones Gestoras* of the Basque provinces approve a proposed Statue of Autonomy by a vote of 249 to 33.

August 11	In a speech at a socialist youth summer camp, Largo Caballero declares that "it is impossible to carry out socialist tasks within a bourgeois democracy."
August 16	An editorial in *El Socialista* seconds Largo Caballero's opposition line to Besteiro.
August 17	It is reported that as of this date some 300,000 peasants in Spain have no work at all, while another 250,000 find employment only three days weekly.
August 22	Disorder in the Seville region causes the government to declare a state of prevention in that locality.
September 4	In municipal elections for the fifteen popular seats on the Tribunal of Constitutional Guarantees, the government once again fares poorly, gaining only one-third of the positions.
September 8	Having seen much of his original program enacted into law, Manuel Azaña tenders his resignation as prime minister in the face of mounting opposition.
September 12	The leader of the Radical party, Alejandro Lerroux, succeeds in forming a government that excludes the socialists.
September 17	The Agrarian party, representing many of the nation's landowners, conducts a national convention in Madrid. The socialist labor union, the UGT, protests the assembly by calling a general strike.
October 2	Following a suspension of its sessions, the Constituent Cortes is presented with the Lerroux cabinet.
October 3	A socialist-sponsored resolution of "no confidence" passes in the Cortes by a vote of 187 to 91. Lerroux resigns, and President Alcalá-Zamora once again begins a search for a prime minister.
October 5	Utility workers in Barcelona stage a strike, forcing the Generalitat to invoke a state of prevention in the city.
October 8	Martínez Barrio, who had only recently split with the Radical party, agrees to serve as prime minister of a caretaker regime that would preside over new elections. Although his government continues to exclude the socialists, Martínez Barrio moves quickly to summon the elections for November 19.
October 15	The electoral campaign officially begins with the CEDA having formed a temporary coalition with the agrarians and monarchist factions.
October 20	The Tribunal of Constitutional Guarantees dismisses the charges that had been brought against Calvo Sotelo.
October 24	CNT officials instruct their followers to boycott the November elections.
October 29	The *Falange Española* is inaugurated at a meeting in Madrid's *Teatro de la Comedia*. The movement's candidates are presented independently in the election rather than join the rightist coalition that embraces Gil Robles, Calvo Sotelo, and Luca de Tena.
November 3	Juan March escapes from his imprisonment and flees to Gibraltar.
November 5	A plebiscite in the Basque provinces overwhelmingly approves a proposed Statute of Autonomy for the region.
November 19	With 67 percent of the electorate participating, a strong conservative trend is evidenced in the returns. CEDA will become the largest single party in the new Cortes, while the socialists will suffer the loss of half of their seats. Even in Catalonia, Francisco Cambó's *Lliga Catalana* wins twenty-five posts in the Cortes compared to the nineteen claimed by Luis Companys' *Esquerra*.
December 2	Violence in Barcelona compels President Alcalá-Zamora to decree again a state of prevention in the region.
December 3	Runoff elections assure rightist control of the new Cortes.
December 4	The president of the Republic extends the state of prevention throughout Spain.
December 7	Fearing violent protests against the election results, the minister of the interior warns all provincial governors to be vigilant against revolutionary insurrection. *FE*, the Falangist newspaper, makes its first appearance.
December 8	The newly elected Cortes convenes.
December 9	Beginning in Barbastro, an anarchist uprising spreads across the nation to Asturias and the Levante.
December 10	President Alcalá-Zamora decrees a state of alarm throughout Spain. Church properties are burned in Granada, strikes grip Valencia, and an express train is derailed in sabotage at Puzol.
December 11	Even though the socialists proclaim their opposition to the insurrection, serious clashes continue. Seven

peasants are killed by the Assault Guards in Villanueva de la Serna (Badajoz), while six perish at the hands of the Civil Guards in Bujalance (Córdoba).

December 14   In spite of CNT calls for a general strike, the insurrection is subdued. The government reports ninety dead and nearly 200 wounded in the violence.

December 16   Once order is restored, Martínez Barrio resigns. Alejandro Lerroux again becomes prime minister with the support of the CEDA in the Cortes. Most of the members of his cabinet are drawn from Lerroux's own Radical party; none are from the CEDA.

Lerroux's government simply ignores the previous Cortes's Law of Congregations, appoints conservatives to chair the *jurados mixtos*, and tempers agrarian reform.

December 25   The most celebrated spokesman for Catalan autonomy, Francesc Macià, dies of natural causes.

December 31   Luis Companys succeeds Macià as president of the Generalitat.

1934

January 3   Regional elections in Catalonia give Companys' *Esquerra* control of the Generalitat. This time the anarchists take part in the electoral process, reversing the trend of the November balloting.

January 11   The appearance of the second edition of *FE* produces a fight on the streets of Madrid which claims the life of a young Falangist.

January 25   Falangists attack the FUE center at the University of Madrid's School of Medicine.

January 27   The Besteiro faction is dismissed from the executive committee of the Socialist party. Anastasio de García becomes president of the committee, and Largo Caballero its secretary.

February 8   The government orders a general disarmament of the civilian population.

February 11   Peasants who had seized cultivated estates are ordered expelled from those localities.

February 12   Civil war erupts in Austria as the Dollfuss regime takes steps to smash its opponents on the Left.

February 13   The Falange merges with Onésimo Redondo's JONS.

February 22   The Generalitat approves the law *Contratos de cultivos*, which permits tenants to purchase lands they had been working for fifteen years or more.

February 28   The resignation of two ministers (Martínez Barrio and Lara at Hacienda) precipitates another Cabinet crisis. The two resigned in protest over the Lerroux government's conservative policies.

March 3   With parliamentary backing from CEDA and the Lliga, Lerroux fashions another cabinet dominated by his own Radical party.

March 12   Workers in Madrid's newspaper industry go out on strike.

March 21   The Cortes approves a major naval construction appropriation.

March 23   The minister of justice introduces legislation in the Cortes that would free those convicted of political crimes before December 3, 1933.

March 27   The Lerroux cabinet votes to reintroduce the death penalty in Spain. In April, the Cortes refuses to endorse this action.

March 28   A general strike is called in Saragossa in protest of the capital punishment decision. The strike movement was inspired by the FAI and seconded by local socialists. The events of the ensuing six-week struggle in the city make a national figure of the FAI leader, Buenaventura Durruti.

March 31   At a meeting at the Quirinal in Rome, representatives of the Spanish Right win Mussolini's support for an armed rebellion against the Republic. Goicoechea, the Carlists, Rafael Olazábal and Antonio Lizarza, and General Barrera earn the Duce's promise of weapons and money. Funds are immediately made available to the conspirators.

April 4   The Cortes votes to exempt the "passive" income of the clergy from the provisions of the Law of Congregations.

April 8   Spanish troops occupy the African territory of Ifni.

April 14   The military stages a grand review in Madrid to celebrate the third anniversary of the Republic.

April 19   An amended amnesty bill is passed in the Cortes. At the insistence of the socialists, the legislation frees all political prisoners sentenced before April 14, 1934.

April 20	President Alcalá-Zamora signs the amnesty bill with the gravest hesitation. Under its provisions, General Sanjurjo is freed and immediately crosses the border into Portugal.
April 22	A mass rally of the *Juventud de Acción Popular* at the Escorial is addressed by Gil Robles. Workers in Madrid stage a general strike in response to the rally and the freeing of General Sanjurjo.
April 25	Smarting from his dispute with the president over the amnesty bill, Lerroux resigns as prime minister. Alcalá-Zamora begins a three-day search for a new head of the government.
April 28	With Lerroux's permission, his colleague in the Radical party, Ricardo Samper Ibáñez, forms a cabinet. It is once again dominated by the Radicals.
May 2	Authorities in Saragossa, contending with the prolonged general strike, appeal to the central government for assistance.
	The Carlist pretender appoints Manual Fal Conde to be general secretary of the Carlist *Communión Tradicionalista*.
May 3	*Acción Española*, suspended from publication since the Sanjurjo uprising, resumes its place on the newsstands.
May 4	Calvo Sotelo returns to Madrid from exile.
	Prime Minister Samper, taking exception to the Generalitat's *contrato de cultivos* legislation, appeals to the Tribunal of Constitutional Guarantees for a ruling on its legality.
May 9	Calvo Sotelo, having been elected to the Cortes "in absentia," takes his seat among the legislators.
May 11	Indalecio Prieto's questions in the Cortes concerning the propriety of trade agreements for rice and corn bring about the dismissal of the governor of the *Banco Exterior de España*.
May 12	The general strike in Saragossa concludes, and peace is restored in the city.
May 24	The 1931 law, *términos municipales*, is repealed by the Cortes.
May 25	A coalition of CNT and UGT farmers threatens an agricultural strike in Andalusia. They demand the reinstatement of the *términos* law and a 12-peseta daily pay increase. The government decides to negotiate.
May 28	The minister of the interior declares that reaping the harvest is a public service, and, therefore, strikes halting that activity would be illegal.
May 29	In the face of the impending crisis with the farm workers, Prime Minister Samper asks the Cortes for a vote of confidence. His government is sustained.
June 1	The Tribunal of Constitutional Guarantees rules that the Generalitat's land distribution plan (the law of *contratos de cultivos*) is unconstitutional since it infringes upon the sovereignty of the central government.
June 5	The Federation of Land Workers (FNTT), a radical branch of the UGT, proclaims its threatened strike in southern Spain. Although the UGT refuses to endorse all of the farm worker's demands, the job action will spread to many rural areas of the country during the ensuing two weeks. Taking unprecedented measures against the movement, the minister of the interior will order the arrest of more than 7,000 persons (including some members of the Cortes) during the period. The strike is eventually broken at a cost of thirteen lives.
June 6	The executive committee of the Socialist party orders local offices of the party to organize for direct action. Socialist *grupos de choque* soon appear on Madrid streets to challenge the Falange.
June 10	A Falangist youth is killed during the day in a street fight with socialists in Madrid. That evening, Juanita Rico is murdered in reprisal. A cycle of vicious street violence begins.
June 12	Basque and Catalan deputies (except those belonging to the Lliga) walk out of the Cortes, angered over the government's confrontation with the Generalitat on land redistribution. Later that day, Companys scores a major victory by gaining the approval of a plebiscite in Catalonia on the land issue.
July 4	The Samper government wins a vote of confidence in the Cortes for its stand against the Generalitat. The assembly also agrees that charges pending against any of its members must be suspended until the expiration of their terms of office.
July 19	Members of the armed forces are forbidden by the government from joining any political parties or syndicates.
August 12	Elections, scheduled on this date in the Basque provinces, are declared illegal by the governor of Vizcaya.

The balloting determines who is to represent the provinces in autonomy negotiations with the central government. Riots immediately occur throughout the region, obliging the government to summon troops. Half of the mayors in the region, including the mayor of Bilbao, resign.

August 13	Bilbao is paralyzed by protests.
August 22	Raising the stakes in its quarrel with Madrid, the Generalitat prohibits the importation of grain into the region from the rest of Spain without the authorization of the Catalan government.
August 26	The representatives elected by the Basques in their illegal voting on August 12 agree to assemble in Zumárraga on September 2 and invite Catalan representatives to attend.
September 2	The Samper government declares the planned Basque assembly at Zumárraga "factious" and uses the Civil Guard to prevent it from convening.
September 3	The executive committee of the Basque leadership meets with representatives of the *Esquerra* and the Socialist party at San Sebastián. In a public statement, they call upon all Basque municipal councilmen to resign.
September 5	The Catalan landowners' organization, the *Instituto Agrícola Catalán de San Isidro*, is attacked by the *rabassaires*.
September 7	The Basque leadership appeals the government's actions with regard to their elections to the Tribunal of Constitutional Guarantees.
September 8	Meeting in Madrid, members of the *Instituto Agrícola Catalán* hear an address by Gil Robles. Workers in the city call a general strike in response. The government, in turn, shuts down Madrid's Casa del Pueblo.
September 9	*Acción Popular* stages a national convocation at historic Covadonga. A general strike in the region succeeds in paralyzing public services. Speaking at Covadonga, Gil Robles accuses the socialists of treason and warns, "We shall no longer suffer this state of affairs to continue."
September 11	Police in Asturias uncover an effort to smuggle arms to the workers of the region aboard the vessel *Turquesa*. Investigation reveals that the former minister, Indalecio Prieto, a Socialist party leader, was involved in the plot. He is obliged to flee the country, and he remains in exile in France until 1935.
September 14	Communist and socialist youth organizations hold a joint assembly in Madrid.
September 23	Responding to the illicit arms trade and rumors of impending insurrection, the government declares a state of alarm throughout the nation.
September 29	The president of the Republic and other ministers attend the inauguration of Miguel de Unamuno as rector of the University of Salamanca.
October 1	After a long recess, the Cortes reconvenes only to hear Gil Robles denounce the Samper government and withdraw his party's support of it. Without CEDA backing, Samper has no choice but to resign.
October 3	In spite of warnings of an impending general strike, President Alcalá-Zamora calls upon Lerroux once again to form a government, this time with CEDA ministers. Gil Robles' followers gain three cabinet posts.
October 4	Socialist call for a nationwide general strike, even though the CNT refuses to take part. Work stoppages follow immediately in Madrid, Barcelona, the Asturias mining region, and most other major Spanish cities.
October 6	In Asturias, the strike becomes a full-scale revolution as armed miners seize towns. In Barcelona, Companys announces the creation of a "Catalan State within the Spanish Federal Republic" in a radio broadcast. Fighting occurs in the Madrid suburbs as the army takes over public services.
October 7	The army in Catalonia remains loyal to the government and at dawn surrounds the Generalitat building, arresting Companys and his fellow councilmen. The revolutionary movement in Oviedo gathers momentum as miners seek to gain control of Oviedo, the provincial capital. The inspector general of the army, General López Ochoa, is ordered with his forces to reestablish the government's authority in Asturias.
October 8	The cruiser *Libertad* bombards Gijón, held by the revolutionaries.
October 9	Former prime minister Azaña is arrested in Barcelona for complicity in the insurrection, while in Madrid the Cortes votes to reinstate the death penalty.
October 10	Along with a wave of arrests in Madrid (as many as 300 persons each day), the government also orders the closing of the offices of *El Socialista*.

The air force attacks Mieres (Asturias), killing twelve persons.

October 11   After having taken Avilés, General López Ochoa's column marches on Oviedo. His forces are supplemented by Foreign Legion units, including native Moroccans. Overall direction of the operations had been mandated jointly to Generals Franco and Goded.

October 12   Backed up by artillery and aircraft, the army launches a successful attack on rebel centers in Oviedo. Atrocities are attributed to both sides in the struggle.

October 14   In the wake of the final events of the general strike in Madrid, Largo Caballero is arrested and imprisoned.

October 17   Mieres, the last center of resistance to government forces in Asturias, succumbs to attack.

October 21   Luis Sirval, a Madrid journalist who reported the shocking treatment of some of the nation's 30,000 rebel captives, is murdered in an Oviedo jail. His stories had touched off international protest over the brutality of the methods employed to crush the rebellion.

November 8   Two ships in Barcelona harbor are converted into floating prisons for the rebels.

November 20   The Cortes sets aside its own rules concerning the prosecution of its members to permit the trial of Teodomiro Menéndez, a socialist deputy captured in Asturias.

December 3   Another member of the Cortes, the socialist delegate Ramón González Peña, is arrested in the Mieres district and charged with insurrection.

December 14   The Cortes votes that autonomy gradually be reintroduced into Catalonia.

December 28   Manual Azaña is set free and the charges against him are dropped.

1935

January 10   The military commander of the Catalan region transfers his authority back to the civilian government—in this case, the governor general, Portela Valladares.

January 15   Ledesma Ramos, Álvarez de Sotomayer, and Onéismo Redondo collectively resign from the Falange.

January 23   Martial law (state of war) is partially lifted in some regions of the nation by the Lerroux government. The prime minister had successfully reorganized his cabinet without producing a crisis of confidence in the Cortes. The task is a delicate one since Lerroux and Gil Robles are badly divided over the issue of what to do with the October revolutionaries.

February 1   A military court in Asturias oversees the execution of two October rebels: Jesús Argüellas and Sergeant Diego Vázquez.

February 9   Teodomiro Menéndez is condemned to death by a court-martial.

February 15   After hearing a speech by Cano López on the infiltration of the army by Masons, the Cortes considers legislation making Masonic membership illegal for any member of the armed forces.

February 16   González Peña is condemned to death by an Oviedo court-martial. In the next few days, seventeen more such sentences are handed down.

February 22   After a noisy demonstration in the assembly's halls by Castilian farmers, the Cortes approves a bill regulating Spanish imports of foreign cereal products. As of this date, domestic grain was twice as expensive as that imported from abroad.

March 10   Manual Azaña and Casares Quiroga are accused in the Cortes of complicity in the *Turquesa* incident.

March 14   The Lerroux government's version of an agricultural reform bill passes the Cortes. The legislation, *arrendamientos rustícos*, is intended to encourage family farming in Andalusia and Estremadura by permitting renters to purchase the plots of land they work. Its immediate effect is to produce a rash of evictions in the two regions.

March 22   The Cortes votes to condemn Azaña and Casares Quiroga on the charges brought against them. Since the vote does not constitute an absolute majority of the assembly, however, the accused are legally freed.

March 26   Cabinet consideration of commuting the death sentences imposed by the courts-martial produces a government crisis. The CEDA insists that the sentences be carried out, while Lerroux refuses, costing him Gil Robles' support in the Cortes.

April 3   Lerroux announces the formation of his fifth cabinet. It excludes the CEDA ministers and is composed of eight persons who were not members of the Cortes.

April 11   Catalonia regains all of its former autonomous powers except control over the police forces.

April 14	On the occasion of the fourth anniversary of the Republic, President Alcalá-Zamora presents the Grand Cross of San Fernando to General López Ochoa.
May 3	Faced with diminishing political support, Lerroux rejects the option of calling for new elections and decides to reform his cabinet with full CEDA participation. This sixth Lerroux cabinet includes five CEDA ministers among whom is Gil Robles in the role of minister of war.
May 8	The new cabinet gains the support of the Cortes by a vote of 198 to 22.
May 15	The remaining socialist deputies in the Cortes decide to boycott its sessions until full freedom of the press is restored.
May 16	General Franco is appointed Chief of the High Central State (*Jefe del Alto Estado Mayor Central*).
May 27	The trial of Companys and his fellow councilmen begins.
June 2	José Díaz, secretary general of the Spanish Communist party, proposes the creation of a Popular Front.
June 6	Those areas of the nation governed under martial law are returned to civil authority acting under a state of alarm. Elsewhere, the government rules under a state of prevention.
	Companys and his associates are found guilty of insurrection and sedition. They are sent to a penal colony at Santa María.
June 29	Popular protests in Barcelona cause the government to reimpose martial law in the city.
July 1	The agency charged with the dissolution of Jesuit property in Spain is itself dissolved.
July 4	The Lerroux government introduces a bill that would have amended the Constitution in forty-two instances. The proposal is rejected by the Cortes.
July 13	Largo Caballero's followers in the Socialist party inaugurate their own publication, *Claridad*.
July 22	The army stages maneuvers in Asturias, with General Franco and Gil Robles on hand to observe.
July 23	The Seventh Congress of the Comintern convenes in Moscow and ultimately endorses the Popular Front concept. An important Spanish delegation attends.
July 26	In its final meeting of the session, the Cortes revises the Republic's Agrarian Reform Law, slashing the budget for the Institute of Agrarian Reform and ending the confiscation of the estates of those involved in the Sanjurjo uprising.
August 12	The government schedules new municipal elections, calling upon all councilmen elected in 1931 to resign their posts.
September 1	Speaking at a JAP convention at Santiago de Compostella, Gil Robles demands a new constitution for the nation.
September 19	The Agrarian party, an organization dominated by the great landowners, withdraws from the government coalition, touching off yet another crisis.
September 22	Lerroux is unable to piece together another cabinet and is obliged to permit one of his political allies, Joaquín Chapaprieta Torregrosa (an independent), to undertake the premiership. The resulting cabinet is composed of agrarians, radicals, a Lliga minister and two members of CEDA, including Gil Robles as minister of war.
October 10	Rumors begin to circulate in the capital about the Straperlo scandal. Allegations link the Dutch businessman, Daniel Strauss, in payoffs to Lerroux's nephew, the former minister of interior, and the current governor of Catalonia, Pich y Pon.
October 11	The government reestablishes constitutional normality in twenty-five provinces, maintaining a state of alarm elsewhere.
October 19	The mayor of Madrid, Salazar Alonso, is dismissed on charges of involvement in the Straperlo scandal.
October 22	The Cortes establishes an investigative commission to inquire into the means used to introduce the Straperlo roulette game into Spain.
October 23	Indalecio Prieto secretly returns from exile.
October 28	The government's opponents in the Cortes succeed in securing the resignation of the mayor of Barcelona and Pich y Pon in connection with the Straperlo scandal.
October 29	Prime Minister Chapaprieta informs President Alcalá-Zamora that his cabinet no longer enjoys the confidence of the Cortes.

October 31	After two days of furious cabinet reshuffling, Chapaprieta wins a vote of confidence in the Cortes, relying on the same parties that had backed his previous government.
November 25	Largo Caballero's trial for insurrection and sedition gets under way.
November 28	The Cortes is obliged to establish yet another investigative commission to look into allegations in the Nombela affair involving improprieties in the Colonial Office.
November 30	Spain's Supreme Court dismisses the charges brought against Largo Caballero.
December 6	The testimony of Captain Nombela implicates Moreno Calvo, subsecretary to President Alcalá-Zamora.
December 7	With new evidence of scandal and a failure to win his allies' support for his proposed budget, Chapaprieta resigns as prime minister.
December 12	President Alcalá-Zamora calls upon his friend, Manuel Portela Valladores (not a member of the Cortes), to create a caretaker government until new elections can be scheduled and conducted. Portela's cabinet excludes CEDA membership.
December 14	Prime Minister Portela promises an end to press censorship over a three-week period.
December 15	*El Socialista* is permitted to resume publication after more than a year of suspension.
December 20	The executive committee of the Socialist party agrees to form a coalition with the bourgeois Republican parties in the forthcoming elections. This victory for Indalecio Prieto causes Largo Caballero to resign from his leadership post in the party.
December 30	Against a background of bitter CEDA attacks upon his government in the Cortes, Portela meets his cabinet only to have the session turn into a shouting match. The president asks Portela to create a new cabinet, which he succeeds in doing by the end of the day. Its centrist composition is much the same as before.

1936

January 4	The Cortes is officially dissolved, and new elections are set for February 16. Gil Robles argues that the dissolution decree is unconstitutional.
January 7	Constitutional normality is decreed for the entire nation.
January 11	An electoral pact is signed by the socialists and communists.
January 15	The Popular Front publishes its electoral platform. Composing the coalition are Azaña's Left Republicans, Martínez Barrio's Republican Union, the Catalan Esquerra, the socialists, and the communists.
January 23	Xavier de Bourbon-Parme assumes the regency powers of the Carlist movement.
January 25	General Franco is selected to represent the Republic at the funeral of England's George V.
February 2	In his final electoral address, José Antonio explains his tactics in not joining the rightist coalition and asserts that the Falange will not respect the results of the February balloting.
February 5	A rightist coalition is formulated for the Madrid elections, calling itself the *Frente nacional contrarrevolucionario*. The Falange is not included except for its maverick member, Giménez Caballero.
February 16	In the midst of relative tranquility, millions of citizens go to the polls for the first round of parliamentary voting. Although Prime Minister Portela announces a Center/Right victory early in the evening, it becomes evident a few hours later that the Popular Front will gain substantially. By evening's end, Calvo Sotelo is asking some deputies how they would feel about a military coup.
February 17	The Popular Front's victory is clear, and the streets are jammed with victory celebrations. The government issues a state of alarm throughout the nation, and General Franco is summoned to consult with the prime minister.
February 19	After meeting with Portela, President Alcalá-Zamora asks Azaña to form a government. Since the socialists refuse to participate in the cabinet, the new prime minister fills those posts primarily with members of his own Left Republican party. That evening it is announced that all the Asturian rebels will be amnestied.
February 21	The permanent commission of the Cortes grants an amnesty to all those in Spain charged with insurrection.
February 22	General Franco is relieved of his command and is dispatched to lead the garrison in the Canary Islands. General Goded is sent to the Balearics.
February 23	The Azaña government suspends rents in Andalusia and Estremadura, restores the Basque municipal

councils suspended in 1934, and reinstates the Companys council in Catalonia. At the same time, however, the prime minister continues ruling with a state of alarm declared throughout the nation.

February 27	Falange headquarters in Madrid are ordered closed.
February 28	General Mola is relieved of his command of the armed forces in Morocco and is reassigned as military governor in Pamplona. Before these recently dismissed officers take up their new duties, they meet in Madrid with General Varela and others to discuss the appropriate conditions for a military rebellion; for example, should Largo Caballero become prime minister. Although no definitive arrangements are reached, Franco does see Azaña and warns him of the army's concern about "communism" in Spain.
February 29	Government decrees order the suspension of all evictions of agricultural tenants and the rehiring of all workers dismissed from their jobs after January 1, 1934, for striking. The decree states that the dismissed workers are entitled to compensation for the lost wages they suffered.
March 1	Runoff elections confirm the February 16 results.
March 4	After his triumphal return to Barcelona, Companys resumes office in Catalonia and the provisions of the statute are completely restored.
March 10	A general strike breaks out in Granada, and several churches are burned. In Pamplona, a clash between peasants and soldiers leaves four dead.
March 11	General Franco is assured of the Falange's support when he meets José Antonio in the home of Ramón Serrano Suñer.
	General López Ochoa is ordered arrested for his culpability in the suppression of the Asturian insurrection of 1934. At the same time, Azaña summons Largo Caballero to his office and orders the socialist to end the victory celebrations that are disrupting national life.
March 13	Falangists attempt to assassinate Jiménez de Asúa. *Mundo Obrero* calls for the "complete elimination of the Falange, and Madrid's church of San Luis burns.
March 14	The government bans the Falange and arrests José Antonio on charges of trafficking in illegal arms. Two more Madrid churches, as well as the printing plant of Calvo Sotelo's *La Nación*, are attacked.
March 16	The estates of those persons involved in the Sanjurjo uprising are ordered subject to confiscation once again.
March 17	An electoral commission of the Cortes, constituted to review the results of disputed returns, rules the balloting in thirty-two districts to have been invalid.
March 20	The newly reorganized Institute for Agrarian Reform declares that it will employ the principle of "social utility" in specifying lands to be confiscated for redistribution to the peasants.
March 22	No longer content to wait for the legalities of governmental land redistribution, peasants in Estremadura begin occupying portions of estates in the region. These actions are often fostered by the FNTT, and in March alone more than 200,000 hectares are seized. The government later sanctions these confiscations.
April 3	In its first formal session, the new Cortes elects Martínez Barrio its presiding officer and hears charges that the president of the Republic illegally dissolved the assembly in 1934. Martínez Barrio rules that Alcalá-Zamora had, in fact, exceeded his authority under Article 81 of the Constitution. In view of this finding, the Cortes postpones scheduled municipal elections until the matter of presidential authority is resolved.
April 4	Prime Minister Azaña presents the Cortes with his legislative program, calling for renewed agrarian reform, intensified school construction, greater authority for municipal councils, autonomy for the Basque region, and reemployment for those dismissed for political activity since the end of 1933.
April 7	Alcalá-Zamora is deposed as president of the Republic on charges of having exceeded his constitutional authority: dissolved the Cortes twice during his term of office. By provision of that same document, he is replaced temporarily by the presiding officer of the Cortes, Martínez Barrio.
April 12	The postponed municipal elections are conducted; runoffs are scheduled for April 16.
April 13	General Quiepo de Llano visits Mola in Pamplona to discuss the eventualities of military insurrection.
April 14	The celebration of the Republic's fifth anniversary touches off bloody clashes in Madrid as the military parades before the president. A bomb explodes under the main reviewing stand, and a member of the Civil Guard is shot when he seems to level a rifle at Martínez Barrio.

April 15	In an angry speech in the renewed session of the Cortes, Calvo Sotelo accuses the socialists of plotting to hand the nation over to communism.
April 16	The funeral of the Civil Guardsman shot during the military review occasions another clash between Falangists and leftists. At least twelve people are killed during day-long fighting.
April 17	Azaña dismisses the minister of *gobernación* and replaces him with Casares Quiroga.
April 18	The Cortes approves a bill forbidding military officers to seek office or to attend secret political meetings. The vote is overwhelming: 200 to 4.
April 20	From exile General Sanjurjo designates General Mola to be his acting delegate in Spain. Mola's first plan for insurrection in Sanjurjo's name had been foiled by General Rodríquez del Barrio, inspector general of the army, whose feigned illness postponed an April insurrection.
April 26	The Popular Front wins the runoff elections for municipal councilmen, even though in many cases less than the 40 percent participation mandated under the law is achieved.
May 1	The CNT proclaims general strikes in most major cities, while working class parades occur throughout the nation. In Cuenca, Indalecio Prieto warns specifically that General Franco might attempt to lead a military insurrection.
May 4	While José Antonio pens a manifesto to the army, more church property is burned in Madrid.
May 8	The Cortes votes to decide a new president of the Republic. Manuel Azaña wins handily. He asks Indalecio Prieto to assume the premiership, but the socialist leader refuses.
May 10	The national congress of the CNT, meeting in Saragossa, denounces the Azaña regime.
May 11	Manuel Azaña is inaugurated as president of the Republic.
May 13	Azaña asks Casares Quiroga to form a cabinet, even though the new prime minister is suffering from tuberculosis. The Gallegan obliges, selecting most of his ministers from Azaña's party.
May 19	In his inaugural address to the Cortes, Casares Quiroga pledges his hostility to fascism.
May 20	The government orders the closing of Catholic schools on the pretense that they are targets of arsonists. In the Cortes, Gil Robles introduces a bill proposing autonomy for León and Castile.
May 24	Largo Caballero assures a rally at Cádiz that the dissolution of the Popular Front will mean the triumph of the proletariat.
May 28	José Antonio is sentenced to five months in prison for trafficking in illegal arms.
May 29	The Civil Guard attempts to supress a meeting at Yeste (Albacete) and finds itself under attack. In the ensuing struggle, the Guard kills nineteen and wounds thirty-eight.
May 31	Raimundo García, a rightist member of the Cortes, arrives at Estoril, Portugal, to confer with General Sanjurjo about the state of planning for the insurrection.
	Speaking at a socialist rally at Ecija, Indalecio Prieto is shot.
June 1	José Antonio promises General Mola at least 4,000 Falangist volunteers should he execute a rebellion against the Republic.
	UGT and CNT syndicates begin a major strike in the Madrid construction industry.
June 2	The Cortes passes a law reversing the eviction of agricultural tenants that had occurred as a result of the Lerroux government's 1935 agricultural legislation.
June 5	General Mola circulates a secret memorandum on the operation of the government that would follow the Republic after a military rebellion.
	José Antonio is moved to the prison in Alicante.
June 9	The socialist and communist youth movements are merged in Catalonia.
	El Sol estimates that, as of this date, one million workers are on strike in Spain.
June 11	General Mola confers with the national delegate of the *Requetés*, Zamanillo, who gives Mola a paper describing the conditions under which his forces would join a military rebellion.
June 16	While Gil Robles darkly warns the Cortes of military intervention, General Mola meets secretly with the

Carlist leadership at the Monastery of Irache. Prime Minister Casares is advised of this gathering by the mayor of Estella.

June 18   A CNT-sponsored general strike disrupts commerce in Barcelona. In Madrid, the former minister, Miguel Maura, begins publishing a series of articles in *El Sol*, calling for a "republican dictatorship."

June 20   The UGT votes to end the construction strike in Madrid, but the CNT unions refuse to return to work.

June 23   General Franco writes Casares Quiroga, warning him that the recent reshuffling of army commands has undermined the discipline of the armed forces.

June 28   A plebiscite in Galicia demonstrates that that region, too, favors a Statute of Autonomy.

June 30   Elections within the Socialist party favor the Prieto faction over the followers of Largo Caballero.

July 1   General Mola circulates a secret memorandum to those who had joined him in conspiracy, advising patience. The Foreign Legion, meanwhile, is staging impressive maneuvers in Morocco.

           Largo Caballero leaves for London to attend a session of the Second International.

July 4   Since the CNT workers insist on continuing their strike in the Madrid construction industry, the UGT advises its members to go to their jobs but not work.

July 6   Luis Bolín, London correspondent for *ABC*, hires a British aircraft to transport General Franco to Morocco.

July 7   Mola meets with General Kindelán in the midst of delicate negotiations with the Carlists. Fal Conde is adamant that the proposed rising take place under the monarchist flag.

July 8   The government arrests hundreds of Falangists throughout the nation. Meanwhile, General Sanjurjo seeks to mediate between Mola and the Carlists.

July 10   Six Falangists invade the studios of *Radio Unión* in Valencia and proclaim that the national-sindicalist revolution will begin within days.

July 11   Captain Bebb leaves London in his *Dragon Rapide* to pick up his passenger in the Canaries.

July 12   Military maneuvers in Morocco end with a brilliant parade and an officers' banquet at which seditious toasts are exchanged. In spite of this display of solidarity on the part of the officers' corps in Morocco, the Carlists are ordered not to obey any orders to rebel except in the name of the Pretender.

           At 9:00 P.M., a Falangist gang murders José Castillo, a lieutenant in the Assault Guards and instructor of the socialist youth. Shortly thereafter, Castillo's friends in the Assault Guards set out on a reprisal raid in a government vehicle. They cannot locate Antonio Goicoechea, and they discover that Gil Robles was on vacation. They then decide on Calvo Sotelo's home, even though his guards had been changed that morning as a security precaution.

July 13   Calvo Sotelo is apprehended at home and shot while being transported in the Assault Guards' vehicle. When the cabinet learns of the assassination, it orders the closing of Madrid's Alfonsist, Carlist, and anarchist headquarters. By noon, Indalecio Prieto is leading socialists, communists, and others in a demand that the population be armed.

July 14   The diplomat Sangroniz arrives at Tenerife to inform General Franco that his transportation to Morocco is ready and to brief him on events in the capital.

July 15   The regular meeting of the Cortes is postponed until July 21, although that body's permanent commission agrees to a decree placing the entire nation on state of alarm status. The Carlists and delegates of *Renovación Española* withdraw from all subsequent sessions of the Cortes.

July 16   With rumors of an impending military revolt abounding, the government takes some precautionary steps, dispatching naval units to the Gibraltar area and arresting General Varela.

July 17   At 4:20 P.M., the Melilla garrison in Morocco rises against the government, followed shortly thereafter by troops in Tetuán. Public buildings are quickly occupied, resistance at the *casa del pueblo* swept aside, and a start of martial law imposed. The supreme commander in Morocco, General Gómez Morato, is arrested when he attempts to restore discipline in the Foreign Legion ranks.

July 18   At 5:15 A.M., General Franco issues a manifesto to the nation which seeks to justify the rebellion. He then departs for Morocco in his British plane. Rising also takes place in Andalusia, but the civil governors refuse to arm the population to resist the rebels.

The Madrid government, confident that the rebellion could be confined to Morocco, reassures the civil population in a radio broadcast and dispatches more naval units to bombard the Moroccan coast. The Texaco Corporation, however, diverts its tankers to rebel-held ports, and volunteers from *Renovación Española* seize several passes in the Somosierra.

July 19   The essentials of a confused situation are as follows:

Morocco—   General Franco lands at Tetuán and assumes command of the armed forces in the colony. Five hundred of his legionnaires cross the Straights in Spanish shipping and march on Seville.

Madrid—   Before dawn, arms distribution begins to the civilian population without government sanction. Prime Minister Casares Quiroga resigns and Azaña asks Martínez Barrio to form a cabinet. This new government is duly announced in the *Gaceta*, but massive street demonstrations against it and the failure of Martínez Barrio's hopes for a negotiated peace bring his resignation before the end of the day. That night government radio announces that José Giral Pereira, an Azaña ally, has formed a cabinet. Its first act is to endorse the distribution of weapons to Madrid's various militias.

Barcelona—After having successfully seized control of Majorca, General Goded flies to the Catalan capital, assuming that the rebellion there had enjoyed equal good fortune. He is arrested as he steps off his plane.

Pamplona—General Mola decrees martial law in the city and is confident enough of his control to dispatch a column under Lieutenant Colonel García Escámez to Madrid.

July 20   While Prime Minister Giral appeals to the French Republic for arms, some military units in the capital attempt to join the rebellion. They are quickly driven back to the Montaña Barracks by loyal troops and armed civilian militia. Later that day, the barracks are stormed and many of its defenders put to death.

In a bold move, General Queipo de Llano gains control of Seville, occupying public buildings and declaring martial law. The ostensible leader of the entire rebellion, General Sanjurjo, is killed in the crash of an aircraft speeding his return from exile in Portugal.

The British Labour party expresses its backing of the Republic, but the London government makes no move to echo those sentiments.

July 21   Government forces surround rebels under command of Colonel Moscardó at the Alcázar in Toledo. Other units counterattack in the Somosierra, and the uprising at Almería is crushed. It turns out, however, that General Aranda at Oviedo has betrayed the Republic and dispatches militia units from that city into the hands of General Mola's armies. From bases in Valladolid and Segovia, Mola's troops march south for Alto de León.

The Comintern seriously considers aiding the Republic while General Franco conducts negotiations with the German businessman, Johannes Bernhardt, to secure aid from the Reich to permit him to invade metropolitan Spain from Morocco.

July 22   Most of Galicia is gained by rebel forces, and García Escámez's column captures Soria. Both sides struggle for control of Alto de León.

Onéismo Redondo, founder of the JONS, is assassinated in Labajos (Segovia), while the revolution he opposed gathers strength in Republican territory. In Barcelona, Companys agrees to the creation of the antifascist militia whose duty it would be to control the war effort in Catalonia. He is, in effect, accepting a collateral government, sharing power with the Marxists and the CNT. Under their influence, nearly 70 percent of the region's industries would be operated under collective ownership ("workers' control"). In time, the same arrangements would appear in Madrid (30 percent) and Valencia (50 percent).

Meanwhile, General Franco reiterates his pleas for German assistance through German officers in Tetuán. The French prime minister, Léon Blum, is at the same time traveling to London to gain British endorsement of his plans to assist the Republic.

July 23   Mola's headquarters announces the formation of a governing council for rebel-held territory, the *Junta de Defensa Nacional*. It is composed entirely of military officers.

The rebellion at Alicante is defeated, and the first shipments of aircraft and pilots leave the Soviet port of Odessa, bound for Spain. At the same time, the Communist party in Catalonia succeeds in merging its organization with that of the socialists, forming the *Partit Socialist Unificat de Catalunya* (PSUC).

The foreign ministers to Britain, France, and Belgium agree to formulate a collective proposal to Hitler and Mussolini concerning Spain and other matters of European security.

July 24   Rebel forces capture Granada, and García Escámez's column reaches the Somosierra and is immediately engaged.

July 25   Mola's troops gain and hold the Somosierra passes. On this date, he is formally designated commander of all rebel armies in the north, while General Franco is assigned operations in the south. There is good news for the Republic, however. The rebel attempt on Albacete is thwarted; an anarchist column, commanded by Durruti captures Caspe (Aragón); and the first shipment of French planes crosses the border.

While Antonio Giocoechea and Sáinz Rodríquez win Mussolini's assurances of a prompt arrival of Italian transport planes, the French government first suggests the idea of nonintervention after a serious split in the Blum cabinet develops.

July 26   The Comintern, meeting in Prague, agrees to seek volunteers to fight for the Republic and to raise a billion francs for its defense.

Hitler decides to assist the rebel cause, ordering the transfer of twenty transport planes to help ferry troops from Morocco.

July 27   Mola's troops are heavily engaged in fighting for the Alto de León, while Queipo de Llano in Seville welcomes much-needed reinforcements.

July 28   Although the Left in Barcelona had passively accepted the cancellation of the forty-hour work week a few days earlier, anarchists noisily protest the central government's efforts to conscript the 1933 and 1934 age contingents, demanding that the Republic continue to rely on militia for its defense.

The ineffectuality of the Republic's efforts in Aragón permits Mola to begin transferring units of the *Requetés* to Guizpúzcoa.

German planes arrive in Morocco and immediately begin transporting Franco's troops into southern Spain. Cementing that relationship, Johannes Bernhardt organizes two trading companies to handle the flow of goods and weapons between the two nations.

July 29   Huelva falls to rebel forces.

July 30   After more than a week of uncertainty, CNT/UGT militias attack the army barracks in Valencia, capturing troops of dubious loyalty. The central government would now treat the leaders of the militia as the de facto authority in the city.

Nine Italian bombers reach Morocco, although three others mistakenly land in French territory.

Meeting in Paris, International Red Help creates a special organization to lend assistance "to the Spanish people."

July 31   Companys unilaterally changes his title from president of the Generalitat to president of Catalonia, increasing the appearance of Catalan sovereignty.

General von Scheele and eighty-five volunteers depart from Hamburg for Cádiz, constituting the advance elements of the Condor Legion.

August 1   Mola's armies occupy Guadarrama.

August 2   The central government, seeking to organize its armies, creates volunteer brigades commanded by regular officers. This step is an effort to gain some control over the militia.
France announces its policy of nonintervention and proposes its European-wide adoption.

August 3   The Republic's air force makes sorties against Majorca and Saragossa, but General Castejón launches a rebel offensive into Estremadura.

The French ambassador in Rome presents his nation's nonintervention proposal to Count Ciano, who promises to study it carefully.

August 5	Five shiploads of legionnaires cross from Morocco into metropolitan Spain under Italian aircover.
	The French ambassador in Berlin presents his nation's proposal for nonintervention to the German government.
August 6	General Franco arrives in Seville where he establishes his headquarters.
	In Barcelona, where preparations are under way for an attempted invasion of Majorca, the government of the Generalitat falls and is replaced by a regime that formally announces its approval of "workers' control" and its intention of appointing representatives to every factory council.
	Ciano agrees "in principle" to the French proposal for nonintervention.
August 7	The Generalitat creates the War Industries Commission, which in a matter of weeks will assume the operation of twenty-four factories in the region and 500 by 1937.
	The French government quietly permits the enlistment of volunteers for service in Spain, while the United States warns all of its consuls to observe the strictest neutrality.
August 8	The Republic launches its invasion of the Balearic Islands, capturing Ibiza and Formentera. This operation coincides with the first conscription of forces in rebel-held territory.
	The French border is closed to arms shipments and volunteers crossing into Spain.
August 10	Indalecio Prieto appeals in a radio broadcast for an end to the Red Terror that has gripped the Republican zone. Estimates vary widely on the incidence of this indiscriminate violence, but the best suggest that 61,000 persons perished in the Republican jurisdiction and 50,000 in the Nationalist zone during the Civil War.
August 11	Republican forces abandon Mérida, near Badajoz, to rebel armies.
August 12	The first International Brigade volunteers arrive in Barcelona. At Montjuich, General Goded is executed.
	The Republic orders the closing of all religious institutions.
August 14	Badajoz falls to rebel armies, and the American reporter, Jay Allen, reports to the world on the atrocities that followed. The action effectively seals off the Portuguese border to the Republic.
August 15	Great Britain bans the export of war matériel to Spain.
August 16	Republican forces in great strength land on Majorca.
August 17	In Asturias, militia units capture the last rebel position in Gijón.
August 19	The internationally acclaimed poet, Federico García Lorca, falls victim to a Falangist firing squad in Viznar (Granada).
August 23	Following a fire at the Model Prison in Madrid, a series of executions of important inmates is carried out. Among the victims are Melquiadez Álvarez, Ruiz de Alda, Dr. Albiñana, and Fernando Primo de Rivera. On the same day, a decree by the Madrid government legitimizes the functioning of the revolutionary courts, one of the instruments of the "Red Terror."
	The Soviet Union announces its adherence to nonintervention.
August 24	The Soviet Union's first ambassador to Spain, Marcel Rosenberg, takes up his post in Madrid.
	Germany and Italy agree "in principle" to the nonintervention proposal.
August 26	Rebel armies occupy the Río Tinto mines. Franco agrees to release 700 legionnaires to Mola to augment Mola's impending offensive against Irún.
August 28	Madrid suffers its first aerial bombardment.
August 29	The red and gold banner is proclaimed to be the new Spanish flag to be displayed in all rebel-held territory.
	The chief of Soviet intelligence in Western Europe, General Krivitsky, is ordered to begin the covert purchase of weapons for the Republic.
August 31	As of this date, most European states have agreed to the terms of nonintervention.

September 3	Talavera de la Reina is captured by rebel forces under the command of General Cabanillas. It was the last significant town between General Franco's advancing columns and Madrid.
September 4	Franco's continued advance obliges the Madrid government to change commanders on the central front once again. Worse news follows from Majorca, where it is learned that the invasion of the island has failed. Prime Minister Giral, recognizing the gravity of the struggle that is about to come, resigns since his Republicans have too little popular backing. Acting against the advice of Indalecio Prieto, Azaña asks Largo Caballero to accept the premiership. Largo Caballero agrees and selects a cabinet that includes six socialists and two communists.
September 5	General Beorlegui's *Requetés* march into Irún after the city is demolished by fleeing anarchist militiamen. Refugees from the Republic flee across the border into France.
September 7	José Antonio Aguirre forms an autonomous Basque government.
September 9	Serving both as prime minister and minister of war, Largo Caballero appoints a commander-in-chief, a general staff, and regional commanders for all Republican forces. Within six weeks he has imposed military discipline upon Republican armies as well.
	Alexander Orlov of the NKVD arrives in Spain. His task is to oversee the effective use of Soviet aid in the Spanish struggle. He interprets this commission broadly, intervening in domestic politics.
	The first meeting of the Non-Intervention Committee convenes in London, although it is unable to take any formal action in the absence of the Portuguese delegation.
September 13	San Sebastián falls to Beorlegui's forces.
	With Madrid in jeopardy, the minister of finance, Dr. Juan Negrín, is authorized to hide the gold reserves belonging to the Bank of Spain. Acting on his own, Negrín selects the Soviet Union as a sanctuary for the gold.
September 14	The Non-Intervention Committee meets again in London, and this time establishes a subcommittee to oversee the routine operation of the policy. The Soviet delegate accuses the Italians of having landed aircraft in Spain, a charge denied by Ambassador Grandi.
	Pope Pius XI, speaking to a crowd of Spanish refugees, deplores the "truly Satanic hatred of God" displayed in the Republic.
September 16	Ronda (Málaga) succumbs to Rebel armies, but an entire shipload of Soviet supplies reaches Barcelona.
September 18	A major Republican effort to break the siege of the Alcázar in Toledo by exploding a mine in the midst of rebel defenses fails.
September 19	The Italian fascist ruler of Majorca, Conde Rossi (Bonaccorsi), successfully employs his forces to dislodge Republican armies from the island of Ibiza.
September 21	Meeting at an estate near Salamanca, the leaders of the rebellion agree that General Franco should be designated *jefe único y supremo* of the forces ranged against the Republic.
September 22	A rebellion sweeps through the indigenous population of Spanish Guinea, requiring extraordinary measures in its suppression.
September 24	The dualistic nature of government in Catalonia ends when the forces that made up the Central Committee of Antifascist Militias (the CNT, the *Partido Obrero de Unificación Marxista* [POUM], and the *Federación Anarquista Ibérica* [FAI]) accept posts in the Generalitat.
September 25	Álvarez del Vayo pleads the Republic's case before the assembly of the League of Nations.
September 26	General Varela's forces arrive before Toledo, heralding an immediate end to the siege of the Alcázar.
	Spain opens its embassy in Moscow.
September 28	Although Varela's diversion to Toledo slows down offensive operations against Madrid, the arrival of his troops in that city touches off joyous celebrations in the rebel camp. Cardinal Gomá seconds that chorus in a radio address.
	Portugal finally manages to send a delegation to the meetings of the Non-Intervention Committee. Lord Plymouth is elected its chairman and the members promptly vote to disallow all charges of the pact's violation before August 28 when Germany and Italy accepted the agreement.

September 29	The *Junta de Defensa Nacional* ratifies the decision taken at the rebel generals' September 21 meeting and designates Franco as *Jefe del Estado y Generalísimo de los Ejércitos*.
	The rebel cruiser *Canarias* sinks a Republican destroyer in the cruiser's first engagement at sea.
September 30	The Republican fleet seeks refuge in Bilbao harbor.
	While Franco arrives in Burgos to assume executive authority over a Nationalist government, the Republic appeals to world opinion by publishing its evidence of German and Italian violations of the nonintervention agreement.
October 1	Before a cheering throng, General Franco is invested with the office of chief of state. He employs the title immediately in decreeing his first law for Nationalist Spain.
	After weeks of delay, an anarchist column reaches the outskirts of Huesca (Aragón).
	Meeting for the first time in Valencia, the Cortes unanimously approves a statute providing for Basque autonomy.
October 3	Franco creates a cabinet (*Junta Técnica del Estado*) composed of three generals, one diplomat, and his brother, Nicolás.
October 4	Republican forces seek to drive Colonel Aranda and his nationalist soldiers from Oviedo.
October 6	The Soviet Union announces that it will abide by the terms of nonintervention only to the same extent as Germany, Italy, and Portugal. The following day, it simply withdraws from the pact and its sessions.
October 7	Vicente Uribe, the communist minister of agriculture, decrees that those lands belonging to persons associated with the rebellion are subject to confiscation. By June 1938, this decree results in the transfer of ownership of nearly one-third of the nation's arable soil to nearly 300,000 peasants.
October 8	General Varela's troops drive to within 11 kilometers of Madrid.
October 9	650 members of the International Brigades arrive at Alicante.
October 10	Militia in the Madrid area are organized into six regular brigades, forming the basis of the future "People's Army." The best are the communist-organized Fifth Regiment volunteers.
October 12	A confrontation occurs at the University of Salamanca during ceremonies marking *El Día de la Raza* between Miguel de Unamuno and the Nationalist general, Millán Astray.
October 17	Nationalist reinforcements reach Oviedo from Galicia, relieving the siege of Colonel Aranda's position in the city.
	The Republic establishes a training base at Albacete for the International Brigade volunteers.
October 20	Franco orders the capture of Madrid by Nationalist armies.
October 22	While President Azaña leaves the capital for a tour of the battlefronts, General José Miaja is given command of the 1st Division, crucial to the defense of Madrid. In Cartagena, Alexander Orlov facilitates the loading of Spanish gold bound for Odessa.
October 24	The first Russian tanks see action in fighting around Aranjuez on the day that German and Italian aircraft join together in attacking Madrid.
	The Generalitat collectivizes all industry owned by rebels or employing more than 100 workers. Less severe terms are announced for smaller industrial operations and foreign-owned businesses.
October 25	510 tons of gold from the Bank of Spain leave Cartagena for Odessa.
October 28	Miguel de Unamuno is dismissed as rector of the University of Salamanca.
October 29	Ramiro de Maeztu, often linked to the "Generation of '98," and Ledesma Ramos, one of Spain's premier fascists, are executed in Madrid.
October 31	The French government once again permits the recruitment of volunteers for service to the Spanish Republic. Hitler, at the same time, decides to provide Franco with an air force of 100 German planes.
November 2	Fighting around Madrid intensifies as Nationalists capture Brunete and Soviet fighter planes appear in the skies to protect the capital from bombing raids. Bilbao suffers aerial bombardment for the first time.

November 4	Franco's troops capture three more suburbs near Madrid (Getafe, Alcorcón, and Leganés). In the face of this peril, Largo Caballero convinces the anarchists to join his government. In the resultant reshuffling of ministers, four representatives of the CNT join the cabinet.
November 5	The central government of the Republic decides to abandon Madrid for Valencia.
November 6	Several more Madrid suburbs are occupied by the Nationalists when General Miaja is placed in charge of the city's *Junta de Defensa*. As the Republic's government moves to Valencia, more German planes land in Seville. Here the Condor Legion was being assembled, composed of four bomber squadrons, four fighter squadrons, and 5,000 to 6,000 troops.
	At the intervention of Cardinal Gomá, Franco orders a halt to the executions of Basque priests, judged to have been supporters of the Republic.
November 7	The assault on Madrid begins with Nationalist troops crossing the Manzanares west of the capital. Captured copies of General Varela's attack plans convince Miaja and Colonel Rojo to commit their forces to University City for the next day's fighting. Anticipating the worst, officials at the Model Prison order the removal of their charges to Valencia. Many are massacred at Paracuellos de Jarama by their guards.
November 8	Furious battle brings General Miaja himself to the front where he steels defenses. During the day, 3,000 troops from the International Brigades arrive in the capital and are positioned promptly against attacks at Casa del Campo.
	Guatemala and El Salvador accord diplomatic recognition to the Franco government.
November 9	General Varela's troops attempt to force the front at University City, where they are met by the International Brigades.
November 10	The Non-Intervention Committee concludes that it has no evidence of foreign intervention in Spain.
November 11	Two more International Brigades arrive in Madrid along with Durruti's anarchist column. Varela confines his attacks to University City.
November 15	Nationalist troops gain control of Madrid's Parque del Oeste.
November 16	Fighting among rubble, Nationalist troops win the School of Engineering at the University of Madrid.
November 17	Even though Varela's artillery drops 2,000 rounds per hour on Madrid, his forces are unable to gain the university's clinical hospital from its defenders.
	The British government instructs its naval commanders not to escort British vessels inside Spain's 3-mile limit.
November 18	In a pause in the fighting around Madrid, both Italy and Germany grant the Franco government diplomatic recognition.
November 19	Buenaventura Durruti is shot (in the back) fighting in University City.
November 20	José Antonio Primo de Rivera is executed by a firing squad in Alicante.
November 24	The Republican government seizes the German and Italian embassies in Madrid.
December 1	The Cortes resumes its sessions in Valencia.
December 2	The Finnish legation in Madrid, which housed more than 1,000 refugees, is attacked.
	In London, the Non-Intervention Committee rejects two Anglo-French proposals: one, calling for mediation of the Spanish conflict; another, suggesting a ban on volunteers as well as supplies to the opposing sides.
December 5	Franco's government orders the dismissal of all governmental employees opposed to the *Movimiento*.
December 6	Barcelona's port comes under heavy aerial attack.
December 13	Catalan communists provoke a crisis in the Generalitat, accusing the POUM of fostering poor discipline among the working classes.
December 14	The cruiser *Canarias* sinks the Soviet supply vessel *Konsomol* after it had departed from Valencia.
December 16	Maneuvering around Madrid begins as Nationalist forces capture Boadilla del Monte. Recognizing the Republic's need for skilled officers, Largo Caballero announces the creation of the *Escuela Superior de Guerra*.

December 17	The Generalitat is reorganized under José Tarradellas and excludes POUM councilmen.
December 20	The first major contingent of Italian volunteers departs from Naples for Spain.
December 23	Advance elements of the Italian forces arrive in Cádiz. Their numbers would eventually reach 70,000.
	The Republic recognizes the anarchist-dominated *Consejo de Aragón* as the legal authority in that region.
December 28	The U.S. government permits the shipment of nearly $3 million of aircraft engines to Bilbao.
December 31	Miguel de Unamuno dies at Salamanca.

1937

January 2	Britain's Anthony Eden signs the "Gentleman's Agreement" with Italy, pledging to maintain the status quo in the Mediterranean.
January 3	The "Battle of the Fog," a nationalist offensive west of Madrid, begins with the capture of Villafrance del Castillo by insurgent forces.
January 4	Nationalist forces continue to gain ground in the "Battle of the Fog."
January 5	The Generalitat imposes food rationing.
January 6	The Congress of the United States strictly forbids the export of arms to Spain. However, the *Mar Cantábrico* had already put to sea with precisely such a cargo.
January 7	The Nationalist vessel *Tutonia* seizes a Soviet ship in the Cantabrian Sea. The Soviet vessel was bound for Bilbao with supplies for the beleaguered city.
January 8	Anthony Eden realizes that 4,000 Italian troops have landed in Spain since the signing of the "Gentleman's Agreement." His notion that the Royal Navy should patrol Spain's coasts to halt all forms of intervention is rejected by Prime Minister Baldwin.
January 10	With Nationalists continuing their advances west of Madrid, the government orders the evacuation of the city's civilian population.
	Cardinal Gomá addresses an open letter to the Basque leader, José Antonio Aguirre, imploring the Basque people not to take up arms against their fellow Catholics serving the Nationalists.
January 11	The United States invalidates all passports issued for travel to Spain.
January 12	An anarchist uprising in Bilbao is easily repressed, while in Barcelona the Generalitat's Finance Ministry issues decrees strengthening regional control over industrial production and further undermining the "workers' control" concept.
January 13	Nationalist forces under Queipo de Llano initiate an offensive in the Málaga region. Five thousand Italian troops take part in the campaign, operating independently under orders of General Roatta.
January 17	Although the Nationalist offensive west of Madrid ends inconclusively (with 15,000 casualties on both sides), Queipo de Llano is able to report the capture of Marbella on the road to Málaga.
January 21	France embargoes arms and volunteers crossing national territory into Spain.
February 6	A Nationalist offensive begins to the southeast of Madrid, commanded by General Luís Orgaz. With 40,000 troops and the assistance of the Condor Legion, it is his goal to reach and cross the Jarama River.
February 7	Málaga falls to the Nationalists as defenses collapse and thousands flee before advancing troops toward Almería.
	Representatives of the Falange and the Carlists convene in Lisbon to seek some basis for unification. Their efforts fail.
February 12	With the help of Russian "Chato" fighters, Republican forces enjoy air superiority over the Jarama battlefields.
February 14	The youth organizations of POUM and FAI stage a mass demonstration in Barcelona, protesting the government's emphasis upon victory over social revolution.
February 15	General Miaja is given command on the Jarama front.
February 20	In its latest session, the Non-Intervention Committee votes to forbid the enlistment of volunteers for service in Spain.

February 21	The Valencia government discharges several important communists from its Ministry of War. This episode occurs when party officials force Largo Caballero to dismiss General José Asensio as undersecretary of war. Other than having commanded at Málaga, Asensio's "error" was to have opposed the mixing of propaganda and tactics in the training of Republican soldiers. In exchange for the dismissal of Asensio, Largo Caballero sacks three communists from his staff and demands the recall of the Soviet ambassador.
February 24	The communist press launches vigorous attacks upon the Largo Caballero government.
February 28	The battle of the Jarama ends inconclusively with 40,000 casualties on both sides. During the course of this action, the Abraham Lincoln Brigade first sees action.
March 3	The Generalitat demands that the militia-controlled *Junta de Seguridad* be dissolved and that all political organizations hand over their weapons. Both the CNT and POUM refuse to comply.
March 4	The Republic accepts the mediation proposal that all foreign volunteers should be withdrawn from Spain.
March 5	The Communist party congress demands that its rival, the POUM, be eliminated.
March 8	With the Italian Black Flames Division in the vanguard, Nationalist forces initiate still another offensive in the Madrid region. In a planned joint operation, the Italians are to attack in the northeast toward Guadalajara, while General Orgaz's forces are to resume their operations on the Jarama. Poor weather delays General Orgaz.
	The *Mar Cantábrico*, carrying supplies from Mexico and the United States, is seized by Nationalist vessels.
	Antonio Goicoechea announces the dissolution of *Renovación Española*.
March 10	After two days of steady advancing, the Black Flames collide with Italians serving the Republic in the Garibaldi Brigade. This civil war within a civil war stems the advance of Mussolini's troops toward Guadalajara.
March 18	A Republican counterattack in the Guadalajara sector brings an end to that campaign. The *Corpo di Truppe Volontaire* claims gains on the ground, while the Republic also proclaims a great victory for its forces and displays evidence of the presence of 50,000 Italians in Spain.
	The *London Times* reports a proposal to the British government from the Spanish Republic, offering to revise the status of Morocco in exchange for a more favorable British posture toward the Largo Caballero regime. Britain, reports the *Times*, rejected the offer.
March 23	Spanish and Republican representations concerning the presence of Italian troops on Spanish soil are met with Grandi's reply that the "volunteers" would not leave Spain until a Nationalist victory had been assured.
March 26	A crisis occurs in the Generalitat concerning CNT objections to conscription to the Peoples' Army. The anarchist councilmen walk out of the Catalan government over the issue (only to return three weeks later).
March 31	General Mola's forces launch an offensive in the Aragón region, while General Franco concludes further negotiations with the Germans, exchanging economic concessions for more arms.
April 4	The official organ of the POUM, *La Batalla*, registers its opposition to the Communist party and its influence over the Republic's government.
April 6	The British steamer *Thorpehall* is halted by Nationalist vessels on its way to Bilbao. British destroyers arrive on the scene to assist the *Thorpehall*, but thereafter the London government instructs its vessels to avoid Bilbao completely.
April 9	Intensified fighting in the northern portion of the nation moves General Miaja to increase Republican operations around Madrid and General Franco to declare a naval blockade of Republican ports on the Cantabrian Sea.
April 12	A surprise attack at dawn gains Santa Quintera Mountain (between Saragossa and Huesca) for Republican troops.
April 13	Nationalist attackers regain Santa Quitera Mountain.
April 16	After long negotiations, the executive council of the Generalitat is reorganized under the leadership of José Tarradellas. CNT and UGT representation is evenly divided, and the Communist party is excluded.
April 17	Acting on orders from Negrín, the newly reorganized *Carabineros* attempt to replace anarchist units serving as border guards. Fighting ensues between the two groups, and eight anarchists are killed.

Meanwhile, Largo Caballero tries to limit the authority of the political commissars assigned to the Peoples' Army in an effort to contain communist influence over the armed forces.

April 19	General Franco orders the unification of the Falange and the Carlists. The resulting organization is to carry the title *Falange Española Tradicionalista y de las Juntas de Ofensiva Nacional-Sindicalista* (FET y de las JONS). General Franco is designated by decree to be the *Jefe Nacional* of this curious amalgam of political forces. This announcement is made only five days after a brawl in Salamanca among the Falange factions contending for the leadership of the movement.

The Non-Intervention Committee agrees to establish patrols to monitor Spain's coasts and borders against potential violators of the pact. Italy and Germany are to observe the Republican ports, while England and France are to monitor the Nationalists. The several fleets are permitted only to determine the destinations of suspected vessels, but have no search and seizure authorization.

April 20	Navarrese troops spearhead the Nationalist offensive into Basque territory.
April 23	The *FET y de los JONS* is structured and is to be directed by a *Junta Política*, half of its members being appointed by the *Jefe Nacional*. Franco first offers the leadership of this *Junta* to the would-be heir to José Antonio's mantle, Manuel Hedilla, who declines.

Largo Caballero dissolves the communist-dominated *Junta Defensiva* of Madrid and returns authority in the capital to the municipal council.

April 24	The fascist salute is officially adopted in Nationalist Spain except in the armed forces.
April 25	The anarchist newspaper *Solidaridad Obrera* joins the POUM in editorial attacks upon the Communist party.

Despairing of hope of gaining Hedilla's support for the *FET y de las JONS*, the Franco government orders his arrest. He remains in solitary confinement for four years.

April 26	The Basque city of Guernica is attacked and obliterated by German bombers. More than 1,600 persons die in the raid since it was launched against the undefended city on its weekly market day.
April 29	Nationalist infantry march into the ruins of Guernica, and the Burgos government announces to the world that the city has been destroyed by communist demolition teams.
April 30	The Republican Navy claims a victory. The Nationalist cruiser *España* is sunk off Santander.

Mounting tensions in Barcelona between the communists and their rivals explode into street fighting in the city.

May 1	Fearing further violence between the anarchists and communists, the Generalitat cancels public observances of the *fiesta de trabajo*.

The Neutrality Act of 1937 becomes legally binding for citizens of the United States, excluding only oil shipments and nonmilitary vehicles.

May 3	Suspecting that the anarchist workers at the telephone company have been monitoring the Generalitat's official communications, Rodríquez Salas, a communist official in the region's security department, demands to inspect the company's censorship office. When the search is initiated, anarchists open fire against the inspectors who then attempt to storm the building. The fighting, once begun, quickly spills over into Barcelona's streets, touching off full-scale battle between the municipal government and the anarchists joined by the POUM. By evening, much of the city is patrolled by armed POUM militia.
May 4	Recognizing the consequences of a one-sided battle between their followers and the regional government, the anarchist ministers, García Oliver and Federica Montseny, urge the CNT/FAI to return to work, leaving Andrés Nin and POUM to face their opponents alone.

The Non-Intervention Committee urges both sides in the Spanish conflict to foreswear the bombing of open cities.

May 5	Although a temporary cease-fire is arranged in Barcelona, the assassination of the UGT minister-designate, Antonio Sese, renews the conflict. The Valencia government dispatches Assault Guards to the embattled city.
May 6	The Valencia government assumes the public order functions of the Generalitat in an effort to restore peace

to Barcelona. These powers, in much reduced form, are not returned to the regional council until weeks later.

The Republic's militiamen in Aragón are disarmed and placed under the command of General Pozas, who only recently joined the Communist party.

May 8	Security forces from Valencia restore order to Barcelona. In the course of the fighting, more than 400 persons are killed and 1,000 wounded.
	A squadron of Republican aircraft, trying desperately to reach Bilbao, touches down at Toulouse, France. Representatives of the Non-Intervention Committee allow them to return to Spain, provided they fly to Barcelona.
May 12	The Spanish delegation to the coronation of England's King George VI is led by the socialist intellectual Julián Besteiro. On instructions from Azaña, Besteiro leaves Spain on a peace mission, returning to find that the government of the Republic has undergone a sudden change. Besteiro is never afforded the opportunity to report on the results of his mission.
May 15	For several weeks, Prime Minister Largo Caballero has found himself increasingly at odds with the communist members of his cabinet over a variety of issues. For example, he urged a military expedition into Estremadura, while the communists were seeking a counterthrust in the vicinity of Madrid. What brings down Largo Caballero's government, however, is the issue of the handling of the POUM. The prime minister urges clemency and as a result, on this date, his communist ministers resign their posts. Azaña asks Largo Caballero to form another cabinet, but his efforts fail.
May 17	The socialist Juan Negrín López succeeds in forming a new government, composed essentially of the same factions as its predecessor. While the new minister of justice, Manuel de Irujo y Ollo, speaks of reestablishing Catholic worship in the Republic, Negrín favors the reduction of "workers' control" and the centralization of governmental authority over industry.
May 29	The German cruiser *Deutschland* suffers an aerial attack by Republican planes while it rests at anchor at Ibiza. The episode touches off an international incident.
May 31	Not only do Germany and Italy withdraw in protest from the Non-Intervention Committee's Maritime Control board in connection with the *Deutschland* incident, but also the cruiser itself exacts reprisal by bombarding the Republican port of Almería.
June 1	General Mola is killed in a plane crash in Burgos province.
June 4	General Fidel Dávila is selected by Franco to replace Mola.
June 6	The air defenses of Bilbao collapse as the last plane in its fighter cover succumbs to the Nationalist Air Force.
June 12	The much-touted "ring of steel" that was to have protected Bilbao from Nationalist attack is pierced.
June 16	POUM's leader, Andrés Nin, is arrested in Barcelona on charges of conspiring on behalf of General Franco.
June 19	Nationalist armies march into Bilbao as refugees crowd vessels in the harbor to leave the country.
June 20	Andrés Nin dies in prison at Alcalá de Henares after having been subjected to torture by NKVD agents.
June 22	An espionage tribunal is established by the Republic. Its primary mission is to try members of POUM.
June 30	Portugal joins Germany and Italy in withdrawing from the Non-Intervention Committee's naval patrol agreement and insists that British observers on its soil depart from that nation.
July 1	A collective letter from the Spanish bishops (excepting the archbishop of Tarragona and the bishop of Vitoria) endorses the Franco regime.
July 2	While heavy fighting is renewed at University City in Madrid, the Franco government officially insists on its rights as a belligerent power.
July 6	Thousands of Republican troops break through Nationalist lines around Madrid and capture the suburb of Brunete. This is the offensive Largo Caballero had opposed.
July 10	The Republican offensive around Brunete continues to gain ground at Nationalist expense, although Franco is quick to dispatch reinforcements to the sector.
July 16	Unprecedented aerial combat takes place over the Brunete battlefields.

July 18	Both Franco and Azaña address the nation on the occasion of the first anniversary of the uprising against the Republic, but Franco's broadcast coincides with a Nationalist counteroffensive at Brunete.
July 26	Nationalist troops regain most of the "bulge" created in their lines by the Republican offensive. As the fighting subsides, casualty figures in the action at Brunete reach 35,000.
July 28	The government of the Generalitat is reorganized to exclude the anarchists.
August 6	The Republic creates the *Servicio de Investigación Militar* (SIM), charged with intelligence duties. It is headed by a socialist of the Prieto wing of the party and takes over some of the functions previously reserved for the NKVD.
August 7	Private religious ceremonies are permitted once again in Republican territory.
August 10	The anarchist-dominated Council of Aragón is dissolved by the Negrín government, its members arrested, and its authority subsumed by the Valencia regime.
August 16	After having banned criticism in the press of the Soviet Union, the Generalitat forbids political meetings of any kind.
August 22	Attempting to relieve mounting Nationalist pressure on Santander, the Republic launches operations in Aragón, threatening Saragossa.
August 24	Fighting in the Aragón offensive focuses upon Belchite where skirmishes continue for weeks.
August 26	Nationalist and Italian troops break through the Republic's defenses and occupy Santander, herding their prisoners into the city's bullring.
	Mysterious attacks begin on neutral shipping making for Republican ports. A British ship is shelled off Barcelona.
August 29	A Republican vessel is attacked off the French coast from an unknown source.
August 30	The Soviet steamer *Tuniyaev* is sunk at Algiers by a "mystery" submarine.
August 31	The British destroyer *Havock* comes under submarine attack and replies with depth charges.
September 1	Pedro Churruca is selected by General Franco to handle negotiations between his government and the Vatican.
	Another unidentified submarine sinks the Soviet vessel *Blagaev* off Skyros.
September 2	The British merchantman *Woodford* is sunk near Valencia by an unidentified submarine.
September 6	Republican forces finally capture Belchite.
	The French government summons a conference of Mediterranean powers (along with Great Britain, Germany, and the Soviet Union) at Nyon to discuss the recent submarine depredations. The session is scheduled for September 10.
September 10	The Nyon Conference convenes and gets off to a disappointing start. The Soviet delegate blames the Germans and Italians for the sinkings. They respond that the entire matter should be handled by the Non-Intervention Committee. When their position is not upheld by the rest of the Conference's delegates, the Germans and Italians walk out. Britain and France, nevertheless, agree to institute naval patrols in the western Mediterranean to attack suspicious submarines.
September 14	The Nyon Conference formally agrees that submarines attacking merchantmen may themselves be attacked by naval patrols.
September 17	The Nyon agreement is extended to aircraft attacking merchantmen.
September 18	Count Ciano is presented with the Nyon accords, and further negotiations ensue.
September 24	The Italian Blue Arrows Division begins operations to counter Republican gains at Belchite.
September 27	The Italian government signs the Nyon accords and agrees to patrol the Balearic Islands and Sardinia in search of the unidentified submarines.
October 1	The Socialist party votes to remove Largo Caballero from its executive committee, replacing him with a Negrín ally, Ramón González Peña.
October 6	Nationalist armies launch a counteroffensive in the Aragón region.

October 7	Salamanca, Franco's headquarters, welcomes the arrival of the papal *nuncio*.
October 17	In a speech in a Madrid cinema, Largo Caballero publicly declares his opposition to Prime Minister Negrín and his conduct of the war.
October 19	After months of struggle, Gijón (Asturias) falls to Nationalist forces.
October 21	The last stronghold of republicanism in the north of Spain, Avilés (Asturias), is overrun by the Nationalists.
October 22	The duke of Alba is dispatched by General Franco to London to take up ambassadorial duties. In return, Great Britain sends Robert Hodgson to Salamanca as its "agent."
October 28	A Republican sally at Madrid's University City is quickly repulsed by the Nationalists.
October 29	Prime Minister Negrín moves his official residence from Valencia to Barcelona.
October 31	The entire Republican government follows Negrín's lead and moves to Barcelona.
November 4	The Non-Intervention Committee votes to create an observer corps to supervise the withdrawal of foreign volunteers from Spain, promising the award of belligerency status to the first side to accept its offer. Ten months of haggling over the specifics of the arrangement follow.
November 12	The CNT recalls all of its representatives from the committees of the Popular Front.
November 18	Álvarez del Vayo resigns his post as *Comisario general de guerra*.
December 1	Japan grants diplomatic recognition to the Franco government.
	The *Junta Nacional* of the *FET y de las JONS* is formally installed in its duties at the Monastery de las Huelgas in Burgos.
December 8	Nationalist aircraft bombard Barcelona, while Republican planes strike at an enemy base in León.
December 11	Ángel Pestaña, leader of the Partido Sindicalista (a breakaway faction of the CNT), dies of natural causes in Barcelona.
December 15	Republican commanders, realizing that Franco is about to attempt another major offensive against Madrid, forestall that effort by mounting an attack on Teruel. The movement catches the Nationalists by complete surprise and does, in fact, indefinitely delay the planned assault on Madrid.
December 22	Republican forces capture most of Teruel from its stubborn defenders commanded by Colonel d'Harcourt. Four thousand are besieged in the city's public buildings. Franco orders Teruel's immediate relief.
December 24	In intense cold and a threatening blizzard, the Nationalist counteroffensive begins on the Teruel front with support from the Condor Legion.

1938

January 3	Franco reorganizes his *Junta* to include some civilian figures.
January 6	The new minister of education in the *Junta*, Pedro Saínz Rodríquez, creates the *Instituto de España*, destined to become a pervasive force in Spanish scholarship.
January 8	Colonel d'Harcourt's garrison surrenders at Teruel.
January 18	General Yagüe's Moroccan troops are committed in the Teruel struggle, while the International Brigades fill Republican ranks in the latter portion of the battle.
January 30	The Nationalist government is completely restructured with the abolition of the *Junta Técnica* and the introduction of a complete cabinet of ministers, most of whom are civilians.
February 1	The Cortes convenes at the Monastery of Montserrat.
February 7	Maneuvering north of Teruel, Nationalist armies begin an assault on Republican positions along the Alfambra River. The operation includes the most significant cavalry action of the Civil War and concludes in two days with heavy losses in territory and lives for the Republican side.
February 21	Facing encirclement, Repbulican forces withdraw from Teruel. They delay their departure so long that El Campesino's column is obliged to execute a fighting retreat.
February 22	Nationalist armies regain Teruel.
March 5-6	In a night engagement off Cartagena, the Nationalist cruiser *Baleares* is sunk by Republican destroyers.
March 9	The Burgos government promulgates a labor charter, the *Fuero de los Españoles*. The document, designed

primarily by the minister of the interior (Franco's brother-in-law, Ramón Serrano Suñer), promises many reforms, but regards strikes as acts of treason. The *Fuero* proposes that Nationalist Spain be organized on a corporate basis.

Nationalist armies in Aragón initiate a massive attack aimed at reaching the Mediterranean coast and cutting the Republic in two. In the first day of fighting, twelve Nationalist divisions break through Republican lines at four points.

March 11	Hitler's armies occupy Austria.
March 12	The Burgos government repeals the Republic's civil marriage law.
March 13	Léon Blum once again becomes the French prime minister, and Negrín leaves immediately to plead with him for the reopening of the border. Blum agrees.
March 16	Italian bombers begin regular night raids on Barcelona.
March 17	The French border is opened to supplies destined for the Republic.
March 22	After seizing Caspe, the Nationalist offensive toward the sea resumes.
March 23	The Republic announces the confiscation of the contents of strong boxes held in private banks within its jurisdiction.
March 28	Indalecio Prieto affirms his desire that peace negotiations begin immediately.
April 3	At a meeting of the Republican cabinet in Barcelona, the communist ministers accuse Indalecio Prieto of defeatism. The news is bad. General Yagüe's Moroccans seize Lérida from El Campesino's veterans on this date, and the Blum government in France is replaced by Daladier. In May, the new French prime minister once again closes the border to Spain.
April 5	Yielding to communist demands, Prime Minister Negrín dismisses Prieto as war minister and reorganizes his cabinet, keeping the War Ministry for himself.
	At Burgos, the Nationalist government officiallly abrogates the Catalan Statute.
April 7	Tremp, a town on the Ebro, falls to Nationalist armies. Its hydroelectric facility had supplied most of Barcelona's electrical power.
April 15	General Alonso Vega's Nationalist armies reach the Mediterranean at Vinaroz.
April 16	After receiving assurances that Mussolini has no permanent designs on the Balearics and will withdraw all of his forces from Spain when the Nationalists are victorious, the British government announces that it has reached a sweeping naval agreement with the Italians.
April 20	Nationalist armies reach the French border after capturing the Arán Valley.
April 22	The Burgos government decrees a press law for its territories, legalizing censorship and forbidding "unauthorized" publications.
May 1	In a major address, designed to reassure the Western democracies about the Republic's objectives, Prime Minister Negrín sets forth his thirteen-point program for the nation's future. The proclamation causes no shift in international policy toward the Republic.
May 3	The Burgos government arranges for the reestablishment of the Jesuit order in Nationalist territory.
May 11	Portugal grants diplomatic recognition to the Franco regime.
May 13	Addressing the League of Nations, the Spanish delegate, Álvarez del Vayo, pleads for an end to the nonintervention policy.
May 31	Franco stages a review of Nationalist naval forces at the newly captured port of Vinaroz.
June 1	Republican forces launch attacks directed toward Tremp and Estremadura.
June 13	Frustrating both Republican initiatives, Nationalist armies resume the offensive and capture the port of Castellón north of Valencia.
June 25	Negrín's government orders that religious services be provided for those Republican troops desiring them.
June 27	The Soviet Union accepts a proposal from the Non-Intervention Committee on the withdrawl of foreign troops from Spain.
July 5	The fortifications at Nules, north of Valencia, are pierced by Nationalist troops.

July 6	The Bank of France announces that the 1,259 millions of francs in Spanish gold, deposited with that agency by the Azaña ministry will not be returned to the Republican regime since the majority of Spain's population now resides in Nationalist territory.
July 18	To commemorate the second anniversary of the uprising, General Franco is presented with the title *Capitán general del Ejército y de la Armada*, an office previously reserved for Spain's monarchs.
July 25	In another surprise offensive, Republican forces recross the Ebro in great strength, threatening Nationalist lines of communication and relieving the danger to Valencia. The fighting that follows in the coming months along the banks of the Ebro becomes the heaviest of the Civil War.
August 1	The initial Republican impetus to the south of the Ebro is contained by Nationalist armies.
August 10	Republican military operations in Estremadura score some local victories.
August 17	As the gains made by Republican troops on the Ebro prove difficult to hold against determined Nationalist attacks, Negrín announces the takeover of all munitions factories in Catalonia by his government. His Basque and Catalan ministers resign in protest, obliging Negrín to reorganize his cabinet once again.
August 18	On the excuse of attending an international conference on medicine meeting in Switzerland, Prime Minister Negrín departs from Barcelona. The real purpose of his trip is to contact the Duke of Alba for the purpose of negotiating a compromise peace. Although the meeting took place, General Franco refuses all initiatives for negotiations.
September 3	Two Nationalist Army corps break through Republican lines at Gandesa, pressing the defenders back on the Ebro.
September 9	Germany suspends military aid to the Burgos government in preparation for its operations against Czechoslovakia.
September 16	Franco's troops force a crossing of the Ebro at Venta de Camposines.
September 21	Negrín informs the League of Nations of his government's assent to the withdrawl of all foreign troops from Republican ranks.
September 29	The Munich Conference begins.
October 1	The Franco government announces the death of José Antonio Primo de Rivera, although the event had taken place two years previously.
	The League of Nations agrees to supervise the withdrawal of the International Brigades from the Republic.
October 4	All foreign troops fighting for the Republic are pulled out of the lines.
October 14	Several major Italian units embark for home aboard ships at Cádiz.
October 24	Trials of the POUM leadership begin in Barcelona.
October 31	The Republic takes its leave of the officers of the International Brigades at an official state dinner.
November 15	The ranks of the International Brigades parade through Barcelona on their way out of the country.
November 16	The battle of the Ebro ends as Nationalist troops reoccupy the territory lost to the earlier Republican offensive and the last Republicans retreat beyond the river.
	Another 10,000 Italian troops leave Spain in compliance with the Anglo-Italian accord.
November 19	Franco agrees to further mining concessions in Spain for Germany. In return, the Germans drop some of their claims for military reimbursements.
November 29	Simultaneous aerial attacks occur on Barcelona and Valencia.
December 6	In a desperate ploy, Republican generals formulate "Plan P," calling for an offensive on the Madrid front to coincide with landings at Motril.
December 8	The Republic creates a *Comisaria general de cultos*, to regulate religious services and practice.
December 11	General Miaja and Admiral Buiza refuse to execute "Plan P."
December 15	The Negrín government claims to have uncovered a Nationalist espionage ring and places 200 persons on trial. In Burgos, meanwhile, the Nationalist government announces the restoration of the properties and citizenship of Alfonso XIII.
December 19	The German-controlled mining corporation, Montaña, is created for operations in Spain. They also gain control of the Mauretania Mining Company of Tetuán.

| December 23 | 350,000 Nationalist troops attack across the Ebro into Catalonia, smashing through Republican lines in four places. |

1939

January 5-6	Attempting to stay the effects of the impending disaster in Catalonia, Republican forces in the central sector attack at Valdesquillo and in Estremadura.
January 13	Tortosa falls to Nationalist armies.
January 15	Tarragona and Reus succumb to Nationalist attacks.
January 22	General Yagüe's troops penetrate Barcelona.
January 23	After thirty months of war, the Republic finally declares martial law.
January 25	The Negrín government abandons Barcelona. At this point, the Burgos government announces that it has interned some 350,000 prisoners.
January 26	Navarrese, Moroccan, and Italian troops march into Barcelona. Negrín establishes his capital at Figueras (Gerona). Thousands of refugees cross the French border.
January 31	Franco's troops enter Gerona province while his air force bombs the remaining concentrations of Republican forces in Catalonia. Refugee columns continue to swarm across the French border.
February 1	In its last session on Spanish soil, the Republican Cortes convenes at Figueras.
February 2	Republican ambassadors formally ask England and France to negotiate an end to the fighting.
February 4	The president of the Republic, Manuel Azaña, crosses the border into exile, accompanied by Martínez Barrio, José Antonio Aguirre, and thousands of his countrymen.
February 6	Colonel Segismundo Casado, commanding Republican forces in the central sector, establishes secret contact with the Nationalists to discuss terms for ending the fighting.
February 7	Prime Minister Negrín and General Rojo depart from Spain by crossing the French border. General Miaja remains in authority over the remaining Republican forces.
February 8	Figueras is captured by Nationalist troops, while the British arrange for the transfer of Minorca's possession to the Nationalists.
February 9	Franco signs the Law of Political Responsibilities, outlining the treatment to be accorded all who opposed the Movement since October 1934.
February 10	Nationalist forces announce their control of all territorial exits into France. Hoping for continued resistance in light of Franco's refusal to compromise, Negrín lands at Alicante.
February 21	100,000 Nationalist soldiers parade before Franco in Barcelona.
February 26	Negrín consults with the general officers still serving the Republic, hoping to foster resistance.
February 27	Manuel Azaña resigns as president of the Republic. His constitutionally designated successor, Martínez Barrio, refuses the post, leaving the Republic a legal shambles. Britain and France announce their recognition of the Franco government.
February 28	The Republican Cortes, convened in Paris, accepts Azaña's decision. Far to the south, Nationalist planes bombard Republican strongholds in Valencia and Cartagena.
March 1	The French Republic designates Marshal Pétain to be its ambassador to Spain.
March 2	Operating from Yeste, Negrín reshuffles armed forces commands, deposing Miaja and placing communist officers in charge of Alicante and Cartagena.
March 4	When the prime minister's commander at Cartagena seeks to take his post, fighting breaks out between communist and noncommunist forces. To add to the confusion, local Falangists join in the fray.
March 5	Colonel Casado creates the National Defense Council, a government committed to peace and opposed to Negrín. His "rebellion" gains the support of General Miaja and Julián Besteiro, who broadcasts the council's goals to the nation. Discovering that his authority has crumbled, Negrín flies to Dakar.
March 6	A Nationalist effort to take the Cartagena naval base by sea fails when a troop ship is sunk.
March 7	Communist-led forces in the Madrid sector revolt against Casado's National Council, and bitter fighting occurs in the streets of the capital. The Republican Navy, meanwhile, steams out of Cartagena for exile in Bizerta.

March 8	With timely assistance from the anarchist commander, Cipriano Mera, Casado's forces defeat their communist opponents. A Nationalist effort to take Madrid in the midst of this disorder fails.
March 15	German forces occupy the remaining independent regions of Czechoslovakia.
March 20	At an airport near Burgos, Casado's representatives meet with Nationalists to discuss peace terms.
March 26	Casado informs Franco that the Republican Air Force will surrender on the following day.
March 27	As the remaining Republican armies begin to disband and surrender, Spain signs the Anti-Comintern Pact.
March 28	Casado's National Defense Council is dissolved and Nationalist troops march into Madrid.
March 29	Franco's troops occupy Cuenca, Ciudad Real, Jaén, and Albacete.
March 30	Valencia and Alicante yield to Nationalist forces.
March 31	Cartagena and the remaining Republican strong points capitulate.
April 1	In a broadcast to the nation, Franco announces the victory of Nationalist forces over the "Red Army" and proclaims, "The war has ended."
	The United States recognizes the Franco government.

For further information, see Gabriel Jackson, *The Spanish Republic and the Civil War, 1931-1939* (Princeton, N.J., 1965); Jesús Lozano González, *La Segunda República: Imagines, cronología y documentos (Barcelona, 1973);* Stanley G. Payne, *The Spanish Revolution* (New York, 1970); and Hugh Thomas, *The Spanish Civil War* (New York, 1977).

A Military History of the Spanish Civil War: 1936-1939

RAYMOND L. PROCTOR

According to plan, the rising of dissident military and political forces was scheduled to start with the military in Africa at 5:00 A.M. on July 18, 1936, and was to be followed by units in Spain on the morning of July 19. It was hoped that the rising of the garrisons would be enough to bring down the government, but in the minds of many there was the disturbing conviction that the rising would result in a bloody civil war.

The rising began prematurely in Melilla, Spanish Morocco, on the afternoon of July 17. The plot was revealed to loyal elements by a member of the Falange, and key officers of the revolt were surrounded in their headquarters by a section of troops under Lieutenant Juan Zaro. The lieutenant, in turn, surrendered when confronted by a unit of the Spanish Foreign Legion. This early action threw many of the army garrison commanders throughout Spain into a state of confusion and doubt that in many instances, resulted in vacillation, timidity, and a dangerous lack of determination which made a violent civil war unavoidable.

The Popular Front minister, Santiago Casares Quiroga, in Madrid, was informed of what had happened in Melilla and, by phone, ordered General Manuel Romerales Quinto (military commander of the area) to arrest Colonels Juan Seguí Almuzara and Dario Gazapo Valdés. The general, however, surrendered in his own office at the point of Colonel Seguí's pistol. These officers now declared a state of war against the Popular Front, and their forces occupied the public buildings in Melilla. Those who resisted the rebellion were shot, including General Romerales.

Colonel Seguí advised Lieutenant Colonel Eduardo Sáenz de Buruaga in Tetuán and Lieutenant Colonel Juan de Yagüe Blanco (with the legion) in Ceuta that they had been forced to move prematurely. The senior military officer, General Augustín Gómez Morato, in Larache, learned from Madrid that something was amis in his command and flew to Melilla only to be arrested on arrival.

In Tetuán, Colonel Sáenz de Buruaga demanded the surrender of the high commissioner, but the latter refused on orders from Madrid. His residence was surrounded by Major Castejón's 5th *Bandera* of the legion. Soon all of Tetuán was in rebel hands. Meanwhile, Lieutenant Colonel Juan Beigbeder, a very intelligent and highly respected Arabist, gained support from the native Moroccan leaders. The Moroccans eventually provided the rebels (or Nationalists) with some of their elite mercenary shock troops.

Shortly after midnight, on July 17, Lieutenant Colonel Yagüe with the legion's 2nd *Bandera* occupied Ceuta without a fight. This was not the case in Larache where the rising did not start until 2:00 A.M. on July 18. But by dawn it was fully under rebel control.

General Francisco Franco, assigned to lead the Army of Africa for revolt, was in Las Palmas and was informed of the necessity for the early action. He declared martial law in the Canaries and issued his manifesto of revolt at 5:15 A.M. on July 18. On the mainland, scattered garrisons began their declarations of war on the morning of July 18. But most rebel leaders were filled with doubt and vacillated for hours, or days, until it was too late either to save themselves or to contribute to the rising.

That same morning the Madrid government ordered three destroyers to Morocco. When the ships' officers heard General Franco's broadcast, they attempted to join the Nationalist revolt. They were overpowered by the ships' crews and disposed of. The minister of marine quickly dismissed all officers of the fleet and gave authority to chief engineers and seamen cells. The crews of the majority of vessels rallied to his orders; as a result, most of the Spanish Navy remained loyal to the Popular Front.

In Madrid, suspect military officers were stripped of their command; troops were relieved of obedience to any officers in revolt; and left-wing officers were soon in full control of the War Ministry and in contact with the union and Left party political leaders who were demanding arms. Lieutenant Colonel Rodrigo Gil, a communist-socialist sympathizer, delivered several thousand rifles to the *Unión General de Trabajadores* (UGT) and the communist-socialist youth who were quickly to dominate the streets of the capital. Those involved in the conspiracy were filled with confusion, doubt, and indecision.

Rebel action was more determined in Seville with an audacious *coup de main* by General Queipo de Llano. By that evening, through sheer bluff and bravado, he had the small garrison on his side, had captured the radio station, broadcasted to all of Spain, and thrown great confusion into the supporters of the Popular Front. The port of Cádiz fell to General José López Pinto (military governor) and to the spectacular General José Varela Iglesias who had only recently been released from prison. Both officers were later to serve the Nationalist Army with distinction. They were aided in Cádiz by a small group of Moroccans who were ferried across the Straits by the destroyer *Churruca*. Jeréz de la Frontera with its important airdrome also passed to the rebels. The towns of Jaén, to the east, and Huelva, near Portugal, remained with the Popular Front. A small unit of the Civil Guard from the latter was ordered against the rebels in Seville. However, on arrival, its commander, Major Gregoro de Haro, cast his force with Queipo de Llano.

In Málaga, on the coast, a company of rebel soldiers fell to loyal Assault and Civil Guards, and to units of the loyal fleet. On this day, the rebels in Granada did not expose themselves, as excited crowds filled the streets. But in Córdoba, Colonel Ciriaco Cascajo Ruiz (the military governor) battered down Popular Front opposition with artillery. By nightfall, rebel control throughout Andalusia was scattered and very thinly held.

The rebel successes in Estremadura were limited to the city and province of Cáceres. The garrison of Badajoz, the communications link with Portugal, remained with General Luis Castelló (the new Popular Front minister of war).

In Madrid, there was a shuffle in the Popular Front cabinet, and during the night of July 18, the new minister, Martínez Barrio, called the arch-conspirator General Emilio Mola Vidal in Pamplona to offer him a post in the new government. The general, who was the "director" of the rising, rejected the offer out-of-hand and advised Martínez Barrio that Pamplona and Navarre had risen in revolt.

Early the next morning, the War Ministry in Madrid distributed 65,000 rifles to the headquarters of the UGT and anarchosyndicalist trade unions (the *Confederación Nacional del Trabajo* [CNT]). Bolts for 60,000 of these, however, were in the Montaña Barracks of Madrid. Colonel Serra, the barracks commander, refused to release the bolts demanded by the ministry. This was the first open act of defiance in Madrid. Still, there was confusion in the ranks of the rising. The arrival of General Joaquín Fanjul Goñi, and officers from other barracks, did not give added direction to their cause. With 2,000 troops and 500 volunteers, they were quickly besieged in the Montaña Barracks by the union militias in the streets. Through the night of July 19, Madrid was at the disposition of the left-wing bands. Fifty churches went up in flames.

Where there was hesitation and indecision in so many regions, General Mola in Pamplona moved with dispatch. His ranks were quickly swollen by thousands of Carlist and Falangist volunteers. On July 19, he dispatched south a battle-column of two battalions and a troop of field guns, under Colonel José Gistau, to hold the vital east Somosierra pass over the Sierra de Guadarrama to Madrid. At the same time, he sent another column of 1,000, mostly volunteers, under Colonel García Escámez y Iniesta, to relieve Guadalajara on the Madrid road. If it could have been held, it would have been possible to approach Madrid without having to cross the Sierra de Guadarrama. En route, Colonel García Escámez secured the risings in the important communications centers of Logroño and Soria. When he arrived at Atienza, on July 22, he learned that the rising had failed in Madrid and that Guadalajara had already fallen to Popular Front forces dashing from Madrid. This column moved north to grasp the Somosierra pass. As a countermove, Colonel García Escámez swung his column to approach Somosierra

from the north of the Guadarrama. It was at Somosierra and the western Guadarrama pass of Alto de León that the first real field-battle of the Spanish Civil War developed.

Mola organized other battle-columns of 200 to 2,000 men. Some were to strike south into Aragón and others northwest into the Basque provinces.

The rising had noted successes northwest of Madrid in Old Castile. Segovia, Salamanca, and Ávila joined without a fight; Zamora and Palencia were quickly captured. There was a contest in the ancient cathedral city of Valladolid, but by nightfall it was under the control of the rebel leader Colonel Ricardo Serrador Santés. He immediately organized a battle-column of one battalion, a company of the Falange, a cavalry squadron, and field guns to head for, and to hold, the passes of Alto de León, the west pass over the Guadarrama, and Navacerrada to its east. The old capital of Burgos fell to the Nationalists with little opposition.

To the west in León, 2,000 miners descended on the military governor, General Carlos Bosch y Bosch demanding arms. He gave up four machineguns and with 200 rifles encouraged them to dash to Madrid. When they were well on their way south, Bosch took the city for the rising.

North in Oviedo, the liberal Colonel Antonio Aranda followed much the same ruse when confronted by 4,000 excited miners. He encouraged them to reinforce their fellow unions and save the capital; that evening he declared a state of war for the revolt. Aranda and Oviedo quickly came under a long and bitter siege by thousands of miners.

A regiment of engineers in the Simancas Barracks in the port city of Gijón, only a few kilometers north, revolted under Colonel Antonio Pinilla. They were also quickly placed under siege.

As July 19 faded, there was no open action from the garrisons or political parties in Galicia. To the east, Santander and Bilbao remained firmly with the Popular Front and the Basque government. In the resort city of San Sebastián, under prodding from General Mola, Lieutenant Colonel Jesús Vallespín Ros in the Loyola Barracks finally revolted. There was bitter fighting, but, by July 28, the garrison supported by the Civil Guard fell before the CNT. The two Basque provinces of Vizcaya and Guipúzcoa remained under government control. This was not the case with Álva and its capital Vitoria. Both were controlled for the Nationalists by General García Benítez and the methodical Lieutenant Colonel Alonso Vega who for so long had been overshadowed by his friend General Franco. In the near future, Alonso Vega (later a general) proved he was an able field commander in his own right.

The most vicious exchange of July 19 was in Barcelona. Here the cavalry general Fernández Burriel was to lead the rising until the arrival of General Manuel Goded Llopis from Majorca. In the various barracks, the army had about 5,000 troops, and the officers assumed that they would be able to hold the city. During the night of July 18, the anarchists stormed several arms depots, and when the troops left their barracks they had to fight a pitched battle with the anarchists and loyal guards. One Nationalist column did reach the Plaza de Cataluña.

With the island of Majorca secured for the rising, General Goded arrived in Barcelona before midday (July 19) and established his headquarters in the old captaincy-general. His headquarters was soon stormed by the anarchists and the loyal security forces. The general was captured and shortly thereafter executed. Other than four army units in the barracks of Atarazanas and San Andrés (with 30,000 rifles) outside the city, all of the Nationalist supporters were overrun. By the evening of July 20 these barracks and the city were in the hands of the anarchists.

Down the coast, in Valencia, on July 19 the anarchists were burning churches, and the left-wing officers of the Guards were distributing arms to the militias—but the rising still had not been announced. The next day the commander of the 3d Division, based in Valencia, decided the issue when he remained with the Popular Front. The revolt was quickly smashed in Alicante and Almería. The government controlled the entire Mediterranean coast. The only bright spot for the rising to the south was in Granada where the Civil and Assault Guards seized the city. For some time, Granada remained an exposed Nationalist salient into government-controlled southern Spain.

Nationalist supporters rose up in Galicia on July 20. In Corunna, General Enrique Salcedo Molinuevo commanded the 8th Division, and General Leandro Pita Romero (the military governor) commanded the 5th Infantry Brigade. Pita convinced Salcedo to stand with the government. But the engineers and Falange, under Colonel Enrique Cánovas Lacruz, declared a state of war and took the city.

That same day, the important naval base of El Ferrol fell to the Nationalists. The Nationalists also gained the battleship *España* and the cruiser *Almirante Cervera* and a number of small ships.

Also on July 20, the decision was made in Madrid. By morning, loyal forces and union militias dominated the city. The rebel troops were under siege and bombardment by aircraft and artillery manned by loyal troops. In midmorning, both General Fanjul and Colonel Serra were wounded in the Montaña Barracks, and by noon it was reduced by storm. There is no point in describing the resulting slaughter. Importantly for the union militias, the 60,000 missing bolts were found in the barracks.

Carabanchel Barracks—a southern suburb of Madrid—surrendered to loyal troops from Getafe. All other facilities were soon overrun or had come out in support of the government, including the important air facilities in the Madrid area. The next day the forces that had seized Carabanchel organized a battle-column of two battalions, four companies, a machinegun battalion, and twelve field guns (under Colonel Enrique Castilló). They skirted Madrid to advance to the west pass of Alto de León. Other columns immediately left for Guadalajara and Toledo. In Toledo, Colonel Moscardó with 1,300 people sought refuge behind the massive walls of the Alcázar and thereby began what was to be one of the most celebrated sieges of the war.

The Nationalists' hold on Aragón was tenacious, with the main strength based on Saragossa. It was siezed by the capable cavalry Colonel José Monasterio Ituarte on July 19.

Jaca and Huesca joined the rebels, and for many months Huesca remained a dangerously exposed salient. Barbastro remained with the government under Colonel José Villalba. To the south, small villages such as strategic Belchite, as well as the large city of Teruel on the Turia River, announced for the rising. In the month to come, both were to be scenes of vicious and costly fighting.

By July 21, vague lines through Spain began to develop which would grow into war fronts. It was through Aragón that the front stabilized between the Nationalists and the Popular Front militias of socialists, communists, but predominantly anarchists, who advanced west from Barcelona.

In the few days of fighting, although there remains mass confusion, it is possible to assess (to a degree) the status of forces and their holdings. The Nationalist failures seem to outweigh their successes. The named leader of the rising (the "Lion of the Riff"), General José Sanjurjo, was killed on July 20 in the flaming wreckage of his aircraft. Thus, while the revolt was in its earliest stages, it was left without a centralized command. There were, in essence, three specific areas of Nationalist authority: Africa, southern Spain, and northern Spain. In each, the commanders acted as "War Lords" and were thrown back on their own initiative and resources. The problem was partially corrected with the formation of the so-called Burgos *Junta* of generals to give direction and unity of purpose. This same *Junta,* on October 1, elected General Franco as the supreme commander and head of the Nationalist government.

But in the first week the most secure area was Morocco under control of the Army of Africa which was by far the best equipped, trained, and disciplined of all the Spanish military. It included the Foreign Legion with its battalion-sized *banderas* and Moroccan *Regulares* in their larger than company-size *tabores*. There were also select Spanish units of cavalry and artillery. The Army of Africa was led by the dedicated, professional battle-scarred veterans of the Riff Wars. General Franco arrived in Tetuán early on July 19 and assumed command.

On the mainland, the Nationalists had a tenuous hold on about one-third of Spain. They controlled less than half the Pyrenees border with France and a wide belt extending through Castile to Portugal. Excluded were the northern Basque provinces, the mining area of Asturias, and two-thirds of the northern coastline. To the east they held about half of Aragón.

Queipo de Llano held Seville in the south and was being reinforced from Africa. For the most part, the Nationalist holdings in Andalusia were enclaves, redoubts, or exposed salients, with much of the land dominated by the Popular Front. He was neither manned nor equipped for any offensive action. In the south, as well as in many other parts of Spain, there were great stretches that were controlled by neither the government nor rebels.

General Mola, in the north, was faced with a war on three fronts: first, against the Basque provinces; second, against Madrid; and third, against the Popular Front militia columns moving into Aragón. His forces were hourly increasing with Carlist, Falangist, and Galician volunteers, but he was critically short of ammunition.

For the Nationalists, the status of forces was trying. The government controlled about two-thirds of the military and paramilitary police. However, the defection of the Army of Africa equalized the number. The greatest share of the fleet as well as most of the aircraft (although obsolete or obsolescent) remained with the government.

Strategically, the government held an overwhelming advantage. With its domination of most of the coastlines and border with France there was no problem of resupply from abroad. It dominated all of Spain's industrial regions, depositories, and production of munitions, largest concentrations of population to draft manpower, and the finances and gold reserves of the country.

The Nationalists had to move the Army of Africa to the fighting. To this end, they requested a limited number of transport-type aircraft from Germany and Italy. At the same time, the government solicited military aircraft from France. Shortly, material began to arrive on each side. Russia contributed greatly to the government, and Germany and Italy to the Nationalists. Eventually, the war became a battleground of many different nationalities and political ideologies.

As noted, the first field-battle as such, was fought for control of the passes over the Sierra de Guadarrama: specifically, the west pass of Alto de León on the Corunna Road, Navacerrada to the east on the road to Segovia, and the most eastern pass of Somosierra, due north of Madrid on the Burgos road. For the Nationalists these passes were the gateways to Madrid, but for the government they were the gateways to the plain of Castile.

A strange column, accompanied by the riffraff from Madrid, under Colonel Julio Mangada headed west to cut Ávila off from the pass of Alto de León. He seized several villages but accomplished little and returned to the cafés of Madrid.

A far more serious effort was made on July 21, when the column commanded by the militant communist Captain Francisco Galán (he later became a general) attacked a small force of monarchists and Falangists who were battling loyal elements for the height of Somosierra. The Nationalists were destroyed the next day, while Colonel José Gistau's relief column (two battalions and a troop of field guns) was but a short distance away. The government column was sizably reinforced, and included were twenty-three pieces of artillery with one battery of 155mm guns. When Gistau attempted to carry the pass (on July 23), the Nationalists were badly mauled and he had to withdraw. He was reinforced that evening by the arrival of Colonel García Escámez's battle-column which had been diverted from its route to Guadalajara. On July 25, the Nationalists outflanked the government force and drove Galán back over the pass. For three days he tried to recarry the pass but suffered heavy losses. The decision was made to dig defensive positions on the Madrid slope. By the end of the month, the government had 5,000 men on the line but made no further effort to attack the pass. Instead, it established a long front to the east and west.

Meanwhile, the government column of Colonel Castilló arrived at Alto de León and prepared to meet the assault of Colonel Ricardo Serrador's column from Valladolid. On

July 22, the government militia panicked before Serrador and fled the heights. Colonel Castilló was shot by his own militiamen. Both sides were quickly reinforced. For the government, included was a communist battalion under Juan Modesto—who in the month to come was to command a full army corps. The militía's lack of discipline again led to government failures the following day. General José Riquelme, from Madrid, attacked Serrador's column for two days with light tanks, twenty additional pieces of artillery, and two air squadrons. Colonel Serrador was wounded in hand-to-hand fighting and many of his officers were killed, but the Nationalists held. Additional reinforcements arrived for Riquelme who tried a flanking maneuver that was countered by his enemy; some of his militia again routed and fled to Madrid. Finally, on August 7, he gave up the effort and also constructed defensive positions on the Madrid slope.

The Nationalists, being critically short of ammunition, could not carry an offensive of their own. Nor could they attempt to carry the pass at Navacerrada.

The Battle of the Passes of the Sierra de Guadarrama, strictly between Spaniards, was indicative of what was to come. The advantage was decidedly with the government. Its forces should have carried the passes. The weakness and indiscipline of its militia, no matter how enthusiastic, were fully demonstrated. The battle ended in a stalemate.

When Mola sent his column to control the passes of the Sierra de Guadarrama, he also dispatched three battle-columns of some 3,400 men into his exposed flank on the Basque provinces. The columns included regular troops and Assault and Civil Guards, but were predominantly *Requetés* and Falangist volunteers. One column (2,000 men), under Colonel Alfonso Beorleguí y Canet, included a section of machineguns, mortars, and a battery of 105mm guns. Colonel Cayuela's column had 830 and Major Latorre's, 600. They faced seemingly impossible odds. Cayuela and Latorre were eventually to lead Navarrese brigades, the Colonel Beorleguí suffered fatal wounds (September 4) at the International Bridge of Fuenterrabia.

To the south, the garrison of Saragossa was reinforced by over 2,000 Carlists. Mola had no intention of launching an offensive to the east, but merely hoped to hold some sort of a front. On the other hand, with the smashing of the rising in Barcelona, the militias were carrying out their social revolution and were enthusiastically preparing battle-columns to seize Aragón. As early as July 24, a 2,500-man anarchist column of the revolutionary Buenaventura Durruti left Barcelona. They were so jubilant in being able to spread their revolution that they left their supplies behind. All the columns from Catalonia had a political base extending from the anarchists through socialists, communists, the Esquerra, to the *Partido Obrero de Unificación Marxista* (POUM) (the Stalinist-communists' hated enemy). The columns numbered some 20,000, including about 2,000 regular soldiers. Facing them in Aragón was a force of less than 10,000 Nationalists strung on an ill-defined front of several hundred kilometers.

The *Partit Socialista Unificat de Catalunya* was based at Tardienta southeast of Huesca. On their left, the POUM was based on Leciñena in the Sierra Alcubierre. Durruti's anarchists, now numbering 6,000, had advanced through Lérida, where they burned the cathedral, to Fraga and Caspe (where there was a sharp battle with the Civil Guard), and to Bujaraloz held by the loyal Colonel José Villalba. Durruti then took positions along the Ebro River, anchored at Pina. To his south was a mixed force, mostly anarchists, based at Montalbán facing the Nationalist front from Teruel to Belchite. The government columns were along the line by the first week in August. They could have carried Saragossa if a concerted effort had been made. Instead, a battlefront was established from north to south. Both sides would fortify high ground, dig in several field pieces, and base 200 to 300 troops in the nearest village to the rear. The opposing forces would then trade blows. This was the procedure for several months.

The great difference between the forces was that the Nationalists were under a structured military command. On the government side, the political columns operated their areas as private fiefdoms. There was little coordination between forces, and it is difficult to determine the command structure. If any consolidated effort was made, it seems to have rested with the anarchist García Oliver in Barcelona.

While Mola was concerned with a war on three fronts, General Queipo de Llano was expanding his hold in Andalusia. On July 19, he was reinforced by 200 *Regulares* who landed at Cádiz from the destroyer *Churruca*. Another detachment arrived on the gunboat *Dato*. The destroyer was lost the next day when its crew disposed of the officers and joined the Popular Front. A small detachment of Major Castejón's 5th *Bandera* was flown to Seville in three Breguet aircraft. Small battle-columns of soldiers, guards, and civilian volunteers, with possibly two field pieces, were organized, which fanned out from points of strength to reduce opposition in the countryside and aid friendly forces under siege. General Varela (twice the winner of Spain's highest decoration for his valor in the Moroccan wars) with a *tabor* of Moroccans drove east to relieve Granada, secure Ronda, and dash north to Córdoba to beat back an attack by a mixed force of 3,000 under General Miaja from Madrid. It was routed on August 20. Although many fought well, militiamen fled the field killing those who tried to stop them.

Thirty-one kilometers north of Andújar, in the Sierra Morena, 2,000 Nationalists, including women and children, established themselves on August 22 in the isolated thirteenth-century Monastery of Sante María de la Cabeza. They were to undergo the longest siege of the war. Although of no strategic or tactical value, the government was determined to destroy the force as an annoyance. In late April 1937, the communist Pedro Martínez Cartón, commanding 20,000 troops, stormed the heights in a fierce, bloody battle. The defenders were overrun on May 1, 1937.

The movement of the Army of Africa gained momentum with the arrival, in Morocco, of eight Italian Savoia bomber-transports and nine German Ju-52 transports. The first Ju-52 delivered its cargo of Moroccans on the evening of July 26. The airlift continued until October 11; by that time, the Germans alone had airlifted 13,000 men and their light equipment.

As early as August 3 and 4, two small battle-columns of the legion and *Regulares* started their drive north from Seville. They were followed on August 9 by a third column; their combined strength was 3,000. Each column, besides machinegun and mortar sections, had a troop of 70mm or 75mm field guns. They moved forward in every type of vehicle that could be seized. The columns were self-contained forces that depended on speed, discipline, and the determination of trained professionals to shatter the undisciplined and poorly led militias being deployed before them. Their objectives were to destroy these militia units, secure the villages, and link with Mola's northern force.

The government assumed that the enemy columns would strike from Seville against the capital via Córdoba. Defensive positions were established with 6,000 men east of that city. Instead, the columns dashed north to Mérida to link with General Mola and clear the enemy out of their concentration at Badajoz and the communications line to Portugal. With this accomplished, the columns were to press on to Madrid from the southwest.

Although there had been skirmishes before many villages on the drive north, the first major contest was at Almendralejo, a short distance south of Mérida, where Lieutenant Colonel (later general) José Asensio Cabanillas halted his forces on August 5 to wait for Major Castejón's column. Asensio's troops suffered heavy losses in an air attack on the following day. With the arrival of Castejón, the columns came under the command of the tough Colonel Yagüe. They dispersed an enemy force almost twice their number and carried Mérida on August 11. The Army of Africa had advanced 320 kilometers in a week. The enemy retired 2,000 of its force to the east and 3,000 to the walled city of Badajoz in the west. The Nationalist columns also joined with General Mola's outriders and delivered needed ammunition. Before the end of July, Mola was in such straits for ammunition that he figured his cause lost and he considered suicide.

Yagüe was reinforced by Lieutenant Colonel de Tella's column which had left Seville on August 9. Tella was to hold Mérida, where he beat back a strong counterattack, while Yagüe, with 3,000 men assaulted Badajoz with its 8,000 well-positioned defenders. The Nationalists pounded the gates through the morning of August 14, and the legionnaires stormed in the afternoon. One company was decimated by machineguns, but the city was carried by bitter hand-to-hand fighting, lasting well into the night. Losses were high on both sides. With the Portuguese border secure, the Nationalists regrouped and turned their columns towards Madrid on August 20.

On August 22, Castejón routed a superior anarchist force attempting to outflank his column along the Guadalupe Sierra, and Asensio's column suffered heavy losses in an air attack by a French squadron at Medellín. Then both columns joined Tella's force at Navalmoral de la Mata and regrouped.

The advance against Talavera de la Reina began on August 28 and reached the city on September 2. The following day, the column accomplished its typical encirclement maneuver and overran the defenses that afternoon. Along with the city, it captured a regiment of artillery. The retreating government force was reinforced from Madrid and from September 5 through 8 attacked the Nationalists in Talavera with 6,000 men, tanks, armored trains, and aircraft. The legion and Moroccans held, and on August 9 they were reinforced by Colonel Monasterio's cavalry from General Mola's army and renewed their drive to Madrid.

The Nationalist columns grew in size, despite losses, through volunteers and reinforcements arriving from Morocco. A fourth column was organized under Lieutenant Colonel Delgado Serrano, and all columns were reorganized. They now constituted 1,500 men in a legion *bandera*, two *tabores* of Moroccans, a troop of field guns, and sections of communications, sappers, and transport. As the advance to Madrid slowly progressed, a fifth column was created under Lieutenant Colonel Fernando Barrón. The five battle-columns numbered 8,500. They were nowhere near equal the strength before them. A vicious battle developed at Oropesa, but to avoid encirclement by Yagüe's columns, the government abandoned its defenses on September 21. The colorful General Varela now replaced Yagüe who had fallen ill.

To protect the Nationalist right flank, General Mola's columns pushed forward from Ávila and east of the Gredos Mountains. Varela's right flank remained exposed.

As the Army of Africa approached Maqueda, Franco made the decision, as a matter of honor, to divert his force and relieve the besieged Alcázar of Toledo. Franco has frequently been criticized for this change of direction because many believe that it delayed an assault on Madrid which, at the time, could have carried the city. The Alcázar was strategically unimportant, but it had become a symbol of Nationalist courage which the government was determined, at great expense, to destroy, as much as Colonel Moscardó's garrison was determined to defend it. With three columns, Varela shattered the forces before him, cut the road to Madrid, and relieved the Alcázar on September 27. The government should have been able to hold the city; there were 16,000 men along with artillery concentrated in the area. But once again, the militias broke and fled the field. The siege had lasted sixty-nine days during which eighty-two defenders were killed and 430 wounded. There were thirty deserters and fifty-seven missing, and seven died of natural causes. The fortress was reduced to rubble, but it had endured thirty aerial bombardments, 15,300 shells of different caliber fired at point-blank range, and explosions of mines, and it had repulsed eight infantry assaults.

In early August, while the government forces crumbled before the Army of Africa, and effort was made to reclaim the Balearic Islands for the Popular Front. A large anarchist force from Barcelona and Valencia, under air force Captain Alberto Bayo and Guard Captain Manuel Uribarri, sailed for the islands. In 1938, Uribarri commanded the dreaded communist-dominated *Servicio de Investigación Militar* (SIM). On August 9, protected by two destroyers, submarine, and aircraft, the invasion quickly eliminated the fifty-man Nationalist garrison of Ibiza. Bayo left Uribarri and some of the anarchists and sailed for Majorca. He landed 8,000 men and ten pieces of artillery at Portocristo to establish a bridgehead 8 miles deep. But his militiamen seemed more interested in celebrating their victory than pressing their advantage. The Nationalists rallied a mixed force of 3,500 supported by Italian aircraft and a unit of Black Shirts. The anarchists fled the field under protection of the guns from the battleship *Jaime I*. They left many dead and much equipment scattered along the beach. The anarchists holding Ibiza also fled after killing 639 prisoners.

The entire government effort was a failure. The islands became strategically important bases from which Nationalist naval craft and air forces, including German and Italian, were to harass the shipping lanes to the ports on the coast and bombard strategic targets from France to south of Valencia.

In this same period, General Mola was determined to seize the initiative in the north. His grave shortage of ammunition, less than a single round per rifle, was corrected with receipt of 600,000 rounds when his forces made the junction with the Army of Africa.

His two small columns of Major Latorre and Colonel Beorleguí (under Colonel José Solchaga) exploded into Guipúzcoa. Latorre drove the anarchists out of Tolosa on August 11, and Beorleguí captured the heights leading to Irún. Three Nationalist ships began bombardment of San Sebastián on August 18 with minimal results.

On August 26, with 2,000 men, supported by artillery, Beorleguí began his assault against Irún. The 3,000 defenders were reinforced by French communists and anarchists from Catalonia. The battle lasted until September 3, and the fighting was savage. The Nationalists would saturate selected enemy positions with artillery fire and follow with an infantry assault. The enemy would withdraw in front of the barrage, regroup, and storm their former positions. Again—as so often was the case in the Spanish war—the struggle was reduced to bitter hand-to-hand fighting. The Nationalist artillery would begin its fire once more and be followed by infantry charging the lost positions. Some of the important heights changed hands four times.

The Nationalists finally carried the immediate height above Irún. Outnumbered two to one, Colonel Beorleguí's column (now 1,500 men) stormed Irún on September 3. The defenders fled to France as anarchists set fire to the city. The Navarrese entered the town the next day, and Beorleguí was fatally wounded. A small force from Navarre had produced a sizable strategic victory for the Nationalists. Besides the valuable land and its industry, the Basque border with France was sealed, and rail and road communications were established from France to Cádiz.

The Nationalists were unable to save the 180-man force of Colonel Antonio Pinilla besieged in the Simancas Barracks of Gijón. Even though covered by the guns of the Nationalist cruiser *Almirante Cervera*, the miners stormed his position on August 16. He radioed the cruiser to fire on his positions, and the request was honored. The miners could now concentrate fully against Colonel Aranda's desperate 3,000 in Oviedo.

It seemed that Colonel Aranda was in a hopeless situation with a city to hold and surrounded by thousands. The strength of his character greatly added to the defense. General Franco dispatched a *bandera* and *tabor*, in a battle-column, to assist the Galician troops attempting to fight through the rugged country to Aranda. The siege lasted for weeks, and when Aranda thought his depleted force was to be overrun, the *tabor* took Mount Naranco (October 16) and brought the militia under deadly fire. The Nationalists fought into the city the next day. The siege had lasted ninety days, but for the next six months Oviedo remained a dangerously held salient.

With the relief of the Alcázar, the Army of Africa regrouped and came under the command of General Mola (Varela and Yagüe remained field commanders) for the advance and frontal assault on Madrid. It had been on the move and in contact with its enemy for sixty days and had inflicted heavy casualties on a vastly superior force. While the Army of Africa had suffered greatly in return, it had captured great stores of military equipment on the battlefield.

Varela resumed his advance up the Toledo road to Madrid on October 7 with five infantry and one cavalry column. To support the Army of Africa, General Mola delayed his operation into Vizcaya and reduced his thin forces even more to bring the columns up to strength. He gave Varela eight light Fiat tankettes that had arrived from Italy and sixteen support guns. To protect Varela's left flank, Mola sent five columns (5,000 men) under General José Valdés Cabanellas to clear the rugged defiles of the Sierra de Gredos. The total Nationalist force was 13,500 with forty guns of various caliber. Other units of Mola's North Army were to invest Madrid in the north in an arch extending from Ávila to near Sigüenza. They were not committed to the assault.

By this time, the government militia units had been brought more directly under military control and were reorganized into Mixed Brigades of 3,850 men. Included were calvary, armor, infantry, artillery, and support units. The force before Varela comprised 25,000 with fifty-one guns. An additional 7,400 with ten guns were dangerously poised on the right flank at Aranjuez.

With his right flank protected by Monasterio's cavalry on the Tagus River and his left screened by the columns of Valdés in the Gredos, the columns advanced with their typical outflanking maneuvers combined with rapid violent thrusts. Their main concentration against Navalcarnero (16 miles west of Madrid) was to be detracted by a drive up the Toledo road by Barrón to Illescas. Madrid assumed this would be the main thrust and strongly reinforced the area. A Madrid force of 15,000, with 155mm guns, slashed at Barrón's column and enveloped his positions. Their encirclement was broken by the Nationalists' reserves thrown in by Varela, and faced with a withering counterattack, the government broke off the attack. Although outnumbered five to one, Barrón carried Illescas on October 18. At the same time, Delgado Serrano and Asensio's columns, now under Yagüe, converged on Navalcarnero.

Yagüe shattered the heavily fortified town on October 21 with 1,500 men and the Fiat tankettes, but could make little progress beyond. The government had assumed that its fortifications were impregnable. Madrid now initiated a powerful three-day counterattack against Barrón's column at Illescas. Barrón held and with a counterattack of his own drove north to Torrejón de la Calzada, 20 kilometers south of Madrid.

Initially, the Nationalists had local control of the air with sixty aircraft, mostly Italian and German. This situation quickly changed with the arrival in Madrid of superior Russian aircraft. At the time, Madrid received the heavy Russian (9 ton) T-26 tanks armed with cannon and machineguns.

By October 28, 9,000 Nationalists were committed on a 50-kilometer front from the Jarama River in the east to west of Brunete. In the same sector, the government had 20,00. The next morning it struck hard at Tella's column on the Toledo road with artillery, aircraft, and armored trains. On the right, Monasterio's cavalry was hit by an oversized brigade (under the communist Lister) supported by fifteen Russian tanks. Lister's infantry failed to follow the armored breakthrough, and the cavalry stopped the tanks at Seseña where they captured two. Varela regained the lost ground, but his columns were badly bloodied. By the first week in November, his effectives were below 6,000, but he had seized Getafe's airdrome from anarchists, Carabanchel, and the height of Cerro de Los Angeles.

Madrid struck hard again on November 4 with forty-eight Russian tanks and nine armored trains. They dented the Nationalist front, but once again their infantry failed to follow through. The cavalry destroyed two more tanks, and the Nationalists resumed the attack on a wide front. Their most forward column took up positions 7 kilometers from the heart of Madrid. The lead columns were now backed by three newly formed columns, and the Nationalists' total strength grew to about 12,000, supported by twenty-four guns and thirty light Fiat and German Mark I and Mark II tanks, armed only with machineguns. But the assault force consisted of only 5,000 men.

Madrid had 33,700 men deployed, but the Popular Front government fled the capital to Valencia. The defense of Madrid fell to General Miaja.

Varela prepared detailed plans for the assault which he hoped would carry the city on the morning of November 8. The main strike would be Castejón's and Asensio's columns between the University City and the Plaza de España. The area through the Casa de Campo greatly favored the defense but was considered to be more desirable than the narrow streets of Madrid and its southern suburbs. Each column was given its objectives down to specific time, buildings to be taken, and what streets to bring under fire. Tella and Barrón were to advance toward the Toledo and Segovia bridges to give the impression that this was the main thrust point. The forces were mainly legionnaires and Moroccans.

After artillery preparation, on November 7, Castejón's column moved into the Casa de Campo but his attack was shattered by a Mixed Brigade, tanks, and artillery. Castejón was wounded and carried from the line. A great boon fell to the defenders that morning when a Nationalist light tank was destroyed. On the body of an officer was found a copy of Varela's complete battle plan. Miaja was thus able to redeploy his forces to place the assault route under raking fire which was to decimate units of the legion and the Moroccans. The same day the 11th International Brigade arrived from Albacete and stopped at Vallecas where the major attack was expected. But the brigade was quickly moved into position to meet the major assault. The force was commanded by a Rumanian/Hungarian communist who was then going by the name of "Kléber."

On November 8, the Nationalists made a major effort all along the line. But with the concentration points strongly reinforced, the advancing columns came under deadly fire. Still, Varela maintained pressure on the entire front throughout the day. The columns in the Casa de Campo were struck by the International Brigade and also had to beat back Miaja's columns attacking on their weak north flank. For the first time, the Moroccans broke, but the battle raged through the night. Once again fighting was reduced to bayonets, knives, and grenades. Varela's columns withdrew slowly and with discipline, leaving their dead but saving their wounded. They had destroyed a third of the International Brigade. By now the government had air, armor, and artillery superiority.

In the face of strong and determined resistance, the Nationalist columns, in spite of their professionalism and discipline, were not able to obtain their objectives and suffered great losses. One column, badly shattered in the Casa de Campo, had to be withdrawn and its survivors used as replacements to other units. The horse cavalry fought an unequal battle with armored cars in the streets of Carabanchel and had to withdraw.

Throughout November 9 and 10, the two armies fought toe-to-toe with each suffering high losses. Yagüe cleared most of the Casa de Campo, and on their right the Nationalists tried to battle their way through the streets of Carabanchel Bajo. It was house-to-house and hand-to-hand fighting which took a dreadful toll of the Moroccans. A twenty-four-hour battle raged in the rooms of the Military Hospital before the International Brigade units were driven out.

Artillery duels were the main effort of November 11-12 as both sides regrouped and replaced their losses. The entire effort was deteriorating to a war of attrition. The government was reinforced by the 12th International Brigade, and the next day, with four additional brigades, the government attempted to storm the flank position of the strongly fortified Cerro de los Ángeles. The bayonet attack was shattered by Nationalist gunners, and the Brigades returned to their point of departure. Had it been successful the attack could have been a disaster for the Nationalists. There was a large attack on the Nationalist left flank which also failed. But the Nationalists did take the high ground of Mount Garabitas in the Casa de Campo and immediately turned it into a powerful artillery position. Small groups of Moroccans also established a narrow front on the Manzanares.

Madrid welcomed 3,000 well-armed anarchists under Durruti on November 14. At their insistence, the anarchists were given their own sector in the Casa de Campo and assigned to lead an assault the next day. Supported by all artillery and aircraft available, but faced with the legion and Moroccans rather than peasants of Aragón, the anar-

chists refused the order to attack. Yagüe's columns struck through the same area to storm the University City. His columns were thrown back from the river three times and suffered greatly. A *tabor* finally carried the river and the far bank to find that the anarchists had deserted their trenches. The Nationalists sent three columns through the narrow gap to join the 800 who were struggling from building to building in the University City. Again it was hand-to-hand fighting. No quarter was asked or given. The 11th Brigade was thrown in by Miaja, and one of its battalions was destroyed to the last man. By November 17, the Nationalist columns were reduced to less than 2,000 and faced the incredible odds of almost 12,000. Still, they slightly widened their gap.

An anarchist unit was routed from the West Park and chased down the Paseo de Rosales and the Calle Princesa by a tank and thirty infantrymen. They had to break off their pursuit in the face of superior forces and withdraw.

Both sides traded heavy blows, but neither could budge the other. Durruti was killed on November 19; it is suspected that he was shot by his own men. Although vastly superior in number, the government could not dislodge the Nationalists from their bridgehead, nor could the Nationalists advance through the narrow streets on their right flank. After a hard struggle, they did take Moncloa and the Hospital Clinic, and repeatedly repelled costly assaults on Mount Garabitas. Franco finally recognized that he did not have the strength to carry the city, and by November 23 he abandoned the effort and attempted to stabilize the front. He hoped to encircle the city and bring it under siege. There were some costly exchanges for the balance of the year, but in essence the Madrid front remained the same until the end of the war.

The Nationalists lost a staggering number of their finest troops. One battalion of 500 volunteers was reduced to only forty effectives. It is believed that the losses of the government forces were even higher.

At first, the Nationalists' air operation was limited and scattered. The German Condor Legion began arriving in Cádiz on November 7, and the German aircraft and crews on hand were placed under its commander. After the middle of the month, the raids were increased to thirty-six aircraft. The lumbering Ju-52 bombers and He-51 fighters proved vulnerble to attacks from the superior Russian aircraft, and the air attacks were moved to the night. From November 14 through 23, 244 civilians were killed and 857 were wounded. The number of military casualties is not known.

Most analysts agree that in the battle for Madrid the Nationalists faced impossible military odds; at the same time, both sides fought with dogged determination. Some feel that had the government concentrated strong attacks on both flanks, the Army of Africa could have encircled and destroyed in detail. Given the Nationalist ability for rapid deployment, this is open to debate. It is suggested that it was a mistake for the Nationalists to have insisted on the frontal assault. Although its control was important psychologically, if Madrid had been captured it would have become a logistical and military liability that would have greatly drained the Nationalists' limited resources.

With the Madrid front stalemated, both sides reorganized their forces. Government militias were converted to Mixed Brigades with at least two brigades comprising a division with its support functions. The front was ultimately divided into five command sectors with their weapons standardized. The Nationalists reformed into three brigades in the so-called Madrid Divison which was to come under General Orgaz when Mola returned to his North Army. For a time the battle-column tactics were still followed. In their secure rear areas, both sides had long before put in motion the procedures to raise, train, and equip forces, not only of tens, but hundreds of thousands. The war was changing from a struggle between columns of a few hundred to massive flows between divisions, army corps, and armies. Both sides received added support in men and equipment from abroad.

Conceding his assault was a failure, General Franco planned a double envelopment which he hoped could place Madrid under siege and bring about its capitulation. He could accomplish this objective by joining the Army of Africa with the North Army east of the city between Guadalajara and Alcalá de Henares. First, he had to secure his weak forces in the Casa de Campo and the University City from the north and west. To that end, on November 29, Varela (with 7,000) attempted to straighten the line west of Madrid from Húmera to Pozuelo. Kléber struck in the area at the same time with twice the force. Their armies met head on, and one of his brigades fled before the legion; it could not be stopped until it reached Pozuelo and Húmera. The few Nationalist tanks were shattered by the Russian tanks, and the survivors had to withdraw. Although the battle raged for six days, Varela could accomplish little. Still, on December 16, he attacked with 10,000, hoping to cut the Corunna Road near Buenavista Height north of the University City. This was to become the battle for Corunna Road.

The ferocity of Varela's attack destroyed a Madrid brigade of 5,000 and enveloped Boadilla del Monte. Here a ruse trapped a battalion of the Internationals, but they succeeded in extracting themselves. The battle raged until December 20, by which time both sides had exhausted themselves. Varela surrendered all positions taken except Boadilla del Monte and Villanueva de la Cañada north of Brunete. The International Brigades were badly damaged, but the Nationalists temporarily lost General Varela who was wounded by fire from a Russian tank.

By early January 1937, General Miaja not only made good his losses but also increased his strength to 80,000. Facing him, General Orgaz's strength had grown to 35,000 holding the line and 22,600 (including reserves) comprising a strike force.

Determined to carry Corunna Road, General Orgaz ordered the offensive resumed on January 3, 1937, with 12,000 men against a well-positioned superior force. A terrible battle raged back and forth until January 19 through a dense winter fog and extreme cold. The mass of the attack shattered the defenses all along the front. Three communist brigades crumbled, and the Thaelmann Battalion, 11th International Brigade, was destroyed near Las Rozas. By January 9, Orgaz held 6 miles of Corunna Road. Miaja pulled battalions from Madrid and committed the 11th and 14th International Brigades. The International Brigades were disengaged from halfhearted attacks against the salient of Granada. Supported by three tank squadrons, on January 11 they launched a powerful attack west of Las Rozas, which smashed through Orgaz's units, and many Nationalist positions were overrun. Most of the credit was due the Russian tanks which reaped a terrible toll of men and equipment. But once again they were not supported by their infantry. The operations for each side were greatly hampered by the fog. One battalion of the Internationals became lost in it and was never seen again; in addition, a Nationalist battalion stumbled into the government lines and was disposed of.

Orgaz repeatedly counterattacked to regain lost positions. Again exhausted, both sides dug in on January 16. Orgaz had advanced 20 kilometers and regained the 10 kilometers of the Corunna Road, and he had stabilized his left flank. But the government had secured its front as well, and Madrid was safe from encirclement from the north and west. The cost for the Nationalists is put at 15,000 of their elite shock troops, with a much higher figure calculated for the government.

In the nature of their assault, the Nationalists showed the influence of the German military hand. Bombardment would be followed by a wave of concentrated tanks and mobile artillery, then a wave of infantry, which was followed by another wave of tanks, and then again more infantry.

While Franco prepared plans to strike from the south to east of Madrid, the fighting momentarily shifted to southern Spain. General Queipo de Llano's South Army was limited in size, but it was well disciplined and relatively well equipped. After the first of the year, he was reinforced by the arrival of Italian units, and the forces easily advanced up the coast to take Estepona and Marbella. They were regrouped to drive up the coast against the government pivot of defense at Málaga and to press beyond as far as possible. The government area commander, Colonel Villalba (formerly of Barbastro in Aragón), had 12,000 men and sixteen guns. He held a front from the ocean on a curve to nearly 35 miles deep into the mountains west of Málaga near Alhama southwest of Granada. The mountain passes and heights were fortified.

On February 3, 1937, the duke of Seville attacked from Ronda and 2 miles east of Marbella, supported by the guns of a cruiser and gunboats. Villalba's artillery was quickly silenced. Believing their flank on the sea would be protected by their own fleet, the government forces had mistakenly constructed their trenches so that they could be brought under enfilading fire by the ships and were quickly emptied. The defenders' flight up the coast was given urgency by the guns from the sea. That evening the duke of Seville occupied Fuengirola. The next day his advance pressed past Torremolinos where it halted for rest and resupply, but also to give time for the Italian columns pressing down from Antequera, Loja, and Alhama to traverse the rugged terrain.

Government forces in Málaga panicked and fled up the coast through Motril, 66 miles from Málaga. The Italians and Spaniards joined at the railroad station, took Málaga on February 8 with only scattered firing, and then pressed past Motril. The combined Nationalist/Italian force scored a decisive victory. Their advance was over 99 miles; with very few casualties, they had captured a major port of the Mediterranean. From this point on, there was no further military effort of any consequence in the south. The general ease of the offensive gave the Italians a false sense of confidence in their equipment and tactics which was to cause problems later.

As the Nationalists and Italians entered Málaga, fighting quickly shifted back to the Madrid front. The left pincer of encirclement was stalled on the Corunna Road, but now the emphasis was shifted to the right pincer which was to crash through the front south on the Jarama River. It was to cut the Valencia road and link, near Alcalá de Henares, with the North Army driving southwest from north of Brihuega. This would be an advance of some 25 miles and would sever communications with Valencia.

General Orgaz assembled south of Madrid a strike force of 40,000 under General Varela who had recovered from his wounds. The army was divided into five brigades which included fifteen cavalry squadrons and 101 guns (with six batteries of 155mm and a battery of the German 8.8 anti-aircraft guns to be used as well for artillery and anti-tank fire). In addition, there were two light tank companies with a total of forty-five tanks and eleven infantry battalions in reserve. Each brigade had a unit of the legion and Moroccans and was under battle-tested commanders.

The forces were assembled from Seseña in the south, to Cerro de los Ángeles in the north. The attack was to cover a 9-mile front. The government was planning an offensive in the same area and had assembled an even larger force; however, the Nationalists had an advantage in artillery. The Popular Front was to quickly gain control in the air over the antiquated German aircraft.

Heavy ranks, with the resulting mass of mud, required the Nationalist effort to be delayed until February 5 when hard mobile attacks shattered the front and were followed by the main offensive the next day. The Popular Front had committed a gross error by not fortifying the series of high ridges that curve from Morata through Arganda.

Colonel García Escámez on the right flank seized the village of Ciempozuelos and destroyed the 15th Brigade which left 1,300 dead. On the left, Colonel Ricardo de Rada's brigade stormed the high ground around Cabeza Fuerte and the peak of La Marañosa which was the key to the Madrid defense line west of the Jarama but was not properly guarded. Here the Nationalists decimated two battalions and quickly installed their 155mm guns on the height. They were later to take a heavy toll of the government forces in their attempted counterattacks. Colonel Rada was held at Coberteras, but Varela, personally leading two reserve brigades, stormed it.

In the center, Nationalist cavalry charged Goźquez de Arriba, but the infantry was held before San Martín de la Vega. On February 7, Colonel Barrón's brigade reached the confluence of the Jarama and Manzanares rivers and brought the Valencia road under fire. But the rains came again and raised the rivers to where they were not fordable. The mud also hampered all operations.

In the early darkness of February 11, a Moroccan *tabor*, with grenades and bayonets, disposed of eighty-six members of a company of the André Marty Battalion defending the Pindoque Bridge. By dawn, most of Barrón's cavalry and infantry were over the river. The bridge was now under heavy fire, which took a heavy toll of the Nationalist troops. In a series of spectacular charges, the Moroccan cavalry, along with infantry, completely wiped out the other companies of the André Marty Battalion. With heavy losses the Poles of the International Brigade managed to hold the line before Arganda.

In the south, Colonel Asensio's Moroccans also captured the damaged bridge near San Martín de la Vega and killed or captured 375 men of an English battalion attempting to hold the bridge and ridge. The Moroccans then had to repel a strong counterattack led by heavy tanks. Here they were aided by accurate artillery fire.

Banderas of the legion stormed Casa Blanca and held it against counterattacks at great cost. By nightfall on February 12, the Nationlist advance was contained in the three main attack zones. It was bitter fighting all day, with both sides realizing staggering losses.

With his reserves exhausted, Varela was still ordered to resume the attack on February 13 in the face of fresh enemy battalions. The lines were somewhat straightened, but the next day as the Nationalists prepared a frontal assault they in turn were almost overrun by units of the International Brigades. It was attack and counterattack throughout the day. When it seemed that the Nationalists might carry the field, their ranks were ripped by fifty Russian tanks and infantry and Colonel Eduardo Saénz de Buruaga's brigade was thrown back to the Jarama. With his *tabores* and *banderas* reduced below half strength, Varela made a desperate attack on February 15 but, faced with the four International Brigades, was unable to carry the heights. The Nationalists were now on the defense.

The Popular Front now regrouped its forces into an army corps of four divisions with a fifth division at Aranjuez. It was placed under a unified command. The corps attacked with a fresh division led by tanks on February 17, between La Marañosa and Cerre le los Ángeles. Other brigades from Arganda struck Barrón's cavalry. When it seemed that the Nationalist front would collapse, they were greatly aided by their air squadrons. As their lines shortened, they stiffened their resistance. The Madrid corps made a costly attack between San Martín de la Vega and the Pingarrón heights on February 19. They carried the heights but were quickly routed by Moroccans who lost 80 percent of their strength. The heights were lost and recaptured at staggering losses to both sides. The government's final effort on February 27 was the climax of the battle of the Jarama. Elements of two divisions led by the American battalion attacked into interlaced machinegun fire. The battalion lost 120 killed and 175 wounded out of 450 men. An anarchist brigade lost 1,100 at the same time. Both sides began digging defensive positions. It was once again a stalemate. The Nationalists had gained some 150 square miles and remained across the Jarama, but Madrid was still connected to Valencia.

The government counted 10,000 casualties and the Nationalists about 6,000. Once again the Russian tanks proved to be a deadly war machine, but again they were not properly supported by infantry. Moreover, the division of command on its side weakened both its offensive and defensive capability. Its almost complete domination of the air greatly aided in containing the Nationalist attack as well as supporting their own counterattacks. The lack of adequate reserves was most telling to the Nationalists, and some of their finest brigades were badly mangled, as well as the International Brigades on the other side. Well-placed and directed artillery was a decided asset to the Nationalists on the defensive.

The story might have been written differently if, while these armies were locked in their deadly struggle, the Italian-Spanish force of 40,000 that was being assembled in the area around Sigüenza had attacked down the road to Madrid. However, at this time, General Roatta would not commit his *Corpo Truppe Voluntarie* (CTV). It was a mechanized force of 31,218 with 2,000 trucks, 216 pieces of artillery and anti-aircraft guns, and ninety whippet tanks and armored cars.

Overconfident with his mobile forces and ignoring Franco's warnings, the Italian prepared his own offensive for early March. The advance was to start 68 miles from Madrid and aimed to advance the front 31 miles on the Saragossa-Guadalajara-Madrid road. They were then to push past Alcalá de Henares and join with the Nationalists driving from the Jarama. General Roatta did not seem to realize that these forces were so weakened that they would be unable to coordinate an attack with his own advance. Thus developed the so-called battle of Guadalajara. It could more accurately be called the battle of Brihuega and Torija, for it was here that the issue was decided. What is important is that the result was a humiliating blow to Italian military prestige.

The topography of the plateau leading down to Madrid lent itself for natural lines of attack with three main lines of thrust. On the right were the Spaniards under General Moscardó; the Italians were concentrated in the center, on the highway, as well as on the left to Brihuega. Initially, the offensive of March 8 led to optimism as the government front defenses were broken. However, as so often was the case on the plateau, the weather turned to cold driving rain with blustering winds and remained so for a week. The plateau turned into a quagmire of mud to the degree that deployment of troops from the main roads was out of the question. Vehicles became hopelessly mired, and entire columns came under demoralizing aerial bombardment and strafing. The Italian-German-Nationalist aircraft could not operate from their improvised muddy fields. Government planes operating from surfaced runways at lower altitudes and many kilometers to the south, and with far more favorable weather conditions, had complete air superiority. Italian resupply became next to impossible.

The Italians did take Brihuega and Trijueque but stalled short of Torija. Moscardó with his Spaniards pressed past Cogolludo in the hills west of Jadraque with its fifteenth-century castle.

Madrid rushed fresh brigades and divisions along with the devastating Russian tanks and artillery to the threatened area. They began their counteraction on March 12. The Italian units began to fall back under heavy pressure, losing Trijueque and Brihuega along with much equipment. On March 23, Spanish brigades stabilized a front 11 miles past the starting point of March 8. To protect his flank, Moscardó pulled back to Jadraque.

It was a great moral victory for the Popular Front, but it was not the disaster for the Nationalists that is frequently painted. The Italian units were to be re-formed and trained, but in the future the Nationalists were reluctant to commit them to given actions. As usual, the casualty figures are confusing, but it appears that the Italians might have lost 1,000 killed, 2,500 wounded, and 800 missing. The Nationalists' losses were 148 killed and 300 wounded. The government losses seem to have been about 6,000.

The government defense was well planned and led, and the counterattack was well coordinated with armor and air support; but it did not exploit its initial successes by pressing on to Alcolea del Pinar and Medinaceli. Strategically, neither side gained anything. But this was to be the last serious attempt of any consequence to capture or encircle Madrid.

In the late winter of 1936-1937, the various fronts in Spain had a total length of 1,821 miles. The Nationalists recognized that before a victory was possible the fronts had to be shortened. In the north, the government-Basque controlled region, besides being politically important, was an area rich in ore, coal, and vital heavy industry. The Nationalists had to secure this area before they could turn their forces against the government strength from the central ranges of the Pyrenees to the Mediterranean. Thus, while many of his brigades were locked in the Jarama (and the Italians were being extricated from the embarrassing debacle at Guadalajara), General Franco, with encouragement from General Sperrle of the German Legion, and with prodding from his Navarre commanders, gave approval for the operation of the North Army against Bilbao. The commander was General Mola.

The northern offensive was initiated between San Sebastián and Bilbao and extended west to Oviedo and Avilés. It was through mountainous terrain, with peaks often shrouded by clouds which formed a perfect defense barrier that the Nationalists had to break through.

The government-Basque forces in the north numbered nearly 150,000, comprising a coalition of Basque nationals, socialists, communists, CNT, and anarchists, all of which were greatly divided in leadership as well as objectives, and largely neglected by the government in Valencia. In the attack zone of Vizcaya, they had a mixed force of forty battalions (27,500 men) with seventy-five guns, which was quickly reinforced, fifty guns were deployed in Santander, and 150 in Asturias. They had a few T-26s and French tanks but only about twenty aircraft.

For the offensive, the Nationalists had 25,000 men led by the four tough Navarre Brigades, with 200 guns, under General Solchaga. They were supported by the German Condor Legion with sixty aircraft operating from Burgos and Vitoria. Some of its squadrons were now equipped with the He-111 bomber and the new Me-109 fighter. In addition, there were about seventy Spanish and Italian planes operating from various fields. All air units were coordinated under General Sperrle and his chief of staff, Lieutenant Colonel Richthofen. The Nationalists had complete control of the air, but the enemy held the strategic positions. The Nationalists were to be reinforced by reorganized brigades of the CTV.

The Nationalists did not have the strength to develop a pincer attack from the east and west. They therefore hoped to establish two breakthrough areas that would be accomplished in waves. The first was directly north of Vitoria and the other at Vergara in a westerly direction. The Germans considered Mola deficient in reserves as well as artillery for quick results. As events developed, the Germans were proven correct.

Much of the tactical planning was made by the German staff. On D-Day, strong points on the front would first be struck by mass bombers. The artillery would follow with saturating fire, then more low-level air strikes at selected targets, followed by the infantry attack that would be directly supported by low flying planes. The ground troops were identified by white panels, and the soldiers wore a white panel on their backs. Enemy strong points to be struck by air were marked with double panels pointing to the positions. Since most Nationalist aircraft were close to the front, they would be able to fly from four to six or more sorties a day.

D-Day was delayed because of poor weather until March 31. The air strikes and artillery performed as planned, but the timetable was not maintained because some of the infantry units delayed their attacks. Others were held up by the rugged terrain and determined resistance. Eventually, they began to carry the heights, but to the Germans the advance was painfully and unnecessarily slow. These repeated delays irritated the German commander and caused friction with General Mola. Supported by twenty-two batteries, including the German 8.8 guns, and all aircraft, the front was ruptured. After a bitter fight, Ochando was taken on April 4. The Nationalist aircraft struck hard at the attempted reinforcements and in one thirty-minute period dropped 60 tons of bombs that inflicted massive casualties. The government forces were in full retreat toward Bilbao. But they were not pursued, which greatly disappointed the Germans who believed that this violation of a basic rule of warfare prolonged the campaign for two and a half months. As it was, the Basques were able to re-form, fortify new positions, and make adjustments to their so-called ring of iron around Bilbao. By April 8, Russian fighters appeared and brought an end to the free operations of Nationalist aircraft.

Bad weather and government spoiling attacks, as well as the most difficult terrain, delayed the second phase of the operation until April 20. Following established artillery and air preparation, the attacking brigades began to envelop defensive positions, some of which were stubbornly defended. At others, defensive units withdrew, such as the CNT units, and thus exposed others. There were instances of friendly aircraft bombing their own forces, but the advance pressed slowly on. Aerial combat increased with aircraft being shot down on both sides, and General Sperrle was forever demanding a faster and more determined ground advance behind his air strikes.

It was during this phase, on April 26, that the historic bombing of the Basque town of Guernica occurred. The controversy generated by this incident rages even today. Guernica created its own library of material, as well as the famous painting by Picasso.

Durango fell on April 28, and Guernica was occupied the next day. After the victories, the Nationalists were shocked by the loss of the battleship *España* off Santander. Still, the Nationalists pressed for semicirclement of the "iron belt." There were moments of setbacks such as the spoiling attack against the CTV at Bermeo. Between March 21 and May 10, the Condor Legion alone dropped 681 tons of bombs. But there were still to be several weeks of heavy fighting. In an attempt to relieve the pressure, the government made two large diversionary attacks, one in Aragón against Huesca and another on the Segovia front which momentarily captured the summer palace village of La Granja. Both efforts were expensive failures. They also called more men to the colors in the north, and additional material arrived from abroad for this force. Introduced were eighty-five cannon, including anti-aircraft, as well as two squadrons of Russian Chato fighters.

The biggest blow to North Army came on June 3, when General Mola died in an aircraft accident. He was replaced by General Dávila, and the attacks gainst the iron belt continued. Through the help of a defector, the Nationalists knew that in many areas the iron belt was a façade, and they organized their assault accordingly.

Massive artillery and air attacks were carried out against the outer ring of defense on June 12 and signaled the second phase of the general assault. Fearful of being cut off, the defenders began to empty their positions. With little cost, the attackers made a breach 1 kilometer wide and pushed to 8 kilometers west of the center of Bilbao and brought it within artillery range. Methodically, the Nationalists closed in on the city and by 6:00 P.M. on June 19, the objective of eighty days' fighting was concluded. The city was in the hands of the Navarre Brigades. Interestingly, a German liaison officer with the 5th Brigade accepted the first enemy forces to surrender.

The weeks of fighting probably cost the Nationalists over 4,000 dead and 25,500 lost to other causes. The government may have realized 10,000 killed out of 35,000 lost. Vast stores of valuable war materials were captured, as well as tens of thousands of prisoners, many of whom would eventually wear the uniform of the Nationalist Army.

As the North Army prepared to continue the northern offensive, the Nationalists were struck by a massive attack by the Popular Front against their forces before Madrid.

This offensive was viewed as politically necessary, and the military reasons were threefold: double envelopment of the enemy army before Madrid and its destruction in detail; severing Nationalist communications with Portugal; and disruption of the northern offensive. To this end, the government committed between 80,000 and 90,000 men with armor, artillery, and aircover. Up to now, it was the largest and best equipped force seen in the war. They hoped to destroy an army of 54,000. The mass of the attack was on a 6-mile front between the Perales and Aulencia rivers west of Madrid. The sector was thinly held by 2,000 troops and a few guns. It was ideal terrain for offense. One of the objectives was the small village of Brunete, 13 miles west of Madrid, which gave its name to the battle.

The battle of Brunete began on July 6 and ruptured the defense in spite of the most determined resistance of a handful of men. The Nationalists quickly disengaged brigades and battalions from the north and other sectors, and rushed them to cut off the breakthrough and then built up for a large counteroffensive. The battle ranged through the terrible heat of July for three weeks. During the counteroffensive, the Condor Legion fighters in spectacular air clashes shot down twenty-one government planes. In all, Madrid lost some 100 planes and the Nationalists twenty-three. The offensive was contained, and the government gains were reduced to a breach of just over a half mile deep and 10 miles wide. Once again the armies were stalemated on the battlefield. The effort was a failure other than for the temporary disruption of the northern offensive. However, the selected Nationalist brigades and battalions quickly returned to that mission.

For the government, it was a costly failure of 23,000 men and stores of new equipment. The Nationalists lost 17,000 of their elite shock troops. Neither side really gained anything from the blood bath.

With the return of the Navarre Brigades before Santander, General Dávila had a force (including 25,000 of the CTV) of 90,000 in 106 battalions supported by fifty batteries and 200 aircraft. In the area, the government had, under General Gamir Ulíbarri, between 70,000 and 80,000, in sixty battalions, but only forty aircraft of all types. To oversee the renewed northern campaign, General Franco moved his headquarters to Aguilar de Campóo 50 miles from the coast on the Santander-Palencia road.

The front extended along the rugged Cantabrian Mountains, and again the heights were held by the government. As on the Bilbao front, concentrated artillery and aerial attacks struck the front on August 14, followed by three Navarrese brigades on the left dashing towards the coast to cut the enemy forces off from Asturias. The defenders were demoralized, and their front collapsed. On August 18, the CTV broke the front to the right, along the coast, and in the center carried the pass of Escudo. Government leaders were soon in flight. The Basque troops withdrew east to the port of Santoña, 35 kilometers from Santander, to surrender to the Italians. With the escape route severed, other than by sea, fighting broke out in Santander between Nationalist supporters and the remaining defenders. General Dávila

entered the city on August 26. Some managed to escape, but an army of 60,000 was captured along with great stores of equipment, including thirty-eight guns. A large portion of this force, along with their weapons, joined the Nationalist army.

As the Nationalists prepared for the final sweep into Asturias, the government shifted five well-equipped communist-led divisions from Madrid to Catalonia. Walter's division included four of the International Brigades. By this time, the Popular Front had experienced its civil war within a civil war in Catalonia, with the resulting destruction of the power of the anarchists and the POUM. Possibly, some of the anarchists remaining on the line would have liked to turn their guns on the communists, but the communists' strength was far too great. With a large offensive against the overextended and thinly held Nationalist front of Aragón, the government hoped, as in the case of Brunete, to withdraw Nationalist strength from the north.

On August 24, with 80,000 men, 100 tanks including the new TB-5s, and 200 aircraft, the government struck the front at eight different points from France to near Teruel in the south. They overran some of the small isolated garrisons in villages and heights which were in the main defended by monarchists, Carlists, and Falangist volunteers. Their furious defense, without asking quarter, appears to have shaken the confidence of the assaulting troops and disturbed the leadership. The Ebro River was crossed near Fuentes del Ebro (16 miles southwest of Saragossa), and after bitter struggles some of the small villages were carried north of the little fortified town of Belchite. It was at Belchite, in the terrible heat of the Aragón sun, that one of the most dogged battles of the breakthrough developed. Now 10 miles behind the battlefront, completely surrounded by the International Brigades, the few hundred defenders, from their walls, stone buidings, and massive stone churches, threw back assault after assault until September 6 when the town was carried by storm and reduced to rubble. This rubble was to be added to not too many months later.

The Nationalists' response was typical: contain the advance, quickly redeploy forces from elsewhere, and with a lightning attack, regain the lost ground. However, to this end they did not dilute their forces in the north other than to fly air squadrons, including many German, into the Aragón. Barrón's 13th Division and Buruaga's 150th Division, being assembled in the Madrid sector, were rapidly redeployed. Barrón quickly contained the advance north of Saragossa, but Buruaga's attempt to relieve the defenders of Belchite to the south was too late. This time the Nationalists did not press for their usual massive counterattack.

The government seized a few small towns and villages and some square miles of ground, but the effort, which should have been a major success, must be considered a military failure. Even before the fall of Belchite, General Dávila began his offensive against Asturias.

In Asturias, the remnant of the government force was about 45,000 troops, with 850 machineguns and about 200 pieces of artillery. Many of the troops were conscripts whose sympathies lay with the other side. They were commanded by Colonel Adolfo Prada who was advised by Russians.

The Nationalist advance was not rapid, but it was methodical and led by fire from 250 field guns. Initially, they lacked some of their former striking power in the air because much of the Condor Legion was in the Aragón, but the offensive pressed through the defended heights of the Leonese Mountains. After six weeks, again being subject to violent bombings by the German squadrons, the defense shattered, and as at Bilbao and Santander, some of its leaders managed to escape by sea. Colonel Prada ordered the execution of three brigade commanders, six battalion commanders, and many other officers but failed to halt the disintegration as Aranda's and Solchaga's pincers closed on Infiesto east of Oviedo. With their leaders in flight, the government forces fell apart, and Gijón surrendered to the Nationalists on October 21. The Russians escaped in the few aircraft available. The Nationalists now controlled all of northern Spain with its vital resources. It was a strategic victory of great magnitude, for they now controlled two-thirds of Spain.

Superior staff planning and coordination of air, artillery, and infantry definitely illustrated the Nationalists' superior military ability in the face of seemingly impossible odds given the defenders by the nature of the terrain. The government forces in the mountains were militarily strong, but, unfortunately, political divisions in the military as well as political leadership set in a decline which the bravery of the individual soldier or unit could not overcome. In six months, the Popular Front suffered 33,000 deaths and 100,000 wounded in the north, with even more being taken prisoner. But the effort cost the Nationalists nearly 100,000 casualties, including 10,000 killed.

During the early winter of 1937-1938, both sides licked their wounds, regrouped their armies, and stockpiled supplies from sources at home and abroad. The Nationalists had a force of half a million in the north, center, and south armies and in strategic reserves. In the air, the government still had superiority of fighters, but the bomber/reconnaissance forces were drawing near parity, with a possible edge for the Nationalists. The Nationalists were also gaining strength at sea, partly by obtaining ships from abroad but largely through the inactiveness of the government fleet. Even with the loss of northern Spain, the government had a quarter of a million more men than the enemy. The forces were concentrated in the armies of the Center (General Miaja), Levante (General Hernández Saravia), East (Catalonia under General Pozas), and the inactive forces of Estremadura and Andalusia.

To the despair of the German commander, Franco began assembling a large force for an offensive through Guadalajara and Alcalá de Henares. His planes were totally disrupted by a massive government offensive against the salient of Teruel. General Hernández Sarabia, with the Army of Levante, struck on December 15, with over 70,000 men in six divisions supported by heavy tanks and air superiority, As the attack started, the typically cold, windy, and snowy weather settled over what was to be the bitter two-month battle of Teruel.

From the north and south of the salient, two government pincers met at Barrios de San Blas to the east and Teruel was surrounded. Rather than develop its wide breakthrough to the largest possible extent, the government diverted most of its forces to reduce the city which the defenders were determined to sell at a dear cost. Franco canceled his own plans, ordered the newly formed corps of Varela and Aranda from the approaches to Madrid to recapture the area at all cost, and diverted all possible air squadrons into the attack area. By Christmas, fighting raged within Teruel, with 2,000 Nationalist soldiers and 2,000 civilians attempting to hold strong points in the city against massive odds. Four days later, after massive artillery and air preparations, the corps of Aranda and Varela struck the front but were not able to break through. On the last day of the year, the Nationalists did take the heights south of the city. What had been nearly impossible weather even worsened (temperatures dropped to well below zero) and took a grim toll of each force in frozen and frostbite. Hundreds of vehicles were trapped in deep snowdrifts, and continued counterattacks were almost impossible. In the city, one Nationalist strong point after another was destroyed by point-blank artillery fire or was stormed with grenades and bayonets. The last position succumbed on January 8, 1938.

At the suggestion of General Volkmann (who had replaced General Sperrle with the Condor Legion), Franco began concentrating his forces for an attack north of Teruel toward the Alfambra River. It was to develop into a three-pronged assault: General Yagüe's Corps Morocco—re-formed from the Army of Africa—would strike from the northwest to Perales de Alfambra; General Monasterio's horse cavalry would charge from Celadas to the village of Alfambra; and Aranda's corps would strike through Muleton Height and wheel south to link with Varela driving east of La Muela. It was hoped to trap a large army in and to the north of Teruel.

With aerial artillery support, Varela and Aranda maintained their pressure, and by January 17 the government forces began to withdraw before them. To prevent a breakthrough, Walter's International Brigades were committed, but Varela's corps carried La Muela. For days, spoiling attacks slowed but did not stop the Nationalist advance, and in some cases government officers shot scores of their own men for rebellion.

Led by artillery barrages, along with strikes from all three air elements, on February 5 the Nationalist front exploded facing the Alfambra River. The Corps Morocco shattered the forces before it, and Monasterio's cavalry broke through with a spectacular saber charge. Aranda's advance was almost as swift.

By February 7, the Nationalists closed the jaws of the trap and were on the Alfambra River. Russian aircraft tried to stem the advance that day, but the Germans alone shot down twelve bombers and one fighter. In three days, the government lost 15,000, plus 7,000 taken prisoner and 50 square miles of territory. Yagüe and Aranda now concentrated their corps for the storming of Teruel. Yagüe crossed the Alfambra on February 17 at Villalba Baja and attacked to the south, with Stuka dive bombers hitting strong points with 250-kilometer bombs. Other crossings were made the next day, and Aranda's corps broke through. Government troops did not collapse but fought very hard, with each position having to be taken by storm even after they had been pounded by artillery and aircraft. Teruel was surrounded with the Nationalists crossing the Turia River to the south. A bloody battle developed for the streets of Teruel which raged until February 23. The goverent managed to pull out many of its forces, but still 15,000 were captured. The total loss for the government cannot be calculated, but it is generally accepted at half again that of the Nationalists, which is put at 14,000 dead and 33,000 wounded and sick, including those lost to frostbite and frozen limbs.

For the Popular Front it was a military disaster. Some then questioned (and some still do) Franco's stubbornness in expending so much effort to win back a city and territory that in reality had little tactical value. The deadly accurate German anti-aircraft guns again proved effective as ground artillery and Nationalist aircraft and crews were proving superior to the Russians. Between January 17 and February 21, the Germans shot down twenty Russian aircraft at a cost of four, with Spanish and Italian fighters accounting for others.

On February 24, as his troops were clearing the streets of Teruel, Franco called all field commanders to his temporary headquarters in the village of Morata de Jiloca. He surprised most of them, particularly the Germans, by announcing that he had abandoned further consideration of an offensive through Guadalajara. Instead, there would be a large offensive to the Levante coast south of the Ebro River. The chosen divisions and all air groups were to begin their deployment.

The objective was to force the enemy into a battle south of the Ebro River by attacking from three directions into the existing bulge between Vivel de Río Martín and Fuentes de Ebro, cut off the bulge, and destroy the enemy within. Then, with a strong right flank on the Ebro, they would make a dash to the Mediterranean Sea. This was to be the well-planned and executed Aragón offensive, which is sometimes called the first battle of the Ebro. The offensive was the mission of the North Army under General Dávila. For the main attack he committed four army corps: Aranda's Corps Galicia (five divisions); the mixed CTV of General Berti (three divisions); Yagüe's Corps Morocco (three divisions); and the reinforced 1st Navarre and cavalry divisions. Spanish air squadrons would support the Corps Galicia; the Italians would cover the CTV; and the Germans would pave the way for the Corps Morocco, Division Navarre, and cavalry.

The spearhead would be Yagüe's Corps Morocco which would strike from the southeast of Cariñena to Escatrón and Caspe. On his right, Monasterio's cavalry would ride from Fuentes de Jiloca and Montón (northwest of Daroca). The Navarre Division would attack from Retascón and Daroca. Based on Olalla, the CTV would advance to Alcañiz. On the right flank would be the Corps Galicia which would drive over Montalbán and swing southeast to press to the sea.

General Varela with his Corps Castile (four divisions) would stand by in the Teruel area. To the north of Saragossa, on Yagüe's left flank, was deployed Moscardó's Corps Aragón (four divisions), and on his left to the French border was the Corps Navarre (four divisions) of General Solchaga.

The attack area was held by the government's weak 12th Corps which was being reinforced. The same International Brigade that had reduced Belchite months before was moved back into the ruins of the town and put on defense. Nationalist air superiority was assured, with 500 aircraft committed against a possible 300 that could be deployed by the government. Dávila had about 200 tanks, some of which were captured Russian T-26s. All Corps had adequate artillery, and the spearhead was reinforced by the batteries of the Condor Legion. The air groups struck air fields and communications centers before the mass attack which started early on March 9. The infantry was delayed for two hours because of the dust raised by troop movements. Then, with their way paved by aircraft and artillery, the troops swept across Aragón, shattering the defenses before them. The air strikes were very intense; on that day alone, the Condor Legion dropped 160 tons of bombs. The speed of the advance was such that, for a time, the command lost contact with a full cavalry brigade. After a sharp exchange, Belchite was recaptured (March 10), and the remains of the International Brigade fled towards Caspe.

Further south, the CTV broke out at Rudilla and drove on to Alcañiz. But Aranda's corps was not able to carry Montalbán until March 16. Caspe was reinforced by the International Brigades, and a bitter battle raged for over two days before the Corps Morocco was able to take the city. The advance now slowed as the Nationalist forces regrouped 70 miles from their starting point. However, to the north of Saragossa, Moscardó and Solchaga broke the front on February 22 and began their drive to the east. For Solchaga, in the hills and valleys, it was no easy task. Eventually, their forces reached the Segre River.

The Corps Morocco crossed the Ebro on March 23 and drove to Fraga and then to Lérida. On the southern flank, Aranda and the CTV made good progress, but in the race to the sea the CTV became stalled at Tortosa. On April 15, the 4th Navarre Division broke out on the Levante coast at Vinaroz. Popular Front Spain was now divided.

General Franco has been repeatedly criticized, and perhaps justly, because he did not continue his successful Aragón offensive against the shattered government forces into Catalonia with Barcelona as the objective. Many analysts believe that such an operation would have been successful and would have shortened the war by months. His decision, however, was to fight down the coast and through the Maestrazgo to capture Valencia. To this end, General Varela with his corps near Teruel was ordered to carry an offensive to the southeast on April 23. Through surprise, his effort might have been a success, but he had to cancel the operation because of bad weather in less than a week. The government forces were also encouraged by the arrival of new war stores which included the latest model high-performance Russian aircraft. They quickly challenged the Nationalists in the skies.

In early May 1938, General García Valiño's corps was committed between Varela and Aranda to the east. In spite of all efforts, including concentration of air and artillery, the three-pronged advance was painfully slow. Days passed with no advance at all, and strong counterattacks were thrown back. After a sharp fight, Castellón on the coast fell to Aranda on June 14, but García Valiño's forces were stalled completely a few kilometers short of Sagunto. The Nationalists massed artillery and aircraft to break General García Valiño's corps through the defenses in the Sierra de Espadán, but he could not breach the defenses. On July 13, Varela's corps, along with the CTV and Navarre divisions, attacked south from Teruel. In the skies, the Germans shot down one Russian bomber and seven fighters, with two more listed as probable. It appeared that the ground attack would roll up the front quickly because it was driven back 56 miles along an 18-mile line. However, the Valencian forces had constructed a strong line of fortifications from Viver into the Sierra de Espadán. The Nationalists were not able to breach this line in costly frontal attacks, nor could the defenses be reduced by heavy air strikes. The divisions suffered heavy losses in repeated attempts to carry the line between July 12 and 23.

The opposing air forces were repeatedly engaged over the battlefields, and each lost aircraft and crews. On July 23, Nationalist reconnaissance aircraft reported large enemy forces forming north of the Ebro River and noted the possibility of an offensive in that area. The warning seems to have been ignored because the government attack of July 25 with the Army of the Ebro had 80,000 men in four army corps, 100 batteries, tanks, and armored cars. It was to disrupt the Nationalist forces along the Ebro in the celebrated battle of the Ebro. The Corps Morocco carried the weight of the attack and at first reeled back under the repeated blows.

The Nationalists responded immediately with heavy air strikes against the bulge and bitterly fought to contain the advance, while redeploying many divisions to build up for their own counterattack. The offensive against Valencia was canceled, with the committed divisions being disengaged and moved into the threatened area of the Ebro. The government assault was largely blunted by August 2, and the Nationalists initiated the first phase of their counteroffensive four days later. This effort cleared the bulge between Mequinenza and Fagón in the north. But for weeks heavy blows were traded along the Ebro in a battle of attrition as the Nationalists cracked the front and by November 18 had driven the government forces back across the Ebro. At Lister's orders, once again Popular Front officers and men were shot for retreating. What had been an initial government success turned into a defeat with great sacrifices on each side. Besides massive losses in men and material, the Popular Front surrendered about 120 square miles of territory which weeks before it had seized in two days.

General Franco immediately ordered the planning and reorganization of his forces for (what many believed should have been done months earlier) a concentrated offensive into Catalonia before the enemy forces would be able to be reorganized and reequipped. Franco now divided his forces into the North Army of General Dávila and the Levante Army under General Orgaz. It was Dávila's mission to reduce Catalonia. For this mission he had the newly formed Army of Urgel with four divisions in the north and anchored with its left flank on the French frontier. It was commanded by the tough veteran General Muñoz Grandes. Then came General García Valiño's Army of the Maestrazgo with three divisions, and on his flank was General Moscardó with three divisions in the Army of Aragón. Next came the mixed CTV, now under General Gambara, with four divisions. To the south was General Solchaga's tough Army of Navarre, which initially had three divisions but a fourth was added later. Finally, there was General Yagüe with the four divisions of the Army of Africa—in fact, his old Corps Morocco. Although called armies, these were in fact the same army corps, with the exception of the Urgel force, that had fought so bitterly over so many months and on so many different fronts. The combined strength was almost 300,000, supported by about 600 guns and the three air groups. Aerial battles were expected, but they were confident of maintaining air superiority. The government could commit about eighty fighters and twenty-six bombers.

The Catalan forces were under Hernández Saravia who had failed so badly at Teruel. He had between 200,000 and 300,000 men divided into the Army of the East under Colonel Juan Perea and the Army of the Ebro under Modesto. The actual combat force is figured at about 150,000. They had nearly 350 pieces of artillery, forty tanks, and eighty armored cars. A massive shipment of equipment was purchased in Russia which might have made the odds more even, but little of it ever arrived in Catalonia.

In his field headquarters at the Castle of Pedrola, near Lérida, Franco divided the front into three sectors: the upper Segre in the Pyrenes; the middle and lower Segre, and the Ebro front. The sectors were to be taken individually, and in each his forces had superiority. He hoped to be able to spare the canal system of the rich Llanos de Urgel.

The main breakthrough areas were to be at Serós and La Baronia. At Serós, the Corps Navarre would attack on the right and the CTV on the left. At La Baronia the Army of the Maestrazgo was to attack on the right and the Army of Urgel on the left. Yagüe's Corps Morocco on the Ebro and the Corps Aragón on the Segre were designed to conduct only limited operations. The offensive was delayed several times but was finally set for December 23. All air groups began their strikes two days before.

The Navarre divisions and the CTV broke across the Segre River north of the Ebro confluence and ruptured the front. In their sectors, Muñoz Grandes and García Valiño had some successes, and the enemy abandoned the Segre. Lister's corps was committed to hold the hills east of Segre and managed to maintain his positions until January 3, 1939, when he withdrew before the CTV. The next day the entire front cracked open. Even with strong resistance, the Navarre divisions could not be slowed as they rolled forward, and the next day Yagüe's divisions crossed the Ebro at Ascó. In a frantic effort to relieve the pressure, the government launched attacks in Andalusia and Estremadura but with only local and very limited success.

In Catalonia, untrained and poorly equipped divisions were committed but were quickly routed by artillery. The advance was now general, and the defenders were fleeing the field. Yagüe took Tarragona on January 14 and linked his forces with Solchaga's to attack to the north. The Nationalists were closing in on Barcelona. Lead elements of Corps Morocco entered the suburbs at 1300 hours on January 26 and were quickly followed by the CTV and Navarre divisions. No real effort was made to defend the city.

Government and party leaders were in flight to France, followed by troops and civilians. Figueras fell on February 8, and the next day Nationalist troops reached the frontier at several points. The offensive of Catalonia was over, and the Popular Front was now reduced to one-third of Spain, with its remaining concentration in the south and Madrid. For all purposes, the issue raised in July 1936 was decided, but it was to be several weeks before there was a complete peace. Before then the Popular Front fought another civil war within a civil war.

The government garrisons on the island of Minorca rebelled and requested surrender.

The Popular Front supreme commander, General Miaja, believing his cause lost, still had a force of almost half a million men divided into four armies which were still intact and undefeated. The command, however, was not only torn with doubt and pessimism but was also fractured from within politically. Many of the former regular officers now tried to cast off their previous adherence to communism, a force which the Nationalists adamantly refused to negotiate. The issue came to a point in Madrid within Colonel Segismundo Casado Lopez's Army of the Center of four army corps. One corps was commanded by the anarchist Cipriano Mera, but the others were under communist command. Casado was a noncommunist officer who wanted peace and was supported by several factions, including anarchists and socialists, who stood in opposition to the minister Negrín. Casado made contact with Nationalist intelligence and was determined to surrender what was left of the Popular Front. But the communists were equally determined that the war would continue.

Casado informed Negrín on February 12 that their cause was tactically and strategically hopeless. At the time, communist leaders were preparing to seize complete control on their own. Through this period, Negrín played out a very dubious role, torn between political factions and with what most of his field commanders viewed as a militarily hopeless situation. Still, he attempted to set up a government at Elda near Alicante to continue the war. Casado continued to expand his contact with the Nationalists for a complete surrender. Although this was still a month in the future, Nationalist Spain was recognized by England and France on February 27.

The navy became party to a revolt against Negrín, and civilians and troops seized Cartagena and asked assistance from the Nationalists. Many ships put to sea and headed toward French ports. Cartagena was retaken by a communist-led division.

In Madrid, Casado ordered the red star torn from army uniforms and suspended communist publications. Some communist leaders were arrested, but many joined Negrín at Elda and from the nearby airfield of Monóvar flew to safety in France. The communist-led divisions near and in Madrid seized strategic points in a fight with Casado's supporters. When it appeared that the communists would be in full control, the 4th Army Corps of the anarchist Mera marched on the capital, seizing Alcalá de Henares and Torrejón de Ardoz. In the second week of March, a serious war was fought in Madrid between the communist and dissident forces. Army commanders in other sectors began arresting the communist leadership. And the Nationalists began to close in on Madrid through the Casa de Campo. Casado was able to suppress the communists on March 11. Several hundred had been killed and wounded, and others were quickly executed. The government forces in Estremadura either took no action or supported Casado, who continued his negotiations with the Nationalists. On March 26, the Nationalists in various sectors began to move and Popular Front forces surrendered; Casado ordered the surrender of the Army of the Center on March 27. Valencia was occupied on March 30, and the next day all major towns remaining were occupied, thus bringing the Spanish Civil War to an end.

The material on the Spanish Civil Was is vast and represents many views. It would be impossible to list all of these works here. These suggestions are merely points of departure. For further information in English, see Louis Bolín, *Spain, the Vital Years* (New York, 1967); R. G. Colodny, *The Struggle for Madrid* (New York, 1958); George Hills, *The Battle for Madrid* (New York, 1977); G. Jackson, *The Spanish Republic and the Civil War* (Princeton, N.J., 1965); P. Broué and E. Témime, *The Revolution and the Civil War in Spain* (Cambridge, 1972); S. G. Payne, *Politics and the Military in Modern Spain* (Stanford, Calif., 1967); and Hugh Thomas, *The Spanish Civil War* (New York, 1977). For works in Spanish, see Manuel Aznar, *Historia militar de la guerra de España (1936-1939)* (Madrid, 1940); Ricardo de la Cierva, *Historia ilustrada de la guerra civil española*, 2 vols. (Barcelona, 1970); Colonel José María Iribarren, *El general Mola* (Madrid, 1945); General Alfredo Kindelán, *Mis cuadernos de guerra* (Madrid, 1945); E. Lister, *Nuestra guerra* (Paris, 1969); General Carlos Martínez de Campos, *Ayer, 1931-1953* (Madrid, 1970); J. Modesto, *Soy del quinto regimiento* (Paris, 1969); General Vicente Rojo, *Alerta los pueblos!* (Buenos Aries, 1939) and *España heroica* (Buenos Aires, 1942); and R. Salas Larrazábal, *Historia del ejército popular de la república*, 4 vols. (Madrid, 1974).

Raymond L. Proctor

Civil War Governments

REPUBLICAN CABINETS

Formed: May 12, 1936

Manuel Azaña	Republican	President
Santiago Casares Quiroga	Left Republican	Prime Minister & War
Juan Moles y Ormella	Esquerra	Interior
Enrique Ramos y Ramos	Left Republican	Finance
Augusto Barcía	Left Republican	Foreign Affairs
Mariano Ruiz Funes	Left Republican	Agriculture
Antonio Velao	Left Republican	Public Works
Francisco Barnés	Left Republican	Education
José Giral	Left Republican	Navy
Manuel Blasco Garzón	Republican Union	Justice
Plácido Alvarez Buylla	Republican Union	Industry
Bernardo Giner de los Ríos	Republican Union	Communications
Juan Lluhí y Vallescá	Esquerra	Labor

Formed: July 20, 1936

Manuel Azaña	Republican	President
José Giral	Left Republican	Prime Minister
Augusto Barcía	Left Republican	Foreign Affairs
Sebastián Pozas	Liberal Republican	War
Luis Castelló	Liberal Republican	War
Plácido Álvarez Buylla	Republican Union	Industry & Commerce
Enrique Ramos y Ramos	Left Republican	Finance
Manuel Blasco Garzón	Republican Union	Justice
Bernardo Giner de los Ríos	Republican Union	Communications & Merchant Marine
Mariano Ruiz Funes	Left Republican	Agriculture
Francisco Barnés	Left Republican	Education
Antonio Velao	Left Republican	Public Works
Juan Lluhí y Vallescá	Esquerra	Labor, Health, & Supplies

Formed: September 4, 1936

Manuel Azaña	Republican	President
Francisco Largo Caballero	Socialist	Prime Minister & War
Julio Álvarez del Vayo	Socialist	Foreign Affairs
Angel Galarza	Socialist	Interior
Anastasio de Gracia	Socialist	Industry & Commerce
Juan Negrín	Socialist	Finance
Indalecio Prieto	Socialist	Navy & Air
Jesús Hernández Tomás	Communist	Education & Fine Arts
Vicente Uribe	Communist	Agriculture
José Giral	Left Republican	Minister Without Portfolio
Mariano Ruiz Funes	Left Republican	Justice
Bernardo Giner de los Ríos	Republican Union	Communications
José Tomás Piera	Left Republican Party of Catalonia	Labor & Health

Formed: November 3, 1936

Manuel Azaña	Republican	President
Francisco Largo Caballero	Socialist	Prime Minister & War
Julio Álvarez del Vayo	Socialist	Foreign Affairs
Angel Galarza	Socialist	Interior
Anastasio de Gracia	Socialist	Labor
Juan Negrín	Socialist	Finance
Indalecio Prieto	Socialist	Navy & Air
Jeśus Hernández Tomás	Communist	Education & Fine Arts
Vicente Uribe	Communist	Agriculture
Juan García Oliver	CNT	Justice
Juan López	CNT	Commerce
Federica Montseny	CNT	Health & Public Assistance
Juan Peiró	CNT	Industry
Carlos Esplá	Left Republican	Propaganda
José Giral	Left Republican	Minister Without Portfolio
Julio Just	Left Republican	Public Works
Bernardo Giner de los Ríos	Republican Union	Communications
Jaime Aiguadé	Esquerra	Minister Without Portfolio
Manuel de Irujo	Basque Nationalist	Minister Without Portfolio

Formed: May 17, 1937

Manuel Azaña	Republican	President
Juan Negrín	Socialist	Prime Minister & Finance
Indalecio Prieto	Socialist	Defense
Julián Zugazagoitia	Socialist	Interior
Jesús Hernández Tomás	Communist	Education & Health
Vicente Uribe	Communist	Agriculture
José Giral	Left Republican	Foreign Affairs
Bernardo de los Ríos	Republican Union	Public Works
Manuel de Irujo	Basque Nationalist	Justice
Jaime Aiguadé	Esquerra	Labor & Social Welfare

Formed: April 5, 1938

Manuel Azaña	Republican	President
Juan Negrín	Socialist	Prime Minister & Defense
Francisco Méndez Aspe	Socialist	Finance
Paulino Gómez Saez	Socialist	Interior
Segundo Blanco	Anarchist	Education & Health
Vicente Uribe	Communist	Agriculture
Julio Álvarez del Vayo	Socialist	Foreign Affairs
Antonio Velao	Left Republican	Public Works
González Peña	Socialist	Justice
Jaime Aiguadé	Esquerra	Labor & Social Welfare
Manuel de Irujo	Basque Nationalist	Minister Without Portfolio
José Giral	Left Republican	Minister Without Portfolio
Bernardo Giner de los Ríos	Left Republican	Transportation

Formed: August 16, 1938

Manuel Azaña	Republican	President
Juan Negrín	Socialist	Prime Minister & Defense
Francisco Méndez Aspe	Socialist	Finance
Paulino Gómez Saez	Socialist	Interior
Segundo Blanco	Anarchist	Education & Health

Vicente Uribe	Communist	Agriculture
Julio Álvarez del Vayo	Socialist	Foreign Affairs
Antonio Velao	Left Republican	Public Works
González Peña	Socialist	Justice
José Moix	Catalan Communist	Labor & Social Welfare
Tomás Bilbao	Basque Nationalist Action	Minister Without Portfolio
José Giral	Left Republican	Minister Without Portfolio
Bernardo Giner de los Ríos	Left Republican	Transportation

(This government served until the end of the Civil War.)

CATALAN GOVERNMENTS
(Generalitat)

Formed: August 1, 1936

Luis Companys	Esquerra	President of Generalitat
Juan Casanovas Maristany	Esquerra	President of Cabinet
José Quero Molares	Esquerra	Justice
José María España Cirat	Esquerra	Interior
Martín Esteve Gual	*Acción Catalana*	Finance
Ventura Gassol Rovira	Esquerra	Culture
Pedro Mestres	Esquerra	Public Works
Luis Prunés	Esquerra	Labor
Juan Comorera	PSUC	Economy
José Calvet	*Unió de Rabassaires*	Agriculture
Martín Rouret	Esquerra	Health
Juan Cerdeña	Esquerra	Public Services
Felipe Díaz Sandino	Lieutenant Colonel Aviation	Defense
Estanislao Ruiz Ponsetti	PSUC	Supplies
Rafael Vidiella	PSUC	Communications
Juan Puig Ferrater	Esquerra	Public Assistance

Formed: August 5, 1936

Luis Companys	Esquerra	President of Generalitat
Juan Casanovas Maristany	Esquerra	President of Cabinet
Felipe Díaz Sandino	Lieutenant Colonel Aviation	Defense
José Quero Molares	Esquerra	Justice
Martín Esteve	*Acción Catalana*	Finance
Ventura Gassol	Esquerra	Culture
José María España Cirat	Esquerra	Interior
José Tarradellas	Esquerra	Economy & Public Services
José Calvet	*Unió de Rabassaires*	Agriculture & Supplies
Pedro Mestres	Esquerra	Public Works
Luis Prunés	Esquerra	Labor
Martín Rouret	Esquerra	Health
Juan Puig y Ferrater	Esquerra	Social Welfare

Formed: September 26, 1936

Luis Companys	Esquerra	President of Generalitat
José Tarradellas	Esquerra	First Councillor & Finance
Artemio Aiguadé	Esquerra	Internal Security
Ventura Gassol Rovira	Esquerra	Culture
Juan P. Fábregas	CNT	Economy
Antonio García Birlan	CNT	Health & Public Assistance
Juan J. Doménech	CNT	Supplies
Juan Comorera	PSUC	Public Services

Miguel Valdés	PSUC	Labor & Public Works
Andrés Nin	POUM	Justice
Felipe Díaz Sandino	Independent	Defense
	(Really Liberal Republican)	
José Calvet	*Unió de Rabassaires*	Agriculture
Rafael Closas	*Acción Catalana Republican*	Councillor Without Portfolio

Formed: December 17, 1936

Luis Companys	Esquerra	President of Generalitat
José Tarradellas	Esquerra	First Councillor & Finance
Antonio María Sbert	Esquerra	Culture
Artemio Aiguadé	Esquerra	Internal Security
José Calvet	*Unió de Rabassaires*	Agriculture
Juan Comorera	PSUC	Supplies
Miguel Valdés	PSUC	Labor & Public Works
Rafael Vidiella	PSUC	Justice
Francisco Isleas	CNT	Defense
Diego Abad de Santillán	CNT	Economy
Juan José Doménech	CNT	Public Services
Pedro Herrera	CNT	Health & Public Assistance

Formed: April 3, 1937

Luis Companys	Esquerra	President of Generalitat
José Tarradellas	Esquerra	First Councillor & Finance
Artemio Aiguadé	Esquerra	Internal Security
Juan Comorera	PSUC	Public Works, Labor, & Justice
José Calvet	*Unió de Rabassaires*	Agriculture & Supplies
Francisco Isleas	CNT	Defense
Juan J. Doménech	CNT	Economy, Public Services, & Health

Formed: April 16, 1937

Luis Companys	Esquerra	President of Generalitat
José Tarradellas	Esquerra	First Councillor & Finance
Antonio María Sbert	Esquerra	Culture
Artemio Aiguadé	Esquerra	Internal Security
José Calvet	*Unió de Rabassaires*	Agriculture
José Miret	PSUC	Supplies
Rafael Vidiella	PSUC	Labor & Public Works
Juan Comorera	PSUC	Justice
Francisco Isleas	CNT	Defense
Andrés Capdevila	CNT	Economy
Juan Doménech	CNT	Public Services
Aurelio Fernández	CNT	Health & Public Assistance

Formed: June 16, 1937

Luis Companys	Esquerra	President of Generalitat
José Tarradellas	Esquerra	First Councillor & Finance
Carlos Pi y Suñer	Esquerra	Culture
Antonio María Sbert	Esquerra	Internal Security
José Calvet	*Unió de Rabassaires*	Agriculture
Miguel Serra Pamiés	PSUC	Supplies
Rafael Vidiella	PSUC	Labor & Public Works
Pedro Bosch Gimpera	*Acción Catalana Republicana*	Justice
Juan Comorera	PSUC	Economy

(This government was the last one to serve the Generalitat.)

BASQUE GOVERNMENT
(Euzkadi)

Formed: October 7, 1936

José Antonio Aguirre y Lecube	PNV	President & Defense
Telesforo Monzón	PNV	Interior
Jesús María de Leizaola	PNV	Justice & Culture
Juan García	PSOE	Public Welfare
Juan de los Toyos	PSOE	Labor
Santiago Aznar	PSOE	Industry
Ramón María de Aldasoro	Left Republican	Commerce & Supplies
Juan Astigarrabía	Communist	Public Works
Gonzalo de Nárdiz	PNV	Agriculture
Heliodoro de la Torre	PNV	Finance

(This government was the only one to serve the Basque government before the Nationalists overran the north in 1937.)

NATIONALIST CABINETS

Note: Party affiliations are not shown since officially only one party, the Falange, was allowed in the Nationalist zone.

Formed: October 1, 1936

Francisco Franco	Chief of State
Fidel Dávila Arrondo*	President of Cabinet
Andrés Amado y Reygonbaud de Villebardet	Finance
José Cortés López	Justice
Joaquín Bau Nolla	Industry, Commerce, & Supplies
Eugenio Olmedo	Agriculture & Agricultural Labor
Alejandro Gallo y Artacho	Labor
José María Pemán y Pemartín	Culture & Education
Mauro Serret	Public Works & Communications

*Drops out of cabinet on June 3, 1937 and is not replaced.

Formed: February 1, 1938

Francisco Franco	Chief of State
Ramón Serrano Súñer	Interior
Francisco Gómez-Jordana y Sousa	Foreign Affairs
Fidel Dávila Arrondo	Defense
Severíano Martínez Anido	Public Order
Pedro Sáinz Rodríguez	Education
Alfonso Peña Boeuf	Public Works
Juan Antonio Suanzes	Industry & Commerce
Raimundo Fernández Cuesta	Agriculture
Andrés Amado y Reygonbaud de Villebardet	Finance
Tómas Domínguez Arevalo*	Justice
Pedro González Bueno	Sindical Organization
Raimundo Fernández Cuesta	Secretary General of the Movement (Falange)

(This cabinet served until the end of the Civil War.)

*Better known as the Conde de Rodezno.

A Select Compendium of Archives and Libraries on the Spanish Civil War

PETER T. JOHNSON

This section identifies major archives and libraries with strong collections of primary and secondary sources devoted to the Spanish Civil War. To merit inclusion, the archive or library must have been recognized by Civil War scholars as holding significant collections. While substantial numbers of collections exist, those with unique or scarce materials are relatively few. Hence, this appendix includes those institutions that hold major collections of principally secondary materials. One may reasonably expect to find such collections at most large research libraries in Europe and the United States. Nor does this section address the question of individual access; regulations governing this and related areas change frequently, and for formalities relating to access researchers should contact each archive or library in advance.

The descriptions for each institution provide as broad, yet specific, information as is available. The entry format generally adheres to that used by the Library of Congress in 1980. Various corporate name changes have occurred over the years which most libraries will indicate through cross-references to the latest form employed. With the expiration of temporal access restrictions, many archives and libraries are in the process of preparing guides to their holdings. Consult the card catalogue of large research libraries, *Libros españoles. ISBN* (Madrid: Instituto Nacional del Libro Español, 1974-) (Z2681.L53), and the Society for Spanish and Portuguese Historical Studies *Bulletin* for full citations. Of course, many finding aids and collection inventories remain unpublished but are available for consultation *in situ*. The guides cited in this appendix contain materials that are broadly relevant to the period, and whenever possible, carry the Library of Congress classification number.

All countries with diplomatic relations with Spain possess consular and other official correspondence. Such sources are gradually becoming available, either within the agency itself or through the country's national archives. In some instances, selective collections of documents have been published and appear in this appendix with the issuing agency or the body holding the papers and responsible for their publication. The ongoing character of these publishing programs suggests increasing accessibility of new materials, and the potential for reassessment and revision of present interpretations.

Within the past decade, various efforts to preserve the documentation generated during the Civil War have been

undertaken successfully. As awareness and availability of technological advances increase, even greater quantities of materials will appear in microformat. For various primary source materials issued by participants and observers and now available in microform, see the Library of Congress's annual *National Register of Microform Masters* (Washington, D.C., 1965-) (Z1033.M5N5) and *Newspapers in Microform: Foreign Countries, 1948-1977* (Washington, D.C., 1973-) (Z6945.U515a). Projects of private sector microfilmers usually appear in these sources as well as in the *Guide to Microforms in Print, Author, Title* (Westport, Conn., Microform Review, 1978-) (Z1033.M5G8). Some national governments actively engage in microfilming projects; for detailed information, consult the specialized guides or catalogues to their publications.

CANADA

Canada. Department of External Affairs. Ottawa

Although Canada had limited interest in the Civil War, this agency possesses materials on Canadians serving in Spain. Selected coverage appears in its *Documents on Canadian External Relatons*, v. 6 (1936-1939), Ottawa, Queen's Printer, 1972 (JX1515.A25).

Public Archives of Canada. Ottawa

The greatest strengths of the Public Archives are in state papers and in those devoted to the Canadians serving in Spain. Among the former are the William Lyon Mackenzie Papers (Secretary of State for External Affairs and Prime Minister), and among the latter are the Mackenzie-Papineau Battalion materials. This International Brigade's collection includes biographical information on nearly 600 Canadian volunteers.

See the *Union List of Manuscripts in Canadian Repositories*, rev. ed:, Ottawa, 1975 in 2 v. plus suppl. 1976 (CD3622.A2U54 1975).

FRANCE

Archives Départementales de l'Ariège. 28 av. Général-de-Gaulle, 09000 Foix

This repository contains materials on frontier relations and surveillance as well as security matters pertaining to refugees. See its *Répertoire numérique de la série O, admin-*

istration et comptabilité communales service vicinal dons et legs (1800-1940), Foix, 1975 (CD1215.A655 1975q).

Archives Départementales de l'Aude. 48 rue Jean-Bringer, 11012 Carcassone

Refugee camps and communications (i.e., post and telegraph) materials form the principal documentation. See its *Guide des archives de l'Aude*, Carcassone, 1976-   . (CD1215.A83A83 1976).

Archives Départementales de la Haute-Garonne. 11 Boulevard Griffoul-Dorval, 31400 Toulouse

This source offers documentation on refugees and surveillance (air and of the frontier), especially by the police. For general background, see its *Petit guide du chercheur aux archives. . .* , Toulouse, 1966 (CD1215.G3A53 1966).

Archives Départementales des Pyrénées—Atlantiques. Blvd. Tourasse, 6400 Pau

Materials devoted to refugees, especially those of the International Brigades, constitute the principal holdings.

Archives Départementales des Pyrénées—Orientales. 11 rue du Bastion Saint-Dominique, 66020 Perpignan

This repository contains documentation on the anarchists (1936-1939), political parties (1935-1939), internment camps, and the International Brigades; limited holdings for 1939.

France. Archives Nacionales. 60 rue des Francs-Bourgeois, Paris 3ᵉ

This major repository contains extensive coverage of such topics as politics, finance, refugees, and police activities. Especially important are post-Civil War negotiations documents. It holds both official papers from government agencies and private sector archives.

France. Ministère de la Guerre. Archives. Pavillon du Roi, Château de Vincennes, 94300 Vincennes

As the major center of French military records, this source is known to contain Civil War materials. Since 1974 called the Ministère des Armées, the archive is also called Archives de l'Armée de Terre.

France. Ministère des Affaires Étrangères. Archives. 37 quai d'Orsay, 75700 Paris

The known strengths of this ministry consist of correspondence of the diplomatic and consular corps. For selected reprints, see France, Commission des Publicacion des Documents Relatifs aux Origines de la Guerre 1939-1945, *Documents diplomatiques français, 1932-1939*, 2d series (1936-1939) tomos 3-12, Paris, Imp. Nationale, 1966-1978.

Paris. Bibliothèque Nationale. 58 rue de Richelieu, Paris 75084.

Extensive holdings of printed materials published during the period encompass all points of view. Various manuscript collections also exist. See its *Catalogue*, Paris, Imp. Nationale, 1897-   (Z927.P2) for works published before 1960; thereafter see its *Catalogue général des livres imprimés, 1960-1964*, Paris, 1965-1967 in 12 v. (Z927.P1957). The Departement des Estampas has photographs and posters.

Paris. Université at Nanterre. Bibliothèque de Documentation Internationale Contemporaine. 2 rue de Rouen, Nanterre

A most important collection of printed materials, generally considered the largest in France, it is particularly strong on the French perspective as documented in newspapers and periodicals. The photograph collection is significant.

GERMANY

Berlin. Geheimes Staatsarchiv. Archivstrasse 12-14, 1 Berlin-Dahlem 33

This repository contains various series of correspondence, including diplomatic and the Nationalsozialistische Deutsche Arbeiterpartei (especially with organizations outside of Germany).

Germany. Auswärtiges Amt. [Politisches Archiv]. Adenauer-Alle 99-103, 5300 Bonn

Vast quantities of documents became the property of the Allied Forces, thereby enabling the preparation of microfilm and printed collections. The U.S. Department of State, Historical Office, *A Catalog of Files and Microfilms of the German Foreign Ministry Archives, 1920-1945*, Stanford, Calif., Hoover Institution, 1962-1972, 4 v. (CD1261.A65) lists filmed and unfilmed materials, albeit captured files of "marginal importance" do not appear. See Vol. I, Appendices I-III, for explanatory matter. These documents were returned to Germany in 1958-1959. For a highly selective group, see its *Documents on German Foreign Policy, 1918-1945: From the Archives of the German Foreign Ministry*, Series D (1937-1945), v. 3, *Germany and the Spanish Civil War, 1936-1939*, Washington, D.C., U.S. Government Printing Office, 1949-1960 (U.S. Department of State, Publication 3838, Department of Foreign Service Series) (JX691.A45). Useful background material appears in v. 9: *The War Years, March 18-June 22, 1940*, Appendix V: Analysis of the Foreign Ministry Archives, pp. 721-723. Film sets are at the U.S. Department of State and the British Foreign Office. For the French selection, see its *Les Archives secrètes de la Wilhelmstrasse*, Tomo III: *L'Allemagne et la guerre civile espagnole*, Paris, Plon, 1952 (JX691.A47). For the German selection of documents, see its *Akten zur Deutschen Auswärtigen Politik 1918-1945*, serie D (1937-1945), v. 3: *Deutschland und der Spanische Bürgerkrieg 1936-1939*, Baden-Baden, Imp. Nationale, 1951 (JX691.A44).

Germany (Federal Republic, 1949-   ). Bundesarchiv. 1, am Wöllershof 12, 54 Koblenz

Spanish coverage includes materials on foreign commerce and trade and related economic papers, as well as notable holdings of photographs. Reparation cases resulting from the Civil War appear here. Also held are Neue Reichskanzlei (1933-1945) files. Strong sections exist for branches of the armed forces. Consult its *Das Bundesarchiv und seine Bestände*, Boppard am Rhein, Boldt, 1977 (CD1226.G47.1977). They also hold the records of central, regional, and local government agencies; for access to the microfilms of these and other seized archives, see the American Historical Association, Committee for the Study of War Documents, *Guides to German Records Microfilmed at Alexandria, Va.*, Washington, D.C., National Archives, 1958-   (D735.A58).

Germany (Federal Republic, 1949-   ). Bundesarchiv Militärarchiv. Wiesentalstrasse 1, 78 Freiburg im Breisgau

This repository holds the files and record groups of the German army, navy, and air force, including German military attachés' reports. Materials pertaining to German involvement in the Civil War, such as the Condor Legion, are limited by substantial losses sustained during World War II.

GREAT BRITAIN

British Library. Department of Printed Books. London

The British Library houses one of Europe's major collections, with substantial strengths in works of the period, especially government documents. See its *General Catalogue of Printed Books*, London, 1965-1966 (Z921.B87) in 263 v. for works to 1955; thereafter see the supplements 1956-1965 in 50 v. and 1966-1970 in 26 v. Now called British Library.

Great Britain. Foreign Office. London

The major documentation relates to the British position; see its *Index to the Correspondence of the Foreign Office for the Year 1936, 1937, 1938, and 1939*, Nendeln, Liechtenstein, Kraus-Thomson, 1969 (CD1051.A13). The materials cited are now in the Public Record Office, London. For publication of selected documents, see its *Documents on British Foreign Policy, 1919-1939*, 2d series, Vol. 17: *Western Pact Negotiations: Outbreak of Spanish Civil War June 23, 1936—January 2, 1937*, London, HMSO, 1979 (DA566.7.A18). For brief histories of agencies and their major publishing series accompanied by bibliographies of publications, see Frank Rodgers, *A Guide to British Government Publications*, New York, H. W. Wilson Co., 1980 (Z2009.R62).

Great Britain. Public Record Office. Chancery Lane. London, WC2

This major archive includes the Admiralty, Cabinet, Foreign Office (for example, general correspondence, 1936-1939), War Office, and Non-Intervention Committee papers, 1936-1939 (microfilmed by Kraus Reprints). Twentieth-century materials are located in the Land Registry building, 18 Portugal Street.

Royal Institute of International Affairs. Library. Chatham House, St. James's Square, London, S.W. 1

This repository contains a general collection of secondary materials and also significant files of selected clippings from English and other non-Spanish papers.

ITALY

Archivo Centrale dello Stato. Plazzale degli Archivi, 00144 Rome

Of major importance for the period are documents of the Partito Nazionale Fascista, Presidenza del consiglio dei Ministri, and from the following ministries: dell'Interno, dell'Aeronautica Militare, and della Marina.

Italy. Ministero degli Affari Esteri. Archivio Storico. Rome

This archive contains the papers of the Gabinetto del Ministro and those of the Direzione Generale degli Affari Politici. For representative correspondence and documents, see Italy, Commissione per la Pubblicazione dei Documenti Diplomatici, *I documenti diplomatici italiani*, series 7 and 8, Roma, Libreria dello Stato, 1952-

Rome (City). Biblioteca Nazionale Centrale Vittorio Emanuele

This library contains the best collection of Italian publications issued during the Civil War.

THE NETHERLANDS

International Institute for Social History, Amsterdam. 262-266 Herengracht, 1016 BV Amsterdam

This institute is a great center for archival material pertaining to leftist movements. The main Civil War collections consist of correspondence, manuscripts, documents, photographs, and publications of various European radical groups. Of special note are holdings of anarchists, the International Workingmen's Association, the Movimento Libertario Español (mainly 1938-1939 but with local and regional coverage), and refugees in France. The Archive of Cipriano Mera is here. Consult its *Alfabetische Catalogus van de Boeken en Brochures van het Internationaal Instituut vor Sociale Geschiedenis, Amsterdam*, Boston, G. K. Hall, 1970 in 12 v. (HN13.A1I5).

PORTUGAL

Portugal. Arquivo Histórico Militar. Largo dos Caminhos de Ferro, Lisbon

This archive contains materials for both the Nationalist and Republican sides. Strengths include documentation of the Missão Militar Portuguese de Observação em Espanha, especially military aspects, intelligence-gathering on military, economic, political, and social issues, and volunteer recruitment. Materials on the status of individuals at the end of the Civil War also appear.

Portugal. Ministério dos Negócios Estrangeiros. Arquivos. Largo do Rilvas, Lisbon.

Materials cover relations with Republican and Nationalist Spain (1931-1942). Holdings include the Portuguese documentation from the International Committee for the Application of the Agreement Regarding Non-Intervention in Spain, principally memorandum, communiques, reports, acts, and documents. Similar coverage exists for the Delegação Portuguesa do Ministério de Assuntos Exteriores (Madrid). See its *Dez anos de política externa (1936-1947) A naçao portuguese e a segunda guerra mundial*, v. 1-6, Lisboa, Imp. Nacional, 1962-1973 (DP680.A47) for a selective presentation of documents.

SPAIN

Agencia EFE, S.A. Ayala 5, Madrid

This press organization holds an extensive photograph collection.

Banco de España, Madrid. Alcalá 59, Madrid

This is a major source for economic activities, especially of a financial nature. Documentation concerning international economic relations is generally excluded, with the major exception being material related to gold and silver mobilization.

The immediate pre-Civil War period located in the Archivo del Servicio de Estudios files has good coverage.

Barcelona. Biblioteca Central

The journal collection is notable. For a general description of holdings, see its *Guía*, Barcelona, 1959 (Z832.B213).

Barcelona. Centre d'Estudis d'Història Contemporània. Calle Numancia 101, Barcelona 14

The private collection of Josep María Figueras Bassols focuses on Spain since the Second Republic, particularly Catalonia's social and political history. It is useful for Civil War research given its strengths in newspapers (over 1,000 titles) and correspondence.

Barcelona. Instituto Municipal de Historia

The Hemeroteca provides access to more than 6,000 titles published in Barcelona and elsewhere. The extensive iconographic archive includes more than 100,000 photographs, of which more than 3,000 pertain to the war. A graphic arts collection contains samples of such items as propaganda fliers and posters. For a general overview of war holdings, consult its "Catálogo" in *Cuadernos de historia económica de Cataluña* 11 [Barcelona, 1974] (HC387.C77C8).

Biblioteca Arús. Barcelona

The principal item held in this library is the Archivos del Consejo Federal de la Región Española de la Primera Internacional.

Fundación Pablo Inglesias. Santa Engracia 90, Madrid

A major center for Socialist party materials, it holds the Largo Caballero papers and is collecting the personal papers of prominent socialist leaders. Very good newspaper runs exist for socialist and left-wing parties. A useful entry point is its *Cien años de socialismo en España*: (*Bibliografía*), Madrid, 1979 (Z7164.S67F87 1979).

Fundación Universitaria Española. Alcalá 93, Madrid 9

This organization will presumably house the remnants of Spanish Republican Government in Exile Archives (1945-1977).

Instituto Español de Moneda Extranjera. Alcalá 59 y Calle Bravo Murillo, Madrid

The archives of the Nationalist Foreign Exchange Authority (Comité de Moneda Extranjera) are major repositories of documents concerned with international economic transactions. Permission to consult them is granted simultaneously by the Department Extranjero in the Bank of Spain and the Dirección General de Transacciones Exteriores in the Ministerio de Economía y Comercio.

Madrid. Biblioteca Nacional. Paso Recoletos 20

Major printed holdings of books, newspapers, journals, and pamphlets (Colección Estelrich) place this repository among the leading ones for such materials. Consult its *Publicaciones periodicas existentes en la Biblioteca Nacional, Catálogo*, Madrid, 1952 (Z6945.M14) for detailed coverage.

Madrid. Hemeroteca Municipal. Plaza de la Villa 3

This repository is widely considered to be the most complete collection of its type. Its holdings are equally strong for the Nationalist and Republican zones, with good coverage of the International Brigades, Republican Army newspapers, and pamphlets.

Montserrat (Benedictine Abbey). Biblioteca. Monestir de Montserrat

This library contains a large collection of printed materials on the Republic and the Civil war.

Seville. Carlist Archives.

This archive holds Falange and Carlist documentation, ranging from correspondence and memoranda to posters, newspapers, and pamphlets.

Spain. Archivo General de la Administración. Alcalá de Henares

This archive has major holdings of the ministries and central authorities, with heavy emphasis on post-Civil War developments. Of particular importance are those materials concerned with ceased departments. Files on censorship, on reconstruction, and on the vertical unions are to be found here. Permission to consult them is through the *secretarios generales técnicos* of present-day ministries.

Spain. Archivo General Militar. Segovia

This archive encompasses a wide range of materials of armed forces issuance. Various official agencies transfer administrative record series to this archive after twenty years.

Spain. Archivo Histórico Nacional. Calle de Serrano 115, Madrid 6

Basic strengths lie with material on the *Causa General* and the files of the Dirección General de Adquisiciones. Correspondence includes that of the secretary general of the head of state. Its *Guía*, Madrid, 1958 (CD1853.A2) offers general information but is incomplete for the twentieth century.

Spain. Archivo Histórico Nacional. Sección Guerra Civil. Gibraltar 2, Salamanca

This archive is a fundamental source for Republican documents. Materials in Sección Militar amount to approximately 10,000 *legajos*. Sección Político-Social has political parties, unions, and governmental agency papers comprising another 7,000 *legajos*, with subdivisions covering major cities. Both series are catalogued. Its collection of pamphlets exceeds 4,000 titles. Graphic documentation is also very strong. Newspaper and journal collections include not only the major Madrid and Barcelona titles, but also many rare local and military publications. This is the best repository for politics and civil aspects of the Republican Zone.

Spain. Ministerio de Asuntos Exteriores. Archivo. Salvador 1, Madrid 12

This absolutely basic source with collections open to 1945 without restrictions holds documents from embassies, legations, and consulates. Of particular importance are sections concerning Republican foreign policy and the holdings of the Republican Embassy to Mexico. It is a major repository for political and diplomatic coverage of the Civil War. For published works in the library, see its *Catálogo de la Biblioteca*, Madrid, 1941-1948 in 9 v. (Z945.M374). María José Lozano Rincon's *Guía del Archivo del Ministerio de Asuntos Exteriores*, Madrid, 1981 provides the organizational divisions for the Republican and Nationalist archives, pp. 39-41; Ch. 4 section 7 "Archivo Reservado" offers detailed coverage of the holding categories.

Spain. Ministerio de Cultura. Sección de Estudios de la Guerra de España. Madrid

This ministry is best known for the pamphlet holdings. It centralizes archival policy in the Subdirección General de Archivos. It was formerly called the Ministerio de Información y Turismo.

Spain. Ministerio de Cultura. [Secretaría General Técnica]. Sección de Documentación. Madrid

A good collection of photographs stands out among an otherwise small collection of sources.

Spain. Ministerio de Hacienda. Archivo Central. Alcalá 11, Madrid 14

Major economic sources such as the records from the Dirección General del Patrimonio del Estado, the Dirección General de Seguros, and the Dirección General de Aduanas reside here, as does the collection pertaining to the Delegación de Hacienda en Burgos which offers materials on the Suscripción Nacional. For economic matters, the Archivos de Hacienda are essential.

Spain. Ministerio de Marina. Archivo Central. Montalbán 2, Madrid 14

This ministry holds the documents of the Dirección General de la Armada and related agencies. In 1977, it joined with others to become the Ministerio de Defensa.

Spain. Ministerio de Marina. Servicio Histórico del Estado Mayor de la Armada

This ministry serves as the repository of both Nationalist and Republican materials on military organization and logistics, but apparently has little on operational plans or political correspondence. Its Archivo Histórico is one of the two most important repositories for military aspects of the war.

Spain. Ministerio del Aire.

Four basic series exist: (1) pesonnel; (2) organizational documentation; (3) supplies and buildings; and (4) administrative. Useful, too, is the Archivo Histórico del Aire. In 1977, this ministry became part of the Ministerio de Defensa.

Spain. Presidencia del Gobierno. Archivo. Alcalá Galiano 10, Madrid 4

Major holdings constitute papers of the Junta de Burgos and documentation of the central authorities. It has major coverage of the political aspects of the Civil War.

Spain. Servicio Histórico Militar. Biblioteca Central Militar. Madrid

This repository was founded in 1932 as the centralized military library. The important divisions include the Hermeroteca Militar with its focus on military journals, and the Archivo which contains original documents, transcriptions, maps, and plans. Its publication is the *Boletín de la Biblioteca Central Militar*.

Spain. Servicio Histórico Militar. Sección de Estudios Históricos. Mártires de Alcalá 9, Madrid

Founded in 1939 to handle the operational and organizational military papers, this service contains documents of both armies, collections of official documents, pamphlets, maps, and plans. In the Archivo de la Guerra de Liberación's section of Documentación Nacional are such groups as the Cuartel General del Generalísimo and Grandes Unidades del Ejército Nacional comprising approximately 2,203 *legajos*. Major emphasis is on military campaigns, recruitment, and associated activities. The section Documentación Roja has major holdings of Republican Army documents. This archive is one of the two principal repositories for documentation on the military aspects of the Civil War.

SWITZERLAND

Fondation Internationale d'Etudes Historiques et Sociales sur la Guerre Civile d'Espagne de 1936-1939 (FIEHS). Geneva

Founded in 1972 to acquire and protect documentation relating to the Civil War, this organization holds a wide range of printed materials and manuscripts. Its research center, formerly located at Perpignan, is in Barcelona.

League of Nations. Historical Collections. Archives. Palais des Nations, CH1211, Genève 10

About seventy files concerning the Civil War remain. The focus is mainly on humanitarian assistance, the league's operation to save Spanish works of art, and the organization of the International Commission to supervise the withdrawal of non-Spanish combatants. The records of the International Commission itself have been destroyed. Consult its *Guide to the Archives of the League of Nations, 1919-1946*, Geneva, 1978 (Publications. Series E: Guides and Studies, 2) [GE78-5051 (8102)-August 1978]. See also its *Journal officiel* and special supplements, as well as the *Resumé mensuel des travaux de la Société des Nations* for contemporary coverage.

UNITED STATES OF AMERICA

Brandeis University. Library. [Special Collections Department]. Waltham, Massachusetts 02154

Brandeis has a notable collection for the International Brigades, especially the archives of the Abraham Lincoln Battalion, 1937-1939, and the Veterans of the Abraham Lincoln Brigade, 1937-1975, which include pamphlets, microfilms, recordings, and photographs. Other materials pertain to Spanish refugees in Mexico and the United States, and the *Partido Obrero de Unificación Marxista*'s (POUM's) reports, documents, and communications, 1936-1938. Documentary films and posters as well as microfilms of news journals constitute significant holdings. About 6,500 volumes of published works exist.

California. University. Bancroft Library. Berkeley 94720

The Leila Jones Leitner Collection contains fifty-one Spanish newspapers, approximately 1,000 issues in all, and various books, pamphlets for 1936-1938, photographs, and posters. Records from the veterans of the Abraham Lincoln Brigade also reside here.

California. University, San Diego. Library. Special Collections. La Jolla 90024

Of major importance is this library's Herbert Rutledge Southworth Collection on the Spanish Civil War, 1936-1939, which has over 11,000 items from the Republican and Falangist perspective. Included are newspapers, magazines, pamphlets, and ephemera. Among the general Civil War collection which contains over 12,000 volumes are materials published by the Spanish Republic prior to the conflict and Spanish exile publications. Various maps and manuscripts also exist. See its *Guide to Selected Ibero-American Holdings*, San Diego, 1975.

Columbia University. Libraries. New York City 10027

The Spanish Refugee Relief Organization, the Medical Bureau to Aid Spanish Democracy, and the North American Committee to Aid Spanish Democracy files consist of correspondence, clippings and scrapbooks, publicity materials, and general office files. Other collections of serials, books, and pamphlets are those of Junius Adams and Manuel Núñez de Arenas. The Archive of the League of American Writers has correspondence, minutes, and press clippings relating to the period.

Franklin D. Roosevelt Library. Hyde Park, New York 12538

This library holds the Franklin D. Roosevelt Papers (Official File, Personal File, and the President's Secretary's File) and the R. Walton Moore Papers; see its *Collections of Manuscripts and Archives in the Franklin D. Roosevelt Library*, Washington, D.C., National Archives and Records Service, 1969.

Harvard University. Library. Cambridge, Massachusetts 02138

Harvard has one of the great collections of materials published during the period, with particular strengths in journals, pamphlets, and newspapers. Extensive coverage exists for refugees, foreign participation, and personal narratives. Many titles have been preserved by microfilming, such as the Blodgett Collection of Spanish Civil War Pamphlets, with the 16-page index (author, title, and place of publication) issued in 1980. See its *Spanish History and Literature; Classification Schedule...*, Cambridge, Mass., 1972 (Widener Library Shelflist, 41) (Z2709.H35).

Harvard University. Houghton Library. Cambridge, Massachusetts 02138

Manuscript collections include William Phillips Journals and Memoranda and the Jay Pierrepont Moffat Papers.

Indiana University. Lilly Library. Bloomington 47401

This library holds the Claude G. Bowers Collection of diaries, clippings, and diplomatic papers.

Michigan University. Library. Department of Rare Books and Special Collections. Ann Arbor 48109

This library has a particularly strong collection of anarchist and Trotskyist materials. It has holdings approaching 40,000 volumes and various photographs and manuscripts. The Labadie Collection contains documents, reports, circulars, and the correspondence of various *Confederación Nacional del Trabajo* (CNT), *Federación Anarquista Ibérica* (FAI), *Alianza Internacional de Trabajadores* (AIT), and POUM committees.

New York (City). Public Library. 5th Avenue and 42d Street, New York City 10018

This library has one of the foremost collections for all forms of documentation. Manuscript holdings include the correspondence of American Friends of Spanish Democracy, the Frank P. Walsh Papers, 1937-1939, Radio Madrid scripts, January 1937-October 1938, David McKelvy White Collection, 1936-1939, for the Veterans of the Abraham Lincoln Brigade, and in the Berg Collection materials concerning George Orwell and Julian Bell. Great strengths exist in newspapers immediately preceding the war and for the period, pamphlets, news bulletins, press releases, 1937-1947, radio addresses, memoranda, and books. Major sections now appear in microformat. See Sam P. Williams, *Guide to the Research Collections of the New York Public Library*, Chicago, American Library Association, 1975 (Z733.N6W54).

Northwestern University. Library. Special Collections Department. Evanston, Illinois 60201

This collection comprises approximately 1,500 volumes, which includes government documents, newspapers, pamphlets, photographs, and maps.

Red Cross. U.S. American National Red Cross. Archives. 18th and D Streets, N.W., Washington, D.C. 20006

Humanitarian relief efforts pertaining to the period exist in correspondence, Central Committee minutes, and the annual reports and records of the Red Cross in other countries.

Stanford University. Hoover Institution on War, Revolution, and Peace. Library. Stanford, California 94305

This important collection documents communist and other leftist parties and movements. The major single holding is the Bolloten Spanish Civil War Collection, a source rich in newspaper clippings, pamphlets, interviews, and correspondence. The overall strengths are in serials. It also contains the Joaquín Maurín Collection of manuscripts and printed materials as well as those of Jay Allen. See its *Guide to the Hoover Institution Archives*, Stanford, Calif., 1980 (CD3119.S7S7 1980) and *The Library Catalog: Catalog of the Western Language Collections*, Boston, G. K. Hall, 1969 in 63 v. and suppl. (Z881.S785 1969Eq).

Tamiment Institute Library. New York University. New York City 10012

These collections emphasize leftist and labor activities, and include the manuscripts and organizational files of the Socialist party, 1938. Notable pamphlet holdings exist. See its *Catalog*, Boston, G. K. Hall, 1980, 4 v.

United States. Department of State. Washington, D.C. 20525

The State Department's archive holds diplomatic correspondence (the department's and Foreign Service Officers') and consular reports, as well as memoranda of the secretary of state and other department officials. For a selection of such items, see its *Foreign Relations of the United States: Diplomatic Papers, 1936* v. 1 and 2, *1937* v. 1, *1938* v. 1 and 2, and *1939* v. 1, Washington, D.C., U.S. Government Printing Office, 1953-1956 (JX233.A3).

United States. Library of Congress. Washington, D.C. 20540

A reasonably well-balanced collection represents all major participants' points of view. The greatest strengths are in the history of the period and military affairs, including foreign intervention, personal narratives, and fiction. Limited numbers of pamphlets exist.

Primary sources include a collection of telegrams sent by R.C.A. Radiogram Communications and the Agence Espagne Informations Télégraphiques et Téléphoniques de Dernière Heure (May 1937-January 1939).

United States. Library of Congress. Manuscript Division. Washington, D.C. 20540

Papers of public figures, especially senators, congressmen, and ambassadors, and private individuals have references to the period. A major collection is the Cordell Hull Papers which includes arms and munitions control material.

United States. National Archives and Records Service. Washington, D.C. 20408

A significant repository given its depth and breadth, the National Archives offer such materials as the records of the Department of State and papers of the Senate Committee on Foreign Relations and the House Committee on Foreign Affairs. Microfilms of captured German and Italian government archives reside here. Various motion picture documentaries also exist. See its *Guide to the National Archives of the United States*, Washington, D.C., 1974 (CD3023.U54 1974).

Veterans of the Abraham Lincoln Brigade. 148 East 30th Street, New York City 10016

This repository collects oral history, films, and posters as specialties; it is also known as the Spanish Civil War Historical Association.

Yale University. Library. New Haven, Connecticut 06520

Civil War materials appear among various collections, including the Ernst Toller Papers (Committee for Impartial Relief in Spain) and the Charles Andrews Fenton Collection which has writings, notes, and serial articles from a literary perspective.

A Selected Bibliography of Bibliographies on the Spanish Civil War

PETER T. JOHNSON

The Civil War witnessed a vast outpouring of writings devoted to the conflict. Virtually all institutions contributed interpretative pieces; individuals expressed their personal and public views; and by 1939 an impressive body of literature documenting the course of the war existed. The significant quality of ephemera renders bibliographic control much more difficult. Speeches, political tracts, and propaganda appearing in pamphlet format, as well as newspapers of short duration, project any detailed bibliographic research into a particularly laborious endeavor. Both combatants issued official publications, often with small press runs and extremely limited circulation. Political parties, trade unions, the Church, and foreign interests account for further diversity. Nearly all these publishing efforts had limited national circulation, usually survived a relatively short time, and utilized poor quality paper. Despite such adverse conditions, the range and depth of Civil War publications in various large research libraries prove remarkable. Major efforts to accurately identify this literature constitute ongoing international projects.

Writers and scholars continue to be fascinated with the conflict experiences. The body of secondary literature drawn from archival and printed sources encompasses all points of view and emanates from many different countries. Precisely because of the geographic spread of current publishing and the restrictions governing access to primary sources, maintaining bibliographic awareness constitutes a specialization in itself. The bibliography in this appendix is the product of a review of the major bibliographies and monographs. Criteria for inclusion were qualitative comprehensiveness, topical coverage unavailable in broader works, or the identification of important precursory studies. Excluded are general bibliographic sources of a purely international scope.

This appendix also contains guides to achives and libraries of entire countries or cities which cite many detailed works valuable for gaining access to their collections. For guides to specific institutions, consult these general guides as well as Appendix D.

For the broadest identification of works published during the period, consult Antonio Palau y Dulcet, *Manual del librero hispanoamericano*...(Barcelona, Librería Palau, 1948-1977 in 28 vols.) (Z2681.P16) and the Instituto Nacional del Libro Español, *Catálogo general de la librería española, 1931-1950* (Madrid, 1957-1965 in 4 vols.) (Z2681.C34). Current production appears in *El Libro español* (Madrid, Instituto Nacional del Libro Español, 1958-) and *Libros españoles. ISBN* (Madrid, Instituto Nacional del Libro Español, 1974-) (Z2681.L53). More specialized coverage appears in the Society for Spanish and Portuguese Historical Studies *Bulletin* (Fredonia, N.Y., 1969-), the *International Bibliography of Historical Sciences* (Paris, 1930-) (Z6205.I61), and *Historical Abstracts, Part B: Twentieth Century Abstracts 1914-* (Santa Barbara, Calif., 1971-).

The following bibliography is arranged by author (personal or corporate) or by title if no single author exists. Each citation carries full bibliographic information, and, whenever available, the Library of Congress classification number. The annotations attempt to describe as succinctly as possible the scope and content of each work. Users should remember that few libraries ordinarily lend bibliographies.

Bardi, Ubaldo. *La guerra civile in Spagna: saggio per una bibliografia italiana.* Urbina: Argalía Editore, 1974. 134 p. (Z2700.B37)

> The best source for Italian contributions on the conflict, arranged by broad subject groups, it draws mainly from works written during 1936-1939 with the greatest strength in serial literature. Many key journals have itemized listings of articles. Nearly all citations are in Italian. Topical coverage includes economics, politics, military operations, fascism and antifascism, diplomatic history, culture, and literature.

Bibliografía general sobre la Guerra de España (1936-1939) y sus antecedentes históricos; fuentes para la historia contemporánea de España. Intro. general y dirección y revision de Ricardo de la Cierva y de Hoces. Madrid: Secretaría General Técnica del Ministerio de Información y Turismo, 1968. 729 p. (Z2700.B52)

> Inclusion of primary and secondary sources published in Spain and abroad reflects a broad interpretation of what is relevant to the period. The wide range of materials and coverage and the absence of annotations result in many citations with no direct relation to the Civil War. Arrangement is by main entry aided by author, geographic, and subject indices. Excluded are newspaper and journal articles.

Bron, Michat. *Wojna hiszpańska, 1936-1939; chronologia wydarzeń i bibliografia.* Warszawa: Wydawn. Ministerstwa Obrony Narodowej, 1964. 516 p. (DP269.B749)

The bibliographic section (pp. 33-455) includes books, journals, documents, pamphlets, and articles published during and after the Civil War. It is most useful for Central and Eastern European imprints, with particular strengths in those offering political interpretations of events. Socialist and communist literature predominates. The remainder of the text is a daily chronicle of events.

Childs, James Bennett. *Spanish Government Publications after July 17, 1936; a Survey.* 3 vols. Washington, D.C., Library of Congress, Reference Department, Serial Division, 1965-1967. (Z663.44.S6)

This extremely valuable work provides the most complete indentification and bibliographic description available of official publications. Organized into three groups—Jefatura del Estado, Presidencia del Gobierno, and the ministries—each agency carries a brief background note on the legal basis of organization and its specific activities, followed by citations of its publications: monographs, serials, pamphlets, and maps. Most entries have complete bibliographic information, and some annotations appear. It serves as a union list of Library of Congress holdings.

Cortada, James, W. *A Bibliographic Guide to Spanish Diplomatic History, 1460-1977.* Westport, Conn.: Greenwood Press, 1977. 390 p. (Z2696.C67)

Organized by chronological period with country subdivisions, the work identifies the principal published sources from books, articles, and dissertations. Citations do not carry annotations. Author index.

Cuadernos bibliográficos de la guerra de España, 1936-1939. Madrid: Universidad de Madrid, 1966-   . (Serie l. Folletos.)

This Work contains citations for pamplets issued by various interest groups. It is arranged alphabetically by author or title; union list information appears for major Spanish repositories. The annotaions range from brief descriptions to detailed summaries. Fascicles appeared in 1966 (792 items) and 1968 (747 items).

Cuadernos bibliográficos de la guerra de España, 1936-1939. Madrid: Universidad de Madrid, 1966-   . (Serie 2. Periódicos.)

An alphabetically arranged list of over 1,300 serials, unannotated, and lacking complete bibliographic information, this work is nevertheless useful for beginning phases of research.

Cuadernos bibliográficos de la guerra de España, 1936-1939. Madrid: Universidad de Madrid, 1967-   . (Serie 3. Memorias.)

An extensively annotated source for eyewitness accounts of the conflict, this source includes publications in various languages. Arrangement is in alphabetical order by author's surname. Fascicles exist for 1967, 1968, and 1969.

García Durán, Juan. *Bibliography of the Spanish Civil War . . .1936-1939.* Montevideo: Ed. El Siglo Ilustrado, 1964. 559 p. (Instituto de Historia de la Guerra Civil Española, 1) (Z2700.G3)

This basic source, given the inclusion of over 6,000 items, contains books and articles published in various languages. Arrangement is in broad subject groups.

Gómez Molleda, María Dolores. *Bibliografía histórica española, 1950-1954.* Madrid: Consejo Superior de Investigaciones Científicas, Inst. Jerónimo Zurita de Historia [e] Inst. Nicolás Antonio de Bibliografía, 1955. 491 p. (Z2696.G6)

This bibliography contains citations of articles and books grouped in the twentieth-century section. It is useful for background material and has an author index.

González Ollé, Fernando. *Manual bibliográfico de estudios españoles.* Pamplona: Ed. Universidad de Navarra, 1976. 1377 p. (Z2681.G58)

Divided by subject and therein by topic, this work offers extensive coverage of the major sources that appear in book or article format. Author and subject indices further enhance the usefulness. As a beginning point for research either on broad or limited topics, the *Manual* should be a high priority. Treatment of guides to archives is particularly strong.

Grimsted, Patricia Kennedy. *Archives and Manuscript Repositories in the USSR: Moscow and Leningrad.* Princeton, N.J.: Princeton University Press, 1972. 436 p. (CD1711.G7)

This work effectively combines descriptions of archives with annotated listings of finding aids. Inclusion of Spanish-related materials appears modest. Updated with Supplement 1: *Bibliographical Addenda* (Zug, Switzerland: Inter Documentation Co., 1976).

Hanson, Carl A. *Dissertations on Iberian and Latin American History.* Troy, N.Y.: Whitston Publishing Co., 1975. 400 p. (Z1601.H32)

This source identifies approximately 3,500 titles written in Canada, Great Britain, Ireland, and the United States between 1889 and 1969. Arrangement is by country or area with topical and chronological subdivisions, accompanied by an author index.

Harvard University. Library. *Spanish History and Literature; Classification Schedule, Classified Listing by Call Number, Chronological Listing, Author and Title Listing.* Cambridge, Mass.: distributed by Harvard University Press, 1972. 771 p. (Widener Library shelflist, 41) (Z2709.H35)

This particularly valuable source for quickly reviewing the range of works published during the Civil War is arranged by author, title, date of imprint, and the library's classification scheme. As one of the world's major collections, early consultation proves useful.

Indice histórico español. Bibliografía histórica de España e Hispanoamérica. 23 vols. Barcelona: Centro de Estudios Históricos Internacionales, Universidad de Barcelona, 1953-1977. (Z2696.I6)

This is the best source available not only for the qualitative selection of citations but also for the authoritative annotations. Organized by chronological period and subdivided by subject area or subfield, this work includes the best available publications from various countries. An excellent starting place, it also proves useful for advanced levels of comparative and interdisciplinary historical research.

Madrid. Biblioteca Nacional. *Publicaciones periódicas existentes en la Biblioteca Nacional; catálogo . . .* Madrid, 1952. 718 p. (Z6945.M14)

> This is a highly useful source for identifying and verifying serials. Arrangement is by broad subject and therein alphabetically by main entry. Most citations carry place, date of publication, and frequency. Its title index is indispensable.

Montes, María José. *La Guerra Española en la creación literaria (ensayo bibliográfico).* Madrid: Universidad de Madrid, 1970. 191 p. (Anejos de Cuadernos bibliográficos de la Guerra de España, 1936-1939, no. 2). (Z6520.S64M65)

> This is a particularly valuable work for the field. Organization is by genre, and citations come from books and articles. Included are author and subject indices for *Hora de España* and *Jerarquía*.

Mouvements ouvriers et socialistes: chronologie et bibliographie. 5 vols. Paris: Editions Ouvrières [1953]. V. 3: *L'Espagne (1750-1936),* by Renée Lamberet. 205 p. (Z7161.M64)

> This basic work organized chronologically cites principally Spanish imprints of books, pamphlets, and official documents. Much of the literature emanates from participants. The absence of an author, title, and subject index places reliance upon the chronological divisions.

Paris. Bibliothèque Nationale. *Répertoire des bibliothèques et organismes de documentation.* Paris: 1971. 733 p. and suppl. 1973. (Z797.A1P35 1971)

> This exceptionally useful work providing a wide range of essential information concerning libraries and archives has sections for the Paris region and Départements. An extensive index facilitates use. Although the Civil War is not directly mentioned, one may identify repositories likely to have holdings. The bibliography of published guides for various archives and libraries should facilitate research. Although less detailed, Erwin K. Welsch's *Libraries and Archives in France: A Handbook*, rev. ed., New York, Council for European Studies, 1979 (Z797.A1W44 1979) is extremely helpful for access questions and identification of principal guides to archives.

Perrino Rodríguez, Fidel. "Bibliografía de la Cruzada Española (1936-1939)," *Boletín de la Dirección General de Archivos y Bibliotecas*, 3:19 supl. (April-May 1954). 14 p. (CD19.S65)

> The perspective of the Movimiento Nacional characterizes most of the approximately 400 works cited. Principal focus is on the military aspects of the war.

Sánchez Alonso, Benito. *Fuentes de la historia española e hispanoamericana; ensayo de bibliografía sistemática de impresos y manuscritos que ilustran la historia política de España y sus antiguas provincias de ultramar.* 3d ed. corr.

3 vols. Madrid: Consejo Superior de Investigaciones Superiores, 1952. (Z2696.S21)

> The fundamental source for background citations drawn from books and journals appears in broad chronological periods with geographic subdivisions. Coverage ends with 1898. Various indices, including author, subject, and manuscript sources, further enhance the work.

Spain, Archivo Histórico Nacional, Madrid. *Bibliografía de archivos españoles y de archivistica.* Madrid: 1963. 340 p.

> Although most entries concern repositories of sources predating the Civil War, it remains an excellent source for extensive bibliography on archival sources.

Spain, Dirección General de Archivos y Bibliotecas. *Los archivos de Barcelona.* Madrid: 1952- . (CD1877.B3A52)

> Organization is by three broad groups: public and private sector archives with the emphasis on the historical, military, and ecclesiastic. Each entry carries background material, comments on the organization, classification systems and finding aids. Civil War holdings are mentioned for various institutions.

Spain. Dirección General de Archivos y Bibliotecas. *Las bibliotecas de Barcelona y su Provincia.* Madrid: 1952. 155 p. (Z832.B24A52)

> Listing both public and private sector libraries, this descriptive guide provides collection size, areas of specialization, and notes about finding aids.

Spain. Dirección General de Archivos y Bibliotecas. *Guía de las bibliotecas de Madrid.* Madrid: 1953. 556 p. (Z832.M168)

> Still the basic source for quick orientation, this guide discusses about 300 libraries of both the public and private sectors. Each entry provides a statistical summary of the types of holdings, a historical background note, availability of catalogues, and policy matters.

Spain. Dirección General de Archivos y Bibliotecas. *Guía de los archivos de Madrid.* Madrid: 1952. 592 p. (Guías de archivos y bibliotecas, 1) (CD1877.M3A52)

> A basic work giving sufficient detail of the major archives in the Madrid metropolitan area, it has notes on the history and comments about the organization, classification, and catalogues of each archive. For government agencies this is particularly helpful.

Spain. Inspección General de Archivos. *Guía de los archivos estatales españoles: guía del investigador.* Madrid: 1977. 142 p. (CD1850.S67 1977)

> This useful source identifies national, regional, and state archives, providing basic information about their collections, personnel, and various published guides to the holdings. Because both books and articles are cited, this guide is a good starting point for developing control over published inventories and descriptions prior to research.

Index

This index covers the Dictionary and Appendix B: A Military History of the Spanish Civil War. It includes references to each of the entries and to the contents of those entries.

The page numbers set in bold face indicate the location of the main entry.

About the Editor

JAMES W. CORTADA, who received his Ph.D. from Florida State University in 1973, is currently employed as a staff instructor for the IBM Corporation. He has authored several books, including *A Bibliographic Guide to Spanish Diplomatic History, 1460-1977* (Greenwood Press, 1977), *Two Nations Over Time: Spain and the United States* (Greenwood Press, 1978), and *Spain in the Twentieth-Century World* (Greenwood Press, 1980), and over fifty articles on Spanish history.